Howe Library
Shenandoah College & Conservatory
Winchester, VA 22601

COMPUTER
CONCEPTS
AND
APPLICATIONS

with *BASIC*

COMPUTER CONCEPTS AND APPLICATIONS

with *BASIC*

Donald H. Sanders
Educational Consultant
Ft. Worth, Texas

McGRAW-HILL BOOK COMPANY

New York | St. Louis | San Francisco | Auckland
Bogotá | Hamburg | Johannesburg | London
Madrid | Mexico | Milan | Montreal
New Delhi | Panama | Paris | São Paulo
Singapore | Sydney | Tokyo | Toronto

COMPUTER CONCEPTS
AND APPLICATIONS
WITH BASIC

Copyright © 1987 by McGraw-Hill, Inc.
All rights reserved.
Printed in the United States of America.
Except as permitted under the United States Copyright Act of 1976,
no part of this publication may be reproduced or distributed
in any form or by any means, or stored
in a data base or retrieval system,
without the prior written permission of the publisher.

1 2 3 4 5 6 7 8 9 0   VNHVNH   8 9 8 7 6

ISBN 0-07-054697-5

This book was set in Times Roman by York Graphic Services, Inc.
The editors were Gerald Gleason, Allan Forsyth, and Peggy Rehberger;
the cover was designed by Nicholas Krenitsky;
the production supervisor was Phil Galea.
The drawings were done by Fine Line Illustrations, Inc.
Von Hoffmann Press, Inc., was printer and binder.

Library of Congress Cataloging-in-Publication Data

Sanders, Donald H.
   Computer concepts and applications with BASIC.

   1. Computers.   2. BASIC (Computer program language)
I. Title.
QA76.S2874 1986   004   86-10371
ISBN: 0-07-054697-5

QA   Sanders, Donald H.
76
.S2874   Computer concepts and
1987   applications with BASIC

004.2 Sa56c, 1987

ABOUT THE AUTHOR

DONALD H. SANDERS is the author of seven books about computers—their uses and their impact—spanning more than 25 years. Over a million copies of his books have been used in college courses and in industry and government training programs.

Dr. Sanders has 20 years of teaching experience. After receiving degrees from Texas A & M University and the University of Arkansas, he was a professor at the University of Texas at Arlington, at Memphis State University, and at Texas Christian University. In addition to his books, Dr. Sanders has contributed articles to journals such as Data Management, Automation, Banking, Journal of Small Business Management, Journal of Retailing, and Advanced Management Journal. He has also encouraged his graduate students to contribute computer-related articles to national periodicals, and over 70 of these articles have been published. Dr. Sanders chairs the "Computers and Data Processing" Subject Examination Committee, CLEP Program, College Entrance Examination Board, Princeton, N.J.

CONTENTS IN BRIEF

Preface

MODULE 1:
BACKGROUND — 2

1 Let's Get Started — 5
2 Computers at Work — 51
3 The Computer Impact — 91

MODULE 2:
COMPUTER CONCEPTS, COMPONENTS, AND SYSTEMS — 126

4 Central Processors — 129
5 Entering Data — 157
6 Storing Data and Receiving Output — 195
7 Personal Computers — 239
8 Data Communications Networks — 273

MODULE 3:
SOFTWARE — 312

9 Prewritten Software:
Single-Function Applications Programs — 315
10 Prewritten Software:
Integrated Packages, Package Selection, and Operating Systems — 345
11 Developing Custom-Made Systems — 369
12 Preparing Application Programs:
Practices and Languages — 397

MODULE 4:
SOCIAL IMPACT — 440

13 Government, Law, and Health Care — 443
14 Education and the Humanities — 473
15 Science, Engineering, and Business — 499

MODULE 5:
PROGRAMMING — 526

16 Programming Analysis: Concepts and Examples — 529
17 A BASIC Beginning — 569
18 More about BASIC — 613

GLOSSARY — 661
INDEX — 671

CONTENTS

Preface

MODULE 1
BACKGROUND   2

CHAPTER 1
LET'S GET STARTED   5

Opening Vignette   The Dawn of a New Age   5

The Need for Computer Literacy | The Purpose of This Book | How This Book Is Organized

Looking Ahead   11

Chapter Outline   11

What's a Computer?   12

Speed and Accuracy Capabilities | Processing Capabilities

Window 1-1   Computer Fingers a Killer   17

Computer System Organization   18

The System Concept | Organization of Computer System Components

The Stored Program Concept: An Example   24

Processing the Beautification Charges

Computer Systems Today: Advances, Differences, and Limitations	27
Computer Advances | *Computer Differences* | *Computer Limitations*	
Feedback and Review 1	37
Looking Back	38
A Closer Look From Abacus to Personal Computer: Our Debt to the Past	43

CHAPTER 2
COMPUTERS AT WORK — 51

Opening Vignette The Things People Do	51
Looking Ahead	53
Chapter Outline	53
Organizing Data for Computer Processing	54
What People Do with Computers: An Introduction to Applications	54
The Byter Family | *Input/Output Applications* | *Calculation Applications* | *Text Manipulation Applications* | *Interactive and Batch Processing* | *A Logic/Comparison Application* | *Storage/Retrieval Applications* | *Sequential and Direct Storage and Retrieval*	
Obtaining Application Software	78
Prewritten Packages	
Window 2-1 Computer Helps Flutie Score Big	79
Development of Custom-Made Software	
Feedback and Review 2	83
Looking Back	84
A Closer Look Controlling Your Home by Computer	89

CHAPTER 3
THE COMPUTER IMPACT — 91

Opening Vignette Asimov Ponders PCs	91
Looking Ahead	93
Chapter Outline	93

Human Thinking and Artificial Intelligence	94
Can Computers Think?	
Window 3-1 Artificial Intelligence and "Fuzzy" Thinking	97
AI in Action: Expert Systems	
The Impact of Computers on People	99
The Positive Impact | The Potential Dangers	
The Impact of Computers on Organizations	109
The Information Processing Industry | The Positive Impact on Using Organizations | The Potential Dangers for Using Organizations	
Let's Summarize	116
Optimistic Views | Pessimistic Views | Another View | A Recap of This Background Module	
Feedback and Review 3	119
Looking Back	121
A Closer Look Computers and the Handicapped	125

MODULE 2

COMPUTER CONCEPTS, COMPONENTS, AND SYSTEMS — 126

CHAPTER 4
CENTRAL PROCESSORS — 129

Opening Vignette Biochips	129
Looking Ahead	131
Chapter Outline	131
Primary Storage Concepts	132
Storage Locations and Addresses | Capacity of Storage Locations	
Coding Data in Storage	135
The Binary Numbering System | Computer Codes	
Storage Components in the Processor Unit	139
Primary Storage Components of the Past | Primary Storage Components of the Present | Primary Storage Components of the Future | Specialized Storage Elements in the Processor Unit	

CONTENTS

xii

Window 4-1 Chips that See, Smell, and Feel	143
The Arithmetic-Logic and Control Functions	144
The Arithmetic-Logic Section | *The Control Section*	
Feedback and Review 4	145
Looking Back	147
A Closer Look Inside Central Processors: The Use of Storage Locations and the Operations of Arithmetic-Logic and Control Sections	150

CHAPTER 5
ENTERING DATA 157

Opening Vignette The Keyboard Stalls the Growth of Japanese Word Processing	157
Looking Ahead	159
Chapter Outline	159
Input Data: Sources and Concepts	160
Sources of Input Data | *Data Entry Methods* | *Input Accuracy and Error Detection*	
Devices for Online Data Entry	168
Visual Display Terminals | *User-Friendly Interfaces for VDTs and Personal Computers*	
Window 5-1 KO for Punched Cards	173
Point-of-Sale Terminals	
Window 5-2 High-Density Bar Codes for Data Input	178
Financial Transaction Terminals | *Teleprinters and Portable Data Entry Terminals* | *Voice Input Systems*	
Media and Devices for Offline Data Entry	180
Magnetic Tape | *Floppy Disks* | *Character Readers*	
Feedback and Review 5	187
Looking Back	188
A Closer Look Smart Cards	193

CHAPTER 6
STORING DATA AND RECEIVING OUTPUT 195

Opening Vignette Preserving the Past on Disks	195

CONTENTS
xiii

Looking Ahead   197
Chapter Outline   197

The Storage Hierarchy: An Overview   198
Elements in the Storage Hierarchy | Storage Selection

Secondary Storage for Direct Access   199
Disk Storage for Direct Access | Direct Access with RAM "Disks" and Magnetic Bubbles | Direct Access with Optical Disks and Tape Strips | Future Direct-Access Developments

Secondary Storage for Sequential Access   212
Disk Storage for Sequential Access | Magnetic Tape Storage

Receiving Computer Output: Some Basic Concepts   215
Why Output is Needed | Output Categories

Printed and Filmed Output   217
Printed Output | Filmed Output

Displayed Output, Computer Graphics, and Voice Response   224
Displayed Output and Computer Graphics

Window 6-1   High-Tech Blackboards   224

Window 6-2   Are Computers Hazardous to Your Health?   225

Voice Response

Feedback and Review 6   229

Looking Back   231

A Closer Look   Facts and Files: Organizing/Storing/Accessing/Processing Concepts   235

CHAPTER 7
PERSONAL COMPUTERS   239

Opening Vignette   Who Needs Personal Computers?   239

Looking Ahead   241

Chapter Outline   241

A PC Introduction   242

PC Concepts

Window 7-1   Multiuser Systems   245

The Classification Dilemma

Hardware Characteristics	244

Microprocessor Characteristics | Factors Affecting Processor Performance | Characteristics of Peripherals | Hardware Standards and System Purchase Considerations

Some Software Considerations	252

Operating System Standards | Prewritten Applications Packages in Homes and Offices | Translating Program Considerations

Feedback and Review 7	260
Looking Back	261
A Closer Look Minis, Mainframes, and "Monsters"	264

CHAPTER 8
DATA COMMUNICATIONS NETWORKS   273

Opening Vignette Radio-Linked Computer Networks Free Traveling Users from Phones and Cables	273
Looking Ahead	275
Chapter Outline	275
The Computing/Communications Setting	276

Data Communications Background | The Converging Computing/Communications Picture

Data Communications Concepts	278

Data Transmission Techniques | Data Transmission Channels | Data Communications Service Organizations | Coordinating the Data Communications Environment

Systems Supported by Data Communications	291

Real Time Processing Systems | Timesharing and Remote Computing Service Systems | Distributed Data Processing Networks | Electronic Mail/Message Systems | Data Base Retrieval Systems | Banking Service Systems | Telecommuting Systems

Window 8-1 Banking on Your Home Computer	303
Feedback and Review 8	304
Looking Back	306
A Closer Look Data Security	311

MODULE 3
SOFTWARE   312

CHAPTER 9
PREWRITTEN SOFTWARE:
SINGLE-FUNCTION APPLICATIONS PROGRAMS   315

Opening Vignette   The People's Firehouse   315

Looking Ahead   317

Chapter Outline   317

Categories of Software Packages: Review and Preview   318

Prewritten Applications Packages | *System Software Packages*

Single-Function Applications Programs   319

Special-Purpose Packages | *General-Purpose Packages*

Window 9-1   Building Simple Spreadsheets   326

Window 9-2   Hypertext   337

Feedback and Review 9   338

Looking Back   339

A Closer Look   How a Word Processing Program Works   342

CHAPTER 10
PREWRITTEN SOFTWARE:
INTEGRATED PACKAGES, PACKAGE SELECTION,
AND OPERATING SYSTEMS   345

Opening Vignette   Live Aid's Backstage Heroes   345

Looking Ahead   347

Chapter Outline   347

Integration of Applications Programs   348

Window 10-1   Memory Resident Software   349

Identifying and Selecting Applications Packages   350

Identifying Suitable Applications Packages | *Narrowing the Field* | *Making the Final Decisions*

System Software: The Operating System 353

Control Programs in an OS | Processing Programs in an OS

Feedback and Review 10 363

Looking Back 364

A Closer Look   Making Computers Easy to Use: Better Software and Hardware Improve the Interface 367

CHAPTER 11
DEVELOPING CUSTOM-MADE SYSTEMS 369

Opening Vignette   On Softer Software 369

Looking Ahead 371

Chapter Outline 371

Examples of Custom-Made Systems 372

Management Information Systems | Hospital Information Systems

The System Development Process 378

Problem Definition | System Analysis | System Design

Window 11-1   Prototyping as an Aid in System Development 388

Feedback and Review 11 391

Looking Back 391

A Closer Look   Expert Systems 395

CHAPTER 12
PREPARING APPLICATIONS PROGRAMS: PRACTICES AND LANGUAGES 397

Opening Vignette   Did the Wrong Programming Language Put New Jersey Motorists in a Jam? 397

Looking Ahead 399

Chapter Outline 399

Program Preparation Practices 400

Conflicting Goals | The Make or Buy Consideration | Programmer Organization Practices

Window 12-1 "Recycling" Used Software	402

Program Construction Practices

Programming Language Classifications	405

Machine Languages | *Assembly Languages* | *High-Level Languages* | *"Fourth-Generation" Languages*

Major High-Level Languages	411

BASIC | *FORTRAN* | *COBOL* | *PL/1* | *RPG* | *ALGOL, Pascal, and Ada* | *Logo and Some Others* | *Selecting a Programming Language*

Software Implementation and Maintenance	422

Program Implementation | *System Conversion and Changeover* | *Program/System Maintenance* | *Post-Implementation Review*

Window 12-2 The Meaning of Software Maintenance	428
Feedback and Review 12	429
Looking Back	431
A Closer Look Careers in Computing	435

MODULE 4
SOCIAL IMPACT — 440

CHAPTER 13
GOVERNMENT, LAW, AND HEALTH CARE — 443

Opening Vignette Streamlining a Federal Bureaucracy	443
Looking Ahead	446
Chapter Outline	446
Computers in Government and Law	447

Housekeeping and Decision-Making Applications | *Computers in Local Government* | *Computers in Regional Organizations and State Governments* | *Computers in the Federal Government* | *Law and Law Enforcement Applications*

Window 13-1 Court Reporting: Going High-Tech to Save Time and Trouble	456
Computers in Health Care	458

Where We've Come From | *Health-Care Systems Today*

Window 13-2 No Place for Guesswork ... 459

Health-Care Systems Tomorrow

Feedback and Review 13 ... 468

Looking Back ... 469

A Closer Look Voting by Computer: Are Systems Vulnerable to Fraud? ... 472

CHAPTER 14
EDUCATION AND THE HUMANITIES ... 473

Opening Vignette A School without Walls ... 473

Looking Ahead ... 475

Chapter Outline ... 475

Computers in Education ... 476

Computer-Managed Instruction | *Computer-Assisted Instruction* | *Computer-Assisted Testing*

Computers in the Humanities ... 483

Art Authenticity | *Authorship Identification* | *Language Translation* | *Computers in the Fine Arts*

Window 14-1 Comic Art by Computer ... 487

Computers and Museums | *Computers in History* | *Computers in Archaeology* | *Skeptics and Dissenters*

Feedback and Review 14 ... 493

Looking Back ... 494

A Closer Look IBM's Writing to Read ... 497

CHAPTER 15
SCIENCE, ENGINEERING, AND BUSINESS ... 499

Opening Vignette Simulating Nuclear Accidents ... 499

Looking Ahead ... 501

Chapter Outline ... 501

Computers in the Sciences ... 502

Planning and Decision-Making Applications | *Control Applications*

Computers in Engineering and Business	508
Computer-Aided Design Applications | *Robotics and Computer-Aided Manufacturing Applications*	
Window 15-1 A Robot Sub Achieves New Depths	512
Control Applications	
Feedback and Review 15	521
Looking Back	522
A Closer Look Information Power	524

MODULE 5
PROGRAMMING — 526

CHAPTER 16
PROGRAMMING ANALYSIS: CONCEPTS AND EXAMPLES — 529

Opening Vignette The Public Library: Public Domain Software	529
Looking Ahead	531
Chapter Outline	531
Programming Analysis Concepts	532
A Program Analysis Approach	
Window 16-1 Useful User Groups	534
General Flowcharting Concepts	
Programming Analysis Examples	538
A Simple Input/Process/Output Example	
Feedback and Review 16-1	539
Gaining Flexibility with Decisions and Loops	
Feedback and Review 16-2	544
A Multiple-Decision Situation | *The Use of Accumulators* | *The Use of Counters*	
Feedback and Review 16-3	553
Benefits and Limitations of Flowcharts	

CONTENTS

Logic Structures and Structured Programming	554
Three Logic Structures | *Structured Programming Concepts* | *Some Benefits of Structured Programming*	
Other Programming Analysis Tools	557
Structured Pseudocode | *Decision Tables*	
Looking Back	561
A Closer Look How about a Computer Program for Dinner?	567

CHAPTER 17
A BASIC BEGINNING — 569

Opening Vignette Computer Software: Today's Shooting Stars	569
Looking Ahead	571
Chapter Outline	571
Some BASIC Necessities	572
Using Your System | *System Commands and Program Statements*	
Window 17-1 The Acronym: A User's Lament	574
Program Entry Elements | *Arithmetic Operations* | *Correcting Errors*	
Program Preparation Examples	579
A Simple Input/Process/Output Example	
Feedback and Review 17-1	583
Gaining Flexibility with Decisions and Loops	
Feedback and Review 17-2	592
A Multiple-Decision Situation | *The Use of Accumulators* | *The Use of Counters*	
Window 17-2 Gauss's Punishment	603
Feedback and Review 17-3	604
Looking Back	605
A Closer Look Programming Style	611

CHAPTER 18
MORE ABOUT BASIC — 613

Opening Vignette A Brief History of Microsoft BASIC	613
Looking Ahead	615
Chapter Outline	615

Nested FOR . . . NEXT Loops	616
FOR . . . NEXT Loops: A Review | Flowcharting FOR . . . NEXT Loops: A Dilemma | Inner and Outer Loops	
The Use of Library Functions	619
The SQR Function | INT and RND Functions	
One-Dimensional Arrays	626
Entering Data into Arrays | Printing Arrayed Data | The DIM Statement | Example Programs Using One-Dimensional Arrays	
Feedback and Review 18-1	635
Two-Dimensional Arrays	636
Example Program Using Two-Dimensional Array	
Feedback and Review 18-2	640
Let's Sort This Out	641
Bubble Sorts	
Feedback and Review 18-3	647
Additional BASIC Statements	648
Statements to Facilitate Structured Programming | A Few Other Statements	
Looking Back	653
A Closer Look Program Debugging	658
Window 18-1 The 10111'rd Psalm	659
GLOSSARY	661
INDEX	671

PREFACE

We woke up the other day and found ourselves smack in the middle of the Information Society . . . . The power of computing brings information to the masses and lets us alter that information . . . A word, a number, a graph, or a set of conclusions is now nothing but a series of electronic pulses, subject to the whims of any individual who intercepts them . . . . Many people view a populace able to find whatever it wants, whenever it needs it, as the ultimate informed society. At the same time, . . . the vulnerability of databases containing information about our private lives haunts us . . . . Are we mature enough to provide access to the information necessary to advance knowledge, yet still manage to protect our privacy, our security, and the information itself, which looms as the most valuable commodity of our new age?

—Pamela Clark, Editor-in-Chief,
Popular Computing, March 1985.
Copyright © 1985 by McGraw-Hill, Inc. All
rights reserved. Reprinted with permission.

Today's students must ultimately answer the broad question just raised by Pamela Clark. In the years ahead, they'll inherit the freedom and responsibilities—and realize the potential for use or abuse—of our Information Society. An important educational goal now is to make sure that today's students are computer literate so that they can participate in such a society, and help shape its policies in humane ways.

The Purpose of This Book

To be computer literate, today's students must know what computers are, what they can and cannot do, how they're put to work to process applications, and how their use in homes, schools, and workplaces can affect society. Thus, the *purpose* of *Computer Concepts and Applications* is to supply information in each of these related computer literacy areas so that readers will:

1 *Know What Computers Are.* Key concepts pertaining to the organization, capabilities, and limitations of computer *hardware* are presented, but unnecessary technical details have been omitted.

2 *Know What Computers Do.* Many uses or *applications* of computers in today's Information Society are considered. For example, the general functions performed by word processing, spreadsheet, data base, graphics, communications, time/project management, and other common applications programs are outlined early in the text and then in later chapters. And dozens of applications found in government and law, health care, education, the humanities, science, engineering, and business are discussed throughout the book.

3 *Know How Computer Systems Are Put to Work.* The emphasis in the text on word processing, spreadsheet, data base, and other common *software* packages (and the similar emphasis in the software supplement that accompanies this text) is designed to support courses that give students "hands-on" experience in putting computers to work to process the kinds of packaged software they'll be working with in the future. In addition, text material shows students how general analysis, design, and program preparation procedures are carried out to produce customized written programs of instruction.

4 *Understand Their Social Impact.* Computers don't operate in a vacuum; they're found in larger systems that include people. Some of the ways that computer usage may impact the people and organizations in our society are considered.

Computer Concepts and Applications provides a well-rounded introduction to these four related topics and is designed for use in the introductory one-term course in computers and information processing that's now taught around the world.

The Organization of This Book

This is the seventh in a series of computer texts that I've written over a period spanning two decades. Several titles have appeared in multiple editions, and have been translated into German, French, Spanish, and Portuguese versions. Over a million of these earlier books have been used in college courses and industry/government training programs.

The organization of *Computer Concepts and Applications* benefits from this earlier experience. For example, this text (like my *Computers Today,* a larger text with a more business-oriented approach) is organized into *modules,* giving it the flexibility to meet the needs of courses with different subject emphasis and with different presentation sequences. There are five modules in this book. The chapters in the first Background Module provide an overview of the four related areas of study mentioned above. (Chapter 1 introduces readers to hardware and stored program concepts and limitations; Chapter 2 presents an overview of what people do with computers and how computers are put to work; and Chapter 3 outlines ways in which people and organizations may be affected by present and future computer applications.) Once these chapters have been completed, readers can then turn immediately to any of the remaining modules shown in the chart (facing page) to meet whatever sequence and depth requirements are needed in a particular course.

Modules 2 through 5 build on the topics introduced in Module 1. Thus, a course can easily be designed so that discussions of prewritten applications packages (Chapters 9–10 in the Software Module) or the concepts needed to write applications programs (Chapters 16–18 in the Programming Module) immediately follow the completion of Chapter 3. Or, readers may be more

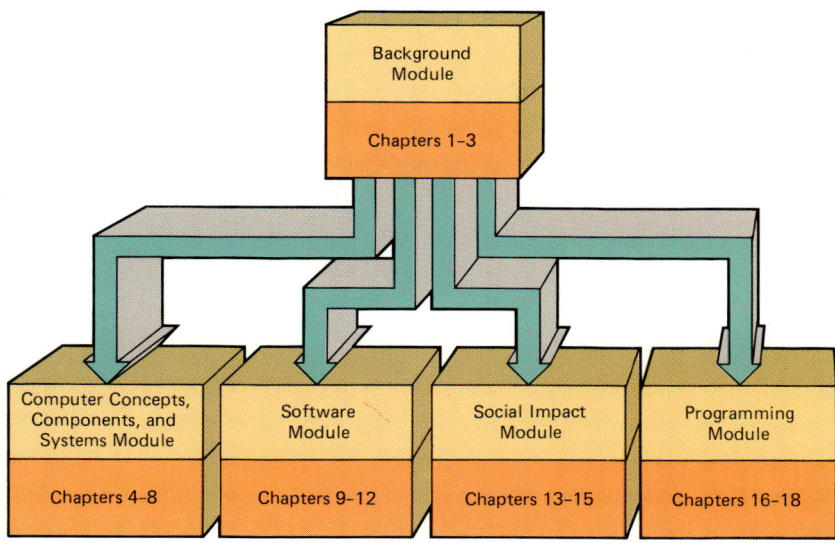

motivated to study other Modules if some time is spent on the Social Impact chapters (13–15) after Chapter 3 is completed. It's also logical to consider hardware concepts and systems in more detail (Chapters 4–8) before moving to another module. Regardless of the path selected, you'll have the flexibility to choose the sequence that's best for your needs, and you'll be able to vary the depth of the material you elect to cover in Modules 2–5.

Computers at Work: A Unifying Theme

Other books give examples of what computers do and how computer systems are put to work. But these examples often involve applications that (1) are unrelated to anything in a student's past, (2) go beyond a beginning student's current interest and experience, or (3) involve solutions to problems that a student never expects to have to deal with. Such examples, of course, are usually viewed as random and boring exercises.

Student interest and motivation is enhanced in this text with the introduction, in Chapter 2, of the computer-using Byter family. The Byters show, by example, how working parents and children in grade school, high school, and college can use personal computers to solve problems related to their work, school, and personal lives. Some of the problems encountered by the Byters in Chapter 2 are solved by using the types of data base, outlining, spreadsheet, graphics, and word processing packages that can be bought at any computer store. But other problems the Byters face use programs written specifically for the task at hand.

What the Byters do with computers is a unifying theme that's carried from Chapter 2 to chapters in the Software and Programming Modules. Further discussion of their use of prewritten applications packages is found in Chapter 9, and *more than 60* programming analysis and BASIC coding examples presented in Chapters 16 through 18 are tied to the Byter family theme. Creating a realistic family that students can identify with, discussing the common applications packages family members use, and then following their analysis, flowcharting, and coding steps as they prepare customized programs is an approach unique to *Computer Concepts and Applications*.

Other Features and Learning Aids

Numerous additional features and learning aids are found in *Computer Concepts and Applications:*

● Hundreds of *full-color* photographs, drawings, and illustrations are used to present concepts effectively and demonstrate useful applications. For example, detailed drawings show how the Byter family uses personal computers to run applications packages and solve problems, and a series of photo galleries reveals the broad range of possibilities created by the use of computers today.

● Each chapter opens with an interesting *vignette* that highlights some aspect of its contents. Each vignette is then followed by a *Looking Ahead* section that lists the *learning objectives* for the chapter, and by an *Outline* section that previews its topics.

● *Boxed inserts* are included in each chapter to provide additional applications, cases, and items of interest to support chapter material. These inserts are effective in stimulating discussions. And important new terms and concepts are highlighted in boldface type in the chapter in which they first appear.

● At least one *Feedback and Review* section is found in every chapter to reinforce reader understanding. Crossword puzzle, scrambled letter, and a variety of other formats are used in these sections, and answers to review material are found at the end of each chapter.

● Readers will also find at the end of each chapter a *Looking Back* section that summarizes the chapter's main points, a *Key Terms and Concepts* listing that includes the chapter page where the term or concept is first mentioned, a number of *review and discussion questions,* a *projects/issues* section that suggests student research topics based on chapter material, and, finally, a *Closer Look* reading that provides additional optional information to stimulate discussion and provide more in-depth coverage of selected subjects.

● Experts in the fields of Government and Law, Health Care, Education, the Humanities, and Science and Engineering were asked to participate in the preparation of the Social Impact Module, and their contributions are included and acknowledged in Chapters 13 through 15.

● A *Glossary* of the terms frequently found in the computer/information processing field is included at the back of the book.

Supplements for Computer Concepts and Applications

Computer Concepts and Applications is more than just a textbook—it's a complete teaching/learning package. Other components of this package include:

● ***Study Guide.*** This student *Study Guide* provides extensive self-tests for each corresponding chapter in *Computer Concepts and Applications.* Each *Study Guide* chapter contains learning objectives; a chapter overview and summary; and varied self-test sections including key term matching, multiple choice, true or false, and completion exercises. Answers for all exercises are included in the *Study Guide*. The *Study Guide* reinforces and integrates text concepts. It's designed for success—no "tricky" questions have been included intentionally—and it's a straightforward, no-frills, implement written for students, not for teachers. Successfully completing the *Study Guide* exercises should increase the confidence of students at all levels.

- **Software.** To provide students with their own inexpensive software which they can use in practical, hands-on applications and exercises keyed to the text, McGraw-Hill, in collaboration with Ashton-Tate, is making available a special, limited version of Framework, the popular integrated software package, for use with IBM systems and compatibles. Framework, which includes word processing, spreadsheeting, data base management, and graphics, is accompanied by an instruction manual which guides students in its use and provides exercises keyed to the text. For those who want software for the Apple II, McGraw-Hill provides an integrated software package of word processing, spreadsheeting, data base management, and graphics.

- **Instructors' Manual.** In addition to sample course outlines and guidance for preparing a syllabus, the *Instructors' Manual* supplies, for each chapter of the text, a chapter overview; teaching objectives; a detailed teaching outline; answers and suggestions for the Topics for Review and Discussion; and comments and suggestions for the Projects/Issues to Consider.

- **Overhead Transparencies.** A set of 64 color transparencies serves as a visual classroom aid which can be used to further explain text concepts.

- **Test Bank.** This complete set of more than 3,000 questions covers all of the important ideas and definitions in *Computer Concepts and Applications*. For your convenience the test bank is available for use with the computer. *MicroExaminer* allows you to generate tests using your Apple IIc or II+, IBM PC, or TRS 80 microcomputer. Questions can be scrambled into two versions, allowing you to create alternative exams for multiple sections of the same course. You also have the option of adding your own questions to the test bank. *The EXAMINER System* contains a magnetic tape which can be installed in your computer center, and offers the same features as *MicroExaminer*.

- **Slide Package.** A package of 80 slides, many of them not found in the text, is available to adopters. This package includes separate 20-slide presentations on history, computer graphics, a tour of a computer center, and computer applications. A descriptive narrative script is provided for each of the four slide presentations.

Acknowledgments

It's particularly appropriate to conclude this Preface with an acknowledgment section because a colorful package of this scope just doesn't happen without the input of many people. For example, the professionals who responded to research studies, participated in focus groups, and reviewed parts of the manuscript made many useful suggestions and helped shape the content and organization of *Computer Concepts and Applications*. These authorities are listed separately following this Preface.

Another debt is owed to the experts who contributed materials used in the module on Social Impact. These subject matter specialists are Donald F. Norris of the University of Nebraska, Omaha, for government and law; Harold Sackman of California State University, Los Angeles, for health care; William Sanders of Indiana University, for education; Andrew Christie of the University of New Hampshire, for the humanities; and William Bulgren and N.D. Francis of the University of Kansas, for science and engineering. Our thanks to them all.

Thanks must also go to the equipment manufacturers, publishers, and photo agencies who furnished materials, excerpts, and photographs for this book. Their individual contributions are acknowledged in the body of the text.

The final tribute and greatest appreciation, however, is reserved for these few: to Allan Forsyth, senior developmental editor, whose research efforts, sense of direction, and ability to condense wordy phrases resulted in improvements on virtually every page; to Marjorie Singer, who kept an author on his toes and assisted in developing the manuscript; to Nicholas Krenitsky, whose striking design helps to bring order to a complex subject; to Phil Galea and Lorinda Morris, whose production and photo research efforts continue to surprise a critical author; to Peggy Rehberger, who efficiently managed this complex project without a hitch; to Christina Mediate, who signed the book and helped guide it to completion; to Rob Fry, Shelly Langman, and Hal Sackman, for their contributions to the *Study Guide,* the *Instructors' Manual,* and the *Test Bank;* to Dr. Gary D. Sanders, University of Illinois, for his programming contributions and suggestions; and to Joyce Sanders for her continuing suggestions and encouragement.

Donald H. Sanders

ACKNOWLEDGMENTS

Professor Robert M. Aiken,
Temple University

Professor Ronald E. Anderson,
University of Minnesota

Professor Anthony Baxter,
University of Tennessee

Professor Ralph B. Bisland, Jr.,
University of Southern Mississippi

Professor Angela S. Blas,
SUNY Farmingdale

Professor Harvey R. Blessing,
Essex Community College

Professor Herbert W. Bomzer,
Fordham University

Blake Carter,
NCR Corporation

Professor Daniel Doud,
University of Pittsburgh

Professor Margaret Easter,
Missouri Western State College

Professor Donald Gaitros,
Baylor University

Professor Rachelle S. Heller,
George Washington University

Professor Charles Herbert,
Business Community College of Philadelphia

Professor John Hirschbuhl,
University of Akron

Professor Peter Irwin,
Richland College

Professor Marcy L. Kittner,
University of Tampa

Professor Daniel W. Kohtz,
University of Nebraska-Omaha

Professor Hans Lee,
Michigan State University

Professor Ruth Malmstrom,
Somerset Community College

Professor Beth McBride,
East Texas State University

Professor Michael E. McLeod,
East Carolina University

Professor Jane Moore,
Texas Wesleyan College

Professor William Moos,
Dallas Baptist College

Professor Barbara B. Owens,
Marcy College

Professor Leonard Presby,
William Paterson State College

Professor Harold Sackman,
California State University, Los Angeles

Professor Marian Sackson,
Pace University

Professor Tom C. Scharnberg,
Tarrant County Junior College

Professor Lynda Sloan,
Iona College

Professor Sandra Stalker,
North Shore Community College

Professor James R. Swanson, Sr.,
University of Florida, Gainesville

Professor Craig Varnell,
University of Texas at Arlington

Professor William Weber,
Southeast Missouri State University

Professor Frank Wright,
Cerritos College

Professor Wayne M. Zage,
Purdue University

MODULE 1

We are crossing the threshold of a new information age. No one knows how this new age will evolve, but it's certain that computer applications will bring about far-reaching changes in our lives. Although we're still feeling our way, we sense that if we are to have some control over our futures we need to know about computers—what they are, what they do, how they are put to use, and the impact they are currently having on the people and organizations in our society. An overview of all these topics is presented in this opening module. The other modules in the book consider these topics in greater detail.

BACKGROUND

1 LET'S GET STARTED

2 COMPUTERS AT WORK

3 THE COMPUTER IMPACT

CHAPTER 1

LET'S GET STARTED

THE DAWN OF A NEW AGE

Imagine for a moment a world where computers exist only in the minds of a few scientists and engineers. Pencils, typewriters, and mechanical calculators are available in this world to help people process facts and figures into useful information. For large processing jobs, there are even some electromechanical machines that can manipulate facts if they've been punched into paper cards. But most of what's done on earth today with computers cannot even be attempted in this imagined world.

As you've probably guessed, we're not describing some planet in a distant galaxy. Rather, we're simply outlining the situation here on earth about 40 years ago, just before the first computer was put into full operation. At that time, only a handful of pioneers had firsthand knowledge of computers.

(We'll identify some of them in the reading at the end of this chapter.) And things didn't change much for most people in the first decade following the introduction of computers. To most people growing up in the 1950s, the few large and expensive computers then available were scientific curiosities that would be used in special ways—ways that would have little direct impact on their lives.

But people growing up in the 1960s and early 1970s acquired a different perspective about computers. The few large computer systems of the 1950s were replaced during this period by tens of thousands of new systems that were more compact, more powerful, and less expensive than their predecessors. These computer systems continued to perform special scientific tasks—people marveled at their role in sending humans to the moon and back. But they were also preparing paychecks, computing taxes and other bills, and processing innumerable other jobs that directly affected people's lives. And during this time, millions joined the early pioneers in gaining firsthand knowledge of computer capabilities and limitations.

Although by 1975 computer systems were found in most medium-sized and larger organizations, they were still too expensive for small groups and individuals. But electronic advances were about to usher in a whole new category of computers—desktop-size machines with the power of earlier giants, at prices that individuals could now afford. A steady stream of these **personal computers** poured out in the late 1970s, and the stream became a flood in the 1980s.

Now, in the last half of the 1980s, personal computers by the tens of millions (and hundreds of thousands of larger systems) inhabit offices, factories, schools, homes, hospitals, government agencies, banks, and retail stores, as well as laboratories. Like automobiles and electricity, these systems exert a daily influence on all our lives that cannot be ignored. And in addition to these visible general-purpose systems, we also encounter other "invisible" special-purpose computers everywhere we turn—in our appliances, automobiles, and wristwatches. In fact, if all computers were suddenly to malfunction today, planes, trains, and many cars and elevators could not move, traffic lights and telephones would be useless, and our world would be plunged into confusion.

People today know that many computer uses, or *applications,* offer definite advantages. The accompanying photos outline a few of these benefits. (Keep in mind as you look at these photos that the machines are able to perform applications only because people have supplied them with detailed sets of instructions called **programs**.) But many people are disturbed by some aspects of computer usage. Some fear that their jobs will be taken over by computerized robots, some feel that they are being numerically coded and molded to fit the needs of cold and impersonal systems, and some worry that personal information about them that has been entered into these systems may be used against them.

The fact that a revolutionary invention like the computer can affect people in positive and negative ways should not come as a surprise. Remember how the harnessing of steam power led to the *Industrial Revolution,* which dramatically increased the amount of goods that could be produced by a worker. While these mass production efficiencies made some factory owners very rich, the assembly line brought deadening monotony and health hazards to thousands of workers. On balance, the Industrial Revolution was beneficial, but it did exact a human toll.

Because we live in a computerized world, we are often unaware of the benefits that computers bring to us daily. When we look at our digital watches, or withdraw cash from a 24-hour automatic teller machine (a), or visit a sick friend in a hospital (b), it's easy to see the benefits of computers because

[(a) Miriam Caravella/The Image Bank]

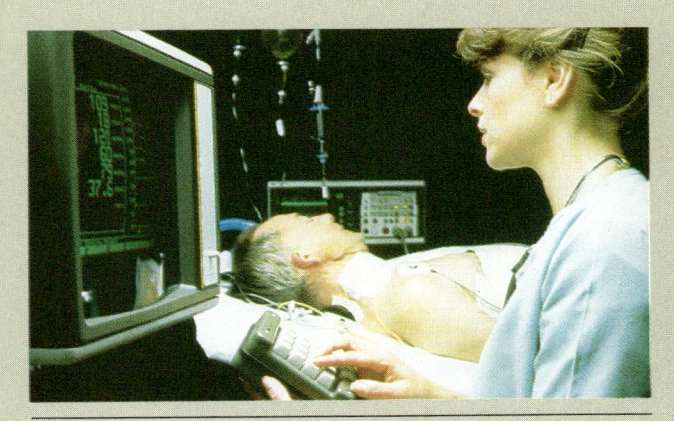

[(b) Courtesy Hewlett-Packard Co.]

[(c) Courtesy Western Union]

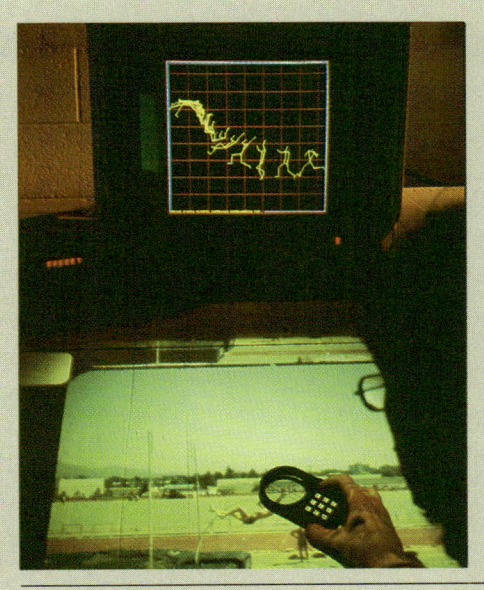

[(d) © D. Kirkland/Sygma]

[(e) © Don Kryminec/Photo Researchers, 1984]

we can watch them at work. Anyone who needs to deal with up-to-the-minute information would be lost without a computer (c), and many athletes now count on computerized analyses of their performances to give them an extra edge in competition (d).

But most of the benefits that computers bring us are invisible. Few of us see industrial robots in action (e), though they play an increasingly important part in manufacturing many of our favorite devices, including our cars, our TVs, our VCRs—and our pc's. Computers help people to design everything from computer circuits (f) to sports cars (g), and computer-generated graphics have opened up new worlds of artistic possibilities (h). Computers help farmers maximize their yields and as a result we pay less for our bacon (i). Whenever we travel, we rely on invisible computers that con-

8

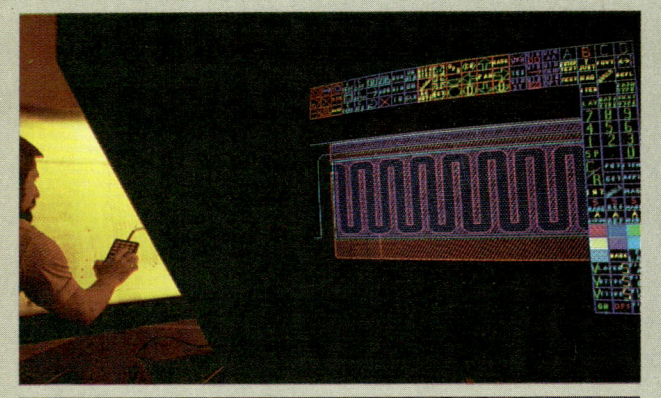

[(f) © Dan McCoy/Rainbow]

[(i) © David Burnett/Contact Press Images, 1984]

[(g) © Hank Morgan/Photo Researchers]

[(j) © Roger Tully/Black Star]

[(h) © Digital Effects]

[(k) © Dennis Brack/Black Star, 1983]

trol everything from traffic lights to the planes and trains we ride in (j). And a vast array of Defense Department computers forms an electronic shield that defends us against thermonuclear attack (k).

Even though some of these computer applications may worry us, we can be certain that computers perform them more quickly, reliably, and accurately than the systems they have replaced. And many computer applications are opening new vistas of education, information, and joy to millions of people of all ages in this whole new computerized world we already live in (l).

[(l) © Lawrence Migdale, 1984]

The Need for Computer Literacy

We're now at the dawn of another era—an era when the emphasis is shifting from the physical labor required by the Industrial Revolution to the mental labor needed to sustain the new *Information Revolution*. Just as gears, gas engines, and electric motors extend our physical power, so do today's computers give us the information we need to extend our thinking power. For the first time, our society is keyed to a resource—information—that's renewable and self-generating. Scientific information is now doubling every 5½ years, but in the years ahead a larger group of scientists, working with increasingly powerful information systems, probably will double the available scientific knowledge every 2 years. Thus, in addition to mass-producing goods, we're now mass-producing information, and this knowledge is the driving force in our economy.

No one knows now how this new information age will evolve. When the first automobiles came clattering over the cobblestones, few people dreamed that their lives would be totally transformed by these awkward machines. Fewer still could imagine themselves speeding over a nationwide network of superhighways at a mile a minute in air-conditioned comfort, at a price that just about everybody could afford. Computer usage will bring about equally far-reaching qualitative changes in our future, and we, too, can barely imagine what those changes will be. We're still feeling our way. Most of us are still puzzled by computer technology, and some feel uncomfortable with it. But we sense that we'll need an understanding of this technology in the years ahead if we are to control it, integrate it into our lives, and turn it to humane ends. In short, we realize that we have a need for **computer literacy**—a need to know about computers and to know when and how to use them so that we can function effectively in an information-rich society.

The Purpose of This Book

Since a broad familiarity with computers is just what you'll need in the years ahead, *the purpose of this book* is to acquaint you with *all four* of the following related areas of knowledge required for computer literacy:

1 *Knowing what computers are.* You should understand the organization, capabilities, and limitations of the various machines, or **hardware,** that make up a modern computer system.

2 *Knowing what computers do.* You should be familiar with some of the more common uses, or **applications,** of computers in today's society. The focus of this book will be on the types of applications used in many areas of society.

3 *Knowing how computer systems are put to work.* You need an understanding of how to use computers, and you need to know the general analysis, design, and program preparation procedures that must be carried out in order to produce written programs of instructions, or **software.** As you've seen, these programs cause the hardware to function in a desired way to process applications. Like television programs and musical scores, computer programs enable people to put lifeless instruments to use.

4 *Understanding their impact.* You should be aware of how individuals and organizations may be affected by present and future computer applications.

How This Book Is Organized

To provide a well-rounded introduction to these four related topics, this text is organized into modules. An overview of *all four areas* of knowledge mentioned above is presented in the three chapters of this Background Module. You should read Chapters 1 through 3 in sequence, but once you've completed them, you can then turn immediately to *any of the other modules.* Further hardware and software details are discussed in Modules 2 and 3, computer applications are spread throughout the book, and the social impact of these applications is outlined in Module 4. We'll begin in the next section with some background information about the computer itself. You'll be surprised at how much you know already and by what you'll learn.

CHAPTER 1

LOOKING AHEAD

The information in this chapter will enable you to:

- Understand your need for computer literacy
- Define the term "computer" and outline some of its capabilities
- Outline the activities involved in data processing and the data processing operations that computers can perform
- Identify the hardware components in a basic computer system and describe the functions of each component
- Explain how a computer can accept and process data, and produce output results, by following the detailed set of instructions in a stored program
- Describe some of the advances that have been made in computer hardware and software, outline ways in which computer systems may differ, and discuss some limiting factors in their use

CHAPTER OUTLINE

LOOKING AHEAD
WHAT'S A COMPUTER?
Speed and Accuracy Capabilities
Processing Capabilities
COMPUTER SYSTEM ORGANIZATION
The System Concept
Organization of Computer System Components
THE STORED PROGRAM CONCEPT: AN EXAMPLE
Processing the Beautification Charges
COMPUTER SYSTEMS TODAY: ADVANCES, DIFFERENCES, AND LIMITATIONS
Computer Advances
Computer Differences
Computer Limitations
Feedback and Review 1
LOOKING BACK

WHAT'S A COMPUTER?

You know that a computer can perform arithmetic operations. But it's much more than just a fast calculator. It's also a machine that can choose, copy, move, compare, and perform other nonarithmetic operations on the many alphabetic, numeric, and other symbols that we all use to represent things. The computer manipulates these symbols in the desired way by following an "intellectual map" called a program. A **program,** we've seen, is a detailed set of instructions that directs the computer to function in a specific way to produce a desired result. And a **computer** is a fast and accurate electronic symbol (or data) manipulating system that's designed to automatically accept and store input data, process them, and produce output results under the direction of a step-by-step stored program of instructions. In the following pages we'll examine the elements in this definition in more detail. At the same time, we'll cover some important computer and data processing concepts.

Speed and Accuracy Capabilities

A computer works one step at a time. It can add and subtract numbers, compare letters to determine alphabetic sequence, and move and copy numbers and letters. There's nothing profound in these operations. What's significant is the computer's *speed*. Measured in the units shown in Figure 1-1, the time required for computers to execute such basic operations as adding and subtracting varies from a few **microseconds** for small machines to 80 **nanoseconds** or less for large ones. Thus small computers can perform hundreds of thousands of operations in a second (Figure 1-2), while larger systems can complete many millions.

In addition to being very fast, computers are also very *accurate*. The circuits in a computer have no mechanical parts to wear and malfunction.

FIGURE 1-1

The minuscule units used to measure computer speed.

Unit of time	Part of a Second	Interpretation
Millisecond (ms)	One-thousandth (1/1000)	A baseball pitched at a speed of 95 miles-per-hour (mph) would move less than 2 inches in a millisecond.
Microsecond (μs)	One-millionth (1/1,000,000)	A spaceship traveling toward the moon at 100,000 mph would move less than 2 inches in a microsecond.
Nanosecond (ns)	One-billionth (1/1,000,000,000)	There are as many nanoseconds in one second as there are seconds in 30 years, or as many nanoseconds in a minute as there are minutes in 1,100 centuries.
Picosecond (ps)	One-trillionth (1/1,000,000,000,000)	Electricity (and light) travels at 186,000 miles-per-second or about 1 foot in a nanosecond. In a picosecond, electricity would move less than 1/50th of an inch. A picosecond is to a second what a second is to 31,710 years.

13

The instructions for the savings accumulation program are located on a small disk that must be inserted into the computer before processing can begin.

```
***SAVINGS ACCUMULATION SIMULATOR***
INITIAL SAVINGS AMOUNT? 2000
INTEREST RATE ON SAVINGS (PERCENT)? 10
NUMBER OF YEARS? 3
      SAVINGS ACCUMULATION MODEL
  YEAR              SAVINGS
   NO.              BALANCE
    1               2,200
    2               2,420
    3               2,662
MORE DATA (YES, NO)?
```

Computer Visual Display Screen

User keys in responses to program queries

FIGURE 1-2

People often like to evaluate many alternatives before making important decisions, and a computer can give them almost instant results. For example, a savings simulation program allows investors to answer "what if" questions by varying savings amounts, interest rates, and years to maturity. Dozens of savings alternatives can be quickly produced and evaluated. The computer's speed frees people to use their time more creatively. Today we can easily obtain information that could not have been produced at all a few years ago or that could have been prepared only after great human effort.

Performing their hundreds of thousands (or millions) of operations every second, these circuits can run errorless for days at a time. *If* the input data entering the computer are correct and relevant and *if* the program of processing instructions is reliable, *then* we can expect that the computer generally will produce accurate output. Perhaps you've heard the phrase **garbage in–garbage out,** or GIGO. Used often by people who work with computers, GIGO implies that "computer errors" can usually be traced to incorrect input data or unreliable programs—both caused by human, not computer, frailties.

Processing Capabilities

Computer processing involves manipulating the symbols that people use to represent things. As Figure 1-3 shows, we create, use, and manipulate many kinds of symbols that represent the facts and concepts of our lives. People have been using letters, numbers, and other "shorthand" symbols for thousands of years, and computer processing is simply the fastest and most accurate way of performing this familiar human task.

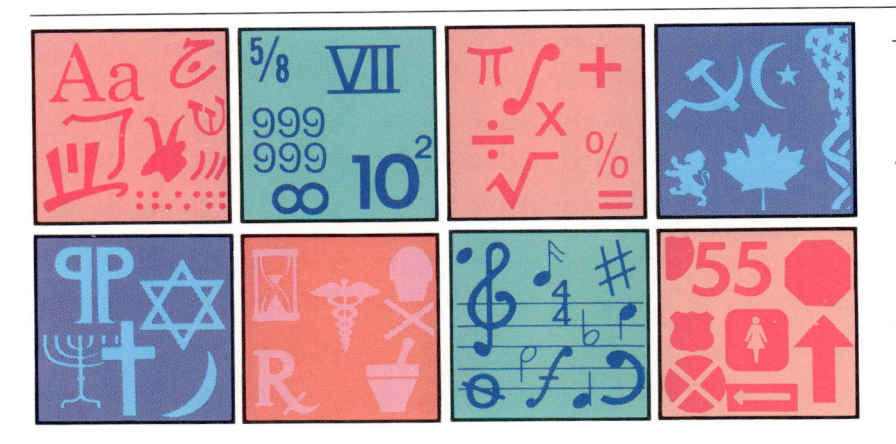

FIGURE 1-3

A few of the symbols used by people to communicate facts and concepts. Early computer experts made an important discovery: A machine that can accept, store, and process numbers can also manipulate nonnumerical symbols, if an identifying code number is assigned to each symbol. Thus the letter "A" can be represented by a code number, as can the addition symbol (+), and so on. Of course, someone must instruct the computer to manipulate the coded and stored symbols in a desired way, such as alphabetizing a stored list of names.

MODULE 1

14

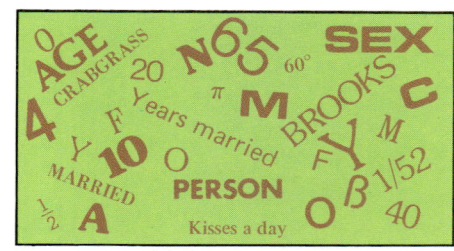

(a) Raw data input

Person	A	B	C
Age	10	65	20
Kisses a day	0	4	40
Sex	M	M	F
Married	N	Y	Y
Years married	0	40	1/52

(b) Selected data have been arranged (processed) in an ordered form to produce information

FIGURE 1-4

Processing converts raw data into information. All information consists of data, but not all data produce specific and meaningful information. Additional data may add new dimensions to existing information. But the interpretation of data generally requires human judgment, and this varies from person to person. Thus what's information to one person may only be raw data to another.

Data versus Information   The word "data" is the plural of datum, which means "fact." **Data**, then, are facts, the raw material of information. Data are represented by symbols, but they are not information except in a limited sense. As used in data processing, information is data arranged in an order and form useful to the people who receive it. That is, **information** is relevant knowledge, produced as the output of data processing operations and acquired by people to enhance understanding and to achieve specific purposes. Figure 1-4 illustrates the distinction between data and information, and Figure 1-5 shows you that information is the result of a transformation process.

Data Processing Activities   You can see in Figure 1-6 that **data processing** consists of three basic activities: capturing the input data, manipulating the data, and managing the output results.

1 *Capturing the input data.*   Data must be recorded or captured in some form before they can be processed. They may initially be recorded on paper **source documents,** as shown in Figure 1-6, or they may be captured by a **direct input device,** such as an automated teller machine, in a paperless, machine-readable form.

2 *Manipulating the data.*   One or more of the following operations may then have to be performed on the gathered data (see Figure 1-6):

(a) *Classifying.*   Organizing similar items into groups or classes is called **classifying**. Classifying is usually accomplished by assigning predetermined abbreviations or codes to the items being arranged. The types of codes used are *numeric* (postal Zip codes used for geographic classification), *alphabetic* (persons A, B, and C in Figure 1-4), and *alphanumeric* (the letters and numbers of the product code in the invoice in Figure 1-6).

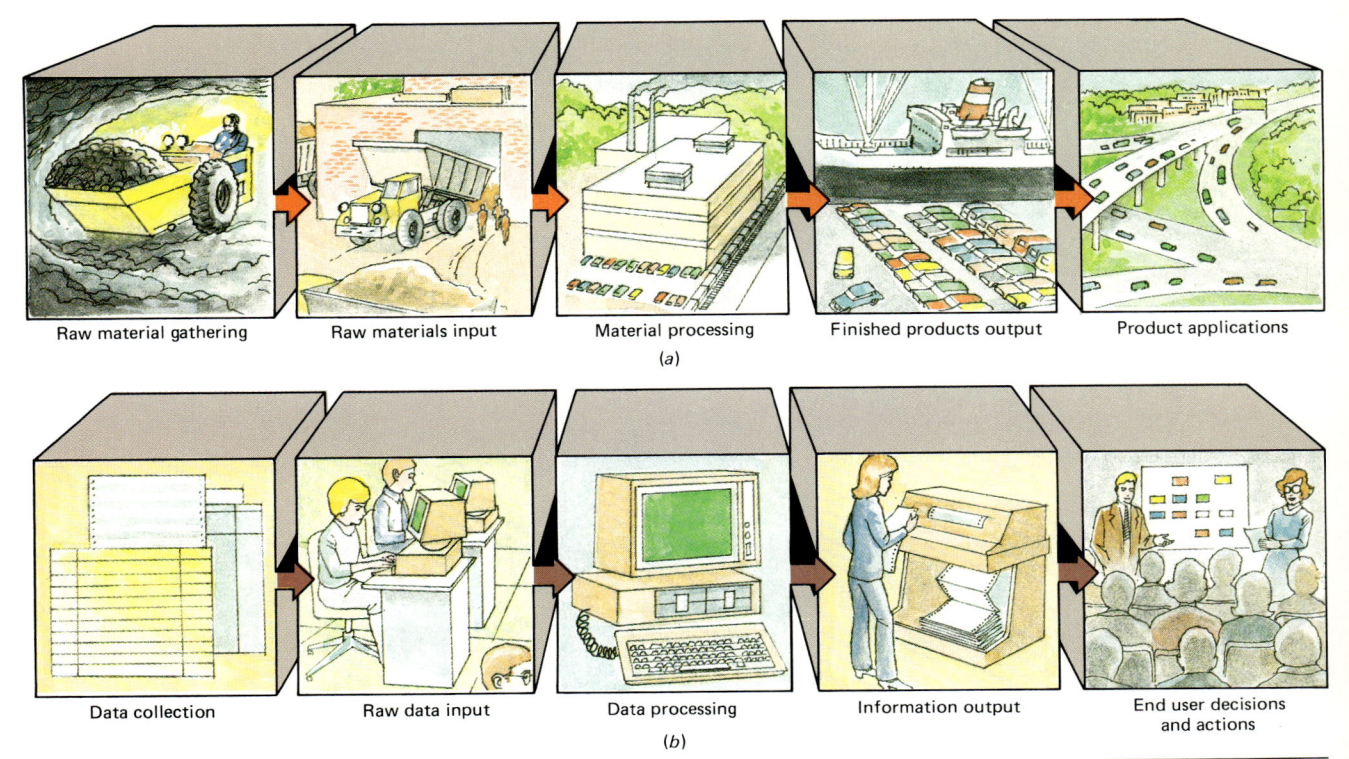

| Raw material gathering | Raw materials input | Material processing | Finished products output | Product applications |

(a)

| Data collection | Raw data input | Data processing | Information output | End user decisions and actions |

(b)

FIGURE 1-5

Just as raw materials are transformed into finished products by a manufacturing process, raw data are transformed into information by data processing. Products produced by a manufacturing process *(a)* have little value until they are used; similarly, information produced by data processing *(b)* is of little value until it supports meaningful human decisions and actions.

(b) *Calculating.* Arithmetic manipulation of the data is called **calculating** and is a common processing activity.

(c) *Sorting.* Usually, it's easier to work with data if they are arranged in a logical sequence. Examples include first to last, biggest to smallest, oldest to newest. Arranging classified data in such a sequence is called **sorting**.

(d) *Summarizing.* Reducing masses of data to a more concise and usable form is called **summarizing**. The pie chart shown in Figure 1-6 is one of the many types of computer-generated graphs and charts that are frequently produced for this purpose.

3 *Managing the output results.* Once data have been captured and manipulated, one or more of the following operations shown in Figure 1-6 may be needed:

(a) *Storing and retrieving.* Retaining data for future reference is **storing**. Recovering stored data and/or information is the **retrieving** activity.

(b) *Communicating and reproducing.* Transferring data from one location or operation to another, for use or for further processing, is **data communication**—a process that continues until information in a usable form reaches the final user. Sometimes, of course, it's necessary to copy or duplicate data. In Figure 1-6, this **reproduction** activity is done by a machine.

1 CAPTURE

The input data must be captured in some form. In this case, a *source document*—a sales invoice—is used, and the data are then keyed into a machine-usable form for processing.

GREEN THUMB NURSERY
Invoice No. 1001

Date	Salesperson	Customer No.	Terms
4/2/8x	J. Alan	10827	30 days

To: Johnson Food Marts, Inc.
4747 East 47th St.
Portland, OR 88888

Quantity	Product Code	Description	Unit Price	Amount
180	P16	Azalea	5.75	$1,035.00
115	P41	Boxwood	3.95	454.25
85	P119	Peony	2.90	246.50
15	C77	12-8-8 Fert.	4.15	62.25
			Total	$1,798.00

2 MANIPULATION

After data have been entered into a computer, they may then be evaluated and arranged in various ways.

Nursery sales results may be organized by product categories (plants, lawn equipment, chemicals), salespersons, customers, or by any other classification useful to managers. In this example, *numeric* (customer numbers), *alphabetic* (salespersons names), and *alphanumeric* (product items) codes are available from sales invoices to classify sales results. A total monthly sales figure has been calculated.

Salespeople could be presented in an alphabetical sequence, but in this case they've been sorted according to the dollar sales volume produced. Numeric sorting is common in computer-based processing systems because it's usually faster than alphabetic sorting.

It's often desirable to replace masses of data with summarized information that's easier to interpret and analyze. For example, the computer can produce this pie chart that summarizes the percentage of the total monthly sales produced by each type of product in the nursery's line.

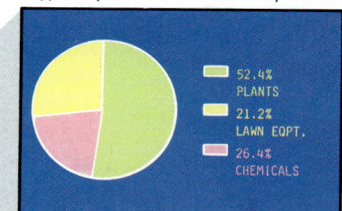

MONTHLY SALES BY TYPE OF PRODUCT

Product Line	Monthly Sales
Plants	$22,676.14
Lawn Eqpt.	$ 9,188.61
Chemicals	$11,414.49
Total	$43,279.24

MONTHLY SALES BY SALESPERSON

Salesperson	Sales
A. Forsyth	$12,449.11
C. Mediate	$11,817.77
J. Alan	$ 9,766.35

52.4% PLANTS
21.2% LAWN EQPT.
26.4% CHEMICALS

CLASSIFYING AND CALCULATING   SORTING   SUMMARIZING

STORING

RETRIEVING

COMMUNICATING

REPRODUCING

Data may be stored on small magnetizeable disks of the type shown here, but larger magnetic disks as well as paper, microfilm, tapes, optical disks, and other storage media are commonly used. A computer can easily retrieve data stored on these media.

Data may be communicated electronically to other locations, or they may be reproduced by printers or other machines.

3 MANAGING OUTPUT

Data that have been captured and manipulated may need to be managed in these ways.

CHAPTER 1

17

Computer Processing Operations   The following four operations are the only ones that a computer can perform, but they enable computers to carry out the data processing activities we've just described.

1   *Input/output operations.*   A computer can accept data (input) from and supply processed data (output) to a wide range of input/output devices. Such devices as keyboards, display screens, and printers make human-machine communicating possible.

2   *Calculation and text manipulation operations.*   Computer circuits perform calculations on numbers, and they are equally able to manipulate the nonnumerical letters and other symbols used in words and sentences.

3   *Logic/comparison operations.*   The computer also has the ability to perform logic operations. As you can see at the top of Figure 1-7, when we compare two data items represented by the symbols A and B, there are only three possible outcomes: (1) A is *less than* B (A < B); (2) A is *equal to* B (A = B); or (3) A is *greater than* B (A > B). The computer is able to perform a simple comparison and then, depending on the result, follow a *predetermined branch*, or course of action, to complete its work. This simple ability to

---

WINDOW 1-1

COMPUTER FINGERS A KILLER

When California police identified the prime suspect in the "Night Stalker" murders, the hero of the story was a computer that matched a fingerprint found on a stolen car.

Matching tiny data from fingerprints found at crime scenes to prints on a file, the NEC Automated Fingerprint Identification System (known as CAL-ID) took 3 minutes to do what might take a human analyst months or even years to do by hand. And it was the computer's first case.

Since installing their computer, San Francisco police have tripled the number of identifications. According to Sgt. Bob Dagitz, head of the San Francisco Crime Scene Investigations unit, the computer has enabled the police to identify perpetrators who would never have been caught under the old system. In cases where investigators have no suspects to narrow the field and must rely solely on fingerprints, the computer has made almost as many identifications in a month as human analysts have made in a year.

Investigators used to identify fingerprint traits like whorls, arches, and loops to narrow the field, then dig through files one at a time, comparing prints to make the identification. Dagitz estimated that one person working 8 hours a day would take 33 years to manually compare a single fingerprint to the more than 300,000 cards the department has on file. The computer does it in an hour.

The CAL-ID computer consists of a fingerprint reader and video screens where investigators can take a closer look at the ridges that form patterns. The investigator places a photograph or a tracing of a fingerprint in the reader, which relays the pattern into the computer's memory.

With red dots, the computer marks the "minutiae points" that distinguish a fingerprint from any other, then links the dots together. The investigator then enters any information known about the person to whom the fingerprint belongs—sex, race, and approximate age. The search takes anywhere from 1 minute to over an hour, depending on how much information the investigator enters, and the system produces a list of candidates. The computer scores the candidates by how many minutiae points coincide, and the investigator can tell from the scores whether the fingerprint matches any on the list. But it still takes a human check to make an absolute identification.

Excerpted from "Computer Fingers Bad Guys," *Gannett Westchester Newspapers*, September 28, 1985. Used by permission of the Associated Press.

⬅ **FIGURE 1-6** *(facing page)*

Data processing activities.

FIGURE 1-7

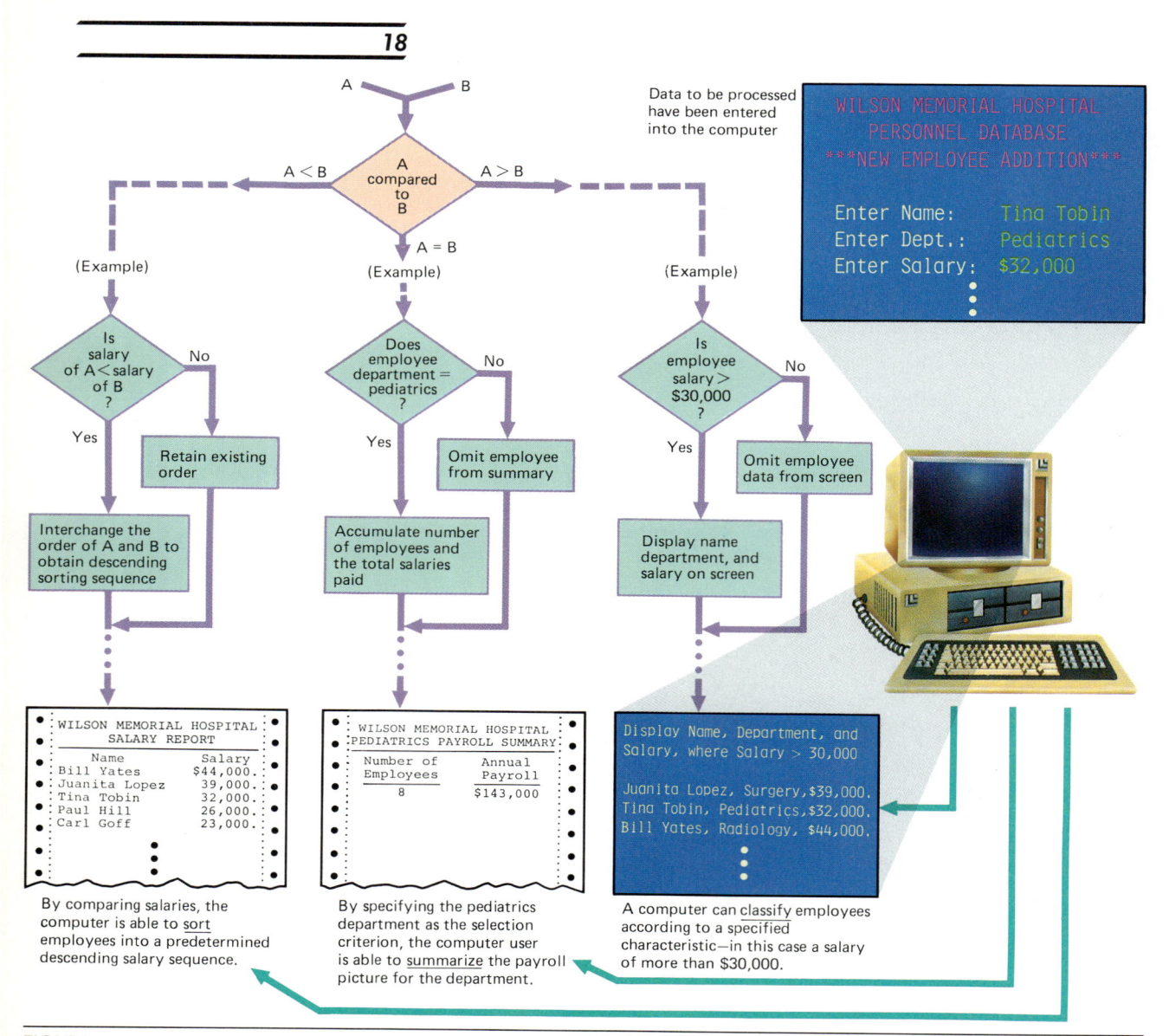

A computer can compare two items and then take an appropriate action branch depending on the outcome.

By comparing salaries, the computer is able to sort employees into a predetermined descending salary sequence.

By specifying the pediatrics department as the selection criterion, the computer user is able to summarize the payroll picture for the department.

A computer can classify employees according to a specified characteristic—in this case a salary of more than $30,000.

compare is an important computer property, because more sophisticated questions can be answered by using combinations of comparison decisions.

4   Storage and retrieval operations.   Both data and program instructions are stored internally in a computer. Once stored, both may be quickly called up, or retrieved, for use.

COMPUTER SYSTEM ORGANIZATION

We've seen that a computer is a fast and accurate symbol-manipulating *system* that's organized to accept, store, and process data and produce output results under the direction of a stored program of instructions. This section explains why a computer is a system and how a computer system is organized.

The System Concept

The term "system" is used in many different ways. Everyone is familiar with such expressions as "Professor Doldrum has an impossible grading system" or "Marty has a system for betting on the horses." But for computer users, a **system** is a group of parts that are integrated for the purpose of achieving some objective. The three following characteristics are key:

1 *A group of parts.* A system has more than one element. A steering wheel is not a system, but it's a vital part of a familiar system called an automobile.

2 *Integrated parts.* A logical relationship must exist between the parts of a system. Mechanical and electronic systems, such as washing machines and video games, have many components that work together.

3 *A common purpose of achieving some objective.* The system is designed to accomplish one or more goals. All system elements should be tied together and controlled so that the system goal is achieved.

Since a computer is a group of integrated parts that have the common purpose of performing the operations called for in the program being executed, it qualifies as a system.

Organization of Computer System Components

Figure 1-8 shows the organization of the basic input, processor, and output elements found in most computer systems. Let's examine each system component in more detail.

Input Devices Computer systems use many devices for input purposes. As shown in Figure 1-9, some **input devices** allow direct human-machine communication, while others require data to be recorded on an input medium,

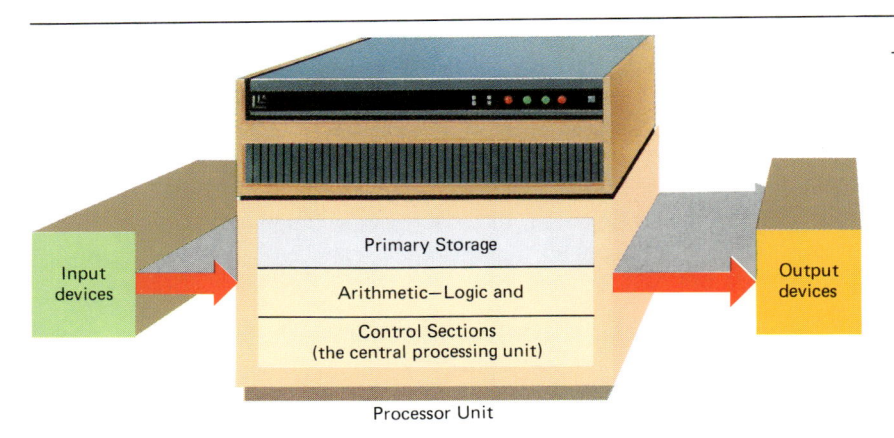

FIGURE 1-8

The basic organization of a computer system includes input, processor, and output elements. The processor unit, in turn, consists of primary storage, arithmetic-logic, and control sections.

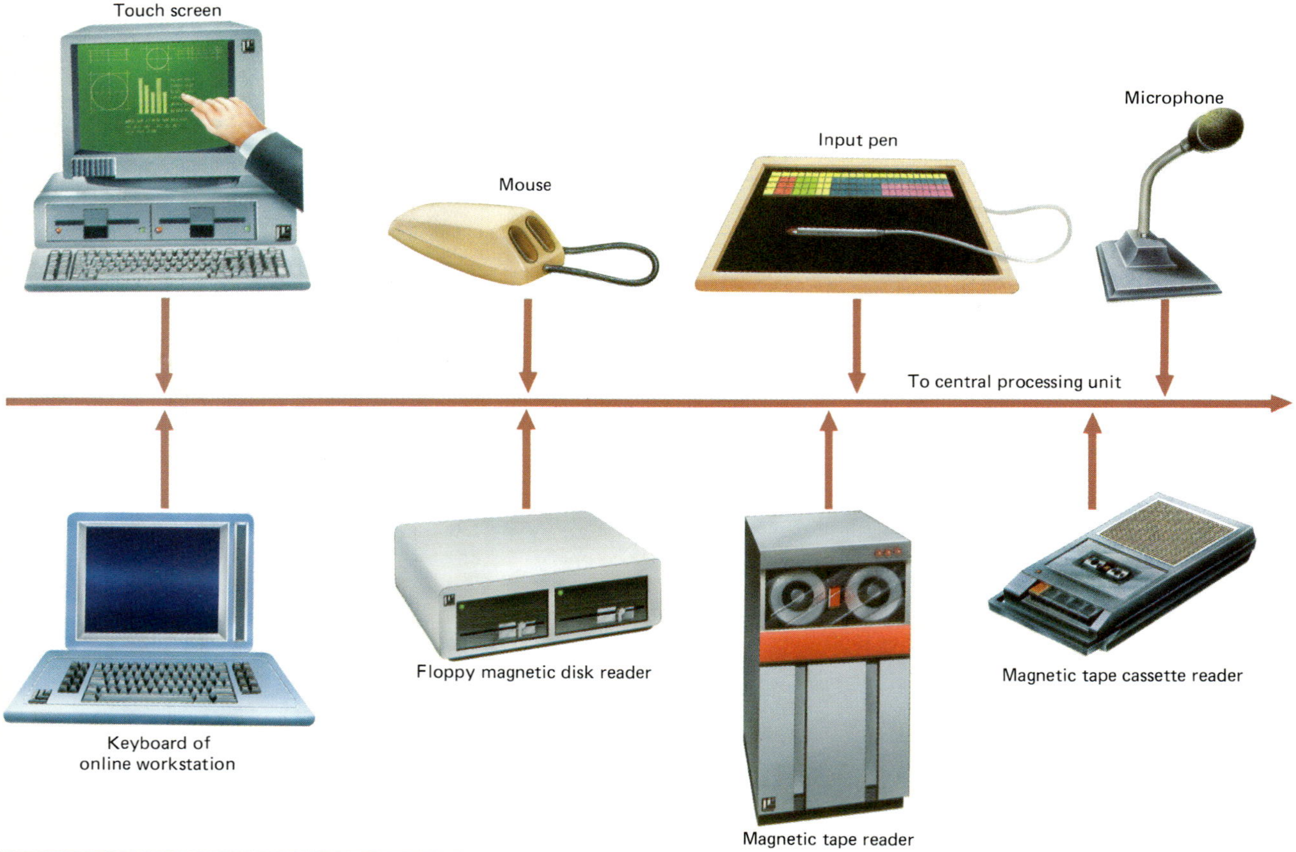

FIGURE 1-9

A few examples of input devices.

such as a magnetizeable material. Devices that read data recorded on specially coated, flexible plastic, or **floppy disks,** and **magnetic tapes** are often used. The keyboard of a workstation connected directly to a computer is an example of a direct input device. Other direct input devices—the mouse, input pen, touch screen, and microphone—are discussed in Chapter 5. All these devices are components used for interpretation and communication between people and computer systems.

Processor Unit   The heart of any computer system is the **processor unit.** As Figure 1-10 shows, there are three main sections found in this unit in a personal computer system. Note that these three sections aren't unique to personal computers: They're found in processors of all sizes.

1   *The primary storage section.* The **primary storage** (also called **main memory**) **section** is used for four purposes. Three of these relate to the data being processed (see Figure 1-10):

(a) Data are fed into an **input storage area** (see the red lines in Figure 1-10) where they are held until ready to be processed.

(b) A **working storage space** that's like a sheet of scratch paper is used to hold the data being processed and the intermediate results of such processing.

(c) An **output storage area** holds the finished results of the processing operations until they can be released.

(d) In addition to these data-related purposes, the primary storage section also contains a **program storage area** that holds the processing instructions (see the green lines in Figure 1-10).

The separate areas used for these four general purposes are not fixed by built-in physical boundaries in the storage section. Rather, they can vary from one application to another. Thus a specific physical space may store input data in one application, output results in another, and processing instructions in a third. The programmer writing the application instructions (or "housekeep-

FIGURE 1-10

The components in the processor unit of a personal computer system. Primary storage, arithmetic-logic, and control sections are found in processors of all sizes. The specific areas of primary storage used for a particular purpose (input storage, program storage, etc.) are *not* physically fixed. Rather, they vary depending on the application program. The dashed lines in the storage section are used to indicate this boundary flexibility. The black, green, and red lines show control, instruction, and data paths.

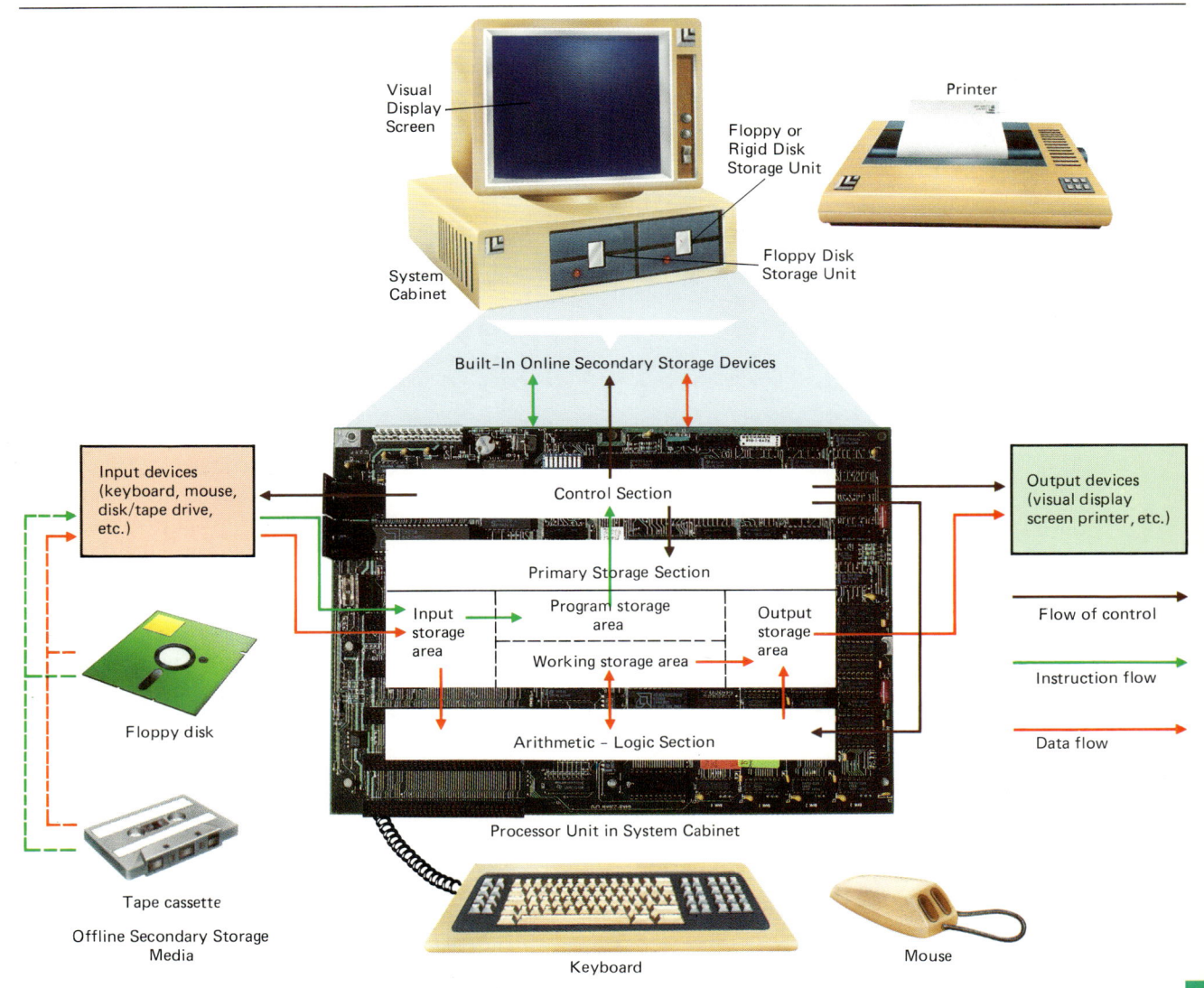

ing" software prepared by other programmers) determines how the space will be used for each job.

2 *The arithmetic-logic section.* The arithmetic-logic and control sections together make up the **central processing unit (CPU)**. All calculations are performed and all comparisons (decisions) are made in the **arithmetic-logic section** of the CPU (see Figure 1-10). Once data are fed into primary storage from input devices, they are held and transferred as needed to the arithmetic-logic section where processing takes place. No processing occurs in primary storage. Intermediate results generated in the arithmetic-logic unit are temporarily placed in a designated working storage area until needed at a later time. Data may thus move from primary storage to the arithmetic-logic unit and back again to storage many times before the processing is finished. Once completed, the final results are released to an output storage section and from there to an output device. The type and number of arithmetic and logic operations a computer can perform are determined by the engineering design of the CPU.

3 *The control section.* How does the input device know when to feed data into storage? How does the arithmetic-logic section know what should be done with the data once they are received? And how is the output device able to obtain finished rather than intermediate results? By selecting, interpreting, and seeing to the execution of program instructions, the **control section** of the CPU maintains order and directs the operation of the entire system. Although the control section doesn't process data, it acts as a central nervous system for the other data-manipulating components of the computer (see Figure 1-10). At the beginning of processing, the first program instruction is selected and fed into the control section from the program storage area. There it's interpreted, and from there signals (shown as black lines in Figure 1-10) are sent to other components to execute the necessary action. Further program instructions are selected and executed, one after another, until the processing is completed.

Secondary Storage Devices

To supplement the limited storage capacity of the primary storage section, most computers also have **secondary** (or **auxiliary**) **storage** capabilities. Secondary storage devices are connected directly to the processor—that is, they are **online** to it. They accept data and/or program instructions from the processor, retain them, and then write them back to the processor as needed to complete processing tasks. In Figure 1-10, these storage devices are built into the system cabinet of the personal computer. Both *floppy disks* and **rigid metal disks** are commonly used for personal computer secondary storage.

Rigid disks often are permanently sealed in their storage devices, but floppy disks are easily removed. The data and/or instructions stored on a floppy disk remain intact after the disk is removed, but since the processor no longer has direct and unassisted access to them, the stored items are said to be **offline** (see Figure 1-10).

Output Devices

Like input units, **output devices** are instruments of interpretation and communication between humans and computer systems of all sizes. These devices take machine-coded output results from the processor and convert them into a form that can be used by people (for instance, printed or displayed reports) or as machine input in another processing cycle. Typical

CHAPTER 1

machine input in this case takes the form of a series of magnetized spots on tapes or disks.

In personal computer systems (Figure 1-10), display screens and desktop printers are popular output devices. Larger and faster printers, many online workstations, and magnetic tape drives are commonly found in larger systems (Figure 1-11). Additional output devices are described in Chapter 6. The

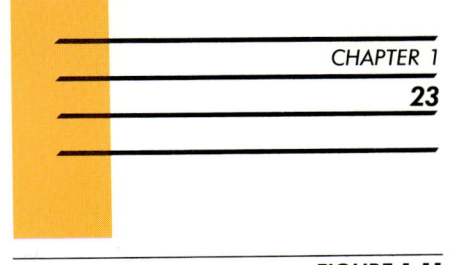

FIGURE 1-11

A summary of some components found in the larger computer systems used in organizations.

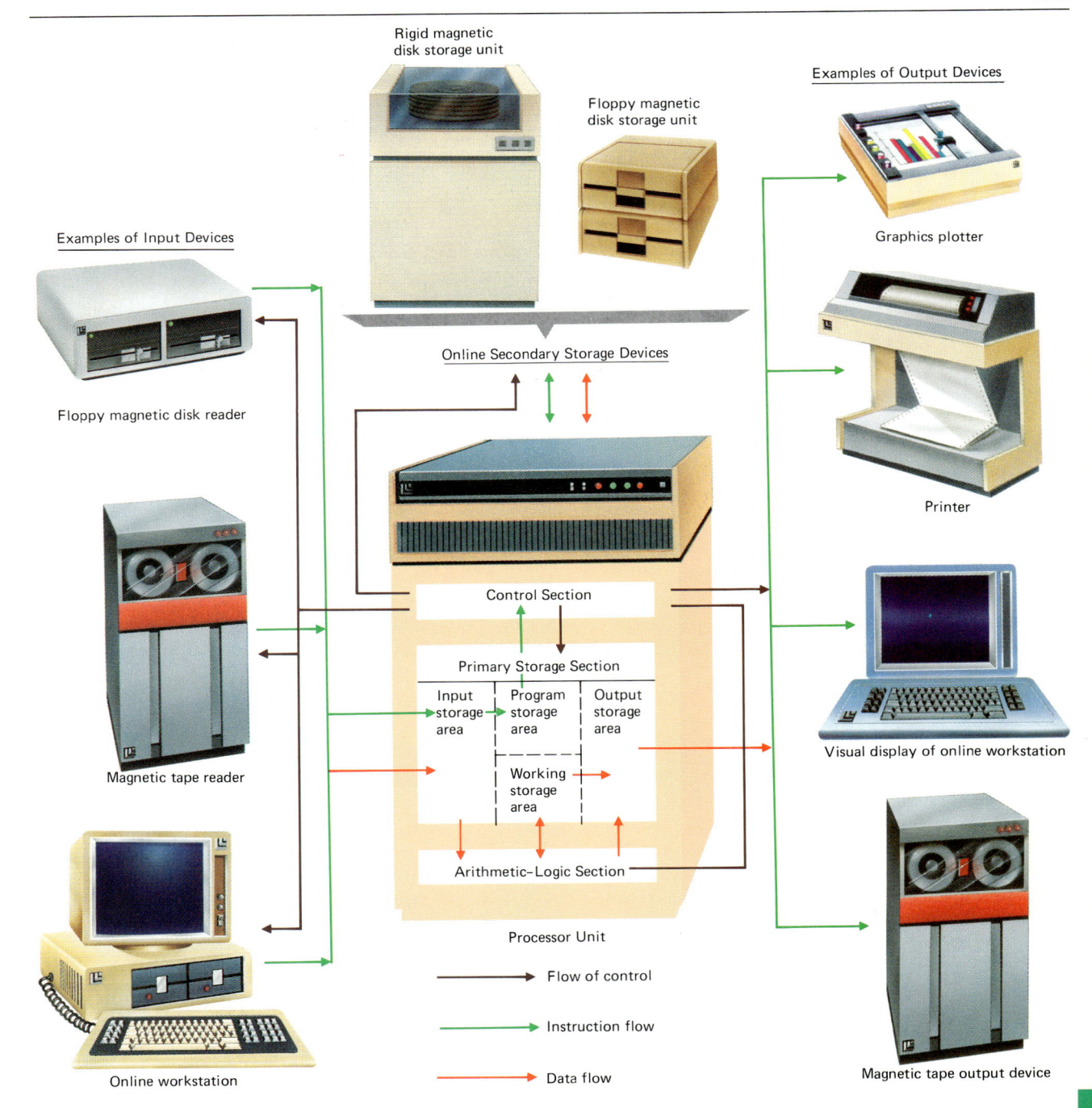

Examples of Input Devices

Floppy magnetic disk reader

Magnetic tape reader

Online workstation

Rigid magnetic disk storage unit

Floppy magnetic disk storage unit

Online Secondary Storage Devices

Control Section

Primary Storage Section

| Input storage area | Program storage area | Output storage area |

Working storage area

Arithmetic-Logic Section

Processor Unit

→ Flow of control

→ Instruction flow

→ Data flow

Examples of Output Devices

Graphics plotter

Printer

Visual display of online workstation

Magnetic tape output device

input/output and secondary storage units shown in Figures 1-10 and 1-11 are sometimes called **peripheral devices** (or just *peripherals*), because they are often located near the processor unit.

THE STORED PROGRAM CONCEPT: AN EXAMPLE

The computer system components just described can accept data, process them, and produce output results *only* by following the instructions contained in a stored program. We'll now see how such a program might be used to process a practical application. Let's assume that Elm Creek runs through the city of Calvin, and the city owns a small strip of land on each bank. The city council decides to clean up the channel, build a jogging path beside the stream, and beautify the city's property with shrubs, flowers, and other plants. Getting into the spirit, some owners of adjacent property offer to buy more plants if city workers will plant them. The property owners also agree to pay an additional charge of 6 percent of the price of the plants to help the city with planting costs. The city manager has approved this arrangement, and planting has started. A program is written to calculate the amount owed by property owners, and a small computer in the city manager's office is used to prepare the charges. The preparation of these charges is shown in Figure 1-12. (You'll want to follow the process shown in this figure as you read the explanation below.)

Processing the Beautification Charges

Input data for each property owner are first entered on job tickets. As shown in Figure 1-12, these facts are then entered via the computer keyboard and stored on a floppy disk. (For illustration purposes, the data are shown on the disk in Figure 1-12, but disk data are actually stored as invisible magnetic patterns.) The first charge statement is to be sent to Bill Byter. The program required to process the charges for Bill and other property owners is also stored on a disk. Let's assume that the 11 steps in this program have now been copied into the program storage area shown in Figure 1-12. After making sure that the disk containing the charge data is properly loaded into a disk device, the operator orders the system to run the program. Processing begins with the first instruction in the program storage area.

The initial program step feeds the first instruction ("Read name, address, quantity planted, and price per plant") into the control section of the processor where it's interpreted. Control signals are then sent to the disk device which executes the instructions and transfers Bill's charge data to an input storage area. (See the lines labeled "1" in Figure 1-12 for the interpretation and execution of this first step. Other program steps are similarly shown, but some lines have been omitted to simplify the figure.)

The control section *automatically* selects program instructions *in sequence* after the initial control setting unless specifically instructed to do otherwise. Thus, as soon as the first instruction has been dealt with, the control unit automatically begins interpreting the second step. This instruction directs the control unit to "read quantity planted into arithmetic-logic section." The control section isn't concerned that Bill has bought 33 plants (the

FIGURE 1-12 (facing page)

Only by following the steps in a stored program can a computer accept and process data and produce output results. In this example, the program is read from a floppy disk into primary storage. The input data to be processed are also found on a floppy disk loaded in the computer. Processing begins with the first program instruction. The program steps are executed automatically. Unless instructed to do otherwise, the computer executes the program steps in sequence.

25

City of Calvin
Job Ticket

Date: 10/2/8x   Number: 1415

Job Description:
Elm Creek Beautification Project

Job Charges:
Bill Byter
622 Hyatt Road
Calvin, Indiana 47631
33 plants @ $4.50 each

Input data from job tickets are keyed onto a floppy disk by the computer operator. The program to process the beautification charges may be stored on this same disk or on a separate disk.

```
City of Calvin
Elm Creek Beautification Project

To:
    Bill Byter
    622 Hyatt Road
    Calvin, Indiana 47631

    Total charges = $157.41
```

Bill Byter 622 Hyatt Road Calvin Indiana 47631   33 450

Control Section
(1) → (2) → (3) → (4) → (5) → (6) → (7) → (8) → (9) → (10) → (11)

Primary Storage Section

Program Storage Area

Input Storage Area	Program Storage Area	Output Storage Area
Bill Byter 622 Hyatt Rd. Calvin, Indiana 47631 33 450	1. Read name, address, quantity planted, and price per plant. 2. Read quantity planted into arithmetic – logic section. 3. Multiply quantity planted by price per plant to get net amount of plants. 4. Duplicate net amount in working storage area. 5. Multiply net amount by .06 to get planting charge. 6. Add planting charge to contents of working storage to get total amount of charges. 7. Move total charges to output storage area. 8. Print charge statement to name and address in input storage area, for amount in output storage area. 9. If last property owner, then branch to step 11. 10. Return control to step 1. 11. Stop processing.	$157.41

Working Storage Area

(4) → $148.50 ← (6)

Arithmetic – Logic Section

33 × $4.50 = $148.50 × .06 = $8.91 + $148.50 = $157.41

Flow of control

Instruction flow

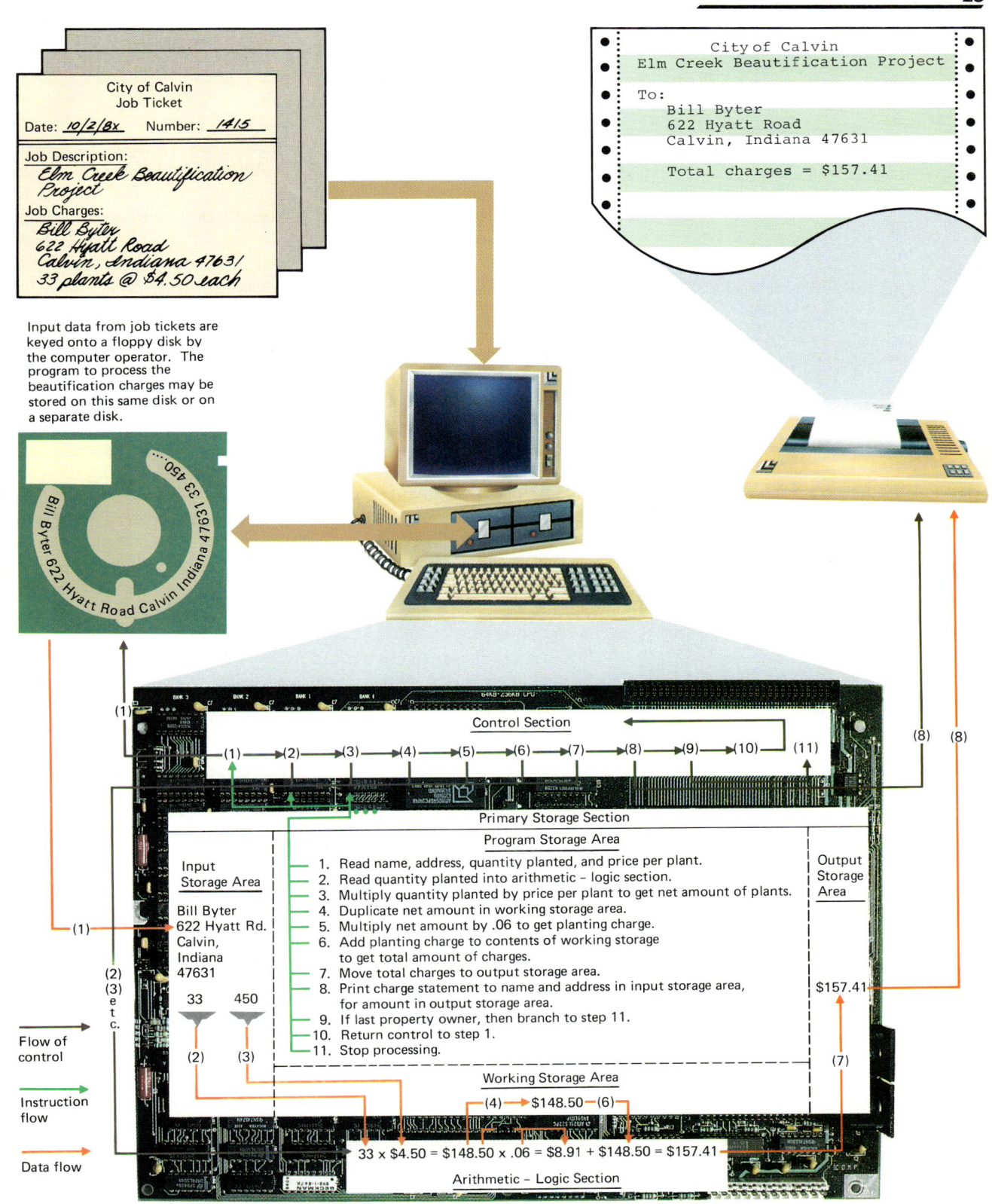

Data flow

next owner's order may differ). It merely carries out program orders, and so places the 33-plant figure in the arithmetic-logic section.

And so the processing continues in sequence: The quantity 33 is multiplied by the $4.50 price per plant to get the net amount of $148.50 (step 3); this amount is duplicated in the working storage area (step 4); the planting charge of $8.91 is found by multiplying the $148.50 plant total by the 6 percent rate (step 5); and this planting charge is added to the $148.50 amount that was temporarily stored in the working storage area to get Bill's total charges of $157.41 (step 6). After the total charges have been computed, the amount is transferred to the output storage area (step 7), and is then sent to a printer which is instructed to print Bill's charge statement (step 8).

At this point in the program a **branchpoint** is reached and a decision must be made. Is Bill the last owner to be charged? The computer follows an appropriate logic/comparison technique, which we'll discuss in Chapter 2, to answer this question. If Bill is the last to be charged, then program control jumps to step 11 and the processing stops. Since he's not the last owner, however, program control moves to the next instruction in the sequence (step 10). This step directs the control section to reset itself to instruction 1 so that the processing may be repeated for the next property owner. Thus the same instructions will be executed over and over again until all the charge statements are prepared. As the data for the next owner are read into the input storage area, they will erase and replace Bill's data just as recording music on a sound tape recorder erases any music that may have previously been stored on the tape. When all charge statements have been prepared, another program can be loaded into the computer and a new application can be processed. This ability to change programs quickly makes the computer a powerful general-purpose machine.

This example demonstrates most of the computer concepts and capabilities discussed in this chapter. To review:

● The various components of a computer system can manipulate and process data automatically and without human intervention by following the directions contained in a stored program of instructions.

● A computer has the built-in ability to obey different types of commands, such as READ, PRINT, MULTIPLY, and MOVE. (Every computer is designed with a particular set of these instruction types.)

● A computer follows program steps in sequence until explicitly told to do otherwise.

● A change in the sequence of steps can result from the computer's ability to follow different paths depending on the answer to a simple question.

As noted earlier, there's nothing difficult about these computer capabilities. What's impressive is the speed with which computer operations are performed and the accuracy of the resulting output.

COMPUTER SYSTEMS TODAY: ADVANCES, DIFFERENCES, AND LIMITATIONS

All computer systems contain hardware components for input, processing, and output. And they all run stored programs (software) to achieve results. We'll look now at the rapid advances being made in hardware and software. But you'll also see that computer systems differ in size and design, and they are subject to certain limitations.

Computer Advances

Hardware Advances

Figure 1-13 summarizes the gains that have been made in computer hardware. Note the dramatic reductions in computer *size*. Electronic components, such as transistors and diodes, are combined to form computer circuits. Thousands of these circuits are now integrated and packaged on a single **silicon chip** (Figure 1-14) a quarter of an inch square. As the size of computers has been reduced, their operating *speed* has increased (see Figure 1-13). In part, this is because smaller size means shorter distances for electric pulses to travel. Figure 1-13 also shows some of the incredible *cost* reductions associated with computer usage.

FIGURE 1-13

A summary of hardware advances. If automobile costs and technological developments had kept pace with the trends in computer hardware, you would now be able to buy a Rolls-Royce for $2.75, and you could drive it 3 million miles on a gallon of gas. The cost as well as the size of many basic computer components will continue to decline in the future while their speeds increase.

	Hardware Development Factors	1950	1960	1970	1975	1980's
Size factor	Number of circuits per cubic foot	1,000	100,000	10 million	1 billion	Many billions
Speed factor	Time to execute an instruction in the central processor	300 microseconds	5 microseconds	80 nanoseconds	25 nanoseconds	5 nanoseconds or less
Cost factors	Cost (in cents) to process 1 million basic computer instructions	2,800	100	2	.1	Less than .01
Cost factors	Cost (in cents) to provide storage for one binary number (a 0 or 1) in the central processor	261	85	5	.1	Less than .01
Storage capacity factors	Primary storage capacity (in characters) of the central processor	20,000	120,000	1 million	10 million	Greater than 100 million
Storage capacity factors	Characters of secondary online storage		20 million	Over 100 billion	Virtually unlimited	Virtually unlimited
Reliability factor	Mean (average) time between failures of some central processors	Hours	Tens of hours	Hundreds of hours	Thousands of hours	Years

FIGURE 1-14

A very large scale integrated chip nestles in a tiny blossom. Since the average number of chip components has doubled each year since 1965, it's now possible through such large-scale integration (LSI) to squeeze billions of circuits into a cubic foot. Nor is there any end in sight to these reductions. Just as yesterday's room-sized computers have been replaced by today's single LSI chips, so will the multiple-chip boards in today's large computers be replaced by a single superchip. Very large scale integration (VLSI) techniques will make tomorrow's circuits far more compact than today's. For example, VLSI chips like that pictured here store over 256,000 bits of information and contain over a half-million electronic devices. But by the 1990s a chip this size will contain 15 to 20 million devices. (Courtesy NCR Corp.)

Finally, Figure 1-13 gives you an idea of what has happened to computer *storage capacity* and *reliability* in the last few decades. The storage capacity of both primary and online secondary storage units has increased thousands of times over the years. And early computers that used to break down every few hours have been replaced by processors that can run for years without failure. For example, in some **fault-tolerant systems,** vital components, such as circuit chips, are backed up by standby spares. A failing chip is detected by a status-sensing device, and the chip is electronically and automatically replaced with its spare.

Software Advances   Great gains have also been made in the development of computer software. In the early 1950s, computer programmers had to write their program instructions in the special machine code numbers that computer circuits can recognize (for instance, the number "21" might mean "add"). Because these strings of numbers were tedious to prepare, they often contained errors. Special **programming languages** were then developed to permit programmers to write instructions in a form easier for humans to understand. For example, a language might permit the word "ADD" or the plus (+) symbol to be used in place of the number "21." But how can the machine execute instructions if they're in a language it can't understand? Just as an American and a German can communicate if one of them uses a translating dictionary, so, too, can the programmer and computer communicate if a separate translation program is employed. A **translation program** is one that transforms programming language instructions into the machine-language codes understood by computers. Almost all problem-solving programs prepared today are first written in languages preferred by people and are then translated into equivalent machine codes. (The translating process is detailed in Chapter 12 of the Software Module.) This easing of hu munication is one reason why computers are having such an impact on society today.

Another factor that's making computers more useful is the greater availability of applications programs. An **application program** is one that has been written to control the processing of a particular task. Although many applications programs must be custom-made for unique jobs, countless other common tasks found in homes, schools, and workplaces can be accomplished with generalized programs. Computer users can now choose from tens of thousands of these prewritten software packages—also called **applications packages** or **packaged programs.** For example, there are scores of these programs that allow users to create and edit text and produce output in graphic form.

Most packages for personal computers and larger machines perform *single* functions, such as processing words, playing games, or updating the records of customers, patients, students, and taxpayers. Since running these prewritten programs isn't nearly as painstaking as writing them, many people have found that a careful selection of available single-function programs has helped them master computer usage.

In addition to these single-function programs, many newer software products combine several functions in a single package. These **integrated software packages** make it possible to share data and move material between several applications. For example, the package's **word processing program** allows a manager to use the keyboard and display screen of a computer to create and edit the text of a sales report (Figure 1-15a). Sales data organized in columns and rows can be manipulated and analyzed by the use of the

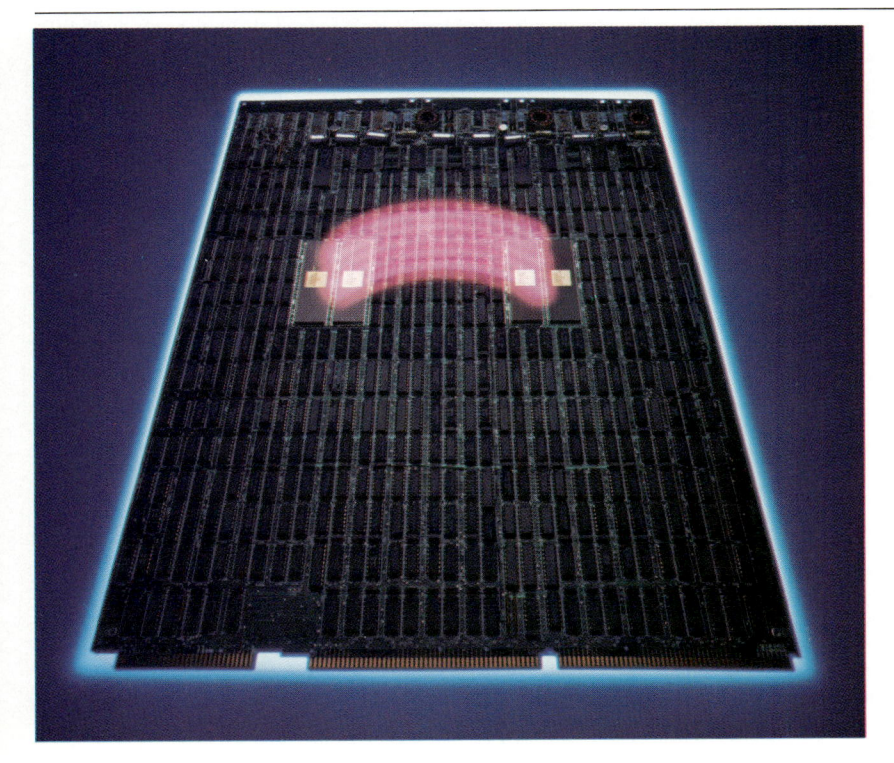

The Stratus/32 fault-tolerant computer checks each operation 8 million times a second, to trap errors before they can corrupt data. The violet arc in this photo of a Stratus/32 circuit board symbolizes the constant cross-checking between duplicate components. (Courtesy Stratus Computer, Inc.)

MODULE 1

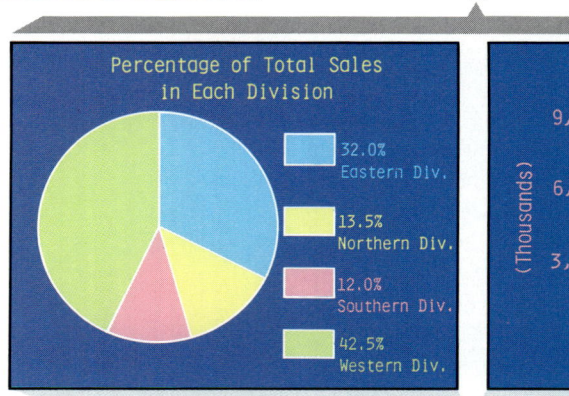

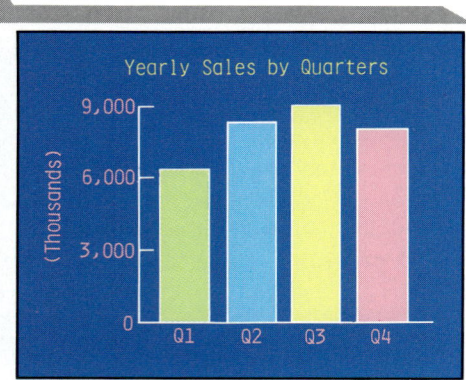

30

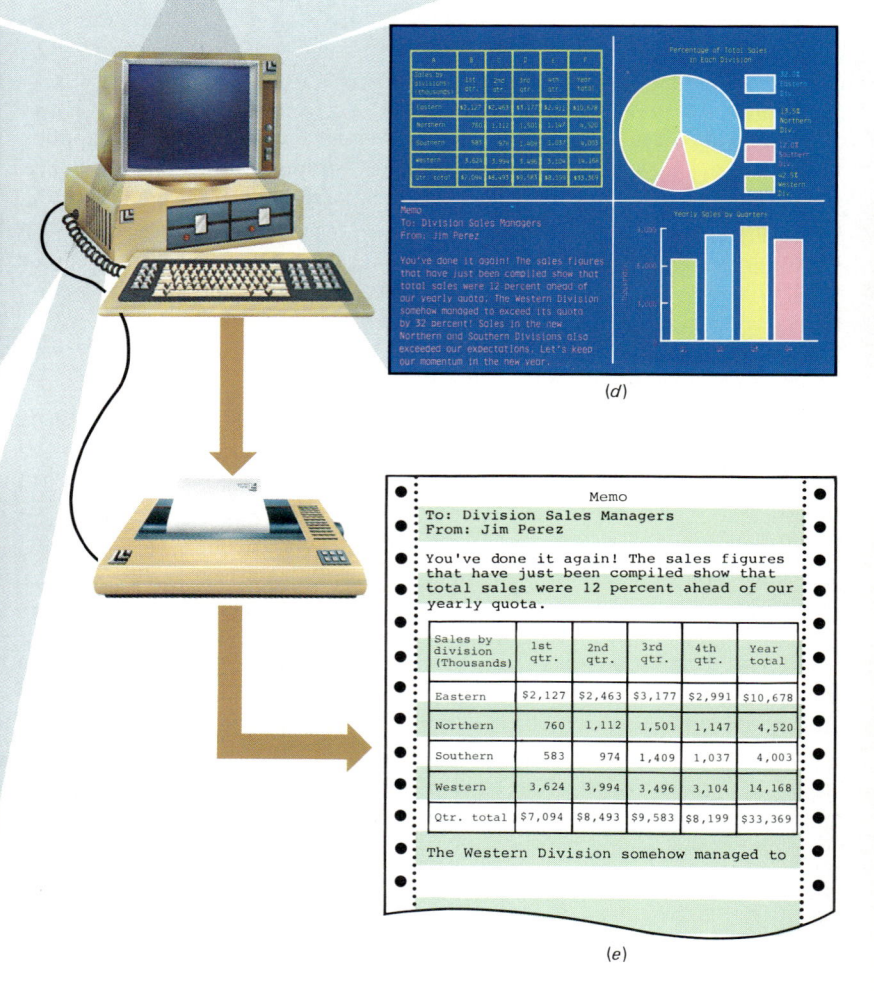

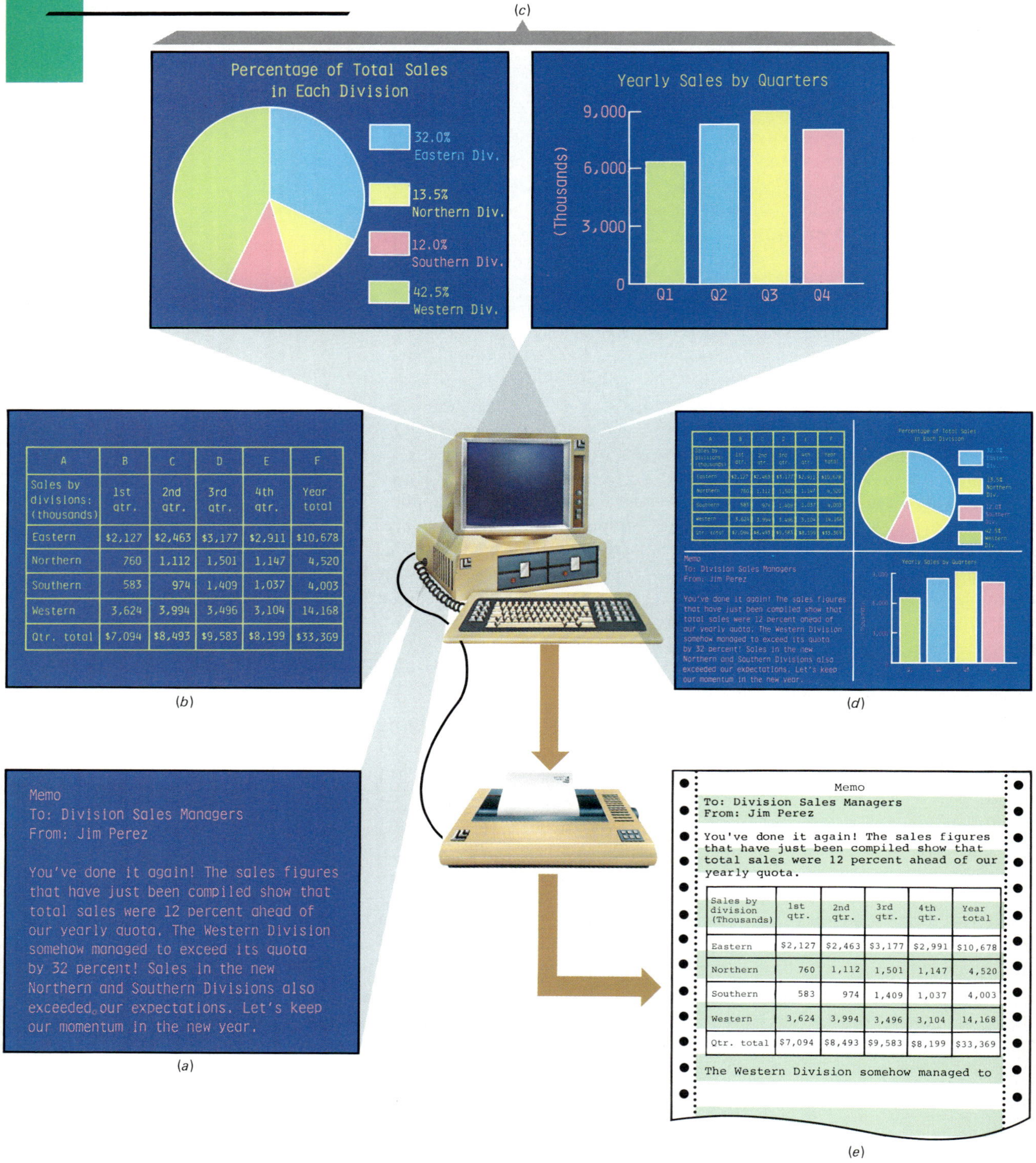

package's electronic **spreadsheet program,** and the results can also be displayed (Figure 1-15b). A **graphics program** in the package can then use the spreadsheet data to produce appropriate sales charts (Figure 1-15c). Further-

◀ FIGURE 1-15 *(facing page)*

(a) Text of a sales report prepared with a word processing program. *(b)* Sales data and formulas are entered by the user, and the spreadsheet program calculates the "Year total" column and the "Qtr. total" row. *(c)* A graphics software program can use the results produced by the spreadsheet program to generate pie charts, bar charts, and other easy-to-understand graphic presentations. *(d)* The screen can be separated into windows to permit the simultaneous display of the output produced by different programs in the integrated software package. *(e)* Printout of the completed report.

more, the current status of each application can be shown *simultaneously* in separate **windows,** or portions of the display screen, as shown in Figure 1-15*d*. Since it's possible to copy information from window to window, the manager can move figures and drawings from the spreadsheet and graphics windows to designated locations in the text window. A copy of the assembled report may then be printed (Figure 1-15*e*).

We've now seen that improvements in translation programs and applications packages have made for a greater use of computers in society. Advances in operating systems have also increased computer productivity and use. An **operating system (OS)** is an organized collection of software that controls the overall operation of a computer. The OS enables the system's hardware to work with the user's applications programs. It allows users to load applications programs into primary storage. It serves these programs by handling the "housekeeping" chores required to move data—between primary and secondary storage units, for example. And it functions in many other "transparent" ways, unseen by the user, that make it easier for people to use the system. In a personal computer system, OS programs are commonly stored on a floppy disk (thus the name **disk operating system,** or **DOS**). These programs are then activated, as shown in Figure 1-16. A further discussion of the functions of a modern OS is presented at the end of Chapter 10.

Computer Differences

Size Differences Modern computer systems vary in physical size from those that fill rooms to those with CPUs that can rest on the nail of your little finger. Generally, the larger the system, the greater is its processing speed, storage capacity, cost, and ability to handle larger numbers of more powerful input and output devices. While the smallest processors are typically used by one person at a time, larger systems can simultaneously serve the needs of many users. For example, a large computer at a health insurance company can process hundreds of customer policies while accepting medical claims from scores of online workstations located in hospitals and doctors' offices.

Systems on the low end of the size scale are called microcomputers or minicomputers. **Microcomputers,** or **micros,** (Figure 1-17) are the smallest units. They may be the tiny special-purpose devices dedicated to carrying out a single task, such as controlling an automobile's ignition system. Or they may be the more visible and familiar *personal computers,* ranging from note-

MODULE 1

32

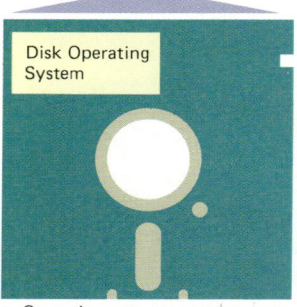

3 After the system is activated and the OS master program has been automatically loaded into primary storage, some symbols are often displayed on the screen to show users that the OS is "alive" and is ready to accept commands. In this example, the OS prompt symbols are A >.

1 Operating system programs are furnished by computer manufacturers and independent software vendors, and are commonly stored on a disk. Users may use the remaining space on the disk to store applications programs and data. A disk with an appropriate OS must be inserted into a disk drive before processing can be accomplished.

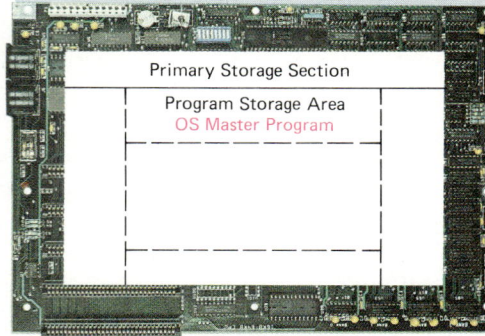

2 When the system is activated, an OS master program is automatically loaded into primary storage. It remains there during processing and copies other specialized OS programs from the disk into primary storage as they are needed.

FIGURE 1-16

An operating system helps people use computers in many ways, but the functions performed by an OS are generally "transparent," or invisible to users.

FIGURE 1-17

Laptop computers like this Hewlett-Packard Portable Computer *(left)* are especially popular with journalists and travelers, who use them to process words at any convenient time and place; the Apple Macintosh *(right)*, like most of today's pc's, can produce text and graphics with equal ease, is powerful and flexible, and can be quickly set up almost anywhere. (Courtesy Hewlett-Packard Co. and Apple Computer, Inc.)

FIGURE 1-18

Though it takes up no more room than a few filing cabinets, this Wang VS 100 super-minicomputer can support up to 128 workstations at once, along with various drives and printers. It typifies the power of today's superminis, and like many larger computers it belongs to a family of compatible machines of varying powers. (Courtesy Wang Laboratories, Inc.)

book size to desktop size, that we can use in countless ways. Microcomputers can perform the same operations and use the same type of instructions as much larger computers. **Minicomputers,** or **minis,** (Figure 1-18) are also small general-purpose systems, but unlike most micros they typically serve multiple users. They are usually more powerful and more expensive than micros, although the performance of some newer micros surpasses the capabilities of some older minis. In physical size, minicomputers vary from desktop models to units the size of small file cabinets.

Continuing up the size scale, **mainframe computers** (Figure 1-19) are systems that offer faster processing speeds and greater storage capacity than a typical mini. A whole series of mainframe models, ranging in size from small to very large, are generally lumped together under a *family designation* by

FIGURE 1-19

This IRS computer center, *(left)* with its Control Data 3500 surrounded by magnetic tape drives, is a classic mainframe computer arrangement. Control Data's current mainframe computer, the Cyber 180 Model 855 *(right)*, puts far more computing power in a trimmer package. (Courtesy Control Data)

mainframe manufacturers. There's quite a bit of overlap possible in the performance of larger minis (those called "superminis") and smaller mainframes.

Finally come the **supercomputers** (Figure 1-20), designed to process complex scientific applications. These are the largest, fastest, and most expensive systems in the world. You'll find more information on computers in each size category in Module 2.

Design Differences Most of today's computers are designed with *single* control, primary storage, and arithmetic-logic sections in the processor unit. Such computers are sometimes called **von Neumann machines** (Figure 1-21a) because they follow the design approach developed in the mid-1940s by John von Neumann and others. (See the reading following this chapter.) A problem with this traditional design is that instructions are interpreted and data are processed and stored in a *single* sequential stream. Since there's only a single channel to carry instructions from primary storage to the control section, and since only one data path is available between primary storage and the arithmetic-logic section, the processing speed—fast as it is—is limited by the speed of the circuits in these channels. Like constrictions in the pipes feeding crude oil to a refinery, these channels can limit the amount of processing achieved.

But there are ways this design, or **architecture,** can be changed to reduce the bottlenecks. For example, large systems may add additional control, storage, and arithmetic-logic elements so that *several* instructions can be processed simultaneously (Figure 1-21b). Such an architecture, in effect, combines two or more processor units into a **multiprocessor** system. And future designs may be able to execute billions of instructions per second by harnessing thousands (millions?) of micro-sized processors in *parallel assemblies* (Figure 1-21c).

Computer Limitations

The computer is one of the most powerful tools ever developed. But we've all

FIGURE 1-20

Today's supercomputers are monsters in computing capacity but modest in size; the blue cabinets behind these computer center workers house a Cray X-MP, one of the most powerful supercomputers currently available. Anyone who has worked arithmetic problems dealing with circles knows that pi (π) has a value of 3.1416. Actually, the true value is 3.14159 . . . and on and on and on . . . . How far on? A team of mathematicians at the University of Tokyo used a supercomputer to calculate pi to 16 million decimal places—a figure that would have required about 6,400 pages if it had been printed! Why bother to compute a gigantic number that nobody will ever see or use? Because "It's just so fascinating," said the editor of *Mathematics of Computation*. (Photo by Joe Gianetti courtesy Cray Research Inc.)

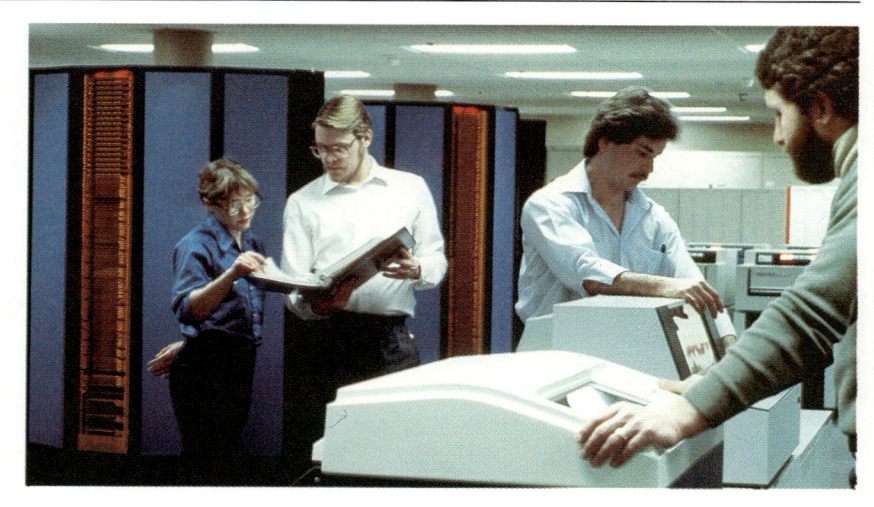

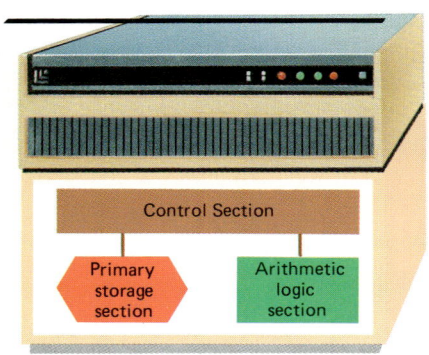

(a) The von Neumann machine has single control, primary storage, and arithmetic-logic sections. Instructions and data flow over single channels, which limits processing speed. But this design approach is the one generally used in small and medium-sized processors.

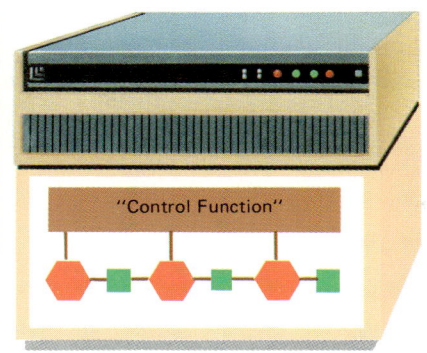

(b) Larger computers may have several powerful arithmetic-logic/storage systems under the guidance of a central control processor (the "control function" box shown here). This multiprocessor design is used to achieve faster computing speeds.

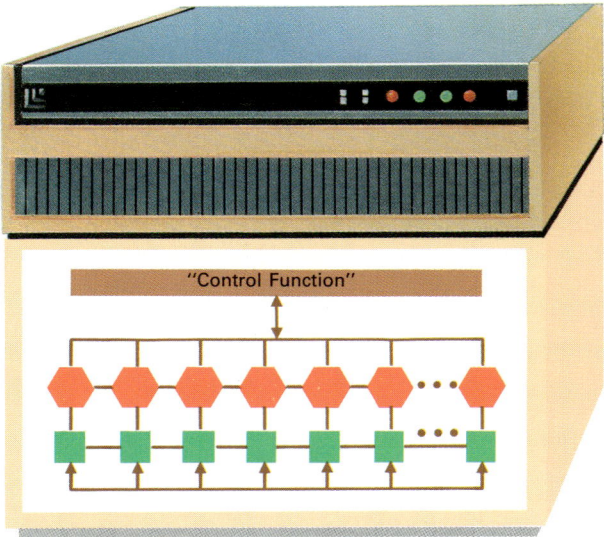

(c) Future computer designs may use huge numbers of processors in a parallel assembly. For example, Columbia University scientists are working on a project to arrange a million processors in a branching, treelike structure. But it's likely that the overall control of these processors will reside in a von Neumann machine (the control function box) that performs like the conductor of an orchestra.

FIGURE 1-21

Computers may differ in the design of the processor unit.

read articles similar to the one about the man who was treated for pneumonia and then charged by the hospital's computer for the use of the delivery room and nursery. Such "computer failures" may be amusing, but most such foul-ups happen because people fail to consider some basic computer limitations. Without reliable programs and sound logic, no computer system will perform adequately.

Programs Must Be Reliable The computer does what it's programmed to do *and nothing else*. This doesn't mean that it must be stupid. A clever program can be written to direct the computer to store the results of previous decisions. Then, by using the program's branching ability, the computer may be able to modify its behavior according to the success or failure of past decisions. But a program that has operated flawlessly for months can suddenly produce nonsense. Perhaps some rare combination of events has presented the system with a situation for which there's *no* programmed course of action. Or perhaps the course of action provided by the programmer contains an error that's just being discovered. Of course, a reliable program that's supplied with *incorrect data* may also produce nonsense.

Application Logic Must Be Understood The computer can only process jobs which can be expressed in a finite number of steps leading to a precisely defined goal. Each step must be specifically and clearly defined. If the steps in the solution cannot be precisely stated, the job cannot be done. This is why the computer may not be helpful to people in areas where subjective evaluations are important. For example, it may not be able to tell a sales manager if a new product will be successful. The market decision may hinge on educated guesses about future social, political, technological, and economic changes. But the computer *can* tell the manager how the product will fare under *assumed* price, cost, and sales volume conditions. These assumed values can be fed into the computer. A spreadsheet program can then manipulate them in response to a series of "what if" questions to project the effects that the manager's questions will have on profits.

Even if program steps are finite and understood, there are still some tasks whose execution could take millions of years, even on a supercomputer. Joseph Weizenbaum, a computer scientist at MIT, has observed that a program could be written to try every legal chess move in a given situation. Every response to a move could then be evaluated, and the subsequent moves and countermoves could all be identified until the computer finds a move which, if suitably pursued, will guarantee a win. Weizenbaum notes that this program would certainly be finite, but the time needed to execute it would be unimaginably large. Although in principle the computer could do the job, in practice it cannot. The term "combinatorial explosion" is given to this type of problem where a finite number of steps generates an impossibly large number of computer operations.

CHAPTER 1

FEEDBACK

Feedback and Review 1

We'll conclude the presentation of new material in each chapter with a brief review exercise that highlights some of the main points made in the chapter. You can use these reviews to test and reinforce your understanding of chapter concepts. The *crossword puzzle* used here is one of a variety of formats you'll see. You'll find the answers to these exercises at the end of each chapter. Fill in the puzzle form here using the sentences and definitions below.

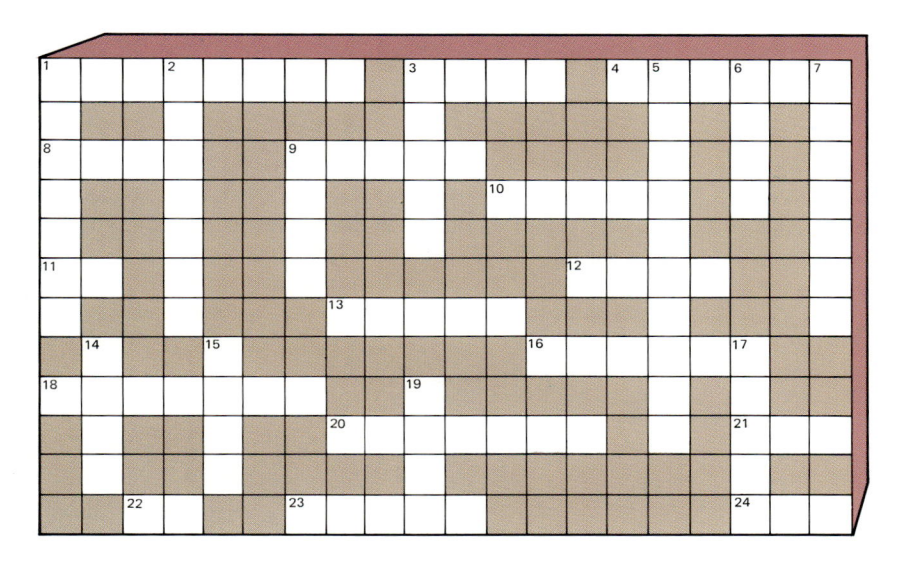

Across

1. A ____ is a fast and accurate electronic symbol (or data) manipulating system that will accept and store input data, process them, and produce output results under the direction of a stored program of instructions.
3. To ____ is to arrange classified data in a predetermined sequence to facilitate processing.
4. In an integrated software package, the status of each current application can often be shown simultaneously in a separate ____ or portion of the display screen.
8. A ____-second is one-billionth of a second.
9. The three types of ____ used to classify data items are numeric, alphabetic, and alphanumeric.
10. To ____ is to retain data for future reference.
11. An abbreviation for the organized collection of software that controls the overall operation of a computer is ____.
12. With the help of a ____ processing program, people can use the keyboard and display screen of a computer to create and edit text.
13. A ____-processor is one with two or more processor units.
16. A ____ is a group of integrated parts that have the common purpose of achieving some objective.

MODULE 1
38

18. A prewritten program that's sold to perform a common task is called an applications _____.
20. Actual data processing operations are performed in the arithmetic-logic section, but not in the _____ storage section or the control section of a processor unit.
21. The abbreviation for the term that's sometimes used to refer to the arithmetic-logic and control sections of a processor unit is _____.
22. Most computers have secondary storage devices that are connected _____-line to the processor and are thus able to accept data directly from, and return data directly to, the processor without human intervention.
23. The computer has the ability to perform _____ operations by comparing data items and then, depending on the results, following predetermined branches or courses of action.
24. If a processor does not have direct and unassisted access to data items, these items are said to be _____-line.

Down

1. Processors of all sizes have primary storage, arithmetic-logic, and _____ sections.
2. A _____ is a detailed step-by-step set of instructions that cause a computer to function in a desired way.
3. A spread-_____ program is an electronic chalkboard that's able to manipulate data organized in columns and rows.
5. An _____ software package combines several functions in a single product and makes it possible for users to share data and move material among the applications in the package.
6. _____ are facts or informational raw materials represented by symbols.
7. The _____ storage area of the primary storage section of a processor is used to hold intermediate processing results.
9. Thousands of computer circuits are packaged on a single silicon _____.
14. A _____-frame computer is generally more powerful than a mini but less powerful than a supercomputer.
15. The word "data" is the plural of datum, which means _____.
17. A personal computer is a general-purpose _____-computer.
19. A _____-computer is generally larger than a microcomputer but smaller than a mainframe model.

LOOKING BACK

1. The use of computers—particularly personal computers—has expanded so rapidly that their presence can no longer be ignored. Everyone needs to feel comfortable with these machines in order to function in modern society. To be a computer-literate person, you need to know about computers themselves, the hardware; what they do, their applications; how they are applied through software; and the social impact of their use. Providing knowledge in these four areas is the purpose of this book.

2. A computer is a fast and accurate electronic symbol (data) manipulating system, designed to automatically accept and store input data, process them, and produce output results under the direction of a detailed stored program of instructions.

3. Computers perform at very high speeds. The time required to execute a basic operation, such as addition, is usually measured in microseconds (one-millionth of a second) for the slowest computers and in nanoseconds (one-billionth of a second) for faster machines. The reliability of computer circuits enables them to run errorless for days and months at a time. Computer "errors" usually reflect faulty programs or inaccurate input data—both generally caused by human and not computer frailties.

4. Computers can manipulate both numeric and nonnumeric symbols. Data are facts or informational raw materials represented by these symbols. Information is the relevant knowledge that results from the processing and arranging of data in an ordered and useful form.

5. Data processing consists of (a) capturing the raw input data; (b) manipulating it by using classifying, calculating, sorting, and summarizing techniques; and (c) storing, retrieving, communicating, and reproducing the output results of the manipulation.

6. These data processing activities are readily carried out by computers. A computer can accept input data from, and communicate processed output to, a large number of devices. The circuits in a computer are designed to perform calculation and text manipulation operations. Classifying, sorting, and summarizing are made possible by the computer's ability to perform simple comparisons and then, depending on the result, follow a predetermined course of action. Split-second storage and retrieval are possible through the use of primary and secondary storage devices.

7. A system is a group of integrated parts that have the common purpose of achieving some objective. Since a computer is made up of integrated components that work together to perform the steps called for in the program being executed, it is a system. A basic computer system is comprised of input and output devices and a processor unit. Processors of all sizes contain primary storage, arithmetic-logic, and control sections.

8. The space in the primary storage section is divided into four areas: input, where data are held for processing; working storage, where intermediate processing results are kept; output, where finished results are kept prior to release; and program storage, which holds the processing steps. In addition to primary storage components, most computers also have secondary storage devices. These devices are usually connected online to the processor; they accept data directly from and return data directly to it without human intervention.

9. All calculations and comparisons are made in the arithmetic-logic section of the processor. Engineering design determines the type and number of arithmetic and logic operations that can be performed. The processor's control section maintains order among the system components and selects, interprets, and sees to the execution of program steps. After an initial control setting, it automatically selects program instructions in sequence until specifically instructed to do otherwise.

10. Computers have the built-in ability to obey different types of instructions. Once job instructions are stored in a computer, the system can process data automatically and without human intervention until the job is completed.

11. There have been dramatic reductions in the size and cost of computer components and equally impressive gains in the speed, storage capacity, and reliability of these same components. In the software area, advances include the development of programming languages and translation programs. Thousands of applications packages are now readily available. Most of these programs perform single tasks, but many newer ones often combine word processing, spreadsheet, graphics, and other functions in a single integrated software package.

12. Computer systems differ in size and in design. Sizes vary from the smallest microcomputers to minis, mainframes, and supercomputers. Computer architecture can vary. Most small systems use single primary storage, arithmetic-logic, and control sections. Some large computers use multiple sections in order to work simultaneously on several program segments and thus speed up processing.

13. Computers have impressive capabilities, but they also have a few important limitations. For example, programs must be reliable and applications logic must be understood.

KEY TERMS AND CONCEPTS

You should now be able to define and use the following terms and concepts (the numbers shown indicate the pages where the terms and concepts are first mentioned):

personal computers 6
programs 6
computer literacy 9
hardware 10
applications 10
software 10
program 12
computer 12
millisecond 12
microsecond 12
nanosecond 12
picosecond 12
garbage in–garbage out (GIGO) 13
computer processing 13
data 14
information 14
data processing 14
source documents 14

direct input device 14
classifying 14
calculating 16
sorting 16
summarizing 16
storing 16
retrieving 16
data communication 16
reproduction 16
system 19
input devices 19
floppy disks 20
magnetic tapes 20
processor unit 20
primary storage (main memory) section 20
input storage area 20
working storage space 20

output storage area 21
program storage area 21
central processing unit (CPU) 22
arithmetic-logic section 22
control section 22
secondary (auxiliary) storage 22
online 22
rigid metal disks 22
offline 22
output devices 22
peripheral devices 24
branchpoint 26
silicon chip 27
fault-tolerant systems 28

programming languages 28
translation program 28
application program 29
applications packages (packaged programs) 29
integrated software packages 29
word processing program 29
spreadsheet program 30
graphics program 30
windows 31
operating system (OS) 31
disk operating system (DOS) 31
microcomputers 31
minicomputers 33
mainframe computers 33
supercomputers 34
von Neumann machines 34
architecture 34
multiprocessor 34

TOPICS FOR REVIEW AND DISCUSSION

1. If computer literacy was a rare skill 20 years ago, why do you need it today?
2. (a) What is a computer program? (b) Why can a computer program be described as an "intellectual map"?
3. (a) What is a computer? (b) What capabilities does a computer possess?
4. (a) Discuss the different views that people may have of computers as they are reflected in cartoons, magazines, newspapers, movies, television, and science fiction. (b) Discuss four ways that computers have affected your life.
5. Electricity can travel about 1 foot in a nanosecond. Does this fact place any upper limits on computer operating speed?
6. Discuss this statement: "If computers are so accurate, why is the phrase 'garbage in—garbage out' associated with their use?"
7. (a) What are data? (b) What is information? (c) What's the difference between these two terms?
8. What additional facts could be supplied to transform the data item "102.2" into useful information?
9. (a) What is data processing? (b) Identify and explain the basic data processing activities.
10. In order to classify data, codes are assigned to the items being arranged. Light trucks are classified with an alphanumeric identification code by General Motors. A code for a particular vehicle is CCL247F153278. How might this code be interpreted and used for classification purposes?
11. Why is the computer's ability to make a simple comparison between two data items important?
12. (a) What is a system? (b) What three hardware components are required in a computer system?
13. "The primary storage section of the CPU is used for four purposes." What are these four purposes?
14. What's the difference between primary and secondary storage devices?
15. (a) What's the function of the arithmetic-logic section of the CPU? (b) What's the function of the control section?
16. What's the typical data flow pattern in a computer system?
17. What's the stored program concept and why is it important?
18. "Society is now in the throes of an information revolution that has been brought on by advances in computer technology." Discuss the advances in (a) hardware and (b) software.
19. How may computers be classified according to size?
20. Discuss some limitations of computer usage.

PROJECTS/ISSUES TO CONSIDER

1. In the mid-October 1984 issue of *Popular Computing*, Dale Peterson writes: "Educational computing, like the Force, is with us. Microcomputers are proliferating in our schools, and unless a lot of people are wrong they're here to stay. But the $64 question is whether these computers will make any difference in the education of our children. When my daughter graduates from high school in the year 2000, will she have received a better education with the help of computers than I did without them? I don't have the answer to that question and nobody else does either."* Prepare a report outlining your views on this issue.
2. Visit your local computer store or other retail outlets that

---

*Reprinted with permission from Dale Peterson, "Nine Issues," Popular Computing, October 1984. Copyright © by McGraw-Hill, Inc. All rights reserved.

sell computers, and write a report describing the hardware characteristics of four of the models you've seen on display.

3. At this writing there are over 100 manufacturers of personal computers. Dozens of these vendors advertise on television and radio and in magazines and newspapers. Make a list of 15 of these vendors you've identified from their ads. You may want to visit your library to check personal computing magazines or other specific sources.

4. Articles reporting new developments in computer technology appear daily in magazines and newspapers. Select a topic from the following list, and locate three recent articles that deal with your subject. Bring your articles to class and be prepared to summarize their contents. (*Topic list*: the information revolution; developments in integrated circuits; computer hardware advances; computer software developments.)

5. Several colleges now require all incoming students to buy their own personal computers so that these machines will become an integral part of their education. Some students, parents, and educators feel that this requirement anticipates the students' future needs. But others worry that students from families with limited financial resources will be denied future educational opportunities. And others argue that the schools should furnish the necessary computing facilities. Do you think that college students should be required to buy computers? Be prepared to defend your position on this issue.

Answers to Feedback and Review Section

The solution to the crossword puzzle is shown below:

	1	2	3	4	5	6	7	8	9	10	11	12	13
1	C	O	M	P	U	T	E	R		S	O	R	T

¹C	O	M	²P	U	T	E	R		³S	O	R	T		⁴W	⁵I	N	⁶D	O	⁷W
O			R						H						N		A		O
⁸N	A	N	O		⁹C	O	D	E	S						T		T		R
T			G		H				E		¹⁰S	T	O	R	E		A		K
R			R		I				T						G				I
¹¹O	S		A		P							¹²W	O	R	D				N
L			M				¹³M	U	L	T	I				A				G
	¹⁴M		¹⁵F									¹⁶S	Y	S	T	E	¹⁷M		
¹⁸P	A	C	K	A	G	E		¹⁹M							E		I		
	I		C			²⁰P	R	I	M	A	R	Y			D		²¹C	P	U
	N		T					N							R				
	²²O	N		²³L	O	G	I	C							²⁴O	F	F		

A CLOSER LOOK

FROM ABACUS TO PERSONAL COMPUTER:
Our Debt To The Past

The abacus and the personal computer are two lap-sized data processing devices separated by thousands of years of history. Let's look at some of the milestones along this lengthy path.

The First Record Keepers and Their Tools

People lived on earth for eons without keeping records, but as tribes grew into nations, trade and commerce developed. By 3500 B.C., Babylonian merchants were keeping records on clay tablets. An early manual calculating device was the *abacus*. Although over 3,000 years old, it's still used today in some parts of the world.

Record-keeping techniques continued to develop through the centuries, with such innovations as record audits (the Greeks) and budgets (the Romans). In 1642, the first mechanical calculating machine was developed by Blaise Pascal, a brilliant young Frenchman. (A modern programming language has been named in his honor.) About 30 years later, Gottfried von Leibniz, a German mathematician, improved on Pascal's invention by producing a machine which could add, subtract, multiply, divide, and extract roots. But no one knew how to manufacture such precision machines.

Even in the 1880s, data processing in the United States was still done with pencils, pens, and rulers. The volume of records during this period was expanding rapidly, and as you might expect, handwritten methods produced information that was relatively inaccurate and often late. To the dismay of the Census Bureau, for example, the 1880 census was not finished until it was almost time to begin the 1890 count! Fortunately for the bureau and for others with a need for improved data processing methods, *electromechanical punched card equipment* was invented at this time.

The Weaver, the Statistician, and Their Cards

The history of the punched card dates back to 1801, when a French weaver named Joseph Marie Jacquard invented them to control his mechanical looms. But it was the problem of completing the 1880 census count that led to the use of cards as a medium for data processing. The inventor of punched card techniques was Dr. Herman Hollerith, a statistician. The Census Bureau hired him to find a solution to the census problem. In 1887, Hollerith developed his machine-readable card concept and designed a device known as the "census machine." Tabulating with Hollerith's methods took only one-eighth of the time previously required, and so his techniques were adopted for use in the 1890 count. Although the population had increased from 50 to 63 million in the decade after 1880, the 1890 count was completed in less than 3 years. (Of course, this is intolerably slow by today's standards. The 1950 census, using punched card equipment, took about 2 years to produce; the computerized 1980 census yielded figures in a few months.)

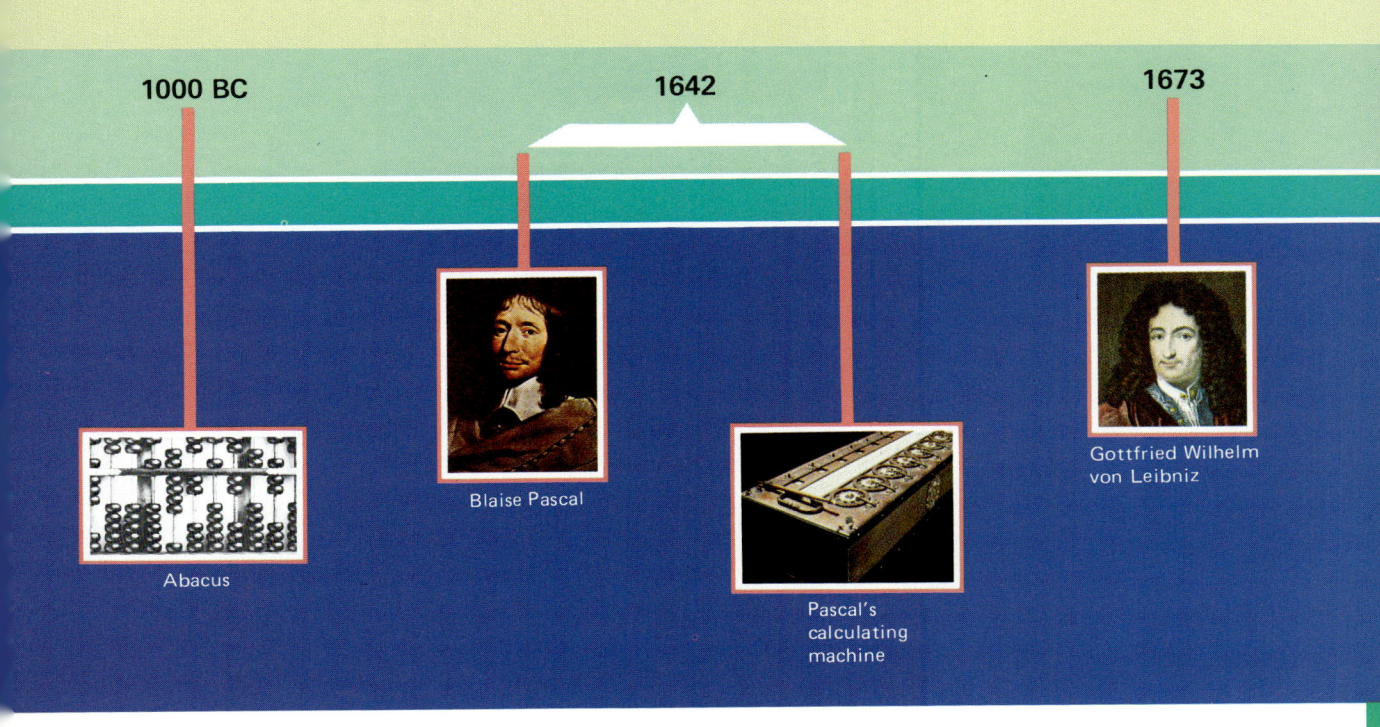

1000 BC — Abacus

1642 — Blaise Pascal / Pascal's calculating machine

1673 — Gottfried Wilhelm von Leibniz

After the 1890 census, Hollerith converted his equipment to commercial use and set up freight statistics systems for two railroads. In 1896 he founded the Tabulating Machine Company to make and sell his invention. Later, this firm merged with others to form the International Business Machines (IBM) Corporation.

Punched card processing was based on a simple idea: Input data were first recorded in a coded form by punching holes into cards. These cards were then fed into a number of electromechanical machines that performed processing steps. Punched card data processing was much faster and more accurate than manual methods. But it still required people to handle trays of cards between each step. Separate machines had to be fed, started, and stopped. This need for human intervention was a major disadvantage. With the computer, of course, this disadvantage disappears: Human intervention isn't required between each step.

Early Computer Development

"Babbage's Folly" About 50 years before Hollerith's efforts, Charles Babbage, Lucasian Professor of Mathematics at Cambridge University in England, proposed a machine, which he named the "analytical engine." Babbage was an eccentric and quick-tempered man who spent much of his life working in vain to complete his incredibly complex machine. Babbage's dream—to many of his contemporaries it was "Babbage's folly"—would have incorporated a punched card input; a memory unit, or *store*; an arithmetic unit, or *mill*; automatic printout; sequential program control; and 20-place accuracy. In short, Babbage had designed a prototype computer that was 100 years ahead of its time. Assisting Babbage in his efforts was Lady Augusta Ada Lovelace, the daughter of Lord Byron, the poet. A brilliant mathematician, Ada corrected some errors in Babbage's work and invented some new approaches to program design using punched cards. She is often referred to as the first computer programmer because of these discoveries. (Another modern programming language, Ada, is named in her honor.) After Babbage's death in 1871, computer development stalled until 1937; punched cards ruled the world of data processing.

ABC, ENIAC, and the Early Pioneers In 1937, Harvard professor Howard Aiken set out to build an automatic calculating machine that would combine electrical and mechanical technology with Hollerith's punched card techniques. With the help of graduate students and IBM engineers, the project was completed in 1944. The completed device was known as the Mark I digital computer. Internal operations were controlled automatically with electromagnetic relays; arithmetic counters were mechanical. The Mark I was thus an *electromechanical* computer; in many respects it was the realization of Babbage's dream.

The first prototype *electronic* computer was conceived in the winter of 1937–1938 by Dr. John Vincent Atanasoff, a professor of physics and mathematics at Iowa State College. Because no available calculating device was adequate for his needs, Atanasoff decided to build his own. Using design

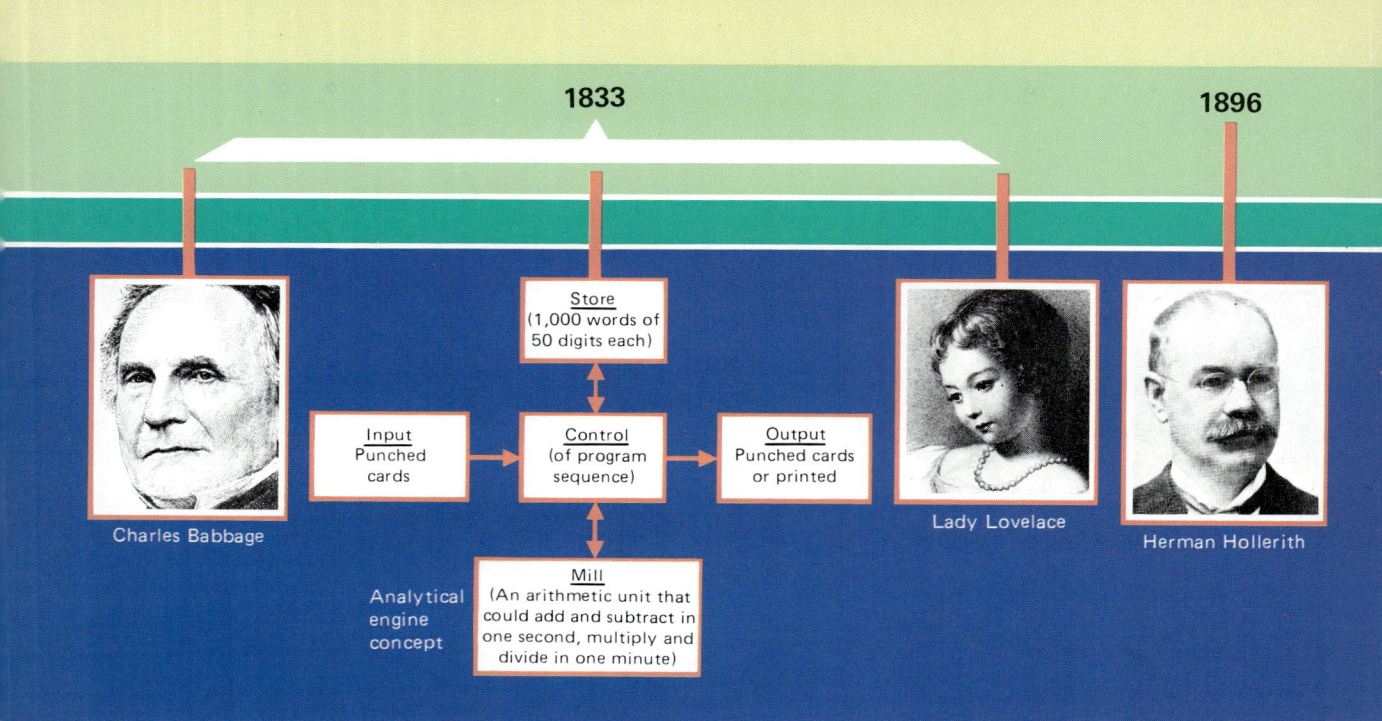

1833

Charles Babbage

Analytical engine concept

- Input: Punched cards
- Store (1,000 words of 50 digits each)
- Control (of program sequence)
- Mill (An arithmetic unit that could add and subtract in one second, multiply and divide in one minute)
- Output: Punched cards or printed

1896

Lady Lovelace

Herman Hollerith

concepts that crystalized in his mind late one winter night in a roadside tavern in Illinois, Atanasoff teamed up with Clifford Berry, his graduate assistant, and began to build the first electronic computer. They called it the "Atanasoff-Berry computer," or ABC. The ABC used vacuum tubes for storage and arithmetic-logic functions.

During 1940 and 1941, Atanasoff and Berry met with John W. Mauchly and showed him their work. Mauchly, working at the Moore School of Electrical Engineering of the University of Pennsylvania, began thinking about how a general-purpose computer might be built. (The ABC was designed for the special purpose of solving systems of simultaneous equations.) Mauchly teamed up with J. Presper Eckert, Jr., a graduate engineering student at the Moore School, to organize the construction of ENIAC in the early 1940s.

ENIAC was the first electronic general-purpose computer to be put into full operation. Funded by the U.S. Army, it was built as a secret wartime project at the Moore School (the Army was interested in the rapid preparation of artillery trajectory tables). Vacuum tubes (18,000 of them!) were also used in ENIAC. Although it weighed 30 tons and occupied the space of a three-bedroom house, ENIAC could do 300 multiplications per second, making it 300 times faster than any other device of the day. Operating instructions for ENIAC were not stored internally; rather they were fed through externally located plugboards and switches. ENIAC was used by the Army until 1955 and was then placed in the Smithsonian Institution.

In the mid-1940s, in collaboration with H. H. Goldstine and A. W. Burks, the mathematical genius John von Neumann wrote a paper suggesting that (1) *binary* numbering systems be used in building computers and (2) computer *instructions,* as well as the data being manipulated, could be stored internally in the machine.

The first of these ideas was used earlier in Atanasoff's ABC, and von Neumann's paper publicized the concept. It's an important idea because the binary numbering system is represented by only 2 digits (0 and 1) rather than the 10 digits (0 to 9) of the familiar decimal system. Since electronic components are typically in one of two conditions ("on" or "off"), the binary concept made equipment design simpler. The second idea—the stored program concept that we now take for granted—was a brilliant breakthrough at the time because it meant that programs could simply be entered into storage like data. There was no longer any need to change countless switches and wires prior to the running of each new application. The origin of the stored program idea is still disputed, but it became a basic part of the philosophy of computer design. As you saw in the chapter, most modern computers can be called *von Neumann machines* because they use these early design concepts.

Although these ideas weren't incorporated in ENIAC, Mauchly, Eckert, and others at the Moore School set out to build a machine with stored program capability. This machine—the EDVAC—was not completed until several years later. To the EDSAC, finished in 1949 at Cambridge University, must go the distinction of being the first *stored program electronic computer.*

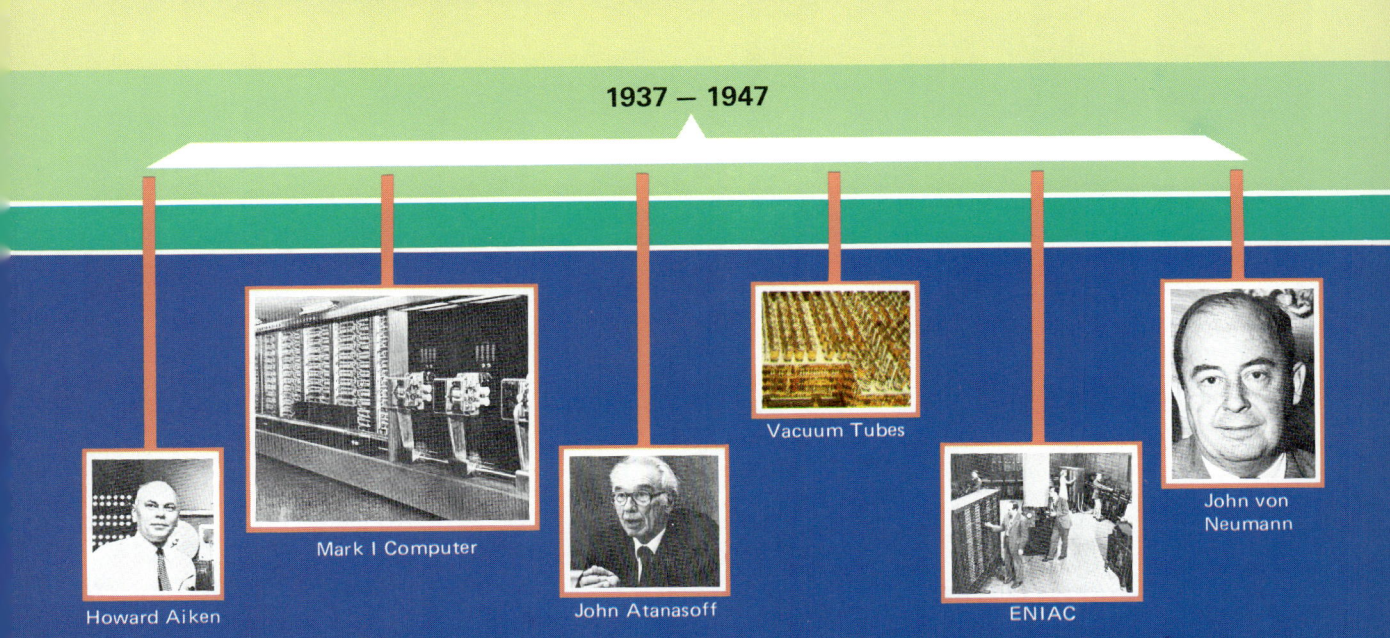

1937 — 1947

Howard Aiken

Mark I Computer

John Atanasoff

Vacuum Tubes

ENIAC

John von Neumann

1948 — Bardeen Shockley Brattain

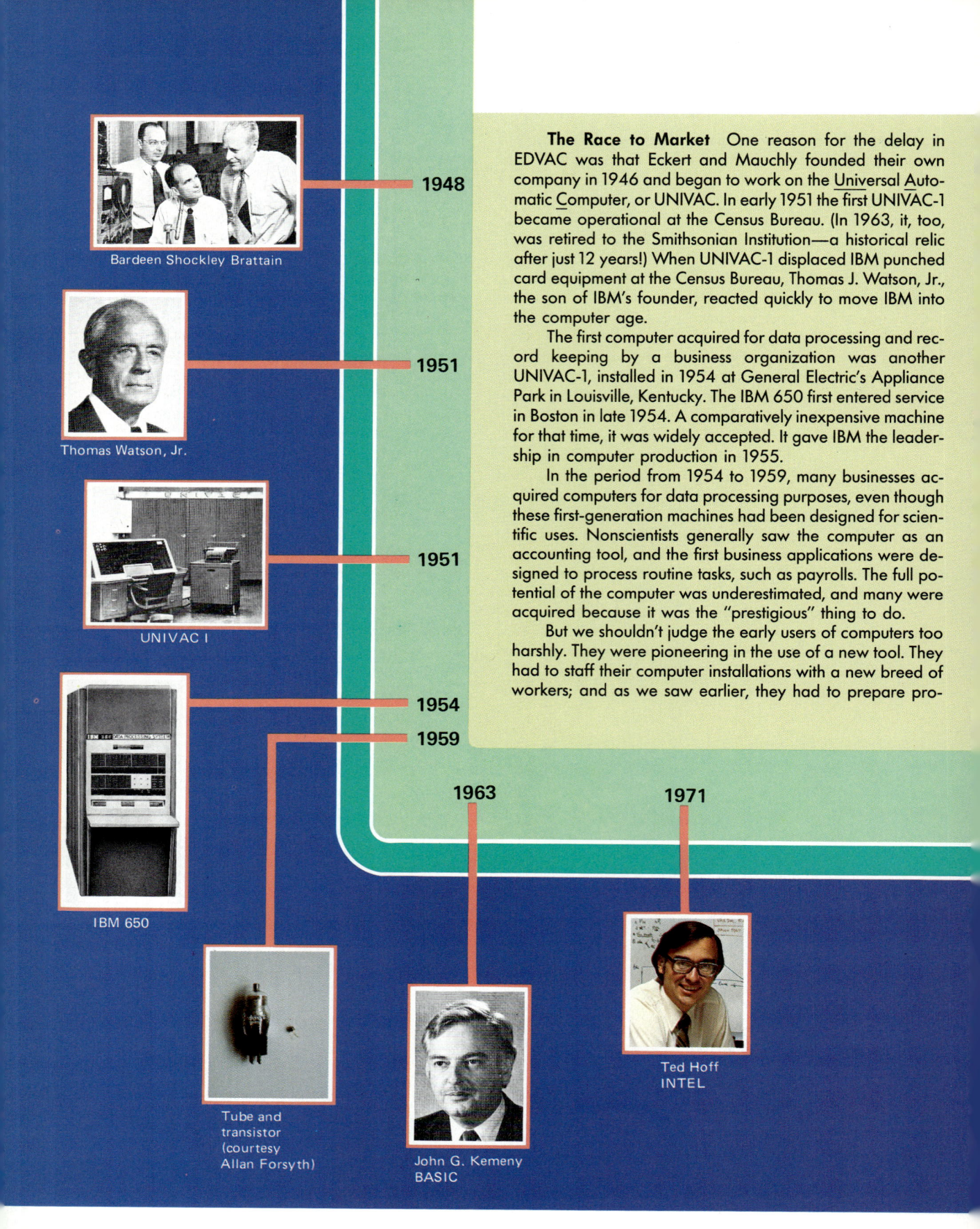

1951 — Thomas Watson, Jr.

1951 — UNIVAC I

1954 — IBM 650

1959 — Tube and transistor (courtesy Allan Forsyth)

1963 — John G. Kemeny, BASIC

1971 — Ted Hoff, INTEL

The Race to Market One reason for the delay in EDVAC was that Eckert and Mauchly founded their own company in 1946 and began to work on the Universal Automatic Computer, or UNIVAC. In early 1951 the first UNIVAC-1 became operational at the Census Bureau. (In 1963, it, too, was retired to the Smithsonian Institution—a historical relic after just 12 years!) When UNIVAC-1 displaced IBM punched card equipment at the Census Bureau, Thomas J. Watson, Jr., the son of IBM's founder, reacted quickly to move IBM into the computer age.

The first computer acquired for data processing and record keeping by a business organization was another UNIVAC-1, installed in 1954 at General Electric's Appliance Park in Louisville, Kentucky. The IBM 650 first entered service in Boston in late 1954. A comparatively inexpensive machine for that time, it was widely accepted. It gave IBM the leadership in computer production in 1955.

In the period from 1954 to 1959, many businesses acquired computers for data processing purposes, even though these first-generation machines had been designed for scientific uses. Nonscientists generally saw the computer as an accounting tool, and the first business applications were designed to process routine tasks, such as payrolls. The full potential of the computer was underestimated, and many were acquired because it was the "prestigious" thing to do.

But we shouldn't judge the early users of computers too harshly. They were pioneering in the use of a new tool. They had to staff their computer installations with a new breed of workers; and as we saw earlier, they had to prepare programs in a tedious machine language. In spite of these obstacles, the computer was found to be a fast, accurate, and untiring processor of mountains of paper.

The Second and Third Generations Arrive

The Second Generation The computers of the *second generation,* which began to appear in 1959, were made smaller and faster and had greater computing capacity. The practice of writing applications programs in machine languages gave way to the use of *higher-level programming languages.* And the vacuum tube, with its relatively short life, gave way to compact *solid-state* components, such as the transistors that had been developed at Bell Laboratories in 1947 by John Bardeen, William Shockley, and Walter Brattain.

Paralleling the development of second-generation systems was the creation of a new industry, built around the idea of integrating transistors and other components into circuits that could be placed on small chips of silicon. An early firm in this industry was Shockley Semiconductor, founded in 1955 by William Shockley in his home town of Palo Alto, California. Some employees of Shockley's firm then left to form Fairchild Semiconductor, and Fairchild people formed a number of other companies including Intel Corporation. Since many of these companies were located in the Santa Clara Valley near Shockley's firm in Palo Alto, the region became known as *Silicon Valley.*

The Third Generation Second-generation systems were rather specialized. They were designed to process either scientific or nonscientific applications, but they weren't meant to do well in both environments. That situation changed in 1964 when IBM announced a *third generation* of computing hardware—its System 360 family of mainframe computers. Each processor in this family had a large set of built-in instructions that it could execute. Some of these instructions were particularly useful in scientific processing, while others were more suited to record-keeping applications. Thus the 360 line could be used efficiently in both environments. Many other upgraded families of processors have been introduced since 1964. Collectively, these processors might be considered a "fourth generation." But the industry failed to agree on a generation designation in subsequent years.

From 1965 to 1974

The Development of Minicomputers The computers built in the early 1960s were mainframes, designed to provide at a central location all the processing power needed by an organization. This approach served the needs of some organizations. But others were unable to afford the larger systems, or they had specialized applications that a large, centralized machine could not process effectively.

Clearly, a need existed for low-cost minimal computers to fill the gaps left by the bigger, faster centralized approach. Several innovators recognized this need and formed new

about 1974
Microprocessor

1975
Steven Jobs

1976
Bill Gates
(courtesy Apple Computer, Inc.)

1985
Integrated software screen
(courtesy Apple Computer, Inc.)

firms in the 1960s to produce these minimal machines. The first processors called *minicomputers* were developed and built in 1965 by Digital Equipment Corporation (DEC)—now the largest producer of minis. Other major suppliers of minis, such as Hewlett-Packard and Data General, quickly followed DEC's lead.

The Introduction of Timesharing In the centralized computing environment of the early 1960s, users prepared their data and programs and then submitted them to the computer center for processing. The computer center collected these user jobs and fed them to the computer in batches at scheduled intervals. The inevitable delay resulting from this *batch processing* approach was very frustrating to some users. The delays were particularly irritating to students with programming assignments, who might have to wait for days to locate and correct a few program errors.

To remedy this situation, John Kemeny and Thomas Kurtz, two Dartmouth College professors, decided to build on some earlier timesharing concepts developed at MIT. *Timesharing* is a term used to describe a processing system with a number of independent, relatively low-speed, online, and simultaneously usable stations. Each station provides the user with direct access to the central processor. Kemeny and Kurtz developed special programs that allow the processor to switch from one student station to another and to do a part of each job in an allocated "time slice" until the work was completed. The intent was to give each student user the illusion that no one else was using the computer.

To further improve the *interactive computing environment* they were creating, the professors developed a programming language that undergraduate students in all fields of study would find easy to learn. The goal was to encourage every undergraduate to use the timesharing stations on a regular basis. This language—BASIC, which stands for Beginner's All-purpose Symbolic Instruction Code—was a success at Dartmouth on both counts. Dartmouth used a General Electric (GE) computer, and the BASIC timesharing system was implemented on this equipment with the help of GE engineers. Following the success of the Dartmouth system, General Electric and others offered timesharing facilities and the use of the BASIC language to customers across the nation.

The Creation of an Independent Software Industry In 1965, computer makers sold or leased their hardware, but they did not charge for the software they provided to customers. From the user's standpoint, this software was "free." A few independent software vendors were around to supply more specialized or more efficient programs than those supplied by manufacturers. But the situation changed in 1969 when IBM and others began to price their hardware and software products separately. This "unbundling" of software gave users an incentive to seek out the best software values, and it led to the creation of many new software houses.

The Microprocessor Arrives The average number of electronic components packed on a silicon chip doubled each year after 1965, and this progress led to a dramatic development: the creation of a microprocessor that could be placed on a single chip. A *microprocessor* contains all the circuits needed to perform arithmetic-logic and control functions. A complete processor unit can be built with a microprocessor, a few additional primary storage chips, and other support circuitry.

The origin of the microprocessor can be traced back to the late 1960s. During this time, Victor Poor, a Datapoint Corporation electronics engineer, was working on the design and development of special-purpose computers. Each time a custom-designed device was needed, Poor and other engineers started the design effort from scratch. This seemed a big waste of time to Poor. Instead, he reasoned, if the basic arithmetic-logic and control elements of a computer could be placed on a single silicon chip, the chip could be mass-produced and then programmed in different ways to perform special jobs.

In 1969, Victor Poor and Harry Pyle, another young Datapoint engineer, developed a model of a microprocessor chip. Since Datapoint Corporation did not make electronic components, Poor took his "chip processor" model to two component manufacturers—Texas Instruments and Intel Corporation—in hopes they would manufacture the chip for Datapoint. No immediate decisions came from these meetings, but the component manufacturers were free to use the microprocessor chip concept—and they did.

Late in 1969, an Intel engineer named Marcian "Ted" Hoff presented his design ideas for a microprocessor chip to representatives from a Japanese calculator company. Calculators were then being built from specialized circuit chips that could perform only a single function. But Hoff's new chip could be programmed to perform several specialized calculator functions. The Japanese customer accepted Hoff's design ideas, and work began on the actual layout of the chip. This first microprocessor—the Intel 4004—could execute only a few instructions, and it could manipulate only tiny amounts of data at one time. But by the fall of 1971, Intel had produced a more powerful chip (the 8008), and Texas Instruments had also delivered a microprocessor. In 1974, Intel produced a third microprocessor—the 8080—and the groundwork was laid for the development of a personal computer (pc).

The Development of Personal Computers

The PC Pioneers The first ad for a pc built around a microprocessor appeared in the March 1974 issue of *QST*, a magazine for amateur radio buffs. The product advertised was the Scelbi-8H, and only about 200 of these processors were sold. Following closely behind the Scelbi was the Altair 8800. Designed around an Intel chip by an Albuquerque,

New Mexico, company named MITS, the Altair was originally offered in kit form for under $400. The lead article in the January 1975 issue of *Popular Electronics* featured this machine, and that article may well have triggered the pc explosion. At that same moment, two young programmers named Bill Gates and Paul Allen were completing a program that could translate instructions written in BASIC into the machine-language codes required by Intel microprocessors. Microsoft Corporation was created to market the Gates-Allen BASIC program, and Microsoft BASIC was licensed to MITS in late 1975. Microsoft is now a leading supplier of pc software.

Many competitors in the pc industry today are multibillion-dollar firms with well-equipped development labs. But the pioneers in 1975 were mostly hobbyists and self-taught engineers who were fascinated with the emerging technology. They built prototype systems, advertised them in magazines, used the money received from orders to buy parts, and assembled their processors in garages. Few of those pioneering companies survived the initial phase. But what they did changed the world.

The Early Successes One company that did grow out of a garage and into American business folklore is Apple Computer. In the spring of 1976, a young Hewlett-Packard technician named Steve Wozniak bought a microprocessor from MOS Technology and set out to build a computer around it. This computer—the Apple I—was shown at the Homebrew Computer Club in Silicon Valley. Wozniak offered his design to Hewlett-Packard, but when it wasn't interested, a friend named Steve Jobs suggested that they form a company to market the Apple. Only about 200 Apple I's were built, but by the end of the summer Wozniak was working on the design for the Apple II. With financial and managerial help from Mike Markkula, a former Intel engineer and marketing executive, Apple suddenly became a major entrant into the computer industry.

By the end of 1977, the dominant machines were the Apple II, the TRS-80 model from the Radio Shack Division of Tandy Corporation, and the dozens of other brands designed to follow the electrical interconnection concepts used in the Altair computer. As you might expect, most application programs in the late 1970s were written for use with these systems.

For example, one important software product introduced in the fall of 1978 was *VisiCalc*, the first electronic spreadsheet program. The idea for this program came from Dan Bricklin, then a student at the Harvard Business School. Bricklin was using the columns and rows on paper worksheets to analyze financial-planning problems. But endless recalculations were needed every time a different financial assumption was made. Bricklin reasoned that if the paper worksheets could be replaced by an "electronic chalkboard" and "electronic chalk," then the computer could take over the task of juggling all the numbers. Bricklin asked a programmer friend named Bob Frankston to help him turn his idea into a marketable product. Frankston added several features and wrote the first program for the Apple II. VisiCalc became a smash hit and was solely responsible for the sale of thousands of Apples. Its success encouraged many other software authors to market spreadsheets and other applications packages.

The Recent Years By the end of the 1970s, the leading machines were being used everywhere—in homes, schools, and workplaces. But as the 1980s began, lower-cost systems intended for home use were produced by such companies as Atari and Commodore. And a whole new generation of more-powerful desktop models for use in schools and workplaces was introduced. IBM entered the market with its IBM PC family of computers and enjoyed huge success, but small start-up firms appeared regularly with new hardware and software offerings.

As you saw earlier, new software products were introduced in the early 1980s that combined several functions in a single package. These integrated software packages, which can show the current status of several applications in separate windows on the display screen, can be traced back to the early 1970s. At that time, researchers at Xerox's Palo Alto Research Center developed the first integrated windowing software. But it wasn't until Xerox brought out its 8010 Star Information System in 1981 that these ideas appeared in a commercial product. Data and programs were represented on the screen by small pictures called *icons*—a picture of a trash can took the place of the typed command DELETE, for example. Data could be passed between applications "through" the multiple windows that could be opened on the screen. Because the Star cost over $15,000, most people were unaware of its capabilities.

But the Star's advantages didn't go unnoticed at Apple Computer. Influenced by the work done at Xerox, Apple engineers designed a lower-cost personal computer that incorporated many of the Star's features. This hardware-software system, named Lisa, was announced in 1983; in 1984 the $2,500 Apple Macintosh was introduced with many of the same hardware-software features. Apple was not alone, of course—dozens of integrated packages designed for popular personal computers were introduced in 1984.

The Dawn of a New Age
We've now come full circle. We're back again to the topic that opened Chapter 1. We've looked at the history of computing, and we've seen how quickly things have changed in the last few decades. But the rate of technological progress outlined in the preceding pages isn't slowing down at all. In fact, the fastest growth period in the history of computing is yet to come.

CHAPTER 2

COMPUTERS AT WORK

THE THINGS PEOPLE DO

Janet has postponed this moment for weeks. But the date for the panic-inducing Scholastic Aptitude Test (SAT) is drawing too close for comfort. Sitting down at her personal computer, Janet slips a magnetic disk with a test program on it into the system and begins to take an SAT diagnostic test. As she proceeds through the sample exam, the test program instructs the computer to tally her responses. After she completes the test, the computer follows program steps to compute her final SAT-equivalent score, analyze her test-taking skills, and suggest a study plan based on her performance. To Janet, the program suggests a sequence of lessons and recommends that she study certain manuals and lesson disks supplied with the SAT software package.

Mark is running for public office. His hopes are high, but his campaign budget is low. To improve his election chances, Mark buys a campaign management software package for $650. This package runs on Mark's personal computer. It contains one program to churn out fund-raising letters, thank-you notes, and mailing labels, another to account for all receipts and expenditures, a third to handle scheduling of Mark's campaign appearances, and a fourth that analyzes opinion poll results and identifies problem areas that need special attention. Mark's campaign has gathered momentum in recent weeks and his incumbent opponent is now running scared.

Millions of people like Janet and Mark are putting their computers to work today. Millions more are joining their ranks every year. Some learn about what they can do with computers in formal classes, some learn in the workplace, and thousands attend computer camps where they mix vacation fun with hands-on training. All these people are discovering that the computer is an intelligence amplifier: It's a powerful tool that permits them to solve problems and perform tasks with unprecedented efficiency. It's little wonder, then, that a few even become information junkies—compulsive computer users addicted by the power of hardware and software. You may now be a tentative observer on the computer scene, but during your lifetime it's likely that you'll use a personal computer to link up with complex networks of huge computers. When that happens, you'll be able to get an answer to practically any question if the answer is known or calculable.

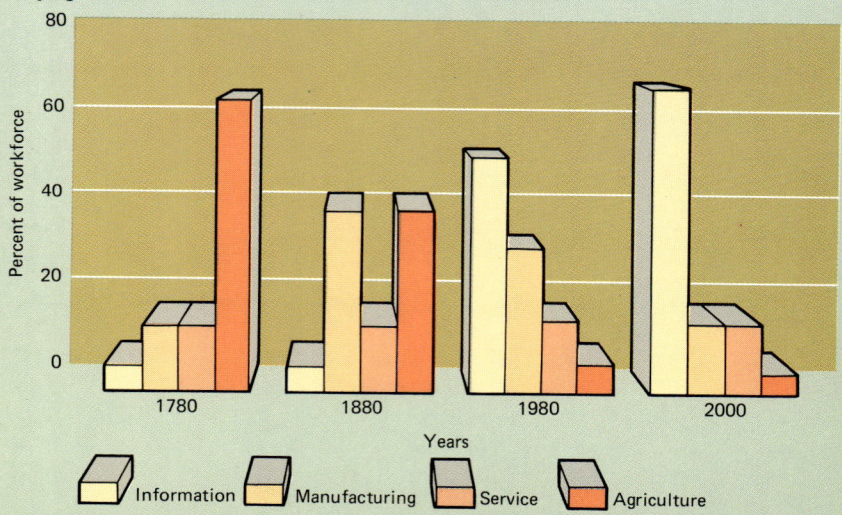

Source: Adapted from David Vincent, "Corporate Culture," *Computerworld*, In-Depth Section, November 5, 1984, P. ID-22. Copyright 1984 by CW Communications, Inc., Framingham, MA 01701.

The tasks people perform in their jobs change over the years. In the last two centuries (see accompanying chart), people first moved away from jobs in agriculture to jobs in manufacturing. Now, more jobs are in information processing than in any other category, and this trend will continue in the future. Scientists, engineers, office workers, decision makers, teachers, health-care and other professionals—information workers in all these overlapping groups are constantly using computers. For example, scientists must perform large and complex calculations; office workers must accept transactions, update data, process large-volume, repetitive applications, and manipulate text; and decision makers must retrieve and evaluate summarized facts and communicate data and information.

Recall from Chapter 1 that the purpose of this book is to give you information about what computers are, what people do with them, how they are put to work, and how they affect society. This chapter focuses on two of these four themes—what people do with computers and how computers are put to work. First, however, you'll learn how data are organized for processing.

CHAPTER 2

LOOKING AHEAD

The information in this chapter will enable you to:

- Describe how data are organized into logical groupings to make computer processing easier
- Identify some common computer applications, and discuss how prewritten software packages can be used to support such applications
- Differentiate between interactive and batch processing and between direct and sequential files
- Outline a few of the characteristics of single-function and integrated software packages, and explain the steps that are followed to develop custom-made software

CHAPTER OUTLINE

LOOKING AHEAD
ORGANIZING DATA FOR COMPUTER PROCESSING
WHAT PEOPLE DO WITH COMPUTERS:
AN INTRODUCTION TO APPLICATIONS
The Byter Family
Input/Output Applications
Calculation Applications
Text Manipulation Applications
Interactive and Batch Processing
A Logic/Comparison Application
Storage/Retrieval Applications
Sequential and Direct Storage and Retrieval
OBTAINING APPLICATION SOFTWARE
Prewritten Packages
Development of Custom-Made Software
Feedback and Review 2
LOOKING BACK

ORGANIZING DATA FOR COMPUTER PROCESSING

Computers operate on data. They accept and process data and communicate results. They cannot directly carry out any physical activities. They cannot bend metal, for example, but they *can* control metal-bending machines.

People receive input data by seeing, hearing, tasting, smelling, and touching, and they are able to interpret these facts in countless ways. But a computer can't match this human ability. Data supplied to a computer must generally be arranged in predetermined ways to satisfy the numeric (numbers), alphabetic (letters), or alphanumeric (letters and numbers) forms demanded by the particular program being used.

Although the required form (or format) of the input data varies from one program to another, these data are generally organized into related groupings to ensure effective processing and useful output. A small unit of data is the **data item** or **data field**.[1] A data item consists of a group of related characters treated as a single unit. Think back to the Elm Creek Beautification Project discussed in the last chapter. The program used by the city of Calvin to assign charges to property owners required the following data items: the name of the property owner, the owner's address, the number of plants used, and the price per plant.

During processing, the data characters in each of these items were treated collectively, as a single unit. Such a collection of related data items treated as a single unit is called a **record.** Thus there's a record made up of four data items for each of the participating property owners.

Records are grouped to form files. A **file** is a number of related records that are treated as a unit. The Calvin Elm Creek owners file consists of the records of all owners who have agreed to participate in the beautification project (see Figure 2-1). Finally, a **data base** is a collection of related data elements that may be structured in various ways to meet the multiple processing and retrieval needs of organizations and individuals. For example, a bank may have created separate checking account, savings account, automobile loan, and personal loan files. The bank's customer data base includes records from each of these files. Using specialized programs, a banker can quickly retrieve and update all of a customer's records that are stored in this customer data base. Figure 2-2 summarizes this data organization hierarchy used by computer-based processing systems.

WHAT PEOPLE DO WITH COMPUTERS: AN INTRODUCTION TO APPLICATIONS

As you'll recall from Chapter 1, the operations which computers perform on data are classified into four categories:

---

[1] Some make the distinction that a data field is a designated physical location for a data item on a storage medium, while the data item itself represents whatever might be contained in the location. This may be a valid distinction, but the terms tend to be used interchangeably.

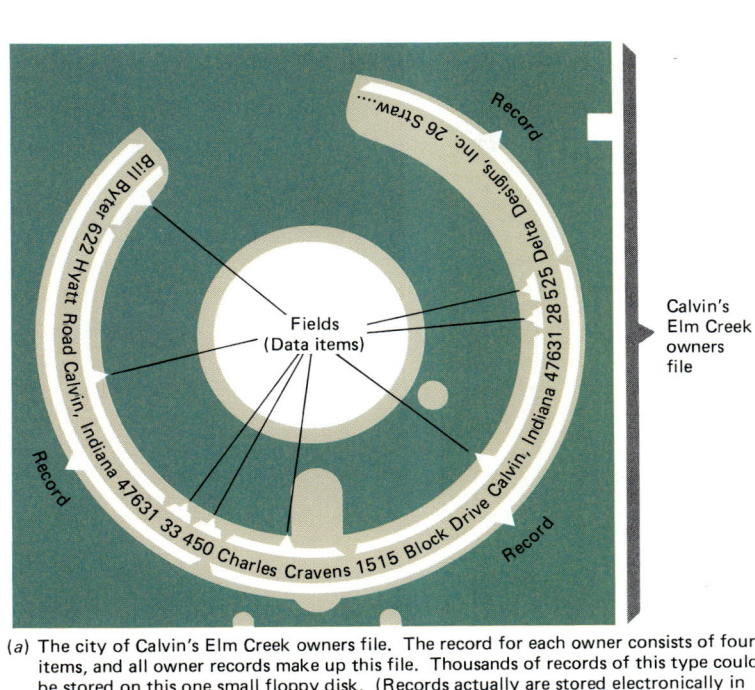

(a) The city of Calvin's Elm Creek owners file. The record for each owner consists of four items, and all owner records make up this file. Thousands of records of this type could be stored on this one small floppy disk. (Records actually are stored electronically in coded form; they are shown here as words for the sake of illustration.)

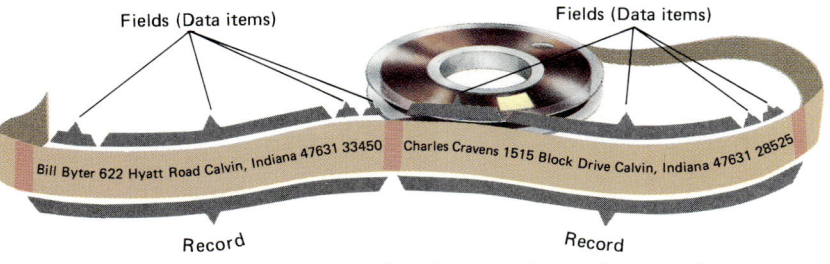

(b) Files are also maintained on other media such as magnetic tape. In a magnetic tape file, a record is stored on a short length of the tape.

FIGURE 2-1
Data organized for computer processing.

1. Input/output
2. Calculation and text manipulation
3. Logic/comparison
4. Storage and retrieval

Because computers can do these four types of operations quickly and accurately, people put them to work performing thousands of different tasks. In this chapter, you'll learn more about computer applications through a series of examples that illustrate each of the four categories. Some of these examples are processed using generalized programs that can be purchased at any computer store; others require programs written specifically for the task at hand. Since most of these applications relate to the computer-using experiences of a particular family, let's pause briefly here to meet the Byters.

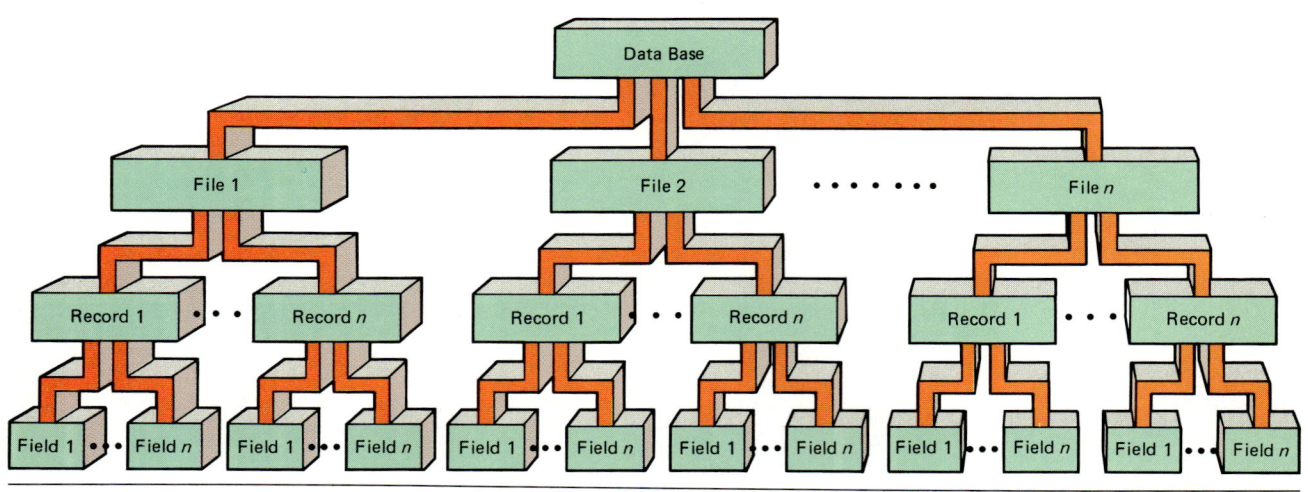

FIGURE 2-2

Data are normally organized into a hierarchy for computer processing. The data item or field is the smallest entity to be processed as a single unit. Related fields are grouped to form records, and related records are combined to form files. The highest level in the data organization hierarchy is the data base, which is a collection of related data elements.

The Byter Family

There are five members of the Byter family. You've already met Bill Byter. Bill is a property owner in Calvin who has participated in the Elm Creek Beautification Project. He's also an employee in the city planning office. Bill's spouse Marie is a social worker. Bill and Marie have three children. Jill is a student in a college's work-study program who also holds down a summer job in a hospital. Her brother Sam is a high school student and a part-time programmer who has an itch to be rich. The youngest Byter is Lisa, who's a student in an elementary school. The Byter family has a personal computer in their home. As you'll see in the following sections and in later chapters, the fictitious Byters often use their computer in very realistic ways.

Input/Output Applications

The Mailing List You saw at the beginning of the chapter that candidate Mark used a computer to print the names and addresses from a mailing list of voters onto gummed labels, to ease the mailing of campaign literature. (The creation of mailing lists is also a basic application of businesses, government agencies, religious groups, schools, and hospitals that solicit support and contributions with the help of computer-produced messages and labels.) Let's assume that Jill Byter is running for a seat in her college's Student House of Representatives. Since she plans to use mailings to gather support for her candidacy, she first compiles a list of the names and addresses of eligible voters from the student telephone directory. Jill uses a personal computer to enter these facts on a floppy disk. Thus the input data for Jill's mailing list application are contained in a file of student records. Each data record consists of the student's name, address, city, state, and Zip code. Jill also writes and stores the program to process the labels on the same disk.

To process the mailing list application and produce the gummed labels, the computer system follows the procedure shown in Figure 2-3. Jill inserts the disk in the disk drive and uses a few keystrokes to copy the program instructions from the disk to the program storage area of the processor. Under program control, a student record on the disk is copied into the input storage area. The data items are arranged in the format specified by the program and moved to the output storage area, and the mailing label is then printed. After a complete label is printed, program control branches back to step 1 and the next student record is processed. When the last record has been printed, the processing stops.

File/Data Base Management Packages Rather than write her own mailing list program, Jill could have bought a file or data base management software package to create and maintain her student voter file. The terms **file management system (FMS)** and **data base management system (DBMS)** are the names given to these packages. Both types of these comparatively easy-to-use packages allow people to define data items for the computer, place these items into designated records, and then combine these records into designated files.

CHAPTER 2

FIGURE 2-3

Using a computer to prepare mailing labels is a basic input/output application. The computer follows these steps to process this application: (1) Program instructions are copied from the disk into the program storage area, and a record from the student voter file on the disk is then read into the input storage area of the processor under program control; (2) the record fields are put in the order needed to produce the mailing label (format details are not shown here); (3) the formatted record is moved to the output storage area in the processor; (4) the mailing label is printed. These steps are repeated until all input records have been processed.

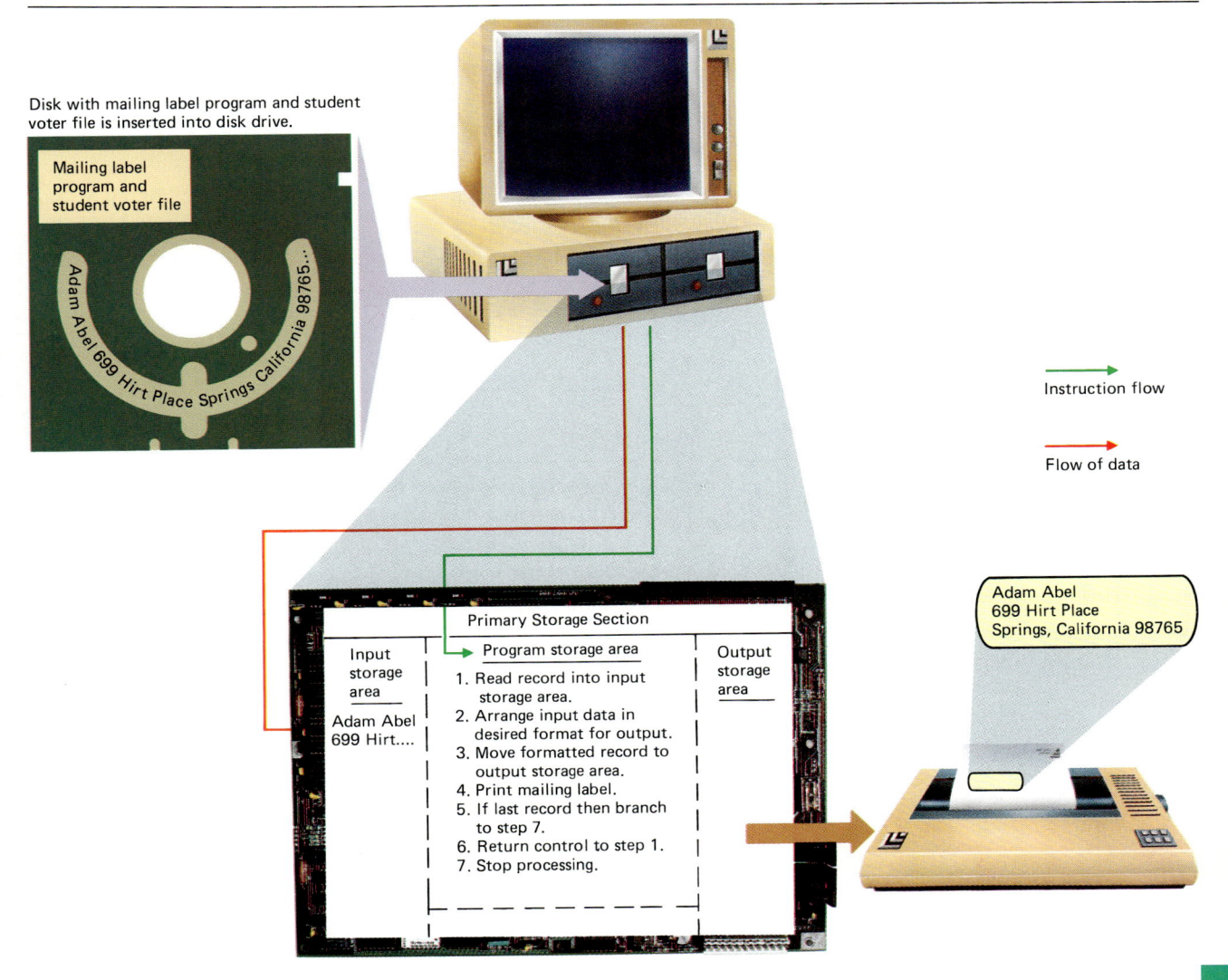

Disk with mailing label program and student voter file is inserted into disk drive.

Mailing label program and student voter file

Adam Abel 699 Hirt Place Springs California 98765...

Instruction flow

Flow of data

Adam Abel
699 Hirt Place
Springs, California 98765

Primary Storage Section

Input storage area

Adam Abel
699 Hirt....

Program storage area
1. Read record into input storage area.
2. Arrange input data in desired format for output.
3. Move formatted record to output storage area.
4. Print mailing label.
5. If last record then branch to step 7.
6. Return control to step 1.
7. Stop processing.

Output storage area

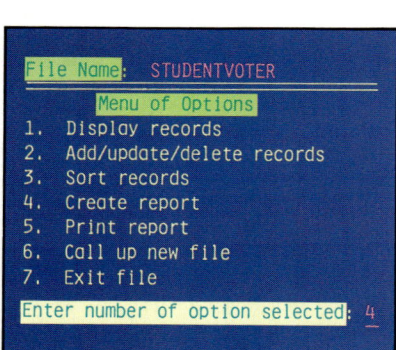

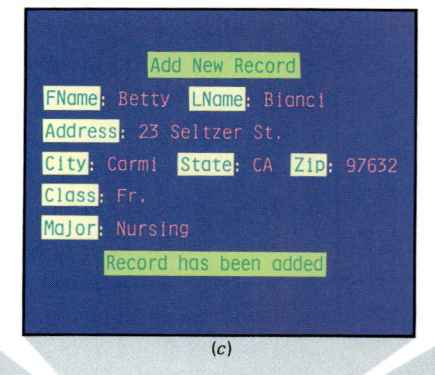

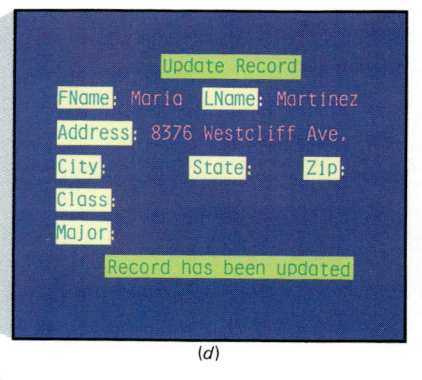

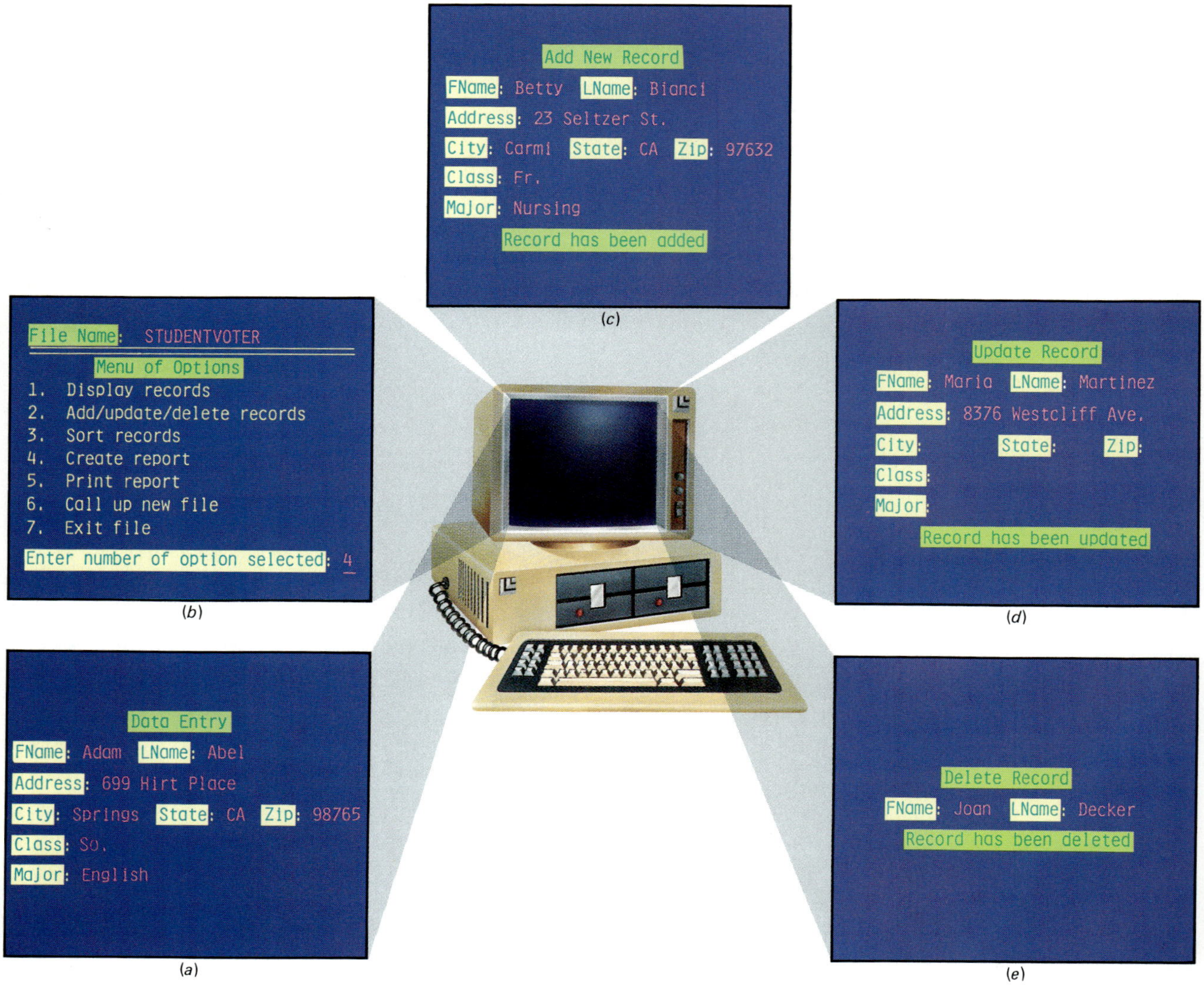

FIGURE 2-4

(a) Data are entered into records by filling in the spaces indicated on the display screen. Additional data such as hobbies, telephone numbers, and birthdays could be placed in the student records. (b) This menu shows how Jill can manipulate the records in the STUDENTVOTER file to achieve her goals. (c) New records can be easily added to the file (the student telephone directory may have omitted some eligible voters.) (d) The file or data base package also permits updating of existing records to reflect changes in names (a student gets married), addresses, classes, majors, and so on. Here the address has been changed and all other items remain the same. (e) Finally, the package allows Jill to delete records as needed (a student transfers or drops out of school).

Both types of packages can also support many separate files, but an FMS can typically access records from only one file at a time, while a DBMS can access appropriate records from two or more files at once.

Jill could use either type package to build her student voter file. For example, by responding to various **menus**—the displayed listings of the package options that users can select—Jill could first name the file (STUDENTVOTER). She could then define the name, address, and any other items she wanted to include in each record. Next, she could key in the data by repeatedly filling in the appropriate spaces on the data entry screen shown in Figure 2-4a. You'll notice that Jill has decided to add each student's class and major field of study to the other data in each record. Once the data are entered into the file, Jill can tell the package what she wants it to do by selecting a choice from a menu of options (Figure 2-4b). By selecting option 4 ("Create Report"), Jill can use package features to specify the output format needed to produce her labels (or "report"). She can then use option 5 to print the labels. Or she can use option 3 to sort records according to the students' class or major, print labels for the selected group, and then send a more personalized campaign appeal to the targeted students.

Jill can also use option 2 in the menu to *add records* to her STUDENTVOTER file (Figure 2-4c), *make changes* to existing records stored in the file (Figure 2-4d), and *delete records* from the file when they are no longer needed (Figure 2-4e). Adding, changing, and deleting file records is a common and necessary data processing task called **file maintenance** or **file updating**. The use of a file or data base management package makes this task much easier.

Outlining Packages We've all prepared outlines to guide us in writing papers or in planning other activities. Typically, our thoughts, and the sequence of those thoughts, undergo many changes before the outline is completed. An **outline processor** is a popular software package that accepts ideas, manipulates them in specified ways, and then produces an organized outline of those thoughts. A package user's first ideas may be entered in a random fashion. As ideas begin to accumulate, they can be labeled and repositioned into an outline structure. The major headings are placed at the left side of the screen, and the subheads are indented.

Let's assume that Lisa Byter is using an outline processor to organize her thoughts before writing a history paper. In Figure 2-5a, you can see that Lisa has picked a topic and has entered some thoughts on what to cover. Entries preceded by a plus sign have subheadings; those beginning with a minus sign have no lower levels. Signs can be changed and entries can be enlarged or rearranged. Lisa uses the program to quickly manipulate, expand, and convert her early ideas into the finished outline shown in Figure 2-5b. Although Lisa has used the outline software in this example, it's also popular with the other family members.

FIGURE 2-5

Outlining packages are designed to process ideas. (a) These flexible programs allow users to type in virtually any idea they may have on a topic in a "brainstorming" session. (b) The original ideas entered at random may then be quickly refined and reorganized to produce a finished outline. Outline processors can handle thousands of entries and levels.

```
+ The Revolutionary War
  - Valley Forge
  - Yorktown
  - Bunker Hill
  - The first battles
  - The last battles
```

(a)
Lisa's initial thoughts

```
+ The American Revolution
  + The war in the north
    + The early years
      - Lexington and Concord
      - Ticonderoga and Crown Point
      - Bunker Hill
      - The siege of Boston
      - Long Island to Princeton
    + The middle years
      - The Pennsylvania campaign
      - Saratoga
      - Valley Forge
    + The last years
  + The war in the south
    + The early years
    + The middle years
    + The last years
      - Charleston
      - King's Mountain
      - Yorktown
```

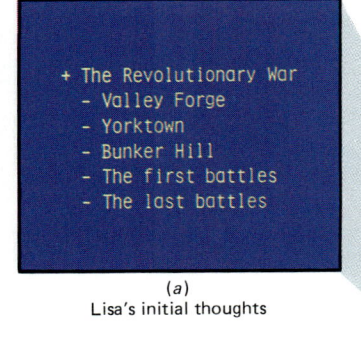

(b)
Lisa's completed outline

Calculation Applications

You may have noticed that no calculations were performed in the preceding examples. Alphanumeric data were merely entered in one form and reproduced as output in another. But some calculations are usually needed in computer applications. Recall that calculations were required before a statement could be sent to Bill Byter detailing his share of the Elm Creek beautification charges (see Figure 1-12, page 25). They are also needed in a report used by Marie Byter.

The Meals Compensation Report The social welfare organization that Marie works for is beginning an experimental program to deliver meals to needy families with preschool children. It's Marie's job to administer this program, and so she hires some part-time employees to prepare and deliver the meals. The workers are paid according to the number of meals they prepare and deliver. The amount earned is 75 cents for each cold lunch and $1.50 for each hot meal. To keep track of employee earnings and meals prepared, Marie has written a program on the family personal computer to produce a Meals Compensation Report. Figure 2-6 shows how this report is processed.

The input data are first transferred from a meals reporting form to the floppy disk that also contains Marie's program. After program instructions stored on the disk have been loaded into the program storage area, the name of the first employee is copied from the disk into the input storage space (step 1). Program control then moves to step 2. The instruction in step 2 compares the employee name to "END OF DATA." To enable the computer to know when the last valid record has been processed, a **dummy record** has been placed at the *end* of the employee data file. The words "END OF DATA" have been put in the field in this record reserved for the employee's name. Since the name of the first employee—R. Barry—obviously doesn't equal "END OF DATA," program control moves on to step 3. But when the last valid employee record is processed and the END OF DATA name field in the dummy record finally enters the input storage area, program control then branches to step 11 and processing stops.

The quantities of cold lunches (Q1) and hot meals (Q2) produced by the employee are read into the input storage area by the instruction in step 3. Program calculations are then carried out in steps 4, 6, and 7 (see Figure 2-6). Finally, the total earnings figure is moved to the output storage area (step 8), and a line is printed on the output report (step 9). Program control then returns to step 1 to begin the processing of the next employee's data.

Spreadsheet Packages Instead of writing a program to prepare her Meals Compensation Report, Marie could have used a prewritten **spreadsheet application package** to achieve the same results. (You've been introduced to this type of program in Chapter 1.) Marie's program was custom-written to process a single report, but a spreadsheet package can cope with almost any problem involving the manipulation of data organized into columns and rows.

When a spreadsheet program is loaded into a computer, the display screen is divided into a series of blank rows and columns. A common format for spreadsheet programs is to identify each row by number and each column by letter. The intersection of a column and row is called a *cell*, or *box*. The package user designates whether a cell should contain the letters in a title, the

FIGURE 2-6 *(facing page)*
Preparation of the Meals Compensation Report. The name of the first employee in the data file is read into the input storage space (step 1), and this name is then compared to "END OF DATA" in step 2. The first employee's name obviously isn't END OF DATA, so processing continues at step 3. But the name field in a dummy record placed at the end of the data file *is* END OF DATA. After all valid records have been processed, this "name" will be entered into the input storage area. Step 2 will then cause program control to branch to step 11 and processing will stop. Until then, the quantities of meals produced by each employee are entered (step 3). The number of cold lunches produced (Q1) is multiplied by $0.75 (step 4), and this earnings figure is moved to the working storage area (step 5). Next, the quantity of hot meals prepared (Q2) is multiplied by $1.50 (step 6), and the earnings amount in working storage is added to this product (step 7) to get the total earnings for each employee. Steps 8 and 9 produce a printed line on the output report, and program control branches back to step 1. The numbers in this diagram show the progression of the program steps.

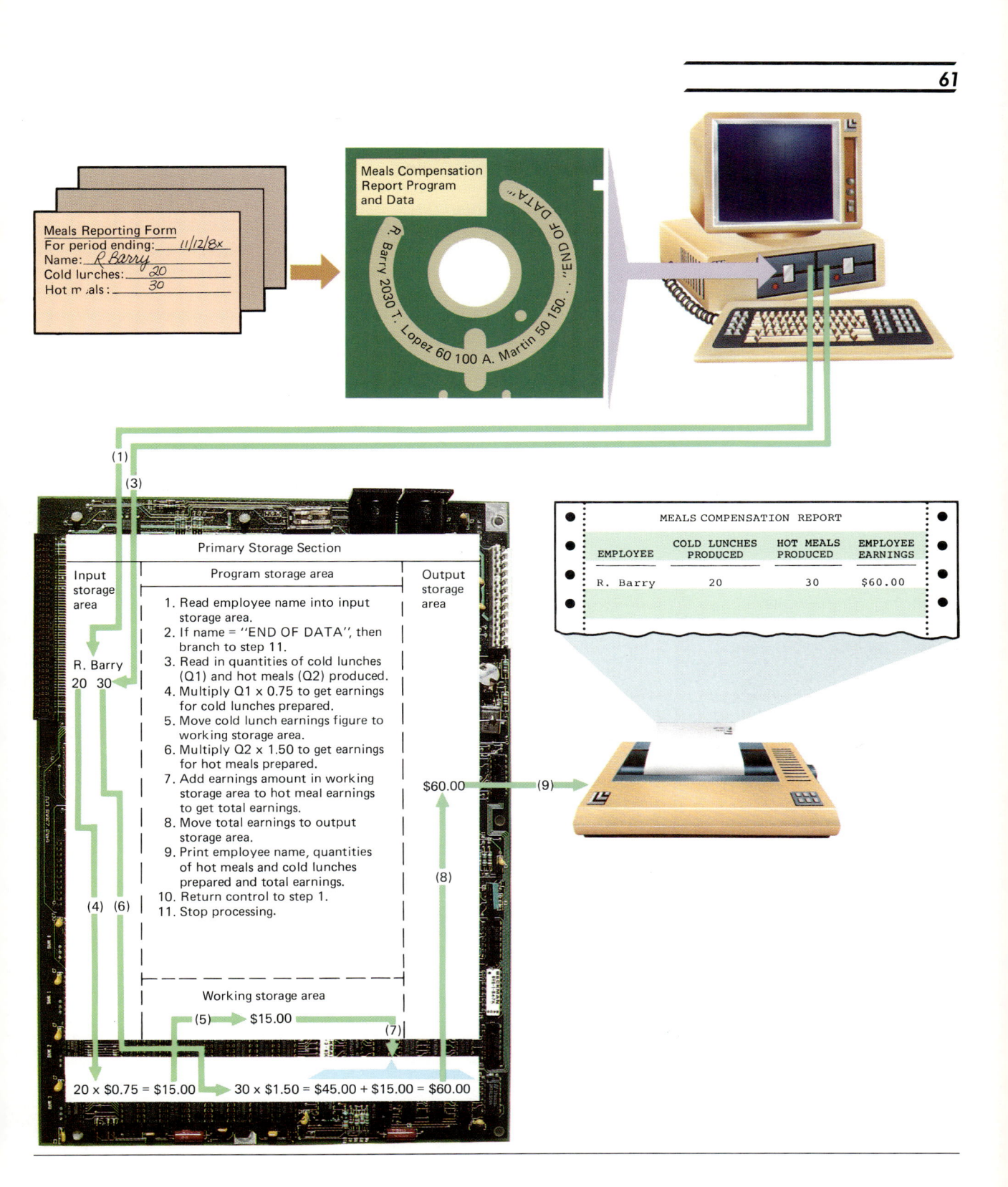

numbers to be manipulated, or the mathematical relationships or formulas that control the processing. Let's look at Figure 2-7 to see how Marie can use a spreadsheet program to produce the Meals Compensation Report.

FIGURE 2-7

A spreadsheet package can be used to produce the Meals Compensation Report. Records for only three employees are shown, but the spreadsheet program can hold thousands of records. Once the user of a spreadsheet program designs the format for the rows and columns and designates the relationships of the cells, new data can be entered and the program will automatically recalculate and display the results. For example, Marie could vary the number of meals produced to see how this would affect her employee labor budget.

Calculations performed by spreadsheet program in response to Marie's instructions.

Marie places her report headings in the first five rows. For example, the EMPLOYEE title is found in cell A4 (the box located at the intersection of column A and row 4), and the EMPLOYEE EARNINGS heading is located in cells D3 and D4 (rows 3 and 4 in the D column). The employee data are then entered in rows 6, 7, and 8, using the spreadsheet format Marie has designed. To calculate the employee earnings values found in column D, Marie specifies a relationship or instruction for box D6 that looks like this:

+(B6 * 0.75) + (C6 * 1.50)

This instruction tells the spreadsheet program to (1) multiply the contents of box B6 by $0.75 (the asterisk means multiply), (2) multiply the contents of box C6 by $1.50, (3) add the products of these two calculations, and (4) place the total in cell D6. The same type of instruction is repeated to produce the other figures in column D.

You'll notice too that Marie has decided to have the spreadsheet program *total* the B, C, and D columns. To get the total for column B, Marie has specified this formula for cell B10:

+(B6 + B7 + B8)

This tells the program to add the contents of rows 6, 7, and 8 in the B column and store the result in row 10 of the same column. The computer totals columns C and D in the same way. You can see from this example that a spreadsheet package can be a powerful calculating and report-generating tool.

Graphics Packages Let's assume that Marie has decided to use a **graphics software package** to bring to life the numbers in her Meals Compensation Report. (You've also seen this type of program in Chapter 1.) After supplying the program with the data to be analyzed, Marie makes a preliminary chart selection from a menu of chart formats supplied by her program (Figure 2-8a). The program will quickly display Marie's data in the chart format she selects (Figure 2-8b). She can vary colors, add descriptive headings, and move these headings around on the screen. If she's not pleased with her first

FIGURE 2-8 *(facing page)*

A graphics package can generate charts and graphs from numerical input. Although data presented in graphic form are easier to absorb and remember, these visual aids were seldom used in the past because their preparation was time-consuming and expensive. Now, however, many inexpensive and easy-to-use graphics packages are available for use with personal computers.

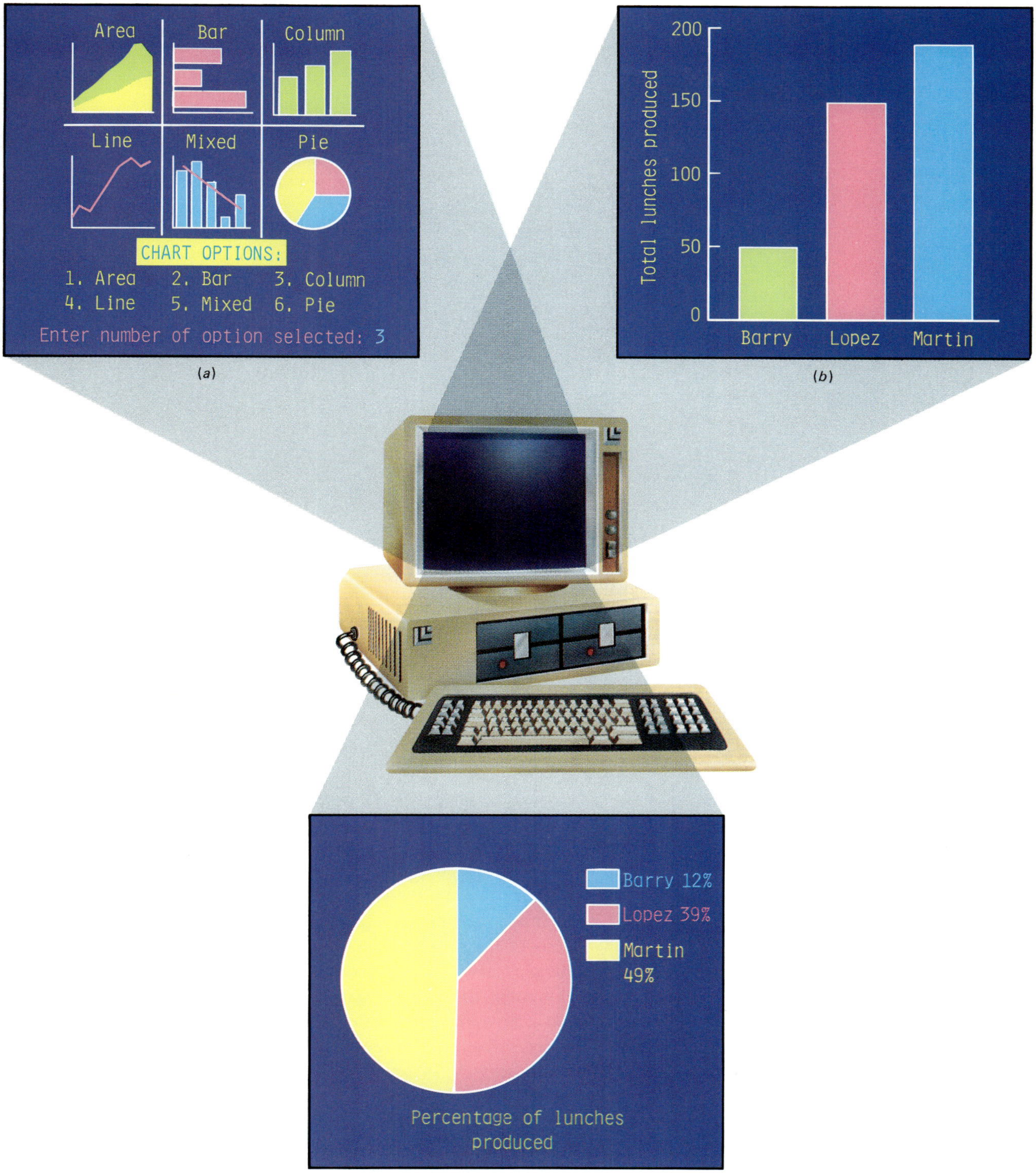

(a)

Area | Bar | Column
Line | Mixed | Pie

CHART OPTIONS:
1. Area   2. Bar   3. Column
4. Line   5. Mixed   6. Pie

Enter number of option selected: 3

(b)

Total lunches produced

Barry | Lopez | Martin

(c)

Barry 12%
Lopez 39%
Martin 49%

Percentage of lunches produced

selection, she can try out other formats (Figure 2-8c). When she has settled on what she wants, Marie can store the chart format on a disk for future use. She can then use an output device, such as a printer or plotter, to put the chart on paper.

Updating Sam's Savings Account Most of us have deposited and withdrawn money from a savings account at a bank, savings and loan, or other financial institution. Such transactions require calculations that are now handled by computer systems. Sam Byter has read about the young entrepreneurs who have made fortunes in the personal computer industry, and he's determined to follow in their footsteps. In fact, he's already making some money as a part-time programmer. Let's assume that Sam has decided to deposit in his savings account a $90 fee he has just earned from a small business in Calvin.

After filling out a deposit ticket, Sam presents the ticket, his savings account passbook, and his $90 check to a teller. The teller inserts the passbook into an online transaction terminal (see Figure 2-9) and keys in the transaction data in response to questions displayed on the terminal screen. The data are then sent to the input storage area of the processor. For Sam's deposit, a transaction code "D" is entered. However, the instructions in the program storage area are also capable of handling withdrawals.

When the input data are received, the computer retrieves Sam's savings account record from an online secondary storage device and adds the $90 deposit to his previous balance of $810. The account number, customer name, and new balance of $900 are then moved to the output storage area. From there the updated record is used to (1) replace the old account record in online secondary storage and (2) print an updated account balance in Sam's passbook that is inserted in the teller's terminal. This entire input/processing/output operation takes only a few seconds.

Text Manipulation Applications

You've already seen how text is manipulated with an outlining package to produce an organized sequence of thoughts. Similarly, a **word processing package** can be used to create, view, edit, store, retrieve, and print text. Before word processing became commonplace, preparing written communications was a time-consuming and expensive process. It's still a big job. But it's a lot easier now that millions of office and home computers are equipped with word processing programs.

For example, an office seeker can write campaign letters and send them to voters to remind them of the outstanding qualities of the candidate. Of course, these letters could be preprinted, but such form letters are often ignored. To personalize each letter, and to create an original copy for each voter, a word processing system can be used. Let's assume that Jill Byter—still seeking election to the Student House of Representatives—wants to use a personal computer and a word processing package to send out campaign letters. (After all, she needs to put *something* in the envelopes addressed with her gummed mailing labels!)

The first step is to create a series of "personalized" campaign letters using the keyboard and word processing program (see Figure 2-10). Since Jill's a nursing student, the first letter in the series will be sent to other nursing

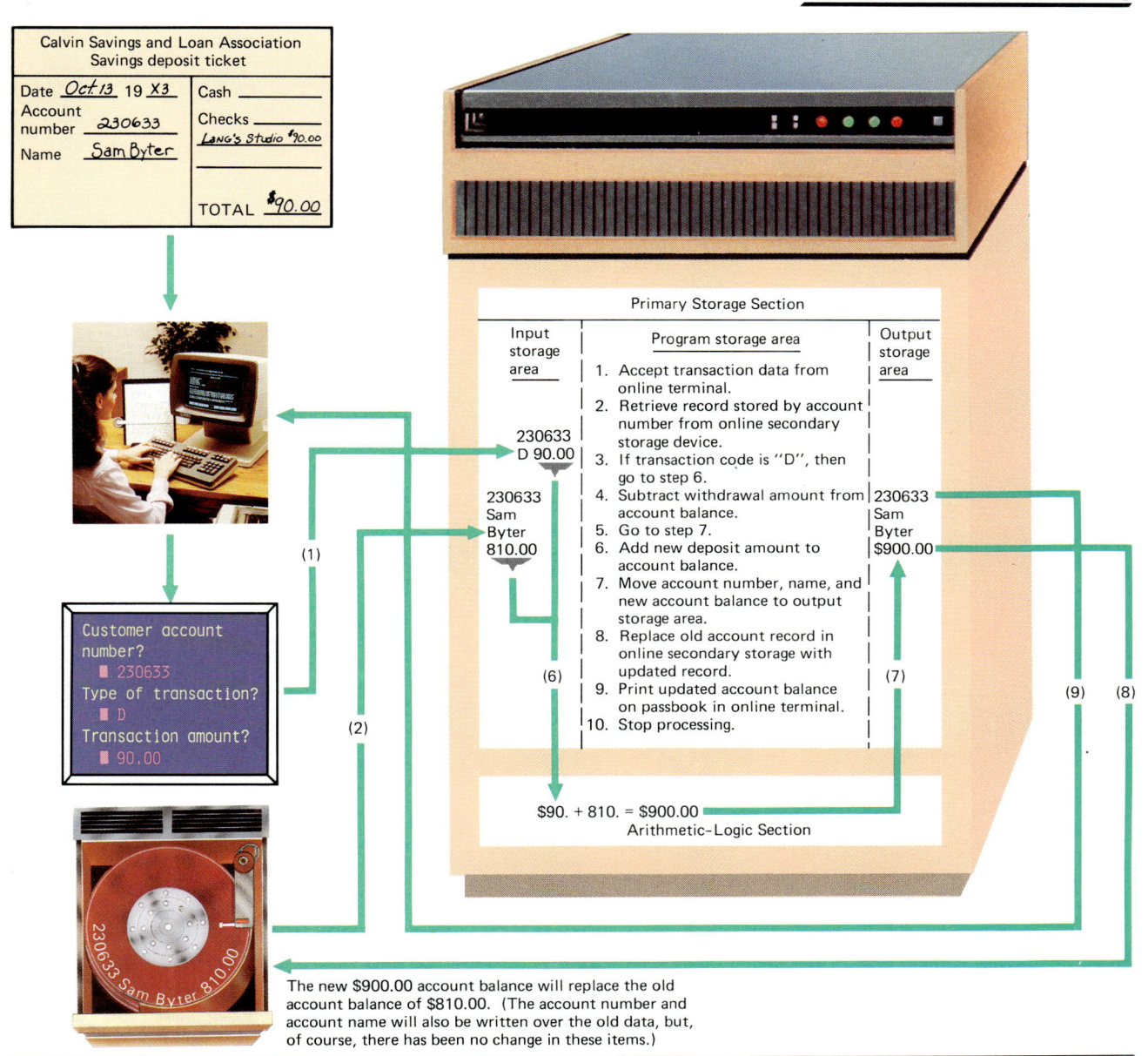

FIGURE 2-9

A computer system may be used to update savings account balances by following the program steps outlined in the program storage area. (The figures in parentheses refer to effects of numbered program steps.)

The new $900.00 account balance will replace the old account balance of $810.00. (The account number and account name will also be written over the old data, but, of course, there has been no change in these items.)

majors. A draft of the text can be written as shown in screen (*a*) in Figure 2-10. Dissatisfied with this original draft, Jill and her campaign manager begin to edit the displayed text. Additional words are quickly *added* (screen *b*), and the program automatically adjusts the screen position of the original text. Finally, some text is *deleted* (screen *c*), to complete the editing process for the first letter. A second letter could be aimed at Jill's classmates. Commuter students who live in certain Zip code areas could be the targets of a third letter, and so on. Once created, these letters can be stored by document name on a floppy disk, as shown in Figure 2-10.

After a letter has been written and stored, it can be easily retrieved. After

(a) The original draft

Dear _____:

The Student House of Representatives election is coming soon. We need a nursing major who'll fight for health-care students.

Please remember, ___, to vote for Jill Byter.

　　　　　　Sincerely,

　　　　　　Campaign Manager

(b) The addition of text

Dear _____:

The Student House of Representatives election is coming soon. We need a nursing major who'll fight for the interests of health-care students.

Please remember, ___, to vote for Jill Byter in the forthcoming election.

　　　　　　Sincerely,

　　　　　　Campaign Manager

(c) The final edited version with text deleted

Dear _____:

The Student House of Representatives needs a nursing major who'll fight for the interests of health-care students.

Please remember, ___, to vote for Jill Byter in the forthcoming election.

　　　　　　Sincerely,

　　　　　　Campaign Manager

② Additions and deletions are easily made to get a final *edited* version of a letter.

Word Processing Program

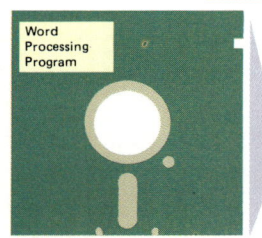

① A personal computer and a word processing program are used to *create* the text of Jill's letters.

③ The text of the letters is *stored* on a floppy disk. This may be the disk that contains the word processing program, or it may be a separate disk.

Jill's letters stored by document name on floppy disk.

④ When a letter is needed, the disk(s) containing the word processing program and stored text is(are) inserted into the computer. The desired letter form is *retrieved* and a name and address is entered through the Keyboard. (With appropriate software, it's possible to *merge* the names and addresses stored in a mailing list file into this operation, thereby eliminating the need to rekey the data.)

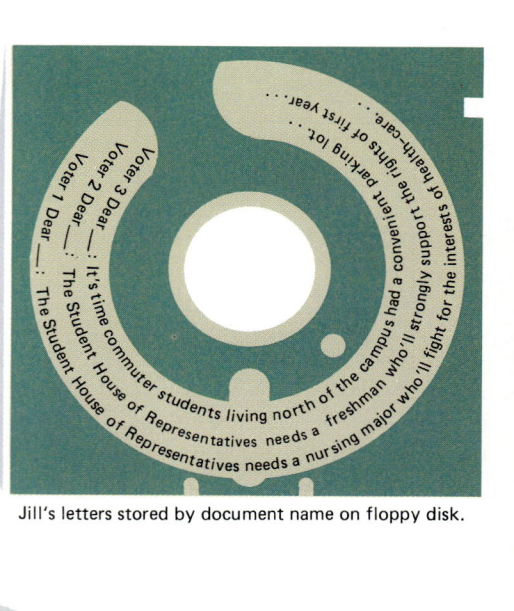

Primary Storage Section

Input storage area	Program storage area	Output storage area
VOTER 1 Dear __: The Student House of Representatives needs a nursing major who'll fight . . . Betty Bianci 23 Seltzer St. Carmi, CA 97632	1. Request data from operator. 2. Read document name into input storage area. 3. Duplicate in input storage area the text stored by document name in online storage device. 4. Read name and address into input storage area. 5. Duplicate contents of appropriate name field in designated text locations. 6. Move name, address, and text to output storage area. 7. Print letter in desired format. 8. Stop processing.	Betty Bianci 23 Seltzer St. Carmi, CA 97632 Dear Betty: The Student House of Representatives needs a nursing major who'll fight . . .

(7) →

Betty Bianci
23 Seltzer St.
Carmi, CA 97632

Dear Betty:

The Student House of Representatives needs a nursing major who'll fight for the interests of health-care students.

Please remember, Betty, to vote for Jill Byter in the forthcoming election.

　　　　　　Sincerely,
　　　　　　John Mahle
　　　　　　Campaign Manager

inserting the disk (or disks) containing the word processing program and the stored text, the operator uses a few keystrokes to load the word processing program into the program storage area and to then notify it that a particular document is needed (steps 1 and 2 in the program storage area). The program locates the needed text and duplicates it in the primary storage section (step 3). Next, the operator keys in the name and address of the person to whom the letter should be sent, and these facts are also read into primary storage (step 4). Finally, the program inserts the addressee's name into the text at appropriate places to personalize the message, and the letter is printed (steps 5 through 7). You can see from Figure 2-10 that efficiency and productivity are enhanced by the use of word processing systems.

Interactive and Batch Processing

"Interactive" and "batch" are terms that describe the *timing* of the processing of applications. Although we haven't used these terms before, we've already examined the concepts.

Interactive Processing **Interactive processing** occurs *immediately* after input data are entered into a computer system, and the output results of the processing are quickly produced. Our *first* interactive processing example in Figure 2-11 is the savings simulation example we saw in Figure 1-2. Here, the user responds to *program queries* to supply savings amount, interest rate, and years-to-maturity input data. The system reacts instantly to process the data and produce the output information, and is then ready to interact further.

Our *second* interactive processing example in Figure 2-11 is the updating of Sam Byter's savings account (from Figure 2-9). The input data in this case—Sam's name, account number, and deposit amount—are entered into an online transaction terminal by a teller responding to questions displayed on a screen. The computer system then immediately locates and retrieves Sam's savings account record, updates his account balance, and prints the transaction on his savings passbook. This type of interactive processing is often called online **transaction processing** (Figure 2-11).

In our *third* interactive processing situation, the system supplies up-to-the-minute information in response to the inquiries it receives from user workstations. In Figure 2-11, a salesperson uses a workstation to answer a customer's question about the availability of a part. Similarly, an airline ticket agent can have immediate access to reservation system records to see if seats are currently available on particular flights. If you purchase a ticket from the agent for flight 205 to Boston, the agent can update the appropriate record instantly by reserving a seat for you.

Batch Processing We've seen that data may be entered into a computer and processed immediately on an interactive basis at the time a transaction occurs.

⬅ **FIGURE 2-10** *(facing page)*

A word processing system. Here the text is created at a personal computer and stored on a floppy disk. (Photo courtesy Apple Computer, Inc.)

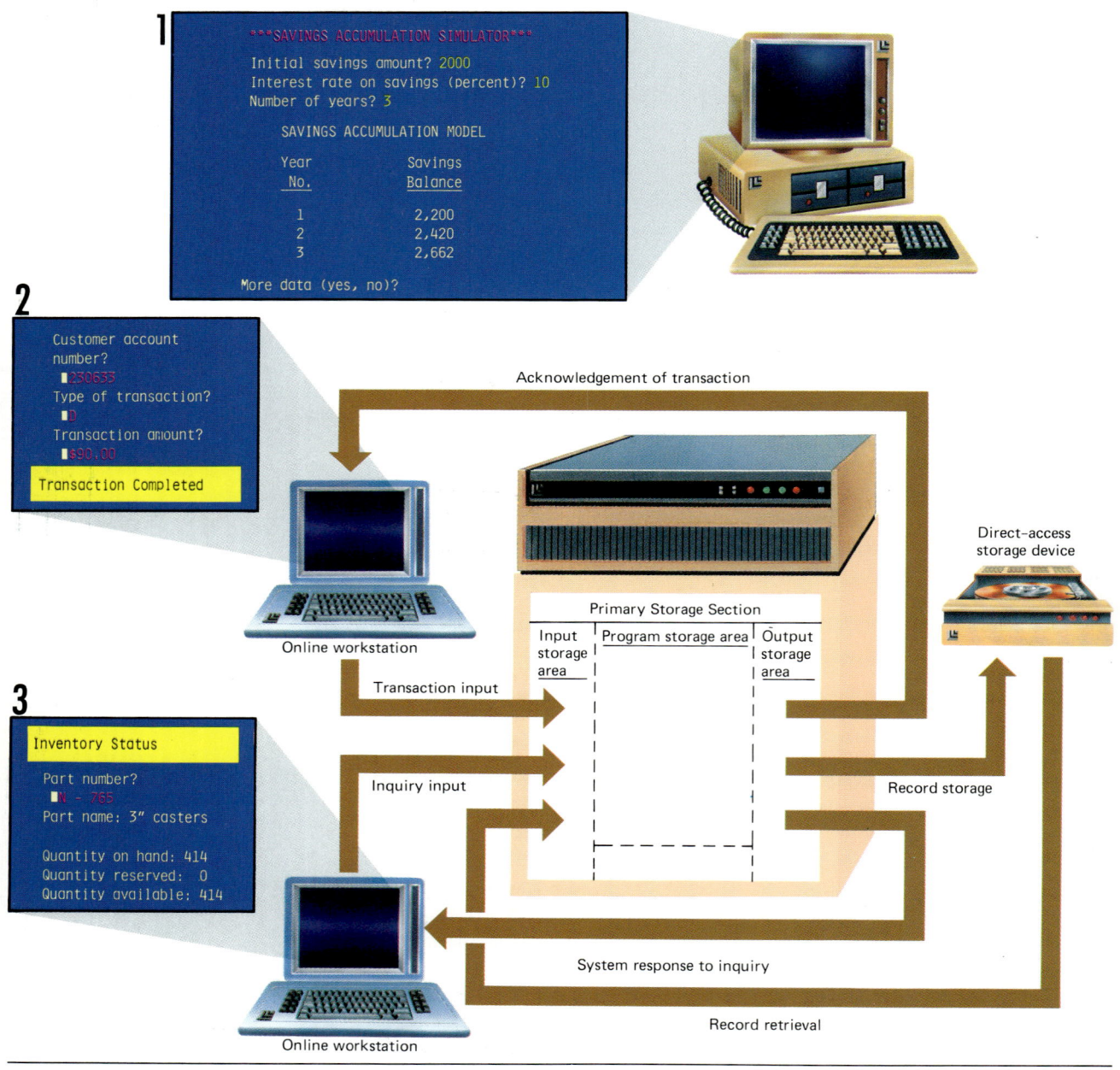

FIGURE 2-11

Three interactive processing examples. (1) The user responds to program queries. (2 and 3) Transactions and inquiries about the current status of records are entered into the processor from keyboards and online workstations. The access to, and retrieval of, a file record stored in an online secondary storage device is accomplished in a fraction of a second. Once the record has been updated or has provided up-to-the-minute information about its contents to the inquiry station, it is returned directly to a designated location in the direct-access storage device.

But in **batch processing,** the data are gathered for a period of time and collected into a group (or *batch*) before they are entered into a computer system and processed. The processing of the Elm Creek beautification charges (Figure 1-12, page 25), the printing of Jill Byter's mailing labels (Figure 2-3), and the preparation of Marie Byter's Meals Compensation Report (Figure 2-6) are all examples of batch processing. When batch processing is used, the input data are typically (but not always) recorded on source documents before being converted into a machine-readable form. (The city of Calvin captured Elm Creek charges on job tickets; Marie's data came from a meals reporting form.) In each of our examples, the accumulated data were stored on floppy disks and were then processed in batches.

Batch techniques were used almost exclusively in the early 1960s to process computer applications. But for many jobs the delay caused by accumulating data into batches was a serious problem. In those days, for example, a sales engineer might know that inventory was available on May 10 to fill an order, but she couldn't assure her customer on May 18 that his order could still be filled. To solve this problem, interactive processing is now replacing batch processing in many situations. The Diebold Group, Inc., a management consulting firm, estimates that the percentage of the computer workload classified as batch processing declined from nearly 50 percent of the total in 1982 to about 33 percent in 1985.

Still, batch processing remains an efficient approach to use in such applications as preparing bills, processing payroll checks, and accounting for credit-card purchases. After all, you don't want to get a water bill every time you take a drink, nor do you expect to get paid every hour. Clearly, it makes sense to accumulate such data as water usage, hours worked, and credit charges made, and then process all the data for a period at once.

Combined Processing Systems It's possible to combine the useful features of interactive and batch processing in a single system. A common practice is to use interactive processing when users are waiting and a quick response is needed. At the same time, data produced by the interactive processing may be captured and accumulated into batches so that it may be processed later. For example, the purchase you make at a department store today may be handled immediately by a clerk using an online workstation. But the data generated by your purchase (the item bought, the purchase amount, the department and store involved, and so on) is accumulated and used to produce management reports at a later time.

A Logic/Comparison Application

You saw in Chapter 1 (Figure 1-7, page 18) that a computer is able to perform logical operations by comparing numbers, letters, or other symbols and then following a prescribed course of action determined by the comparison. Logical operations have played a part in several of our earlier applications. For example, the program in Figure 2-3 (Jill's mailing label application) contains a step that reads: "If last record then branch to step 7." You know that the purpose of such an instruction is to determine whether the last valid record in a file has been processed. If the last record *has* been processed, the computer is directed to the steps necessary to stop the processing. Otherwise, program control branches back to an earlier step to process another record.

How does the computer know when the last valid record has been processed? One approach was shown in Figure 2-6 (Marie's Meals Compensation Report). You'll recall that the *dummy record* placed at the end of Marie's employee file has "END OF DATA" in the employee name field. Each employee name was then compared to "END OF DATA." When a match was made, the program knew that all valid records had been read, and the processing stopped.

Let's look briefly now at another logic/comparison example—one that relates to Bill Byter's job in the Calvin City Planning Office. Bill is managing

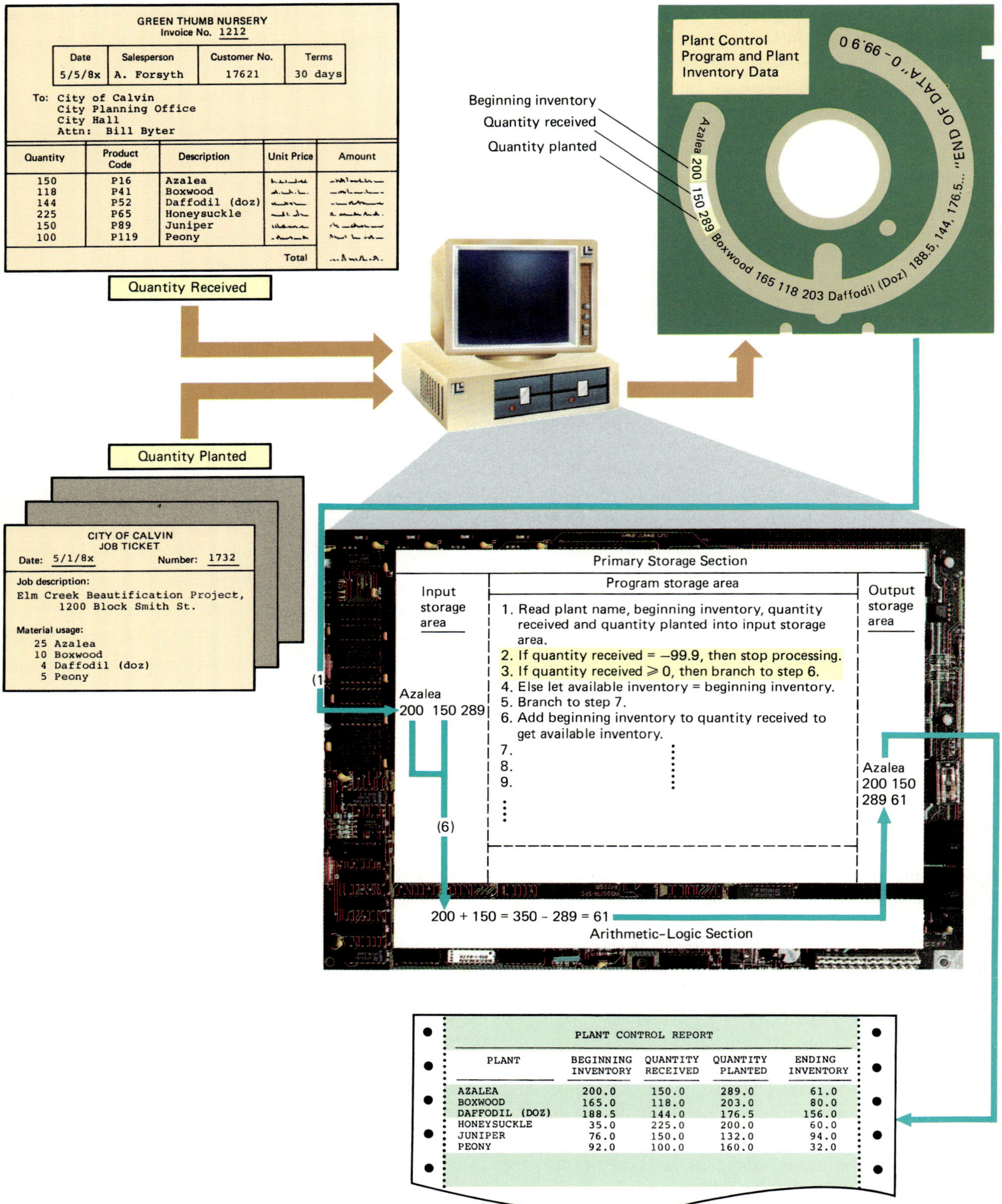

70

GREEN THUMB NURSERY
Invoice No. 1212

Date	Salesperson	Customer No.	Terms
5/5/8x	A. Forsyth	17621	30 days

To: City of Calvin
City Planning Office
City Hall
Attn: Bill Byter

Quantity	Product Code	Description	Unit Price	Amount
150	P16	Azalea		
118	P41	Boxwood		
144	P52	Daffodil (doz)		
225	P65	Honeysuckle		
150	P89	Juniper		
100	P119	Peony		
			Total	

Quantity Received

CITY OF CALVIN
JOB TICKET

Date: 5/1/8x   Number: 1732

Job description:
Elm Creek Beautification Project,
1200 Block Smith St.

Material usage:
  25 Azalea
  10 Boxwood
   4 Daffodil (doz)
   5 Peony

Quantity Planted

Plant Control Program and Plant Inventory Data

Azalea 200 150 289 Boxwood 165 118 203 Daffodil (Doz) 188.5 144 176.5... "END OF DATA" 0 -99.9 0

Beginning inventory
Quantity received
Quantity planted

Primary Storage Section

Input storage area

(1)

Azalea
200 150 289

(6)

Program storage area

1. Read plant name, beginning inventory, quantity received and quantity planted into input storage area.
2. If quantity received = −99.9, then stop processing.
3. If quantity received ≥ 0, then branch to step 6.
4. Else let available inventory = beginning inventory.
5. Branch to step 7.
6. Add beginning inventory to quantity received to get available inventory.
7.
8.
9.
⋮

Output storage area

Azalea
200 150
289 61

200 + 150 = 350 − 289 = 61

Arithmetic-Logic Section

PLANT CONTROL REPORT

PLANT	BEGINNING INVENTORY	QUANTITY RECEIVED	QUANTITY PLANTED	ENDING INVENTORY
AZALEA	200.0	150.0	289.0	61.0
BOXWOOD	165.0	118.0	203.0	80.0
DAFFODIL (DOZ)	188.5	144.0	176.5	156.0
HONEYSUCKLE	35.0	225.0	200.0	60.0
JUNIPER	76.0	150.0	132.0	94.0
PEONY	92.0	100.0	160.0	32.0

the inventory of plants that the city is buying to beautify Elm Creek. To keep track of this inventory, Bill has written a program that produces a Plant Control Report. A few of the steps required to process this report are shown in the program storage area in Figure 2-12.

Let's just concentrate on the two logic/comparison operations presented in Figure 2-12. As you can see, source documents provide Bill with quantity-planted and quantity-received data. These facts are keyed onto a floppy disk and are then entered into Bill's computer under program control (step 1 in the program storage area). The *first* logic/comparison operation in step 2 is a test to see if all valid records have been processed. The value stored in the quantity-received field of the input record is compared to a value of −99.9. If this quantity is not −99.9, the processing continues in sequence. If the quantity received is −99.9, the processing stops. A quantity of −99.9 plants will never be received, of course. But such a value is used in a last dummy record at the end of Bill's data file to indicate that all valid records have been processed. Naming the plant in the last record "END OF DATA" and then making a test against that field would produce the same result.

It's a common practice to include steps in programs to detect errors in data entry, and this is the purpose of the *second* logic/comparison operation found in step 3. The inventory available for planting *should* be found by adding the plants received to the beginning inventory (step 6). To help prevent a data error, Bill has set up the logic/comparison operation in step 3. This step tells the computer what to do if the quantity-received value in some record other than the dummy record is found to be a negative number. If any record is *not* greater than or equal to (≥) zero, a provision in the program keeps the available inventory equal to the beginning inventory (steps 4 and 5).

Additional program steps (not shown in Figure 2-12) are used to process a plant record and print a line on the Plant Control Report shown in Figure 2-12. Program control then branches back to step 1, and processing begins on the next plant record which will produce another line on the report.

Storage/Retrieval Applications

We've seen how computers are used to perform input/output, calculation, text manipulation, and logic/comparison operations on data. The computer's ability to store and retrieve programs and data was obviously vital in each of these applications. Let's look now at some popular software packages that emphasize these storage/retrieval functions.

Communications Packages   A **communications package** is software that speeds the flow of data throughout a network of computers and workstations. Data stored at one office can be distributed electronically to other locations (Figure 2-13a). Users in the other locations can retrieve and examine the data at their convenience and fire off responses if necessary. We'll discuss the use of such **electronic mail** systems in Chapter 8.

In addition to providing the programs needed to support the flow of data between offices, communications packages also provide easier access to data stored in the huge online libraries of outside information services. Computer users can subscribe to such services and then use regular telephone lines to retrieve vast amounts of information stored in over 1,000 data banks. But instead of dialing a 10-digit number and then keying in a password and a user

FIGURE 2-12 (facing page)

The system designed by Bill Byter to prepare his Plant Control Report. Source documents provide data on the number of plants received and planted. These facts are keyed onto a floppy disk and are then read under program control into the computer's program storage area. After reading in the input data for the first plant ("Azalea") in step 1, the program sets up the *first* logic/comparison operation (step 2). If the value of the quantity-received field in the input record is equal to −99.9, processing will stop. (This will occur when the last dummy record at the end of the data file which has a quantity-received value of −99.9 is read.) Since the quantity-received value in the first input record isn't −99.9, the program moves to step 3. This *second* logic/comparison operation is designed to detect an error in data entry. If the quantity-received value in some record other than the dummy record is found to be a negative number (*not* ≥ 0), step 4 will keep the available inventory equal to the beginning inventory. Of course, the normal progression through the program should be to branch from step 3 to step 6 because the inventory available for planting *should* be found by adding the plants received to the beginning inventory (step 6).

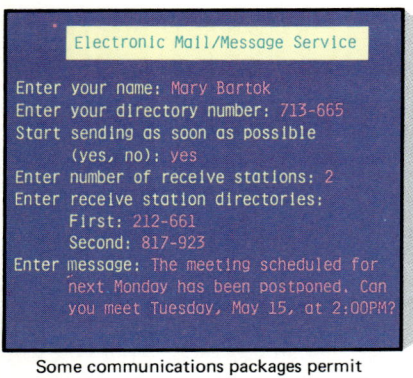

```
Electronic Mail/Message Service

Enter your name: Mary Bartok
Enter your directory number: 713-665
Start sending as soon as possible
     (yes, no): yes
Enter number of receive stations: 2
Enter receive station directories:
     First: 212-661
     Second: 817-923
Enter message: The meeting scheduled for
     next Monday has been postponed. Can
     you meet Tuesday, May 15, at 2:00PM?
```

Some communications packages permit users to send and receive electronic mail.

(a)

```
Data Bank Selection Menu
1. Dow Jones News/Retrieval
2. The Source
3. CompuServe
4. BRS/Search
5. Dialog
6. NEXIS
7. Orbit Search Service
8. Exit

Enter number of selection: 2
```

Communications packages can also put computer users in touch with a world of stored information with just a few keystrokes.

(b)

FIGURE 2-13

Communications packages make it easier for users to get the information they need. Electronic mail allows users to exchange data and messages, while information services give subscribers access to huge libraries of stored facts.

number every time a data bank is accessed, a subscriber can use a communication package that will automatically run through all the necessary log-on procedures (Figure 2-13b). Log-off procedures are also handled automatically by the package.

Project Management Packages   A *project* is a special task that must usually be completed over a relatively short period of time. All organizations have projects that must be managed: A hospital or school must build a new wing, a government must beautify its property along a creek (sound familiar?), an archaeologist must prepare a site for study, a company must develop and introduce a new product, and so on. A **project management package** is software that helps managers plan, schedule, and control the human and material resources required to complete such projects on time and for a reasonable cost. A manager identifies the project activities that must be performed, determines the sequence in which those tasks must be carried out, and estimates the time needed to complete each task.

Once these initial steps have been entered and stored in the system, the project management package then identifies the *longest* sequence of events in the project. The sum of the individual activity times in this sequence becomes the total project time, and this sequence of tasks is known as the **critical path.** Figure 2-14 shows how a package can help an engineer identify the critical path jobs required to complete the laying of electrical cable under a downtown street. By focusing on the tasks in the critical path, the engineer can quickly pinpoint potential problems. If a critical activity begins to fall behind schedule, she can retrieve the stored data to determine what steps can be taken to correct the situation. For example, she can simulate a different mix of resources to commit to the job, and she can then ask the program to determine project time after each change. Project management software packages were first used on large machines, but they are now readily available for personal computers.

Time Management Packages   We've seen how busy people use spreadsheets, graphics packages, and word processing programs to streamline their activities. But many busy people are frustrated because they lack the time

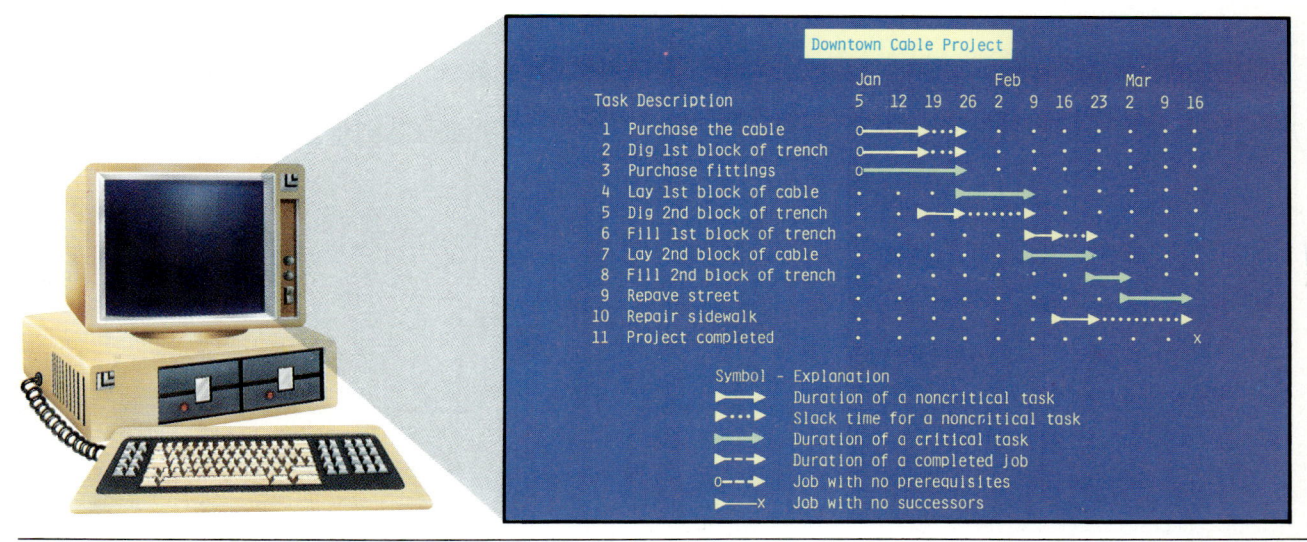

```
                        Downtown Cable Project
                                  Jan              Feb            Mar
   Task Description      5   12  19  26   2   9  16  23   2   9  16
    1  Purchase the cable
    2  Dig 1st block of trench
    3  Purchase fittings
    4  Lay 1st block of cable
    5  Dig 2nd block of trench
    6  Fill 1st block of trench
    7  Lay 2nd block of cable
    8  Fill 2nd block of trench
    9  Repave street
   10  Repair sidewalk
   11  Project completed

        Symbol  -  Explanation
          ▶        Duration of a noncritical task
          ▶···▶    Slack time for a noncritical task
          ▶        Duration of a critical task
          ▶--▶     Duration of a completed job
          o---▶    Job with no prerequisites
          ▶---x    Job with no successors
```

FIGURE 2-14

Project management packages can be used in most organizations. In a construction project, for example, such a package improves *planning* because it forces engineers to identify all the project tasks that must be performed. *Control* is also improved because engineers can direct their attention to the sequence of tasks in the critical path. If a task slips behind schedule, the data on project resources can be retrieved and checked to see how the situation can be corrected. The program can be asked to determine how the addition of extra resources will affect the critical path. By a greater commitment of resources, managers can often reduce the time required to complete a task in the critical path and thus reduce project time.

each day to do what needs to be done. It's not surprising that many of them turn again to their personal computers for help.

A **time management package** (also called **accessory software**) is an aid that you can employ to plan and control your use of time more effectively. It takes over several time-consuming office tasks and allows you to carry out most or all of the following activities:

1 You can store the wealth of material that you may need to have at your fingertips, such as names, addresses, phone lists, expenses, things to do, ideas that need to be followed up, appointments, and so on. All this material can be retrieved with a few keystrokes.

2 You can have your own private "telephone operator" that will retrieve and then dial telephone numbers, and will remind you with a chime and a note on the display screen when it's time to make an important call.

3 You can display a "desk calculator" on the screen along with an electronic paper tape that permits you to perform and record calculations.

4 You can press a few keys every morning to retrieve your appointment calendar along with your notes that remind you of the time, place, and subject of the day's activities (Figure 2-15a). The program can sound a chime to let you know when you should leave for a meeting.

Time management packages typically reside in a quiet corner of the computer's primary storage area while the user is preparing a spreadsheet, working on a document, or doing other work. But these programs and the data entrusted to their care are always available with a few keystrokes. For example, if you're preparing a document with a word processing program and you want to total a column of figures in the text, you can retrieve the screen calculator, make your computations, and then return to your place in the document with a keystroke (Figure 2-15b). Or if you're working on a spreadsheet and someone calls to cancel a meeting, you can quickly retrieve your appointment calendar and review your planned activities before rescheduling

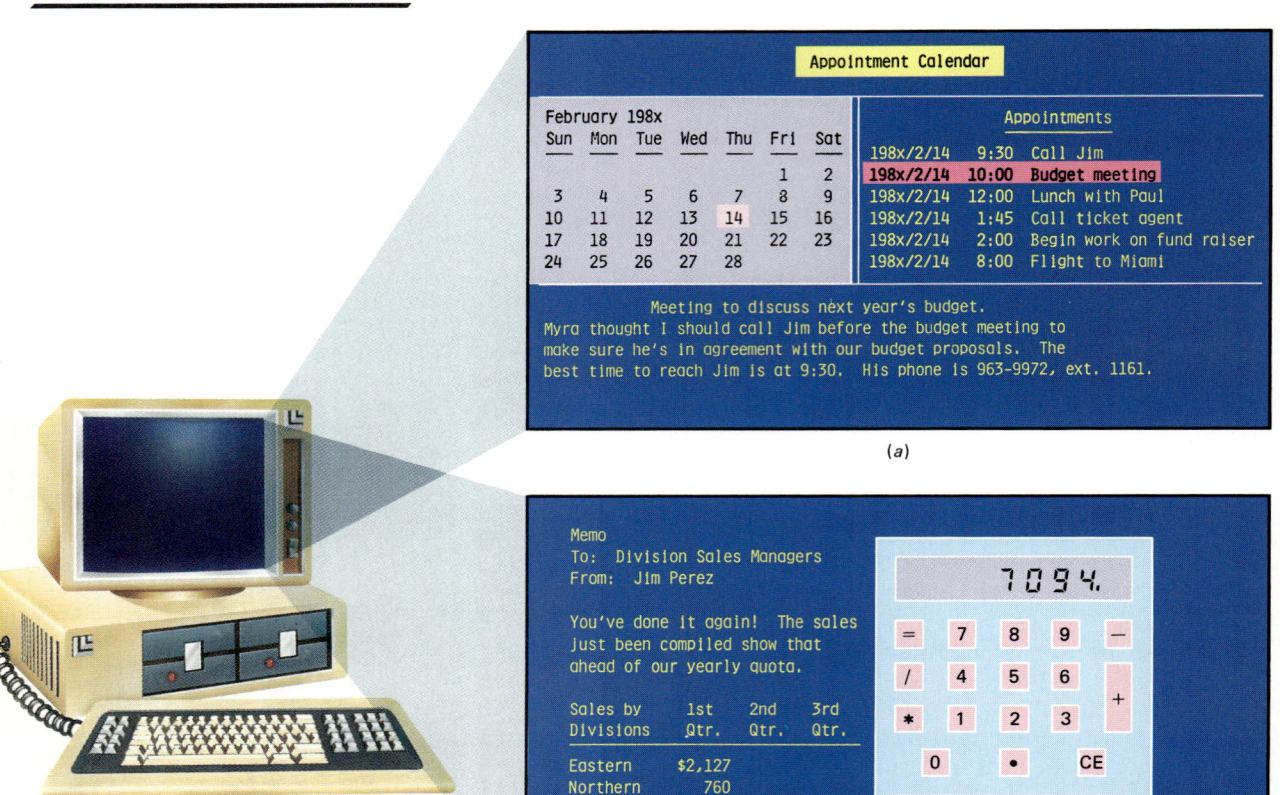

FIGURE 2-15

A time management package can carry out a number of the time-consuming tasks usually found in offices. (a) One such task is keeping track of appointments and other daily activities. (b) And another is calling up and using a visual calculator to check figures being recorded in a text.

the meeting. As you store the new appointment in your calendar, you can also store any thoughts that occur to you about this meeting. A keystroke then takes you back to where you were in the spreadsheet when the phone rang. The popularity of time management packages is due in large part to their instant storage and retrieval capabilities.

Sequential and Direct Storage and Retrieval

Data to be processed are either recorded on a secondary storage medium, such as a disk or tape, prior to processing (Figures 2-3, 2-6, and 2-12) or entered directly into the system through an online input device (Figures 2-9 and 2-11). Implicit in all the applications that we've studied is the fact that the data items placed in secondary storage must be *organized* in some way before they can be stored and retrieved. In most cases, the data are placed in files organized in either a *sequential* way or a *direct* way.

Sequential Storage and Retrieval A **sequential file** is one in which records are stored one after another. The storage sequence is generally determined by a **record key**—an identifying field or value that's found in every

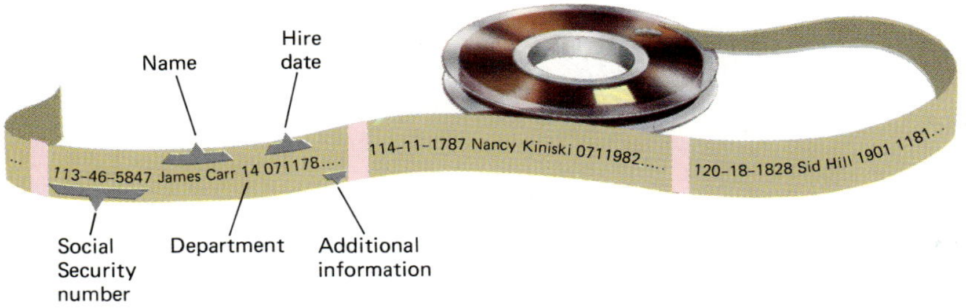

FIGURE 2-16

A sequential file of employees. Records in this file are stored in an ascending sequence as determined by the Social Security number key of each employee. To retrieve and update any record in this file, the computer must begin with the first employee and then search every record in the sequence until the desired record is reached. Such a procedure is fine for processing payrolls since the computer will be updating most employee records in a single pass through the file. But it's an inefficient way to look up the hire date of a specific worker.

record in the file. The contents of each key value or field must be unique for each record because duplications would cause serious problems. This key may be some number, such as an account number or a Social Security number, or it may be a name. In Figure 2-16, for example, the records are stored on a tape in an ascending Social Security number sequence. In Jill's mailing label application in Figure 2-3, the key is each student's last name, and the file is stored on a disk in an alphabetical sequence. When tape is the storage medium, records must be stored in a sequence; when disks are used, sequential storage may be employed, but it isn't required.

Sequential processing consists of retrieving and processing the first record stored in the file sequence, then the second record in the order, and so on until the entire file has been searched. The applications illustrated in Figures 2-3, 2-6, and 2-12 are all examples of sequential processing. This type of processing is suitable for the periodic updating of files if a large number of records need to be processed. (Batch processing is often accomplished with sequential files.) For example, we've seen that it's an efficient way to process payroll data (Marie's Meals Compensation Report) or maintain inventory records (Bill's Plant Control Report), because many records may be updated during a processing run.

But sequential processing has some *limitations*. As Figure 2-17 shows, the transactions (additions, deletions, or changes) that affect the records in the sequential master file must first be sorted into the same key sequence as the master file. (A separate computer sorting program is used to do this.) And when processing a sequential file, records near the end of the file cannot be retrieved until all preceding records in the sequence have been read into the computer. Thus if there's a need to update only a few records near the end of the file, processing will be delayed until all earlier records have been read. It's obviously inefficient to enter transaction data on an interactive basis into a sequential file because the file search to find the affected record will have to begin with the first record in the sequence each time a transaction is entered.

Direct Storage and Retrieval In a **direct** (or **random**) **file,** records are stored in such a way that the computer can go directly to the key or identifying value of the record needed without having to search through a sequence of other records. Records to be retrieved in a direct file must be stored on a medium such as a hard or flexible disk, and these disks must be kept in a **direct-access storage device (DASD)** if the processor is to have access to their contents.

Direct processing (also called **direct-access** and **random processing**) consists of directly locating, retrieving, and updating any record stored in a file without the need to read preceding or succeeding file records. When a

The additions, deletions, and changes made to file records are recorded on a machine-readable medium—e.g., a magnetic tape or disk.

Computer program used to sort transactions by record key

Sorted transactions in master file sequence

Old master file

Primary Storage Section
Program storage area

Program instructions to update master file

Payroll checks, bills, reports, etc.

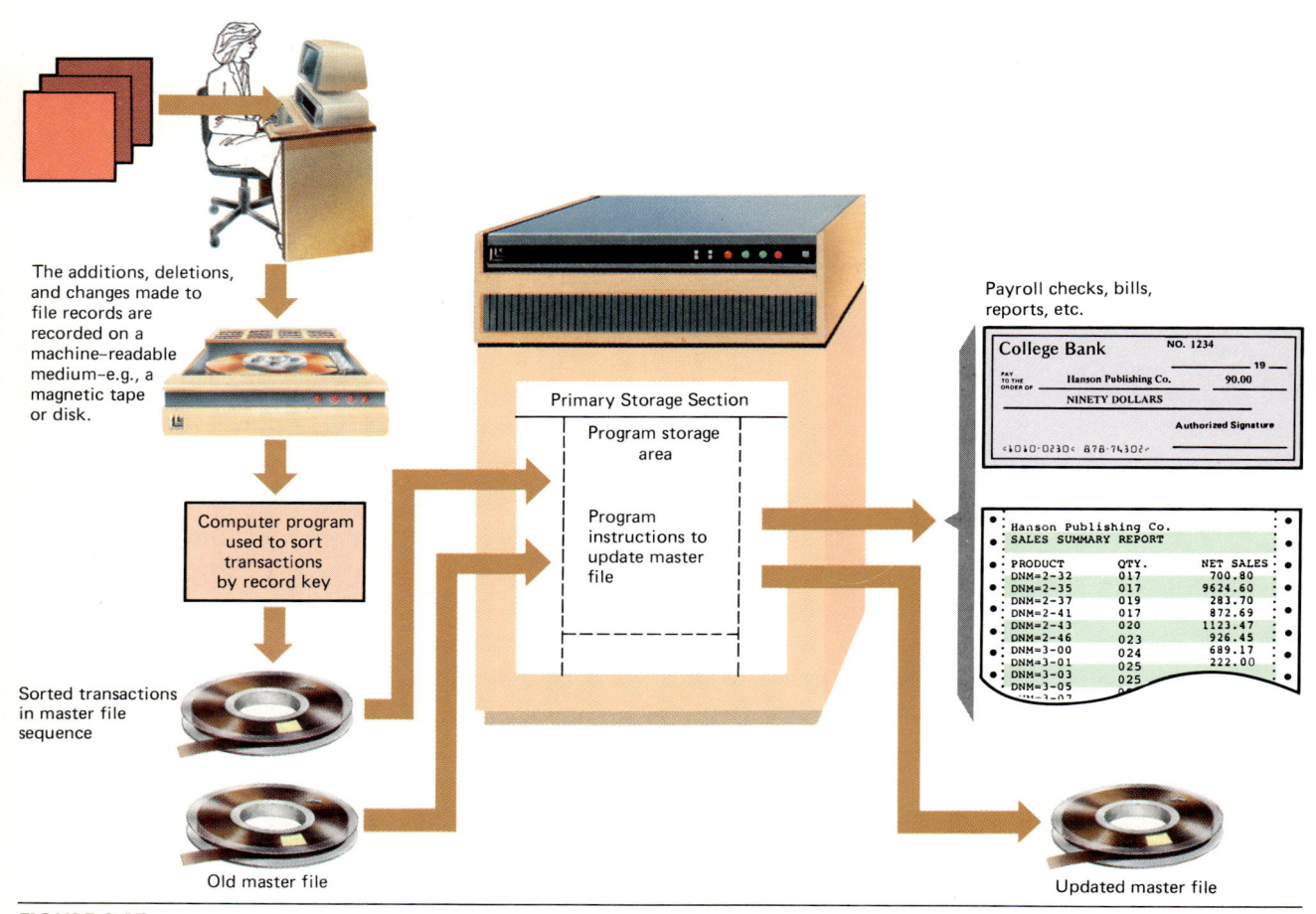

Updated master file

FIGURE 2-17

The sequential file processing approach. Transactions affecting file records are identified by a record key, and these transactions are arranged into the same ascending or descending sequence as the master file before processing can begin. Transaction data and old master file records are then read into the processor unit. The record key is used to match a new transaction with the appropriate old file record. The old record is updated by program instructions and a new file record is created and written on an output medium. Various documents such as checks, bills, and reports may also be prepared during the processing.

computer system is performing direct processing, it typically accepts input data from an online keyboard or some other transaction-recording device. This was what was done to update Sam's savings account in Figure 2-9. Sam's record was retrieved from a DASD by the use of an account number key. Accessing the record was quick and direct. It was retrieved in a fraction of a second, without a sequential search of the file. After processing was completed, the updated record was returned to its storage location in the DASD.

We've seen that updating Sam's savings account is an example of an interactive application. Direct files must be used to store interactive data input when the objective is to process transactions quickly and give fast response to users. But as you saw earlier, interactive data input can also be stored and accumulated in direct files to support a later batch processing operation. And

FIGURE 2-18 (facing page)

A summary of data input, processing, and file storage/retrieval concepts. Remember as you study this illustration that batch and interactive are terms that describe the timing of the processing, while sequential and direct are terms that describe the method of storing and retrieving data.

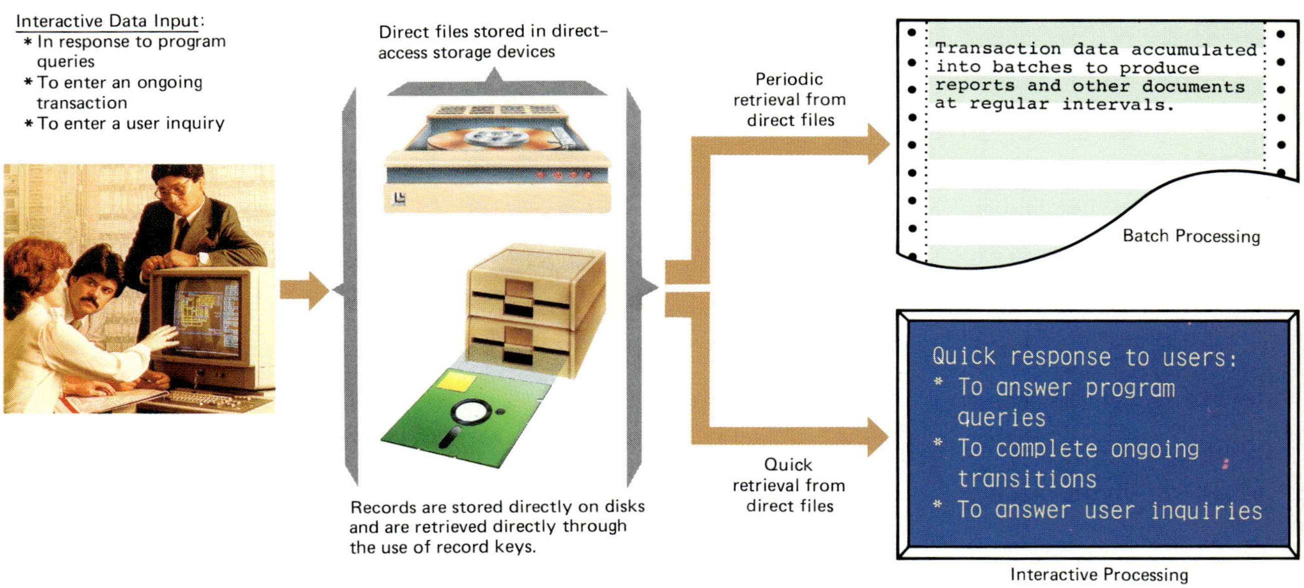

Interactive Data Input:
* In response to program queries
* To enter an ongoing transaction
* To enter a user inquiry

Direct files stored in direct-access storage devices

Records are stored directly on disks and are retrieved directly through the use of record keys.

Periodic retrieval from direct files

Quick retrieval from direct files

Transaction data accumulated into batches to produce reports and other documents at regular intervals.

Batch Processing

Quick response to users:
* To answer program queries
* To complete ongoing transitions
* To answer user inquiries

Interactive Processing

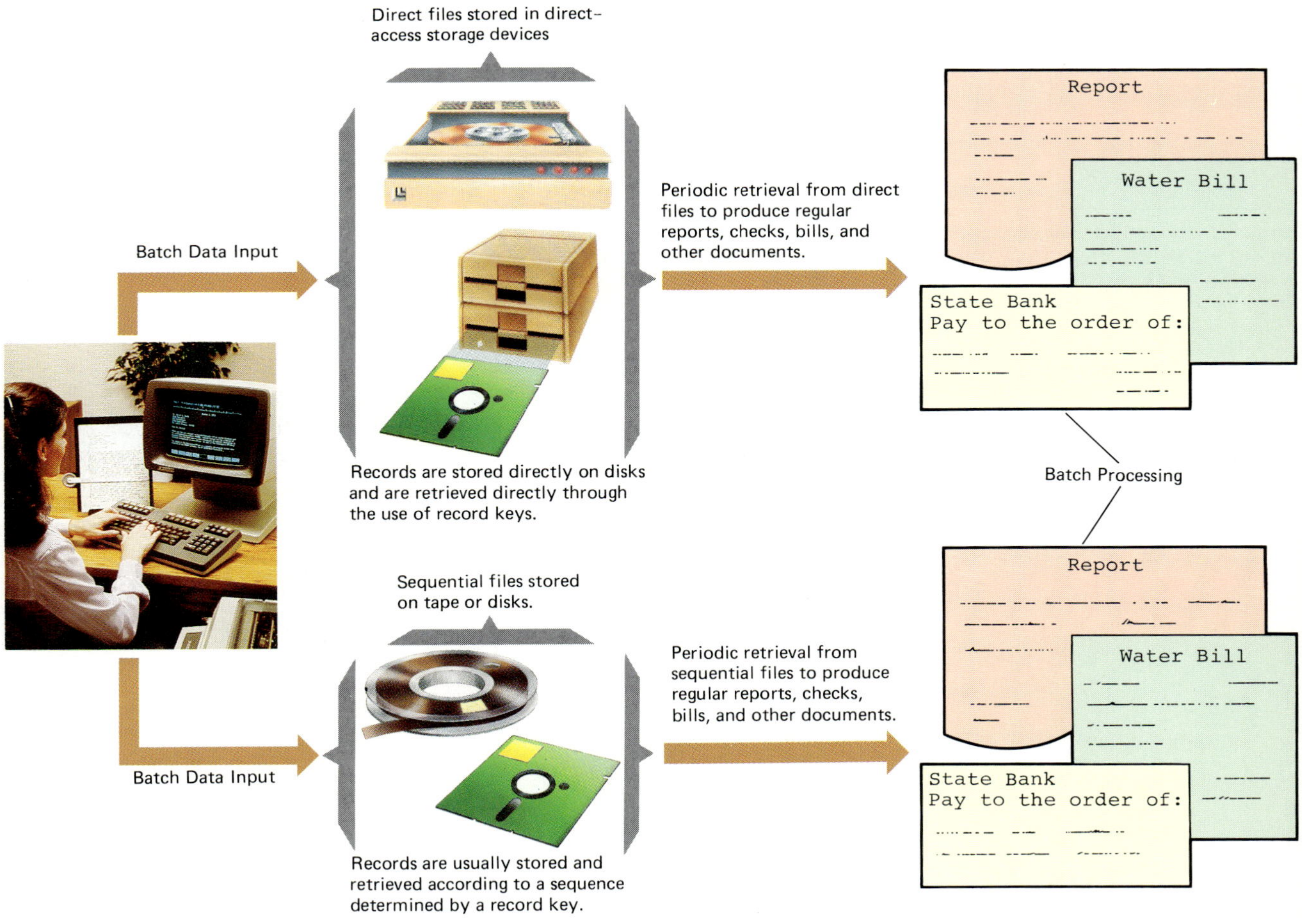

Batch Data Input

Direct files stored in direct-access storage devices

Records are stored directly on disks and are retrieved directly through the use of record keys.

Periodic retrieval from direct files to produce regular reports, checks, bills, and other documents.

Report
Water Bill
State Bank Pay to the order of:

Batch Processing

Batch Data Input

Sequential files stored on tape or disks.

Records are usually stored and retrieved according to a sequence determined by a record key.

Periodic retrieval from sequential files to produce regular reports, checks, bills, and other documents.

Report
Water Bill
State Bank Pay to the order of:

batch data can also be entered by a record key into a direct file. After the data are accumulated for a period, they may be processed against master records stored in another direct file. Sorting of records isn't necessary in this case. Figure 2-18 summarizes many of the data input, processing, and file storage/retrieval concepts presented in this chapter.

OBTAINING APPLICATION SOFTWARE

You've just seen a few of the thousands of computer system applications that exist. We classified these few examples rather arbitrarily according to one of the functions that they perform: input/output, calculation and text manipulation, logic/comparison, and storage/retrieval. But you can see that in most applications the computer system will execute more than one function.

Our selected applications are limited but not random. Recent studies have identified the types of applications that account for the greatest use of computing resources by individuals and organizations. These applications are those that can be carried out with spreadsheet, word processing, file/data base management, graphics, communications, outlining, mailing list, and project/time management software. Also included are the accounting applications used by business, government, health-care, and educational organizations to send out bills, pay employees, and control inventories. You'll recognize, of course, that *our selection includes applications in all these areas*.

You'll also recognize that our selection has included the use of (1) *prewritten applications packages* and (2) *custom-made programs* written by members of the Byter family.

This kind of single-function, special-purpose software package is highly interactive, as computer game players know. (Courtesy Sony Corp. of America)

Prewritten Packages

Prewritten applications packages are created by skilled programmers who usually work for equipment suppliers and independent software firms. These packages may be obtained at computer stores and other retail outlets, or from mail-order houses. Some perform *single functions*, while others *integrate* several functions in a single package.

Single-function packages can be classified into special- and general-purpose categories. One such *special-purpose* package is a game program that only allows a user to do battle with aliens from outer space. Another example is the pharmacy package that determines the possibility of dangerous interactions between the ingredients in a customer's old prescriptions and those in a new prescription. All the packages discussed earlier in this chapter, however,

---

WINDOW 2-1

COMPUTER HELPS FLUTIE SCORE BIG

When Heisman Trophy winner Doug Flutie was about to turn pro, he faced a unique problem: How to choose from among the 69 agents, lawyers, and wheeler-dealers who wanted to negotiate a contract for him with a professional football league.

Fortunately, Flutie had some computer help from his father, a computer technician at a microchip company. Mr. Flutie, Sr., felt that there had to be a better way than interviewing all the agents. Because he wanted some objective data to back up his feelings, Mr. Flutie wrote a computer program to evaluate each of them.

The program ranked each agent in categories from 1 to 10, weighing each category according to its importance. Experience in direct negotiations with the National Football League, tax expertise, and "chemistry" were some of the factors he programmed into this analysis. The computer selected Bob Woolf, a Boston attorney, who immediately launched into negotiations with the New Jersey Generals. The Generals offered a contract estimated at $1.3 million per year for 4 years, which would make Flutie the highest paid rookie in professional football.

Then Mr. Flutie began the next phase of his computer analysis. He programmed his personal computer to examine the contracts of all players drafted by the 28 NFL teams in 1982 and 1983. This program produced a curve on which the total value of each contract was plotted. From this output, Mr. Flutie got an exact idea of how his son's contract should be structured, and he evaluated the Generals' offer in light of this information.

When this process was over and the restructured contract was signed, even the agents who were not selected suggested that Mr. Flutie should write a book. If he ever does, says Flutie, "it will recommend a computer as the best way to save time, organize thoughts, and come to a conclusion which is backed by objectivity."

Adapted from Gerald Eskanazi, "The Computer Search for Flutie's Agent," *New York Times*, 1984, and from Sue Mott, "The Computer Fortunes of Doug Flutie," *Personal Computing*, April 1985. Photo courtesy Focus on Sports.

have been *general-purpose* programs. For example, a word processing package only manipulates text, but it can support any activity that requires written communication.

You've seen in Chapter 1 that people can also buy an *integrated applications package* that *combines* several functions. Most or all of the following general-purpose functions are typically integrated in such packages: manipulating spreadsheets, processing words, managing files or data bases, preparing graphics, sending communications, and creating outlines. Each of these functions is available in separate applications programs, of course. And many users are better served with separate programs that are tailored to their needs. But successful integrated packages are designed so that data may be easily moved between the component programs. Also, a common set of instructions allows all tasks to be performed in a similar way.

Since the topic of Chapters 9 and 10 is prewritten software packages, we'll defer further discussion of this subject until that time. You'll also find information there to help you identify and select appropriate applications packages for your own use.

Development of Custom-Made Software

Custom-made programs are prepared for specific individuals or organizations to meet precise needs. Sometimes, the custom program addresses a problem that's unique so no application package exists to solve it. In other cases, packages are available to solve similar problems, but so many modifications are needed to adapt the package to the situation that it's easier to start fresh and build a custom solution. And in still other situations, the problem is simple enough that some people prefer to write a short program to do the job rather than spend time and money acquiring a package. (This last reason may explain why the Byters write their own software rather than using available packages that would quickly produce the same results.)

Most of us who use personal computers can now find suitable packages to do just about anything we want to do. And many of us will spend a lifetime

The study team at work. (Courtesy Honeywell Corp.)

making productive use of computers without ever writing a custom program. But most large organizations have applications that are either unique or quite unlike other applications, and so they employ a staff of computer specialists to create and maintain custom software.

It's the people in organizations who put computers to work. It's people working together who determine processing needs, provide input data, design processing steps, select hardware and software, write programs, and use processed output. Some are computer specialists. But contributions from *end users*—clerks, secretaries and assistants, managers and professionals—who enter the data and use the output are equally essential to the creation of a custom software system.

People in organizations typically use a system study approach to develop custom-made software. A **system study** is a step-by-step process used to

Program preparation (© Robert J. Witkowski/The Image Bank)

The last step: working with users to maintain and improve the software. (Courtesy Sperry Corp.)

identify and then develop specific improvements in an organization's information system. The steps or stages in the system study process are:

Step 1: Defining the Need End users, computer specialists, and managers usually work together to define the problem and spell out the specific goals to be achieved.

Step 2: System Analysis Next, a study team gathers and then analyzes data about current processing operations. An end user and a **system analyst**—an information specialist who's knowledgeable about the technical aspects of analyzing, designing, and implementing custom-made software—are usually included in this team. System analysis occurs after data about current operations have been gathered. **System analysis** is the study of existing operations to learn what they accomplish, why they work as they do, and what role (if any) they may have in future processing activities.

Step 3: System Design **System design** is the process of creating alternative custom solutions to satisfy the study team's goals, evaluating these proposed solutions, and then drawing up the specifications for the chosen solution.

Step 4: Programming Analysis After the decision has been made to create custom software, the design specifications provide the input for this step. **Programming analysis** is the process of breaking down the design specifications into the specific input/output, calculation and text manipulation, logic/comparison, and storage/retrieval operations required to produce the custom software.

Step 5: Program Preparation One or more programmers convert the operations identified in the preceding step into a custom program (or programs) of instructions written in a language and form acceptable to the organization's hardware.

Step 6: Implementation and Maintenance The last step is to test the new custom software for errors, place it in operation, and revise and maintain it as necessary to meet changing conditions.

Every step in the system study process should be a joint effort between those served by the system or application and those who create it, because computer hardware, by itself, cannot solve a single problem. These six steps in the system study process will be considered further in the Software Module.

FEEDBACK

FEEDBACK AND REVIEW 2

You've seen a few of the things that people do with computers, and you've learned a number of new concepts. You can test your understanding of the chapter contents by using the following sentences and definitions to fill in the crossword puzzle.

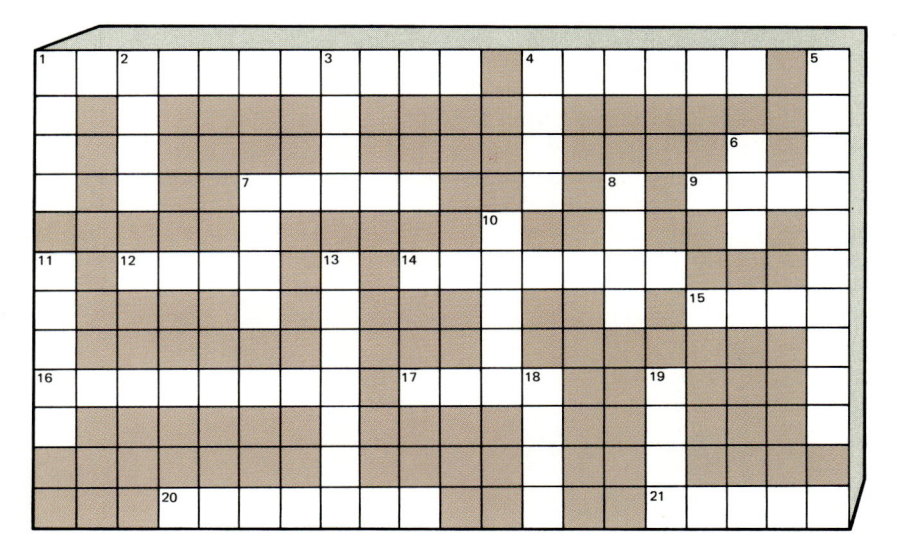

Across

1. _____ processing occurs immediately after input data are entered into a computer system and the output results are quickly produced.
4. A _____ or random file is one in which records are stored in such a way that the computer can go directly to the key or identifying value of the record needed without having to search through a sequence of other records.
7. The smallest logical data entity is called a data item or data _____.
9. A _____ is a displayed listing of program options that users can select.
12. The intersection of a column and row in a spreadsheet is called a box or _____.
14. A _____(s) software package allows users to prepare a variety of charts for analysis and presentation purposes.
15. The names and addresses from a mailing _____ of voters are often printed on gummed labels by computer systems.
16. A project management package can help engineers and others identify the _____ path so that they can direct their attention to the sequence of activities in that path.
17. An abbreviation for the online secondary storage devices required to support direct storage and retrieval is _____.
20. A _____ is a special task that must usually be completed in a relatively short period of time.
21. A special field can be used in a _____ record placed at the end of a file to indicate when all valid records have been processed.

MODULE 1

Down

1. The smallest logical data entity is a data field or data ___.
2. ___ management packages are also called accessory software.
3. A directly accessible appointment calendar is a feature of a ___ management package.
4. ___ is an abbreviation for a type of software package that allows users to create, retrieve, and maintain records in a data base.
5. In a ___ file, records are stored one after another, and they must be retrieved in the same order.
6. A unique identifying value that's found in every record in a file is called a record ___.
7. Periodically adding, changing, and deleting file records is called ___ maintenance.
8. Communications packages permit people to send electronic ___ to designated users along a network of computers and workstations.
10. Huge online libraries are maintained by information services in over 1,000 data ___.
11. In ___ processing, the data are gathered for a period of time and collected into a group before they are subsequently entered into a computer and processed.
13. A ___ processor is a software package that accepts ideas, manipulates them in specified ways, and then produces an organized outline of those thoughts.
18. A ___ base is a collection of logically related data elements that may be structured in various ways to meet the multiple processing and retrieval needs of organizations and individuals.
19. A ___ processing package can be used to create, view, edit, store, retrieve, and print text material.

LOOKING BACK

1. All that computers do is operate on data, and these data are organized into logical groupings. The smallest data entity is a data item or data field consisting of related characters that are treated as a unit. Fields are grouped together to form records, and related records are then grouped to produce a file. A collection of logically related elements may then be organized into a data base.

2. Computers are able to perform four types of operations on data: input/output, calculation and text manipulation, logic/comparison, and storage/retrieval. Example applications emphasizing each of these types of operations have been presented in this chapter.

3. The preparation of mailing labels for Jill Byter was one application used to emphasize basic input/output operations. A file of prospective voters was created and maintained on a machine-readable medium. Rather than write her own mailing list program, Jill could have used a file or a data base management package to achieve the same results. Such a package would offer Jill several additional features. For example, she could sort and retrieve her records in a number of different ways and then send a more personalized cam-

paign appeal to the targeted voters. The file or data base package could print the mailing labels, and a word processing program could be used to create, edit, and print the personalized messages. A file or data base package also improves file management by making it easy to add, change, or delete records. Another popular software package is an outline processor that accepts input ideas, manipulates them in specified ways, and then produces an organized outline of those thoughts.

4. Marie Byter's Meals Compensation Report program shows how calculations may be carried out. A dummy record was placed at the end of Marie's employee file to tell the processor when the last valid record had been processed. But Marie could have used a spreadsheet application package to achieve the same result. A spreadsheet package would give Marie a number of additional features, such as the ability to conduct "what if" simulations to evaluate the effects of changes made to selected variables. The chapter also shows how Marie could use a graphics software package to bring life to the numbers in her report. Another example of a calculation application was the updating of Sam Byter's savings account.

5. Batch processing was used to prepare Marie's report, while interactive processing was used to update Sam's record. The terms "interactive" and "batch" describe the timing of processing. Interactive processing occurs as soon as input data are entered into a computer system. In batch processing, the data are gathered for a period of time and collected into a group before they are entered into a computer and processed. It's possible to combine interactive and batch processing in a single system.

6. Bill Byter's Plant Control Report demonstrates the logic/comparison capabilities of computers. Storage/retrieval capabilities are shown through the use of such popular software as (1) communications packages with the ability to store messages in an electronic mail network and retrieve data from the large data banks maintained by information service firms; (2) project management packages that help engineers and other planners use stored data to keep better control over project resources; and (3) time management packages that help people store and retrieve a wealth of material so that they can plan and control their use of time more effectively.

7. The terms "sequential" and "direct" refer to the methods used to store and retrieve data. A sequential file is one in which records are stored one after another. The storage sequence is generally determined by a record key—a unique identifying value that may be a number or a name. Records must be sorted sequentially if magnetic tape is used. Sequential processing consists of retrieving and processing the first record in the sequential file, then the second record, and so on until the entire file has been searched. The limitations of sequential processing are pointed out in the chapter. A direct file is one in which records are stored in such a way that the computer can go directly to the key of the record needed without having to search through a sequence of other records. Records to be retrieved in a direct file must be stored on a medium, such as a disk, and the disk must be kept in a direct-access storage device (DASD) if the processor is to have access to their contents. Direct processing consists of directly locating, retrieving, and updating any record stored in a file

without the need to read preceding or succeeding file records. Figure 2-18 summarizes many of the data input, processing, and file storage and retrieval concepts presented in this chapter.

8. The applications selected for this chapter are the same types of applications that account for the greatest use of computers by individuals and organizations. Our selection has included the use of prewritten applications packages and custom-made programs. Prewritten applications packages may be obtained from retail stores or mail-order houses. They may perform single functions or they may integrate several functions in a single package. Custom-made software is written for many organizations because their applications are either unique or so unlike other applications that no packages exist that will do what's needed. These organizations employ computer specialists and conduct systems studies to develop their own custom-made programs.

KEY TERMS AND CONCEPTS

data item (data field) 54
record 54
file 54
data base 54
file management system (FMS) 57
data base management system (DBMS) 57
menus 58
file maintenance (file updating) 59
outline processor 59
dummy record 60
spreadsheet application package 60
graphics software package 62

word processing package 64
interactive processing 67
transaction processing 67
batch processing 68
communications package 71
electronic mail 71
project management package 72
critical path 72
time management package (accessory software) 73
sequential file 74
record key 74

sequential processing 75
direct (random) file 75
direct-access storage device (DASD) 75
direct processing (direct-access processing, random processing) 75
prewritten applications packages 79
custom-made programs 80
system study 81
system analyst 82
system analysis 82
system design 82
programming analysis 82

Topics for Review and Discussion

1. "When computers operate on data, the data will normally be organized into logical groupings so that processing will be effective and output results will be useful." Identify these logical groupings and discuss the relationship that exists between them.
2. Computers are able to perform four types of operations on data. What are these four types?
3. (a) How was a computer used to prepare Jill Byter's mailing labels? (b) How could Jill have used a file or data base management package to create and maintain her student voter file?
4. "The use of a file or data base management package greatly facilitates file maintenance." Discuss this statement.
5. (a) What is an outlining package? (b) How are such packages used?
6. (a) How was a computer used to prepare Marie Byter's Meals Compensation Report? (b) How could Marie have used a spreadsheet application package to achieve the same results? (c) How could Marie have used a graphics package to chart the values in her report?
7. (a) What's a dummy record? (b) How are such records used for logic/comparison purposes?
8. (a) How was a computer used to update Sam Byter's savings account? (b) Discuss the use of interactive processing and a direct file in this application.
9. (a) What is a word processing package? (b) How did Jill use such a package to prepare her campaign letters? (c) Do you think it's appropriate for politicians to use file management packages to identify special-interest groups and to then use word processing packages to personalize the messages sent to such groups?
10. (a) Define interactive processing and give two examples of its use. (b) Define batch processing and give two examples of its use.
11. "It's possible to combine the timing characteristics of both interactive and batch processing in a single system." Discuss this statement and give an example of a combined processing system.
12. How was a computer used to prepare Bill Byter's Plant Control Report?
13. (a) What is a communications package? (b) Discuss two ways that such packages may be used.
14. (a) What's a project management package? (b) What is the critical path? (c) How can project management packages help people plan and control projects?
15. Discuss three ways that a time management package can help you plan and control your use of time.
16. (a) What's a sequential file? (b) What function does a record key play in such a file? (c) How are sequential files processed? (d) Give two examples of the use of sequential processing. (e) What are the limitations of sequential processing?
17. (a) What is a direct file? (b) What function does a record key play in such a file? (c) How are direct files processed? (d) Give two examples of direct processing.
18. "Direct files must be used to store interactive data input, but such files can also be used in batch processing." Discuss this statement and give examples to support your discussion.
19. "'Batch' and 'interactive' are terms that relate to the timing of processing, while 'sequential' and 'direct' are terms that relate to the method of storing and retrieving data." Explain this statement.
20. (a) What functions are likely to be included in an integrated software package? (b) What is a special-purpose application package? (c) A general-purpose package?
21. (a) Why is custom-made software needed? (b) What is the purpose of a system study? (c) What are the steps in such a study?

Projects/Issues to Consider

1. Contact an organization in your area, and see how it uses a computer to process one of the applications discussed in this chapter. Summarize your findings in a report to the class. Prepare drawings to show the class how the organization processes the selected application.
2. Thousands of brand-name, prewritten applications programs are currently offered for sale by equipment manufacturers and independent software firms, who advertise their products in magazines and newspapers. Many of these programs are designed to process the types of applications discussed in this chapter. Visit your library or a retail computer store, and identify three program products that can process the types of applications discussed in this chapter. Prepare a report for the class that summarizes some of the features of the programs you've selected.

ANSWERS TO FEEDBACK AND REVIEW SECTION

The solution to the crossword puzzle is shown below:

	1 I	2 N	T	E	R	A	3 C	T	I	V	E		4 D	I	R	E	C	T		5 S
	T	I					I						B							E
	E	M					M						M				6 K		Q
	M	E		7 F	I	E	L	D					S		8 M		9 M	E	N	U
					I					10 B				A			Y		E
11 B		12 C	E	L	L		13 O		14 G	R	A	P	H	I	C					N
A					E		U			N				L		15 L	I	S	T
T							T			K										I
16 C	R	I	T	I	C	A	L		17 D	A	S		18 D		19 W					A
H							I						A		O					L
							N						T		R					
			20 P	R	O	J	E	C	T				A		21 D	U	M	M	Y	

MODULE 1
88

A CLOSER LOOK

CONTROLLING YOUR HOME BY COMPUTER

After using their home computer to streamline their work, monitor their personal finances, and entertain them with some games, a family like the Byters might put their computer to work on a more demanding task—control of their home. Home computers don't yet scrub floors, but many are being used to regulate air conditioners, turn down thermostats at night and turn them up in the morning, brew the morning coffee, turn out the lights, and detect intruders and fires.

Most such systems now in use aid homeowners by minimizing energy costs and functioning as security systems. They reduce energy consumption by being programmed to run appliances during off-peak hours, to turn on heaters for fixed amounts of time, and to monitor lights so that they turn off automatically when a person leaves a room. They increase security by sounding an alarm or calling the police or fire department when sensors signal a break-in or a fire.

One system that controls a solar home uses a personal computer to calculate the exact angle at which the sun's rays are the strongest and then tilts the solar panels on the roof to gain optimum power.

Most home control systems consist of a controller, modules, sensors, and a computer program. An appliance, like a lamp or air conditioner, is plugged into a module that, in turn, is plugged into a wall socket. The modules receive instructions over existing house wiring from the controller. The controller can be a special unit dedicated to running a specific program or it can be directed by a personal computer program. Adding sensors to this system gives the program the ability to compare temperature, pressure, wind direction, and so on, to a specific value. If, say, the temperature falls below 60 degrees, then the program turns the furnace on.

Most home control systems are designed to be easy to program. In addition, hardware and software developers offer preprogrammed systems designed solely for home control. One such program, Smarthome, works with an IBM PC or Apple computer. A homeowner draws a floor plan of his or her home, with assistance from the program, and inserts values in the Smarthome program by moving symbols on the computer monitor. For example, the user can move a light symbol to the wall where the light is plugged in, then connect

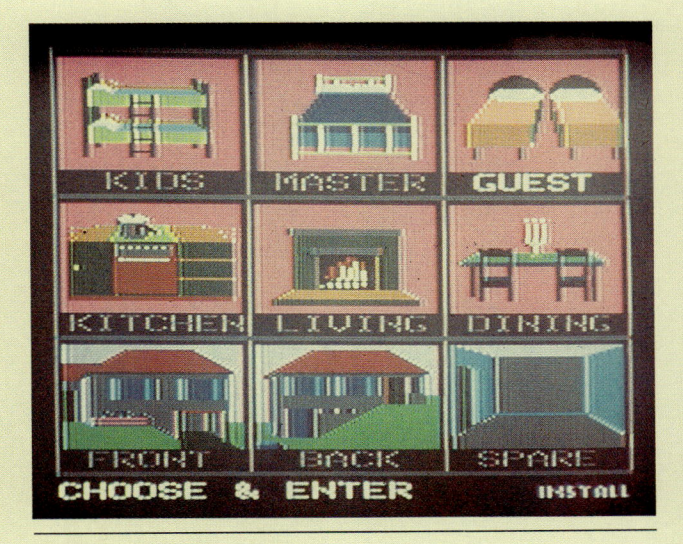

(Courtesy X-10 (USA) Inc.)

a module to that wall and plug the lamp in. The computer will turn the lamp on and off at whatever times the homeowner inserts in the program. General Electric has developed a program called HomeMinder that controls a home from a computer monitor or TV screen. The program displays rooms in the house and specific functions that the computer will perform, such as turning an appliance on or off. This system can be operated by touch-tone phone so that the user can work with the program from a distance—perhaps to turn on the microwave oven so dinner will be ready just as the computer user arrives home.

Are there any drawbacks to such systems? To keep them affordable, home control systems use existing power lines to link appliances to the controller. This eliminates the expense of running wires all over the house, but it results in power lines that are full of electrical traffic that can confuse a computer signal. Such electrical glitches can cause the system to malfunction—to turn on the sprinklers during a garden party, for example. In addition, some home appliances already can regulate themselves and linking them to computer control may damage them.

Although the technology for home control is still in its infancy, it offers the computer owner yet another way to make the personal computer into an electronic servant.

CHAPTER 3

THE COMPUTER IMPACT

Asimov Ponders PCs

Every advance in problem-solving tools must have given rise to vague fears. One can well imagine predynastic Egyptian architects suspiciously viewing the first measuring sticks. "People will grow dependent on these mechanical contrivances," they might have said disapprovingly. "They will forget how to judge distance with a keen eye and mind and will place responsibility for decisions on these inanimate pieces of wood. Instead of making a slow, good decision, they will make a quick, bad one."

Now it is the personal computer—and its "intelligent" software—that seemingly will shield us from responsibility and allow our minds to wither.

However, the spectre of GIGO—garbage in, garbage out—stalks us. If your name has ever been bulk-mangled in a piece of "personalized" mail, or if you've ever tapped in the wrong numbers on an adding machine, you've discovered that the inevitable answer can be explicitly wrong. The personal computer is as prone to this kind of error as any other problem-solving device and will hand you the wrong answer just as calmly. There is danger in trusting the computer, but so is there danger in trusting your finger to alight on the proper line of a multiplication table. The flaw, as always, lies with the human being.

There are many ways to check answers, but the best way to sift the gems from the garbage is simply recognizing when an answer looks wrong. Here the human brain tellingly outperforms the computer. Computers can solve astoundingly complex problems, but the human brain has an ability far beyond this—call it intuition, if you will.

It is, of course, conceivable that computers will someday exhibit all the complexities of the human brain, but not in the foreseeable future. The human brain has 10 billion neurons and nearly 100 billion subsidiary cells connected in an astronomically complex wiring scheme.

Besides, why should we build a computer to do what humans already do so satisfactorily?

The personal computer, then, in the course of its development, will remain a tool, ever more complex and perhaps ever more able to question the instructions given it. Yet however complex, I doubt the computer will ever match the intuition and creative powers of the remarkable human mind.

In my opinion, the future will see computers and humans, each representing totally different forms of intelligence, working in cooperation rather than in competition and accomplishing more together than either could possibly achieve alone.

Excerpted from "Asimov Ponders PCs," by Isaac Asimov, *PC World*, Sept. 1985. Reprinted by permission of the author.

CHAPTER 3

93

LOOKING AHEAD

You've seen some examples of what computers can do in Chapter 2. But it's not enough just to be familiar with a few specific applications. You should also be aware of the social impact of computer usage. That is, you should have an understanding of the ways in which people and organizations may be affected by present and future computer applications. We'll look first in this chapter at how research in artificial intelligence is having an impact on all of us. We'll then consider some of the positive and negative effects that computer usage is having on people and organizations. The information in this chapter will enable you to:

- Describe some of the developments that have taken place in the field of artificial intelligence

- Outline some of the positive and negative effects that computer usage may have on individuals

- Discuss the rapid changes taking place in the information processing industry, and explain how computer usage can both benefit and endanger other organizations

- Summarize the optimistic and pessimistic views about the future impact of computer systems on people

CHAPTER OUTLINE

LOOKING AHEAD
HUMAN THINKING AND ARTIFICIAL INTELLIGENCE
Can Computers Think?
AI in Action: Expert Systems
THE IMPACT OF COMPUTERS ON PEOPLE
The Positive Impact
The Potential Dangers
THE IMPACT OF COMPUTERS ON ORGANIZATIONS
The Information Processing Industry
The Positive Impact on Using Organizations
The Potential Dangers for Using Organizations
LET'S SUMMARIZE
Optimistic Views
Pessimistic Views
Another View
A Recap of This Background Module
Feedback and Review 3
LOOKING BACK

HUMAN THINKING AND ARTIFICIAL INTELLIGENCE

The superhuman thinking computers found in science fiction don't exist. But science fiction has a way of becoming science fact. Scientists are now looking for ways to make computers solve unstructured problems. These are the types of problems that people solve by trying various approaches and learning from their mistakes. Until now, only a human intelligence could do this—but intelligent computer programs are beginning to compete with us. Efforts to design computer systems that exhibit the characteristics we associate with human intelligence are classified under the heading of **artificial intelligence (AI).** Using concepts from such disciplines as psychology, linguistics, and computer science, researchers are learning how to prepare programs or construct systems that do tasks that no machine has ever done automatically before.

For example, computers have been programmed to play checkers and to modify their programs on the basis of past successes and failures against human opponents. In one such program, the computer has continually improved its game to the point where it easily defeats the author of the program. Thus the machine has "learned" what not to do through trial and error.

Hundreds of chess-playing programs have been written that can run on machines ranging from small micros to huge supercomputers (see Figure 3-1). As you learned in Chapter 1, the possible number of moves in a chess game is so large that all the moves could not possibly be stored or analyzed by any computer. Thus the only workable approach is to program the computer to evaluate possible moves and formulate a playing strategy.

At the *beginning* of a chess game, proven approaches to minimize losses and, perhaps, to create openings are often followed for the first 7 to 10 moves. Much less predictable is the *middle part* of the game. Good chess players must adopt a strategy and "look ahead" to determine the future consequences of a move. If the middle game is complicated, the *end game* is absolutely baffling. Each player may have six or seven pieces left. The sides of the board

FIGURE 3-1

Belle, the chess-playing computer, takes on two human challengers as part of a continuing research program in artificial intelligence. (Courtesy Bell Labs)

have generally lost their meaning, and the pieces may be positioned in ways that have *never occurred before* in the history of the game. In a few moves, a strong attack can result in an impossible defense. People may develop new strategies at this time. A computer program, of course, must also try to adapt to end-game situations.

Given this brief summary of chess, a natural question is, How have computer programs fared against humans in this very intellectual game? This question can be answered by looking back at the "Levy challenge." In 1968, David Levy, a Scottish chess champion with an international master ranking (that's one rank below the top grandmaster rank), beat John McCarthy, a Stanford University professor of AI, in a chess game. McCarthy remarked that although he couldn't beat Levy, there would be within 10 years a computer program that could. A bet of 250 British pounds was made between Levy and McCarthy. Levy would win the bet unless a computer program won a match against him before the end of August 1978.

During the next few years, other AI professors and computer programmers joined McCarthy in betting against Levy. In 1977, Levy played a match against a Northwestern University program named Chess 4.5 that had just won the Minnesota Open championship against human opponents. Levy won the match and later in the year beat Kaissa, a Russian program. As the 1978 deadline approached, a final six-game match was arranged between Levy and Northwestern's Chess 4.7 (a successor to Chess 4.5). The first game was a draw (each side received ½ point). Levy won the second and third games, the computer won the fourth game, and Levy won the fifth game. (A sixth game was unnecessary since Levy had already scored 3½ points out of a possible 6.)

The human won this round in the late 1970s, but the rivalry continues today. A prize of $100,000, being offered through Carnegie-Mellon University, awaits the creator of the first computer program to wrest the world chess championship from a human. Carnegie-Mellon professor Hans Berliner has written a program that defeated the world backgammon champion. Berliner believes that a program will be the chess champion by the year 2000. Others aren't so sure.

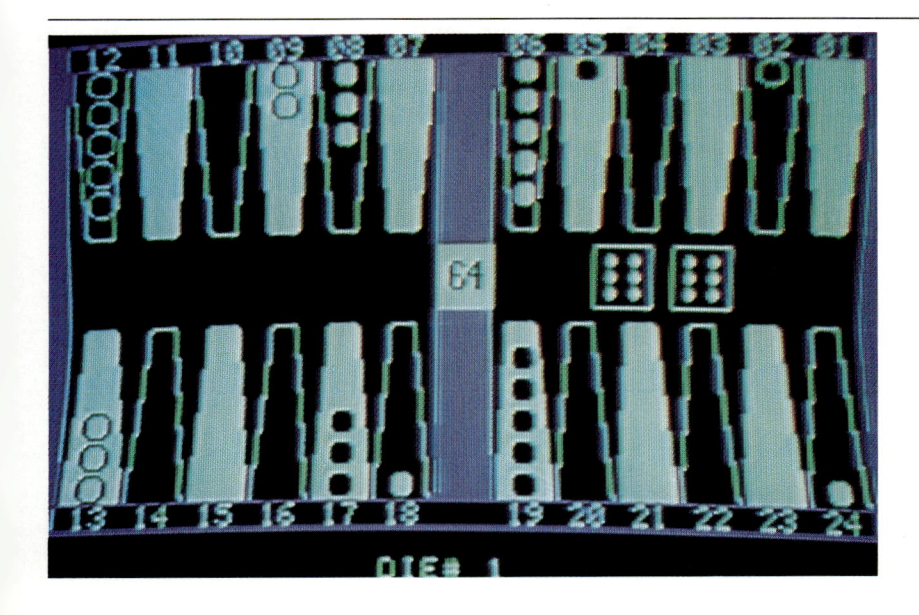

A computer backgammon program like this has defeated the world's human champion. Will a computer be the world's champion chess player by the year 2001? (© Dan McCoy/Rainbow)

Can Computers Think?

Much has been written pro and con about whether computers can be programmed to "think" and "learn." Most of the controversy stems from (1) a lack of understanding about the processes involved in human thinking and learning and (2) the absence of acceptable definitions of such words as "think" and "learn."

One test to find out if a computer might be considered to possess intelligence and the ability to think was a game proposed by Alan Turing, a British mathematician. The game requires two respondents—a machine and a human—and a human interrogator who tries to determine which of the unseen respondents is the human. Communications terminals are used to answer questions posed by the interrogator. The machine tries to deceive while the human tries to convince the interrogator of his or her true identity. Intelligence and the ability to think would, according to **Turing's test,** be demonstrated if the machine succeeds in fooling the interrogator.

Have machines passed Turing's test? Not yet, but they *have* passed incomplete versions. Several years ago Joseph Weizenbaum, an MIT professor, wrote a program with which one could "converse" in English. The program—Weizenbaum named it *Eliza*—plays the role of a psychotherapist engaged in an interview with a patient. A hypothetical conversation between patient and "doctor" might go like this (computer entries are in capital letters):

DO YOU HAVE ANY PROBLEMS?
Yes, I am depressed
I AM SORRY TO HEAR YOU ARE DEPRESSED
My boyfriend makes me unhappy
TELL ME ABOUT YOUR BOYFRIEND

In a variation of Turing's test (people tested didn't know it was a test, and the program wasn't competing with a human), staff members at Massachusetts General Hospital let a number of people "talk" to Weizenbaum's program for a time. When asked if they had been talking with a human or a machine, most thought they had been in contact with a human. David Levy, the chess master, believes that since the Chess 4.7 program he competed against is stronger than 99.5 percent of all human chess players, it has already passed the stage where he could correctly identify it as a human or computer opponent under Turing-test conditions.

Where's the current research in AI likely to lead us? No one knows. Researchers use the term **heuristic** (pronounced hew-'ris-tik) to describe the judgmental, or *commonsense,* part of problem solving. That is, it describes that part of problem solving which deals with the definition of the problem, the selection of reasonable strategies to be followed, and the formulation of hypotheses and hunches. Human beings are now *far superior* to the computer in the heuristic area of intellectual work. As people's thinking and learning processes become better understood, however, it will be possible to develop new programs and machines with improved heuristic abilities. Some very able researchers are working toward this end.

AI in Action: Expert Systems

In fact, some earlier heuristic problem-solving research efforts have already led to the development of commercial products called expert systems. An

WINDOW 3-1

ARTIFICIAL INTELLIGENCE AND "FUZZY" THINKING

In most computer programs, a decision is made on a yes or no, black or white basis. There is no gray, no maybe—unless the program is using a new concept called fuzzy set theory. Fuzzy logic, as it is more commonly called, introduces the element of probability to computer operations.

Lacking the option of choosing "maybe," a computer is at a disadvantage against a human in many contests of logic. For example, consider the game of backgammon. At a 1978 tournament, a computer program for backgammon which had taken four years to develop was promptly defeated by its first two human opponents.

When the program's originator, Carnegie-Mellon University professor Hans Berliner, revised the system using fuzzy set theory, it succeeded in defeating the world's backgammon champion. "When you're forced to make black or white decisions," Berliner explains, "you cannot afford to be wrong, because when you're wrong, you lose. The other way is more forgiving. If you figure that something is 80% gray, but it turns out to be 90% gray, you're not going to get punished very much."

Lotfi A. Zadeh, professor of computer science at the University of California at Berkeley, is credited with first codifying the principles of fuzzy logic: forsaking the traditional series of tidy yes-no decisions made in computer programs and substituting a percentage-probability assessment. The computer thus decides which alternatives are most and least likely to yield the desired result—a way of solving problems that was revolutionary when introduced in computer circles. "It takes people a while to accept these ideas," says Zadeh, "but once they do, fuzzy logic is more comfortable than the abstract concepts of classical logic."

Foreign computer experts have been, if anything, more receptive than Americans to this new approach. In Japan, Hitachi Ltd. is preparing Tokyo commuter trains to run on an automatic control system, using fuzzy logic, in 1987. In Britain, two companies—Tymshare and ICL PLC—are producing and selling fuzzy logic software. And West German researchers are exploring possible banking applications of fuzzy logic.

Having succeeded at backgammon, Hans Berliner is now at work on a fuzzy logic chess program. His ultimate goal is "to devise computer software that can do strategic planning in a fuzzy way. Instead of rigidly analyzing every tactic for hundreds of moves, a chess playing computer could quickly narrow the scope of a given situation in a game. This would have all kinds of applications, Berliner believes. Numerous business and scientific problems, from making the most of an airline's flight schedules to forecasting the weather, cannot be solved quickly [using classical logic] because of information overload." Fuzzy logic would bypass this obstacle.

The development of an integrated circuit for processing fuzzy data, brainchild of Yamakawa Takeshi at Kumamoto University in Japan, opens new possibilities for a fuzzy-logic computer. "Such a machine might be the ultimate computer described by Patrick H. Winston, director of the AI Laboratory at Massachusetts Institute of Technology: a machine that reasons from analogy, not deduction, and applies experience gained from past situations to new ones. In the process, it would formulate new insights and new knowledge—and learn."

Excerpted from Otis Port, "Where 'Fuzzy' Thinking is an Asset," *Business Week*, April 22, 1985. Copyright © 1985 by McGraw-Hill, Inc. Reprinted by special permission.

---

expert system is a software package that includes (1) a stored base of knowledge in a specialized area and (2) the capability to probe this knowledge base in order to recommend solutions to specific problems. Although expert systems have only recently appeared in selected areas, their future applications seem almost limitless.

To develop the knowledge base for an expert system, AI researchers spend many months picking the brains of specialists to extract and structure the knowledge that's the basis for the specialists' expertise. Once a knowledge base is created, programmed techniques for efficiently representing and processing the stored facts and ideas are then used to probe the base. Different approaches are used by different expert system packages to deduce factual relationships and arrive at conclusions. Knowledge may be expressed in a natural language (English, French, Spanish), and a series of exchanges between the user and the expert system is usually needed. As the user supplies input facts, the expert system responds as an intelligent assistant by giving advice and suggesting possible decisions.

Some examples of expert systems include:

- *Medical diagnostic packages.* Several expert system programs have been developed to diagnose diseases and recommend treatments. These expert systems include *Mycin,* which specializes in blood diseases, and *Puff,* which measures lung functions. *Caduceus* is a more generalized package, programmed to evaluate over 4,000 symptoms and other data in order to recognize over 600 diseases. Developed at the University of Pittsburgh, Caduceus accepts the initial data on a patient from a doctor at a terminal. After considering these facts, the program begins asking questions about the patient. During this questioning, Caduceus tells the doctor what diagnosis it's considering and what data it's temporarily disregarding. The program may provide its diagnosis for the doctor in a few minutes. To avoid unnecessary lab tests, Caduceus is programmed to consider the least costly diseases first.

- *A geology package.* An expert system called *Prospector* asks the user about an area's geologic formations and then gives advice on the possible location of mineral deposits. Prospector has accurately predicted the location of a multimillion-dollar molybdenum deposit under Mount Tolman in eastern Washington.

- *Troubleshooting and repair packages.* General Electric (GE) has an expert system that helps mechanics identify and repair problems with its diesel locomotives (see Figure 3-2). And France's Elf Aquitaine oil company

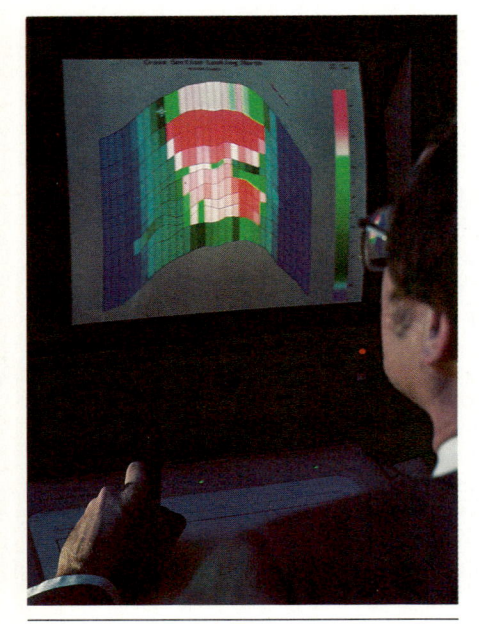

This petroleum engineer is working with an expert system to determine the best way to extract oil from a geologic formation. (© Hank Morgan/Photo Researchers)

FIGURE 3-2

General Electric's locomotive repair expert system uses data supplied by a mechanic to home in on a problem. It can then display locomotive components on a screen, and demonstrate repair procedures on a video monitor by calling up filmed instructions stored on a videodisk. (© 1984 Lynn Johnson/Black Star)

Fujitsu's FACOM VP-100 supercomputer is a first stage in the Japanese effort to become world leaders in artificial intelligence by the year 2000. (Courtesy Fujitsu)

uses an expert system that can evaluate more than 500 variables to diagnose problems at drilling sites. General Electric's system is available to its railroad customers. But Elf officials believe their system gives them a major advantage over competitors, and so they are keeping its details secret.

Much of the earlier work in expert systems has occurred in the United States, but Japan plans to spend hundreds of millions of dollars over the next decade to develop advanced new computers aimed specifically at AI applications. (Some believe that four generations of computers have been developed since the 1940s. The Japanese effort has thus been described as an attempt to produce "fifth-generation" machines.) Before the year 2000, the Japanese expect to achieve leadership in AI technology with a supercomputer capable of storing a knowledge base of up to 20,000 rules and 100 million data items. On a much smaller scale, packages for personal computers are beginning to appear that give users expert legal and financial advice, as well as assistance in other categories.

For the foreseeable future, however, the role of the computer should continue to be that of an intelligence amplifier in an alliance with humanity. This alliance combines the current superiority of the human brain in matters involving creativity, judgment, and intuition with the computer's superiority in processing speed, accuracy, and tireless attention to detail. The word **synergy** refers to the ability of two entities to achieve together what each is incapable of achieving alone. As Figure 3-3 indicates, the alliance between humans and computers can produce a synergistic effect. The potential achievements of such an alliance seem almost limitless.

THE IMPACT OF COMPUTERS ON PEOPLE

The computer is one of the most powerful forces in society today. It is being put to use everywhere—in homes and in organizations of all sizes—and no

FIGURE 3-3

The strengths of humans and computers differ.

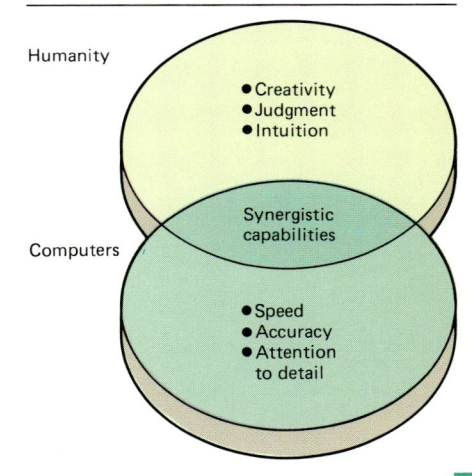

Humanity
- Creativity
- Judgment
- Intuition

Synergistic capabilities

Computers
- Speed
- Accuracy
- Attention to detail

one can doubt that this usage is having a strong impact on many people. The computer is the driving force behind an information revolution, and as in any revolution, some innocent people may be harmed. Let's look briefly here at some of the positive and negative effects that computer usage may have on individuals.

The Positive Impact

Many people enjoy challenging careers in the computing field, and these career opportunities are outlined in detail at the end of Chapter 12. But we all benefit in other ways from the use of computers. We benefit *on the job* even though we aren't computer specialists. We benefit as the *consumers* of the goods and services provided by computer-using organizations. And we benefit *at home* by using personal computers for work and for play.

Employment Benefits   Each day, computers are helping millions of people to do their jobs more effectively. For example, computers can help *managers* decide on a future course of action (the **planning** function), and they can then help with the follow-up checks on performance to see if planned goals are being achieved (the **control** function). By using the more accurate and timely information supplied by a *data base management system (DBMS),* a manager can do a better job of identifying problems and recognizing opportunities. The information retrieved by a DBMS can then be manipulated by a *spreadsheet* software package to help the manager plan alternate courses of action. And managers may no longer need to spend as much time in controlling because a computer can be programmed to signal with a triggered report whenever actual performance varies from what was planned. The time saved in controlling may enable managers to give more attention to employee concerns, and this, in turn, may result in improved morale.

But employment benefits certainly aren't restricted to managers. *Healthcare investigators and other scientists* now use computers to research complex problem areas that could not otherwise be considered. *Lawyers* are using legal data banks to locate precedent cases in order to serve clients better. *Sales personnel* can now receive more timely information about customers and product inventories, can promise more efficient handling of sales orders in order to serve their customers better, and can thus improve their sales per-

Design engineers and architects now use computers to simplify design work and increase the space usage and layout alternatives that they can study. Structural engineers use computer models to predict the effect of stresses on different structural configurations. (Courtesy Intergraph)

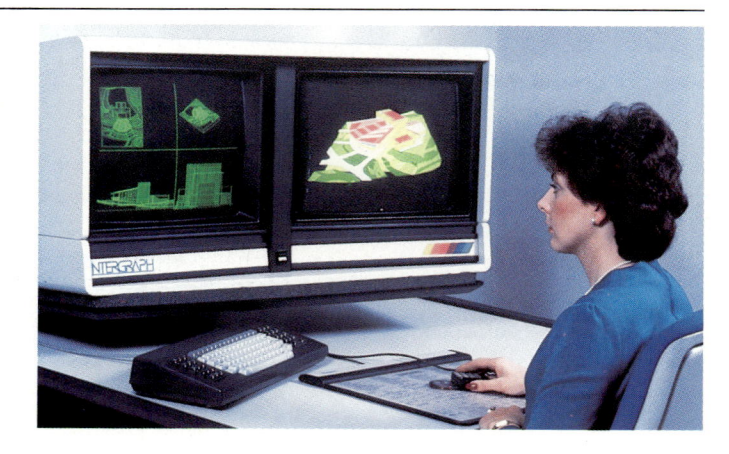

formance because of computer systems. And the job duties of some *clerical employees* and *factory workers* have changed from routine, repetitive operations to more varied and appealing tasks through computer usage.

Benefits from Organizations Using Computers   A few examples of the possible benefits that people may receive from their dealings with computer-using organizations are discussed below. (You'll find many additional examples in the chapters in Module 4.)

● *Greater efficiency.*   Because public and private organizations have avoided waste and improved *efficiency* through the use of computers, the prices and even the taxes we now pay are less than they would otherwise have been. For example, about one-third of all the dairy cows in the nation are now bred, fed, milked, and monitored for productivity with the help of computers. The dairy industry today can produce all the milk that was supplied 15 years ago with only half as many cows. Computer uses like this can significantly improve **productivity**—the amount of goods or services possessing economic value that people and machines (and cows) can produce in a given time period. And such productivity gains usually lead to higher levels of real income for more people.

● *Higher-quality products.*   Computers may also help improve the *quality* of the products and services we receive. For example, microcomputers are now installed in cars to provide a more efficient means of controlling the engine's fuel mixture, ignition timing, and exhaust emissions. And computer-controlled manipulators or **robots** can be used to assemble products or components with closer tolerances than were previously feasible.

● *Better service.*   Individuals may now receive *better service* from *government agencies*. In contrast to the bureaucratic runaround that often accompanies a call to city hall, a Long Beach, California, system enables citizens calling city hall with an inquiry or complaint to dial a single number, get the

Today's instant, worldwide reservation services for airlines, hotels, and car rentals would be impossible without computers. (© H. Scott Heist/Sperry Corp.)

right department, and be guaranteed a response. The computer creates a record of each call, prints a letter to the caller, and sends a copy to the appropriate city council representative. If a final disposition on a call is not received within a given time period, the computer triggers a follow-up procedure. Service benefits from computers in *businesses* include (1) shorter waiting lines at banks and airline ticket offices and at the reservation desks of hotels and car-rental agencies, (2) faster and more accurate answers to the inquiries of people served by the businesses, and (3) more efficient customer service and control of inventory in retail outlets. Service benefits from computers in *health care* include (1) faster and more thorough approaches to the preparation and analysis of medical histories, (2) faster and more thorough testing to detect and identify disease, (3) more accurate methods of physiological monitoring, and (4) better control of lab test results and the dispensing of drugs.

- *Recreational and educational benefits.* Some organizations are using computers solely to amuse and entertain people. As you read this, personal computer game programs probably are being prepared by hundreds of producers. **Computer animation** is being used to give the illusion of movement to inanimate objects, and the results of this animation are now seen regularly in movies and on TV. And the potential for computers in education has barely been tapped (see Figure 3-4).

- *Aid to the handicapped.* Microcomputers can be used to control devices that permit severely handicapped persons to feed themselves even though they have no upper-limb responses. Computer-based human-machine analyses are making it possible to develop more effective artificial limbs for amputees. And computer workstations in homes, linked to outside office systems by communications lines, expand job opportunities for handicapped people. The Closer Look section following this chapter describes several other computer applications that aid handicapped people.

- *Improved safety.* Computers contribute to safety in many ways. Computer-controlled braking systems in aircraft and in cars help prevent dangerous skids and produce the optimum stopping distance in all weather condi-

FIGURE 3-4

Computers are helping many preschool and older children learn how to write. The computer displays and then speaks the words they type. Bank Street Writer, a word processing program designed for children in the elementary grades, has become a popular educational tool for children—and a popular writing tool for adults as well. (© Sal DiMarco/Black Star)

tions. Computers permit gas utility companies to do a better job of controlling the pipeline leaks that can seriously jeopardize public safety. And state and local governments are using computers to design safer roads and control air and water pollution.

- ● *Better information retrieval.* A New York surgeon contacted a medical library when a near-term pregnant woman lapsed into a hepatic coma. He needed immediate information on exchange blood transfusions for the woman. Using a computer terminal and a retrieval program, the librarian was able to search more than a half-million medical documents in a few minutes to get the information needed by the surgeon to perform an emergency blood transfusion. The patient recovered fully from the hepatitis. Although most information retrieval projects obviously don't involve life-or-death decisions, quick computer-assisted retrieval can save time and aggravation for many people.

Benefits from Personal Computing You've already seen a few of the benefits that can come from the use of personal computers in Chapter 2, and Chapter 7 will provide additional examples. Thus the following brief listing of benefits will suffice here.

- ● *Entertainment and hobby benefits.* A personal computer (pc) can entertain you with hundreds of challenging games. And pc users can compose music, store and maintain stamp and coin collection records, and polish their foreign language and programming skills.

- ● *Educational benefits.* Educators agree that the home pc can be a powerful motivating and learning tool. Thousands of educational programs are available in such categories as reading, languages, science, mathematics, social studies, art, and music. The National Education Association (NEA) reviews educational programs and puts its "teacher certified" NEA seal on those packages that meet its standards.

- ● *Benefits of greater personal efficiency.* You've already seen how a

Managing your money is much easier with personal computers. In many cities, you can bank at home, as this woman is doing. Other programs help you to budget your expenses, balance your checkbook, analyze the stock market, and prepare your tax return. (© Kim Steele/Black Star)

time management package can help people save time and use time more efficiently. But a pc can also help individuals put up a better fight for their social concerns against well-heeled bureaucracies. With his wife and neighbors, Richard Bach, author of *Jonathan Livingston Seagull,* forced the U.S. Bureau of Land Management to cancel a timber sale in Oregon that they felt would have damaged the environment. The group used pc's to gather information from public data banks and to prepare the documents needed for their successful protest.

The Potential Dangers

In spite of the countless benefits that people receive from computer usage, such usage can also lead to potential dangers and problems.

Employment Problems   Computer usage has sometimes produced displacement and unemployment—which aren't the same. **Unemployment** refers to the total number of people involuntarily out of work. **Displacement** occurs when jobs are eliminated as a result of technological change. *If* displaced workers can't find similar jobs elsewhere and *if* they can't find work in other occupations, then there is, indeed, an increase in the unemployment figures.

Some managers whose decisions were structured and repetitive found that those decisions were programmable on a computer. Once programs have been written to take over those duties, fewer administrators may be needed to perform the remaining job functions. During the first half of the 1980s, the middle-management ranks of many large organizations grew much thinner. And clerical employees have often been displaced by computers too. A few years ago, for example, Los Angeles County installed a new Welfare Case Management Information System that was designed to increase efficiency and eliminate 900 jobs over a 3-year period.

A more serious displacement problem, however, is likely to result from the increased use of computer-controlled *robots* in assembly operations. The automobile industry is a leading user of robots; for several years they have performed such production tasks as stamping, welding, and spray painting. Robots perform these dreary, dirty, and dangerous tasks without complaint, so robots were usually applied first in such areas of worker discontent. But production techniques are now changing rapidly in the automobile industry, and auto builders are replacing both workers and old machines with a new generation of programmable robots (see Figure 3-5).

Nor are professional workers immune from the effects of computer usage. The advancement in scientific and engineering knowledge (which may be attributed in part to the expanding use of computers) makes it increasingly difficult for scientists and engineers to keep abreast of their fields. They must have the ability and willingness to learn about computing, adopt new techniques, and, perhaps, go through several "retreading" periods in their careers simply to retain marketable skills. The anxiety associated with this continuing threat of technical obsolescence is something that some professionals may have to learn to live with.

Data Gathering Problems   A staggering volume of personal information has been gathered by government agencies and private organizations. The federal government alone maintains over 4,500 data systems containing over 3.4 *billion* records and dossiers on individuals. These thousands of federal

FIGURE 3-5

Robots like these welders, assembling vans in a plant seemingly empty of people, have already displaced 20% of the people who once were needed to assemble cars. As programmable robots take over, the number of manufacturing workers in the United States will drop from today's 25 million to an estimated 3 million by the year 2010. (Courtesy Chrysler Corp.)

data banks, when combined with the thousands of others maintained by states, counties, and cities, provide governments with specific information on virtually every citizen. Hundreds of private organizations, such as credit bureaus, also collect personal information about people and sell it to other organizations.

There are several problems associated with all this data gathering. Included in these problems are:

- ***Gathering data without a valid need to know.*** For years, the Justice Department maintained a computer-based Inter-Divisional Information System (IDIS) to gather data about the "agitational activities" of political dissidents. However, after examining IDIS files, Senate investigators concluded that "massive amounts of irrelevant information had been compiled on innocent individuals." Another example of questionable data gathering involves the private firms that collect personal data about people for insurance companies, employers, and credit grantors. These data about a person are frequently gathered by an interviewer from two or three of the person's neighbors or acquaintances. In 10 or 20 minutes, the interviewer may ask questions about the subject's reputation, use of alcohol or narcotics, and lifestyle, and probe for any news of domestic troubles or reports of dubious business practices. Questions calling for such detailed, subjective, and impressionistic responses in such a short time are an open invitation to gossip and faulty moral assessments. But this is a data gathering method that has been used by a large consumer reporting service. Once stored in a computer data bank, the contents of a person's file are available to data bank users for a small fee.

MODULE 1

These banks of magnetic tape drives at the FBI's National Crime Information Center contain millions of arrest records—and at least a quarter of these records contain no information about the final outcome of the cases. (Courtesy The FBI)

● *Gathering inaccurate and incomplete data.* It isn't just questionable methods that introduce inaccuracies into a computer data bank. Unintentional mistakes in filling out input forms and keying records are common enough to any record-keeping system. But the consequences may be more serious in a computer-based system. There may be fewer people to catch errors—and the speed with which inaccurate information is made available to system users may be much faster than the speed with which errors are detected and corrected. For example, in converting data on a questionnaire into machine-readable form, a data entry operator may hit the "1" key instead of the "2" key (where 1 is the code for "yes" and 2 the code for "no") on a question concerning a felony conviction, a prior bankruptcy, or a history of mental disorder or venereal disease. Imagine the possible consequences of this simple mistake! Finally, input data are also subject to serious errors of omission. If, for example, a person is arrested and accused of, say, auto theft, this fact will be entered into several law enforcement data banks. But if the person is later found innocent of the charges, this very important fact that's needed to complete the record may *not* be entered into the data banks.

If the input data important to people are accurate and complete when they are gathered and entered into a computer system, are processed correctly, and don't become inaccurate through subsequent errors, we could be confident about the integrity of the data. But even if we were successful in controlling **data integrity,** this wouldn't be enough to eliminate all the adverse effects that computer systems may have on the private lives of people. It doesn't help people to know that the information about them that's gathered and stored in a data bank is accurate and complete if they also know that the information isn't *secured and protected* against theft, fraud, or malicious scrutiny and manipulation.

The Systems Security Issue   For our purposes, **systems security** involves (1) the protection of stored *data* against accidental or malicious disclosure and

(2) the *physical* protection of hardware and software against damage or destruction. It's important for us to know that our confidential records are preserved and used only for approved purposes and that the equipment and programs needed to store and retrieve them are protected against damage or penetration.

The vulnerability of computer systems has increased in recent years, and so the security issue has become more critical. Early computers were accessible only to a few specialists and were used to process batches of data in a single stream. As computer systems increased in number and became more sophisticated, however, the use of shared resources and jointly used data became common, and direct interaction with a computer became routine for even casual users. Such an open environment has obviously increased the difficulty of maintaining security. The vulnerability of systems has also increased for two other reasons: (1) The information found in a relatively complete and up-to-date data bank may be of sufficient value to tempt outsiders to seek access to it and (2) more and more people are mastering the skills required to program, penetrate, and manipulate computer systems.

Unfortunately, the computer hardware in general use today wasn't designed with security provisions in mind. Thus the provisions that do exist are found in the software and in the organizational policies and data processing controls of a particular system. But when it comes to security, existing software is indeed soft. Clever interlopers have had no difficulty in breaking through the security provisions of most computer operating system programs. It's happened frequently enough, in fact, that the use of personal computers to gain unauthorized access into organizational systems is a popular story line today for television and movie writers. Today's computer operating systems aren't completely predictable. Furthermore, there's no guarantee that an operating system hasn't been programmed to perform unauthorized acts. Thus there's no guaranteed defense against several known techniques by which a programmer can corrupt a system.

The lack of control over computer system security has had unhappy consequences for many people. Individuals as well as organizations lose money to the computer thief. In one instance, a computer was used to send out phony invoices to people. The thief knew that some people pay authentic-looking bills automatically. When a phony bill was questioned, the thief would merely send back a form letter saying, "Sorry, our computer made an error." A person's finances can also become fouled up in other ways (see Figure 3-6).

The Privacy Issue *Both* information *integrity and security* are needed to protect a person's **right to privacy**—to protect the legitimate right of an individual to limit access to personal and often sensitive information. If a lack of integrity in a law enforcement data bank permits the arrest of an innocent person and then results in the creation of an arrest record that may not be purged from the system, and if a lack of systems security subsequently permits the circulation of this arrest record to prospective employers and credit agencies, these deficiencies have certainly contributed to an invasion of the individual's privacy. In short, data integrity, information security, and personal privacy are interrelated, as shown in Figure 3-7.

A few examples and speculations will demonstrate how a computer system or network could be used to violate a person's legitimate right to privacy.

FIGURE 3-6

Automatic teller machines make life more convenient for customers—and for thieves. For example, a Chicago woman was mailed a bank money card and a personal identification number without having requested them. Both were intercepted by a thief who used them to empty the woman's $600 account and run up an overdraft of $1200. The bank then froze the woman's other account because she was overdrawn. It took an attorney and 2 months of wrangling with the bank to get her money released. (Courtesy NCR Corp.)

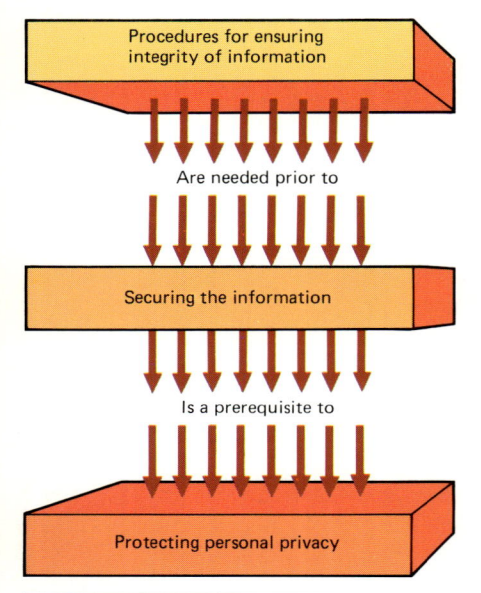

FIGURE 3-7

The relationship among data integrity, systems security, and personal privacy.

[Diagram: Procedures for ensuring integrity of information → Are needed prior to → Securing the information → Is a prerequisite to → Protecting personal privacy]

- *Surveillance possibilities.* People often use a plastic "money card" to pay for goods and services. Electronic signals may be sent between computers and online financial terminals to adjust the accounts of the parties involved in a transaction. No cash or checks are used in such an **electronic funds transfer system (EFTS).** Although the EFTS used by banks and other financial institutions aren't intended for *surveillance,* they could be easily adapted to this purpose. The use of *cash* in a transaction reveals nothing about the parties to the transaction. When a *check* is written, a record is created of the payer, the payee, and the transaction amount. And when a *money card* is used, all this information, along with the transaction time, location, and nature of the transaction, is recorded. Thus if all your transactions were normally processed through EFTS computers, a *daily record* of much of *what* you do and *where* you do it could be prepared.

  Of course, EFTS proponents maintain that adequate laws can prevent surveillance abuse. But critics point out that existing check authorization systems can "flag" accounts so that if a "flagged" person tries to cash a check, someone (police perhaps?) can be told of the person's exact location. These critics fear that future operators of EFTS networks would be unable to resist the pressures from governments to use the EFTS for surveillance purposes.

- *List-compiling abuses.* Mailing lists giving details about people are regularly compiled and sold by both private and public organizations. State auto licensing agencies, for example, sell lists to auto equipment suppliers. There's not much harm in this if it results only in your receiving literature that tries to persuade you to buy seat covers a few weeks after you've registered your new car. But what about the computer dating service that sold its list of female clients to a publishing organization that then printed and sold through local newsstands lists of "Girls Who Want Dates"? Try to tell one of those women that her privacy hasn't been invaded!

EFTS keys or surveillance tools? A few years ago, a group of U.S. computer, communications, and surveillance experts was given the following problem: If they were advisers to the Russian secret police, how would they design an unobtrusive system to monitor the activities of all citizens and visitors in the U.S.S.R.? As one of these experts put it in a congressional hearing, ". . . this group decided that if you wanted to build an unobtrusive system for surveillance, you couldn't do better than an EFTS."

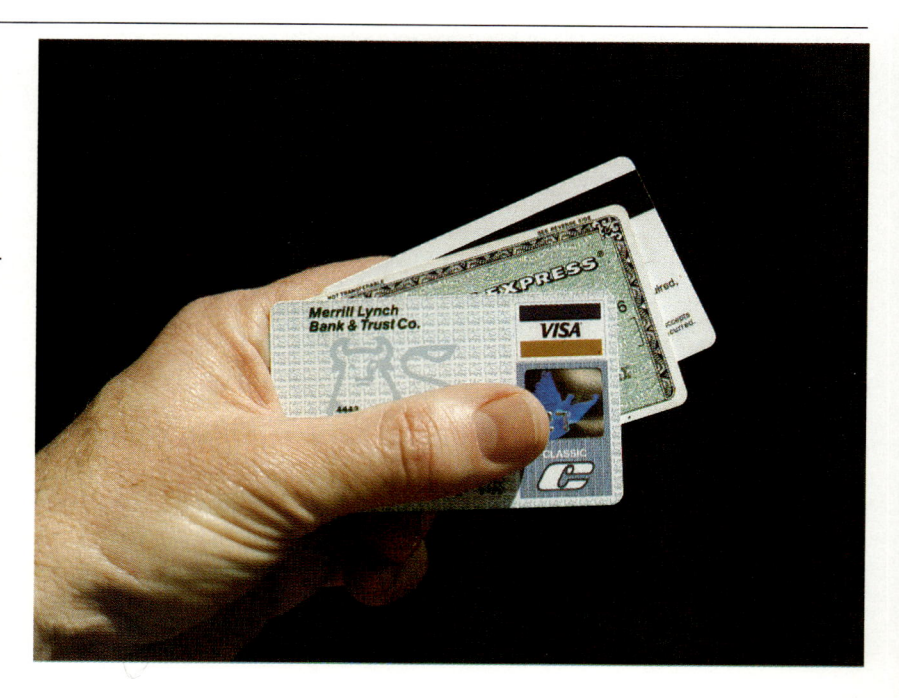

- *Freedom restrictions.* Thousands of law enforcement officers and credit clerks have easy access to networks containing information on millions of people. Many of these officers and clerks without any real "need to know" may be tempted to browse through the records of friends and acquaintances just to see what they can uncover. And most categories of personal information gathered for legitimate research purposes by reputable social, political, and behavioral scientists aren't protected by any laws. Thus sensitive personal information gathered by these researchers may be obtained through a subpoena issued by a court or other government body and put into data banks for future use. Such facts may make many people more cautious. It may restrict their actions even when the data are accurate, the use of the data is authorized by law, and controls on the use of the data are imposed. You may favor the use of computers to curtail crime, but you may also resent being listed with felons in an unsecured data bank. And you may believe that a professor should conduct a study that requires the gathering and analyzing of personal data, but you may not feel free to let your personal data become part of that study. In short, you may behave differently (and less freely) than you once would have because of your increasing awareness of what you say and do may become part of some computer record.

Privacy Controls   We've been discussing an individual's "right" to privacy, but the word "privacy" doesn't appear anywhere in the Constitution. What, then, is the legal status of privacy? In 1928, Supreme Court Justice Louis Brandeis wrote in a minority opinion: "The right to be let alone is the most comprehensive of rights and the right most valued by civilized men." But what one person considers a privacy right may be judged by others to be an item of genuine public concern. For example, if a newspaper reporter finds that a member of Congress has put a number of unqualified relatives on the government payroll, and if the reporter then reveals this fact and prints the names and salaries of the relatives, she has undoubtedly infringed on their privacy. But she has also used rights guaranteed to her in the Bill of Rights (the First Amendment's freedom of speech and freedom of the press) to perform a public service. Thus, there may be legitimate rights operating against privacy in some situations.

In short, since privacy is not one of the specific constitutional rights, and since a balance has to be struck between the personal need for privacy and society's need for legitimate information, *the extent to which individuals are given privacy protection must depend on judicial and legislative decisions.* That is, the *continuous task* of balancing human rights against basic freedoms in order to establish privacy controls is the responsibility of the judicial and legislative branches of government.

THE IMPACT OF COMPUTERS ON ORGANIZATIONS

After noting that "the world is too much with us, late and soon," William Wordsworth took a stroll along a sandy beach to calm his ruffled sensibilities. He could not know that tiny silicon chips made from the sand he was walking on would cause feverish activity 200 years later. These chips have dropped into our midst like small stones into a lake, but they are causing waves rather than ripples! And the waves caused by computers are having both positive and

U.S. lawmakers have been restoring some balance in favor of privacy in recent years, passing numerous federal statutes and about 150 state laws to control invasions of privacy. Examples include:
The Fair Credit Reporting Act of 1970. This federal law gives people the right to know what information is kept on them by credit bureaus.
State "Fair Information Practice" laws. Laws in many states spell out the rights of people when dealing with state government data banks.
The Privacy Act of 1974. This federal law is aimed at correcting some of the abuses of federal data banks.
State Cable Television Privacy acts. Several states have passed laws forbidding cable TV companies from monitoring subscribers' sets or their selection of programs. (Courtesy The Social Security Administration)

negative effects on the organizations that make them and on those that use them.

The Information Processing Industry

Computers have created a dynamic industry which produces and maintains the machines and supplies much of their software. The growth curve has been climbing so rapidly in the information industry that sales statistics and other measuring data become outdated almost as soon as they are published. The latest figures available at this writing show that industry sales had grown nearly 20 percent from the preceding year, and total revenues for just the top 100 U.S.-based firms were over $90 *billion*. The revenues of Japanese and European businesses added many additional billions to these figures. The industry leader is IBM with revenues of about $50 billion. The next 11 U.S. firms in the industry also had data processing revenues that topped the $1 billion mark.

Rapid Change Is the Rule Since it's technology-driven and subject to short product cycles and rapid obsolescence, the information processing industry is one in which rapid change is the rule. Competitive pressures aren't limited to the pc market. Large and well-financed companies, such as General Electric, RCA, and Xerox, have tried to compete in the mainframe market sector and have failed.

Entrepreneurs with technical and managerial skills have started many small companies with money supplied by venture capitalists, have nursed these start-up operations into thriving businesses, have sold out to larger organizations at attractive prices, and have then started a second, third, or even fourth high-technology company. Makers of integrated circuits are putting the mainframes of a few years ago on one or a few silicon chips. And the independent software sector of the industry is experiencing explosive growth. Software houses are now selling billions of dollars of off-the-shelf packages each year.

The merging of data processing, word processing, and data communications technologies has made competitors out of firms that a few years ago were not even included in the "computer industry." For example, AT&T, shorn of its Bell Telephone operating companies, has now moved into the unregulated and competitive information processing industry.

Competition from Japanese and European companies is also growing. We've seen that the Japanese have embarked on an ambitious "fifth-generation" national development push to build supercomputers. Other Japanese efforts pose a threat to those who build smaller systems. To meet this overseas competition, U.S. computer, communications, and semiconductor firms have launched a wave of joint ventures, research cooperatives, technology exchanges, and ownership agreements. For example, a number of companies are supporting the Semiconductor Research Cooperative and the Microelectronics and Computer Technology Corporation (MCC).

As you can see, the speed with which new technology is being applied produces a challenging competitive environment in the information processing industry. The rewards are great for those who respond quickly to opportunities, but the penalties are also severe for those who fall behind. Let's look now at how the products of this industry can produce similar benefits and dangers for those organizations that use them.

Cashing in your chips has a new meaning in the information processing industry, where company rankings can change dramatically in a single year. Recently, one pc maker jumped past 15 other top-100 companies; others have grown almost overnight into $100 million giants. And some firms fall even faster than they grew. For example, Osborne Computer Corporation was started, achieved an annual sales rate of nearly $100 million, and then filed for bankruptcy—all in just 2½ years! (Courtesy Sperry Corp.)

The Positive Impact on Using Organizations

Computer-using organizations are generally active in government, law, health care, education, the humanities, science, engineering, and business. We'll briefly mention a few examples of benefits in these areas here and leave further details to Chapters 13 through 15.

Computers in Government, Law, and Health Care Computers are helping governments with their *planning and decision-making, control,* and *law enforcement* activities. For example:

● Computer simulation models have helped planners in the Department of Health and Human Services study the cause-and-effect relationships of water pollution so that preventive action can be taken to protect rivers. Military planners sharpen their analytical skills and gain experience in decision making through the use of computer-based "war games." Members of Congress and the state legislatures use computer systems to retrieve statutory material and other data to support planning and decision making. Urban planners have developed computer programs to evaluate the different transportation systems, traffic-flow patterns, and alternative recreational, housing, and other land-use needs of communities. And California uses computers to control the movement of water through hundreds of miles of canals and tunnels.

● A nationwide police information network connects the FBI's National Crime Information Center (NCIC) computers in Washington with the computer systems maintained by states and many larger cities. The New York Statewide Police Information Network (NYSPIN) is just one element in the national net. NYSPIN has a central computer complex that serves hundreds of online terminals located in state and municipal agencies, criminal justice departments, the FBI, the National Auto Theft Bureau, and the Federal Bureaus of Narcotics and Customs. NYSPIN is also linked with many other computers including those at the NCIC, the National Law Enforcement Telecommunications System in Phoenix, Arizona, and the Department of Motor Vehicles in Albany.

The Internal Revenue Service uses computer matching programs to compare income reported by taxpayers (such as interest earned) against the filed reports of income paid to the taxpayer (such as the interest paid by banks). Without computers, such control activities would be impossible. (Courtesy The IRS)

Several computer systems are being used to monitor patients in hospitals. The system shown here watches over patients who have just had surgery or suffered heart attacks. These patients are connected to computer-monitored sensing devices that immediately detect dangerously abnormal conditions and flash warning signals to doctors and nurses. Similar systems watch the vital signs of premature babies in neonatal intensive care units. (Courtesy Hewlett-Packard Co.)

Computers are also being used for *planning and decision making* and *control* purposes by health-care professionals and organizations. For example:

● Some doctors are using the computer as a diagnostic tool in hospitals and clinics. Patients are given physical exams consisting of a series of basic tests at a number of screening centers around the country. The testing equipment may be linked directly to a computer for an automatic transfer of results. Once the data are received, the computer can compare test measurements against the standards established in the program. Within a few minutes, the test results are reported. If they fall outside prescribed limits, the program suggests procedures that should be repeated and additional tests that should be conducted. The computer may also be running an expert system program to suggest tentative diagnoses to explain abnormal test results. The patient's physician, of course, is responsible for the final diagnosis.

We'll look at other ways government and health-care organizations can benefit from computer usage in Chapter 13.

Computers in Education and the Humanities Computers bring to the educational process such attributes as untiring patience, around-the-clock availability, and individualized and student-paced instruction programs. And their use *can* lead to improved student performance in thinking logically, formulating problem solution procedures, and understanding relationships. The following examples merely scratch the surface of the computer's potential:

● High school physics students in Lexington, Massachusetts, have written a program that simulates a landing on the moon. The object of the program is to have a physics student land the spacecraft safely—an operation requiring the student to apply information that she or he has learned about gravitational effects and Newton's laws of motion (see Figure 3-8).

● History students may be paired up (one representing the North, the other the South) to make decisions about the tactics, troops, supplies, etc., prior to the beginning of a specific Civil War battle. The object of the simulation is to win the battle. Since the simulation program is based on actual Civil War conflicts, the history student is motivated to learn about the clashes because he or she will be "participating" in them. It's possible for an informed

CHAPTER 3

113

FIGURE 3-8
High school students like these developed a lunar landing game that begins with the spacecraft traveling 3,600 miles per hour 120 miles above the moon. Every 10 seconds the program takes a "radar" check of altitude and measures velocity and remaining fuel. The student then tells the computer how much fuel to use in the next 10 seconds. A safe landing requires a touchdown speed of a tenth of a mile per hour, with all fuel burned. Most students crash at first, and must make new calculations to improve their next landing. These calculations reinforce the physics concepts being taught. (© 1984 by Joseph Nettis/Photo Researchers)

"southern general" to defeat an uninformed northern opponent at the battle of Gettysburg.

A growing number of people with interests in history, literature, music, graphic arts, and other branches of the humanities have turned to computer usage in recent years to (1) ease manuscript preparation, (2) save research time and effort, (3) conduct studies that would otherwise be impractical, (4) discover significant stylistic patterns in texts, and (5) apply their artistic talents to a new medium. We'll look at examples in these categories in Chapter 14.

Computers in Science, Engineering, and Business   We'll look at some of the ways that scientific and business organizations are benefiting from computer usage in Chapter 15. For now, let's just focus on how computers can help produce significant gains in productivity.

Economists tell us that productivity is dependent on such factors as (1) the attitudes, health, and training of people and (2) the amount of capital equipment available and the technological sophistication of this equipment. Since computers are sophisticated tools that can significantly improve productivity, and since the overall U.S. productivity gains in recent years have trailed the gains made in many other nations, there's now a concerted effort under way in this country to apply computers in design and production processes. Let's consider here how **flexible manufacturing systems (FMS)** and **computer-aided design (CAD)** improve productivity.

● *Flexible manufacturing systems.* Unlike a *fixed automation system* which follows a rigid series of steps to produce a product, an FMS can be programmed to *alter* its procedures to suit different production needs. Thus, small-lot manufacturing may become nearly as economical as mass produc-

A computer program that stores musical compositions and plays them back on command is one of the many ingenious computer applications created for the humanities. (Courtesy Verbatim Corp.)

MODULE 1

114

This computer-guided drill press is a first-generation flexible manufacturing system. An FMS like this can be quickly reprogrammed to produce new items, so it can make a variety of specialized products with scarcely a pause between runs. As a result, it is almost as efficient as a mass-production assembly line. (© 1982 Morton Beebe/The Image Bank)

tion is today. In fact, computers and robots may reduce overall costs in small-lot manufacturing by more than 50 percent between 1980 and 1990. Future "parts-on-demand" FMS production facilities may be able to turn out different products on different days or even different hours.

● *Computer-aided design.* Certain steps are generally required in the development of a wide range of items. These steps are (1) preliminary design, (2) advanced design, (3) model development, (4) model testing, (5) final testing, and (6) production and construction. All these steps are made quicker and simpler by the use of computers. In the past, preliminary sketches, design drawings, and engineering drawings were usually prepared early in the design and development of new products and projects. When designers or engineers had a new thought, they would make some preliminary sketches to get the idea down on paper so that it could be analyzed more thoroughly. As the design was modified, additional drawings would be required. When the design was finally approved, further detailed production drawings were prepared. Today, special computer input devices, such as *electronic pens* and *graphic tablets,* permit engineers to make quick changes in their sketches. Once the initial drawings are finished and displayed to the engineer's satisfaction, the computer may then be instructed to test a computer "model" of the displayed design and report on its characteristics. Interactive communication between designer and computer continues until a design with a desirable set of characteristics is produced. Ships, aircraft, automobiles, highways, electronic circuits—these and many other items are now developed in this way. In addition, it may soon be common to have the computer prepare (1) detailed engineering blueprints from the stored design and (2) control tapes that program automatic machine tools and robots to produce component parts of new products precisely according to the blueprint specifications. In other words, in such a **computer-aided design/computer-aided manufacturing (CAD/CAM)** environment, the computer may interact with the engineer from the time of the initial idea until the final production step is completed.

The Potential Dangers for Using Organizations

Although organizations receive many benefits from computer usage, they may also encounter some computer-related problems.

The Threats to Systems Security People in charge of an organization's computer systems must guard against the following dangers:

- *The threats to assets.* In the absence of proper controls, knowledgeable employees (or a skilled outsider) can steal data and/or programs and sell them. They can fraudulently add, delete, or change transactions in the data in order to embezzle a firm's assets. And they can do these things at the computer site or from a remote station. Thieves are interested in computerized records today because the job of accounting for the assets of many organizations has now been entrusted to computer systems. When paper money was introduced, thieves used printing presses to copy it. Now plastic money (credit cards) and magnetic money (money cards with magnetic strips, and magnetic tapes and disks) are used, and thieves are using computers. Measures must be taken to protect the system against the electronic theft of assets.

- *The threats of attack and penetration.* As Figure 3-9 indicates, organizational computer systems are vulnerable to attack and penetration from many sources if adequate controls aren't provided. The motivation for such penetration sometimes comes from simple curiosity and the challenge of solving a puzzle or playing a joke. (This type of thinking may be a carryover from a penetrator's school days when he or she played the disturbing "game" of

FIGURE 3-9

Programmers, operators, maintenance people, and online users can penetrate system security. Programmers may insert instructions into operating system programs that provide a "trap door" for later penetration. Outsiders may also attack online systems. Penetrators can obtain the passwords of legitimate users by wiretapping, and can then use these passwords to masquerade as authorized users to browse in a data base. The piggybacking approach attaches a small "bootleg" processor or terminal to a tapped line to intercept and modify legitimate messages. Transmissions between branch banks could be intercepted, for example, and credits to the tapper's account could be added to the message. Numerous other techniques that don't require wiretapping are also available to the penetrator.

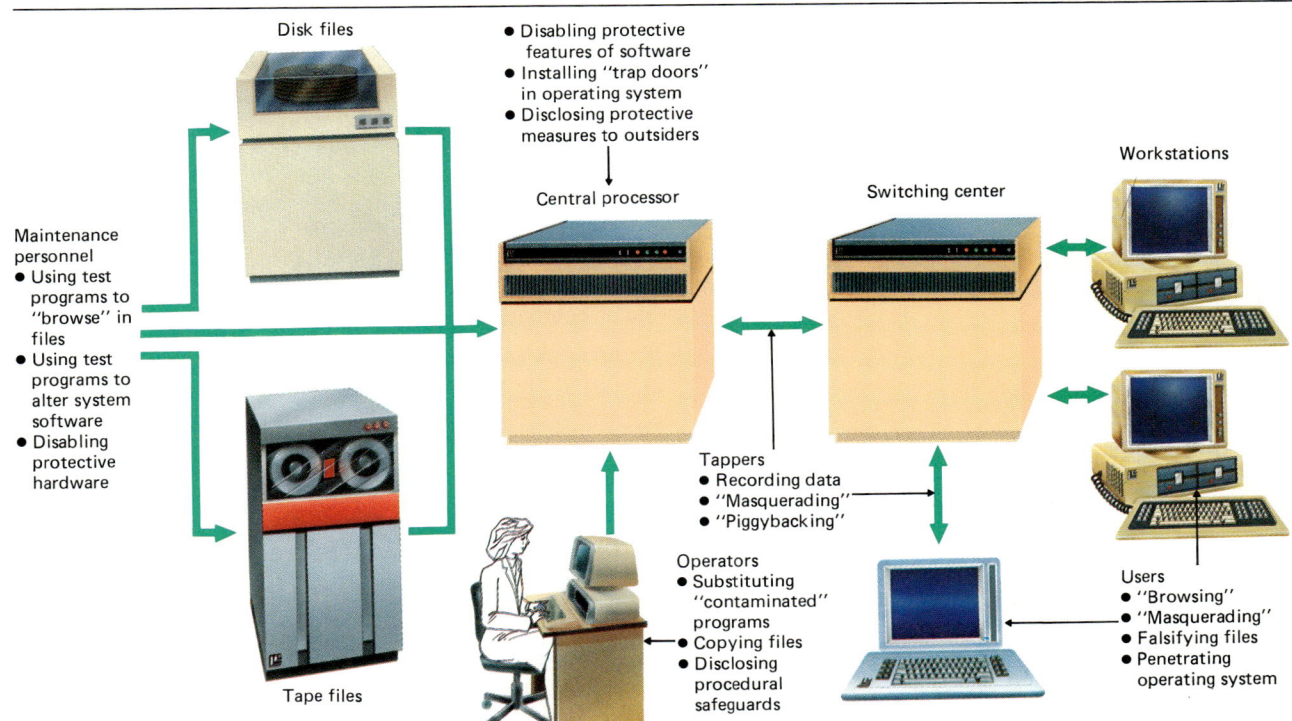

Maintenance personnel
- Using test programs to "browse" in files
- Using test programs to alter system software
- Disabling protective hardware

Disk files

- Disabling protective features of software
- Installing "trap doors" in operating system
- Disclosing protective measures to outsiders

Central processor

Tape files

Operators
- Substituting "contaminated" programs
- Copying files
- Disclosing procedural safeguards

Tappers
- Recording data
- "Masquerading"
- "Piggybacking"

Switching center

Workstations

Users
- "Browsing"
- "Masquerading"
- Falsifying files
- Penetrating operating system

penetrating the control programs of the school's computer.) Or the purpose may be to steal the secrets of an individual or competitor, or to cause a competitor's system to "crash," or become inoperable. Regardless of the motivation, penetrating a typical system today is about as difficult as solving the crossword puzzle in a Sunday paper. The ease with which 12 Milwaukee teenagers—dubbed the "414 hackers" because of Milwaukee's Area Code—gained access into over 60 systems, including computers at the Defense Department, the Los Alamos Scientific Laboratory, and the Memorial Sloan–Kettering Cancer Center, tends to support that claim. Obviously, controls must be designed to make attack and penetration more difficult than that.

- *The threats to the physical security of the computer site.* Many organizations can no longer carry out some of their day-to-day operations without computer help. Thus it's vital that their hardware and software be *physically protected* against damage or destruction from such hazards as *fire, flood,* and *sabotage.* Thousands of military records were destroyed in a fire at the Army Records Center in St. Louis. A severe tropical storm flooded numerous computer centers in the eastern United States. And computers have been bombed, shot, knifed, and bathed with milk shakes by radical students, disgruntled employees, and frustrated programmers. Provisions must be made to store important programs and data at a backup site and to protect the computer site against disasters of this type.

The Dangers of Organizational Stress

Organizations group people and other resources into logical and efficient units in order to carry out plans and achieve goals. In a manufacturing organization, for example, people may be grouped by *type of work* (production, marketing), by *geographic area* (district sales offices), and by *product line* produced or sold. As new computer systems are designed and implemented, however, decision-making powers and data processing activities may move from one group to another. And computing resources and stored data may be centralized or dispersed.

When such changes are introduced, organizational stress is likely to appear. Work groups may be created, disbanded, or realigned. Existing departments may be added to or eliminated. The people affected by such changes may react in different ways. At one extreme, they may temporarily feel threatened, but after a brief adjustment period, they resume their previous behavior. At the other extreme, they may resort to open opposition and even sabotage of the system. Between these extremes, a number of other stress symptoms appear, including withholding facts, providing inaccurate data, and displaying an attitude of indifference. Resisting employees and managers have been able to scuttle a number of computer system efforts in the past. Thus it's important that managers take steps to reduce the organizational stress that may occur when they introduce or change computer systems.

LET'S SUMMARIZE

Optimistic Views

Optimistic forecasters believe that computer usage will result in greater freedom and individuality and a more human and personalized society. They point to many of the computer applications we've described here to prove their contention that the benefits to be obtained far outweigh any temporary difficulties and inconveniences.

The optimists hold that the computer-assisted manufacturing trends described in this chapter, and the resulting outlook for productivity gains, will lead to a higher standard of living, a shorter workweek, and increased leisure time. And personal computers may be used to stimulate the analytical and intellectual abilities of people and add to their enjoyment of this increased leisure time. Of course, these optimistic views don't go unchallenged.

Pessimistic Views

The pessimists doubt that computer usage will lead to greater freedom and individuality. On the contrary, pessimists examine many of the same applications as optimists and come to the opposite conclusion: that computer usage will (1) dominate our lives as a society and as individuals and (2) sweep us along in a tide over which we—the harassed and exposed victims of a depersonalized and dehumanized process that places greater value on efficiency than on the more noble qualities of life—shall have little control.

Pessimists agree with optimists about certain points. They agree, for example, that computer-assisted manufacturing techniques will result in enormous gains in productivity. But the pessimists argue that when humans must compete with robots, the humans will lose—they'll lose their jobs, they'll lose their security, and they'll lose their personal dignity. And pessimists can also see dangers in educational applications. For example, it seems possible to install voice-print analyzers into future computerized teaching systems. These analyzers would be able to determine the student's identity—and also his or her mental stability and emotional state. Optimists say that this voice analysis will enable the system to determine if a student is unhappy, angry, nervous, or cheerful so that a teaching program may be selected automatically to respond in a more personal way to the student's mood. But pessimists are convinced that such monitoring of individual emotions is the ultimate danger to privacy, and an Orwellian prophecy come true.

The optimist's view: The computer is a liberator. (Courtesy Verbatim Corp.)

Another View

Is it possible to draw conclusions from the different viewpoints that have been presented? Perhaps. We can conclude, for example, that there are at least three different contemporary views of computers and technological change:

1 *Computers and technology are an unblemished blessing.* This uncritical, optimistic view holds that technology is the source of all progress for the individual and society, that social problems will inevitably be solved through the application of technology, and that every new technological possibility will automatically be beneficial.

2 *Computers and technology are an unbridled curse.* This pessimistic view holds that technology increases unemployment, leads to depersonalization and bewilderment, threatens an individual's right to dignity and privacy, and threatens to pollute or blow up the world.

3 *Computers and technology are undeserving of special attention.* This unconcerned view holds that technology has been with us forever, and

The pessimist's view: The computer is a depersonalizer, capturing all our private lives in banks of electronic data. (© Gary Gladstone/The Image Bank)

we are now better educated and more able than ever before to adapt to the new ideas and changes which it has brought and will bring.

Each of these views is deficient, although each probably contains an element of truth. The optimists are correct when they conclude that new technology often creates new opportunities for society. The pessimists are correct when they conclude that new problems are often created by new tools. And the unconcerned are correct when they conclude that social institutions (such as schools) can, and often do, play an important role in tempering the effects of technology.

No one can be sure about the future effects on employment of technological advances. Computers have caused displacement. But has the development of the computer caused a larger number of people to be unemployed than would otherwise have been the case? In other words, have computers reduced the total number of jobs available in the labor market? Many observers think not. They point out that the number of unemployed who found jobs because of new technology, plus those who would have been jobless if new technology had not appeared, equals or exceeds the number forced onto the unemployment rolls. Others disagree with this assessment. They join economist Wassily Leontief (a Nobel Prize winner) in wondering if investment in high technology can replace the number of industrial jobs likely to be lost in the years ahead. In spite of the growing uneasiness, though, we may have little choice in the matter. Since other nations are committed to the concept of factory automation and the goal of higher productivity, the U.S. alternative to technological progress is apt to be economic stagnation and a declining standard of living.

Pessimists have definitely pointed out influences and possibilities that the concerned citizen should keep in mind. Many pessimists *don't* disagree with the optimistic position that computer technology *could* increase freedom, individuality, social justice, and well-being. But the pessimists doubt that the effort to increase social awareness and give adequate attention to necessary safeguards will be made.

The predictions of optimists or pessimists will become facts or fables if people make them so. We cannot know what people will do in the future. They *could* achieve the optimistic vision. But if in using computers they choose procedures that are impersonal and coldly efficient, they should not be surprised if the results are inhumane and inflexible. Thus, in the years ahead, it will be up to concerned and informed citizens who have an awareness of the potential dangers to see that the optimistic view prevails.

A Recap of This Background Module

You've come a long way in just three chapters. In Chapter 1, you were introduced to the computer itself. You saw that it's a very fast and accurate machine with the ability to handle input/output, calculation and text manipulation, logic/comparison, and storage/retrieval operations. You saw the types of hardware components that are organized to make up a working computer system. You saw how a detailed set of instructions could be stored within the processor to cause it to accept input data and produce the desired output results. And you saw that although significant advances have been made in hardware and software, computer systems still differ widely in size and design, and they are still subject to certain limitations.

In Chapter 2, you gained a better understanding of what computers actually do. You saw how data are organized for computer processing, and many examples showed you how computer systems process the most common applications. And you saw how prewritten applications packages and custom-made programs work, and how they may be obtained.

Finally, in this chapter you've learned that what computers do has a profound impact on the people and organizations in a society. Because you've learned all this, you're not restricted now to following all the remaining chapters in sequence. Instead, you can turn immediately to the first chapter of any of the remaining modules in this book. Each of these modules builds on what you've already learned.

The realist's view: The computer is an increasingly powerful tool, but the people and organizations that use it will decide whether that power is put to humane uses. (Courtesy Atari)

FEEDBACK

FEEDBACK AND REVIEW 3

To test and reinforce your understanding of the impact that computer systems may have on the people and organizations in a society, place a T or an F in the space provided in the following *true-false questions*.

____ 1. A computer can store and analyze all the moves possible in a chess game.
____ 2. A computer program is now the world chess champion.

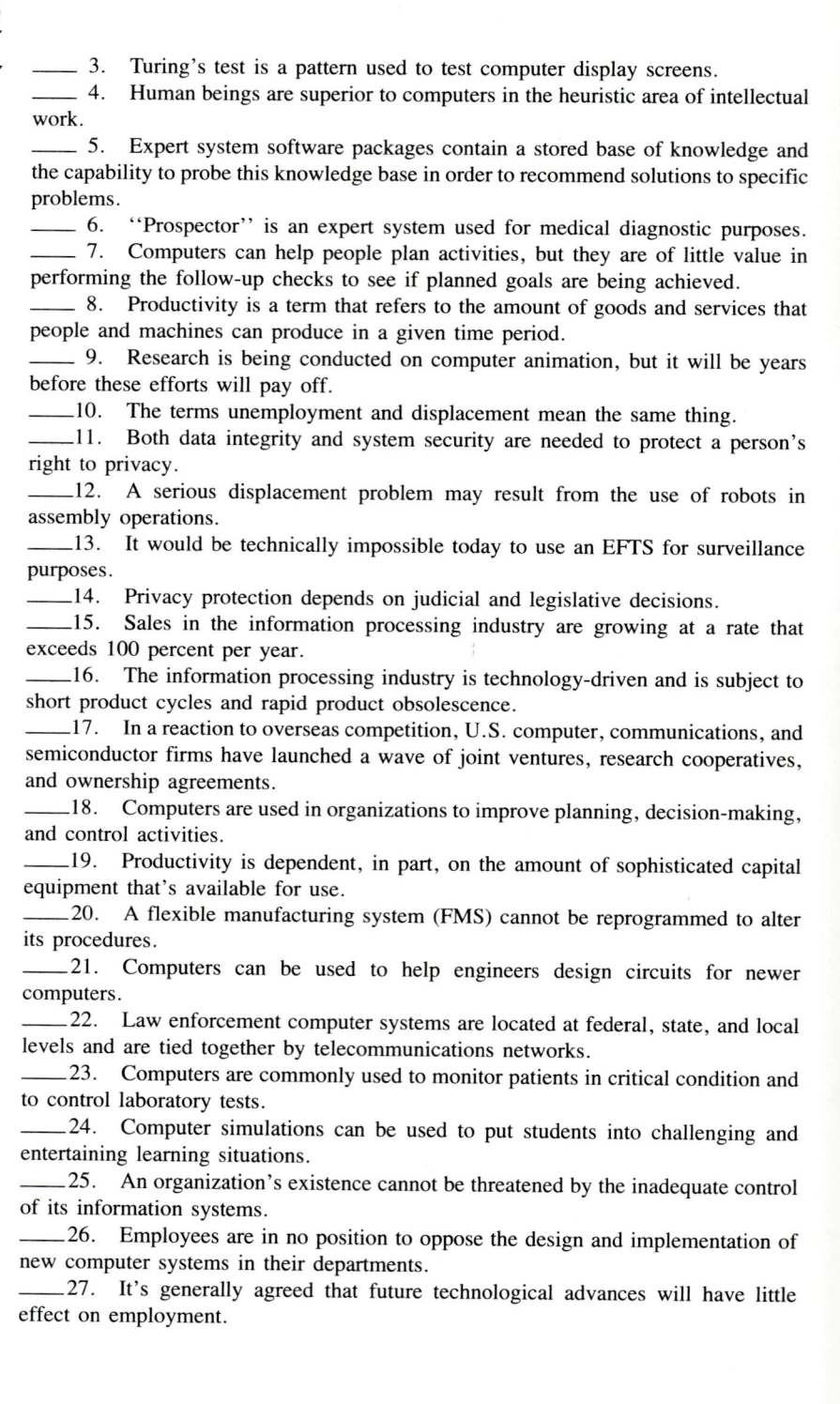

_____ 3. Turing's test is a pattern used to test computer display screens.

_____ 4. Human beings are superior to computers in the heuristic area of intellectual work.

_____ 5. Expert system software packages contain a stored base of knowledge and the capability to probe this knowledge base in order to recommend solutions to specific problems.

_____ 6. "Prospector" is an expert system used for medical diagnostic purposes.

_____ 7. Computers can help people plan activities, but they are of little value in performing the follow-up checks to see if planned goals are being achieved.

_____ 8. Productivity is a term that refers to the amount of goods and services that people and machines can produce in a given time period.

_____ 9. Research is being conducted on computer animation, but it will be years before these efforts will pay off.

_____10. The terms unemployment and displacement mean the same thing.

_____11. Both data integrity and system security are needed to protect a person's right to privacy.

_____12. A serious displacement problem may result from the use of robots in assembly operations.

_____13. It would be technically impossible today to use an EFTS for surveillance purposes.

_____14. Privacy protection depends on judicial and legislative decisions.

_____15. Sales in the information processing industry are growing at a rate that exceeds 100 percent per year.

_____16. The information processing industry is technology-driven and is subject to short product cycles and rapid product obsolescence.

_____17. In a reaction to overseas competition, U.S. computer, communications, and semiconductor firms have launched a wave of joint ventures, research cooperatives, and ownership agreements.

_____18. Computers are used in organizations to improve planning, decision-making, and control activities.

_____19. Productivity is dependent, in part, on the amount of sophisticated capital equipment that's available for use.

_____20. A flexible manufacturing system (FMS) cannot be reprogrammed to alter its procedures.

_____21. Computers can be used to help engineers design circuits for newer computers.

_____22. Law enforcement computer systems are located at federal, state, and local levels and are tied together by telecommunications networks.

_____23. Computers are commonly used to monitor patients in critical condition and to control laboratory tests.

_____24. Computer simulations can be used to put students into challenging and entertaining learning situations.

_____25. An organization's existence cannot be threatened by the inadequate control of its information systems.

_____26. Employees are in no position to oppose the design and implementation of new computer systems in their departments.

_____27. It's generally agreed that future technological advances will have little effect on employment.

LOOKING BACK

1. Computer chess programs can now defeat 99.5 percent of all human chess players. Experiments are being conducted by researchers in the field of artificial intelligence to improve the machines' heuristic capabilities. One result of this research is the development of a number of expert systems. But humans still remain far superior to computers in this area of intellectual work. The potential of an alliance between humans and computers, however, seems limitless.

2. Some managers and employees in organizations have found their jobs more rewarding because of computer systems, and consumers have received benefits from the ways in which organizations use computers. Increased efficiency, higher quality, improved safety, and better service are benefits described in the chapter. Without computers many recreational and educational benefits wouldn't be feasible, handicapped persons would be denied tools that make their lives more meaningful, and retrieving needed information would be a more tedious task.

3. Although some managers and employees have benefited by the use of computers on the job, others haven't been so fortunate. Some have lost their jobs or have suffered a loss of status and prestige when computer systems were installed. Clerical employees, for example, have often been displaced by computers, and production employees are being threatened by the rapidly growing use of computer-controlled robots.

4. In private life some people have been inconvenienced and confused by computer information systems employing questionable data processing practices. Data are sometimes gathered without a valid reason or a careful check on their accuracy, and many people have also been victimized by systems errors and inaccurate data input.

5. Information integrity and security are needed to protect a person's legitimate right to privacy. Systems security involves the protection of both the data and the hardware and software used to process the data. Computer security difficulties are caused by the fact that many skilled people may have access to the system, and by the fact that the value of the stored data may warrant the attempt to penetrate the system. Although there are hardware and software security provisions in a typical system, these provisions are seldom capable of blocking a skilled penetrator. The lack of control over computer systems security has resulted in economic loss, inconvenience, and a loss of privacy for people.

6. There are many benefits to be obtained from the creation of data banks, but there's also a concern about the threat these data banks might present to an individual. Ways in which computers are used (or could be used) for surveillance, for the creation of a climate that restricts individual freedom, and for other abuses are presented

in the chapter, along with a discussion of the controls that have been used to restore some balance in favor of privacy.

7. Computer systems are obviously having a profound impact on the dynamic information processing industry that produces them. This industry is technology-driven, and its products are subject to rapid obsolescence. The competition can be fierce, and company positions in the industry can change dramatically in a year's time.

8. Government planners at all levels have a mandate to use public funds and resources efficiently in ways that best serve the needs of society. Federal government decision makers are actively using computers in such areas as environmental planning and military planning. One concern of state and municipal planners is urban planning. Members of Congress and legislators are finding legislative data systems to be of value. And the control function is being performed at all levels of government by computer systems. Millions of dollars have been channeled into the development and use of law enforcement computer systems. Many of these systems are tied together at the state levels, and the state systems are, in turn, linked to the FBI's NCIC system. Computers and expert system programs are being used to assist doctors in diagnosing illnesses. The control of the physiological status of patients and the monitoring of laboratory tests are also important applications of computers. Chapter 13 presents more information on the use of computers in government, law, and health-care organizations.

9. Computers can bring to the educational process such attributes as patience, around-the-clock availability, and individualized and student-paced instruction programs. And people with interests in the humanities are finding many uses for computers. All of Chapter 14 is devoted to computer usage in education and the humanities.

10. A concerted effort is now under way in industrial nations to apply computers in design and production processes in order to improve productivity. Computer-aided design techniques are used to speed up product development, and robots and flexible manufacturing systems are used during production. Chapter 15 presents more information on the use of computers in the areas of science, engineering, and business. In addition to productivity and other benefits, however, the use of computer systems can also lead to difficulties. Organizations can be vulnerable to computer systems that aren't adequately controlled, and the introduction of new computer systems can produce organizational stress and employee resistance to change.

11. The future uses of computers are viewed by some people with optimism, while others believe that computers and technology are likely to be the curse of humanity. Which view—optimism or pessimism—will prevail? No one knows. Predictions of each group will become facts or fables only if people make them so. An enlightened citizenry, aware of the dangers, can help bring about the optimistic version.

KEY TERMS AND CONCEPTS

- artificial intelligence (AI) 94
- Turing's test 96
- heuristic 96
- expert system 97
- synergy 99
- planning 100
- control 100
- productivity 101
- robots 101
- computer animation 102
- unemployment 104
- displacement 104
- data integrity 106
- systems security 106
- right to privacy 107
- electronic funds transfer system (EFTS) 108
- flexible manufacturing system (FMS) 113
- computer-aided design (CAD) 113
- computer-aided design/computer-aided manufacturing (CAD/CAM) 114

TOPICS FOR REVIEW AND DISCUSSION

1. Why does controversy surround the question of whether computers can be programmed to "think"?
2. Robert Jastrow, director of NASA's Goddard Institute for Space Studies, has written that the alliance between humans and computers will not last very long. He states: "Computer intelligence is growing by leaps and bounds, with no natural limit in sight. But human evolution is a nearly finished chapter in the history of life." Jastrow believes that a new kind of intelligent life will probably emerge on the earth, and this life "is more likely to be made of silicon." (a) What's your reaction to this opinion? (b) Are your views changed by the fact that Jastrow believes the evolution of the new silicon species will take about a million years?
3. (a) What's an expert system? (b) Identify and discuss two examples of expert systems.
4. (a) How have managers of organizations benefited from computer usage? (b) Identify employees of organizations who have benefited, and explain how they've been helped.
5. Discuss how the following individuals in organizations may benefit from computer usage: (a) law enforcement officers, (b) members of Congress, (c) school teachers, (d) nurses, and (e) district office managers.
6. Identify and discuss three ways in which consumers may benefit from the use of computers (a) by businesses, (b) by nonprofit organizations, and (c) in the home.
7. (a) How have managers been the victims of computer usage? (b) How have employees been victimized?
8. A few years ago, Westinghouse Electric Corporation received a grant from the National Science Foundation to experiment with the use of robots to replace people in low-volume or batch-manufacturing operations—the types of operations that account for about 75 percent of all U.S. manufacturing. According to a Westinghouse spokesperson, "Complex assembly tasks will continue to be performed by people, but many repetitive, boring tasks, and those performed in an unpleasant environment can and should be automated." Discuss this statement.
9. How may a lack of control over data gathering lead to undesirable results for people?
10. "Data integrity, information security, and personal privacy are interrelated." Define these terms and discuss this statement.
11. Explain how a lack of data security and physical security can lead to undesirable consequences for people.
12. Discuss the EFTS surveillance possibilities.
13. In George Orwell's *1984*, Big Brother controls individuals through sensors housed in the two-way (send-receive) TV screens located in all homes, offices, and public squares. The sensors tune in on people and monitor their heartbeats. Recently, a young physiologist, seeking to measure the physiological activities of salamanders, created a delicate instrument that can detect and record from a distance an animal's heartbeat, respiration, and muscle tension. Orwell described 137 "futuristic" devices in *1984* (which was published 4 decades ago). About 100 of these devices are now practical. Do you think that a democratic society has anything to fear from such technology?
14. "What one person may consider to be a privacy right may be judged by others to be an item of public concern." Discuss this statement.
15. "The information processing industry is one in which rapid change is the rule." Explain why this statement is true and give examples to illustrate your points.
16. Discuss and give examples of how government computers have been used for planning and decision-making and control purposes.
17. "Some doctors are now using the computer as a diagnostic tool in hospitals and clinics." Discuss this statement.
18. How are computers used for physiological control?

19. Discuss ways in which computer simulation can be used for instructional purposes.
20. (a) Identify two factors that help determine productivity. (b) How can computer-aided design improve productivity?
21. (a) Identify and discuss the types of threats that can be aimed at an organization's computer systems. (b) How may people react to the introduction of new computer systems?
22. (a) Are you an optimist or a pessimist about the future impact of computer systems on people? (b) Defend your answer.

Projects/Issues to Consider

1. Identify a topic of interest in the field of artificial intelligence—game-playing programs, "thinking" computers, Turing's test, expert system packages, AI pioneers—and research the topic you've selected. Present your findings to the class.
2. Visit your library, identify a computer-based activity by a government or private organization that you believe may threaten an individual's right to privacy, and prepare a report about it.
3. Visit your library and identify and then research three cases of computer-related fraud or embezzlement. Share your findings with the class.
4. Consider the following case: A few years ago a Decision Information Distribution System (DIDS)—a low-frequency radio network to warn people quickly of impending attack—was under development in the Pentagon. Planners expected all citizens to buy a specially designed unit capable of receiving DIDS warning broadcasts. The DIDS would also warn listeners of impending floods, hurricanes, and similar emergencies and would provide other services. Because of the warning functions of DIDS, the receiving units in the homes could be turned on *automatically* by the message-sending agency (the circuitry to do this is available). Under questioning by a congressional subcommittee member, a Pentagon delegate admitted that the DIDS receiver could also be converted into a *transmitter*. A subcommittee staff member commented: "They'll ultimately decide to go ahead with DIDS because they'll be evaluating only its *technical* performance, not its *political* possibilities." Plans were made to seek funds to install DIDS units on new radio and TV sets. A coast-to-coast network could be in operation in a few years. *Question:* On balance, is DIDS a good idea? Defend your answer to this question in a class presentation.
5. People placing anonymous calls to police may be surprised to learn that the "enhanced 911" telephone systems serving police departments in Redondo Beach, California, and other areas around the country will flash the caller's whereabouts and telephone number on computer screens the instant the dispatcher answers the phone. Check with your local law enforcement agencies to see if similar systems are in use in your area. Share your findings and your evaluation of such systems with the class.
6. In the March 1984 issue of *Popular Computing,* Michael Kurland, a well-known science fiction writer, made the following prediction: "In a few short years computers will become bionic. At the age of six a child will receive his/her first computer-chip implant. As the child grows up, the biocomputer will be enlarged and its capability increased. These chips will not only increase memory capability and logic processing (with built-in calculus, trig, matrix algebra, and all that other good stuff), but they will also monitor blood serum for hormone levels, signs of disease, and mental instability. 'Give me a child's mind at seven, and I'll have him at seventy,' the old saying goes. This is a way to *really* control a child's mind."* On balance, would such implants be desirable? Be prepared to defend your conclusions in class.

---

*Michael Kurland, "Computers in Science Fiction," *Popular Computing,* March 1984. Copyright © 1984 by Michael Kurland.

Answers to Feedback and Review Section

1. F 2. F 3. F 4. T 5. T 6. F 7. F 8. T 9. F 10. F 11. T 12. T 13. F 14. T 15. F 16. T 17. T 18. T 19. T 20. F 21. T 22. T 23. T 24. T 25. F 26. F 27. F

A CLOSER LOOK

COMPUTERS AND THE HANDICAPPED

Although society as a whole may debate the benefits and costs of computer applications, one group has unquestionably benefited from the changes that computers, particularly microcomputers, have brought.

More than 4 million school-age children have physical, mental, or sensory disabilities, and 14 million people of working age are also disabled. A growing number of these people are using pc's to enrich their lives and secure the education and training they need to compete for good jobs.

The most common additions to computers designed to assist the handicapped are peripherals that aid in speech synthesis and speech recognition, and modified keyboards. These souped-up computers can read for the physically blind or dyslexic, write for paralyzed or mobility-limited students, speak for the vocally handicapped, move for the disabled, and, to some extent, hear for the deaf. They dramatically enhance the ability of the handicapped to learn and to communicate.

Speech synthesis is a technology you may have encountered in automobiles that advise you to fasten your seatbelts, or soda machines that tell you they are empty. To the visually or vocally handicapped, speech synthesis is the tool that permits them to hear and "speak" information typed on the computer keyboard, to hear digitized lessons, text, and instructions that allow them to tap commercial data bases, and to send and receive electronic mail (including banking and shopping) by voice over the telephone.

An ordinary microcomputer can become a speech synthesizer with the addition of a relatively inexpensive circuit board. The quality of synthetic speech, however, is directly related to the cost of this peripheral device. A more expensive model might offer features such as variation in speed from 120 to 350 words per minute along with sharper speech quality. Clear speech and high speed are important for the blind, who must read a great deal of computer-stored information.

Speech synthesizers also provide a voice for nonvocal individuals. People paralyzed by cerebral palsy or stroke can use a computer with a speech synthesizer to communicate with others or to compose a message on a computer and send it via telephone to others.

A sister technology to speech synthesizing is voice or speech recognition, which enables a computer to hear. Computers can recognize and respond to a few hundred words—enough to allow a handicapped computer user to log on to a data base, such as the Source, or to enter data orally into a computer program.

Severely disabled children have difficulty manipulating

This experimental, computer-guided kitchen robot is being developed to enable paralyzed people to cook their own meals and feed themselves. It may be guided by speech recognition, puff and sip switches, or other types of emulators. (© Diego Goldberg/Sygma)

standard computer keyboards. Alternative input devices called emulators offer them a way to enter information into a computer. Two devices, the Express 3 and Minspeak, permit fine-motor-disabled individuals to control input by mouth stick, tongue switch, or a pneumatic puff and sip switch. People with disabilities such as cerebral palsy or quadriplegia can operate these devices with no more than brow wrinkling.

Much of the equipment used to adapt computers for people with disabilities, like the voice synthesizer, was developed for the general computer market. And some equipment designed especially for disabled users may have applications in business and industry. The Minspeak emulator can be equipped with a keyboard that shows pictures instead of letters, allowing quick retrieval of common sentences. This device is being considered for use at nuclear power plants, where quick retrieval of data is essential.

Computers, with and without special enhancements, are very useful in the education of the retarded. Retarded people seem to learn better with computers than with any other educational technology, possibly because of the computer's patience and the interactive nature of good computer instruction that offers immediate feedback to the user.

Despite the positive impact enhanced microcomputers have made on the lives of the handicapped, computers can do still more for disabled people. The quality of the software for the handicapped has been criticized, for instance, because much of it doesn't meet the needs of special education. Yet the technological breakthroughs generated by the computer revolution already have enabled many handicapped people to live more independent and productive lives.

MODULE 2

The Background Module introduced you to the computer itself. You saw that the key elements in the basic organization of a computer system include input, processing, and output components.

The purpose of this module is to examine the way computers and their components work. We'll also consider some computer systems that are supported by data communications networks.

4 CENTRAL PROCESSORS

COMPUTER CONCEPTS, COMPONENTS, AND SYSTEMS

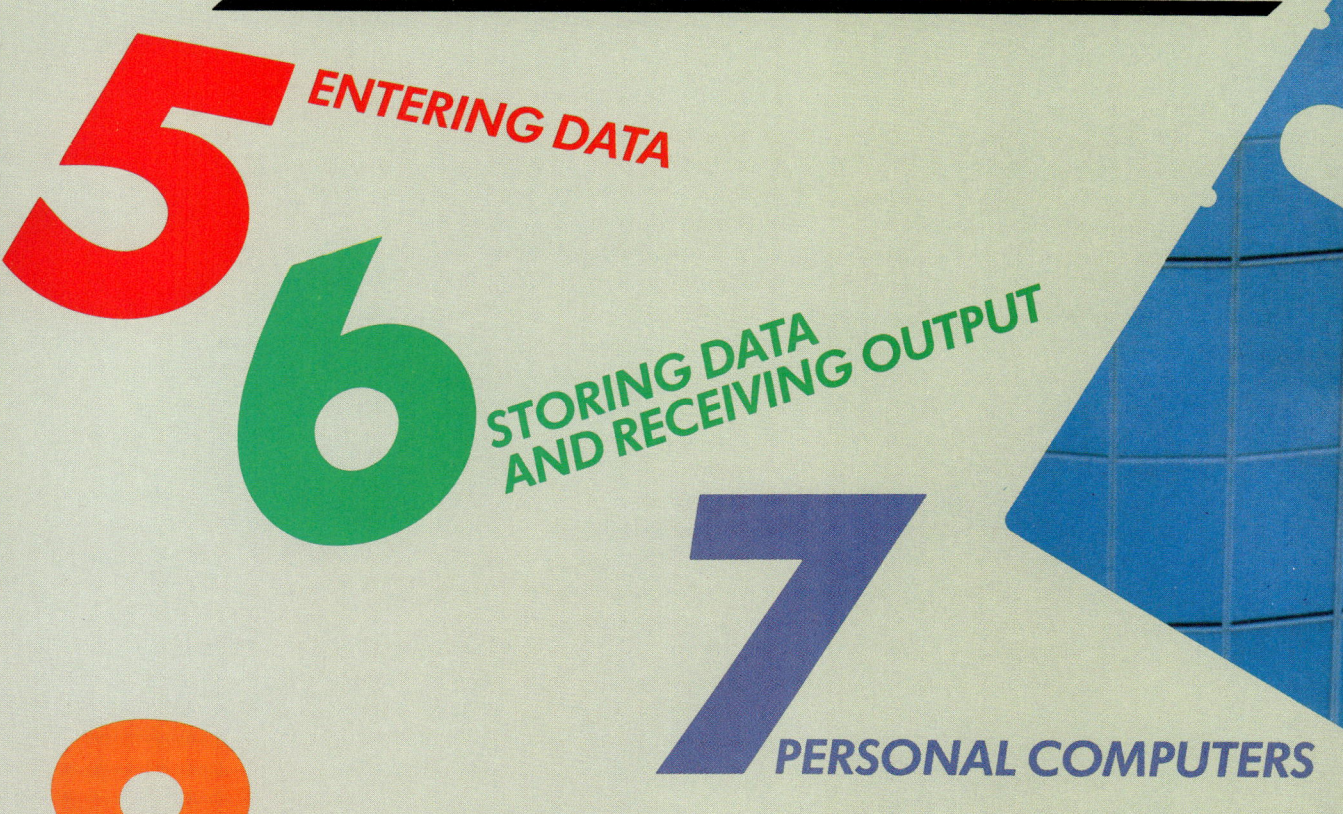

5 ENTERING DATA

6 STORING DATA AND RECEIVING OUTPUT

7 PERSONAL COMPUTERS

8 DATA COMMUNICATIONS NETWORKS

CHAPTER 4

CENTRAL PROCESSORS

Biochips

Creating a biological computer that can emulate the human brain is an idea that has been with us since the 1950s, when computers became a reality.

Although this may seem like science fiction, researchers are already working to merge biological and computer technologies. Their goal is to produce a computer chip that is a million times smaller and millions of times faster than the human brain; a computer chip that can eat, think, and even reproduce itself—a biochip.

Like a nerve cell, an individual circuit component of a computer chip is made of thousands of molecules. These thousands of molecules all combine to form one transistor on a chip, or one cell in a brain, which can process one bit of information or perform one function at a time. But imagine the capabilities of a computer using individual *molecules* as its circuit elements. A particle of matter the size of a single transistor on a computer chip could perform thousands of functions, one to each molecule. Using living molecules that function as electronic components, a computer with the power of today's largest mainframe computer would be only the size of a bacterium.

Protein molecules are the likely candidates for the building blocks of a biochip. They can self-assemble, and via genetic engineering, bacteria could be produced that actually build a biochip computer using their own DNA as an instruction set.

Dr. James McAlear of Gentronix Laboratories is working on a biological computer that would have the capabilities of the human brain and be so small that you would need a microscope to see it. It would derive its power from oxidation. McAlear thinks that in its primitive form it could restore sight to the blind by processing information from a miniature camera and directly stimulating the visual cortex. In its most sophisticated form, a biochip computer might represent a new life-form.

Computer and brain functions are strikingly similar. They are both based on the flow of energy in one direction and the resistance to that flow in the opposite direction. The main differences between a human brain and a solid-state computer are size and complexity. The human brain has millions more neurons than there are transistors in the CPU of even the most complex computer.

One of the biggest problems with using computers in conjunction with the human brain has been the gross size of wires when compared with delicate individual neurons. This also presents a problem for biochips, as the circuit elements are so much smaller than any physical wire. Current research techniques for getting information into and out of a biochip involve *growing* progressively larger semiconductor ''wires'' from strategic points on the biochip and the use of conducting biological substances, which are grown into junctions with wires.

There are many technical problems to overcome before biochips become a reality, but researchers around the world are racing to be the first to develop these amazing computers of the future.

Adapted from Thom Hartmann, ''Advanced Technology: Molecular Computers,'' *Popular Computing* March 1984. Copyright © 1984 by McGraw-Hill, Inc. Reprinted with permission. All rights reserved.

CHAPTER 4

LOOKING AHEAD

The heart of any computer hardware system is its processor unit. This chapter explains what the processor is and how it works. The information in this chapter will enable you to:

- Explain how primary storage locations are identified
- Discuss the capacity of storage locations, understand how data are coded in storage, and identify the types of storage components found in the processor unit
- Explain the general functions of the arithmetic-logic and control sections in a processor unit

CHAPTER OUTLINE

LOOKING AHEAD
PRIMARY STORAGE CONCEPTS
Storage Locations and Addresses
Capacity of Storage Locations
CODING DATA IN STORAGE
The Binary Numbering System
Computer Codes
STORAGE COMPONENTS IN THE PROCESSOR UNIT
Primary Storage Components of the Past
Primary Storage Components of the Present
Primary Storage Components of the Future
Specialized Storage Elements in the Processor Unit
THE ARITHMETIC-LOGIC AND CONTROL FUNCTIONS
The Arithmetic-Logic Section
The Control Section
Feedback and Review 4
LOOKING BACK

MODULE 2

PRIMARY STORAGE CONCEPTS

You learned in Chapter 1 that primary storage is used for four activities. Data are fed into an *input storage* area. A *working storage* space is used to hold intermediate processing results. An *output storage* area holds the final processing results. And a *program storage* area contains the processing instructions. You also saw that the separate locations used for these four tasks don't have built-in physical boundaries. Rather, a specific storage location can hold input data in one application and output results or program instructions in another. Now let's take a closer look at these storage locations.

Storage Locations and Addresses

Primary storage has a lot in common with post office mailboxes. In your local post office, each mailbox is identified by a specific number. Each box can hold different items. A letter containing instructions on how to tune an engine may have been placed in the box yesterday, and an electric bill for $86.18 may be put there today. Instructions are stored one day and data the next. The contents change, but the box and its number remain the same. A post office may have many such boxes that differ only in their identification numbers.

The primary storage section of a computer also has many small storage areas. Each one is assigned an **address**—a built-in and unique number that identifies the location. Like a mailbox, a storage location can hold either a data item or an instruction, and its identifying number remains the same regardless of its contents.

Comparing storage locations with mailboxes is convenient, but *this analogy breaks down in several important ways*. For one thing, a mailbox can hold several different messages at once while an address location only holds one item at a time. Another difference is that when a new item is placed in a mailbox, the previous contents remain undisturbed. But when new data are stored in an address location, the previous contents are erased and replaced. When the contents of a mailbox are retrieved, the box is emptied. But when a computer system needs an item in a storage location, it merely reads it and then duplicates the item elsewhere; it does not remove the item from its original location.

To summarize, retrieving data *from* a storage location is **nondestructive**, but entering data *into* a location is **destructive**. The act of *retrieving* existing data from storage is called *read out, read from,* or simply *read*. The act of *entering* new data into storage is called *read in* or *write*.

There are 65,536 or more storage locations in the primary storage sections of most personal computers. (A machine with 65,536 primary storage locations is often called a "64K" machine, where "K" is an abbreviation that represents slightly more than 1,000 storage areas. More about this later.) The addresses in one such computer may then be numbered from 00000 to 65,535 (or more). Thus one unique address is designated 00017. There's an important difference between the address number and the contents of the address. Suppose that $157.41 is the data item stored in address 00017. If the programmer wants that amount printed, she will *not* instruct the computer to print $157.41. Rather, the machine will be ordered to print 00017, and it will interpret this instruction to mean that it should *print the contents of address*

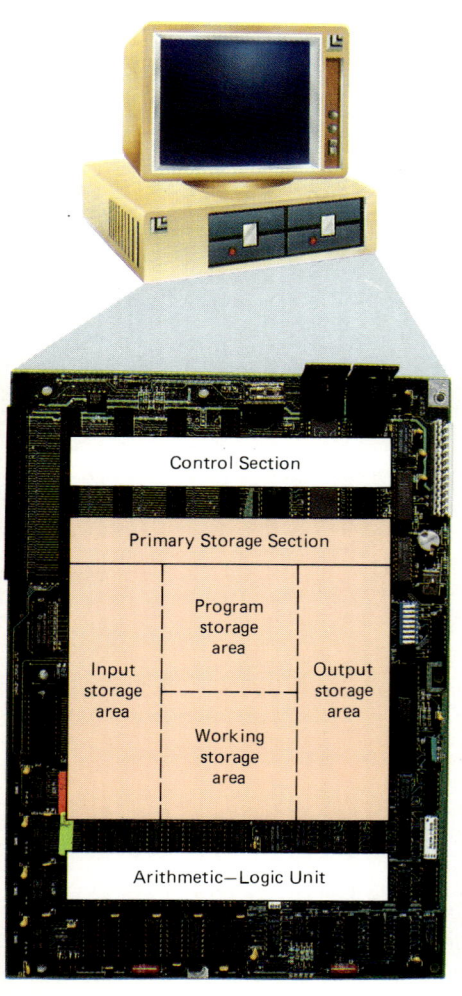

00017. Just as you can locate friends in a strange city if you know that their home address is 4009 Sarita Drive, so too can the computer locate the desired data item if it knows the location number.

Computers ultimately require specific instructions to process data stored in these numbered locations. An explanation of how such instructions and addresses are used by central processors during data processing is given in the Closer Look reading at the end of this chapter.

Capacity of Storage Locations

We've not yet considered the storage capacity of *each address*. All we've seen is that an address holds a specific data or program element. Actually, the storage capacity of an address is *built into* the computer. Over the years, computer manufacturers have used several different design approaches to partition the primary storage section into addresses.

One approach is to design the primary storage section to store a *fixed number of characters* in each numbered address location. These characters are then treated as a single entity or **word.** Thus BYTER might be treated as a single data word, and MULTIPLY might be a single instruction word. Machines built to store a fixed number of characters in each address are said to be **word addressable,** and they employ a **fixed word-length storage** approach.[1]

The primary storage section can also be organized so that *each* numbered address can only store a *single character* (8, B, $). Machines designed in this way are said to be **character addressable.** Thus a sequence of characters such as BYTER would require five storage addresses while $157.41 would occupy seven addresses (the dollar sign and decimal point require two locations). Character-addressable machines are said to employ a **variable word-length storage** approach. Figure 4-1 summarizes the difference between the fixed-length and variable-length storage approaches.

---

[1] The number of characters that can be stored in each address varies depending on the make of computer. One modern design (the Control Data Corporation Cyber 170) can hold 10 alphanumeric characters in each address. Other machines have fixed word-lengths of two, four, six, and eight characters.

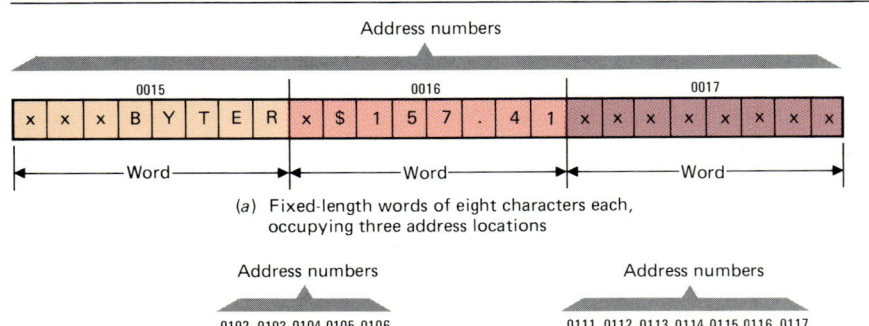

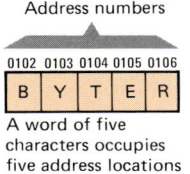

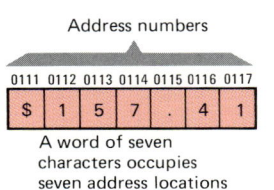

FIGURE 4-1

Fixed word-length storage compared with variable word-length storage. Each approach has distinct advantages. (a) Fixed-length words of eight characters each, occupying three address locations. (b) Variable-length words of varying lengths. (Some leading zeros have been deleted in the address numbers.)

(a) Fixed-length words of eight characters each, occupying three address locations

(b) Variable-length words of varying lengths

A word of five characters occupies five address locations

A word of seven characters occupies seven address locations

Each of these ways of organizing the primary storage section has advantages and limitations. Variable word-length processors generally make the most efficient use of the available storage space, since a character can be placed in every storage cell. But if the storage capacity in each address of a fixed word-length processor is eight characters, and if many data words containing only two or three characters are placed in each address, then many of the storage cells cannot be used. However, fixed word-length machines have faster calculating capabilities. Such a machine can add two data words in a single operation. If the fixed-length word is eight characters, 2 eight-digit numbers can be added in a single operation. With a character-addressable processor, only one digit in each number is added during a single machine operation, so eight steps would be needed to complete this calculation.

Some of the largest and most powerful modern computers use *only* a fixed word-length storage approach. These giant processors are used primarily for scientific calculations and need the faster calculating capability of the fixed word-length design. Some personal computers, on the other hand, are variable word-length machines that operate *only* on one character at a time during processing.

In between these two size extremes are the hundreds of personal computer, minicomputer, and mainframe models that have built-in flexibility. Most of today's business and scientific processing is handled by these flexible machines that can be operated as *either* variable *or* fixed word-length computers. Available program instructions permit these models to operate on either single characters or fixed-length words.

Let's first look at how a flexible computer operates as a variable word-length machine. Each address in this type of computer holds one alphanumeric character. Each character is represented in a storage location by a string of adjacent binary numbers (0s and 1s) that are treated as a unit. This unit or set of binary digits, or **bits**, is called a **byte**, and a byte typically consists of a grouping of 8 bits. Since a byte usually represents a single alphanumeric character, a flexible computer is often said to be **byte addressable.** By using an appropriate set of instructions, a programmer working with such a machine can retrieve a stored data item by identifying the address of the first character in the data word and by then indicating the number of address locations to be included in the word (see Figure 4-2). Since variable-length data words are common in files, instructions of this type are frequently used for file processing applications.

But bytes representing characters can also be grouped together in a flexible computer and operated on as a unit. Let's assume that a scientific application calling for numerous calculations is to be processed. To achieve faster calculating speeds, programmers can choose other available instructions that will cause the computer to automatically retrieve, manipulate, and store as a

---

FIGURE 4-2

A variable-length word in a byte-addressable computer is identified by the address number of the *first* character in the word. The number of characters included in the word must also be specified in a program instruction. (Some leading zeros have been deleted in the address numbers.)

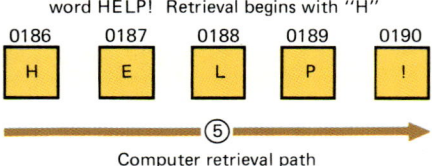

Address 0186 is used to identify the word HELP! Retrieval begins with "H"

| 0186 | 0187 | 0188 | 0189 | 0190 |
| H | E | L | P | ! |

⑤ Computer retrieval path

single unit a fixed word of 4 bytes. Or they may choose to group 8 bytes into a single unit and have the machine function in this fixed word format. Figure 4-3 illustrates the word arrangements that are possible with many of today's computers.

Coding Data in Storage

Although the capacity of their storage locations can vary, every computer stores numbers, letters, and other characters in a coded form. As you saw in the last section, every character in storage is represented by a string of 0s and 1s—the only digits found in the binary numbering system. Let's see how it's possible to use just two digits to represent any character.

The Binary Numbering System

There's nothing mysterious about numbering systems. The first ones used an *additive* approach. That is, they consisted of symbols such as I for 1, II for 2, III for 3, etc. Each symbol represented the *same value* regardless of its position in the number. Since arithmetic is difficult when such systems are used, *positional* numbering systems were developed as the centuries passed. In a positional system, there are only a few symbols, and these symbols represent different values depending on the position they occupy in the number. For example, 5 equals the Roman numeral V, but 51 does not equal VI because the meaning of 5 has changed with the change in its position. The actual number of symbols used in a positional system depends on its *base*. The familiar decimal system has a base of 10, and it thus has 10 symbols (0 to 9). In any positional numbering system, the *highest* numerical symbol always has a value of *one less* than the base.

Any number can be represented by arranging symbols in various positions. You know that in the decimal system the successive positions to the left of the decimal point represent units, tens, hundreds, thousands, etc. But you may not have given much thought to the fact that *each position represents a specific power of the base*. For example, the decimal number 1,684 (written $1{,}684_{10}$) represents:[2]

$$\underbrace{(1 \times 10^3)}_{1{,}000} + \underbrace{(6 \times 10^2)}_{600} + \underbrace{(8 \times 10^1)}_{80} + \underbrace{(4 \times 10^0)}_{4} \leftarrow \text{decimal point} = 1{,}684$$

The principles that apply to the decimal system apply in *any other* positional system. An *octal* numbering system, for example, is one with a base of 8. In such a system, the possible symbols are 0 to 7 (8 and 9 don't exist in this case). Since each position in the octal number 463 (written 463_8) represents a power of the base, the decimal equivalent of 463_8 is:

$$\underbrace{(4 \times 8^2)}_{256} + \underbrace{(6 \times 8^1)}_{48} + \underbrace{(3 \times 8^0)}_{3} \leftarrow \text{octal point} = 307_{10} \text{ the decimal equivalent}$$

---

[2] Just in case you've forgotten, n^0 is, by definition, 1. That is, any number raised to the zero power equals 1.

FIGURE 4-3

Word formats permitted with many byte-addressable computers.

1 byte = 1 coded alphanumeric character

(a) *Variable word format: a variable number of bytes make up a word*

2 bytes
(This is the only fixed word format available with some personal computers and smaller minicomputers)

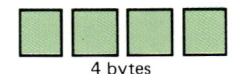

4 bytes
(This is the standard word size used by larger minis and many mainframe models)

8 bytes
(This is a "doubleword" size used by many mainframe models)

(b) *Fixed word formats permitted*

Similarly, the **binary numbering system** uses a base of 2. The possible symbols, therefore, are just 0 and 1. Again, each position in a binary number represents a power of the base, and the decimal equivalent of the binary number 1001 (written 1001_2) is:

$$\underbrace{(1 \times 2^3)}_{8} + \underbrace{(0 \times 2^2)}_{0} + \underbrace{(0 \times 2^1)}_{0} + \underbrace{(1 \times 2^0)}_{1}. \leftarrow \text{binary point}$$

$= 9_{10}$ the decimal equivalent

And the decimal number 202 is represented in binary as:

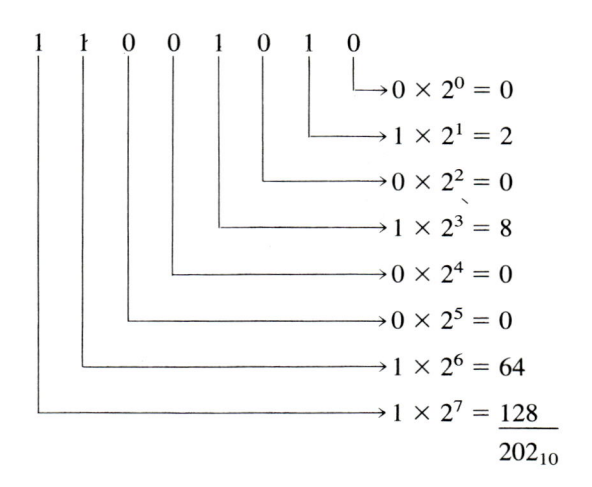

$$
\begin{aligned}
1\ 1\ 0\ 0\ 1\ 0\ 1\ 0 &\\
0 \times 2^0 &= 0\\
1 \times 2^1 &= 2\\
0 \times 2^2 &= 0\\
1 \times 2^3 &= 8\\
0 \times 2^4 &= 0\\
0 \times 2^5 &= 0\\
1 \times 2^6 &= 64\\
1 \times 2^7 &= \underline{128}\\
&\ 202_{10}
\end{aligned}
$$

or:

Binary number	1	1	0	0	1	0	1	0
Power of base	2^7	2^6	2^5	2^4	2^3	2^2	2^1	2^0
Decimal equivalent	128	64	32	16	8	4	2	1

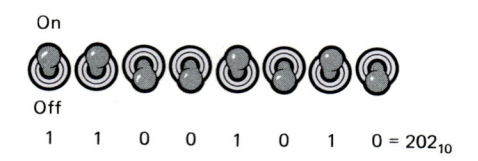

On

Off

1 1 0 0 1 0 1 0 = 202_{10}

As you can see, the use of a smaller base may require more positions to represent a given value ($1001_2 = 9_{10}$). In spite of this fact, however, all but the very first computers have been designed to use binary numbers. Why the rush to binary? *One* reason is that computer circuits only have to handle 2 binary digits (bits) rather than 10. Design is simplified, cost is reduced, and reliability is improved. A *second* reason that computers use the binary system is that electronic components naturally operate in a binary mode. A switch is either open (0 state) or closed (1 state); a transistor either is not conducting (0) or is conducting (1). *Finally*, the binary system is used because everything that can be done with a base of 10 can also be done in binary.

Computer Codes

Up to now we've been discussing true or "pure" binary numbers. But most computers use a *coded* version of true binary to represent letters and special symbols as well as decimal numbers. Although many coding schemes have been developed over the years, the most popular of these use a **binary coded decimal (BCD) approach.**

The BCD Approach   With BCD, it's possible to convert *each* decimal number into its binary equivalent rather than convert the entire decimal value into a pure binary form. The BCD equivalent of each possible decimal symbol is shown in Figure 4-4. Since 8 and 9 require 4 bits, *all* decimal digits are represented in BCD by 4 bits. You've just seen that 202_{10} is equal to 11001010_2 in a pure binary form. Converting 202_{10} into BCD, however, produces the following result:

$$202_{10} \text{ in BCD} = \underbrace{0010}_{2} \, \underbrace{0000}_{0} \, \underbrace{0010}_{2} \text{ or } 001000000010$$

When 4 bits are used, there are only 16 possible configurations (2^4). As you saw in Figure 4-4, the first 10 of these combinations are used to represent decimal digits. The other six arrangements (1010, 1011, 1100, 1101, 1110, and 1111) have decimal values from 10 to 15. These arrangements *aren't used* in BCD coding. That is, 1111 doesn't represent 15_{10} in BCD. Instead, the proper BCD code for 15_{10} is 0001/0101.

Six-Bit BCD Code   Instead of using 4 bits with only 16 possible characters, computer designers first used 6 bits, and then moved to 7 or 8 bits to represent characters in alphanumeric versions of BCD. In the **6-bit code,** the four BCD *numeric* place positions (1, 2, 4, and 8) are retained, but two additional *zone* positions are included (Figure 4-5a). With 6 bits, it's possible to represent 64 different characters (2^6). This is a sufficient number to code the decimal digits (10), capital letters (26), and other special characters and punctuation marks (28). Figure 4-5b shows you how a few of the 64 possible characters are represented in a standard 6-bit BCD code. (You can observe the systematic arrangements of the bits, but it's certainly *not* necessary that you remember these or any of the following BCD patterns.)

Seven- and Eight-Bit Codes   Since 64 possible bit combinations aren't sufficient to provide decimal numbers (10), lower-case letters (26), capital letters (26), and a large number of other characters (28+), designers have extended the 6-bit BCD code to 7 and 8 bits. With 7 bits, it's possible to provide 128 different arrangements (2^7); with 8 bits, 256 variations are possible (2^8). In addition to the four numeric place positions, there are three zone bit positions in a **7-bit code,** and four zone bit positions in an **8-bit code.** The 7-bit American Standard Code for Information Interchange (**ASCII**) is widely used in data communications work and is the code used to represent data internally in personal computers. The ASCII format and the coding used to represent selected characters are shown in Figure 4-6.

There are also two popular 8-bit codes in common use. One is the Extended Binary Coded Decimal Interchange Code (**EBCDIC**). This code is

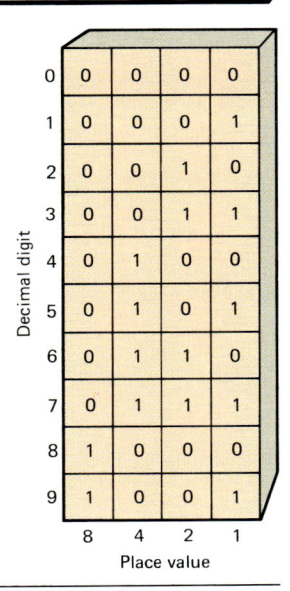

FIGURE 4-4

BCD numeric bit configurations and their decimal equivalent.

Decimal digit	8	4	2	1
0	0	0	0	0
1	0	0	0	1
2	0	0	1	0
3	0	0	1	1
4	0	1	0	0
5	0	1	0	1
6	0	1	1	0
7	0	1	1	1
8	1	0	0	0
9	1	0	0	1

Place value

FIGURE 4-5

The 6-bit BCD code.

Zone Bits		Numeric Bits			
B	A	8	4	2	1

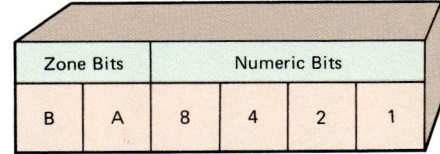

(a) Format for 6-bit BCD code

Character	Standard BCD Interchange Code
0	00 1010
1	00 0001
2	00 0010
3	00 0011
4	00 0100
5	00 0101
6	00 0110
7	00 0111
A	11 0001
B	11 0010
C	11 0011
D	11 0100
E	11 0101

(b) The coding used to represent selected characters in a standard 6-bit code used in IBM mainframe models and in similar machines produced by other manufacturers. The other 8-bit code is **ASCII-8,** an 8-bit version of ASCII that is frequently used in the larger machines produced by some vendors. Figure 4-7 presents the 8-bit format and shows how selected characters are represented in these 8-bit codes. The main difference is in the selection of bit patterns to use in the zone positions.

Detecting Code Errors

Computers are very reliable, but they're not infallible. If just one bit in a string of 6, 7, or 8 bits is lost during data input, processing, or output operations, an incorrect character code will be created. Such an error can be caused by dust particles on storage media, by improper humidity levels near the computer, or by many other factors.

Computer designers have developed a method for detecting such errors by adding an extra *check bit* or *parity bit* to each 6-, 7-, or 8-bit character represented in storage. Thus, as you can see in Figure 4-8, a total of 7, 8, or 9 bits may actually be stored. The designers of a particular computer model may then use the check bit to make sure that every valid character code will *always* have an *even* number of 1 bits. The 7-bit ASCII coding used to represent selected characters was presented earlier in Figure 4-6. Several of these characters have been reproduced in Figure 4-9. You'll notice that if the *basic code* for a character such as 1 or 2 requires an odd number of 1 bits, an additional 1 bit is added in the check-bit location so that there should always be an *even* number of such bits. If an odd number of 1 bits is detected by special **parity checking** circuits, the system will know that a character code is incorrect.

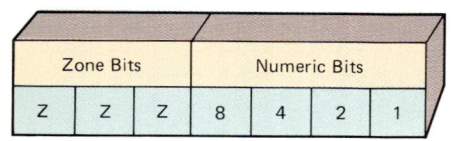

FIGURE 4-6
The 7-bit ASCII format and selected ASCII character codes.

(a) Format for 7-bit ASCII code.

Character	ASCII
0	011 0000
1	011 0001
2	011 0010
3	011 0011
4	011 0100
5	011 0101
6	011 0110
7	011 0111
A	100 0001
B	100 0010
C	100 0011
D	100 0100
E	100 0101

(b) The coding used to represent selected characters in the ASCII 7-bit code.

FIGURE 4-7
The format for EBCDIC and ASCII-8 8-bit codes and selected characters represented by these codes. Each 8-bit unit used to code data is called a *byte*.

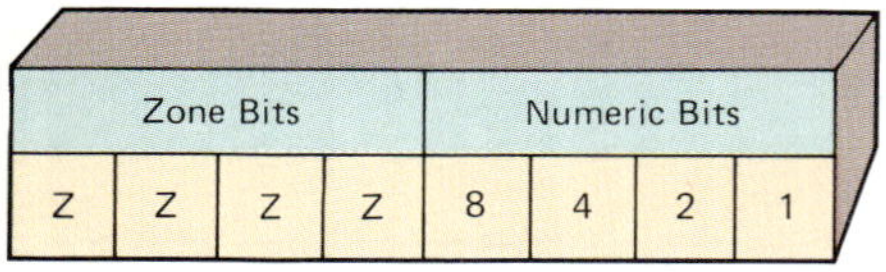

(a) Format for 8-bit EBCDIC and ASCII-8 codes

Character	Extended BCD Interchange Code (EBCDIC)	ASCII-8
0	1111 0000	0101 0000
1	1111 0001	0101 0001
2	1111 0010	0101 0010
3	1111 0011	0101 0011
4	1111 0100	0101 0100
5	1111 0101	0101 0101
6	1111 0110	0101 0110
7	1111 0111	0101 0111
A	1100 0001	1010 0001
B	1100 0010	1010 0010
C	1100 0011	1010 0011
D	1100 0100	1010 0100
E	1100 0101	1010 0101

(b) The coding used to represent selected characters in the EBCDIC and ASCII-8 8-bit codes

FIGURE 4-8
(a) Format of 6-bit BCD code with check bit included. (b) Format of 7-bit ASCII code with check bit included. (c) Format of 8-bit codes with check bit included.

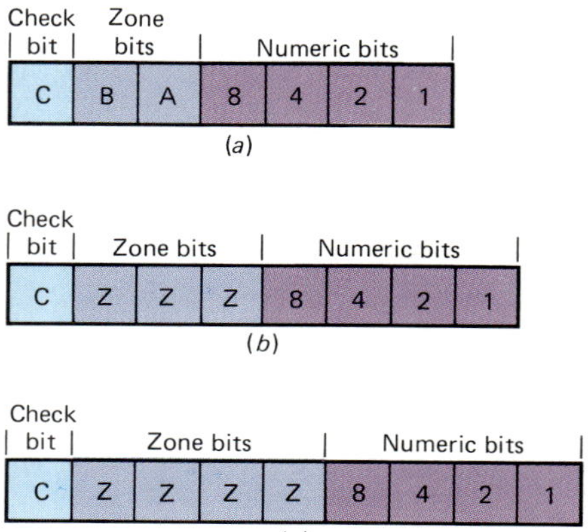

CHAPTER 4

139

	(Check bit)	(Zone bits)			(Numeric bits)			
A	0	1	0	0	0	0	0	1
1	1	0	1	1	0	0	0	1
3	0	0	1	1	0	0	1	1
2	1	0	1	1	0	0	1	0

Primary Storage Section

FIGURE 4-9

An example of parity checking. A check bit is used to make sure that every stored character in the part number entered by the user has an even number of 1 bits. We've used an *even-parity* format in this example, but some computers use the check bit to produce an *odd parity*. Since every valid character in a computer that uses even parity must always have an even number of 1 bits, circuits for parity checking are built into the computer to constantly monitor the data moving through the system. The computer operator may be notified if a bit is lost or gained and a parity error is detected. Of course, parity checking will only detect coding errors. It cannot signal the fact that incorrect data have been entered into the system if the data are properly coded. As you can see here, each 8-bit byte in a personal computer *can* be designed to code a 7-bit ASCII character and provide for a parity check. But some pc's don't perform such checks, and so the leftmost bit isn't used.

STORAGE COMPONENTS IN THE PROCESSOR UNIT

Primary Storage Components of the Past

The first general-purpose electronic computer built in the 1940s (the ENIAC) used vacuum tubes. These tubes were relatively large and each was able to hold only a single bit. Storage capacity was thus tiny by present standards. The most popular computer in the mid-1950s (the IBM 650) used a rotating drum coated with a magnetizeable material as the primary storage instrument.

During the 15 years between 1960 and 1975, however, the dominant computer storage design used tiny rings or *cores* of magnetizeable material in the primary storage section. Current flowing in one direction produced a 0-bit magnetic state; flow in the opposite direction caused a 1-bit state. Since the core permanently retained its magnetic state in the absence of current, it was a **nonvolatile storage** medium. Core storage was popular for 15 years because

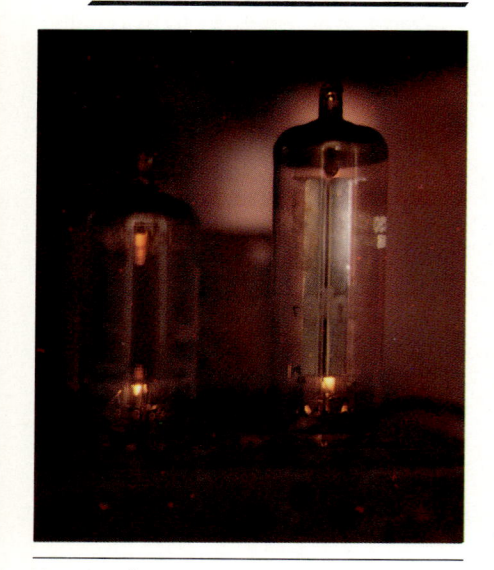

Vacuum tubes in action; each tube can store only a single bit. (© Bert Tanner)

it was safe, durable, and reasonably fast. But the new storage devices that appeared in the 1970s offered even faster performance at a lower cost, and so the popularity of cores quickly faded.

Primary Storage Components of the Present

Virtually all computers made today use semiconductor elements in their primary storage sections. **Semiconductor storage** elements are tiny integrated circuits. Both the storage cell circuits and the support circuitry needed for data writing and reading are packaged on chips of silicon. There are several semiconductor storage technologies currently in use. It's not necessary to consider the physics of these different approaches in any detail. It's enough just to mention that faster and more expensive *bipolar semiconductor* chips are often used in the arithmetic-logic and certain other sections of the processor while slower and less expensive chips that employ *metal-oxide semiconductor (MOS)* technology are usually used in the primary storage section. These primary storage components are often referred to as random access memory **(RAM) chips** because any of the locations on a chip can be randomly selected and used to directly store and retrieve data and instructions.

RAM chips may be classified as dynamic or static. The storage cell circuits in **dynamic RAM chips** contain (1) a transistor that acts in much the same way as a mechanical on-off light switch and (2) a capacitor that's capable of storing an electrical charge. Depending on the switching action of the transistor, the capacitor either contains no charge (0 bit) or does hold a charge (1 bit). Figure 4-10 shows how 64 bits might be arranged in a section of a chip. To locate a particular cell for writing or reading, row and column addresses (in binary) are needed. The storage location of the shaded cell in Figure 4-10 is the row numbered 0011 (3) and the column numbered 0101 (5). Since the charge on the capacitor tends to "leak off," provision is made to periodically "regenerate" or refresh the storage charge. Unlike a magnetic core, then, a dynamic RAM chip provides **volatile storage.** That is, the data stored are lost in the event of a power failure.

These 256K dynamic RAM chips are only a quarter-inch long—less than a pencil width—but they can store more than a quarter of a million bits. (Courtesy AT&T/Bell Labs)

Static RAM chips are also volatile storage devices, but as long as they are supplied with power they need no special regenerator circuits to retain the stored data. Since it takes a total of six transistors and other devices to store a bit in a static RAM, these chips are more complicated and take up more space for a given storage capacity than do dynamic RAMs. Static RAMs are thus used in specialized applications while dynamic RAMs are used in the primary storage sections of most computers. Because of the volatile nature of these storage elements, a backup **uninterruptible power system** (UPS) is often found in larger computer installations. Personal computer users can also invest a few hundred dollars and get a small battery-powered UPS. This device will supply current for a period long enough for users to save data on a disk and then shut down the system in an orderly way.

Semiconductor memory chips have found their way into modern computers for three good reasons:

1 *More storage at lower costs.* For the last decade, the number of bits that can be stored on a chip has quadrupled every 3 years. During the same period, the cost per bit of storage has been cut in half every 3 years. There seems to be no end in sight to these cost reductions. We've seen that the symbol **K** is often used when the storage capacity of chips is discussed. One K represents 2^{10}, or 1,024 units. Today, many chips are able to store 256K, or 262,144 bits. But as you can see in Figure 4-11, these chips are being surpassed by others that will each store 1 *megabit* (or 1M, where M is equal to 1.048 million bits), and the cost per bit will drop once again. It's then anticipated that the trend will continue with the development of first a 4-megabit (4M) chip and then a 16-megabit chip.

2 *Compact size.* Semiconductor chips require a small fraction of the space needed by earlier storage devices of similar capacity.

3 *Faster performance.* Semiconductor devices are capable of faster performance than earlier storage units. Their more compact size contributes to this faster speed.

Primary Storage Components of the Future

Scientists in the United States, Japan, and Europe are working on primary storage approaches that promise to be much more compact and much faster than anything in current use. For example, to pack more circuits on storage chips, engineers are working to create "trenches" in the thin oxide material that coats the silicon base. The walls of the trenches then give engineers more surface area on which to place the storage transistors and capacitors.

It has also been found that speed advantages can be obtained by replacing silicon with a semiconductor material called **gallium arsenide (GaAs)**. Electronic pulses can move through GaAs five to seven times faster than they can through the best silicon devices currently available. And GaAs chips may consume less power. Farther into the future, scientists are dreaming of replacing silicon and GaAs chips with **biochips** made of large organic molecules and genetically engineered proteins.

Although we can't know what technology will dominate in the future, we can be sure that future storage devices will be smaller, faster, and cheaper than those in use today.

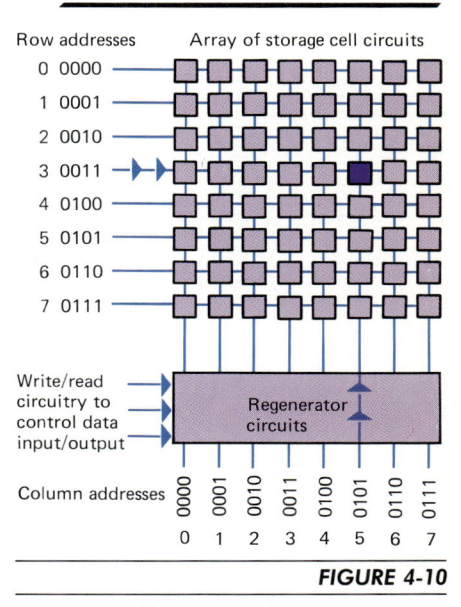

FIGURE 4-10

Dynamic RAM storage concepts.

FIGURE 4-11

The number of bits that can be stored on a silicon chip has quadrupled every 3 years, and the cost per bit of storage has been cut in half every 3 years. This trend in semiconductor storage is expected to continue.

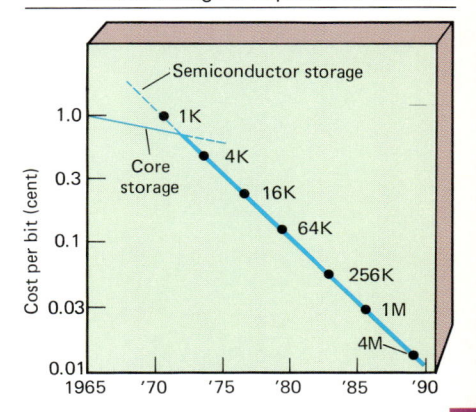

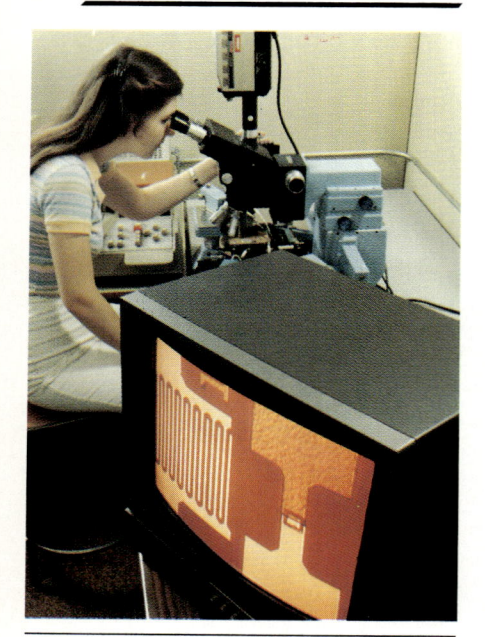

A researcher studies an experimental gallium arsenide chip under a microscope that incorporates a color TV camera. Because they are faster than silicon chips and require less power, gallium arsenide chips may soon displace silicon chips. (Courtesy Sanders Associates, Inc.)

Specialized Storage Elements in the Processor Unit

You know that every processor has a primary storage section that holds the active program(s) and data being processed. In addition to this *general-purpose* storage section, however, many processors also have built-in *specialized* storage elements that are used for specific processing and control purposes (Figure 4-12).

One element used during *processing* operations is a **high-speed buffer** (or **cache**) memory that's both faster and more expensive per character stored than primary storage. This high-speed circuitry is used as a "scratch pad" to temporarily store data and instructions that are likely to be retrieved many times during processing. Processing speed can thus be improved. Data may be transferred automatically between the buffer and primary storage so that the application programmer may be unaware of its use. Once found only in larger systems, cache memory is now available in some of the tiny microprocessor chips used in personal computers.

Other specialized storage elements found in many processors are used for *control* purposes. The most basic computer functions are carried out by wired circuits. Additional circuits may then be used to combine these very basic functions into somewhat higher-level operations (e.g., to subtract values, move data, etc.). But it's also possible to perform these same higher-level operations with a series of special programs. These programs—called **microprograms** because they deal with low-level machine functions—are thus essentially substitutes for additional hardware.

Microprograms are typically held in the processor unit in special control storage elements called read-only memory **(ROM) chips.** Unlike RAM chips, which are volatile, ROM chips retain stored data when the power goes off. Microprogram control instructions that cause the machine to perform certain operations can be repeatedly read from a ROM chip as needed, but the chip will not accept any input data or instructions from computer users.

The most basic type of ROM chip is supplied by the computer manufacturer as part of the computer system, and it can't be changed or altered by users. Such chips have found wide application as a program storage medium in video games and personal computers. Of course, it's possible for a user to "customize" a system by choosing the machine functions that will be per-

FIGURE 4-12

In addition to the primary storage section, many processors also contain specialized storage elements that are used for processing and control purposes.

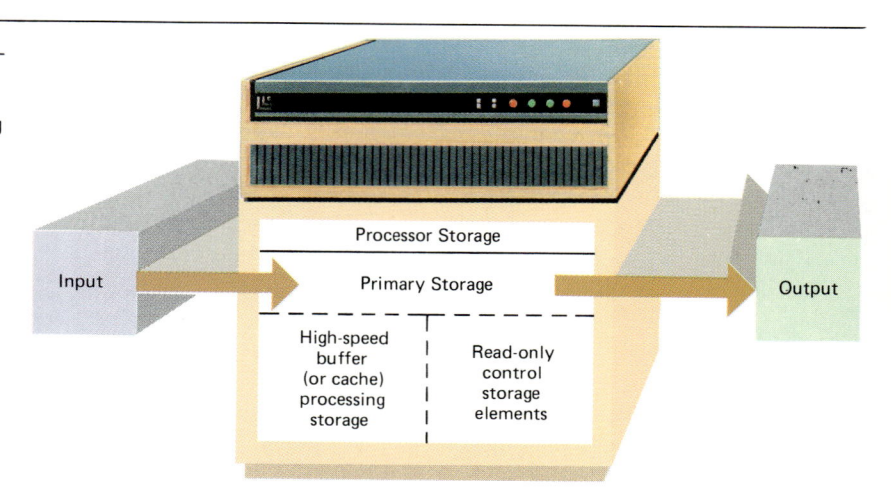

formed by microprograms and by then using a second type of ROM chip. For example, critical or lengthy operations that have been slowly carried out by software can be converted into microprograms and fused into a <u>p</u>rogrammable <u>r</u>ead-<u>o</u>nly <u>m</u>emory **(PROM) chip**. Once they are in a hardware form, these tasks can usually be executed in a fraction of the time previously required.

PROM chips are supplied by computer manufacturers and custom ROM vendors. Once operations have been written into a PROM chip, they are permanent and cannot be altered. There are other types of ROM control chips available, however, that *can* be erased and reprogrammed. Since one type of <u>e</u>rasable and <u>p</u>rogrammable <u>r</u>ead-<u>o</u>nly <u>m</u>emory **(EPROM) chip** needs to be removed from the processor and exposed for some time to ultraviolet light before it can accept new contents, it's hardly suitable for use by application programmers. Another type of <u>e</u>lectrically <u>e</u>rasable <u>p</u>rogrammable <u>r</u>ead-<u>o</u>nly <u>m</u>emory **(EEPROM) chip** is also available that can be reprogrammed with

WINDOW 4-1

CHIPS THAT SEE, SMELL, AND FEEL

A new generation of sensor technology is on the way. Microchip sensors have been in use for several years; recently, however, new sensor technology is being developed that could revolutionize medicine, manufacturing, and defense, to name just some of the possible applications.

In medicine, for example, a biosensor has been developed that is capable of detecting critical amounts of sodium, potassium, and chloride in a drop of blood in less than half a minute. In manufacturing, Honeywell Inc. has developed a sensor which precisely measures gaps in machine parts, to be used by robotic equipment in automobile factories, costing less than 1/10 as much as existing computer systems that perform a similar task. In defense, Honeywell is developing a sensor that can detect sound and vibration, to be used in a fuse for land mines. The new sensors would also be a vital component of any Star Wars defense system.

The sensors are made by combining a computer chip with materials that will initiate a change in electrical current when exposed to various stimuli such as sound, chemical pollutants, or even cancer cells, depending on the sensor. For example, biosensors such as those mentioned above, manufactured by Toshiba Corp., work with enzymes or antibodies bonded to the surface of the chip. When the enzyme or antibody combines with its designated protein or chemical, an electrical signal is generated and transmitted to the chip.

The most promising immediate uses for the new sensor technology are in medicine. Several groups are working on sensors to detect cancer, and Toshiba has come out with a device to monitor glucose levels in diabetics. While the prototype unit cannot operate for periods of time long enough to make an implant practical, it is expected that soon a sensor will be available that could be implanted and would automatically control the level of insulin to be administered into the patient's circulatory system.

In dentistry, a company called Integrated Ionics Inc. is marketing an oral sensor, capable of measuring acid and calcium levels in a patient's mouth. The sensor, which is described as "as small and flexible as toothbrush bristles," would be placed in an oral retainer. The company is also working on a disposable sensor that could detect and prevent gum disease.

Business experts expect the new sensor technology, more than other innovations such as artificial intelligence or biotechnology, to show immediate profit and expansion. In 1982, sales of smart sensors barely topped $8 million, estimates Business Communications Co., a Stamford (Conn.) market researcher. But by 1990, the market is expected to approach $250 million. The effort is already so competitive that few companies are willing to talk about laboratory projects under way—thus estimates may well be quite conservative. Integrated Ionics alone hopes to consolidate a $100 million market on the disposable gum-disease sensor it is developing.

It is difficult to predict what the new sensor technology will be capable of. While specialists are convinced that smart sensors will soon routinely perform a broad range of tasks, from monitoring pollutants in water supplies to shutting household windows when it rains, what happens after that is anybody's guess.

Excerpted from Emily T. Smith et al., "Chips that See, Smell, and Feel," *Business Week*, May 13, 1985. Copyright © 1985 by McGraw-Hill, Inc. Reprinted by special permission.

FIGURE 4-13

Semiconductor storage chips and their use.

Memory Type		Some Applications
Random-access memories (RAMs)	Dynamic RAM	Main primary storage device for mainframes, minicomputers, and personal computers.
	Static RAM	Microcomputers requiring a small storage capacity; high-speed versions for minicomputer buffer storage; low-power versions for portable computers.
Read-only memory categories (ROMs)	ROM	Program storage for personal computers; character set storage for visual displays and printers.
	PROM	Microprogram control instructions for minicomputers; military and automobile uses.
	EPROM	Same as for ROM. Ability to reprogram makes it easier to correct errors during software development.
	EEPROM	ROM and EPROM applications needing occasional program or data modifications.

special electrical pulses. Regardless of the type of ROM chip used, however, they all serve to increase processor efficiency by controlling the performance of a few specialized tasks. Figure 4-13 summarizes the list of semiconductor storage chips that we've now encountered.

THE ARITHMETIC-LOGIC AND CONTROL FUNCTIONS

Up to now, we've concentrated almost exclusively on the storage function of the processor unit. It's logical to spend so much time on this function because the data that people are interested in must be stored in a coded form before they can be processed. But you know that to process data every computer must have components to perform the arithmetic-logic and general control functions. Let's now take a quick look at these components.

The Arithmetic-Logic Section

You'll recall that the arithmetic-logic section is where the actual data processing occurs. All calculations are made and all comparisons take place in this section (also called the arithmetic-logic unit, or **ALU**). A detailed explanation of how an ALU operates on data is given in the Closer Look reading at the end of the chapter.

Every arithmetic step requires two numbers and produces a result. Multiplication, for example, uses a multiplicand and a multiplier to get a product. Although *every* ALU must be able to manage the two data words and the result, different processing and storage techniques are used in different models.

In addition to arithmetic functions, the ALU also handles logic operations. Logic operations usually involve comparisons. Circuits in the ALU are generally used to compare two numbers by subtracting one from the other. The sign (negative or positive) and the value of the difference tell the processor that the first number is equal to, less than, or greater than the second number. Branches are provided in the program for the computer to follow, depending on the result of such a comparison. Alphabetic data may also be compared according to an assigned order sequence.

The Control Section

The control section of the processor selects and interprets program instructions and then sees that they are executed. The ALU responds to commands coming from the control section. A detailed discussion of the control section's operation is also presented in the Closer Look reading at the end of the chapter.

The operations of the ALU and the control unit are performed with incredible speed. These operations are usually synchronized by an *electronic clock* that emits millions of regularly spaced electrical pulses each second. Commands are interpreted and then executed at proper intervals, and the intervals are timed by a specific number of these pulses. Thus the speed with which an instruction is executed is directly related to the computer's built-in **clock speed**—that is, the number of pulses produced each second. This clock speed is measured in **megahertz (or MHz),** where mega means million and hertz means times per second. Most of today's popular personal computers have clock speeds in the 2- to 8-MHz range. But microprocessors are now being built with ratings of over 15 MHz. Larger machines are even faster.

FEEDBACK

Feedback and Review 4

The following *multiple-choice* review questions will test and reinforce your understanding of the material presented in this chapter. Place the letter of the best response in the space provided.

 ____ 1. A single primary storage location in the processor unit
   a) can hold several different data items at the same time.
   b) is identified by a built-in and unique number called an address.
   c) can hold data items but not program instructions.
   d) is identified by a number that varies with the contents in the location.
 ____ 2. Entering data into a storage location
   a) is likely to cause variation in its address number.
   b) adds to the contents of the location, but has no effect on data previously held there.
   c) is destructive of previous contents.
   d) is called a readout operation.

___ 3. The storage capacity of each numbered address in the processor unit
   a) can never hold more than a single data character.
   b) must always hold more than a single data character.
   c) depends on the storage design approach built into the processor.
   d) is always able to hold a word consisting of four characters.

___ 4. A large computer designed to handle complex scientific calculations
   a) may use only a fixed word-length storage approach.
   b) will likely require a character-addressable storage unit.
   c) must use fixed-length words of four characters each.
   d) will not use numbered address locations.

___ 5. An 8-bit unit used to code data is called a
   a) word.
   b) data set.
   c) byte.
   d) K.

___ 6. ASCII is a
   a) 6-bit BCD code used by mainframe computers.
   b) 7-bit BCD code used by personal computers and minis.
   c) 8-bit BCD code used in IBM mainframes.
   d) 9-bit BCD code used in supercomputers.

___ 7. A parity bit
   a) is a check bit added to each 6-, 7-, or 8-bit character represented in storage.
   b) is what farmers use to set grain prices.
   c) always produces an odd number of 1 bits in a stored character.
   d) is used to detect human keying errors.

___ 8. In studying numbering systems, you've learned that
   a) the first numbering systems used a positional approach.
   b) in a positional numbering system, the highest numerical symbol always has a value one more than the base.
   c) the possible symbols in the binary numbering system are 0 to 9.
   d) each position to the left of the binary point in the binary numbering system represents a specific power of the base of 2.

___ 9. As you read about primary storage components, you learned that
   a) a volatile storage medium retains its magnetic state in the absence of power.
   b) a static ROM chip is the primary storage device of choice for use with personal computers.
   c) a dynamic RAM chip is a nonvolatile storage device.
   d) the number of bits that can be stored on a silicon chip has quadrupled about every 3 years, and this trend is likely to continue in the next decade.

___10. A specialized storage element often found in a processor unit is
   a) the nonvolatile dynamic RAM chip.
   b) the high-speed buffer or cache unit that's used as a "scratch pad" during processing.
   c) the volatile ROM chip that's used to store user data and programs.
   d) the gallium arsenide chip used to slow down processing speeds.

LOOKING BACK

1. Storage locations in the primary storage section of a processor unit are identified by address numbers. These locations are able to hold either data or program instructions. When the contents of an address are needed by a program, the machine must be given the address number so that it can locate the desired item. The act of retrieving existing data or instructions from an address is nondestructive, but entering new contents into an address will erase the previous contents.

2. The storage capacity of an address is built into a computer. Some computers can only store a fixed number of characters in each numbered address location. They then treat these characters as a single entity or word. Such systems are said to be word addressable, and they use a fixed word-length storage approach. Other computers can only store a single character in each address location. These machines are said to be character addressable, and they employ a variable word-length storage approach. There are advantages and limitations to each of these approaches. Many of today's computers have been built with the flexibility to operate on either single characters or fixed-length words. Such systems are said to be byte addressable.

3. Every computer stores numbers, letters, and other characters in a coded form. Each character is represented by a coded string of binary digits (bits) that are treated as a unit. Binary numbers (0s and 1s) are used to simplify computer design. A 4-bit binary coded decimal (BCD) coding system can be used to represent decimal numbers, but 6-, 7-, or 8-bit codes are used to represent characters in alphanumeric versions of BCD. Since the 64 possible characters permitted by the older 6-bit BCD format aren't enough for many applications, the 7- and 8-bit formats are generally used. The ASCII 7-bit code is used in personal computers, and two popular 8-bit codes (EBCDIC and ASCII-8) are used in many larger machines.

4. To detect any code errors that may occur, an extra check bit or parity bit may be added to each 6-, 7-, or 8-bit character represented in storage. The check bit is used to make sure that every valid character in a computer that uses even parity will always have an even number of 1 bits.

5. Many types of primary storage devices have been used. Between 1960 and 1975, the dominant storage medium was magnetic cores. Since then, however, volatile RAM semiconductor storage chips have been used because of economic and performance factors. And future storage devices promise to be much more compact and faster than anything in current use.

6. In addition to the primary storage section, many processors also have built-in specialized storage elements that are used for specific processing and control purposes. A high-speed buffer or cache

memory may be used to improve processing speed. And microprograms that deal with special machine functions may be held in nonvolatile read-only memory (ROM) chips. Microprogram instructions are repeatedly called on to control the processor as it performs certain basic operations.

7. The arithmetic-logic section does the actual processing under program control, and the control section selects, interprets, and sees to the execution of program instructions in their proper sequence. The speed with which an instruction is executed is directly related to the computer's built-in clock speed.

KEY TERMS AND CONCEPTS

address 132
destructive read in (or write) 132
nondestructive read out 132
word 133
word addressable 133
fixed word-length storage 133
character addressable 133
variable word-length storage 133
bit 134
byte 134
byte-addressable computer 134
binary numbering system 136
the binary coded decimal (BCD) approach 137

6-bit BCD code 137
7-bit BCD code 137
8-bit BCD code 137
ASCII 137
EBCDIC 137
ASCII-8 138
parity checking 138
nonvolatile storage 139
semiconductor storage 140
RAM (random access memory) chip 140
dynamic RAM chips 140
volatile storage 140
static RAM chips 141
uninterruptible power system (UPS) 141
K 141

gallium arsenide (GaAs) 141
biochips 141
high-speed buffer (or cache) storage 142
microprograms 142
ROM (read-only memory) chip 142
PROM (programmable read-only memory) chip 143
EPROM (erasable and programmable read-only memory) chip 143
EEPROM (electrically erasable and programmable read-only memory) chip 143
ALU 144
clock speed 145
megahertz (MHz) 145

TOPICS FOR REVIEW AND DISCUSSION

1. (a) How is an addressable storage location similar to a post office box? (b) How do storage locations differ from mailboxes?
2. Discuss this statement: "Over the years, computer manufacturers have used several different design approaches to partition the primary storage section into addresses."
3. (a) Distinguish between word-addressable and character-addressable computers. (b) What is an advantage of each of these computer types?
4. (a) What is a byte-addressable computer? (b) How does it achieve its flexibility?
5. (a) What is the difference between an additive and a positional numbering system? (b) Give examples of both types of numbering systems.

6. Identify two principles that apply to any positional numbering system.
7. Why have computers been designed to use the binary numbering system?
8. (a) What is the decimal equivalent of 1101011_2? (b) Of 11010_2?
9. (a) What is 150_{10} in 4-bit BCD code? (b) What is 75_{10} in BCD?
10. Why has a 6-bit BCD code been extended to 8 bits?
11. Identify and discuss (a) the 7-bit BCD code and (b) the two popular 8-bit codes.
12. How can a computer detect whether a bit in a character code is lost during processing?
13. (a) What types of primary storage devices have been used in the past? (b) What is the dominant primary storage technology at the present time? (c) What technology may emerge in the future?
14. Why are semiconductor chips popular as storage devices?
15. (a) Identify the specialized storage elements that may be found in a processor unit. (b) How may these elements be used?

PROJECTS/ISSUES TO CONSIDER

1. Let's assume that you have a friend who is thinking of buying a personal computer to use at work. Your friend asks you to help identify some models that might be suitable. Identify three possible personal computer candidates, and determine the following characteristics for each: word length; type of primary storage; minimum capacity of primary storage; maximum capacity of primary storage; ROM storage available (if any); type of microprocessor chip used; clock speed of the microprocessor; purchase price range. Prepare a report outlining your findings.

2. The Santa Clara valley in northern California is called "Silicon Valley" because of the hundreds of semiconductor and computer companies that are located there. The manufacture of silicon chips requires the use of chemicals that are hazardous to human health. Some California citizens became alarmed in the early 1980s about the possibility that the earth and water in the valley were being polluted by toxic wastes. At this writing, a state regulatory agency has identified 136 contaminated sites in the valley, the majority of which are linked to electronics firms. And the U.S. Environmental Protection Agency has recently added 19 contaminated areas in the valley to its list of priority cleanup sites. Toxic chemicals have apparently seeped into underground water supplies and have then contaminated some of the public and private wells used by valley residents. Research this issue and report your findings to the class.

ANSWERS TO FEEDBACK AND REVIEW SECTION

1. b   2. c   3. c   4. a   5. c   6. b   7. a   8. d   9. d   10. b

A CLOSER LOOK

INSIDE CENTRAL PROCESSORS
THE USE OF STORAGE LOCATIONS AND THE OPERATIONS OF ARITHMETIC-LOGIC AND CONTROL SECTIONS

The Use of Storage Locations

To get a general idea of how storage locations are used, let's take another look at the application to process Elm Creek beautification charges that was discussed in Chapter 1. You'll recall that property owners agreed to pay the city of Calvin to improve their property along the stream. Input data for each property owner are first entered on city job tickets and are then keyed onto a floppy disk. The first input record was for Bill Byter. The processing of this application was shown in Figure 1-12, page 25. But that figure showed the stored program concept in only the most general way. It made no reference to addressable storage locations.

Figure 4-A presents a more realistic version of the processor shown in Figure 1-12 because it illustrates the use of storage addresses. (Although we're concentrating here on the characteristics of a personal computer, keep in mind that larger systems possess these same characteristics.) The program steps shown in Figure 4-A are identical in purpose to those discussed in Chapter 1. These instructions have been read into addresses 04 through 14[1] in the primary storage section of Figure 4-A. This choice of addresses for the *program storage* area is arbitrary; any space in primary storage could have been used.[2] Let's now trace through the program steps shown in Figure 4-A to see how storage locations are used to prepare Bill's charges. (The circled address numbers shown in the figure indicate how the computer responds to the instruction stored in that address. Some flow lines have been omitted to simplify the figure.)

After the computer operator has loaded the charge data in a disk drive in the pc system cabinet and has set the computer to the instruction in address 04, the processing starts. The first instruction (04) is fed into the control section of the CPU where it's interpreted. Control signals are sent to the disk drive which executes the instruction and transfers a record to the *input storage* area identified in the instruction. Thus Bill's charge data are read into addresses 00, 01, 02, and 03.[3] The data could easily have been assigned to other unused addresses, and so this is also an arbitrary choice.

The control unit will interpret the instructions automatically and in sequence after the initial control setting until directed to do otherwise. Thus after the instruction in address 04 has been executed, the control unit begins to interpret the instruction in address 05. This instruction sets up a type of logic/comparison operation discussed in Chapter 2. It requires that the contents of address 02 be compared to a value of −99 plants. This value of −99 plants is placed in a last dummy record at the end of the property-owner file to indicate that all valid data have been processed. If the contents do not equal −99 plants, the processing continues in sequence. If the quantity in the plant field does equal −99, program control will branch to address 14 and processing will stop. Since Bill has received 33 plants, program control moves on to address 06. This instruction tells the control unit that the contents of address 02 are to be copied into the arithmetic-logic section, and so 33 plants is duplicated there.

By now you should be able to trace through the remaining program steps in Figure 4-A. The 33-plant figure in the arithmetic-logic section is multiplied by the $4.50 price per plant stored in address 03 to get the net amount of the plants (instruction in address 07). This net amount figure is copied (instruction, 08) in address 15, which is the *working storage area*.[4] The amount of the planting charge is computed (in-

---

[1] Leading zeros—e.g., 00004 or 00014—in the address numbers have been deleted here to simplify the figure. And the 18 addresses used—00 to 17—are a much smaller number than actually exist in the primary storage area but are enough to illustrate the concept.

[2] Programmers who write applications instructions in higher-level languages, such as BASIC, Pascal, and COBOL, do not worry about address selection. Instead, they use prewritten, specialized programs provided by computer manufacturers and others to assign storage locations to the different possible purposes.

[3] As you've seen in the chapter, the capacity of storage locations can vary. A few additional storage locations would be needed to hold all our input data. This would be no problem for the computer, but it would add unnecessary detail to our example.

[4] Why address 15 instead of 16 or some other unused location? Again, the choice is arbitrary.

FIGURE 4-A (facing page)

This figure illustrates the use of storage locations. The application is the processing of Elm Creek beautification charges discussed in Chapter 1 and illustrated earlier in Figure 1-12. The areas used for input storage (addresses 00 through 03), program storage (addresses 04 through 14), working storage (address 15), and output storage (address 17) are shown. The selection of specific addresses to use for these purposes was arbitrary. The circled numbers in this figure refer to address numbers in the program storage area. The actions taken by the system in response to specific program steps are indicated by the circled numbers.

151

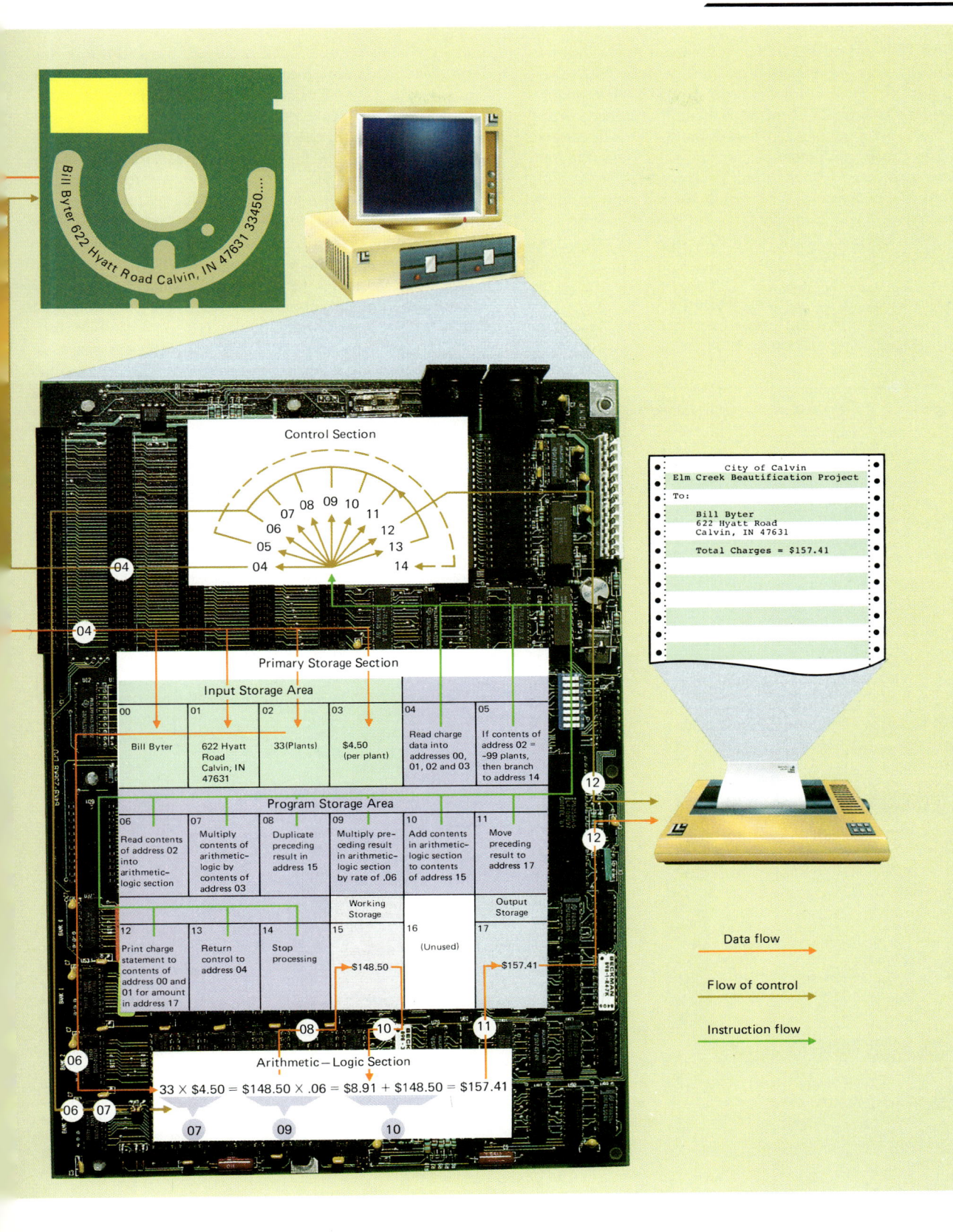

Control Section

07 08 09 10 11
06　　　　　　12
05　　　　　　13
04　　　　　　14

Primary Storage Section

Input Storage Area

00	01	02	03	04	05
Bill Byter	622 Hyatt Road Calvin, IN 47631	33 (Plants)	$4.50 (per plant)	Read charge data into addresses 00, 01, 02 and 03	If contents of address 02 = -99 plants, then branch to address 14

Program Storage Area

06	07	08	09	10	11
Read contents of address 02 into arithmetic-logic section	Multiply contents of arithmetic-logic by contents of address 03	Duplicate preceding result in address 15	Multiply preceding result in arithmetic-logic section by rate of .06	Add contents in arithmetic-logic section to contents of address 15	Move preceding result to address 17

			Working Storage		Output Storage
12	13	14	15	16	17
Print charge statement to contents of address 00 and 01 for amount in address 17	Return control to address 04	Stop processing	$148.50	(Unused)	$157.41

Arithmetic—Logic Section

33 × $4.50 = $148.50 × .06 = $8.91 + $148.50 = $157.41

City of Calvin
Elm Creek Beautification Project
To:
Bill Byter
622 Hyatt Road
Calvin, IN 47631

Total Charges = $157.41

Data flow →
Flow of control →
Instruction flow →

struction, 09) and added to the net amount figure that was temporarily stored in the working storage area (instruction, 10) to get Bill's $157.41 total charge. This $157.41 amount is then moved to address 17, which is the *output storage area*.[5] From there, the amount is sent to a printer which is directed to print Bill's charge statement (instruction, 12). Finally, the control unit is directed to reset itself to address 04 (instruction, 13), and the processing is repeated for the next property owner. When the charge data for the next owner are entered into addresses 00 through 03, they will erase Bill's data.

The Operation of the Arithmetic-Logic Unit

Let's look again at the Elm Creek beautification charges application to see how an arithmetic-logic unit (ALU) operates

---

[5] You guessed it: Any unused location would have been acceptable.

on data. We won't need all the program instructions from this application to demonstrate ALU operation. The ones from Figure 4-A that we *will* need are reproduced in Figure 4-B*a*. These instructions are written so that we can understand them, but they cannot be interpreted in this form by the computer. A more machinelike version of these same instructions is shown in Figure 4-B*b*.

The instruction in address 06—CLA 02—calls for the computer to first CLear the ALU of all previously stored data and then Add (store) the contents of address 02 to that section. Both the ALU and the control section have special-purpose storage locations called **registers**. The number of registers varies among computers as does the data-flow pattern. In the city manager's computer, the contents of address 02 are entered into an ALU register known as the **accumulator**. Thus, as Figure 4-C illustrates, Bill's 33 plants—the contents of address 02—are now held both in address 02 and in the accumulator. (Once again, the circled address

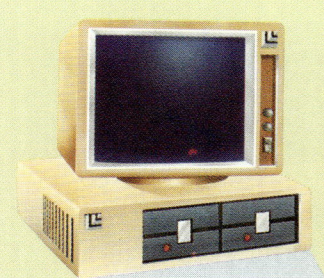

06	07	08	09	10
Read contents of address 02 into arithmetic-logic section	Multiply contents of arithmetic-logic section by contents of address 03	Duplicate preceding result in address 15	Multiply preceding result in arithmetic-logic section by rate of .06	Add contents in arithmetic-logic section to contents of address 15

(a)

06	07	08	09	10
CLA 02	MUL 03	STO 15	MUL RATE	ADD 15

(b)

FIGURE 4-B (above)

(a) Five of the program steps needed to prepare the Elm Creek beautification charges application illustrated in Figure 4-A. (b) The five program steps presented in Figure 4-A in a form the computer can interpret.

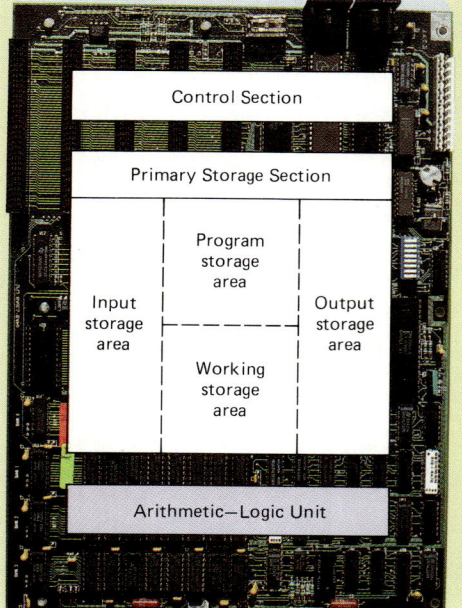

FIGURE 4-C (facing page)

(a) The operation of an arithmetic-logic section in a processor. Every arithmetic-logic section uses special storage locations, or registers. In this example, two such registers—the accumulator and storage register—are used to hold the data items being processed. All arithmetic functions are handled by the adder. The adder is also used in logic operations involving comparisons. By subtracting one value from another, the adder can tell if the first value is equal to, less than, or greater than the second value. The circled address numbers in the data flow lines indicate how the computer responds to the instructions stored in those addresses. (b) The execution of the instruction found in address 09. (c) The execution of the instruction found in address 10.

153

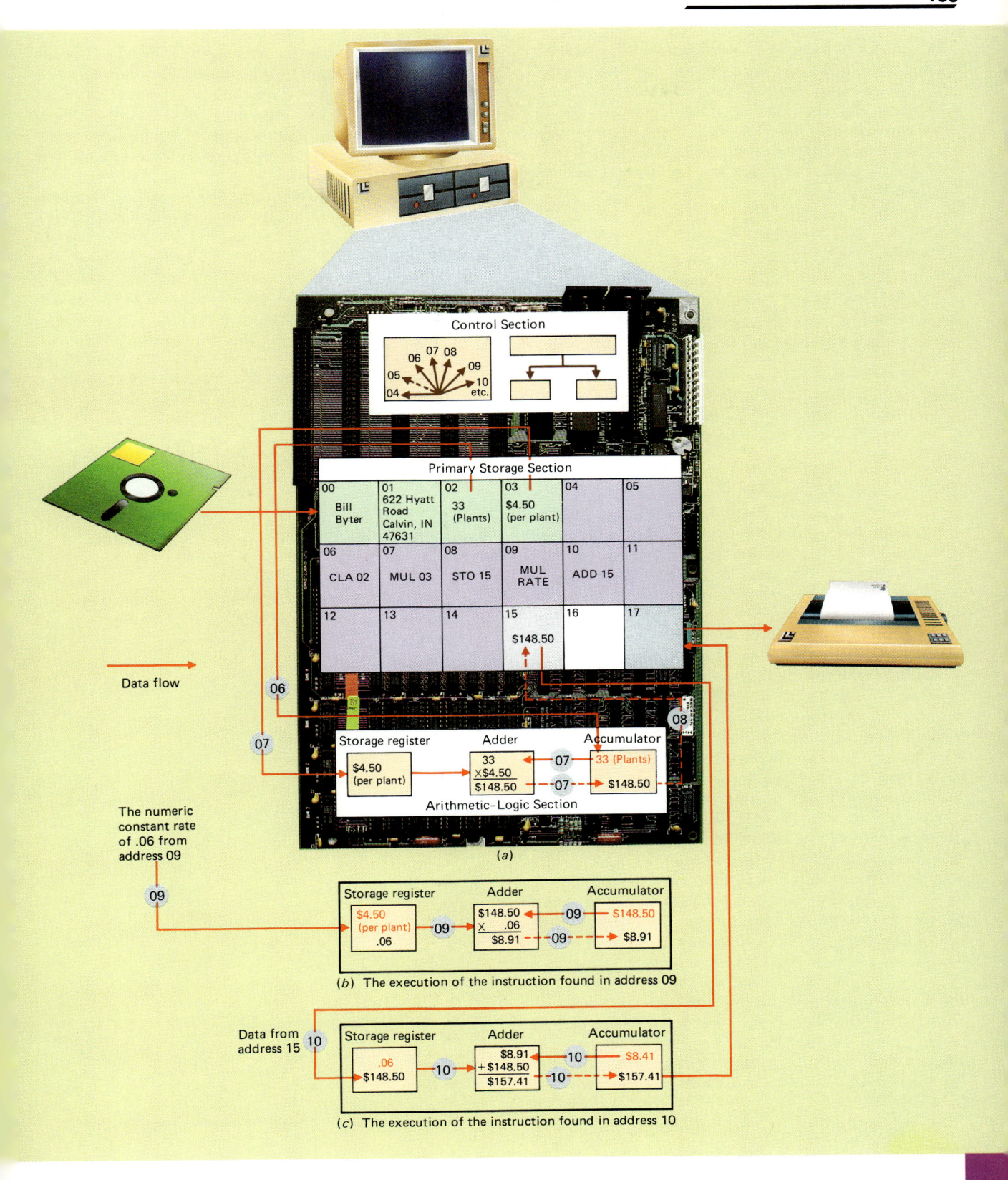

Control Section

00 Bill Byter	01 622 Hyatt Road Calvin, IN 47631	02 33 (Plants)	03 $4.50 (per plant)	04	05
06 CLA 02	07 MUL 03	08 STO 15	09 MUL RATE	10 ADD 15	11
12	13	14	15 $148.50	16	17

Primary Storage Section

Data flow

⑥

⑦

Storage register: $4.50 (per plant)

Adder: 33 × $4.50 = $148.50

Accumulator: 33 (Plants) → $148.50

07 ----- 07

Arithmetic–Logic Section

(a)

The numeric constant rate of .06 from address 09

⑨

Storage register: $4.50 (per plant) .06

Adder: $148.50 × .06 = $8.91

Accumulator: $148.50 → $8.91

09 ----- 09 ----- 09

(b) The execution of the instruction found in address 09

Data from address 15 ⑩

Storage register: .06 → $148.50

Adder: $8.91 + $148.50 = $157.41

Accumulator: $8.41 → $157.41

10 ----- 10 ----- 10

(c) The execution of the instruction found in address 10

numbers shown in the figure indicate how the computer responds to the instruction stored in that address.)

The next instruction in address 07 is MUL 03. This is interpreted to mean that the contents of address 03 ($4.50 per plant) are to be MULtiplied by the contents in the accumulator (33 plants) to get the net amount of Bill's plants. The following steps are carried out in the execution of this instruction (see Figure 4-Ca):

- The contents of address 03 are read into a *storage register* in the ALU.

- The data that are now in the accumulator (33 plants) and the storage register ($4.50 per plant) are copied in the **adder**—the arithmetic element in the ALU that also performs subtractions, multiplications, and divisions on binary digits.

- The multiplication is executed in the adder and the $148.50 result is *entered into the accumulator*. As you know, the act of writing the $148.50 result into the accumulator erases the 33 plants that was previously stored in that register.

After executing the instruction in address 07, the computer moves to the one in address 08. This instruction—STO 15—tells the machine to STOre the *contents of the accumulator* in address 15, the working storage location. Entering the $148.50 amount into address 15 is destructive to any previous data that might be there, but the readout from the accumulator is nondestructive.

Figures 4-C*b* and *c* show how the ALU will execute the instructions found in addresses 09 and 10. In Figure 4-C*b*, the MUL RATE instruction in address 09 causes the planting rate of .06 to be entered into the storage register,[6] thereby destroying the previous contents of $4.50 per plant. The contents of the accumulator ($148.50) and the storage register (.06) are now multiplied in the adder. The $8.91 result is entered back into the accumulator, thereby erasing the $148.50 amount. Figure 4-C*c* shows what happens when the instruction in address 10—ADD 15—is executed. The data stored in address 15 ($148.50) are read into the storage register, and you know what this does to the .06 rate figure that was there. The adder then ADDs the $8.91 in the accumulator to this $148.50 amount in the storage register to get Bill's $157.41 charge total, which is entered back into the accumulator. From there, the $157.41 amount is first read into address 17 and then printed on Bill's statement.

The Operation of the Control Section

You've just seen that a basic instruction that can be interpreted by a computer generally has at least two parts. The first part is the *operation* or *command* that is to be followed (MUL, STO, ADD, etc.). The second part is the *address* which locates the data or instructions to be manipulated. The basic components contained in the control section of the city manager's computer (shown once again in Figure 4-D) are the *instruction register, sequence register, address register,* and *decoder.*

Let's follow an instruction from the Elm Creek application through the control section to see how it's handled. We'll assume that the CLA 02 instruction in address 06 has just been executed and that 33 plants is stored in the accumulator of the ALU. The following steps are then carried out (the circled letters in the lines in Figure 4-D correspond to these steps):

(a) The instruction in address 07 (MUL 03) is selected by the **sequence register** and read into the **instruction register** in

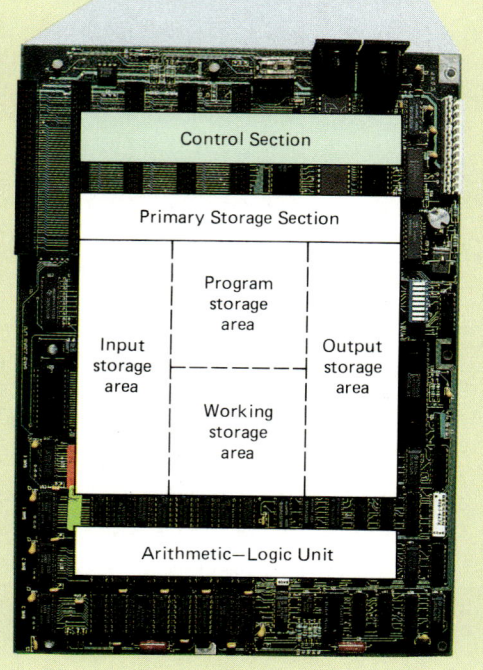

---

[6]The name "RATE" is defined to be the numeric constant value of .06 in another program step that we've omitted, to avoid unnecessary detail.

155

Control Section

Sequence register: 04, 05, 06, 07, 08, etc. (e, a)

Instruction register: MUL 03
- b → MUL (Decoder)
- c → 03 (Address register)

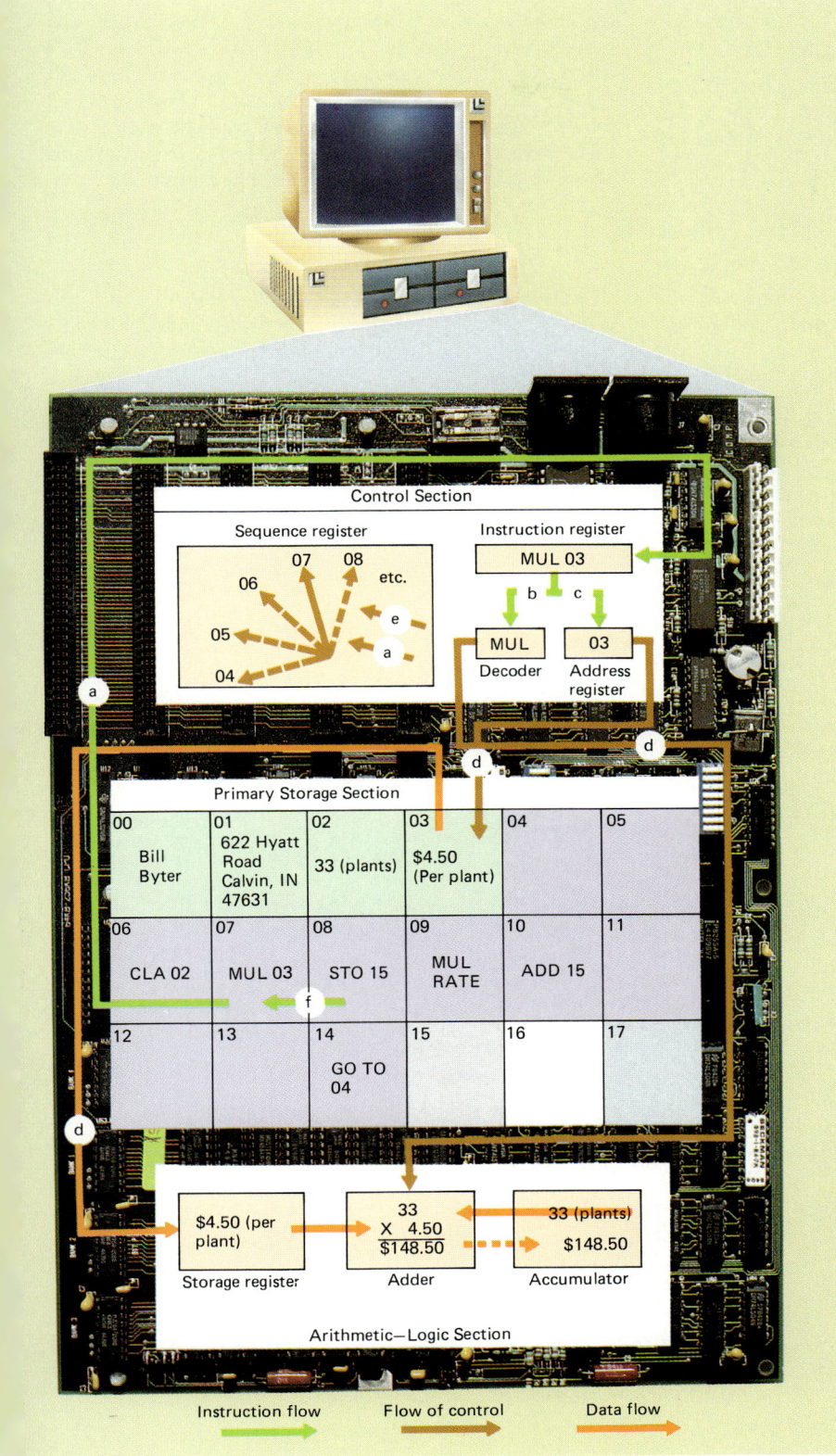

Primary Storage Section

00 Bill Byter	01 622 Hyatt Road Calvin, IN 47631	02 33 (plants)	03 $4.50 (Per plant)	04	05
06 CLA 02	07 MUL 03	08 STO 15	09 MUL RATE	10 ADD 15	11
12	13	14 GO TO 04	15	16	17

Arithmetic–Logic Section

- Storage register: $4.50 (per plant)
- Adder: 33 × 4.50 = $148.50
- Accumulator: 33 (plants) $148.50

Instruction flow → Flow of control → Data flow

FIGURE 4-D

The operation of a control section in a processor. An instruction to be executed is selected by a sequence register and read into an instruction register. The function to be performed is sent to a decoder where it is interpreted. The location of the data or other instruction to be manipulated is sent to an address register. A signal may then be sent to the ALU to execute the specified function using the contents of the specified address. These steps occur as each program instruction is considered. The circled letters in the lines refer to the steps discussed in the text.

the control section. (We'll have more to say about the sequence register in step e below.)

(b) The operation part (MUL) and the address part (03) of the instruction are separated. The operation is sent to the **decoder,** where it is *interpreted*. The computer is designed to respond to a number of commands, and it now knows that it's to multiply.

(c) The address part of the instruction is sent to the **address register.**

(d) The signal is sent to enter the contents of address 03 into the ALU. The command to multiply also goes to the ALU where the instruction is *executed*.

(e) The processing began when the sequence register was set to address 04, the location of the first program instruction. As each earlier instruction was executed, the sequence register automatically moved to the next instruction in the processing sequence. Now as the multiplication in address 07 is being executed, the sequence register is again automatically moved to address 08. Note, however, that when the sequence register gets to address 14, it encounters an instruction that reads GO TO 04. This instruction alters the advance of the sequence register and resets it to address 04.

(f) The instruction in address 08 moves into the instruction register, and the above steps are repeated.

There are two cycles or phases that occur as each program instruction is considered. Step *d* is the **execution cycle.** The other steps comprise the **instruction cycle.** Most computers are *synchronous* machines, and the steps mentioned above are synchronized by an electronic clock that emits millions of electrical pulses each second.

CHAPTER 5

ENTERING DATA

***THE KEYBOARD STALLS THE GROWTH
OF JAPANESE WORD PROCESSING***

The keyboard is the premier data entry device, with hundreds of millions in use on every sort of machine from typewriters to personal computers to mainframes to machine shop lathes. While increasing numbers of American office workers are adapting to the computer keyboard after years spent at the familiar typewriter, their Japanese counterparts face a more fundamental question: How do you use a keyboard?

The answer, if it is a keyboard for the Japanese language, is not easy. Some versions, with hundreds of keys and thousands of characters, are enough to give a typist nightmares.

As the Japanese struggle to automate their offices and develop their computer industry, one of the most formidable obstacles has been their own written language. Only recently have Japanese companies managed to develop practical word processors for Japanese. Now, they say, the door is open for office automation.

The most obvious obstacle facing office-equipment makers is how to squeeze 2,000 or more language characters onto a keyboard. Because of the difficulty and expense, typewriters never became commonplace in Japan. Most correspondence has either been handwritten or sent to a professional printer. But now, with the equipment available, Japanese office workers face the task of leaping directly from an age of handwriting to an age of word processors.

Devising a workable keyboard and teaching the Japanese how to use it are only parts of the problem. Compounding the difficulty of manufacturing for the Japanese market is the fact that the computers, printers, and display screens needed to handle Japanese characters must be far more powerful and have more capacity than machines used in the West.

The Japanese language uses about 7,000 Chinese characters known as *kanji*, although only about 2,000 are needed for day-to-day communication. In contrast, an English-language word processor need only store 128 characters. And where a Roman letter can be represented on a computer screen by 35 or 72 pixels, or dots, Japanese characters require 256 or 576 dots.

A big breakthrough in Japanese keyboard design came in 1978, when Toshiba introduced the first word processor to use a simpler set of Japanese characters known as *kana*. Kana, which represent the basic syllables of the Japanese language, are roughly akin to letters in English—any Japanese word can be represented by stringing enough kana together. With kana, it is possible to represent the entire language on only 50 keys. The Toshiba word processor allowed the user to type in a version of kana and have the computer change it to kanji. Nearly all Japanese computer and office automation companies that have since entered the market have produced keyboards that are variations of the kana system.

The ability to convert kana to kanji does not solve the entire problem. Japanese is full of words that sound alike but are written differently. The sound "yo," for instance, can be represented by 81 different kanji, each with a different meaning. The computer does not know which kanji to pick, so it presents a list of choices to the operator.

Makers of Japanese word processors are trying to make the computer do more of the work by programming it to analyze the sentence or look at previous situations in which the same word choice was made. Nevertheless, the process is tedious by American standards. The best word processor operators in Japan can type 60 words a minute, while an expert American typist can type more than 100 words a minute. So the drive is on to find improved solutions for entering the Japanese language into computers.

One approach would allow information to be fed into computers by handwriting. Machines capable of recognizing handwriting are starting to appear, but they are expensive and only work well when handwriting is near-type quality. Speech recognition is also a focus of research.

There is a positive side to the Japanese language problem. In developing computers to handle their language, the Japanese have gained an advantage in certain technologies. The Japanese are strong in printers and video displays in part because of the difficulties of printing and displaying kanji.

Adapted from Andrew Pollack, "The Keyboard Stymies Japan," *New York Times* June 7, 1984. Copyright © 1984 by The New York Times Company. Reprinted by permission.

LOOKING AHEAD

Chapter 5 introduces the input devices and media used to enter data into computer processing systems. The information in this chapter will enable you to:

- Describe the sources of input data, the location of data entry activities, and the methods for entering data in interactive and batch processing applications
- Explain the importance of input accuracy
- Outline the characteristics and applications of the several types of devices used for online data entry
- Identify the media and devices used for offline data entry

CHAPTER OUTLINE

LOOKING AHEAD
INPUT DATA: SOURCES AND CONCEPTS
Sources of Input Data
Data Entry Methods
Input Accuracy and Error Detection
DEVICES FOR ONLINE DATA ENTRY
Visual Display Terminals
User-Friendly Interfaces for VDTs and Personal Computers
Point-of-Sale Terminals
Financial Transaction Terminals
Teleprinters and Portable Data Entry Terminals
Voice Input Systems
MEDIA AND DEVICES FOR OFFLINE DATA ENTRY
Magnetic Tape
Floppy Disks
Character Readers
Feedback and Review 5
LOOKING BACK

INPUT DATA: SOURCES AND CONCEPTS

As you saw in Chapter 1, the information people need from a computer system to support their decisions and actions is produced by a series of data processing activities. The first step is to capture the necessary input data. Data processors may enter these data *directly* into the computer system (usually from the keyboard of an online workstation), or they may capture the data on some machine-readable medium *before* entering them into the system. Once in the computer, the data are manipulated to produce the desired information. Much of this chapter deals with the direct input devices and the media used for entering data. But before we look at these devices and media, let's briefly consider the sources of input data and then discuss some important concepts associated with the data entry function.

Sources of Input Data

Organizations obtain their input data from internal and external sources. The *internal* sources are the people in an organization who (1) respond to program questions, (2) enter inquiries, and (3) produce the data that must be processed.

When a salesperson asks whether a certain item is available, the inventory manager calls up the information on a computer screen and responds immediately. (Courtesy Texas Instruments Inc.)

Numerous examples of internal sources are found in Chapters 1 and 2. A banking officer supplies data in response to program queries and instantly receives needed information (see Figure 1-2, page 13). A salesperson inquires about the inventory status of a product and quickly receives information about the quantity available for sale (Figure 2-11, page 68). And Calvin city employees capture data on job tickets that are later used to process Elm Creek beautification charges (see Figure 1-12, page 25).

External sources of input data are the people and groups located outside the organization. These sources include patients, students, taxpayers, clients, customers, government agencies, suppliers, competitors—this list could go on and on. For example, hospitals need input data from patients and their doctors in order to submit health insurance claims, and these claims represent external data to the insurance companies processing them. And Sam Byter was an external data source to his savings and loan association when he made a deposit to his savings account (Figure 2-9, page 65).

Data Entry Methods

The *locations where the data are entered* into the computer system and the *timing of the processing required* usually determine which of the many possible data entry methods will be selected in a given situation.

The Location of Data Entry Activities
In some applications, an organization's data entry function is scattered or distributed to the sites where transactions occur. (The terms **source data automation** and **distributed data entry** are used to describe this approach.) In other applications, the data entry function is performed by a group of skilled operators located at a *central* computer site. Of course, some organizations use distributed data entry for some applications while maintaining a centralized data entry group for others.

The Timing of the Processing
You'll recall from Chapter 2 that *interactive processing* produces output results *immediately* after input data are entered into a computer system. When a computer system relies on scattered online data entry stations, such a quick response is often needed. For example, shoppers are waiting to make purchases at point-of-sale terminals, passengers are waiting to make reservations at airline or car rental stations, and depositors are waiting to deposit or withdraw money at teller machines—and none of these people like to be kept waiting!

Distributed *data collection stations* and interactive processing are also often used in factories, as shown in Figure 5-1. Let's assume that a manufacturer receives an order from a customer to make 10,000 picture frames. These frames are made out of strips of wood that are cut to length, fastened together, and painted. First, a shop order is prepared, and then the identical order data are entered into a work-in-process file in a direct-access storage device (DASD). (You'll recall from Chapter 2 that interactive processing requires direct files stored in DASDs.) A job control number is used to identify the order in the DASD. A copy of the shop order is sent to a shop supervisor and the job is put into production. As each activity is completed, workers use data collecting stations on the shop floor to *interact* with a computer program in order to update the job record in the DASD. Messages may be flashed under program control to a screen at the data collection station to guide the worker

162

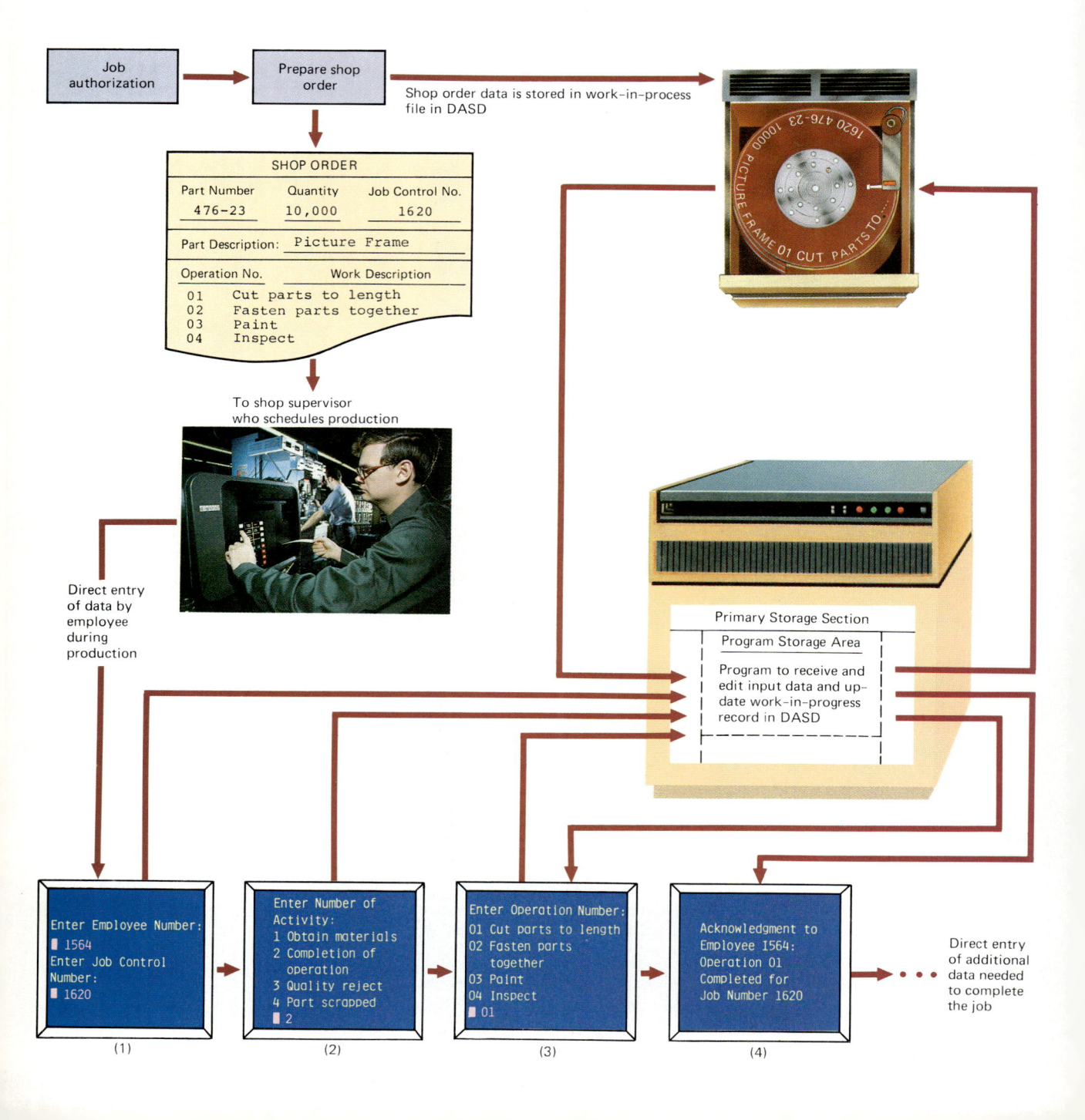

through the data entry activity. The caption of Figure 5-1 explains these messages.

When the timing isn't so critical, data at scattered locations may be gathered and stored for a period at **remote batch stations** (Figure 5-2). For example, a wildlife research agency headquartered in Maryland may have branches in Minnesota and Louisiana. The data gathered at the Minnesota site may be collected in a direct transaction file stored on a disk (Figure 5-2a), and the data at the Louisiana site may be captured in a sequential transaction file stored on a tape (Figure 5-2b). (Refer back to Figure 2-18, page 77, to refresh your memory about direct and sequential files.) The data accumulated at these sites are then periodically sent to headquarters in Maryland to update master files (Figure 5-2c). As shown in Figure 5-2, a *master file* is a relatively permanent file that contains all the existing records for a particular application. A *transaction file,* on the other hand, is one that's periodically created during the data gathering process to reflect the changes made to file records. A transaction file is used to update a master file.

Centralized data entry groups are generally created to support large batch processing applications. One such application is the **order entry/shipping/billing system** used by organizations that sell products to credit customers. Let's assume that Educator Supply Inc. (ESI) uses such a system to record orders, ship products, and send bills to its school customers. As you can see in Figure 5-3, the customer order is the first document generated in the *order entry* step. Typically prepared by an ESI salesperson or order clerk, this document provides the necessary input data. The display screens shown in Figure 5-3 will give you an idea of how the ESI data entry system works.

The entry of order data begins when the system displays the single line shown in screen 1. The operator enters the customer number and the codes used by ESI to designate different types of customers and orders (codes identify credit limits, normal or emergency orders, and so on). After the system automatically checks to see that the customer number is valid and the codes entered agree with those allowed for this customer, the second screen appears on the operator's display unit. The system uses the customer number to locate the customer's record in a file stored in a DASD, and then displays the **de-**

⬅ **FIGURE 5-1** *(facing page)*

Data entry in an interactive processing application used by manufacturing firms. Production order data are entered on a shop order and are stored in a work-in-process file in a DASD. When production begins, workers use *data collection stations* on the plant floor to update the job record in the work-in-process file. In our example, the worker is first asked to enter an employee number and the job control number (screen 1). The job control number is used to retrieve the job record from the DASD. A *menu* of possible activities related to the particular job is the next message displayed (screen 2). The worker keys in the correct activity number (here, the completion of a job task). The program then reads the job record and displays a menu of the operations required to finish the job (screen 3). In our example, the worker has indicated that the wood for the frames has now been cut to length. To check the accuracy of the data received, the program sends an acknowledgment message to the worker who can then correct any errors (screen 4). The same procedure is followed as additional tasks are completed. Such a system permits an up-to-the-minute account of the production status of each job in the work-in-process file. It can also be used to assign labor and material costs to each job. Managers can thus use the information produced by such a system to plan and control work flow and to analyze how efficiently people and machines are being utilized. (Photo © Ellis Herwig/The Image Bank™)

164

(a) Data entry approach used in Minnesota.

Remote batch station.

Transaction data stored in direct file.

Minnesota data are transmitted to Maryland.

Minnesota transaction data are loaded into DASD at central site.

Old master file kept in Maryland.

Louisiana transaction data are copied onto tape at central site.

(c) Processing carried out at central headquarters in Maryland.

Magnetic tape drive

Magnetic disk unit

(b) Data entry approach used in Louisiana

Printer

Remote batch station.

Transaction data may be keyed to a disk and then sorted into a proper sequence before being transferred to a tape.

Louisiana data are transmitted to Maryland.

Transaction data stored in sequential file in proper order.

Updated master file kept in Maryland.

Documents and reports that include Minnesota and Louisiana data.

Updated master file kept in Maryland.

→ Louisiana data

→ Minnesota data

← FIGURE 5-2 *(facing page)*

Interactive processing is often needed when the data entry function is distributed to the sites where the transactions occur. When the timing isn't so critical, data at scattered locations may be gathered at remote batch stations as shown here. The data at a Minnesota site (a) are collected in a direct transaction file stored on a disk, while the data at the Louisiana branch (b) are captured in a sequential transaction file stored on a magnetic tape. The data accumulated at both these sites are then periodically transmitted to headquarters in Maryland to update master files (c). (Photos courtesy Motorola/Four Phase Systems; Sperry Corp.)

fault data you see on screen 2 of Figure 5-3. Default data are values that will be correct *most* of the time, and these values are automatically supplied by the system to minimize keystrokes and improve an operator's productivity. In screen 2, the "bill to" and "tax code" default data won't change, but the operator must replace the "ship to" default item with the correct information. When screen 2 has been completed, the system displays screen 3 so that the items ordered can be entered. As you can see, the operator only needs to enter the item number and quantity data. The system is programmed to supply the rest of the order data. Once the keyed data have been captured on a machine-readable medium, such as a disk, they are then used to prepare ESI's *shipping* order and customer *bill* shown in Figure 5-3.

The same data are also used in several important *follow-up tasks*. One such ESI application is an **accounts receivable** (A/R) operation to keep track of the amounts owed by and the payments received from its customers. An-

A sales analysis computer program allows merchants to spot fast-selling items and reorder them before they run out of stock. (Courtesy Texas Instruments Inc.)

166

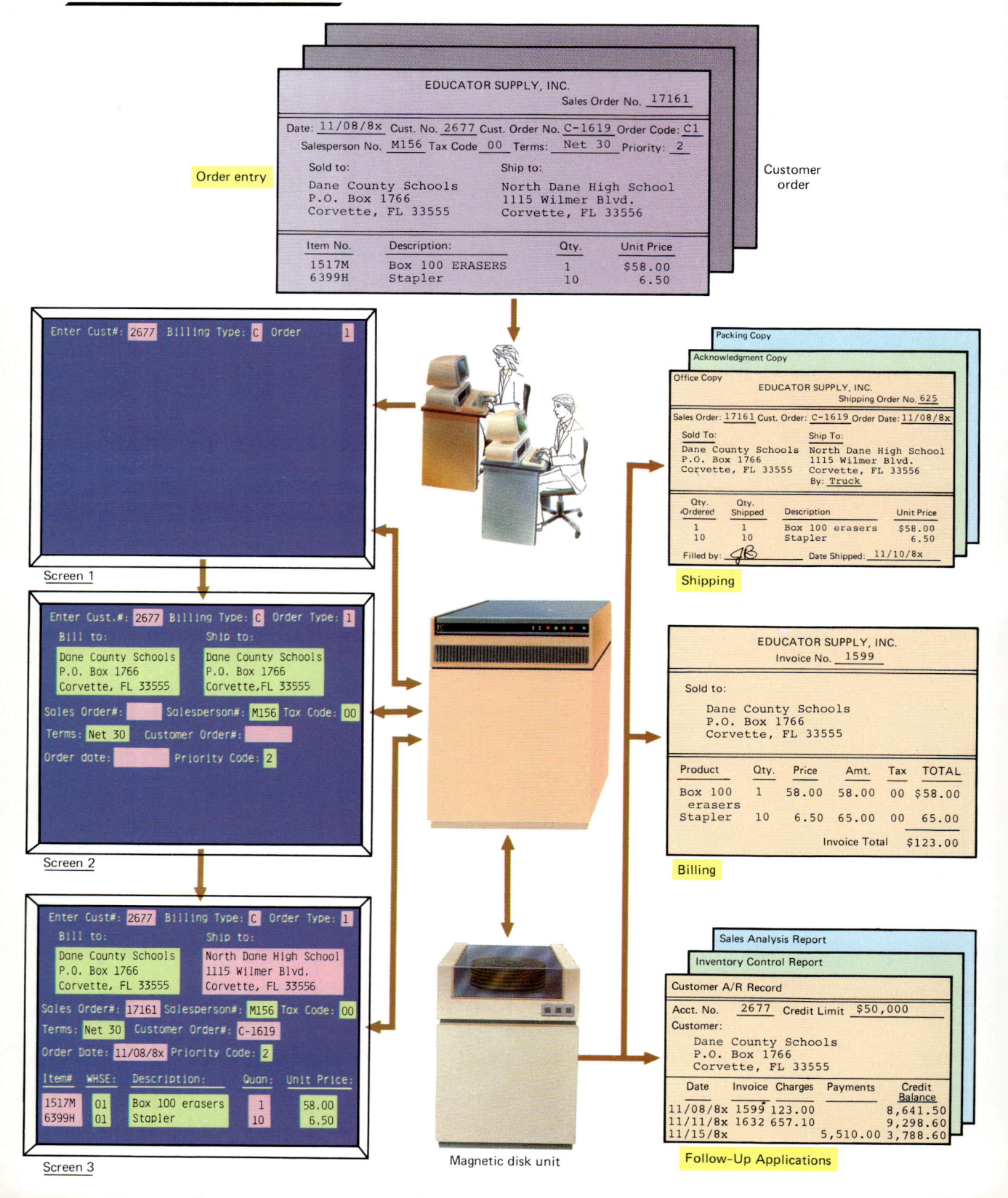

FIGURE 5-3 (facing page)

An example of the *order entry/shipping/billing* and *follow-up applications* supported by ESI's centralized data entry group. The input data are captured on customer order forms and are keyed into ESI's system by data entry operators. This system is controlled by ESI's central computer. Once the data have been keyed, they are then sent to a transaction file in a DASD. From there, they are subsequently processed by the central computer system to produce the *shipping orders, customer bills,* and other *follow-up documents* shown here. Multiple copies of the shipping order are made: One is needed by those filling and shipping the order, another is sent to the customer to acknowledge the order, and a third is packed with the shipment. After the order is shipped, a bill is sent to the customer. *Accounts receivable, inventory control,* and *sales analysis* applications then make use of the data that have been gathered.

other **inventory control** application uses quantity-sold data to (1) keep an up-to-date record of the availability of individual inventory items and (2) prepare reports that show which items to reorder or discontinue. And in a third **sales analysis** application, the data are examined and reports are prepared to show who's buying, what they're buying, how much they're ordering, where they're located, and so on.

In all of these ESI applications, batches of data are gathered for a time in a direct transaction file stored in a DASD. They are periodically retrieved and processed as a group to update master files and produce shipping orders, bills, and reports. The data entry stations used in this example are connected directly to ESI's central computer, and the trend in batch processing today is toward such online systems. (You saw in Chapter 2 that interactive processing is replacing batch processing in many applications.) If a small computer dedicated to data entry operations is used at a central location, this system may not be connected directly to the main processor unit. In this case, the central data entry system often uses the approach shown in Figure 5-2*b*. Data are first captured in sequential transaction files and are then used to update master files.

Input Accuracy and Error Detection

People have a greater effect on the quality of output of a data processing system than do the data processing machines. It's people who prepare the input data for the machines and thus determine the output quality. You've seen that if reliable programs are used, processors, storage units, and output devices generally produce predictable results. But these results will be correct only if the input prepared by people is accurate.

People can introduce data errors into a computer system in several ways. One way is to record data incorrectly on source documents. Suppose a customer orders an item with a code number of 6783, and the sales order is written to ship product number 6873. If this *transposition error* isn't caught in time, the wrong item will be shipped and an unhappy customer may be billed for an unwanted product. Errors with similar consequences occur when employees strike the wrong keys at online transaction-recording stations or when data entry operators make keying mistakes while copying accurate source document data on an input medium.

It's important to catch these errors as early as possible. The Institute of Computer Sciences & Technology of the U.S. Commerce Department estimates that an error detected at the time of data entry can be corrected at a cost of about 10 cents per character in error. Mistakes found after they are entered into a file, however, may cost $2 or more per character to correct. Of course, if errors cause people to ship the wrong product or if they cause other inappropriate actions, the possible costs can be much greater.

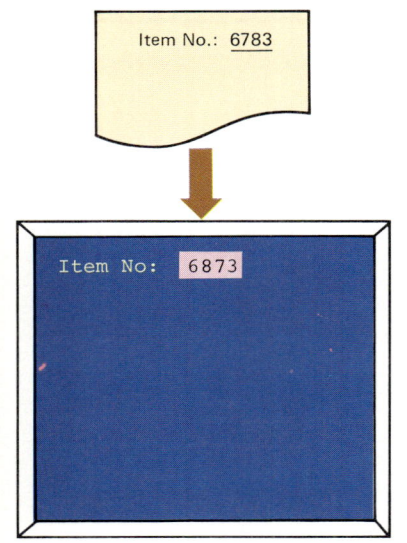

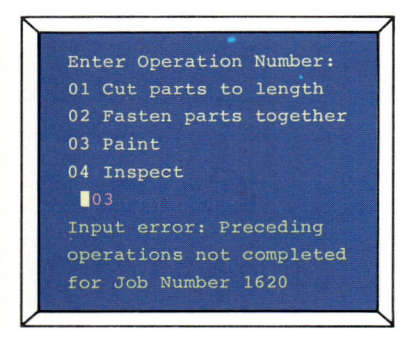

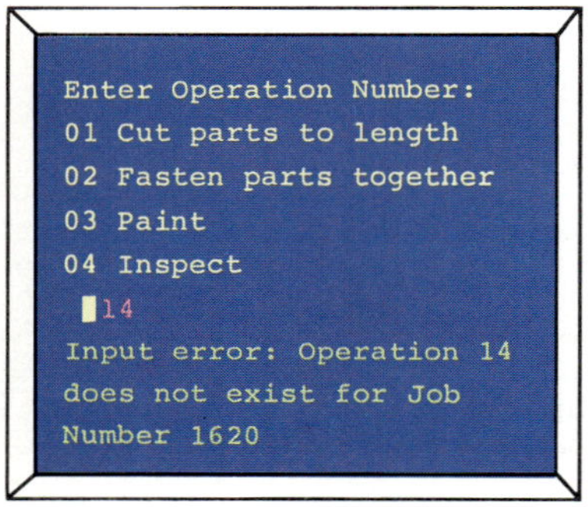

Input data are normally checked for errors before they are used in a processing application. The goal of an error-checking system is control. That is, the goal is to make sure that all transactions are identified, that these transactions are accurately recorded at the right time, and that all recorded transactions are then entered into the system.[1] A few of the possible error-detecting procedures are:

- *Accounting for prenumbered source documents.* A missing number in a batch of consecutively numbered source documents signals a missing form.

- *Using control totals.* After knowledgeable people have inspected and edited source documents, a **control total** can be prepared for each batch that is to be entered into the system. For example, the total number of items shipped to all customers can be computed for a batch of shipping orders before the orders are recorded on an input medium. The same total can then be obtained from the input medium to see if the figures match. This procedure allows people to detect the presence of one or more transcription errors.

- *Using programmed tests.* Instructions can be written in applications programs to check on the reasonableness of data as they enter the processing operation. The number of such checks is limited only by the programmer's imagination. In the manufacturing example shown in Figure 5-1, for example, **edit checks** can be made to ensure that workers don't enter letters in numeric data spaces, don't use inactive job control numbers, or don't indicate that picture frames have been painted *before* the parts have been cut to length. **Range checks** can also be written to ensure that numbers fall within an acceptable range of values. If a worker in Figure 5-1 entered an operation number of 14 for a job that only has 4 acceptable operations, a range check would cause an error message to be displayed on the screen of the data collection station. Finally, programmed **limit checks** can be used to verify that input data don't exceed reasonable upper or lower values. Such a check can catch inexcusable errors, such as the one that resulted in a high school student in Utah receiving a state tax refund check for $800,014.39 when the correct amount should have been $14.39.

Devices for Online Data Entry

There were about 8 million online data entry devices in use in the United States in 1983, and this number is expected to grow to 22 million by 1987. These devices are connected directly to and are under the control of the computer that will process the data. You've already encountered several of these

---

[1] Most organizations must try to strike a balance between input accuracy and cost control. From a control standpoint, an ideal system would catch every error. But such a system (assuming it could be built) would be slow and expensive. The total costs of operating this "errorless" system might easily top the costs required to operate a less accurate system and then correct at a later time the few errors that managed to slip through.

online stations in this book. In Chapter 2, an online financial transaction terminal updated Sam Byter's savings account. And you've just seen how factory data collection stations track the production status of jobs, and how data entry terminals process orders. The online data entry devices we'll now examine possess the following characteristics:

- They're able to enter data directly into the processor; intermediate data recording isn't required.

- They may be located at or near the data source, and this can be far away from the processor.

- They create a direct and interactive relationship between people and computers.

- They handle economically a low and/or irregular volume of input data.

Visual Display Terminals

By far the most popular input device used today for interactive processing and for the online entry of data for batch processing is the **visual display terminal (VDT).** A keyboard is used to enter data into a processor, and a video display unit—called a **cathode-ray tube (CRT)** or **monitor**—that looks like a television picture tube is used to display the keyed data and to receive messages and processed information from the computer (Figure 5-4).

Dumb, Smart, and Intelligent VDTs Several hundred VDT models currently are being offered by over 100 manufacturers. In an attempt to classify the bewildering range of available products, the computer industry has divided VDT offerings into dumb, smart, and intelligent categories. **Dumb terminals** are simple devices that immediately transmit each keyed data character to the processor. When a keying error occurs, the operator may need to backspace to the error and then rekey all later characters.

FIGURE 5-4

A visual display terminal (VDT) is made up of a keyboard and a video display unit, often called a cathode-ray tube (CRT) or monitor. VDTs are by far the most popular input devices for interactive processing and for the online entry of data for batch processing. About 2 million more CRT-based terminals are installed in U.S. organizations each year. (Courtesy Hewlett-Packard Co.)

Smart terminals provide additional features. They are designed with a *microprocessor chip* that contains the circuits needed to perform arithmetic-logic and control functions, and they have an internal storage capability. They can move the **cursor**—a highlighted screen symbol (usually a rectangle or an underline mark) that points to the placement of the next character—in all directions to add, delete, and change keyed characters. If there's an error in a line of text, the operator can move the cursor to the place where the correction is needed, and the change can be made without disturbing the rest of the line. Special **function keys** may be included in the keyboard. For example, let's assume that smart terminals are used in Figure 5-3 to enter Educator Supply's order data into the ESI system. When the operator has keyed the necessary data shown in screen 3 of Figure 5-3, a single stroke of a function key might be used to (1) transmit all those facts to the processor and (2) present the operator with a fresh screen 1 display so that data can be entered for the next order. This example shows that smart terminals can store and consolidate input data prior to sending them to the processor. But smart terminals can't normally be programmed by users.

Intelligent terminals combine VDT hardware with built-in microprocessors that *are* user-programmable. They can be used to process small jobs without the need to interact with a larger computer. Online secondary floppy-disk storage devices are often used to process these jobs. Programmed checks can be used to test the validity of input data being entered at the intelligent terminal or at dumb terminals linked to the intelligent station. After data have been collected and edited, they can be stored for later transmission to a larger computer. The cost of adding microcomputer components to a dumb terminal has now dropped so low that almost all new VDTs have smart or intelligent features to help make data entry and retrieval easier for people.

What's the difference between an intelligent terminal and a personal computer (pc)? There's very little difference. The keyboards, screens, storage/processor chips, and online floppy-disk units are just like those used in many pc's. The intelligent VDT is designed with circuits that permit it to communicate with other terminals and larger processors, while most pc's have been designed primarily to operate alone. But plug-in hardware and appropriate software both allow interaction between mainframes and many popular pc's. And other plug-in modules are available to convert existing dumb and smart terminals into full-fledged microcomputers. For example, Digital Equipment

An intelligent terminal. Because most VDTs now include intelligent features that make them user-programmable, they often resemble personal computers in looks and functions. (Courtesy Wang Laboratories, Inc.)

Corporation produces a slide-in circuit board that turns its VT100 terminal into a micro, and IBM has an attachment that gives its 3278 terminals many of the capabilities of its PC family. Technology has blurred the distinctions that once existed between some types of terminals and pc's.

User-Friendly Interfaces for VDTs and Personal Computers

An **interface** is a shared boundary. It may be the boundary between two systems or devices, but in the context used here it's the hardware or software connection that permits communication between people and computers. This connection was accomplished in the past when computer specialists keyed in the types of cryptic codes shown in Figure 5-5. But most people who work with computers today aren't computer specialists. They may have limited computer experience, or they may be knowledgeable users who are too busy to learn a new set of interface rules for every new hardware or software package. In either case, what these people want is an interface that's **user friendly**—one that has hardware that's easy and comfortable to use and software that's easy to learn.

Most people interact with VDTs or pc hardware/software packages. And most suppliers of these packages regularly claim user-friendly features for their products. *When* these claims are true, the products are likely to include many of the hardware and software properties discussed in the following sections.

Keyboard/Display Features Since data are typically entered through keyboards and displayed on screens, VDT and pc users welcome improvements in these interface components. Some features that make *keyboards* easier and more comfortable to use are:

- **Function keys.** Some keyboards have less than 60 keys while others add dozens more. Some of these extra keys carry labels to indicate the types of functions they perform. For example, HOME and END keys allow users to move instantly to the beginning or end of a stored document; CURSOR keys move the screen pointer up, down, left, and right; the PAGE UP and PAGE DOWN keys allow users to move through a stored document a page at a time; the INSERT and DELETE keys permit users to add and erase stored characters; and the PRINT SCREEN key can be used to produce a printed copy of the information displayed on the screen. Other function keys are merely stamped F1, F2, F3, and so on, and are used in many different ways by the programs being run. For example, a word processing program can use the F7 key to underline text and the F8 key to designate that text should be printed in a bold typeface. As long as this word processing program is being used, these keys will always perform the same functions. But different software will program the same keys to perform other functions.

- **Numeric keypads.** A row of numeric keys appears near the top of almost all keyboards. But many VDT and pc units also include a separate numeric keypad. These keys are arranged like those on a calculator to permit rapid entry of numeric data.

- **Detached keyboards.** **Ergonomics** is the science of designing machines so that the human-machine interface is comfortable, convenient, and effi-

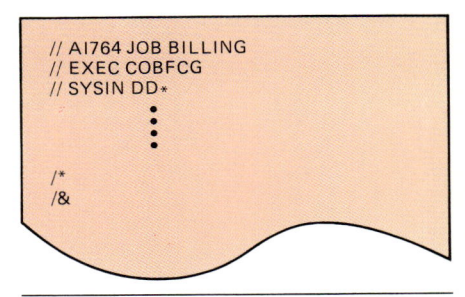

171

```
// A1764 JOB BILLING
// EXEC COBFCG
// SYSIN DD*
    .
    .
    .
/*
/&
```

FIGURE 5-5

A few of the cryptic codes that might be used to tell a computer to process a billing program. Such communication between people and machines may be satisfactory when the people are computer specialists. But it hardly represents a "friendly" interface for most of today's computer users.

The detached keyboard of this personal computer includes both function keys, in grey, and a numeric keypad at the right. The color monitor enhances the graphics display. (Courtesy Zenith Data Systems)

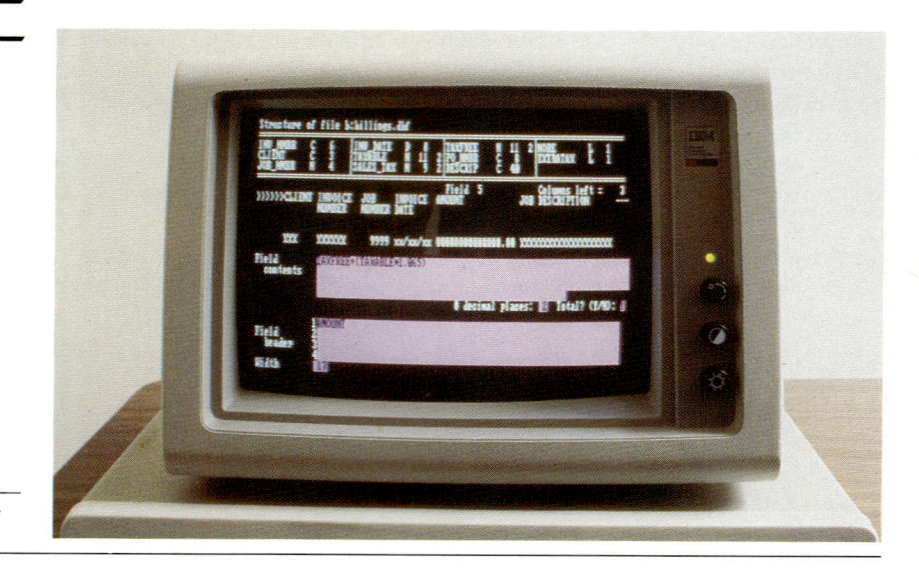

Reverse video highlights an on-screen color display. (Courtesy Ashton-Tate)

The light-colored boxes on this touch screen act like function keys on a keyboard. (Courtesy Hewlett-Packard Co.)

cient. A few years ago, it was common to find a VDT or pc keyboard and screen housed in a common cabinet. Nowadays, though, nearly every new VDT and pc designed for desktop use has a separate keyboard so that the operator can move it to any desk or lap position that's comfortable. Many of these detached keyboards are "low-profile" versions that provide tilt adjustments.

Some features that make *screens* easier and more pleasant to use are:

- ***Reverse video.*** Monochrome (one-color) screens often display characters in a single color (e.g., green, amber, or white) on a dark background. Let's assume that we have a screen that displays green characters. When the **reverse video** feature is programmed, a section of this screen is shaded with a green background, and the characters displayed on this background are dark. Reversing the normal screen pattern in this way serves to highlight areas of the screen that require operator attention.

- ***Color.*** Reverse video can also be used to good effect with color displays. For example, the feature can be used in the order entry screens shown in Figure 5-3 to highlight the places where entries are needed. The growing popularity of color CRTs is partly explained by recent dramatic price reductions. In addition, many operators prefer them and report fewer instances of eye fatigue and blurred vision.

- ***Enhanced graphics capabilities.*** Many intelligent VDTs and pc's are designed to display *alphanumeric* data and are used to enter and retrieve letters, numbers, and special characters. But other systems also possess *graphics* capabilities. Such graphic systems permit the display screen to be divided (or "mapped") into thousands of picture elements. Each picture element, or **pixel,** is controlled by the contents of a specific location in storage. By turning each pixel on or off, the processor is able to paint a graphic image on the screen. A screen capable of displaying a large number of pixels can give users high-resolution images in multiple colors.

- *Touch-screen capabilities.* Some VDT and pc systems allow users to enter limited amounts of data simply by touching sensitive areas of the screen. For example, small boxes displayed on a **touch screen** may perform like special function keys. Touching one of these boxes may cause the system to store a document, center a line, or carry out some other preprogrammed task. Touch screens are also used for *menu-driven* applications where the operator can simply point to a menu choice and receive a response from the system. Although "user friendly," touch screens cannot be used to enter large amounts of data.

- *Improved ergonomic designs.* Newer screens can swivel and tilt so that operators can move them to comfortable positions. Monochrome displays using white characters on dark backgrounds are being replaced by screens featuring green or amber characters that are easier on the eyes. The sharpness or resolution of the displayed characters has been improved, and special screen coatings are being used to reduce glare.

Other Hardware Interfaces The mouse, light pen, and input tablet are input devices that are often used with VDT and pc systems. A **mouse** is a pointing device about the size of a tape cassette. It usually rolls on a small bearing and has one or more buttons on the top. When a user rolls the mouse across a flat surface, such as a desk, the screen cursor moves in the direction of the mouse's movement. For example, if the user rolls the mouse forward and to the right, the cursor moves up and to the right on the screen. Perhaps this movement positions the cursor on a menu choice that the user has selected. With a click of the mouse's button, the system can then be notified of this choice.

Because the cursor follows the way the user's hand moves the mouse, the user has a sense of pointing at something on the screen. Positioning a cursor with a mouse is easier for nontypists than pressing various key combinations

---

WINDOW 5-1

KO FOR PUNCHED CARDS

Modern computers accept data entered directly by users or stored on magnetic media, but these media and the devices that accept input have changed radically in the last few decades. A typical computer center 25 years ago relied on a different type of input device from those shown in Figure 1-9: the card reader. Data were entered on punched cards.

Punched cards were first used in the nineteenth century to program weaving looms and they were used in the first computer systems to code data and programs. A firm that later became one of the foundations of IBM was founded by the man who developed the punched card coding scheme: Herman Hollerith. At the height of card demand in the 1960s, eight IBM plants and several competitors produced tons of cards used in the batch processing systems that dominated data processing at that time. In the 1970s, the prices of online terminals dropped and personal computers were born. As more users were able to work directly with central processors, punched card sales plummeted. IBM closed the last of its punched card plants in 1984 due to lack of demand.

Punched cards had many drawbacks. They were slow to process, cumbersome, and easily damaged. A few data processing centers still rely on punched cards from other suppliers because they use older equipment to process data. But the U.S. government, which relied on punched cards to pay its bills for 40 years, switched to multicolored paper checks in 1985. Before long, when the last few holdouts switch to the reliability and speed of online processing, the punched card's stern warning not to bend, fold, spindle, or mutilate it will be a thing of the past.

Source: Edward Warner, "The Bell Tolls for Punch Cards at IBM Production Plants," *Computer World,* September 7, 1984.

and is similar to using the **joystick** game controllers found in video arcades and home computer systems. With the proper software, a mouse can also be used to "draw" pictures on the screen and edit text.

A **light pen** is another pointing device that can be used to choose a displayed menu option. The pen consists of a photocell placed in a small tube. As the user moves the tip of the pen over the screen surface, it's able to detect the light coming from a limited field of view. The light from the screen causes the photocell to respond when the pen is pointed directly at a lighted area. This electrical response is transmitted to a processor, which can identify the menu option that's triggering the photocell. The light pen is also useful for graphics work. The user "draws" directly on the screen with the pen. By using the pen and a keypad attached to the VDT or pc, the user can select different colors and line thicknesses, can reduce or enlarge drawings, and can add or erase lines.

Input tablets are also graphics instruments. These tablets come in different sizes and are usually classified as **digitizer tablets** or **graphics tablets**. A typical tablet is a work surface that contains hundreds of copper lines that form a grid. This grid is connected to a computer. Each copper line receives electrical pulses. A special pen or *stylus* attached to the tablet is sensitive to these pulses and is used to form the drawings. (A device with crosshairs can also be used to copy existing drawings into a computer.) However, the pen does not mark directly on the tablet. Instead, a designer, architect, or other user traces a sketch on a piece of paper placed on the tablet. The tablet grid senses the exact position of the stylus as it moves and transmits this information to the processor.

The developing sketch is displayed on the screen. But there's a difference between the drawings and the display. Poorly sketched lines are displayed as straight; poor lettering is replaced by neat printing; and poorly formed corners become mathematically precise. Changes and modifications in the drawing can be quickly made. For example, a line can be "erased" from, or shifted on, the display unit with a movement of the stylus. Once the initial sketching is finished and satisfactorily displayed, the computer may then be instructed to analyze the design and report on certain characteristics. For example, the computer might be asked to work out the acoustical properties of a theater design or evaluate the flight characteristics of an aircraft design. The user may then use this analysis to modify the sketch. This interactive graphics capability helps people save valuable time for more creative work.

A designer uses a graphics tablet and its stylus to create the graphic design shown on the color monitor. (Courtesy Computervision)

Software Features   Hardware that's easy and comfortable to use is a desirable part of the human-machine interface. But the best keyboards and screens are of questionable value to most VDT and pc operators if they have to follow difficult procedures to enter programs and then memorize complex commands in order to accomplish any useful work. Recognizing this fact, software developers have reduced the frustration for VDT and pc users by producing packages that are easier to learn and simpler to use than those of just a few years ago. Most of these packages incorporate menus, and many use icons and simulate a desktop environment. Let's look at each of these features.

In contrast to **command-driven programs** that often require VDT or pc users to learn complex and confusing interface "languages," **menu-driven programs** lead users through a series of data entry and processing procedures, giving and requesting information as necessary *at each program level* to complete a task. As you can see in Figure 5-6, a **main menu** is typically followed by second-level menus, then third-level menus, and so on. As users move through these lower-level menus (called **submenus**), the choices become more detailed. Menus at all levels typically include a title, the possible options, and some type of **prompt**, or message, telling the user how to respond. Reverse video is often used to highlight the prompt.

In Figure 5-6 the user has selected the word processing function from the main menu of an integrated software package by entering the number 2 in response to the prompt message. A second-level word processing menu then appears on the screen. (Other submenus are called up when other main-menu selections are made.) This word processing menu has seven selections. The caption in Figure 5-6 explains how the user can make selections in order to retrieve and then print a stored document.

Figure 5-6 shows you one way that menus can be presented so that users can make their selections. But there are many other program formats to present selections to users. For example, the main menu shown at the top of Figure 5-6 could be replaced with a screen that shows the options as drawings on a **simulated desktop** (Figure 5-7). These drawings, or **icons,** are pictures

FIGURE 5-6

Menu-driven programs lead users through a series of procedures so that they can accomplish useful work. Here the operator is using the word processing function in an integrated software package to retrieve and then print a stored document. The word processing option is selected in response to the main-menu prompt. A word processing submenu is then flashed on the screen and the operator selects the fourth option—the GET/SAVE choice—to retrieve the document (screen A). There are two prompts on the GET/SAVE submenu. The *first* tells the program that the user wants to retrieve a stored document; the *second* tells the program that the document is stored on a disk in drive B under the TAXLTR name the user has given it. The program then retrieves the document and returns the user to the word processing menu. Next, the user selects DEFINE PAGE (option 2) from this menu (screen B). The margin spacings shown in the DEFINE PAGE menu are the *default values* assigned by the program. The user decides to leave these values unchanged and returns to the word processing menu to select the PRINT function (option 3). Since TAXLTR is a five-page document, the program assumes that the user wants to print it all. That happens to be correct in this case, so the user moves to the PAUSE BETWEEN PAGES prompt. The default value is N (for no), but since the user wants to load each blank sheet of paper into the printer, this value is changed to Y (for yes). The other default values are correct, so the user turns on the printer and presses a function key on the keyboard to begin the printing operation. Such a menu-driven procedure can be learned quickly and easily.

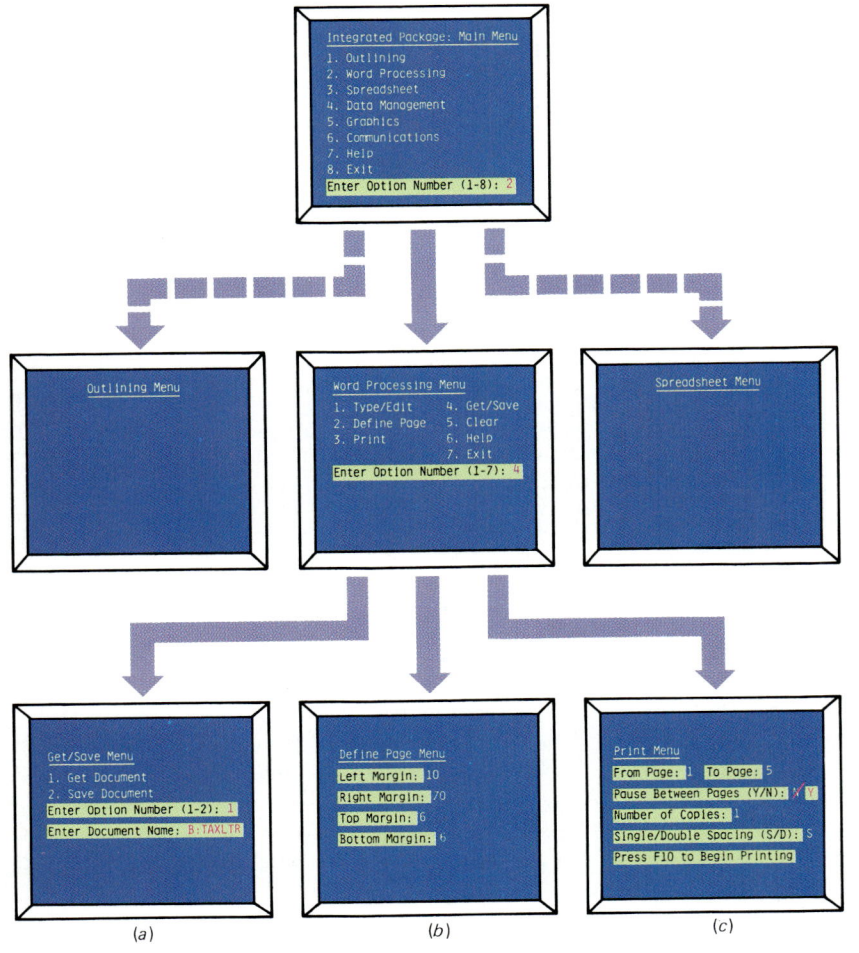

(a) (b) (c)

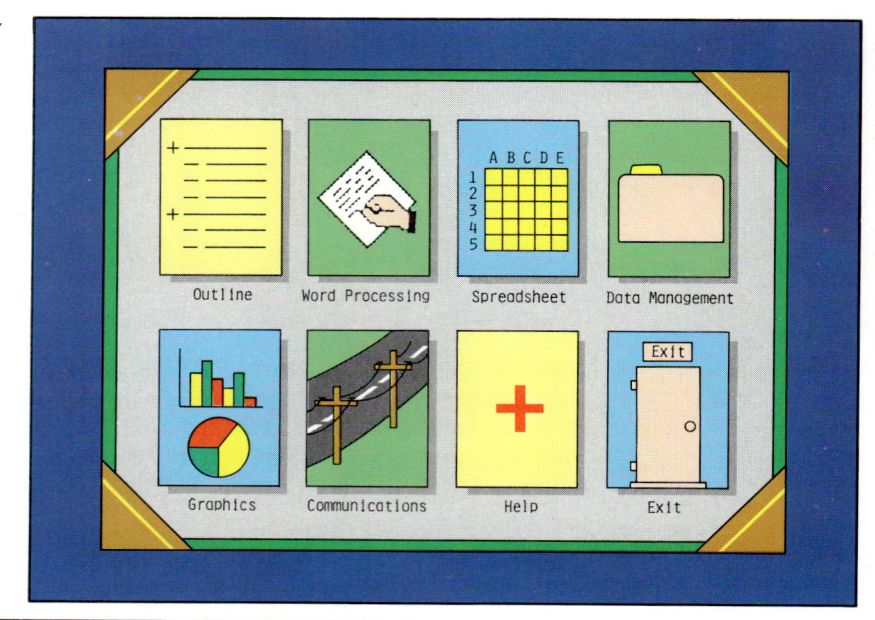

FIGURE 5-7

Users can select a program option by identifying the appropriate icon on a simulated desktop. In this case, a mouse is used to position the screen cursor symbol (an arrow here) near the word processing icon, and the word processing function is then selected by clicking the mouse's button.

FIGURE 5-8

An alternative to the full-screen word processing menu shown in Figure 5-6 is the menu line shown at the top of this screen. This line remains displayed throughout the time the word processing program is being used. The "Get" command in the menu line is used to retrieve a stored document, and a pull-down menu appears under this word to facilitate retrieval. The word "Format" in the menu line corresponds to the DEFINE PAGE option shown in the word processing menu in Figure 5-6, and the pull-down menu shown here corresponds to the DEFINE PAGE menu shown in Figure 5-6. The default options shown in the braces can be changed by the user. After retrieving the stored document and checking the page format, the user can select the word "Print" in the menu line, call up its pull-down menu, and then print the document.

that represent the options that can be picked. Users can select an option by pressing a designated function key or by pressing a button on a mouse used to position the screen cursor near the icon representing the desired choice.

Another approach that's often used is to display a **menu line** of key words across the top or bottom of the screen. The words in the line represent available options. The menu line for a particular program generally remains displayed throughout the time that program is being used. The user can select an option from this line at any time, and when a choice is made, a **pull-down** (sub)**menu** may then be displayed. For example, the full-screen word processing menu shown in Figure 5-6 can be replaced by the equivalent menu line shown in Figure 5-8, and the DEFINE PAGE submenu in Figure 5-6 can be replaced by the pull-down version shown in Figure 5-8.

Icons are often combined with menu lines and pull-down menus. And when integrated software packages are used, the main-menu line may be displayed at all times; the current contents of the word processing, spreadsheet, and other functions supported by the package may be shown simultaneously in separate *windows,* or portions of the display screen, just as sheets of paper might be scattered about on a desk; and icons and pull-down menus may be used to enter data and then move them from window to window. Software that simulates a desktop in this way eases the human-machine interface for many people.

Menus can speed the learning process and help people become productive users in a short time. But once a system has been learned, many users prefer to enter a few commands and get on with their work rather than page through several menu levels. For this reason, some software packages provide menus and on-screen help messages and tutorials for infrequent users, but give others the option of bypassing those menus and messages.

Most people who enter data into computer systems use the types of keyboards, screens, and interface software that we've now discussed. But there are a number of other important online data entry devices that we can't ignore.

Number System Character
0 = Grocery products
3 = Drugs and health-related products, etc.

Manufacturer's Identification Number
16000 = General Mills
21000 = Kraft Foods, etc.

Product/Part Code Number
66210 = 18-ounce box of Wheaties
67670 = 10-ounce box of Buc Wheats, etc.

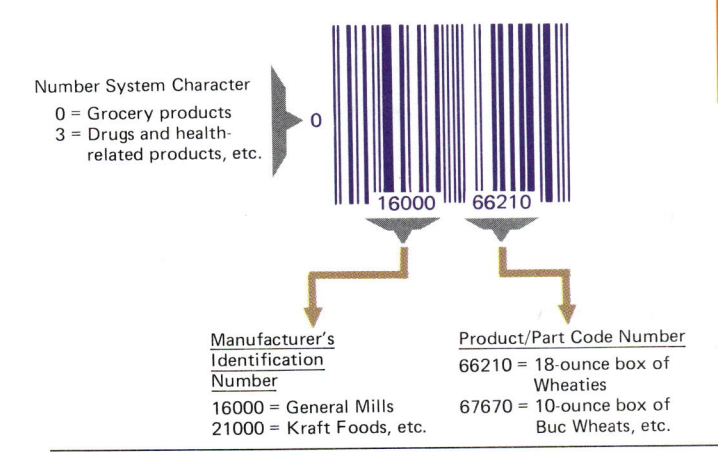

FIGURE 5-9

The Universal Product Code used to represent an 18-ounce box of Wheaties.

Point-of-Sale Terminals

Data can be coded in the form of light and dark bars, and these **bar codes** are commonly used today to identify merchandise in retail stores. For example, manufacturers print a **Universal Product Code (UPC)** on most items sold in grocery stores. The next time you spring out of bed at 6 A.M. to have a hearty breakfast before your eight o'clock class, be sure to notice that your cereal box has a code similar to the one shown in Figure 5-9. When bar-coded items are received at a supermarket's automated checkout stand, they are pulled across a fixed scanning window. As items are scanned, the bars are decoded by a device called an **optical character reader.** Reflected light patterns are converted into electrical pulses and then transmitted to recognition logic circuits. There they are compared with the patterns the reader has been programmed to recognize. If a suitable comparison is made, the data are transmitted to a computer that looks up the price, possibly updates inventory and sales records, and forwards price and description information back to the checkout stand.

Besides using optical readers at checkout stands, store personnel can also use hand-held "wands" attached to portable recording devices to replenish the store's inventory. When an item must be restocked, the wand reads the item's bar code that's fastened to the shelf where the item is displayed. This reading accurately enters the item description into the recorder. The clerk keys the quantity needed into the recorder. The recorder can then be connected by telecommunications lines to a warehouse computer system to complete the reordering procedure.

But **point-of-sale (POS) terminals** aren't restricted to reading bar codes. They can also read printed information. By passing a wand across a special tag attached to department store merchandise, a clerk can read the item description and price into a terminal. Under computer control, the terminal displays the scanned data and then prints an itemized sales receipt that shows the total amount of the purchase including taxes. If a credit card is used, the wand can read and enter the credit card numbers into the computer to update the customer's account. Transaction data can also be used to update inventory records and provide sales data to managers for analysis.

The scanning window in this supermarket's automated checkout stand uses a laser beam to read UPC bar codes. (Courtesy IBM Corp.)

WINDOW 5-2

HIGH-DENSITY BAR CODES FOR DATA INPUT

The question of how to distribute computer programs and data has long been debated among manufacturers of microcomputers. Originally, floppy-disk drives were too expensive to be practical for storing data and programs; a single drive cost more than a basic personal computer itself.

At the time, audio cassettes were trumpeted as the most cost-effective answer. Though exceedingly slow, they were still a decided improvement on the punched paper tape that had been used to load software into a personal computer.

The idea of programs on paper did not die, however. Around 1978 some computer experts predicted that bar codes would become the preferred method of distributing software. They expected to see entire magazines containing nothing but page after page of those black lines of uneven width now familiar as the Universal Product Code label and seen on everything from breakfast cereals to packages of pantyhose. The computerist, they foretold, would take one of these magazines home, run a reading wand down the columns one after the other, and thereby feed the computer the latest exciting program from the Top 40 chart.

There were three things wrong with this outline. First, people did not buy programs the way they bought magazines and boxes of cereal. Second, using a reading wand to scan the bar codes was a tedious and imprecise process. The final blow to the bar code movement was dealt by the floppy disks. The price of both the drives and the disks began to plummet.

Because a floppy-disk system permits the user to load data from a disk into the computer, and provides storage for computer-generated data on disks as well, this superior arrangement won out over both cassettes and bar codes. The idea of paper-conveyed software was buried once and for all. Or so it seemed.

Now, however, the concept has surfaced again in Softstrip, from Cauzin Systems of Waterbury, Connecticut. Softstrip is the old bar code in new attire, its most significant innovation being that it can hold 30 or 40 times as much information per square inch of surface area as traditional bars do.

A Softstrip is $5/8 \times 9 1/2$ inches—a size chosen to conform to the requirements of most magazines—and stores the equivalent of 5,000-plus characters. A letter-size paper covered with such strips could hold close to 50,000 characters, the equivalent of 30 double-spaced typed pages.

A major use of the Softstrip is loading data from magazines and newspapers into a pc. The Wall Street stock tables, if listed in this format, could be loaded into a computer's memory in minutes, more quickly and cheaply than downloading this information from some distant data base via telephone channels. Some publishers are planning to reproduce the indexes of scientific publications in bar-coded format so that listed articles could be loaded into data bases instantly.

Will the Softstrip remove some of the tedium of entering repetitive data into a computer? Will it be challenged by optical character scanners that can read the same print as humans do? It provides an inexpensive alternative to the job of data entry, and it should prove popular until our ever-changing technology offers a cheaper, faster substitute.

Adapted from Erik Sundberg-Diment, "Supermarket Bar Codes are Applied to Software," *New York Times*, October 15, 1985. Copyright © 1985 by The New York Times Company. Reprinted by permission.

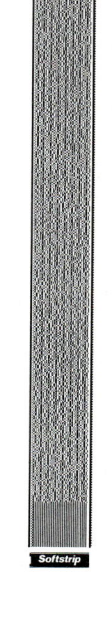

Financial Transaction Terminals

In addition to the online teller terminals used to handle customer deposits and withdrawals, there are several other types of **financial transaction terminals** in common use. Some of these devices are used in the electronic transfer of funds. One such **electronic funds transfer (EFT)** station is the **automated teller machine** (or **ATM**).

An ATM is an *unattended* device that's located on or off the financial institution's premises to receive and dispense cash and to handle routine financial transactions 24 hours a day. To date more than 70 million plastic "currency" or "debit" cards have been issued for use in ATMs. Your account number and credit limit are magnetically encoded on a strip of tape on the back of the card. When the card is inserted into the ATM, the terminal reads and then transmits the tape data to a processor which activates your account. By following instructions displayed on a screen and pushing a few keys, you direct the computer to carry out transactions.

A technological alternative to ATMs is used in Europe (see the Closer Look reading at the end of this chapter). Instead of a magnetic strip, the card has a built-in microcomputer chip. This chip can store a considerable amount of information. Data representing a specific amount of cash can be encoded in the chips before the cards are issued to customers. As the cards are used to make purchases, parts of the stored data are destroyed by special electronic registers used by merchants. These electronic registers are not connected to a computer. In effect, customers gradually "cash in their chips" and use up their electronic money. These "smart cards" also can store a record of more than 100 purchases. Look for competition between ATM/magnetic strip technology and smart cards in the future.

An ATM isn't the only type of EFT station that's connected directly to financial computers. Other stations owned by financial institutions are located at the checkout counters of stores, hotels, hospitals, and in railroad and airline terminals. These EFT stations are used to verify that a customer's check or credit card transaction will be honored. They can also be used to electronically transfer funds from a shopper's account to a merchant's account. A Touch-Tone telephone can also become an EFT terminal. A depositor can call up a bank computer, enter data through the telephone buttons, and transfer funds to or from an account.

Teleprinters and Portable Data Entry Terminals

A **teleprinter terminal** has a keyboard for data entry and a built-in printer that records typed input and produces computer-processed output. Tens of thousands of small portable teleprinters are being used today by salespeople, managers, newspaper reporters, engineers, and others on the move.

A portable teleprinter (or a portable terminal or microcomputer that substitutes a small flat display screen for a printer), in effect, lets these people take a computer with them wherever they go. For example, a sales representative can attach the terminal to a customer's telephone, dial in to a company computer system, key in questions about the availability of stock, and receive immediate confirmation on the terminal printer that the customer's order can be filled. If a sale is then made, the sales order can be keyed directly into the system from the customer's office. Similarly, a lawyer can carry a terminal along on a business trip and keep up with office work during airport layovers or hotel stays. And a reporter can type and file a story into a computer system from a remote location.

Some portable terminals are battery-powered, weigh less than 2 pounds, and are small enough to fit in the palm of your hand. These terminals have small keyboards and are used to send data to a computer, but they often have little or no ability to receive information from the processor. Such devices are often used by salespeople as electronic order books. For example, a route salesperson calling on retailers can carry a terminal through a customer's store. When items are found to be in short supply, the salesperson can key in the product number and quantity needed into the terminal. (Or, as we've seen, bar codes may be read by a penlike optical reading wand that may be attached

A traveling sales representative uses his portable terminal to send sales information to his home office over the telephone while waiting for his flight. (Courtesy Texas Instruments Inc.)

to the terminal.) Semiconductor storage chips are then generally used to hold the data that have been entered in the terminal. Every few hours, or at the end of the day, the salesperson can attach the terminal to a telephone and send the orders in to a company computer system.

Voice Input Systems

Input devices do nothing more than convert human language into machine language. Why, then, doesn't someone invent a machine that will let a person talk to the computer in English? As a matter of fact, a few manufacturers have done just that. A *microphone* or telephone is used to convert human speech into electrical signals. The signal patterns are then transmitted to a computer where they are compared to a "dictionary" of patterns that have been previously placed in storage. When a close match is found, a word is "recognized" and the computer then produces the appropriate output.

Most voice recognition systems are **speaker-dependent.** That is, they can't be used until after the speaker has repeated a word several times to "train" the system to recognize his or her particular voice pattern. Recently, however, **speaker-independent** systems have been developed that can recognize words spoken by anyone. But no existing system can recognize an unlimited number of words spoken in a continuous stream. Vocabularies of all systems are very limited, users must speak distinctly, and they must pause between each word or each short phrase. In one experiment, the words "recognize speech" were interpreted as "wreck a nice beach" by the computer. Other problems in speech recognition are caused by speaker accents and dialects (people's voice prints are as unique as their fingerprints), and the fact that the meaning of words can vary depending on the context in which they are used.[2]

Although speech recognition is in its infancy, it's likely to be used much more often in situations where a person's hands are busy, where a worker's eyes must remain fixed on a display or measuring instrument, or where telephone input is desirable. For example:

● A "hands busy" loading dock employee at a Ford Motor Company warehouse can pick up a package, read the package destination into a microphone, and then put the package on a conveyor belt. The system then moves the package to the correct storage location. A similar United Parcel system zips packages into the right trucks as workers read destinations aloud.

● A state employee in Illinois gets clearance to make a long-distance phone call on the state's private lines by calling a computer and reciting his or her authorization number into the system. If the number is accepted, the computer then switches the employee to the next available long-distance line.

MEDIA AND DEVICES FOR OFFLINE DATA ENTRY

You saw in Figure 5-3 how data entered directly into a computer system from *online* terminals can be accumulated into batches for later processing. But you

---

[2] Scientists from IBM have been working for a decade on a word processing system that can take dictation. However, a commercial product that can do this seems at least another decade away.

also saw in Figure 5-2 that data for batch processing may be transferred from source documents to a machine-readable medium through the use of *offline* devices.

For decades, card punch machines were the most popular offline data entry device, and **punched cards** were used as the machine-readable input and storage medium. A batch of cards was punched, sorted into the sequence used by the master file being updated, and then carried to the computer where it was processed. A few punched card systems are still in use, but the card essentially passed into history in December 1984 when IBM closed the last of its punched card manufacturing plants.

Magnetic Tape

Magnetic tape has been used for years as an input/storage medium for batch processing, and it remains a preferred choice today for high-speed, large-volume batch applications. Its **data density** (the number of characters that can be stored in a given physical space) is high, and its **transfer rate** (the speed with which data can be copied into processor storage) is fast.

FIGURE 5-10

The magnetic tape input medium is packaged in different ways. (Photos courtesy 3M)

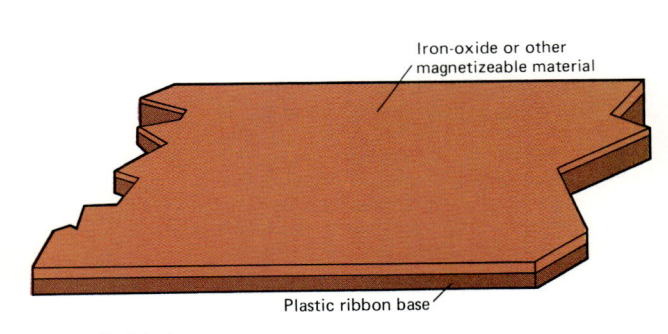

(a) The tape in large reels is used in mini- and mainframe computer systems. This tape is usually ½ inch wide and 2,400 feet long. (Lengths of 300, 600, and 1,200 feet are also available.) The coating is applied to one side of the plastic ribbon base.

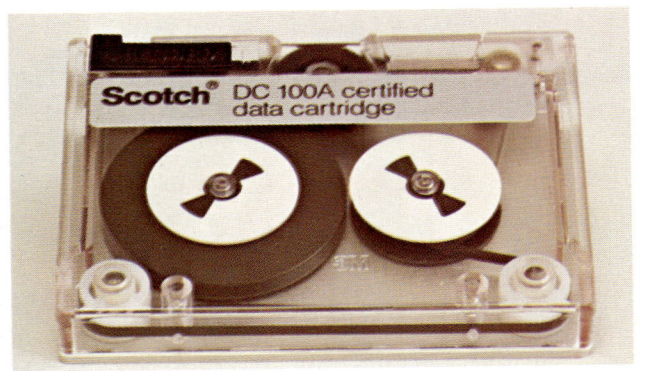

(b) Magnetic tape cartridges of the type shown here are used in minicomputers. This tape is ¼ inch wide and varies from 140 to 450 feet in length. Some newer mainframe cartridges use a ½ inch tape with a chromium dioxide coating to hold as much data as the largest reel shown above.

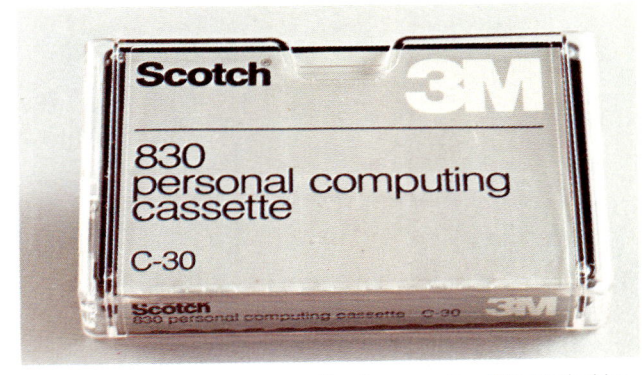

(c) Magnetic tape cassettes are used in microcomputers. This tape is either 150 or 300 feet long.

MODULE 2

182

You'll notice in Figure 5-10 that the tape itself may be in a large **reel** or a small **cartridge** or **cassette.** However packaged, the tape is similar to the kind used in a sound tape recorder. It's a plastic ribbon that's coated on one side with iron oxide or some other material that can be magnetized. Tiny invisible spots representing data are recorded by electromagnetic pulses on the coated side of the tape, just as sound waves are converted to magnetic patterns on the tape of a sound recorder. Both the data and the sound can be played back many times. Like voice (or sound) recording tape, computer tape can be erased and reused indefinitely. Old data on a tape are automatically erased as new data are recorded in the same locations.

Data Entry Although offline devices that enable operators to key data directly onto a tape were popular in the past and are still available, most magnetic tape data entry systems in use now employ multiple **key-to-disk stations.** As you can see in Figure 5-11, a minicomputer controls the input coming from the keystations and prepares it for processing. Note that this computer *doesn't process* the data; the entry system it controls is offline from the computer that has that task. But the minicomputer *does* provide the same type of operator support supplied by the main computer in the example in Figure 5-3. For example, it allows operators to call up frequently used data fields stored on the system's disk unit, to eliminate unnecessary keying. If the names and addresses of customers are stored on the disk by their account numbers, an operator keying data from order entry forms can call up this information merely by entering a customer number.

As data are keyed and displayed at the stations, the types of programmed checks mentioned at the beginning of the chapter can be made to ensure that the data are reasonable. After the data for a particular batch processing job have been copied from the source documents, checked, and stored on the system disk, the minicomputer program transfers the disk data to a magnetic tape for later processing by the main computer.

FIGURE 5-11

A multistation key-to-disk data entry system. Such systems may have dozens of keystations and may be quite expensive. A minicomputer is usually located in a supervisory console to control the system operation. In addition to its editing, storage, and retrieval functions, this minicomputer can also keep track of such statistics as records keyed, number and types of errors detected, and so on.

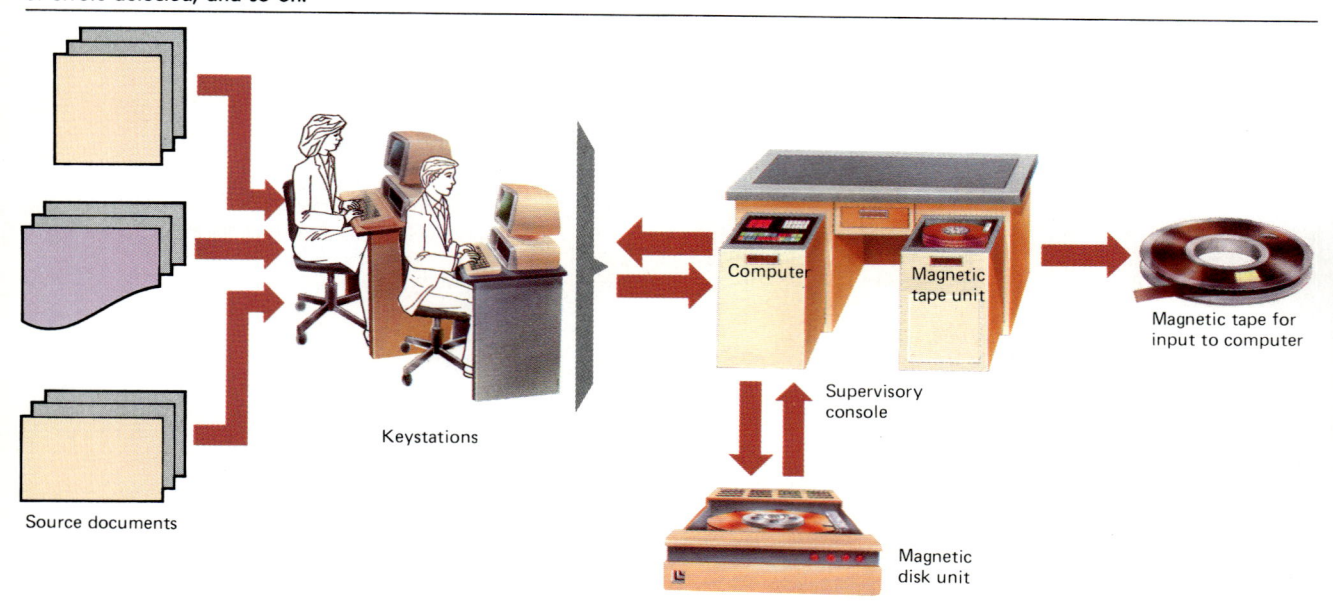

Source documents → Keystations → Computer / Magnetic tape unit → Magnetic tape for input to computer

Supervisory console ↕ Magnetic disk unit

Magnetic Tape Equipment Before the data on a magnetic tape can be processed by a computer, the tape must be placed in a machine called a **tape drive** or **tape transport.** This machine can either read data from a tape into the processor or write the information being produced by the computer onto a tape. Reading data from a tape into the processor does not destroy the tape data, but writing data from the computer onto a tape erases previous tape contents.

You can see in Figure 5-12 that tape moves through a tape drive in much the same way that film moves through a movie projector. The tape movement during processing is from the supply reel past a read/write head assembly to the take-up reel. Several tape drives are used in a typical installation. In most applications, a tape is either read or written in a single pass. Therefore, to update a file of student records, one unit may read in the old master file while another feeds in update transactions and a third writes the updated master file. If the update program is kept on tape, a fourth drive will be needed to enter the processing instructions.

Floppy Disks

The IBM 3740 data entry system (see Figure 5-13) allows source document data to be keyed directly onto a floppy magnetic disk. The **floppy disk** (also called a **diskette**) gets its name from the fact that it is made out of a flexible plastic material. This plastic base is coated with an iron-oxide recording substance that's similar to the material applied to the plastic ribbon of a magnetic tape. Data are recorded as tiny invisible magnetic spots on this coating. Each data entry disk in this system is 8 inches in diameter and is packaged in a protective paper or plastic envelope from which it is never removed.

A **key-to-diskette** data entry station records the keyed data directly onto a floppy disk. The disk is loaded in this station in its protective envelope. As the disk is rotated inside the envelope, a read/write head assembly accesses the disk surface through a slot in the envelope to record the data. A small display screen shows the data being entered and helps the operator perform data editing and verification functions.

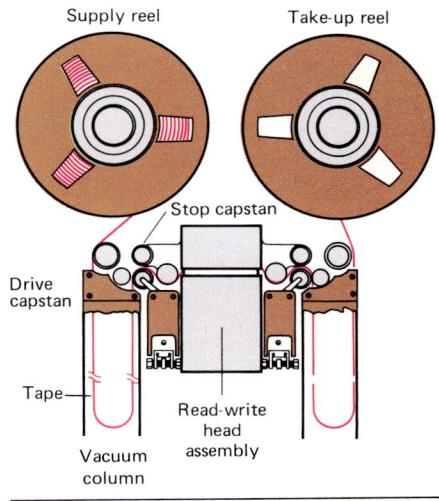

FIGURE 5-12

The movement of the tape during processing is from the supply reel to the take-up reel. Tapes may move at speeds up to 200 inches per second, and they achieve this rate in a few milliseconds. Several methods are used to prevent tape damage from sudden bursts of speed. One such method is to use vacuum columns to hold slack tape.

FIGURE 5-13

The IBM 3740 data entry system. Source document data are keyed directly onto the floppy magnetic disk. (Courtesy International Business Machines Corporation)

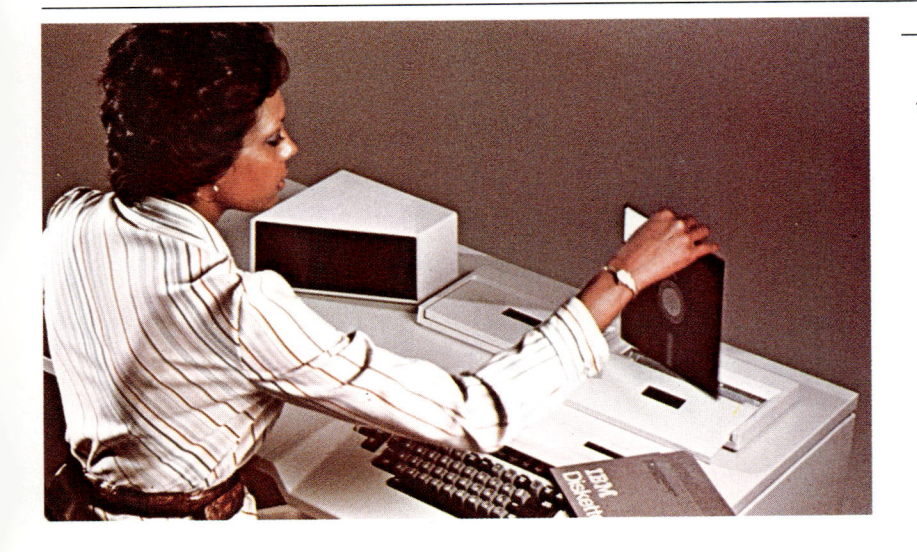

MODULE 2

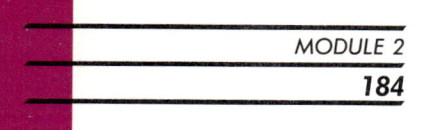

Once the data have been recorded, a **floppy-disk reader** can be used to enter the data into the processor. Again, the disk is loaded and rotated inside its envelope. Tiny electromagnetic heads in the disk reader access the data through the slot in the jacket. Like magnetic tape, a diskette is inexpensive and can be erased and reused many times. The erasable feature makes it easy to make changes and corrections during data entry.

In addition to being an input medium for batch processing, the floppy disk has also become the most common online secondary storage medium used with intelligent VDTs and pc's. These storage disks are scaled-down 5¼-inch (or smaller) versions of the original 8-inch floppy.

Character Readers

Although improvements have been made in offline data entry media and devices, the transcribing activities carried out by the operators of these devices are still expensive and time-consuming. To eliminate the need to recopy transaction data, several devices have been built to read the characters printed on the source documents and to then convert these data *directly* into computer-usable input. Let's now examine some of these character readers that are used in high-volume batch processing applications.

Magnetic Ink Character Readers **Magnetic ink character recognition (MICR)** is widely used by banks to process the tremendous volume of checks being written each day. The sample check in Figure 5-14 is precoded along the bottom with the bank's identification number and with the depositor's account number. These numbers and other special symbols are printed with a special ink that contains magnetizeable particles of iron oxide. Employees at the first bank to receive the check after it has been written use the same ink to encode the amount in the lower right corner. The check can then be processed by machines.

Checks are accumulated into batches and placed in the input hopper of a **reader-sorter unit.** As they enter the reading unit, the checks pass through a magnetic field which causes the particles in the ink to become magnetized. Read heads are then able to interpret the characters as the checks pass through

FIGURE 5-14

A sample check encoded with MICR characters. These characters are printed with a special ink that contains particles of magnetizeable material.

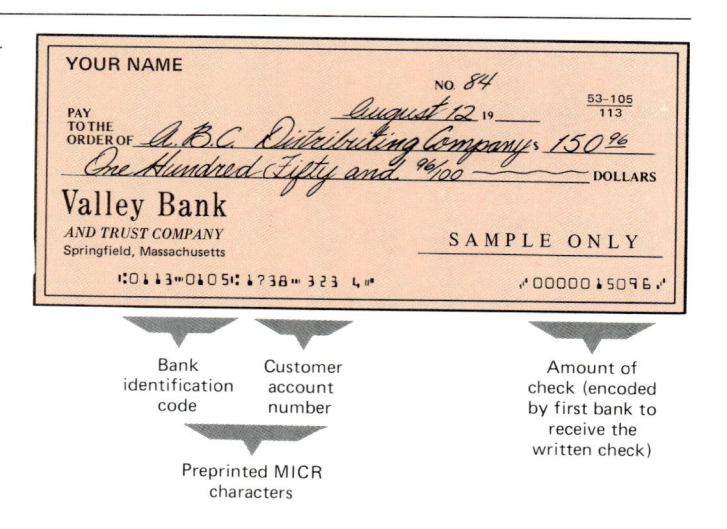

Bank identification code

Customer account number

Preprinted MICR characters

Amount of check (encoded by first bank to receive the written check)

the reading unit. The data being read can be entered directly into a computer, or they can be transferred to magnetic tape for later processing. As up to 2,600 checks pass through the machine each minute, they are also sorted into pockets according to their identification code numbers. Several sortings may be required to move a check from (1) the initial bank receiving the check to, perhaps, (2) a Federal Reserve Bank, to (3) the depositor's bank, to (4) the depositor's account.

There are several *advantages* associated with the use of MICR:

- Checks may be roughly handled, folded, smeared, and stamped, but they can still be read with a high degree of accuracy.

- Processing is speeded because checks can be fed directly into the input device.

- People can easily read the magnetic ink characters.

The main *limitation* of MICR is that only the 10 digits and 4 special characters needed for bank processing are used. No alphabetic characters are available.

Optical Character Readers

Unlike MICR, **optical character recognition (OCR)** techniques permit the direct reading of any printed character (not just 14). No special ink is required. This OCR flexibility makes it possible for organizations to eliminate or reduce the input keying bottleneck. You've already seen how *optical character readers* can read bar codes and merchandise tags to enter data directly into a computer system. But readers designed to interpret *handmade marks* and *machine-printed characters* are also commonly used in offline operations to prepare data for processing.

For example, you've probably taken tests and marked your answers to questions on a special test-scoring sheet (Figure 5-15a). An *optical mark reader* was then used to interpret your marks for immediate or later processing. Optical scanners can also read certain handmade letters and numbers, but these characters must usually be precisely written (Figure 5-15b). The automatic reading of handwritten script is still some years in the future. (Your penmanship is undoubtedly beautiful, but mine presents a formidable challenge to the equipment designers.)

Figure 5-16 shows an optical reading system that's capable of scanning handmade characters. This system also has the flexibility to read entire pages of machine-printed alphanumeric symbols. These symbols are often printed in the standard type font shown in Figure 5-17. Most optical character readers of this type scan the printed matter with a photoelectric device that recognizes characters by the absorption or reflectance of light on the document (characters to be read are nonreflective).

Such readers are used in many large-volume batch processing applications. For example, the computer-printed bills sent to customers by many public utilities, credit card companies, and other businesses are prepared with characters that can be read by optical scanners. When customers make their monthly payments, they are instructed to return the bill or a remittance stub with their checks. These documents are then entered directly into optical readers to update accounts receivable records. Little or no human keying is needed. Other large-volume applications of scanners include the reading of Zip codes by the U.S. Postal Service, the reading of passenger tickets and

FIGURE 5-15

Machine-readable handmade marks and characters.

(a) A portion of a completed test-scoring sheet

Correct and readable

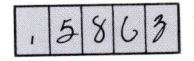

Incorrect and probably unreadable

(b) Handprinted numeric characters

MODULE 2
186

FIGURE 5-16

An optical page reading system. Several thousand machine-printed characters and up to 1,200 handprinted characters can be read each second by this type of data entry system. (Courtesy Recognition Equipment, Inc.)

Programmed controller directs input operation

Pages containing character patterns such as are placed in an input hopper

freight bills by airlines, and the processing of social security forms and motor vehicle registrations by governments.

The primary *advantage* of OCR is that it eliminates some of the duplication of human effort required to get data into the computer. This reduction in effort can improve data accuracy and can increase the timeliness of the information processed. However, *difficulties* in using OCR equipment may be encountered when documents to be read are poorly typed or have strikeovers or erasures. Also, form design and ink specifications may become more critical than is the case when people key the data from the forms. Finally, optical readers do not pay their way unless the daily volume of transactions is relatively high.

FIGURE 5-17

This standard type font (designated OCR-A) is currently used in about three-fourths of the applications that rely on optical character reading for data entry.

ABCDEFGHIJKLMNOPQRSTUVWXYZ
1234567890:;.,=¬?"$%|&'{}*+

After moving beneath a reading system, the character data are transmitted to integrated circuit chips for recognition. The data may then be recorded on magnetic tape.

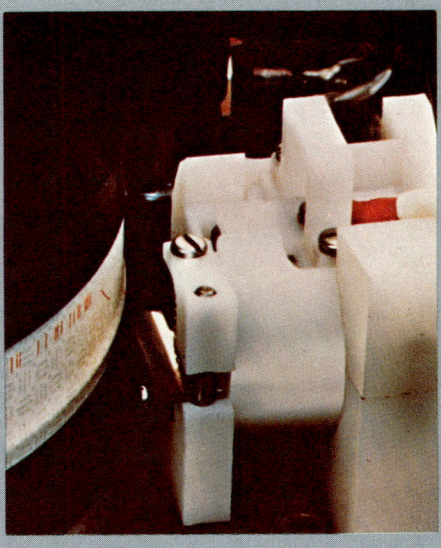

As each document is processed, a high-speed ink-jet printer capable of spraying 106,000 droplets of ink per second may be used to imprint a control code on the document.

Documents may then be directed to output pockets.

FEEDBACK

Feedback and Review 5

The following *matching questions* will test and reinforce your understanding of the material presented in this chapter. A number of terms are listed below. Place the letter of the appropriate term beside the definition or concept to which it belongs.

A) visual display terminal B) ergonomics C) data collection station D) mouse
E) reverse video F) cursor G) distributed data entry H) limit check
I) data density J) order entry/shipping/billing K) intelligent terminals
L) interactive M) interface N) pull-down O) touch screen P) stylus
Q) Universal Product Code R) light pen S) teleprinter T) magnetic U) icons
V) floppy disk W) key-to-disk station X) prompt Y) dependent
Z) automated teller machine

____ 1. A term used to describe the placement of the data entry function at the scattered locations where the transactions occur.
____ 2. A type of processing that produces output results immediately after input data are entered into a computer system.
____ 3. Input devices that are often used in a factory setting.
____ 4. One type of large batch processing system maintained by organizations that sell products to credit customers.
____ 5. An error-detection control that's used to verify that input data don't exceed reasonable upper or lower values.

____ 6. The most popular input device used today for interactive processing and for the online entry of data for batch processing.
____ 7. The name given to the highlighted screen symbol that points to the placement of the next character.
____ 8. User-programmable terminals that combine VDT hardware with built-in microprocessors.
____ 9. The hardware/software boundary that permits communication between people and computers.
____10. The science of designing machines so that people will find them comfortable, convenient, and efficient.
____11. A display feature that highlights areas of the screen that may require operator attention.
____12. Small boxes displayed on a ____ may perform much like special function keys.
____13. This screen pointing device rolls on a small bearing and has one or more buttons on the top.
____14. Another screen pointing device that uses a photocell placed in a small tube.
____15. This special pen is used to form drawings on an input tablet.
____16. Menus at all levels typically include a title, the possible options, and some type of ____.
____17. Screen drawings or pictures that represent program options that users can select.
____18. When a user selects a choice from a menu line, a ____ menu may then be displayed.
____19. A code used to identify merchandise in retail stores.
____20. An online electronic funds transfer station.
____21. A type of online terminal equipped with a keyboard and a built-in printer.
____22. Most voice input systems are speaker-____.
____23. The number of characters that can be stored in a given physical space.
____24. A device used in magnetic tape data entry systems.
____25. Another name for a diskette.
____26. Character readers used in banks require this type of ink.

LOOKING BACK

1. Input data are either entered into a computer system directly or first captured on some machine-readable medium before being entered into the system. Data used by organizations are obtained from both internal and external sources. The data entry method followed in a given application is often determined by the locations where the data are entered and the timing of the processing required. In some applications, the data entry function is likely to be distributed to the sites where the transactions occur. In other situations, the data entry function is performed by operators located at a central computer site. Interactive processing is often required when data originate at scattered sites. An example of distributed data collection stations and interactive processing in a factory setting is presented in the chapter. When the timing requirements aren't critical, data at scattered locations may be gathered for a period and collected into groups at remote batch stations. These data may then be processed by a computer at a central location. Centralized data entry groups have generally been created to support large batch processing applications. One such application is the order entry/shipping/billing system used by organizations that sell products to credit customers. An example of such a batch system (using online data entry stations) is shown in the chapter.

2. The quality of output of a data processing system is more dependent on people than on machines. This is because people prepare the data input (and programs) for the machines. Mistakes entered on source documents or errors made during keying are not uncommon, and it's important to catch them as early as possible. Several error-detecting techniques are described in this chapter.

3. Millions of online data entry devices are now in use, and additional millions are being installed every year. By far the most popular device for interactive processing and for the online entry of data for batch processing is the visual display terminal (VDT). There are dumb, smart, and intelligent VDTs. Smart VDTs have a microprocessor and some internal storage, and they can edit, store, and consolidate input data. But they aren't user-programmable. Intelligent VDTs are user-programmable, and there's very little difference between them and many personal computers.

4. The hardware/software boundary that permits communication between people and computers may be considered an interface. And what most people need and want is an interface that's user friendly—one that has hardware that's easy and comfortable to use and software that's easy to learn. VDT and personal computer (pc) users have found that detached keyboards with function keys and numeric keypads offer advantages. And screens that feature reverse video, the use of color and enhanced graphics, and touch capabilities are "friendlier" than those that lack these properties. Other VDT and pc hardware interfaces that facilitate human-machine communication are the mouse, light pen, and input tablet.

5. The best keyboards and screens are of questionable value to VDT and pc users if they have to follow difficult procedures to accomplish useful work. Thus software developers have produced packages that are easier to learn and use than those of just a few years ago. Most of these packages incorporate menus, and many use icons and simulate a desktop environment. A menu-driven program leads users through a series of data entry and processing procedures, giving and requesting information as necessary at each program level to complete a task. A main menu is typically followed by a number of submenus. There are many ways that programs can present menu selections to users. Options can be listed, presented as drawings or icons, or displayed on a menu line at the top or bottom of the screen. Most menu lines include pull-down submenus. Integrated software packages may use a combination of menu lines, pull-down menus, icons, and screen windows to simulate a desktop environment.

6. Point-of-sale (POS) and financial transaction terminals are special-purpose devices used by retail stores and financial institutions. POS terminals can reduce customer waiting time at checkout

counters and can directly update the online files used in accounts receivable, inventory control, and sales analysis applications. Automated teller machines can handle routine financial transactions 24 hours a day. Other electronic funds transfer terminals can be used by stores and hotels to verify that a customer's check is good. Portable teleprinters are particularly useful to people who do a great deal of traveling. The use of other types of portable data entry devices is also expanding rapidly.

7. Voice input systems convert human speech into electrical signals that a computer can recognize. Although speech recognition technology is in its infancy, and many problems remain to be solved, it's now being used in applications where keyboarding isn't a practical way to enter data.

8. Magnetic tape has been used for years as an input/storage medium for batch processing. It remains a preferred choice today for high-speed, large-volume batch applications because its data density is high and its transfer rate is fast. Magnetic tape is packaged in reels, cartridges, or cassettes. Data are generally entered from source documents by key-to-disk systems. A tape drive is used to read data from a tape into the processor.

9. A key-to-diskette station may be used to enter source document data on a floppy disk. A floppy-disk reader may then be used to enter the data into a processor. Magnetic ink and optical character readers have been developed to eliminate the need to recopy transaction data from source documents. Magnetic ink reader-sorter units are special-purpose devices used to process checks in the banking system. They only recognize the 14 characters needed for check processing. Optical character readers, on the other hand, can directly read handmade and machine-printed letters, numbers, and special characters, as well as bar codes and handmade marks. Such readers are often used in large-volume processing applications such as billing. They are also frequently used at POS stations to scan the items marked with the bars of the Universal Product Code.

Key TERMS AND CONCEPTS

source data automation 161
distributed data entry 161
remote batch stations 163
order entry/shipping/ billing system 163
default data 165
accounts receivable 165
inventory control 167
sales analysis 167

control total 168
edit checks 168
range checks 168
limit checks 168
visual display terminal (VDT) 169
cathode-ray tube (CRT) 169
monitor 169
dumb terminal 169
smart terminal 170
cursor 170

function keys 170
intelligent terminal 170
interface 171
user friendly 171
ergonomics 171
reverse video 172
pixel 172
touch screen 173
mouse 173
joystick 174
light pen 174
digitizer tablet 174

CHAPTER 5

191

graphics tablet 174
command-driven program 174
menu-driven program 174
main menu 175
submenu 175
prompt 175
simulated desktop 175
icons 175
menu line 176
pull-down menu 176
bar codes 177
Universal Product Code (UPC) 177
optical character reader 177
point-of-sale (POS) terminal 177
financial transaction terminal 178
electronic funds transfer (EFT) 178
automated teller machine (ATM) 178
teleprinter terminal 179
speaker-dependent 180
speaker-independent 180
punched card 181
magnetic tape 181
data density 181
transfer rate 181
reel 182
cartridge 182
cassette 182
key-to-disk stations 182
tape drive (tape transport) 183
floppy-disk (diskette) 183
key-to-diskette device 183
floppy-disk reader 184
magnetic ink character recognition (MICR) 184
reader-sorter unit 184
optical character recognition (OCR) 185

TOPICS FOR REVIEW AND DISCUSSION

1. "The input data used by an organization are obtained from internal and external sources." Discuss this statement.
2. "The locations where the data are entered into the computer system and the timing of the processing required play an important role in determining the data entry approach used in a given situation." Explain this statement and give examples to support your points.
3. What advantages are there to capturing data at the transaction source?
4. (a) What's an order entry/shipping/billing system? (b) What follow-up applications are likely to use the data produced in such a system?
5. "People have a greater effect on the quality of output of a data processing system than do the data processing machines." Discuss this statement.
6. (a) How are data errors introduced into a computer system? (b) Why is it important to catch these errors as soon as possible?
7. How can errors be detected in input data?
8. Discuss the general characteristics of the devices used for online data entry.
9. (a) What is a visual display terminal? (b) How may visual display units be used? (c) How may data be entered at such terminals?
10. (a) What is an intelligent terminal? (b) How may intelligent terminals be used? (c) What's the difference between an intelligent terminal and a personal computer?
11. (a) What's the difference between a dumb terminal and a smart terminal? (b) Why are almost all new VDTs smart or intelligent?
12. "What most VDT and pc users want and need is an interface that's user friendly." Discuss this statement.
13. Identify five keyboard/display features that make VDTs and personal computers easier to use.
14. (a) How may a mouse be used? (b) A light pen? (c) An input tablet?
15. (a) What is a menu-driven program? (b) What's the relationship between a main menu and a submenu? (c) What's a prompt?
16. "There are many approaches that programs can use to present menu selections to users." Identify and discuss two of these approaches.
17. (a) What's the relationship between a menu line and a pull-down menu? (b) How do these program features support a desktop environment?
18. (a) What is the Universal Product Code? (b) How is it used?
19. (a) What's the purpose of a POS terminal? (b) Of financial transaction terminals?
20. (a) What is a teleprinter terminal? (b) How may portable teleprinters be used?
21. "Voice input systems may be speaker-dependent or speaker-independent." How do these systems differ?
22. (a) How is magnetic tape packaged? (b) How are data entered on magnetic tape?
23. (a) How are data recorded on a floppy disk? (b) How are floppy disks similar to magnetic tape? (c) How are they different?
24. MICR and OCR devices are similar in that both types of machines convert source document data directly into computer-usable input. How do these machines differ?

Projects/Issues to Consider

1. Identify and prepare a class presentation on four sources of input data used by an organization that you know about, belong to, and/or work for. Include in your presentation a report on the input media and/or devices used to enter the data into the organization's computer system.

2. Go to the library and/or a computer store and identify by brand name four data entry devices used with personal computers. Prepare a report describing the characteristics of the devices you select.

Answers to Feedback and Review Section

1. G 2. L 3. C 4. J 5. H 6. A 7. F 8. K 9. M 10. B 11. E 12. O
13. D 14. R 15. P 16. X 17. U 18. N 19. Q 20. Z 21. S 22. Y
23. I 24. W 25. V 26. T

A CLOSER LOOK

SMART CARDS

The Smart Card is a multifunctional microprocessor and memory on a computer chip embedded in a plastic card—literally a "computer in a card" for your wallet. This specimen card has the inner workings—the computer—exposed for you to see. (Courtesy SmartCard International, Inc.)

Soon it will be possible to carry much of the power of a personal computer in one small compartment of a billfold. It will reside in a device called a smart card: one or more microelectronic chips mounted in a piece of plastic the size of a credit card.

Smart cards that have slightly less computing power than a personal computer are already being produced and used in France in a number of applications. In September 1985, Mastercard began issuing some 50,000 cards to American users in Washington, D.C., and Palm Springs, Fla., as part of a field trial. Eventually there may be many types of smart cards, each having a different level of sophistication. The most advanced of these might carry small liquid-crystal-display readouts and have the capability to encrypt and decrypt any dialogue with an external device; they will be powered by solar panels. The least sophisticated card might consist of little more than a simple processor and a small memory; it could serve, for example, as a "debit card" for long-distance calls on public telephones or as a complete personal medical history. It is not inconceivable that within a few years smart cards will be able to store digitized versions of their owners' signatures, retina prints or fingerprints; personalized smart cards could be used as highly secure keys, allowing access to telephone networks, corporate data banks and secure buildings.

In what is perhaps their most natural application, smart cards may replace credit cards and the cards that function in automatic banking machines. In a typical smart-card transaction, a cardholder puts the card in a "point-of-sale terminal": a special card-reading cash register. The terminal supplies the card with electric power and communicates with its microcircuitry through eight metal contacts on the card's surface. The cardholder is asked to enter a password on a keyboard, and the terminal verifies that the card is valid and the user is legitimate. When the sale is rung up, the amount of the transaction is stored in the card's memory, credited to the retailer's account and deducted from the cardholder's credit balance, which is also stored in the card's memory. The cardholder may be able to replenish the credit balance at an automatic banking machine.

Smart cards have properties that make them invulnerable to the most common kinds of fraud and abuse. First, a smart card has a nonvolatile, programmable, read-only memory into which information can be placed after the card has been issued and that will remember any such information even when it is not connected to a power source. Second, each smart card contains its own central processing unit—essentially a small computer—which controls all the interactions between the memory and the various external devices that read the card and enter data onto it.

Through the central processing unit the card itself can examine any proposed password and compare it with the correct password, which is stored in a secret location in the card's memory. The card never has to reveal the correct password to any outside system. Even the company that issues the card does not need to know the correct password. When the card is first issued, the cardholder can program the password directly onto it by means of a card-reading/writing machine. After the password has been entered and checked (the cardholder is asked to enter the password two or three times to ensure that it is not entered incorrectly), the card stores it in the memory's "secret zone."

In addition to the password the secret zone stores the cardholder's account balance, the card's serial number and a sequence of letters or numbers, chosen by the card's issuer, that can be used to determine whether the card is legitimate. Another zone of the programmable, read-only memory, called the open zone, might store the cardholder's name, address, telephone number and account number. The open zone can be read by any card-reading machine, but it cannot be altered; the card's cpu will not obey instructions to change any information in the open zone.

Whenever the card is used to make a purchase, such information as the amount of the purchase, the name and address of the store and the date is stored in a third zone of the memory, called the working zone. Information can be written there only under certain conditions (when the card is in a legitimate cash register, say) and can be read or written only with the cardholder's permission. A cardholder can buy a separate card-reading machine, which, when it is connected to a home computer, a television set or a printer, displays a complete record of all purchases made with the card.

The smart card may effect major changes in the economic functioning of society. As keys, for example, smart cards may provide the degree of security necessary to make true computer networking a viable proposition; a complete data-bank-exchange and electronic-funds-transfer network can exist only if there is a way to ensure that no unauthorized users have access to the system. Smart cards may bring about this true union between telecommunications and computing.

Smart cards will also change the way simple commercial transactions are carried out. It has been quite some time since the system of barter, of trading one commercial item directly for another, was replaced by a system of trading items for standard units of wealth (say shells or pieces of gold). Eventually the units of wealth themselves were replaced by receipts: certificates that represented a certain amount of gold or silver. Those certificates have now been replaced by cash and checks. Not too far in the future paper money itself may be replaced by "units of purchasing power" stored electronically on smart cards.

Excerpted from Robert McIvor, "Smart Cards," *Scientific American*, November 1985. Copyright © 1985 by Scientific American, Inc. All rights reserved.

CHAPTER 6

STORING DATA AND RECEIVING OUTPUT

Preserving the Past on Disks

Any scholar who has descended into the morass of a poorly maintained archive—rotting papers in boxes, mildewed photos in decaying albums, and other mementos of great intellects—has experienced horrors worse than any described by Edgar Allan Poe.

A system consisting of a digitizing camera, a pc, off-the-shelf software, videodisks, a videodisk player, and a high-resolution printer could be the solution to this research nightmare. This combination of hardware and software makes it easy for any photograph, drawing, or paper document to be digitally encoded, stored, retrieved, and widely distributed, with all the handwritten notes and curlicue typefaces preserved. It has drawn rave reviews from museum directors and other archive dwellers, for it makes messy, disorganized archives as accessible as any top-quality online data base.

The system was assembled by Hernan Otano and Rob Martella of the advanced projects division of the Smithsonian Institution's Air and Space Museum in Washington, D.C., who pursue their work in a museum basement 50 feet beneath Lindbergh's *Spirit of St. Louis* airplane.

The heart of the Smithsonian's aviation collection consists of over 2 million photos—everything from the Wright brothers' flight to *Voyager*'s photographs of Saturn—and countless millions of schematic drawings and written documents. Aviation scholars coming to look at the collection had to go through the standard archival retrieval process, which involves asking a librarian to dig through the stacks of paper until the desired item is found. If the researcher wanted a photo, a copy would cost $5. The whole search-and-copy process required days, even weeks, and perhaps hundreds of dollars.

Otano decided he wanted a computerized system to store photos and documents electronically. His system had to incorporate five principles: easy acquisition, mass storage, automatic indexing, easy retrieval, and cheap distribution.

The first device acquired for this system was a digitizing camera. Point it at a photograph or document, press a button, and the whole page is encoded digitally (or, more precisely, bit mapped) in less than 3 seconds at a resolution of 200 dots per inch. The captured images can be stored on hard disks, reel tape, or any other high-capacity memory device.

The storage system begins with an easel, illuminated by two high-intensity lights, with the digitizing camera aimed at it. The document is placed on the easel, the operator presses a button to capture the image digitally, then checks it on a high-resolution monitor. The image is stored on a Winchester hard disk in a pc and on a reel-tape backup. The disk image is then transferred to an optical disk for easier transportation. A videodisk master is made from the optical disk and videodisk copies can then be created. Each videodisk can hold copies of 50,000 photographs or 100,000 documents on each side.

Photographs can be located on the videodisk using a specialized application of DBase II, a popular commercial data base package. When the researcher selects the photo he or she is looking for, the print option will produce a copy of it. The Air and Space Museum has several videodisk-pc-monitor-keyboard-printer setups in its research library. Scholars can enter their requests and receive prints for 40 cents each.

Futurists have predicted a paperless world as a result of computers, but our planet is overflowing with documents that have accumulated for centuries. A system such as this organizes them, makes them easy to retrieve, and preserves them for future generations.

Adapted from Brad Lemley, "Preserving the Past on Disk," *PC Magazine*, June 25, 1985. Copyright © 1985 Ziff-Davis Publishing Company.

CHAPTER 6

LOOKING AHEAD

You've seen in Chapter 5 how data are entered into computer systems. Now, in Chapter 6, you'll encounter the secondary storage and output components found in such systems. You'll learn first that most computer systems can use various storage methods, and one type of method is usually selected for a particular task on the basis of retrieval speed, storage capacity, and storage cost. Next, you'll learn about output media and devices that are used to print, film, display, and capture in other ways the information computer systems produce. The information in this chapter will enable you to:

- Identify the elements in the storage hierarchy and discuss the factors to be considered in storage selection
- Summarize the characteristics of those secondary storage media and devices that provide quick and direct access to stored records and those that store data that are sequentially organized and processed
- Summarize the types of computer output that may be produced and the devices used to prepare this output

CHAPTER OUTLINE

LOOKING AHEAD
THE STORAGE HIERARCHY: AN OVERVIEW
Elements in the Storage Hierarchy
Storage Selection
SECONDARY STORAGE FOR DIRECT ACCESS
Disk Storage for Direct Access
Direct Access with RAM "Disks" and Magnetic Bubbles
Direct Access with Optical Disks and Tape Strips
Future Direct-Access Developments
SECONDARY STORAGE FOR SEQUENTIAL ACCESS
Disk Storage for Sequential Access
Magnetic Tape Storage
RECEIVING COMPUTER OUTPUT: SOME BASIC CONCEPTS
Why Output Is Needed
Output Categories
PRINTED AND FILMED OUTPUT
Printed Output
Filmed Output
DISPLAYED OUTPUT, COMPUTER GRAPHICS, AND VOICE RESPONSE
Displayed Output and Computer Graphics
Voice Response
Feedback and Review 6
LOOKING BACK

THE STORAGE HIERARCHY: AN OVERVIEW

By now you know that all computers store and retrieve data. Some small personal computer systems may need to store only a few thousand characters. But large systems need access to billions of characters stored in a computer-readable form. When computer specialists refer to the **storage hierarchy** of a particular computer system, they have in mind a range of different storage methods. These different methods are found in all but the smallest computer systems and are ranked according to the following criteria:

1   *Retrieval speed.*   The **access time** of a storage device is the time it takes to locate and retrieve stored data in response to a program instruction. A fast access time is preferred.

2   *Storage capacity.*   A device's ability to store the amount of data needed now and in the future must be considered. A large capacity is desired.

3   *Cost per bit of capacity.*   An obvious goal is to minimize this cost.

Elements in the Storage Hierarchy

Figure 6-1 gives you a general idea of the ranking of different storage devices and media. At the top of the storage hierarchy pyramid are the *primary storage* components found in the processor unit. The principal component is the primary storage section which was discussed in Chapter 4 along with the other specialized processing and control storage devices that may be found in the processor unit. The semiconductor storage chips commonly used in the processor have the fastest access times. Relative to other available storage devices, however, chips have the smallest storage capacity and the highest cost per bit of capacity.

Secondary (or **auxiliary**) **storage** components supplement primary storage in most computer systems. Included in the secondary storage classification, and located below primary storage in the hierarchy of Figure 6-1, are *direct-access storage devices* (DASDs). The data retained in these secondary storage units are *online* and are available to the processor at all times. Compared with primary storage, the storage capacity of a DASD is larger and the cost per bit stored is lower. Although the access time of a DASD may be only a few milliseconds, primary storage speed is thousands of times faster. Different DASDs provide different levels of cost and performance, as you'll see later in this chapter.

At the base of the storage hierarchy is another type of secondary storage. The data retained on **sequential-access storage media** are periodically accessed and updated by the sequential processing techniques discussed in Chapter 2.[1] These stored data are *offline* from the processor except when loaded on an input device. The storage capacity of these media is virtually unlimited, and the storage cost is very low. But before the processor can gain access to a particular record, a computer operator must locate the sequential file and load it on an input device. The processor must then read all preceding

---

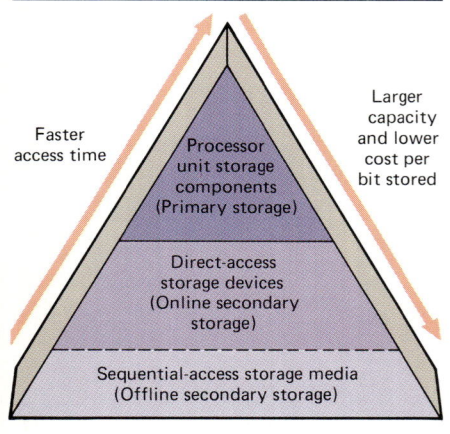

[1] A review of the Chapter 2 section "Sequential and Direct Storage and Retrieval" might be helpful here. The Closer Look reading at the end of the chapter may also be helpful.

FIGURE 6-1

The storage hierarchy pyramid. A faster access time is obtained by moving up the pyramid. A larger storage capacity and a lower cost per bit stored are the results of moving down the pyramid. Thus processor unit storage components generally have the *fastest* access times, the *smallest* storage capacity, and the *highest* cost per bit stored. The *primary storage* of a computer system consists of the components in the processor unit. Supplementing primary storage is the *secondary* (or *auxiliary*) *storage* of a computer system. This broader classification includes all the online direct-access storage devices and all the offline sequential-access storage media that hold data in a computer-readable form.

Faster access time ← Processor unit storage components (Primary storage) / Direct-access storage devices (Online secondary storage) / Sequential-access storage media (Offline secondary storage) → Larger capacity and lower cost per bit stored

records until the desired one is found. This procedure alone takes several minutes.

Storage Selection

If a single storage component were superior in speed, capacity, and cost, there would be no need for a storage hierarchy. Since this isn't the case, computer system designers must study each application and then choose the best storage approach for the job. That is, the way the data are organized and processed determines the approach they select. If a file can be organized sequentially, and if records require only periodic updating, then the lowest-cost option is likely to be the use of a sequential-access secondary storage medium. On the other hand, the need for quick access to any file record requires a quick processing response, and a DASD must be used. These ideas are covered in the Closer Look reading at the end of the chapter.

In selecting a DASD, designers must usually make compromises between performance and cost. For example, in specialized scientific applications where processing speed is paramount and cost is secondary, the system selected may have a large primary storage section linked to a very fast DASD. In many file processing applications, however, a slower DASD with larger capacity may be picked over a faster and more expensive device that has less capacity.

SECONDARY STORAGE FOR DIRECT ACCESS

Disk Storage for Direct Access

Magnetic disks are the most popular medium for direct-access secondary storage. A magnetic disk is a metal or plastic platter that resembles a grooveless phonograph record. Let's use this phonograph record analogy to get an idea of how a disk storage device works. Suppose you have both a sound tape player and a record player. Suppose, too, that 10 songs are recorded on your favorite tape, and your favorite record has seven pieces of music. Now what must you do if you only want to listen to (or access) the sixth song on the tape and the fourth song on the record? To get to the sixth tape song, you must put the tape on the player and wait until the tape used to record the first five songs has moved through the player. Although your player may "fast forward" the tape quickly past the first five pieces, there's still a delay of several seconds. To get to the fourth song on the record, you can do one of two things. You can place the record on the player, position the pickup arm at the beginning of the first song, and wait until the arm has played the first three pieces. (Following the stored sequence in this way is logically similar to accessing the music on a tape.) Or you can *directly* move the pickup arm across the record to the groove where the fourth song begins.

Like the songs on a sound tape, the data records organized on a magnetic tape *must* be retrieved according to the storage sequence. And like the music, the data recorded on a magnetic disk *can* also be accessed in a sequence if they have been organized in a way that supports such retrieval. **Read/write heads** are tiny electromagnets that can read, write, or erase the polarized spots that represent data on magnetic media. When such heads are fastened to an

MODULE 2
200

FIGURE 6-2

Removable rigid disks are packaged in a number of ways. There are three sizes of disk packs shown here in front of two types of disk cartridges. The storage capacity of the single cartridges shown here usually varies from about 5 million to 28 million characters. For a single disk pack, the storage capacity usually ranges from about 30 million to 300 million characters. A disk pack equal in storage capacity to a reel of magnetic tape may be about 25 times more expensive, but the cost per bit stored is still modest. (Courtesy Memorex)

FIGURE 6-3

Portable packs of rigid magnetic storage disks being loaded into multiple disk storage devices. (Photo courtesy Sperry Corporation)

arm in a disk storage device, they can be moved quickly and directly to any disk location in order to store or retrieve data. The facts stored on a disk can be read many times. They will remain indefinitely or until the disk surface is erased and reused.

Types of Magnetic Disks   All magnetic disks are round platters coated with a magnetizeable recording material, but their similarities end there. They come in different sizes. They can be portable or permanently mounted in their storage devices (called **disk drives**). And they can be made of rigid metal or flexible plastic. Here are some of the possible options:

● *Larger (14-inch) metal disks permanently housed in sealed, contamination-free containers.*   Read/write heads and access mechanisms are also sealed in with the disks they serve. These sealed disks are used in all but the smallest computer systems. Their containers are usually not removed from the disk drive. High-capacity storage units that use these sealed housings are called **Winchester disk drives.**

● *Other 14-inch metal disks packaged in removable cartridges or disk packs.*   Removable disk devices use one- or two-disk **cartridges** or **disk packs** of three or more disks mounted on a single shaft (see Figure 6-2). These are also used in all but the smallest systems, but they aren't sealed in contamination-free containers. Multiple disk storage devices, each capable of holding one or more cartridges or packs, may be connected to a processor unit (Figure 6-3).

● *Smaller 8-inch and 5¼-inch rigid disks permanently housed in Winchester disk devices.*   These are used in minicomputer and microcomputer systems (see Figure 6-4). Some 5¼-inch disk drives are also available with sealed but removable Winchester-type *cartridges.*

● *Smaller 8-inch and 5¼-inch portable floppy (flexible) disks individually packaged in protective envelopes.*   In addition to their data entry uses, these diskettes are currently the most popular online secondary storage medium used in personal computer and intelligent terminal systems (see Figures 6-5 and 6-6).

FIGURE 6-4

Winchester was the code name used by IBM during the development of this technology. The story is told that IBM designers originally planned to use dual disk drives to introduce the new concepts. Each drive was to have a storage capacity of 30 million characters. The product was thus expected to be a "30-30." Since that was the caliber of a famous rifle, the new product was nicknamed "Winchester." The dual-drive plans were later dropped, but the name stuck. Many other vendors now make Winchester disk drives. (Photo courtesy Seagate)

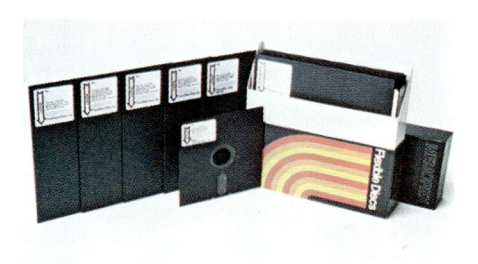

FIGURE 6-5

The floppies shown here are 8-inch and 5¼-inch sizes. The 5¼-inch disk is used in most systems today, but smaller sizes are gaining in popularity. (Courtesy Memorex)

FIGURE 6-6

Personal computer systems often use floppy disks for online secondary storage as well as for data entry. (Photo courtesy International Business Machines Corporation)

- ***Even more compact floppy and rigid disks measuring less than 4 inches in diameter.*** There are several competing *floppy* sizes. Disks with diameters of 3-inch, 3¼-inch, and at least three incompatible 3½-inch sizes have led to a confusing "aflopalypse now" situation with several vendors vying for a leading market position. But all the floppy versions are individually packaged in a nonbendable shirt-pocket-sized plastic case. This hard case has a dust-sealing and fingerproof shutter that opens automatically when the case is inserted in its disk drive. These disks are used in desktop and portable personal computers and word processing units. For example, Apple Computer

MODULE 2

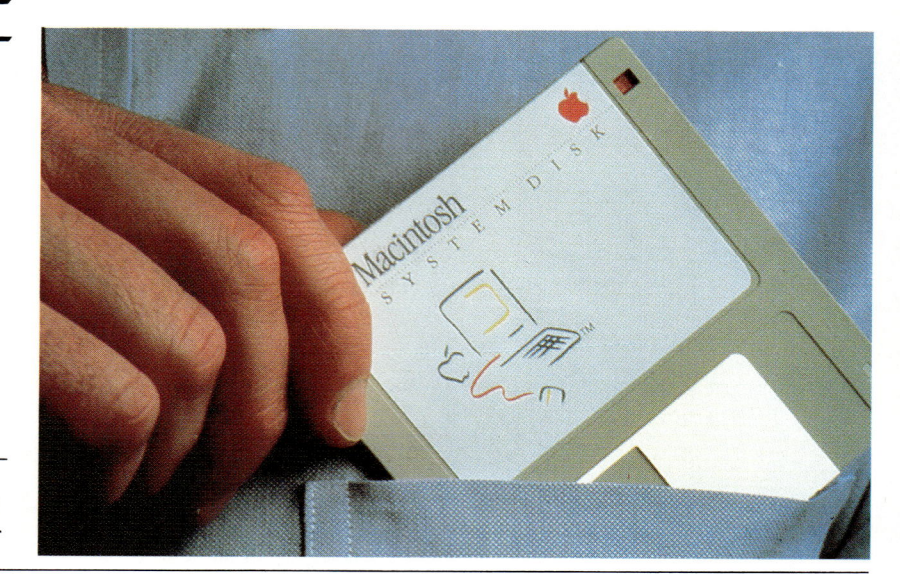

202

The 3½-inch floppy disk, with its hard case and protective shutter, is far better protected than 5¼-inch floppies. (Courtesy Apple Computer, Inc.)

FIGURE 6-7

Removable Winchester-type hard-disk cartridges are a fairly recent innovation in hard-disk applications. (Reprinted with permission from David Powell, "How a Hard Disk Works," *Popular Computing*, May 1984, p. 121. Copyright © 1984 by McGraw-Hill, Inc. All rights reserved.)

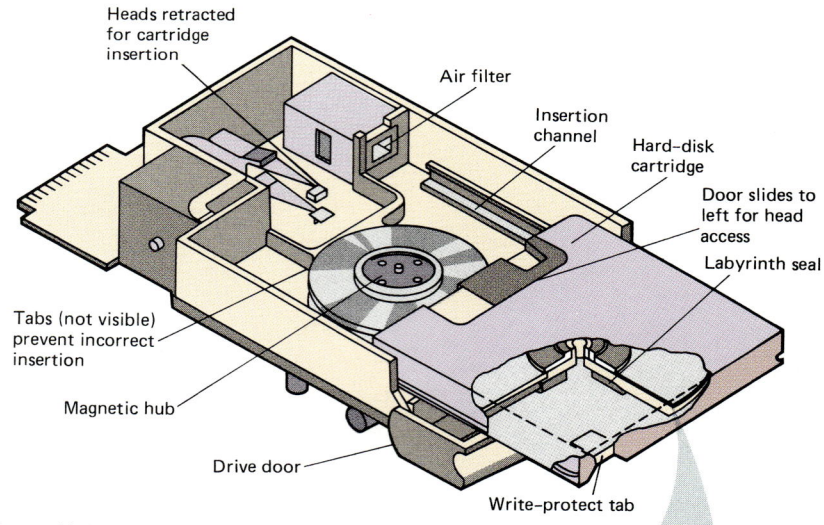

Heads retracted for cartridge insertion
Air filter
Insertion channel
Hard-disk cartridge
Door slides to left for head access
Labyrinth seal
Tabs (not visible) prevent incorrect insertion
Magnetic hub
Drive door
Write-protect tab

Removable Hard-Disk Cartridge

As a hard-disk cartridge is inserted into its drive, the cartridge door slides open to allow access by the read/write heads. When the cartridge is seated on the drive spindle, the disk is held in place by a magnetic hub.

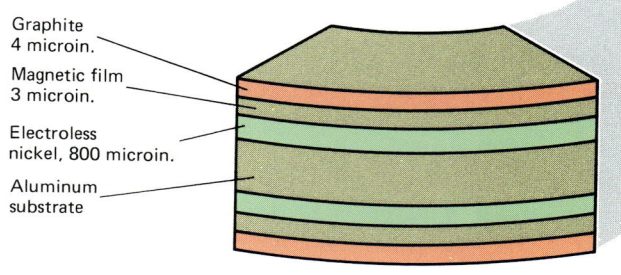

Graphite 4 microin.
Magnetic film 3 microin.
Electroless nickel, 800 microin.
Aluminum substrate

Disk Cross Section (not to scale)

uses a 3½-inch version in its Macintosh models. *Rigid* disk drives with sealed but removable Winchester-type *cartridges* have also been developed in a compact 3.9-inch size (see Figure 6-7).

Storing Data on Magnetic Disks   Music is stored on a phonograph record in a continuous groove that spirals into the center of the record. But there are no grooves on a magnetic disk. Instead, data are stored on all disks in a number of invisible concentric circles called **tracks.** These tracks, like the rings in a tree, begin at the outer edge of the disk and continue toward the center without ever touching (see Figure 6-8). Each track has a designated number.

A motor rotates the disk at a rapid speed.[2] Data are recorded on the tracks of a spinning disk surface and read from the surface by one or more read/write heads. If a floppy disk is used, the head is in contact with the disk. If hard disks are used, the heads "fly" on a cushion of air a few microinches (or millionths of an inch) above the surface. When multiple disks are packaged together, a number of **access arms** and read/write heads are used (see Figures 6-9 and 6-10). Data are written as tiny magnetic spots on the disk surface. A 1-spot is magnetized in one direction, a 0-spot in another. The 7- or 8-bit BCD codes discussed in Chapter 4 are generally used to represent data. Writing new data on a disk erases data previously stored at the location, but otherwise magnetic spots remain indefinitely. Reading of recorded data is accomplished as the magnetized spots pass under a read head and induce electrical pulses in it.

The more disk surfaces a particular system has, the greater its storage capacity will be. For example, many floppy disks are designed to store data on just one surface. Access to the surface of a **single-sided** disk is through a single slot or window on one side of the disk jacket. But **double-sided** floppy disks with slots for both surfaces are available with some systems. As you would expect, the storage capacity of a double-sided disk is about twice that of a single-sided one.

---

[2]Most floppy disks turn at a constant speed of between 300 and 600 revolutions per minute (rpm), but the Apple Macintosh system varies the rotational speed between 390 and 600 rpm depending on the track being used. Hard disks rotate at a constant speed from 2,400 to 4,700 rpm, with 3,600 being common.

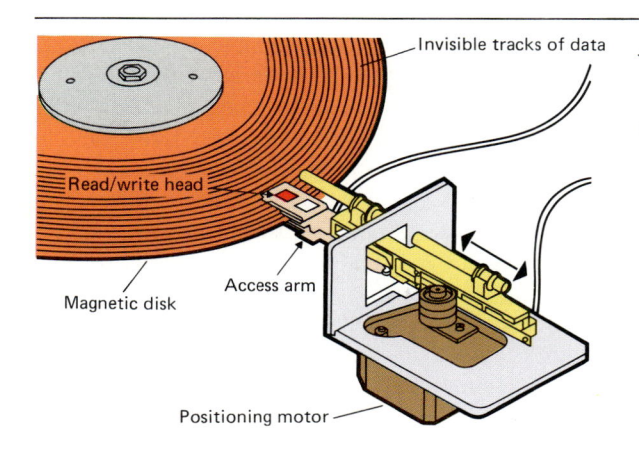

FIGURE 6-8

Data are stored on invisible tracks on the surface of a disk. There may be from 35 to over 100 tracks on a floppy-disk surface, and from about 200 to over 800 on hard-disk surfaces. Both the top and bottom of a hard disk are generally used for data storage. One or more read/write heads are assigned to each storage surface to record and retrieve data. These heads are fastened to access arms or actuators which are moved in and out over the spinning disk surfaces by positioning motors. The heads can thus be quickly located over any track to read or write data.

MODULE 2

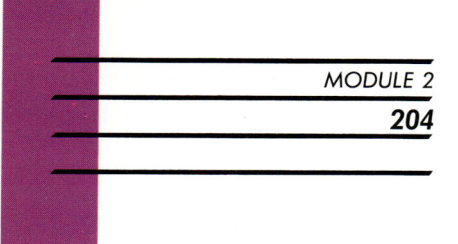

204

FIGURE 6-9

Multiple access arms and read/write heads are used with disk packs. The arms move in and out in unison among the individual disks. Two heads are frequently mounted on each arm to access two surfaces. In this example, the heads on the top arm access the bottom of the top disk and the top of the second disk. Data aren't stored on the top surface of the top disk or the bottom surface of the bottom disk because these surfaces are easily scratched. In this illustration, the pack has ten recording and two protective surfaces.

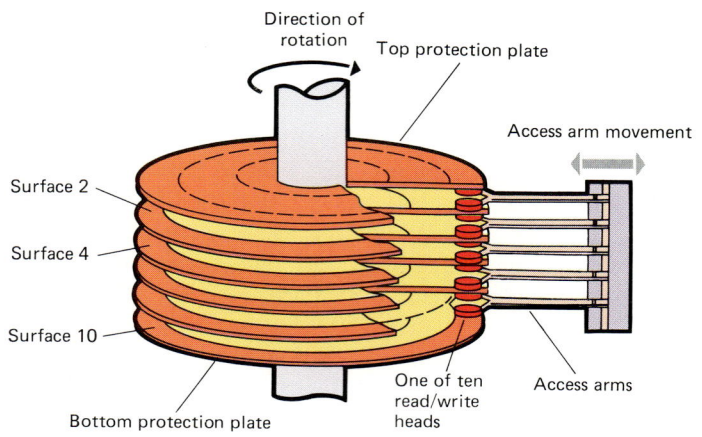

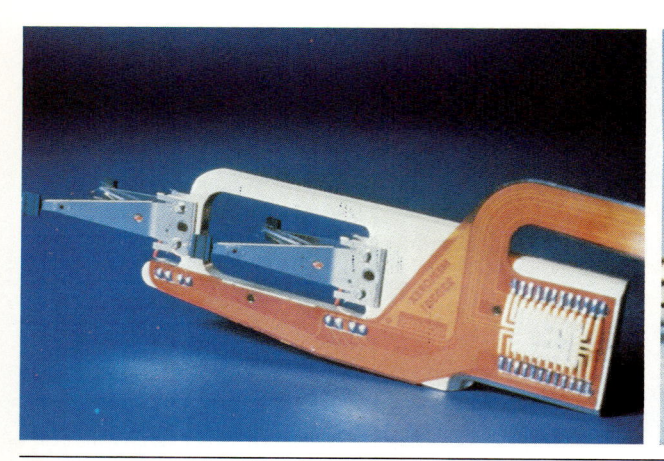

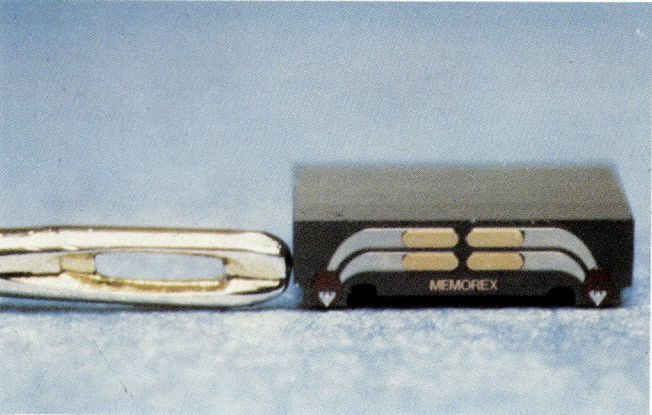

FIGURE 6-10

(*left*) A head-arm assembly used in a hard-disk drive. (*right*) One of the four thin-film read/write heads on the arm assembly shown next to a needle's eye for perspective. (Courtesy Memorex)

The storage capacity of a disk system also depends on the **bits per inch of track** and the **tracks per inch of surface.** That is, the storage capacity depends on the number of bits that can be stored on an inch of track and the number of tracks that can be placed on an inch of surface (see Figure 6-11). A constant goal of hard-disk-drive designers is to increase the data density of a disk surface by increasing the number of tracks. To accomplish this goal, they must reduce the distance between the read/write head and the disk surface so that smaller magnetized spots can be precisely written and then retrieved. But as designers found ways to reduce this distance and increase the data density, they ran into a problem. As Figure 6-12 shows, they moved the read/write head so close to the disk surface that a human hair or a dust particle on the disk loomed like a mountain in the path of the flying head. The resulting collision caused the head to bounce up and then **crash** on the far side of the particle. This often damaged the head, the disk, and the data.

Winchester technology was developed to reduce this problem. Sealing the disks and their heads in contamination-free containers reduced head crashes, permitted smaller distances between head and disk, and increased disk storage capacity. Of course, disk problems can't be totally eliminated.

FIGURE 6-11

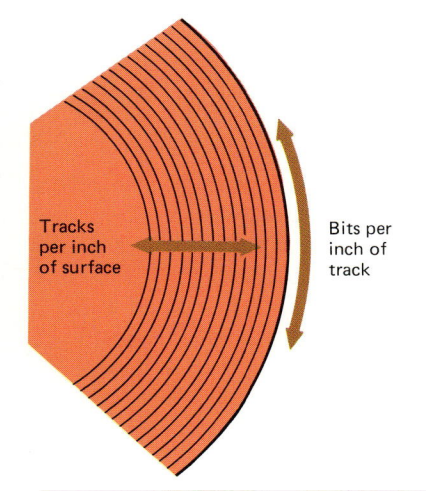

the storage capacity of a magnetic disk system include bits per inch of track, and tracks per inch of surface. Some Winchester hard-disk systems can store well over 10,000 bits on an inch of track and have over 400 tracks on an inch of disk surface. Their high data density permits compact 3.9-inch Winchester-type disk devices to store over 6 megabytes (a *megabyte* is roughly a million bytes or characters). Some 5¼-inch Winchester systems can store over 60 megabytes. Similar 8-inch systems can store over 100 megabytes, and up to one gigabyte (a *gigabyte* is roughly a billion bytes or characters) can be held on a 14-inch Winchester disk system. The 14-inch disks packaged in removable cartridges and packs usually have a much lower data density than Winchester disks. Floppy-disk systems come in either single- or double-density versions and record on one or both surfaces of a diskette. Thus the capacity of an earlier system using a single-sided 5¼-inch diskette may only be a little over 100 kilobytes (a *kilobyte* is about a thousand bytes or characters), while the capacity of a later system using a double-density, dual-sided 5¼-inch or smaller diskette may be over 3 megabytes.

And if there's a failure, let's say, in a Winchester device with a permanently mounted disk, the information stored isn't available for some time or it may even be lost. Thus **backup copies** of the information stored on the fixed Winchester disk—or any other important disk—need to be saved periodically.

One popular approach is to make backups using the magnetic tape *cartridges* discussed in Chapter 5. These cartridges are inserted into a **streaming tape drive** that may be built into the hard-disk unit or housed in a separate cabinet. As the 600 feet of ¼-inch tape in a single cartridge ''streams'' through the tape drive, it can store over 60 million characters of information. Another approach is to write the Winchester information onto the removable disks used with other disk drives. For example, the information on a personal computer's Winchester disk can be transferred to the computer's floppy-disk system and saved on diskettes. However, it may take from a dozen to well over a hundred 5¼-inch floppies to hold the information stored on a single 5¼-inch Winchester disk, so this backup method is expensive and time-consuming.

Accessing Data on Magnetic Disks Just as the pickup arm of a record player can be moved directly to the location of a specific song without playing

FIGURE 6-12

Data density can be improved and storage capacity can be increased by reducing the flying height of read/write heads over disk surfaces. Each reduction in height allows an increase in bits per inch of track and tracks per inch of surface. The reason Winchester technology was developed to control the disk environment is obvious in this illustration. A smoke particle 250 millionths of an inch in diameter can't begin to fit in the space between head and disk. And a human hair looks like Pike's Peak to the flying head. The head flies 20 millionths of an inch above the disk at speeds of over 100 miles per hour. That's comparable to an airplane flying 600 miles per hour around the circumference of a lake at an altitude of ¼ inch.

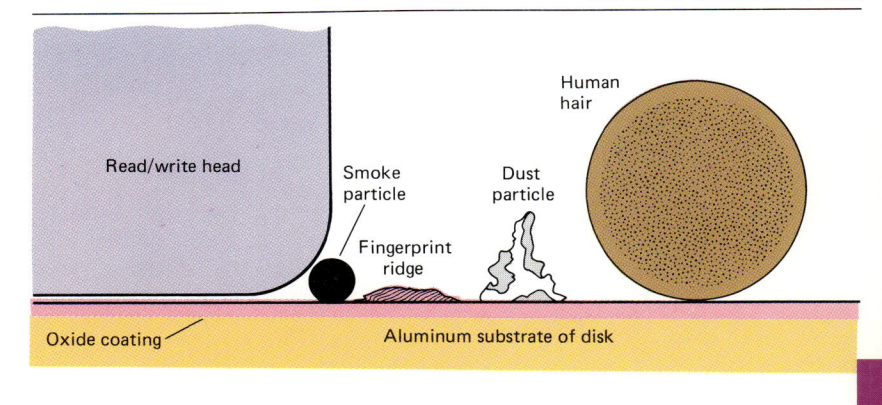

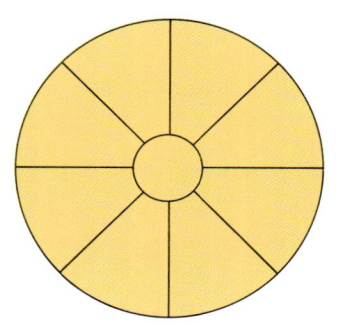

(a) Segments on a disk surface are often arranged like cuts of pie. The number of these segments varies, but there are generally 8 or more.

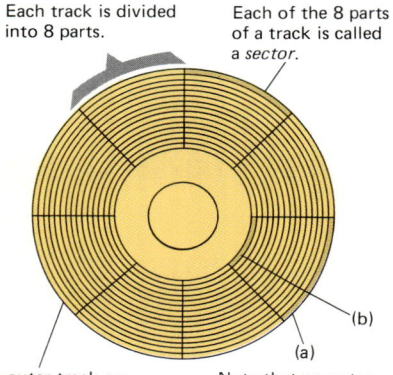

Each track is divided into 8 parts.

Each of the 8 parts of a track is called a *sector.*

The outer track on the disk surface. (Although not all are shown, there are 80 such tracks on the disk.)

Note that an outer sector (a) is longer than an inner sector (b) though both hold the same number of characters.

(b) If a floppy disk with 80 tracks is divided into 8 pie-slice wedges, each track is divided into 8 parts, and each of these 8 portions of a track is called a *sector*. Thus, if there are 8 sectors per track, and if there are 80 tracks on the disk, then there are 80 x 8 or 640 sectors on the disk surface. Each sector holds a specified number of data characters, typically from 256 to 1,024.

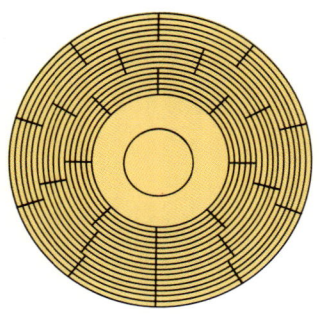

(c) A newer disk storage method adds sectors to the outer tracks so that all sectors occupy approximately the same space over the entire disk surface. This approach is used with the Apple Macintosh disk system, and Apple was able to increase the storage capacity of its 3 ½-inch floppy disk by about 40 percent.

other music, an access arm can move a read/write head directly to the track that contains the desired data without reading other tracks. Disk-drive manufacturers use either the *sector method* or the *cylinder method* to organize and physically store data on disks.

The sector method This method is used with single disks (including floppies) as well as with cartridges and packs of multiple disks. A disk surface is often divided into invisible segments shaped like "pie cuts" (see Figure 6-13a). Although the number varies with the disk system used, there are generally at least eight of these segments on a disk. Let's suppose that a floppy disk with 80 tracks is divided into eight of these equal segments. Each track is thus divided into eight parts (Figure 6-13b), and each of these eight portions of a track is called a **sector.** Each sector holds a specified number of characters. You'll notice that the sectors on the outer tracks are longer than those on the inner ones. Since the same number of characters is held in each sector, the size of the inner sectors determines the storage capacity for all other sectors on the disk. This means that storage space remains unused on the outer tracks, and this is a disadvantage of dividing disks into pie-shaped segments. To avoid this wasted space, disk control programs used with some newer Apple, Commodore, and other personal computers partition the disk so that all sectors occupy approximately the same amount of space (Figure 6-13c).

Before a disk drive can access any sector record, a computer program must provide the record's **disk address.** This address specifies the track number and sector number (and surface number when double-sided diskettes or hard disks are used). Let's look at Figure 6-14 to see how data may be read from a floppy disk (some of the same general concepts apply when hard disks are used). You'll notice in Figure 6-14a that a typical floppy disk has a small hole to the right of the larger center hole. This small hole in the *jacket* is called the **index-hole window** (or **sector sight hole**). There's also a small hole in the *disk itself,* although you can't see it unless it's aligned with the jacket hole. This hole in the disk is called the **index hole** (or **begin-sector hole**). The index hole enables the disk controller to locate disk sectors, as shown in Figure 6-14b.

Access begins in step 1 of Figure 6-14b when a read/write head is moved to the track specified in the disk address. Next, the disk-drive controller looks for an index reference so that it can determine sector locations (step 2). In a floppy-disk system, this reference is the index hole that marks the location of the first sector on a track. (Other arrangements are used with hard disks.) The alignment of the index hole in the disk with the index-hole window in the jacket allows a light to pass through the disk. This light triggers a light-sensing device to mark the hole's location. When the index hole is detected, the disk controller begins reading data (step 3), and when the sector specified in the disk address begins to pass under the read/write head, the controller starts

FIGURE 6-13

Although there are no standard ways for sectors to be arranged on disk surfaces, variations of the arrangements shown here are commonly used.

(a) A closer look at a floppy disk

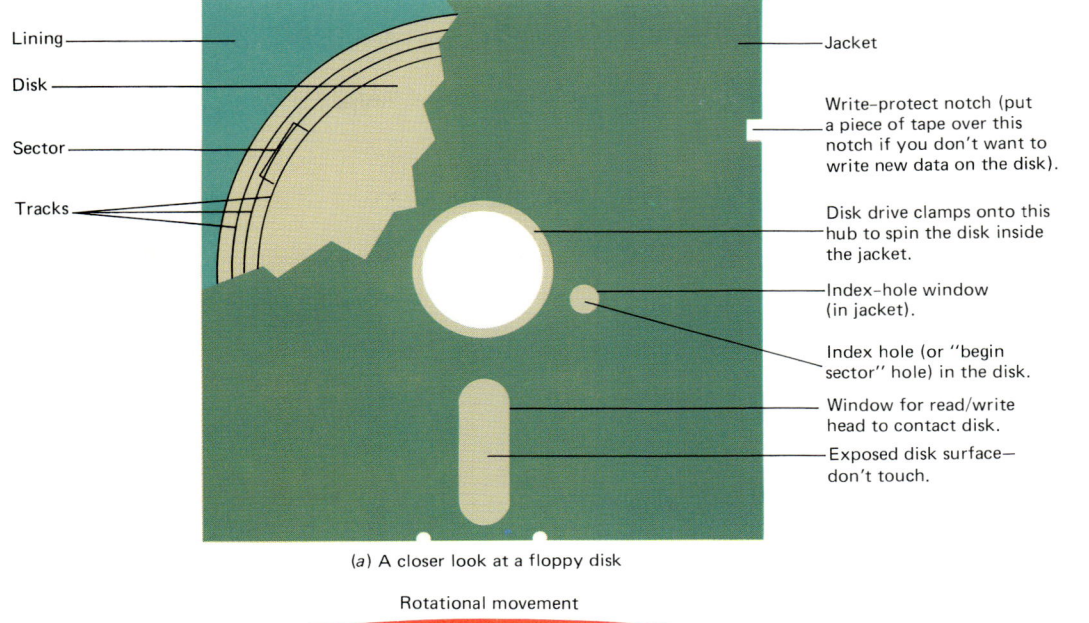

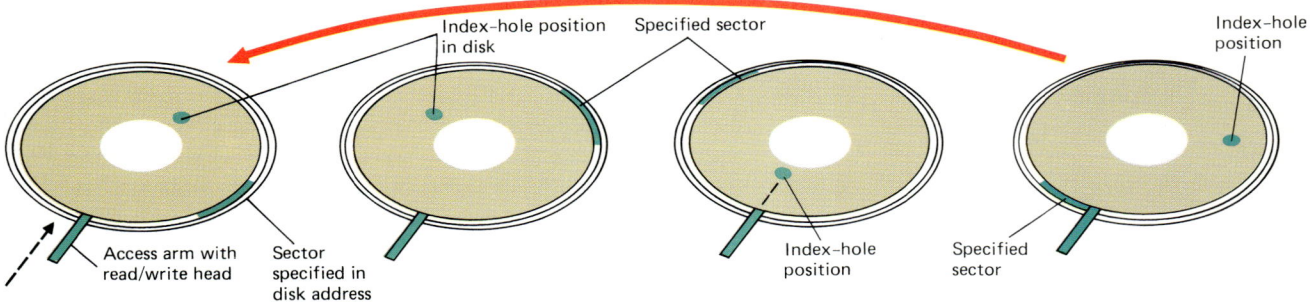

(b) Reading data from a floppy disk

FIGURE 6-14

transmitting data to the processor unit (step 4). Earlier floppy-disk drives used **hard-sectored** disks that were punched with an entire ring of holes so that each hole marked the beginning of a different sector, but such disks aren't used much today. Instead, a single hole is punched and software is then used to **format** the disk—that is, to determine the number of sectors per track and the number of characters that can be stored in each sector. Such a disk is said to be **soft-sectored.**

The cylinder method This method of organizing disk data is used with packs of removable disks and is shown in Figure 6-15. Access arms move in unison in and out of a disk pack. Thus if the read/write head that serves the top recording surface is positioned over the twentieth track, each of the heads on the arms that serve other surfaces is similarly positioned over the same track.

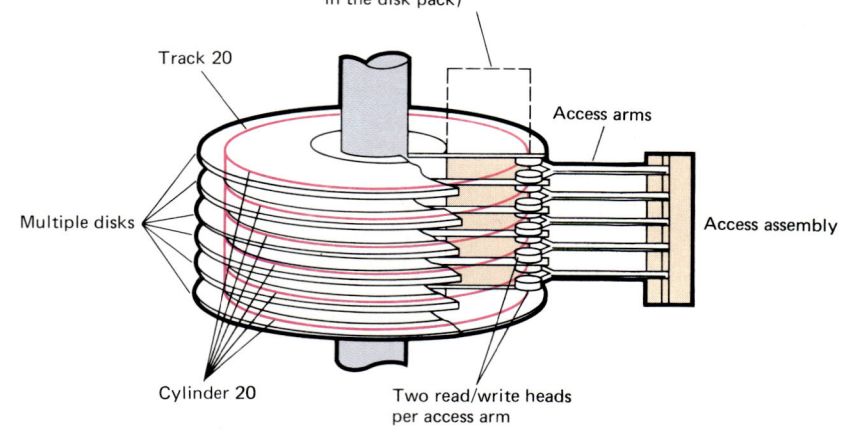

FIGURE 6-15

When data are organized by cylinders, the cylinder number, surface number, and record number are needed to access the stored data. All tracks with the same number in a disk pack form a cylinder with the same number. Each invisible cylinder passes vertically through the pack.

All the twentieth tracks together comprise the twentieth **cylinder** of the disks. If there are 200 or more tracks on a single hard-disk surface, there are also 200 or more cylinders in a multiple stack of the disks. Before a record can be accessed, a computer program must again give the disk drive the record's address. This address supplies the cylinder number, the surface number, and the record number. Thus a desired record might be on a cylinder (track) 20, on surface 1, in record location 5. If a large number of related records are typically processed in sequence after record 5, they can be organized to follow record 5 on this same track and surface and can then be continued on the same track of other surfaces in the cylinder. In one revolution of the disk, the data on track 20 of surface 1 is read. In the next revolution, control is instantly switched to the read/write head over surface 2, and a full track of data can be read in a single revolution. This procedure can continue down the cylinder without any delays caused by the movement of access arms.

Access speed The access time for data stored on a disk is basically determined by:

1 The **seek time**—the time required to position a head over the proper track

2 The **search** (or **latency**) **time**—the time required to spin the needed data under the head

The average access time for most hard-disk storage systems is usually between 10 and 100 milliseconds.[3] For floppy-disk systems, the average time usually ranges from 70 to 600 milliseconds.[4] Most disk drives have a single

---

[3]Technically speaking, disk drives have *direct* but not *random* access to records. Random access refers to a storage device in which the access time is independent of the physical location of the data. Since the disk access time does vary with the data location, it's more correct to say that disks provide direct access. This distinction is not always observed, however, and disk drives are sometimes referred to as random access units.

[4]Floppy disks rotate much more slowly than hard disks and so their search time is much longer. A floppy can't turn too fast or centrifugal force will bend it out of shape and damage the stored data. A rigid metal disk doesn't have this problem.

read/write head for each disk surface. But some of the faster hard-disk systems either have a *fixed-head* for *each* track of a surface, or they use *multiple heads* on each movable access arm to service a number of adjacent tracks. A **fixed-head-per-track device** has *no* seek time delay, and multiple heads reduce the average length of horizontal movement of the access arms and thus decrease the seek time. Of course, these faster systems are more expensive than the single-head-per-arm devices.

Once the data have been accessed, they are copied from the disk to the processor. The transfer rate depends on the density of the stored data and the rotational speed of the disk. For floppy systems, the maximum transfer rate is typically between 30,000 and 150,000 characters per second. For hard-disk systems, the maximum rate usually ranges between 200,000 and 2 million characters per second.

Advantages and Limitations of Magnetic Disks

Let's summarize a few disk *advantages:*

- Disk records can be stored sequentially and processed like magnetic tape records, or they can be stored for direct-access processing.

- Any online disk record can be accessed and updated in a few milliseconds. No sorting of transactions is necessary.

- A single input transaction can be used to simultaneously update the online disk records of several related files.

But disks also have some *limitations:*

- When a magnetic tape file is updated, the old master tape usually remains unchanged and is available for a period of time in case of system malfunctions. When the records in a disk file are updated, however, the old records may be erased when the new records are written on the disk. And information stored on a fixed Winchester disk could be unavailable or lost if there's a drive failure. We've seen that special backup procedures are thus required to protect disk records from malfunctions.

- People have broken through security provisions and gained access to sensitive online disk files from remote terminals. These files have been manipulated and destroyed. It's easier to maintain the security of magnetic tape files.

Direct Access with RAM "Disks" and Magnetic Bubbles

RAM "Disk" Storage

In this direct-access storage approach used with personal computers, a block of semiconductor RAM chips is used as a *simulated* "disk" to replace the mechanical operations of rotating disks. Sometimes referred to as a *silicon disk* or a *pseudo-disk,* a **RAM disk** isn't really a disk at all, and it has no moving parts. Rather, it's a bank of RAM chips set up to look like a disk drive to the computer. The extra RAM chips may be placed on add-on circuit boards that fit inside the computer, or they may be housed in separate cabinets. Either way, these extra chips look just like a disk drive to the control programs used in the personal computer's operating system.

MODULE 2

This RAM "disk" board fits inside a computer and imitates the functions of a disk drive, giving the user extremely fast access to programs stored in its chips. (Courtesy Quadram Corp.)

FIGURE 6-16

Magnetic bubble chip. (Courtesy Intel Corporation)

The main advantage of a RAM disk is its speed; it turns a slow processor into a "hot rod." Instead of waiting seconds while data or instructions are loaded from a floppy disk, RAM disk users have nearly instant access. Even Winchester disks are slow by comparison. To gain speed during a processing session, then, users can copy their programs from floppies or some other permanent medium into a RAM disk and avoid most of the delay that might be caused by frequent calls to a disk. However, a problem with the volatile RAM chips commonly used today is that the stored contents are lost when power is removed. Thus programs and the data files produced during a processing session must be stored on a permanent disk before the power is shut off.

Magnetic Bubble Storage **Magnetic bubble storage** devices are also semiconductor chips that have no moving parts and are thus reliable (see Figure 6-16). But unlike the chips used for RAM disk storage, bubble chips retain their stored contents when power is removed. When they were introduced in the late 1970s, some researchers expected that they would eventually replace many magnetic disk systems. But bubble devices have failed to live up to these optimistic expectations. Disk storage costs fell much faster than expected while bubble storage costs remain higher than predicted.

Still, large numbers of bubble chips are now being used in specialized areas. They are found in portable computers. Portable terminals use bubble devices to store data until they can be transmitted to a larger system. And bubble chips are also being used in machine tools, robots, and military computers. The data density of these chips is high. About 240 typewritten pages of information can be stored on a chip the size of a thumbnail.

Direct Access with Optical Disks and Tape Strips

Optical Disk Technology You're probably aware that **optical disks** are now used by consumer electronics companies to record movies, concerts, sporting events, and other audio/visual presentations for playback on television sets. Some of these platters are grooveless "videodisks" that are created by **laser recording systems.** A beam of laser light may be used to burn tiny holes (or pits) into a thin coating of metal or other material deposited on a spinning disk. Visible only under a powerful microscope, these holes are used to represent images and sounds. Of course, they can't be erased and the disk can't be reused. A less powerful laser light beam in a videodisk player may be used to read the hole patterns, convert these patterns into audio/visual signals, and transmit the signals to a television set. (Other laser writing techniques exist, but all produce marks that are only about one-fiftieth the thickness of a human hair.)

The same optical disk technology that's used to record and play back sound and images can also be used to store and retrieve data. The storage density of optical disks is enormous (100 or more times greater than a typical rigid magnetic disk of the same size), the storage cost is extremely low (e.g., less than 5 cents to store the contents of this book), and the access time is relatively fast. Laboratory systems already can store on a single disk the contents of a library of several thousand volumes. Permanent archives now stored on microfilm and magnetic tape may soon be placed on optical disks. One small inexpensive disk can already replace 15 reels of magnetic tape (Figure 6-17). And the future storage capacity of a single disk is expected to be much greater. Disk players will be able to access any data on these disks in a few milliseconds. And newer techniques have been developed to permit optical disks to be erased and reused.

FIGURE 6-17

A single Hitachi optical disk provides the same memory capacity as 15 magnetic tapes. (Photo courtesy Hitachi, Ltd.)

Mass Storage with Tape Strips A single reel of magnetic tape costing less than $20 will hold the contents of about 200 books of this size. Wouldn't it be nice to combine these magnetic tape advantages of low cost and high storage capacity with the advantages of direct record accessibility? This is the objective of **tape strip devices** used for mass storage. The storage medium may be considered to be a length of flexible plastic material upon which short strips of magnetic tape have been mounted. These strips are then placed in cartridges, and the cartridges are loaded into a storage device that's online to the processor unit. An example of such a device is the IBM mass storage system (see Figure 6-18). Honeycomb storage compartments are used to hold the data cartridges. It requires several seconds for this device to locate the cartridge specified by an instruction from the processor. Once the cartridge has been located and placed in a position to be read, several more seconds are needed to transfer the data to a magnetic disk and then to the processor. That's an eternity compared to other online devices in the storage hierarchy. But the storage capacity is huge and the cost per bit stored is very small.

FIGURE 6-18

(*top*) IBM mass storage system. (*bottom*) Honeycomb storage compartments are used in this system to hold data cartridges. Over 400,000 books the size of this one can be stored in this system. (Courtesy International Business Machines Corporation)

Future Direct-Access Developments

Direct-access storage devices will continue to be improved for years to come. Such devices will be developed to provide virtually unlimited online secondary storage at a very modest cost. Storage hierarchies will continue too; the fastest auxiliary storage utilizing the latest technology will likely be more expensive and may have less storage capacity than slower and less expensive alternatives.

Perpendicular recording techniques (Figure 6-19) and other methods that significantly increase the density of data storage on a given *magnetic* disk surface may be developed in the near future. Soon, the contents of over 600 books of this size can be stored in a magnetic disk device occupying the space of two small present-day floppy-disk drives. Over 15 million bits of data are currently being stored on a square inch of some disk surfaces. In the next 6

FIGURE 6-19

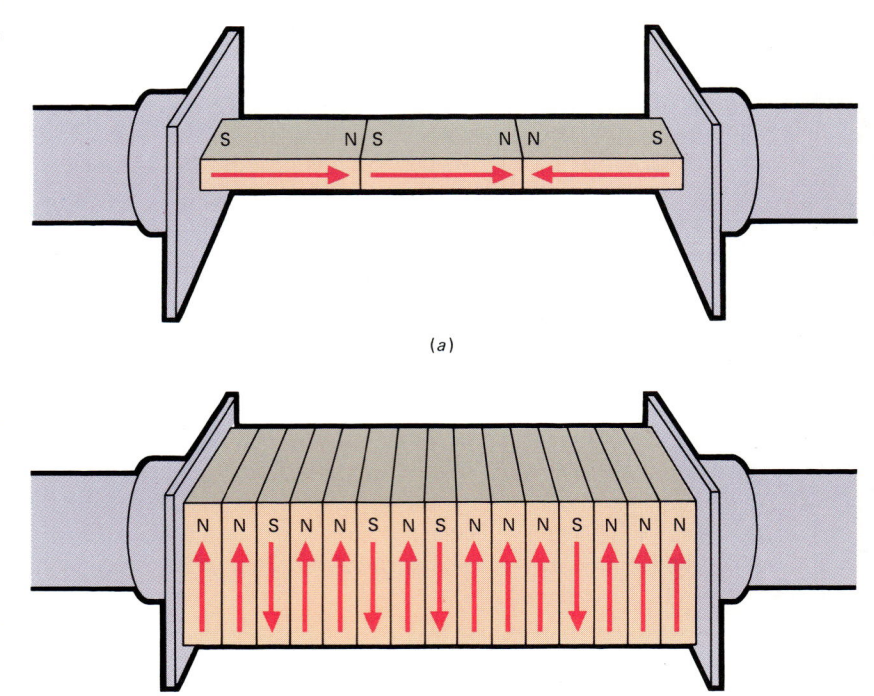

The perpendicular recording techniques now being developed promise to significantly increase the density of data storage on a disk surface. (a) When the conventional horizontal recording approach is used, the bits of stored data resemble bar magnets laying end to end. (b) In contrast, the perpendicular recording technique stands the recorded bits upright in a crystal structure made from cobalt and chrome. (Copyright 1982 by CW Communications, Inc., Framingham, Mass. 01701. Reprinted from *Computerworld*.)

or 7 years, there may be a tenfold improvement—to 150 million bits or more. The costs of disk storage will also drop dramatically. A 100-million-character hard-disk drive for personal computers will soon be available for less than $1,000. Finally, it's likely that both erasable and nonerasable *optical* disk systems will replace magnetic and microfilm media in applications where enormous amounts of data must be retained.

SECONDARY STORAGE FOR SEQUENTIAL ACCESS

You'll recall from Chapter 2 that the records in a sequential file are typically stored one after the other in an ascending or descending order determined by the record key. To access records, the computer starts with the first one in the sequence. This record is read and is either processed or passed over. The second record is then accessed, followed by the third, and so on. Files of sequential records were maintained for years in decks of punched cards, but the storage media used for sequential access today are magnetic disks and magnetic tape.

Disk Storage for Sequential Access

We've already considered how music on a phonograph record can be recorded in a particular sequence and then replayed in the same sequence if that serves our purpose. Similarly, data recorded on a magnetic disk can be stored and then retrieved in a predetermined order to support a sequential processing

FIGURE 6-20

Large computer systems make use of extensive tape libraries, which contain thousands and thousands of reels of stored information and occupy entire rooms in an organization. (Courtesy AT&T)

application. But when records on a disk are sequentially organized and processed, the direct-access capability of the disk drive really isn't used. The first record in the sequence may be directly retrieved, but all others are then read and processed in order as if they were stored on a magnetic tape.

Magnetic Tape Storage

Magnetic tape is often the medium selected to store large files that are sequentially accessed and processed. Thousands of reels of stored data are maintained in the magnetic tape libraries of large computer systems (see Figure 6-20).

Storing Data on Magnetic Tape You saw in Chapter 5 that data are stored as tiny spots on the magnetizeable material that coats one side of a plastic tape. The coated side of the tape is divided into vertical columns (or **frames**) and horizontal rows (called **channels** or **tracks**). An 8-bit BCD code of the type discussed in Chapter 4 is used with a **nine-track magnetic tape** format in many tape systems today. Figure 6-21 shows a few characters coded in a nine-track arrangement.

It's popular now to use nine tracks to record data on standard ½-inch-wide *reels* of tape. But newer tape systems have recently been introduced that record 18 tracks of data on the same ½-inch-wide surface. The tape in these newer systems is stored in 4- by 5-inch cartridges. A nine-track tape is coated with an iron-oxide magnetizeable material, but the new cartridges use a chromium dioxide coating. Up to 6,250 characters can be stored on a single *inch* of nine-track tape, but 38,000 characters can be squeezed onto the same space when an **18-track cartridge system** is used.

Since any magnetic tape is a continuous-length medium, how can different file records be identified on a tape? The answer is that records may be

Despite its small size, the IBM 3480 18-track tape cartridge holds as many characters as the older 9-track reel of tape it rests upon here. (Courtesy IBM Corp.)

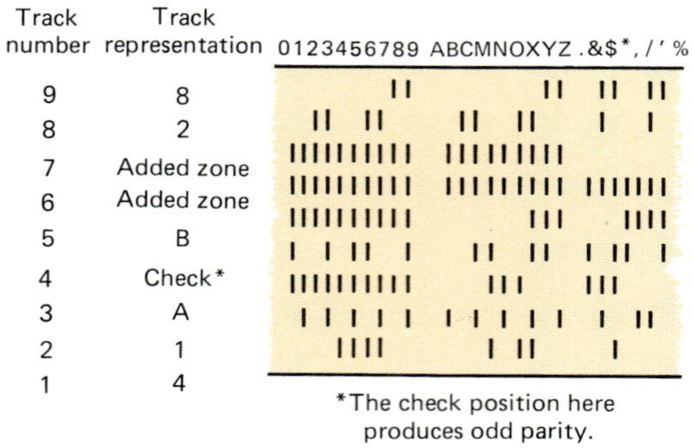

MODULE 2

214

FIGURE 6-21

A nine-track tape code used with many modern computers. An 8-bit EBCDIC format is used in this example.

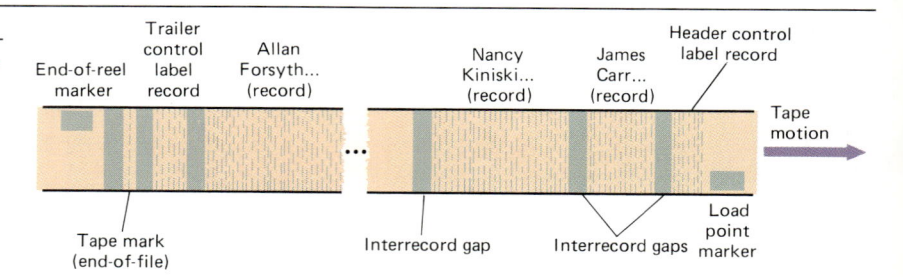

Track number	Track representation
9	8
8	2
7	Added zone
6	Added zone
5	B
4	Check*
3	A
2	1
1	4

0123456789 ABCMNOXYZ .&$*,/'%

*The check position here produces odd parity.

FIGURE 6-22

A file of employees (first introduced in Figure 2-16). The first several feet of tape are unrecorded to allow for threading on the equipment. A reflective marker known as the *load point* indicates to the equipment the beginning of usable tape, while a similar *end-of-reel* marker signals the end of usable tape. The markers are placed on opposite edges of the tape for machine identification purposes. Between the load-point marker and the first data record is a *header control label*, which identifies the tape contents, gives the number of the program to be used when the tape is processed, and supplies other control information that helps to prevent an important tape from accidently being erased. Following the last data record in a file is a *trailer control label*, which may contain a count of the number of records in a file. A comparison between the number of records processed and the number in the file may be made to determine that all have been accounted for. The end of a file may be signaled by a special one-character record. This special character is called a *tape mark*.

End-of-reel marker | Trailer control label record | Allan Forsyth... (record) | Nancy Kiniski... (record) | James Carr... (record) | Header control label record

Tape mark (end-of-file) | Interrecord gap | Interrecord gaps | Load point marker

Tape motion →

separated by blank spaces on the tape called **interrecord gaps.** These gaps are automatically created when data are written on the tape. When record data are read from a moving tape into the processor, the movement stops when a gap is reached. The tape remains motionless until the record has been processed and then moves again to enter the next record into the computer. This procedure is repeated until the file has been processed. Figure 6-22 shows how an employee file could be represented on tape. Tape records can be of varying lengths. If a tape contains a large number of very short records and if each record is separated by an interrecord gap, then more than half the tape could be blank and there would be a constant interruption in tape movement. To avoid this inefficient situation, several short records can be combined into a tape **block** (see Figure 6-23).

Accessing Data on Magnetic Tape To access data stored on an offline magnetic tape, the computer operator must first locate the tape and load it on a tape drive (Figure 6-24). The tape is then moved past read/write heads in the drive. There's a separate head for each tape track. Figure 6-25 explains how these heads are used to read data from a tape and to write data onto a tape.

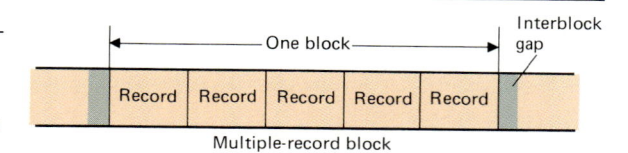

FIGURE 6-23

Several short records are commonly combined into a block and read into the processor as a single unit to save tape space and speed data input. The program of instructions in the computer separates the records within a block for processing.

← One block → | Interblock gap

| Record | Record | Record | Record | Record |

Multiple-record block

Advantages and Limitations of Magnetic Tape   The following *advantages* are possible with magnetic tape storage:

- *High data density.*   A typical 10½-inch-diameter reel of tape is 2,400 feet long and is able to hold 800, 1,600, or 6,250 characters in each inch of this length, depending on the tape drive used. Thus if 6,250 characters are held in each inch of tape and if the tape is 28,800 inches long (2,400 feet times 12 inches), then the maximum capacity of the tape is 180 million characters. And as we've seen, newer 18-track tape cartridges can achieve a sixfold improvement in data density.

- *Low cost and ease of handling.*   A 10½-inch reel of tape costs less than $20. A removable disk pack with comparable storage capacity may be 25 times more expensive. And since a reel is compact and weighs less than 3 pounds, it takes up little storage space and is easy to handle.

But there are *limitations* to the use of magnetic tape for secondary storage. Included among these are:

- *Lack of direct access to records.*   Magnetic tape is a sequential storage medium that's used for batch processing. The entire tape must be read and processed to update the sequentially organized records in a file. If frequent access to file records is needed on a rapid and random basis, then the file should not be stored on magnetic tape. Too much operator time would be required to load and unload tapes, and too much machine time would be wasted in reading records that aren't needed.

- *Environmental problems.*   Specks of dust and uncontrolled humidity or temperature levels can cause tape-reading errors. Tapes and reel containers must be carefully labeled and controlled so that an important file isn't erased by mistake.

FIGURE 6-24

To retrieve data stored offline on a magnetic tape, the computer operator must locate the appropriate file and load it on a tape drive. (Photo used with permission of Nixdorf Computer Corporation, Burlington, Mass.)

RECEIVING COMPUTER OUTPUT: SOME BASIC CONCEPTS

Why Output Is Needed

Computer data processing transforms input data into the output information that people can use to improve their understanding of issues and achieve specific goals. For example, you've seen in Chapter 2 that the output of personal computers is helping people manage data files, outline thoughts, manipulate spreadsheet data to answer "what if" questions, generate graphs for analysis and presentation, process text, communicate with others electronically, and manage projects and time.

Besides being helpful to individuals who use it to achieve personal ends, computer output is often vital to decision makers in organizations. To achieve organizational goals, these people must usually:

1   *Plan* for the future use of scarce human and capital resources. (Capital is money and the things money can buy.)

FIGURE 6-25

A read/write head. There are nine read/write heads in a nine-track tape drive. When a tape is being read, the magnetized patterns on the tape induce pulses of current in the read coils and these pulses are transmitted as data into the processor. In the writing operation, electrical pulses flow through the write coils at the appropriate tracks causing the iron-oxide coating of the tape to be magnetized in the proper pattern.

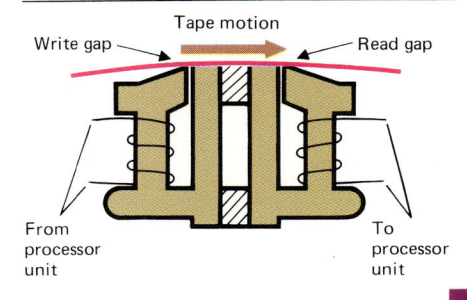

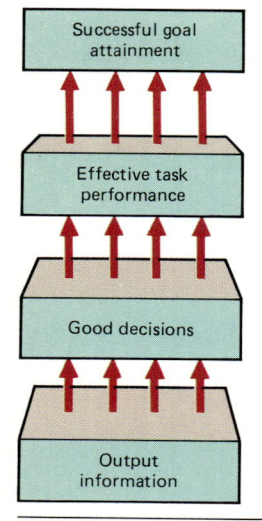

FIGURE 6-26

The success of an organization may depend on its output information.

2   *Organize* these resources into logical and efficient units.

3   *Control* these resources.

An organization's success is determined by how well its people perform these three tasks. And how well these tasks are carried out often depends, in part, on the quality of the available computer output. This is true because each task involves decision making, and decision making must generally be supported by output information that's as accurate, timely, complete, concise, and relevant as possible.

In summary, as Figure 6-26 shows, good output information in the hands of those who can effectively use it will support good decisions. Good decisions will lead to the effective performance of organizational tasks, and effective task performance will lead to success in reaching the organization's goals. Of course, decision makers must often use important information that's not produced by their organization's computers. But as Figure 6-26 suggests, computer output is now an important bonding agent that helps hold many organizations together.

Output Categories

Computer output produced by organizations may appear in various forms. The type of output that's likely to be generated in a particular application depends on such factors as (1) *who uses the output,* (2) *how fast it's needed,* and (3) *how much is needed.*

Output can be grouped into internal and external categories to identify those who use it. **Internal output** is information that's intended solely for the use of people within an organization, while **external output** is produced for those outside the organization. Organizations support *interactive* processing systems to give fast response to both internal and external users. For example, employee inquiries must be answered promptly, and the system must accept ongoing transactions from employees, check those transactions for accuracy, and send confirmation or error messages back to employees. Similarly, external users such as bank customers at automated teller machines expect quick and accurate responses to account-balance inquiries and deposit/withdrawal transactions.

The output volume produced for both internal and external users in an interactive processing situation is likely to be low and irregular. Therefore, the output itself is usually produced by display screens, small printers, or voice response units. It's important that interactive systems be easy to use for all who enter data and receive output. Menu-driven software generally guides external users and many internal users to the desired results. But internal output can be in a more coded and detailed form. For example, the internal output sent in response to a salesperson's inquiry about the availability of parts can include part code numbers and other information that a customer wouldn't understand.

When the timing requirements are less critical, internal and external output are produced by batch processing operations. The *internal* output is often in the form of reports that help decision makers do a better job. For example, a report can be prepared for the manager of the children's department in a store. This **detail report** might list each product offered by the department, and then give the sales for each product for a period. Such information might help the department manager make day-to-day operating decisions. However, the store manager doesn't need such detailed information.

What the store manager may need, however, is a **summary report** that condenses and sifts the detailed data so that sales patterns and trends emerge and appropriate actions may be taken. The type of information printed in summary reports is also frequently presented in the form of **computer graphic output** (see Figure 6-27). It's thus often possible to further condense several pages of summary information into a few pictures.

Unlike detailed and summary reports that are prepared at regular intervals, **exception reports** are usually triggered to supply computer output to people only when operating data fall outside the normal limits specified in a program. The purpose of an exception report is to alert someone to the need for decisions and actions. For example, such a report can be triggered to tell a pharmacist when the supply of certain drug items falls below a specified level. Exception reports save human time by permitting people to concentrate on the important exceptions.

The *external* output produced by batch processing can be the bills and statements sent to patients, clients, and customers, the checks issued to suppliers, or the income tax withholding forms sent to the Internal Revenue Service. These and other output documents issued by the organization must often be prepared on designated forms. Colorful trademarks are often preprinted on many of these forms to present a favorable image of the organization.

Since the output volume generated during the preparation of internal reports and external bills, checks, and other documents may be large, high-speed line and page printers are often used. When large-volume output is to be retained for some time, it may be recorded directly on microfilm. And when graphic output is produced, printers and plotters designed for this purpose are used. Let's now take a closer look at the devices and media mentioned in this section that are used to produce computer output.

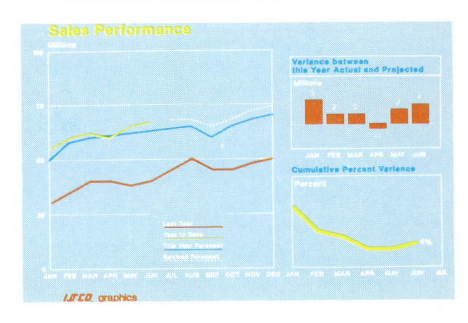

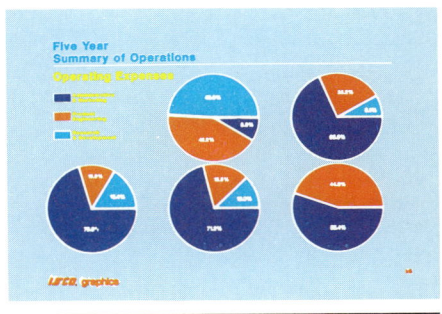

FIGURE 6-27

Output created by using graphic software packages makes mountains of data easier to understand. (Reprinted with permission from ISSCO, San Diego, Calif.)

PRINTED AND FILMED OUTPUT

Printed Output

Printers are the primary output devices used to prepare permanent documents for human use. Printers are classified by how they print and by how fast they operate.

Low-Speed Character Printers **Character printers** are one-character-at-a-time devices used with microcomputers, minicomputers, and teleprinter terminals for low-volume printing jobs. The techniques used to print characters vary widely. **Impact printers** operate like a typewriter, pressing a typeface against paper and inked ribbon. Impact printers often use a **daisy-wheel** or a **dot-matrix** printing mechanism (see Figure 6-28).

In the daisy-wheel printer (Figure 6-29*a*), each "petal" of the wheel has a character embossed on it. A motor spins the wheel rapidly, and when the desired character spins to the correct position, a print hammer strikes it to produce the output. (Some printers substitute print "thimbles" or "cups" for

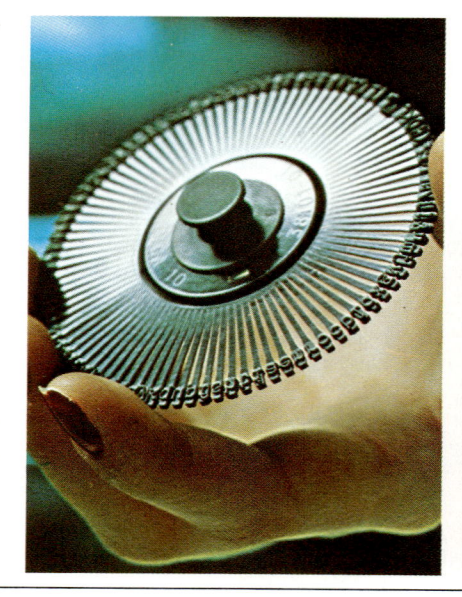

MODULE 2

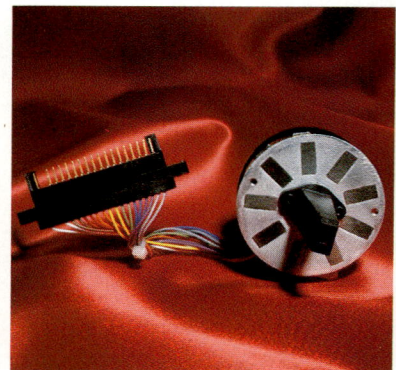

218

FIGURE 6-28

Print elements for (*left*) daisy-wheel and (*right*) dot-matrix character printers. [Photos supplied by Dataproducts Corporation, Woodland Hills, Calif. (*left*) and Datasouth Corporation (*right*)].

FIGURE 6-29

Two of the mechanisms used in character printers. (*a*) The daisy-wheel mechanism. Daisy print wheels are easily removed and replaced with wheels having different type fonts. The speed of a daisy-wheel printer is usually in the 10 to 60 characters-per-second (cps) range. (*b*) The dot-matrix printer. Dot-matrix printer speeds usually range between 50 and 400 cps. The printing head contains a vertical array of pins. As the head moves across the paper, selected pins "fire" against an inked ribbon to form a pattern of dots on the paper. In the example shown, the *capital* letters are formed by using 5-dot rows and 7-dot columns. Such a pattern is called a 5 × 7 matrix. You'll notice in our example, though, that there are nine pins in the print head. The bottom two pins are used to form the *descenders* of *lowercase* letters, such as *p, g, q,* and *y.* Many inexpensive dot-matrix printers don't provide descenders, but print quality is improved when they are used. A 5 × 7 matrix produces readable text, but many other matrix sizes are used. The print quality is also improved when larger matrices are used. Some slower daisy-wheel printers are available for personal computer systems at prices beginning at less than $500, and dot-matrix printers are available for less than $300. Both daisy-wheel and dot-matrix printers are noisy output devices.

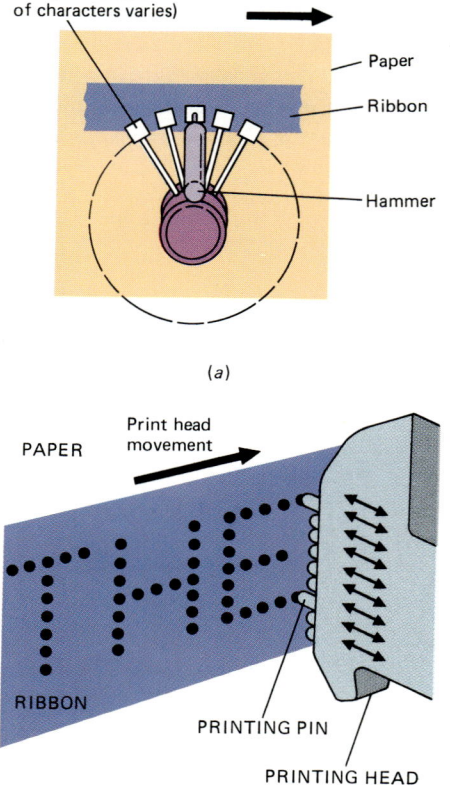

(*a*)

(*b*)

CHAPTER 6

219

```
     !  "  #  $  %  &  '  (  )  *  +  ,  -  .  /
  0  1  2  3  4  5  6  7  8  9  :  ;  <  =  >  ?
  @  A  B  C  D  E  F  G  H  I  J  K  L  M  N  O
  P  Q  R  S  T  U  V  W  X  Y  Z  [  \  ]  ^  _
  `  a  b  c  d  e  f  g  h  i  j  k  l  m  n  o
  p  q  r  s  t  u  v  w  x  y  z  {  |  }  ~
```
(a)

```
Get sharp and smart letter quality characters using a high
density 40x18 dot array matrix font. You may think this was
printed with an office typewriter or a daisy wheel printer,
but it is actually dot matrix.
```
(b)

```
THIS IS NORMAL.
THIS IS NORMAL.ITALICS.
THIS IS NORMAL,DOUBLESTRIKE.
THIS IS NORMAL,DOUBLESTRIKE,ITALICS.
THIS IS NORMAL,EMPHASIZED,DOUBLESTRIKE.
THIS IS NORMAL,EMPHASIZED,DOUBLESTRIKE,ITALICS.
THIS IS SUPERSCRIPT.
THIS IS SUPERSCRIPT.ITALICS.
```
(c)

```
A B C D E F G H I J K L M N O P Q R S T U V W X Y Z
a b c d e f g h i j k l m n o p q r s t u v w x y z
1234567890  ¼ ½         [(!@#$%¢&*+=?/_-"':;,.)]
```
(d)

FIGURE 6-30

Which print quality is right for you? Impact character printers now offer quite a range. (a) Printing produced by a basic 5 × 7 dot-matrix printer priced under $300. (b) Much better quality can be produced with a 40 × 18 dot-matrix array formed by the $600 Mannesmann Tally MT 160 printer with two passes of its print head. (c) Dot-matrix printers such as the Epson MX models can easily vary the appearance of the printed characters. (d) The highest quality comes from the fully formed characters produced by a daisy-wheel printer. (From "The Top 40 Low-Cost Printers," by David B. Powell, appearing in the July 1983 issue of *Popular Computing* magazine. Copyright © 1983 Byte Publications, Inc. Used with the permission of Byte Publications, Inc.)

print wheels, but their operation is essentially the same.) In the dot-matrix printer (Figure 6-29b), an arrangement of tiny hammers strikes to produce the desired characters. Each hammer prints a small dot on the paper. Thus the letters are formed as shown in Figure 6-29b.

Dot-matrix printers are usually faster than daisy-wheel devices and are often less expensive, but their print quality isn't as good. Thus some organizations use dot-matrix printers for internal reports and daisy-wheel printers for external output. Figure 6-30 shows the print quality possible with dot-matrix and daisy-wheel models. All impact printers can produce multiple copies by using carbon paper or its equivalent.

There are also **nonimpact** character printers available that use thermal, electrostatic, chemical, and inkjet technologies. For example, when **continuous-stream inkjet printers** are used, droplets of ink are electrically charged after leaving a nozzle (Figure 6-31a). The droplets are then guided to the proper position on the paper by electrically charged deflection plates. The print quality is good because the character is formed by dozens of tiny ink dots. Continuous-stream printers may produce better text and graphics, and they may be somewhat faster than the **drop-on-demand inkjet printers** that are used with personal computer systems (Figure 6-31b).

Low-Speed Page Printers Nonimpact desktop printers that use a laser beam to produce the dots needed to form pages of characters recently have become popular personal computer output devices. Blending printer and office-copier technologies, these **laser printers** write the desired output image on a copier drum with a beam of laser light that operates under computer control (Figure 6-32). A difference in electrical charge is created on those parts of the drum surface exposed to the laser beam. These laser-exposed areas attract a toner (an ink powder) that attaches itself to the laser-generated

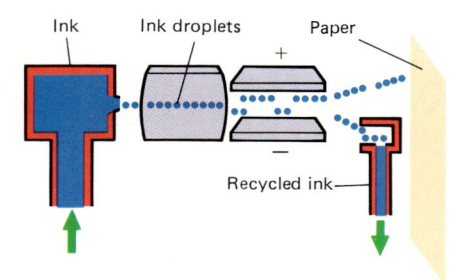

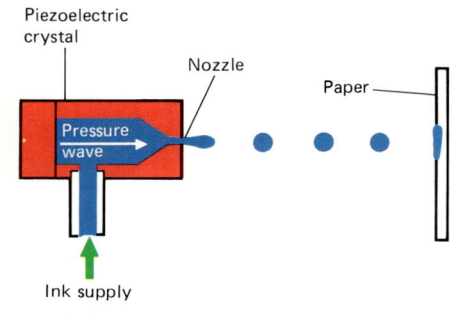

FIGURE 6-31

(a) The *continuous-stream* inkjet approach. One or more nozzles in the print head emit a steady stream of ink drops that are guided to the paper by deflection plates. A nozzle for black ink may be all that's needed to print text, but full-color printing is also possible with the addition of three extra nozzles for the cyan (blue), magenta (red), and yellow primary colors. If a droplet isn't needed for the character or image being formed, it's recycled back to its input nozzle. (b) The *drop-on-demand* inkjet approach. Ink drops are only produced when needed. No deflection plates or recycled ink channels are used. A drop is produced when a brief voltage causes a crystal to shudder and to send a pressure wave through an ink chamber. When this pressure reaches the tip of a nozzle, a drop of ink is forced to fly straight at the paper. Multiple nozzles are generally used in a drop-on-demand print head just as multiple pins are used in a dot-matrix print head. Full-color printing is possible. Inkjet printer speeds usually range between 40 and 300 cps. Prices vary from a few hundred dollars for single-color drop-on-demand printers to tens of thousands of dollars for continuous-stream models with full-color capabilities. Inkjet printers are virtually silent during operation and have few moving parts. The average life expectancy of an inkjet print head is estimated at about 10 billion characters, while the print head life of many dot-matrix printers is only one-fiftieth as long.

(a) The continuous-stream inkjet approach

(b) The drop-on-demand inkjet approach

FIGURE 6-32

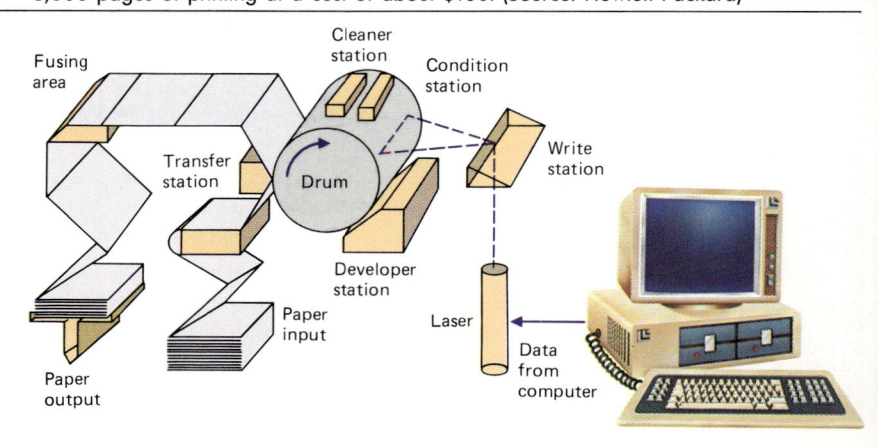

Operation of a laser printer. The bits of data sent by the computer to the printer act as "triggers" to turn the laser beam on and off. To produce a page of output, the modulated laser beam scans back and forth across the surface of a drum that has been cleaned at a cleaner station and given a positive electrical charge at a condition station. This electrical charge is changed on just those parts of the drum surface exposed to the laser beam. As the drum rotates past the developer station, these laser-exposed parts of the drum attract the toner particles that are then transferred to paper at the transfer station. As the paper moves to the fusing area where the toner particles are permanently fixed to the paper with heat or pressure, the drum rotates back to the cleaner station where a rubber blade cleans off any excess toner and prepares the drum for the next page. The laser beam sweeps across the drum at a constant speed, and the drum rotates at a constant speed. A fixed number of pages (usually 8 to 12 for desk-sized models) can thus be printed each minute, and it makes no difference how many characters happen to be placed on each page. Pages of single-spaced text are produced just as quickly as pages of double-spaced text. Small desk-sized laser printers are currently priced at about $3,000. Many of them put expendable items such as the print drum and the toner in a cartridge, and this cartridge must be replaced after about 3,000 pages of printing at a cost of about $100. (*Source:* Hewlett-Packard)

charges on the drum. The toner is then permanently fused on the paper with heat or pressure. Laser printers are quiet, and they produce a high-quality output.

Spooler Programs and Printer Buffers The speed of the printers we've discussed thus far is incredibly slow compared with the processing speed of the computer to which it's connected. Even though the slowest personal computer is loafing along while it's sending text to these printers, it can't normally be used for any other productive work until printing is completed. But two approaches used by larger systems for years are now available to allow users to continue to operate their personal computers while printing is in progress. One option is a **spooler program** that allows the processor to alternate between processing a user's ongoing activity and controlling the printing process. Of course, disk space or a dedicated block of primary storage must be available to store the text to be printed by the spooler. If the ongoing activity uses most of the system storage, there may be none left for the spooler to use. To overcome this possibility, a second option is **printer buffer** hardware. This buffer is an additional storage device that can accept text to be printed as fast as the computer can send it. The buffer then slowly releases the text data to match the printer's speed while the computer is free to do other things.

High-Speed Impact Line Printers **High-speed line printers** use impact methods to produce *line-at-a-time* printed output. They typically use rapidly moving *chains* or *bands* of print characters or some form of a print *drum* to print lines of information on paper (see Figure 6-33). From 300 to over 2,000 lines can be printed each minute depending on the printer used. Figure 6-34*a* illustrates the concept of a **print chain.** The links in the chain are engraved character-printing slugs. The chain moves at a rapid speed past the printing positions. Hammers behind the paper are timed to force the paper against the proper print slugs. A **band printer** (Figure 6-34*b*) is similar in operation to a chain printer. But instead of using a print chain, a band printer has a rotating scalloped steel print band. Hammers force the paper against the proper print

FIGURE 6-33

A scalloped steel print band (*left*) is used in a high-speed impact band printer (*middle*). The print drum (*right*) used in a high-speed drum printer. (Photos courtesy Dataproducts Corporation, Woodland Hills, Calif.)

FIGURE 6-34

Some of the mechanisms used with the impact line printers. (a) The print chain approach. Print hammers are located at each print position. Speeds of over 2,000 lines per minute are reached with chain printers. (b) The band printer approach. Similar in operation to a chain printer, a band or belt printer uses a rotating scalloped steel print band rather than a print chain. The print bands can be removed and replaced with bands using different type fonts. Speeds of up to 2,000 lines per minute are possible. (c) The print drum approach. Print hammers are located opposite each print band. Speeds of over 2,000 lines per minute are possible with drum printers.

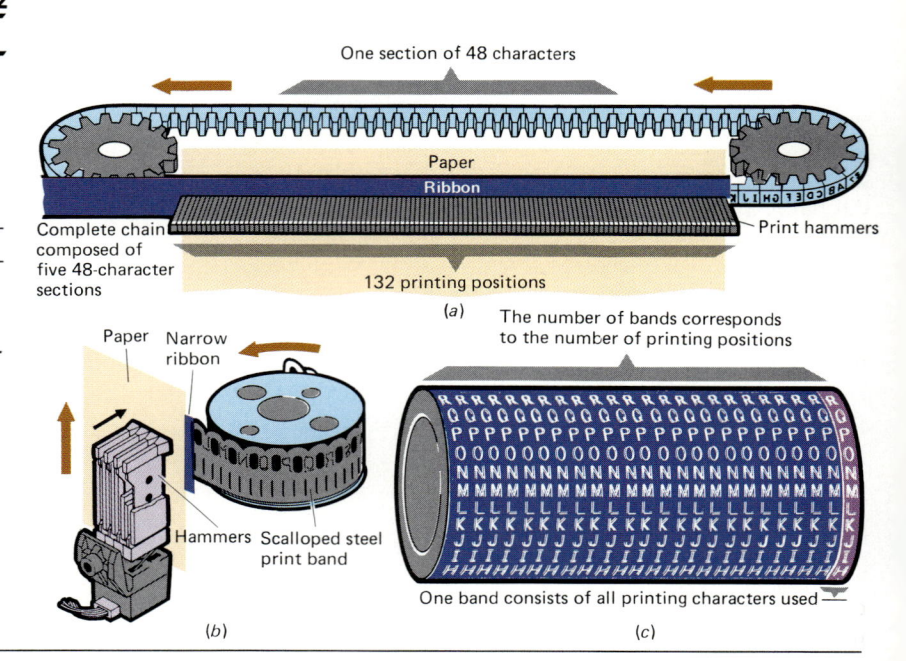

FIGURE 6-35

A high-speed laser page printer. (Photo courtesy Hewlett-Packard)

characters. Speeds of up to 2,000 lines per minute are also possible with band printers.

In the **drum printer,** raised characters extend the length of the drum (Figure 6-34c). There are as many bands of type as there are printing positions. Each band contains all the possible characters. The drum rotates rapidly, and one revolution is required to print each line. A fast-acting hammer opposite each band strikes the paper against the proper character as its passes. Thus, in one rotation, hammers of several positions may "fire" when the A row appears, several others may strike to imprint D's, etc. At the end of the rotation, the line has been printed.

High-Speed Nonimpact Page Printers **A high-speed page printer,** as shown in Figure 6-35, can produce documents at speeds of over 20,000 lines per minute. (That's fast enough to print this entire book in about one minute!) Electronics, xerography, lasers, and other technologies have made these high-volume systems possible. Each page is an original since there are no carbon copies. Although they come with a five- or six-figure price tag and thus cost more than many entire computer systems, high-speed printers can be economical when hundreds of thousands of pages are printed each month. The costs of special report forms can also be reduced since these devices can print both the form layout and the form contents at the same time.

Filmed Output

Organizations prepare many reports for internal use. These reports and any other documents that need to be filed away for future reference can be printed on paper or they can be stored on film. **Computer-output-to-microfilm (COM)** technology is used to record computer output information as microscopic filmed images. The information that can be printed on a page of paper

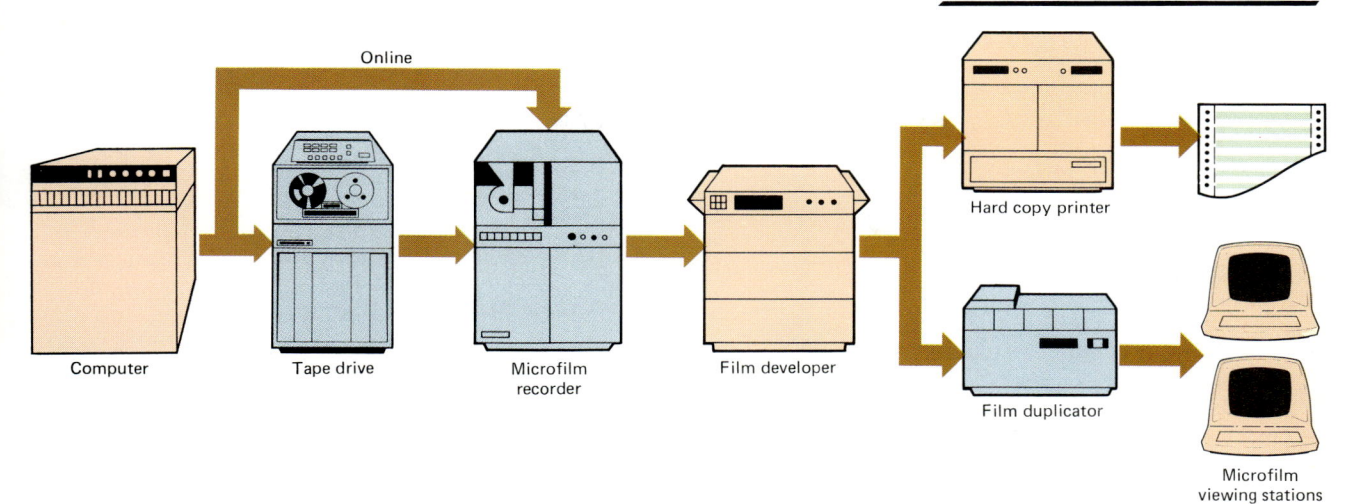

FIGURE 6-36

A computer-output-to-microfilm (COM) system. Computer output is read onto magnetic tape and then, in an offline operation, entered on film by a *microfilm recorder*. Or the recorder may receive the information directly from the computer. Most recorders project the characters of output information onto the screen of a cathode-ray tube. A high-speed camera then photographs the displayed information at speeds of up to 32,000 lines per minute. That's 10 to 20 times faster than a high-speed impact printer can print it. Thus a single COM recorder can do the work of a dozen line printers. But a COM recorder is expensive, and a high-volume workload is needed to justify its cost. In some systems, the recorder processes the film from the camera; in other systems, a separate, automated film developer is used. Film duplicators can make as many copies of the developed film as needed. The information on the sheets or rolls of film is then read by users from the screens of small desktop microfilm viewing stations. A 1-ounce microfiche can hold the equivalent of 10 pounds of paper, and so film storage and mailing costs are low. The cost of the film itself is also low (the cost of the paper needed to print a 1,000 page, three-copy report is about 30 times greater than the cost of the film needed to do the same job). But people who like to write notes on the margins of paper reports may feel uncomfortable when using a COM system. Also, the loss or misplacement of a few microfiche can create a significant gap in an organization's records.

can be reduced in size 48 or more times and recorded on a sheet or roll of microfilm. A 4- by 6-inch sheet of film is called a **microfiche.** (*Fiche* is a French word meaning "card," and is pronounced "fish" as in "fiche or cut byte.") A typical microfiche reproduces up to 270 page-sized images, but some ultrafiche systems can store 1,000 standard pages in the same space. Rolls of 16- and 35-millimeter film packaged in cartridges are also used. The COM approach is shown in Figure 6-36.

In some COM systems, users must locate and then manually search through the film cartridge or card to find the needed information. In other COM systems, however, a **computer-assisted retrieval (CAR)** approach is used (see Figure 6-37). Each microfilmed document is assigned an "address" that gives its cartridge or fiche drawer location. An index of document locations is stored in the memory of a small computer connected to the viewer stations. To retrieve a document, a user calls up this index, quickly locates the

FIGURE 6-37

A computer-assisted retrieval system. (Courtesy 3M)

> **WINDOW 6-1**
>
> **HIGH-TECH BLACKBOARDS**
>
> For those who have discovered with dismay that the vital information they wrote on the blackboard was erased overnight by the janitor, the answer is at hand. New high-technology blackboards can make paper copies of what is written on them.
>
> Whiteboards were introduced 10 to 15 years ago as a replacement for slate blackboards. They were made of porcelain and steel and had a smoother surface than chalkboards. Whiteboards that make paper copies were pioneered in Japan in 1984 and are being manufactured by several U.S. firms. The image on the board is scanned and the pattern of white and dark spots is recorded electronically. That information allows a printer to reproduce the image on paper.
>
> The next step is a combination of computer screens and blackboards, designed to automate the office meeting room. Such a room might contain a computer terminal for each desk where a person could type or draw something on his or her own monitor, which would then appear on a central board and be seen by everyone. Or someone standing in front of the room could draw on the central board and have that appear on the individual screens. One way to draw on the board is with a finger. Beams of laser light sweeping in front of the screen determine the position of the finger and relay it to the computer. As an alternative, a penlike device with buttons on it—a sort of mouse for the blackboard—could be used for input. With Liveboard, a prototype of this computerized blackboard developed at the Xerox Palo Alto Research Center, the user presses buttons on such a pen (called electronic chalk) to activate windows and make choices from a menu. If developments like these take over, the screech of chalk on a chalkboard may soon be only an uncomfortable memory.
>
> Adapted from Andrew Pollack, "The High-Tech Black-boards," *New York Times*, October 24, 1985. Copyright © 1985 by The New York Times Company. Reprinted by permission.

correct film magazine, and waits a few seconds for the viewing station to pick out the correct document from the thousands of pages that may be recorded on the film. If a paper copy of the document is needed, a reader-printer is used to provide full-size prints. This may be the first time the output information has been placed on paper.

DISPLAYED OUTPUT, COMPUTER GRAPHICS, AND VOICE RESPONSE

You've seen that the output from interactive processing usually comes from character printers or visual display screens. Computer-prepared voice responses are also used to reply to inquiries entered from online terminals. Let's look at each of these methods of output more closely.

Displayed Output and Computer Graphics

Alphanumeric Output The screens of visual display terminal and personal computer (VDT and pc) systems are used to receive output in alphanumeric form—as letters, numbers, and special characters. The viewing surface of a typical desktop VDT or pc screen is about equal to that of a 12- to 15-inch television set, but the number of characters that can be shown at any one time varies among VDT and pc systems. The display format of many monitors is 24 or 25 lines with up to 80 characters on a line. About 2,000 characters can thus be displayed. But some pc formats include 16 lines of 64 characters per line or 16 lines of 40 characters per line. Some VDT screens have the precise resolution needed to display 132 characters on each of many lines.

WINDOW 6-2

ARE COMPUTERS HAZARDOUS TO YOUR HEALTH?

Among the controversies surrounding computer use are the side effects of prolonged sessions at a computer monitor or visual display terminal (abbreviated VDT).

Although recent government studies indicate there are virtually no health risks associated with VDT use, there are those who feel that VDTs are a health hazard because of radiation from the terminal that they think causes cataracts and birth defects; eye problems such as irritations, pain, fatigue, and reduced acuity; and muscular problems such as arm, back, and neck pains. One union, the Computer Workers of America, has even produced data that support a link between VDT use and angina—the chest pains that often precede a heart attack.

VDTs emit low levels of radiation in the form of x-rays and ultraviolet radiation. Computer terminals and monitors operate in the same manner as a television picture tube. A beam of high-velocity electrons scans the face of the tube. These electrons activate a coating on the inside of the tube, causing the picture or data on the screen to appear, along with ultraviolet rays and x-rays. To meet government standards, most manufacturers use lead-impregnated glass on VDTs to absorb most stray radiation. Tests sponsored by the National Institute for Occupational Safety and Health (NIOSH) show that VDTs send out minute amounts of radiation, but these emissions are very low—one-thousandth that of current federal standards for safe exposure. The only problems that researchers have confirmed are disorders such as backaches and eye strain, which can be corrected with changes in lighting and equipment design.

Radiation from VDTs has caused workers and their unions to question the safety of workers spending the better part of their day working on computer terminals. The unions base their claims on cases in which an unusually large percentage of female workers experienced pregnancy problems or spontaneous abortions, or had babies with birth defects, and the large number of VDT workers who complain of eye strain, headaches, backaches, and stress. The unions feel that the data in current studies are insufficient and that this is a major health threat to the 15 million workers who currently use computer terminals and the 100 million who are projected to use them by 2000.

To address this issue, many businesses are employing ergonomists—people who study the impact of machinery and the job environment on workers—to redesign computer workplaces and make them more suitable for workers' needs. A professional group of ergonomists is preparing voluntary guidelines for industry to help combat fatigue and other VDT-related problems.

Firms that manufacture VDTs are working on low-voltage computer displays to replace the current high-voltage monitors. IBM is working on a "gas plasma" flat-panel display that uses low-voltage ionized gases instead of an electron beam to generate its orange characters. The Japanese have produced a number of monitors using liquid-crystal displays that produce no radiation. In addition, new display screens often have nonglare surfaces and they tilt and swivel to adapt to a worker's requirements.

Various state legislatures are considering bills to ensure VDT worker safety. Several long-term studies on the relationship between pregnancy problems and VDTs also are underway, sponsored by the federal government and private agencies.

Until more conclusive data on VDT use and health become available and until changes in VDT design become more widespread, there are several steps that you can take to relieve any discomfort you may encounter from working with a microcomputer or a terminal.

1 Sit as far from your VDT as possible. Detachable keyboards make this easier to accomplish. Experts advise a distance three times that of the screen's diagonal measurement.

2 For a margin of safety, attach a nonglare screen to your monitor.

3 Arrange your work area so that the keyboard is clearly illuminated while the light is directed away from the display screen.

4 Sit in a chair that supports your lower back and promotes good posture. Adjust the height of your chair so your hands rest comfortably on the keyboard and the screen is at eye level.

5 Every 30 minutes or so, take a break from your computer to stretch and walk around. Exercise your eyes by focusing on objects at different distances from you.

MODULE 2

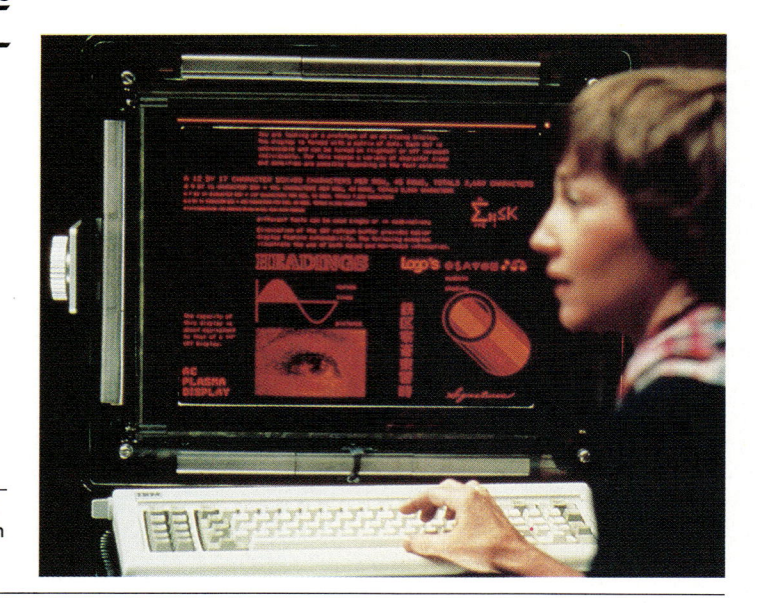

This experimental flat VDT screen uses a gas plasma to make its display more brilliant than the black-on-gray LCD screens in use today. (Courtesy IBM Corp.)

A *cathode-ray tube* (CRT) screen is generally found in desktop VDT and pc systems and in the larger transportable pc models. These tubes operate much like those in television sets. But CRT screens are too heavy and bulky for lap-sized portable computers. These notebook-sized portable pc's use flat-panel **liquid-crystal display (LCD)** screens that operate like the small silver-gray displays found on some digital watches and pocket calculators. Today, these cells produce black images on a gray background. But color LCD panels have been developed, and more brilliant monochrome and color LCD displays doubtless will grow popular in the years ahead.

Graphic Output   A study made by a computer manufacturer indicates that people can read at rates of up to 1,200 words per minute. When pictures are used, however, the rate of comprehension leaps. Maybe the old saying that one picture is worth a thousand words understated the true ratio! Graphs, charts, maps, and other visual presentations prepared from pages of statistical data are better able to capture and hold the interest of a user. Data showing the relationships, changes, and trends that are often buried in piles of alphanumeric reports can be highlighted with a few graphic presentations. Although some loss of precision often results when tabular information is presented in graphic form, this is usually not a problem.

You'll recall from Chapter 5 that people can use light pens and graphics tablets to enter drawings into computer systems. The screen of a VDT designed for graphics work is often used by designers, engineers, and architects to display preliminary sketches. Computers can be programmed to analyze the sketches and report on certain characteristics. Designers can then interact with their computers to produce finished drawings. A growing market for graphic terminals and personal computers capable of producing high-resolution color images has also developed in government, health-care, and business organizations. Using alphanumeric data as input, people in these offices can use graphic software packages to create colorful and informative pictures on the screens of their terminals and pc's. After engineering drawings or office graphic presentations have been displayed on a screen to a user's satisfaction, permanent copies can be prepared using the following graphics devices:

- **Printers.** A *dot-matrix printer* can produce effective pictures through its ability to generate hundreds of lines of tiny dots on an inch of paper. Many of the inexpensive dot-matrix printers used with personal computers have **dot-addressable graphics capability.** That is, with appropriate software, users can control each wire in the print head and thus determine where each dot is printed (see Figure 6-38a). Furthermore, when the print head can handle multicolor ribbons, it's possible to produce color images. Nonimpact **electrostatic printers** using processes similar to photocopying are also available. And some *inkjet printers* have impressive multicolor graphics capabilities (Figure 6-38b). **Thermal-transfer printers** use ribbons that hold the ink in a wax binder. As the hot pins in a thermal-transfer print head press the ribbon against the paper, the wax melts and the ink is transferred to the paper. The wax transferred along with the ink helps give an image a glossy look.

- **Plotters.** Special plotters are also available that use pen or inkjet approaches. **Pen plotters** generally use drum or flatbed holders (see Figure 6-39). When a **drum device** is used, the paper is placed over a drum that rotates back and forth to produce an up-and-down motion. A carriage holding one or more pens is mounted horizontally across the drum, and the pens can move along this carriage to produce motion across the paper. Under computer control, the carriage and drum movements act together to produce a picture. When several pens are mounted on a carriage, each pen can be filled with a different ink color. Since each pen is program-selectable, the plotter has the ability to produce color pictures. Some newer "paper mover" plotters do away with the drum and hold the paper on both sides with pinch wheels that provide the back and forth paper movement. When a **flatbed** (table) **plotter** is used, the paper doesn't move and the pen-holding mechanism must provide all the motion. **Inkjet plotters** are able to produce large drawings containing many colors. The paper is again placed on a drum, and jets with different-colored ink are mounted on a carriage. The computer program controls the color and amount of ink placed on the paper.

- **Film recorders.** The CRT screen can be photographed with black and white or color film to produce prints and 35-millimeter slides. Videotape copies can also be made.

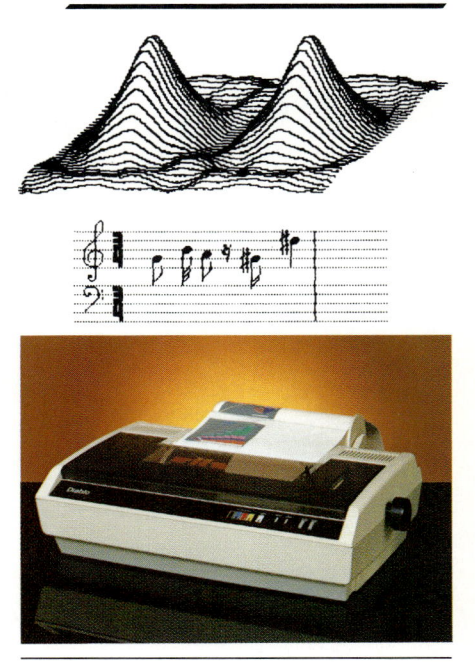

FIGURE 6-38

(*above*) Many inexpensive dot-matrix printers used with personal computers can produce effective graphics. This example was prepared using a horizontal resolution of 160 dots per inch and a vertical resolution of 144 dots per inch. The price of the printer used is less than $600. Although this printer can't produce color images, others are available for less than $600 that *do* have the ability to use four-color ribbons. (From "The Top 40 Low-Cost Printers," by David B. Powell, appearing in the July 1983 issue of *Popular Computing* magazine. Copyright © 1983 Byte Publications, Inc. Used with the permission of Byte Publications, Inc.) (*below*) This inkjet printer can print 120 dots per inch and is capable of producing seven colors. (Courtesy Diablo Systems, Incorporated)

Voice Response

Just as a voice recognition system will allow you to talk to a computer, so, too, will a **voice response system** permit a computer to talk back to you. In fact, a computer has probably "talked" to you many times. For example, when you try to call a telephone number that has been changed, a signal is sent to a telephone company computer. You then hear: "The number you have dialed has been changed to 9-2-6-2-5-6-3." The first part of this response is a conventional recording, but the new number is given in the "voice" of the computer's audio-response unit. This voice may be choppy and unnatural, but it's easily understood.

Many other organizations use audio-response systems to respond to

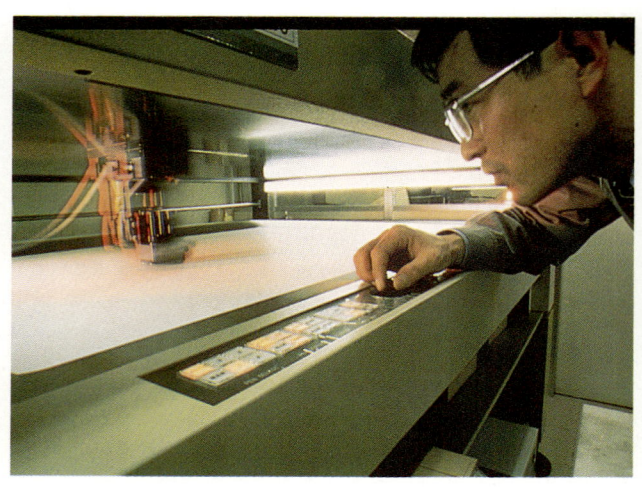

FIGURE 6-39

(*left*) This electrostatic color plotter can produce complex, full-color plots in a matter of minutes. (*right*) Close-up view of a high-speed plotter in action. (Photos courtesy Xerox Corporation; The Bohle Company)

FIGURE 6-40

Texas Instruments' Speak & Spell is an interactive teaching device and a specialized type of microcomputer. A voice synthesizer chip like that in Speak & Spell is used to make safety announcements in some new cars. (Courtesy Texas Instruments, Inc.)

human inquiries that are transmitted over telephone lines to a central computer. All the sounds needed to process the possible inquiries are prerecorded on a storage medium. Each sound is given a code. When inquiries are received, the processor follows a set of rules to create a reply message in a coded form. This coded message is then transmitted to an audio-response device, which assembles the sounds in the proper sequence and transmits the audio message back to the station requesting the information.

Audio-response techniques, combined with briefcase-sized (or smaller) terminals, turn every telephone into a potential computer I/O device. A traveling engineer, for example, can check on a project's status by keying an inquiry directly into the home-office computer. A computer-compiled audio response then gives the engineer the necessary output information. Similarly, construction personnel can enter and receive labor, material, and equipment information.

Audio-response systems can be inexpensive. Many are available now for use with personal computers. Such a system is also used in Texas Instruments' Speak & Spell product to teach children to spell and pronounce over 200 basic words (see Figure 6-40). A single integrated circuit chip costing a few dollars synthesizes the selected sounds that are used for audio response. Thus the spoken word in machine-usable form is now cheap enough to be installed in your microwave oven or washing machine—if you want talking appliances.

CHAPTER 6
229

FEEDBACK

Feedback and Review 6

To test and reinforce your understanding of the secondary storage and output concepts presented in this chapter, rearrange the *scrambled letters* to spell out the correct word for the space indicated in the following sentences.

1. A series of different storage elements is found in most computer systems, and these different elements make up the storage ___.   R A H Y H I E R C
2. The ___ time of a storage element is the time it takes to locate and retrieve stored data in response to a program instruction.   C S E S C A
3. Magnetic ___ are the most popular medium for direct-access secondary storage.   S I D S K
4. Magnetic disks may be packaged in removable cartridges or packs, or they may be housed in sealed, contamination-free containers that employ ___ technology.   H C W I S T N E E R
5. Data are stored on all magnetic disks in a number of invisible concentric circles called ___.   R S A K C T
6. The storage capacity of a disk system depends on the bits per inch of track and the tracks per inch of ___.   S R F E C A U
7. A dust particle on a magnetic disk can cause a flying head to bounce up and then ___ on the disk surface.   H S A C R
8. The disk ___ specifies the track number and other information to enable the access mechanism to pinpoint the exact location of stored data.   S S D A E R D
9. Either the ___ method or the cylinder method is used to organize and physically store disk data.   E S C T R O
10. An ___ hole is used to mark the location of the first sector in a soft-sectored disk.   D X E N I
11. The access time for data stored on a disk is determined by the seek time and the ___ time.   S R E H C A
12. Magnetic ___ storage chips have no moving parts, and they provide nonvolatile direct-access storage of data.   U L B E B B
13. A beam of ___ light is used to record and retrieve data on optical disks.   E L R S A
14. Data stored on disks can be accessed in either a direct or ___ way.   E Q N E L S U A T I
15. An advantage of magnetic tape is that it has a high data ___.   D N T Y I S E
16. Good output information in the hands of those who can effectively use it will support good decisions; good decisions will lead to the effective performance of tasks; and effective task performance will lead to success in reaching an organization's ___.   A L G O S
17. ___ output is information that's intended for use solely within an organization, while external output is information that will be used outside the organization.   T E I N R L A N
18. A ___ report condenses detailed data to help decision makers spot patterns and trends.   M A R Y S U M

19. _____ reports are triggered to supply information only when operating data fall outside specified limits.   C E E X O N P T I

20. _____ are the primary output devices used to prepare permanent documents for human use.   I E P R R S N T

21. Unlike inkjet printers, daisy-wheel and dot-matrix printers are character-at-a-time devices that use _____ methods to produce printed characters.   P A I C T M

22. The use of spooler programs and/or _____ hardware allows personal computer operators to do other processing work at the same time a printing operation is in progress.   E U F R B F

23. Some low-speed page printers use _____ light to write the desired output image on a copier drum.   R A E L S

24. High-speed impact line printers typically use rapidly moving chains or bands of print characters or some form of a print _____ to print lines of information on paper.   M U D R

25. High-speed nonimpact _____ printers are fast enough to print this entire book in about 1 minute.   A P E G

26. _____ plotters are computer graphics devices that use either drum or flatbed paper holders.   E P N

27. Some organizations use _____-response systems that directly respond to human inquiries that are transmitted to a central computer over telephone lines.   E I C V O

LOOKING BACK

1. Most computer systems have a storage hierarchy. The different components in the hierarchy are usually ranked according to their access time, storage capacity, and cost per bit of capacity. Primary storage generally has the fastest access time, the smallest storage capacity, and the highest cost per bit stored. Supplementing primary storage is the secondary storage of a computer system. This classification includes the online DASDs and the offline storage media that hold data in a computer-readable form.

2. Computer system designers must study each application to be processed and then select a storage approach to use. This approach is determined by the way the data are to be organized and processed. Sequentially organized files that require only periodic updating can be stored on an offline secondary storage medium. But if quick access to any file record may be needed at any time, a DASD must be used. In selecting an appropriate DASD, designers must usually make compromises between performance and cost.

3. Magnetic disks can be used for sequential processing, but their popularity is largely due to their direct-access capabilities. Disks come in different sizes, are either portable or permanently mounted in their disk drives, and are made of rigid metal or flexible plastic. Disk storage systems come in a wide price range and provide an equally wide range of access times, storage capacities, and transfer rates.

4. Data are stored on the surface of all magnetic disks in a number of invisible concentric circles called tracks. Tiny magnetic spots representing data are recorded on, and read from, these tracks by one or more read/write heads. The data density is determined by the bits per inch of track and the number of tracks that can be placed on each disk surface. Winchester disk systems have very high densities. Program instructions specify the disk address of a needed record. Sector and cylinder approaches are used to organize and physically store disk data. A read/write head is then moved directly to the specified address to access the data. The access time is determined by the seek time needed to position the head over the proper track and the search time needed to spin the needed data under the head.

5. Other devices used for direct-access secondary storage include RAM "disks," magnetic bubble chips, optical disks, and magnetic tape strips. Each of these storage approaches has been briefly outlined in the chapter.

6. Magnetic tape is often the medium selected to store large files that are sequentially accessed and processed. An 8-bit BCD code is generally used to represent data on magnetic tape. Interrecord gaps are used to identify different tape records. Frequently, however, several records are combined into a block and read into the

processor as a single unit to save tape space and speed data input. A tape drive is used to access data stored on a magnetic tape. Although its data density is high and its cost is low, magnetic tape can't provide rapid and random access to file records.

7. Computer output is vital for decision makers who must plan, organize, and control to achieve their goals. Output is internal or external; internal output is information intended for use within an organization, whereas external output is meant for outside use. In interactive processing applications, the output is usually produced by display screens, small printers, or voice response units. The internal reports and external documents created during batch processing operations in larger organizations are likely to be produced by high-speed printers or microfilm recorders. Printers and plotters also produce graphic output.

8. Printers are the primary output devices used to prepare permanent documents for human use. Impact or nonimpact character-at-a-time printers, or low-speed page printers, are used for low-volume printing jobs. When impact mechanisms are used, a typeface strikes against paper and inked ribbon to create a character. Daisy-wheel and dot-matrix devices are examples of impact character printers. Nonimpact printers use thermal, electrostatic, chemical, inkjet, and laser technologies to produce their output. Low-speed page printers blend printer and office copier technologies and use laser light to create the desired output image. High-speed impact line printers typically use rapidly moving chains or bands of print characters, or some form of print drum, to print at speeds that can exceed 2,000 lines per minute. And even faster nonimpact page printers use xerography, lasers, and other technologies to produce output at speeds that can exceed 20,000 lines per minute.

9. Internal documents to be filed away for possible future reference are sometimes recorded on film by a computer-output-to-microfilm process. Hundreds of page-size images can be recorded on a single 4- by 6-inch microfiche. Once information has been placed on film, it can be recovered by people using desktop viewing stations and manual search or computer-assisted retrieval techniques. Full-sized documents can be printed from the filmed images.

10. Visual display screens are used to receive alphanumeric and graphic output information. Many VDT and pc systems only display alphanumeric characters, but many professionals require terminals and personal computers with graphic capabilities. In addition to displaying engineering drawings, graphic terminals and personal computers can also show the relationships, changes, and trends that often lie buried in piles of alphanumeric reports through the use of graphs, charts, maps, and other visual aids. And when graphic presentations are displayed on a screen to a user's satisfaction, permanent copies can be prepared using printers, plotters, and film recorders.

11. Voice response systems permit computers to talk to people. In many cases, such a system responds directly to human inquiries that are transmitted to a central computer over telephone lines.

KEY TERMS AND CONCEPTS

storage hierarchy 198
access time 198
secondary (auxiliary) storage 198
sequential-access storage media 198
magnetic disks 199
read/write heads 199
disk drives 200
Winchester disk drives 200
disk cartridges 200
disk packs 200
tracks 203
access arms 203
single-sided disk 203
double-sided disk 203
bits per inch of track 204
tracks per inch of surface 204
crash 204
backup copies 205
streaming tape drive 205
sector 206
disk address 206
index-hole window (sector sight hole) 206
index hole (begin-sector hole) 206
hard-sectored disk 207
format a disk 207
soft-sectored disk 207
cylinder 208
seek time 208
search (latency) time 208
fixed-head-per-track device 209
RAM "disk" 209
magnetic bubble storage 210
optical disks 210
laser recording systems 210
tape strip storage devices 211
perpendicular recording techniques 212
frames 213
channels (tracks) 213
nine-track magnetic tape 213
18-track cartridge system 213
interrecord gaps 214
tape block 214
internal output 216
external output 216
detail report 216
summary report 217
computer graphic output 217
exception report 217
character printers 217
impact methods 217
daisy-wheel printer 217
dot-matrix printer 217
nonimpact printer 219
continuous-stream inkjet printer 219
drop-on-demand inkjet printer 219
laser printer 219
spooler program 221
printer buffer 221
high-speed line printer 221
print chain 221
band printer 221
drum printer 222
high-speed page printer 222
computer-output-to-microfilm (COM) 222
microfiche 223
computer-assisted retrieval (CAR) 223
liquid-crystal display (LCD) 226
dot-addressable graphics capability 227
electrostatic printer 227
thermal-transfer printer 227
pen plotters 227
drum device 227
flatbed plotter 227
inkjet plotters 227
voice response system 227

TOPICS FOR REVIEW AND DISCUSSION

1. "In a storage hierarchy, it's generally necessary to make compromises between retrieval speed, on the one hand, and storage capacity and cost per character stored, on the other." Explain this statement and give examples to support it.

2. What components make up the storage hierarchy of your school's computer system?

3. What storage elements are included in the secondary storage classification?

4. "The storage approach selected for a particular application is determined by the way the data are organized and processed." Discuss this statement.

5. Identify and discuss the types of magnetic disks used for direct-access secondary storage.

6. (a) How are data stored on magnetic disks? (b) What factors determine the storage capacity of disks?
7. (a) What causes head crashes? (b) How can Winchester technology reduce the head crash problem?
8. (a) How can data stored on magnetic disks be accessed? (b) What determines the time required to access the needed data?
9. What are some advantages and limitations of magnetic disks?
10. (a) What's a RAM "disk"? (b) How is a RAM disk used?
11. What are the characteristics of magnetic bubble storage?
12. What are the potential storage benefits of optical disk technology?
13. (a) How are data stored on magnetic tape? (b) How are these data retrieved? (c) What are some advantages and limitations of magnetic tape?
14. (a) How can computer output benefit the users of personal computers? (b) Why is computer output likely to be needed by decision makers in most organizations?
15. (a) What's the difference between internal and external output? (b) What should a system designer consider when planning the type of output to be produced by a computer?
16. Identify and discuss the three types of output reports mentioned in this chapter.
17. (a) Identify four output devices used in interactive processing applications. (b) Identify four output devices used in batch processing.
18. (a) What's an impact printer? (b) Identify and discuss two types of impact character printers. (c) Identify and discuss three types of impact line printers.
19. (a) What's a nonimpact printer? (b) Identify and discuss the inkjet approach to nonimpact printing. (c) How do low-speed laser printers operate?
20. (a) What types of internal documents are typically placed on microfilm? (b) How is computer output placed on microfilm? (c) How are microfilm images retrieved?
21. (a) What's the display format of a CRT screen available to you? (b) What's the maximum number of characters that can be displayed?
22. Why have computer graphics become so popular in recent years?
23. How can pictures displayed on a screen be permanently preserved?
24. How are voice response systems used?

Projects/Issues to Consider

1. Visit a computer store and/or your library's periodical section and identify three suppliers of products in each of the following categories: Winchester disk drives; 5¼-inch floppy-disk drives; 5¼-inch floppy disks; disk drives for disks measuring less than 4 inches in size; daisy-wheel printers; dot-matrix printers; inkjet printers; plotters. Prepare a summary of your findings for the class.
2. Let's assume that you've just been hired to prepare television commercials for three of the suppliers you've identified in the preceding project. Select a storage/output product manufactured by each of these suppliers, and write commercials for these products. Your time is limited, of course, so you'll want to emphasize the main competitive strengths of each product. "Broadcast" your commercial messages to the class.
3. Collect your junk mail for a few weeks, and then examine each document to see what type of printer was used in its preparation. Present your findings to the class.
4. Identify a business or some other organization you're familiar with (such as a bank, newspaper, clinic, library, or admissions office), and determine how some of the organization's records are stored and maintained. Prepare a report of your investigation.

Answers to Feedback and Review Section

1. hierarchy 2. access 3. disks 4. Winchester 5. tracks 6. surface 7. crash 8. address 9. sector 10. index 11. search 12. bubble 13. laser 14. sequential 15. density 16. goals 17. internal 18. summary 19. exception 20. printers 21. impact 22. buffer 23. laser 24. drum 25. page 26. pen 27. voice

A CLOSER LOOK

FACTS AND FILES
Organizing/Storing/Accessing/Processing Concepts

You'll recall from Chapter 2 that data are typically organized into different levels ranging upward from data items or fields to records, files, and data bases. And you've seen in this chapter how data are stored on and then retrieved from magnetic disks and magnetic tapes. Let's take a closer look now at the *sequential, direct,* and *indexed sequential* approaches that may be used by information system designers to organize and store, access, and then process files consisting of records and data items (see Figure 6-A).

Sequential Files
You know that sequential files may be *organized* so that records are *stored* one after another in an ascending or descending order determined by the record key. There are likely to be tens of thousands of these records in customer account number sequence in the files of electric, telephone, and oil companies. Once a file is sequenced according to a designated key field, however, it's almost certain to be out of any sequence in every other field. A file sequenced by customer account number, for example, will not be in a Zip code sequence or an alphabetical sequence. Other files could be sequenced on these record keys, but maintaining multiple files of duplicate data can be expensive.

When computer processing is used, the stored records in a sequential file are usually kept on magnetic tape or magnetic disk. To *access* these records, the computer must read the file in sequence from the beginning. To locate a particular record, the computer program must read each record into primary storage in sequence and compare its record key to the one that's needed. Only when the record keys match will the retrieval search end and processing begin. If only a single record in a sequential file is needed, the computer would read, on the average, about half the file before it found the one it wanted.

Since an entire sequential file may need to be read just to retrieve and update a few records, it's desirable to accumulate transactions of a similar type into batches, sort these batches into the record key sequence used in the file, and then *process* the entire batch in a single pass through the file (see Figure 2-17, page 76). System designers have found that this is a very efficient processing approach to use when a high proportion of the file records in an application need to be updated at regularly scheduled intervals. Applications such as payroll processing, billing and statement preparation, and bank check processing meet these conditions.

Direct Files
There are many other applications, however, that don't meet these conditions. In these applications, the proportion of file records to be processed is often low, the timing of record transactions and/or inquiries is often unpredictable, and the processing delays caused by accumulating transactions into batches is often unacceptable.

When a **direct file** (also called a **random** or **relative** file) *organization* is used, the computer can directly locate the key of the needed record without having to search through a sequence of other records. This means that the time required for interactive inquiry and updating of a few records is much faster than when batch techniques are used. Of course, this also means that direct file records must be kept in a direct-access storage device (DASD). A record is *stored* in a direct file by its key field. Although it might be possible to use the storage location numbers in a DASD as the keys for the records stored in those locations, this is seldom done. Instead, an arithmetic procedure called a **transform** is frequently used to convert the record key number into a DASD storage location number. For example, the record key number might be divided by a value determined by the transform. The record could then be stored in the DASD location that corresponds to a value calculated by the division operation. Sometimes a transform produces **synonyms**—i.e., two or more records whose keys generate the same DASD location number. Several methods are followed to overcome this difficulty when it occurs. One approach is to include a **pointer** field at the location calculated by the transform. This field points to the DASD location of another record that has the same calculated transform value.

When the computer is given the key of a record to be processed at a later date, it reuses the transform to locate the

FIGURE 6-A
System designers can choose to organize, access, and process records and files in different ways depending on the type of application and the needs of users.

File Organization	Record Access Method	Processing Approach
1. Sequential 2. Direct (or random) 3. Sequential (but with an index)	1. Sequential 2. Direct 3. Indexed sequential	1. Sequential 2. Direct 3. Indexed sequential

stored record. If the record is at the location calculated by the transform, the search is over and the record is *directly accessed* for processing. If the record at the calculated location does not have the correct key, the computer looks at the pointer field to continue the search. Thus direct files are direct-accessed and *directly processed* (see Figures 2-9 and 2-11, pages 65 and 68). It's also possible to process direct file records in a record key sequence. But if a large number of file records need to be processed in sequence, the computer may have to repeatedly use the transform algorithm and constantly reposition the reading mechanism of the DASD to retrieve and process these records.

Indexed Sequential Files

You've now seen that there are some processing situations that are best suited to the use of sequential files, and there are others that need the benefits to be obtained from a direct file organization. To further complicate the lot of system designers, there are also some files that are commonly used to support both sequential and direct processing operations. An inventory file, for example, may be updated each week. Transactions involving quantities of parts received and quantities sold may be batched, sorted by part number, and used to produce a new report each week of the inventory available for sale. The purchasing department may use this report for reordering purposes. However, the same inventory file may also be used to provide availability data in response to inquiries coming from online terminals in the sales department. Similarly, an organization may want to use sequential processing techniques to update an accounts receivable file and at the same time use that file to give quick answers to customer inquiries.

When both batch and interactive processing must be supported, an **indexed sequential file** may be used. The records in this type of file are *organized in sequence* for the efficient processing of large batch jobs, but an **index** is also used to speed up access to the records. This file organization is thus a compromise approach that combines some of the advantages (and avoids some of the limitations) of both the sequential and direct approaches. Records are *stored sequentially* by a record key in a DASD. When these records are periodically updated during a batch run, the direct-access capability of the DASD really isn't used. The *first* record may be directly *accessed,* but all others are then read in sequence as if they were stored on a magnetic tape.

Indexes are used to permit access to selected records without requiring a search of the *entire* file. The use of an index is already familiar to you. If you wanted to find information on one or a few topics in this book, you would not begin on page 1 and read every page until you came across the topic(s) of interest. Rather, you would find the subject by turning to the index at the back of the book to locate the page number, and then by turning directly to that page to begin reading. In the same way, a computer can use an **indexed sequential access method (ISAM)** to locate a record by using an index rather than by starting every search at the beginning of the file. In an accounts receivable file, for example, customer records may be sequentially organized by account number. One or more indexes of these account numbers can then be stored in the DASD as shown in Figure 6-B. The account number key represents the *highest* customer account number in the storage area. Thus to locate customer number 1932, the computer is instructed to access storage area 12. Another index for storage area 12 would probably then be used to further pinpoint the location of the record. A sequential search, involving only a tiny fraction of the entire file, may then be made to retrieve the desired record. In summary, then, records in indexed sequential files can be batch processed or accessed quickly through the use of indexes.

Advantages and Limitations of These File Approaches

Which of the above file organization approaches should system designers use? There's no single answer to this question, of course, unless the answer is "all of them." The best approach to use in a given application is the one that happens to meet the user's needs in the most effective and economical manner. In making the choice for an application, designers must evaluate the distinct strengths and weaknesses of each approach. These advantages and limitations are summarized in Figure 6-C.

FIGURE 6-B

Account Number Key	Storage Area for Customer Data
1492	10
1776	11
1945	12
2232	13
2565	14
•	•
•	•
•	•

SEQUENTIAL FILES

Advantages
- Simple-to-understand approach
- Locating a record requires only the record key
- Efficient and economical if the *activity rate* — i.e., the proportion of file records to be processed — is high
- Relatively inexpensive I/O media and devices may be used
- Files may be relatively easy to reconstruct since a good measure of built-in backup is usually available

Disadvantages
- Entire file must be processed even when the activity rate is very low
- Transactions must be sorted and placed in sequence prior to processing
- Timeliness of data in the file may deteriorate while batches are being accumulated
- Data redundancy is typically high since the same data may be stored in several files sequenced on different keys

DIRECT FILES

Advantages
- Immediate access to records for inquiry and updating purposes is possible
- Immediate updating of several files as a result of a single transaction is possible
- Transactions need not be sorted

Disadvantages
- Records in the online file may be exposed to the risks of a loss of accuracy and a breach of security; special backup and reconstruction procedures must be established
- May be less efficient in the use of storage space than sequentially organized files
- Relatively expensive hardware and software resources are required

INDEXED SEQUENTIAL FILES

Advantages
- Permits the efficient and economical use of sequential processing techniques when the activity rate is high
- Permits quick access to records in a relatively efficient way when this activity is a small fraction of the total workload

Disadvantages
- Less efficient in the use of storage space than some other alternatives
- Access to records may be slower using indexes than when transform algorithms are used
- Relatively expensive hardware and software resources are required

FIGURE 6-C

Factors to consider in evaluating file alternatives.

CHAPTER 7

PERSONAL COMPUTERS

Who Needs Personal Computers?
By J. Presper Eckert

I must confess that I don't own a personal computer. I have no reason to. I suppose I could use a computer for my hobby, electronic musical instruments, and conduct research on how to generate an accurate replica of a piano note (today's electronic pianos lack warmth in their tones). But I would need a pretty fast computer to handle the sampling of a note's characteristics in a reasonable amount of time.

We've come a long way since the day when Dr. Howard Aiken, designer of the pioneering Mark series of computers at Harvard, could say that just a half-dozen electronic machines would be enough to fulfill the world's needs (a statement he later retracted). On the other hand, I remember my colleague John Mauchly talking about the importance of personal computers long before they existed.

During the late 1950s I was involved in trying to build what would now be called a personal computer, probably the first machine to fit on a desktop. We used hundreds of magnetic core amplifiers and diodes, a few transistors and tubes, and a motor-driven drum for memory storage. The same motor powered a flyprinter, which typed the computer's output onto a moving strip of paper.

Often I am asked whether computers have had a dehumanizing influence on society. This may be so in some cases, but mostly it just isn't true. If anything, computers can free you from tedium. And they allow you to exercise your individuality. You can go into a dealer's showroom and order a car with your choice of colors and options, thanks to a computerized assembly system. This is a far cry from Henry Ford's Model T and its choice of any color as long as it was black.

There are problems, of course. Computers are replacing humans on the assembly line, but bolt-stuffing a machine chassis, for instance, could hardly be thought of as a particularly humanizing activity. Progress always brings problems, and we should be working on solutions to those problems. You've got to be for progress or go back to eating bark in the forests.

Who needs personal computers? Society at large. Overall, personal computers are the greatest development since the first electronic computers. They are important not for their individual use, but for their long-term educational effect. Home computers will surely awaken some young geniuses who will make a tremendous difference in the future. It's this long-shot effect, this gamble on the next step in our evolution, that defines our real need for personal computers.

J. Presper Eckert, one of the pioneers in the development of the electronic computer, was the chief engineer on ENIAC (see the Closer Look following Chapter 1).

Source: Adapted from J. Presper Eckert, "Who Needs Personal Computers?", *Digital Deli*, Steve Ditlea (ed.), Workman Publishing, New York, 1984. Used by permission.

CHAPTER 7

LOOKING AHEAD

Chapters 4 through 6 in this Hardware Module gave you a general introduction to the processor unit, to I/O, and to information storage. Now Chapter 7 will give you more specific information about real computer systems. The chapter itself focuses on personal computers because these are the systems you're most likely to encounter in your everyday activities. But some characteristics and uses of minis, mainframes, and supercomputers are examined in the reading at the end of the chapter. The information in this chapter will enable you to:

- Explain what personal computers are
- Describe some general hardware characteristics and software considerations applicable to personal computers
- Discuss some functions that applications packages can perform in homes and offices
- Identify representative "home" and "office" personal computer systems

CHAPTER OUTLINE

LOOKING AHEAD
A PC INTRODUCTION
PC Concepts
The Classification Dilemma
HARDWARE CHARACTERISTICS
Microprocessor Characteristics
Factors Affecting Processor Performance
Characteristics of Peripherals
Hardware Standards and System Purchase Considerations
SOME SOFTWARE CONSIDERATIONS
Operating System Standards
Prewritten Applications Packages in Homes and Offices
Translating Program Considerations
Feedback and Review 7
LOOKING BACK

MODULE 2

A PC INTRODUCTION

PC Concepts

You'll recall from Chapter 1 that the smallest computer systems are called *microcomputers*. Some microcomputers are tiny *special-purpose* devices dedicated to carrying out a special task, such as controlling the ignition and fuel systems in an automobile. But other microcomputers are *general-purpose* systems that can be used in countless ways. A **personal computer (pc)** is such a system: It's a general-purpose microcomputer system that can execute program instructions to perform a wide variety of tasks.

A pc has all the functional components found in any larger system. That is, it's organized to perform the input, storage, arithmetic-logic, control, and output functions. Some special-purpose microcomputers may package all these functions on a *single* silicon chip, but personal computers are generally much larger and employ several chips mounted on a **main circuit board,** or "**motherboard**" (see Figure 7-1). A **microprocessor chip,** for example, contains the circuits and storage registers needed to perform the arithmetic-logic and control functions discussed in Chapter 4 (see Figure 7-2).[1] Several *random access memory (RAM) chips* are available to handle the primary stor-

---

[1] The origin and development of microprocessor chips and personal computers is outlined in the reading at the end of Chapter 1.

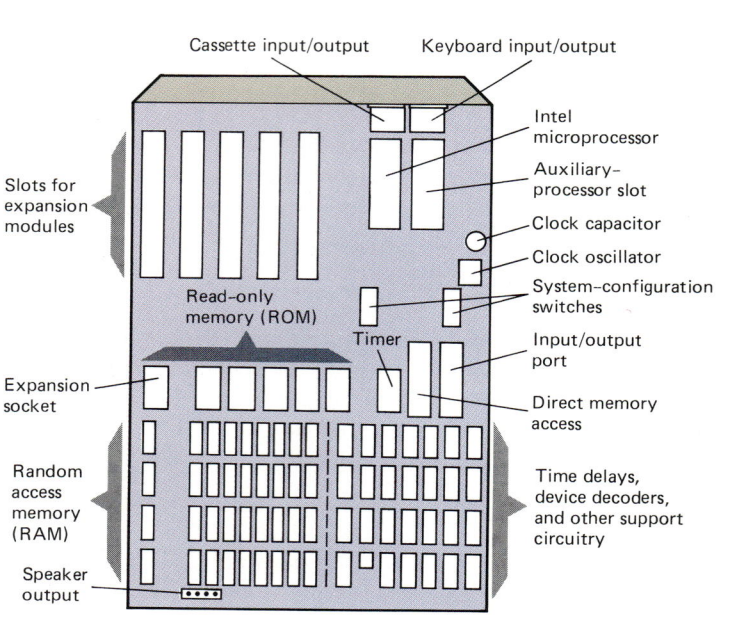

FIGURE 7-1

Personal computers typically employ a number of chips mounted on a main circuit board. (a) The motherboard shown here is used in the IBM Personal Computer. It's slightly larger than a standard sheet of typing paper (it measures 8½ by 12 inches). (b) The major components mounted on the main circuit board are identified in this drawing. The microprocessor shown on the upper-right side of the board is an 8088 chip made by Intel Corporation. The RAM and ROM chips are shown on the lower-left quarter of the board. Additional boards containing more RAM chips and other support circuitry can be plugged into the expansion slots located on the upper-left side of the motherboard. (*Source:* Hoo-min D. Toong and Amar Gupta, "Personal Computers," *Scientific American,* December, 1982, p. 86. Copyright © 1982 by Scientific American, Inc. All rights reserved.)

(a)

(b)

FIGURE 7-2

The world's first microprocessor chip, the Intel 4004 (left), seemed amazingly intricate in 1971, but it looks simple when compared with today's 32-bit microprocessor chips, like the National Semiconductor 32032 (right). (Courtesy Intel Corp. and National Semiconductor Corp.)

age function. Additional *read-only memory (ROM) chips* are generally used to permanently store preprogrammed data or instructions. And still more chips are used to carry out timing, input/output, and other support functions.

The various components on the main circuit board of the pc processor unit are linked together by sets of parallel electrical conducting lines called **buses** (Figure 7-3). Different collections of these internal bus lines are used for different purposes and are given different names, as we'll see later in the chapter. These internal buses also provide an electrical interconnection between processor components and the interface devices used with peripheral equipment (more about this later).

Personal computers come in a variety of shapes and sizes. Some portable hand-held models are notebook-sized or smaller and weigh less than 4 pounds. Other briefcase-sized portables weigh a little more, but they frequently have a larger display screen and more secondary storage capability. Then come the suitcase-sized "transportables" that usually substitute small cathode-ray tube display screens for the liquid-crystal displays used with the smaller models. Since these transportables may weigh in at about 30 pounds, they are sometimes referred to as "luggables" by those who have tried to carry them any distance. Finally, there are the desktop models. These are easily moved, but they weren't designed for constant travel.

Most personal computers are designed to be used by one person at a time; that is, they are **single-user oriented.** But another class of microcomputer

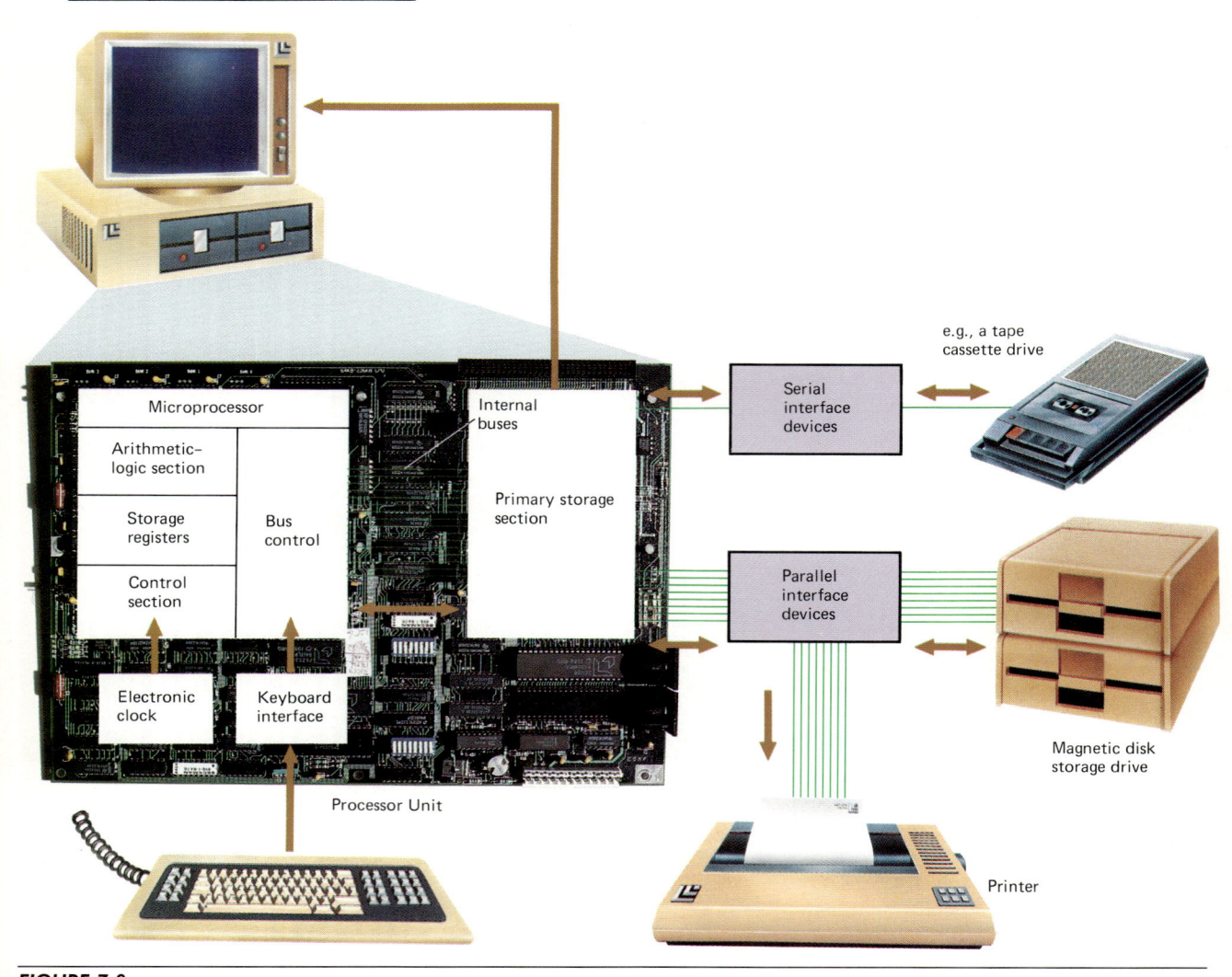

FIGURE 7-3

Sets of parallel electrical conducting lines called buses link the components mounted on the main circuit board of the pc processor unit. Buses also provide an electrical interconnection between processor components and the interface devices that may be used with peripheral equipment.

system has emerged in recent years that isn't restricted to a single user. These **multiuser supermicros** employ many of the same microprocessor and RAM/ROM chips found in single-user systems, but they can handle a number of tasks concurrently and can thus support several user workstations.

The Classification Dilemma

You'll recall from Chapter 1 that the computer industry classifies computers as micros (pc's), minis, mainframes, and supercomputers. But the development of supermicros proves once again that these classifications are arbitrary. The fact is that the size, cost, and performance capabilities of machines in different classifications are likely to overlap. As Figure 7-4 indicates, for example, a model sold as a large pc or supermicro by its maker may have more processing capability (and cost more) than a machine sold as a small mini. And as you'll see in the Closer Look reading following this chapter, a powerful supermini may also outperform a small mainframe system.

Experts don't agree on computer classifications. If you conducted a survey now among a dozen computer experts, asking each of them to tell you the difference between pc's and minicomputers, or between minis and mainframe family models, you would likely get a dozen very different answers. The problem is that computer technology is changing so fast. Within a matter of months after a new computer model comes on the market, it's faced with two potential successors. One costs the same and has a much higher performance; the other has the same performance and costs much less. Thus a recently introduced small system can outperform the large models of a few years ago, and a new pc can do the work of an earlier minicomputer at a much lower cost. This rapid technological pace plays havoc with classification schemes.

Experts agree that the greatest growth in personal computing is yet to come. In studying the potential U.S. market for pc's, analysts note that over 80 million homes have TV sets, over 50 million white-collar employees and over 25 million professionals are in the workforce, and over 4 million small businesses process data. If every home and desktop represents a potential pc site, in 10 years there could be 80 million pc's in use in the United States. Let's look now at some of the hardware characteristics of these micro miracles.

Hardware Characteristics

Microprocessor Characteristics

The first pc's were built in the mid-1970s around microprocessor chips that could operate on **8 bits** of data at a time. Upgraded versions of these first 8-bit

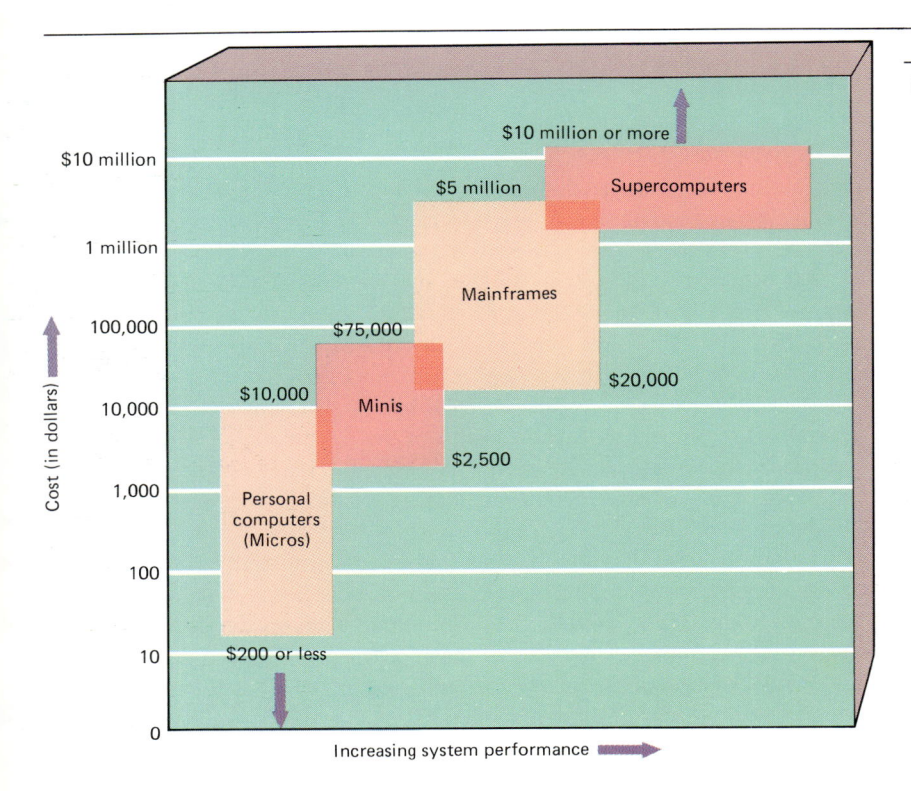

FIGURE 7-4

Computer systems may be classified into personal (micro), mini, mainframe, and supercomputer ("monster") categories depending on size, cost, and system performance. Any such classification is arbitrary. Since categories overlap, the most powerful systems in one category may exceed the capabilities (and cost) of the least powerful systems in another.

> ## WINDOW 7-1
>
> ### MULTIUSER SYSTEMS
>
> Personal computers have sprouted on millions of desks and taken a vital role in thousands of small businesses. But some companies have stopped buying additional computers as their businesses grow. Instead they are buying multiuser systems. Such a system consists of a powerful microcomputer connected to several terminals and a hard disk, which stores the company's data. With this system, several workers can use the same computer, sharing information on the disk without having to copy it separately for each computer.
>
> A multiuser microcomputer is a cross between the minicomputer and the personal computer, combining some of the features of both. A typical multiuser system allows from three to twelve terminals to share a central processor unit, memory, a hard disk, and a printer.
>
> Multitasking is a term often used with multiuser systems. A multitasking computer can perform more than one duty simultaneously for a single user, such as sorting the names in a large data base while the user continues to write a report. More exotic uses might include having the computer monitor several online information services for electronic mail while the user performs some other task. Multiuser computers are really an extension of the multitasking idea: Allowing a second person to use the machine means that the computer must run a specialized second task. A multitasking computer need not be linked in a multiuser system, however. Apple's first 16/32-bit computer, the Lisa, was a multitasking computer designed for a single user. Most of the powerful personal computers now on the market, such as IBM's AT and the AT&T personal computer, have the ability to be linked in multiuser networks.
>
> Despite these advantages, there are some drawbacks to multiuser systems that are similar to problems encountered when several stations use the same minicomputer. Too many people using the system simultaneously may slow it down. Users worry that their private files may be read by others despite the use of code words. And if a multiuser system breaks down, several workers are idled, not just one.
>
> Nevertheless, multiuser systems give the small business the computing power that was only available on mini- or mainframe computers just a short time ago and extend the capabilities of the personal computer.
>
> ---
>
> Adapted from Jim Bartimo, "Multiuser Systems Returning," *InfoWorld*, September 20, 1984, published at 1060 Marsh Road, Menlo Park, CA 94025. Copyright © 1984 by Popular Computing Inc., a subsidiary of CW Communications, Inc. And from William M. Bulkeley, "Multiuser Computer Systems Seen Emerging as a Big Force in Market," *The Wall Street Journal*, August 6, 1984. Copyright © 1984 by Dow Jones and Company, Inc., 1984.

chips were soon introduced, but *all* pc's built during the 1970s were 8-bit systems. Some models (the Apple II systems, the Commodore 64, and some Radio Shack TRS-80 systems) continue to use 8-bit microprocessors today.

All 8-bit pc's use a few popular microprocessor chip designs. These chips—Zilog's Z80, MOS Technology's 6502, Intel's 8080, and Motorola's 6809—have built-in 8-line data paths, or **data buses.** This means that these chips can only retrieve from storage, manipulate, and process a single 8-bit byte of data at a time. A 16-line **address bus** is also built into these chips to determine the primary storage locations of the instructions and data that are needed. With 16 address lines, it's possible for these chips to identify a maximum of 2^{16}, or 65,536, separate storage locations. That's a maximum of 64K bytes in pc lingo.

To improve the data handling and addressing capabilities of their products, microprocessor suppliers introduced improved chips in the early 1980s. These chips operate on **16 bits** of data at a time, and they became the heart of a new generation of pc models. All these 16-bit pc's are also built around a few popular microprocessors. For example, the Intel 8088 is found in IBM PC models and in dozens of other machines. The data path between the 8088 and primary storage is only 8 bits wide, and so all operations to and from storage are done 8 bits (1 byte) at a time. Once retrieved, however, data are processed 16 bits at a time internally in the 8088. The 8088 is thus referred to as an **8/16-bit chip;** it functions like a fast 8-bit microprocessor with an extended set of instructions. A stablemate of the 8088 is Intel's 8086. Unlike the 8088, the internal and external data paths of the 8086 are all 16 bits wide. The 8086 is thus a true **16/16-bit chip.** An expanded built-in address bus with 20 lines permits both the 8088 and the 8086 to identify about a million separate primary storage locations ($2^{20} = 1,048,576$ bytes, or 1 megabyte).

A third popular microprocessor found in the Apple Macintosh and many other systems is the Motorola 68000 (Figure 7-5). A 16-bit external bus is used to move data between this chip and primary storage, but processing is done internally 32 bits at a time. The 68000 is thus a **16/32-bit chip** and is more powerful (and more expensive) than the 8088 or 8086. The 68000's address bus has 24 lines and permits a primary storage capacity of up to 16 megabytes ($2^{24} = 16,777,216$ bytes). The Intel and Motorola microprocessors discussed above were the first 16-bit chips to appear on the market, but enhanced versions of these earlier products are now found in many pc's. For example, the Intel 80186 chip operates about twice as fast as the 8086, but it also incorporates the circuits found in a number of 8086 support chips. And the Intel 80286, which is about six times faster than an 8086, can support a primary storage capacity of up to 16 megabytes. Other suppliers such as Zilog (with the Z8000 chip), National Semiconductor (with its 16032 chip), and Western Design Center (with its 65816—a 16/16-bit version of the chip used in Apple IIs) are in the 16-bit market.

But progress hasn't stopped with 16/32-bit chips. Powerful pc's and supermicros designed in the mid-1980s use chips with internal and external data paths that are *all* 32 bits wide. These **32/32-bit chips** allow desktop systems to perform like the mainframes of a few years ago. Some of the competitors (and

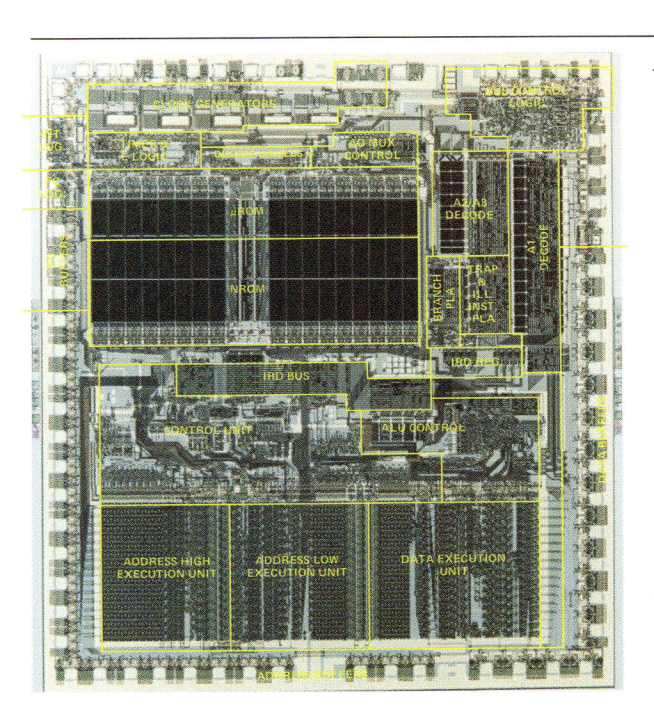

FIGURE 7-5

The data path between this Motorola 68000 microprocessor chip and primary storage is 16 bits wide. Once data are retrieved, they may be processed 32 bits at a time. The 68000 chip is used in the systems of many vendors including Apple Computer's Macintosh, Atari's 520 ST, Commodore's Amiga, and Radio Shack's TRS-80, model 16. (Courtesy Motorola, Inc.)

their chips) in this latest round of microprocessor development are Intel (80386), Motorola (68020), Zilog (Z80000), and National Semiconductor (32032). These chips are sold to the manufacturers of pc systems. Other 32/32-bit chips are produced by companies such as Data General, Digital Equipment, Hewlett-Packard, NCR, and Western Electric for use only in their own products.

Microprocessors with *64-bit* data paths should be available by 1990. The head of microprocessor design at Bell Laboratories estimates that the 1990 equivalent of the processor in a current $20,000 minicomputer will be available on a chip costing less than $1!

Factors Affecting Processor Performance

A number of factors determine the performance characteristics of all pc systems. You can get an idea of the processing capability of a particular model by answering the following questions:

- *Is an 8-, 16-, or 32-bit microprocessor used?* An 8-bit processor can manipulate only a single 8-bit byte of data in a given period. A 16-bit chip can handle 2 bytes in the same unit of time while a 32-bit chip can deal with 4 bytes. If short program segments dealing only with *calculations* are being processed, the execution speed of a 16-bit machine may be two or more times faster than that of an 8-bit model. In processing program segments involving I/O, logic/comparison, and storage/retrieval operations, the 16-bit model may have less of an advantage. In general, a 16-bit pc will be faster than an 8-bit system, but it won't be twice as fast. A 32-bit machine, of course, will have an edge over 8- and 16-bit models.

- *What's the clock speed of the microprocessor?* It's noted in the Closer Look reading at the end of Chapter 4 that there are two cycles that occur during the processing of each program instruction. These *instruction* and *execution* cycles are synchronized by a specific number of electrical pulses produced by an electronic clock that's built into the processor (see Figures 7-1 and 7-3). Thus the speed with which an instruction is executed is also directly related to the chip's *clock speed,* or number of pulses it uses each second. Different versions of a particular chip, such as the Motorola 68000, are produced with different clock speeds. The 68000 used in Apple's Macintosh system runs at 7.83 million pulses per second (that's 7.83 megahertz, or 7.83 MHz). This chip, of course, is faster than the 6 MHz version of the 68000 used in Radio Shack's TRS-80, model 16. The Intel 8088 used in IBM's PC has a slower clock speed of 4.77 MHz. Although most of today's pc models function in the 2- to 10-MHz range, the newest chips can operate at speeds up to 25 MHz.

- *How much primary storage capacity is available?* The more data and program segments that can be kept in primary storage, the fewer time-consuming disk operations may be necessary. Processing speeds up. Even when a Winchester disk drive is used, it's 1,000 times faster to access data located in primary storage. More sophisticated word processing, data base management, and scientific programs can thus be processed on a pc without lengthy waits. You know that a 16-line address bus is used with 8-bit microprocessors to provide a maximum of 64K bytes of primary storage. But it's possible to increase the *apparent* size of primary storage in an 8-bit pc by using software-controlled switches and additional banks of RAM chips. Memory-management software keeps track of the location of needed data items. The microprocessor is always directly connected to only 64K bytes of storage, but there may be 128K bytes of data in the storage blocks (see Figure 7-6). Of course, the time used by the microprocessor to execute the instructions needed to support this **bank-switched memory** approach is time that's not available for other processing tasks. With 20 or 24 lines in its address bus, a 16-bit chip doesn't have to resort to bank switching since it's able to directly address from 1 to 16 megabytes of primary storage. Although many 16-bit systems are currently equipped with 256K bytes of primary storage, additional capacity can easily be added.

● *What instruction sets are available?* Every microprocessor has the built-in ability to respond to a particular set of machine instructions. These instructions are quite similar in 8-bit chips. In fact, the designers of the Zilog Z80 chip incorporated the Intel 8080 instruction set into their design and then extended the Z80 set to include other functions. But incredible as it may seem, these and other 8-bit chips have no single built-in multiplication or division instruction. Rather, these arithmetic functions are carried out at the most basic machine level by a programmed series of other instructions. In contrast, 16-bit processors *do have* single built-in multiplication and division instructions and are able to perform these operations 10 to 20 times faster than 8-bit chips. Thus the composition of the instruction set (and the efficiency of the software used to manage the pc system) can have a significant effect on pc performance.

Characteristics of Peripherals

Input Whatever other devices are used for input—mouse, light pen or joystick, microphone or touch-sensitive display screen, all discussed in Chapter 5—virtually all personal computers include an operator *keyboard* for data entry. And all these keyboards follow the typewriter pattern of placing the letters QWERTY . . . in the top row of alphabetic characters. But there the similarities stop. Some keyboards are permanently housed with the processor unit and display screen, while others are detachable and adapt easily to individual work habits. Most have individual keys, but others substitute flat plastic membranes for keys and are suitable only for hunt-and-peck typing. Some have special-function keys, separate numeric keypads, and adequate spacing between keys, while others don't have any of these features. Some have more than 100 keys, while others have less than half as many. And there are no standard locations for the placement of the keys used to control the location of the cursor on the display screen. These and other differences create problems for people who use several different keyboards.

Storage Floppy-disk drives are generally used to enter data and programs and receive the processed output of office pc systems. Magnetic tape cassette players sometimes perform the same functions for home pc's. Small magnetic tapes and floppy disks are also used for offline secondary storage, and small rigid disk drives employing Winchester technology are available to vastly

FIGURE 7-6

The bank-switched memory approach found in some 8-bit personal computers. Blocks of 16K-byte RAM chips are often used. A combination of hardware and software additions is needed to "trick" the 8-bit microprocessor into accepting data from additional storage blocks.

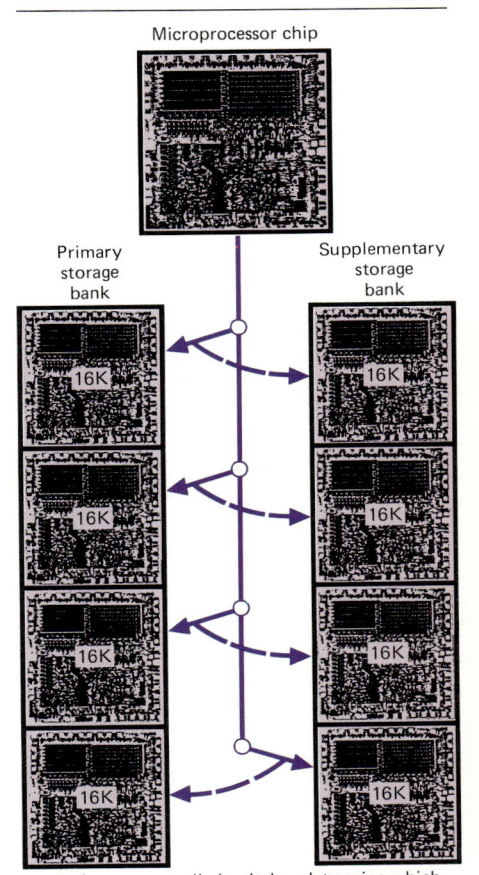

Software-controlled switches determine which blocks are active at any given time

enlarge online secondary storage. Online secondary storage can also be provided by a RAM "disk"—a bank of RAM chips set up to look like a disk drive to the pc. All these storage concepts are discussed in Chapter 6.

Output   The visual display screens, character printers, plotters, and speakers also considered in Chapter 6 are among the devices used to produce output in a humanly usable form. A cathode-ray tube (CRT) is used in most desktop pc display monitors. Some CRT screens are monochrome (one color), while others produce many colors. You saw in Chapter 5 that some pc systems have a graphics mode of operation that permits the display screen to be mapped into thousands of picture elements, or *pixels*. When a pc system with a large number of pixels is connected to a high-resolution color CRT, it can produce quality color graphics. A CRT is reliable, flexible, and easy to use. But it's also bulky and consumes a lot of power. Thus, as we've already seen, battery-powered portable pc's use liquid-crystal displays that are compact, lightweight, and durable and use little power.

Hardware Standards and System Purchase Considerations

Let's suppose that you want to buy a pc system that will fit your budget and meet your needs. If all of your pc components come from the same manufacturer, there may be no problems with the shared connections, or *interfaces*, between various pieces of equipment. But if you want to connect a brand M printer to a brand N computer, you may run into trouble.

Printer M may not work with Computer N because of a lack of **interface compatibility**—the ability to plug various components together and have them function in an acceptable way. Stereo components from different manufacturers have this compatibility, but pc components often don't because many pc makers have developed proprietary standards that are unique to their own products. (Of course, this may help them shut out competitors and sell complete systems.) Uniform and industrywide interface standards are needed by pc users, but they've been slow to appear. Some of the official and *de facto* (unofficial but industry-acknowledged) standards that have emerged for pc hardware over the years are discussed next.

Parallel Interface Standards   A **parallel interface** is one that moves information 8 or more bits at a time. (We've seen that a pc can also operate internally on 16 or 32 bits at a time depending on the microprocessor.) The S-100 internal bus design used with some of the earliest pc's was originally a *de facto* parallel standard that has now been officially designated as the *IEEE-696* by the Institute of Electrical and Electronics Engineers. Another official interface—the *IEEE-488*—was developed by Hewlett-Packard in the early 1970s to connect a computer with as many as 14 other devices on a single cable or bus. Standard cables and sockets are used.

Another *de facto* parallel standard is the *Centronics printer interface*. In the early 1970s, Centronics Data Computer Corporation developed this interface for its popular Series 100 printers. As more Centronics printers were sold, other vendors designed their printers to be compatible with the Centronics interface in order to gain greater market acceptability. (These competitors sometimes used the term "industry standard parallel interface" to avoid the Centronics name.) Many of today's pc systems have a built-in Centronics parallel printer connection. An interface connection is often called a **port.** If both the computer and the printer that a user selects have compatible Centronics parallel ports, then a hardware link-up can be made. But problems can still be encountered if the program instructions (or **driver program**) used by the computer to communicate with a printer cannot be recognized by the selected printer. It's thus wise for a purchaser to insist on a demonstration to prove that the selected computer, printer, and programs will work together.

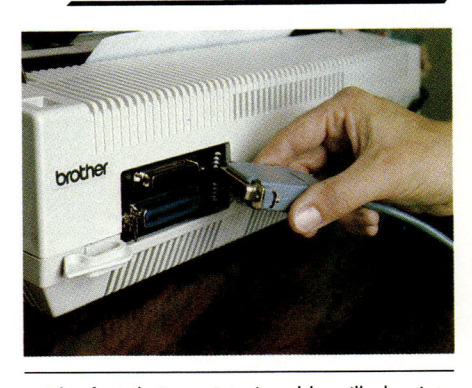

Serial Interface Standards   Unlike a parallel *printer interface* that uses eight wires to transmit all 8 bits in a byte at the same time, a **serial interface** transfers the various bits in sequence over a single wire. When a pc uses an output serial interface port, the 8-bit bytes produced in parallel by the pc are then lined up into a single stream of bits for serial transmission to a printer or other device.

The most popular serial interface is the *RS-232C*, a standard originally established by the Electronic Industries Association to facilitate the transmission of data over telephone lines. Most of the serial ports installed on the processors, printers, and some other devices found in a pc system follow this RS-232C standard. But about all this "standard" guarantees is that a cable connecting two devices will usually plug into both units. Frequent problems arise with wiring cable, synchronizing the number of bits transmitted per second, and letting the computer know when to slow down to avoid overrunning the printer. Assorted software incompatibilities are common too. Again, a demonstration prior to purchase is needed to prove that selected hardware and software will work together.

The fact that a printer's cable will plug into this RS-232C port does NOT guarantee that the printer will work with the computer. (Courtesy Allan Forsyth)

System Purchase Steps   The pc marketplace offers a bewildering range of choices. There are hundreds of different processor units, thousands of peripheral devices of all descriptions, tens of thousands of software packages, and many square miles of retail showroom space. Somewhere in this maze there's likely to be a hardware/software package that's just right for practically any situation. But how do you find what's right for you? There's no foolproof answer to this question, but the following checklist will help you make a wise selection.

1   *Define your needs.*   Is your objective to improve personal productivity, or is it to explore education, entertainment, or other interests?

2   *Identify your primary applications.*   What are likely to be your primary applications? If improving personal productivity is your goal, will your primary applications be the use of word processing, spreadsheet, time management, data base management, or other similar packages? (We'll consider some specific steps to identify and select suitable applications packages in Chapter 9.)

3   *Identify your general hardware needs.*   What hardware features are needed to support the primary applications you've identified? For example, a word processing emphasis may call for a daisy-wheel printer, a graphics interest may require a color display screen, and the manipulation of large data bases and spreadsheets may require a substantial amount of primary and secondary online storage.

4   *Consider the compatibility issue.*   Will the system you select need to

If you are buying a pc it's wise to shop around for the best combination of price and service—and for a demonstration that the hardware items you have selected will actually work together. (Courtesy Computerland)

interface with those of friends, work associates, or others? Will it need to support a particular piece of I/O equipment? If so, remember the interface problems mentioned earlier.

5 *Investigate those systems that satisfy your general hardware and software needs.* Can it be demonstrated to your satisfaction that each system will run the types of primary applications you've identified? Do the systems of interest have keyboards and screens that possess the user-friendly features outlined in Chapter 5? Are the instruction manuals easy to understand? Can friends or colleagues help with system recommendations? Are the warranty terms satisfactory?

6 *Consider the need for future expansion.* Are you likely to need more computing power in the future? If so, are future storage upgrades and other improvements possible with the systems you're considering?

7 *Shop for the best buy.* Have you priced comparable systems at different suppliers? Does a supplier offer satisfactory service arrangements and maintenance contracts? There may be significant differences in the prices quoted by retail stores. Mail-order houses often sell for less than retail stores, but they usually give fewer services.

Some Software Considerations

You learned in Chapter 1 that computer software can be classified into *operating system, application program,* and *translating program* categories. Let's briefly consider a few topics in each of these categories.

Operating System Standards

An *operating system (OS)* is the overall set of program instructions that are needed to manage and coordinate the various parts of a computer system. An OS controls I/O housekeeping operations, keeps track of where facts are stored, and orchestrates in other ways the operation of each pc component. After an OS is loaded into a pc, the user communicates with it, supplies applications programs designed to run with the particular OS in use, furnishes input data, and receives output results. From the user's viewpoint, it would be desirable to have a few pc operating systems that conform to official industry standards, but these *official* standards don't exist.

There are numerous *proprietary operating systems* just as there are many proprietary hardware standards. For example, Apple's DOS (Disk Operating System) and Radio Shack's TRSDOS (TRS Disk Operating System) are intended for use only with specific machines. Since applications programs must work in harmony with a pc's OS, software written for an Apple II running DOS can't be used with a TRS-80 running TRSDOS. Thus the thousands of programs that have been written to run on these two operating systems can't be used without modification on other operating systems.

The CP/M-80 de facto Standard

Because of its widespread acceptance, Digital Research's **CP/M-80** (Control Program/Microprocessors) is a *de facto* OS standard for 8-bit pc systems using Z80 and 8080 microprocessors. Developed in the early 1970s, CP/M-80 has been updated several times.[2] The CP/M-80 OS was adopted for use by dozens of pc manufacturers in the 1970s. As these brands poured into the marketplace, independent software suppliers saw an opportunity and developed thousands of applications programs for the pc systems running CP/M-80. The wealth of 8-bit software that's compatible with CP/M-80 has, in turn, forced the builders of later 8-bit machines to make the OS available to their customers. Plug-in hardware kits are even available to allow the users of some Apple and Radio Shack models to run software written for this OS.

Operating system disk

The MS-DOS de facto Standard

Applications programs are still being prepared for 8-bit machines, but the earlier flood has now become a trickle. Most independent software suppliers have now turned their attention to writing programs for 16- and 32-bit models. And the 16-bit machines that have received the most attention in the mid-1980s are those designed around Intel's 8088 and 8086 microprocessors. The dominant OS for these machines, and one whose acceptance has also made it a *de facto* standard, is **MS-DOS** developed by Microsoft Corporation. The popularity of MS-DOS is due to the fact that it's the one IBM selected to use with its popular Personal Computer (IBM calls it PC-DOS). After IBM selected MS-DOS, more than 50 other hardware manufacturers also picked it. Many of the popular programs first written for 8-bit CP/M systems have now been adapted to a 16-bit MS-DOS environment. And much of the best new business and professional software prepared by independent suppliers is written for this environment first. Other machines get the programs later, if at all.

UNIX and Other Important Operating Systems

The **UNIX** OS was first developed at Bell Laboratories in 1969 for larger machines. It was later adapted for pc systems, and its recent acceptance is rapidly turning it into

---

[2] A 1976 upgrade (version 1.4) improved on the original bare-bones disk OS, a 1979 revision (version 2.0) made further improvements, and a 1982 update (version 3.0, also called CP/M-Plus) was designed to be used with bank-switched memory systems.

another *de facto* standard. Other 16-bit OSs include the proprietary versions offered by some pc makers, the CP/M-86 version developed by Digital Research for 8088/8086 microprocessors, the Oasis-16 from Phase One Systems, the Pick OS from Pick Systems Inc., and the p-System developed at the University of California at San Diego.

Prewritten Applications Packages in Homes and Offices

The OS software controls the overall operation of a computer, but *application programs* control the processing of a particular task. Many application programs are custom-made for unique jobs, but countless other programs have been written and packaged for pc users. Tens of thousands of these prewritten applications packages exist. Simply look at the ads in any of the dozens of pc magazines, and you'll get an idea of the scope and variety of available pc software packages.

Applications Packages in Homes Like all computers, the millions of pc systems installed in homes are general-purpose symbol manipulators. And symbols can be manipulated in countless ways to entertain, educate, and serve people. Thus there's virtually no limit to the number of possible applications that can be developed. Since the demand for good home software is large and growing, it's no wonder that many package suppliers are working hard to serve this market.

For example, with the right applications packages, your home pc system can be used to:

● Entertain you with hundreds of challenging games, many of which have impressive graphic and sound features.

● Balance your budget and checkbook.

● Monitor your home's energy usage.

● Help you learn a new subject, such as a foreign language or auto repair techniques. Game strategies are being incorporated into educational software to increase student motivation.

● Help you compose music.

● Produce better typed documents through the use of word processing programs.

● Maintain automobile and other expense records, and accumulate income data by categories.

● Keep track of the performance of your investments by categories, monitor the coverages and costs of your insurance policies, and prepare your tax returns.

● Compute and keep track of your installment payments.

● Control your household appliances and security devices.

● File for easy retrieval and reference such information as recipes, price lists, names and addresses, telephone numbers, and dates of birthdays and anniversaries.

● Give you information from the data bases of a number of information retrieval networks. For example, you can call a local telephone number, connect your personal computer to one of the information networks discussed in Chapter 8, and access up-to-the-minute information from a wide variety of data banks.

You can add many additional examples to this brief list.

Applications Packages in Offices Personal computers are flooding into offices today. In many large organizations, people tired of waiting for the computer center to process their applications have obtained their own pc systems to do the work. The relatively low cost of a pc system has meant that even the smallest organizations can now afford one. There are thousands of file processing and accounting packages available for use on pc systems. And this doesn't count the additional thousands of educational, health-care, and scientific software packages that are available.

With the right applications packages, a pc system can be used in an office to:

● Link up with the data bases maintained in an organization's mainframe system in order to tap a vast reservoir of information about people, financial assets and liabilities, products and services, and many other topics.

● Manipulate columns and rows of spreadsheet data in order to get quick answers to "what if" questions.

● Compute payrolls and process orders; maintain student, patient, customer, or client records; pay debts and collect receipts; analyze sales and market research data; and process other necessary general accounting tasks.

● Keep track of appointments, schedule meetings, plan daily activities, and maintain an online alphabetical and subject file showing office locations of original letters and documents.

● Schedule production, route jobs, analyze production costs, and control machine tools and other production equipment.

● Control inventory levels of thousands of different items.

● Produce personalized letters, mailing labels, and other documents through the use of word processing software. And then use other software to check the spelling in the documents prior to printing.

● Supply students and employees with educational and retraining opportunities through the use of innovative computer-assisted instruction techniques.

● Monitor and compare the costs of fuel, oil, and repairs for many vehicles, prepare maintenance schedules for these vehicles, and produce vehicle cost reports.

- Prepare the graphic images that are used (to cite just a few examples) by (1) managers to analyze financial data, (2) engineers for stress analysis and interactive design, (3) clinical laboratory technicians to plot quality-control data, and (4) anthropologists to plot the length of bones of prehistoric humanoids.

This listing of tasks performed by applications packages could go on and on, but you get the idea: The actual and potential uses of pc systems in homes and offices can be as numerous and varied as human ingenuity and imagination will permit. We'll consider prewritten software packages again in Chapters 9 and 10.

Translating Program Considerations

A *translation program* is one that transforms the instructions prepared by people using a convenient language into the machine-language codes required by computers. Each programming language requires different translating software. Some pc manufacturers support the use of only one programming language, while others offer users a choice. Independent software vendors compete with manufacturers by offering translators for additional languages or by offering translators that may provide benefits not available with those supplied by pc builders. The translating programs themselves are packaged in various ways. Some may be permanently fused into the ROM chips located on the pc motherboard; others may be stored in plug-in cartridges or on supplied disks.

Many pc users buy their systems so that they can run prewritten applications programs, but they have no interest in developing their own custom-made software. For these users, the translating software is essentially invisible. For program developers, however, the choice of programming languages and the speed and efficiency of the available translating software are important matters. We'll consider translating programs again in Chapter 12.

PERSONAL COMPUTER SYSTEMS

Now that we've considered some of the general hardware and software characteristics of pc systems, let's quickly examine a few examples of the systems found in homes and offices.

Personal Computing Systems in the Home

General-interest pc systems are usually found in the home. They are used to entertain, educate, and increase personal productivity. Millions of these systems have been produced by manufacturers such as Apple, Atari, Commodore, IBM, and Radio Shack. Prices range from less than $100 to about $2,000. The least expensive models have limited keyboards, and a TV set may be used to display output. Primary storage capacity is relatively limited, although 64K bytes are available in machines selling for less than $300. Cassette tape may be used for offline secondary storage of programs and data. It's a slow process to write output onto a cassette tape and to read programs and data from a tape, but cassette recorder/players and tapes are inexpensive. Dot-matrix and nonimpact character printers, and connections that permit communication over telephone lines, are available options for many of these systems.

Since most home systems use the same microprocessor chips found in many larger systems, they can perform complex computations. Originally, many consumers bought home computers to run game programs. But these same systems enabled users to achieve a measure of computer literacy by giving them "hands-on" computer operating experience and by giving them the opportunity to become familiar with the rudiments of computer programming.

Personal computers, as shown in these pages, contain all the elements found in any larger system, and people are taking advantage of the technology in every imaginable way. At home, at school, or on the road, more and more Americans are relying on pcs. [Courtesy Apple Computer, Inc., (above), Verbatim Corp., (above right), and Texas Instruments, Inc. (bottom right)]

Personal Computing Systems in the Office

The costs of the additional hardware and software usually needed in an organizational or professional setting generally mean that the price of office pc systems will range between $2,000 and $10,000. For example, more complete keyboards, larger primary storage sections, significant online secondary storage in the form of floppy and, perhaps, Winchester disk drives, easy to read display screens, and letter-quality printers are needed with *desktop* systems designed to do serious word processing, spreadsheet calculating, and data base managing. The *portable* pc systems used by professionals also need most of these same features. Either 8- or 16-bit machines can be effective in a working system. Many thousands of business-type programs are written for the Apple DOS, CP/M-80, TRSDOS, and the other operating systems used with 8-bit models. These 8-bit programs generally perform *single functions* such as controlling inventory or creating graphic presentations.

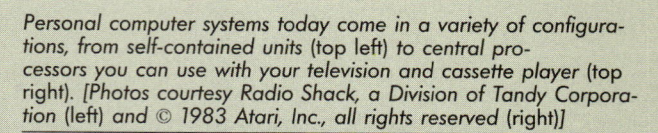

Personal computer systems today come in a variety of configurations, from self-contained units (top left) to central processors you can use with your television and cassette player (top right). [Photos courtesy Radio Shack, a Division of Tandy Corporation (left) and © 1983 Atari, Inc., all rights reserved (right)]

Almost all the important 8-bit single-function programs have now been adapted for use on 16-bit pc systems. And the best new organizational/professional software is being written for 16- and 32-bit machines. These newer programs often *integrate several functions* in a single package. You saw in Chapter 1 that these integrated packages allow users to simultaneously show the current status of several ongoing applications in separate "windows" on the display screen. One window can show the preparation of text, another can show the results of manipulating columns and rows of figures, and a third can show work being done to create graphics. Data can be moved from window to window (and from application to application) as needed. Expensive resources such as 256K (or more) bytes of primary storage, floppy and Winchester disk drives, a system that permits the display screen to be divided into tens of thousands of addressable picture elements, and a printing/plotting output device are often needed to support these more sophisticated software packages.

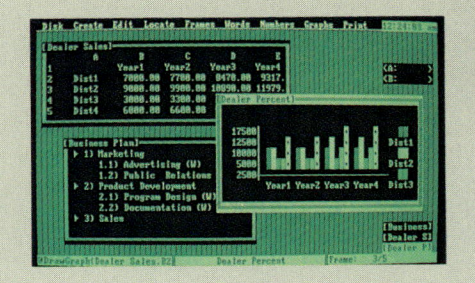

No matter what size the organization, professionals and business people with pc systems have found that the computer regularly pays for itself within a year. [Courtesy Apple Computer, Inc., and © Richard Falco/Photo Researchers, 1985, (page 258); courtesy Hewlett-Packard Co., (top left and top right); IBM Corp., (middle and bottom right); and © Ashton-Tate, 1984, all rights reserved, (bottom left)]

FEEDBACK

FEEDBACK AND REVIEW 7

The following *multiple-choice* questions will test and reinforce your understanding of the material presented in this chapter. Place the letter of the most nearly correct answer in the space provided.

_____ 1. A recently introduced personal computer system
   a) can often do the work of an earlier minicomputer, but it costs much more.
   b) may cost the same as an earlier pc system, but it's likely to offer improved performance.
   c) differs very little from earlier pc systems in terms of cost and performance.
   d) is defined to be a personal computer by rigid industry standards.

_____ 2. Which of the following *isn't* likely to be found on a pc main circuit board:
   a) RAM chips
   b) microprocessor chip
   c) ROM chips
   d) liquid-crystal display clocks

_____ 3. A microprocessor chip used in a pc system
   a) performs the arithmetic-logic and control functions.
   b) is the only chip found in most pc models.
   c) almost always operates on 64 bits of data at a time.
   d) performs the primary storage function.

_____ 4. The popular pc systems produced in the 1970s
   a) were made by Intel Corporation.
   b) use 16-bit microprocessor chips.
   c) use 8-line data buses and 16-line address buses.
   d) are able to identify a maximum of 32,000 separate primary storage locations.

_____ 5. Most of the more powerful pc systems designed today use
   a) 16- or 32-bit microprocessor chips.
   b) over 300 different types of microprocessors.
   c) microprocessors with 128-line data paths.
   d) microprocessors with 16 address lines.

_____ 6. A multiuser supermicro system
   a) uses 6-bit data buses
   b) cannot use the same type microprocessor chips found in single-user systems.
   c) can handle a number of processing tasks concurrently.
   d) is likely to be more powerful than a new mainframe model.

_____ 7. All 16-bit pc systems
   a) are built around a few popular microprocessor chips.
   b) can address a maximum of 1 megabyte of primary storage.
   c) use the microprocessor chip designed by IBM for its Personal Computer.
   d) use a true "16/16-bit" chip.

_____ 8. Which of the following is *not* a factor affecting the processing capability or performance of a pc system:
   a) the clock speed of the microprocessor
   b) the revolutions per minute of the printer disk
   c) the primary storage capacity of the processor
   d) the built-in instruction set available to the microprocessor

_____ 9. A set of official industrywide standards has been approved
   a) for the layout of pc keyboards.
   b) to permit any printer to interface with any pc.
   c) for pc operating systems.
   d) for none of the choices mentioned above.
_____10. A parallel interface
   a) is one that moves information one bit at a time over a single wire.
   b) is used with the RS-232C standard.
   c) moves information 8 or more bits at a time.
   d) is never used to connect printers to personal computers.
_____11. Two of the most popular operating systems for 8- and 16-bit personal computers are (in 8- and 16-bit order):
   a) MOSES and ADAM
   b) MOS and CMOS
   c) CP/M-80 and MS-DOS
   d) CP/M-86 and TRSDOS
_____12. Most pc systems designed for home use
   a) have a relatively limited primary storage capacity.
   b) are 16-bit models with Winchester disk drives.
   c) come equipped with display screens and letter-quality printers.
   d) are priced above $2,000.
_____13. Most pc systems designed for office use
   a) use a TV set to display output.
   b) are limited to the use of programs that are only able to perform single functions.
   c) need a significant amount of online secondary storage capacity.
   d) are unable to produce graphic images.
_____14. Suitable applications packages
   a) are available for home use, but office programs must be custom-made.
   b) may be single-function programs, or they may be programs that integrate several functions in a single package.
   c) are easy to identify and select because of the limited number of such packages.
   d) should be considered only after you've acquired the hardware you'll need to do the work.

LOOKING BACK

1. Personal computer systems are the smallest general-purpose symbol manipulators that can be programmed to process a countless number of applications. Built around a single microprocessor chip (which is an 8-, 16-, or 32-bit device), a pc also uses RAM and ROM storage chips in the processor unit. The various components on the pc main circuit board are connected by sets of parallel conducting lines called buses. Most pc's are single-user oriented, but a new class of multiuser supermicros has emerged in recent years.

2. Technological changes are occurring so rapidly in the computer industry that it's now very difficult to classify the broad range of available machines on the basis of size and computing capabilities. The models discussed in this chapter are arbitrarily classified as personal computers. Larger machines are considered in the reading that follows.

3. All 8-bit pc systems have built-in 8-bit data buses and are thus able to process a single 8-bit byte of data at a time. They also have 16-line address buses, and so they can directly identify a maximum of about 65,000 separate storage locations. The built-in data paths between primary storage and the microprocessors used in 16-bit machines are either 8 or 16 bits wide, and data are processed internally 16 or 32 bits at a time depending on the microprocessor. The 20- or 24-line address buses permit primary storage capacities of 1 megabyte and 16 megabytes. A superior performance may be expected from a pc system that has a 16- or 32-bit microprocessor running at a high clock speed, a large primary storage capacity, and an efficient instruction set.

4. Various I/O and secondary storage devices are available for pc systems. Most of these devices are discussed in detail in Chapters 5 and 6. But combining the I/O and storage components made by several vendors to produce a pc system can lead to problems because of a lack of interface compatibility. Some official and de facto parallel and serial interface standards do exist, but they don't guarantee that selected hardware and software will work together. A checklist is provided in the chapter to help you improve your chances of buying a pc system that meets your needs.

5. An OS is the overall set of program instructions that are needed to manage and coordinate the various parts of a computer system. The user of a pc interacts with an OS, supplies applications programs designed to run with that particular OS, furnishes input data, and receives output results. There are many proprietary OS packages, such as Apple's DOS and Radio Shack's TRSDOS. And because of its widespread usage, CP/M-80 has become a de facto standard for 8-bit systems. Likewise, MS-DOS has become a de facto standard because of its use in most 16-bit systems. Several representative pc systems and their applications are classified into home and office categories and are discussed in the chapter. Translation programs are available for all pc systems to transform the program instructions prepared by people into the machine-language codes required by computers. These programs are important to software developers, but they are essentially invisible to pc users who don't create their own software.

Key Terms and Concepts

personal computer (pc) 242
main circuit board (motherboard) 242
microprocessor chip 242
buses 243
single-user-oriented pc's 244
multiuser supermicros 244
8 bits 246
data bus 246
address bus 246
16 bits 246
8/16-bit chip 247
16/16-bit chip 247
16/32-bit chip 247
32/32-bit chip 247
bank-switched memory 249
interface compatibility 250
parallel interface 250
ports 251
driver program 251
serial interface 251
CP/M-80 253
MS-DOS 253
UNIX 253

Topics for Review and Discussion

1. (a) What is a personal computer? (b) What is a motherboard? (c) What's the difference between a microcomputer and a microprocessor?
2. "Most personal computers are standalone, single-user-oriented machines used by people at work and at play." Discuss this statement and point out any exceptions you're aware of.
3. (a) What's an 8/16-bit microprocessor chip? (b) What's a 16/32-bit chip? (c) Can the microprocessor in an 8-bit pc be considered to be an 8/8-bit chip?
4. Why do some 16-bit pc systems have a maximum primary storage capacity of 1 megabyte, while others can manage up to 16 megabytes?
5. Identify and discuss the factors that affect processor performance in a pc system.
6. (a) Identify four ways to supply input data to a pc system. (b) Identify four ways that output may be received from a pc system. (c) Identify three devices that may be used to provide a pc system with secondary storage capabilities. (You may want to review the I/O and storage media and devices discussed in Chapters 5 and 6 to answer this question.)
7. (a) What is meant by the term "interface compatibility"? (b) What's the difference between a parallel interface and a serial interface?
8. "People may follow a series of steps that may help them avoid unwise system purchases." Identify and discuss these steps.
9. (a) What's a translation program? (b) What's an operating system? (c) Identify three operating systems used with 8-bit machines and three used with 16-bit models.
10. (a) Give three examples of pc systems used primarily in the home, and provide three examples of professional pc models. (b) Discuss four ways that applications packages may be used in the home and four ways that these packages may be of use in organizations.

Projects/Issues to Consider

1. Conduct a survey among five people in the computer/data processing field and ask them these two questions: (a) How would you differentiate between a pc and a minicomputer? (b) How would you differentiate between a minicomputer and a small mainframe model? Present the results of your survey to the class.
2. Select a type of application of interest to you (word processing, accounting, entertainment, educational, scientific, and so on). Identify three possible packages that could be used to process your application. List the features and hardware requirements of each package. Identify the pc systems that you could use to process your application, and describe how you would buy such a system. Summarize your findings for the class.

Answers to Feedback and Review Section

1. b 2. d 3. a 4. c 5. a 6. c 7. a 8. b 9. d 10. c 11. c 12. a 13. c 14. b

A CLOSER LOOK

MINIS, MAINFRAMES, AND "MONSTERS"

Minicomputer Systems

Though it's almost impossible to define a minicomputer anymore, we'll resort to an arbitrary definition. A **minicomputer** is a small general-purpose computer ranging in price from about $2,500 to $75,000. It can vary in size from a small desktop model to a unit about the size of a four-drawer file cabinet. There's obviously an overlap between the more powerful personal computer systems and the low-end minicomputers in terms of cost and processing capability. The same overlap also exists between the most expensive minis and small mainframe models. In fact, the makers of minicomputers are finding that their traditional market is being attacked on the low end by pc vendors and is being squeezed on the high side by mainframe builders.

Most of the minis produced in the 1970s are **16-bit machines.** They are able to simultaneously move and manipulate data words consisting of two 8-bit bytes. This 16-bit capability gave minis an edge in performance over the 8-bit personal computers that were also introduced in the 1970s. Of course, much of the performance advantage enjoyed by the older 16-bit minis was lost when 16-bit pc systems were introduced early in the 1980s.

But the mini makers did not rest on their 16-bit designs and wait for the pc vendors to catch up. Rather, many of them were busy in the 1970s developing a new generation of 32-bit **supermini** models. Able to operate on 4 bytes at a time rather than 2, these superminis gave users the performance of small mainframe models in less expensive packages. Today, mainframe makers are bringing out lower-priced models to counter the supermini threat, both mini and mainframe suppliers are producing personal computers in an effort to ward off the advances of other pc builders, and users are benefiting from the competitive dogfight.

Some Characteristics of Typical Minis Today's typical mini system carries a higher price tag and will surpass the typical pc in storage capacity, speed of arithmetic operations, and ability to support a greater variety of faster-operating peripheral devices. For example, the larger hard-disk units used for online secondary storage in some mini systems have a much greater capacity and are faster operating than the small Winchester and/or floppy devices used in most professional pc systems.

While most pc systems remain oriented toward single users, mini systems are usually designed to simultaneously handle the processing needs of *multiple* users. Minis may support dozens or even hundreds of terminals. Thus they are almost always found in organizations. And in addition to processing the tasks submitted from multiple workstations, minis can also serve as a communications link between these stations and a central mainframe. One of the first mini applications was to handle the flow of information between mainframes and outlying terminals. Thus early minis were designed to interact with mainframes, and this capability has been improved over the years. Current pc systems generally lack the communications hardware/software resources available to minis.

Some of the more advanced 16-bit minis, and many of the superminis, achieve faster processing speeds by employing a special *high-speed buffer,* or *cache,* storage section in the processor. As noted in Chapter 4, the cache temporarily stores very active data and instructions during processing. Since the cache storage unit is faster than the primary storage section, the processing speed is increased. The capacity of this high-speed buffer typically ranges from 4K to 128K bytes. But it's interesting to note, too, that the newest microprocessor designs now include a small cache unit on the chip.

MINICOMPUTER GALLERY

Some 16-bit traditional models and some 32-bit superminis are represented in the Minicomputer Gallery. As mini systems get larger, primary and online secondary storage capacities increase, the peripheral devices that can be supported become more numerous and more powerful, and there's an increase in the number of users that can be simultaneously supported.

Many Uses for Minis

Organizations have found many uses for minicomputers. The early minis were used primarily for single specialized applications—to monitor instruments and test equipment in a laboratory or to control a machine tool or a flow process in a factory—or they were used to process a number of general applications in a small organization. They are still widely used for these purposes. In addition, dedicated minicomputers are also used to control the data input received from multiple key-to-disk encoding stations (see Figure 5-11, page 182).

Although pages could be filled with other examples of minicomputer uses, perhaps one more very important type of application will be enough. Over the years many organizations have decided to establish **distributed data processing (DDP) networks.** Typically, in a DDP network, a larger central **host computer** communicates with, and exercises some control over, **satellite** (or **node**) **processors.** A satellite may, in turn, act as a host to subordinate processors and/or terminals. The satellite processors are likely to be minicomputers that handle much of the data processing done locally in offices and on factory floors. Connected to these satellite minis may be other subordinate minis, personal computers, intelligent terminals, and/or dumb terminals. And in addition to the dozens of minis that are used in some large DDP networks to process data, still more minis are used to control the flow of communications between network stations. We'll look at DDP networks in more detail in Chapter 8.

Most minis were originally 16-bit machines, as shown here, and have filled the data processing needs of business since the 1970s. Minicomputers originally gained popularity by filling a gap created by a move toward centralized processing facilities geared to large organizations which could afford mainframe power. (Photos reproduced by permission of Data General Corporation, Westboro, Mass., and courtesy Wang Laboratories, Inc.)

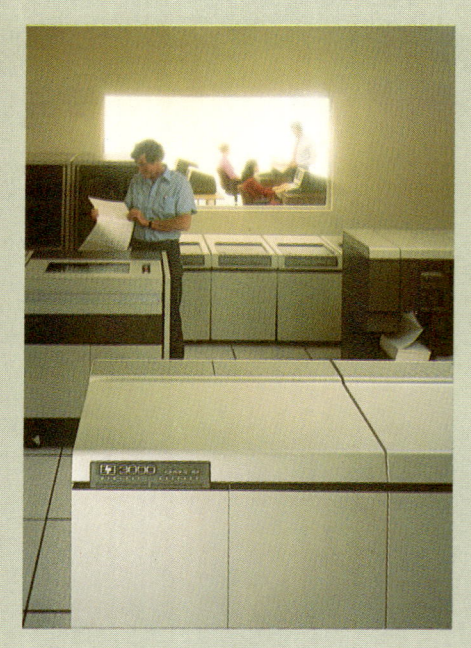

Minicomputers perform a vast array of applications, from data processing for a small organization to controlling production processes to high-speed transaction processing in the financial industry. Many newer mini systems are 32-bit machines which provide for increased processing power and multiuser capabilities. [Photos courtesy Hewlett-Packard Company and Digital Equipment Corporation (top); provided by Datapoint Corporation, all rights reserved, and courtesy AccuRay Corporation (above); and courtesy Perkin-Elmer Corporation (right).]

Mainframe Family Models

A computer that's generally *more powerful* than a typical mini is now often called a **mainframe.** Models carrying the mainframe designation vary widely in cost and performance capability. And we've already seen that there's considerable overlap possible in the cost and performance of large minis and small mainframes.

Some Characteristics of Typical Mainframes A whole series of mainframe models ranging in size from small to very large are typically lumped together under a *family designation* by mainframe manufacturers. It's usually possible to run programs prepared for one machine on other models in the same family with little or no modification. This **software compatibility** between family models makes it easy for users to move up to larger systems in the same family if they outgrow their smaller machines. However, it's usually not as easy to convert programs to a larger system in a different product line, a fact that helps maintain the stability of a mainframe manufacturer's customer base.

What was true of the other computer categories we've now considered remains true of mainframe families: Primary and online secondary storage capacities increase as the systems get larger. Furthermore, in the larger mainframe models it's likely that an alternative computer system architecture will be substituted for the **single processor** (or **uniprocessor**) **approach** in design used in smaller machines. For example, several arithmetic-logic and control units may be used in a larger **multiprocessor mainframe** to process several tasks at the same time. A multiprocessor design, in effect, creates a system with two or more processing units. Also, high-speed cache storage sections with large capacities are routinely used in the more powerful mainframes. The result of these and other features, of course, is that larger mainframes can process applications faster than smaller computers.

Another characteristic that improves their performance is the fact that most of the *smaller* mainframes are basically **32-bit machines** and can manipulate 4-byte words in a single machine cycle. In *larger* mainframes, the length of the data word that can be manipulated in a given instant is increased to 48, 60, or 64 bits, depending on the model. Most mainframes also have large instruction sets that give them the flexibility to automatically operate on from 2 to 8 bytes in the same unit of time. Of course, we've seen that superminis now use a 32-bit design, and 32-bit microprocessor chips are available in personal-sized computers. The trend toward cheaper, smaller, and more powerful systems continues unabated!

MAINFRAME GALLERY

Well over half of all the mainframes installed in the 1970s were IBM System/370 machines. The 370 line consisted of about a dozen models. Although thousands of 370 machines are still in use, IBM is now concentrating its efforts on several newer mainframe families. One family of small- to medium-sized systems—the IBM 4300 series—also has about a dozen models. Another IBM family—the 308X series—currently includes seven large-scale systems. Prices of processors in the 4300 series range from about $60,000 to $500,000, while prices for the 308X series processors start at $1 million and go to $7 million.

Note that these and other figures given in this section don't include the price of peripherals. But for an idea of the cost/performance improvements that have occurred in the last decade, consider this: A medium-sized System/370 model (the 158) with 1 megabyte of primary storage was priced at about $1.6 million in the mid-1970s. A 4300 series processor (the 4361-4) with about the same performance and 12 times as much storage now costs about $200,000. Other mainframe vendors pictured here can point to similar cost/performance improvements.

Mainframe Uses and Applications

For years, virtually everything that was done with computers was done on mainframes. Even as late as 1975, 83 percent of the money spent for computers went to buy mainframes. By 1988, however, it's expected that only 30 percent of industry sales will be for these models. Some observers reading these figures have concluded that mainframes are becoming obsolete and will be replaced by minis and pc systems. What they fail to notice, though, is that mainframe sales have continued to grow—from about $10.6 billion in 1975 to an expected $26 billion in 1988. The confusion results from the fact that sales of smaller systems have been growing at a much faster rate.

Mainframes are available in models that fill rooms—the IBM 4300 series shown above—or that take up no more room than a filing cabinet—the NCR 9300 system shown at the left and below. Regardless of their physical size, mainframes will continue to play a vital role in information processing in the coming years. (Photos courtesy IBM Corporation and NCR Corporation)

Although a number of major processing categories will require mainframe capabilities for an indefinite period, we'll mention just three. The *first* category is the processing of periodic *high-volume batch applications*. Most medium-sized and larger organizations in the country with a history of computer usage have one or more mainframes to prepare thousands (and even millions) of paychecks, invoices, welfare checks, mailing labels, and so on. Mainframes are designed to control the multiple printers and banks of disk and tape drives that are needed for large-scale batch jobs. A *second* type of application that calls for mainframe capabilities is the *management of very large centralized data bases*. Scores of people in many locations may need access to all or part of the data for update and/or inquiry purposes. The power of a mainframe is needed to control access, interpret queries, and retrieve and update records. And a *third* mainframe use is as the *central host computer in a large DDP network*. The mainframe communicates with, and exercises some control over, smaller satellite processors and workstations. At Blue Cross Insurance Company of Virginia, for example, a large mainframe is used for claims processing. Over 200 workstations in hospitals and doctors' offices are used to enter medical claims into the computer. The system prompts users on how to enter claims, notifies them immediately of any errors, and tells them when to expect payment.

Mainframe systems supply the processing power many organizations need to get their work done—running high-volume batch jobs, managing large centralized data bases, or acting as the host processor in a large distributed data processing network. (Photos courtesy Social Security Administration, top, and Honeywell, Inc.)

Supercomputer Systems

As you've probably guessed, **supercomputers** are the most powerful and most expensive computers made. Only a few of these computing monsters are produced each year because only a few organizations need (and can afford) their processing capabilities. But supercomputers are far more important to a nation than their numbers would indicate. They are a national resource. The calculations needed in some scientific research and development areas simply can't be managed without supercomputers. A nation's leadership role in energy, space exploration, medicine, industry, and other critical areas is unlikely to continue if its scientists must use computers that are less powerful than those available to their counterparts in other lands. For example, today's supercomputers aren't fast enough to simulate the airflow around an entire aircraft. Builders of new airplanes must therefore simulate the passage of air around separate pieces of the plane and then combine the results to produce an effective aerodynamic design. Scientists at the National Science Foundation (NSF) believe that the first nation to build a supercomputer capable of simulating the airflow around a complete airplane will be the country that develops planes with superior performance.

Recognizing the importance of supercomputers, Japanese leaders have launched a high-priority national effort to develop by 1989 a machine that will be 1,000 times faster than current United States models. Several responses have been made in the United States to this effort. Research and development consortiums funded by companies in private industry and supported by universities have been created to do basic research. Government agencies such as the Advanced Research Projects Agency of the Defense Department, the NSF, and the National Aeronautics and Space Administration have taken renewed interest in supercomputer projects. And conferences have been called to allow the exchange of views between supercomputer makers and users.

Some Characteristics of Supercomputers Since supercomputers are designed to process complex scientific applications, the computational speed of the system is most important. To maximize the speed of computations, each address location in a supercomputer holds 64 bits of information. Thus, in a single machine cycle, two 64-bit data words can be added together. The **cycle time**—the time required to execute a basic operation—may be as low as 4 nanoseconds (billionths of a second). That's about six times faster than the largest mainframes considered in the last section. One of today's supercomputers has the computing capability of approximately 40,000 IBM Personal Computers. And as we've seen, efforts are underway in the United States and Japan to produce a machine with the power of 40 *million* IBM PCs.

The entire primary storage section of some supercomputers consists of the types of expensive components that are generally reserved *only* for a high-speed cache section in less powerful machines. This usage, combined with the large number of circuit chips required to process the large (64-bit) fixed-length words, makes a supercomputer very expensive. Prices range from about $4 million to about $15 million.

SUPERCOMPUTER GALLERY

Cray Research and Control Data Corporation (CDC), two firms located in the Minneapolis/St. Paul area, are the primary builders of supercomputers in the United States. Cray has sold about 55 of its Cray-1 and X-MP models, while CDC has installed about 15 of its CYBER 205 systems. In one recent year, Cray sales totaled—are you ready for this?—21 systems! But Cray received about $220 million for these 21 machines. Cray, CDC, and the Japanese are planning new efforts in the supercomputer field. Cray is building a new Cray-2 model that is one-tenth the size of its current line and at least six times faster. Control Data has announced a new subsidiary—ETA Systems, Inc.—that will concentrate on supercomputers, and the Japanese are expected to offer competitive models in the years ahead.

Supercomputer Applications

Some of the supercomputers that have been delivered are making top-secret weapons-research calculations for the federal government at the Los Alamos Scientific Laboratory in New Mexico and at the Lawrence Livermore Laboratory in California. (There are five Cray-1s at Los Alamos.) A Cray-1 is providing complex calculations for petroleum and engineering companies at a Kansas City data processing service. Still other Cray-1s are working on weather-forecasting problems at the European Center for Medium Range Weather Forecasts in England and at the National Center for Atmospheric Research in Boulder, Colorado. The National Weather Service has also bought a CYBER 205.

In weather forecasting and in research involving the earth's atmosphere, weather data supplied by a worldwide network of space satellites, airplanes, and ground stations are fed into supercomputers. These data are analyzed by a series of computer programs to arrive at forecasts. Although current programs certainly provide forecasts that are more accurate than unaided human guesses, there's still room for considerable improvement. It's not that scientists don't understand the principles involved well enough to be able to prepare programs that *could* provide much better forecasts. Rather, the problem is that even with the power of a Cray or CDC machine, the thousands of variables involved cannot now be evaluated to the satisfaction of scientists in the time available for forecasting. Nobody cares if a computer produces a storm warning hours after the storm has hit. In short, the current forecast programs being run on supercomputers are crude models of what meteorologists would use if much more powerful computers were available. This is just another incentive for supercomputer builders to make ever-larger machines.

Over the past 10 years, electronic design engineers have pushed the state of the art to produce faster and faster computers. Once the sole province of United States firms, advanced supercomputer technology gave the U.S. advantages in, for example, weapons research (top). Now the Japanese are entering the supercomputer market with machines that challenge their American counterparts (bottom). (Photos courtesy Los Alamos National Laboratory and Toshiba America, Inc., OEM Division)

But not all supercomputer applications involve serious scientific work. Digital Productions Inc., a Hollywood filmmaker, uses a Cray X-MP to produce computer-generated images that can be incorporated into its movies. When smaller machines were used, it took Digital Productions about a year to produce the images needed to fill a 2-minute strip of film. Now they are able to produce 4 minutes of film each month and thus substantially compress the time needed to produce a feature-length movie.

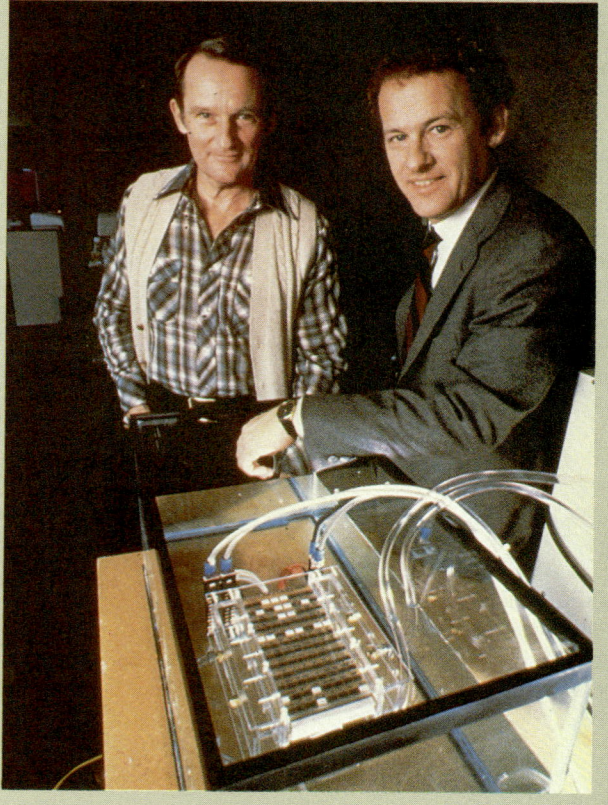

Today's supercomputers can perform in hours simulations that only a few years ago took weeks to complete. But users continue to devise tasks more complex than even the fastest computers can readily handle—so designers like Seymour Cray, at the left, are developing even mightier supercomputers like the Cray 2 in the foreground. (Photos courtesy Cray Research, Inc., by Joe Gianetti, and Control Data Corporation)

CHAPTER 8

DATA COMMUNI-CATIONS NETWORKS

RADIO-LINKED COMPUTER NETWORKS FREE TRAVELING
USERS FROM PHONES AND CABLES

The first reporter to a telephone usually beats the competition on a breaking story. But scrambling for phones may soon be a thing of the past at papers like the *Seattle Times,* where journalists are beginning to work with portable devices that combine word processing with radio communications.

Times reporters, using lap computers grafted to mobile phones, can type stories at the scene of the action and send them instantly to the paper via radio waves. The devices are now used mainly by sportswriters but are expected to improve coverage of other fast-breaking news far from phones.

As the technology for radio-linked computers makes possible smaller and cheaper systems, it is inspiring new applications. Like that at the *Times,* most involve a number of small mobile computers communicating with a fixed central unit. Federal Express, for example, has installed computers in its delivery trucks for tracking and dispatching couriers. Police officers use similar equipment in their cruisers to check data bases for information on stolen vehicles and wanted persons. And taxi companies will soon be able to use radio-linked computers to facilitate credit card payment of fares.

As lap computers become smaller and cheaper, more people are getting interested in carrying computing power around with them. This will increase the demand for wireless links. Linking computers by radio is technologically tricky, however. Walls reinforced with metal can interfere with transmissions, hills can block them, and thunderstorms and electrical devices can distort them. A partial solution is to transmit data in short bursts, which minimizes the signal's exposure to disruptive influences. But this technique can't always guarantee that a signal will get through. Many radio-communications devices have the ability to check for the reliability of the data being transmitted. These methods usually involve sending error-checking signals along with the data; if these signals arrive distorted, the receiver instructs the transmitting computer to resend the data.

To guard against eavesdropping, data are also frequently translated before sending into a special code, which is unscrambled by the receiver.

The initial wireless systems were expensive, but as with all other computer technology, vendors of wireless computer networks are designing new systems that are smaller and cheaper. They envision real estate agents using portable units to check prices and availability of houses while talking to clients at their homes, and see sales representatives using computers in the field to retrieve information on customers' orders.

Cellular, or mobile, telephones provide ready-made radio systems that can be used to link computers. Some of the most futuristic hybrids of cellular phones and computers are designed as radio navigation devices. Such systems carried in a boat or car can calculate its whereabouts and relay the data to a central computer, which would show the location on a video-display map. This system could help find a vessel stranded at sea or track a stolen boat or car.

Adapted from David Stipp, "Radio-Linked Computer Networks Free Traveling Users from Phones and Cables," *The Wall Street Journal,* November 5, 1985. Copyright © 1985 by Dow Jones and Company, Inc. Reprinted by permission. All rights reserved.

CHAPTER 8

LOOKING AHEAD

Data communications is an integral part of many information systems. And while communications systems date back to the beginning of history, we'll focus in this chapter on rapidly emerging data communications systems that are vital to any modern society. The information in this chapter will enable you to:

- Understand the converging computing/communications setting
- Describe the data transmission techniques and channels, and identify the types of organizations that provide these services for groups and individuals
- Outline the components used to coordinate a complex computing/communications network
- Give specific examples of information systems supported by data communications

CHAPTER OUTLINE

LOOKING AHEAD
THE COMPUTING/COMMUNICATIONS SETTING
Data Communications Background
The Converging Computing/Communications Picture
DATA COMMUNICATIONS CONCEPTS
Data Transmission Techniques
Data Transmission Channels
Data Communications Service Organizations
Coordinating the Data Communications Environment
SYSTEMS SUPPORTED BY DATA COMMUNICATIONS
Real Time Processing Systems
Timesharing and Remote Computing Service Systems
Distributed Data Processing Networks
Electronic Mail/Message Systems
Data Base Retrieval Systems
Banking Service Systems
Telecommuting Systems
Feedback and Review 8
LOOKING BACK

THE COMPUTING/COMMUNICATIONS SETTING

You've become familiar with the term interactive processing in many earlier chapters. This type of processing, as shown in Figure 8-1, generally involves online stations located at or near the data sources, and these sources can be far away from the processor. To cite just a few examples, teller and point-of-sale terminals are spotted in locations away from computers; airline, car rental, and hotel reservation systems have thousands of terminals located many miles from their processors; and factory data entry stations may not be near a computer. **Data communication** refers to the means and methods whereby data are transferred between such processing locations. It's the "glue" that permits a direct interactive bond between the people at these stations and the central processing systems.

Data Communications Background

There's nothing new about data communications. The ancient Greek runner carrying the message of victory on the plains of Marathon inspired a present-day athletic event. Pony Express riders carried messages and won the admiration of a nation in the brief period before they were replaced by telegraph service. For 30 years, telegraph companies enjoyed a monopoly on the use of electrical impulses to transmit data between distant stations. But in 1876, Alexander Graham Bell demonstrated that electrical signals could be used to transmit voice messages along telephone lines, and so a second data communications, or **telecommunications,** channel was established.

In the 75 years after the introduction of the telephone, a complex network of telecommunications systems was established to link locations throughout the world. The first linkage of computing and communication devices occurred in 1940 when Dr. George Stibitz used telegraph lines to send data from Dartmouth College in New Hampshire to a Bell Laboratories calculator in New York City. But it wasn't until the late 1950s that the computing/commu-

FIGURE 8-1

Two types of interactive processing: *(left)* hotel reservation system; *(right)* shop control at a factory. (Photos courtesy Bunker Ramo Information Systems and NCR Corporation)

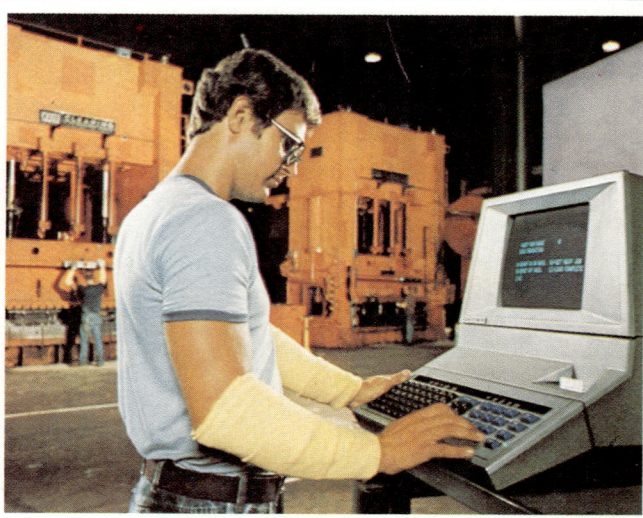

nications linkage began in earnest. Telegraph lines were used first to connect teleprinter terminals with computers, but telephone lines were quickly pressed into service. An early large-scale business application was the Sabre passenger reservation system developed in the late 1950s and early 1960s by American Airlines and IBM. Hundreds of scattered terminals were linked to a central processing center. Communications usage has grown steadily since then. Today, most minis and larger machines are able to communicate with outlying terminals. And with available attachments, most personal computers can use telephone lines to access the data bases maintained by information retrieval services.

The Converging Computing/Communications Picture

Twenty years ago computing capability was obtained from computer vendors, and communications service was supplied by telecommunications firms. The communications firms used some computer-controlled message-switching devices to improve their services, and the computer vendors offered limited communications packages to sell data processing services. But it wasn't difficult to differentiate between the two groups.

As the years passed, however, computer vendors began to offer a larger package of communications services to their customers while telecommunications suppliers furnished more computing resources to those who used their networks. Prior to this convergence of computing and communications technologies, government regulation of the many organizations that offered computing and communications services was reasonably clear. An *unregulated* legal status applied to organizations whose communications offerings were only incidental to their competitive computing services. And a *regulated* legal status generally applied to firms whose data processing services were only incidental to their furnishing of communications channels. But as many "hybrid" organizations arose to offer expanded computing and communications services, regulatory status became an uncertain—and often heated—issue (Figure 8-2).

Attempting to keep up with technological advances and perform regulatory functions, Federal Communications Commission (FCC) actions served to pit rich and powerful organizations in the unregulated computing industry against equally rich and powerful regulated communications groups. Federal antitrust lawsuits brought against the largest firms in each sector—IBM and American Telephone and Telegraph Company (AT&T)—dragged on for years.

Recent FCC rulings tend to favor a greater degree of unregulated competition in the evolving data communications field. Settlements were also reached in the antitrust suits. The suit against IBM was dropped. And after agreeing to split off its regulated Bell Telephone subsidiaries into separate companies, AT&T has now entered the competitive and unregulated computing/communications environment.

Today computers are an essential part of a modern communications network, and such a network is vital to the operation of many modern computer-based information systems. Many of the same electronic circuit chips are now used in both computing and communications devices. Computer vendors can offer a large package of communications services, and they are committing more research and development funds to communications technology. Not to

FIGURE 8-2

As computing and communications technologies converged, the issue of government regulation in the data communications field became unclear.

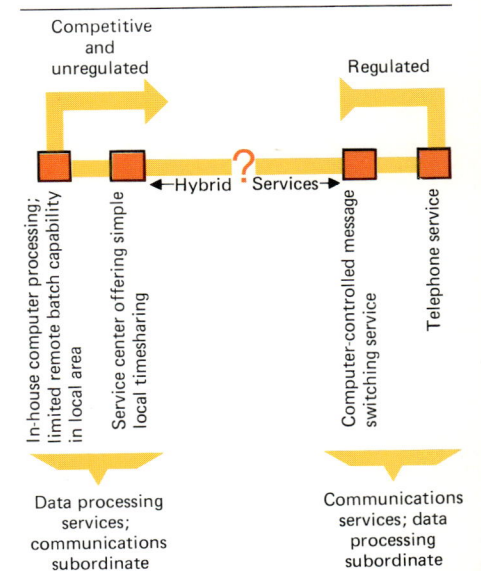

Competitive and unregulated → ← Hybrid ? Services → ← Regulated

In-house computer processing; limited remote batch capability in local area | Service center offering simple local timesharing | Computer-controlled message switching service | Telephone service

Data processing services; communications subordinate | Communications services; data processing subordinate

FIGURE 8-3

A simple data communications system typically links I/O devices at remote locations with one or more central processors. Interface elements such as modems and front-end processors are used to bridge and control the different data communications environments. Modems are used to permit the system to switch back and forth from computer digital data to analog signals that can be transmitted on voice communication lines. A front-end processor is a computer used to monitor and control the data transmission channels and the data being transmitted. In this system, data to be sent to a processor are entered into a workstation through a keyboard. On command from the operator, the data in digital form are sent in a serial (one bit at a time) fashion to a nearby modem to be converted into an analog signal. This signal is a warbling sound composed of frequencies ranging from 1070 to 2225 cycles per second—tones that are well within the range of the human voice. The converted data are then transmitted over telephone lines to another modem near the central processor. This modem converts the analog signal back to a digital form. The data in digital form are then sent to a front-end processor which may check them for possible errors and then temporarily store them or route them to the main processor for immediate processing. The same route is followed when output information is sent from the central processor back to the remote location. The entire data communications activity is controlled by program instructions stored in communications processors and/or central processors.

be outdone, suppliers who formerly concentrated on telecommunications equipment are now offering storage chips, workstations, software, pc's, and many other computer products.

Several new terms have been coined to reflect this merger of computing and communications technology. (The French use the word "telematique," the English use "telematics," and "compunications" has been suggested by a Harvard professor.) As more personal computers are attached to communications networks, and as more of the equipment in an organization is linked together by data communications, the distinctions between computing and communications will become even more blurred.

DATA COMMUNICATIONS CONCEPTS

In a simple data communications system, terminals and other remote I/O devices are linked with one or more central processors to capture input data and receive output information. Connecting equipment and software, sometimes referred to as **interface elements,** are used to bridge the different physical and operating environments of I/O devices and central processors. And a variety of data transmission channels carry data from one location to another. In the next few pages we'll concentrate on some interface elements, data transmission channels, and related data communications concepts.

Data Transmission Techniques

You'll notice that an interface element called a modem is shown at *each* end of the data transmission channels in Figure 8-3. A **modem** is a modulation-demodulation device that converts the discrete stream of digital "on-off"

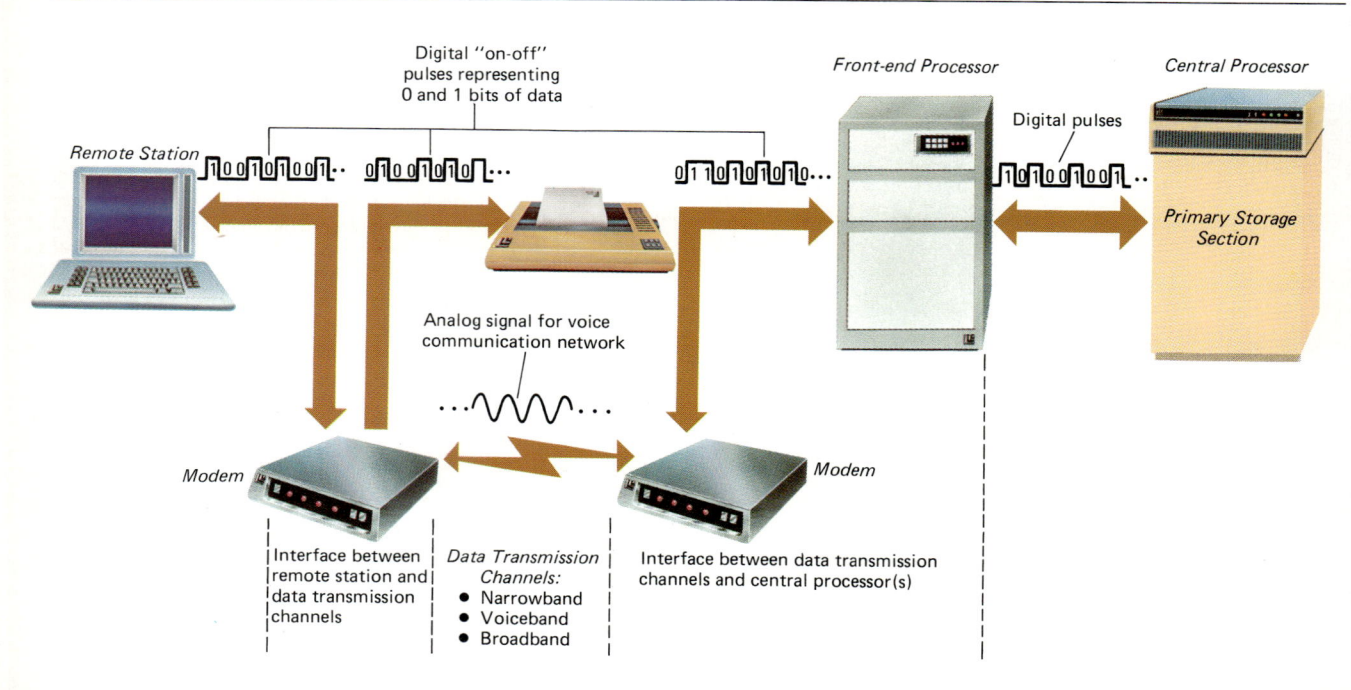

electrical pulses used by computing equipment into the type of continuously variable analog wave patterns used to transmit the human voice over many existing telephone lines. Digital pulses cannot effectively travel any distance over lines that were designed years ago for voice communications. Thus a modem is needed to *modulate,* or convert, the digital pulses when older telephone lines are used to transmit data. For example, when data from a terminal are sent over these lines to a processor, a modem is needed at the transmitting end to convert the digital pulses into analog signals. And another modem is needed at the receiving end to *demodulate,* or recover, the digital data from the transmitted signal. Of course, when output from the processor is sent back to the remote site, the process is reversed. The modem at the processor location modulates the output, and the modem at the remote location demodulates the transmitted signal.

The modems shown in Figure 8-3 are wired directly to the I/O equipment at the remote and central locations. These devices have their own cabinets and are called **external direct-connect modems.** But **internal direct-connect modems** are also available. These devices, on plug-in circuit boards, are installed inside personal computers that are designed to accept them. Figure 8-4 shows how external and internal direct-connect modems can be connected to personal computers. Both these types of modems may be equipped with built-in microprocessors, storage chips, and specialized communications chips. Such **intelligent modems** can be programmed to automatically perform dialing, answering, and disconnecting functions.

But not all modems use direct-wiring connections. You'll recall in Chapter 5 that large numbers of portable terminals are now used by salespersons,

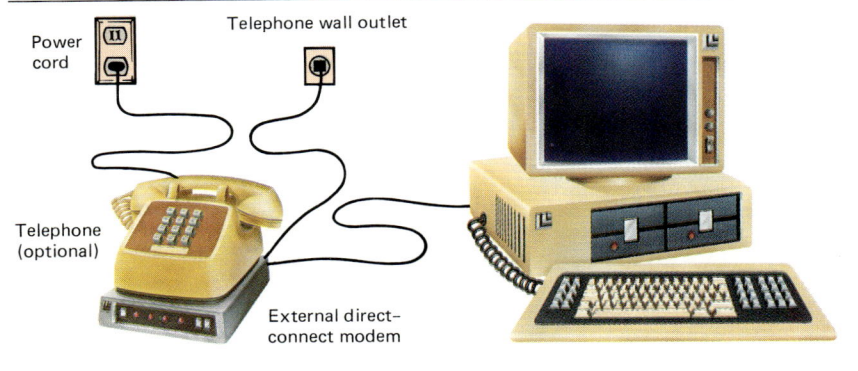

FIGURE 8-4

Direct-connect modems can be housed in separate external cabinets (a). Or they can be placed on circuit boards and plugged into expansion slots inside a personal computer (b). An external modem can be used with virtually any pc, while the internal modem is designed to fit a specific model. A user who changes equipment would probably have to buy another modem to replace an internal device; an external modem would likely save that expense. But since an internal modem draws its power from the pc and needs fewer cables, it's a less expensive and neater alternative.

managers, engineers, and others to communicate with distant processors. A special type of modem called an **acoustic coupler** is used in these situations to provide the necessary interface. The acoustic coupler is attached to (or built into) a portable terminal, and a standard telephone handset fits into rubber cups located on the coupler. The digital pulses produced by the terminal are converted into audible tones that are picked up by the handset receiver. The

FIGURE 8-5

Direct-connect modems and acoustic couplers can be used to link personal computers. Data are transmitted as a serial stream of bits using the ASCII code (Chapter 4). An RS-232C serial interface connection (Chapter 7) is generally used to link the personal computers to the modems. In addition to the data bits, each character transmitted may also be accompanied by a "start" bit and a "stop" bit. When start and stop bits are used to coordinate communications, an asynchronous transmission mode is being used. Synchronous transmissions are also possible, using special codes and equipment that carefully time the data flow to the receiving computer. Start and stop bits for each character are then unnecessary. Most pc systems use asynchronous transmission because the necessary communications equipment is simpler and less expensive. If asynchronous transmission is used, 10 bits may be sent over the telephone lines for each character transmitted. Data may be transmitted at various speeds. Some standard rates are 300, 1200, 2400, 4800, and 9600 bits per second (bps). Thus a 300 bps transmission rate (also called a 300 baud rate) gives 30 characters per second, while a 1200 bps rate represents 120 characters per second. The slower bps rates (2400 and under) are normally used with personal computer systems.

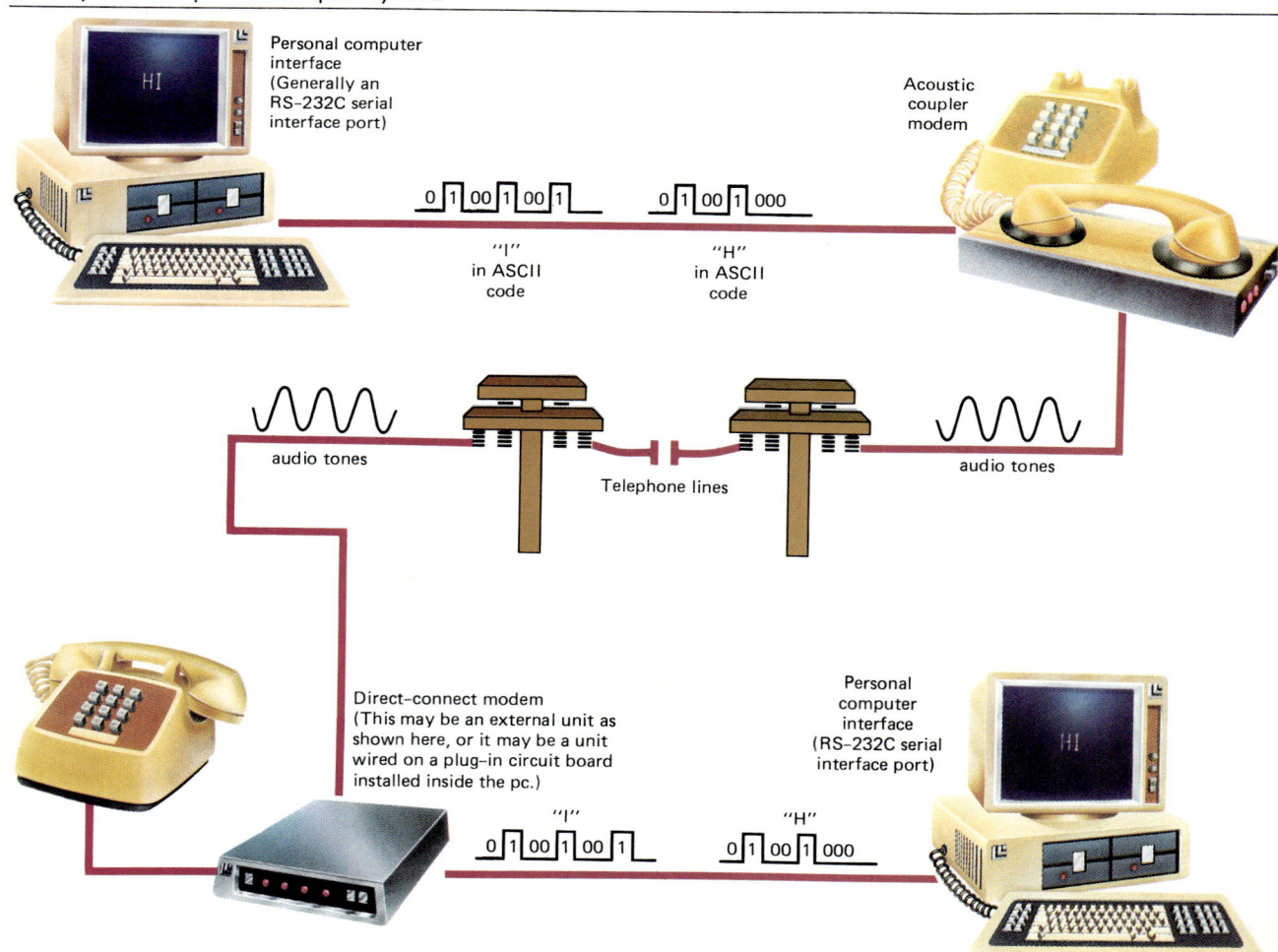

signals from these tones are then sent to the processor location where another modem converts them back to digital pulses. Figure 8-5 shows how both direct-connect modems and acoustic couplers can be used to link distant personal computers.

The need to transmit large volumes of computer data over long distances has developed in a short period of time. Organizations in the United States, Japan, and most of Europe are currently making large investments to build communications networks designed for *all-digital transmission*. Such networks eliminate the need for modems because analog signals aren't used. Until these systems are more fully developed, however, the vast public network of telephone lines (and modems) will continue to handle much of the transmission workload.

Data Transmission Channels

Figure 8-3 indicates that the **data transmission channels,** or "highways," used to carry data from one location to another are classified into narrowband, voiceband, and broadband categories. The wider the bandwidth of a channel, the more data it can transmit in a given period of time. *Telegraph lines,* for example, are **narrowband** channels, and their transmission rate is slow (from about 5 to 30 characters per second, or cps). This is adequate to directly accept data being keyed into a terminal. Standard *telephone lines* are **voiceband** channels that have a wider bandwidth. They are able to speed up the transmission rate to over 1,000 cps.

In many cases, a terminal operator at a remote location uses the regular dial-up telephone switching network, calls a number at the central processor location, and enters the data. For large volumes of data, however, it's often cheaper for an organization to acquire its own **dedicated** or **leased line** which can be used for both voice and data transmissions.

Different types of telephone and telegraph transmission circuits can also be selected to meet the needs of people and organizations. As Figure 8-6 shows, a **simplex** circuit permits data to flow in *only one* direction. A terminal connected to such a circuit is either a *send-only* or a *receive-only* device. Simplex circuits are seldom used because a return path is generally needed to send acknowledgment, control, or error signals. Thus a **half-duplex** line that can *alternately* send and receive data, or a **full-duplex** connection that can *simultaneously* transmit and receive, is usually used. A full-duplex line is faster since it avoids the delay that occurs in a half-duplex circuit each time the direction of transmission is changed.

Broadband channels are used when large data volumes must be transmitted at high speeds (over 100,000 cps is possible). Coaxial cables, microwave circuits, and communications satellites are commonly used to provide these channels. **Coaxial cables** are groups of specially wrapped and insulated wire lines that are able to transmit data at high rates. **Microwave systems** use very high frequency radio signals to transmit data through space. When microwave facilities are used, the data may be transmitted along a ground route by repeater stations that are located about 25 miles apart. The data signals are received, amplified, and retransmitted by each station along a route. Or the data may be beamed to a **communications satellite** that acts as a reflector by accepting signals from one point on earth and returning the same signals to some other point on earth. The satellite appears from the earth to be a station-

FIGURE 8-6

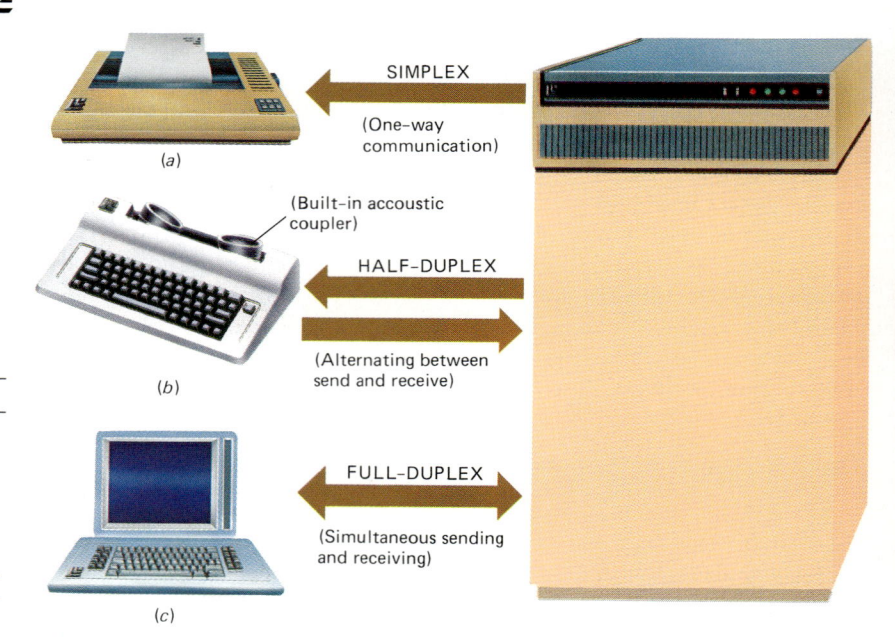

Data transmission circuits. (a) A simplex line permits communication in only one direction. That direction may be from the processor to an I/O device, as shown here, or it may be from a terminal to a processor. (b) A half-duplex circuit permits data to be sent in both directions but not at the same time. (c) A full-duplex connection does permit the simultaneous sending and receiving of data.

Thin as a human hair, able to bend light around corners, each thread in a fiber-optic cable can transmit vast amounts of data at the speed of light. (Courtesy AT&T/Bell Labs)

ary target for the microwave signals because it's precisely positioned 22,300 miles above the equator with an orbit speed that matches the earth's rotation. Dozens of satellites are now in orbit to handle international and domestic data, voice, and video communications. Figure 8-7 lists some of these satellite systems.

Existing broadband channels are expensive and are generally used only by large organizations. However, the rapidly maturing use of **fiber-optic cables** and **laser technology** allows huge amounts of data to be routinely transmitted at the speed of light through tiny threads of glass or plastic. Teamed with a laser, a single glass fiber the size of a human hair can transmit across the country in a single second all the characters in dozens of books the size of this one. (It would take about 21 hours to send the same information over a copper telephone line.) Since thousands of these fibers can be packaged in a single cable, the future cost of broadband transmission capability should fall within the reach of small organizations and individuals. It's expected that by 1990 30 percent of the metropolitan transmissions in the United States will be over fiber-optic links.

Data Communications Service Organizations

The data transmission channels that we've just examined are furnished by a number of data communications organizations. You're familiar, of course, with the large public telephone and telegraph networks offered for use by **common carriers.** These carriers include the local and regional facilities of the seven "Bell Telephone" operating companies, the long-distance network of the AT&T Communications division (formerly the Long-Lines Division), and the networks maintained by General Telephone and Electronics and Western Union.

In addition to these common carriers that offer a broad range of facilities,

INTERNATIONAL

INTELSAT system. This **I**nternational **Tele**communications **Sat**ellite Consortium includes about 130 member nations on six continents. INTELSAT is headquartered in Washington D.C., which is also the home of the **Com**munications **Sat**ellite **Corp**oration (COMSAT), an organization that was chartered by Congress in 1962 to be the United States representative to INTELSAT. COMSAT performs a management function for INTELSAT. Beginning with Early Bird in 1965, several generations of satellites have now been launched by INTELSAT, and these now form a global communications system that accounts for a major proportion of all long-distance international communications.

DOMESTIC

RCA Americom system. The first to offer domestic satellite service, RCA has several SATCOM satellites in orbit. Major transmitting/receiving stations are located in large cities from New York to California.

Western Union system. The first satellite in Western Union's Westar system was launched in 1974. Several more have now been placed in orbit, and additional "Advanced Westar" satellites are now available. Western Union has major ground stations in several cities and, of course, a nationwide network of telegraph lines.

American Telephone & Telegraph system. AT&T currently leases several COMSTAR satellites from COMSAT. The system also has its own Telestar satelites.

General Telephone and Electronics system. GTE also has access to COMSTAR satelites and has its own GSTAR units.

Satellite Business Systems. Developed by IBM, Aetna Life and Casualty Insurance Company, and COMSTAT at a cost of $400 million, SBS provides all-digital transmission services at very high speeds. SBS began operations in 1981 after a successful satellite launch late in 1980. The SBS network is now a part of MCI Communications.

American Satellite Corporation. Jointly owned by Fairchild Industries and Continental Telecom, Inc., American Satellite provides high-speed all-digital transmission services. It leases satellite capacity from Western Union, owns a 20 percent interest in the existing Westar system, and has contracted for 50 percent ownership of the Advanced Westar satellites.

Hughes Communications Corporation. Hughes has two GALAXY satellites in orbit to serve the needs of Cable TV organizations.

FIGURE 8-7

Satellite data transmission systems. (Photo courtesy Western Union Corporation)

---

there are also **specialized common carriers** whose public networks are often restricted to a more limited number of services. Included in the specialized carrier category are several of the satellite-using organizations listed in Figure 8-7 as well as:

- *MCI Communications Corporation.* MCI is a long-distance carrier that employs microwave, fiber-optic, and satellite facilities to serve people and organizations. It offers dedicated leased lines that are arranged exclusively for data transmission. It also offers long-distance voice communications between selected domestic cities, and has acquired Western Union International Inc. to gain entry into the international communications market. An alliance between MCI and IBM was established in 1985.

- **Southern Pacific Communications Corporation.** A subsidiary of the railroad company, the original SPCC network followed the right-of-way of the tracks from San Francisco through Dallas. SPCC now offers a nationwide private line service to 80 metropolitan areas. Microwave stations and broadband cables are used, and two SPACENET satellites are in orbit.

- **ITT World Communications.** ITT Worldcom offers long-distance circuits between 88 cities in the United States. Services between the United States and other countries are also provided.

Another type of data communications service organization is the **value-added carrier.** This type of carrier offers specialized services, but it may not have its own transmission facilities. For example, GTE Telenet and Tymnet, Inc., both have computer networks that receive customer data coming in over telephone lines. These data are temporarily stored and organized into "packets" of characters. These packets are then computer-routed and transmitted at high speed over dedicated common carrier channels to Telenet and Tymnet offices near the final data destination. At these offices, data in the packets are reassembled into the complete message for transmission to the final destination (Figure 8-8). The transmission cost of a **value-added network (VAN)** is frequently less than directly utilizing common carrier channels, which are often less efficient. Telenet and Tymnet are sometimes referred to as **packet-switching networks,** and each serves over 250 cities in more than 35 countries. The Uninet system of United Telecom Communications Inc. is another VAN that serves over 200 cities in the United States.

Finally, there are data communications organizations that can provide a wealth of on-demand information services to *people at home*. Customers of these organizations use special terminals with their TV sets or use personal computers to receive the information requested. Two types of services—teletext and videotex—may be received. A **teletext system** continuously transfers information in one direction only, and the information is generally received on a TV set. An example of teletext usage is the closed-caption system supported by some television networks that displays words on a TV screen so that hearing-impaired viewers can follow the program. A **videotex**

FIGURE 8-8

When packet switching is used, the packets of data originating at one source can be efficiently routed through different network lines. The packets are then reassembled in their original order when they reach their destination. (Adapted from John G. Posa, "Phone Net Going Digital," *High Technology*, May 1983, p. 45)

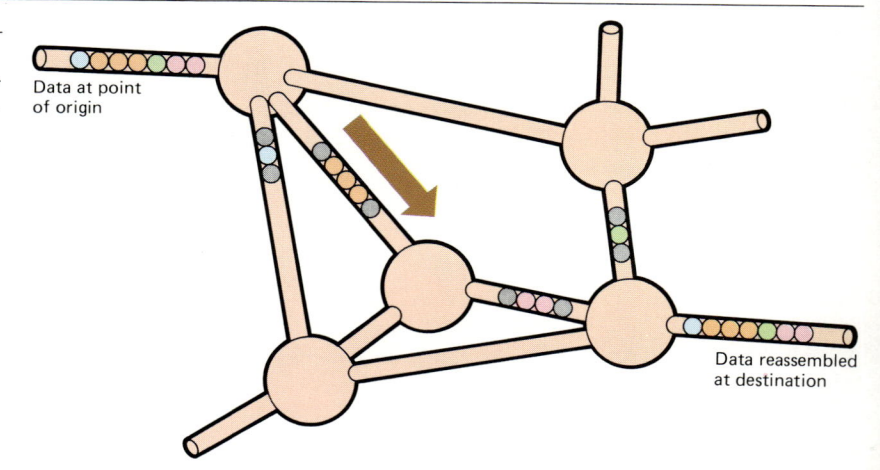

Data at point of origin

Data reassembled at destination

A videotex home information system links home video terminals to computerized data banks providing reviews and advertising. The system can also be used for shopping and banking from home—or for calling up recipes when an impulse to make a pie strikes suddenly. (© David Burnett/Contact Press Images, 1982)

system is one that (1) stores a vast amount of graphic and alphanumeric information at a central computer facility, (2) receives customer requests for stored information over telephone lines and other channels, and (3) retrieves the requested information and forwards it electronically to customers equipped to receive it. Videotex is thus an *interactive* (two-way), graphics-rich service that permits users to select what they want. Predictions are that videotex home information networks will experience explosive growth in the next decade, and many large organizations are planning now to participate in this growth.

But you've seen in Chapter 7 that personal computer users can already transmit and receive electronic mail messages and can participate in many other videotex services through the facilities of personal computing/communications networks. Figure 8-9 shows the linkages used and describes some of the available networks.

Coordinating the Data Communications Environment

The simple data communications system shown in Figure 8-3 was typical of the types used in the late 1960s, and it's still appropriate for many organizations. But the data communications environment has changed rapidly since then. As Figure 8-10 indicates, much larger computing/communications networks are now in service, and the coordination required for efficient network use is complex. Such networks may have hundreds of terminals and many small processors located at dozens of dispersed sites. These sites, in turn, may be linked by different transmission channels to larger computers. The task of network designers is to select and coordinate the network components so that the necessary data are moved to the right place, at the right time, with a minimum of errors, and at the lowest possible cost.

Communications Processors Figure 8-10 shows that a number of **communications processors** (typically micros or minis) are used by network design-

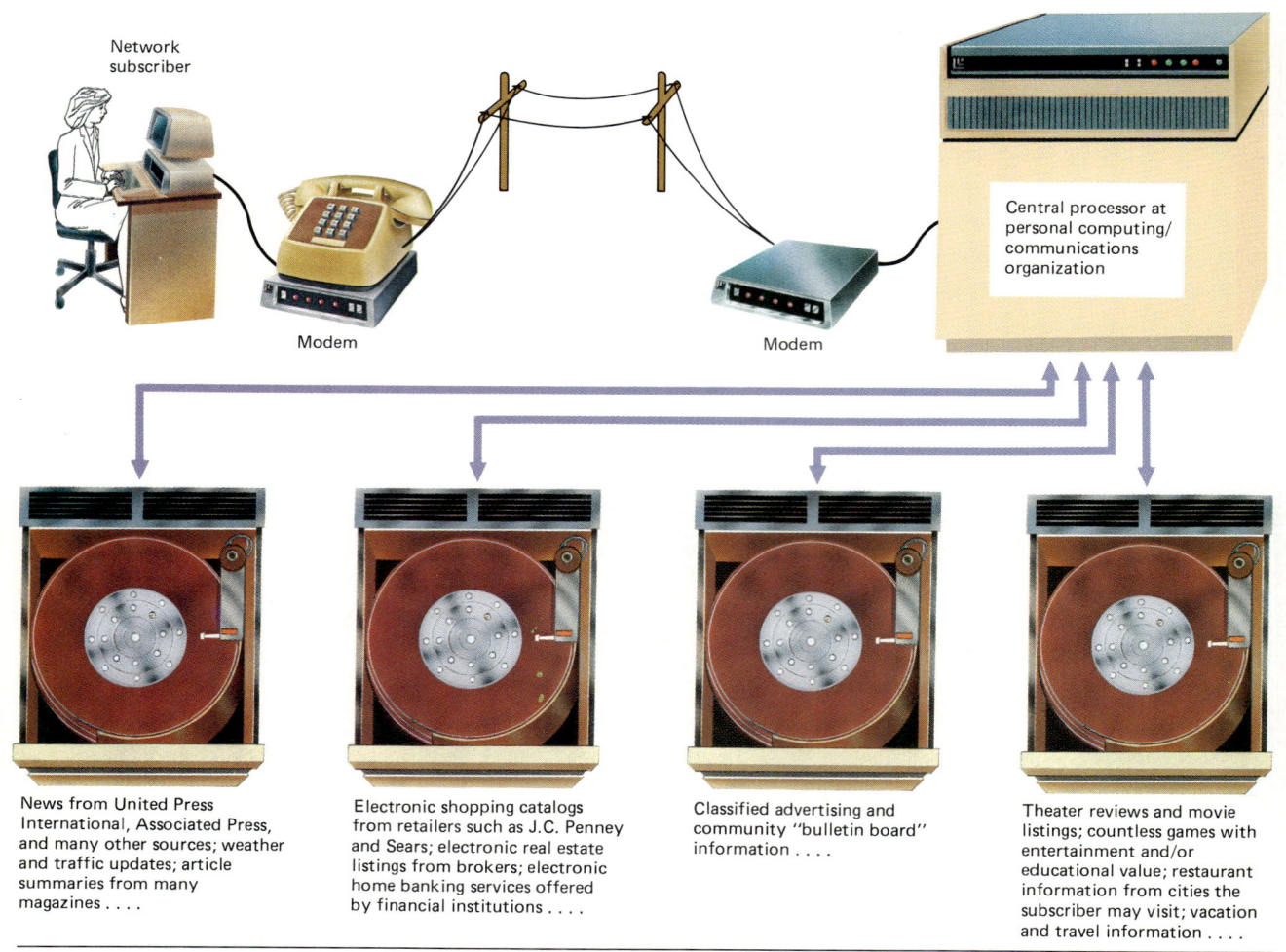

News from United Press International, Associated Press, and many other sources; weather and traffic updates; article summaries from many magazines . . . .

Electronic shopping catalogs from retailers such as J.C. Penney and Sears; electronic real estate listings from brokers; electronic home banking services offered by financial institutions . . . .

Classified advertising and community "bulletin board" information . . . .

Theater reviews and movie listings; countless games with entertainment and/or educational value; restaurant information from cities the subscriber may visit; vacation and travel information . . . .

FIGURE 8-9

An enormous wealth of information is available to those who subscribe to the services offered by personal computing/communications network organizations. Some of these organizations are:

- *The Source.* This is a network of Source Telecomputing Corporation, a subsidiary of *Reader's Digest.* Its Source Mail service allows an individual to use his or her personal computer to exchange messages with any other Source subscriber. Instant access to over 1,000 other information and communications services is available. A $100 one-time subscription fee is charged, and an hourly hookup rate is levied that varies according to the time of day. Transmission is over local telephone lines and the GTE Telenet and Tymnet value-added networks.
- *CompuServe Information Service.* CompuServe is owned by H&R Block Inc., the income tax service firm. It's similar to The Source, offering an electronic mail system and access to scores of large data bases. (A detailed description of what's available from The Source and CompuServe would fill up the rest of this book!) Subscriptions to the service are sold at many computer stores, and subscribers may hook into the network by using readily available software. A variable hourly hookup fee is charged. Transmission is over local telephone lines and the Tymnet network.
- *Dow Jones News/Retrieval.* This service, offered by the publisher of *The Wall Street Journal,* gives subscribers business and economic news, historical and current stock market quotations, and other investment information.

FIGURE 8-10

A computing/communications network. The remote concentrators, message switchers, and front-end processors in such networks are typically microcomputers or minicomputers used for communications purposes.

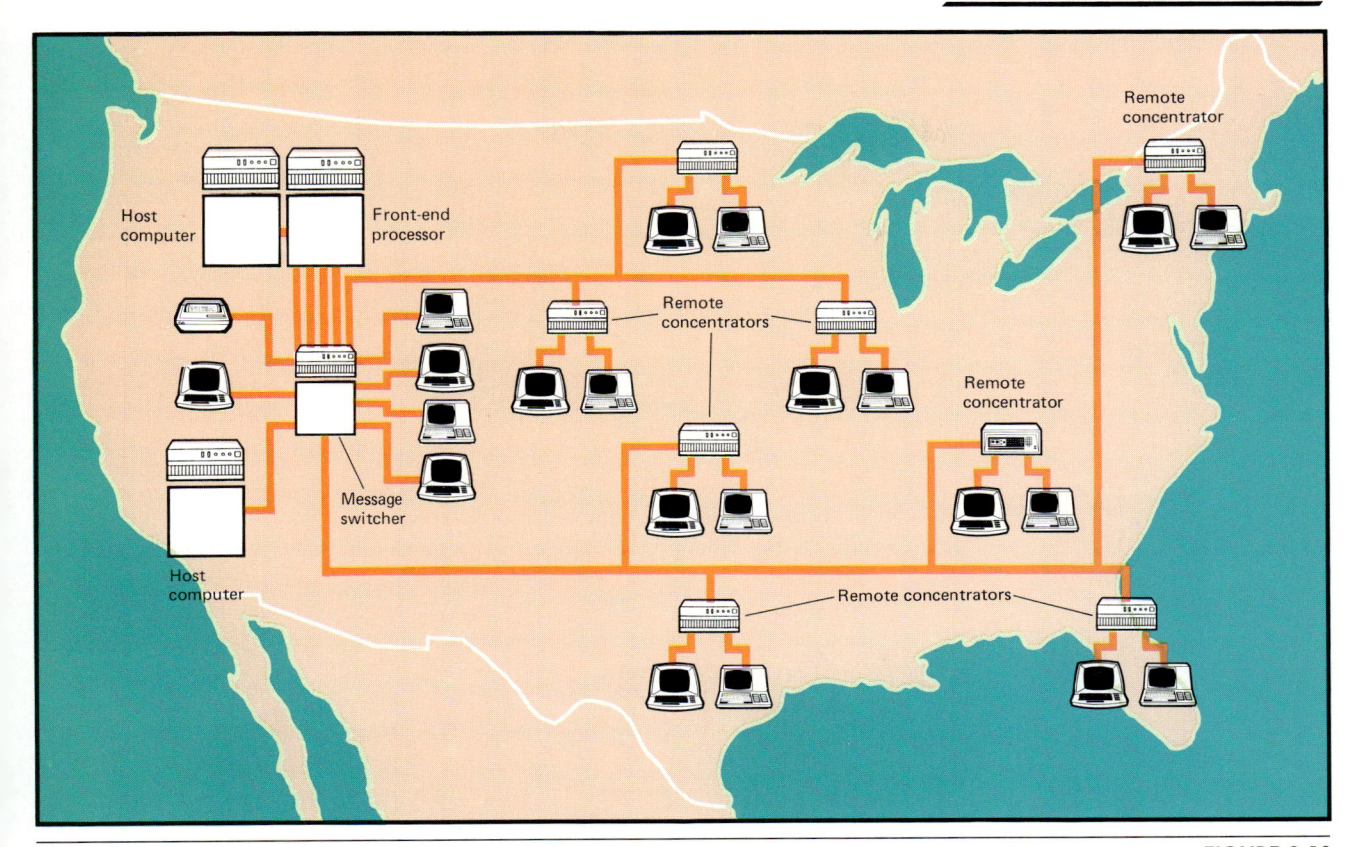

ers to achieve their goals. These processors are used for the following purposes:

1 *Remote concentration of messages.* The **remote concentrator** reduces transmission costs by receiving terminal input from many low-speed lines and then concentrating and transmitting a compressed and smooth stream of data on a higher-speed and more efficient transmission channel (Figure 8-11). Although faster communications channels are more expensive, they can do more work, and thus the cost per character transmitted may well be reduced. Devices called **multiplexers** also perform this concentration function. Multiplexers are less expensive than concentrators, but many of the earlier ones weren't programmable and thus didn't have the flexibility of concentrators. However, today's microprocessor-equipped multiplexers perform much like concentrators.

2 *Message switching.* The **message switcher** receives and analyzes data messages from points in the network, determines the destination and the proper routing, and then forwards the messages to other network locations. If necessary, a message may be stored until an outgoing line is available.

3 *Front-end processing.* The **front-end processor** is usually located at a central computer site. Its purpose is to relieve a main computer—called a **host computer**—of a number of the functions required to interact with and control the communications network.

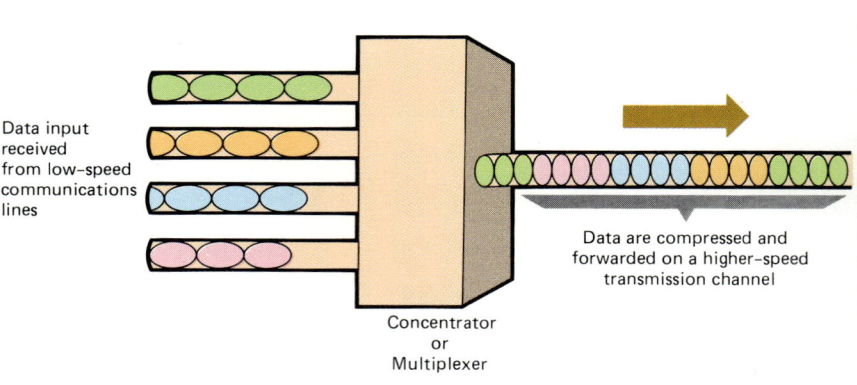

FIGURE 8-11

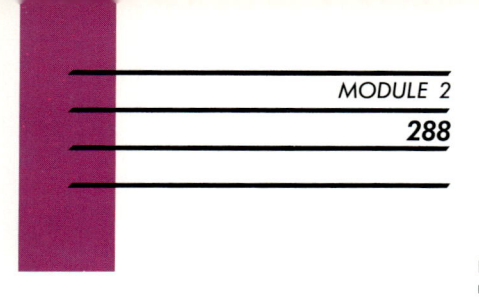

The function of a remote concentrator, or multiplexer, is to concentrate the output from many low-speed terminals into a single data stream that can be transmitted over a higher-speed channel. (Adapted from John G. Posa, "Phone Net Going Digital," *High Technology,* May 1983, p. 45)

Data input received from low-speed communications lines

Concentrator or Multiplexer

Data are compressed and forwarded on a higher-speed transmission channel

The functions of communications processors differ from one network to another, and there may be an overlapping of functions. A message-switching processor, for example, may also function as a remote concentrator; a front-end processor may perform message-switching functions; and, in less complete networks, the host computer may perform most or all of the functions of the front-end processor.

Local-Area Networks   Up to now we've been looking at communications situations in which data are transmitted between distant sites. But in many organizations data are also transmitted between computers, terminals, word processing stations, and other devices that are all located within a compact area such as an office building or a campus. The communications system used to link these nearby devices is referred to as a **local-area network (LAN).** A LAN is owned by the using organization, and these LANs use a star, bus, or ring physical configuration. A **star LAN** has a central controller, and all network station hookups radiate out from this central node like the points of a star (Figure 8-12a). In a **bus LAN,** however, a single cable (or "bus") is routed from station to station to provide the network linkage (Figure 8-12b). In the third "lay of the LANs," each piece of equipment is hooked together to form a circle, or **ring,** configuration (Figure 8-12c).

Transmission channels may use everything from pairs of twisted wires to coaxial and fiber-optic cables. Special hardware/software elements are used in place of modems and outside telephone lines. The speed of transmission and the network cost varies widely depending on the type of LAN used. Some LANs allow the integration of peripherals and computers made by different vendors, while others are restricted to the components made by a single supplier.

Although there are dozens of LAN offerings available to organizations, most of them can be placed in one of the following categories:

● *High-speed networks.*   Over 20 million bits per second (Mbps) can be transmitted over these LANs that are designed to provide links between large mainframes. Examples of these high-speed networks are Control Data Corporation's *Loosely Coupled Network* and Network Systems Corporation's *Hyperchannel.* It costs about $40,000 to attach each mainframe to the Hyperchannel LAN.

FIGURE 8-12 (facing page)

Common LAN configurations. (a) A star LAN has a central controller that provides the hardware/software interface resources needed by the network stations. Thus a failure of the central controller shuts down the network. (b) A bus LAN has no central controller and so each network component must be equipped to handle interface problems. The network vendor generally supplies these hardware/software interface elements for specific types of equipment. (c) A ring LAN is one in which all stations are linked to form a continuous loop. Data may flow around the ring in only one direction. A coded electrical signal called a "token" passes around the ring from station to station. When a station has data to transmit, it waits until it receives the token before sending its message to a programmed destination. The failure of any station in the ring may shut down the entire network.

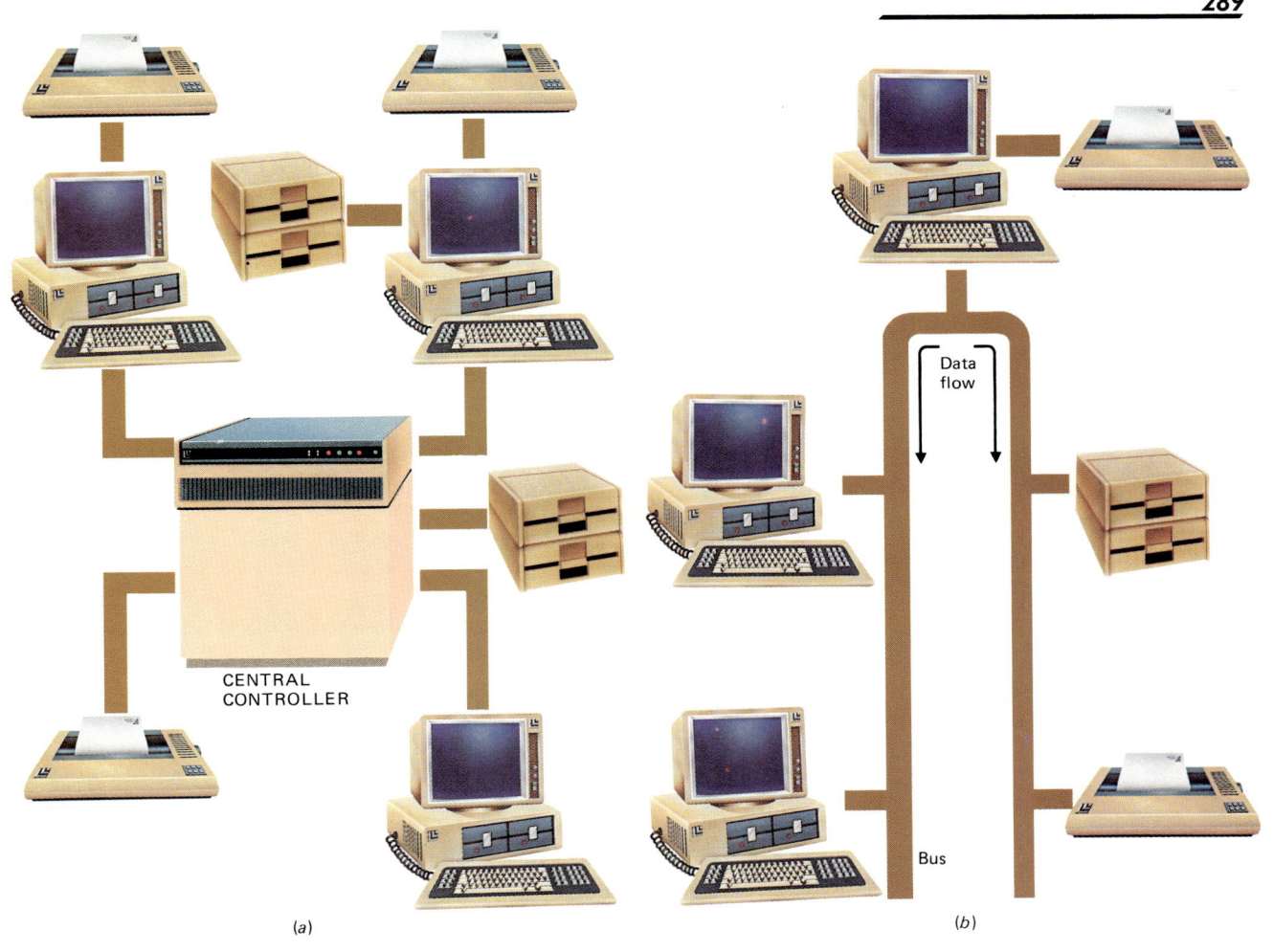

CENTRAL CONTROLLER

(a)

Data flow

Bus

(b)

(c)

- *Medium-speed networks.* The transmission speed of these LANs varies between 1 Mbps and 20 Mbps. Suitable for use with smaller mainframes and minicomputers, some of these LANs can support a few hundred workstations and other devices, while others can theoretically accommodate tens of thousands of these peripherals. The cost of attaching each device averages a few hundred dollars. One example of these medium-speed LANs is *Ethernet.* Developed by Xerox, this 10 Mbps network uses a coaxial cable in a bus configuration for data transmission. Special integrated circuit chips called controllers are used to connect equipment to the cable, and small boxes called transceivers transmit and receive cable data at each workstation. Each station can exchange data with any other station or group of stations. Other medium-speed bus-type LANs are Datapoint Corporation's *ARCnet,* Wang Laboratories' *Wangnet,* Sytek's *LocalNet 40,* and Ungermann-Bass' *Net/One.*

- *Low-speed personal computer networks.* The transmission speeds of LANs in this category are generally less than 1 Mbps. Prices and capabilities vary considerably. For example, some bus networks require only the purchase of a cable and a few interface elements, while others come furnished with a hard-disk drive and other peripherals. You saw in Chapter 7 that personal computer (pc) users often have difficulty connecting different brands of equipment because of the lack of hardware and software standards in the industry. Thus there are no LANs that will link all brands of personal computers together. Also, some of the LANs that support more than one brand will allow the different makes to share printers and other peripherals, but they may not allow the different makes to talk to each other. A few examples of the available LANs are Corvus Systems' *Constellation,* a star-type network with a central controller and a hard-disk drive that supports Apple, Radio Shack, and other pc makes; Corvus Systems' *Omninet,* a bus-type LAN that also allows a number of different pc's—e.g., Apple, IBM, Radio Shack, Digital Equipment, Zenith, Texas Instruments—to share hard-disk drives and other peripherals; Davong Systems' *Multilink,* a ring-type LAN that supports IBM PCs; and Nestar Systems' *PLAN 4000,* a network that uses Datapoint's ARCnet technology to support Apple and IBM machines.

- *Low-speed digital PBX networks.* For years the initials PBX (for private branch exchange) described the familiar telephone switchboard installed in office buildings and other places. The PBX was the central controlling device in a voice-only, star-type network, and an operator used pluggable cords and a board full of sockets to route network calls. The old operator-managed PBXs have been replaced by computer-controlled **digital PBX**s that automatically manage thousands of individual lines. A digital PBX network still uses a star configuration, but both voice and data transmissions can now be handled simultaneously. No modems are needed for local data exchanges, and existing telephone wires are used so that no special cables need be installed. The use of existing telephone wires is an attractive feature for organizations located in older buildings because it may be difficult and expensive to string new cable to numerous network locations. However, a disadvantage of using the standard telephone lines wired into a building is that these lines can't transmit data at the high speeds permitted by cables. Thus a LAN based on a digital PBX system is a low-speed network that's designed to link together devices that have relatively light data communications requirements. But many believe that the computer-controlled PBX is rapidly becoming the hub around which future office communications systems will be designed. A few examples of digital PBX network offerings are AT&T's *Systems 75* and *85*, InteCom's *IBX*, Mitel's *SX-2000*, Northern Telecom's *SL-1*, and Rolm's *CBX*s.

In summary, a network designer must select and coordinate the communications elements that link far-flung sites with central locations. And within the central locations, the designer may also need to coordinate the intrafacility local-area networks. Figure 8-13 illustrates a few of the possible options.

SYSTEMS SUPPORTED BY DATA COMMUNICATIONS

You're already familiar with many applications supported by data communications. To cite one example, a teller at a branch bank may update online savings account records stored at a central computer site through the use of data communications facilities. Let's take a brief look now at a few additional examples.

Real Time Processing Systems

A **real time processing system** is in a parallel time relationship with an ongoing activity and is producing information quickly enough to be useful in

FIGURE 8-13

A modern data communications network may use broadband satellite transmission channels to link the major East and West Coast offices of an organization. Various intracity data channels may include ground microwave stations, fiber-optic and other telephone and telegraph circuits, and the coaxial cables furnished by cable television companies. Within each major office, data may move over intrafacility local-area networks. Telephone and telegraph channels may be used to connect smaller offices to one or both of the major facilities.

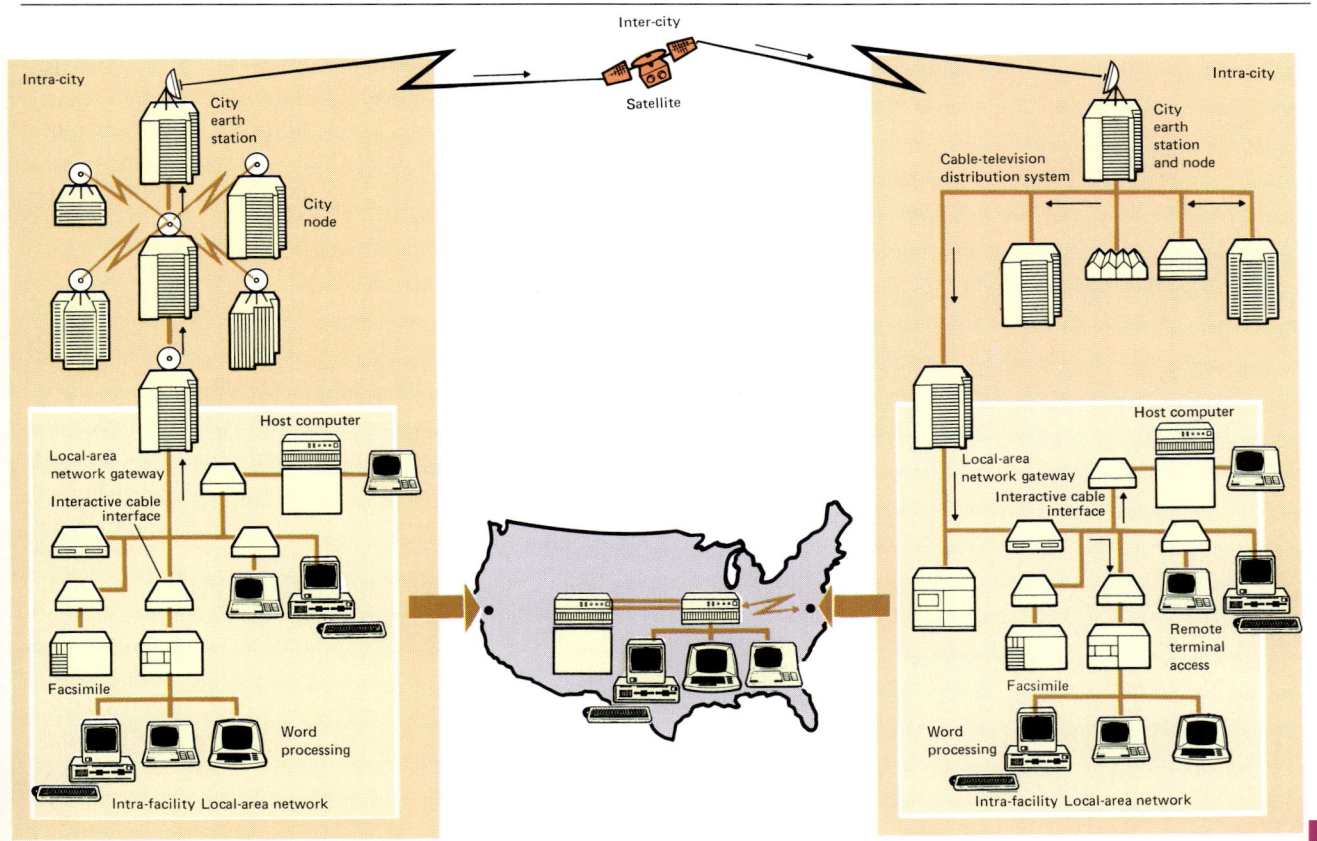

controlling this current live and dynamic activity. Thus the words "real time" describe an interactive processing system with severe time limitations. A real time system uses interactive processing, but an interactive system need not be operating in real time. The difference is that real time processing requires *immediate* transaction input from all input-originating terminals. Many stations are tied directly by high-speed telecommunications lines into one or more processors. Several stations can operate at the same time. Files are updated each minute and inquiries are answered by split-second access to up-to-the-minute records. But it's possible to have an interactive system that combines immediate access to records for inquiry purposes with *periodic* (perhaps daily) transaction input and updating of records from a central collecting source. Such an interactive system would meet many needs and would be simpler and less expensive than a real time system.

The reservation systems used by airlines, hotels, and car rental agencies are examples of real time systems that have been mentioned earlier. A few other examples of real time systems supported by telecommunications are:

- *Military systems.* A World Wide Military Command and Control System has been developed for U.S. military commanders from the President on down. The system links 35 large computers at 26 command posts around the world. And over a dozen computers at the North American Air Defense Command accept, store, and constantly update masses of data from worldwide radar installations. Every humanly produced object in earth orbit is tracked. If a rocket is launched, the computers quickly calculate its trajectory.

- *Air traffic control systems.* Millions of aircraft flights are tracked across the nation each year by air traffic controllers. These flights are monitored by computers and are switched to different control jurisdictions as they move across the continent (Figure 8-14). When a flight approaches Chicago's O'Hare International Airport, for example, a control system sends out special "beacon" signals. Answering signals from the aircraft give the plane's identity, altitude, and speed. These data are processed by computer and are instantly displayed on a controller's screen next to a "blip" of light that represents the plane. Over 100 aircraft can be tracked and controlled simultaneously by the system.

Timesharing and Remote Computing Service Systems

Timesharing is a general term used to describe a processing system with a number of independent, relatively low-speed, online, and simultaneously usable stations. Each station, of course, provides direct access to the processor. The use of special programs allows the processor to switch from one station to another and to do a part of each job in an allocated "time slice" until the work is completed. The process is frequently so fast that a user has the illusion that nobody else is using the computer.

A number of organizations sell timesharing and remote computing services to their customers. These organizations may install terminals or personal computers in customer offices and then use telecommunications channels to link these workstations to their central processors. Or they may link their processors to customer-owned personal computers. A broad range of jobs may be processed, or the service organization may specialize in the needs of a

FIGURE 8-14

This U.S. Air Force air traffic control system covers air space in a 4,000 square mile area. (Photo courtesy Sanders Associates, Inc.)

particular group. Other remote computing services (sometimes referred to as *service bureaus*) may accept a customer's input data over telecommunications lines, do custom batch processing for the customer, and then transmit the output information back to the customer's terminal. Timesharing and remote computing service organizations generally offer a library of online applications programs to their clients who need only supply the input data and access the programs to obtain the desired information. Customers pay transaction charges that vary (like long-distance telephone calls) according to usage.

Distributed Data Processing Networks

Timesharing isn't new. The relatively high cost of computer hardware in the 1960s spurred many organizations to establish a central computer system and to then achieve economies by sharing the time of that system among many users. When one or two processors handle the workload of all outlying terminals, the word "timesharing" is probably still accurate. But as you know, it's possible now for an organization to buy many computers for the price of just one earlier large machine. And when *many* geographically dispersed or *distributed* independent computer systems are connected by a telecommunications network, and when messages, processing tasks, programs, data, and other resources are transmitted between cooperating processors and terminals, the timesharing term may no longer be broad enough.

Distributed data processing (DDP) network is the term often used today to describe this extension of timesharing. For our purposes, a DDP arrangement may be defined as one that places the needed data, along with the computing and communications resources necessary to process these data, at the end user's location. Such an arrangement may result in many computers and significant software resources being shared among dozens of users. Figure 8-15 shows some of the possible DDP network configurations. You'll recognize the similarities between these configurations and the LAN network designs shown in Figure 8-12.

A DDP network, like a timesharing system, may be intended for the use of a *single* organization, or it may be available for use by *many* organizations.

Single-Organization DDP Networks   Two of the many organizations with private DDP networks are:

- *Hewlett-Packard Company.* Figure 8-16 shows the worldwide DDP network that Hewlett-Packard has developed for its internal business applications. Five mainframes and over 500 Hewlett-Packard superminicomputers are scattered around the network to handle processing, data entry and retrieval, and telecommunications work. Over 28,000 terminals and pc's are used. This network links manufacturing facilities and sales offices at over 100 sites to corporate offices in California and Switzerland. Although overall control of the network is maintained by the California center, division computers operate autonomously to process local jobs. The hierarchical variation of the star network is used.

- *Bank of America.* The Bank of America in California has a network of over 50 minicomputers to support online inquiries from 6,000 teller terminals located in the 1,000 branch offices in the state.

(a) Star network

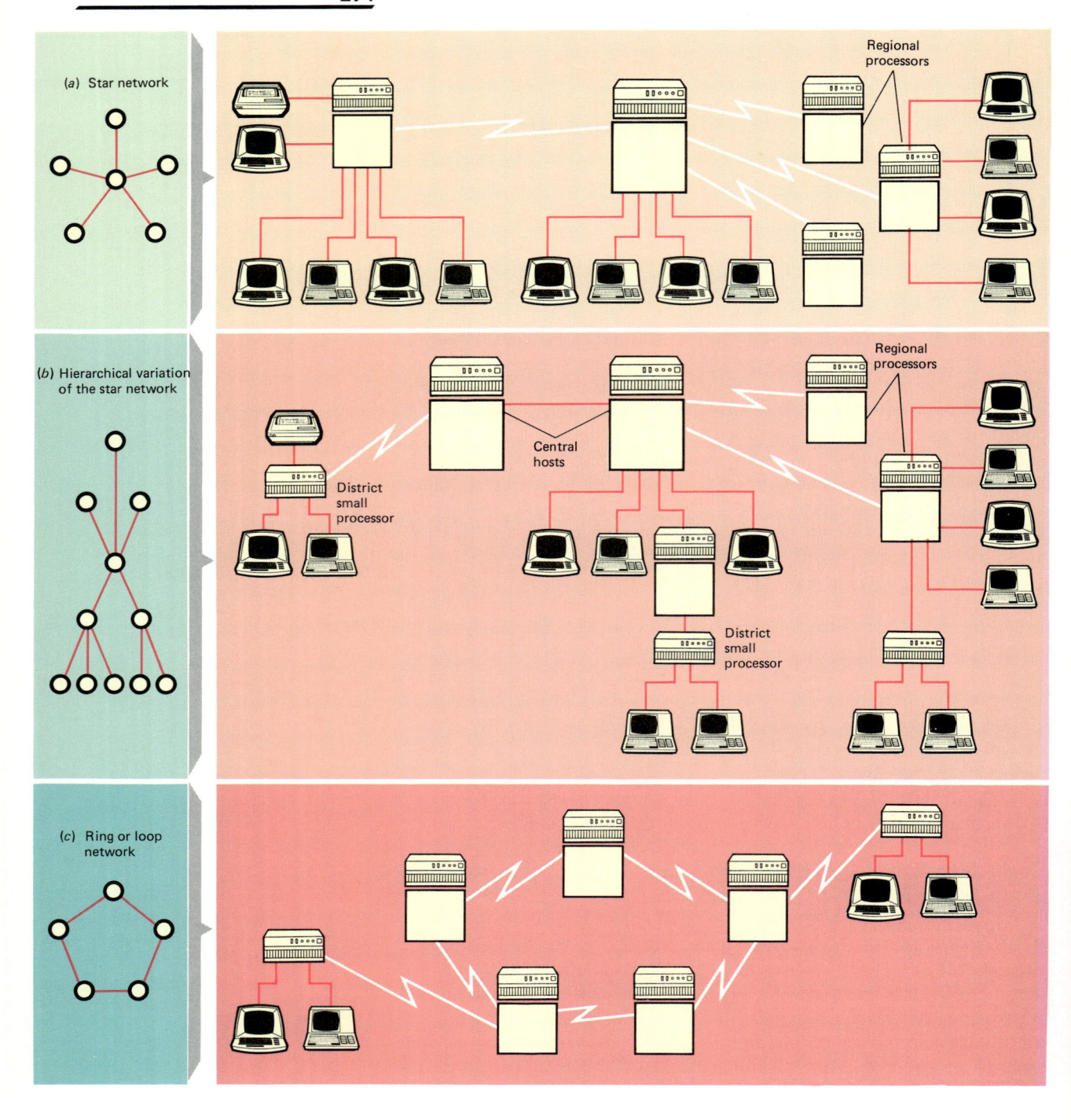

(b) Hierarchical variation of the star network

(c) Ring or loop network

Regional processors

Central hosts

District small processor

District small processor

Regional processors

FIGURE 8-16

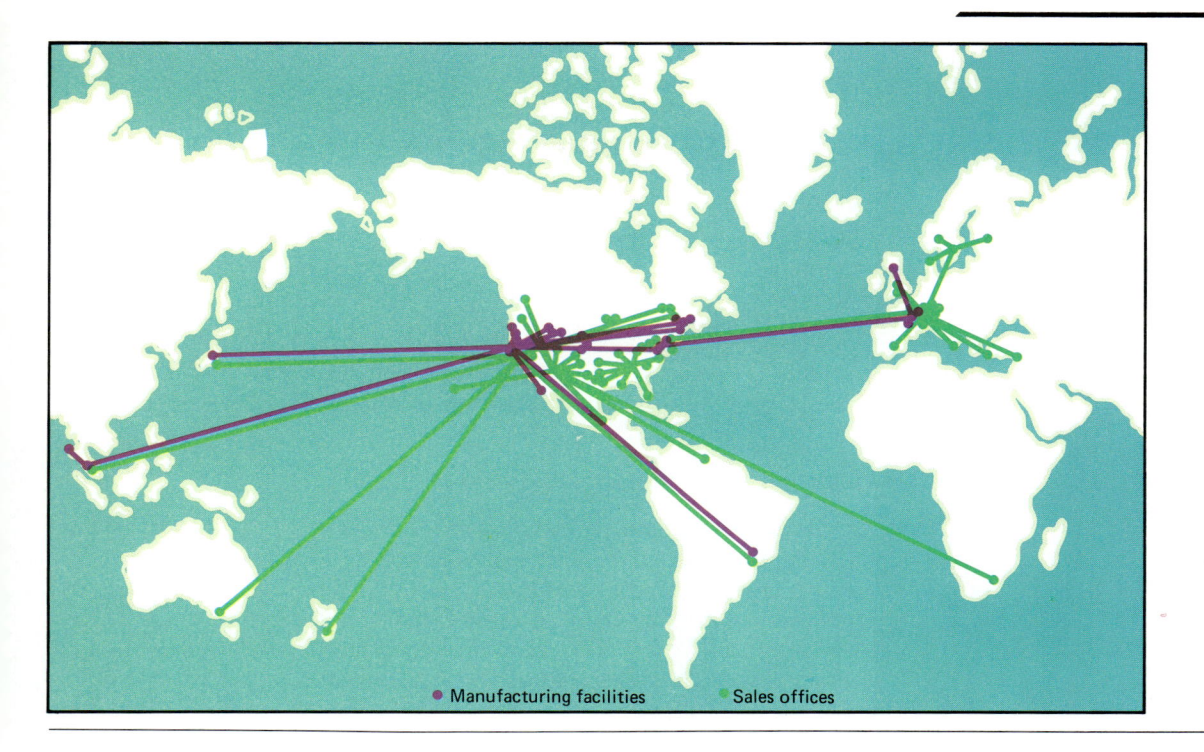

Single-organization DDP network. Hewlett-Packard Company's distributed data processing network links hundreds of computers and thousands of terminals at over 100 manufacturing plants and sales offices to corporate centers in Palo Alto, Calif., and Geneva, Switzerland.

⬅ **FIGURE 8-15**

Possible DDP network configurations. (a) In the *star* DDP configuration, a central host, or star computer, communicates with and controls a second level of satellite or node processors. These nodes, in turn, communicate with I/O terminals and pc's. (b) In the *hierarchical variation of the star* DDP network, the central host computer is still linked to regional node processors. But these regional nodes may, in turn, act as hosts to subordinate small district processors. In addition to processing local applications, the small third-level processors in the hierarchy (usually minicomputers) may support local-level intelligent terminals and pc's that are also able to independently process small jobs. The higher-level computers in the hierarchy are used to manage large data bases and to serve the lower-level processors by executing jobs that require extensive computations. Most current DDP networks use the star arrangement or some hierarchical variation of it. (c) The *ring* DDP network is a "no-host," or ring, arrangement of communicating equals. Each ring processor may have communicating subordinates, but within the ring there's no master computer.

Multiple-Organization DDP Networks Two DDP networks that serve a number of organizations are:

- *The DARPA Network.* The Pentagon's Defense Advanced Research Projects Agency (DARPA) connects about 40 universities and research institutions throughout the United States and Europe with about 50 computers ranging in size from minis to supercomputers. A few of the schools included are Harvard, MIT, Carnegie-Mellon, Case, Illinois, Utah, Stanford, UCLA, and USC.

- *The Tymshare Network.* This system (Figure 8-17) offers computing resources to customers in business, government, health care, and education. It serves over 400 cities and 40 countries with over 60 computers.

Electronic Mail/Message Systems

An **electronic mail/message system (EMMS)** is one that can store and deliver, by electronic means, messages that would otherwise probably be forwarded through the postal service or sent verbally over telephone lines. The postal service is relatively slow and messages are sometimes lost. The term "mailroom drag" describes the delays encountered in using this message delivery system. And using the telephone requires that (1) the message recipient can be located and (2) the recipient is willing to be interrupted to take the call. Studies have shown that only about one in four calls made to people in organizations goes through on the first try. Three out of four times, then, a call isn't completed, and a frustrating game of **telephone tag** may then begin. Ms. Johnson leaves a message requesting that Mr. Burke return her call; Burke calls back to find that Johnson is in a meeting; Johnson tries again and learns that Burke has been called away from his desk. And so it goes—sometimes for days.

EMMS concepts have been developed in response to the shortcomings in other message delivery systems. An EMMS can perform a number of func-

FIGURE 8-17

Multiple-organization DDP network. The DDP network of Tymshare, Inc., serves organizations in over 400 cities and 40 countries.

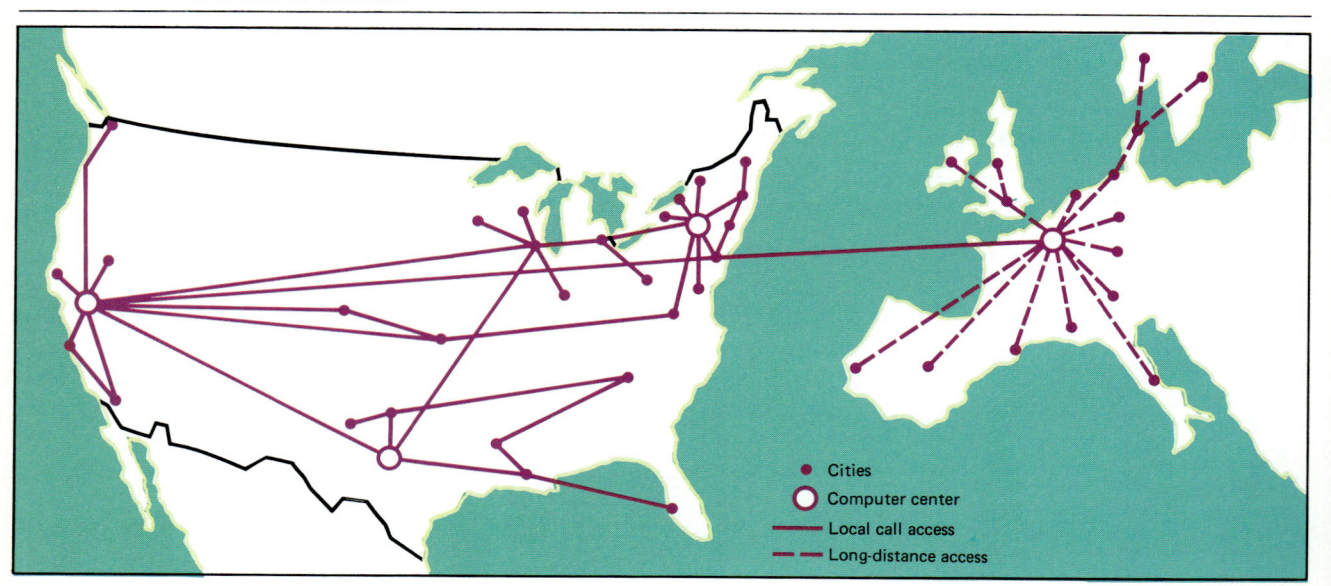

tions. It can, for example, provide *message distribution services, transmission of documents and pictures,* and *computerized conferences.*

Message Distribution Services   A keyed or spoken message is sent on the first try, and at any time of the day or night, to a *specified individual* who has a storage "mailbox" in the message system. (And it's just as easy for the sender to transmit a message to an identified *group of people* as it is to send it to a single person.) It's not necessary to locate the receiver(s) or interrupt him or her at a bad time. Rather, the receiver can periodically review stored messages at a time that *is* convenient.

Some EMMSs handle *spoken* messages, while others are designed to manage *keyed* text. When a **voice mail** approach is used, the sender calls the system's phone number, logs into the system, and then transmits the message to one or more recipients. The spoken sound waves produced by the sender are converted into digital pulses and are then stored on a hard disk for later retrieval. When message recipients call the **voice store-and-forward system,** they are notified that messages are waiting. After listening to the messages produced as reconstituted speech, they can then delete them, save them for future reference, or forward them to other parties. Figure 8-18 shows the features available to the users of the Wang DVX voice mail system.

Keyed messages are generally entered and received on teleprinter and visual display terminals or on personal computers. After reading (not listening to) the stored messages, a receiver can fire off responses and, if necessary, make a printed copy of the communication (see Figure 8-19).

Users of EMMSs can also receive and send messages at home during the evening, or during business trips, by using a portable pc or terminal and/or a telephone. Beyond reducing interruptions, message distribution systems also provide *other benefits*. For example, people at remote sites no longer feel isolated because they can and do receive messages from headquarters as easily and quickly as do those who are located in the headquarters building. And people in different time zones can often communicate more easily since widely scattered offices may not be open at the same times. Another possible benefit is that EMMS messages tend to be brief and to the point, thus saving time.

Transmission of Documents and Pictures   In this EMMS function, an original document can be placed in a sending **facsimile,** or **fax, machine** (see Figure 8-20). A communications link-up is then made with a receiving fax device at another location. As the sending machine scans the document, the receiving device reproduces the scanned image. Thus, when the transmission is completed, the receiving device has produced a duplicate, or "facsimile," of the original. The use of fax machines isn't new, but manufacturers are striving to improve fax systems by increasing transmission speeds, by reducing transmission costs, and by integrating fax equipment into an automated office setting. A number of data communications service companies also provide fax transmission facilities. Satellite Business Systems, for example, offers high-speed fax services, and the Domestic Transmission Systems unit of ITT offers a Faxpak service for users. Faxpak rates permit users to send a page anywhere in the United States for a few cents.

Of course, copies of printed documents can also be sent electronically between intelligent copying machines or between **communicating word pro-**

Voice mail system menu tree

- Log on
  - (1) Mailbox access
    - (1-1) Message scan
    - (4) Play message
      - (1) Disable touch tone
      - (7) Rewind
      - (9) Advance
    - (5) Act on message
      - (7) Reply to message (record a reply)
        - (*) DVX directory
        - (4) Review reply
        - (5) Send reply
        - (6) Re-record reply
      - (8) Forward a message (record intro)
        - (4) Review intro
        - (5) Send intro and message
        - (6) Re-record header
        - (*) DVX directory
      - (9) Save message
    - (6) Go to next message (deletes message if not saved)
  - (1-1) Message scan
  - (2) Message creation
    - Enter recipient ID or phone no.
    - Enter delivery Time/date recorded
      - (4) Review message
      - (5) Send message
      - (6) Re-record message
    - (*) Directory
      - (#) Return to creation
      - (1) No ID no.
      - (*) Reverse directory
  - (3) Administrative functions
    - (4) Change tel. delivery no. — (*) Password-protect telephone delivery (optional)
    - (5) Enter extended absence notification
    - (6) Specify no. of delivery attempts (0-5)
    - (7) Program message waiting unit
    - (8) Change DVX password
  - (4) Message confirmation — Enter recipient ID — (*) Review message
  - (8) Prompt creation
  - (9) Name response
  - (*) Begin another session
  - (#) Log off

FIGURE 8-18

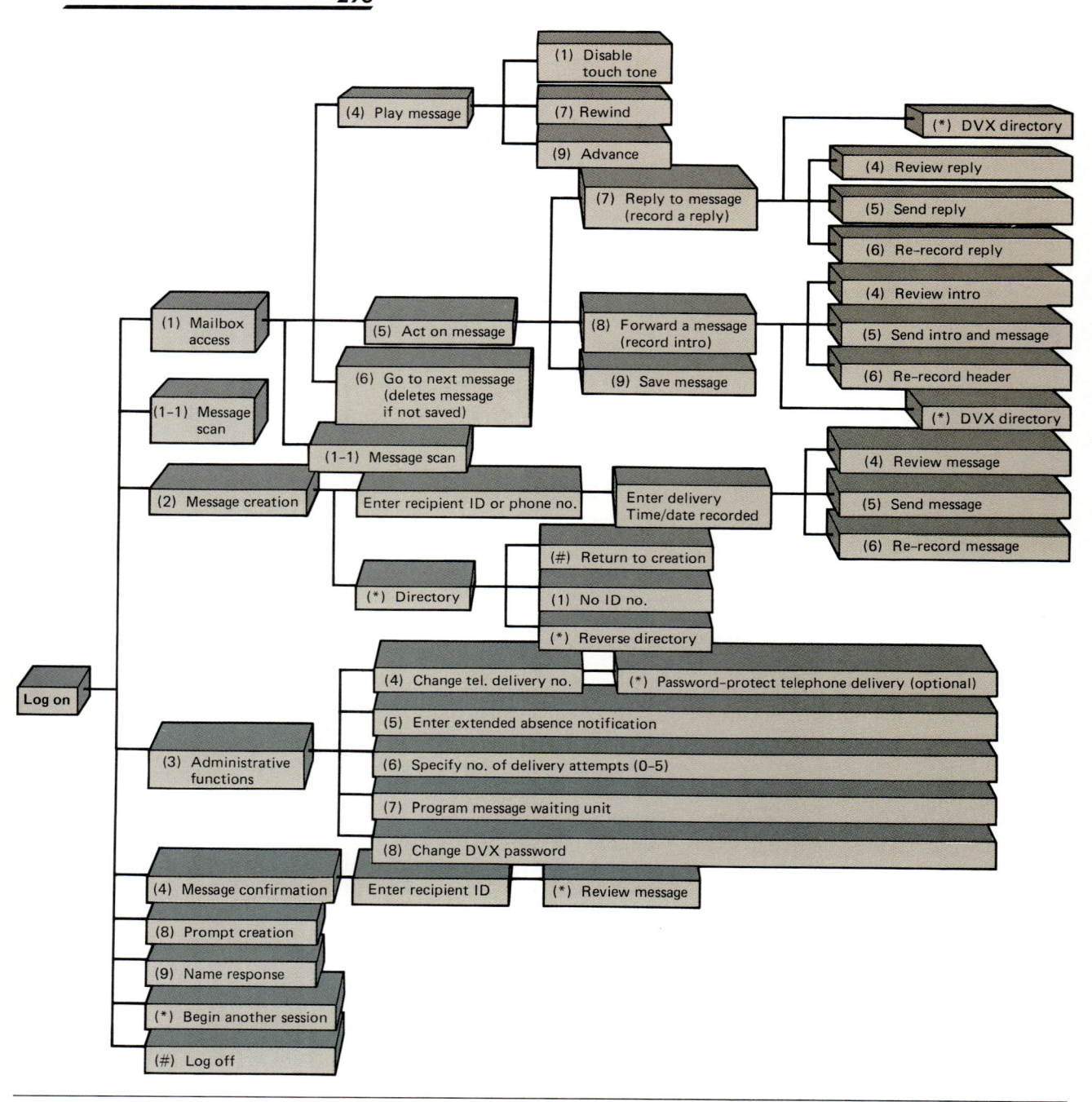

The features possible in the Wang DVX voice mail system. Users control the system with Touch-Tone signals. The numbers shown here refer to the keys on a Touch-Tone phone. Such numerical prompts are common, but some voice mail systems also use the letters that designate certain keys. (*Source:* Michael Orzech, from Geoff Lewis, "Voice Mail Struggles to Be Heard," *High Technology*, October 1984, p. 24. Used by permission of the artist.)

cessing stations. In a typical example, a Digital Equipment Corporation salesperson on the West Coast sat down with a customer in front of a visual display. As sections of a proposed contract were displayed on the screen, changes were agreed on and then entered into the document stored in a word processing (WP) station. After the contract had been revised, the communicating WP station forwarded it to a similar station at DEC's headquarters on

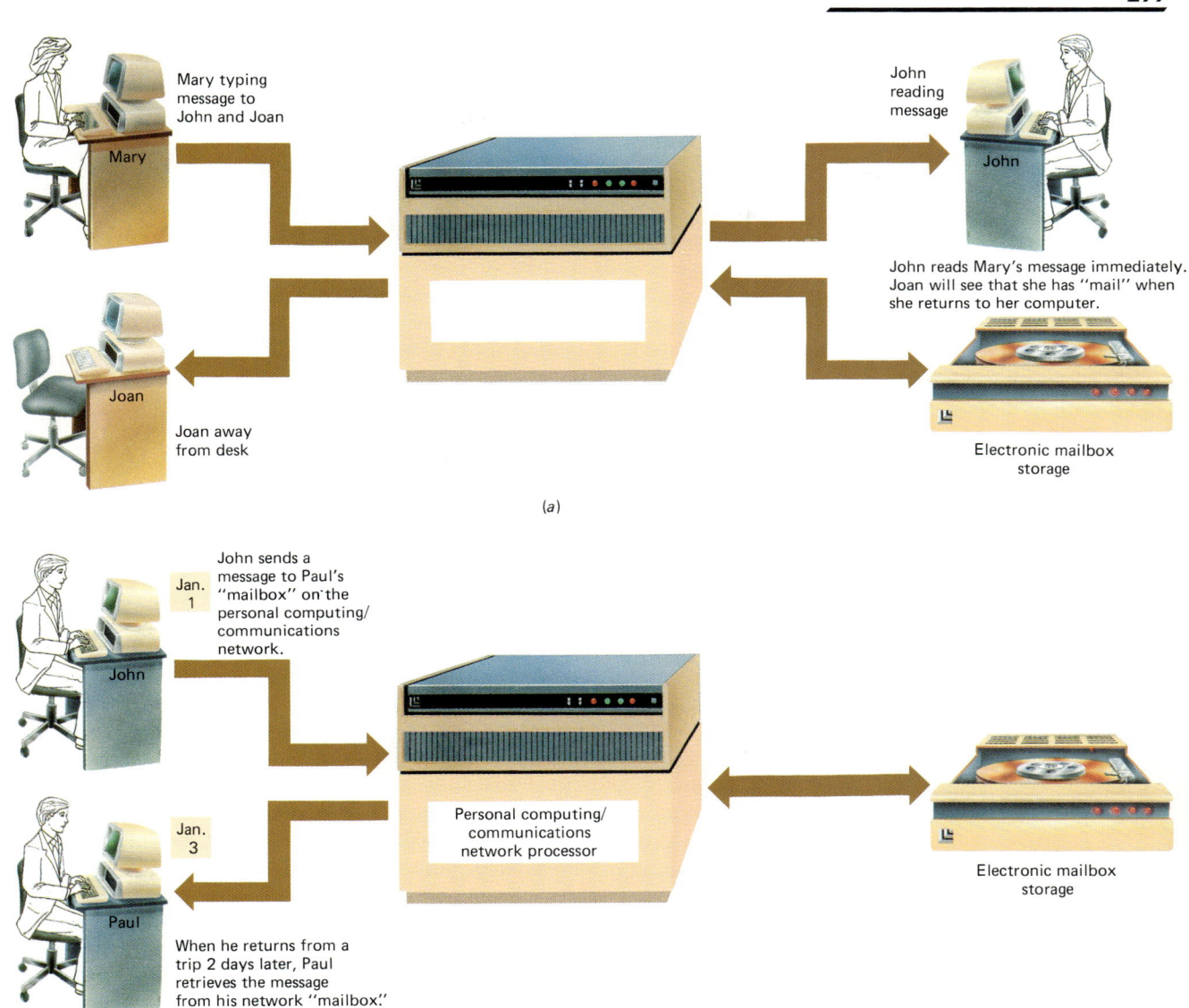

FIGURE 8-19
Using electronic mail (a) within an organization and (b) with the aid of a personal computing/communications network system.

the East Coast. Corporate lawyers made a few alterations and then sent the contract back to the West Coast. This contract was printed by the West Coast WP station and signed by the salesperson and customer. The entire transaction was completed in less than one afternoon.

Computerized Conferences A computer-based EMMS permits "conferences" to be held at the convenience of the participants. Since the conference dialog may be stored, it's *not* necessary for all participants to be online at their terminals or pc's *at the same time*. And, of course, it's also not necessary that they be physically present at the same place. Instead, a person can sit down at a terminal or pc at a convenient time, call up any conversations she or he

MODULE 2

300

FIGURE 8-20

This tabletop digital facsimile machine can transmit high-resolution copies worldwide in as fast as 35 seconds. (Courtesy Business Communication Products Division/3M)

hasn't seen, make additional comments, respond to questions, and then sign off. Several conference participants can "talk" at the same time. Once again, interruptions of other important work can be avoided. And a permanent history of all conference discussions can be recorded.

Infomedia Corporation of Palo Alto, California, offers two computer conferencing services called Planet and Notepad. To use these services, a group member dials a Tymnet local-access telephone number, couples the telephone to a terminal, and accesses a central computer file that's shared by all group members. Another computer conferencing network is the Electronic Information Exchange System sponsored by the New Jersey Institute of Technology. Subscribers are organized into groups devoted to specific topics such as technology for the handicapped. Many subscribers belong to more than one group. Group members come from corporations, governments, and nonprofit foundations. Access is generally through the GTE Telenet system.

The term **computer conferencing** refers to the types of EMMSs that we've just considered that permit people to participate at *different* times. An alternative to computer conferencing is **teleconferencing**—a term that refers to the electronic linking of geographically scattered people who are all participating at the *same* time. Facsimile devices, electronic blackboards that can cause chalk markings to be reproduced on distant TV monitors, the Picturephone Meeting Service supplied by AT&T—these and other technologies allow people to communicate over wide distances in real time. Of course, there are advantages in face-to-face meetings that teleconferencing can't replace. Facial expressions and "body language" can convey information that might be missed with teleconferencing. But time, energy, and money are saved when people don't have to travel long distances to conduct a meeting.

Data Base Retrieval Systems

You'll recall from Chapter 2 that a data base is a collection of logically related data elements. Organizations and individuals maintain countless data bases in computer-accessible form for their *private* uses. But many data base producers amass and update information on specific subjects for *public* use. Some producers of these public data bases set up their own online computer/communications systems to electronically distribute specialized information to their subscribers. But many other producers choose to sell the distribution rights to an online service organization. The service organization typically enters a data base into its computer storage facilities, provides instructions to online users on how to access it, and pays the producer royalties when subscribers use it.

Over 1,400 of these public data bases are stored and maintained in online computer systems in the United States. Public personal computing/communications network organizations such as *The Source* and *CompuServe Information Service* were discussed in Figure 8-9. These two services (and others) enable people to retrieve information *in their homes* from scores of these data bases. In addition, these networks maintain public bulletin boards to allow members to exchange messages.

People *at work* also have telecommunications access to electronic libraries of information that are stored in central computers. These **data banks** tend to fall into statistical, bibliographic, and computational categories. *Statistical* data banks are compilations of numeric data. Included in this category are The Conference Board Data Base that provides information on capital spending and purchasing power for 20 different industries, the Standard & Poor's *Compustat* service that gives online access to financial statistics on U.S. and Canadian firms, and the American Statistics Index that furnishes citations and abstracts about U.S. government statistical documents.

Bibliographic data banks contain text-based information abstracted from books, newspapers, magazines, and professional journals. Hundreds of these data banks are maintained by their producers. Most of the important ones are then indexed and stored on computers by a few large distributors. The distributors also provide the telecommunications links to their customers. Some of the largest information retrieval distributors are:

- ***Dialog Information Services.*** A division of the Lockheed Corporation, the *Dialog* system provides online access to about 200 data bases in such fields as government, health, education, social and physical sciences, humanities, and business. Many of the resources of the Dialog system are available at reduced rates to personal computer users after business hours and on weekends. The name of this pc-oriented service is *Knowledge Index*.

- ***SDC Information Services.*** SDC's *Orbit Search Service* has over 70 online data bases, many of which are also found in the Dialog system.

- ***Bibliographic Retrieval Services.*** *BRS/Search* offers over 60 different online data bases. Its *BRS/After Dark* service is aimed at pc users and is similar to Dialog's Knowledge Index.

- ***Mead Data Central.*** Unlike the distributors above, Mead is both the producer and distributor of its LEXIS and NEXIS services. LEXIS is a vast library of legal information including federal and state codes and millions of court opinions. NEXIS, shown in Figure 8-21, is a computerized news research service that carries information produced by over 100 major publications and news services.

Computational data banks allow users to manipulate raw data in order to produce economic models and forecasts. These data banks are prepared with data supplied by Standard & Poor's, Chase Econometric Associates, Data Resources, Inc. (DRI), and others. DRI, a division of McGraw-Hill, Inc., has joined with a producer of a popular spreadsheet program to give pc users access to DRI resources. A user can supply data to the spreadsheet program from over 50 DRI data bases and then use the program to manipulate the data.

Banking Service Systems

Banks communicate with each other and send funds-transfer instructions over telecommunications networks. The Fed Wire transfer network, for example, is operated by the Federal Reserve System for use by member banks. Hundreds of member banks and the Federal Reserve banks are linked together. Dozens of computers and hundreds of terminals are used to handle over 25 million messages each year. Over $50 *trillion* is annually transmitted by Fed Wire. A cooperative funds-transfer network called BankWire also serves several hundred banks in the United States. And a cooperative international network called SWIFT (Society for Worldwide Interbank Financial Telecommunications) links banks in over 20 countries.

Bank-at-home systems also use telecommunications lines to permit people to interact with their individual banks. Personal computers or special input devices attached to television sets use telephone or two-way cable TV lines to access a bank computer. (See "Banking on Your Home Computer," page 303).

Telecommuting Systems

Millions of people do much of their work on desktop devices such as word processors and personal computers. And we've seen that these devices can be located in the home and linked to outside office systems by telecommunications networks. Thus a growing number of people are questioning the need to commute to downtown office buildings to perform tasks they could easily do at home. In fact, tens of thousands of professionals are now doing some or all of their work in home and neighborhood work centers and are then forwarding the results in an electronic form to the office of an employer or client. This **telecommuting** approach isn't for everyone, of course, and some people prefer the social life of an office. But telecommuting benefits those who prefer flexible working hours and regular days at home. In the years ahead, it's expected that millions of telecommuters will be working in "electronic cottages" and forwarding their results to other sites.

FIGURE 8-21

Subscribers to the NEXIS system enjoy access to a vast news research data base. (Courtesy Mead Data Central)

WINDOW 8-1

BANKING ON YOUR HOME COMPUTER

Being able to sit at the home computer and do a week's banking in privacy and comfort is a dream that has come true for customers of many major banks. Home banking's time has come, say proponents, and home computer owners can use the service as easily as they use prepackaged software to arrange their household finances.

To initiate a home banking session, the user dials a local or toll-free number to reach the service's computer, which communicates with a home personal computer or videotext terminal through a modem. Menus displayed on the home screen help the user obtain account balances, transfer money between accounts, track checks, and pay bills to previously specified merchants. Some services also let the user apply for loans, purchase certificates of deposit, balance home budgets, and query bank officials by electronic mail. Interfacing with stock brokers and other investment avenues is projected as another major convenience.

The home terminal talks to the bank's computer via an intermediate computer called a gateway, which takes care of all the networking details like verifying passwords and enforcing protocols. Some gateways remain continuously tied in to the bank's computer so they can adjust account balances as transactions occur, with little or no delay. Most gateways, however, deal with "strip files," sets of working records adjusted nightly to reflect the day's transactions. In most cases, therefore, the user can access information current only to the previous afternoon.

Bill paying is less direct. For institutions or merchants that receive a large number of payments—utility companies, say—the bank sends payments daily in the form of a single lump-sum check accompanied by a computer tape detailing who paid what. Otherwise the bank must write and mail an individual check, verifying the payee against a list of approved businesses (most will not pay to an individual) previously submitted by the customer.

As of 1985, about two dozen banks in ten states had programs in full operation; another 35 had pilot programs or well-developed plans. It is estimated that by 1990 over 1,000 banks (and multi-facet institutions such as Sears and J. C. Penney) will be offering the service.

Customers for home banking are, of course, limited to those who can afford a computer and modem. For the first year or two, users tended to be "first on the block" types who enthusiastically adopt electronic gadgetry in general. Still, feedback is quite positive—and with good reason.

Banks sink a large investment into preparing a home

Bank-at-home systems enable users to check on their accounts, transfer funds, and even pay bills. (Photo courtesy Chemical Bank)

banking system. Since about 15% of customers must subscribe to make the service viable, incentives to users are generous. Besides keeping the monthly subscription fee to a minimum, some banks offer drastic discounts on the hardware and/or software for their systems. Users have commented that their savings in postage (not having to mail checks) and greater interest earnings (due to more efficient management) more than pay for the service.

Drawbacks of home banking include, above all, its inability to deliver cash, forcing the user to make trips as usual to the automated teller machine or the bank. Another major question is security (see "Data Security," p. 311). "Smart cards," plastic plates with embedded computer chips, are a possible solution to both problems. (See "Smart Cards," p. 192.) The user would insert the card into a reader connected to the terminal, where a code stored in the card's memory, in combination with the user's identification number, would work as a unique "signature" to open the system for business. The card's logic chip could also encrypt data, giving extra security. Some experts theorize that smart cards could replace cash by serving as a universally acceptable charge card.

Will home banking by pc become as commonplace as credit cards, travelers' checks, and automated teller machines? Many say yes, pointing out that initial acceptance of these banking innovations was equally spotty. Others are skeptical, but most agree it is too early to tell.

Adapted with permission from David H. Freedman, "Your Check is in . . . the Phone Line," *High Technology,* August 1984. Copyright © 1984 by High Technology Publishing Corporation.

FEEDBACK

Feedback and Review 8

This chapter has introduced you to a number of data communications concepts and networks. To test and reinforce your understanding of this material, use the following clues to fill in the *crossword puzzle*.

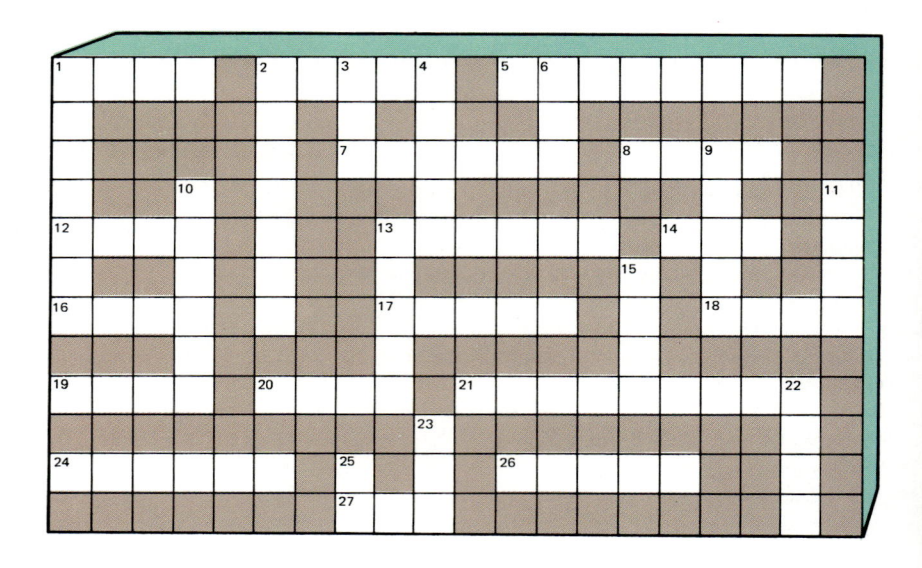

Across

1. _____ communication refers to the means and methods whereby data are transferred between processing locations.
2. A _____ is an interface device that converts the stream of "on-off" electrical pulses used by computing equipment into the type of analog wave patterns used to transmit the human voice over telephone lines.
5. Another name for the computing/communications networks that provide information retrieval services to personal computer users is _____ systems.
7. "Value-added" telecommunications carriers that receive customer data over telephone lines and then organize these data into groups for transmission over high-speed channels are sometimes referred to as _____-switching networks.
8. A _____-duplex transmission circuit is one that can simultaneously transmit and receive messages.
12. Data communications by means of electrical signs is also referred to as _____-communications.
13. The companies that offer a broad range of telegraph and telephone services to the general public are referred to as _____ carriers.
14. _____ is the acronym for the government agency that has held hearings to determine the extent of regulation and competition that will be permitted in the telecommunications industry.

16. Customers often pay for timesharing services in much the same way they pay for ____-distance telephone service.
17. ____-band transmission channels use coaxial cables, microwave systems and satellites, and fiber-optic cables to transmit large volumes of data at high speeds.
18. A standard telephone ____ is a voiceband channel that has a wider bandwidth and a faster transmission rate than a telegraph line.
19. In the ____ type of DDP network configuration, a central host computer communicates with and controls a second level of node processors.
20. ____-sharing is a term used to describe a processing system with a number of independent, relatively low-speed, online, and simultaneously usable stations.
21. A communications ____ is precisely positioned in space and acts as a reflector by accepting signals from one point on earth and returning the same signals to other points on earth.
24. An internal ____-connect modem is wired on a plug-in circuit board that's then installed inside a personal computer.
26. When a ____ mail EMMS is used, the user calls the system's phone number, logs into the system, and then transmits a verbal message to one or more recipients.
27. A digital ____ network uses existing telephone wires in a building to link together computing devices that have relatively light data communications requirements.

Down

1. Modems convert ____ "on-off" pulses into analog wave patterns.
2. ____ switchers are communications processors that receive and analyze data from points in a network, determine the destination and routing, and then forward the data to other network locations.
3. A ____ network is an extension of timesharing that employs many geographically dispersed computers and a telecommunications system to place data and computing resources at end-user locations.
4. ____-wave transmission systems use radio signals to transmit data through space.
6. A specialized common carrier that offers long-distance circuits to 88 U.S. cities and to other countries is ____ World Communications.
9. A ____-area network is used to transmit data between computers and I/O devices that are all located within a compact area such as an office building.
10. A ____ is taking place today between computing and communications technology.
11. Data ____ retrieval organizations tend to supply data that fall into statistical, bibliographic, and computational categories.
13. A coaxial or fiber-optic ____ can be used to transmit data at high speeds.
15. ____ time processing systems are in a parallel time relationship with ongoing activities and are producing information quickly enough to be useful in controlling these current live and dynamic activities.
22. An abbreviation for a system that can store and deliver, by electronic means, messages that would otherwise probably be forwarded through the postal service or sent verbally over telephone lines.
23. A type of machine that can use communications networks to transmit duplicate copies of documents and pictures.
25. Communicating ____ stations can also be used to transmit copies of printed documents.

LOOKING BACK

1. Data communication refers to the means and methods whereby data are transferred between processing locations. There's nothing new about telecommunications; telephones have been around for over 100 years. What's relatively recent, though, is the merging of computing and telecommunications technology and the increased competition permitted in the data communications field.

2. When older telephone lines are used to transmit computer data, one modem must be used at the sending station to modulate the digital "on-off" pulses into the analog wave patterns used to transmit the human voice. And a second modem is needed at the receiving location to demodulate, or recover, the digital data from the transmitted signal. A special type of modem called an acoustic coupler is often used with portable machines, but internal and external direct-connect modems are generally used at permanent stations.

3. In addition to medium-speed telephone lines, narrowband telegraph channels and high-speed broadband channels are also used to transmit data. The broadband channels use coaxial or fiber-optic cables, and microwave/satellite systems. Transmitted data can move along simplex, half-duplex, or full-duplex lines depending on the needs of the user.

4. Most organizations offering telecommunications services can be classified into common carrier, specialized common carrier, or value-added carrier categories. Common carriers provide large public telephone and telegraph networks and a broad range of services. Specialized common carriers often use broadband facilities such as microwave/satellite systems to offer public networks that provide a limited number of services. Value-added carriers generally use the telephone lines and transmission facilities of other carriers. Customer data are received, temporarily stored and organized into packets of characters, and then routed over high-speed leased channels to their destinations. There are also service firms that offer computing/communications networks and/or videotex systems for home use.

5. Large computing/communications networks use a number of communications processors to coordinate network components. Remote concentrators or multiplexers receive terminal input from low-speed lines and then concentrate and transmit the data on higher-speed facilities. Message switchers receive data from points in the network, determine destination and proper routing, and then forward the data to other locations. And front-end processors are used to relieve main computers of a number of the functions required to interact with and control the network.

6. Local-area networks (LANs) are communications systems that are used to link the terminals, computers, word processing stations, and other devices located within a compact area. LANs typically

follow a star, bus, or ring configuration, and they can be classified into high-, medium-, and low-speed categories. Some low-speed LANs designed for use with personal computers use special cables, while other low-speed networks use telephone wires and digital PBX controllers. Regardless of the type of LAN used at a local site, it must often be coordinated with the communications elements that link geographically dispersed processing centers.

7. A real time processing system is in a parallel time relationship with an ongoing activity and is producing information quickly enough to be useful in controlling this current live activity. A real time system uses interactive processing, but an interactive system need not be operating under the severe time limitations of a real time system.

8. Timesharing is a general term used to describe the interleaved use of the time of a processor by a number of independent, online, and simultaneously usable stations. A number of firms sell timesharing services to their customers.

9. A distributed data processing network consists of many geographically dispersed independent computer systems connected by a telecommunications network. It places the needed data, along with the computing/communications resources necessary to process these data, at the end user's location. As examples in the chapter show, DDP networks may be intended for the use of a single organization, or they may be available for use by many organizations. The possible DDP network configurations include the star, a hierarchical variation of the star, and the ring arrangements.

10. An electronic mail/message system is one that can store and deliver, by electronic means, messages that would otherwise probably be forwarded through the postal service or sent verbally over telephone lines. The use of EMMSs is growing rapidly, due to postal service delays and the frustrations caused by "telephone tag." An EMMS can provide electronic message distribution services, a means of transmitting copies of documents and pictures, and computerized conference functions. A message distribution system allows messages to be sent at any time to specified individuals or groups. Recipients periodically review stored voice or keyed-text messages at convenient times. Interruptions are reduced, people may feel less isolated, and communication between time zones is facilitated. Facsimile machines are used to transmit copies of documents and pictures. Computer conferencing and teleconferencing are both used to link people who are geographically separated, but computer conferencing permits people to participate at different times, while teleconferencing requires participants to be online at the same time.

11. Telecommunications has also made it possible to develop systems to provide banking services and retrieve information from numerous statistical, bibliographic, and computational data bases. Some people also enjoy the benefits of telecommuting through the use of telecommunications networks.

KEY TERMS AND CONCEPTS

data communication 276
telecommunications 276
interface elements 278
modem 278
external direct-connect modems 279
internal direct-connect modems 279
intelligent modems 279
acoustic coupler 280
data transmission channels 281
narrowband channel 281
voiceband channel 281
dedicated (leased) line 281
simplex circuit 281
half-duplex circuit 281
full-duplex circuit 281
broadband channel 281
coaxial cable 281
microwave systems 281
communications satellite 281

fiber-optic cable/laser technology 282
common carriers 282
specialized common carriers 283
value-added carriers 284
value-added network (VAN) 284
packet-switching networks 284
teletext system 284
videotex system 284
communications processors 285
remote concentrator 287
multiplexer 287
message switcher 287
front-end processor 287
host computer 287
local-area network (LAN) 288
star LAN 288
bus LAN 288
ring LAN 288

digital PBX 290
real time processing system 291
timesharing 292
distributed data processing (DDP) network 293
electronic mail/message system (EMMS) 296
telephone tag 296
voice mail 297
voice store-and-forward system 297
facsimile (fax) machine 297
communicating word processing stations 297
computer conferencing 300
teleconferencing 300
data banks 301
bank-at-home systems 302
telecommuting 302

Topics for Review and Discussion

1. (a) What is data communication? (b) What can you tell a friend who is under the impression that data communications is a new phenomenon?
2. (a) Why are computing and communications technologies merging? (b) What are likely to be some of the effects of this merger? (c) In your opinion, which computing/communications services should be regulated and which should be open to unregulated competition?
3. What components are typically found in a simple data communications system?
4. (a) What's a modem and why is it needed? (b) What's a direct-connect modem? (c) An intelligent modem? (d) An acoustic coupler?
5. Identify and discuss the three basic types of data transmission channels.
6. "A full-duplex line is faster since it avoids the delay that occurs in a half-duplex circuit." Explain this sentence.
7. (a) How are communications satellites used? (b) Identify four domestic satellite data transmission systems.
8. Identify, discuss, and give examples of three types of organizations that offer data communications services.
9. "A giant home information industry is being built around the development of videotex systems." Discuss this statement.
10. Identify and indicate the purpose of the communications processors used to coordinate the operations of a data communications network.
11. (a) What is a local-area network? (b) What's the difference between a star LAN and a bus LAN? (c) Identify and discuss three types of LAN offerings.
12. (a) Explain this sentence: "A real time system uses interactive processing, but an interactive system need not be operating in real time." (b) Give some examples of a real time system.
13. What is timesharing?
14. (a) What's a DDP network? (b) Give an example of a DDP network used by a single organization. (c) Give an example of a DDP network used by multiple organizations.
15. (a) What's an EMMS? (b) What are the limitations of the alternatives to an EMMS?
16. (a) What are the benefits of an electronic message distribution system? (b) How are such systems used?
17. (a) How are fax machines used? (b) Can other devices perform the same function?
18. (a) What is computerized conferencing? (b) What is teleconferencing?
19. "People at work may use public electronic libraries of information that are stored in central computers. These libraries tend to fall into three categories." Identify these categories, and give three examples of organizations that supply data bank information.
20. Identify three banking service systems that use telecommunications networks.
21. What is telecommuting?

Projects/Issues to Consider

1. Investigate a data base retrieval system—one whose services interest you—and research the current charges it makes for (a) initial hookup and (b) delivery of information. Write a brief report of your findings and explain how you would make use of the selected service.
2. Identify an organization (your school, a business, a hospital, a government agency) that uses a LAN or some other communications network during its data processing operations. Outline the results of your study in a report to the class.
3. Data base retrieval organizations such as those that offer the *Dialog*, *BRS/Search*, and *LEXIS/NEXIS* data banks are paid to gather and/or retrieve vast amounts of information for their customers. But technology is now available to permit huge quantities of data to be stored on a few inexpensive optical disks. And future fiber-optic cables will permit large blocks of data to be transmitted in a brief time period. Thus the technology will soon be in place to permit a subscriber to copy entire data banks at a low cost. For example, a law firm could copy the entire LEXIS data bank and then update it at regular intervals. Research the effects that such technological change is likely to have on information retrieval organizations, and summarize your findings and predictions in a class presentation.
4. Some computer "hackers" have used public and private bulletin boards to share surreptitiously gathered telephone numbers and computer codes that permit access to the processors in some organizations. In some cases, a message left on the bulletin board asks for information that could be used to penetrate the system of a specific organization. Research the literature to see what is currently being written about this security issue, and present your findings in a report.
5. To help organizations manage their truck fleets, TRW, Inc., is developing a system that will use satellites to detect drivers who are speeding or sitting idle when they should be hauling a cargo. The technology is available now for such an application. Organize a debate on this use of technology. Some of your classmates could play the role of managers in favor of such a system, while others could take the role of truck drivers who resent being monitored at all times.

MODULE 2

Answers to Feedback and Review Section

The solution for the crossword puzzle is shown here:

	1 D	2 A	T	A		2 M	3 O	D	4 E	M		5 V	6 I	D	E	O	T	E	X	
	I					E		D	I				T							
	G					S	7 P	A	C	K	E	T		8 F	U	9 L	L			
	I			10 M		S			R						O			11 B	
12 T	E	L	E		A			13 C	O	M	M	O	N		14 F	C	C		A
A			R		G			A				15 R		A					S
16 L	O	N	G		E		17 B	R	O	A	D		E		18 L	I	N	E
			E					L			A							
19 S	T	A	R		20 T	I	M	E		21 S	A	T	E	L	L	I	T	22 E
							23 F									M		
24 D	I	R	E	C	T		25 W		A		26 V	O	I	C	E		M	
					27 P	B	X										S	

A CLOSER LOOK

DATA SECURITY

"He's a good kid. He means no harm. He just accessed your computer data base," reads the advertisement for a data security system. Appearing in the pages of major business periodicals, ads like this are increasingly common as computer networking—and the threat of its misuse—proliferates among the general public.

Although the chances of "hacker" break-in are statistically very low for any given system, events like the 1985 "New Jersey Hack Sack," in which seven teenagers were arrested for conspiracy and computer theft, have raised concern. Using their modem-equipped home computers to exchange stolen credit card numbers and supposedly secret phone numbers, purchase computer and stereo components, and circulate such information as a letter-bomb recipe, the youngsters had acquired some $30,000 worth of hardware and hundreds of floppy disks full of software when police apprehended them. A much-publicized rumor, quickly refuted by AT&T and Comsat, alleged that the hackers had succeeded in altering the orbit of one or more communications satellites. Had they done so, they would have interrupted telephone and telex connections over two continents.

Nor was this crime without precedent. In the summer of 1983, the FBI discovered unauthorized entry into over sixty databases, including those belonging to the Sloan-Kettering Cancer Center, the Los Alamos National Laboratory, and the Defense Department, by an amateur network calling itself the "414 Gang" after the area code of the members' home city, Milwaukee. A worst-case scenario for hacker mischief was played out in the movie "War Games," where a high school whizkid uses his computer to penetrate the Pentagon's database and narrowly avoids setting off World War III.

The painful truth is that many massive government and business computer databases are vulnerable to invasion by personal computer. Obvious targets are credit and charge card numbers; the "Hack Sack" case came to light when a credit card customer complained of being charged for a piece of equipment he had never purchased. With the increasing availability of electronic banking, electronic shopping, and "bulletin boards" which exchange all kinds of information, no networking computer is safe from intruders.

And teenage hackers are not the only computer criminals. According to IBM's director of security, Harry De Maio, an honest user may accidentally discover a weakness in a system and find the temptation irresistible. Whether it is a government employee harboring a petty grudge, or an office worker yearning for a better car, someone who finds that theft is possible may be seduced. Many experts advise taking the common-sense precaution of examining software for errors and leaks: Can money be transferred to a made-up account number? Is the password an obvious one like "password"? Is a computer left on 24 hours a day rather than being programmed to let users call in for data only during certain hours? Finally, urges lawyer August Bequai, author of several books on the subject, the human factor should not be overlooked. Both employees and amateur bulletin board buddies should be screened for personal reliability.

For more clear-cut protection, data security packages can be purchased for prices less than $1,000. Some of the most versatile packages involve sophisticated passwords, both in multiple layers and in guess-limit setups, where the would-be user must insert the correct password within a certain number of tries. The system hangs up on anyone who fails and will not answer again for some time.

Other systems place a "flag" on every transaction made by a new user, not incorporating it until it is approved by a previously authorized user. This is a variant of the audit trail, a feature that was once commonplace but was eliminated from the first personal computer packages due to the need to strip down software to fit the machines' limited memories. With the expanded capabilities of newer personal computers, audit trails are again being used in recording transactions, allowing the origins of suspicious data to be traced.

Data security can also be protected through a dialback service, which hangs up after receiving a caller's ID number, then redials only the authorized telephone number corresponding to that ID. Some systems also make use of encryption devices, which scramble output into gobbledygook illegible to all but authorized receivers equipped with the proper de-scrambler.

Data protection systems are expensive—American businesses spent $600 million on them in 1984—and they make computers less "friendly," or harder to use. Yet experts agree that they are necessary, and that computer crime will remain a threat in spite of them. Maintaining data integrity, for personal computer owners as well as for large businesses and government, will be a matter of common-sense caution and endless vigilance.

MODULE 3

Software is the name given to the written programs of instructions (and associated documents) that cause computer hardware to function in a desired way. Like television programs, computer programs turn lifeless machines into something useful. We'll begin this Software Module with two chapters that focus on prewritten software packages. Next, we'll take a look at the procedures required to develop custom-made systems. Then we'll consider some of the practices and languages used to prepare applications programs for these systems.

SOFTWARE

9 PREWRITTEN SOFTWARE: SINGLE-FUNCTION APPLICATIONS PROGRAMS

10 PREWRITTEN SOFTWARE: INTEGRATED PACKAGES, PACKAGE SELECTION, AND OPERATING SYSTEMS

11 DEVELOPING CUSTOM-MADE SYSTEMS

12 PREPARING APPLICATIONS PROGRAMS: PRACTICES AND LANGUAGES

CHAPTER 9

PREWRITTEN SOFTWARE:
SINGLE-FUNCTION APPLICATIONS PROGRAMS

THE PEOPLE'S FIREHOUSE

With the aid of a computer, residents of a resurgent New York City neighborhood are rallying to fight arson and bolster the business life in their community.

In Greenpoint and Northside, working class communities in Brooklyn, woodframed homes coexist with industrial warehouses and factories. During New York's severe fiscal crisis of the mid-1970s, the city attempted to close a local firehouse, Engine Company 212. Coming on the heels of a slew of other cutbacks in vital municipal services, this closing provoked the largely Polish and Hispanic population to take action. The community protested the cutbacks vehemently.

Fred Ringler, executive director of the People's Firehouse, recalls, "community volunteers organized to stop the closing. We took the firehouse over and held it hostage for a year and 4 months. We lived in it and operated it as what became known as the 'People's Firehouse.'" Eventually, the city relented and reopened the firehouse. But the organization that Ringler and other volunteers formed has continued. Today the "People's Firehouse" has evolved into a grant-supported 41-employee, computer-assisted operation that includes an arson outreach center and a community education service.

Since 1984, a Texas Instruments Portable Professional personal computer has been the heart of the group's arson awareness program: the Arson Data Information System. "We've used the dBase II program to collect thousands of housing and fire datum on structural fires over the last 5 years," said Ringler in 1985. "This has helped us pinpoint high arson risks in the neighborhood."

Some of the information stored in the data base includes: the locations of buildings; the names of their owners, insurance companies and tenants; and statistics on housing, fire, and industrial trends. Having such information readily available has made arson-prone properties easier to identify. When a threat to "burn the building down" was overheard in one apartment house, for example, the People's Firehouse turned to its computerized records to put together a background profile on the property, explained Felice Jergens of the arson prevention project. Tenants association members guarded the building 24 hours a day until the city foreclosed on its negligent owner, and turned management over to the People's Firehouse.

Locating these arson-prone properties is only half the battle, though. Outreach workers from the People's Firehouse train tenants and community groups to recognize the early warning signs of arson: poor security, instances of past fires, and generally rundown conditions.

The latest project formed by the People's Firehouse is the Business Assistance Project. This is essentially an economic development program that utilized a minicomputer set up in the office. The minicomputer has been used mainly for fiscal management and word processing by staff members. An accounting and word processing package are used for internal management information. The system is now open to businesses in the community; "The business people that want the service can come into our office to set up financial records and the like," Ringler notes.

As the People's Firehouse demonstrates, dedicated people in neighborhood organizations can harness the power of computers to make their neighborhoods safer, cleaner, and more productive.

Adapted from Nancy Huscha, "The People's Firehouse," *Personal Computing*, February 1985.

CHAPTER 9

LOOKING AHEAD

A wide range of prewritten software is available to computer users. This software processes user applications and controls the operations within the computer itself. Our purpose in Chapter 9 is to classify software packages and examine some prewritten applications programs designed to perform single tasks. (Chapter 10 then discusses other packages that integrate several applications, outlines a way to select prewritten applications packages, and summarizes the tasks carried out by operating system software.) The information in this chapter will enable you to:

- Classify the types of prewritten software packages that are available
- Describe and give examples of some popular types of single-function applications programs

CHAPTER OUTLINE

LOOKING AHEAD
CATEGORIES OF SOFTWARE PACKAGES: REVIEW AND PREVIEW
Prewritten Applications Packages
System Software Packages
SINGLE-FUNCTION APPLICATIONS PROGRAMS
Special-Purpose Packages
General-Purpose Packages
Feedback and Review 9
LOOKING BACK

CATEGORIES OF SOFTWARE PACKAGES: REVIEW AND PREVIEW

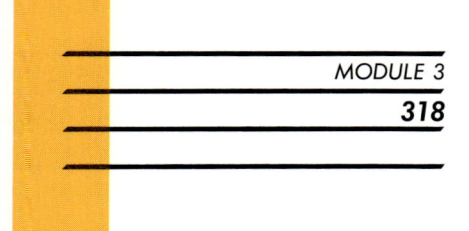

Computers are to computing as instruments are to music. Software is the score, whose interpretation amplifies our reach and lifts our spirit. Leonardo da Vinci called music "The shaping of the invisible," and his phrase is even more apt as a description of software.

Alan Kay, "Computer Software," *Scientific American*, September 1984, p. 53.

Just as "invisible" notes in a composer's mind may become beautiful sounds when written and then played on an instrument, so, too, may invisible symbols in a programmer's mind be put to useful purpose when written and then processed by a computer. Computer software, like music, can be classified into several categories (see Figure 9-1). For example, users can elect to use **prewritten software packages** to perform specific tasks, or they can "compose" their own **custom-made programs** to do the work. Our interest in Chapters 9 and 10 is on the prewritten packages created by the skilled people working for equipment suppliers and independent software houses. We'll look at the development of custom-made systems and programs in Chapters 11 and 12.

It's also possible to classify prewritten software packages into *applications* and *system software* categories. Let's make sure we understand each of these categories.

Prewritten Applications Packages

You've seen in earlier chapters that an *application program* is one that allows the computer to solve a specific data processing task for a user. And you've also seen in Chapters 1 and 2 that prewritten applications packages may perform *single* functions or they may *integrate* several functions in a single package.

Single-function applications packages can be further classified into special-purpose and general-purpose categories. Examples of single-function **special-purpose packages** are game programs (such as programs to play chess) and packages designed for a specific class of user (such as programs used by religious organizations to account for member contributions). We'll look at a few more examples of special-purpose packages in the next section.

Examples of single-function **general-purpose packages** are word processing and spreadsheet programs. These programs only manipulate text or numbers in columns and rows, but they can be used in any home or office to make writing and calculating faster and more accurate. We'll also look at examples of general-purpose programs in the next section. **Integrated-function packages** are written to include a number of these general-purpose applications.

System Software Packages

A **system software package** is a collection of complex programs designed to operate, control, and extend the processing capabilities of the computer itself. Computer users often write customized applications programs, but the preparation of intricate system software is almost always left to computer manufacturers and independent software suppliers. An important system software package found in almost all computer installations is the *operating system* (OS). Some of the basic functions of an OS were discussed in Chapter 1. We'll look at the tasks performed by OSs and related utility programs in the next chapter.

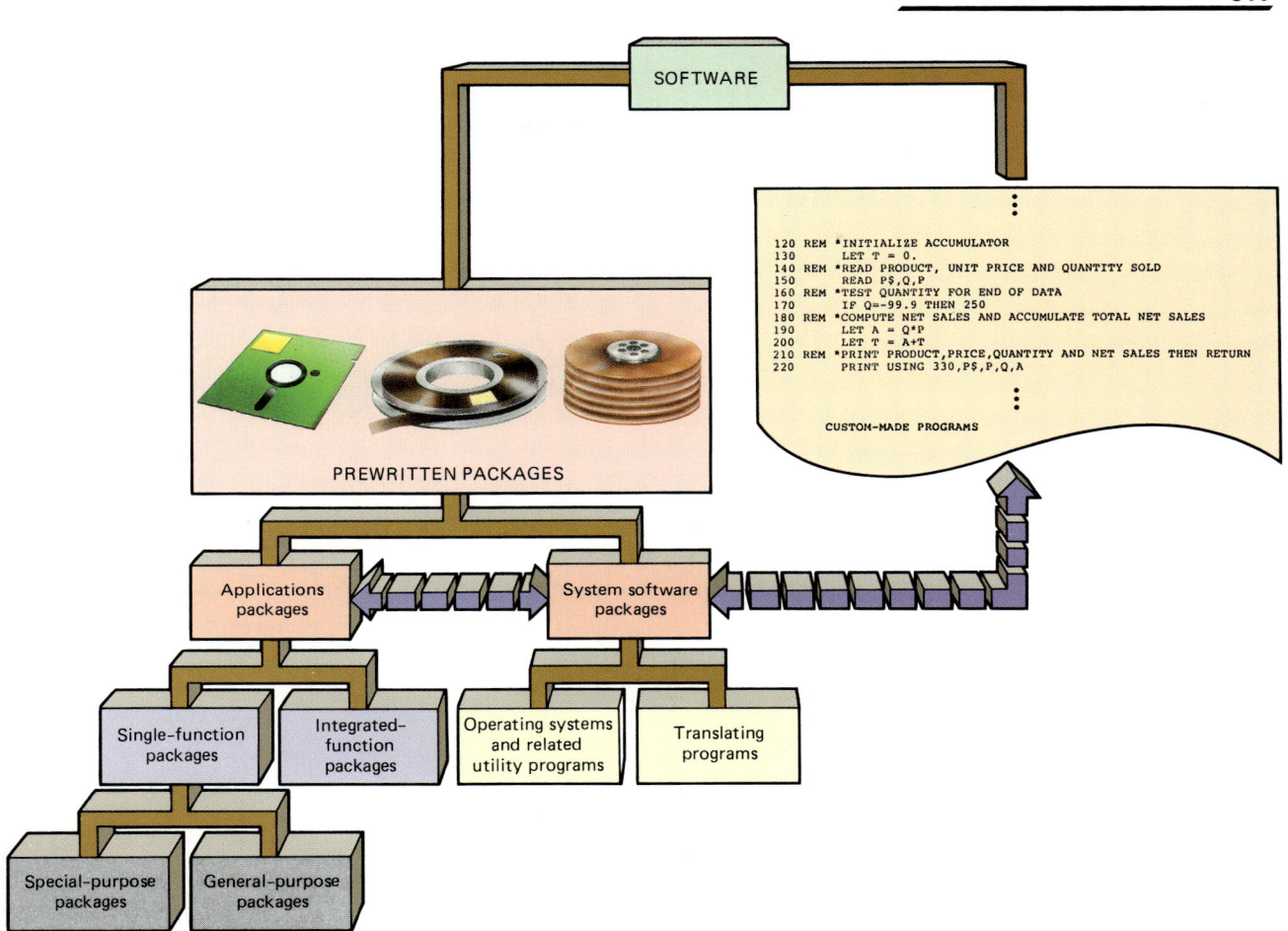

```
120 REM *INITIALIZE ACCUMULATOR
130     LET T = 0.
140 REM *READ PRODUCT, UNIT PRICE AND QUANTITY SOLD
150     READ P$,Q,P
160 REM *TEST QUANTITY FOR END OF DATA
170     IF Q=-99.9 THEN 250
180 REM *COMPUTE NET SALES AND ACCUMULATE TOTAL NET SALES
190     LET A = Q*P
200     LET T = A+T
210 REM *PRINT PRODUCT,PRICE,QUANTITY AND NET SALES THEN RETURN
220     PRINT USING 330,P$,P,Q,A
```

FIGURE 9-1

Software can be classified into prewritten packages and custom-made programs. The prewritten package category includes various types of applications and system software packages. You'll see in Chapter 10 that prewritten system software packages are used to control the operation of the computer itself. The dashed lines show that system software supports the use of both prewritten applications packages and completed custom-made programs. System software is also used during the development of custom-made programs, as you'll see in Chapter 12.

Another system software component discussed in Chapter 1 is the *translating program*. These programs transform the instructions prepared by people using convenient languages into the machine-language codes required by computers. Translating software is essentially invisible to the many computer users who use prewritten applications programs but have no interest in developing their own custom-made software. For program developers, however, the choice of programming languages and the availability of efficient translating software is important. We'll consider these matters again in Chapter 12.

SINGLE-FUNCTION APPLICATIONS PROGRAMS

Special-Purpose Packages

The key to success for many package producers has been to identify a specialized market that's (1) large enough to be profitable and (2) uniform enough so that packages need not be customized for each user. For example, it's unrealistic to attempt to address the inventory control needs of *all* retail stores in a single program because these needs would be so varied. But an industry-specific package could meet the needs of thousands of florists, who have similar requirements.

In Organizations   The following list describes a few of the thousands of special-purpose packages available to organizations:

- ***Political campaign packages.***   Large computers have been used for years to help manage well-funded campaigns for national and statewide offices. But now *any* office seeker can choose from a number of campaign software packages that run on personal computers. The functions performed by these packages are described in the reading at the beginning of Chapter 2. Some packages are sold only to candidates of a designated political party, while others are available to any campaign organization.

- ***Law-office software.***   There are over 1,000 personal computer (pc) software packages designed specifically for the legal profession. More than 120 suppliers offer packages in legal accounting to help attorneys keep track of their time and expenses for client billing purposes. Calendar and docket-control programs remind lawyers of document filing dates and court-related deadlines and appearances. Other packages include those used for customizing standard legal forms.

- ***Medical-office software.***   Over 1,500 pc software packages are available for doctors, dentists, and other health-care professionals. Medical insurance companies and others are offering hardware/software packages that allow doctors' offices to generate a patient bill and an insurance claim with a single data entry. Diagnostic packages are also available. For example, a doctor can enter a patient's allergy history and the results of allergy tests, and a package can then respond with the most likely diagnosis and recommendations for treatment.

- ***Educational packages.***   There are over 6,000 educational packages for pc's, and the number grows daily. Many packages used in schools can be purchased for home use. Some are administrative programs—those used by teachers to keep student records, calculate grade averages, and so on. But most are used for instruction. In **computer-assisted instruction (CAI),** a student interacts with, and is guided by, a program through a course of study aimed at achieving specific instructional goals. A student sits at a terminal or pc and communicates with the educational package. Interaction may occur in this way: (1) The package presents instructional information and questions; (2) the student studies this material, answers questions, and, perhaps, asks questions; and (3) the program then accepts, analyzes, and provides immediate feedback to the student's responses, and it records the student's performance for later evaluation. The simplest and most-used form of CAI is the **drill-and-practice approach** that's designed to *complement* instruction received from teachers, printed materials, and other noncomputer sources. Students respond to package questions, and learning is facilitated because the package instantly supplies correct answers as feedback to student mistakes. Thousands of drill-and-practice programs are available in learning areas such as science, mathematics, languages, reading, and spelling where substantial memorizing is needed. A more complex **tutorial CAI package** plays the role

Special-purpose software packages are popular in law offices, which use them to process the lengthy and specialized forms required for such tasks as real estate closings and the management of trust funds. (Courtesy Verbatim Corp.)

Playing Blackjack with this home computer software package saves you the expense of a trip to Las Vegas—and saves you the expense of losing as well. (Courtesy Coleco)

of a private and very patient tutor as it presents *new* material to a student. And challenging **educational games and simulations** allow students to assume roles and make decisions. For example, a student may take the part of a genetic scientist who's responsible for the controlled breeding of animals. The simulation package allows the student to formulate and test hypotheses, design experiments, gather and analyze data, and draw conclusions—all important scientific activities.

In Homes   A few of the thousands of special-purpose programs available for home use are described below:

● *Hobby and entertainment packages.*   People with interests in *music* can use available pc packages to enhance their musical knowledge and write their own compositions. These compositions can then be played through a pc speaker. Programs called **paint systems** offer a range of colors and screen lines (called ''brushes''), and they permit the user to fill in screen areas and zoom in on a section of the screen ''canvas'' for more detailed graphics work. Amateur astronomers can use other packages to see on their display screens how the night sky looked on any night in history, from any position on earth. And people can entertain themselves with a huge variety of shooting games, board games, maze chases, and action and strategy simulations. In one night you can pilot a simulated aircraft, command the troops at the Civil War battle at Shiloh, and build a transcontinental railroad line in the late 1800s.

● *Home educational software.*   Many home entertainment programs offer substantial educational value as well. For example, you can learn scientific principles while piloting a simulated airplane, and you can gain a better understanding of history by ''participating'' in historical events. Entire catalogs of home educational software are available. (A recent *Weekly Reader Family Software* catalog had over 80 pages of educational programs offered by scores

FIGURE 9-2

A personal financial management package can give you a clear picture of your financial affairs. (a) Some of the financial management tools available in a typical package are shown on this *main-menu* screen. The user first makes a selection from the main menu. This selection could be to enter and store the amount and purpose of checks written to cover household budget expenses (option 1), but the financial calculator (option 4) has been selected in our example. (b) Several options can be displayed to give the user a choice of financial calculating tools. In this example, the user can enter data on several lines, and the program will then calculate the figures for the remaining lines.

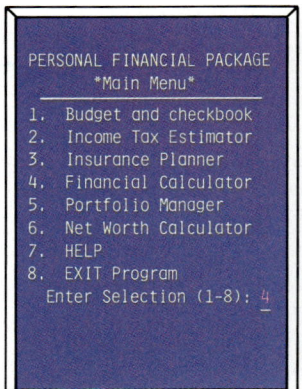

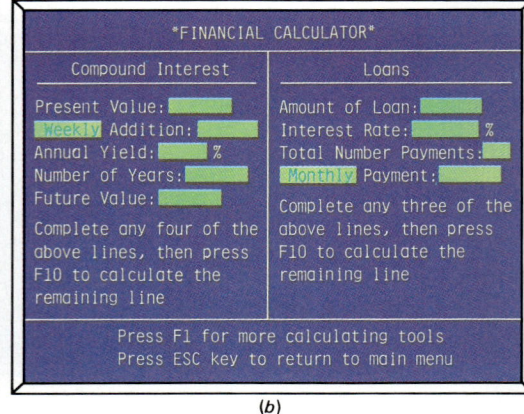

```
PERSONAL FINANCIAL PACKAGE
       *Main Menu*

1.  Budget and checkbook
2.  Income Tax Estimator
3.  Insurance Planner
4.  Financial Calculator
5.  Portfolio Manager
6.  Net Worth Calculator
7.  HELP
8.  EXIT Program
    Enter Selection (1-8): 4
```
(a)

```
          *FINANCIAL CALCULATOR*
  Compound Interest        Loans

Present Value:         Amount of Loan:
Weekly  Addition:      Interest Rate:      %
Annual Yield:      %   Total Number Payments:
Number of Years:       Monthly Payment:
Future Value:
Complete any four of the   Complete any three of the
above lines, then press    above lines, then press
F10 to calculate the       F10 to calculate the
remaining line             remaining line

    Press F1 for more calculating tools
    Press ESC key to return to main menu
```
(b)

of suppliers.) People can also use the educational packages described at the beginning of Chapter 2 to prepare for the Scholastic Aptitude Test (SAT).

● *Personal financial management packages.* There are many packages that help people monitor their finances. They can keep track of how much money is coming in, how much is being spent and for what purpose, and how much (if any) is left over. Figure 9-2 shows some of the capabilities of these packages.

● *Home health advisory programs.* These programs quickly evaluate your answers to health-habits and family-history questionnaires and then give immediate advice about the health risks they detect.

General-Purpose Packages

Let's look now at the most popular types of single-function general-purpose applications packages.

Word Processing Packages You saw in Chapter 2 that a *word processing (WP) package* is used to create, view, edit, store, retrieve, and print text material. Figure 9-3 repeats a Chapter 2 figure and shows how all of these WP text-manipulating capabilities are used to prepare Jill Byter's campaign letters. Many organizations are now introducing computing/communications technology into their offices to reduce labor costs and improve the productivity of their workers. Word processing is often the "backbone" application in these new **electronic offices.**

Both individuals and organizations find WP to be an amazingly flexible tool. You can see in Figure 9-3 that as text is keyed into the system, it's also

FIGURE 9-3 *(facing page)*

Word processing packages can be used to streamline the creation and production of letters, reports, and other documents. The text-manipulating capabilities of such packages allow users to create, view, edit, store, retrieve, and print text material efficiently.

323

(a) The original draft

Dear _____:

The Student House of Representatives election is coming soon. We need a nursing major who'll fight for health-care students.

Please remember, ___, to vote for Jill Byter.
        Sincerely,

        Campaign Manager

(b) The addition of text

Dear _____:

The Student House of Representatives election is coming soon. We need a nursing major who'll fight for the interests of health-care students.

Please remember, ___, to vote for Jill Byter in the forthcoming election.
        Sincerely,

        Campaign Manager

(c) The final edited version with text deleted

Dear _____:

The Student House of Representatives needs a nursing major who'll fight for the interests of health-care students.

Please remember, ___, to vote for Jill Byter in the forthcoming election.
        Sincerely,

        Campaign Manager

② Additions and deletions are easily made to get a final *edited* version of a letter.

Word Processing Program

① A personal computer and a word processing program are used to *create* the text of Jill's letters.

③ The text of the letters is *stored* on a floppy disk. This may be the disk that contains the word processing program, or it may be a separate disk.

④ When a letter is needed, the disk(s) containing the word processing program and stored text is(are) inserted into the computer. The desired letter form is *retrieved* and a name and address is entered through the Keyboard. (With appropriate software, it's possible to *merge* the names and addresses stored in a mailing list file into this operation, thereby eliminating the need to rekey the data.)

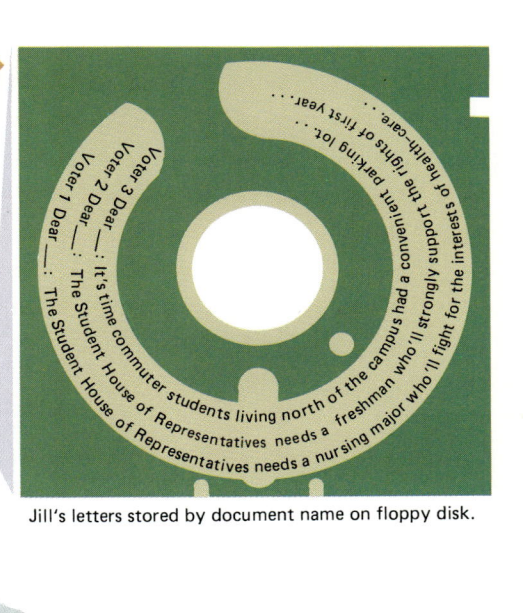

Jill's letters stored by document name on floppy disk.

2 3 4

Primary Storage Section

Input storage area	Program storage area	Output storage area
VOTER 1 Dear___: The Student House of Representatives needs a nursing major who'll fight . . . Betty Bianci 23 Seltzer St. Carmi, CA 97632	1. Request data from operator. 2. Read document name into input storage area. 3. Duplicate in input storage area the text stored by document name in online storage device. 4. Read name and address into input storage area. 5. Duplicate contents of appropriate name field in designated text locations. 6. Move name, address, and text to output storage area. 7. Print letter in desired format. 8. Stop processing.	Betty Bianci 23 Seltzer St. Carmi, CA 97632 Dear Betty: The Student House of Representatives needs a nursing major who'll fight . . .

(7) →

Betty Bianci
23 Seltzer St.
Carmi, CA 97632

Dear Betty:

The Student House of Representatives needs a nursing major who'll fight for the interests of health-care students.

Please remember, Betty, to vote for Jill Byter in the forthcoming election.

        Sincerely,
        John Mahle
        Campaign Manager

displayed on the screen. "Carriage returns" are automatic, and corrections are easy. Words, sentences, paragraphs, and larger blocks of text can be added, deleted, or moved around in the document being prepared. When the displayed text is correct, the text and output format instructions can then be saved on a storage medium such as a floppy disk. For example, the package can be instructed to automatically put headings and numbers on each page of a report, center headings on the page, and produce specified top, bottom, left, and right margins. Finally, the document or report can be printed or, with the proper equipment, it can be transmitted electronically to another WP station. Thus, in an electronic office, letters and reports need not be mailed; they can be printed for the first time on receiving equipment in a nearby office—or thousands of miles away.

In addition, some WP packages permit users to call up prerecorded paragraphs from the dozens that may be in storage. These paragraphs can then be *merged* to create a new document. Then a "dictionary," or **spelling checker,** element in the package can be called up, to check every word in the document against a list of correctly spelled words. Words that don't match any of the tens of thousands stored in the dictionary are highlighted or flagged with a special character. The entire document can then be searched, and these highlighted or flagged words can be automatically presented to the operator for action. Some spelling checkers display suggested spellings for words that aren't on the stored list. If the word is spelled correctly, it can be added to the dictionary list; if it's misspelled, it can be corrected. This **global search** capability can also be used to search for words or phrases specified by the operator. When found, they can be deleted or replaced with other words or phrases. This **search-and-replace** feature can also be used to substitute names in documents or replace an abbreviation or acronym with a longer phrase. For example, if you are frequently typing some phrase such as "New York Economic Development Council" in a document, you can use substitute keystrokes such as "@@" in your text and then tell the package to replace these keystrokes with the desired phrase. Finally, a package may also include an **in-context thesaurus** element that will suggest synonyms for the words you've created in a document. See the Closer Look reading at the end of the Chapter for more information on WP programs.

Electronic Spreadsheet Packages

You've seen in the Background Module how a *spreadsheet package* may be used to manipulate data that have been organized into columns and rows. For example, Figure 9-4 shows again how Marie Byter's Meals Compensation Report (discussed in Chapter 2) could be produced with such a package.

The spreadsheet created by a typical package can be visualized as a huge chalkboard that's divided into dozens (or hundreds) of columns and hundreds (or thousands) of rows. There are thus thousands of intersections where columns and rows meet. At each intersection in this matrix is a *cell,* or *box,* that can be filled with letters, mathematical symbols, numbers, and formulas. Cell B6 in Figure 9-4 is at the intersection of column B and row 6. A user can designate a particular cell in the spreadsheet "chalkboard" and then enter a title, number, or formula.

A *standard-size* cell may be set to display a certain number of characters, but cell sizes can be expanded or reduced. A cell may be a *value cell* or a *label cell* in any given application depending on the first character that's entered

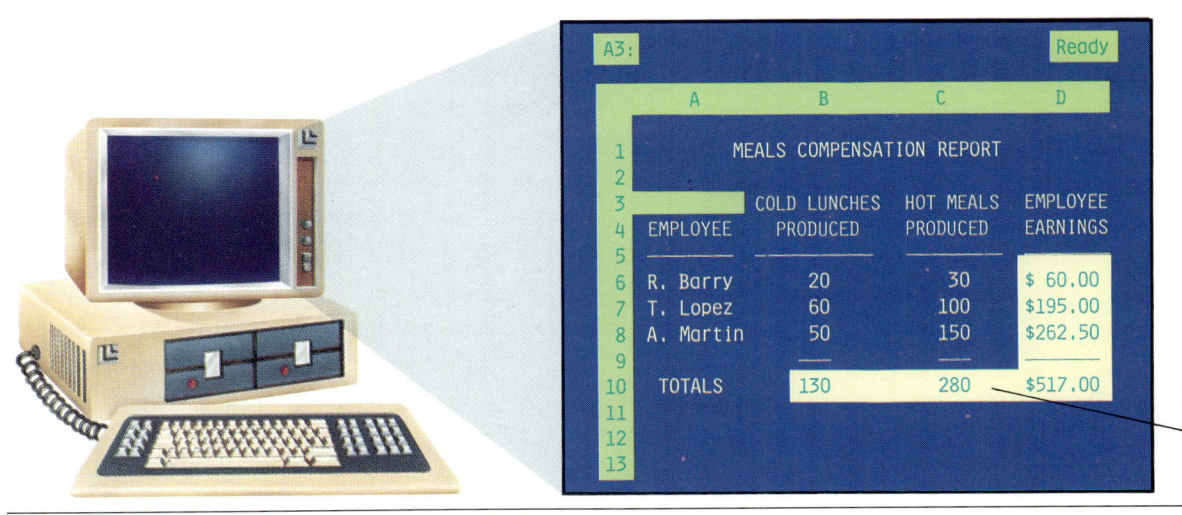

	A	B	C	D
1		MEALS COMPENSATION REPORT		
2				
3		COLD LUNCHES	HOT MEALS	EMPLOYEE
4	EMPLOYEE	PRODUCED	PRODUCED	EARNINGS
5				
6	R. Barry	20	30	$ 60.00
7	T. Lopez	60	100	$195.00
8	A. Martin	50	150	$262.50
9				
10	TOTALS	130	280	$517.00

FIGURE 9-4

Output produced by an electronic spreadsheet package. When a spreadsheet program is loaded into a computer, it displays a set of blank rows and columns. A common format is to identify each row by number and each column by letter. The intersection of a column and row is called a *cell*, or *box*. The package user designates whether a cell should contain the letters in a title, the numbers to be manipulated, or the mathematical relationships or formulas that control the processing. In this example, report headings have been placed in the first five rows. The user (Marie Byter) has then entered employee data in rows 6, 7, and 8 of columns A, B, and C. To calculate the employee earnings values found in column D, the user has placed an instruction in cell D6 that looks like this:

+(B6 * 0.75) + (C6 * 1.50)

This instruction tells the spreadsheet package to (1) multiply the contents of cell B6 by $0.75, (2) multiply the contents of cell C6 by $1.50, (3) add the products of these two calculations, and (4) place the total in cell D6. The same type of instruction is repeated to produce the other figures in column D. To get the total for column B, the user places the following formula in cell B10:

+(B6 + B7 + B8)

The package then knows it must add the contents of rows 6, 7, and 8 in the B column and store the result in row 10 of the same column. The totals in columns C and D are found in the same way.

Calculations performed by spreadsheet program in response to Marie's instructions.

into the cell. Numbers and mathematical symbols may create value cells; letters and quotations produce label boxes. Value cells do the calculating; label boxes are used for headings and descriptions. With a few keystrokes a user can tell a spreadsheet program to add cells B6, B7, and B8, and store the total in box B10. Many other mathematical functions can be performed on other identified value boxes. Users can create their own spreadsheet layout designs and specify the relationships that exist between cells, or they can purchase layout designs complete with the formulas needed to process common applications. If one of these available **templates** fits a user's requirements, the user need only enter the data and review the output results.

After a spreadsheet layout has been designed and the relationships needed to control the processing have been given to the package, the spreadsheet can then provide quick answers to "what if" questions. For example, the data in cells B6, B7, and B8 may change in response to different assumptions made by the user, and the total in cell B10 will automatically be adjusted to reflect these changes. To plan for the introduction of a new product, a manager often wants to consider what will happen if different raw material prices, labor costs, and sales volume figures are assumed. If the assumed figures are fed into a pc, the spreadsheet package will manipulate them to project the effect that different values will have on profits.

Graphics Packages   We've also seen examples in the Background Module of how graphics packages may be used. Figure 9-5 shows again how such a package can visually portray the spreadsheet data presented in Figure 9-4. After supplying the graphics program with the data to be presented, the user may make a trial selection from a menu of chart layouts supplied by the package (Figure 9-5*a*). The package then quickly displays the data in the selected format (Figure 9-5*b*). The user can vary chart colors and the positions and typefaces of chart labels. If not satisfied with one format, the user can go back to the layout menu and select another (Figure 9-5*c*). When a final layout is approved, the user can store it on a disk for future use and then use an appropriate output device to capture it in a visual form. For example, a printer

WINDOW 9-1

BUILDING SIMPLE SPREADSHEETS

A fact that novice spreadsheet users may not be aware of is that many useful models are possible employing only the most basic math and logic functions.

Software developers have for years competed to make their spreadsheet programs as powerful and function-rich as possible. Today's most popular sellers, such as Lotus 1-2-3 and Multiplan, succeeded in part by offering the functions required by heavily number-oriented professionals, in particular managers and accountants, for financial analysis and budgeting applications. These users were accustomed to working with higher math and statistical tools on paper. Thus, their transition to using the same concepts on a personal computer was relatively simple.

But the versatility of the spreadsheet concept means that these products can be used for a lot more than pure number-crunching. A random survey of 2,000 households conducted by the market research firm Software Access found that 39 percent of spreadsheet users do financial and budget analysis. The other 61 percent represents such a diverse mix of applications that Software Access' Mary Ellen Dick found it difficult to group them. "We found people doing production scheduling, personnel records, investments, project formulation, home accounting and all sorts of things," she says. "Spreadsheets really are an all-purpose tool."

The Software Access survey showed that many people use spreadsheets to develop their own application even when off-the-shelf application-specific programs are available to them.

One of the reasons that so many people choose to use spreadsheets for so many different applications is that they give you the versatility to structure the application your own way. When you build your own model to do a particular job, you understand the relationships involved because you've built them in yourself. If they have to be changed, it can be a lot easier to rewrite a few formulas in your spreadsheet model than it would be to reconfigure or reprogram a vertical applications package whose inner workings you may have never understood. You will also tend to have a lot more faith in conclusions when you know how the numbers were produced.

A spreadsheet model does not have to be complicated to be useful. David Phares, a judge with the Chandler Justice Court in Chandler, Ariz., has developed a simple model that demonstrates this point amply to his fellow judges. (He teaches at a 1-week judicial applications course during National Judicial College sessions at the University of Nevada at Reno.) Phares has each judge set up a spreadsheet program that allows them to track their own sentencing record and detect any biases they may have in terms of age, sex, and race of the defendants.

Using the Microplan spreadsheet program from Chang Labs, Phares suggests each judge take 50 sample cases of the same offense in which they have passed sentence and then enter the case name or number in the row label column. Columns are created across the worksheet for each subcategory of age, sex, and race being considered. The judge then enters the length of the sentence in the three columns which describe the defendant. So a 32-year-old white male who had received 90 days for burglary would have 90 entered in the columns headed age 30–35; sex male; race Caucasian.

Phares shows the judges how they can write formulas under each column to develop comparative statistics for themselves such as averages and percentages. "You might find, for example, if you enter 50 marijuana possession cases that you're sentencing people in the 18 to 22 age group much more severely than those found guilty of the same crime in the 26 to 30 group," says Phares. One of the big advantages that the judges can see immediately, according to Phares, is that they can set the model up for themselves and keep the results private. Since they are in control of the numbers and are doing it for their own awareness, they can also be certain that the cases they treat in the model are relevant and not use particular cases.

It is not hard to see how a relatively simple spreadsheet model like Phares' judicial application can not only provide a great deal of useful information to the novice user immediately but can also be built upon in the future as the user gains experience. "Novice users find it an easy leap to make if they start out by taking the jobs they do all the time on paper to the rows and columns of a spreadsheet," says Tod Riedel, president of First Micro, a training and consulting firm. People often start using spreadsheets as little more than a tabular word processor, a tool for quickly setting up a table of words or numbers in presentable form. While that may not be taking great advantage of the program's capabilities, Riedel believes that most users will quickly graduate to using formulas and what-if manipulations once they become comfortable with their electronic worksheet.

"People put just about anything on a spreadsheet," says Riedel. "Any application that you can do with paper, pencil and a calculator you should be able to do better with a spreadsheet."

Source: Edward Foster, "Building Simple Spreadsheets," *Personal Computing*, January 1985, pp. 61–62.

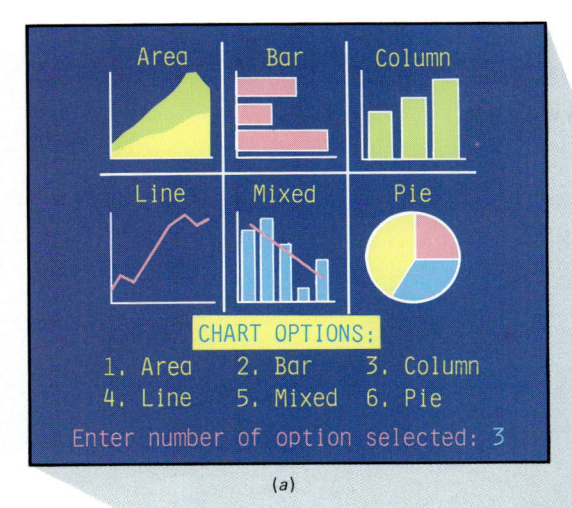

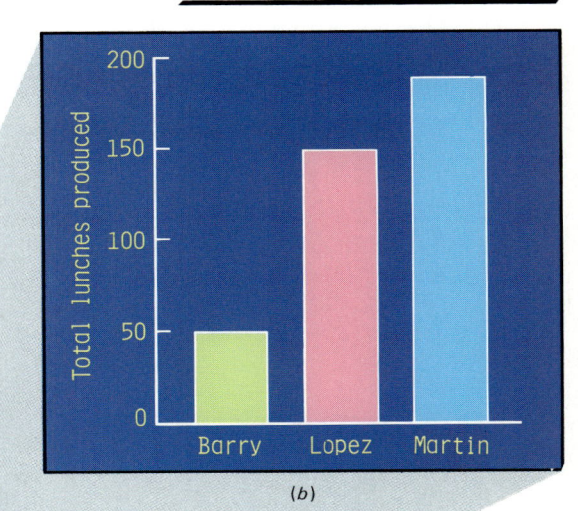

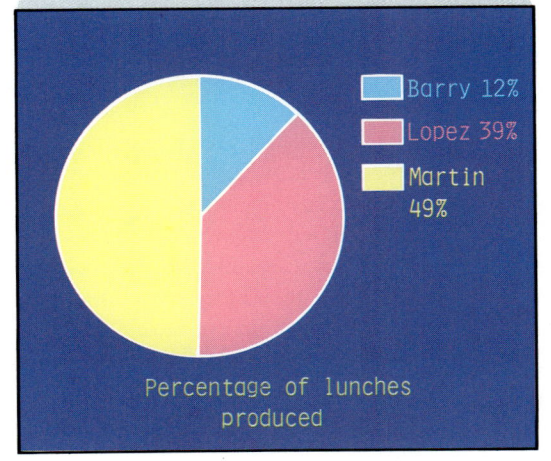

FIGURE 9-5

A graphics package can be used to bring numbers to life. Although data presented in graphic form are easier to absorb and remember, these visual aids were seldom used in the past because preparing them was time-consuming and therefore expensive. Now, however, many inexpensive and easy-to-use graphics packages are available for use with personal computers. The output of these packages may be effectively used to summarize and analyze data. In addition, the visual aids they produce are very helpful in making presentations to others.

or plotter can put the chart on paper, or a special camera can film the image presented on the display screen.

Data Base Management System Packages *File management systems (FMS)* and *data base management systems (DBMS)* were introduced in Chapter 2. These software packages allow people to (1) define data items, place these items into designated records, and then combine these records into designated files; (2) store these files on a direct-access storage medium such as a magnetic disk; and (3) access, retrieve, and maintain record and file contents as needed. Both types of packages can support many separate files. An FMS typically accesses records from only one file at a time, while a DBMS may access appropriate records from two or more files at once. We'll simplify matters here by using the broader DBMS designation for all packages that handle the tasks of creating, storing, accessing, and maintaining file and data base records.

DBMS packages are available for machines of all sizes. Some mainframe packages cost tens of thousands of dollars, are used to develop and support hundreds of applications in an organization, and are considered to be a part of the essential system software required by the installation. At the other extreme, a pc package may cost less than a hundred dollars and be used by an individual for a single purpose.

Uses of DBMS packages in organizations Let's go back a few years to see how departments in organizations often created their own computer applications. Each application typically had its own master file and processing program. The records in each file were generally organized according to a single key field. When this key field wasn't relevant to the information needed, the entire file might have to be searched. For example, to get the names of employees with a certain educational background from a personnel file organized by employee number might require a search of all file records. If the personnel department's need for such information became routine, a new file structured on an educational background key (and a new program to process it) might be created. Of course, this new file would duplicate much of the data stored in the first file. The problems created by this departmental file-oriented approach were (1) a great deal of data redundancy occurred and the cost of entering and storing the same data in many files was expensive; (2) it was also expensive to update many separate files, and changes in data items were made in some files and neglected in others; and (3) processing programs tied closely to specific files often had to be rewritten every time a data field in a file was added, deleted, or changed.

Dissatisfied with the problems caused by the departmental file-oriented approach, software designers began looking for ways to consolidate activities. The results of their efforts are found today in DBMS packages. When a data transaction is introduced into a DBMS, all the records affected by this transaction may be updated at the time of input. These updated data then become available as needed to all authorized users of the DBMS package. The package permits people to search and probe data base contents in order to extract answers to nonrecurring questions. These questions might initially be vague or poorly defined, but people can "browse" through the data base until they have the needed information. In short, the DBMS "manages" the needed data items and assembles them from the common data base in response to the queries of those who aren't programmers. In a file-oriented system, a user needing special information has to communicate this need to a programmer, who, when time permits, writes one or more programs to extract the data and prepare the information. A DBMS package gives all authorized users a much faster alternative (see Figure 9-6).

To illustrate the flexibility of a DBMS in an organization, let's assume that a personnel manager of a large multinational corporation has just received an emergency request to send an employee to a foreign country to fix a hydraulic pump that the company stopped making 6 years ago. The person needed must be a mechanical engineer, must have knowledge of the particular pump (and, therefore, let's assume, must have been with the corporation for at least 8 years), must be able to speak French, and must be willing to accept an overseas assignment. In the past, the manager might have spent hours going through a lengthy printout of the entire personnel file in order to locate employees who match the requirements. With a DBMS package, however, the manager can use an online station to request that personnel records be searched for the names and locations of French-speaking engineers with 8 or

FIGURE 9-6

An organization's DBMS package can give fast response to users with special information needs.

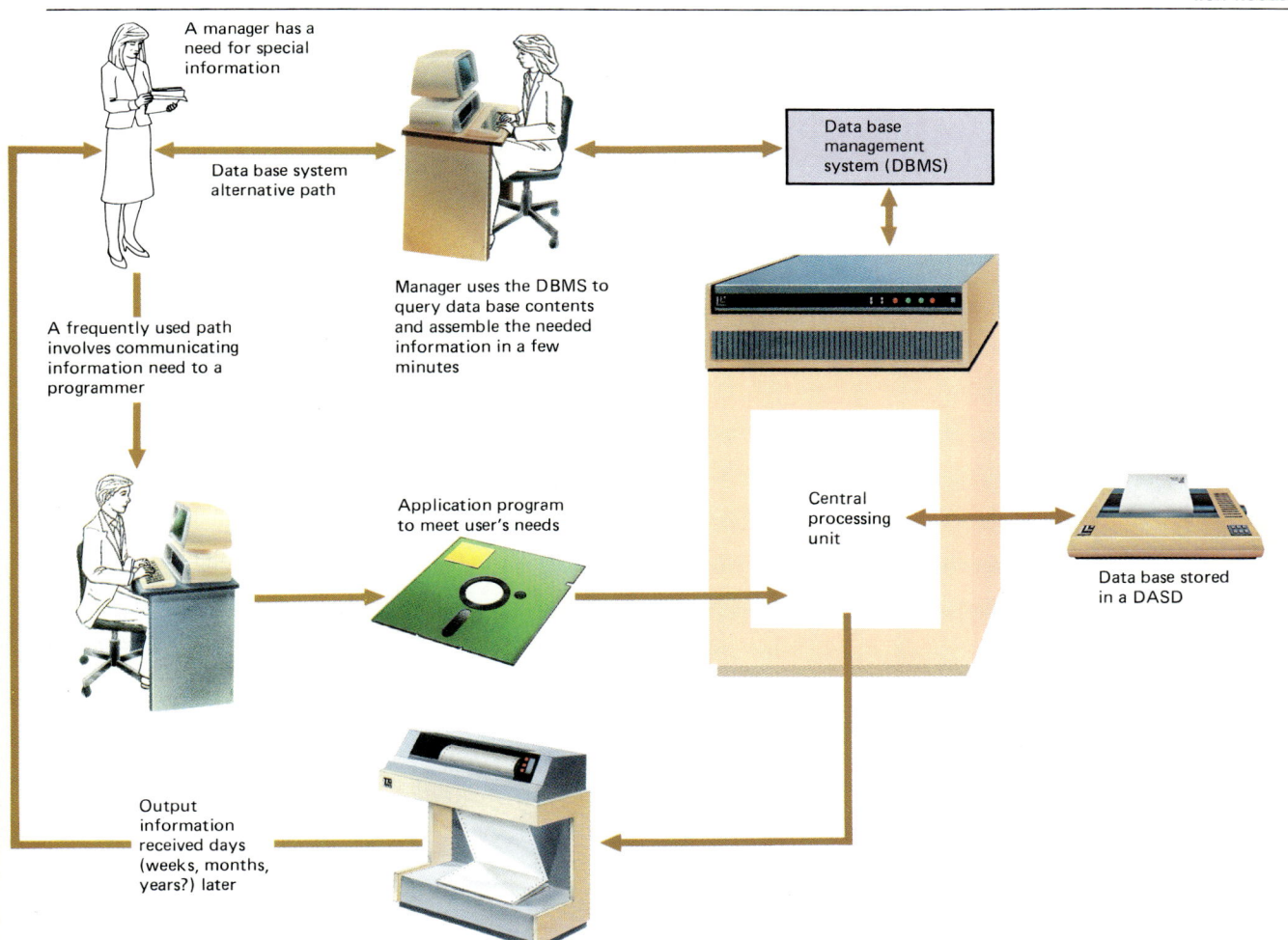

more years of company experience. Armed with such information obtained by the package in a few minutes, the manager can then contact the named employees to fill the overseas assignment.

Uses of DBMS packages by individuals If Jill Byter had used a DBMS package during her race for a seat in her college's Student House of Representatives (discussed in Chapter 2), her first step might have been to respond to DBMS package menus similar to those shown in Figure 9-7. The "create file" option is selected from the MAIN MENU (Figure 9-7a), and the CREATE FILE menu is then displayed on Jill's pc screen (Figure 9-7b). Jill gives the name STUDENTVOTER to the file she wants to build and then supplies a name and description for each of the data items that will be included in each file record.

After naming the file and defining the data items to be included, Jill can key in the data for each record by repeatedly filling in the appropriate spaces on the data entry screen shown again in Figure 9-8a. These records are stored on a floppy or hard disk in Jill's pc. After the data are entered into the file, Jill can tell the package what she wants it to do by selecting a choice from another menu (Figure 9-8b). Finally, as shown in Figures 9-8c through e, menu options can be used to maintain the STUDENTVOTER file by adding new records and changing and deleting existing ones.

You can use a pc and a DBMS package anytime you have facts that you need to store, manipulate, and retrieve. To name just a few examples, you can use DBMS software to keep automobile and other expense records; maintain records on your stamp, coin, or other collections; and file for easy retrieval and reference such information as recipes, price lists, names and addresses, telephone numbers, and dates of birthdays and anniversaries.

The logical structures of DBMS packages A DBMS package ties together the logically related data in one or more files by using one of the following structuring techniques during storage, access, and retrieval operations:

1 *List structures.* When a **list structure** is used, records are linked together by the use of pointers. A *pointer* is a data item in one record that identifies the storage location of another related record. The records in a

FIGURE 9-7

Users often respond to various menus to create and manipulate the files that are managed by DBMS packages. (a) In this example, the "create file" option is selected from a main menu. (b) The CREATE FILE menu allows the user to first enter the new file name and then give names and descriptions to each data item that will be included in the records of this file. Data Item 1, for example, is named "FName." The "A, 12" description means that the package should allocate room for 12 Alphanumeric characters in the FName field of each record. Similarly, Data Item 6 is named "Zip," and the package is told to make room for 5 Numeric characters in the Zip field of each record.

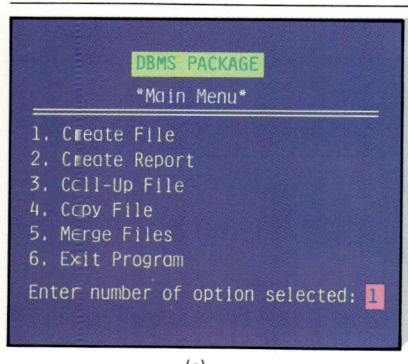

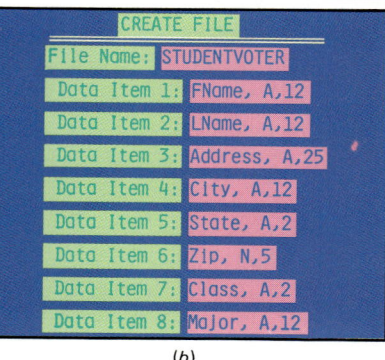

(a)
DBMS PACKAGE
Main Menu
1. Create File
2. Create Report
3. Call-Up File
4. Copy File
5. Merge Files
6. Exit Program
Enter number of option selected: 1

(b)
CREATE FILE
File Name: STUDENTVOTER
Data Item 1: FName, A,12
Data Item 2: LName, A,12
Data Item 3: Address, A,25
Data Item 4: City, A,12
Data Item 5: State, A,2
Data Item 6: Zip, N,5
Data Item 7: Class, A,2
Data Item 8: Major, A,12

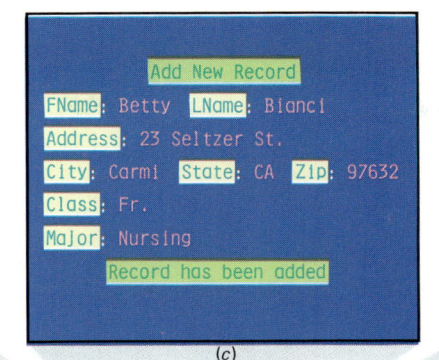

(a) Data Entry
FName: Adam LName: Abel
Address: 699 Hirt Place
City: Springs State: CA Zip: 98765
Class: So.
Major: English

(b) File Name: STUDENTVOTER
Menu of Options
1. Display records
2. Add/update/delete records
3. Sort records
4. Create report
5. Print report
6. Call up new file
7. Exit file
Enter number of option selected: 4

(c) Add New Record
FName: Betty LName: Bianci
Address: 23 Seltzer St.
City: Carmi State: CA Zip: 97632
Class: Fr.
Major: Nursing
Record has been added

(d) Update Record
FName: Maria LName: Martinez
Address: 8376 Westcliff Ave.
City: State: Zip:
Class:
Major:
Record has been updated

(e) Delete Record
FName: Joan LName: Decker
Record has been deleted

FIGURE 9-8

There are many ways that individuals can use DBMS packages. (a) After a file has been named and the data items for each file record have been identified and described, the user of a DBMS package enters the records into the file. Although not shown here, additional data such as hobbies, telephone numbers, birthdays, and so on, could have been placed in the student records. (b) This menu shows how the DBMS package can manipulate the records in a file to achieve the user's goals. By selecting option 4 and then option 5, the user can specify the output format desired and can then print mailing labels or many other kinds of documents. As we've seen in Chapter 2, the user can also select option 3 in the menu to sort records according to the students' study major, class standing, and/or Zip code, and then direct personalized appeals to the targeted students. (c) New records can be easily added to the DBMS file. (d) The package permits updates to existing records. (e) And it also allows the user to delete records stored in a file.

store's customer master file, for example, will contain the name and address of each customer, and each record in this file is identified by an account number. During an accounting period, a customer may charge a number of items on different days and pay on a monthly basis. Therefore, the company maintains an invoice file to reflect these transactions. A list structure could be used in this situation to show the unpaid invoices at any given time (see Figure 9-9).

2 *Hierarchical (tree) structures.* In this technique, data units are structured in multiple levels that graphically resemble an "upside-down" tree with the root at the top and the branches formed below. There's a superior-subordinate relationship in a **hierarchical (tree) structure** (see Figure 9-10).

3 *Network structures.* Unlike the tree approach, which does not permit the connection of branches, the **network structure** allows the linkage of the subordinate elements in a multidirectional manner (see Figure 9-11).

4 *Relational structures.* A **relational structure** is made up of many tables. Data are stored in the form of "relations" in these tables. For example, relation tables could be established to link a college course with the instructor of the course and with the location of the class (see Figure 9-12).

Relational structures are popular today because they are simple and adaptable. It's easy to ask a relational DBMS new and unusual questions because anything may be related to anything else. If the data are in storage, the user can generally get to them. But a purely relational DBMS package has no preexisting links, and so it may take longer to locate the needed data. Hierarchical and network models are likely to be faster when the necessary data linkages are present, but they may lack the flexibility of the relational structure.

Communications Packages There are several types of *communications packages* that facilitate the flow of data throughout a network of computers and workstations. One type allows communication *between* pc's and other stations so that the *electronic mail/message activities* described in Chapter 8 can be carried out. A second type of package permits communication between pc's and the online data banks that were also discussed in Chapter 8. Figure 9-13 shows again the use of these two types of packages.

A third type of communications package provides a linkage between pc's and mainframe systems. These **micro-to-mainframe linkage programs** access the data stored in an organization's mainframe system. These facts may be retained in a format used by the mainframe, and the pc may then use appropriate hardware and software to imitate a mainframe terminal. Or the mainframe data may be converted into a format used by the pc. Many micro-to-mainframe packages access mainframe data through the mainframe's DBMS software. These facts are then supplied to the pc in a form that's immediately usable by some popular spreadsheet and integrated software packages.

Data from central data bases can be copied and stored on floppy disks at many different locations. People can then enter this "real data" into their spreadsheet models and manipulate them for planning and decision-making purposes. Serious problems could develop, however, if pc users are allowed to change the contents of important central data files. Maintaining the security

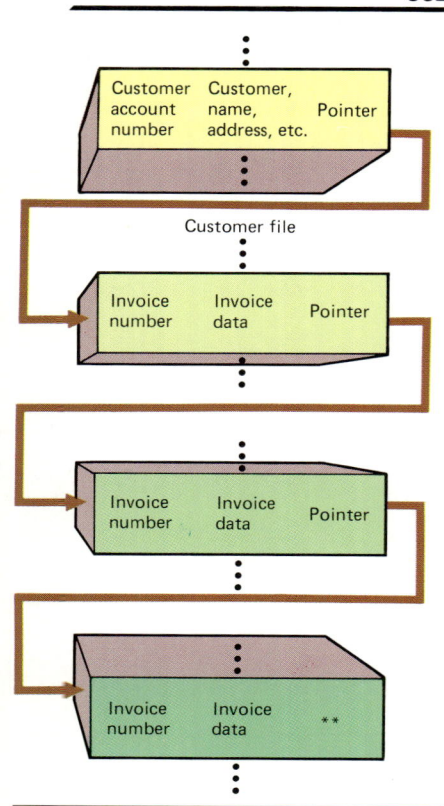

FIGURE 9-9

A list structure. Each record in the customer file would contain a field that points to the record location of the first invoice for that customer in the invoice file. This invoice record, in turn, would use a pointer (or link field) to show the record location or address of the next invoice record for the customer. The last invoice in the chain would be identified by the use of a special character as a pointer.

CHAPTER 9

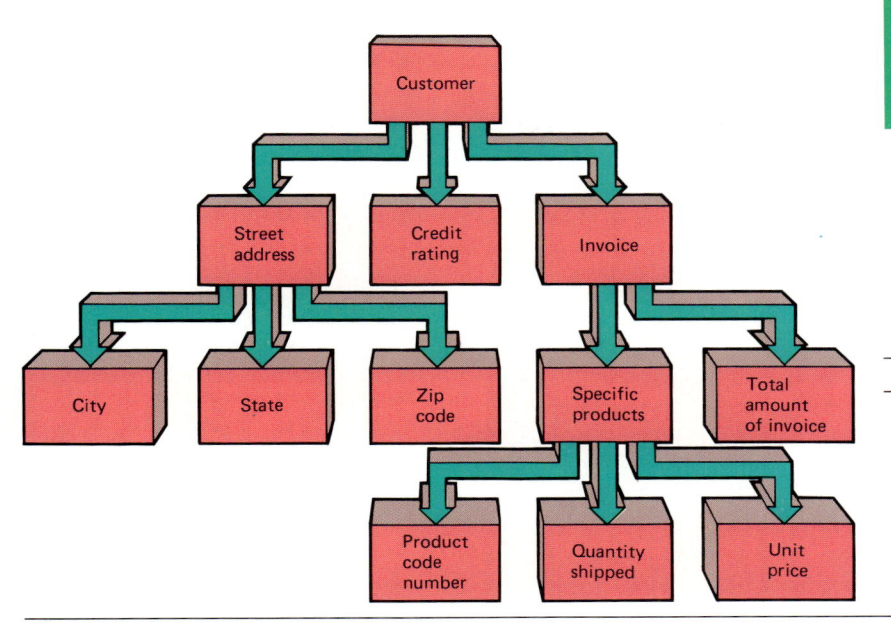

333

FIGURE 9-10

A hierarchical (tree) structure. Below the single-root data component are subordinate elements or nodes, each of which, in turn, "owns" one or more other elements (or none). Each element or branch in this structure below the root has only a single owner. Thus a customer owns an invoice, and the invoice has subordinate items. The branches in a tree structure are not connected.

FIGURE 9-11

A network structure. Each node may have several owners and may, in turn, own any number of other data units. Data management software permits the extraction of the needed information from such a structure by beginning with any record in a file.

FIGURE 9-12

A relational structure. To find the name of the instructor and the location of the English class, the course/instructor relation is searched to get the name ("Fitt"), and the course/location relation is searched to get the class location ("Main 142"). Many other relations are, of course, possible.

| Course/Instructor Relation ||
COURSE	INSTRUCTOR
ENGLISH 103	FITT
SCIENCE 116	GOMEZ
MATH 101	PIRELLI
⋮	⋮

| Course/Location Relation ||
COURSE	LOCATION
ENGLISH 103	MAIN 142
MATH 101	SCIENCE 125
SCIENCE 116	SCIENCE 111
⋮	⋮

Other Relations

For example, course related to time of meeting, days of meeting, hours of credit, etc.

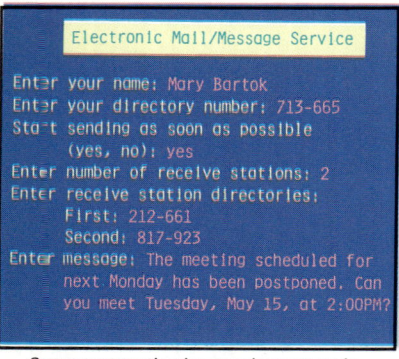

```
        Electronic Mail/Message Service
Enter your name: Mary Bartok
Enter your directory number: 713-665
Start sending as soon as possible
      (yes, no): yes
Enter number of receive stations: 2
Enter receive station directories:
      First: 212-661
      Second: 817-923
Enter message: The meeting scheduled for
      next Monday has been postponed. Can
      you meet Tuesday, May 15, at 2:00PM?
```

Some communications packages permit users to send and receive electronic mail.

(a)

```
        Data Bank Selection Menu
    1. Dow Jones News/Retrieval
    2. The Source
    3. CompuServe
    4. BRS/Search
    5. Dialog
    6. NEXIS
    7. Orbit Search Service
    8. Exit

    Enter number of selection: 2
```

Communications packages can also put computer users in touch with a world of stored information with just a few keystrokes.

(b)

FIGURE 9-13

(a) With the help of an appropriate communications package, data available at one location can be distributed electronically to other locations. Users in the other locations can retrieve and examine the data at their convenience and then fire off responses and other messages if necessary. (b) Communications packages also facilitate the retrieval of data stored in the huge online libraries maintained by outside information services. Instead of dialing a 10-digit number and then keying in a password and/or user number every time a data bank is accessed, a subscriber to the data bank can use a communications package that will automatically dial and log on. Log-off procedures are also handled automatically by the package.

and integrity of those files is a major concern for any organization. Thus linkage packages should provide close control over which pc users can access specific data.

Project/Time Management Packages   You saw in Chapter 2 that a *project management package* helps people plan, schedule, and control the human and material resources required to complete projects on time and for a reasonable cost, while a *time management package* is an aid that people can use to plan and control their own use of time more effectively. Figures 9-14 and 9-15 summarize again the use of such packages.

Outlining Packages   An example of an *outlining package* was also presented in Chapter 2, and is summarized again here in Figure 9-16. The ability to outline a document with headings and subheadings and then expand, col-

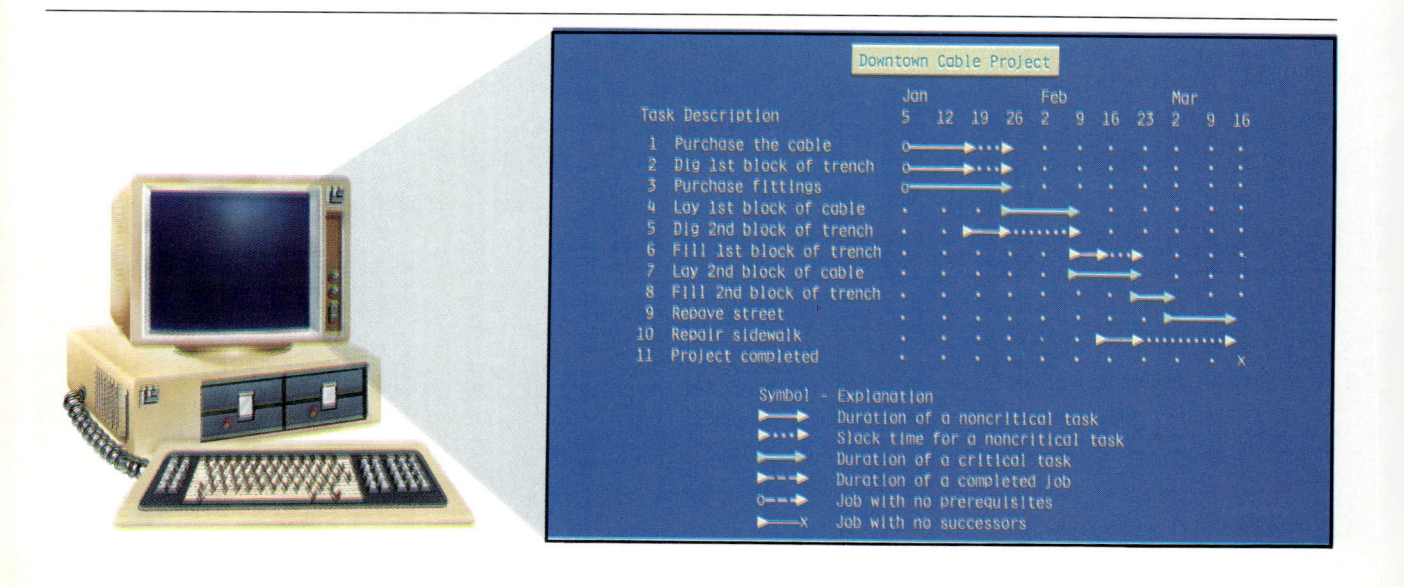

```
                    Downtown Cable Project
                         Jan           Feb           Mar
Task Description         5  12  19  26  2   9  16  23  2   9  16
 1  Purchase the cable
 2  Dig 1st block of trench
 3  Purchase fittings
 4  Lay 1st block of cable
 5  Dig 2nd block of trench
 6  Fill 1st block of trench
 7  Lay 2nd block of cable
 8  Fill 2nd block of trench
 9  Repave street
10  Repair sidewalk
11  Project completed

Symbol - Explanation
  ───▶    Duration of a noncritical task
  ····▶   Slack time for a noncritical task
  ═══▶    Duration of a critical task
  ---▶    Duration of a completed job
  o──▶    Job with no prerequisites
  ───x    Job with no successors
```

335

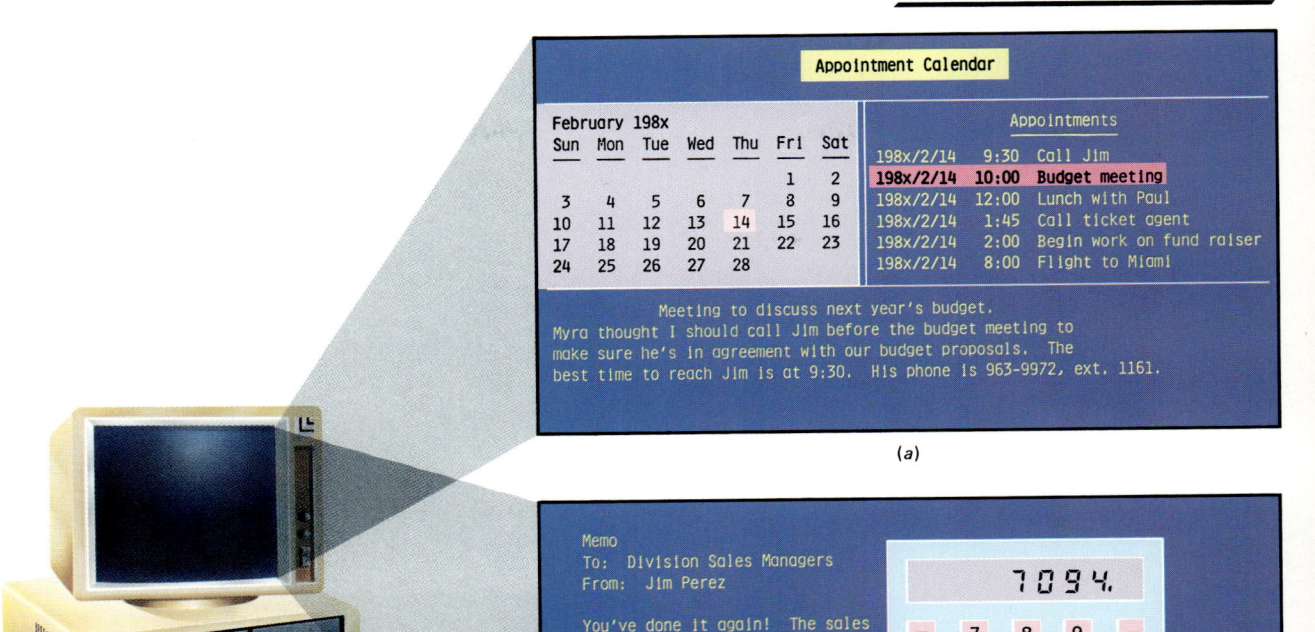

(a)

(b)

FIGURE 9-15

(a) With a time management package, a user can store appointments, names, addresses, phone lists, expenses, things to do, ideas that need to be followed up, and so on. The time management program typically resides in an out-of-the-way place in the computer's primary storage area while the user is doing other things, but the program and the data entrusted to its care are always available to the user with a few keystrokes. (b) For example, if a user is preparing a document with a WP program and wants to total a column of figures in the text, he can retrieve the time management package's visual desk calculator, make his computations, and then return to his place in the document with a keystroke. Or if a user is working on a spreadsheet and someone calls to cancel a meeting, she can quickly retrieve her appointment calendar and view her future plans before rescheduling the meeting. As she stores the new appointment in her calendar, she can also store any thoughts that occur to her about this meeting. A keystroke then takes her back to where she was in the spreadsheet before the phone rang.

◀ **FIGURE 9-14** *(facing page)*

A project management package can help an engineer plan, schedule, and control an underground electrical cable project. The package user identifies the project activities that must be performed, determines the sequence in which those activities must be carried out, and estimates the time interval needed to complete each activity. Once these steps have been entered and stored in the system, the program then identifies the *longest* sequence of events in the project. The sum of the individual activity times in this sequence becomes the total project time, and this sequence of activities is known as the *critical path*. By focusing attention on the activities in the critical path, the user can quickly pinpoint potential problems. If a critical activity begins to fall behind schedule, stored data can be retrieved to determine what steps can be taken to correct the situation.

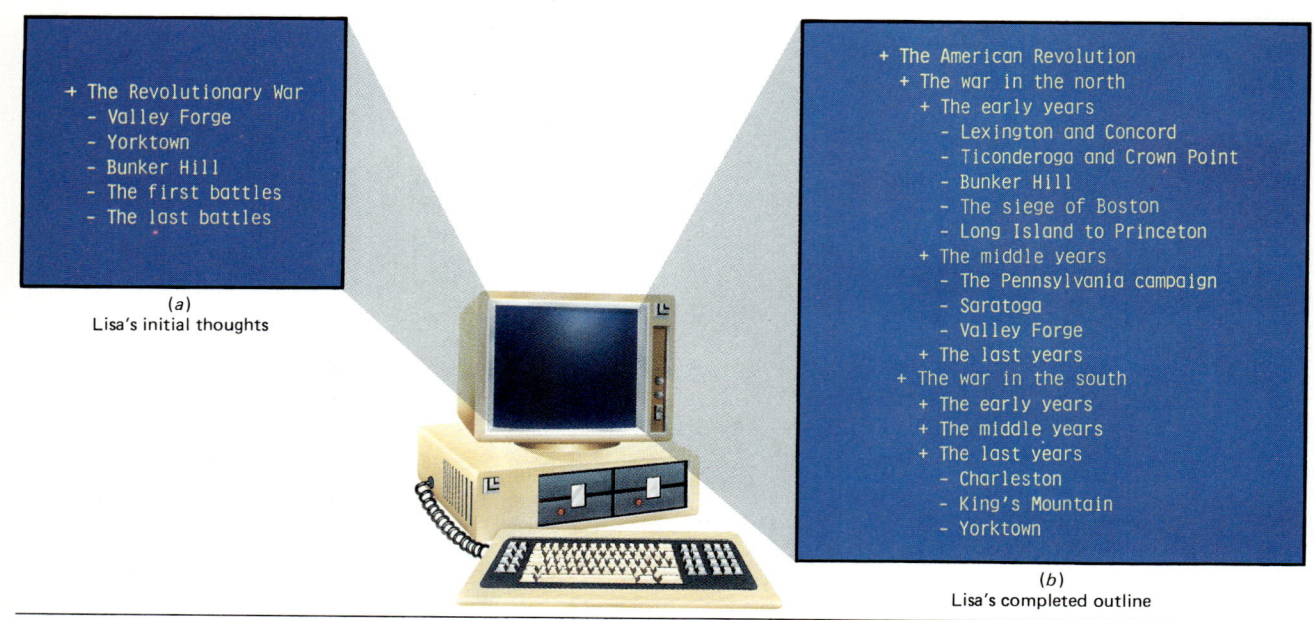

```
+ The Revolutionary War
  - Valley Forge
  - Yorktown
  - Bunker Hill
  - The first battles
  - The last battles
```
(a)
Lisa's initial thoughts

```
+ The American Revolution
  + The war in the north
    + The early years
      - Lexington and Concord
      - Ticonderoga and Crown Point
      - Bunker Hill
      - The siege of Boston
      - Long Island to Princeton
    + The middle years
      - The Pennsylvania campaign
      - Saratoga
      - Valley Forge
    + The last years
  + The war in the south
    + The early years
    + The middle years
    + The last years
      - Charleston
      - King's Mountain
      - Yorktown
```
(b)
Lisa's completed outline

FIGURE 9-16

Outlining packages are designed to process ideas. (a) The user (Lisa Byter) has picked a subject for a history paper and has entered some preliminary thoughts on the topics she'll cover. Entries preceded by a plus sign have subheadings; those beginning with a minus sign have no lower levels. Signs can be changed and entries can be enlarged or rearranged. (b) The original ideas entered at random may then be quickly refined and reorganized to produce a finished outline.

lapse, or move these headings around is an important characteristic of outline processors. Some suppliers of WP packages have built outline programs into their software, just as they have merged spelling checkers into their products. In one WP package, for example, the text associated with an outline heading moves along with the heading every time the outline is changed.

"Mindware" Packages A number of controversial **"mindware" packages** with psychological overtones have been introduced. Some packages allow users to flash messages of their choice on display screens so fast that while the eye can't transmit them to the conscious brain, they are allegedly picked up and retained by the subconscious mind. One purpose of these packages is presumably to alter the user's bad habits (the message flashed might be "Stop Smoking").

The goal of some other packages is to help users get what they want from "opponents" (clients, customers, bosses, employees, teachers, and so on) during meetings and negotiating sessions. Designed with *expert system* overtones (remember the discussion in Chapter 3 on artificial intelligence?), these programs ask users dozens of questions about themselves and their opponents. After processing all the user answers, mindware packages may then summarize the negotiating situation, analyze the personalities involved, and recommend the tactics and strategies that the user can employ during the actual meetings. Many psychologists question the effectiveness and desirability of mindware programs, as you'll see in the Projects/Issues section at the end of this chapter.

WINDOW 9-2

HYPERTEXT

Text written on paper must be in a specific order. This chapter, for instance, has a particular order of paragraphs, and you will normally read it from beginning to end in sequential fashion.

But computer-based information is not bound by the restrictions imposed by paper. With computers it is possible to call up small packets of information in any order the reader desires. This concept has been called nonsequential text, or "hypertext," and it is slowly gaining adherents in computer science. With hypertext, a document can be prepared that people can look at at various levels.

The concept of nonsequential text is not easy to grasp, but one analogy might be tours through a museum. Some provide a single route that takes a visitor past all the exhibits. Others concentrate on certain exhibits and by-pass others.

Similarly, an electronic hypertext document would offer choices. For instance, a person reading a hypertext article about a company would have a choice of how much detail he or she wanted on the company's history and how much on finances. The concepts have been used in some electronic novels and computer games, in which the plot changes depending on the choices made by the player.

But hypertext would also allow users to link different documents. Encyclopedias, for instance, now often contain cross-references to other articles, which in turn contain cross-references to still others. But following the cross-references is tedious. With a hypertext encyclopedia, a reader could press a button and jump to the relevant parts of the cross-referenced article and from there to another cross-referenced article. In short, one could hop from article to article following a given idea. Similarly, instead of just seeing a reference to another book in a footnote, a reader could move immediately to the relevant part of that book.

This system is more advanced than traditional data banks, which permit the retrieval of documents quickly, but do not allow movement from one document to the middle of another.

Although the first hypertext system was developed in the 1960s, it is only now that computer technology has improved enough to allow such programs to become more widespread. Brown University has developed a system for use on the Macintosh computer that will be used in English courses as a way of providing students with information and comments on the literature being read.

Another system for managing information in software development is being tested by Tektronix, an electronics company. Such software projects involve huge numbers of documents and when a change is made, such as in a design specification, it often requires changing many documents. Using the hypertext system, with the relevant parts of the various documents connected by electronic links, it is easy to make those changes.

Hypertext might also be used in computer programs to help people write papers. Simple concepts related to hypertext are appearing in personal computer programs such as Thinktank by Living Videotext and Framework by Ashton-Tate. These programs, sometimes called outline processors or idea processors, allow users to manipulate blocks of data into outline form.

Notecards, a program developed at Xerox Corporation's Palo Alto Research Center, also aims at this market and is more sophisticated. It is the electronic version of the system, long used by college students, of taking notes on index cards. But paper index cards must be arranged in sequence. And the student writer may not know at first whether George Washington's battles will be in the section of the report dealing with George Washington's life or with the Revolutionary War. With paper index cards, the student must choose or else make duplicate cards. With the Notecards program, however, ideas do not have to be organized in a linear outline. The system allows any card to be connected to any other in a complex network. The writer can envision a system of cards with lines between them, like a map of cities and connecting highways.

Of course, the report writer eventually must organize the various thoughts into a sequential pattern, so they can be printed on paper. But the Notecards program makes all of the possible alternatives instantly available so that the writer may choose the organization that works the best.

Adapted from Andrew Pollack, "Technology: Data Retrieval Improvements," *The New York Times*, Aug. 29, 1985. Copyright © 1985 by The New York Times Company. Reprinted by permission.

FEEDBACK

Feedback and Review 9

Let's test and reinforce your understanding of the prewritten software material presented in this chapter. Answer the following *true-false* questions by placing a T or an F in the space provided.

_____ 1. An application program performs the same functions as a system software program, and both are generally written by users.

_____ 2. Single-function applications programs can be classified into special-purpose and general-purpose categories.

_____ 3. An example of a general-purpose package is a program to play chess.

_____ 4. A system software package is designed to operate, control, and extend the processing capabilities of the computer itself.

_____ 5. System software packages are seldom written by their users.

_____ 6. An operating system is an example of a system software package.

_____ 7. Special-purpose applications programs are available for law offices but not medical offices.

_____ 8. Computer-assisted instruction (CAI) is a learning method in which a student interacts with, and is guided by, a program through a course of study aimed at achieving certain instructional goals.

_____ 9. The most complicated form of CAI is the drill-and-practice approach.

_____ 10. A tutorial CAI package imitates the actions of a private and patient tutor.

_____ 11. A paint system is a software package that may be used in graphics applications.

_____ 12. A personal financial management package may be designed to help people monitor their financial condition.

_____ 13. A word processing (WP) program is often the backbone application package in an electronic office.

_____ 14. A spelling checker element in a WP package will catch all the typographical errors made by users.

_____ 15. A WP package may include either a spelling checker or an in-context thesaurus, but both elements aren't possible in the same program.

_____ 16. Spreadsheet templates provide layout designs complete with the formulas needed to process common applications.

_____ 17. A graphics package is always combined with a spreadsheet program.

_____ 18. A file management system typically accesses records from only one file at a time, while a data base management system (DBMS) may access appropriate records from two or more files at once.

_____ 19. DBMS packages are used exclusively on personal computers.

_____ 20. All DBMS packages use the relational structuring technique during storage and retrieval operations.

_____ 21. A relational structure in a DBMS is made up of many tables.

_____ 22. Communications packages can be used to support electronic mail systems.

_____ 23. A micro-to-mainframe linkage program should permit pc users to browse through central data bases and manipulate any of the records in the central files.

_____ 24. Project and time management programs may be helpful in planning and controlling the use of scarce resources.

LOOKING BACK

1. Software can be classified into prewritten packages—the subject of Chapters 9 and 10—and custom-made programs—the topic of Chapters 11 and 12. Included under the prewritten package category are various types of applications and system software packages. This chapter has concentrated on single-function applications packages that are written for special and general purposes. A discussion of integrated packages and operating system software is presented in the next chapter.

2. Examples of the types of special-purpose packages used in organizations and in homes are given in the chapter. These examples include law- and medical-office software, educational programs for schools and homes, and hobby and entertainment packages. As their classification suggests, general-purpose applications are likely to be used in both homes and offices. The general-purpose packages considered in the chapter are those used to process words, manipulate spreadsheets, prepare graphics, manage files and data bases, communicate information, manage projects and time, and prepare outlines. A controversial "mindware" category has also been included.

3. Word processing (WP) packages are used to create, view, edit, store, retrieve, and print text material. An amazingly flexible tool, a WP package may permit a user to call up prerecorded paragraphs from the dozens that may be in storage. These paragraphs may then be merged to create a new document. A spelling checker may be used to locate suspicious words, and an in-text thesaurus may be used to call up suitable synonyms for words in a document.

4. A spreadsheet package manipulates data that have been organized into columns and rows. The spreadsheet created by a typical package may have dozens of columns and hundreds of rows. There are thus thousands of intersections, or cells, where columns and rows meet. Users can create layout designs and specify the relationships that exist between cells, or they can buy templates of common layouts complete with the formulas needed to process specific applications. Spreadsheets are particularly useful in providing quick answers to "what if" questions. Graphics packages may be used to portray visually the relationships revealed by spreadsheet analysis, but graphics packages can also be used to chart data from many other sources.

5. A data base management system (DBMS) package handles the tasks associated with creating, storing, accessing, and maintaining file and data base records. Originally designed to reduce expensive data duplication and other problems in organizations, DBMSs now are available to individuals as well as organizations. Examples of DBMS usage are given in the chapter, and the structures employed by DBMS packages are briefly described.

6. Several types of communications packages are discussed. One type facilitates electronic mail/message activities, another permits communication between pc's and online data banks, and a third provides a micro-to-mainframe linkage. The project and time management packages that are helpful in planning and controlling the use of scarce resources are considered, outlining packages are reviewed, and "mindware" packages are discussed.

KEY TERMS AND CONCEPTS

prewritten software packages 318
custom-made programs 318
single-function applications packages 318
special-purpose packages 318
general-purpose packages 318
integrated-function packages 318

system software package 318
computer-assisted instruction (CAI) 320
drill-and-practice approach 320
tutorial CAI package 320
educational games and simulations 321
paint systems 321
electronic offices 322
spelling checker 324

global search 324
search and replace 324
in-context thesaurus 324
spreadsheet templates 325
list structure 330
hierarchical (tree) structure 332
network structure 332
relational structure 332
micro-to-mainframe linkage programs 332
"mindware" packages 336

TOPICS FOR REVIEW AND DISCUSSION

1. (c) How may software be classified? (b) Give an example of software in each of the categories you've identified.
2. (a) What's a system software package? (b) What's the difference between applications packages and system software packages?
3. (a) Give two examples of ways that special-purpose packages may be used in organizations. (b) And give two more examples of how such packages may be used in homes.
4. (c) What's computer-assisted instruction? (b) How may student and program interaction take place in a CAI setting?
5. What's the difference between drill-and-practice CAI and tutorial CAI?
6. "Both individuals and organizations find WP to be an amazingly flexible tool." Discuss this statement.
7. "A spelling checker will catch all the typographical errors made by users of WP packages." Explain why this statement is false.
8. (a) What are electronic spreadsheets? (b) How are these spreadsheets used? (c) What's a spreadsheet template?
9. What control does a user have over the output produced by a graphics package?
10. (a) What functions are performed by data base management systems (DBMSs)? (b) Why were DBMSs introduced into organizations? (c) How are DBMSs used in organizations? (d) How are they used by individuals?
11. Identify and discuss three logical structuring techniques used in DBMS packages.
12. Identify and discuss three tasks performed by communications packages.
13. (a) How are project management packages used? (b) How are time management packages used? (c) How are outlining packages used?
14. Why do you think "mindware" packages have provoked controversy?

Projects/Issues to Consider

1. In discussing mindware packages, Jerry Pournelle, a science-fiction writer with a Ph.D. in psychology, noted in the November 1984 issue of *Popular Computing* that expert systems claims were being made for the programs designed to help users "win" in negotiating sessions. The problem with these claims and with these programs, he noted, is that in the areas covered by the programs there are no *human* experts. The programs claim to do what people can't do. He agrees that computers can certainly do some things that people can't manage in the time allotted for the tasks. But he writes that there's quite a difference between a medical diagnosis and a psychological diagnosis. In a medical diagnosis, scientific and objective facts (such as the presence or absence of bacilli or the measurement of bodily functions) underlie the diagnosis, but similar objective facts are often unavailable to support a psychological diagnosis. His conclusion is that mindware programs running on pc's won't produce scientific facts when they are based on unproven social theory. Program producers, of course, dispute Pournelle's position. Research the mindware package controversy, form your own opinions about the effectiveness and desirability of such programs, and present your findings to the class.

2. Sales figures for prewritten software packages are published regularly. The problem with these figures, even when they are released at about the same time, is that they often vary by billions of dollars. Gather current software sales figures from several sources, and note the variations in current and projected totals. Write a report outlining your findings and suggesting some reasons for these huge variations.

3. Select a type of application of interest to you—word processing, accounting, entertainment, educational, scientific, and so on. Identify three possible packages that could be used to process your application. List the features and hardware requirements of each package. Which package would you buy and how would you buy it?

Answers to Feedback and Review Section

1. F 2. T 3. F 4. T 5. T 6. T 7. F 8. T 9. F 10. T 11. T 12. T 13. T 14. F 15. F 16. T 17. F 18. T 19. F 20. F 21. T 22. T 23. F 24. T

A CLOSER LOOK

HOW A WORD PROCESSING PROGRAM WORKS

By Paul Lutus, author of the Apple Writer word processing program

Computers do word processing almost naturally, and nearly every personal computer installation includes some kind of word processing program. When the computer is manipulating text, the keyboard and display take the place of a typewriter, putting us on relatively familiar terrain.

Basic word processing functions can be broken into two main categories: text editing and print formatting. Text editing features include the ability to enter, edit and delete text with ease, speed and flexibility. Also necessary is the ability to find any arbitrary character string and replace it with another. Advanced functions include the ability to automate completely certain text editing tasks and to define sentences or control sequences that are then made available with a single keystroke.

Print formatting functions include the ability to print the file created with the text editor, read embedded formatting commands and carry them out, and provide various margins and text justifications (e.g., left and right flush, centered, fill). Early text editors intended for use by programmers were mated with print formatters and sold as word processors. The newer products are fully integrated software packages in which the text editor and print formatter functions are simultaneously available without changing program environments.

Following is a description of the simplest text editing function and the computer's accompanying actions. In this example, the cursor (the text editor's point of action) is moved into a line of text, then a word is added. The text editor's file is normally retained in the computer's memory while the work is being performed. Each typed character is placed, as a number, in the next available memory location.

Display
The quick brown fox

Memory Address	Number	Character
1	84	T
2	104	h
3	101	e
4	32	
5	113	q
6	117	u
7	105	i
8	99	c
9	107	k
10	32	
11	98	b
12	114	r
13	111	o
14	119	w
15	110	n
16	32	
17	102	f
18	111	o
19	120	x
20	32	

Note that spaces in the example are represented by the number 32. Each character or text formatting action has a number. The command to move the printer's carriage down and to the left, for instance, is assigned the number 13. When you press RETURN, the number 13 is placed in the computer's memory.

Now the cursor is moved left along the typed line. When the cursor position is changed, some of the characters are moved up into higher memory locations to make room for subsequent text insertions:

Display
The very quick brown fox

Memory Address	Number	Character
1	84	T
2	104	h
3	101	e
4	32	
985	113	q
986	117	u
987	105	i
988	99	c
989	107	k
990	32	
991	98	b
992	114	r
993	111	o
994	119	w
995	110	n
996	32	
997	102	f
998	111	o
999	120	x
1000	32	

Now a new word is typed at the cursor position:

Display
The very quick brown fox

Memory Address	Number	Character
1	84	T
2	104	h
3	101	e
4	32	
5	118	v
6	101	e
7	114	r
8	121	y
9	32	
985	113	q
986	117	u
987	105	i
988	99	c
989	107	k
990	32	
991	98	b
992	114	r
993	111	o
994	119	w
995	110	n
996	32	
997	102	f
998	111	o
999	120	x
1000	32	

Even though the file has two memory segments, the display shows them as an integrated whole. This has the advantage that in most common text manipulation actions only one character needs to be moved or saved, adding to program speed. Most text editing functions include this basic scheme. Text search and replacement involves moving characters between the file's high and low memory segments, searching for the desired text, then performing deletions and insertions as instructed by the user's entry.

Placing the text in the computer's memory makes it possible to perform fast text manipulation and display. The drawback is that file length cannot exceed available memory. The normal solution to this problem is to break the file into segments, each of which can fit in memory. An alternate method is to read and write to a mass storage device as text editing takes place. This method shields the user from memory limitations but is often very slow.

The word processor should work consistently no matter which function is being performed. There should also be consistency in how the characters are typed in or moved or deleted. And while the cursor is being moved about, it should not be necessary to shift from one function to another. This type of "mode-free" design is included in only about a quarter of personal computer word processors. In order to be mode-free, a word processor must work overtime. For example, pressing a key in Apple Writer often changes only one displayed character, but 1,920 characters are drawn from memory, formatted and placed on display. (This is always done, even for functions that don't need it, so the user won't have to think about modes.) Such a display requirement mandates the use of the fastest possible computer code: assembly language. Other functions, such as search and replace, greatly benefit from fast coding. For these and other reasons, word processors written in slow high-level languages are almost never mode-free.

Let's discuss program control for a moment, using Apple Writer as an example. In its normal state, the program takes keyboard entries and adds them to a memory buffer, updates the display, then awaits the next typed character. This sequence accompanies the typing of normal characters such as upper- and lower-case alphabetic, numeric and punctuation characters.

Another kind of keyboard entry is accompanied by the control key. Control entries, and the use of the arrow keys on Apple II computers, cause special control subroutines to be executed. The selected control subroutine may move the cursor, load or save a file, change display characteristics, format and print a file or perform some more exotic function. These subroutines are designed to be unobtrusive in direct proportion to their likelihood of use. Text search, file loading and saving, and a handful of other functions carry out their tasks without erasing the text display, while other less frequently used commands may display a selection menu of their own.

There are many fundamental improvements yet to be made in word processing. The most important is to replace the keyboard with the human voice, a task that is currently receiving a lot of attention in computer labs across the country. Some improvements will have to wait for faster machines with more memory, although a few existing programs seem to have resigned themselves to making you wait.

Remember this about word processing: If the program mystifies you, if its actions aren't obvious, if it displays cryptic error messages, if an hourglass appears and stays like a dying relative, it's not your fault. Computers are powerful enough, and programmers get paid well enough, to no longer excuse program actions that are comprehensible only to another computer. If the program won't hold your hand, don't turn in your hand—turn in the program.

Source: Paul Lutus, "How a Word Processing Program Works," *Digital Deli*, Steve Ditlea, ed. Copyright © 1984 by Steve Ditlea. Workman Publishing, New York. Reprinted by permission of the publisher.

CHAPTER 10

PREWRITTEN SOFTWARE:
INTEGRATED PACKAGES, PACKAGE SELECTION, AND OPERATING SYSTEMS

LIVE AID'S BACKSTAGE HEROES

Scheduling hundreds of rock performers on two stages an ocean apart and broadcasting the concert, live and on tape, to the planet for 16 consecutive hours had all the makings of a logistical nightmare of global proportions. But before the first guitar note was played at the 1985 Live Aid benefit for Ethiopia famine relief, a volunteer corps of personal computer users helped turn the event into a nearly seamless spectacle seen by millions of people around the world.

Susan Secord, Live Aid's scheduling systems manager, started with two Macintosh computers and a printer at Philadelphia's Four Seasons Hotel the week of the concert. Only days before the July 13, 1985 event, the producers of Live Aid put out an urgent call for more help. Students at nearby Drexel University, where there are more Macs than freshmen (thanks to a computer literacy requirement), came to the rescue with their machines.

Jazz software was used to produce a minute-by-minute schedule. Using the Jazz worksheet, Secord constructed a grid of almost 1,000 rows, listing each minute from 7 A.M. (EST), the time of singer/organizer Bob Geldof's opening in England, through 11 P.M., the curtain close in Philadelphia. Occupying the columns to the right were the names of performers in both Britain and the United States, which acts were being shown on the Diamond Vision giant screen in the Philadelphia stadium, and what video was being sent to the various networks including MTV, ABC, a syndicated service to stations in the United States, and a "World Truck" transmission overseas. A separate column noted which bands needed to be taped for delayed showing in instances where a group in England was performing at the same time as a group in America. Such details as televising the landing of Phil Collins' Concorde in New York and slotting the Led Zeppelin reunion and Mick Jagger/Tina Turner act all had to be entered on the worksheet. The printout filled 32 pages.

Secord used the Macintosh's mouse to drag each column to the appropriate width. She only had to type in the minutes for the first hour, since she was able to copy progressively larger blocks to fill out the rest of the worksheet. Last-minute changes were easily accomplished as in the case when the group Tears for Fears dropped out and was replaced by George Thorogood And The Destroyers. When one operator repeatedly spelled Mick Jagger's name "Mik," a universal search and replace corrected the error.

One of the Drexel volunteers, Denise Wall, a third-year mechanical engineering student, helped supervise the transcribing of hundreds of pages of script from Thursday afternoon until dawn Saturday. Things were so hectic that at one point she had both her hands on mice connected to a pair of Macs. Exclaimed Wall, "Our motto was: Anytime someone swears, save it!" (Saving work on-screen averaged once every seven minutes, she added.)

Mike Mitchell, president of Worldwide Sports & Entertainment Inc., which managed the event, commented, "Because of its complexity, there is no way that Live Aid could have been produced without the aid of computers."

From Michael Antonoff, "Live Aid's Backstage Heroes," *Personal Computing*, November 1985.

CHAPTER 10
347

LOOKING AHEAD

The discussion of prewritten software we began in Chapter 9 is continued in this chapter. Our first purpose in Chapter 10 is to examine software that's designed to integrate several applications in a single package. Next, we'll outline some steps you can follow to select prewritten applications packages. Finally, we'll summarize the tasks carried out by operating system software. The information in this chapter will enable you to:

- Explain the reasons for the integration of applications programs and outline the forms of integration used
- Identify and select applications packages of interest
- Outline the role of operating system software and describe some of the tasks performed by such software

CHAPTER OUTLINE

LOOKING AHEAD
INTEGRATION OF APPLICATIONS PROGRAMS
IDENTIFYING AND SELECTING APPLICATIONS PACKAGES
Identifying Suitable Applications Packages
Narrowing the Field
Making the Final Decisions
SYSTEM SOFTWARE: THE OPERATING SYSTEM
Control Programs in an OS
Processing Programs in an OS
Feedback and Review 10
LOOKING BACK

*I*NTEGRATION OF APPLICATIONS PROGRAMS

Some people find that one program allows them to do all they want to do with a computer. But others need to run several programs on a regular basis, and that need can produce some frustrating moments. Let's assume that a user is writing a report with a word processing (WP) package and decides to include some spreadsheet data in the report. With separate WP and spreadsheet programs, the user may have to store the document, shut down the WP program, change disks, load the spreadsheet program and data, and retrieve the data with a set of program commands that bear no resemblance to those used with the WP program. Having finally retrieved the spreadsheet information, the user may then have to print it out and paste it into the report at a later time because it's often cumbersome or impossible to share data between separate single-function packages.

Software integration reduces frustrations. It lets people perform similar tasks with similar commands, and it lets them pass information freely between applications. Integrated software may take the following forms:

- *Integrated software series.* The user selects from a set of separate but coordinated packages created by a single supplier. The available programs in an **integrated software series** generally include those used to manipulate spreadsheets, process words, manage files or data bases, prepare graphics, and control communications. Other functions such as project/time management and outlining may also be available. All these packages are designed to share data and use a common set of commands. Of course, some programs in such a series may satisfy a user's needs better than others, and these separate programs are generally not used simultaneously.

- *Integrating software "shells."* In this integration approach, the user may continue to rely on a library of familiar single-function programs ac-

The on-screen windows of this multifunction integrated software package show its ability to produce graphics, spreadsheets, and text at the same time. (Courtesy Ashton-Tate)

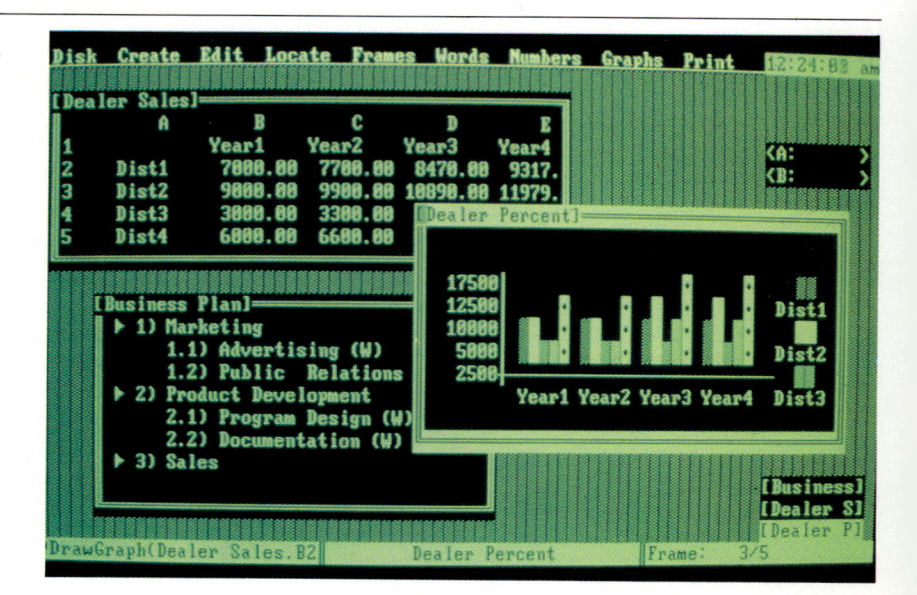

WINDOW 10-1

MEMORY-RESIDENT SOFTWARE

Personal computers are becoming able to keep more things on their "minds" at once. But as with people, having too many things on one's mind sometimes leads to trouble.

The reason is a relatively new type of software known as memory-resident software. Memory-resident programs usually do not handle mainstream applications such as word processing or financial spreadsheets. Rather, they provide accessory functions such as calculators, note pads, and phone lists. And as their name implies, they do not have to be loaded from a disk each time they are needed. After being loaded once, they sit quietly in the back of the computer's memory while the main application is running and pop up to the surface instantly when they are called upon.

Such programs are popular because they are inexpensive, useful, and easy to use. But as more of these programs are used, they are beginning to interfere with one another and with the main program. The result is that sometimes the memory-resident programs do not work when they should. At other times, the entire computer can come to a halt as the memory-resident programs battle for control of the computer.

Despite the problems, memory-resident programs are popular because they have expanded the usefulness of personal computers. One best-seller, Sidekick, provides "desktop accessories" such as a note pad, phone list, electronic appointment calendar, and calculator. A person working on a spreadsheet who gets a phone call, for example, can instantly pop up the note pad and take down a message, or pop up the calendar to schedule an appointment, and then return to the spreadsheet.

Keyboard enhancers, such as Prokey and Superkey, are another category of memory-resident software. They allow the user to replace a sequence of keystrokes with a single key or word. By typing "logon," for instance, a user can activate the computer to automatically enter the keystrokes necessary to sign on to an electronic data base. Still another type of memory-resident program is the print spooler, which stores data waiting to be printed and feeds it to the printer at a rate the printer can handle, freeing the computer for other tasks. Others recently introduced include outlining programs, spreadsheet annotating programs, spelling checkers, and electronic thesauri. With computers coming with more memory, software developers envision more and more uses for memory-resident programs.

One problem that arises is that the main application sometimes blocks out the memory-resident program. The resident programs usually work by watching, as it were, which keys on the keyboard are hit. When the special key combination that activates the background program is hit, the program springs to life. But a few programs, such as older versions of some word processing software, seize total control of the keyboard in such a way that memory-resident programs cannot "see" what keys are hit.

Yet another type of interference occurs where there are several programs residing in the memory at once. All the programs are trying to look at the keyboard at the same time and, like a crowd at a parade, they sometimes block one another's view. Thus, providers of resident programs try to insure that their program gets a clear view. In extreme cases, however, the computer can be immobilized as the resident programs vie to get in the front of the line.

The main problem behind all this is the lack of operating standards. The existing IBM computer, the machine for which most of the memory-resident programs are designed, and the MS-DOS operating system were only designed for one application at a time. Designers of many applications programs, such as word processing programs, assumed that their programs would have complete control of the computer and never considered that they would have to cohabitate with others. But developers of memory-resident programs figured out ways to circumvent this limitation and, as often happens, the technology rushed ahead before standards could be developed. Many of the older programs are being upgraded or modified so that memory-resident programs can work with them.

In the longer run, future versions of the MS-DOS operating system will be "multi-tasking", meaning that they will be able to run several programs at once. Running at the same time is a step beyond merely sharing the memory at the same time, and the technical challenges are even more daunting.

From Andrew Pollack, "Technology: Cutting Clutter in Memories," *The New York Times*, Nov. 28, 1985. Copyright © 1985 by The New York Times Company. Reprinted by permission.

---

quired from different suppliers. A **software shell** (or **system integrator) package** is purchased to manage the exchange of data between the user's separate applications programs. The shell package thus performs an integrating function. When a system integrator is used with many older programs, there's obviously not going to be a consistent command structure between the various applications. But applications packages designed specifically to operate in a given shell environment may be purchased from a number of suppliers, so that all of a user's packaged programs will respond to the same commands and queries. For example, a common set of *icons*—pictures on the display screen that represent user options—may appear in all these programs, and a consistent style of *pull-down menus* may also be employed to give users other program choices. (Icons and pull-down menus are discussed in Chapter 5, and in the Closer Look reading at the end of this chapter.)

● *Multifunction integrated packages.* In this approach, the users buy a single all-in-one package from a supplier. This **multifunction integrated package** typically combines most or all of the types of programs found in an integrated software series. A common user interface is provided, and similar commands are given to all package elements. Data may be easily moved between functions. Figure 10-1 shows again the use of a multifunction package. Of course, there may be a rather lengthy learning period while the user adapts to the style of work imposed by the structure of the package. And some package elements may not meet user needs, or they may be used infrequently or not at all.

IDENTIFYING AND SELECTING APPLICATIONS PACKAGES

Let's assume that you have a problem to be solved or a need to be satisfied. Let's further assume that you have a clear understanding of the nature of this problem or need. Let's suppose next that you suspect that the problem or need can best be handled through the use of a pc system. And let's finally assume that you believe that the most economical solution to your problem or need lies in acquiring one or more applications packages.

Unless you're already locked into a particular hardware system, your best bet is probably to follow the **software-first approach.** That is, you should find the applications package(s) that will do exactly what you want to do and then acquire the hardware needed to run the package(s). (Don't stop here if you already have a computer. Most of what follows is still relevant for you.) So how do you go about identifying prospective packages and then deciding on the "best" selection? That's not a simple question, given the past and expected growth in the pc software market. Some guidelines are given in the following pages to help you identify a list of appropriate packages, narrow the field to a few suitable choices, and then make the final purchase decision. But you should remember that even the pros have trouble picking software for themselves because programs are complicated products.

Identifying Suitable Applications Packages

Some of the sources of information you can use in this first step are outlined below:

● The advertisements published in pc magazines and software mail-order catalogs give general descriptions of packages, and the members of local

FIGURE 10-1 (facing page)

(a) Text of a sales report prepared with a word processing program. (b) Sales data and formulas are entered by the user, and the spreadsheet program calculates the "Year total" column and the "Qtr. total" row. (c) A graphics software program can use the results produced by the spreadsheet program to generate pie charts, bar charts, and other easy-to-understand graphic presentations. (d) The screen can be separated into windows to permit the simultaneous display of the output produced by different programs in the integrated software package. (e) Printout of the completed report.

CHAPTER 10
351

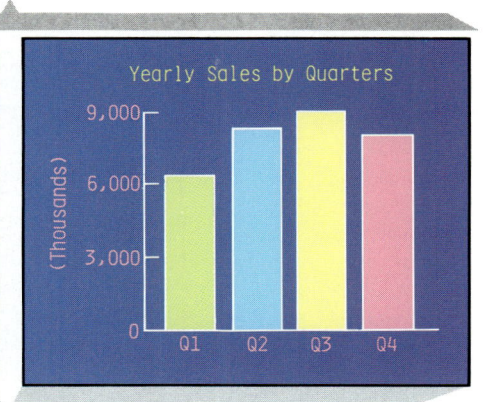

Once you have identified the type of software you need, it's a good idea to discuss the alternatives with people in computer clubs and retail stores before you buy a packaged program. (Courtesy Hewlett-Packard Co.)

computer clubs can give specific accounts of the performance of competitive products. (There are hundreds of clubs and many knowledgeable members.)

● The reviews of software products published in many pc magazines go beyond the advertising descriptions and give more information on the functions and features of selected packages. Books containing software reviews are also available.

● People in retail stores that carry software packages should be able to demonstrate their products, answer questions, and furnish promotional literature. Most retail outlets also sell pc hardware, but *software-only* stores are springing up around the country.

● Vendors of software packages can often supply **demonstration disks** and literature for their products. The demo disks cost a few dollars. Some offer little more than advertising hype, but the better ones give you a realistic idea of the capabilities of the programs they represent. It may also be possible to buy the manual that explains the use of a package. If the package is popular, independent publishers will also offer books specifically aimed at present and potential users. (These books are often more clear and helpful than the vendor's manuals.) But if you do buy a vendor's demo disk or manual and then order the complete package, the vendor may give you credit for the price of the evaluation materials. A problem with this data-gathering approach, of course, is that the manuals and books can be expensive.

● Computer consultants and acquaintances with problems similar to yours can answer questions and make package recommendations.

● Several *software-searching firms* have appeared. Some sell *directories* cataloging thousands of packages. Others such as Softsearch International use computers to store and retrieve information on over 30,000 packages. This electronic library is available for a fee to pc users, retailers, and consultants.

Narrowing the Field

Once you've identified suitable package candidates, use this *selection* checklist to further narrow the field:

● Is the package really available, or is it just another example of **"vaporware"**—a product announced well in advance of the time when it's actually ready for use?

● Is the *output* produced by the package suitable in form and content?

● Can the package accept the *input data* you need to process in the format that you need to use?

● Can the package support an acceptable range of I/O devices?

● Are the *files* created and/or processed acceptable in terms of size, contents, storage media, record formats, access restrictions, and degree of permanency?

● Does the package have an *adequate response time,* or must you wait for lengthy periods while the program digests your last data entry?

● Is the package "user friendly"—is it easy to learn and easy to use?

What's the quality of the *documentation?* That is, are the manuals and other documents in the package complete, clearly written, and well organized?

● Does the package have good *error-handling controls?* Are system errors reported to the user in clear messages or cryptic codes?

● Can duplicate program backup copies be stored on disks to protect against the loss or destruction of the original program?

● If multiple programs are needed, will they all run on the same hardware using the same operating system? Is an integrated software series available that will satisfy your needs? Can a multifunction integrated software package be substituted for several single-function programs? Is the package supplier likely to survive in a competitive marketplace?

Making the Final Decisions

The following questions may help you make the best package choice:

● Can it be demonstrated to *your* satisfaction that the package works with *your* data, in the format *you* use, to solve the problem that *you* specified?

● What's the *warranty period* for the package? What's the *level of support* you can expect to receive from the vendor and/or the vendor's representative? Is some knowledgeable person able and willing to help you with any problems that may develop as you use the package?

● Does the package represent a good value for the money? Can an alternative, but acceptable, package be obtained for a significantly lower outlay?

Once you've decided on a package, where do you go to buy it? There are likely to be three outlets for the software. The *first* source is a *retail store*. Although stores vary in the amount of software they carry, they *should* be familiar with the packages they sell. When that's true, they should be able to demonstrate the program, answer your questions about it, and provide support for it. Obviously, though, a dealer can't begin to carry all the packages that are available. And perhaps what isn't carried is exactly what you need. In that case, the dealer may be able to order the package for you. The price charged by the retailer is likely to be close to the list price, but this is reasonable *if* you can depend on the retailer for help before and after the sale.

A *second* possible package source is a *mail-order distributor*. If you're buying a relatively simple package and don't need any support help, then you can usually save money by ordering it from this source. And a *third* way to buy the selected package is to order it *directly from the producer*. This may be about the only way to get a copy of a program supplied by the firm whose only office is located above the owner's garage. Prices are often negotiated, and the firm may not be around later if you need help.

SYSTEM SOFTWARE: THE OPERATING SYSTEM

An **operating system (OS)** is an integrated set of specialized programs that's used to manage the resources and overall operations of a computer (Figure

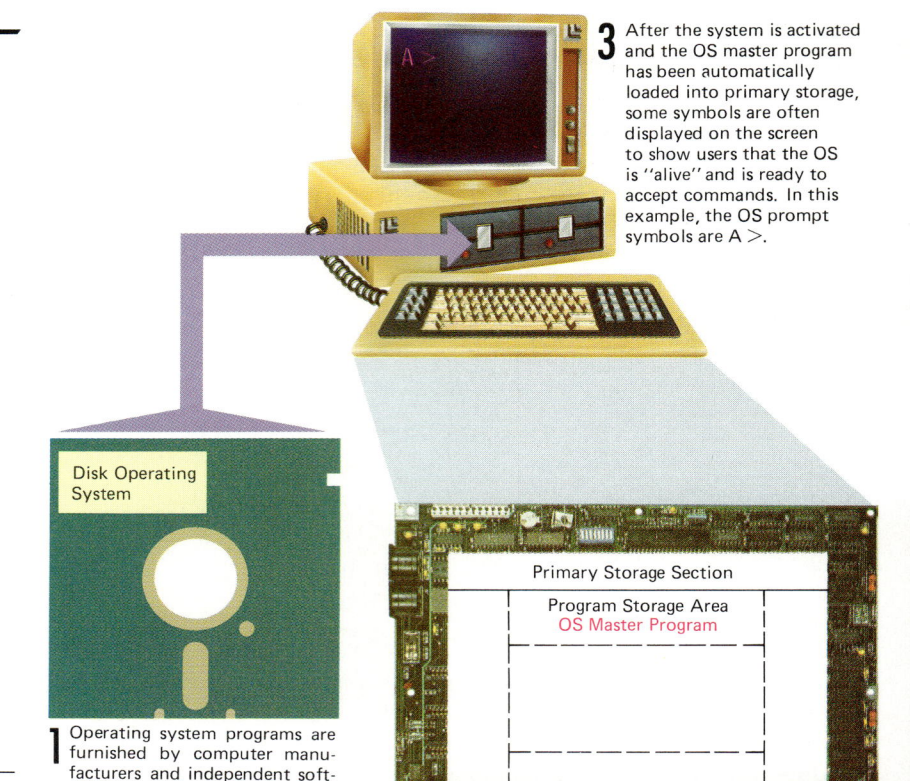

FIGURE 10-2

An operating system is an important system software package that's found in almost all computer installations. The OS helps people use computers in many ways, but users are seldom aware of the functions being performed for them by the OS.

1 Operating system programs are furnished by computer manufacturers and independent software vendors, and are commonly stored on a disk. Users may use the remaining space on the disk to store applications programs and data. A disk with an appropriate OS must be inserted into a disk drive before processing can be accomplished.

2 When the system is activated, an OS master program is automatically loaded into primary storage. It remains there during processing and copies other specialized OS programs from the disk into primary storage as they are needed.

3 After the system is activated and the OS master program has been automatically loaded into primary storage, some symbols are often displayed on the screen to show users that the OS is "alive" and is ready to accept commands. In this example, the OS prompt symbols are A >.

10-2). The OS permits the computer to supervise its own operations by automatically calling in the applications programs, translating any other special service programs, and managing the data needed to produce the output desired by users. Thus, as Figure 10-3 indicates, the OS tends to isolate the hardware from the user. The user communicates with the OS, supplies applications programs and input data that are in a language and format acceptable to the OS, and receives output results. But the user is usually not concerned with the hardware specifics of the system, or with how the OS will direct the hardware to handle certain tasks.

The computer systems running under OS control today range in size from small personal computers to the largest mainframes and supercomputers. The general goal of OS developers has been to devise ways to operate a computer with a minimum of idle time and in the most efficient and economical way during the execution of user programs. In pre-OS days, computer operators would go through the same ritual to process each job. The job program and input data would be loaded on input devices, the storage locations in the processor would be cleared of any data remaining from the previous job, appropriate switches would be set, and the job would run alone in the processor until it was completed. After completion, the job program, input data, and output results would be unloaded by the operator, and the entire ritual would begin again for the next job.

Because the computer sat idle while the operator loaded and unloaded jobs, a great deal of processing time was lost. The early OSs reduced this idle time by allowing jobs to be stacked up in a waiting line. When one job was finished, system control would branch back to OS software which would automatically perform the housekeeping duties needed to load and run the next job. This automatic job-to-job transition is still one of the major functions performed by a modern OS.

Although there are numerous programs in an OS today, most OS elements can be classified as either *control* or *processing* programs.

Control Programs in an OS

You've just seen that one of the functions of an OS is to control *input/output housekeeping operations*. By shifting the control of these operations from human operators to specially prepared programs, the earlier OSs reduced operator drudgery. They also cut down on the need for programmers to rewrite certain I/O instructions for each program, provided relatively nonstop operation (operators could load data for the next job while the current job was being processed), and therefore speeded up the amount of processing that could be accomplished. But a modern OS does much more than just control I/O housekeeping activities. Other sophisticated control programs are required to keep ever-faster and more powerful hardware occupied.

The Role of the OS Supervisor The overall management of a computer system is under the control of an OS master program. This master program is referred to by such names as **supervisor, monitor,** or **kernel.** The supervisor program coordinates all other parts of the OS, and it resides in the primary storage section of the processor. Other programs in the OS are kept in an online **system residence device** (usually a magnetic disk drive) so that the supervisor can call them up and temporarily store them in the processor when they are needed.

In many pc systems, the OS supervisor, other specialized OS programs, and one or more applications programs selected by the user are all stored on a single floppy disk. This disk is inserted into a disk drive (let's call it drive A) and the OS supervisor is automatically loaded into primary storage (Figure 10-4a). The other specialized OS programs on this disk are called into primary storage as needed. For example, the user can first request that a specialized program that translates instructions written in a programming language be loaded from the disk in drive A into primary storage. The OS supervisor oversees this operation (Figure 10-4b). Then the user can instruct the supervisor to copy into primary storage a billing application program that's stored on the same disk with the OS software (Figure 10-4c). The supervisor consults a specialized file directory to determine the size of the billing program, and the primary storage section is checked to see if enough storage space is available. If so, the supervisor calls in and then turns control over to a specialized basic input/output system (BIOS) program that sees to the loading of the billing program. This billing program may then be modified, or it may be used to process data stored in disk drive B.

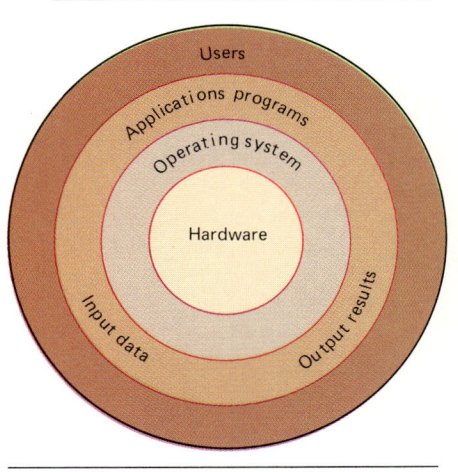

FIGURE 10-3

An OS is a set of programs that, in a sense, disguises the hardware being used. For example, popular OSs used with personal computers are Digital Research's CP/M-80, Microsoft's MS-DOS, and AT&T's UNIX. (For more information about personal computer OSs, see Chapter 7, pages 252–254.) A person who knows how to communicate with CP/M-80, MS-DOS, or UNIX may be able to process applications programs written to run on these OSs on a number of personal computers without being concerned about the hardware specifics of the various machines. Likewise, programs written for use with CP/M-80, MS-DOS, or UNIX can often be run on the systems produced by many different manufacturers whose machines will accept these operating systems.

(a) The operating system and a billing program are stored on a floppy disk. This disk is inserted into disk drive "A." A "bootstrap" program permanently located in ROM storage may be used to automatically load the OS supervisor into the primary storage section of the processor.

A disk containing the "Billing" application data may be inserted into a second, or "B," drive

Disk operating system/ billing program

Billing application data

A > Basic

A > Basic
Load "Billing"

(b) The user requests a program on the OS disk that translates instructions written in a programming language, and the OS supervisor sees that the program is loaded into primary storage.

(c) Next, the user instructs the OS supervisor to copy the billing program stored in drive A into primary storage. After determining from a file directory program that enough space is available, the supervisor calls up another special OS program that sees to the loading of the billing software. Control over the processing of the billing application data stored in drive B is then turned over to the billing program.

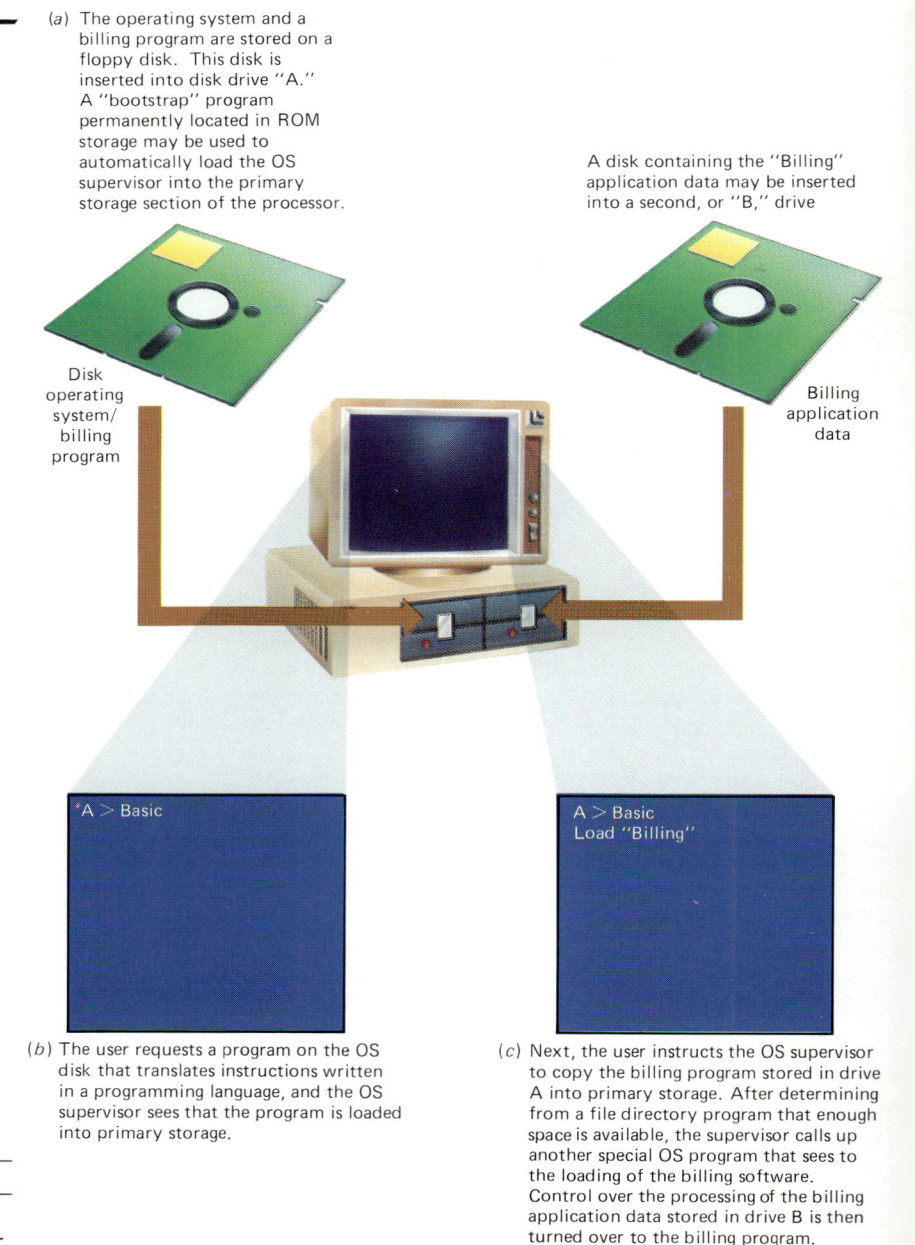

FIGURE 10-4

The operating system software controls the overall management of a personal computer.

After a specialized task has been completed, system control branches back to the supervisor. The following discussion of the use of job control programs illustrates this fact and shows the supervisor's role in maintaining system control in a larger installation.

Job Control Programs Let's consider once again the OS function of providing automatic job-to-job linkages during the processing of applications programs. These linkages are handled by a job control program. When a number of jobs are to be run in a *batch processing* (or **stacked job**) environment, instructions to the OS are written in the codes of a **job control language (JCL)**. These coded statements tell the OS such things as the name of the job, the user's name and account number, the I/O devices to use during processing, the assembler or compiler to use if language translation is needed (see Chapter 12), and so on.

In Figure 10-5a, let's assume that the job control instructions for Job 1 have been read, the Job 1 program has been loaded into the processor from a

FIGURE 10-5

The role of the OS supervisor and the job control program in providing job-to-job linkages.

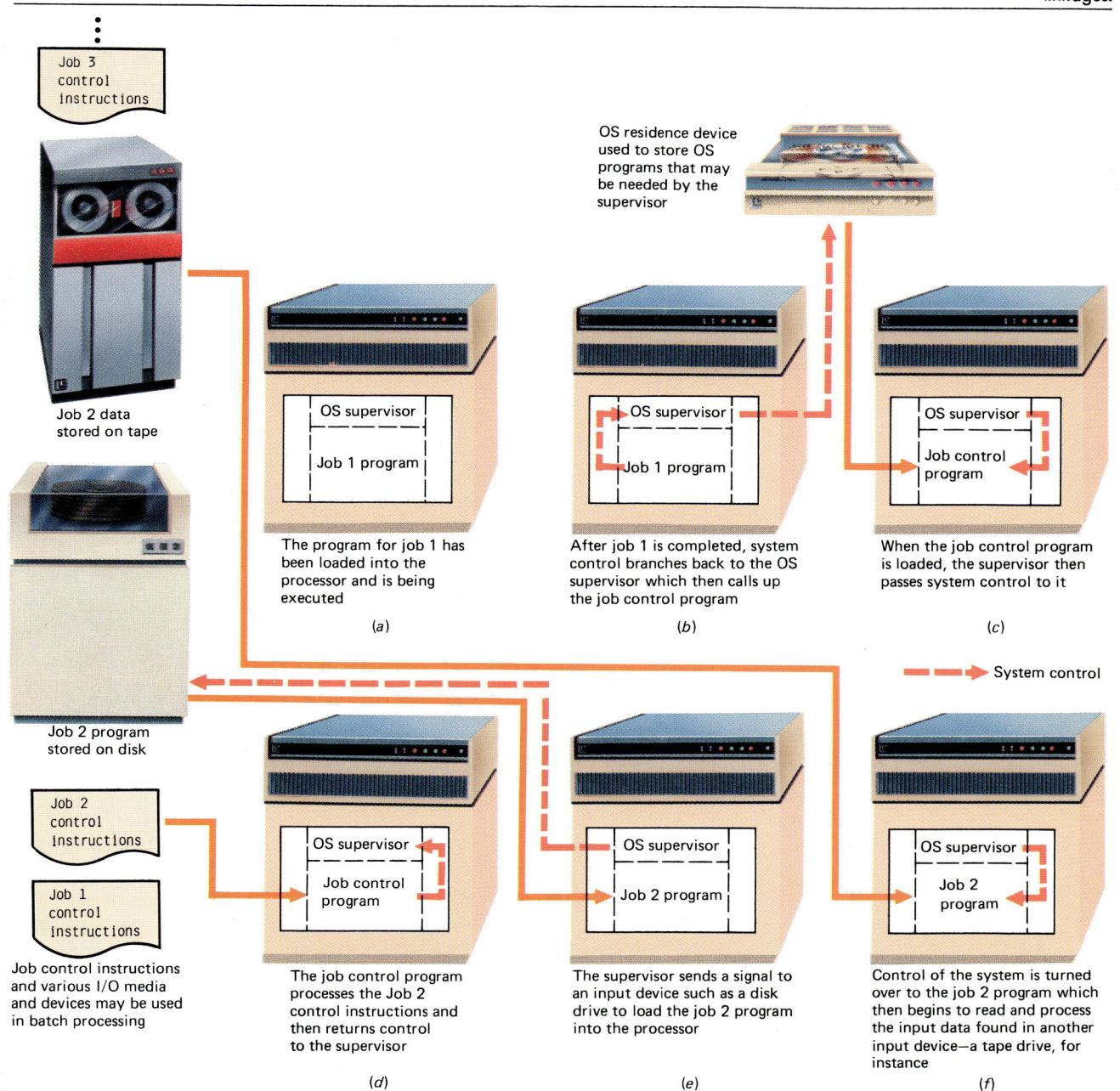

Job 3 control instructions

Job 2 data stored on tape

OS residence device used to store OS programs that may be needed by the supervisor

(a) The program for job 1 has been loaded into the processor and is being executed

(b) After job 1 is completed, system control branches back to the OS supervisor which then calls up the job control program

(c) When the job control program is loaded, the supervisor then passes system control to it

Job 2 program stored on disk

Job 2 control instructions

Job 1 control instructions

Job control instructions and various I/O media and devices may be used in batch processing

(d) The job control program processes the Job 2 control instructions and then returns control to the supervisor

(e) The supervisor sends a signal to an input device such as a disk drive to load the job 2 program into the processor

(f) Control of the system is turned over to the job 2 program which then begins to read and process the input data found in another input device—a tape drive, for instance

- - - ▶ System control

magnetic disk drive, and the input data stored on a reel of magnetic tape are being processed. When the processing is completed, system control branches back to the OS supervisor which then sends a signal to the OS residence device to load the **job control program** into the processor (Figure 10-5*b*). When this program is loaded, the supervisor branches control to it (Figure 10-5*c*). The *function of the job control program* is to read and process the special codes that have been written in the JCL for Job 2. The job control program then returns control to the supervisor (Figure 10-5*d*). Since the program for Job 2 also happens to be stored on a magnetic disk, the supervisor sends a signal to the disk drive to load the Job 2 program into the processor (Figure 10-5*e*). After this operation is completed, the supervisor turns system control over to the Job 2 program which then begins to read and process the input data found on a magnetic tape mounted on a tape drive (Figure 10-5*f*). At the end of Job 2 processing, control is returned to the supervisor, which calls the job control program, which reads the Job 3 control instructions . . . and so it goes.

Other Job/Resource Control Activities   Figure 10-5 showed the processor processing one job at a time. But since processors of almost any size today can process far more data in a second than a single set of I/O devices can supply or receive, it's common to **overlap** processing jobs. When this happens, the OS must be ready to:

- Perform *system scheduling* tasks
- Handle *system interruptions*
- *Monitor system status* and supply appropriate messages to people

System scheduling   Whenever possible, multiple tasks are scheduled to balance I/O and processing requirements. As noted above, this often involves overlapping I/O and processing operations. The channels shown in Figure 10-6 are used to facilitate overlapped processing.

A **channel** consists of hardware that, along with other associated monitoring and connecting elements, controls and provides the path for the movement of data between relatively slow I/O devices and the high-speed processor. A channel may be a separate, small, special-purpose control computer located near the processor, or it can be a physical part of the computer which is accessible to both I/O devices and other processor elements. Once a channel has received appropriate instruction signals from the OS, it can operate independently and without supervision while the processor is engaged in performing computations.

For example, Figure 10-7 shows that in **time slice** 5 when the processor is working on the record labeled 2 for Task A, Channel 1 can be accepting another Task A input record, Channel 2 can be receiving processed information from Task A for an output device, Channel 3 can be accepting an input record for Task B, and Channel 4 can be transmitting Task B information to an output device. The OS switches control back and forth between Tasks A and B (and, perhaps, between Tasks C, D, . . .) throughout their execution. You'll notice in Figure 10-7 that the processor would be idle in time slice 6 if it did not branch to Task B.

In addition to channels, small high-speed storage elements called **buffers** also play an important role in overlapping input, processing, and output operations. Buffers may be located in peripheral devices (printer buffers are discussed in Chapter 6), or they may be reserved sections of primary storage. Data from input devices are fed under channel control into an *input buffer*. This input buffer has an important characteristic: It can accept data at slow input speeds and release them at electronic speeds. (The reverse is true of the *output buffer:* It accepts data from the processor at electronic speeds and releases them at the slower operating speeds of output devices.)

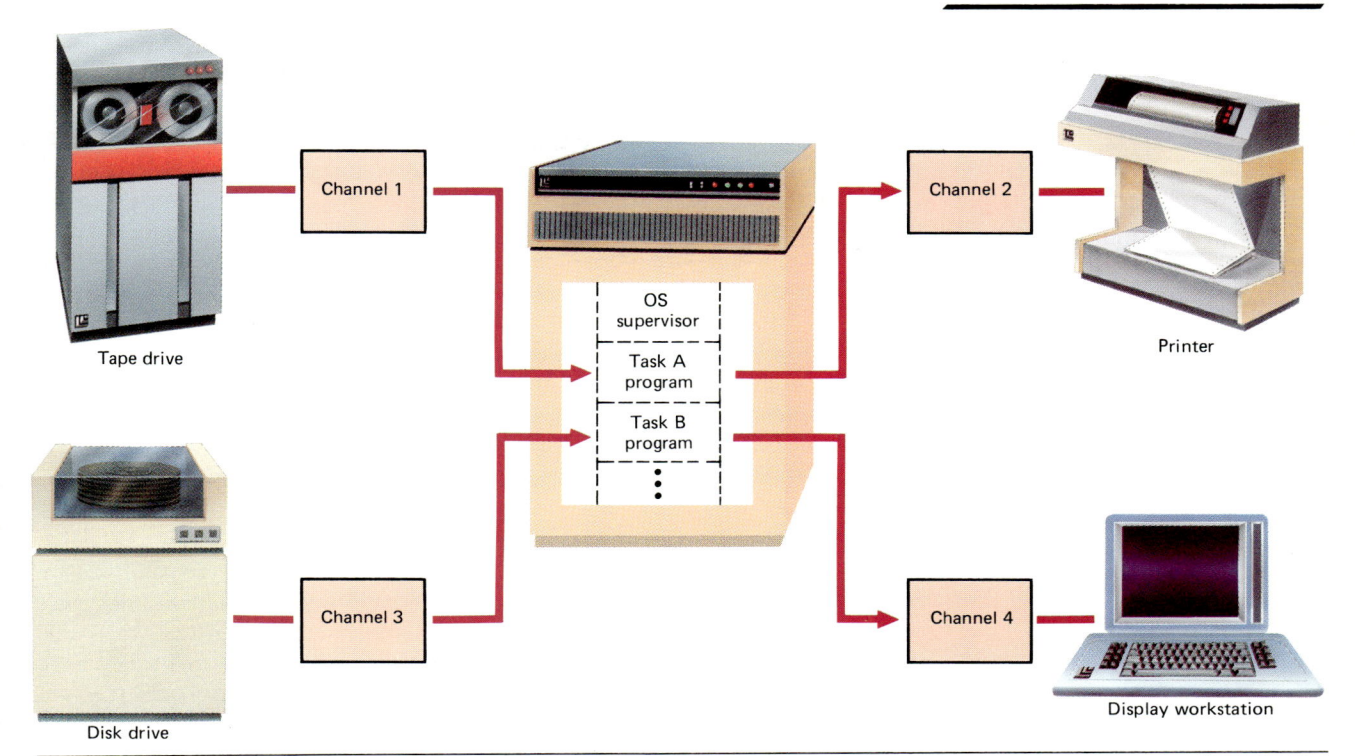

FIGURE 10-6

Channels control the execution of I/O instructions and thereby facilitate the scheduling of system resources.

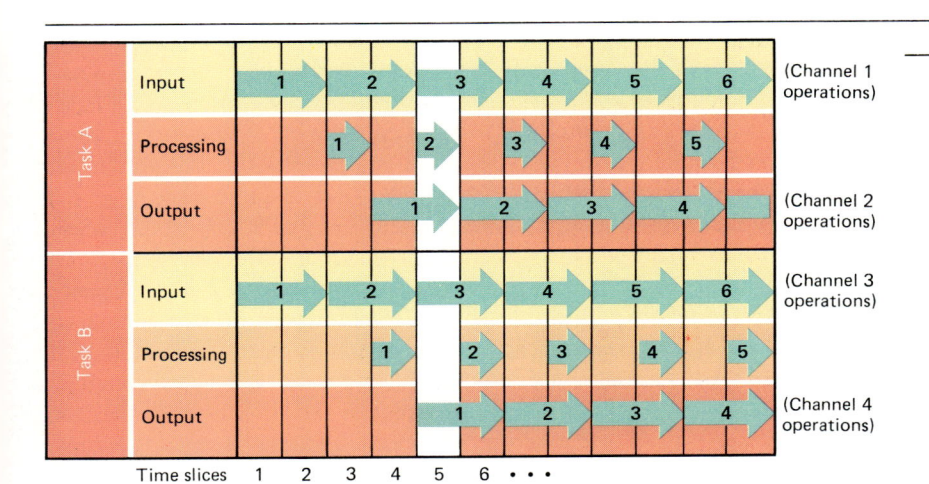

FIGURE 10-7

The OS uses channels to balance system input, output, and processing capabilities.

Thus, in Task A in Figure 10-7, the first two time slices are required to read record 1 into the input buffer. Once in the buffer, however, there is virtually *no delay* in releasing record 1 to the computer for processing in time slice 3. While the first record is being processed, a second record starts to enter the input buffer. As soon as the first record is processed, it's immediately transferred under channel control to the output buffer. Two more time slices are then required before the output device can complete the writing operation. But during this time (see slices 4 and 5), the computer processes a Task B record and another Task A record.

Multiprogramming (or **multitasking,** or **concurrent programming**) are names given to what we've been examining in Figure 10-7. These terms refer to the *interleaved* execution of two or more different and independent programs by the same computer. Notice, however, that multiprogramming is *not* defined as the execution of instructions from several programs at the same instant in time. Rather, it does mean that there may be a number of programs available to the processor from one or more users, and the processor executes a portion of one program, then a portion of another, and so on. As we've seen, the OS switches control from one program to another almost instantly. The processor can thus keep busy while channels and buffers are occupied with the job of bringing in data and writing out information.

If a number of programs are being processed, the OS may allocate only a small amount of time—say 150 milliseconds per second—to each program being executed. Fifteen-hundredths of a second may not seem like much time to you, but that's enough to calculate the amounts owed to hundreds of employees for a given pay period. The result of such speed is that people whose programs are being processed often feel that they have the undivided attention of the computer. In some multiprogramming systems, only a *fixed* number of jobs can be processed concurrently (multiprogramming with a fixed number of tasks, or MFT), while in others the number of jobs can *vary* (multiprogramming with a variable number of tasks, or MVT).

Multiprocessing is the term used to describe a processing approach in which two or more independent processors are linked together in a coordinated system. In such a system, instructions from different and independent programs can be processed at the same instant in time by different processors. Or the processors may simultaneously execute different instructions from the same program. Again, it's the job of the OS to schedule and balance the input, output, and processing capabilities of these systems. This is no easy task! In fact, in distributed data processing networks with multiple processors, small computers called *front-end processors* are often dedicated to the single function of scheduling and controlling all work entering the system from remote terminals and other input devices. The front-end processor(s) thus permit one or more larger *host computers* to devote their time to processing large and complex applications programs. (If you've read Chapter 8, you already know about distributed data processing networks and front-end processors.)

The larger processors in a multiprocessing system may have separate primary storage sections, they may share a common primary storage unit, or they may have access to both separate and common memories. A common OS may control all or part of the operations of each processor, and each computer may be dedicated to specific types of applications. For example, one can process interactive jobs while another is concentrating on batch applications.

However, it's common for one processor to be able to take over the workload of another malfunctioning machine until repairs are made.

As you would expect, scheduling and coordinating the input/processing/output activities of multiple processors requires a very sophisticated OS. In fact, the *largest* OSs need a primary storage size of between 4 and 6 million characters before they can get out of their own way and allow the system to produce results for users.

Handling system interruptions Priorities are typically assigned to the programs in a multiprogramming system. A high priority is given to the programs used in interactive processing that manipulate data and respond to inquiries coming from people at online terminals. A lower priority is assigned to batch processing programs that don't require such quick response. Thus, it often happens that a high-priority program will interrupt the processing of a lower-priority program. When a **program interrupt** occurs, the OS must see to it that the data, instructions, and intermediate processing results of the interrupted program are kept separate from any other job. The storage *partitions* reserved for each job must be properly handled, shifted, and protected. After the higher-priority program(s) have been processed, the OS must restore the interrupted program and continue with its processing (Figure 10-8).

In addition to protecting and restoring interrupted low-priority programs, the OS in many installations is also able to partition the programs being executed into primary and online secondary storage portions. This is an important capability. For many years, the size of an application program was effectively limited by the size of the computer's primary storage section because the complete program was held in primary storage during its entire execution. If the program size didn't exceed the limited primary storage capacity, then there was no problem. But if, on the other hand, the task required thousands of instructions, then the programmer might be forced to find ways to trim the program or to divide it into separate jobs. This can be a tedious and time-consuming chore.

To avoid this situation, OSs with **virtual storage** capability have been developed. The basic approach is to divide total programs into small sequences of instructions called either **pages** or **segments.** Then only those program pages or segments that are actually required at a particular time in the processing need be in the primary (or *real*) storage. The remaining pages or segments may be kept temporarily in online (or *virtual*) storage, from where they can be rapidly retrieved as needed following a program interruption (see Figure 10-9). The OS handles the swapping of program pages or segments between primary and online secondary storage units. Thus, from the applications programmer's point of view, the effective (or "virtual") size of the available primary storage appears unlimited.

Monitoring system status The OS constantly monitors the status of the computer system during processing operations. It may respond to user "HELP" commands and supply information about its functions and operation. It also directs the computer to send messages to an operator's station when I/O devices need attention, when errors occur in the job stream, or when other abnormal conditions arise. When an error in a job is detected in a larger computer system, however, the computer usually doesn't stop and wait for the

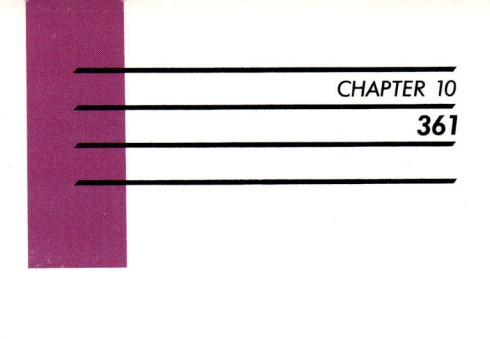

FIGURE 10-8

Handling system interruptions is a function of the OS.

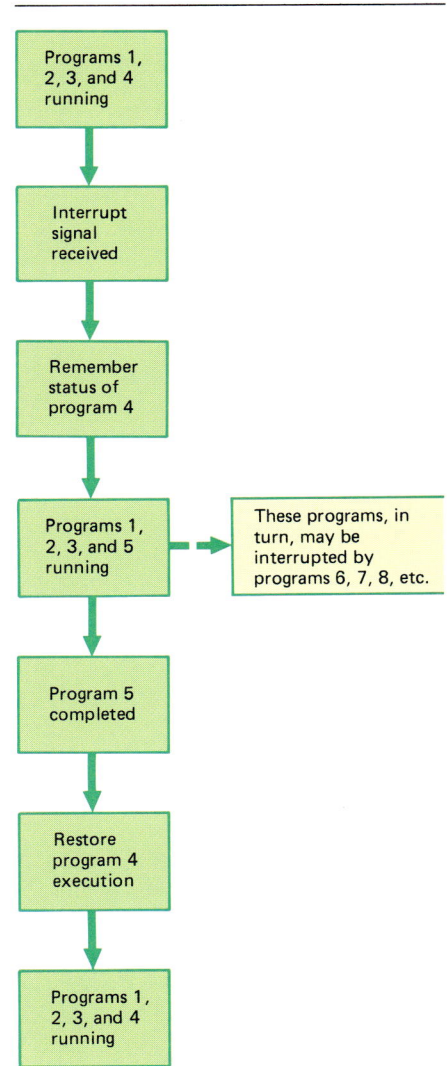

Programs 1, 2, 3, and 4 running
↓
Interrupt signal received
↓
Remember status of program 4
↓
Programs 1, 2, 3, and 5 running → These programs, in turn, may be interrupted by programs 6, 7, 8, etc.
↓
Program 5 completed
↓
Restore program 4 execution
↓
Programs 1, 2, 3, and 4 running

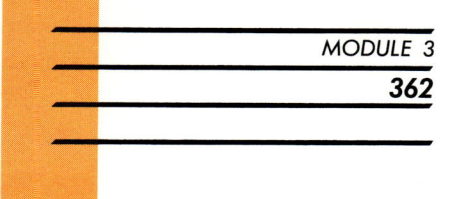

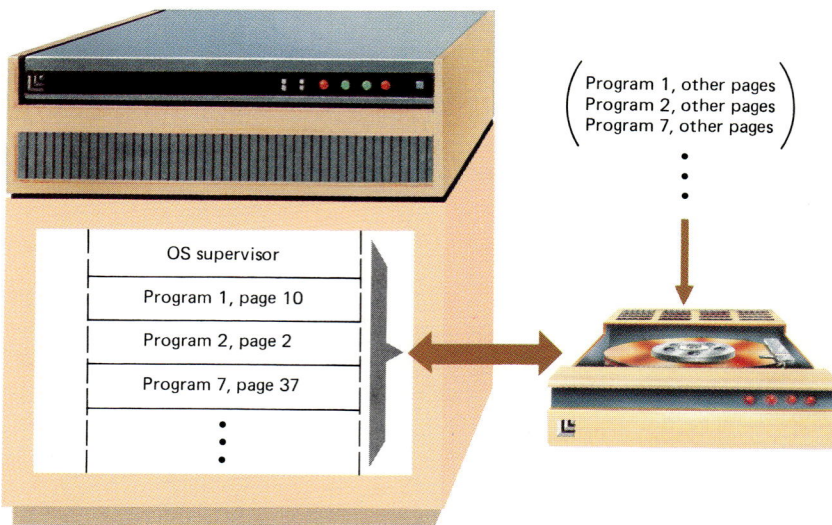

FIGURE 10-9
Virtual storage capability.

operator to take appropriate action. Rather, the message is printed and control passes on to the next job without delay.

The OS also keeps a log of the jobs that have been run in larger systems. These jobs are clocked in and out of the system. The elapsed time required to run programs may be recorded and printed. The security of the system may also be monitored. Any attempt to use unauthorized passwords from online terminals may be recorded. And the OS may print a warning message if suspicious activity is occurring at one or more terminal sites.

In addition to control routines, an OS also includes or has access to a number of programs designed to simplify *processing* operations. These programs can reduce the time and expense of program preparation.

Processing Programs in an OS

The **program call-up capability** of an OS gives it access to a number of programs that can simplify processing operations. Translating programs, utility (or service) programs, and library programs are examples of OS-controlled software that can reduce the time and expense of preparing applications programs. *Translating programs* transform the instructions written in a humanly convenient form by applications programmers into the machine-language codes required by computers. These translating programs are loaded into the computer where they control the translation process. As you saw in Figure 10-4, they are often stored in a direct-access storage device (DASD) and are called up when the user informs the OS supervisor of what's needed. (See Chapter 12 for more details on the use of translating programs.)

Utility (service) programs are also available for call-up by the OS. These routines perform needed services such as sorting records into a particular sequence for processing, merging several sorted files into a single large updated file, or transferring data from one I/O device to another. Job control statements again tell the OS supervisor which utility programs are needed.

A library of frequently used subroutines can also be stored on a DASD. These tested **library programs** are stored in a machine-language form. They are then called up by the OS whenever they are required in the processing of other programs. This eliminates the need for a programmer to rewrite these modules every time they are used. A **librarian program** controls the storage and use of the programs in the system library. The "librarian" maintains a program directory. It also spells out the procedures used to add and delete programs from the library.

FEEDBACK

Feedback AND REVIEW 10

To test and reinforce your understanding of the prewritten software material presented in this chapter, answer the following *true-false* questions by placing a T or an F in the space provided.

_____ 1. An integrated software series is generally produced by a single supplier.
_____ 2. Integrating software "shells" allow users to exchange data between separate programs produced by different suppliers.
_____ 3. A multifunction integrated program combines several standalone applications packages in a single unit with a common user interface.
_____ 4. You should always buy a computer first and then look around for applications that will run on your choice.
_____ 5. All software packages adhere to a rigid documentation format to ensure that user-friendly features are consistently applied.
_____ 6. Software packages for personal computers must be purchased in retail stores.
_____ 7. An operating system is an integrated set of specialized programs that's used to manage the resources and overall operations of a computer.
_____ 8. An OS tends to isolate the hardware from the user.
_____ 9. A modern OS is restricted to running on a single machine model.
_____10. A goal of OS developers is to devise ways to operate a computer with a minimum of idle time.
_____11. Automatic job-to-job transitions were performed by early OSs, but are no longer needed in a modern system.
_____12. Most OS elements can be classified as either control or processing programs.
_____13. The overall management of a computer system is under the control of an OS master program called the job controller.
_____14. The OS supervisor resides in primary storage while other OS programs are kept in an online system residence device.
_____15. The OS supervisor may call up a job control program to read and process the special codes written in a job control language.
_____16. Whenever possible, multiple tasks to be processed are scheduled to balance I/O and processing requirements.
_____17. Only one channel is needed for multiprogramming systems.

MODULE 3

_____18. Small high-speed storage elements called buffers play a role in overlapping input, processing, and output operations.

_____19. Multiprogramming (or multitasking) is defined to mean the execution of instructions from several programs at the same instant in time.

_____20. A multiprocessing system can execute instructions from several programs at the same instant in time.

_____21. In a multiprogramming system, a higher priority is assigned to batch processing than to interactive processing.

_____22. The effective size of the primary storage available for programs may appear to be unlimited when virtual storage concepts are used.

_____23. The program call-up capability of an OS gives it access to programs that can simplify processing.

LOOKING BACK

1. Some people find that a single-function application program satisfies all their computing needs. But others run several programs on a regular basis. Integrated applications packages can reduce some of the frustrations experienced by multiple-program users. An integrated package lets people perform various tasks with a single set of commands, and it lets them pass information freely between applications. Software integration may be accomplished by an integrated software series, by an integrating software "shell," or by a single multifunction integrated package.

2. Sources that can be used to identify suitable applications packages include ads, software reviews, and listings in magazines and directories; advice from members of computer clubs, people in computer stores, and computer consultants; and demonstration disks and literature from software suppliers. Once suitable package candidates have been identified, a selection checklist presented in the chapter may be used to further narrow the field. Another chapter checklist can then be used to help you make the "best" package choice.

3. An operating system (OS) is an integrated set of specialized programs that's used to manage the resources and overall operations of a computer. Users communicate with an OS, supply input data and applications programs, and receive output results. An automatic job-to-job transition procedure was devised for early OSs, and this is still one of the major functions performed by a modern OS. Other activities carried out by an OS can generally be placed in control or processing categories. The OS supervisor controls and coordinates all other parts of the OS, and it resides in primary storage. Other programs in the OS are kept in an online system residence device so that the supervisor can retrieve them when they are needed. In a large batch processing (stacked job) environment, statements may be presented to the OS in the codes of a job control

language. A job control program in the OS is then used to read and execute these codes.

4. It's common now to overlap processing tasks in larger systems. Whenever possible, multiple tasks are scheduled to balance I/O and processing requirements. Channels and buffers facilitate the overlapping of processing tasks. Multiprogramming or multitasking is the interleaved or concurrent execution of two or more different and independent programs by the same computer. Multiprocessing describes a system in which two or more processors are linked together in a coordinated way. Instructions from two or more programs can be processed at the same instant in a multiprocessing system, but not in a multiprogramming environment. Priorities are typically assigned to the programs in a multiprogramming system. When a high-priority program interrupts the processing of a lower-priority program, the OS must see to it that the data, instructions, and intermediate processing results of the interrupted program are kept separate from other jobs. The execution of the interrupted program must then be restored at a later time.

5. A computer with virtual storage capability keeps active program pages or segments in primary storage and assigns other program parts to an online storage device. The OS handles the swapping of program pages between primary and online secondary storage units as needed. The program call-up capability of an OS gives it access to a number of translating programs, utility programs, and library programs that can be used to simplify processing operations.

KEY TERMS AND CONCEPTS

integrated software series 348
software shell (system integrator) package 349
multifunction integrated package 350
software-first approach 350
demonstration disks 352
vaporware 352
operating system (OS) 353
supervisor (monitor, kernel) 355

system residence device 355
stacked job environment 357
job control language (JCL) 357
job control program 358
overlap 358
channel 358
time slice 358
buffers 358
multiprogramming (multitasking, concurrent programming) 360

multiprocessing 360
program interrupt 361
virtual storage 361
pages (segments) 361
program call-up capability 362
utility (service) programs 362
library programs 362
librarian program 363

Topics for Review and Discussion

1. "Integrated software may take several forms." Identify and discuss these forms.
2. (a) What sources are available to help you identify suitable pc applications packages? (b) What questions should be considered in selecting a specific package?
3. What's an operating system?
4. "The OS tends to isolate the hardware from the user." Discuss this comment.
5. (a) Into what two categories can most OS programs be classified? (b) Give an example of an OS program from each category.
6. Explain the role of the OS supervisor.
7. (a) How are channels used to facilitate overlapped processing? (b) How are buffers used?
8. (a) What is multiprogramming? (b) What is multiprocessing?
9. Why must an OS be prepared to handle system interruptions in a multiprogramming environment?
10. (a) What is virtual storage? (b) Why was it developed?
11. How can the program call-up capability of an OS be used to simplify processing operations?

Projects/Issues to Consider

1. The software industry is convinced that it's being "ripped off" to the tune of hundreds of millions of dollars each year by people who illegally copy programs. Elaborate copy protection schemes are placed on package disks by some software producers only to have other producers write and sell packages designed to unlock the protection features. A group of software producers has banded together to fight the illegal copying of their products, and several lawsuits have been filed. Research the issue of software piracy, determine the consequences of this issue, and outline your findings in a class presentation.
2. Visit your library and/or a computer software store to identify three OS packages. Gather the following information on each package: (a) name and supplier of the package, (b) primary storage requirements of the package, and (c) price of the package. Present your findings in a report.

Answers to Feedback and Review Section

1. T 2. T 3. T 4. F 5. F 6. F 7. T 8. T 9. F 10. T 11. F 12. T 13. F 14. T 15. T 16. T 17. F 18. T 19. F 20. T 21. F 22. T 23. T

A CLOSER LOOK

MAKING COMPUTERS EASY TO USE
BETTER SOFTWARE AND HARDWARE IMPROVE THE INTERFACE

With more sophisticated software and improving hardware, microcomputer designers have the freedom to develop new interfaces—new ways of giving a computer information and of receiving information from it.

Interface design has always been torn by the conflicting demands of ease of use versus ease of programming. The simplest interfaces to use are also the hardest to program, so traditionally, the choice has been ease of programming. Thus the operating systems of most computers, whatever their size, use command-line interfaces. In the microcomputer world, such operating systems include Apple DOS, CP/M, and MS-DOS (or PC-DOS on IBM PCs or compatible computers).

For a new user, command-line interfaces pose a major hurdle, as they offer virtually no information; the screen shows A> or something equally cryptic. Because of hardware restrictions, most efforts to improve them have been limited to additional on-screen text, in the form of prompt lines or menus.

For certain tasks, command-line interfaces will survive a long time. For example, a programming language is really a command-line interface with hundreds or even thousands of variations possible at each program step. Similarly, command lines will continue to be used to ask for information from data bases, because data base query systems are too complex for menus.

New command-line interfaces will be able to understand natural language—ordinary English—eliminating the need for rigid codes or syntax. But natural language isn't suitable for many common computer functions; we should never have to type

DELETE THE NEXT SENTENCE

Old-fashioned interfaces on large mainframe computers present no insuperable problems for data processing specialists trained to use them. And when a microcomputer user must access the mainframe, a modern interface on the micro can act as a buffer, converting the user's commands into the form needed by the mainframe.

Command-line interfaces have survived partly because they will run on any kind of computer terminal, even one without a CRT screen. But today's microcomputers with bit-mapped screens (on which every point has its own memory location) have sufficient graphics resolution to display any image. Such hardware developments herald the end of the command-line interface for the average user; operating systems like CP/M and MS-DOS may be the last of their type. They are being replaced by visual interfaces.

Visual interfaces owe their development mainly to Xerox's Palo Alto Research Center, which produced the Xerox Star, the first commercial computer with such an interface. Former Xerox employees at Apple were instrumental in putting the visual interface on the Lisa and the Macintosh.

A visual interface is more intuitive and therefore much easier and quicker to operate than older designs. The essence of the visual interface is that you manipulate icons—graphic symbols—rather than type commands. To copy a disk file onto a second disk with one command-line interface version, you must type without error,

PIP B:=A:TEXTFILE.EXT

With a visual interface, you merely point at a file icon and move it to an icon for the second disk. A mouse is the most common pointing device for selecting and moving the symbols.

Not every command can be put into icons. Symbols work best for choices that have clear visual attributes, such as left and right text margins. But what is an icon for "search"? All visual interfaces therefore combine icons and menus. These menus are typically "pulled down"; only the heading is visible until selected, then the rest of the menu appears. Because pull-down, or pop-up, menus take up only a portion of the screen at a time, they don't obliterate your working area. And by pointing at different menu headings in turn, you can scan the menus much more quickly than with older full-screen designs.

Improved screen graphics can display different typefaces, sizes, and styles, giving users access to 500 years of typography that until now was available only on printing presses.

Most visual interface packages also include windows, which let users divide the screen into different working areas.

Still, no interface is perfect for all situations and visual interfaces have their problems. They are slow for some operations. Common commands, such as "undo," just take too many steps. To remedy this, most visual interfaces add function keys for common commands. For example, "undo" on the Macintosh is achieved by pressing the command key and Z.

As more and more noncomputer specialists learn about and work with computers, the demand will increase for both software and hardware that is easier to use.

From Cary Lu, "Making Computers Easy to Use," *High Technology*, July 1984. Copyright © 1984 by High Technology Publishing Corporation. Used by permission.

CHAPTER 11

DEVELOPING CUSTOM-MADE SYSTEMS

O<small>N SOFTER SOFTWARE</small>

Today's software is too hard. Usually designed to work well for any and all potential buyers, a few years and hundreds of hours of interaction later a software package will still interface with you exactly as it did at the time of purchase. Your special use may make some uncommon program command the one most often employed, but you'll have to punch any number of extra keys every time you invoke it. Today's software fails to remold itself to express a history of use, and this can lead to incredible inefficiency.

There are programs that allow the advanced user to adjust default values, which are those responses the programmer decided would be most typical for users of a specific application when the software was first booted up. There are also programs that can store a series of often invoked keystrokes and can tell the machine to take the sequence you've named and perform it again.

These keyboard macros, the most trivial form of softer software, force you to go through a special set of operations to enter and record changes to the program.

Why shouldn't software automatically adapt to your needs, e.g., learn from experience to change the interpretation of a command, when this is done on a human level all the time? In human-to-human communication, we adapt our terminology and our method of understanding to our previous history of interaction with each individual. There's no reason computer software should not be as flexible.

"Softer software" is the term I invented to avoid using the poorly understood term "artificial intelligence." In fact, it is a *form* of artificial intelligence, though not like speech recognition or the expert data base systems that are based on specific algorithms and do not really learn dynamically. Softer software is capable of getting better and better because it has advanced pattern recognition capabilities and can change its performance accordingly.

In general, making software softer requires storing information about a user's history of program commands and analyzing its patterns. This is a form of learning, since the software can build expectations of what the user may do later. Individual characteristics of users, what they're good at and what they're not good at, can be used to establish a reasonably unique dialogue with the computer.

A data management program, for example, could recognize that you always query its files by employee name rather than by an individual's address or hair color. Taking advantage of this pattern and predicting what will be your most common operations on data, the program could customize its query file structure to put information within easier reach. Or maybe it could learn to be forgiving of your most common keyboard mistakes by ignoring misspellings.

Software softness becomes very difficult when recognizing semantics rather than specific operations is required. Say you go into a document, move the mouse to bring the cursor to a certain position and make a word boldface, then go to another position and do it again. Instead of storing up the exact positions where this takes place and trying to match them to later entries pixel by pixel, you may want your software to draw the general conclusion that you boldface the first word in a paragraph and to position the cursor appropriately. Matching things, recording and playing them back at the semantic level: This is the hard part of softening software.

It is possible to say that we have certain types of softness built into software today and that over time we will see a clear progression as programs record a greater number of user events, recognizing more general patterns and building up the dialogue throughout the computer's history. Truly softer software is still some years away, but we are on an evolutionary path where at some point soon this term will be fully justified.

Source: Excerpted from Bill Gates, "On Softer Software," Digital Deli, Steve Ditlea, ed., Workman Publishing, 1984. Used by permission.

CHAPTER 11

LOOKING AHEAD

Although the prewritten software packages considered in Chapters 9 and 10 can perform many special and general functions, there are unique situations where these packages don't fit the need. In such cases, a custom-built system or application must be created. Our purpose now is to look at examples of custom-made systems and the process used to develop such systems. The information in this chapter will enable you to:

- Explain the need for custom-made systems and give examples of systems with customized elements
- Outline the steps required to develop custom-made systems and applications
- Describe procedures that may be followed to define a system problem, and explain how data are gathered and then analyzed during the system analysis step
- Summarize system design issues and note the specifications produced during the system design step

CHAPTER OUTLINE

LOOKING AHEAD
EXAMPLES OF CUSTOM-MADE SYSTEMS
Management Information Systems
Hospital Information Systems
THE SYSTEM DEVELOPMENT PROCESS
Problem Definition
System Analysis
System Design
Feedback and Review 11
LOOKING BACK

EXAMPLES OF CUSTOM-MADE SYSTEMS

You saw in Chapter 1 that a *system* is a group of parts that are integrated to achieve some objective. In the context of this chapter, the "parts" are the procedures and computer programs that people and organizations use to meet their informational needs. These needs may be met in much the same way that people satisfy their clothing needs. General information needs may be served by prewritten off-the-shelf software packages just as general clothing needs may be met with off-the-rack clothes. Sometimes these packages or clothes aren't quite "right" when bought, but are useful after a few alterations.

All the software or clothing needs of many may be satisfied in these ways. But not all software or clothing needs are general; some are unique and cannot be met by existing products. Just as a custom-tailored garment is designed to fit a specific person, a **custom-made system** is designed and built by or for a specific individual or organization to meet exact requirements. Such systems are developed by or for individuals with singular needs; they are found in large organizations that combine procedures in unparalleled ways; and they are designed by small organizations whose activities are so specialized that they haven't attracted the attention of package developers. Anything that's custom-made is likely to cost more and take longer to put into service than an off-the-shelf item. There's also the risk of errors and an improper fit with a customized product. We'll look at some suggestions for reducing these dangers later in the chapter. Right now, though, let's briefly look at two examples of larger custom-made systems used by business and health-care organizations. Many other customized systems designed for smaller organizations in these and other fields, such as government and education, are presented in the chapters of Module 4.

Management Information Systems

A **management information system (MIS)** is a network of computer-based data processing procedures, developed in an organization and integrated with manual and other procedures for the purpose of providing *timely* and *effective* information to *support decision making* and other necessary management functions. We'll use a business example to illustrate some of the elements in this definition, but MIS concepts certainly aren't restricted to businesses.

Timely Information The growth of many businesses and the speed with which new technological discoveries are now being applied for competitive purposes combine to produce a complex and challenging management environment. At the beginning of this century, for example, there was an average wait of 33 years between an invention and its application. But the laser was invented in 1958 and was being used just 7 years later for surgical and manufacturing purposes. And as this application rate continues to accelerate, less reaction time is available to managers (see Figure 11-1). Thus, as pressures increase from foreign and domestic competitors, businesses find that previously acceptable systems no longer give managers the timely information they need. This is why some organizations have pushed hard in recent years to develop proprietary MISs that will give them a timing edge.

Effective Information What information does a person need to manage ef-

FIGURE 11-1

A major decision that might have taken several years to implement 10 years ago must now be carried out in a shorter period if the organization is to remain competitive. But while the available management reaction time is shrinking, each decision may carry a greater risk and be valid for a shorter time period. Furthermore, as reaction time shrinks, profitable opportunities are lost because preoccupied managers fail to recognize them.

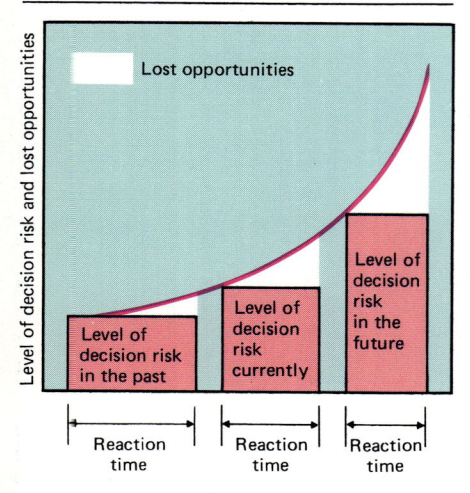

fectively? This question can be answered only in broad general terms because people differ in the ways they view, analyze, organize, and use information. An added complication is the *organizational level* of the managerial job. In smaller organizations there are few levels, and the managers at those levels often have a general understanding of the whole organization's activities. But as organizations grow, more levels are added and specialists are hired. Information sufficient for generalists is often not detailed enough for these specialists. It thus becomes necessary to supply different types of information to people at different levels.

Top-level managers still must have a general understanding of the organization's activities. Since they are charged with weighing risks and making major policy decisions on such matters as new product development and new plant authorizations, they need the type of information that will support these long-range **strategic plans and decisions.** *Middle-level managers* are responsible for making the **tactical decisions** that will allocate the resources and establish the controls needed to implement the top-level plans. And *lower-level managers* make the day-to-day **operational decisions** to schedule and control specific tasks. The actual results of an operation may be checked daily against planned expectations, and corrective actions may be taken as needed. In short, as Figure 11-2 shows, managers use their time differently, need

FIGURE 11-2

(a) More time is generally spent at the lower managerial levels performing control activities (e.g., checking to make sure that production schedules are being met), while at the upper levels more time is spent on planning (e.g., determining the location and specifications of a new production plant). (b) Lower-level managers need detailed information relating to daily operations of specific departments, but top executives are best served with information that summarizes trends and indicates exceptions to what was expected. (c) The higher a manager is in an organization, the more likely it is that he or she will use information obtained from external sources. A supervisor uses internally generated feedback information to control production processes, but a president studying the feasibility of a new plant needs external information about customer product acceptance, pollution control, local tax structures, and labor availability.

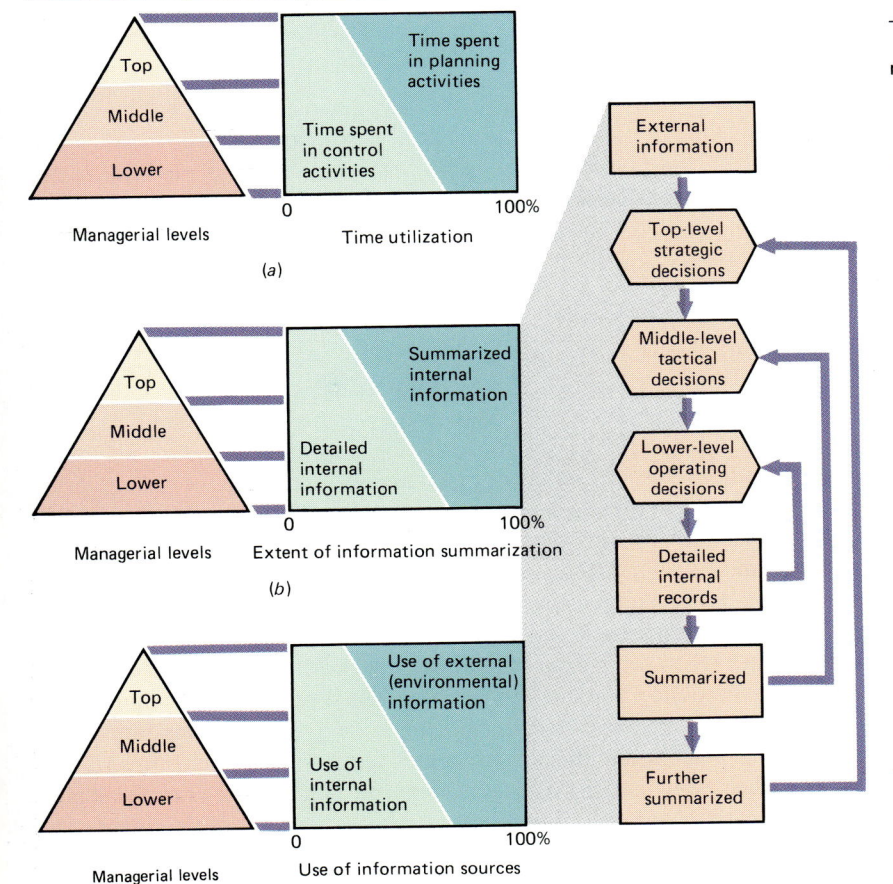

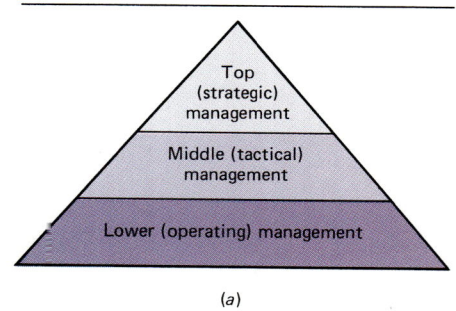

internal information with varying degrees of detail, and need different mixes of internal and external information in order to make their decisions. Thus most MIS designers first develop customized conceptual models for their organizations, and then begin to upgrade and integrate existing information-producing systems into their long-range plans. This integration and system-building continues today in many organizations.

Although MIS models differ, most of them recognize the concepts shown in Figure 11-3. In addition to what might be termed the *horizontal* management structure shown in Figure 11-3*a*, an organization is also divided *vertically* into different specialties and functions which require separate information flows (see Figure 11-3*b*). Combining the horizontal managerial levels with the vertical specialties produces the complex organizational structure shown in Figure 11-3*c*. Underlying this structure is a data base consisting, ideally, of internally and externally produced data relating to past, present, and predicted future events.

The formidable task of the MIS designer is to develop the information flow needed to support decision making (see Figure 11-4). Generally, much of the information needed by managers who occupy different levels and who have different responsibilities is obtained from a collection of existing information systems (or subsystems). Prewritten software packages may be used to process many of these subsystem applications. These systems may be bound together very closely in an MIS. More often, however, they're more loosely coupled. Either way, though, there's likely to be a need for custom software to tie elements together.

Decision Support   Computer-based MISs regularly support the planning and decision-making activities of managers in a number of business areas (see Figure 11-5). The components of an MIS that assist managers in these activities are often called **decision support systems (DSSs)**. Included among the planning and decision-making practices that may be supported are the uses of *simulation, expert systems,* and *information centers*.

● *The use of simulation.*   As Figure 11-6 shows, the simulation concept rests on reality or fact. Few people (if any) fully understand every aspect of a complex situation. Theories are thus developed which may focus attention on only part of the complex whole. Models may then be built in order to test or represent a theory. Finally, **simulation** is the use of a model in the attempt to identify and/or reflect the behavior of a real person, process, or system. Managers may evaluate proposed projects or strategies by using spreadsheet software to construct theoretical models. They can then determine what happens to these models when different values are plugged into the spreadsheet cells or when various assumptions are tested. Simulation is thus a trial-and-error problem-solving approach that's very useful in planning. Simulation models serving managers at different levels may also be integrated into an overall **corporate modeling** approach to planning and decision making. For example, a model can receive estimates from top executives about economic conditions and capital expenditures for the next 5-year period. Simulation runs may then produce estimated financial statements for each of the 5 years. Managers next analyze the simulated financial statements. If results are disappointing, the managers can change variables in the model that are under their control, such as future capital spending, and then repeat the simulations. When accept-

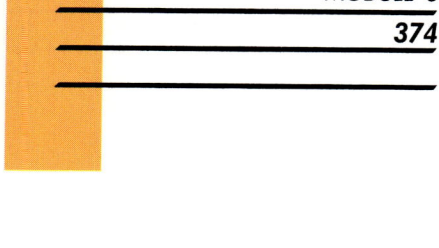

FIGURE 11-3

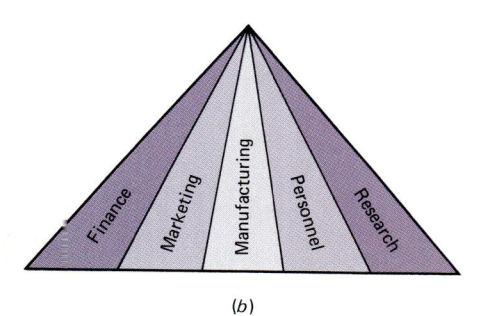

MIS design considerations.

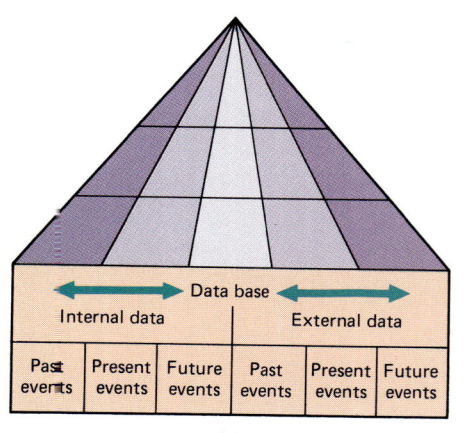

Information flow needed to support decision-making and other management functions

Representative tasks

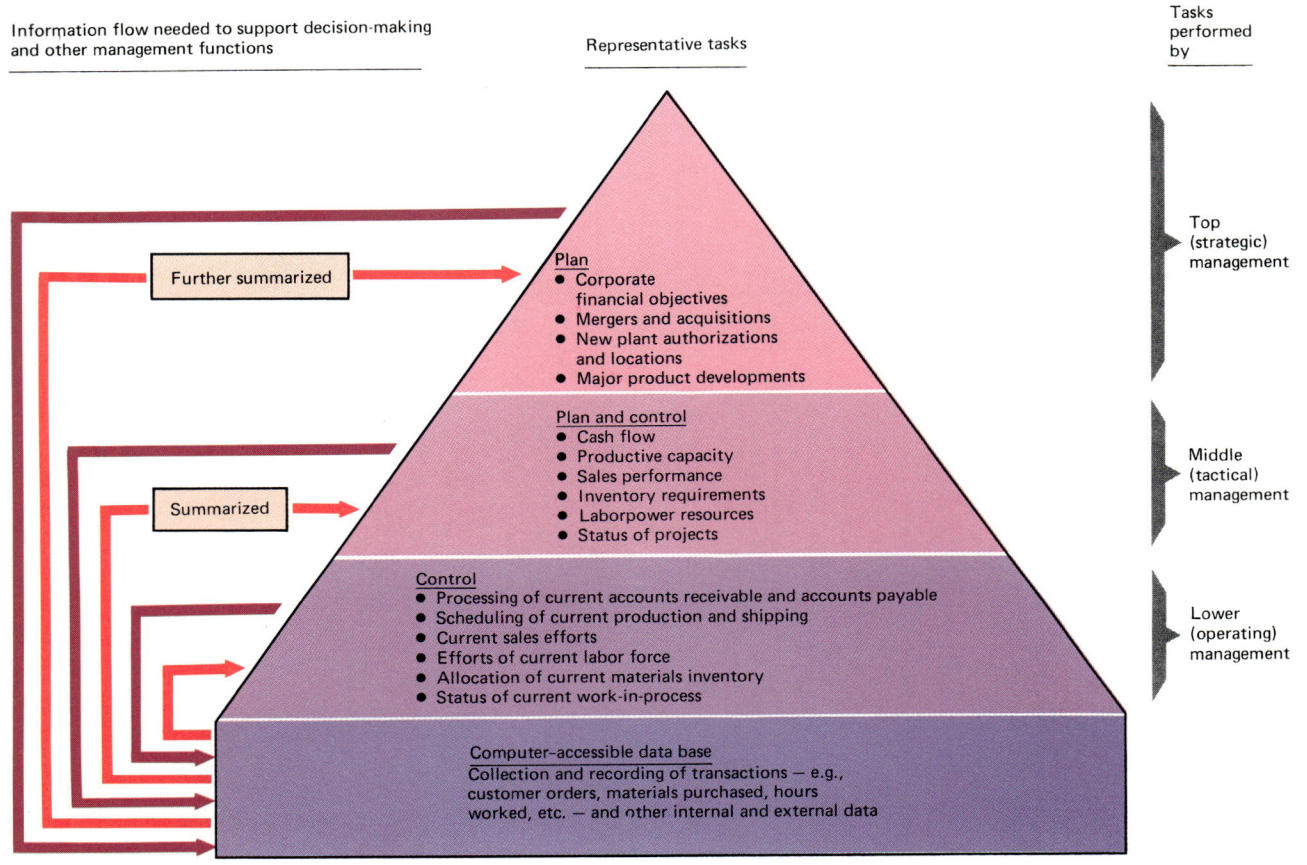

Tasks performed by

Further summarized →

Plan
- Corporate financial objectives
- Mergers and acquisitions
- New plant authorizations and locations
- Major product developments

Top (strategic) management

Summarized →

Plan and control
- Cash flow
- Productive capacity
- Sales performance
- Inventory requirements
- Laborpower resources
- Status of projects

Middle (tactical) management

Control
- Processing of current accounts receivable and accounts payable
- Scheduling of current production and shipping
- Current sales efforts
- Efforts of current labor force
- Allocation of current materials inventory
- Status of current work-in-process

Lower (operating) management

Computer-accessible data base
Collection and recording of transactions — e.g., customer orders, materials purchased, hours worked, etc. — and other internal and external data

FIGURE 11-4

The task of MIS designers is to develop the information flow needs to support decision making.

able financial results are obtained, they become the targets for planning at lower levels in the company (see Figure 11-7). As you would expect, software that meets such specific needs must often be custom-made.

- ***The use of expert systems.*** As you saw in Chapter 3, an *expert system* is a software package that includes (1) a stored base of knowledge in a specialized area and (2) the capability to probe this knowledge base and make decision recommendations. The products of years of research in the field of *artificial intelligence,* expert systems are beginning to appear in selected areas, and their future applications seem almost limitless. Some expert systems such as the one prepared at General Electric to help mechanics repair diesel engine locomotives may be purchased. But other custom-written programs such as the one used by a French oil company to diagnose problems at drilling sites are considered to be competitive tools, and so their details remain closely guarded secrets. You'll find further information on expert systems in the Closer Look reading at the end of this chapter.

- ***The use of information centers.*** Many organizations with large mainframe computers have established information centers to support the planning and decision-making activities of their employees. Generally set up as a service branch of an MIS department, an **information center** gives its users a

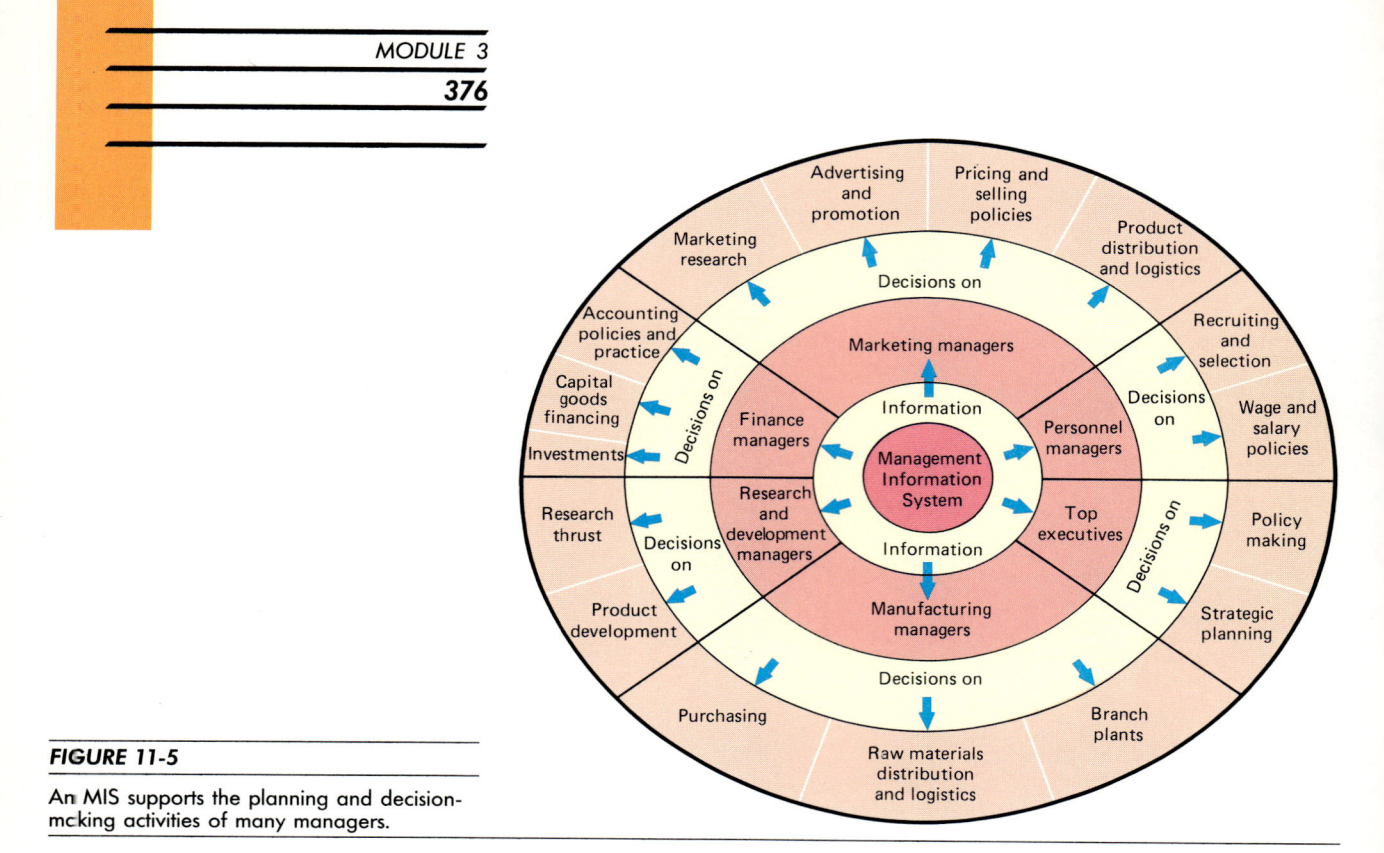

FIGURE 11-5

An MIS supports the planning and decision-making activities of many managers.

FIGURE 11-6

The simulation concept.

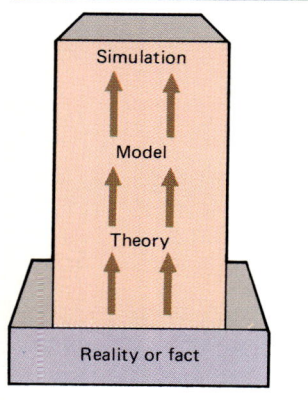

direct online path into the organization's data bases to retrieve the facts they need. Center personnel show people how to employ available software to develop their own custom-made applications and generate their own reports. Instead of channeling their information requests through analysts and programmers in the MIS department, end users can thus produce their own output to support their planning and decision-making activities. Since analysts and programmers are often trying to cope with a huge backlog of applications requests, this do-it-yourself approach allows people to cut through the backlog and get a quicker response to their needs.

Hospital Information Systems

The development of **hospital information systems (HISs)** in health-care organizations has paralleled the development of MISs in business settings, and an HIS shares many common elements with a business MIS. An HIS provides management and clinical information to administrative and health-care professionals throughout a hospital. An integrated data base management system is used, and software modules are designed for key administrative and clinical applications.

Some of the key applications on the *administrative* side of an HIS are those in the financial, personnel, materials and facilities, and medical record storage areas. The financial subsystem in an HIS manages patient billing, payroll, and other financial matters; the personnel subsystem keeps track of employee skills and other records; the materials and facilities applications deal with room use and occupancy, length of stay, food service, and so on;

FIGURE 11-7

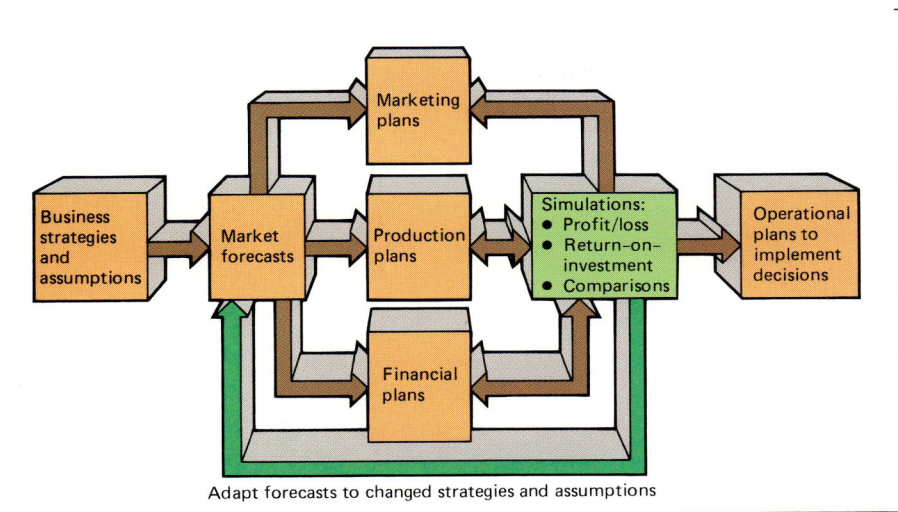

The strategies, goals, and economic assumptions of managers serve as the basis for *market forecasts*. This expectation of how many items can be sold then becomes the basis for determining (1) how and when to acquire materials and make the items (the *production plans*), (2) how and when to have the money on hand to pay for the acquired materials and produced items (the *financial plans*), and (3) how and when to promote and distribute the items (the *marketing plans*). And these plans are then used in simulations to estimate such variables as profit and return on investment. Of course, the results of these simulations may bring about changes in established plans and/or the results may cause changes in strategies and assumptions. Once initial simulations have been concluded and high-level plans have been made, operational plans at lower levels are often needed to implement the decisions.

and the medical record storage and retrieval functions include maintaining patient and research data bases and clinical and administrative files.

On the *clinical* side of an HIS, the applications subsystems include those associated with (1) data collection and analysis for diagnostic purposes,

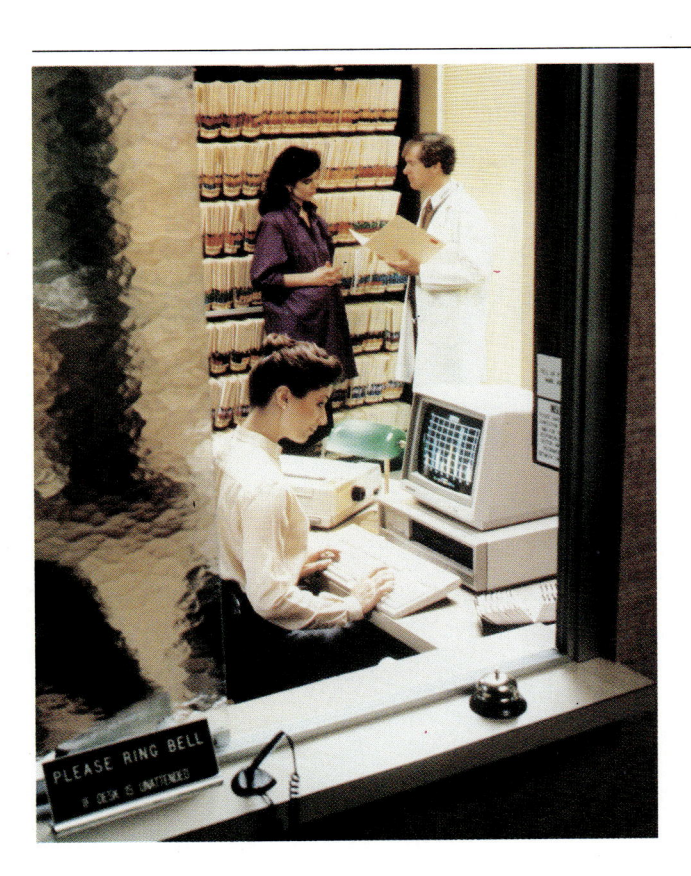

Hospital information systems organize and manage many administrative functions in a hospital, including the storage of patients' medical records in a way that makes them available for research studies as well as for later treatment when that is needed. (Courtesy Texas Instruments, Inc.)

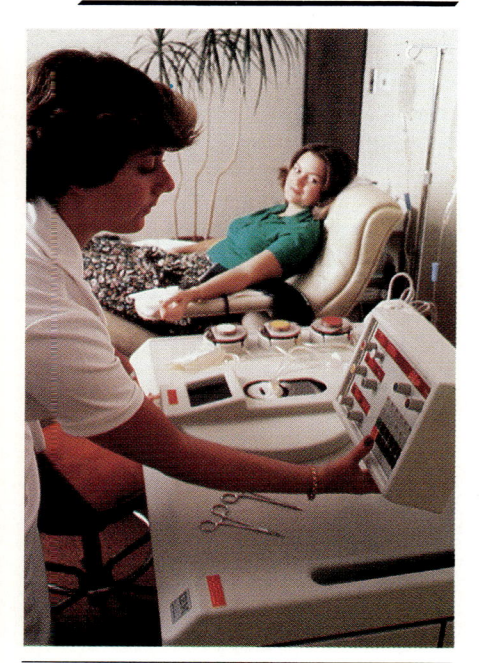

Hospital information systems also include many clinical subsystems, including those that monitor the various drugs being given to each patient. (Courtesy IBM Corp.)

(2) lab testing procedures and the analysis of lab data, (3) patient monitoring and intensive care, (4) pharmacy control, and (5) specialized research functions associated with such topics as assistance for the handicapped, occupational diseases, and preventive and community health programs. As in the case of MISs, many subsystem elements may be performed with prewritten software packages, but it's also likely that custom software is needed to tie elements together. Let's look now at how custom-made systems are developed.

THE SYSTEM DEVELOPMENT PROCESS

As you saw in Chapter 2, information users and data processing specialists must often work together to complete a series of steps in a *system study*. The object of such a study is to develop and/or acquire the software needed to control the processing of specific applications. Although some study steps may be bypassed if suitable software packages are available, the six steps shown in Figure 11-8 are needed when custom-made programs are written. (The first three steps are generally also needed before a suitable software package can be identified.) These six steps may be classified into two development stages. Steps 1 through 3 make up the **system analysis/design stage,** while steps 4 through 6 represent the **programming stage.** We'll look at system analysis/design steps in this chapter. General programming concepts are outlined in the next chapter.

Problem Definition

Problem definition is the first and perhaps the most important step in the system study. After all, people must recognize that a need or problem exists before they can create a solution. A clear and accurate problem definition—one that's not open to misinterpretation by people with different backgrounds—isn't easy to prepare. But since it's the foundation for all the system study steps that follow, such a definition must be created.

The Problem Definition Survey
A preliminary **problem definition survey** is often conducted to identify the problem or need. There's certainly nothing new about such surveys. In the Bible in chapter 13 of the Book of Numbers, Moses sent out a team to survey the Promised Land and report back their findings. Three important prerequisite principles were observed in this early survey:

1 *The survey had support at the highest levels.* God told Moses: "Send men to spy out the land of Canaan . . . from each tribe of their fathers shall you send a man, every one a leader among them." Moses certainly had support at the highest level! Although requests for system changes or additions may originate from many sources, top-level management support is important to the success of the effort.

2 *The survey team consisted of highly respected people.* Only tribal leaders were sent on the mission. Members of the team seeking to define the

1 The first step in the system study is to clearly *identify the particular problem* to be solved or the tasks to be accomplished. Managers departmental employees, and data processing personnel jointly participate in determining the problem and setting system goals.

2 The second step involves *system analysis*. After the problem has been identified, a study team works closely together to *gather* and then *analyze* data about current data processing operations.

3 The third step is *system design*. After analyzing the procedures currently being followed, the people in the study team must then cooperate in the design of any new systems or applications that may be required to satisfy the need. As a part of the system design phase, people must settle on the most feasible design alternative to achieve the study goals. And they must prepare new design specifications that include the output desired, the input data needed, and the processing procedures required to convert the input data into the output results.

4 The fourth step is *programming analysis*. The new system or application specifications may be turned over to one or more programmers. These specifications are then broken down into the specific input/output, calculating, logic/comparison, and storage/retrieval operations required to satisfy the need.

5 The fifth step is *program preparation*. At this stage, one or more programmers translate or code the required operations into a language and form acceptable to the computer hardware.

6 The sixth step involves the *implementation* and *maintenance* of the system or application. People must first make sure that the coded program(s) is checked for errors and tested prior to being used on a routine basis. After programs appear to be running properly and producing correct results, the changeover to the new approach is made. The cooperation of the many people who may be involved in the preparation of input data and the use of output results is needed at this if the new approach is to be successfully implemented. Finally, implemented systems and programs are usually subject to continual change and must therefore be maintained. This modification and improvement must be a cooperative effort between those served by the system of program and those responsible for maintaining it.

FIGURE 11-8

A summary of the six steps people follow to develop custom-made systems. These six steps may be classified into system analysis/design and programming stages. This chapter deals with steps 1 through 3 that make up the system analysis/design stage. Steps 4 through 6 represent the programming stage. General programming concepts are presented in the next chapter. (Photos courtesy Hewlett-Packard Company; Honeywell, Inc.; Teletype Corporation; General Electric Information Systems Company; Edith G. Haun Stock, Boston; and Control Data Corporation)

problem should also be qualified people selected for the offsetting talents they can bring to the job. At least one member (and very possibly the leader of the survey team) represents the interests of the end users of any new system that will be developed. Another member should be familiar with system development and the technical side of data processing. An auditor may also be included to evaluate the effects of any proposed changes on existing data integrity and system security controls.

3 *The scope and objectives of the survey were clearly stated.* Moses specifically told his team to investigate the richness of the land and the strength of the occupants. In a problem definition survey, the nature of the operation(s) that is (are) to be investigated, and the objectives that are to be pursued, should be specifically stated. The organizational units that are to be included should also be identified.

The biblical survey team returned to Moses after 40 days. The team members agreed on the richness of the land, but not on the strength of the occupants. Sessions were held to present the differing viewpoints. It's also usually necessary for the problem definition team to hold preliminary sessions with those who are likely to be affected by any changes. These **requirements sessions** allow the people who are most familiar with existing methods to make suggestions for improvement and to help define specific system goals.

A repeating (or *iterative*) process may be necessary before the problem definition step is completed. There's no definite procedure to be followed before detailed system analysis can begin. A top executive may believe that informational deficiencies exist. He or she may prepare a general statement of objectives and then appoint a manager to conduct a survey. A number of requirements sessions may be held to translate general desires into more specific goals. The scope of the survey may be enlarged or reduced, and objectives may also change as facts are gathered. When it appears that approval has been reached on the problem definition, the survey team should put the detailed definition *in writing* and send it to all concerned for written approval. If differences remain, they should be resolved in additional requirements sessions. There are those who may become impatient with the "delays" in system development caused by these additional sessions. But wiser heads know that the really lengthy and expensive delays occur when users discover very late in the development process that the designed system is unsatisfactory because of earlier requirements oversights (see Figure 11-9).

FIGURE 11-9

The cost of correcting an oversight in problem definition can mushroom later in the process. It's estimated that an oversight that's not detected until the implementation stage can cost 10 to 100 times more to fix than one that's found during the definition step.

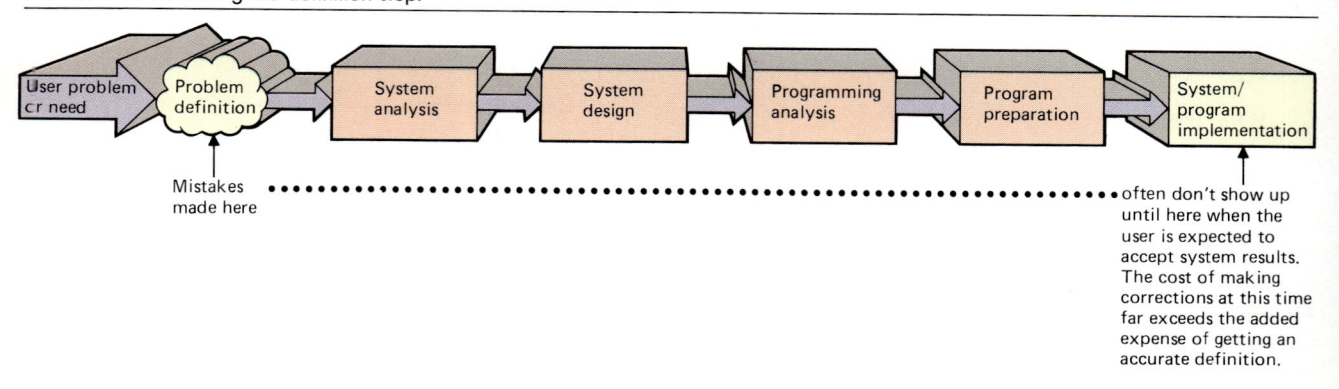

The System Study Charter As a final act before the detailed system analysis step begins, the survey leader should prepare a *written charter* for approval by a high-level executive or steering committee. This **system study charter** should include:

- A detailed statement of the scope and objectives of the system study
- A list of those who should be assigned to the system study team
- A grant of authority to permit this team to use some of the working time of specified individuals
- A development schedule giving a target date for the completion of the study, and interim "checkpoint" dates for the presentation of progress reports to interested parties (These progress reports give users, managers, and auditors a chance to determine the accuracy and completeness of the study effort.)

System Analysis

Since most new systems in organizations are based to some extent on existing procedures, a first step for the study team analysts is often to gather data on current operations. In short, they must find out where they are before they can figure out where they want to go.

Data Gathering It's likely that preliminary facts were gathered during the problem definition step. But more details are now needed to determine the strengths and weaknesses of current procedures. The data to be collected will vary, of course, from one study to another. But in most cases the study team members should answer the following general questions about current operations:

1 *What output results are currently being achieved?* The content, purpose, and use of reports and other output results should be determined, and the accuracy and timeliness of the output should be checked.

2 *What processing procedures and resources are being used to produce this output?* The records and files being processed, the frequency, volume, and accuracy of this processing, the sequence of steps being followed, the people and departments doing the work, the processing and storage equipment being used, the cost of the processing—these and other matters should be checked.

3 *What input data are used to produce output results?* The source, form, and volume of input data should be understood. The frequency of input, the accuracy of the input, and the input cost should also be known.

You recognize that these questions refer to the input/processing/output components found in any data processing system. But the input to output sequence is often reversed during system analysis because the analysts need an early understanding of current output before they can properly separate and analyze the processing and input functions that are relevant to the output.

Data-gathering aids The following tools and techniques are often used during data-gathering operations:

- **System flowcharts.** A **system flowchart** is a diagram that shows the basic data flow and sequence of operations in a system. The emphasis is on input documents and output reports. Only limited detail is furnished about how a workstation or machine converts the input data into the desired output. Standard symbols are used in all flowcharts to record and communicate information clearly. The basic symbols representing input/output and processing are shown in Figure 11-10*a*. Although the input/output (I/O) symbol may be used to show any type of medium or device, it's often replaced in system charts by other symbols whose shape suggests the particular medium or device being used (Figure 11-10*b*). Additional symbols are shown in Figure 11-10*c*. System flowcharts are often drawn up during the data-gathering stage. They are used to record the flow of data in a current procedure from the originating source, through a number of processing operations and machines, to the output report. The flowchart may help an analyst acquire a better understanding of the procedure than would otherwise be possible. It can also help point out possible bottlenecks in the data flow of the system. In complex systems, there's likely to be an overall "macro chart" that describes the general input/processing/output components of the system. There may then be a hierarchy of more detailed "micro charts," each of which describes a module in a higher-level chart. This breakdown of a system into a series of detailed input/processing/output graphics is a frequently used analysis technique.

- **Questionnaires and special-purpose forms.** Analysts often use printed forms to obtain answers to commonly asked questions. These questionnaires and other specialized data-gathering forms are often keyed to the activities presented in a system flowchart. They supply the details about processing frequencies, I/O volumes and materials, and the time needed to perform each activity. One forms-driven approach to data gathering is shown in Figure 11-11.

- **Interviews and observations.** Interviews are needed to gather data, prepare charts, and fill in questionnaires and forms. Analysts can watch as people perform the tasks required by the system being studied. An analyst can also take an input document and "walk it through" the processing procedure. Such a walkthrough gives the analyst a chance to obtain suggestions from people about ways in which a procedure can be improved.

Analysis of the Problem   After the necessary data have been gathered, the analysts must study their findings to determine the strengths and weaknesses of the existing procedures. During data gathering, the emphasis was on learning *what* was being done. Now, the focus is on learning *why* the system operates as it does. The purpose of this analysis is to develop suggestions on how the study goals may best be achieved.

Analysis aids The following tools and techniques may be used to analyze the current system and develop suggestions for improvement:

- **Checklist of questions.** Questions dealing with procedural, personnel,

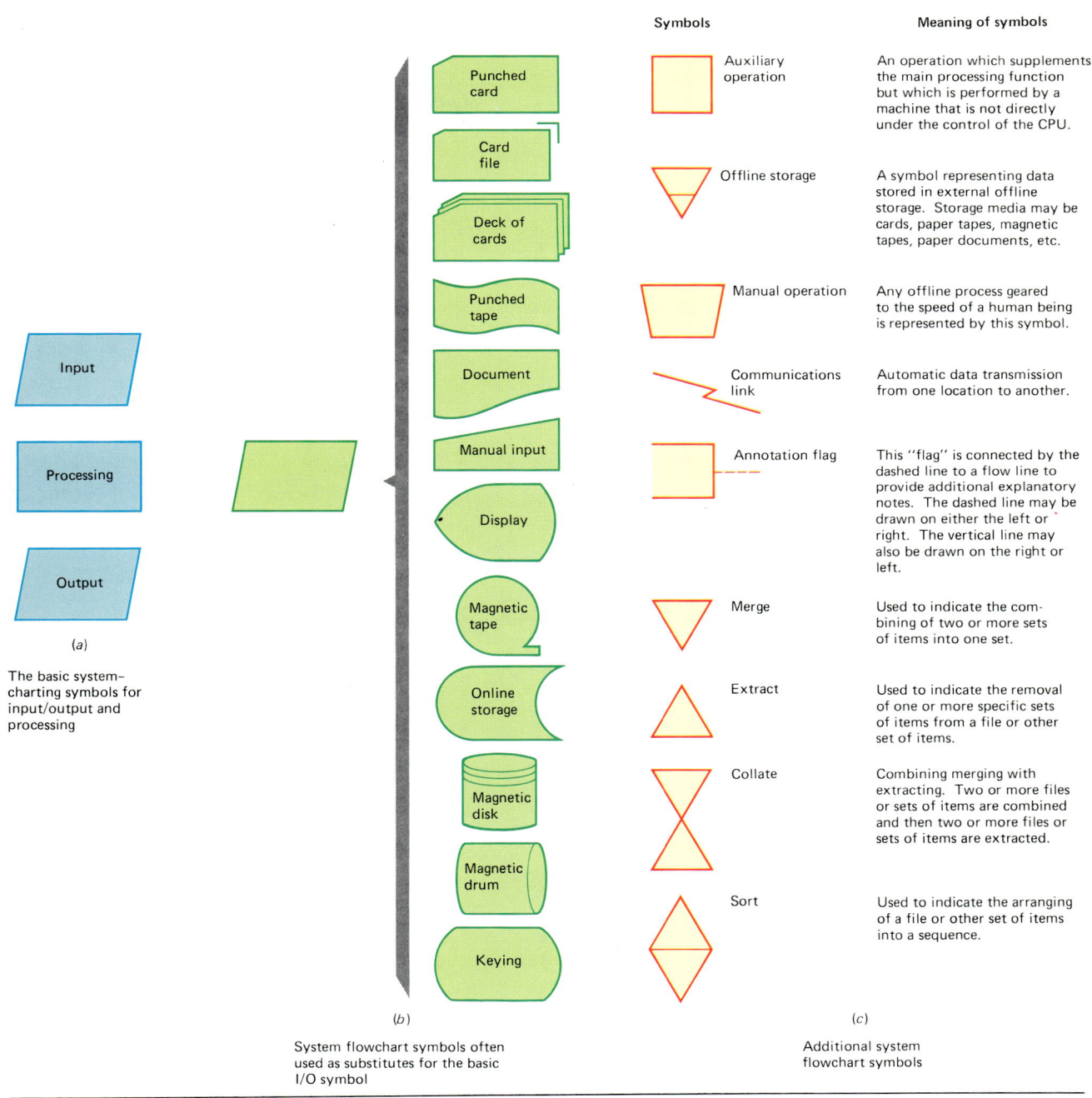

FIGURE 11-10

The standard symbols used in system flowcharts. (a) The basic system-charting symbols for input/output and processing. (b) System flowchart symbols often used as substitutes for the basic I/O symbol. (c) Additional system flowchart symbols.

(a) The basic system-charting symbols for input/output and processing:
- Input
- Processing
- Output

(b) System flowchart symbols often used as substitutes for the basic I/O symbol:
- Punched card
- Card file
- Deck of cards
- Punched tape
- Document
- Manual input
- Display
- Magnetic tape
- Online storage
- Magnetic disk
- Magnetic drum
- Keying

(c) Additional system flowchart symbols:

Symbols	Meaning of symbols
Auxiliary operation	An operation which supplements the main processing function but which is performed by a machine that is not directly under the control of the CPU.
Offline storage	A symbol representing data stored in external offline storage. Storage media may be cards, paper tapes, magnetic tapes, paper documents, etc.
Manual operation	Any offline process geared to the speed of a human being is represented by this symbol.
Communications link	Automatic data transmission from one location to another.
Annotation flag	This "flag" is connected by the dashed line to a flow line to provide additional explanatory notes. The dashed line may be drawn on either the left or right. The vertical line may also be drawn on the right or left.
Merge	Used to indicate the combining of two or more sets of items into one set.
Extract	Used to indicate the removal of one or more specific sets of items from a file or other set of items.
Collate	Combining merging with extracting. Two or more files or sets of items are combined and then two or more files or sets of items are extracted.
Sort	Used to indicate the arranging of a file or other set of items into a sequence.

organizational, and economic considerations should be answered. A few representative questions are shown in Figure 11-12.

- **System flowchart analysis.** Charts can be examined to help locate essential data and files. And they can also be used to identify bottlenecks and unnecessary files. For example, a chart may show a file where information is being stored, but from which little or nothing is being retrieved.

MODULE 3

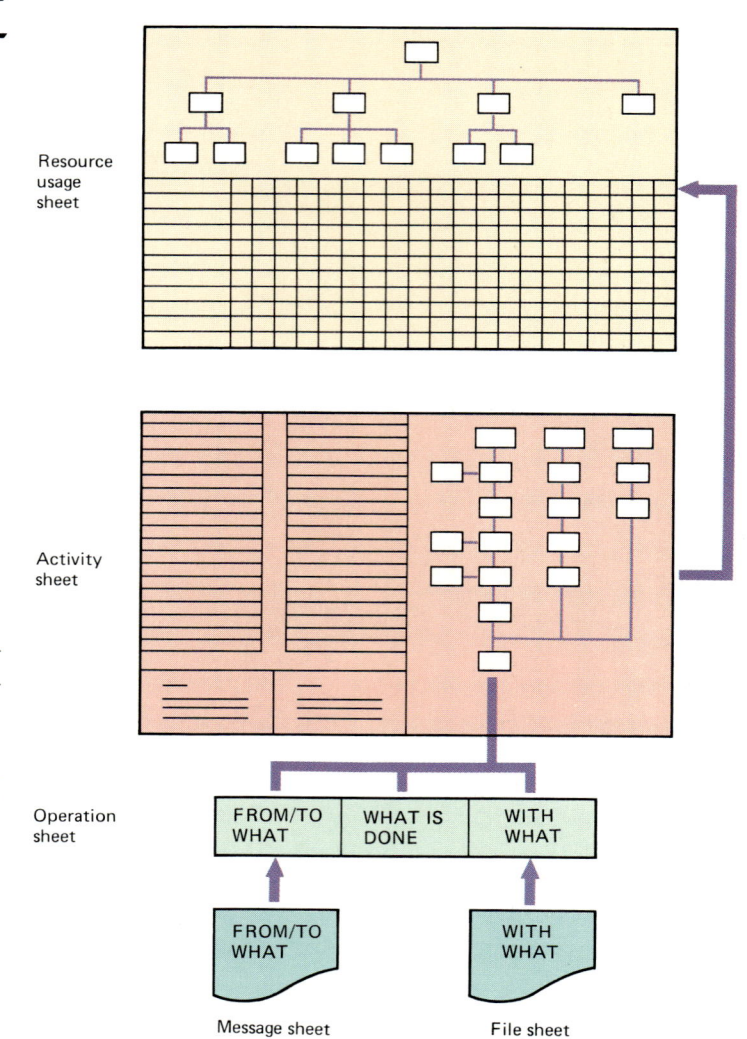

FIGURE 11-11

In IBM's study organization plan (SOP), five data-gathering forms are used to describe the existing system. When completed, the *message sheets* provide detailed facts on current output and input. The *file forms* show the data stored in the system. And the *operation sheets* present the detailed processing steps performed by the system. A separate operation sheet is typically keyed to each step outlined by the system flowchart on the *activity sheet*. Finally, the organizational environment of the current system and the costs of the system are presented on the *resource usage sheet*. (Courtesy International Business Machines Corporation)

- *Forms analysis.* The input/processing/output forms, such as those shown in Figure 11-11 that describe I/O documents and processing logic, are also helpful both in identifying key data items and in uncovering those items that are processed and stored but are seldom used.

- *Grid charts.* Special **grid** (or **input/output**) **charts** may be used to show the relationship that exists between system inputs and outputs. Input documents are listed in rows on the left of the chart (see Figure 11-13), while the output reports produced by the system are identified in the chart columns. An "x" is placed at the intersection of a row and column when a particular document is used to prepare a specific report. For example, in Figure 11-13 form A is used to prepare reports 1 and 4. The chart enables the analyst to identify independent subsystems for further study. This is done by (*a*) drawing a vertical line down any single report column and then (*b*) drawing a horizontal line across any row with a covered x, etc., until further vertical and horizontal lines are impossible. For example, if we draw a line down column

Procedural Considerations

- Is faster reporting desired? Is faster reporting necessary? Can the processing sequence be improved? What would happen if any documents were eliminated?
- Is greater accuracy needed?
- What monetary value do users place on the output? Are they willing to have their budgets charged with all or part of the cost of preparation?
- Is the output in a useful form? Has writing been minimized?
- Does an output document cause action when it's sent to a manager? If not, why is it sent?
- Is the output stored? If so, for how long? How often is it referred to?
- Can documents be combined? Is the same information duplicated on other reports? In other departments? If so, can procedures be integrated?
- Is unnecessary output generated? Do current reports clearly point out exceptions?
- Is system capacity adequate? Do bottlenecks exist? Is customer-service adequate?

Personnel and Organizational Considerations

- Is the output being prepared in the proper departments? By the right people? Could departments be combined? What effects would organizational change have on people?
- What effect would any procedural changes have on people? What would have to be done to reduce resistance to change? What would be done with those whose jobs would be eliminated or changed? If new jobs were created, what consideration would have to be given to selecting and training workers to staff these vacancies?

Economic Considerations

- What is the cost of the present system? What would be the cost of processing with revised current procedures? Approximately what would it cost to satisfy needs using other alternatives?

FIGURE 11-12

Questions for analysis.

1, we cover only one x—the one indicating that form A is used in preparing report 1. If we then draw a horizontal line along the form A row, we cover the x in column 4. We then draw a vertical line down column 4 and a horizontal line along any row with a covered x. The result of this procedure is that forms A, B, and E and reports 1, 2, and 4 combine to form an independent subsystem.

- *The top-down analysis methodology.* If the system being analyzed is complex, a "divide and conquer" methodology is often used to break the system down into smaller components. A top-level function is identified, analyzed, and then broken down into a series of second-level components. Each of these components, in turn, may be further reduced into still lower-level elements. A hierarchy of understandable subfunctions may be the result of this **top-down analysis methodology.**

The Analysis Report   Regardless of the aids used, the final product of the system analysis step should be a *documentation package* and a report of the analysts' findings. The documentation package should include copies of all forms, charts, questionnaires, I/O documents, and written procedural descriptions that have been gathered and analyzed. The **analysis report** should include:

- A restatement of the problem

Input Source Documents	Output Reports							
	1	2	3	4	5	6	7	8
Form A	x			x				
Form B		x		x				
Form C			x					
Form D						x		
Form E		x		x				
Form F			x					x
Form G					x		x	

FIGURE 11-13

An example of a grid chart.

- A summary of current procedures and a statement of present problems or opportunities

- A list of the general specifications needed to solve the problem along with some preliminary suggestions for solution alternatives that could be considered

- An evaluation of the operational feasibility of the project from a personnel and organizational standpoint

- An estimate of the economic feasibility of the project

After evaluating the analysis report, responsible managers may decide to revise the study goals, cancel the project, postpone development until later, or proceed to the system design phase.

System Design

During the system design phase, designers must decide *how* to produce an efficient (economical) and effective (relevant and useful) system. To do this, they must first *determine feasible alternatives* and then settle on a single set of *detailed specifications* for the problem solution. This isn't easy! As Figure 11-14 shows, many factors have a bearing on the design task. These factors present practical limits to the number of system alternatives that can actually be evaluated.

Design Tools and Techniques   The following tools and techniques are among those used during system design:

- *Top-down design methodology.* The **top-down design** technique requires the early identification of the top-level functions in the proposed system. Each function is then broken down into a hierarchy of understandable lower-level modules and components as shown in the **hierarchical charts** in Figure 11-15. After a top-level chart showing the total structure of the system

FIGURE 11-14

Some factors having a bearing on the design process. The detailed design specifications depend on such input factors as user needs, the skill of system designers and the tools they use, the external environment, and the organization's resources. Design specifications may also depend on existing methods and equipment and on the hardware/software alternatives that may be obtained.

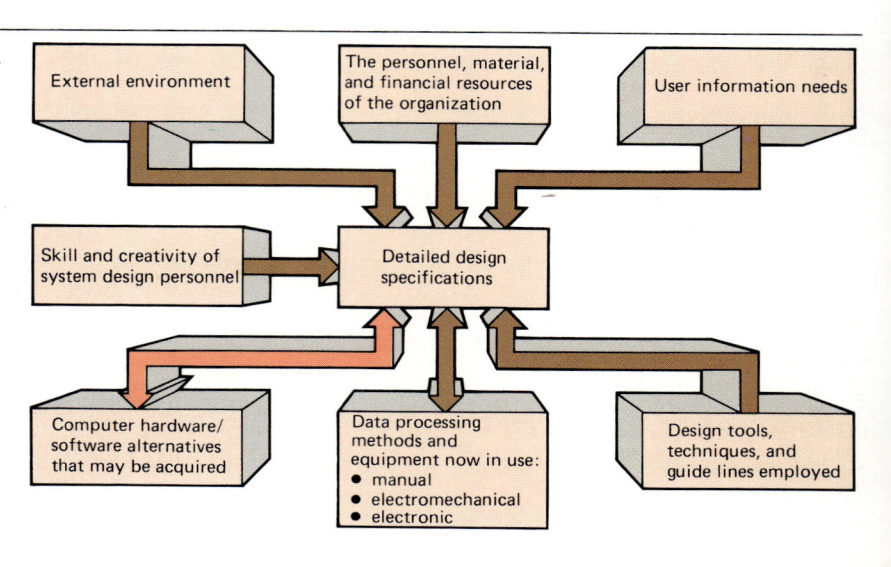

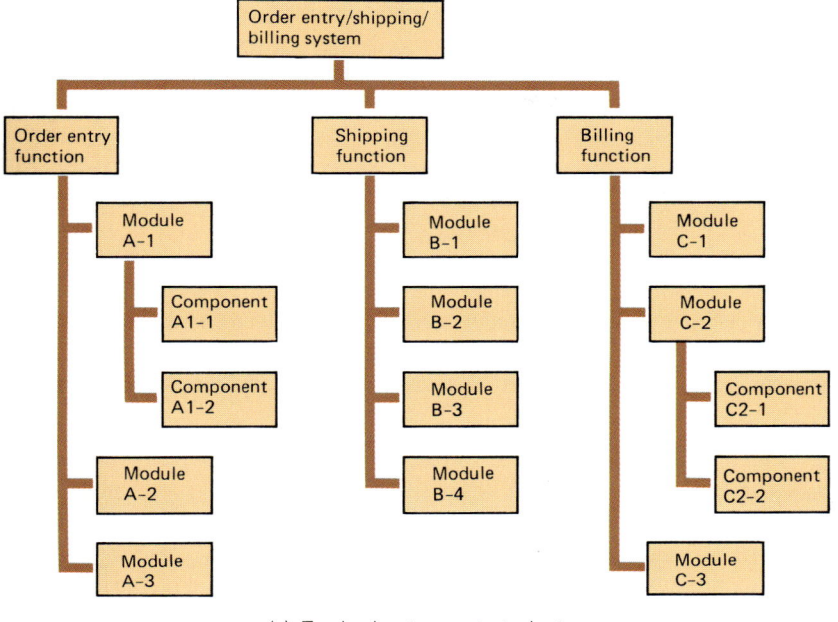

(a) Top-level system contents chart

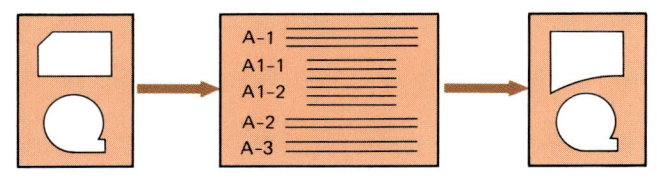

(b) Order entry function input/processing/output overview

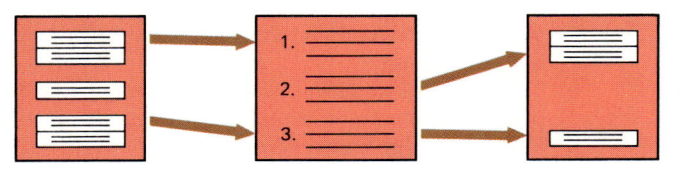

(c) Order entry module/component input/processing/output detail

FIGURE 11-15

Hierarchical charts used in top-down design.

is prepared, lower-level diagrams are created to show the input/processing/ output details of each function, module, and component. Several iterations will usually occur in this design and charting process. Designers may start with simple diagrams showing general solutions. This first effort is then refined to produce more complete charts as the design requirements become clearer.

- *Design reviews and walkthroughs.* Periodic sessions may be held so that interested users can review the design progress. Designers can present sample outputs and "walk through" the input and processing operations to describe the handling of data. Users can be encouraged to look for errors and to make comments during this **design walkthrough.**

- *Special charts and forms.* The charts and forms prepared during the system analysis phase are very helpful in the design stage. Weaknesses spotted during analysis can now be corrected. And the existing input/processing/output relationships may now be used to design a more integrated system.

Determining Alternatives: Some Design Issues Issues involving methodology and the use of resources usually influence the alternatives that are selected. These issues include questions about:

1. *The long-range design plans that are followed.* Many organizations have developed conceptual models or long-range plans for the evolution of their information systems. The alternatives that designers can consider in implementing specific projects must conform to the overall design plan that has been adopted.

2. *The control provisions that should be included.* Designers must make sure that procedures and controls are built into any alternative to ensure that the integrity of the data and the security of the system are not impaired. An "audit trail" that permits the tracing of transactions through the system from input to output must be included in the design. A basic issue facing designers is how to balance the control need against the possibility of creating an "overcontrolled" system that's expensive to operate and that produces delays in getting information into the hands of users.

Experienced system designers encourage the people who will use their new system to look for potential problems in it during a series of design walkthroughs. (Courtesy Sperry Corp.)

WINDOW 11-1

PROTOTYPING AS AN AID IN SYSTEM DEVELOPMENT

A technique called prototyping helps software developers to design custom-made systems. When this technique is used, a prototype, or preliminary version, of the computer system is developed quickly—typically in 1 to 3 months. The system user operates it for a time, analyzes feedback and makes refinements, and continues this process until a stable set of requirements can be established. Then the prototype is discarded, and a more conventional development process begins, using the results of the prototyping process as the actual specification.

In this case, prototyping is used only for requirements analysis, leaving the remainder of the application development process intact. This type of prototyping, called requirements prototyping, is often used by businesses to create computer systems during rapidly changing market conditions or during the establishment of a new business function or department.

Another type of prototyping is known as evolutionary development. This approach is also characterized by a quick approximation of the problem, but the prototype becomes the nucleus of the evolving system. Each evolutionary cycle simply adds more features to it. In this case, prototyping becomes a replacement for the entire development process.

The most important outcome of either prototyping approach is that a working model or prototype serves to help define the final system solution.

Prototyping sometimes is blamed for problems in system development. Such problems usually reflect a casual approach to the system development process, or a misunderstanding of the prerequisites for a successful prototyping project. For example, requirements prototyping should be used only when no conventional or alternative technique for requirements analysis can identify and validate the true requirements of the computer system. And some users may not realize the limited scope of the prototype and thus they have unrealistic expectations of the prototype system. But when it is properly implemented and clearly understood, prototyping provides an effective tool for designers of custom-made systems.

Adapted from Wayne Smith, "Alternative Approaches for Successful Prototyping," *Computerworld,* Sept. 16, 1985. Copyright © 1985 by CW Communications, Inc., Framingham, MA 01701.

3 *The advisability of "making" the system in-house or of "buying" it from an outside supplier.* Designers must often choose between creating a new in-house design or buying a custom-built system from an outside supplier.

4 *The attention that should be given to human factors.* Will the proposed alternatives be easy for people to understand and use? Will the alternatives give prompt response, relieve people of unnecessary chores, and be pleasant to use? These and many other questions bearing on the operational feasibility of a system must be considered. A nonresponsive design that harasses users and wastes their time will be resisted.

5 *The economic tradeoffs that should be made.* The question of economic feasibility underlies the whole system development effort. The decisions made by designers in considering all the above issues can be reached only after a careful study has been made of the available economic resources.

So many variables affect the design process that it's impossible to establish exact rules to follow in selecting alternatives. The issues we've examined are resolved in different ways by different designers using different resources in different environments.

Choosing an Alternative   By this stage, the designers also have prepared a detailed set of written and documented system specifications to achieve the system study goals. These specifications should include:

1 *Output requirements.* The form, content, and frequency of output are needed.

2 *Input requirements.* The necessary new input data should be identified along with the stored file data that are required.

3 *File and storage requirements.* The size, contents, storage media, record formats, access restrictions, and degree of permanency of any affected files should be known.

4 *Processing specifications.* The procedures needed for the computer to convert input data into desired output results should be indicated. Manual processing procedures should also be noted.

5 *Control provisions.* The steps required to achieve system control should be specified, and the later system testing and implementation procedures should be outlined.

6 *Cost estimates.* Preliminary estimates of the costs of different alternatives should be made.

We've seen that there are no exact rules to follow in selecting alternatives. Likewise, there aren't any precise guidelines to follow in choosing from among the alternatives selected. But the system specifications listed above should give the team the information it needs to pick the alternative that best suits its goals.

The Design Report   Guided by a written charter which defined the problem, people have analyzed relevant facts. The design of a detailed set of system specifications has evolved from this analysis, and the team has settled on the alternative that it thinks will result in the "best" problem solution. The team has made many decisions. But the final decisions are made by top-level managers. It's now the team's job to prepare a system **design report** and make recommendations. It's the responsibility of top executives to decide on system implementation.

The report of the study team should include the following points:

- A restatement of study scope and objectives

- The design specifications for procedures and operations that will be changed

- The anticipated effects of such changes on organizational structure and physical facilities

- The anticipated effects on people, and the personnel resources available to implement the change

- The economic effects of the change, including a cost-benefit analysis

- A summary of the expected problems and benefits arising from the change

If managers decide to continue with the development of a custom-made system or application, the project enters the programming stage, and the next steps are programming analysis, program preparation, and system implementation and maintenance. As noted earlier, we'll look at these steps in the next chapter.

FEEDBACK

FEEDBACK AND REVIEW 11

The following *matching questions* will test and reinforce your understanding of the material presented in this chapter. A number of terms are listed below. Place the letter of the appropriate term beside the definition or concept to which it belongs.

A) tactical B) information center C) requirements sessions D) system flowchart E) programming F) top-down G) simulation H) external I) decision support systems J) custom-made K) hospital information system L) system M) artificial intelligence N) system design O) operational P) management information system Q) system study charter R) grid charts S) problem definition T) expert system U) system analysis/design

_____ 1. A group of parts that are integrated to achieve some objective.

_____ 2. A type of system that's designed and built by or for a specific individual or organization to meet exact requirements.

_____ 3. A network of computer-based data processing procedures, developed in an organization and integrated with manual and other procedures for the purpose of providing timely and effective information to support decision making and other necessary functions.

_____ 4. Top-level managers need information to support strategic plans and decisions, while middle-level managers need information for _____ decisions.

_____ 5. The use of a model in the attempt to identify and/or reflect the behavior of a real person, process, or system.

_____ 6. A software package that includes a stored base of knowledge in a specialized area and the capability to probe this knowledge base and make decision recommendations.

_____ 7. People in this service branch of an MIS department show users how to develop their own custom-made applications and generate their own reports.

_____ 8. Management and clinical information are provided to the users of this type of health-care system.

_____ 9. This stage of a system study consists of the first three system development steps.

_____ 10. This stage of a system study consists of the last three system development steps.

_____ 11. The first step in a system study.

_____ 12. Meetings held to allow people to participate in setting or revising specific system goals.

_____ 13. A final act before the detailed system analysis step begins may be to prepare this document.

_____ 14. A diagram that shows a broad overview of the data flow and sequence of operations in a system.

_____ 15. Charts that show input documents in rows and output reports in columns.

_____ 16. Hierarchical charts are often used in a _____ approach to system design.

_____ 17. Lower-level managers make these types of day-to-day decisions.

_____ 18. The higher a manager is in an organization, the more likely it is that she or he will use information obtained from _____ sources (see Figure 11-2).

_____ 19. Components of an MIS that assist managers in planning and decision-making activities.

_____ 20. Expert systems are the products of years of research in this field.

_____ 21. The third step in a system study.

LOOKING BACK

1. Although prewritten software packages can perform many special and general functions, there are unique situations where these packages don't fit the need. In such cases, a custom-built system or application—one designed and built by or for a specific individual or organization to meet exact requirements—must be created.

2. A management information system (MIS) often includes many custom-made elements. An MIS is a network of computer-based data processing procedures developed in an organization and integrated with manual and other procedures for the purpose of providing timely and effective information to support decision making and other necessary management functions. The formidable task of the MIS designer is to develop the information flow needed to support decision making. Different types of information are needed by people at different levels in an organization. Top-level managers need information to support long-range strategic planning, middle-level managers need information for tactical decisions, and lower-level supervisors need information to support their day-to-day operational functions.

3. The components of an MIS that help improve planning and decision making are often called decision support systems. Simulation is a trial-and-error problem-solving technique that's also very useful in planning. Simulation models can be used by managers to evaluate proposed projects or strategies. Managers can see what happens to these models when certain conditions are given or when certain assumptions are tested. An expert system is a software package that includes a stored base of knowledge in a specialized field. As a user supplies input data, an expert system responds as an intelligent assistant by giving advice and suggesting possible courses of action. And information centers can give users a direct online path into an organization's data base(s) to retrieve the facts they need to make plans and decisions.

4. Custom-made elements are also found in hospital information systems (HISs). The development of these systems paralleled the development of MISs in business settings, and an HIS shares many common functions with a business MIS. An HIS provides management and clinical information to administrators and health-care professionals throughout a hospital.

5. The six steps followed in the system development process are (1) problem definition, (2) system analysis, (3) system design, (4) programming analysis, (5) program preparation, and (6) system/program implementation and maintenance. Steps 1 through 3 make up the system analysis/design stage, while steps 4 through 6 represent the programming stage. This chapter has considered the system analysis/design stage. Steps in the programming stage are discussed in the next chapter.

6. A preliminary system survey is often conducted during the prob-

lem definition stage to identify the need. This survey should have high-level support and should be conducted by qualified people. A number of requirements sessions are often held to allow people to participate in setting or revising system goals. At the conclusion of the problem definition step, a detailed written statement of the scope and objectives of the study should be prepared.

7. Analysts gather data on current operations during the system analysis stage. Some of the tools they use during data gathering are system flowcharts, questionnaires, special-purpose forms, and interviews. After data have been gathered, analysts study these facts to develop suggestions on how the study goals may be achieved. The analysis tools they may use include checklists of questions, a hierarchy of system flowcharts, and grid charts. An analysis report is written at the end of this step.

8. During the system design phase, designers decide how to produce an efficient and effective system. Feasible alternatives are identified, and a set of detailed specifications for the problem solution is prepared. Issues involving methodology and the use of resources surface at this time. Five of these issues are discussed in the chapter. Design tools such as the top-down design approach, special charts and forms, and design walkthroughs are used. Since so many variables bear on the design process, it's impossible to establish exact rules for selecting alternatives or choosing from among the alternatives selected. After considering the design report prepared by the study team, top executives decide if a new system or application should be implemented. If the decision is to go forward, then the steps in the programming stage must be carried out.

KEY TERMS AND CONCEPTS

custom-made system 372
management information system (MIS) 372
strategic plans and decisions 373
tactical decisions 373
operational decisions 373
decision support systems (DSSs) 374
simulation 374
corporate modeling 374
information center 375
hospital information system (HIS) 376
system analysis/design stage 378
programming stage 378
problem definition 378
problem definition survey 378
requirements sessions 380
system study charter 381
system flowchart 382
grid (input/output) charts 384
top-down analysis methodology 385
analysis report 385
top-down design 386
hierarchical charts 386
design walkthrough 387
design report 390

Topics for Review and Discussion

1. "Software needs may be met in much the same way that people satisfy their clothing needs." Discuss this statement.
2. (a) What's a custom-made system? (b) What are some examples of these systems? (c) Why are such systems developed?
3. (a) What is an MIS? (b) Why have traditional information systems failed to meet the needs of managers?
4. "A factor that complicates the subject of the information needed by managers is the organizational level of the managerial job." Discuss this statement.
5. (a) What is simulation? (b) How can it be used in planning and decision making?
6. (a) What is an expert system? (b) Identify one example of such a system.
7. (a) What is an information center? (b) What functions may be performed by such a center?
8. (a) What are some of the key administrative applications performed by an HIS? (b) What are some of the key clinical applications?
9. (a) What are the steps in the system development process? (b) Which step do you think is most important? (c) Which steps make up the system analysis/design stage? (d) The programming stage?
10. What principles should be observed in conducting a problem definition survey?
11. Why is it important to not become impatient with "delays" that occur during problem definition?
12. (a) What tools and techniques may be used to gather data about current operations? (b) To analyze the current system and develop suggestions for improvements?
13. "There are a number of issues that have a bearing on the design alternatives that are finally selected." What are four of these issues?
14. What tools and techniques are used during system design?
15. What should be included in the written design specifications?

Projects/Issues to Consider

1. Visit an organization with a central computing facility (your school, your job, a nearby business, a hospital, or a government facility). Prepare a class report outlining two ways that the facility supports the planning and decision-making activities of people in the organization.
2. Visit your library and locate some articles on system analysis tools and/or system design techniques. Select a tool or technique of interest to you for further research, and then prepare a summary report of your research findings.
3. Identify a system you're involved with at school, work, or home. Analyze this system, and point out ways that it could be redesigned to serve you better. Present your analysis and redesign thoughts to the class.

Answers to Feedback and Review Section

1. L 2. J 3. P 4. A 5. G 6. T 7. B 8. K 9. U 10. E 11. S 12. C 13. Q 14. D 15. R 16. F 17. O 18. H 19. I 20. M 21. N

A CLOSER LOOK

EXPERT SYSTEMS

At Boeing Aerospace Company, new product lines do not roll off the assembly line every month. The typical large aircraft design project has a lifespan of 10 years. Back in 1975–1976, Boeing management realized that two of its key aircraft designs would reach the anticipated end of their design lifespans just as several senior tool-design engineers were due to retire. The coincidence raised an unsettling prospect: Boeing would have to rely on a young, untried generation of designers to prepare its next cycle of aircraft designs.

Boeing's first pass at the problem, initiated in 1977, was to create design teams that paired senior and junior engineers, with each team having its own computer-aided design (CAD) workstation. None of the engineers had previously used design graphics software, but all took to it immediately and helped Boeing gain a double benefit. The first was an increase in design productivity, as engineers could use the CAD system to test a design's feasibility without having to build physical models. Second, pictorial representations of design projects made it much easier for the older engineers to pass on their knowledge to the new generation. By the time the older engineers finally retired, the young engineers had absorbed enough of their seniors' expertise to carry on the new aircraft design cycle.

The intergenerational design teams proved to be a good short-term solution, but Boeing wanted more effective and dependable ways of disseminating expertise among its knowledge workers, to prevent valuable knowledge from retiring with the worker. The result has been the development of some dozen expert systems: computer programs that mimic the problem-solving and goal-oriented thought processes of human experts. Such systems make valuable knowledge and experience accessible throughout a firm.

Expert systems are one application of artificial intelligence (AI). Boeing was one of a small band of innovators that explored the uses of AI during the last decade, often pooling their knowledge with AI laboratories at universities such as Stanford and Carnegie-Mellon. In 1983, Boeing opened its Artificial Intelligence Center. Besides supporting research in robotics, expert systems development tools, natural languages, and voice simulation, the center encourages employees from any Boeing division to take classes and develop expert systems for their departments. At least 12 systems are currently under development, including a helicopter repair adviser, a deep space station designer, a system to diagnose airplane engine troubles, and a program that advises division managers on data base management system purchases.

Other U.S. companies seeking ways to combat their own knowledge-worker shortages would love to imitate Boeing's effort. In an increasingly complex and cutthroat business world, the demand for specialized expertise keeps growing—and so companies battle for a dwindling supply of available experts. Expert systems could ease this problem by making valuable expertise available to any knowledge worker with a computer terminal. But expert systems are still at the stage where expectations usually outweigh their abilities.

A number of promising systems have been developed, like the Boeing example, but they required the resources of Fortune 500 companies with large staffs and multimillion dollar AI laboratories. The products and services that will put major-league expert systems within smaller firms' reach are mostly down the road. What is available are development tools or "shells," expert system building blocks that include a knowledge editor for constructing the "knowledge base," and an "inference engine" that decides how to use the knowledge to reach conclusions and solve problems. Developing an expert system around a prefabricated shell takes far less time than doing it from scratch with an AI programming language such as LISP or PROLOG.

But even these shells require the presence of "knowledge engineers" to perform the crucial job of extracting an expert's knowledge and converting it into rules-of-thumb that can be loaded into a knowledge base. Right now, these knowledge engineers are hard to find and expensive to keep.

Many businesses would like to see expert systems they can buy off the shelf and use at once. But by definition an expert system must contain knowledge unique to a specialized domain and the collected expertise of the firm that will be using it. Thus, expert systems vendors include in the price of their offerings the time it takes for their consultants to sit down and help the customer load proprietary knowledge into the system.

Before embarking on the expensive course of developing an expert system, a company must decide whether the unique uncertainties of these products are offset by unique capabilities far beyond those of ordinary software—particularly of decision support systems (DSSs), which come closest to expert systems in purpose. A good example of how the two types of products differ is a project underway at Boeing's AI Center: an expert system that will work in concert with a DSS program called Structural Design Language (STRUDL).

Both decision support and expert systems products are designed to help boost engineers' productivity by speeding the process of testing prototype designs, performing stress analysis, and so on. But STRUDL is a passive tool whose effectiveness depends on the user's abilities. By feeding the right data into the appropriate STRUDL stress-analysis formula or graphic modeling application, a design engineer can gain insight into a design prototype's potential. However, STRJDL cannot help the engineer decide what questions to ask or what data to key in, nor can it suggest further actions based on the results of an analysis. Only an expert system that assumes the role of teacher/partner can do this.

The foundation of an expert system's authority is its knowledge base, which contains all the relevant expertise that can be extracted from human experts in a given field. This expertise is generally stored in the form of rules-of-thumb or "heuristics"—typically, "if/then" statements. Given an initial set of circumstances, the system can map out a set of contingencies, and further contingencies that might arise from the first set, and so on. A heuristic does not guarantee results. Rather, it suggests a general direction that is likely to prove fruitful.

A structure of interlocking heuristics, called a "decision tree," is one way an expert system represents knowledge. Some expert systems perform "backward inferencing," starting with a goal and trying different combinations of rules and/or actions until they reach it. The other major category of expert system performs "forward inferencing": reasoning from initial information until it reaches useful conclusions. Most expert systems combine both types of inferencing, searching for a way to reach a goal within certain constraints.

In developing an expert system, the more complex and amorphous the expertise to be captured, the longer it takes for an expert and a knowledge engineer to reach an acceptable approximation. Often they put together a working prototype and try it out with a sample problem to see if the system and the expert come up with the same answer. If not, they will have to figure out where the system made a wrong turn.

Expert systems are typical programs in the sense that the original designers are unlikely to uncover all of the bugs. There will always be exceptions to rules that they did not think of. Like a human expert, the system must be able to learn from experience, not just during the development process, but throughout its lifetime.

One simple way of learning involves discarding decision tree branches when they do not pan out. A much more sophisticated expert system capability is the continual formulation of new heuristics based on the system's experience.

Human input to expert systems remains a crucial element in their development. Expert systems are used as consultants, not decision makers; the human users must decide how to make use of a system's knowledge. As long as expert systems serve their human operators, humanity can put aside its nightmares of intelligent computers taking over the world, or of dim-witted computers making terrible mistakes. While expert systems already are solving extremely complex problems, researchers are still a long way from developing systems that can mimic how even a 3-year-old learns to deal with the world.

Adapted from Elizabeth Horwitt, "Exploring Expert Systems," *Business Computer Systems*, March 1985. Reprinted with permission of *Business Computer Systems* Magazine, a Cahners Publication.

CHAPTER 12

PREPARING APPLICATIONS PROGRAMS:
PRACTICES AND LANGUAGES

DID THE WRONG PROGRAMMING LANGUAGE PUT NEW JERSEY MOTORISTS IN A JAM?

A bureaucratic gridlock of epic proportions entangled New Jersey motorists, due to a system design consultant's inappropriate choice of a fourth-generation computer language to program the state's Motor Vehicle computer system.

As a result, more than a million drivers were unable to register their cars, or were incorrectly listed in New Jersey's computers as operating unregistered vehicles. So many drivers were forced to drive without registrations that the New Jersey Attorney General's office ordered police to stop citing drivers for the offense.

The controversial system was designed for the New Jersey Department of Motor Vehicles using Ideal, a new computer language, and a relational data base management system produced by Applied Data Research. The system was designed to process automatically New Jersey's 5 million drivers' license and registration renewals and to update daily, instead of weekly, New Jersey's merit rating surcharge system. This system keeps track of traffic violation points and penalizes careless drivers with higher insurance rates.

The Department of Motor Vehicles wanted to expand to 1,000 the number of terminals able to access the system. Instead, they found the new system foundering with 200 terminals. Response times went from the 3 to 5 seconds targeted to as long as 5 minutes. The result was a backlog in recording motor-vehicle registrations that cost New Jersey $160,000 a month in overtime to correct from July 1985, when the project began, until 1986 when reprogramming in COBOL produced a system that operated properly.

Disagreement about the cause of the computer problem put the manufacturer of the computer language and data base and New Jersey on one side of the argument and the systems consultant on the other. New Jersey claimed that the consultant used Ideal, a language developed in 1983, for the entire project because it is cheaper, easier, and faster to code programs in it than in COBOL. Applied Data Research, the manufacturer of Ideal, claimed that it should have been used for only 85 percent of the project. It was not designed to handle the daily transferral of all registrations into the central data base. ADP argued that COBOL, which is used for similar systems in New York and Connecticut, is better suited for this heavy volume of batch transactions.

The system was finally repaired by reprogramming it in COBOL, but the problem could have been avoided by more careful planning in the system analysis/design stage of the project.

Source: Charles Babcock, "New Jersey Motorists in Software Jam," *Computerworld*, Sept. 30, 1985. Copyright © 1985 by CW Communications, Inc., Framingham, MA 01701.

CHAPTER 12
399

LOOKING AHEAD

In this chapter dealing with the programming process, you'll learn about some of the practices followed during program preparation. The different categories of programming languages are then identified and discussed. Next, you'll be introduced to some of the major high-level languages used in program coding. Finally, the implementation and maintenance of coded software are presented. The information in this chapter will enable you to:

- Identify and discuss several of the practices followed during program preparation
- Outline the features and uses of machine languages, assembly languages, and high-level languages
- Identify some major high-level languages and describe their characteristics
- Summarize the steps that are taken during software implementation and maintenance

CHAPTER OUTLINE

LOOKING AHEAD
PROGRAM PREPARATION PRACTICES
Conflicting Goals
The Make or Buy Consideration
Programmer Organization Practices
Program Construction Practices
PROGRAMMING LANGUAGE CLASSIFICATIONS
Machine Languages
Assembly Languages
High-Level Languages
"Fourth-Generation" Languages
MAJOR HIGH-LEVEL LANGUAGES
BASIC   RPG
FORTRAN   ALGOL, Pascal, and Ada
COBOL   Logo and Some Others
PL/1
Selecting a Programming Language
SOFTWARE IMPLEMENTATION AND MAINTENANCE
Program Implementation
System Conversion and Changeover
Program/System Maintenance
Post-implementation Review
Feedback and Review 12
LOOKING BACK

PROGRAM PREPARATION PRACTICES

You'll recall from Chapter 11 that the six steps required to develop custom-made software are:

1 Define the problem(s) to be solved or the task(s) to be accomplished.

2 Gather and analyze data pertaining to the problem or task.

3 Design the new system(s) or application(s) required to satisfy the need.

4 Break down the design specifications into the specific computer input/output, calculation/text manipulation, logic/comparison, and storage/retrieval operations required to satisfy the need.

5 Program these specific computer operations into a language and form acceptable to an available machine.

6 Implement and maintain the completed system(s) or application(s).

The first three steps—the *system analysis/design stage*—were considered in Chapter 11. The last three steps—the *programming stage*—are presented here. Let's look first at some of the practices followed during steps 4 and 5. We'll then describe the programming languages that may be used in step 5 and outline the software implementation and maintenance concepts associated with step 6.

Conflicting Goals

Preparing computer programs has historically been a painstaking art. It still is. Whether programming for an organization or a personal application, programmers generally share similar objectives:

1 To serve user needs

2 To reduce the time and money needed to develop and implement programs

3 To produce programs with minimal errors

4 To produce programs that are easy to implement and maintain

In trying to achieve one desirable goal, however, programmers are often faced with tradeoffs: Should we reduce the time spent in the analysis/design stage and then run the risk of producing programs that are more error-prone and harder to maintain? And in any case, programmers must often deal with a number of issues involving methodology and the use of resources: Should we create our own custom software, or should we contract with a vendor to adapt a package to our needs? How should programming tasks be assigned? What program design methods should we use? One reason programming is still an art rather than an exact science is that people with the same types of problems to solve follow different practices when answering these and other questions.

In the next few pages we'll look at a few of the practices used by those who prepare programs. The field of **software engineering** has emerged in the last decade to apply scientific principles to the development of computer programs. As a result, it's likely that the practices used by professional programmers will follow a more scientific approach in the years ahead.

The Make or Buy Consideration

Sometimes there's no choice but to create custom software for a unique application. But often an outside supplier is willing to adapt an available package to meet a user's needs. The user then faces a "make or buy" decision that usually involves tradeoffs. The modified package may achieve the goals of lower cost (the development costs for major package elements may be shared by many customers), faster implementation, and reduced risk of error (it may be possible to test the package before a final purchase is made). The in-house, custom-made program has the possible advantages of greater operating efficiency and the ability to satisfy user needs more effectively. Whenever feasible, however, most organizations seriously consider the available packages before beginning in-house program development projects.

Programmer Organization Practices

The output of a program preparation project should be an effective product at an economical price. Programmers are currently assigned to such projects in various ways. Each organizing practice differs in significant ways from the others. There's no agreement on which approach is best. Some organizations are trying to develop other options for organizing programmers that combine some of the features of the three practices presented here:

Traditional Hierarchical Grouping   A programming manager assigns tasks to programmers and exercises overall control over the project. But the manager does not normally participate in the actual coding. Rather, individual programmers code, test, and document the programs to which they are assigned. They may be shifted from project to project as the workload dictates.

Chief Programmer Teams   In the **chief programmer team** approach, each project is assigned to a team consisting of a senior-level *chief programmer,* a skilled *backup programmer,* and a *librarian.* Applications programmers and other specialists are added to this nucleus as needed. In many ways, this team is like a surgical team in a hospital. The chief programmer (surgeon) has responsibility for the project and is the key coder of the program(s) being prepared. The backup programmer (assisting doctor) is ready to take the chief programmer's place, if necessary, and is expected to develop important elements of the program. Other team members (like nurses and an anesthesiologist) perform special tasks for the chief programmer. The librarian, for example, gathers and organizes the records and documents associated with the project. And applications programmers code modules that have been mapped out by the chief programmer.

"Egoless" Programming Teams   We've seen in the traditional approach that

WINDOW 12-1

"RECYCLING" USED SOFTWARE

Regardless of the booms and busts of the economy or the computer industry, there always has seemed to be an insatiable demand for used hardware—everything from reconditioned personal computers to Cray supercomputers.

Now the nation's leading aerospace companies hope to do the same with software—slightly used software that can be "recycled"—as they write programs for new airplanes, weapons, and communications systems. The aim is to cut drastically the time it takes to develop new equipment for the Pentagon, which recently concluded that 80 percent of the labor content in "mission critical" systems lies in the design of increasingly unwieldy programs.

Proponents of recycled software, chiefly the Software Productivity Consortium in Reston, Va., boast that it could save more than half the time now required to design and write some of the largest programs used by the Defense Department and its contractors. But other computer experts are wary and say that a host of obstacles—mostly technical, some legal—will have to be surmounted before program "modules" can be snapped into place like headlights.

In the mid-1960s, when airplanes and communications systems were far simpler, so little depended on computers that the average military system required less than 5 months of software development time. Today, hardly a landing gear is locked in place or a navigation system turned on without the oversight of one or more computer systems, usually communicating constantly with other computers in the air and on the ground. By most estimates, it now takes 8 years to develop the software for a complex military system.

The frustrating part for programmers is that much of their time is spent reinventing the wheel, writing computer code very similar to programs written many times before.

"Probably 70 percent of the software developed by the major aerospace manufacturers has been written sometime, somewhere before," according to V. Edward Jones, president of the consortium. "But there has never been a library where those programs can be cut up into pieces, indexed by function, and then stored."

Building that library has become the first task of the consortium. Once that system is operating, Mr. Jones hopes that it would be possible for a programmer to isolate the program fragment he or she needs, place it into a larger program under development, and rest assured that it has already been debugged, or rid of errors.

But programs, unfortunately, are rarely written in neat modules that can be snapped on and off like hubcaps. Instead, they are ridden with interdependencies—logical loops that rely on information gained elsewhere in the execution of the program. The troubles do not end there. Only recently has the Pentagon settled on a single computer language, called ADA, for all of its systems. But the consortium's library, which is really just a large computer data base, will be filled with programs written in a dozen computer languages. "In most cases, we won't have the tools for translation," said Mr. Jones. "In those cases, it would probably be faster just to write the program again, in the language you need."

Moreover, not all the programs in the library will be available for loan. The participants in the consortium, which consists of 12 aerospace companies, say they expect no antitrust objections from the Justice Department over joint research, but sharing proprietary computer programs among the companies might be tempting fate. As a result, TRW, for example, will be able to catalog all of its own programming work, but it will not have access to programs written by the other consortium members.

In time, access to the programming code may be less important than access to the concepts underlying it. Researchers studying recycled software are looking for ways to reuse generalized designs and program specifications, so that they can be translated into virtually any language.

More than efficiency and cost savings are at stake in the recycling effort. Computer experts often bemoan the fact that the pace of software development has not kept up with advances in hardware, particularly microelectronics. One reason is that chip designers rarely spend time worrying about the design of individual circuits. Rather, they borrow an arithmetic unit from one chip, the memory section of another, and the telecommunications sections of another to build a whole system on a single chip.

Right now, there is no equivalent of that process in software.

Adapted from David E. Sanger, "'Recycling' Used Software," *New York Times*, October 31, 1985. Copyright © 1985 by The New York Times Company. Reprinted by permission.

CHAPTER 12
403

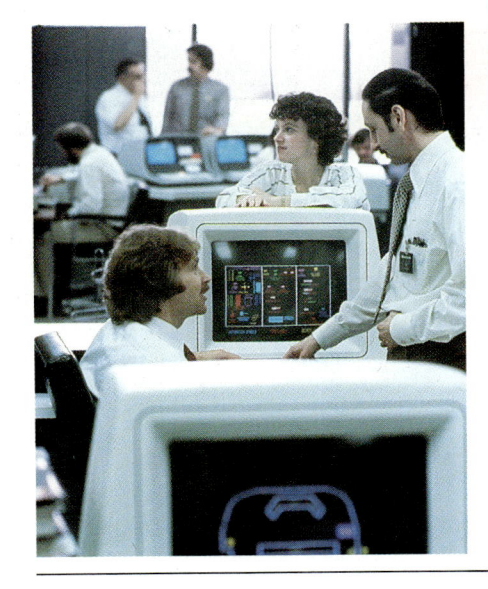

Because members of "egoless" programming teams check each other's work throughout the coding process, the finished program is truly a product of the entire team. (Courtesy Honeywell, Inc.)

a programmer may often be responsible for coding and implementing an entire program. This close association with the program may serve to make it an extension of the programmer's ego. If errors are then discovered in the program (and they often are), the programmer may consider the discovery to be a personal attack. To avoid this situation, an **"egoless" programming team** is assigned to a project. Membership in the close-knit team seldom changes, and there's no designated chief. Assignments are determined in a democratic way with each member doing that part of the work for which he or she is best suited. During coding, team members check the work of each other to help locate and correct errors. The completed code is then not the responsibility of a single person but is rather the product of the entire team.

Program Construction Practices

Different program construction techniques have been developed to help achieve the four goals listed earlier. Again, different organizations often use a varying mix of the following practices:

Modular (Top-Down) Program Design   A **main-control program** may be used to outline the major segments, or **modules,** needed to solve a problem. The main-control program specifies the order in which each subordinate module in the program will be processed. When the **modular (top-down) program design** practice is used, an instruction in the main-control program branches control to a subordinate program routine (**subroutine**) or module. When the specific processing operation performed by the module is completed, another branch instruction may transfer program control to another module or return it to the main-control program. Thus the modules or subroutines are really programs within a program. Each module typically has only one entry point and only one exit point. Many programmers believe that modules should be limited in size to about 50 lines of code—the amount that can be placed on one page of printer output. Figure 12-1 summarizes the

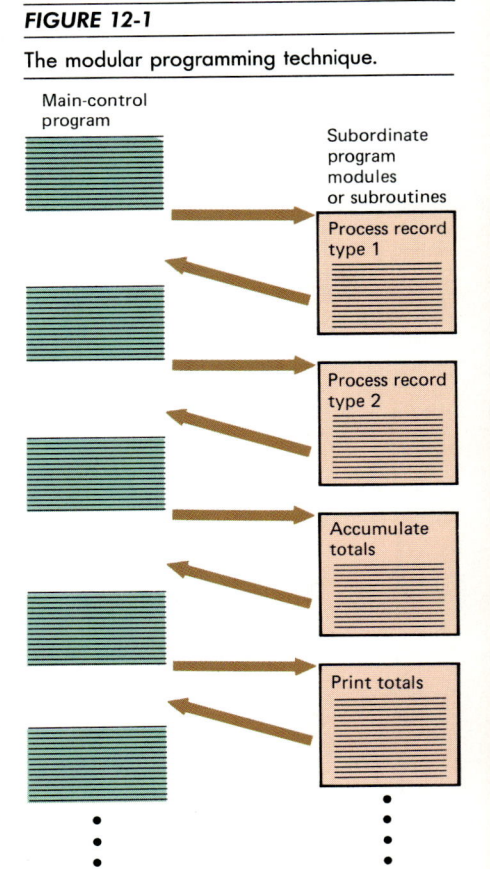

FIGURE 12-1

The modular programming technique.

MODULE 3

modular technique. Some of the advantages of using this construction practice are:

1 Complex programs may be divided into simpler and more manageable elements.

2 Simultaneous coding of modules by several programmers is possible.

3 A *library* of modules may be created, and these modules may be used in other programs as needed.

4 The location of program errors may be more easily traced to a particular module, and thus implementation and maintenance may be simplified.

5 Effective use can be made of tested subroutines prepared by software suppliers.

The Use of Basic Coding Structures Computer storage capacity grew throughout the 1960s, and so did the size of the programs being stuffed into the machines. During this time, clever programming "artists" often wrote ever-larger programs with mazes of branches that altered the sequence of processing operations. These programs worked at first. But since the artists were often the only ones who understood their convoluted logic, these programs quickly became nightmares for those responsible for their maintenance. The difficulties encountered in creating and maintaining large programs gave researchers an incentive to look at how programs were being organized and produced. Factors contributing to unnecessary program complexity were identified. It was discovered in the mid-1960s that any program operation, no matter how complex, could be expressed by using just three simple logic structures. The identification of these three structures (used to follow a sequence of steps, to select alternative program paths, and to establish program loops) allowed researchers to develop new concepts and tools in the late 1960s. The term **structured programming** was used to describe these concepts and tools that were designed to handle and tame program complexity. The figure illustrates the three logic structures.

Many organizations now require the use of the three basic coding struc-

---

The three standard logic patterns shown here are all that are necessary to prepare any program. The **simple sequence structure** (a) merely consists of one step followed by another. The **selection structure** (b) requires a test for some condition followed by two alternative program control paths; the path selected depends on the results of the test. This pattern is sometimes referred to as an **IF-THEN-ELSE structure**.

The **loop structure** (c) causes the program to execute one or more operations while a condition is *true*. When the condition becomes false, the looping process is ended. If the condition is initially false, the operation found in this **DO WHILE structure** isn't executed. A variation of this third basic pattern, called a **DO UNTIL structure** (d), is one in which the operation is repeated *until* a condition is found to be true. Notice that the condition test is made at the beginning of a DO WHILE loop and at the end of a DO UNTIL loop.

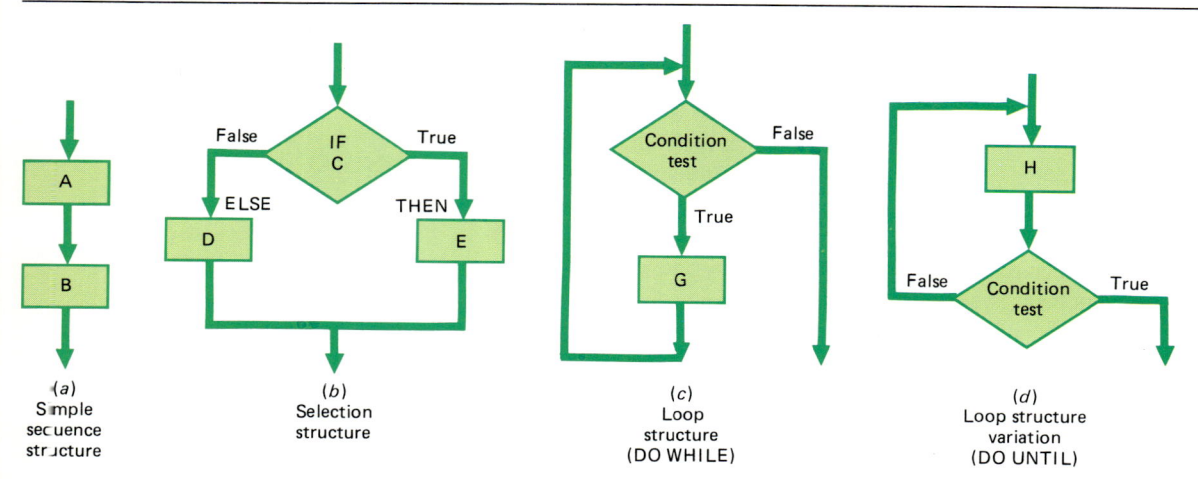

(a)
Simple sequence structure

(b)
Selection structure

(c)
Loop structure (DO WHILE)

(d)
Loop structure variation (DO UNTIL)

tures in all programs. These organizations have found that when programs are so structured, and when modular techniques are used, programs can be read from top to bottom and are easier to understand. This greater clarity can help reduce (1) program errors, (2) the time spent in program testing, and (3) the time and effort spent on program maintenance.

Peer Reviews   The practice of holding a **peer review** during program construction to detect software errors is called a **structured walkthrough.** Each review is initiated by the programmer whose work is to be checked. Materials are handed out in advance of the review session, and the objectives of the session are outlined to participants. (Programmer managers are not invited.) The role of the participants is to detect errors, but no attempt is made during the session to correct any errors that are discovered.

A walkthrough session will typically include three to five of the programmer's colleagues. (These colleagues will have their own work reviewed in other similar sessions.) During the session, the reviewee will walk through, step by step, the logic of the work. One participant will keep a record of any errors that are uncovered so that proper corrective action can be taken by the reviewee. The tone of the session should be relaxed, and there should be no personal attacks.

The possible advantages of the peer review technique are:

1   Fewer errors are likely to get through the development process.

2   Faster implementation, a reduction in development costs, and greater user satisfaction may then be possible.

3   Better program documentation may be obtained.

4   Later program maintenance efforts may be easier and less expensive.

5   Higher programmer morale may result from the spirit of cooperation that can exist.

These same advantages, of course, are possible when programmers are organized into the egoless programming teams described earlier.

Peer reviews, like "egoless" programming teams, allow programmers to review each other's work to catch errors and suggest improvements. (Courtesy AT&T/Bell Labs)

PROGRAMMING LANGUAGE CLASSIFICATIONS

A language is a system of communication. A programming language consists of all the symbols, characters, and usage rules that permit people to communicate with computers. There are at least several hundred, and possibly several thousand, different programming languages and dialects. Some of these are created to serve a *special purpose* (controlling a robot), while others are more flexible *general-purpose* tools that are suitable for many types of applications. However, every programming language must have instructions that fall into the familiar input/output, calculation/text manipulation, logic/comparison, and storage/retrieval categories.

But even though all programming languages have an instruction set that permits these familiar operations to be performed, there's a marked difference to be found in the symbols, characters, and syntax of machine languages, assembly languages, and high-level languages.

Machine Languages

A computer's **machine language** consists of strings of binary numbers (0s and 1s) and is the only one the processor directly "understands." An instruction prepared in any machine language will have at least two parts. The *first part* is the *command* or *operation,* and it tells the computer what function to perform. Every computer has an **operation code,** or "op code," for each of its functions. The *second part* of the instruction is the **operand,** and it tells the computer where to find or store the data or other instructions that are to be manipulated. The number of operands in an instruction varies among computers. In a *single-operand* machine, the binary equivalent of "ADD 0184" could cause the value in storage location or **address** 0184 to be added to a value stored in the arithmetic-logic unit. In a *two-operand* machine, the binary representation for "ADD 0184 8672" could cause the value in address 8672 to be added to the number in location 0184. The single-operand format is popular in the smallest microcomputers; the two-operand structure is found in most other machines.

By today's standards, early computers were intolerant. Programmers had to translate instructions directly into the machine-language form that computers understood. For example, the programmer writing the instruction to "ADD 0184" for an early IBM machine would have written:

00010000000000000000000000010111000

In addition to remembering the dozens of code numbers for the commands in the machine's instruction set, a programmer had to keep track of the storage locations of data and instructions. The initial coding often took months, was therefore expensive, and often resulted in error. Checking instructions to locate errors was about as tedious as writing them initially. And if a program had to be modified at a later date, the work involved could take weeks to finish.

Assembly Languages

To ease the programmer's burden, *mnemonic* operation codes and *symbolic* addresses were developed in the early 1950s. The word "mnemonic" (pronounced ne-mon′-ik) refers to a memory aid. One of the first steps in improving the program preparation process was to substitute letter symbols—mnemonics—for the numeric machine-language operation codes. Each computer now has a **mnemonic code,** although, of course, the actual symbols vary among makes and models. Figure 12-2 shows the mnemonic codes for a few of the commands used with some IBM mainframe computers. (The complete instruction set has about 200 commands.) Machine language is *still* used by the computer as it processes data, but **assembly language** software first translates the specified operation code symbol into its machine-language equivalent.

This improvement set the stage for further advances. If the computer could translate convenient symbols into basic operations, why couldn't it also

FIGURE 12-2

Partial instruction set for some IBM mainframe computers.

Command Name	Mnemonic (Symbolic) Operation Code
Input/Output Commands	
Start I/O	SIO
Halt I/O	HIO
Calculation Commands	
Add	A
Subtract	S
Multiply	M
Divide	D
Logic/Comparison Commands	
Compare Register	CR
Compare	C
Compare Logical Character	CLC
Branch on Condition Register	BCR
Branch on Condition	BC
Branch on Count	BCT
Storage/Retrieval and Movement Commands	
Load Register	LR
Load	L
Move Characters	MVC
Move Numerics	MVN
Store	ST
Store Character	STC

perform other clerical coding functions such as assigning storage addresses to data? **Symbolic addressing** is the practice of expressing an address *not* in terms of its absolute numerical location, but rather in terms of symbols convenient to the programmer.

In the early stages of symbolic addressing, the programmer assigned a symbolic name and an actual address to a data item. For example, the total value of merchandise purchased during a month by a department store customer might be assigned to address 0063 by the programmer and given the symbolic name TOTAL. The value of merchandise returned unused during the month might be assigned to address 2047 and given the symbolic name CREDIT. Then, for the remainder of the program, the programmer would refer to the *symbolic names rather than to the addresses* when such items were to be processed. Thus an instruction might be written "S CREDIT, TOTAL" to subtract the value of returned goods from the total amount purchased to find the amount of the customer's monthly bill. The assembly language software might then translate the symbolic instruction into this machine-language string of bits:

011111	011111111111	000000111111
Mnemonic op code	2047	0063
(S)	(CREDIT)	(TOTAL)

Another improvement followed. The programmer turned the task of assigning and keeping track of instruction addresses over to the computer. The programmer merely told the machine the storage address number of the *first* program instruction, and the assembly language software then automatically stored all others in sequence from that point. So if another instruction was added to the program later, it was not necessary to modify the addresses of all instructions that followed the point of insertion (as would have to be done in the case of programs written in machine language). Instead, the processor automatically adjusted storage locations the next time the program ran.

Programmers no longer assign actual address numbers to symbolic data items. Now they merely specify where they want the first location in the program to be, and an assembly language program takes it from there, allocating locations for instructions and data.

This **assembly program,** or **assembler,** also enables the computer to convert the programmer's assembly language instructions into its own machine code. A program of instructions written by a programmer in an assembly language is called a **source program.** After this source program has been converted into machine code by an assembler, it's referred to as an **object program.** It's easier for programmers to write instructions in an assembly language than to prepare instructions in machine-language codes. But two computer runs may be required before source program instructions can be used to produce the desired output. These separate *assembly* and *production* runs are outlined and discussed in Figure 12-3.

Assembly languages have *advantages over machine languages.* They save time and reduce detail. Fewer errors are made, and those that are made are easier to find. And assembly programs are easier for people to modify than machine-language programs. But there are *limitations.* Coding in assembly language is still time-consuming. And a big drawback of assembly languages

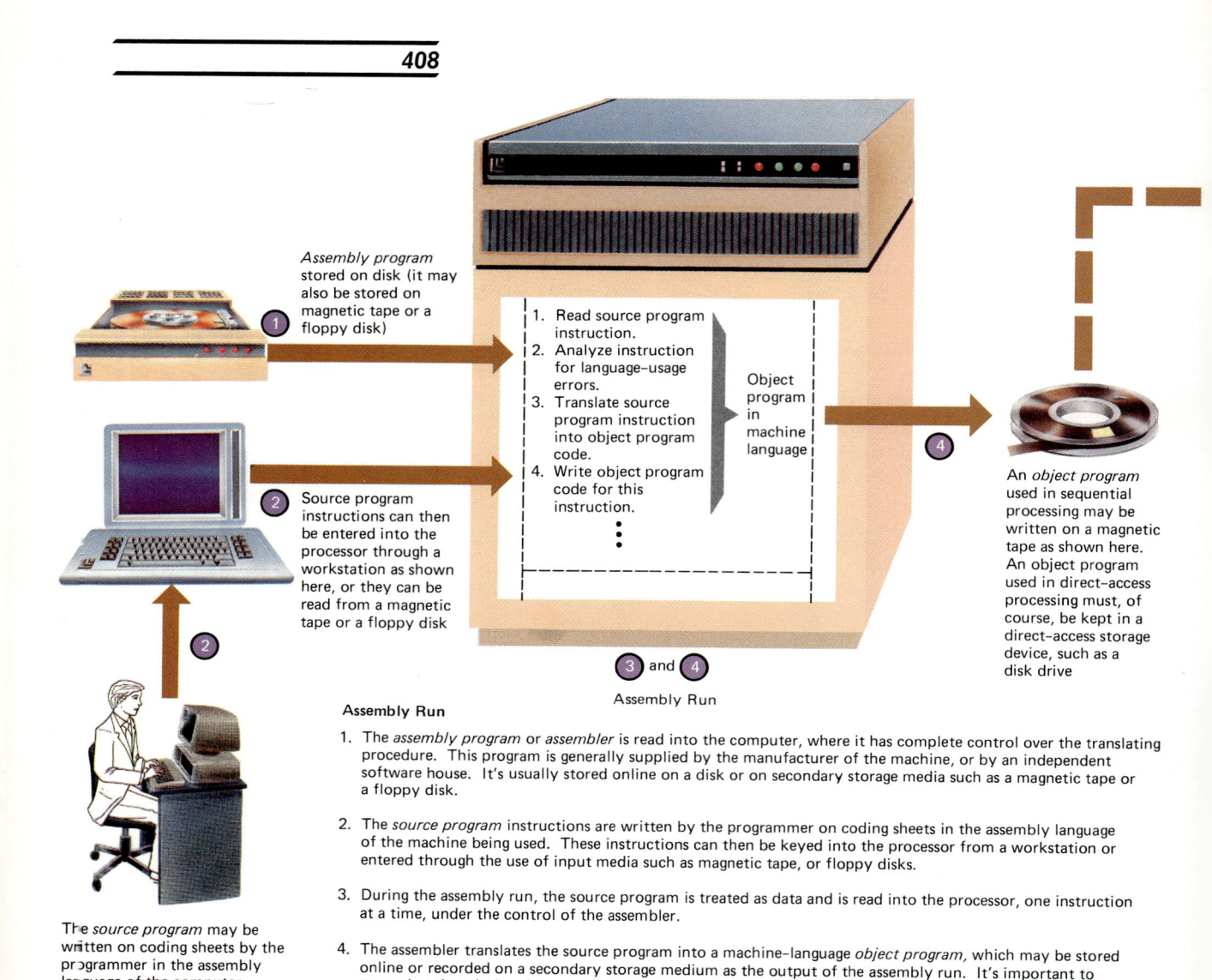

Assembly Run

Assembly program stored on disk (it may also be stored on magnetic tape or a floppy disk)

Source program instructions can then be entered into the processor through a workstation as shown here, or they can be read from a magnetic tape or a floppy disk

1. Read source program instruction.
2. Analyze instruction for language-usage errors.
3. Translate source program instruction into object program code.
4. Write object program code for this instruction.

Object program in machine language

An *object program* used in sequential processing may be written on a magnetic tape as shown here. An object program used in direct-access processing must, of course, be kept in a direct-access storage device, such as a disk drive

③ and ④ Assembly Run

The *source program* may be written on coding sheets by the programmer in the assembly language of the computer system being used

Assembly Run

1. The *assembly program* or *assembler* is read into the computer, where it has complete control over the translating procedure. This program is generally supplied by the manufacturer of the machine, or by an independent software house. It's usually stored online on a disk or on secondary storage media such as a magnetic tape or a floppy disk.

2. The *source program* instructions are written by the programmer on coding sheets in the assembly language of the machine being used. These instructions can then be keyed into the processor from a workstation or entered through the use of input media such as magnetic tape, or floppy disks.

3. During the assembly run, the source program is treated as data and is read into the processor, one instruction at a time, under the control of the assembler.

4. The assembler translates the source program into a machine-language *object program,* which may be stored online or recorded on a secondary storage medium as the output of the assembly run. It's important to remember that *during the assembly run no problem data are processed.* That is, the source program is *not* being executed. It's merely being converted into a form in which it can be executed by the processor.

FIGURE 12-3

Assembly language source program instructions are translated into machine-language code during the assembly run (steps 1–4). The machine-language object program is then used to process problem data during a production run (steps 5–7).

is that they are *machine-oriented.* That is, they are designed for the specific make and model of processor being used. Programs might have to be recoded for a different machine.

High-Level Languages

The earlier assembly programs produced only one machine instruction for each source program instruction. To speed up coding, assembly programs were developed that could produce a *variable* amount of machine-language code for *each* source program instruction. In other words, a single **macro instruction** might produce *several* lines of machine-language code. For example, the programmer might write "READ FILE," and the translating software might then automatically provide a detailed series of previously prepared

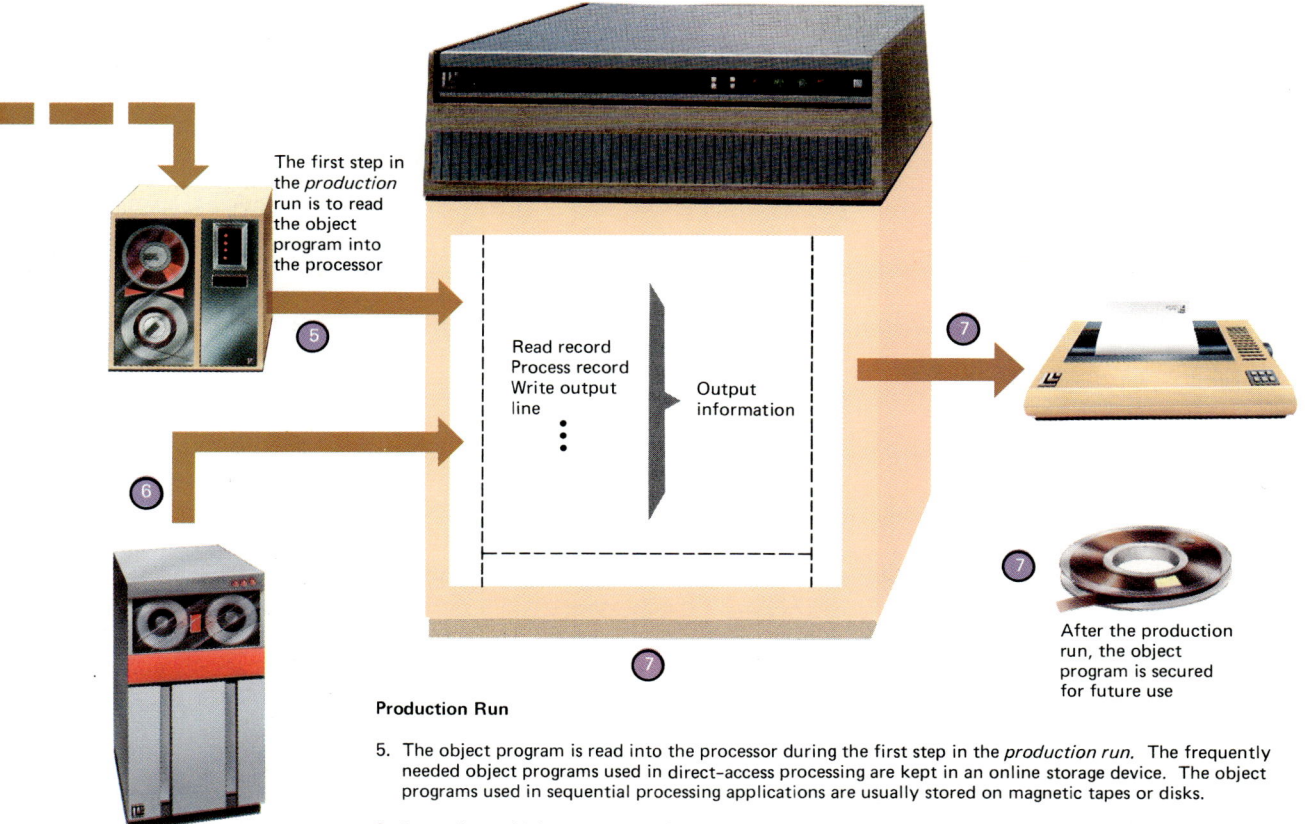

The first step in the *production* run is to read the object program into the processor

⑤

Read record
Process record
Write output line
⋮

Output information

⑦

After the production run, the object program is secured for future use

⑥

Input data to be processed are read into the processor under object program control (In this example, data are stored on magnetic tape, but many other input options are available

⑦

Production Run

5. The object program is read into the processor during the first step in the *production run.* The frequently needed object programs used in direct-access processing are kept in an online storage device. The object programs used in sequential processing applications are usually stored on magnetic tapes or disks.

6. Input data, which may be recorded on a suitable input medium or entered from an online terminal, are read into the processor under object program control.

7. The data are processed, information output may be produced, and the object program is secured for future use.

---

machine-language instructions which would copy a record into primary storage from the file of data being read by the input device. Thus the programmer was relieved of the task of writing an instruction for every machine operation performed.

The development of mnemonic techniques and macro instructions led, in turn, to the development of **high-level languages** that are often oriented toward a particular class of processing problems. For example, a number of languages have been designed to process scientific-mathematic problems, and other languages have appeared that emphasize file processing applications.

Unlike assembly programs, high-level language programs may be used with *different makes of computers* with little modification. Thus reprogramming expense may be greatly reduced when new equipment is acquired. Other advantages of high-level languages are:

- They are easier to learn than assembly languages.
- They require less time to write.
- They provide better documentation.
- They are easier to maintain.
- A programmer skilled in writing programs in such a language is not restricted to using a single type of machine.

Compiler Translation   Naturally, a source program written in a high-level language must also be translated into a machine-usable code. A translating program that can perform this operation is called a **compiler.** Compilers, like advanced assembly programs, may generate many lines of machine code for each source program statement. A *compiling run* is required before problem data can be processed. With the exception that a compiler program is substituted for an assembly program, the procedures are essentially the same as those shown in Figure 12-3. The production run follows the compiling run.

Interpreter Translation   An alternative to using a compiler for high-level language translation is often employed with personal computers. Instead of translating the source program and permanently saving the object code produced during a compiling run for future production use, the programmer merely loads the source program into the computer along with the data to be processed. An **interpreter** program stored on the computer's operating system disk or permanently wired inside the machine then converts each source program statement into machine-language form as it's needed during the processing of the data. No object code is saved for future use.

The next time the instruction is used, it must once again be interpreted and translated into machine language. For example, during the repetitive processing of the steps in a loop, each instruction in the loop will have to be reinterpreted every time the loop is executed. The interpreter eliminates the need for a separate compiling run after each program change to add features or correct errors. But a previously compiled object program should obviously run much faster than one which has to be interpreted each step of the way during a production run.

"Fourth-Generation" Languages

The machine, assembly, and high-level languages we've just examined are given "generation" designations by some people in the computer field. They note that the move from first-generation machine languages to second-generation assembly languages brought approximately a seven-to-one improvement in programmer productivity. A similar improvement occurred when high-level (third-generation) languages were introduced. Now, a number of software vendors are producing a variety of application development tools that may offer further improvements in productivity, and these tools are often referred to collectively as **fourth-generation languages (4GLs).**

A clear-cut definition of a 4GL isn't possible because each tool, or "language," is the product of a specific vendor, and these suppliers don't agree on definitions. Some vendors tie their tools to the data base management system (DBMS) software they also produce. Such products may increase productivity by allowing professional programmers to simply specify *what* the application output should be without spelling out all the details of *how* the data should be manipulated to produce that result. Other vendors may also tie their 4GLs to popular DBMS packages. These suppliers often emphasize how their tools allow end users (who aren't professional programmers) to query data bases, develop their own custom-made applications, and generate their own reports with a minimum amount of training. (Such 4GLs may be found in the *information centers* discussed in Chapter 11.) And some 4GLs have productivity and flexibility features that can be adapted to the needs of both programmers and end users.

Although the use of 4GLs is increasing, a large majority of the new applications programs prepared today are written in a high-level language. Let's look now at the major languages in this category.

MAJOR HIGH-LEVEL LANGUAGES

BASIC

BASIC (<u>B</u>eginner's <u>A</u>ll-purpose <u>S</u>ymbolic <u>I</u>nstruction <u>C</u>ode) is a popular interactive language that has wide appeal because it's easy to use. An **interactive language** permits direct communication between user and computer system during the preparation and use of programs. A problem-solver with little or no knowledge of computers or programming can learn to write BASIC programs at a personal computer (pc) or terminal keyboard in a short period of time. Entering data is easy, and the problem-solver need not be confused about output formats because a usable format may be automatically provided. It's also easy to insert changes and additions into a BASIC program.

Because of its simplicity, BASIC was used in the first pc to gain commercial success. It's now by far the most popular high-level language used in pc systems. This fact makes it one of the most widely installed computer languages in the world. Interpreters are frequently used in pc systems to translate BASIC instructions into machine-language code. But BASIC language compilers are also available for these systems. Recreational and educational programs are published in many pc magazines, and these programs are usually documented in BASIC. The development and early use of BASIC is discussed in the reading following Chapter 1.

By 1974, BASIC was available for most computers, and it's now offered by virtually all computer manufacturers. Although the original BASIC had a well-defined syntax, numerous extensions to the language have been made over the years. Because their developers seldom tried to make these extensions compatible with other versions of the language, "BASIC" today is really a generic name for a group of dialects with many similar features. There's an American National Standards Institute **(ANSI) standard** for a minimal version of BASIC that was published in 1978. But this standard is so simple that it has been extended in virtually every available BASIC dialect. (A more complete version is forthcoming.)

Users of BASIC range from public school students to aerospace engineers to business managers. A BASIC version of a simple billing program designed to process bills for multiple customers is shown in Figure 12-4.

```
10 REM *BILLING PROGRAM
20 REM *
30 REM *VARIABLE NAMES
40 REM * N$   NAME
50 REM * S$   ADDRESS
60 REM * C$   CITY AND STATE
70 REM * Q    QUANTITY PURCHASED
80 REM * P    UNIT PRICE
90 REM * A    NET AMOUNT
100 REM *
110 REM *READ NAME,ADDRESS,QUANTITY PURCHASED AND PRICE
120     READ N$,S$,C$,Q,P
130 REM *TEST QUANTITY FOR LAST INPUT
140     IF Q=-99.9 THEN 400
150 REM *COMPUTE NET AMOUNT
160     LET A = Q*P
170 REM *PRINT NAME,ADDRESS AND NET AMOUNT
180     PRINT N$
190     PRINT S$
200     PRINT C$
210     PRINT TAB(3);"NET = ";A
220     PRINT
230     PRINT
240     GO TO 120
260 REM *INPUT DATA
270     DATA "PIERRE'S RECORD SHOP"
280     DATA "6453 ORLEANS STREET"
290     DATA "BOOGIE,LOUISIANA 54321"
300     DATA   300.0,25.00
310     DATA "ROCKY COLLEGE STORE"
320     DATA "1563 BEETHOVEN DRIVE"
330     DATA "ROCKTOWN,MARYLAND 20765"
340     DATA   3.25,25.00
350     DATA "WYNN D.TOOTS,INC."
360     DATA "120 BROWNING STREET"
370     DATA "GONG,CALIFORNIA 98765"
380     DATA   2.00,25.00
390     DATA "L","L","L",-99.9,0.
400     END
```

> Computer listing of the BASIC program

```
PIERRE'S RECORD SHOP
6453 ORLEANS STREET
BOOGIE,LOUISIANA 54321
   NET =     7500

ROCKY COLLEGE STORE
1563 BEETHOVEN DRIVE
ROCKTOWN,MARYLAND 20765
   NET =     81.2500

WYNN D.TOOTS,INC.
120 BROWNING STREET
GONG,CALIFORNIA 98765
   NET =     50
```

> Output produced by the computer as the program is executed

FIGURE 12-4

An example of a BASIC program. At the top is a computer listing of a simple billing program designed to process bills for multiple customers. At the bottom is the output produced by the computer when the program is run.

FORTRAN

A FORTRAN program listing for this same simple billing problem is shown in Figure 12-5. When supplied with the data shown in the BASIC program, this FORTRAN version will produce the same output, as you can see in Figure 12-5. We can trace the origin of **FORTRAN** (FORmula TRANslator) back to 1954 when an IBM-sponsored committee headed by John Backus began work on a scientific-mathematic language. The result of this effort was FORTRAN, which was introduced in 1957 for the IBM 704 computer. It's

```
C ...BILLING PROGRAM
      INTEGER ADDR1,ADDR2
      DIMENSION NAME(20),ADDR1(20),ADDR2(20)
C...READ NAME,ADDRESS,QUANTITY PURCHASED AND UNIT PRICE
   10 READ(5,70) NAME
      READ(5,70) ADDR1
      READ(5,70) ADDR2
      READ(5,75) QTY,PRICE
C ...TEST QTY FOR LAST CARD
      IF(QTY.EQ.-99.9) GO TO 20
C ... COMPUTE NET PRICE
      ANET = QTY*PRICE
C ...PRINT NAME,ADDRESS AND NET PRICE
      WRITE(6,80) NAME,ADDR1,ADDR2
      WRITE(6,85) ANET
      GO TO 10
   20 STOP
C ...FORMAT STATEMENTS
   70 FORMAT(20A4)
   75 FORMAT(2F10.2)
   80 FORMAT(//3(/3X,20A4))
   85 FORMAT(6X,6HNET = ,F10.2)
      END
```

Computer listing of the FORTRAN program

```
PIERRE'S RECORD SHOP
6453 ORLEANS STREET
BOOGIE,LOUISIANA 54321
   NET =     7500.00


ROCKY COLLEGE STORE
1563 BEETHOVEN DRIVE
ROCKTOWN,MARYLAND 20765
   NET =       81.25


WYNN D. TOOTS,INC.
120 BROWNING STREET
GONG,CALIFORNIA 98765
   NET =       50.00
```

Output produced by computer as program is executed. The same input data used in the BASIC program were punched on cards and read into the computer under program control.

FIGURE 12-5
A computer listing of the simple billing program written in the FORTRAN language.

estimated that the cost of producing the 25,000 lines of detailed machine instructions that went into the first FORTRAN compiler was $2.5 million. FORTRAN is noted for the ease with which it can express mathematical equations. It has been widely accepted and has been revised a number of times. Several of its features were later incorporated into the first BASIC language.

The vast majority of all computers now in service—from small pc's to the largest number-crunchers—can use FORTRAN. Compilers rather than interpreters are used. Because of its early widespread acceptance, work began in 1962 on FORTRAN standard languages. Two standards—a basic or minimal version of FORTRAN and a "full" or extended version—were approved by ANSI in 1966. FORTRAN thus has the distinction of being the first standardized language. The current FORTRAN standards were published by ANSI in 1977.

As you can see in Figure 12-5, a FORTRAN program consists of a series of *statements*. These statements supply input/output, calculation, logic/comparison, and other basic instructions to the computer. The words READ, WRITE, GO TO, and STOP in the statements mean exactly what you would expect. FORTRAN programs are executed sequentially until the sequence is altered by a transfer of control statement.

FORTRAN has the *advantage* of being a compact language that serves the needs of scientists and business statisticians very well. Huge libraries of engineering and scientific programs written in FORTRAN are available to scientists and engineers. The language is also widely used for business applications that don't require the manipulation of extensive data files. Because there are established FORTRAN standards, programs written for one computer are usually easily converted for use with another. *However,* it may be more difficult to trace program logic in FORTRAN code than in some other high-level languages. And FORTRAN is not as well suited for processing large business files as the next language we'll discuss, COBOL.

COBOL

As its name indicates, **COBOL** (COmmon Business Oriented Language) was designed specifically for business-type data processing. And it's now the most widely used language for large business applications. The group that designed the language gathered at the Pentagon in Washington, D.C., in May 1959, with the official sanction of the U.S. Department of Defense. Members of the COnference of DAta SYstems Languages (**CODASYL**) represented computer manufacturers, government agencies, user organizations, and universities. The CODASYL Short-Range Committee, which prepared the COBOL framework, consisted of representatives from federal government agencies and from computer manufacturers. From June to December 1959, this committee worked on the language specifications. Its final report was approved in January 1960, and the language specifications were published a few months later by the Government Printing Office.

Since 1961, COBOL compilers have been prepared for virtually all processors used in business data processing. And they are available now for use with pc's. Other CODASYL committees have continued to maintain, revise, and extend the initial specifications. An ANSI COBOL standard was first published in 1968, and a later version was approved in 1974. A new standard—COBOL 85—was approved in 1985.

Figure 12-6 shows a computer listing of a COBOL program. This program is a COBOL version of the BASIC and FORTRAN simple billing programs illustrated in Figures 12-4 and 12-5. If the same input data used in the earlier language examples are read into a computer under the control of this COBOL program, the output results will be essentially the same as you can see in Figure 12-6.

COBOL is structured much like this chapter. *Sentences* (analogous to statements in FORTRAN) direct the processor in performing the necessary operations. A varying number of sentences dealing with the same operation are grouped to form a *paragraph*. Related paragraphs may then be organized into a *section*. Sections are then grouped into a *division,* and *four divisions* complete the structural hierarchy of a COBOL program.

The *first* entry, line 1 in Figure 12-6, is IDENTIFICATION DIVISION—the first of the COBOL divisions. A required paragraph identifies the program, and additional optional paragraphs are included for documentation purposes. The *second* division, line 7, is the ENVIRONMENT DIVISION,

```
00001                    IDENTIFICATION DIVISION.                              BILLING
00002                    PROGRAM-ID.    BILLING PROGRAM.                       BILLING
00003                    AUTHOR.        CRAIG ELDERS.                          BILLING
00004                    REMARKS.       THIS PROGRAM PRODUCES A PRINTOUT CONTAINING: BILLING
00005                                   NAME, ADDRESS, AND NET PRICE.          BILLING
00006                                                                          BILLING
00007                    ENVIRONMENT DIVISION.                                 BILLING
00008                    CONFIGURATION SECTION.                                BILLING
00009                    SOURCE-COMPUTER.    XEROX-SIGMA-9.                    BILLING
00010                    OBJECT-COMPUTER.    XEROX-SIGMA-9.                    BILLING
00011                                                                          BILLING
00012                    INPUT-OUTPUT SECTION.                                 BILLING
00013                    FILE-CONTROL.                                         BILLING
00014                        SELECT CARD-INPUT ASSIGN TO CARD-READER.          BILLING
00015                        SELECT PRINTOUT   ASSIGN TO PRINTER.              BILLING
00016                                                                          BILLING
00017                    DATA DIVISION.                                        BILLING
00018                    FILE SECTION.                                         BILLING
00019                    FD  CARD-INPUT                                        BILLING
00020                        RECORD CONTAINS 80 CHARACTERS                     BILLING
00021                        LABEL RECORD IS OMITTED                           BILLING
00022                        DATA RECORDS ARE CARD-NAME-ADDRESS-RECORD         BILLING
00023                                         CARD-QUANTITY-PRICE-RECORD.      BILLING
00024                    01  CARD-NAME-ADDRESS-RECORD.                         BILLING
00025                        05  CARD-NAME-ADDRESS         PICTURE X(30).      BILLING
00026                        05  FILLER                    PICTURE X(50).      BILLING
00027                                                                          BILLING
00028                    01  CARD-QUANTITY-PRICE-RECORD.                       BILLING
00029                        05  CARD-QUANTITY             PICTURE 999V99.     BILLING
00030                        05  CARD-PRICE                PICTURE 999V99.     BILLING
00031                        05  FILLER                    PICTURE X(70).      BILLING
00032                                                                          BILLING
00033                    FD  PRINTOUT                                          BILLING
00034                        RECORD CONTAINS 132 CHARACTERS                    BILLING
00035                        LABEL RECORD IS OMITTED                           BILLING
00036                        DATA RECORD IS PRINTER-RECORD.                    BILLING
00037                    01  PRINTER-RECORD.                                   BILLING
00038                        05  FILLER                    PICTURE X(10).      BILLING
00039                        05  PRINT-AREA                PICTURE X(30).      BILLING
00040                        05  FILLER                    PICTURE X(92).      BILLING
00041                                                                          BILLING
00042                    WORKING-STORAGE SECTION.                              BILLING
00043                    77  NET-COST                      PICTURE 99999V99.   BILLING
00044                    77  END-OF-DATA-FLAG              PIC X(3)   VALUE 'NO'. BILLING
00045                    77  MISSING-CARD-FLAG             PIC X(3)   VALUE 'NO'. BILLING
00046                    01  NET-COST-PRINT-LINE.                              BILLING
00047                        05  FILLER  VALUE SPACES      PICTURE X(10).      BILLING
00048                        05  FILLER  VALUE IS 'NET = ' PICTURE X(6).       BILLING
00049                        05  PRINT-NET-COST            PICTURE $$$,$$$.99. BILLING
00050                        05  FILLER  VALUE SPACES      PICTURE X(106).     BILLING
00051                                                                          BILLING
00052                    PROCEDURE DIVISION.                                   BILLING
00053                    OPEN-UP-FILES.                                        BILLING
00054                        OPEN INPUT   CARD-INPUT.                          BILLING
00055                        OPEN OUTPUT  PRINTOUT.                            BILLING
00056                                                                          BILLING
00057                        PERFORM READ-LOOP THRU READ-LOOP-EXIT             BILLING
00058                            UNTIL END-OF-DATA-FLAG = 'YES'.               BILLING
00059                                                                          BILLING
00060                        CLOSE CARD-INPUT.                                 BILLING
00061                        CLOSE PRINTOUT.                                   BILLING
00062                        STOP RUN.                                         BILLING
00063                                                                          BILLING
```

FIGURE 12-6 (Continued on next page)

The computer listing of the simple billing program written in the COBOL language is numbered from 1 to 102. The four required divisions in any COBOL program are shown. The same input data used in the BASIC and FORTRAN examples were read into the computer under the control of this program. The output results are similar.

which consists of two required sections that describe the specific hardware to use when the program is run. If the application is to be processed on different equipment, this division will have to be rewritten, but that usually presents no problem.

The DATA DIVISION (line 17 in Figure 12-6), the *third* of the four

```
00064              READ-A-CARD.                                              BILLING
00065                  READ CARD-INPUT                                       BILLING
00066                      AT END MOVE 'YES' TO END-OF-DATA-FLAG.            BILLING
00067                                                                        BILLING
00068              READ-LOOP.                                                BILLING
00069                  PERFORM READ-A-CARD.                                  BILLING
00070                  IF END-OF-DATA-FLAG = 'NO'                            BILLING
00071                      MOVE ALL SPACES TO PRINTER-RECORD                 BILLING
00072                      MOVE CARD-NAME-ADDRESS TO PRINT-AREA              BILLING
00073                      WRITE PRINTER-RECORD AFTER ADVANCING 2 LINES      BILLING
00074                      PERFORM READ-A-CARD                               BILLING
00075                      IF END-OF-DATA-FLAG = 'NO'                        BILLING
00076                          MOVE CARD-NAME-ADDRESS TO PRINT-AREA          BILLING
00077                          WRITE PRINTER-RECORD AFTER ADVANCING 1 LINES  BILLING
00078                          PERFORM READ-A-CARD                           BILLING
00079                          IF END-OF-DATA-FLAG = 'NO'                    BILLING
00080                              MOVE CARD-NAME-ADDRESS TO PRINT-AREA      BILLING
00081                              WRITE PRINTER-RECORD AFTER ADVANCING 1 LINES BILLING
00082                              PERFORM READ-A-CARD                       BILLING
00083                              IF END-OF-DATA-FLAG = 'NO'                BILLING
00084                                  COMPUTE NET-COST =                    BILLING
00085                                      CARD-QUANTITY * CARD-PRICE        BILLING
00086                                  MOVE NET-COST TO PRINT-NET-COST       BILLING
00087                                  WRITE PRINTER-RECORD FROM             BILLING
00088                                      NET-COST-PRINT-LINE AFTER ADVANCING BILLING
00089                                      1 LINES                           BILLING
00090                              ELSE                                      BILLING
00091                                  MOVE 'YES' TO MISSING-CARD-FLAG       BILLING
00092                          ELSE                                          BILLING
00093                              MOVE 'YES' TO MISSING-CARD-FLAG           BILLING
00094                      ELSE                                              BILLING
00095                          MOVE 'YES' TO MISSING-CARD-FLAG.              BILLING
00096                                                                        BILLING
00097                  IF MISSING-CARD-FLAG = 'YES'                          BILLING
00098                      DISPLAY 'THERE ARE NOT ENOUGH DATA CARDS TO BE PROCESSED' BILLING
00099                          UPON PRINTER.                                 BILLING
00100                                                                        BILLING
00101              READ-LOOP-EXIT.                                           BILLING
00102                  EXIT.                                                 BILLING
```

```
PIERRE'S RECORD SHOP
6453 ORLEANS STREET
BOOGIE, LOUISIANA 54321
NET =   $7,500.00

ROCKY COLLEGE STORE
1563 BEETHOVEN DRIVE
ROCKTOWN, MARYLAND 20765
NET =      $81.25

WYNN D. TOOTS, INC.
120 BROWNING STREET
GONG, CALIFORNIA 98765
NET =      $50.00
```

Output produced by the computer as the program is executed

FIGURE 12-6 (Continued)

divisions, is divided into file and working storage sections. The purpose of this division is to present in detail a description and layout of:

● All the *input data* items in a record and all the records in each file that's to be processed

- All *storage locations* that are needed during processing to hold intermediate results and other independent values needed for processing

- The format to be used for the *output* results

The *last* COBOL division, the PROCEDURE DIVISION (line 52), contains the sentences and paragraphs that the computer follows in executing the program. In this division, input/output, calculation, logic/comparison, and storage/retrieval and movement operations are performed to solve the problem.

One *advantage* of COBOL is that it can be written in a quasi-English form that may employ commonly used business terms. Because of this fact, the logic of COBOL programs may often be followed more easily by the nonprogrammers in business. Thus there may be less documentation required for COBOL programs. COBOL is better able to manipulate alphabetic characters than FORTRAN, and this is important in business processing where names, addresses, or descriptions are frequently reproduced. Also, a standard version exists; the language is relatively machine-independent; and it's maintained, updated, and supported by its users. Finally, there are large libraries of COBOL business applications modules and packages available today from vendors. A *limitation* of COBOL, however, is that it's obviously not a compact language. It's not the easiest high-level language for most of us to learn, and it's not as well suited for complex mathematical computations as FORTRAN.

PL/1

We've seen that early languages such as FORTRAN and COBOL were written to solve *either* scientific or business data processing problems. But in the early 1960s, IBM and a committee of users of the IBM System/360 family of computers began development work on what was promoted as a "universal language." This **PL/1** language (Programming Language/"One") was implemented in the mid-1960s to solve all types of business and scientific problems. As a scientific language, PL/1 was designed to include some of the features of FORTRAN; however, COBOL-type file processing techniques are also used. An ANSI committee produced a PL/1 standard in 1976. A "Subset G" of this full standard is also available for use with pc's.

Since it has features found in both FORTRAN and COBOL, PL/1 is a flexible and sophisticated language. A portion of a PL/1 program to average test grades is shown in Figure 12-7. Although this program was written on a general-purpose coding sheet, PL/1 programs can be prepared in a rather free-form way. The basic element in PL/1 is the *statement* which is concluded with a semicolon. Statements are combined into *procedures*. A procedure may represent an entire small program or a "building block" or module of a more complex program.

Because of its modular structure, a novice programmer need only learn a small part of the language in order to prepare applications programs of a particular type. Also, modular procedure blocks and other features of the language support the use of structured programming concepts. And a PL/1 compiler has built-in features—called *default options*—that can detect and correct common programming errors. But a *limitation* of PL/1 is that it's more difficult to learn in its entirety than either FORTRAN or COBOL.

MODULE 3

418

FIGURE 12-7

A portion of a program written in PL/1.

FIGURE 12-8

The processing logic built into RPG.

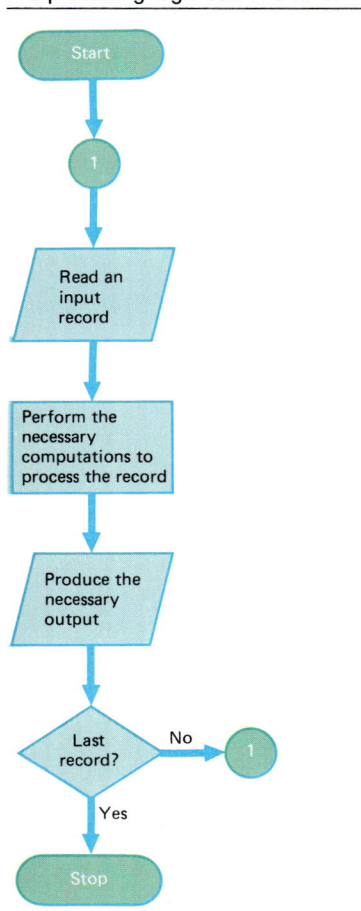

RPG

RPG (Report Program Generator) was introduced in the 1960s, primarily to process business applications on small business computers. As the name suggests, RPG is designed to generate output reports, but it can also be used to periodically update files.

In spite of its file-updating capabilities, RPG is a *limited-purpose* language because object programs generated by the RPG compiler follow a basic processing cycle without deviation. The general form of this cycle is shown in Figure 12-8. Since the processing logic is built into the language and never varies, the RPG programmer is concerned only with *file description* and with specifications about *input, calculations,* and *output.* Very detailed coding sheets are used by programmers to write these specifications.

One *advantage* of RPG is that it's relatively easy to learn and use. Since program logic is fixed, there are fewer formal rules to remember than with many other languages. RPG is well suited for applications where large files are read, few calculations are performed, and output reports are created. It has been an important language of small business-oriented computers for years, but it's not yet available for pc's. Of course, the limited purpose for which it was designed is also a *disadvantage* of the language: RPG has restricted mathematical capability and cannot be used for scientific applications.

ALGOL, Pascal, and Ada

ALGOL (ALGOrithmic Language) was introduced in 1958. It was designed by an international group of mathematicians and developed by groups in Europe and the United States. John Backus of FORTRAN fame assisted in this development. As you might expect, ALGOL was intended for use in scientific and mathematical projects. Several versions of the language have been created, and the current version is ALGOL 68. FORTRAN has generally been used instead of ALGOL in the United States, but ALGOL is very popular in

Europe. Like PL/1, ALGOL is a block-structured or modular language that's well suited for use in structured programming.

An offspring of ALGOL is **Pascal.** Named in honor of Blaise Pascal, a seventeenth-century French mathematician, philosopher, and inventor, this language was developed in the late 1960s and early 1970s by Professor Nicklaus Wirth at Switzerland's Federal Institute of Technology. Pascal was the first major language to be created after the concepts associated with structured programming became widely disseminated.

A Pascal version of a simple billing program similar to those presented earlier in other languages is shown in Figure 12-9. The output produced by

FIGURE 12-9

A computer listing of the simple billing program written in the Pascal language.

```
(* BILLING PROGRAM
   VARIABLE NAMES:

   Q:  QUANTITY PURCHASED
   P:  UNIT PRICE
   A:  NET AMOUNT *)

PROGRAM PROGRAM1 (INPUT,OUTPUT);
VAR CH:CHAR; Q,P,A:REAL; I:INTEGER;
BEGIN
WHILE NOT EOF (INPUT) DO
BEGIN
FOR I:= 1 TO 3 DO
    BEGIN

        (*  READ AND WRITE NAME AND ADDRESS *)

        WHILE NOT EOLN DO
        BEGIN READ (CH);
        IF NOT EOF THEN WRITE (CH);
        END;
        IF NOT EOF (INPUT) THEN
             BEGIN READLN; WRITELN;
             END
    END;
    IF NOT EOF (INPUT) THEN
    BEGIN
              (* READ QUANTITY AND PRICE *)
        READ (Q,P);
        A := Q * P;
        WRITE ('   NET = ',A);
        READLN;
        WRITELN;
        FOR I := 1 TO 2 DO WRITELN;
    END
END
END.
```

Computer listing of the PASCAL program

```
PIERRE'S RECORD SHOP
6453 ORLEANS STREET
BOOGIE, LOUISIANA  54321
    NET =       7500


ROCKY COLLEGE STORE
1563 BEETHOVEN DRIVE
ROCKTOWN, MARYLAND  20765
    NET =        81.25


WYNN D. TOOTS, INC.
120 BROWNING STREET
GONG, CALIFORNIA  98765
    NET =         50
```

Output produced by the computer as the program is executed

CHAPTER 12
419

this program when three input records are supplied is also shown. Like ALGOL, Pascal is block-structured. Programs are composed of *blocks* starting with BEGIN and terminating with END. Program *statements* proceed in a logical flow from start to finish. All variables are identified at the beginning of the program.

Pascal can be used for both scientific and file processing applications. A growing number of high school and college instructors are using it to teach programming to their students. And Pascal is now one of the major languages running on pc and minicomputer systems. Pascal became an ANSI standard language in 1983. It's also the language used by the College Entrance Examination Board to test students seeking college credit for their programming skills.

Another language in the ALGOL/Pascal lineage is **Ada**. This language is named in honor of Lord Bryon's daughter, Lady Augusta Ada Lovelace. Ada worked with Charles Babbage on the concepts for an "analytical engine" in England during the first half of the nineteenth century. Because of her writings, she is considered by many to be the first programmer.

The Ada language is sponsored by the U.S. Department of Defense (DOD) for use by the military services. In 1975, the DOD began a series of studies to specify and design a new common language to be used by computer vendors and military programmers. The new language—Ada—was presented by the design team late in 1980. Critics called it unwieldy and inefficient, while supporters labeled it a breakthrough in software technology. It's still too early to know which view will prevail. Since the DOD will require military computers to have Ada capability, however, the language will endure. Ada became an ANSI standard language in 1983.

Logo and Some Others

Logo was developed in the late 1960s by Seymour Papert and his colleagues at MIT. Although it's used in universities for serious scientific work, Logo has been popularized as a first educational language that children can use to achieve intellectual growth and develop problem-solving skills. The easy-to-learn graphics features, for example, give children an opportunity to communicate and experiment with a computer and draw, color, and animate images. Children create these images by writing programs to move a Logo **turtle** (a small triangle of light) around on the display screen (Figure 12-10).

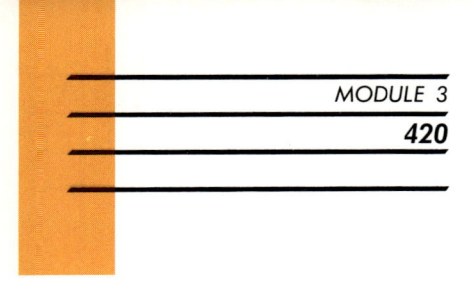

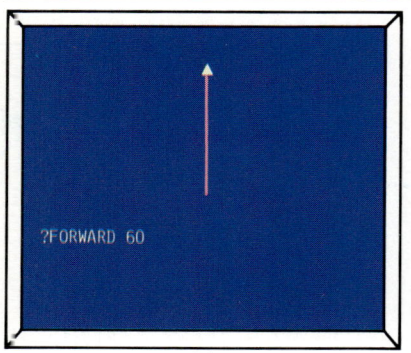

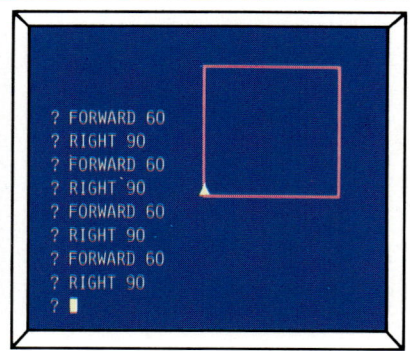

FIGURE 12-10

Children can easily learn to draw images by using the built-in Logo commands that a turtle already knows. (a) Starting at the center of the screen, the command "FORWARD 60" tells the turtle to move forward 60 "turtle steps." As it moves, the turtle leaves a trail in its path (a "PENDOWN" instruction given earlier makes this possible, but if a "PENUP" instruction is used the turtle will move without leaving a trail). (b) After the turtle has moved the designated distance, the second command ("RIGHT 90") causes it to turn 90 degrees to the right. Another "FORWARD 60" instruction completes the top side of the square and another "RIGHT 90" points the turtle downward. When all commands shown on the screen have been executed, the turtle will be back to its starting point. All the commands shown on this screen can be condensed into the following form:
    REPEAT 4 [FORWARD 60 RIGHT 90]
And a child can teach the turtle how to make a square with the following commands:
    TO SQUARE
    REPEAT 4 [FORWARD 60 RIGHT 90]
    END
In the first line, the student names the procedure "SQUARE," but any name could be used. The second line, we've seen, outlines the procedure required to produce the square, and the third line signals the end of the procedure. Once a procedure has been made a part of the turtle's vocabulary, it can be called up at any time. The next time the student uses "SQUARE" in a program, the turtle will automatically produce a square with 60 turtle steps on each side. Children quickly learn how to place procedures within procedures to create interesting geometric shapes.

(a)

(b)

As they produce images, students may establish new goals, tinker with different shapes, and build on what they've done earlier. And they do these things with the computer on an interactive and almost personal basis. Although the Logo turtle is obviously useful in teaching geometry and art, there's much more to Logo than turtles and drawings. Logo runs on pc's and is also used in elementary grades and college classes to manage data, compose music, and manipulate text.

Dozens of other programming languages have been developed. Some of the more important examples are summarized in alphabetical order in Figure 12-11.

Selecting a Programming Language

As you've seen, many languages are available that permit the programmer to write instructions to control the computer during the processing of an application. Which language should be used? Obviously, a selection must be made prior to program coding. Obtaining answers to the following questions will generally help in the selection process:

1 Are programmers familiar with the language? In many cases, the language used is simply the one that's best known to the programmers. If a language is not familiar, can it be learned quickly? Is it easy to use?

2 What's the nature of the application? Does the language perform well in applications of this type?

3 Does the language support structured programming concepts? COBOL, PL/1, ALGOL, and Pascal are better able to support structured programming than most existing BASIC or FORTRAN dialects.

4 Is satisfactory translating software available? There's an important distinction between a language and a compiler or interpreter. A language is a

> There is no best programming language any more than there is a best natural language. "I speak Spanish to God, Italian to women, French to men and German to my horse," said Charles V (presumably in French). A programming language too must be chosen according to the purpose intended.
>
> *Lawrence G. Tesler*

FIGURE 12-11

A summary of additional major programming languages.

APL (*A* *P*rogramming *L*anguage) is a powerful interpreted language that's used with personal computers and larger systems. It uses many curious symbols such as squashed squares and bent arrows, but it can often perform complex arithmetic-logic operations with a single command.

APT (*A*utomatically *P*rogrammed *T*ooling) is used in manufacturing applications to control machine tools.

C was developed at Bell Laboratories and was used to produce the Unix operating system discussed in Chapter 7. It is a favorite of systems programmers and others who develop software packages for small computer systems. It is also used to create graphics and special effects in films (e.g., *Star Trek II* and *Return of the Jedi*). Code that approaches machine language in density and efficiency may be written, but C also offers some high-level language features.

FORTH, like C, resembles a high-level assembly language. It's used by systems programmers for in-house software development projects. It's also used to control astronomical telescopes on observatories around the world.

LISP (*LIS*t *P*rogramming Language) was developed by John McCarthy in 1959-1960 to support research in the field of artificial intelligence (AI). It's designed to manipulate nonnumeric data, and has remained the language of choice among AI researchers in the United States.

Modula-2 is a new language developed by Nicklaus Wirth, the creator of Pascal. Although it retains the advantages of Pascal, Modula-2 is expected to be more powerful and easier to use. It's relatively easy to translate Pascal programs into Modula-2 code.

PILOT (*P*rogrammed *I*nquiry *L*earning *O*r *T*eaching) is used by the developers of computer-assisted instruction materials to prepare programs that emphasize drills, tests, and dialogs.

PROLOG is an AI language that was developed in France. It has been chosen by the Japanese to be the standard language for their "fifth-generation" computer project (discussed in Chapter 3).

SNOBOL (*S*tri*N*g *O*riented Sym*BO*lic *L*anguage) is a text-manipulating and information retrieval language used by researchers in the humanities.

humanly convenient set of rules, conventions, and representations used to convey information from human to machine. A compiler or interpreter is a translator written by one or more programmers. It's entirely possible that a good language, when used with an inefficient translator, will yield unsatisfactory results.

5 *How often will the application be processed?* An assembly language program written by a clever programmer usually has a shorter production run time and takes less storage space than does a program of the same application written in a high-level language. If the job is run often enough, the value of the operating time saved may be more than enough to offset the cost of additional time spent in program preparation. For limited-life jobs, however, the faster the possible programming time is (with high-level languages), the more economical the approach.

6 *Will the program be changed frequently?* The ease of program modification varies with different languages. A high-level language is typically easier to modify than an assembly language.

7 *Is a hardware change anticipated during the life of the application?* Conversion of standardized high-level language programs is easier and faster. Machine-oriented programs may have to be completely rewritten.

8 *Is the language being supported, improved, and updated?* Are resources being committed to the support of the language? Will new computers continue to accept the language source programs? Who's sponsoring the language, and what's their commitment to it?

SOFTWARE IMPLEMENTATION AND MAINTENANCE

So far we've looked at some program preparation practices, considered programming language categories, and discussed several major high-level languages. All these topics occupy an important place in the programming stage. But this stage also includes the actual writing (or coding) of the instructions needed to process an application into a language and form acceptable to a computer. In **program coding,** people must follow specific rules with respect to punctuation and statement structure.

Once software has been written, the final step in the system/program development process is to see that it's implemented and then maintained. The time and effort required for the activities shown in Figure 12-12 will often be determined by the practices followed during system/program development. For example:

● The use of tested prewritten package elements may make it possible to bypass many implementation problems.

● The use of modular system/program design to divide complex problems into more manageable elements may make it easier to trace errors and to insert tested and proven subroutine modules as needed.

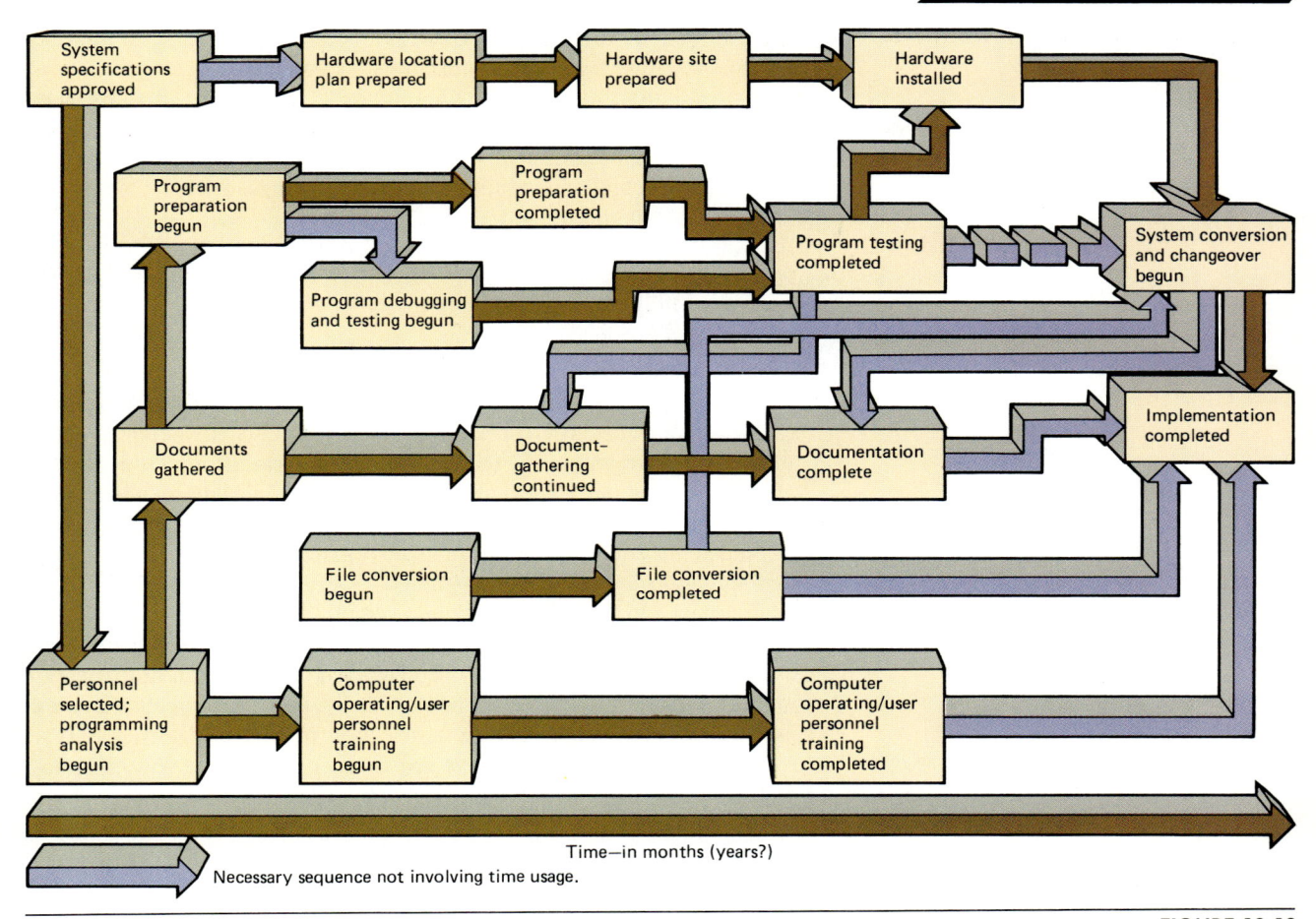

FIGURE 12-12

System/program implementation considerations.

- The use of simple coding structures can lead to programs that are easier to understand and that are thus easier to test and maintain.
- The use of peer reviews can result in fewer errors, faster testing, better documentation, and easier maintenance.

Program Implementation

The first step in **program implementation** is to *debug* the program, to detect and correct errors that prevent the program from running. *Testing* the results produced by the program to see if they are correct is the next implementation step. And ensuring that a complete *documentation* package is available for the application is a third implementation step.

Debugging   There are days when nothing seems to go quite right. Such days may be more common for programmers than for other mortals. *Bugs* are the clerical mistakes and errors that crop up in programs. These bugs or "glitches" (bugs have also been defined as "sons of glitches") just seem to occur even under the best of circumstances. It's unusual for complex programs to run to completion on the first attempt. In fact, the time spent in **debugging** and testing often equals or exceeds the time spent in program coding. Failure to provide for a possible program path, keying errors, mistakes in coding punctuation, transposed characters—these are but a few of the bugs that can thwart the programmer.

To reduce the number of clerical and logical errors, the programmer should carefully check the coding for accuracy before entering it into the computer. This **desk-checking** process should include an examination of program logic and program completeness. Furthermore, typical input data should be manually traced through the program processing paths to identify possible errors. In short, the programmer attempts to play the role of the computer.

After programs have been desk-checked for accuracy, an attempt is made to convert the source program into object program form. Compiler programs and interpreters contain error-diagnostic features, which detect (and print messages about) mistakes caused by the incorrect application of the language used to prepare the source program. In many organizations, a programmer can sit at a workstation and key in the program code from his or her coding sheets. The programmer can then call up an online compiler program to immediately convert the source code into object code. Next, a listing of the detected language-usage (or **syntax**) **errors** may be displayed on the screen of the workstation. The programmer may interact with program development software and use the editing features of the workstation to correct detected errors. When changes have been made in response to detected errors, a new compilation can be ordered. This process may continue until all detected syntax errors have been remedied.

You should realize, however, that compiler/interpreter diagnostic checks will *not* detect the presence of **logical errors** in a program. If an instruction should be "LET A = B*C" but has been coded "LET A = B + C," this error will not be noticed since no language rules have been broken. Thus an "errorless" pass of the program through the compiler or interpreter *does not* mean that the program is perfected or that all bugs have been eliminated. But it usually does mean that the program is ready for testing.

Testing A program to be tested has generally demonstrated that it will run and produce results. The purpose of **testing** is to determine whether the results are correct. The testing procedure involves using the program to process input test data that will produce known results. *The items developed for testing should include:*

- Typical data, which will test the generally used program paths

- Unusual but valid data, which will test the program paths used to handle exceptions

- Incorrect, incomplete, or inappropriate data, which will test the program error-handling capabilities

A testing procedure that's often followed is to separately test different portions of a program. This helps to isolate detected errors to a particular program segment. The use of a modular programming approach, of course, eases this procedure. Another technique that's often used is to entrust much of the testing to someone other than the programmer who wrote the code. A fresh outlook is often helpful, and errors that are missed by a programmer who is "too familiar" with the code may be easily picked up by someone else. There are also many specialized software packages available today that are designed to help people test applications programs.

If the program passes the tests, it may be released for use. However, errors may still remain. In complex programs there may be tens of thousands of different possible paths through the program. It simply isn't practical (and maybe not even possible) to trace through all these paths during testing. For example, the flowchart in Figure 12-13 looks rather simple, but the number of different possible paths is an astounding 10^{20}. If we could somehow check out one path per nanosecond, and if we had started our testing in the year 1, we would only be about half done today! This is why programs may suddenly produce nonsense months after they've been released for use. Some unique and unanticipated series of events has produced input or circumstances that turn up an error for the first time. The error was always there; it simply remained undetected. It's thus impossible to certify that very complex systems are error-free.

If the program does not pass a test, the programmer may:

1 Call for a **trace program** run. The trace program prints out the status of storage registers after each operation. Errors may be discovered by noting register contents after each program step.

2 Call for a **storage dump** when the program "hangs up" during a test run. That is, obtain a printout of the contents of primary storage and registers at the time of the hangup. The programmer can then study this listing for possible clues to the cause of the programming error(s).

Testing ends when users and programmers are satisfied that the software is running properly and producing correct results.

Documentation   **Documentation** is the process of collecting, organizing, storing, and otherwise maintaining on paper (or on some relatively permanent medium) a complete record of *why* applications were developed, for *whom*, *what* functions they perform, and *how* these functions are carried out. Producing documentation is an important—but often neglected—activity of programmers. A number of special prewritten software packages are available to help people carry out this function.

The *documentation package* for software used in an organization should include:

1 *A definition of the problem.* Why was the software prepared? What were the objectives? Who requested it and who approved it?

2 *A description of the system.* The system or subsystem environment in which the software functions should be described. Broad systems specifications outlining the scope of the problem, the form and type of input data to be used, and the form and type of output required should be clearly stated.

3 *A description of the program(s).* Program flowcharts, program listings, test data and test results—these and other documents that describe the program(s) and give a historical record of difficulties and/or changes should be available.

FIGURE 12-13

Errors can remain hidden in an obscure path in a program for years without being detected. This is possible because complex programs contain billions of possible paths. In this simple-looking flowchart, for example, there are 10^{20} possible paths.

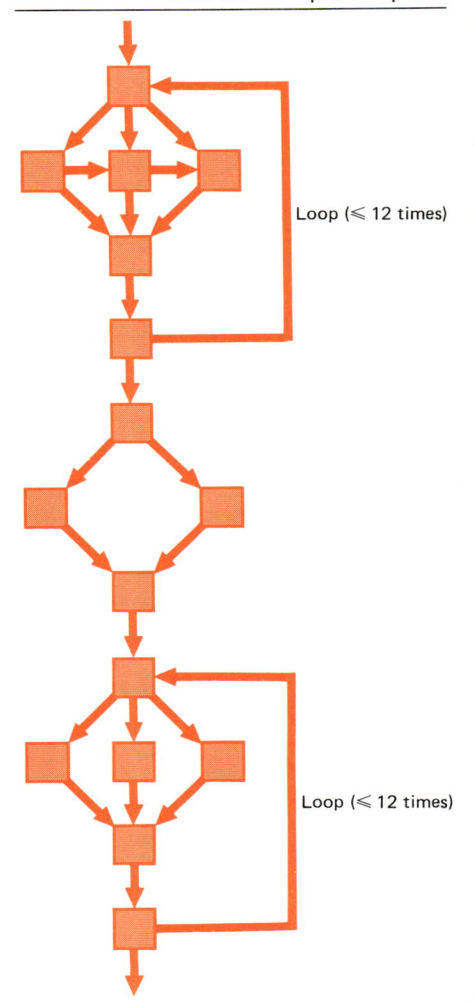

Loop ($\leq$ 12 times)

Loop ($\leq$ 12 times)

4 *A recitation of operator instructions.* Among the items covered should be computer switch settings, loading and unloading procedures, and starting, running, and terminating procedures.

5 *A description of program controls.* Controls may be incorporated in a program in a number of ways. For example, programmed controls may be used to check on the reasonableness and propriety of input data. A description of such controls should be a part of the documentation.

System Conversion and Changeover

If new systems are to be implemented, the system conversion and changeover may begin after programs appear to be producing correct results. This conversion period is almost always a period of personnel and organizational strain. Data processing people may work long hours under pressure to complete the conversion. Unforeseen problems, last-minute corrections, and the disruption of data processing services to using departments often add to these pressures. It's at this time that cooperation is badly needed between data processing specialists and system users. Yet it's precisely at this time that cooperation frequently breaks down because of preoccupation with technical conversion matters at the expense of good human relations.

Everyone who will be affected by the new system should receive training prior to the conversion period to become familiar with the changes. This training is likely to become more intense as new procedures are phased into operation, as old forms are replaced by new ones, as old input devices are retired in favor of new hardware, and as last-minute changes are made in manual methods and personnel assignments.

During system conversion, it may be necessary to change current files into a form acceptable to the processor. This can be a tremendous task, and it's one that's often underestimated. Files should be consolidated and duplicate records eliminated. Errors in current files must be detected and removed.

Converting to a new system is often a stressful event, both for the programmers who have developed the system and for the end users who must adapt to it. (© John Terence Turner/The Image Bank)

And file inconsistencies must be found *before* the changeover rather than later when they can cause system malfunctions.

There's frequently a transitional changeover or shakedown period during which applications are processed by both currently used and new procedures as a final check before the cutover to the new system occurs. A **parallel running** conversion involves the processing of *current* input data by old and new methods. If a significant difference appears, the cause must be located. Various **pilot testing** approaches may also be used during conversion. For example, input data for a *previous* month's operations may be processed using new methods, and the results may be compared with the results obtained from existing operations. A pilot conversion approach is often used when a system is to be installed in a number of different locations over a period of time. One location—say a regional warehouse—may be selected for the initial conversion effort. Once the start-up problems have been solved and the system has been proven under actual operating conditions, the organization can then convert other warehouses to the new procedures.

Regardless of the conversion approach, final changeover to computer production runs comes from satisfactory performance during this shakedown period.

Program/System Maintenance

Changing operating conditions, the revised needs of computer users, new laws—these and many other factors require that existing programs and systems be continually *maintained* and modified. **Program maintenance** is an important duty of programmers and may involve all steps from problem definition through analysis, design, and program preparation. In some installations there are programmers who do nothing but maintain existing programs. It generally takes less time for these programmers to make a change than it does to find the program location(s) where changes are needed.

When an organization first acquires a computer, much of the custom programming effort goes into the development of new applications. But as the number of installed programs in the organization grows, it's not unusual to find that more programming time is being spent on maintenance than on new development work. In fact, in many organizations well over half the total programming effort is spent on maintenance. Over the life cycle of a typical application, the maintenance and enhancement costs may be two to four times larger than the initial development costs (see Figure 12-14). To reduce maintenance costs and improve programmer productivity, many organizations have invested in prewritten software packages that can automatically go through programs and identify poorly written or unnecessary lines of code.

Post-Implementation Review

Once the program/system is implemented and in operation, a thorough audit or **post-implementation review** should be made. This follow-up is commonly conducted by people who have an independent viewpoint and are not responsible for the development and maintenance of the software. Some of the questions that should be considered in the audit are:

- How useful is the software to decision makers? How enthusiastic are they about the services they receive? Do they receive output in time to take action?

FIGURE 12-14

Cost pyramid of the program life cycle.

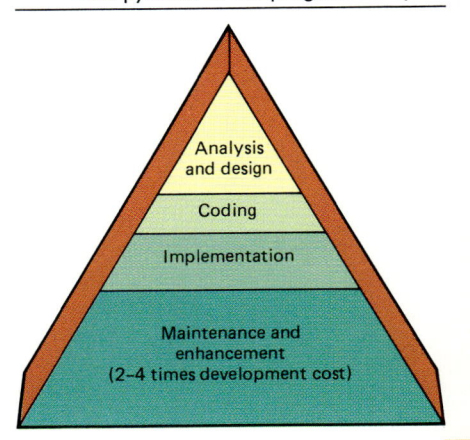

WINDOW 12-2

THE MEANING OF SOFTWARE MAINTENANCE

Hardly a week goes by without our being treated to a prediction of how the onslaught of computers will affect employment. It's easy to get the impression that soon we'll all be programming computers or serving fast food. Such predictions are naive, unrealistic, and myopic. You might think that programming would win hands-down for individuals who could choose between the two activities, but there are some distinct advantages to serving fast food. When you slap together a hamburger, for example, at least you know when you're done. Not so with software development—as the following distortion of a well-known saying illustrates:

A fast food job lasts from bun to bun
But a programming job is never done

It's obvious that a programming job can be a long one, especially if the object is to develop a large software system, but many people don't realize just how long it can take. One reason for that is the term "software maintenance."

Although we don't blame a car when it crashes, computers are often the scapegoat when humans cause them to work improperly. There is one legitimate reason for blaming computers, however: insufficient or faulty maintenance. Some car parts need occasional attention to keep them working properly, and others need occasional replacement. If these needs are neglected or improperly met, a crash may ensue.

Can insufficient or faulty maintenance be blamed for a software crash? No, at least not in the same sense. Cars and other products need maintenance because they wear out with use. But software has no physical properties, only logical properties. When you run the same program a thousand times, some of the hardware components may wear out and require maintenance, but the software can't wear out.

A program can work properly a thousand times and fail suddenly the next time. It might thereby give the appearance of having worn out, but what really happened is that an unusual set of circumstances was encountered for the first time. A program doesn't fail because you wear it out; it fails because it didn't work properly to begin with and you finally have occasion to notice that fact. Software is one of the few products of engineering that can truly be said to last forever. This is a marketing dream; unfortunately, few software products are good enough to take advantage of it.

Although the term "software maintenance" is inappropriate, it's common enough to hear it. Indeed, when most customers buy a large program, they usually enter into a maintenance contract. In return for a monthly or yearly payment, the customer receives occasional revisions of the program. The revisions contain fixes for some of the bugs that were in the original product and perhaps some improvements. The maintenance contract may also provide access to consultants who can help customers work around bugs that they may encounter. To a large extent "maintenance" is a software euphemism for "continued development." This language doesn't fool anyone, but it's a convenient fiction. It allows software developers to declare, in analogy with equipment contractors, that a software product has been "developed" and is ready to enter service and be "maintained." If software products were never accepted until they were error-free, few companies could ever finish their development contracts.

From John Shore, "The Meaning of Maintenance," *The Sachertorte Algorithm and Other Antidotes to Computer Anxiety*, Viking, New York, 1985, pp. 168–169. Copyright © 1985 by John E. Shore. Reprinted by permission of Viking, Penguin, Inc.

- Are planned processing procedures being followed? Are all new procedures being processed on the computer? Have old procedures been eliminated? If not, why not?

- Are system controls being observed? Is documentation complete? Have procedures to control program changes been established? Are any modifications or refinements indicated as a result of operating experience? If so, are they being made?

- How do operating results compare with original goals and expectations? Are economic benefits being obtained? If variations exist, what's the cause? What can be done to achieve expected results?

CHAPTER 12

429

FEEDBACK

Feedback and review 12

You should now have an understanding of some of the practices followed during program preparation. You should also be aware of some of the general characteristics of programming languages. And you should be able to outline the steps followed during the implementation and maintenance phase of the programming process. To test and reinforce your understanding of the material presented in this chapter, fill in the following *crossword puzzle*.

Across

1. A computer's ____ language consists of strings of binary numbers and is the only one it directly understands.
2. One of the first high-level languages designed for scientific applications, and still one of the most popular, ____ was designed in the mid-1950s by an IBM-sponsored committee headed by John Backus.
5. The ____/1 language was designed to solve all types of business and scientific problems. It includes features found in both FORTRAN and COBOL, and it facilitates the use of structured programming concepts.
7. The ____ division is the third of the four divisions required in a COBOL program. This division presents a detailed description of the input data to be processed, the working storage locations that are needed, and the format to be used for the output results.
9. After a program has demonstrated that it will run and produce results, the next step is to ____ it to see if the results are correct.
10. The first part of a machine-language instruction is called the command or operation, and it tells the computer what function to perform. Every computer has an ____ code for each of its functions.
13. A ____ review is also called a structured walkthrough. The purpose of this review is to allow a programmer's colleagues to check his or her work in order to detect errors.

MODULE 3

430

15. A block-structured scientific language that's very popular in Europe. Pascal is considered an offspring of this language.

18. ____ languages use mnemonic operation codes and symbolic addressing, and they are designed for a specific make and model of computer.

21. A program that translates the source code of a high-level language into the machine-language object code of a computer is called a ____. Unlike the object code produced by an interpreter, the object code produced by this program is saved for repetitive use.

22. Whenever feasible, the purchase of an appropriate ____ program should be considered as an alternative to the creation of an in-house custom-made program.

23. Changing conditions require that production programs be continually ____ and updated. The effort spent on this activity can easily exceed the time spent on new program development.

Down

1. In a modular program, a main-control program specifies the order in which each ____ (or subroutine) in the program will be processed.

3. An assembler or compiler is used to translate a source program written in the language used by the programmer into a machine-language ____ program that the computer can understand.

4. An acronym for the organization that publishes programming language standards.

6. When ____ programming is used, three simple logic structures are employed to handle and tame program complexity.

8. Named after Lord Byron's daughter, this recent language in the ALGOL/Pascal line is sponsored by the U.S. Department of Defense.

9. If a program fails to pass a test, the programmer can call for a ____ program run to check on the status of registers after each program operation.

11. The first major language to be created after structured programming concepts became widely disseminated, ____ is an offspring of ALGOL and is now running on many micros and minis.

12. Designed specifically for business-type data processing applications, ____ is a standardized language that requires the use of four divisions in every program. Programs can be written in a quasi-English form, and the language is suited to manipulating large files.

14. ____ is a language used with small business computers to generate output reports. These reports result from the processing of common business applications.

16. The most popular language used with microcomputers and timeshared minicomputers, ____ is an easy-to-use high-level language.

17. When a programmer is responsible for coding an entire program, the program may become an extension of the programmer's ____.

19. The inelegant term used to describe a clerical mistake or logical error that crops up in programs.

20. RPG is a language that uses built-____ processing logic.

LOOKING BACK

1. Programmers generally want to write programs that meet user needs, are produced on time and with a minimum cost, are accurate, and are easy to implement and maintain. In trying to achieve these goals, however, they must usually deal with a number of issues involving methodology and the use of resources. Included among these issues are: Should custom software be written or should an existing program package be adapted to meet the need? How should programming tasks be assigned? What program design methods should be used? Which programming language(s) should be selected?

2. When compared with custom-made programs, prewritten packages generally cost less and may be put into use in a shorter time period. But the custom-made program can be designed to better fit the unique needs of users. The responsibility for preparing a program can be assigned to a programmer who codes and implements the task. Or a programming project can be assigned to a chief programmer or to egoless programming teams. Each of these practices for organizing programmers differs from the others, and they are all used today.

3. Different organizations also follow different program construction practices. Modular (top-down) program design, the use of basic coding structures, and the use of peer reviews—a mix of these and other practices is often followed.

4. Assembly, high-level, and "fourth-generation" programming languages are selected for program coding. Most applications today are coded in a high-level language. Before the source program instructions written in the programmer's language can be used by the computer, however, they must be translated into the machine-language object code that the computer understands. This machine language consists of strings of binary numbers (0s and 1s). An assembly program (used with assembly languages) or a compiler or interpreter (used with higher-level languages) is used to translate source programs into object programs.

5. An overview of some of the most popular high-level languages in use today is presented in this chapter. These languages include BASIC (an easy-to-use, general-purpose language), FORTRAN (a popular language for scientific-mathematic applications), COBOL (the most widely used language for large business applications), PL/1 (a language suitable for both business and scientific applications), RPG (a limited-purpose language used to prepare business reports), ALGOL (a scientific-oriented language that's popular in Europe), Pascal (a general-purpose language that supports the structured programming approach), Ada (a language sponsored by the U.S. Department of Defense), and Logo (a popular educational language with easy-to-learn graphics features). Other important languages are summarized.

6. After software has been written, the final step in the system/program development process is to see that it's implemented and then maintained. Implementation consists of debugging the program(s), testing the results produced to see if they're correct, and preparing a complete documentation package for the software. If new systems are to be implemented, the system conversion and changeover may begin after programs appear to be producing correct results. Parallel running and pilot testing conversion approaches are often used. Program maintenance consists of revising and updating existing programs to meet changing conditions. Much of the programming effort in organizations with mature data processing operations is spent on maintenance. Once a system/program is implemented and in operation, a post-implementation review should be made.

KEY TERMS AND CONCEPTS

software engineering 401
chief programmer team 401
"egoless" programming team 403
main-control program 403
modules 403
modular (top-down) program design 403
subroutine 403
structured programming 404
peer review (structured walkthrough) 405
machine language 406
operation code 406
operand 406
address 406
mnemonic code 406
assembly language 406

symbolic addressing 407
assembly program (assembler) 407
source program 407
object program 407
macro instruction 408
high-level languages 409
compiler 410
interpreter 410
fourth-generation languages (4GLs) 410
BASIC 411
interactive language 411
ANSI standard 411
FORTRAN 412
COBOL 414
CODASYL 414
PL/1 417
RPG 418
ALGOL 418
Pascal 419

Ada 420
Logo 420
turtle 420
program coding 422
program implementation 423
debugging 424
desk-checking 424
syntax errors 424
logical errors 424
testing 424
trace program 425
storage dump 425
documentation 425
parallel running 427
pilot testing 427
program maintenance 427
post-implementation review 427

Topics for Review and Discussion

1. "During program preparation, programmers must usually deal with a number of issues involving methodology and the use of resources." Discuss this statement and identify three of the possible issues.
2. What are the possible advantages and limitations of adapting a packaged program to meet user needs?
3. Identify and discuss three ways that programmers can be assigned to program preparation projects.
4. (a) What is a modular program? (b) What advantages might there be to the use of modular programming techniques?
5. What advantages might there be in requiring that programmers use only basic coding structures in their programs?
6. (a) What's a peer review? (b) What advantages does this practice offer?
7. "Every programming language has instructions that fall into four categories." Identify and discuss these categories.
8. "An instruction prepared in any machine language has at least two parts." Identify these parts and discuss the function of each.
9. (a) How does an assembly language differ from a machine language? (b) How is an assembly language source program translated into a machine-language object program?
10. (a) What advantages do high-level languages have over assembly languages? (b) Discuss two approaches used to translate high-level languages into machine languages.
11. What are the possible advantages of using a "fourth-generation" language?
12. (a) What is BASIC? (b) How is it used today?
13. (a) What is FORTRAN? (b) How did it originate? (c) How is it used today?
14. (a) What is COBOL? (b) How did it originate? (c) How is it used today?
15. (a) What is PL/1? (b) What advantages does it possess?
16. (a) What is RPG? (b) How is it used? (c) Why is it a limited-purpose language?
17. Discuss the development and current use of (a) ALGOL, (b) Pascal, and (c) Ada.
18. (a) What is Logo? (b) How is it used today?
19. What questions should be considered in determining the programming language to use in given situations?
20. What steps can be taken during debugging and testing to locate and remove program errors?
21. What should be included in a program documentation package?
22. (a) What's a parallel running conversion? (b) What's meant by the pilot testing approach to system conversion?
23. Why is program maintenance needed?

Projects/Issues to Consider

1. Visit a computer center in your area and identify the programming languages supported by the center. Prepare a report that (a) lists these languages, (b) describes the reason for their selection in given applications, and (c) outlines the extent to which each language is used.
2. People who hire programmers and systems analysts don't always agree on the characteristics that are likely to identify an ideal employee. In a recent editorial in *Datamation* magazine, a West Coast data processing manager for a major retail chain said: "The number one question I ask job applicants is: 'Do you play a musical instrument or do you have such an interest?' I've found that a proficiency in music has the highest correlation with excellence in programming—both require a person to be creative within a structure." Others may not agree with this manager's statement. Interview five computer center managers to (a) get their reactions to this statement and (b) determine the educational backgrounds and experience they look for in hiring programmers and systems analysts. (You may get some ideas for additional questions after you've examined the Closer Look reading at the end of this chapter.) Present your research findings to the class.

Answers to Feedback and Review Section

The solution to the crossword puzzle is shown below:

	1 M	A	C	H	I	N	E		2 F	3 O	R	T	4 R	A	N		5 P	L		6 S
	O									B			N							T
	D		7 8 D	A	T	A				J		9 T	E	S	T		10 O	11 P		R
	U			D			12 C		13 P	E	E	R		I		14 R		A		U
	L		15 A	L	G	O	L		C		A					P		S		C
	E		16 B			B			T		C		17 E		G			C		T
			A			O					E		G					A		U
18 A	S	S	E	M	19 B	L	Y		20 I			21 C	O	M	P	I	L	E	R
			I		U				N											E
22 P	A	C	K	A	G	E	D			23 M	A	I	N	T	A	I	N	E	D

A CLOSER LOOK

CAREERS IN COMPUTING

We've now completed the four chapters in the Software Module. In these chapters we've often referred to those who create prewritten packages and develop custom-made software solutions to satisfy user needs. Every issue of *Computerworld*, a weekly newspaper for the computer industry, contains many pages of "help wanted" ads with enticing captions (see Figure 12-A). These ads are aimed at finding people to fill the occupational categories presented in the following sections. As you read these sections, perhaps you'll find a path that will lead to future opportunities.

Information System Managers

Like all managers, a *manager of a department* such as system analysis/design or program preparation must perform the functions of planning, organizing, staffing, and controlling. To be able to plan effectively and then control his or her department activities, such a manager must possess technical know-how in addition to managerial ability. But too much emphasis on technical competence at the expense of management skills can cause problems. Too often in the past, the most skilled technician was promoted to group manager only to demonstrate, very soon, a lack of competence in management techniques. It's likely that the larger the department, the more important managerial skills become in the total mix of skills required by a manager (Figure 12-B).

The *management information system (MIS) director* must also possess technical knowledge, for he or she is responsible for planning and controlling the information resources of an organization. In addition, however, the MIS director must:

- Clearly understand the organization's purpose and goals, and its unique data processing needs.

- Be able to communicate with, motivate, and lead a number of highly skilled people

- Possess the poise and stature to command the respect of other executives as well as data processing employees

People planning to seek a career in information system management should acquire a college degree. Courses in business administration, economics, personnel management, computer science, and statistics are desirable. And practical experience is also required to attain the maturity that's needed.

Data Base Administrators

Larger organizations typically rely on sophisticated DBMS packages to manage much of their data. The person respon-

---

FIGURE 12-A

A small sampling of ads from an issue of *Computerworld*. Scores of ads covering dozens of pages were included in this issue.

IBM has career openings in

**SYSTEMS PROFESSIONALS...
ADVANCE YOUR CAREER WITH
A DYNAMIC LEADER!**

**CAREER OPENINGS
With
World-Wide Travel Opportunity**

**CHALLENGING CAREER
OPPORTUNITY
IN
OPERATING SYSTEM
SOFTWARE SUPPORT**

**PHOENIX, ARIZONA
MIS OPENINGS**
The City of Phoenix has immediate openings in the MIS Department for well qualified persons in the following key areas.

FIGURE 12-B

Total mix of skills required by an information systems manager.

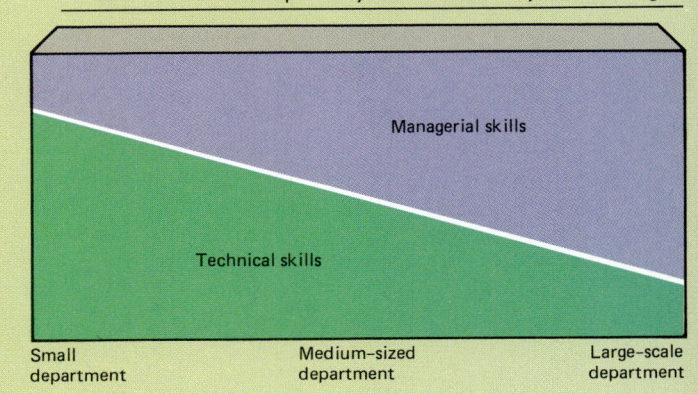

Managerial skills

Technical skills

Small department — Medium-sized department — Large-scale department

sible for the operation of a DBMS is often called a *data base administrator* (DBA). The role of the DBA is to:

- Establish a data dictionary that records organization-wide data definitions and standards

- Coordinate the data collection and storage needs of users

- Act as a file design and data base consultant to others in the organization

- Design the data base security system to guard against unauthorized use

To perform these duties, a DBA must have a high degree of technical knowledge. He or she must also have the political skills needed to balance conflicting user needs, and the ability to communicate effectively with users who have dissimilar backgrounds.

Given this job description, it's not surprising that the DBA has sometimes been called the "superperson" of the data processing installation. Educational backgrounds vary, but a college degree that emphasizes computer science, management, and communications skills is appropriate. In large organizations, there can be several DBAs working under the direction of a manager of data base administration.

Systems Analysts

The title of *systems analyst* is given to those who are responsible for analyzing how computer data processing can be applied to specific user problems and for designing effective data processing solutions. Although there are often several grades of systems analyst (lead, senior, junior), the job consists of:

- Helping users determine information needs

- Gathering facts about, and analyzing the basic methods and procedures of, current information systems

- Designing new systems, integrating existing procedures into new system specifications as required, and assisting in the implementation of new designs

Senior systems analysts are often chosen to act as leaders of system study teams (discussed in Chapter 11).

Analysts must usually be very familiar with the objectives, personnel, products and services, industry, and special problems of the organizations that employ them. They must also know the uses and limitations of computers as well as other types of data processing equipment, for they are the interpreters between users and other data processing specialists. They must understand programming basics and be able to determine which jobs are candidates for computer processing. In addition to logical reasoning ability, they must also have initiative and the ability to plan and organize their work since they will frequently be working on their own without much direct supervision. And they must be able to communicate with and secure the cooperation of operating employees and supervisors. Educational backgrounds vary, but a college degree or the equivalent is generally needed. Courses that have proven valuable to the types of system analysts described above are the same ones mentioned for data processing managers.

Programmers and Programmer Team Personnel

Programmers may be classified here into two categories: applications programmers and systems programmers. The job of an *applications programmer* is often to take the systems specifications of analysts and transform them into effective, efficient, and well-documented programs of instructions for computers. However, there are different applications programmer categories, and their duties can vary. In some organizations, for example, the duties of system analyst and applications programmer are combined into an *analyst/programmer* job. In other organizations, some applications programmers work primarily on new program development while others devote their time almost exclusively to maintaining existing programs. A single programmer may be assigned to develop a new program, or a team of program-

FIGURE 12-C

Jobs for trained programmers are expected to double from their 1978 level of a quarter million to half a million by 1990. Others in high demand will be software engineers, systems analysts, and management-level personnel with computer knowledge, including data base managers and managers of information service systems. (Bureau of Labor Statistics)

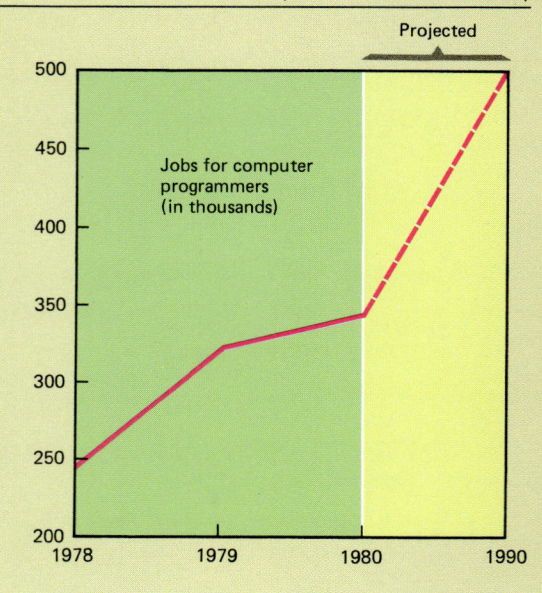

mers may be given the task. As Figure 12-C shows, job opportunities for programmers are expected to grow throughout the 1980s. The National Science Foundation expects a shortage of over 100,000 programmers and analysts in 1987.

The organizing of programmers into *chief programmer teams* and *"egoless" programming teams* is discussed in the chapter. When chief programmer teams are used, a highly skilled *lead* or *"chief" programmer* is in charge of the team, another senior programmer acts as the chief's *backup programmer,* and a *team librarian* is assigned to gather and organize the records and documents associated with the project. Other applications programmers are assigned to the project team as needed.

The job of a *systems programmer* is to select, modify, and maintain the complex system software packages discussed in Chapter 10. Systems programmers thus perform a support function by maintaining the system software environment in which applications programmers and computer operators work. They also participate in decisions involving hardware/software additions or deletions.

Since programmer job descriptions vary, the educational requirements for these jobs also vary. A systems programmer is likely to need the courses offered in a computer science degree program or the equivalent in professional training. The educational background needed by applications programmers depends on such factors as:

• The degree of separation between the systems analysis and programming functions

• The complexity of the data processing systems in the organization

• The industry in which the organization operates

Completion of a 4-year college program isn't an absolute condition for employment in many applications programming groups, but the skills required from a 2-year college program are often needed.

Regardless of the educational background requirements, however, all programmers need the following basic skills:

• Analytical reasoning ability and the ability to remember and concentrate on small details

• The drive and motivation to complete programs without direct supervision

• The patience and perseverance to search for small errors in programs and the accuracy to minimize the number of such errors

• The creativeness to develop new problem-solving techniques

Telecommunications Personnel

Telecommunications specialists are responsible for the design of the local-area and external data communications networks described in Chapter 8. They work with others such as systems programmers to evaluate and select the communications processors to be used in the network. The analysis of network traffic and the preparation of data communications software are included in their duties. They may also establish the standards for network operation. Nondata communications links used for voice and picture transmission are also likely to be included in their responsibilities. Like systems programmers, telecommunications specialists perform a support function. And also like systems programmers, they need a strong technical background.

Computer Operations Personnel

As Figure 12-D shows, about 40 percent of the people in a typical MIS division in a large company perform computer operations functions. The duties of *computer operators* include setting up the processor and related tape and disk drives, starting the program run, checking to ensure proper operation, and unloading equipment at the end of a run. Some knowledge of programming is needed. Programs at some 2-year colleges are designed to train computer operators. But on-the-job training and experience are often all that's required to hold operating jobs.

Data entry operators transcribe data from source documents into a magnetic media form that's suitable for input into

FIGURE 12-D

How people are classified in a typical MIS division in a larger company. (International Data Corporation)

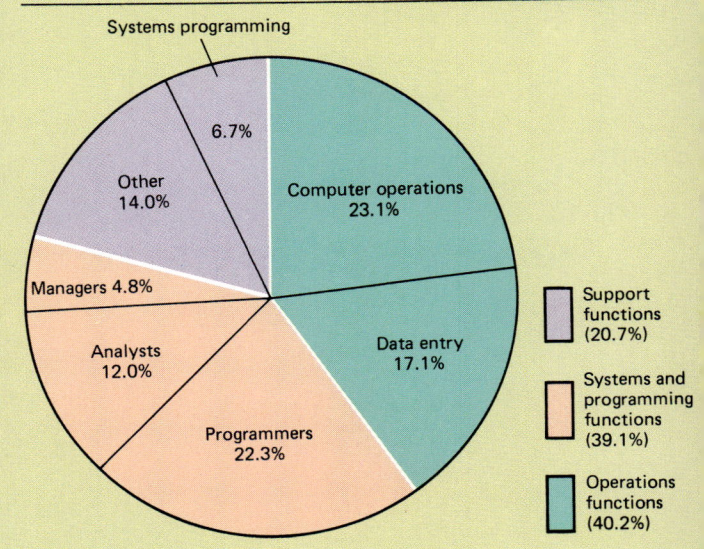

Systems programming 6.7%
Other 14.0%
Managers 4.8%
Analysts 12.0%
Programmers 22.3%
Data entry 17.1%
Computer operations 23.1%

Support functions (20.7%)
Systems and programming functions (39.1%)
Operations functions (40.2%)

438

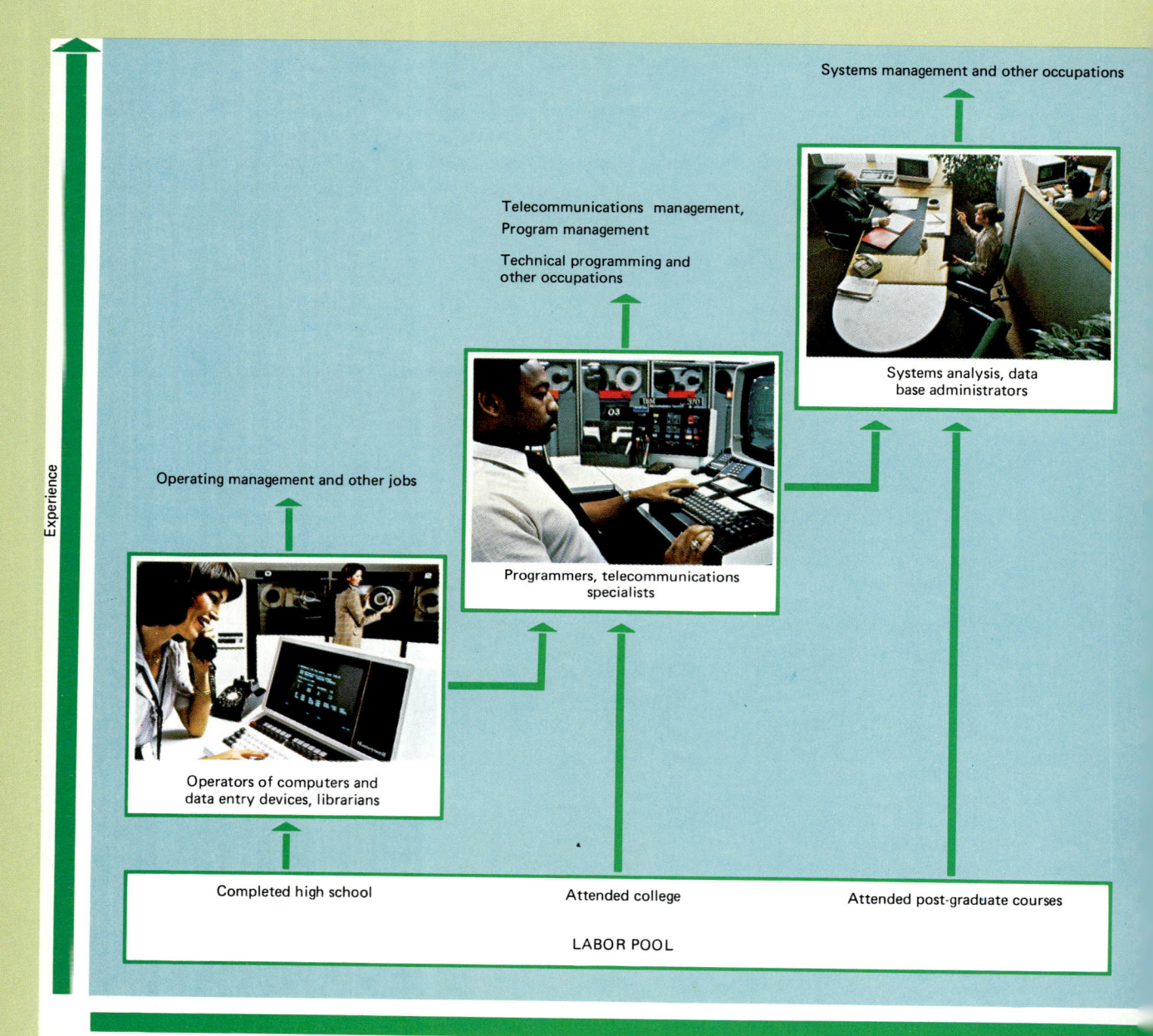

Systems management and other occupations

Telecommunications management,
Program management

Technical programming and
other occupations

Systems analysis, data
base administrators

Operating management and other jobs

Programmers, telecommunications
specialists

Operators of computers and
data entry devices, librarians

Experience

Completed high school Attended college Attended post-graduate courses

LABOR POOL

Education

FIGURE 12-E

Some of the possible career paths in computing. (Courtesy Honeywell, Inc., and General Electric Information Systems Company)

a computer system. Skill at a keyboard is usually needed, and intelligence and alertness are required to recognize and correct errors. A formal educational background is usually not necessary, but careful on-the-job training is needed to minimize data entry errors. Data entry operators may be grouped together at a centralized site or dispersed at remote terminal locations. The demand for data entry operators at central sites is likely to decline in the future.

Program and media librarians are often found in the computer operations section. They have the very important task of maintaining and protecting the installation's programs and data. The documentation of programs and procedures is controlled by a librarian. Magnetic tapes and disks are cataloged, stored, and supplied to authorized people by a librarian. Computer operators and programmers must get a librarian's approval to check out programs and data, and charge-out records are kept. Media cleaning and inspection are also a librarian's responsibility. Clerical record-keeping skills are needed. On-the-job training is generally used to prepare people for librarian jobs.

Figure 12-E summarizes some of the possible career paths for those who choose opportunities in the computer-related jobs we've considered. Many other computer-related jobs are held by those who *design, manufacture, sell,* and *service* computer hardware. *Technical writers* often produce users manuals and other software documentation. And *educators* are employed to teach computing concepts at thousands of public and private schools. You can probably add more computer-related job categories to the ones listed in this reading (what about the jobs building and running computer-controlled robots, the need for artificial intelligence specialists . . . ?).

MODULE 4

Early in the Background Module you saw that one purpose of this book is to show you how computer applications are affecting people and organizations in a modern society. Thus in this module we'll look at the impact of computer usage in various areas that involve us all, including government and law, health care, education, the humanities, science, engineering, and business.

SOCIAL IMPACT

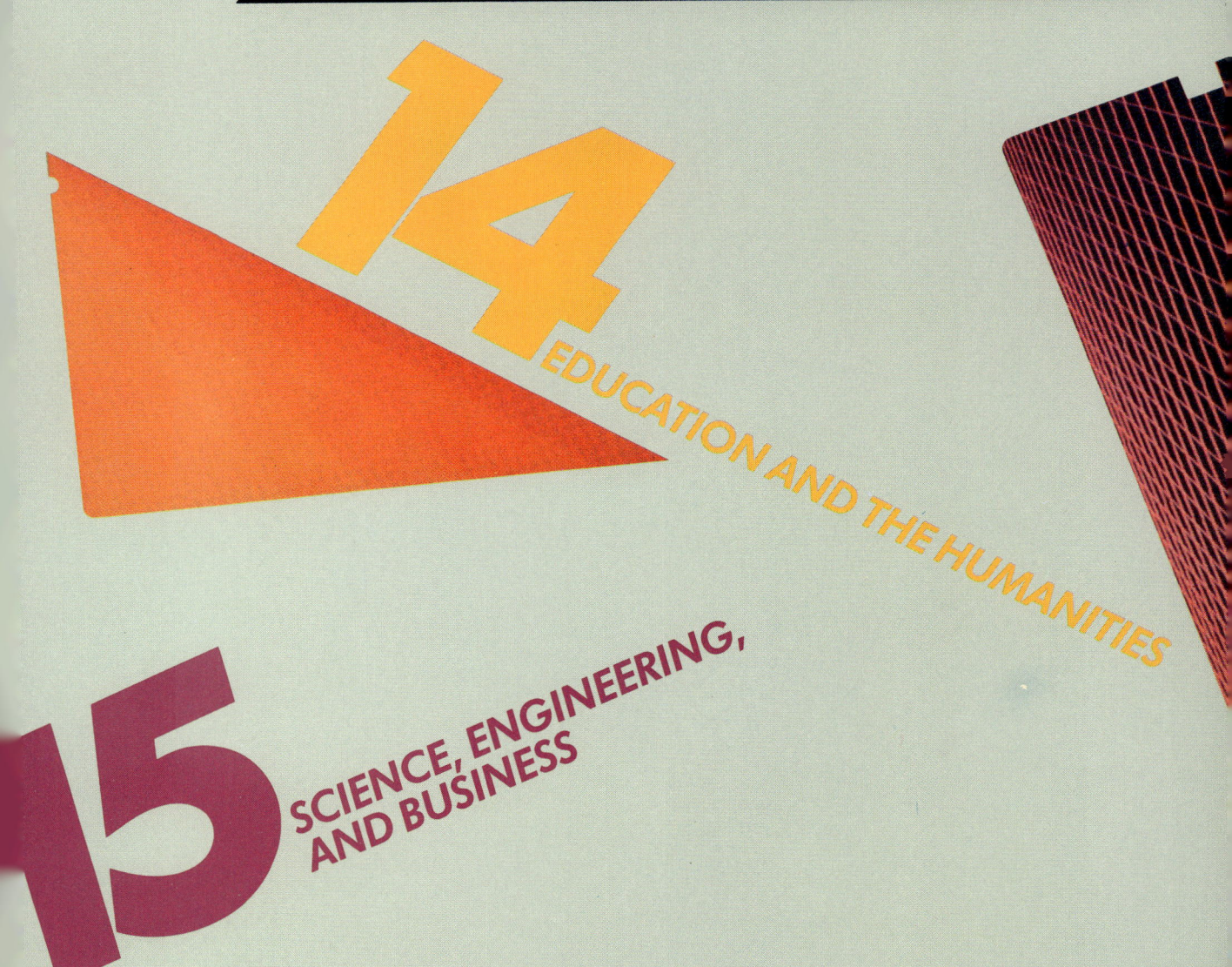

13 GOVERNMENT, LAW, AND HEALTH CARE

14 EDUCATION AND THE HUMANITIES

15 SCIENCE, ENGINEERING, AND BUSINESS

CHAPTER 13

GOVERNMENT, LAW, AND HEALTH CARE

STREAMLINING A FEDERAL BUREAUCRACY

Suite 2127 at the General Services Administration (GSA) building in Washington, D.C., is a riddle in time. The ceilings are high and the furniture old-fashioned. There is a cool quality about the rooms, a quality enhanced by the half-drawn shades and dim lighting. Walking into Suite 2127, one feels catapulted back to the pre-air-conditioned days of 1955, possibly even 1934. It could be any time.

But it isn't. It's the mid-1980s and the shades are drawn, not to cool the occupants but to protect two IBM PC/XTs from overheating. In the past 2 years, according to office director M. Scott Downing, these computers have caused a revolution in the way this federal agency works.

GSA is a mammoth arm of the federal bureaucracy, employing nearly 26,000 people nationwide. It functions as a large diversified corporation, acting as landlord and builder, business manager, telecommunications and data processing consultant, and purchasing agent for most of the U.S. government.

If that task seems formidable, consider that the GSA's revenues for these chores, in 1985, logged in at $5 billion, with appropriations from Congress for special, one-shot deals totaling an additional $496 million. Managing those moneys—getting and spending them—is the responsibility of the GSA's Office of Budget. Keeping a paper trail of that management is Scott Downing's job, a job that, before the arrival of personal computers, frequently took on the quality of "a nightmare."

There is, for instance, the issue of the President's budget, a report put together annually for the White House, that summarizes how revenues are to be spent. These reports are prepared under a tight deadline and with constant revisions. Putting out the presidential budget used to call for as many as sixty 23-column spreadsheets, and a rainbow of colored pencils to keep track of the revisions. "Only you got to the point," said Downing, "where you eventually ran out of colors."

An online Planning System for the President's report, which had been set up by another federal agency, only made matters worse. Among other things, this mainframe-based system offered no way of catching mistakes—of checking to see if figures matched—until all the data were entered. And there were no printouts at the reporting agencies, only dumb terminals, so that once mistakes had been factored by the mainframe, a user had to sit before a moving screen, scribbling frantically to take down the list of errors by hand.

In self-defense, Downing turned to the personal computer, devising a routine that permitted the GSA's budget analysts to draw up an irrefutable draft for the Planning System mainframe program. Since Downing's computers perform all the math and pick up for repeat use figures already entered, they cut down on errors of calculation and mistaken input.

In addition, they compare data from competing parts of the report, so analysts can frequently tell while they are still entering data whether something is out of whack. Downing estimates that the time GSA users spend entering and re-entering their data on the Planning System has now been cut by half.

But that's hardly where the technological gold mine stops. A happy by-product of Downing's bid to unhook from the mainframe system is a reduction of mistakes and of time management spent on other reports. For example, GSA's annual budget to Congress used to cause as much tooth-gnashing as the President's budget. Today, Downing's program sets up the congressional report using figures already entered and laboriously checked for the presidential budget, permitting the former to be produced "untouched by human hands."

And after that is done, there are still reports to be generated for GSA's management: long-range budgets; scenarios projecting the impact of GSA's immense spending on the national economy at various times; monthly reports comparing current to projected expenditures on items as varied as paper clips and motorcycles; quarterly reports justifying spending changes; the list goes on and on. But not the data entry process. With the new program, figures once entered are picked up automatically by the computer for use on all subsequent reports.

GSA uses IBM XTs and Victor 9000s at its Washington headquarters and 11 regional offices. To communicate with one another long distance, the offices employ commercial communication packages, as well as electronic mail.

Downing has tried to simplify software matters by relying, wherever possible, on the Lotus 1-2-3 spreadsheet package. He has even used that program as a primitive word processing program. Now, users in the regional offices can justify, in text, their requests for approval of budget changes on the same Lotus 1-2-3 system that they use for the accompanying numerical report. The text is then transmitted via electronic mail to Washington, where it can receive immediate attention.

At GSA these days, the wheels of bureaucracy may continue to grind slowly, but the reports come out fast.

Excerpted from Mary Nelson, "Streamlining a Federal Bureaucracy," *Personal Computing*, October 1985.

We would like to acknowledge and thank the experts who have contributed a wealth of detailed information to this chapter. Donald F. Norris of the Center for Applied Urban Research of the University of Nebraska, Omaha, has provided materials for the government and law section, and Harold Sackman of the Business Information Systems Department, California State University of Los Angeles, has supplied materials for the health-care section.

MODULE 4

LOOKING AHEAD

Since computer usage is having a profound impact on the ways we are governed and the health care we receive, this chapter gives you a glimpse of some computer applications in the government and health-care sectors of society. We'll first look at a few of the ways that computers are being used in local, state, and federal governments and in law enforcement agencies. We'll then examine a number of key health-care applications that make effective use of computers today. The information in this chapter will enable you to:

- Discuss several ways that computers are used by local, state, and federal government organizations
- Describe the role of computers in law enforcement
- Summarize some major uses of computers in the health-care field

CHAPTER OUTLINE

LOOKING AHEAD
COMPUTERS IN GOVERNMENT AND LAW
Housekeeping and Decision-Making Applications
Computers in Local Government
Computers in Regional Organizations and State Governments
Computers in the Federal Government
Law and Law Enforcement Applications
COMPUTERS IN HEALTH CARE
Where We've Come From
Health-Care Systems Today
Health-Care Systems Tomorrow
Feedback and Review 13
LOOKING BACK

COMPUTERS IN GOVERNMENT AND LAW

Housekeeping and Decision-Making Applications

The use of computers in government organizations most often involves either housekeeping or decision-making activities. **Housekeeping activities** include the everyday tasks that organizations must perform just to keep going, such as billing, budgeting, accounting, payroll, record keeping, and word processing. Most housekeeping activities, such as the preparation and updating of inventory and taxpayer records and the processing of bills, relate to the financial management of an organization. Small governmental organizations and small agencies within larger government units still perform some of their housekeeping functions manually. But larger governmental organizations are extensively computerized, because to perform housekeeping activities without computers would require hiring armies of clerks—something their budgets don't permit.

Decision-making activities may use information developed in housekeeping activities, but the purpose of decision-making activities is to support future courses of action. For example, the purpose of *budgetary accounting,* a routine housekeeping activity, is to compare information about current revenues and expenditures to budgeted (or projected) figures and to the previous year's amounts. But *budget preparation,* a decision-making activity, differs from budgetary accounting because its purpose is to determine future financial conditions. Using data from budgetary accounting reports, budget preparers ask "what if" questions to create alternative financial projections. Officials then choose among these projections to establish next year's budget. During budget preparation, planners may ask such questions as, "What if all employees receive a 5 percent salary increase, or the cost of medical insurance increases 10 percent, or the number of employees decreases by 5 percent while tax revenues decline by 2 percent?" Answers to these hypothetical questions help budget planners anticipate future revenues and expenditures. Decision makers can then decide which set of projections to choose for next year's budget.

Computers in Local Government

Local governments run nearly 7,000 cities and over 3,000 counties in the United States. Nearly all large U.S. cities and counties now use computers for such housekeeping tasks as financial management and record keeping, while the second most frequently computerized area is law enforcement. This law enforcement use of computers can be explained by two facts. The first is that law enforcement agencies in large cities and counties produce huge volumes of data. Managing these data without computerization would be difficult. Second, a great deal of federal funding has been provided to help local governments computerize their law enforcement activities.

The introduction of powerful yet inexpensive personal computers (pc's) has put computer hardware within the financial reach of even the smallest governments. And today's easy-to-use packaged software enables computers to be used by organizations that cannot afford to hire and support staffs of

Most state and local law-enforcement agencies now rely on computers to manage their operations and to give them access to national crime data bases. (Courtesy AT&T Technologies Inc.)

technical experts. As a result, even small cities are becoming sophisticated computer users.

Example 1 The city of Seward, Nebraska, population 5,000, owns an electricity distribution system. In 1982, Seward installed a pc system to monitor customer demand for electric power. The system was programmed to display and print power demand levels at 15-minute intervals. At peak levels, the city has to pay premium rates for the electricity it buys. When usage begins to approach peak levels, the city takes action to reduce the demand for this expensive electricity.

City employees call major electricity users and ask them to shut off pumps, air conditioners, and electric motors. Once the load has been reduced and the city is no longer in danger of incurring higher rates, users are told that they can resume their previous consumption of power. During its first year of operation, this $16,000 system saved Seward $82,000, and over $100,000 was saved in the second year. These savings were passed along to electricity customers; electricity rates remained steady in the face of mounting costs.

Numerous other communities have adopted computer-assisted electric utility load management systems. Some are more sophisticated than Seward's and use radio signals to stop and restart electrical equipment at user locations.

Example 2 Another innovative use of computers by local government is found in the public library system in Iowa City, Iowa. Before moving to a new facility, the Iowa City library contracted with a vendor to develop an online catalog employing touch-sensitive display screens. When the system was implemented in the new building, the old card catalog was replaced by terminals.

At first, results were mixed. The library saved over 3,000 personnel hours by not updating the old card catalog, but the need to use terminals upset some users and the touch-sensitive screens seemed awkward to people accustomed to using keyboards. In addition, the system's software wasn't simple to use. But the library staff felt the system was worth saving, so changes were made. Program logic was improved and simplified to reduce the number of

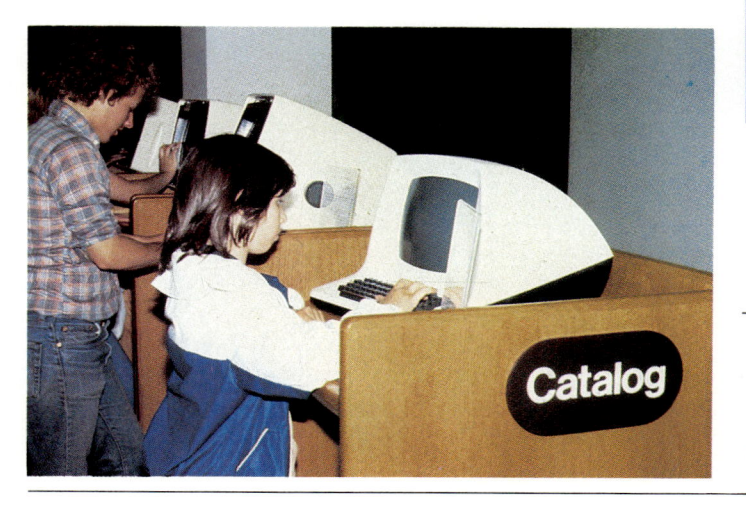

The Iowa City Public Library's computerized catalog is far more popular than its old card catalog, but the touch-screen terminals in the background are being replaced because users prefer keyboard terminals like the one in the foreground. (Courtesy Iowa City Public Library)

steps needed for book searches, and easier-to-use software and keyboard terminals were installed. Despite the early problems, there are now about three times more electronic catalog users than there were users of the old card catalog.

Example 3 One of the nation's fastest-growing areas is Fairfax County, Virginia, near Washington, D.C. The county has implemented an automated land development system on its mainframe computer. Developed to streamline the county's land development regulation process, the system consists of online programs that track rezoning applications, plans and agreements, and inspection services information.

But a major data collection problem surfaced when the system was first implemented. The volume of construction inspection data was so large that it couldn't be entered into the system until several days after it was collected. This meant that issuance of occupancy permits by the county's department of environmental management was needlessly delayed. To speed up the data flow, the county provided hand-held computer input devices to collect on-site inspection data and transfer it to the inspection records on the mainframe. Each portable data entry device is the size of a pocket calculator and can store about 64,000 characters of information. Although field inspectors had their doubts about the devices at first, field experience has demonstrated the reliability of the units and they have cut data entry time to a day in most cases.

Example 4 Control Data Corporation, a pioneer in many areas of the computer industry, is also a leader in providing an online data base for local governments. LOGIN (LOcal Government Information Network) contains over 20,000 "data units." Most of these units are examples and brief case studies of innovative practices in governmental administration. The data units are fed into the LOGIN data base by academic researchers, LOGIN staff and consultants, public interest groups, and governmental agencies.

The data base is accessed through a local telephone number that connects with the nationwide Cybernet communications network. By keying in their identification code, users gain access to LOGIN and can browse at their leisure through the data base. They can read data units on their screens, and they

If LOGIN's online data base doesn't suggest a solution for a local government problem, local officials can use LOGIN's electronic mail service to question a nationwide interest group of officials coping with similar problems. (© John Blaustein/Four-Phase Systems)

can get printouts of them. Furthermore, most data units list the names and telephone numbers of persons to contact for additional information.

Another important LOGIN service is electronic mail (see Chapter 8 for more information on communications networks and electronic mail). Users can place questions on the general network bulletin board or can address them to members of one of LOGIN's special-interest groups (such as governmental managers, reference librarians, and people with city, county, and municipal league interests). LOGIN staff members estimate that about 300 questions are asked each month, about 75 percent of these questions receive answers, and the time required to produce answers is usually less than a week.

As computers continue to become more powerful and less expensive and as more packaged local government software becomes available, local government use of computers will increase. Administrators of these public units will thus need to be far more knowledgeable about computer applications than their predecessors.

Computers in Regional Organizations and State Governments

At the Regional Level **Regional organizations**—often called regional planning or development districts or commissions and councils of government—are governmental units with jurisdictions that cross city and county lines within a given geographic area. The range of powers of regional governments varies depending on state requirements, enabling legislation, and local participation.

Many regional entities participate in the federally mandated Areawide Waste Water Treatment Planning program. This program requires that water pollution control be planned on a watershed or river basin basis, rather than within the political boundaries of cities and counties. The reason is that sources and effects of water pollution ignore political boundaries. They can be dealt with systematically only if they are addressed throughout the watershed or river basin in which they occur. Regional organizations, because of their "areawide" nature, are more suited to such planning efforts than individual local governments.

One regional organization that makes innovative use of computer technology to aid in water pollution control planning is the West Michigan Regional Planning Commission ("Region 8," as it's known). To begin its program, Region 8 had aerial photographs taken of its nine-county, 6,000-square-mile area. The photographs were interpreted within grids of cells set up for rural and urban areas. Each data cell included information on all observable land uses in its area, as well as the predominant soil type and the slope condition. All this information was then entered into a mainframe computer. Region 8 soon produced a land-use data base of over half a million data cells.

This data base is used for two purposes: (1) to model or simulate the water quality of the region's rivers under various conditions (such as heavy rainfall in an agricultural watershed or direct discharge from wastewater treatment plants) to determine the types and locations of water pollution control measures needed to meet federal standards and (2) to identify environmentally sensitive lands (such as shoreline areas) to prepare local land-use plans and regulations.

The ability to process the wealth of data in the Region 8 data base helps many governments in the region develop land-use plans. It also helped one of

Dade County, Florida's, computerized traffic control system is one of many similar regional control systems in urban areas throughout the United States. (Courtesy Dade County Department of Transportation)

the cities in the region to show that a proposed (and expensive) sewage treatment system wasn't necessary. State water-quality authorities had argued that the city's sewage plant didn't adequately treat the wastewater it dumped into a river. They claimed that the city's water discharge lowered the dissolved oxygen content of the river to dangerously low levels. But by simulating the behavior of the river on a computer, Region 8 planners showed that only "worst case" low-flow conditions, such as occurred only once every 50 years or more, would put the river below the state's minimum standards. These findings showed that a costly new sewage treatment plant wasn't needed.

At the State Level **State governments** use computers for internal housekeeping and decision-making activities. But states also provide computer-related services to other governmental agencies, and they support programs to improve the use of computer technology by local units of government. In Nebraska, for example, the state computer center, located in the capitol building, maintains payroll and personnel records for 13,000 state employees and processes financial management data for over 80 state departments. But the data center also supports Nebraska's legislature by maintaining complete histories of the 700 or more bills introduced in each legislative session. And other software packages available at the computer center—graphics packages, statistical programs, and data base managers—are available for use by state agencies and local online users.

Other examples of state government uses of computers include:

- *The use of computer matching to prevent welfare fraud.* Massachusetts compares names in its welfare file against names in the account files of several Massachusetts banks. The first time this comparison was made, it uncovered $125 million in welfare, food stamp, medicaid, and general assistance fraud. The matching program also identified welfare recipients who had bank accounts with deposits that exceeded the maximum allowed by law.

- *A system for controlling participation in a food stamp program.*

Eligible people in Michigan are issued participation cards which can be read by computer terminals in food stamp centers. Once authorized by the central computer, food stamps are issued to the participant. This system is projected to save $2.5 million per year by reducing postage costs (cards are issued once per participant and the previous monthly mailings are no longer needed) and by reducing the fraudulent uses of authorization cards.

● *A distributed system to handle the processing of motor vehicle records.* Each of New Mexico's five motor vehicle regions has a data processing center, and each center is equipped with a minicomputer system. All field offices are also equipped with terminals and printers that are linked interactively to their regional centers. This system makes it possible to issue vehicle and driver's licenses efficiently. It also permits law enforcement agencies to get current information from the motor vehicle department instantly.

Computers in the Federal Government

The **federal government** is the world's largest computer user, because it must deal with countless complex social, economic, political, and physical issues and because it must retain and analyze enormous amounts of information. Indeed, computing is so widespread in the federal government that it's hard to choose among examples. But the following five illustrate the range of federal computer applications:

Example 1 The U.S. Air Force's Strategic Air Command (SAC) provides a strategic air capability to deter an attack and, if required, to retaliate against such an attack. To perform its mission, SAC makes extensive use of computers. At SAC headquarters near Omaha, Nebraska, over 2,500 people are involved in computer systems activity and support. SAC's Directorate of War Planning Systems is responsible for the computer systems that support what's known as the "SIOP," or Single Integrated Operational Plan. SIOP is the nation's set of planned responses, involving all branches of the military, to a hostile attack. The SIOP determines targets and routes for U.S. land- and sea-launched ballistic missiles, strategic bombers, and cruise missiles. Planning the targeting for all these systems involves many alternative routes and response scenarios.

The development of the air-launched cruise missile has forced SAC to expand its computer capability, to control the hundreds of cruise missiles in the arsenal and the many possible attack routes for each missile. Planning these routes, from many possible launch points to their targets, is a complex computer-based operation. The routes must be chosen to avoid enemy defenses, to follow a low-altitude course that dodges mountains and other obstacles, and to prevent interference with other U.S. weapons and aircraft. The guidance system in these missiles is based on a digitized map of the whole world that's made up of data points at 100- and 300-foot intervals. Each data point lists its own altitude, longitude, and latitude.

Example 2 The U.S. Army Corps of Engineers' Missouri River Division relies on computer programs to control the Missouri River. These programs govern the long-range planning and analysis of river flow patterns to regulate reservoirs, maintain river navigability, control floods, and provide for power generation, irrigation, and recreation. The Corps maintains historical flow

This Corps of Engineers planner is using computer graphics to illustrate the costs of satellite data collection—a key element in the Corps' Missouri River control program. (Courtesy U.S. Army Corps of Engineers, Missouri River Division)

records dating back to 1898 and adds new information that's collected daily at numerous points on the river. These data are fed by satellite to a computer in Portland, Oregon, where they are used in regular analyses to establish reservoir levels at river dams for flood control, navigation, and irrigation purposes.

The Corps also uses several computerized models to simulate the behavior of the river. Models exist for flood control, sediment allowance in reservoirs, and the impact of storms on the river. These large and complex models are used for such tasks as forecasting reservoir behavior under various conditions (such as heavy snow melt, rainfall, drought), predicting river flow, and estimating the downstream economic effects of floods.

Corps personnel use the Telenet communications network to send and receive electronic mail. Information from Corps headquarters in Washington, D.C., can be sent quickly to the district office, which uses electronic mail to send orders to the river dams to regulate reservoir levels. Current plans call for full automation of the dams so that they can be operated from one remote site. (Perhaps the plot in a future movie will show a teenage computer wizard penetrating this automated system from a pc to unleash a flood!) And computer graphics are used by Corps planners to provide visual representations of flow patterns. Graphic aids are especially handy when planners are conducting public information meetings because they provide a visual picture of data that may otherwise be difficult to understand.

Example 3 The federal government's General Services Administration (GSA) is in charge of motor pools, procurement schedules, and the management of government buildings. But the GSA also has an Office of Software Development and Information Technology that collects and disseminates information about computer software. This office publishes a catalog of abstracts of computer programs submitted to it by other federal agencies. The catalog lists about 1,000 abstracts each year, and data entries are continually updated. New ones are added, old ones are dropped, and a list of ''top sellers''—listed software for which the center receives frequent requests—is maintained.

The catalog is issued twice a year and is available to anyone for the $75 subscription cost. Federal agencies can buy the abstracted software directly from GSA, while other persons or organizations can buy programs through the National Technical Information Service. Sales to nonfederal organizations and persons run three to four times that of federal purchases.

Example 4 The Department of Transportation's Transportation Systems Center (TSC) in Cambridge, Massachusetts, uses computers for many activities. For example, the TSC builds computer models of transportation systems. These models are then used to observe system behavior under various conditions and to plan changes in system operation. One such model is called RUCUS II (RUn CUtting System, version II). RUCUS II is used by planners to examine municipal and regional public transit systems in order to create new routes, redesign old ones, and identify the effects of routing changes.

A major user and supporter of pc's, the TSC has developed several pc projects for highway and transportation user groups. One supports pc use by state and county highway engineers and planners in rural areas. And a second project supports urban traffic engineers and planners in metropolitan planning agencies. Each project develops pc application software for transportation engineering and planning, distributes user-produced software, provides a telephone hotline to supply information to users, and publishes a newsletter for its user group.

Example 5 Information management in the White House has grown significantly in the 1980s. The computing needs of the staff of the President currently require three mainframes, three minicomputers, 200 dedicated word processors, and 50 pc's equipped with hard disks. Two mainframes are used for large applications such as correspondence management. Hundreds of thousands of mail items received by the White House are cataloged, filed, and tracked. In this way, the White House can maintain a complete history of all correspondence from receipt through response and possible follow-up action. The third mainframe is used to develop and test software for use on other machines.

One minicomputer tracks the thousands of political patronage or appointment jobs that can be filled by every president—ambassadorships, federal judgeships, subcabinet-level positions, and others. The minicomputer has access to the records of current jobholders and potential appointees. A second White House minicomputer is used with a large word processing system that contains standard paragraphs stating the administration's positions on scores of issues. If you write to the President about the problem of acid rain, for example, the letter will go to a correspondence analyst who selects appropriate paragraphs from the system for use in a reply. The third minicomputer is dedicated to a system that controls and supports the two White House libraries.

Personal computers are most visible as executive workstations for staff officials up to and including the White House chief of staff. The pc's allow users to dial up and use data bases such as LEXIS, NEXIS, and online news services. As a White House staff member has noted, "The pc's are one-stop shopping terminals for instant access to large data bases." The pc's are also used to support an electronic mail/message system in the White House (see Chapter 8 for more information on dial-up data bases and electronic mail/message systems).

Law and Law Enforcement Applications

Lawyers and Computers As you might expect, law firms use computers for housekeeping and decision making. Common housekeeping functions include word processing, client billing, and accounting. Word processing (WP) is an especially useful tool for lawyers. Standard documents like wills and contracts can be developed and stored on a WP system for selective retrieval and modification to fit a particular client or case. This reduces both the amount of legal work needed to create the documents for each client and the time needed to type the documents each time they are used. Certain types of legal documents also contain what is known as **boilerplate language.** Boilerplate may be clauses, paragraphs, or entire sections that rarely change. Storing this language in a WP system for easy retrieval can save much time and expense in a law office.

Computers affect the legal profession in other ways. One of the most promising uses of computers is for legal research. Online data bases such as LEXIS provide case law citations, while WESTLAW catalogs federal and state court cases (see Chapter 8). By subscribing to one or more of these services, a legal researcher can enter inquiries through online computer terminals and receive instant responses. For example, a lawyer can ask for a list of all cases between 1980 and 1986 in which the words "computer," "fraud," and "bank" appear. The lawyer may then ask for summaries of all these cases. Such a retrieval system is faster and is likely to provide more comprehensive results than a manual search of law books.

Automated criminal justice information systems that keep records of the contacts that people have with police and other criminal justice agencies also affect the legal profession. Lawyers may find these systems helpful in preparing cases for trial—or they may be involved in actions to remove derogatory information from such systems.

Courts in larger jurisdictions often use computers to manage dockets and

Online data bases such as LEXIS give lawyers instant access to a library of case law citations and can provide summaries of all the cases in which one or more key words are cited; such services typically save days of research time. (Courtesy Mead Data Central)

WINDOW 13-1

COURT REPORTING: GOING HIGH TECH TO SAVE TIME AND TROUBLE

For fans of Perry Mason, the stenotypist who reads back crucial testimony is a familiar fixture in the courtroom. Now a Detroit courtroom is adding a new twist to the plot. In the Wayne County Circuit Court, computer terminals have been installed on the bench of Circuit Judge Robert J. Colombo Jr., on the tables of both counsels, and on a mobile stand outside the jury room. Almost as soon as the stenographer takes down the testimony, the key strokes are translated into words on all of the video screens.

"Now we have the capability to recall the testimony and print it out" on a moment's notice, says Judge Colombo, and the mobile terminal can be wheeled into the jury room to assist in deliberations. Moreover, the system will help shorten appeals by eliminating delays in preparing transcripts of major trials, which takes at least three months, says Judge Colombo. The $50,000 tab for the equipment was picked up by the National Shorthand Reporters Assn. "Our five-year goal is to computerize the majority of courts in this country," says Raymond F. De Simone, president of the NSRA and of De Simone Computer Reporting Inc. in New York.

(© Don Kryminec/Photo Researchers, 1984)

Adapted from "Court Reporting: Going High Tech to Save Time and Trouble," *Business Week*, Feb. 4, 1985. Copyright © 1985 by McGraw-Hill, Inc. Reprinted by special permission.

---

select juries, and computer use by courts and lawyers is growing and will continue to grow. As a result, attorneys must prepare to service their clients' needs more efficiently through the use of computers. Many attorneys must also be prepared to handle cases involving conflicting claims about computers and computer crime, and they must be prepared to try cases with the aid of computers.

Cops, Criminals, and Computers We've seen that only the housekeeping activities of governments are more computerized than law enforcement. The increasing number of police/citizen contacts related to crime prevention, suspect identification, and apprehension demands timely and efficient ways of keeping and sorting through the resulting deluge of data. The computer is the only choice for this purpose, and so large federal grants have been given to establish automated criminal justice information systems.

Example 1 The **National Crime Information Center (NCIC),** operated by the Federal Bureau of Investigation in Washington, D.C., is a massive data base containing criminal history files, records of missing and wanted persons, and records of stolen property. Over 5 million records are maintained by NCIC's computers, and state and local police agencies have online access to these records. Let's assume, for example, that a person is stopped by a police officer for a traffic violation. The officer asks for the driver's license and auto registration and radios the person's name and the auto registration number to the dispatch office. The officer may also have the license plate number checked. A dispatcher then keys this information into an NCIC terminal and cross checks it with data on file at NCIC. After a few minutes, either the driver and car are "cleared" (there's no outstanding arrest warrant or report that the car is stolen) or an arrest can be made on the spot.

NCIC is obviously a valuable tool for law enforcement. It provides police officers with information for apprehending suspects, and it also provides a degree of security for those officers. But NCIC's records also pose potential threats to personal liberty. One problem is that incorrect or outdated information may remain on file and may result in the arrest of an innocent person. A second concern is the "Big Brother" nature of a large criminal information file that compiles dossiers on millions of people. To what extent may these dossiers offer potential threats to personal liberty? You can be sure that these issues will continue to be debated hotly in coming years.

Example 2 REJIS, the REgional Justice Information System, maintains a comprehensive criminal justice data base for the St. Louis, Missouri, metropolitan area. The REJIS operation is supported by three mainframes and is linked to over 100 user agencies. Law enforcement application software includes programs to process arrest and booking, wanted and missing persons, stolen property records, criminal history and regional summons files, and traffic tickets. REJIS also provides specialized programming for courts, prosecutors' offices, and correctional and juvenile services agencies. REJIS is connected to computers maintained by the Missouri and Illinois state police, the Missouri department of revenue, and the NCIC.

Example 3 The Long Beach, California, police department uses a computer-assisted dispatch system. When a call is received by a dispatcher, the name and address of the caller and the problem type and code are entered into the system. The system verifies the address, checks for duplicate calls, executes a site information search (looking for such information as previous complaints, number of children and invalids present, relative danger of the

Computer terminals in squad cars allow police officers to check a suspect's name immediately against the files of the National Crime Information Center. This procedure makes for more effective police work, but it also leads to more arrests of innocent people because the NCIC files are often inaccurate. (© Bill Varie, 1982)

area), and informs the dispatcher of the available units to be sent to the address. This system has improved police response time to emergency calls by 50 percent and has enabled the department to deploy its officers much more efficiently. It's also connected to the NCIC system.

Example 4 Scottsbluff, Nebraska, uses a law enforcement software package purchased from a vendor. This package runs on the city's minicomputer and consists of a complaints, arrests, and case history module, collision and citation records, and field investigations. Comprehensive law enforcement software packages that run on pc's are also available to small police departments.

COMPUTERS IN HEALTH CARE

Just as computers were first used for housekeeping purposes in most government organizations, so, too, were they initially applied to process billing, accounting, payroll, and medical records in hospitals and other health-care organizations. Housekeeping applications still account for much of the health-care computing time, but the medical profession is now using computers in scores of new ways to improve health care.

Where We've Come From

Several recent computerized innovations in health-care applications can be traced back to the manned spaceflight program. Instant medical monitoring of astronauts was needed, both for flight safety and to obtain physiological data about the effects of weightlessness and other novel stresses of space flight. At the beginning of the space age, however, remote and continuous physiological monitoring was a new concept and no suitable instruments were available. But a biosensor system was developed to measure respiration, oral temperature, and blood pressure, and the first U.S. astronauts were wired with these devices. Signals from these biosensors were relayed from space capsules back to earth stations, where doctors monitored the physiological status of astronauts on a computer screen.

These space-age developments encouraged the creation of optimistic projects to develop new computer applications in medicine. Although some projects were expensive failures, successful hospital information systems (see Chapter 11) and powerful computer-aided diagnostic tools were introduced in the 1970s. Cheaper, faster, and more powerful hardware and versatile software packages tailored to health-care needs began to appear. And these developments led to a flood of new health-care systems in the 1980s. Some of the features of these new systems are described below.

Health-Care Systems Today

Health care-systems may be classified into five categories:

1 **Diagnostic systems** that collect data and identify the cause of illness.

2 **Lab automation systems** that perform medical imaging and testing procedures and analyze the data gathered

---

John H. Glenn, Jr., first American astronaut to orbit the earth, is wired with biosensors for his 1962 flight. These pioneering remote sensing devices have led to many of today's computer-aided medical systems. (Courtesy NASA)

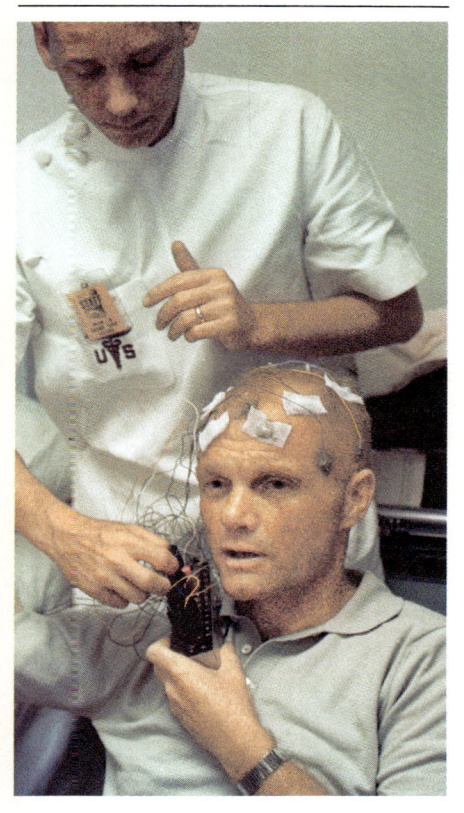

WINDOW 13-2

NO PLACE FOR GUESSWORK

A rare coincidence sets the stage for a possible mix-up of patients. Two baby girls with the same last name are born within hours of each other. One has a slight lung infection. A doctor prescribes antibiotics, and the nurse orders the medication through the hospital's computer terminal.

The computer system has a record of two babies with the same last name and requires the nurse to enter the infant's identification number.

Six months later the baby without the lung infection takes the same antibiotic for an ear infection and has an allergic reaction. If she had been mistakenly given the antibiotic at birth, the reaction would have been life-threatening.

The system that helps avoid that kind of scenario at the Northwest Mississippi Regional Medical Center in Clarksdale is IBM's System/38 Hospital Patient Management System (HPMS). This system helps run the hospital and is a good administrative and patient-care tool.

One area where the computer system assists in patient care is the hospital's lab. Orders for lab work are entered on terminals at nurse stations throughout the 194-bed hospital and are printed instantly in the lab. When lab tests are completed, results are keyed in and transmitted back to the appropriate station. People in the lab used to average 5 to 6 hours a day manually posting lab results; now it is done automatically, with results getting to the hospital floor instantly.

Another area where the HPMS helps provide quality care is in the pharmacy. When a drug is ordered from a nurse station, HPMS pulls the patient record to check the order for possible harmful drug interactions, patient allergies, and the appropriateness of the dosage for that particular patient's body weight.

For professionals working here, patient care also means having a low-cost, efficiently run hospital. The S/38 and HPMS are critical to these efforts. One motivation for installing the system was cost control. Most of the hospital's patients are poor, and there isn't a big margin of profit.

The system at the Northwest Mississippi Regional Medical Center is involved in most aspects of hospital operations including admissions, discharge, and transfers; patient billings and accounts receivable; order communications and results reporting; general ledger and accounts payable; pharmacy management; medical records; case mix, reporting systems, and personnel and payroll. Other benefits are the system's flexibility, ease of use, and expandability. For example, the system can accommodate easily changes in government regulations and other requirements. The system's programs are easy to understand and modify, and the types of data produced are useful as management decision tools. Plans for expanding this system include adding IBM PCs that can operate alone or as terminals for the S/38.

Hospital administration has changed over the past few years, with more changes in sight. Computerized hospital management systems enable health professionals to meet the challenges of running a hospital efficiently and effectively.

Adapted from Krista Brewer, "No Place for Guesswork," *Viewpoint*, published by International Business Machines Corporation, vol. 13, no. 3, May/June 1985. Copyright © 1985 by International Business Machines Company. Used by permission.

---

3 **Patient monitoring systems** such as those found in postoperative and intensive care units that constantly check a patient's vital signs for abnormalities

4 **Pharmacy information systems** that monitor drug labeling, alert pharmacists to possible harmful drug interactions, and control drug inventories.

5 Other specialized systems such as those that provide assistance to the handicapped, those that support medical research, and those used in preventive and community health-care projects

An ever-increasing range of health-care applications is found in each of these categories. We'll focus first on diagnostic and medical imaging systems because these are some of the most advanced applications of medical computer technology. But we'll also review applications found in some of the other categories.

Medical Diagnosis and Expert Systems

MYCIN, a software system that assists medical diagnosis, is an example of an *expert system*. You'll recall from Chapter 3 that an expert system is an application of artificial intelligence. Such a system gathers information based on the experience and judgment of experts in their specialty, places this information in a knowledge base, and uses programmed guidelines and decision rules to produce results that are useful to practitioners. MYCIN, developed at Stanford University, is used to diagnose bacterial blood disease and then recommend appropriate antibiotic therapy for patients.

The user interacts with MYCIN in a conversational manner, starting out with general information on the patient, such as symptoms and lab results, and then proceeding to fine details. There are about 400 decision rules in MYCIN, and a search technique is used to attempt to solve the problem posed by the user. MYCIN's suggested solutions include probability levels to indicate strong or weak confidence in results. MYCIN can be challenged by the user to defend its rationale and its conclusions. This feature is very useful as a training device.

MYCIN can also be tested against known cases to determine its accuracy and to fine-tune the knowledge base with improved feedback. At the conclusion of the diagnostic encounter, MYCIN attempts to identify the infective microorganism and the recommended course of therapy, qualified by probability estimates of the level of confidence in the diagnosis. MYCIN has been tested against expert physicians, and has demonstrated an accuracy rate of 65 percent versus a range of 42 to 63 percent for doctors. But it hasn't been put into widespread use because it doesn't yet know enough to say "I don't know" when it lacks an appropriate response in its knowledge base. Instead, it makes a best fit to whatever it does have. Keeping up with the latest medical knowledge is a continuing major problem for medical expert systems.

In addition to MYCIN, there are other diagnostic expert systems such as Caduceus (an internist program), Puff (a program for pulmonary or lung diseases), and ONCOCIN (a cancer diagnostic tool). The trend is away from broad diagnostic systems toward more specialized and limited areas to avoid "shallow" interpretations and foster detailed and more tightly reasoned analyses. As exciting and promising as these expert systems are, they'll remain experimental until they become professionally acceptable and commercially viable.

Medical Imaging Systems

Unlike computer-aided diagnosis, **medical imaging techniques** that provide pictures of anatomic structures are already part of established medical practice and are in widespread use. Let's look at five leading imaging technologies.

Computerized axial tomography (CAT) scanning **CAT scanning** is essentially taking rapid, successive x-ray pictures, or "slices," and integrating the results into well-defined composite pictures that give the physician a clear visualization of anatomic structures and abnormalities (see Figure 13-1). The CAT scans are so much clearer than ordinary x-rays that it's often unnecessary to conduct exploratory surgery to confirm a diagnosis. This is a great boon for the anxious patient.

CAT-scan equipment uses sensitive crystal detectors instead of film to indicate the degree of x-ray absorption by body tissues. This absorption is

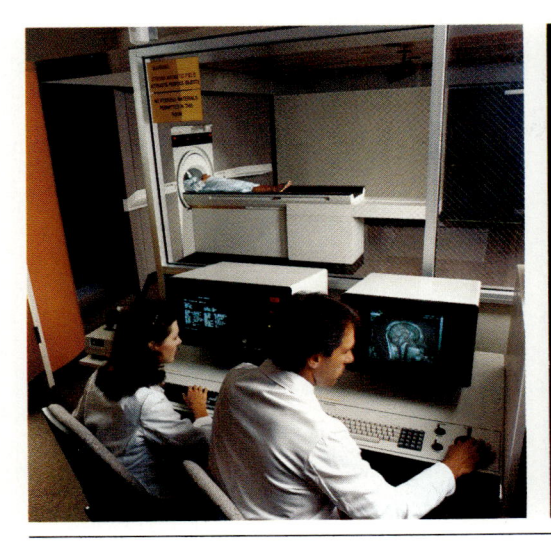

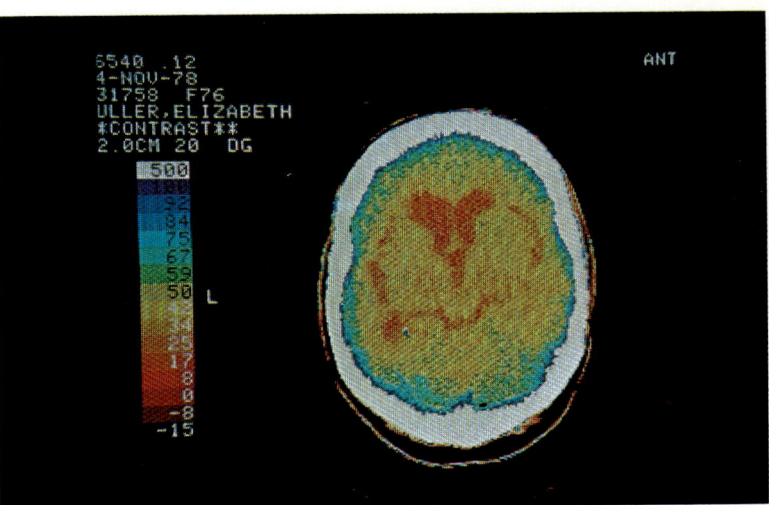

FIGURE 13-1

As the x-ray machine rotates around the patient in the background, technicians monitor the computer-integrated CAT scan. The right-hand photo shows the graphic display of a brain scan produced by a CAT scanner. (Courtesy Picker International; © Dan McCoy/Rainbow)

calculated by a computer. The computer uses pattern recognition programs in assembling and integrating the differential absorption of x-rays by the patient's organs and tissues as the x-ray machine rotates around the patient. The crystal detectors are directly opposite the x-ray machine, with the target area of the patient in between. The differential x-ray absorption levels are translated into different colors to highlight tissues and organ boundaries more clearly on the hard-copy output and the computer display (see Figure 13-1). These color-enhanced pictures provide the basis for more accurate diagnoses of abnormal conditions. The typical CAT lab consists of two rooms, one for the x-ray scanner and associated equipment and the other housing the computer system. The cost of the entire facility is about $1 million. But virtually all large American hospitals have adopted CAT scanners in spite of this high cost.

Nuclear magnetic resonance (NMR) Medical specialists claim that **nuclear magnetic resonance** offers even clearer pictures than CAT scanners for soft tissues in the body. NMR permits specialists to observe "in vivo" body chemistry; that is, they can watch actual living chemical processes. Since it uses a magnetic field, NMR doesn't have the liabilities of x-rays, which may increase the risk of cancer.

The heart of the NMR scanner is a doughnut-shaped magnet large enough to surround the patient (see Figure 13-2). The patient is exposed to a strong magnetic field, and elements in the body such as hydrogen or phosphorus that have an odd number of neutrons or protons are magnetized. These elements physically point themselves toward the power source, just as your pocket compass points to the North Pole. This means that all the hydrogen atoms in the patient's body are oriented toward the magnetic field. A radio wave perpendicular to the magnetic field is then beamed at the patient. This causes the hydrogen atoms to flip, or do a 90-degree turn toward the radio wave. This flip in each hydrogen atom in the patient's target area produces a detectable electromagnetic signal.

Each type of tissue and organ has a characteristic signal pattern that is picked up by receivers and fed into a computer. Pattern recognition software

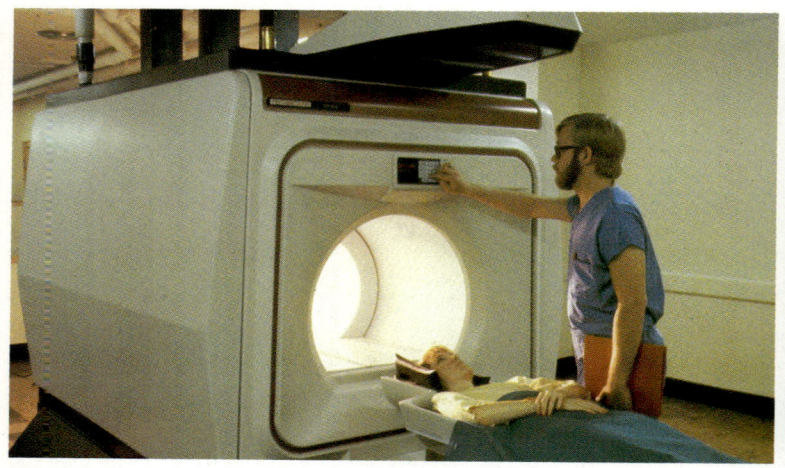

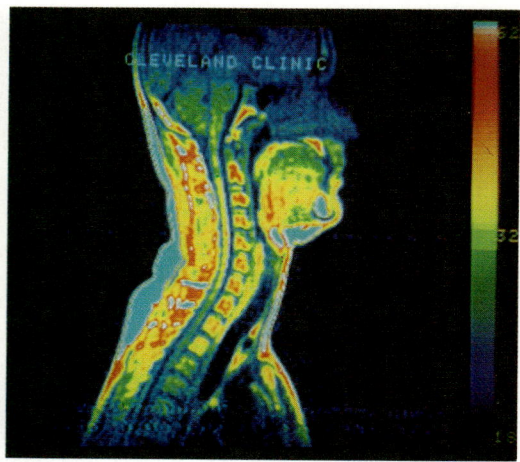

FIGURE 13-2

The NMR scanner at the left produces detailed, color-enhanced cross-sectional pictures of the human body, such as the one shown at the right. (Courtesy the Cleveland Clinic)

translates signal pattern data into color-enhanced pictures on a video screen to portray vivid, cross-sectional images of the human body. Though still an emerging technology, NMR has received rave reviews for observing live biochemical activity levels and for detecting early multiple sclerosis (with almost 100 percent accuracy), lung tumors, and plaque buildup in arteries around the heart. Over 100 NMR units already are installed in U.S. hospitals, at a cost of $2 million apiece.

Ultrasound A descendant of the World War II sonar equipment used to detect underwater sound waves from submarines, **ultrasound** is a relatively inexpensive imaging technique that doesn't use potentially hazardous radiation. It's especially effective in gynecological and obstetrical explorations and in diagnosing gallbladder problems. It's also quick and safe for imaging infant brains. Ultrasound is thus popular with radiologists and hospital administrators. The main drawback is its fuzzy image—a drawback that's being reduced in new generations of ultrasound equipment.

Positive emission tomography (PET) With a $3 million price tag which involves a nuclear cyclotron, **positive emission tomography** scanners are designed to show metabolic changes in any desired cross-section of the body. The patient ingests a radioactive substance that's attracted by the organ to be examined. The radioactive compound emits positrons that interact with nearby electrons, producing gamma rays. The gamma ray activity is picked up by PET, and the results are analyzed by the system computer and colorfully displayed on a screen.

The PET scanner is used to study metabolic problems in the pancreas, liver, lungs, heart, and brain. For example, in cardiac cases the scanner provides information on the damage that has been inflicted by a heart attack. PET is in the experimental stage, and it remains to be seen how well it will compete with other imaging techniques.

Digital subtraction angiography (DSA) Angiography refers to x-ray examination of blood vessels, and **digital subtraction angiography** is a computer-

CHAPTER 13

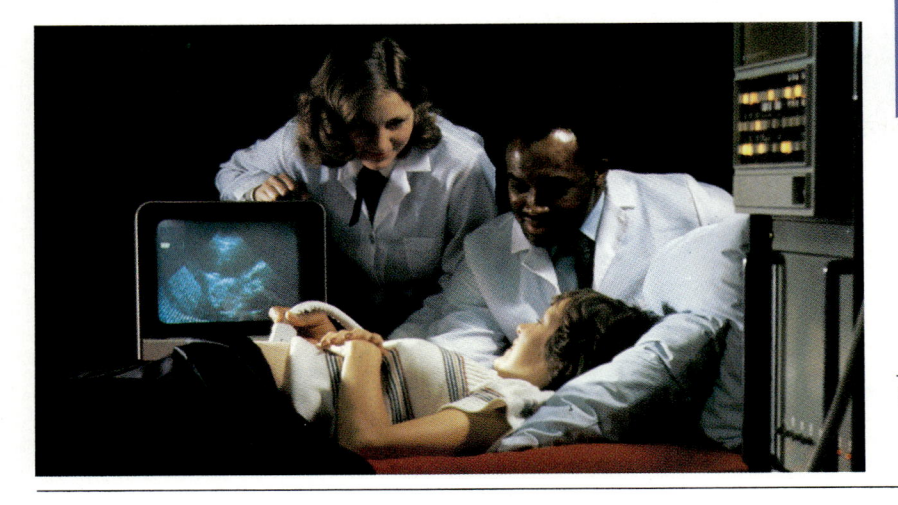

463

Ultrasound images, integrated by a computer, allow doctors to examine infants in the womb without exposing them or their mothers to dangerous radiation.

based technique to facilitate this activity. Before DSA came along, arterial x-rays required insertion of a small plastic catheter, or tube, into the artery being examined. Contrast material that shows up in x-rays was then injected into the artery. With DAS, an initial x-ray photo is taken of the target artery, a contrast substance is then injected, and a second photo is taken. No catheter is needed. The computer then subtracts, or drops out of the picture, everything except the walls of the artery being examined. The computer can enlarge the picture to provide an unusually clear image of the artery.

A DSA system costs about $700,000 and is useful in preventing strokes, detecting high blood pressure, monitoring postoperative progress, and studying heart conditions. DSA is an experimental imaging technique.

Patient Monitoring in Intensive Care Units   **Intensive care units** (ICUs) are designed to monitor critically ill patients. Computer-aided ICUs are becoming more affordable and more popular with the advent of inexpensive microcomputers. Bedside biosensors are attached to the patient for tracking and recording vital signs, such as heart rate, blood pressure, temperature, respiration, and electrocardiogram waveforms. This information is relayed to a central computer where a monitoring program checks for abnormalities and issues warnings to nurses, physicians, and rescue teams. The ICU must provide highly reliable 24-hour monitoring with adequate "failsoft" backup operations that will take over automatically in the event of system failure.

Figure 13-3 shows some of the key elements of an automated patient monitoring system. Bedside monitors are linked to a central computer, and radio transmitter/receiver links are used with ambulatory patients who aren't confined to their beds. Edit terminals permit the collection, display, and analysis of data over extended time periods to evaluate treatment effectiveness. Patient data may be copied for future use. And pattern recognition software establishes baseline waveforms (such as the heartbeat pattern shown in Figure 13-4) in the form of "templates" and detects abnormal beats that deviate from the template or baseline pattern. This is a key element in monitoring for irregular heartbeats.

Automated patient monitoring devices and systems are continually im-

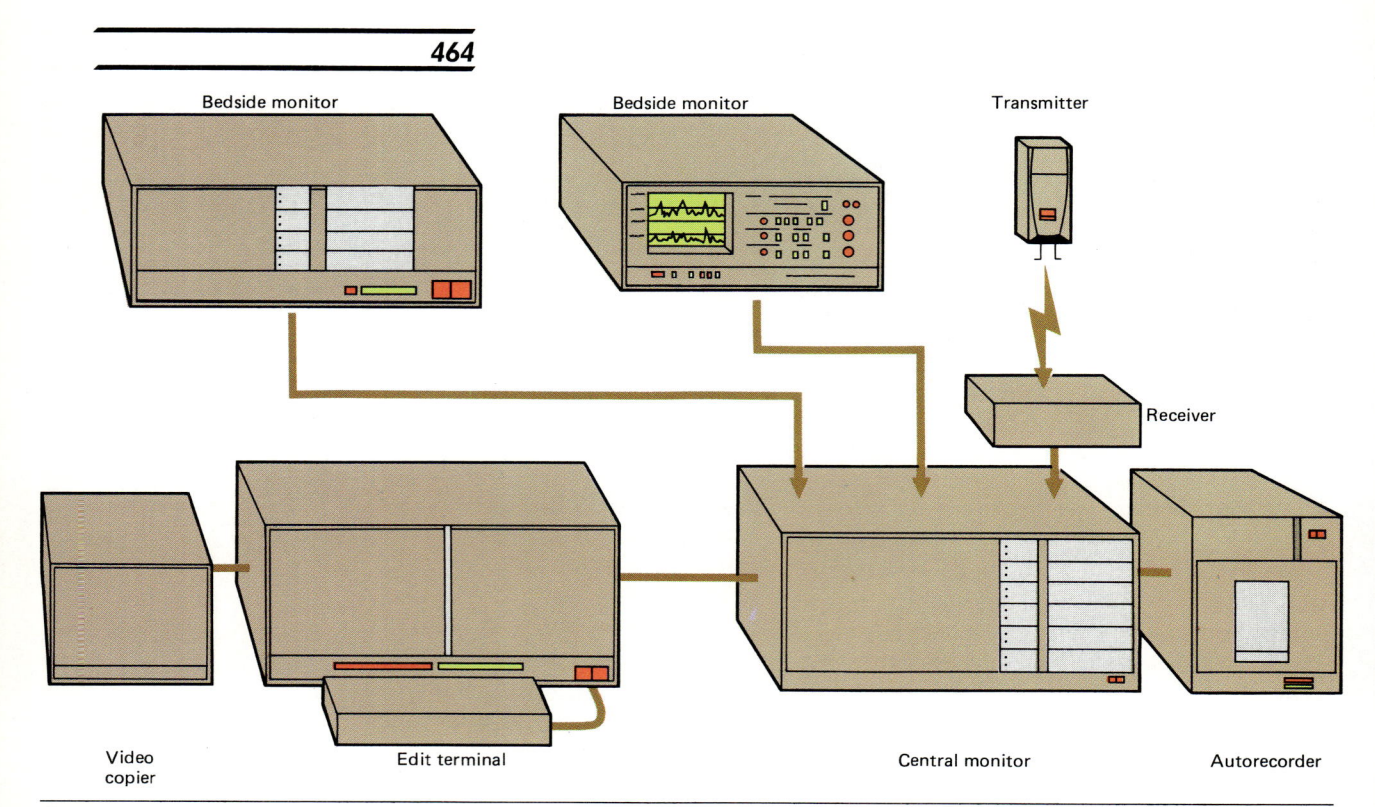

464

FIGURE 13-3

An automated patient monitoring system configuration.

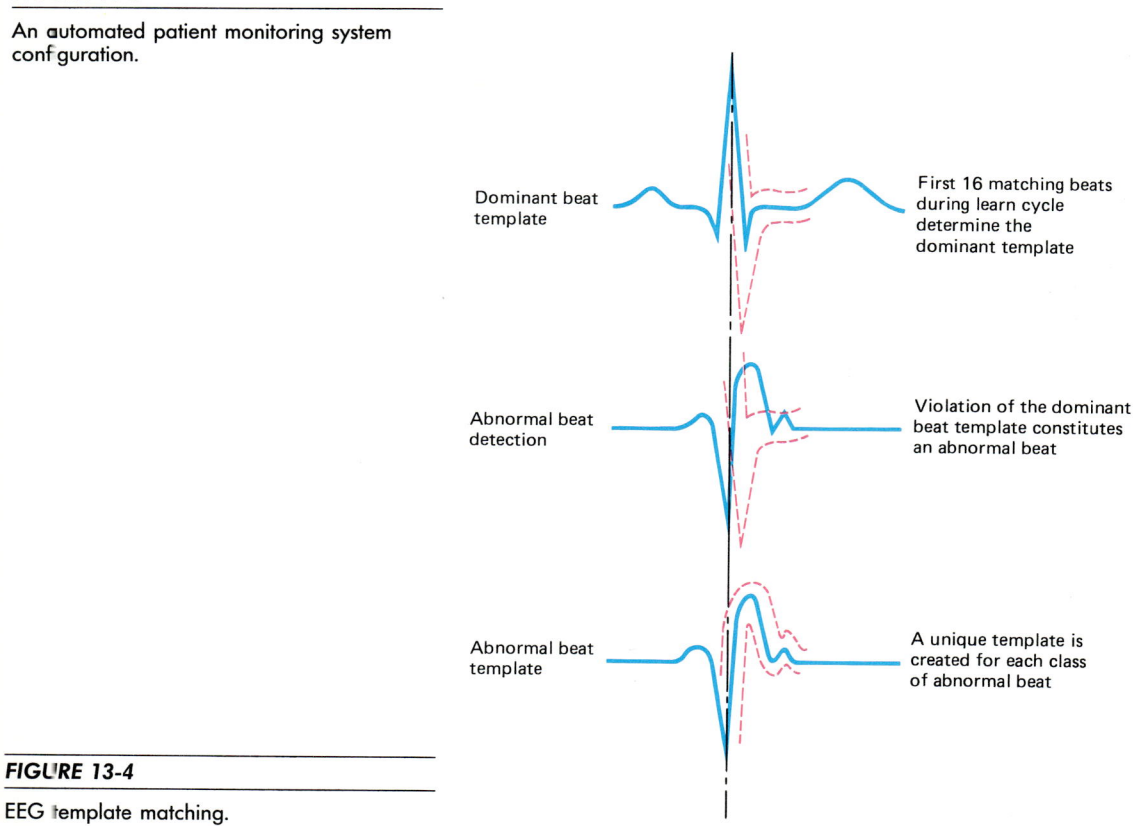

FIGURE 13-4

EEG template matching.

- Dominant beat template — First 16 matching beats during learn cycle determine the dominant template
- Abnormal beat detection — Violation of the dominant beat template constitutes an abnormal beat
- Abnormal beat template — A unique template is created for each class of abnormal beat

proving, and hospitals report increasing success in saving and extending human life. For example, in one study of a coronary ICU, computer-assisted patient monitoring helped cut mortality rates in half. In the care of terminally ill patients, however, there's growing public controversy over the patient's right, and the immediate family's right, to refuse such assistance. In any case, we can look forward to continuing improvements in life-saving ICU automation, made possible by new medical discoveries and new computer technology.

Computers for the Handicapped At least 10 percent of the total population of the world suffers from some form of disabling physical handicap. Let's look at some of the things computers can do to help these people.

Computers and the visually handicapped The **Kurzweil Reading Machine (KRM)** translates printed text into spoken words. The user places printed material face down on a glass surface. An optical scanner goes through the page word by word and line by line. A computer program transforms words into speech sounds called phonemes that approximate the spoken word, and a voice synthesizer generates the audio output. Although the spoken output isn't as clear as natural speech, it's intelligible to an experienced user. The KRM can read about 300 different type fonts with its scanner system. Reading speeds of up to 300 words per minute can be controlled by the user. The voice tone and volume can be adjusted as desired. Special features include spelling out words and tagging particular words, phrases, or passages for later reference. Some KRM features can be used in conjunction with pc's.

Another aid for the visually handicapped is a talking computer terminal that permits people to hear everything keyed into the terminal including letters, punctuation marks—and the mistakes we all make at a keyboard. The keyboard system has a standard set of typewriter keys identified by raised dot, or braille, characters, and it helps users write computer programs and gain more effective access to computer services.

The Kurzweil Reading Machine uses an optical scanner to "read" a book and a computer program to translate what it sees into recognizable spoken output.
(© Dan McCoy/Rainbow)

Sightless people can also use the **Versabraille system** to write braille characters more quickly and easily. Such characters are represented by raised six-dot patterns that are typically embossed on heavy paper. Each pattern represents an alphanumeric character. The Versabraille is, in effect, a braille word processor that allows the user to preview output by touch-reading it on a special display before it's embossed on paper. Corrections and modifications are thus easily made.

Computers and the hearing impaired A major frustration for deaf people is the inability to use the telephone. But standard teleprinter and visual display terminals equipped with modems permit deaf users to transmit printed messages to others over telephone lines (see Chapters 5 and 8 for information about terminals and modems). Other computer-aided devices extend communication for the deaf by transforming audio signals into visual displays or by converting beeper signals into physical vibrations.

Captioning of TV newscasts and educational/entertainment programs makes TV more accessible to the hearing-impaired. Captioning can be transmitted two ways. The simplest is direct broadcast where everyone receives the caption messages on their screens. A second method is **closed captioning** where only those users who have the required microprocessor-controlled equipment can see the captions. Thus closed captioning doesn't distract the hearing audience. The Public Broadcasting Service has been active in captioning for the hearing impaired.

Computer-aided prosthetics Prosthesis refers to the replacement and substitution of limbs and organs by artificial aids to correct physical defects and to the amplification of natural human capabilities through the use of artificial devices. Eyeglasses and dental bridges are common examples of prosthetics. Computers are being used to help design and produce artificial human joints, such as hip joints, that can be surgically implanted to replace defective joints. The New York Hospital for Special Surgery has developed a procedure for designing and producing such joints. In the design phase, the computer analyzes patient x-rays in three dimensions and suggests possible designs based on the x-rays and on patient biographical data and medical history. The surgeon makes a final design decision after evaluating the key design alternatives. Computer-assisted manufacturing techniques are used to produce the desired artificial joint, following the design specifications. This computer-aided procedure enables patients to get their artificial joints in about half the time previously required.

Computer-Aided Medical Research Computer simulation is helping to stimulate medical research. For example, researchers at the University of Pennsylvania have developed a simulation of the cardiovascular system based on hundreds of variables that influence cardiac function. By changing specific variables, the investigators can determine possible effects on other factors and on overall cardiac performance. This type of analysis is facilitated by the use of computer graphics based on computer simulation of the heart.

As we've seen, researchers are using imaging techniques for real time "in vivo" studies of the living heart with CAT and NMR scanners. And a recent invention combines a CAT scanner with an electron microscope to allow scientists to produce three-dimensional pictures of living cells. This new process, called **microtomography,** can be used to observe the way cancer cells grow and how embryos develop. Microscopic effects of drugs on living cells can also be observed.

Perhaps the most remarkable breakthrough in biology this century has been the deciphering of the genetic code at the molecular level. The genetic code for all plant and animal life is found in the self-duplicating **DNA** (deoxyribonucleic acid) **molecule.** Intense research into the mysteries of DNA has led to the development of **genetic engineering**—the natural and synthetic development of DNA for an enormous variety of biological purposes.

A recent development is the use of **gene machines** that synthesize DNA. The earlier manual process to synthesize DNA was time-consuming and expensive. But with new microcomputer-controlled gene machines, researchers can complete the task in less than a day at a small fraction of the earlier cost and with fewer errors. Current gene machine technology can synthesize only short segments of DNA that are inserted into longer segments taken from living organisms. But future developments are likely to lead to longer DNA segments and more versatile manipulation of genetic codes.

Health-Care Systems Tomorrow

The health-care industry is undergoing dramatic change. Established hospitals are competing with 24-hour emergency care centers, minor surgical walk-in centers, alcohol and drug treatment centers, community mental health centers, multidoctor clinics, and health maintenance organizations. And since all segments of the health-care industry are looking for ways to become more effective and efficient, they are increasingly turning to computers for help. This is partly because government (which pays about half of the bill for health care in the United States) is exerting strong regulatory pressures on the health-care industry, and this pressure is propelling the industry toward increasing computerization to meet financial, legal, and quality-control accountability.

More new technologies have been introduced into medicine in the last 12 years than in the previous 100 years. As we've seen, the marriage of medicine and computers has led to remarkable inventions that are revolutionizing specialties in medicine and health care. CAT scans and nuclear magnetic resonance have transformed medical imaging, and online physiological monitoring devices that produce automatic crisis warnings have changed patient-care procedures. The imminent breakthrough in practical expert systems for computer-aided diagnoses is another potentially revolutionary development. And major advances in computer-aided genetic engineering are likely to lead to entirely new fields of medicine and biology. As computer power and software versatility increase, as computer networks proliferate, and as the costs of emerging computer-based health-care systems decrease, the frontiers of medicine will be pushed back. Research will lead to discovery, to development, and finally to improved health-care practices.

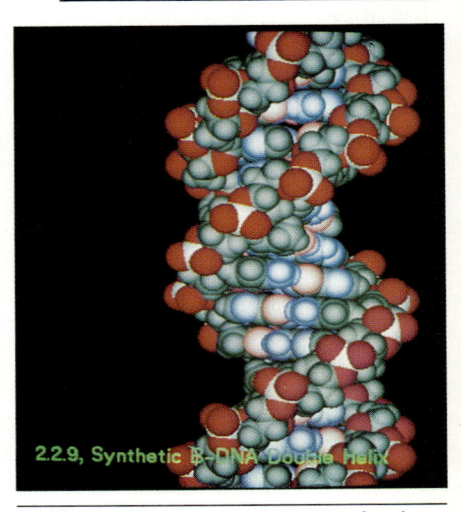

Research in genetic engineering has been aided by computer-generated images of the DNA double helix, which can be viewed from any angle by researchers. (© R. Feldmann & Dan McCoy/Rainbow)

FEEDBACK

FEEDBACK AND REVIEW 13

To test and reinforce your understanding of the applications and concepts presented in this chapter, rearrange the *scrambled letters* to spell out the correct word for the space indicated in the following sentences.

1. Most housekeeping activities relate to the ____ management of an organization. A I A N F N C I L
2. Budget preparation is an example of a ____-making activity that's commonly performed in government and nongovernment organizations. I I N D C S E O
3. The second most frequently computerized area in local government is ____ enforcement. W L A
4. Some local governments use computer-assisted ____ utility load management systems. L C E T R E C I
5. A ____ organization is a governmental unit whose jurisdiction may cover several cities and counties in a given area. G N R A I E O L
6. States have used computer ____ to help prevent welfare fraud. H I G M T N A C
7. The U.S. Army Corps of Engineers uses computerized models to simulate the behavior of a ____. I V E R R
8. A minicomputer at the ____ House keeps track of political patronage jobs. I H T E W
9. Certain types of legal documents contain ____ language that is often stored in WP systems. B E R L L O P T E I A
10. An automated ____ justice system keeps track of the contacts people have with police and other law enforcement agencies. C I N R M L A I
11. The FBI's ____ is a massive online data base that contains over 5 million records. C C I N
12. Some of the impetus for innovations in computerized health care can be traced to the government's ____ program. C P E S A
13. ____ systems are health-care systems that collect data and identify the cause of illness. I D N S T A G O I C
14. MYCIN is an example of an ____ system. X E P R T E
15. Medical ____ techniques provide pictures of anatomic structures for diagnosis and research purposes. G I N I M A G
16. CAT and nuclear ____ resonance scanners offer clear pictures of body structures. A M G E N I T C
17. The origin of ultrasound imaging devices may be traced to ____ equipment used in World War II. R A N O S
18. When a PET scanner is used, the patient ingests a ____ substance. D I O R A A C I V E T
19. Bedside biosensors are attached to critically ill patients housed in ____ care units. I E S I E N T N V
20. Kurzweil Reading Machines, talking terminals, and Versabraille systems are available to help the ____ handicapped. U V S A Y I L L
21. The genetic code for all plant and animal life is found in the DNA molecule, and research into the mysteries of DNA has led to the development of ____ engineering. E T C G E N I

CHAPTER 13

LOOKING BACK

1. The use of computers for information management in government organizations most often involves either housekeeping or decision-making activities. Housekeeping activities include everyday financial management tasks such as billing, budgeting, accounting, and payroll processing. Decision-making activities support future courses of action.

2. Local governments run nearly 7,000 cities and over 3,000 counties in the United States. The most common use of computers in local governments is for housekeeping tasks, while the second most frequently computerized area is law enforcement. The introduction of powerful pc's, and the availability of suitable packaged software, has put computer usage within the reach of even the smallest government organization. Four examples of how computers are used in local governments are presented in the chapter.

3. Regional government units have jurisdictions that cross city and county lines within a given geographic area. Computers are used for a variety of regional purposes including the control of water pollution over the area of a watershed or river basin. State governments use their computers for their own internal needs, and they support and provide computer services to other governmental entities.

4. The federal government is the world's largest user of computers because it must deal with complex problems and retain enormous amounts of information. Five representative examples of federal computer usage have been selected from the thousands of possible choices.

5. Lawyers use computers for word processing and client billing. Standard documents containing boilerplate language are stored in WP systems for fast and easy retrieval. Lawyers also use computers to search online legal data bases. And police, attorneys, courts, and citizens are also affected by the automated criminal justice information systems that keep records of the contacts people have with police and other law enforcement agencies.

6. Several recent computerized innovations in health-care applications can be traced back to the manned spaceflight program. Today, health-care system developments are advancing in diagnostic, lab automation, patient monitoring, pharmacy information, and other specialized areas. For example, experimental diagnostic expert systems such as MYCIN have met with some success and have attracted wide attention. These expert systems are based on the reasoning that specialists follow in reviewing symptoms, developing alternative diagnoses, and arriving at a likely diagnostic choice.

7. Medical imaging systems are computer-aided lab automation tools that use pattern recognition procedures to clarify and enhance x-ray, gamma ray, radio wave, and other electromagnetic and

acoustic pictures of the human body. CAT-scan technology using x-rays is a widely practiced procedure. Nuclear magnetic resonance, using strong magnetic fields, and positron emission tomography, using a nuclear cyclotron, are promising new technologies.

8. Computers now help monitor patients in intensive care units. Computerized bedside monitors constantly track patient vital signs. If the patient's condition deteriorates, the system sets off alarms to alert the medical staff.

9. Computers are also helping the handicapped. For example, there are reading machines for visually handicapped people that accept printed input and produce intelligible, spoken output. There are also braille-oriented computer systems that accept touch input and produce hard-copy braille output. Useful computer aids for hearing-disabled people include portable terminals and modems that connect to telephones. These devices enable deaf people to call others with similar devices and converse with them via typed messages. People with hearing handicaps may also use low-cost computerized decoding devices to watch special TV programs transmitted with printed captions. And computers can also be used to design and control prosthetic devices, such as artificial joints.

10. Medical research is facilitated by computers in many ways. For example, computer simulation makes it possible to perform highly complex analyses of heart, brain, and metabolic disorders using a large number of variables. And genetic engineering is receiving a boost from "gene machine" computer systems that permit faster, cheaper, and more accurate production of segments of genetic material. More new technologies may have been introduced into medicine in the last 12 years than in the previous 100 years, but the frontiers of medicine are constantly changing. Current research will lead to discovery, to development, and then to improved health-care practices.

KEY TERMS AND CONCEPTS

housekeeping activities 447
decision-making activities 447
local governments 447
regional organizations 450
state governments 451
federal government 452
boilerplate language 455
automated criminal justice information system 455

National Crime Information Center (NCIC) 456
diagnostic systems 458
lab automation systems 458
patient monitoring systems 459
pharmacy information systems 459
medical imaging techniques 460
CAT scanning 460
nuclear magnetic resonance 461

ultrasound 462
positive emission tomography 462
digital subtraction angiography 462
intensive care units (ICUs) 463
Kurzweil Reading Machine (KRM) 465
Versabraille system 466
closed captioning 466
microtomography 467
DNA molecule 467
genetic engineering 467
gene machines 467

Topics for Review and Discussion

1. "Computers are used in government for housekeeping and decision-making activities." Define and give examples of housekeeping and decision-making activities.
2. (a) What is a local government? (b) What is a regional government organization? (c) Give examples of computer usage in each of these types of government.
3. Give three examples of how computers are used by state governments.
4. Give four examples of how computers are used by the federal government.
5. "Word processing is a useful tool for lawyers." Discuss this statement.
6. (a) What's an automated criminal justice information system? (b) Give two examples of such systems and discuss their use.
7. What contributions to computer-aided medicine were made by the manned spaceflight program?
8. (a) What is an expert diagnostic system? (b) Give an example of such a system.
9. (a) What functions are performed by medical imaging techniques? (b) Identify and discuss four imaging technologies.
10. How can computers save lives in intensive care units?
11. (a) How can computer usage aid the visually handicapped? (b) The hearing impaired? (c) The person needing an artificial hip joint?
12. How can computers aid those engaged in medical research?
13. How can computers help genetic engineers?

Projects/Issues to Consider

1. Go to your library and identify five uses of computers in government that were not discussed in this chapter. Research these applications and present a report to the class.
2. Identify and research three computer applications in the health-care field that weren't discussed in this chapter and present a report to the class.
3. It was noted in the chapter that the FBI's National Crime Information Center is a valuable law enforcement tool, but it's also a tool that could pose a threat to personal liberty. Research the pros and cons of automated criminal justice information systems and report your findings to the class.
4. Genetic engineering is a rapidly changing field. Research current genetic engineering developments and prepare a report summarizing your findings.

Answers to Feedback and Review Section

1. financial 2. decision 3. law 4. electric 5. regional 6. matching 7. river 8. White 9. boilerplate 10. criminal 11. NCIC 12. space 13. diagnostic 14. expert 15. imaging 16. magnetic 17. sonar 18. radioactive 19. intensive 20. visually 21. genetic

A CLOSER LOOK

VOTING BY COMPUTER: ARE SYSTEMS VULNERABLE TO FRAUD?

When political bosses of the past set out to steal an election, they ordered their ward heelers to cast votes for the residents of the local cemetery. More than once, historians say, this "silent majority" gave the bosses their margin of victory.

Today, experts in and out of government warn that elections could be stolen less dramatically but more effectively through the manipulation of computerized voting systems, which are used in thousands of local and county jurisdictions throughout the country.

One weakness of computerized voting systems, says Gary Greenhalgh, director of the International Center on Election Law and Administration, is that they centralize the opportunity for fraud. While lever-type voting machines could have their counts rigged only machine by machine, counting votes by computer is done at one central site in most counties.

With computer voting systems, the voter usually punches holes in a thin cardboard ballot and the computer program reads the holes in the cards and totals them, presumably counting all votes and counting them only once, on command from an operator. Extra votes may be entered in the form of bogus ballots on punched cards, or vote totals may be altered through the use of control cards. According to one authority, either method could be performed successfully by a computer novice. Someone with more computer knowledge could turn off the portion of the program designed to document any changes made in either the program or the votes being counted by the program.

An early warning about computerized voting came more than 25 years ago, when a group of computer experts on the West Coast contended that the computer system that Los Angeles had purchased to count votes in the 1968 election was vulnerable to vote rigging. An official investigation found the allegations were technically accurate but said that the administrative procedures of the city provided good protection. The investigators said stealing an election would have required a conspiracy among several city officials.

Partly as a result of the dispute in Los Angeles, Congress approved a law in 1977 calling upon the Federal Election Commission to develop a model program to improve the integrity of computerized voting systems. The model program has not yet been developed, and little has changed except that computers are counting more votes.

Experts cite these reasons for inaction or lack of improvement on computerized voting systems:

- Many local election officials are baffled by computers and are unable to understand, question, and challenge the computer systems.
- Election system vendors are often forced by competitive bidding pressures to offer jurisdictions the cheapest possible systems, which include only minimal fraud protection.
- Many House and Senate members believe that congressional oversight of the voting apparatus should be limited, despite a provision of the Constitution giving Congress broad authority over elections.

The Federal Election Commission's efforts to develop standards have been handicapped by a lack of federal money for research. And the computerized voting industry has been competing to produce low-cost systems that can tally voting results quickly. So far, the industry has not provided features such as audit trails to make fraud difficult. Audit trails can be established if the computers are programmed to record the names of individuals who enter the system, the changes that are made, and the times that entries occur.

Deborah Seiler, a senior election official in California, says she does not know of any state or local jurisdiction that has the expertise or the resources to test the vulnerability of the programs. Moreover, many equipment vendors insist that their programs must be kept secret, or they will lose their competitive advantage.

Robert Naegele, a computer expert with more than 20 years of experience in testing election systems, says that most state laws require tests for the mechanical accuracy of voting systems but do not require checks on the system's abilities to resist manipulation.

"Many voting officials shrug their shoulders and tell you there is no way to build a perfect system," according to Mr. Naegele. "But I don't recall that the Mosler Company has started building its safes out of cardboard."

Mr. Naegele is developing three separate voluntary standards for the Federal Election Commission. One standard would establish minimal requirements for equipment. The second would set standards for the instructions that tell the computer how to count the votes. The third would suggest procedures for the administration of elections.

But these standards are useless until states adopt them and institute a way of testing systems to ensure that standards are being met. Some have suggested that an independent, licensed, and professional group certify programs for all states or that the National Bureau of Standards be made responsible. But even without standards, reliance on computerized voting systems is increasing. In 1984, over 60 percent of American voters used some type of computerized system. As this trend continues, the need to make these systems tamper-proof and reliable will continue to increase.

Adapted from David Burnham, "Vote by Computer: Some See Problems," *The New York Times*, Aug. 21, 1985; and "Computerized Systems for Voting Seen as Vulnerable to Tampering," *The New York Times*, July 29, 1985. Copyright © 1985 by The New York Times Company. Reprinted by permission.

CHAPTER 14

EDUCATION AND THE HUMANITIES

A SCHOOL WITHOUT WALLS

You won't find any ivy-colored halls at the Electronic University (EU). Here, students and instructors meet via software and telephone lines without the distractions of a bustling campus. Students focus on the course material, communicate via modems with their profs, and progress at their own pace.

EU combines hardware, software, and a communications network to create an online correspondence school. The software turns a pc into an electronic tutor that calls you by name, asks questions to test your understanding, and gently corrects your errors. It also allows you to communicate with the instructor, who monitors your progress and answers your questions.

The Electronic University, which is produced by TeleLearning Systems, works together with 2,000 participating schools that will grant college credit to students who complete an EU course and pass a proctored final exam.

The same communications network that processes your coursework and allows message exchange with your instructor gives you access to TeleLearning's Electronic Library. This library consists of a set of more than 60 online data bases such as the United Press International Wire Service, the Medlars medical data base, and the Academic American Library.

When an Electronic University course begins, the students write a short essay to introduce themselves and to describe what they hope to get out of the course. Using that information, the instructor can tailor the course to each student's individual needs—so the teacher-student interaction may be more personal via computer than it is likely to be in a conventional classroom.

Each Electronic University course begins with lecture notes that emphasize key concepts in the reading assignments. In addition, many lessons include an electronic workbook that asks the student questions about course material and comments on the student's answers. Most lessons conclude with a progress evaluation or a quiz to test understanding. When the student is satisfied with the answer, the quiz is sent to the instructor via electronic mail and the software unlocks the next lesson on the disk. In a day or two, the student can check his or her electronic mailbox to read the instructor's responses. Or the student can arrange a modem-to-modem chat, where questions are typed in and the instructor's responses appear on the monitor.

The greatest advantage of the Electronic University is convenience. Colleges can offer courses for credit to students who otherwise could not enroll because of time, work, distance, financial constraints, or physical disability.

Adapted from Dara Pearlman, "A School Without Walls," *Personal Computing*, April 1985. Copyright © 1985 Ziff-Davis Publishing Company.

Our thanks to the experts who have contributed the detailed information that is at the heart of this chapter: William H. Sanders of Indiana University, who provided the materials for the education section, and Andrew Christie of the University of New Hampshire, who supplied materials for the humanities section.

CHAPTER 14

LOOKING AHEAD

This chapter looks at some computer applications in education and the humanities. You'll see how computers are used in education to control learning, deliver student instruction, and evaluate learning. And you'll see how computers are used in the humanities to help evaluate the authenticity of art objects and the authorship of literary works. Computer applications to translate language, create new sounds and pictures, and support research in history and archaeology are also studied. The information in this chapter will enable you to:

- Discuss how computers are used by educators to control learning, deliver instruction, and evaluate learning
- Give specific examples of how computers are used by humanists to help solve mysteries, create new art, and support scholarly research

CHAPTER OUTLINE

LOOKING AHEAD
COMPUTERS IN EDUCATION
Computer-Managed Instruction
Computer-Assisted Instruction
Computer-Assisted Testing
COMPUTERS IN THE HUMANITIES
Art Authenticity
Authorship Identification
Language Translation
Computers in the Fine Arts
Computers and Museums
Computers in History
Computers in Archaeology
Skeptics and Dissenters
Feedback and Review 14
LOOKING BACK

MODULE 4

Computers in Education

Computers have had a strong impact on such educational functions as research, administration, and instruction. Most early computer developments took place in the research labs of major universities, and university researchers continue to push ahead at the computing frontiers. Many processing techniques so valuable to government and industry have also found their way into the offices of educational administrators. Few school districts operate today without computer support for budget, payroll, inventory, grade reporting, and other types of record keeping. And with the advent of microcomputers, an increasing amount of computing capacity has become available to teachers for classroom use.

The instructional uses of computers fall into two broad categories. The first category involves instruction "about" computers. The computer is itself a subject of study in computer science and other departments offering courses in computer usage. In the second category are activities involving instruction "with" computers. Computers are used here as tools for instruction—another medium of learning similar in function to textbooks, lectures, and films. Earlier chapters in this book have focused on material about computers, so we'll concentrate here on new instructional techniques made possible with the help of computers.

The uses of a computer as a tool in the instructional process are generally referred to as **computer-based education (CBE).** The goals and objectives of CBE are the same as those of instruction in general: the control, delivery, and evaluation of learning. CBE may be subdivided into the following three areas (see Figure 14-1): (1) computer-managed instruction for the *control* of learning; (2) computer-assisted instruction for the *delivery* of learning; and (3) computer-assisted testing for the *evaluation* of learning.

In order to master a computer application, students must learn the mechanics of working with a computer. These American Airlines trainees are learning to use computers in order to master the art of making reservations by computer. (Courtesy Telex Corp.)

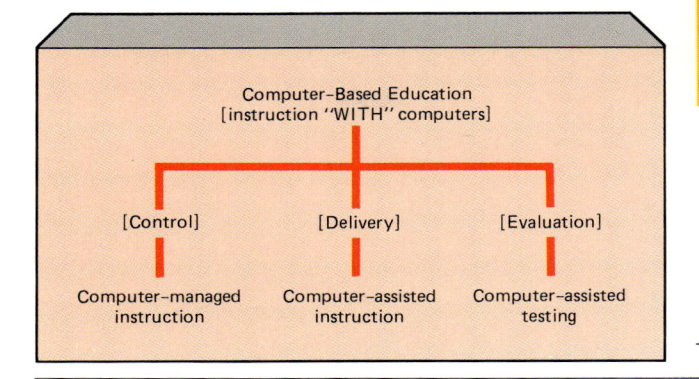

FIGURE 14-1

Computer-Based Education [instruction "WITH" computers]
- [Control] → Computer-managed instruction
- [Delivery] → Computer-assisted instruction
- [Evaluation] → Computer-assisted testing

Computer-Managed Instruction

Computer-managed instruction (CMI) is the use of a computer to control the instruction received by students. To help you understand CMI, let's assume that Jean is taking a high school course in U.S. history. Let's also assume that Jean's teacher has organized the course into different modules with clearly defined objectives and has prepared tests to ensure that students have met the criteria of each module. When students complete all modules, they're given credit for the course.

In a CMI environment, students need not march together through the materials. Rather, they can work individually and move ahead at a more flexible pace. Enrichment materials may be provided for faster students, and remedial materials can be made available to slower ones. If Jean is working through a 1-week module on the legislative branch of the government, she might be assigned preliminary readings in her text and then be required to take a short computer-based test on the structure and function of the legislative branch. When she completes the test, the CMI software package might direct her to a computerized lesson which identifies all the steps in the passage of a bill through the House and Senate. Perhaps the lesson draws a picture of the lawmaking process and asks Jean to specify each step in advance through her computer. Successful completion of the lesson allows her to move ahead.

CMI packages usually have built-in reporting mechanisms. When the teacher wants a report of student progress, the system generates a class roster listing the modules completed by each student. Thus the teacher may quickly observe the progress of each student in the course and may observe the quality of the student's work as well. Because this evaluation is performed by the computer, the teacher has more class time to work directly with students. Although we've used a high school example, CMI systems are more likely to be found in higher education where they are often developed by interested faculty. They also are commonplace in business training programs.

Computer-Assisted Instruction

Computer-assisted instruction (CAI) refers to the use of a computer to deliver instruction to students. CAI has its roots in the fields of educational psychology and instructional technology. In the 1950s, educational psychologists began to experiment with the concept of "programmed instruction."

They divided a course's content into "frames" which allowed students to master materials by completing specified sequences of frames in workbook fashion. Psychologist B. F. Skinner was an early champion of programmed instruction.

In the late 1950s, researchers in education and industry began to implement instructional strategies (including programmed instruction) on computers. These experiments continued throughout the 1960s. The computers of that day were expensive, and few of the early projects worked well in an educational setting. But those that survived made significant contributions to CAI.

CAI Strategies and Techniques   Most of today's computer-based educational strategies and techniques are just computerized versions of teaching techniques usually performed without computers. The CAI applications now in use can usually be classified by the strategies they use: *drill and practice, dialogue, problem solving, simulation, game,* or *discovery learning.*

Drill and practice   **Drill and practice** is an instructional strategy that's well suited to the acquisition of basic knowledge that requires rote memorization. Lower-level drill and practice activities typically involve memorizing such information as multiplication tables, foreign-language vocabulary, and the spelling of words. But drill and practice is also useful in more complex learning tasks since the acquisition of almost any knowledge or skill requires repetitive practice. It has continued to increase in popularity as a computer-based teaching strategy for two reasons. First, its tasks are quantifiable and therefore may be implemented on computers. And second, the computer delivery of drill and practice materials requires no teacher to monitor a student's learning activity.

The three major parts of any drill program are the *item selection, item delivery,* and *record-keeping* methods used. The computer offers several op-

CAI applications aren't limited to the classroom; this giant periodic table in Berkeley, California's Lawrence Hall of Science uses an Apple II+ to manage interactive educational dialogues with visitors. (Courtesy the University of California, Berkeley)

tions in item selection. For example, it can store many items (such as words and their meanings) in files and present them to students, or it can be programmed to generate different problems of the same type, such as math problems. Computers also allow both sequential and random delivery of items. In sequential presentation, the computer presents materials to students in a specified order. For example, a series of problems or activities might be arranged so that success on later items depends upon successful completion of early items. When the order of presentation isn't critical, computers can present problems in random order. This reduces the possibility that students can successfully complete problems based on cues related to sequence. In keeping records, the computer may be programmed to track all problems of all types and to keep careful records of student performance.

In the presentation and tracking of drills, the computer is capable of a level of detail and sophistication rarely possible with human tutors. For example, medical and legal students are required to memorize large numbers of terms and their definitions. In this situation, it's possible for the computer to select small pools of test items from large pools, present them in random order, identify and clear up confusions, track results, and provide detailed information to both the learner and the teacher concerning items mastered as well as those which require more practice.

Dialogues The idea of a dialogue between teacher and pupil has been a fundamental concept of western education since the days of Socrates. CAI dialogues cast the computer in the role of a teacher who possesses knowledge or information that the student must acquire. Most CAI dialogues take one of two forms. In a **tutorial dialogue,** the computer presents information, asks questions, and controls the flow of instruction. Most computer-based dialogues are of this type. When **inquiry dialogue** is used, though, the computer possesses knowledge and information which students must extract. Students must ask questions, select the sequence of activities, and take active steps toward analysis and problem solving. A geology tutorial dialogue, for instance, systematically explains various aspects of soil and rock strata, asks questions, and presents short quizzes at the end of each section. But an inquiry dialogue provides students with basic facts and concepts of geology and leads them to deduce additional information concerning rock and soil strata by asking questions and evaluating new information received from the computer.

Tutorials have also been a popular form of computer instruction, but they have always been difficult to write. Early problems encountered in writing tutorials led practitioners to develop special programming languages. These languages, usually referred to as **authoring languages,** differ from many other languages in that they have special capabilities for handling and analyzing English text. Some of the more popular authoring languages, such as PILOT, are now available for use with pc's.

The biggest drawback to the use of dialogues is the problem of analyzing student answers. Because no instructional programmer can anticipate all possible student responses to any question, special techniques are used to control and limit the range of those responses. Simpler dialogues allow only multiple-choice or single-word responses, while more sophisticated programs include language analysis techniques that can handle a broader range of student input. (Perhaps the most famous system of this type is PLATO, developed by the computer-based education research laboratory at the University of Illinois.)

MODULE 4
480

The evolving techniques of artificial intelligence and natural language processing should greatly improve authoring languages and dialogue techniques in the future.

Problem solving Math and science teachers often look at a student's ability to solve problems as a key indicator of learning. And in art and music, problem-solving exercises are frequent. In recent years, various problem-solving programs have become available for pc's. Examples of such software include statistical analysis packages, electronic spreadsheets, and accounting packages. Such packages allow instructors to assign problem-solving exercises so that students may focus on correctly formulating a solution without getting bogged down in calculations. It's often far more important for a student to demonstrate the ability to collect and organize information and set up the solution to a problem than to carry out manually all the calculations involved. The most significant benefit of such problem-solving exercises is that they allow students to work with complex and challenging problems. By relieving students of the drudgery of computation, the computer allows them to spend their class hours on the process of problem solving.

Simulation An **instructional simulation** gives students classroom exercises that closely approximate real world experience. For example, law students participate in "moot court," driver education students use driving simulators, and Junior Achievement students use simulations that help them understand business operations. Simulations are particularly useful in situations where firsthand experience is unavailable, inappropriate, too expensive, or too risky. Let's look now at three types of instructional simulations.

Task performance simulations help students acquire the psychomotor skills related to specific tasks. Obvious examples include flight and driving simulators that often use special equipment attached to a computer. Realism is important in these simulations to ensure that student learning will transfer to the activity itself.

This computer simulation of a distillation experiment allows students to see the effects of temperature changes on the system without going near a chemistry lab. (PLATO screen courtesy Control Data Corp.)

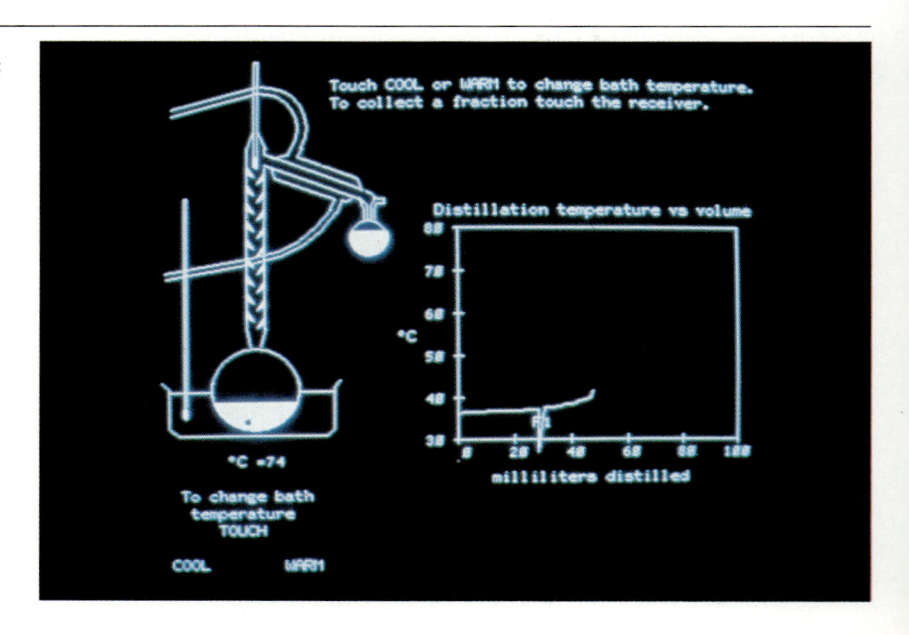

Systems modeling simulations contain information required to describe the state of a system as well as rules which govern system activity. Given a working model, students can introduce changes to system parameters and study their effects. By manipulating various aspects of the model, students gain an appreciation and understanding of system components and concepts. Most teachers hope that their students not only will memorize facts and ideas but that they also will be able to integrate such learning into broader, more sophisticated concepts. It's one thing to understand the physiological characteristics of fish and other marine life; but the understanding of oceanic ecosystems, and the interrelationships among living things in the sea, represents learning of a different order. Weather systems, economic and political systems, human anatomy, and the flow of traffic on city streets all represent examples of systems. In fact, the world may be described as a vast network of interlocking systems of various types. Providing students with a meaningful understanding of such systems is the goal of systems modeling simulations.

Experience/encounter simulations differ from systems models in that the experiences which they simulate may not be formalized and structured enough to be represented in a system. Examples include simulations of foreign travel, first-year teaching experiences, or job interviewing encounters. In these cases and others, programs provide students with hypothetical problems and opportunities that require some decision or action. Students gain increased understanding of such situations by observing the consequences of their actions. The rules which govern progress in an experience/encounter simulation are likely "qualitative" rather than "quantitative." Such simulations are useful in bringing to the classroom a feeling for and an appreciation of activities and experiences that would otherwise be unavailable.

Games Games have long been a part of human recreation, and they are also believed to be valuable in shaping mental processes. Unfortunately, the connection between games and learning isn't always clear. For example, a relationship undoubtedly exists between good chess playing and certain highly developed mental skills, but our understanding of that relationship is vague. And the difference between instructional and recreational games isn't clear either. But the degree to which the mental tasks and activities of a game can be related to specific learning objectives represents a good measure of its instructional value. For example, the game of tick tack toe isn't clearly tied to any learning objective, but the popular children's game of hangman has educational content that's related to word recognition, spelling, and vocabulary building. Playing hangman helps students sharpen their skills in recognizing patterns and combinations of letters and learning the details of spelling.

Identifying and selecting games with instructional value is only part of the problem. Games are difficult to use in classrooms because they usually require that students be taught how to play according to the rules before instructional benefit is obtained. But the concepts of most existing games aren't important enough to justify the investment of such a large effort. When a computer can be programmed to serve as both referee and as another player in the game, however, much of the need for preparation is eliminated.

Games may be divided into games of "cooperation" and "competition." Most computer games are games of competition that pit one player or team against another. Games of cooperation usually require students to work together toward a common objective in order to win. These games are often

MODULE 4

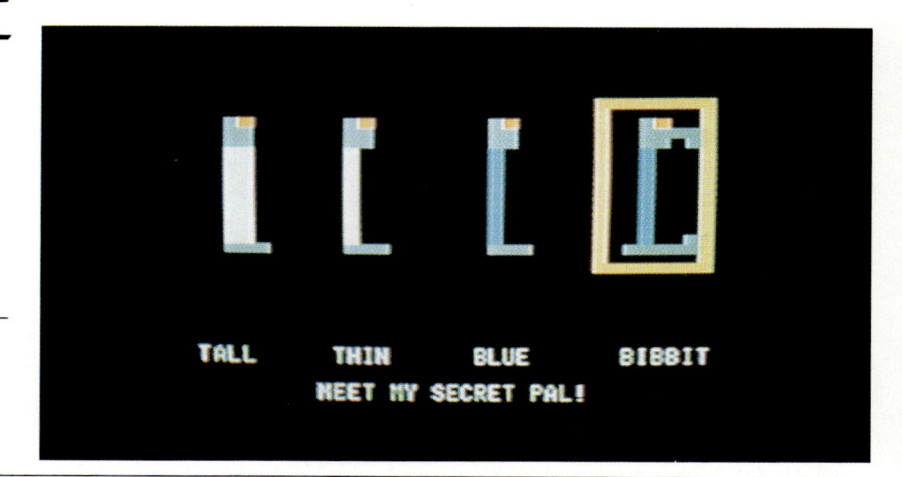

482

Do educational computer games like Moptown Hotel actually help young children to learn and retain such concepts as tallness, thinness, or color? Nobody knows for certain—but the kids have fun playing the games. (Courtesy The Learning Company)

used when team building and interdependence among people need to be encouraged. Regardless of the type, most computer games provide a goal-directed activity which is fun for participants. In addition, competitive computer games lack the drawbacks which make competing inappropriate for some students. For example, some students find that the stress and tension of direct interpersonal competition can greatly reduce the effectiveness of the game for them. But when these students compete against a skillfully prepared computer program (one that adjusts its play and responses to those of the student), many tensions and anxieties disappear. As educators and researchers sharpen their skills at designing and producing computer games of instructional value, we'll see more games in the mainstream of teaching.

Discovery learning   Most classroom teaching involves lectures, exercises, quizzes, and other activities of short duration. Because instructors need to maintain control and monitor progress for many students, it's rare for students to have any say over the timing and sequencing of learning events. But computer-based learning environments can give students much more control. A **discovery learning environment** fosters the acquisition of knowledge by encouraging experimentation by trial and error. It also encourages students to choose the time and manner in which they tackle ideas and concepts, and it allows the sequence of learning events to be controlled by the student's own internal motivation. Clearly, there are many similarities between simulations, games, and discovery learning. In a sense, simulations and games represent different types of discovery learning environments. But all of them allow students considerable latitude in the timing and sequencing of their work.

Computer-Assisted Testing

Computer-assisted testing is the use of computers to evaluate student learning. The heart of a computer-based testing system is the item bank—a data base which contains not only a large number of test questions but also a statistical history of the use of each item. In constructing a test with such a system, a teacher may select appropriate questions from the item bank. After the test has been given, student answer sheets are submitted to the computer for analysis. These sheets are graded, and student performance is reported for entry in the gradebook. The test itself is then analyzed to determine the behavior of individual test items. For example, if a particular question is answered correctly by all those who failed the test but is answered incorrectly by all those with high scores, then something may be wrong with that question. These analysis results are entered into the data base and are combined with the past history of each item. Over time, successful items are maintained, new items are introduced, and unsuccessful items are weeded out.

Computers in the Humanities

Asked to choose a field of study that would probably remain unaffected by computers, many would select one of the humanistic disciplines. After all, the humanities are concerned with human judgment and creativity, and with the expressive, moral, and contemplative aspects of life, while computers deal with quantitative and relatively depersonalized data. It's true that computers are having less impact in the humanities than in areas such as engineering, science, business, and medicine. Nonetheless, the impact of computers in the humanities is significant and developing.

Several factors are leading to the increased acceptance and use of computers in the humanities. Advances in software, spurred by more powerful hardware, have made it much easier to work with nonnumerical data such as texts, musical scores, and pictures. Computer power is becoming much less expensive. And the exponential growth in the quantity of scholarly and artistic material being produced is forcing increased reliance on computers simply to keep up with the deluge. Let's look now at a few examples of how computers are being used in the humanities.

The art of restoring great paintings has always required a deft and knowledgeable touch—and computers have enabled art historians to make their knowledge bases far larger and more accessible in recent years. (Courtesy IBM Corp.)

Art Authenticity

At New York's Metropolitan Museum of Art, Carl Dauterman has used a computer to study the sets of coded marks found on Sevres porcelain—a valuable eighteenth-century French porcelain that's often copied by forgers. Pieces of genuine porcelain have coded sets of painted and incised marks that identify such things as workers, dates, and types of paste. There can be 10 different painted and incised marks on a single piece of porcelain. The computer program compares and cross-correlates the combinations of painted and incised marks found on genuine articles and flags as suspicious any pieces of pottery with markings that deviate from the normal patterns. The computer cannot settle the issue of whether a marking is genuine; after all, a deviant pattern might have been made by an especially creative (or depressed) artisan. But the computer aids researchers by focusing attention on noteworthy cases. One printout, for example, revealed 13 pieces of porcelain with suspiciously deviant markings.

Authorship Identification

A writer is constantly making choices, among them how to start an article, story, or poem, or whether to describe the noise as "loud," "thunderous," "deafening," or "blaring." For centuries, humanists have tried to identify the telltale choices that uniquely identify a writer. For example, in 1897 a Polish scholar published a list of 500 facets of style that he believed could be used in identifying authors. **Computer stylistics** is the field of study that uses computers to find reliable, measurable indicators of style.

The *Federalist Papers* consist of 77 essays written in 1787 and 1788 to persuade New York citizens to ratify the U.S. Constitution. Although they were published anonymously, it's generally agreed that John Jay wrote 5 of the essays, Alexander Hamilton wrote 43, James Madison wrote 14, and Hamilton and Madison collaborated on 3. A quick tally (without a computer) tells us that the authorship of 12 essays hasn't been determined. In spite of the fact that after Hamilton's death in a duel, Madison claimed to have written the 12 papers, scholars have debated the issue for decades. Since the writing styles of Hamilton and Madison were similar, it appeared that the matter would remain unresolved. But with the aid of a computer, Frederick Mosteller of Harvard and David Wallace of the University of Chicago have determined that it's probable that Madison was, as he claimed, the author of all 12 disputed essays.

How was this done? After a computer-readable version of the *Federalist Papers* was prepared, the computer was asked to determine the frequency of word usage typical of Madison and Hamilton. Mosteller and Wallace found 28 significant differences in usage. One such difference concerned the words "while" and "whilst." In the 14 essays known to be by Madison, "while" never occurs, and "whilst" occurs 8 times. By contrast, "while" occurs in 14 of the 48 essays known to be by Hamilton and "whilst" never occurs. Thus the presence of "whilst" in five of the disputed papers points to Madison as the author. A similar pattern was found with the words "on" and "upon." Two such usage differences are significant but hardly decisive. But when 28 such cases are present, the evidence becomes overwhelming. Without the computer, it would likely be impossible to achieve the high standard of proof demanded by scholars.

Computers have also been used in studies attempting to identify the authors of portions of the Old Testament of the Bible. The authorship of the Book of Isaiah, for example, has vexed scholars for centuries. The first 12 chapters are generally attributed to Isaiah; the authorship of the remaining 54 chapters is disputed. Some scholars contend that Isaiah wrote the entire work; others believe that the last 54 chapters were written by anywhere from two to four anonymous prophets. To shed new light on this emotionally charged controversy (disputants long ago ceased to be on speaking terms), Y. T. Radday, lecturer in charge of Hebrew studies at the Israel Institute of Technology, used a computer in an authorship study. Although Radday was convinced at the beginning of his analysis that Isaiah had written the entire book, his final conclusion was that multiple authors were involved. The chance that the author of Chapters 1 to 35 wrote Chapters 40 to 66 was computed to be only 1 in 100,000. Similar studies of authorship have also been made of the New Testament. Reverend Andrew Q. Morton and James McLeman have published a controversial analysis maintaining that of the 14 epistles traditionally attributed to the Apostle Paul, only Corinthians, Galatians, and Romans I and II were written by Paul and not extensively revised by others.

Computer stylistic and authorship studies aren't confined to the classics.

Disputes concerning authorship may make headlines. In the early 1970s, Patty Hearst, the daughter of a wealthy newspaper magnate, was kidnapped. Held captive for several months by the so-called Symbionese Liberation Army, she allegedly wrote and read a number of tape-recorded "communiques" claiming participation in several bank robberies. When she was later brought to trial, her defense lawyers attempted to use computer stylistics to demonstrate that she wasn't the author of the incriminating messages. The presiding judge, fearful that jurors might be overly impressed by statistics and computer-generated graphs, disallowed the evidence. But as the methods become more reliable and familiar, they're likely to find acceptance even in courts of law.

In summary, computers are now widely used to show that one or another pattern in A makes it much more like B than like C. In situations like that of the *Federalist Papers,* where there's a great deal of data and only two possible authors, the computer can help scholars settle disputes. More frequently, the computer adds important evidence but leaves basic questions unresolved. A fundamental limitation in computer stylistics is that while a computer can spot significant patterns, it can't explain *why* the patterns exist.

Language Translation

In 1954, a computer with a stored vocabulary totaling 250 words and 6 rules for determining word relationships in sentences was programmed to translate a few Russian sentences into English. This small demonstration program was widely publicized, and it was then predicted that computers would soon be used to translate documents from one natural language into another. The reasoning was that since computers could hold a large number of, say, Russian-English synonyms in storage and since grammar rules for the two languages could probably be programmed, there should be a substantial amount of machine translation in the future.

Relative to 1954, it's now "the future." Are computers used for lan-

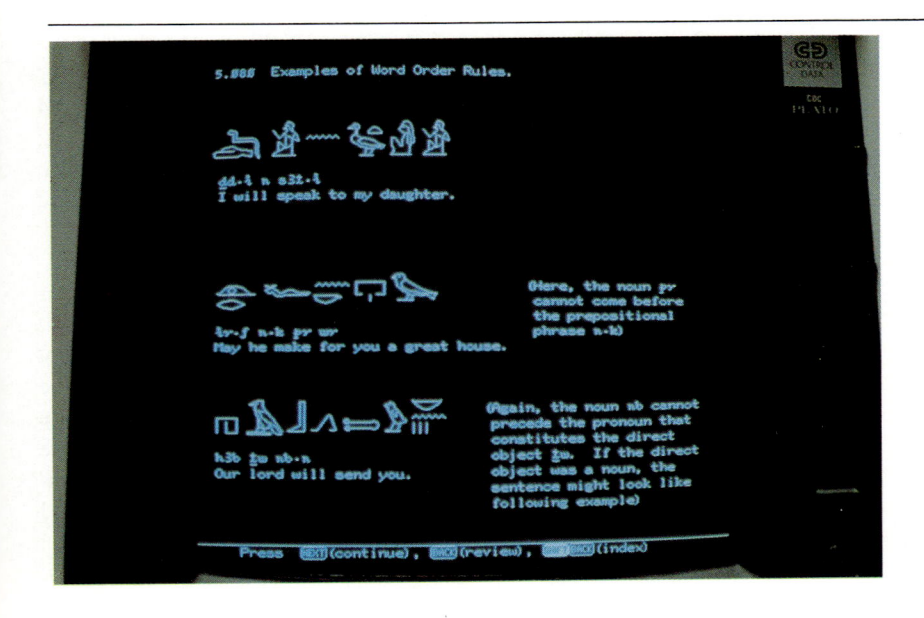

This PLATO program not only translates the hieroglyphs of ancient Egypt but also deciphers the rules of grammar that govern the placement of these icons in a sentence. (Courtesy Control Data Corp.)

guage translation today? Well, yes and no. Despite the optimism of the 1950s, it's not now possible (nor is it expected to be within this century) to present a computer with a text in a foreign language and receive as output a flawless translation. There are at least two reasons for this. First, grammarians haven't managed to determine all the rules of grammar for any language. Language has turned out to be far more complex than anyone used to imagine. Second, a good translation requires an understanding of how the meaning of words depends on the context in which they're used. This isn't easy. One story, perhaps apocryphal, is that a computer translated the English sentence, "The spirit is willing, but the flesh is weak," into a Russian sentence meaning, "The vodka is good, but the meat is rotten." More seriously, consider the sentence, "Time flies like an arrow," which may seem clear at first, but is subject to several interpretations. One incorrect translation, for example, is, "Time the speed of flies as quickly as possible." Another inappropriate interpretation is, "One type of fly—a time fly—likes to have an arrow." For a computer to avoid these foolish interpretations, it would need to be told that the activity of timing flies is unusual at best and that there are no insects called time flies. Of course, a programmer could easily write rules to give a correct interpretation in this particular case. But then how would the machine interpret the sentence, "Fruit flies like a banana"? With the word "flies" treated as a verb in this sentence, the translation into another language would be ridiculous to us—but not to a computer.

Pronouns present further difficulties for translation programs. It's common sense, not word order or anything readily accessible to a computer, that tells us what the word "it" means in the following sentences:

She dropped the bowl on the table and broke it.

She dropped the bowl on the egg and broke it.

"There's a man in the room with a green hat on" is unambiguous because everyone knows that rooms don't wear hats. But computers don't know what everyone knows.

In spite of such limitations, researchers have succeeded in writing usable translation programs. Presented with technical texts, in which words and sentences tend to have fewer ambiguities and are somewhat more independent of context, these programs make an acceptable first-draft of, for example, a Russian-to-English translation. A skilled translator can then polish the draft. One reason that the programs are useful is that they're quite good at identifying and flagging (but not resolving) problematic situations.

Computers in the Fine Arts

The very idea of "computer art" might seem a contradiction in terms. After all, art is at the center of human expression, creativity, and passion, while computers are relentlessly mechanical and unemotional. But this apparent incompatibility between computers and art is easily dispelled once one realizes that the artists who work with computers are simply using another medium of artistic expression. The artist remains the creator. It is as it always has been. Creative artists, eager to explore and to present us with new ways of seeing, hearing, and reacting, are often quick to use the latest technologies.

> **WINDOW 14-1**
>
> ### COMIC ART BY COMPUTER
>
> Cartoonist Jeff Danziger has replaced his pencils with an Apple Macintosh to create the comic strip *McGonigle*. This strip, which Danziger created in 1984, is carried by the News America Syndicate and runs in about a dozen daily papers.
>
> *McGonigle* is about a fictional newspaper. The Macintosh is integral to the strip's look: The words of the strip's characters are hand-lettered, but Danziger uses the computer's print output to provide humorous newspaper-page backdrops for *McGonigle* panels. "One of the drawbacks of hand-lettering is that when it gets too small, it gets hard to read and you lose readers," says Danziger. "The Macintosh has opened up a whole new world for me—getting the typographer right next to my desk."
>
> But clean type and neat-looking graphics aren't the only reasons Danziger has fast become a computer enthusiast. He feels that the computer really has contributed to his writing. "A lot of people don't agree with me, but the computer tends to make you write more and make the writing better. It makes you want to edit, improve, and go back and take a look at what you've written."
>
> It may be only a matter of time before other cartoonists follow Danziger's lead and use computers to create their strips. In 1985, the comic book *Shatter*, produced entirely on the Macintosh, debuted. Artist Michael Saenz created the graphics on the Macintosh, printed the panels out on an Imagewriter printer, and then colored them. *Shatter* is the story of a twenty-first-century police officer in a world where everything is computerized.
>
> Danziger hopes to add a laser printer and digitizing gear to his system. The laser printer would enable him to draw backgrounds, and the digitizing equipment would allow him to alter images on the computer screen.
>
> If Danziger's dreams come true, his syndicate will go on line. Almost all of his work now travels express mail. "If I could send my work electronically, I could be right on top of the news. If I read something in the morning paper that struck me as funny, I could get a cartoon down and it would be off the same day."
>
> ---
>
> Adapted from Nancy Huscha, "A Comic Strip Artist and His Computer," *Personal Computing*, July 1985; Michael J. Miller, "Comics by Computer," *Popular Computing*, June 1985. Copyright © 1985 by McGraw-Hill Inc. All rights reserved.

The impressionists' masterful scenes of nature quickly followed the invention of high-quality oil-based paints in tubes—a technological advance that freed painters from their studios. Beethoven wrote his majestic symphonies for the large concert halls being built and for the new instruments loud enough to be heard within them.

Computers and Music Computers may be programmed to produce (or "synthesize") a wide variety of musical tempos, sounds, and harmonies. **Synthesizers** (computers dedicated to producing sound) are often used to imitate the sounds of traditional instruments. For example, some of the advertising jingles you hear on the radio that sound as if they were produced by musicians playing instruments were actually "played" by a single computer. But creative musicians do more than imitate. Walter Carlos used a synthesizer to produce *Switched-On Bach*, the best-selling classical album of all time! This album includes synthesizer versions of many of Bach's best-known pieces. Some criticized the album as a gimmick, which only sold because it exploited Bach's indestructable melodies. But others noted that Bach often wrote music without indicating which instrument it should be played on, and that the synthesized versions of Bach should join the piano, organ, classical guitar, and harpsicord versions as equally valid and exciting ways of highlighting aspects of Bach's genius.

Several possibilities are attracting creative musicians to computer music. With its mechanical precision and unparalleled ability to do just what it's told, the computer can produce sounds with rhythms, changes, and leaps that are

MODULE 4

When Herbie Hancock makes music, his instruments include a computer-driven Fairlight synthesizer and an Apple II PC. (© David Burnett, Contact Press/Woodfin Camp, 1983)

beyond the reach of even the most talented orchestra, jazz combo, or rock group. Many of the eerie, dramatic, and sometimes pleasing sounds in contemporary movie soundtracks (especially science-fiction thrillers like *Star Wars*) are computer-generated. Yale's J. C. Tenney uses a computer to compose and then play music. He provides certain constraints in his program; the computer then selects notes at random and plays the resulting piece. The results often surprise the artist. Artistry hasn't been eliminated; rather, it takes the unusual form of selecting worthwhile constraints for the computer.

Another possibility opened up by the computer involves the use of unfamiliar scales. Most familiar music uses so-called major and minor scales. Scales differ in the pitch between successive notes. Major scales sound bright and are appropriate for songs of joy and triumph, while music employing a minor scale often sounds subdued, sad, or reflective. Much of the distinctive sound of music from India and Japan comes from the use of unfamiliar scales. It's now possible to instruct a computer to play scales previously unexplored by human composers. But it's far too early to know if the new sounds, rhythms, scales, and harmonies created by the computer will open up a whole new era in music. Will there be a Bach or Beethoven in computer music? Let's hope so!

Computers in the Visual Arts   Computers are also opening up new possibilities in the visual arts. Perhaps without recognizing it, you've already seen a great deal of computer-generated art. For example, artists use powerful graphics software to create dramatic pictures of key moments during televised sports events. Television station breaks are frequently filled with computer-generated logos undergoing complex transformations. And science-fiction movies use computers to display fantasy worlds and produce striking visual effects.

Computers and Museums

The preservation of materials is an important function of any museum, and

Computer artist Paul Xander at work with his electronic paintbrush (*left*), and one of his startlingly realistic computer-generated images, entitled "Moss Water" (*right*). (Courtesy New York Institute of Technology)

computers are often used to keep track of a museum's collection. For example, the Smithsonian's Museum of Natural History has over 50 million specimens of such items as fossils, flowers, fish, and birds. A million new specimens are added each year. In one section alone, crustacean specimens in 500,000 bottles occupy more than 10 miles of shelves. Detailed information about the museum's holdings is of interest to researchers in colleges, hospitals, and other museums. To help scientists locate specimens (and information

A light bulb orbits amid a host of planets in this computer-generated advertising image for Philips/Westinghouse, created by Al Cerullo and Margaret Twomey. (Courtesy Feigenbaum Productions/New York Institute of Technology)

MODULE 4

"What's in your lunch?" Tell this interactive computerized exhibit at the Lawrence Hall of Science what you ate and it will tell you about the nutritional value of your meal. (Courtesy the University of California, Berkeley)

about the specimens), the museum has developed an electronic data base. A further value of electronic cataloging is the possibility of linking data bases together using sophisticated telecommunications equipment. Using a network of computers, museum personnel planning an exhibit can find out which participating museums have items that would supplement the showing.

The combined use of video and computer technologies is adding a new dimension to museum cataloging and record keeping. Photographs (perhaps the phrase ''video images'' would be more accurate) of the National Gallery of Art's entire collection have been recorded on a single optical disk. By controlling a laser disk player with a computer, a user can access pictures by whatever category and in whatever order is desired.

Museums throughout the country are playing a role in educating the public about computers by providing access to computing facilities. The Museum of Science in Boston offers a variety of courses introducing people to pc's. A large selection of these machines is available for interested users. Computers are also used to personalize several exhibits. For example, the computers in one exhibit devoted to energy conservation make detailed projections of the probable energy savings one would achieve using various conservation techniques. And the Lawrence Hall of Science, a science museum on the Berkeley campus of the University of California, has two computer rooms with multiple terminals where workshops are offered to school children and others. In addition, Lawrence Hall personnel load a van each morning with a dozen pc's and set up a temporary computer laboratory at a school somewhere in the San Francisco Bay area.

Computers in History

The computer and the statistical techniques it supports are important tools in studies of electoral and legislative behavior. At the University of Michigan, for example, an enormous computer data base, containing data about virtually every national election on a county by county basis, has been established for the use of historians throughout the country. More than ever before, it's now possible to make reasonable estimates of how particular ethnic, religious, and social groups voted and how they changed their allegiances over time.

Legislative bodies have long kept detailed records about the passage and defeat of bills. Especially useful for historians are the records of roll call votes that show how each member of the legislature voted. Computer analysis of these records makes it possible to examine to what extent such factors as party affiliation, personal wealth, regional interests, and religion influence legislative behavior. Quantitative historians hope to shed new light on the century-old dispute between economic determinists (who maintain that people vote their pocketbook) and followers of German historian Max Weber (who stress the independent importance of religion and personality). Although the computer hasn't put an end to such scholarly debates, it has improved the quality of the discussion.

Census data, tax lists, marriage licenses, birth records, and similar data often stored (and usually decomposing) in the basements of town halls make possible numerical estimates of social mobility. Who were the winners and losers over a particular period? To what extent was there room at the top for newcomers? Has the possibility of improving one's lot in America increased or decreased since the 1800s? Stephen Thernstrom used a computer analysis of such records to trace the lives of several hundred residents of Newburyport, Massachusetts, from 1860 until 1900. He found that the chance for an unskilled manual laborer to attain a more prestigious white-collar job was very low, but the children of unskilled laborers fared somewhat better. Thernstrom's results ignited a flurry of similar computerized studies on social mobility.

Historians are also interested in producing theories that may be useful in predicting future trends. In 1918, British meteorologist Lewis Richardson returned from World War I shocked by the violence and destruction he had seen. Since an arms race had preceded the war, Richardson turned his attention to constructing a predictive model (a reasonable task for a weatherman). He hoped that politicians would learn to avoid wars by knowing when they were likely to occur. His model, while by no means perfect, has an excellent track record at distinguishing "unstable" arms races that lead to war from "stable" arms races that are much less volatile. Philip Schrodt of Northwestern University has written a computer program that makes it possible to explore Richardson's model in detail. Scholars can show that the arms race between Iran and Iraq in the late 1970s was particularly unstable, and in 1980 a deadly conflict erupted between the two nations. More cheering is the fact that the 40-year arms race between the Soviet Union and the United States is, according to Richardson's model, a stable one.

Computers in Archaeology

Statistical techniques and simulation methods have been developed by archaeologists and statisticians to analyze and classify archaeological data, and several computer data banks have been created for the storage and retrieval of archaeological information. Some examples of computer usage in archaeology are described below:

1 Building on decades of archaeological research, Ned and Lou Heite created a program called POTS that gives an estimate of when a site was occupied. The program works by comparing the type and quantity of ceramic fragments found at the site with a data base containing information on pottery producers, including when they were at peak production and when they closed. The estimates generated by the POTS program matched closely the exact dates of site use, when they were independently available.

2   George Cowgill of Brandeis University has studied the origin and growth of the pre-Aztec city of Teotihuacan in central Mexico. Using a computer programmed to sketch a map of the city on the basis of the site information presented, Cowgill has been able to show the types of neighborhoods that existed in a city that covered an area 8 or 9 square miles. For example, an *almena* is a ceramic roof decoration that was found in the upper-class neighborhoods. Since the computer can produce a map showing the number of almenas discovered on every site, it's possible to see that an elite neighborhood was located near the "main street." The computer mapping for various time periods shows that building density was high and that there was a high degree of planning.

3   Ray Winfield Smith has used a computer to solve the puzzle of 35,000 decorated blocks of stone found in Egypt. The blocks were originally thought to be the remains of a single temple, but after classifying the blocks the computer showed that there had been a large complex of temples and buildings stretching across the desert for over a mile.

4   James Strange of the University of South Florida has worked to restore an ancient synagogue in the village of Khirbet Shema that was destroyed around A.D. 417. The site is located 90 miles north of Jerusalem. When most of the dimensions of the building site were known, a computer was used to make engineering calculations to determine the missing structural parameters. The computer was also used to make drawings of what the building probably looked like.

Skeptics and Dissenters

Not all artists and humanists are enthusiastic about computers. Some insist that we keep the current uses of computers in perspective. Knowing how many authors wrote which parts of Isaiah is interesting but doesn't address the central question of what the work means and what it has to teach twentieth-century humanity. And graphing the fine details of election results can distract scholars from discussing how much difference the election made in the flow of history. In short, these people worry that the computer is a time-consuming distraction which only throws light on relatively minor questions. Clearly, not everyone agrees, and computer usage in the humanities continues to increase.

   Other humanists and artists go beyond questioning the value of specific computer applications. In their view, the humanities, theology, and the arts represent vital areas of human life that shield us from too much science and technology. What are we to make of the wedding, recently reported on the news, in which a computer was programmed to read in its mechanical voice, "Do you solemnly swear . . . " and the couple responded by typing the letter "Y" at a keyboard? Is this a clever publicity stunt? Or a sign of a culture that's so in love with technology that it has lost sight of its values? Many eloquent voices within the humanities are questioning the wisdom of having computers enter every walk of life.

CHAPTER 14

493

FEEDBACK

Feedback and Review 14

To test and reinforce your understanding of the uses of computers in education and the humanities, fill in the following *crossword puzzle*.

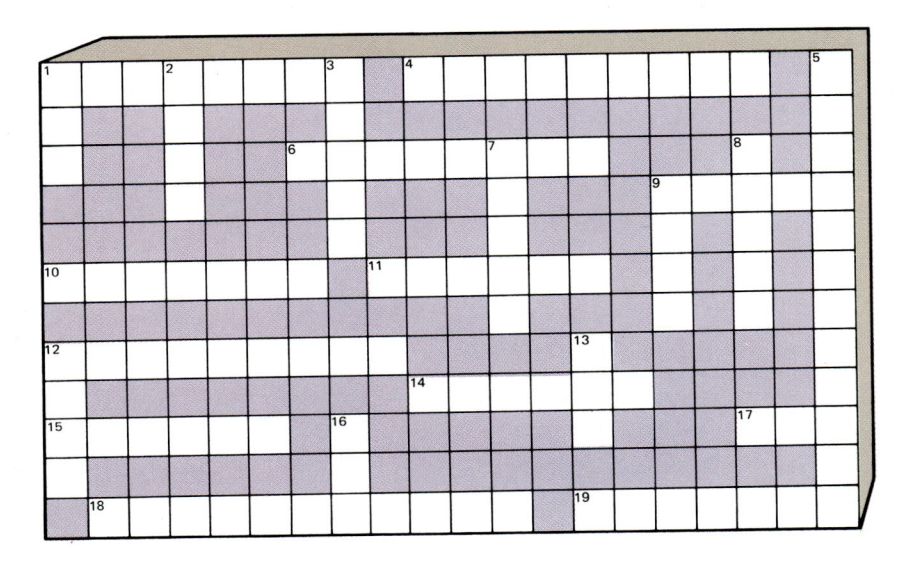

Across

1. Computer-_____ testing is the use of computers to evaluate student learning.
4. Early problems in writing computer-based dialogue programs led to the development of special programming languages called _____ languages.
6. A CAI _____ program attempts to cast the computer in the role of a teacher who possesses knowledge or information that the student must acquire.
9. _____ is an example of an authoring language.
10. Computer-managed instruction is the use of a computer to _____ the instruction received by students.
11. An _____ is a ceramic roof decoration found at archaeological sites in Mexico.
12. In the 1950s, it was expected that computers would soon be used to _____ documents from one natural language to another.
14. Computers are opening up many new possibilities in the _____ arts.
15. Historians use census data, tax lists, birth records, and other data to make numerical estimates of _____ mobility.
17. The goals and objectives of _____ [an acronym] are the control, delivery, and evaluation of learning.
18. Games may be divided into games of cooperation and games of _____.
19. _____ modeling simulations contain information required to describe the state of a system and the rules which govern its activity.

MODULE 4

Down

1. Computers have been used at the New York Metropolitan Museum of Art to gain further information about the authenticity of ____ objects.
2. The heart of a computer-assisted testing system is the ____ bank, a data base that contains a large number of test questions.
3. ____ and practice is a CAI instructional strategy that's well suited to the acquisition of basic knowledge that requires rote memorization.
5. ____ are often used to imitate the sounds of traditional musical instruments.
7. Long a part of human recreation, ____ are also believed to be valuable in shaping mental processes.
8. ____ is an example of a system that uses CAI dialogue techniques.
9. New Testament epistles attributed to the Apostle ____ have undergone authorship identification studies.
12. ____ performance simulations help students acquire psychomotor skills.
13. The authors of the *Federalist Papers* are Hamilton, Madison, and ____.
16. ____ is an acronym that refers to the use of a computer to deliver instruction to students.

LOOKING BACK

1. Educational applications of computers include activities in research, administration, and instruction. Educators have historically been involved in the research and development of computers and in the development of techniques for their use. Instructional applications of computers may be divided into two categories: instruction "about" computers and instruction "with" computers (also called computer-based education). Instruction "with" computers is an attempt to use the computer as a tool in the teaching process.

2. Computer-based educational activities can be classified by the way they relate to control, delivery, and evaluation of instruction. Computer-managed instruction (CMI) deals with control activities, computer-assisted instruction (CAI) consists of delivery activities, and computer-assisted testing embraces evaluation activities.

3. Most early CAI educational strategies were based on teaching techniques similar to those used in the traditional classroom, such as drill and practice, student/teacher dialogue, and problem solving. More sophisticated techniques, including the use of several types of instructional games and simulations, have developed as computers have become more powerful, less expensive, and easier to use.

4. Humanists are using computers more than anyone might have thought possible a few years ago. For example, computers are being used to help scholars form judgments about the authenticity of art objects and the authorship of literary works. And although machine-language translation techniques have failed to live up to earlier optimistic predictions, considerable use is now being made of specialized programs that generate acceptable first-draft translations of some materials.

5. Artists are exploring the new possibilities opened up by the computer for creating music and for producing images. There's also a bright future for computers in museum information storage and retrieval. And computers permit historians and archaeologists to manipulate masses of data to arrive at relationships and insights that might otherwise remain undetected.

6. Critics of the current use of computers in the humanities include those who think that too much money and energy is being spent on insignificant projects and those who think that the humanities ought to remain one area of life in which technology does not dominate human expression.

KEY TERMS AND CONCEPTS

computer-based education (CBE) 476
computer-managed instruction (CMI) 477
computer-assisted instruction (CAI) 477
drill and practice 478
tutorial dialogue 479
inquiry dialogue 479
authoring languages 479
instructional simulation 480
task performance simulations 480
systems modeling simulations 481
experience/encounter simulations 481
discovery learning environment 482
computer-assisted testing 482
computer stylistics 484
synthesizers 487

TOPICS FOR REVIEW AND DISCUSSION

1. (a) What is computer-based education (CBE)? (b) Into what three categories can CBE be divided?
2. Define computer-managed instruction and give an example of its use.
3. (a) What is computer-assisted instruction (CAI)? (b) Identify and discuss four CAI instructional methods.
4. "Drill and practice continues to increase in popularity as a computer-based teaching strategy for two reasons." What are these reasons?
5. What are the three major parts of any drill program?
6. "Most CAI dialogues take one of two forms." Identify and discuss these two forms.
7. (a) What's an authoring language? (b) Give an example of such a language.
8. What benefits may be obtained from the use of problem-solving software packages?
9. Identify and discuss three types of instructional simulations.
10. "The connection between games and learning isn't always clear." Discuss this statement.
11. Games may be divided into two categories. What are these categories?
12. What is a discovery learning environment?
13. How is an item bank used in computer-assisted testing?
14. What impact are computers having on the humanities?
15. Give examples of the use of computer stylistics in authorship identification studies.
16. (a) Why were earlier optimistic predictions for machine-language translation techniques wrong? (b) How are current programs for machine translation being used and what are some of their limitations?
17. Discuss the new possibilities computers are creating in the fine arts.
18. What are some principal uses of computers by museums?
19. Discuss ways in which computers have been applied in historical research.

MODULE 4

20. How have computers been applied in archaeological research?

21. Not all humanists are welcoming computers. Explain two frequent objections to the use of computers in the humanities.

PROJECTS/ISSUES TO CONSIDER

1. Go to your library and identify three examples of computer usage in education that weren't discussed in this chapter. Research these examples and present a report to the class.

2. Identify and research three computer applications in the humanities that weren't mentioned in this chapter, and prepare a report for the class.

ANSWERS TO FEEDBACK AND REVIEW SECTION

The solution to the crossword puzzle is shown below:

1 A	S	2 S	I	S	T	E	3 D		4 A	U	T	H	O	R	I	N	G		5 S
R			T				R												Y
T			E		6 D	I	A	L	O	7 G	U	E				8 P		N
			M				L			A				9 P	I	L	O	T
							L			M				A		A		H
10 C	O	N	T	R	O	L		11 A	L	M	E	N	A	U		T		E
								S						L		O		S
12 T	R	A	N	S	L	A	T	E			13 J							I
A							14 V	I	S	U	A	L						Z
15 S	O	C	I	A	L		16 C				Y				17 C	B	E
K							A											R
	18 C	O	M	P	E	T	I	T	I	O	N		19 S	Y	S	T	E	M	S

A CLOSER LOOK

IBM'S WRITING TO READ

Writing to Read, an experimental, computer-based educational program developed with IBM's support, is a radical departure from the way most of us learned to read and write. Instead of teaching the ABCs, then transforming those printed characters into spoken sounds, and finally showing how to convert those sounds back into writing, Writing to Read uses computers, typewriters, and tape recorders to teach kindergarteners and first-graders to read and write. Writing to Read is based on the principle that these children, whose spoken vocabulary may comprise 4,000 or 5,000 words, can easily learn to write anything they can say—and to read anything they can write—using a simplified phonetic spelling.

Because 5-year-olds have a short attention span, children using Writing to Read spend only 15 minutes on the computers during a 1-hour daily program. The computer uses color images, accompanied by spoken words, to help children recognize and type the 42 phonemes (sounds) of the English language. After the computer session, children move on to 15 minutes at a tape recorder, listening to the same lesson while entering responses in a workbook. They then listen to a story, also recorded, as they follow along in a book. The fourth stop is at a typewriter, on which they may type whatever they wish. The children in test groups learned to type narratives, stories, and poems at an age when other children are still learning how to write their names.

Writing to Read was created by John Henry Martin, an educator who has spent 40 years working with the problems of teaching reading. Martin recognized the potential of personal computers in this area as soon as they were introduced.

In 1945, high school principal Martin discovered what he thought was a new phenomenon: high school boys who could not read. He began to study alternative theories of reading instruction. By 1963, Martin was experimenting with teaching machines and working with Omar Khayam Moore, the professor who invented the talking typewriter. In 1975 Martin tried out some of his theories of reading education in grade schools, using such novel materials as clay, sand, and plastic letters. This led him to the idea of using tape recorders and typewriters. Martin favored the IBM Selectric typewriter for children because it can't jam, and began his association with IBM when he requested some Selectrics for use in local schools. But Martin felt that personal computers, if they could talk, would provide the best way to put his theories into practice. When IBM released its first personal computers in 1981, he enlisted the corporation's support in developing his Writing to Read program.

Children easily adapt to the irregular spellings of English after first using Writing to Read. But a writing program that openly embraces misspelled words, as Writing to Read does, is not likely to appeal to most elementary school teachers. Martin says, "What we really have to do is teach a whole adult generation that they don't know how to write. When they're writing, they're only writing the first draft. The process of writing is called rewriting. The finest piece of political literature by the greatest political stylist is called The Declaration of Independence, and it went through 17 drafts before Jefferson felt it was good enough to show to Franklin and Adams. And they rewrote it some more.

"We've got to get rid of this notion that a child's first draft should be neat and clean so they can put it on the wall with a doily for parents' night. This premature insistence that you have to be able to spell the best words in your vocabulary is one of the great inhibitors of adults. You should just write it the way it sounds until you see it in a book.

"We let the children in on the secret from day one that the way the word is spelled in a book is what they're going to get eventually. They don't have a problem with that."

Children who have completed the program have been more enthusiastic and eager to learn to read and write than their counterparts in more traditional courses of study. Perhaps this is partly due to the nature of a computer, which is endlessly patient. In situations where a human teacher may become frustrated and show impatience to the student, the computer simply repeats instructions as often as necessary, calmly and without a hint of disapproval. One teacher using the program believes that her students begin by treating Writing to Read like a video game. As they get more involved in the program, it becomes a learning game. Perhaps it is this atmosphere that promotes the competence that Writing to Read seems to produce in its graduates.

Adapted from Ron White, "Writing to Read: 25,000 Kids Help IBM Test Unconventional Learning Theory," *Softalk for the IBM PC*, June 1984. Copyright © 1984 by Ron White. Used by permission.

CHAPTER 15

SCIENCE, ENGINEERING, AND BUSINESS

SIMULATING NUCLEAR ACCIDENTS

The Brookhaven National Laboratory's nuclear reactor towers above the trees of its bucolic Long Island setting, visible for miles around. But the reactor is not the Brookhaven Department of Nuclear Energy's only sophisticated research tool: It also has some familiar IBM PCs. Dr. Wolfgang Wulff and his group of scientists use several of the PCs, with customized software, to simulate possible nuclear power plant accidents. The nuclear reactor behavior simulation has real life-protecting value, because its ultimate use is to prevent a nuclear power plant accident. It can also help designers alter plant architecture and procedures to minimize the dangers of a critical situation.

Most procedures at a nuclear power plant are automated. In the event of an accident, many automated steps occur in rapid succession: Pumps are shut off, valves are closed, and emergency coolant is injected. The plant's computer system also eliminates unlikely possibilities. That is, it gives the operator only two or three possible explanations for what has occurred. The operator can then call up the emergency procedures for these situations on the screen.

"At the Three Mile Island nuclear plant," according to Dr. Wulff, referring to the accident that occurred there on March 28, 1979, "a lot of these things were automatic, but then 6 hours later there were still the high pressures and high temperatures. It was a condition that we hadn't seen before, and we didn't have the procedures on how to recover. When you are in a situation that no one has thought of before—one not written up in the procedures—that's when you need a computer simulation." The status of the plant at the critical moment can be input into the simulation program and the effects of alternative actions simulated.

Fortunately, a plant does not have to be in such dire straits before a simulation program is useful. By running simulations of a plant as it is currently designed and administered, plant managers can consider possible preventive measures. "Based on the results," explains Dr. Wulff, "a plant may do what is called backfitting, but that costs a lot of money. Many times plants make administrative changes or change the control system to create another safety trip." Like the simulators used in training pilots, a nuclear reactor simulator is an invaluable training tool for plant staff.

Calculation programs, rather than full-fledged simulation programs, have been available for some time, but these programs may take several months or a year to arrive at an answer to a problem. According to Dr. Wulff, it took groups of researchers 3 months to compute how to fix the reactor after the accident at Three Mile Island. Such intensive effort, which requires long number-crunching programs, is very expensive. After Three Mile Island, researchers began exploring different approaches.

The Brookhaven group began looking for smaller, special-purpose computers. They chose the AD 10, built by Applied Dynamics International. These computers run a customized simulation program called High Speed Interactive Plant Analyzer (HIPA), written by the Brookhaven team to simulate a boiling water nuclear reactor. When simulating a reactor, some laboratories examine thermal stresses or the nuclear physics (neutronics) interactions. Brookhaven concentrates on hydraulics—the behavior of the coolant and the resulting temperatures—so it uses a simplified model of the neutronics.

Even with this simplifying set of assumptions, a simulation program is extraordinarily complex. HIPA is dynamically solving the conservation laws of mass, momentum, and energy; integrating some 250 differential equations; and computing 4,000 parameters. It requires the combined computer power of two AD 10s, a PDP-11 minicomputer, and an IBM PC/XT.

The input data to HIPA (called transients) are the elements in a nuclear plant's processes that are temporary and can be altered. For instance, steam flow and pressure are both transients that the system can alter by opening or closing valves. When the simulation is run, two of these transients are set to a steady state. Then an element such as a valve is varied to see how it affects the transients. HIPA produces graphs of the output, labeling the axes and scaling the graphs to fit on the PC monitor screen. In one run, a valve was set to remain stuck in the open position. The graph of the power line rose and continued upward until it went off the top of the screen, demonstrating vividly that HIPA is a safe way to simulate a nuclear power plant accident.

Adapted from Stephanie Stallings, "Simulating Nuclear Accidents," *Personal Computing,* May 28, 1985. Copyright © 1985 Ziff-Davis Publishing Company.

CHAPTER 15
501

LOOKING AHEAD

The purpose of this chapter is to outline a few ways that computers are used for scientific and engineering applications. As you'll notice, most of the engineering applications take place in business settings. (If you've read Chapter 11, you've also seen other examples of how businesses use computers to manage their operations and plan for the future.) In the first section of this chapter, you'll see how scientists use computers for planning, decision making, and control purposes. Then you'll see how engineers and others use computers for computer-aided design, computer-aided manufacturing, and operational and traffic control. The information in this chapter will enable you to:

- Summarize some of the ways that scientists are using computers to plan and control research activities
- Give examples of how computers may be used in computer-aided design and computer-aided manufacturing
- Outline how computers may be used in operational and traffic control applications

CHAPTER OUTLINE

LOOKING AHEAD
COMPUTERS IN THE SCIENCES
Planning and Decision-Making Applications
Control Applications
COMPUTERS IN ENGINEERING AND BUSINESS
Computer-Aided Design Applications
Robotics and Computer-Aided Manufacturing Applications
Control Applications
Feedback and Review 15
LOOKING BACK

MODULE 4

COMPUTERS IN THE SCIENCES

Thousands of scientific applications are processed each day on the world's computers. We'll look at a few of these here in the important areas of *planning and decision making* and *control*.

Planning and Decision-Making Applications

You saw in Chapter 3 that the *planning* function looks to the future; to plan is to decide in advance on a future course of action. The **planning steps** followed by scientists, business managers, and others in arriving at rational decisions are (1) identify the problem or opportunity, (2) gather and analyze relevant facts, (3) determine suitable hypotheses or alternatives, (4) evaluate and select the most appropriate hypothesis or alternative, and (5) follow up on the decision(s). As you'll see in the following applications, computers are helping scientists perform one or more of these steps every day.

Weather Forecasting *Simulation* is the art of building and testing a computer model of some real or theoretical object or system. Unlike the scaled-down physical models of cars or airplanes that people build, most **computer models** are expressed as symbols that lend themselves to quantitative analysis. Many factors can be entered into these computer models, where they can then be examined under a variety of experimental conditions. By interacting with a model to explore the consequences of various input factors, scientists can gain insight into how real or hypothetical systems respond to these factors. For example, a mathematical weather model has been in existence for decades with equations that describe how changes in such atmospheric factors as air pressure, temperature, humidity, and velocity of the air occur over time.

Our thanks to the experts who supplied the detailed information upon which this chapter was built: William Bulgren and N. D. Francis of the Computer Science Department, University of Kansas, Lawrence.

Monitoring the weather is an exceptionally challenging task of database management, because huge amounts of fast-changing data must be processed quickly and organized for easy access as well. (© Hank Morgan/Photo Researchers)

Scientists knew back in 1911 that the weather could be predicted by solving these equations. If pressure, temperature, and other factors are simultaneously known at many points around the world, the equations can accurately predict what these quantities will be an hour or a day later. Weather stations around the world can make the necessary measurements for these calculations, but the model requires a tremendous number of computations. Without a computer, these calculations required months of work—and there was obviously no reason to predict the weather if it was already over!

When computers became available, however, mathematicians and meteorologists reexamined their predictive model. Although the first results of model use were crude, by 1962 a useful system was in routine operation. This early system used about 2,000 measurement reports to establish the initial conditions, and then a large computer required 1 hour to make a 1-day prediction. Forecast programs today are more sophisticated and more accurate than the early ones, but there's still room for considerable improvement. In fact, the current programs that tax the capabilities of the world's largest computers are crude models of what meteorologists would use if only more powerful computers were available. Our supercomputers still aren't super enough.

Weather data are collected by federal government scientists several times each day from thousands of input points scattered around the world. The data come from aircraft, Coast Guard ships, ocean buoys, ground stations, and space satellites. These data are processed at a Suitland, Maryland, computer center. Processed forecast information is distributed by the National Weather Service and generally reaches the public by radio and television broadcasts and newspaper accounts.

Water Planning A nationwide system of computers is helping U.S. Geological Survey scientists find answers to problems of water supply. For example, what major alterations of a river's flow pattern will occur if an electric power company builds a dam for generating purposes? What will be the effect on sewage and waste assimilation, on aquatic life, and on other current users of the water? Computer simulation models are helping planners arrive at answers to such questions.

Another system, designed by scientists at the Soil Conservation Service of the Department of Agriculture, uses radio signals to relay data on snowfall and rainfall from sensors located at 160 remote stations in 10 western states to central data collection sites in Boise, Idaho, and Ogden, Utah. The data are processed by minicomputers at these sites, forwarded to the Conservation Service's Portland, Oregon, center, and then distributed to farmers, ranchers, and government irrigation agencies in the 10-state area. The data on the amount of snowfall in the mountains are important to these agricultural planners because about 85 percent of the annual water supply in the 10-state area comes from melting snow.

Agricultural Planning A team of scientists from the Department of Agriculture, the National Oceanic and Atmospheric Administration (NOAA), and the National Aeronautics and Space Administration (NASA) is using *Landsat* earth-orbiting satellites to view the croplands containing wheat and other grains in such important growing regions as the United States, the Soviet Union, Canada, Australia, and India. The satellite photos (Figure 15-1) allow these scientists to estimate the acreage under cultivation, and the worldwide weather data supplied by NOAA during the growing season permit them to

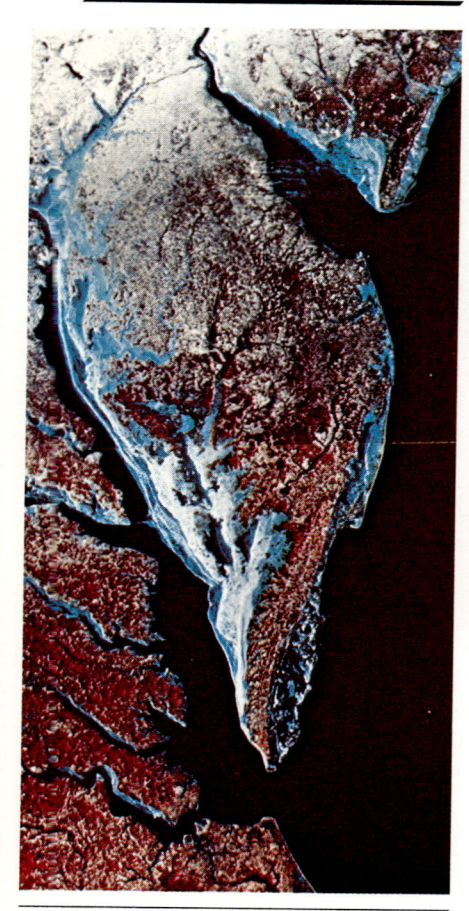

FIGURE 15-1

Data from satellite photos are fed into computers and analyzed for planning and research purposes. (*left*) Two Landsat satellite photos are combined to show the ice patterns that have formed along the western shore of the Delmarva Peninsula. Factory smoke from the northeastern shore of the peninsula is also visible as the winds drive the pollution eastward. (*right*) An infrared photo of the Finger Lakes region of New York was taken from an altitude of over 500 miles by NASA's Earth Resources Technology Satellite. Healthy crops and vegetation show up bright red. Areas with sparse vegetation appear light pink. Clear water is black. Lake Ontario is at the top left of the picture, and the Finger Lakes appear at the bottom of the image. (Courtesy National Aeronautics and Space Administration)

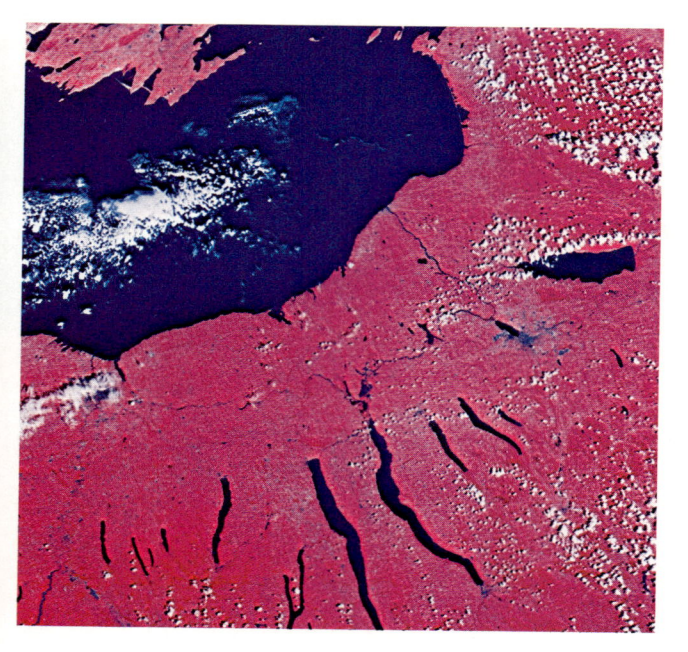

develop computer-based crop yield models and make harvest predictions. An accurate prediction of worldwide crop yields is vital to those who must make decisions about domestic agricultural policy.

Other Satellite Applications Computers at NASA's Goddard Space Flight Center at Greenbelt, Maryland, reduce telemetry data from orbiting scientific satellites into proper form for study and analysis by scientists. Instruments in satellites perform experiments and transmit the results to earth. The data are received from worldwide tracking stations and are processed, and the information is forwarded to scientists located throughout the United States, Canada, and Europe. This information, in turn, adds to the storehouse of scientific knowledge, leads to plans for additional space experiments, and serves to reinforce or change existing scientific theories.

Scientists at the Laboratory for Applications of Remote Sensing at Purdue University have used a computer to analyze the multispectral scanner data obtained by Landsat satellites passing over the Great Lakes region of the United States and Canada. Maps produced as a result of this analysis pinpoint industrial and agricultural areas that seem to be dumping pollutants into the lakes. Once pollution sources are identified, plans can be made to minimize further environmental damage.

University of Toledo scientists have used data from NASA's Orbiting Astronomical Observatory to "see" more stars than can be observed from earth. Material floating in space between stars has been studied for clues to the possible existence of life elsewhere in the universe. Other studies are seeking to determine the nature of stars and their locations in space. Complex simulation models of the universe can predict the lives of stars. Rapid advances have been made in the field of astronomy in the past two decades, and much of the current work in the field couldn't be attempted without computers. At the University of Toledo, for example, one job containing 7.2

billion calculations would have taken 250 operators at desk calculators 30 years to complete (working 8-hour days). A computer did the job in 10 hours.

Applications in Medical Research   The computer is a research tool that's helping medical scientists gain insights into the following:

1   *Causes and prevention of stroke.*   A stroke usually occurs suddenly and is due to a disruption in the normal flow of blood in the brain. Statistical research to correlate many of the factors suspected of causing stroke has been conducted by the Iowa Heart Association. By isolating the most important causes of stroke, scientists hope to educate the public on possible preventive measures.

2   *Ways drugs affect people.*   Dr. Peter Witt has conducted studies at North Carolina's Department of Mental Health to determine how such drugs as LSD and mescaline affect the web-weaving ability of spiders. A computer compared the webs produced by drugged spiders against the characteristics of a normal web. Results of the comparisons were used to gain insight into the possible effects of drugs on the human brain and body. Other studies have focused on drug side effects. Although every new drug is tested extensively before it's placed on the market, unexpected side effects can still occur. Combining a new drug with other medications and administering the drug to patients in situations not encountered during the testing period can produce surprising results. Some scientists are interested in using computers to gather data on the experiences of many physicians with a particular drug. Computer analyses may then reveal a relationship between drug use and unfortunate results. Tragedies such as the one that occurred some years ago when a number of babies were born deformed because their mothers were given thalidomide during pregnancy could thus be reduced.

3   *Ways in which the brain stores and retrieves information.*   At UCLA's Brain Research Institute, computer analysis of brain waves has improved the understanding of brain function and has made it possible to analyze subtle patterns that indicate information transfer.

4   *Possibility of bringing sight to the blind.*   University of Utah scientists are working on an electronic vision system that, it's hoped, will enable blind people to ''see'' well enough to move about safely and read ordinary printed material. Images from a tiny electronic camera in an artificial eye would be scanned by a microprocessor (located in the frame of the user's glasses), which then computes a pattern and sends the data to an array of electrodes implanted in the blind person's brain to re-create the image.

5   *Study of the defects of the inner ear.*   A series of mathematical equations has been developed by IBM scientists at the Ear Research Institute of Los Angeles to learn more about hearing defects that originate in the nearly inaccessible cochlea, or inner ear. A computer model uses the equations to simulate experiments that could not be performed on the cochlea itself.

Looking much like a colorful snail, this computer-generated image of the human cochlea, or inner ear, was developed to simulate research experiments that cannot be performed on live humans. (Courtesy Frank R. Galey, PhD./The House Ear Institute)

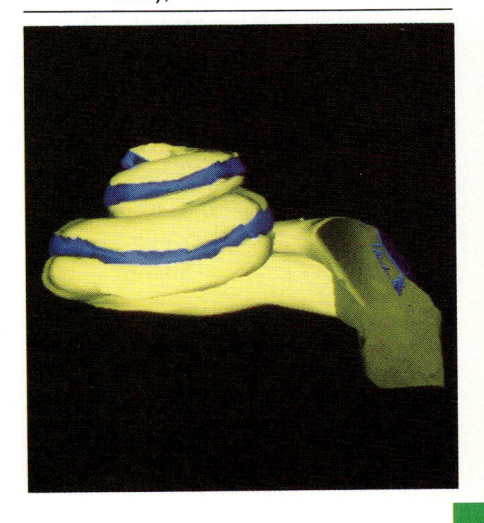

Applications in the Social Sciences   Computers are also used by social scientists to:

1   *Gain economic insights.*   The Federal Reserve System is the nation's central banker. A member of its board of governors may use a computer in researching the tradeoffs between inflation and unemployment at given times before making monetary policy judgments. Or the governor may use the computer to research the concentration of banks in a particular market area before making a decision on a merger application. Federal Reserve economists have worked to develop and refine a large-scale research model of the U.S. economy. This model may help social scientists gain new insights into the economy's structure; it may also prove valuable in predicting what the possible effects of alternative monetary policies may be.

2 *Plan political campaigns.* Computers are used to plan and schedule campaign activities to make the best use of a candidate's time and resources. Campaign trips are planned using concepts developed by transportation organizations to eliminate unnecessary travel and ensure that key geographical regions are given effective coverage. Electronic mail/message systems are used by presidential and vice presidential candidates traveling their separate ways to ensure that there's no conflict in their public statements. And the results of frequent random samples of the voting public are transmitted to a computer by campaign workers so that political scientists can quickly detect shifts in voter opinion and gauge the effects of an opponent's campaign.

3 *Support social welfare and urban planning.* In *social welfare* agencies, as in other organizations, computers can improve administrative planning and decision making. For example, in the administration of one social welfare agency—Family Service of Metropolitan Detroit—computer-processed data have speeded up administrative analysis and improved program planning. Caseloads of social workers, size and composition of families, family stress caused by divorces and unemployment—all this information is used by Detroit social scientists to analyze the effects of possible changes in agency policies and services. Social welfare simulations have also been designed for planning purposes. At New York University, for example, Dr. Isidor Chein has built a model to estimate the effects of housing developments and social welfare efforts on juvenile delinquency. The model incorporates dozens of socioeconomic factors, and gauges the quality of the living units in hundreds of neighborhoods. The incidence of delinquency in a neighborhood is compared with the number and type of public housing units and with existing social programs. The model can thus give planners an idea of what may happen to the delinquency rate if more public housing is built or if a mix of social programs is implemented. And *urban* planners have used simulation techniques to tackle traffic congestion and land-use problems. For example, urban scientists use computers to simulate *traffic flow patterns*. Variables such as the expected distribution of trips, the type of vehicles used, and the routes traveled are analyzed to plan proposed roads and use existing roads in the most efficient way. All too often in the past, urban planners began road construction without considering recreational, housing, and other alternative land-use priorities. The need to consider alternative uses of land as a vital input of traffic models has, in fact, resulted in the development of local and regional *land-use models*. Included in land-use simulation equations are future expectations about population, employment, number of households, income, and distribution of available land for commercial and residential purposes. In the Washington metropolitan area, such a computer land-use system is used for planning. This system receives data from continuously updated files and is of value to adjoining governments as well as Washington planners.

Control Applications

The control function is a follow-up to planning; it's a check on past and current performance to see if planned goals are being achieved. The **control steps** followed by scientists and others are (1) set standards, (2) measure actual performance, (3) compare actual performance with standards, and (4) take appropriate control action. Computers help scientists perform these steps, as you'll see in the following applications.

Pollution Control   Scientists in federal, state, and local government agencies use computers to evaluate and control the levels of pollution. To cite just one example from the many that exist, the Empire State System of New York collects water and air data from monitoring stations located at critical sites around the state. Data from the stations are automatically forwarded to a central computer. Each air-monitoring station reports every 15 minutes, and each water station transmits once every hour. Upon receiving transmitted data, the computer edits the message, sends any necessary operating instructions to the station, and compares edited information to acceptable environmental standards. If standards aren't met, the computer sends an appropriate alarm message to either the Air Resources or Pure Waters Division of the Department of Environmental Conservation. Corrective action may then be taken.

Conservation of Natural Resources   Scientists and engineers have also developed computer systems that help conserve natural resources. California's State Water Project, for example, is designed to conserve water by moving it from abundant areas in northern California to needy areas in the south and west. Water is moved hundreds of miles through a network of canals, tunnels, gates, pipelines, pumping stations, and power plants. All these facilities are monitored by computers located at five remote control centers. In an emergency, a control center quickly shuts down the affected part of the system. For example, if a canal is broken by an earthquake, check gates in the affected section are closed immediately to prevent water loss.

South Carolina scientists use a computer to identify, track, and help conserve rare or irreplaceable natural and human-made resources in more than 400 areas across the state. These areas range from the breeding ground of the rare loggerhead sea turtle near the Atlantic coast to scattered stands of virgin timber. And scientists at the Ministry of Natural Resources in Ontario, Canada, use a computer system to predict the location and time of forest fires. A network of lightning sensors throughout the province records the number of lightning discharges within a 20-mile radius. With a formula that considers forest inflammability and weather conditions, it's then possible to predict the number and location of expected fires. Early detection is, of course, important in controlling fire damage.

Using a computer program called SPLASH to simulate ocean current flows, scientists can identify safe offshore dumping sites that will not send pollutants flowing into areas where fish breed. (© Ira Block/The Image Bank)

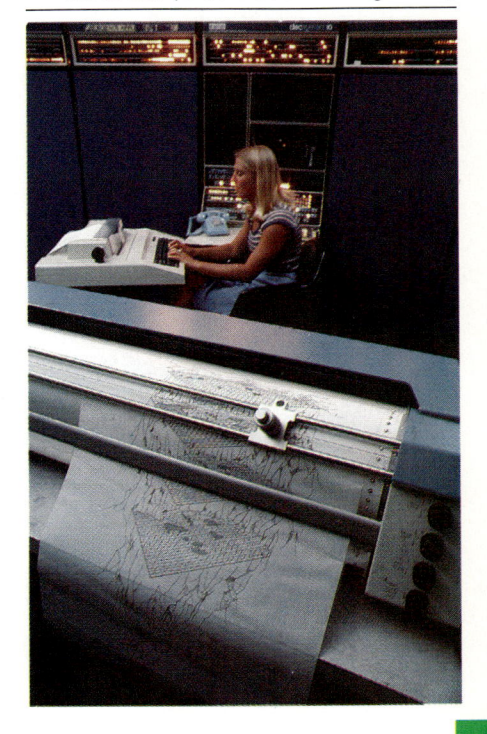

COMPUTERS IN ENGINEERING AND BUSINESS

Computer-Aided Design Applications

Computer-aided design (CAD) refers to the integration of computers and graphics-oriented software in order to automate the design process. A typical CAD system includes a computer, a color graphics display unit, a printer and/or a plotter, and a variety of input devices such as keyboards, light pens, and graphics tablets. The CAD software records the input data in a data base and is able to manipulate these facts interactively and display the results on a graphics screen. This interactive human-machine capability is important because, as you saw in Chapter 3, the design process consists of defining the specifications for an item (such as functional requirements and cost and size limits), creating a preliminary design, and then redesigning, testing, and developing the item until the specifications are satisfied and it's ready for production. In short, CAD systems accept a model of the item in graphic or numerical form. The designer then studies and improves the item and ultimately identifies a design that's suitable for implementation. For example, a CAD system allows an automobile designer to check the tire clearances of an automobile body in motion, evaluate possible interior features to improve driver comfort, and detect sources of vibrations and the effects of repositioning engine mounts to reduce these vibrations.

As relatively low-cost CAD systems are now available, many smaller businesses are switching to this technology to remain competitive by producing better designs in less time and at lower cost. Let's look now at a few CAD applications in *structural, architectural,* and *industrial engineering* and in the design of *integrated circuits* and *machined parts.*

This engineer is using a CAD system to work out the most efficient way for a robot welder to weld a car body as it moves past the robot's station. (Courtesy Computervision)

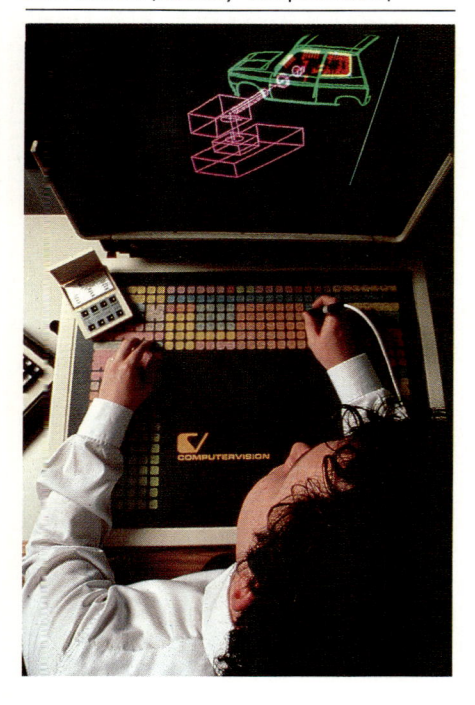

Structural Engineering   Stress analysis is required in the design of such things as buildings, bridges, airplanes, and ships, where adequate strength is critical to the design. The **finite element method (FEM)** is the name given to a technique used by engineers to analyze stress. In this technique, the structure to be analyzed is geometrically represented by a mesh of regular interconnecting elements. The position and interconnection of the mesh elements, the structural material used, and the loads on the structure are combined to generate a set of structural equations. By solving these equations, engineers can predict the strength and behavior of the structure. Without the aid of computers, however, it's almost impossible to cope with the amount of data produced by the mesh generation process.

The FEM approach is widely used in the automobile industry to optimize structural design. A simple model of a car is first used for FEM analysis. Later, a more complete model is developed to produce a detailed analysis of mechanical strength in critical areas. Structural engineering software packages are available for larger computer systems, and structural engineers regularly use several low-cost mini- and micro-based FEM packages.

Architectural Engineering   Many architects are now using CAD systems to plan towns, design buildings, arrange buildings on a site, or organize rooms within a building. Architects communicate with surveyors, mechanical engineers, and structural engineers through the use of a set of two-dimensional

CHAPTER 15

509

Architectural CAD systems turn a two-dimensional drawing into a three-dimensional on-screen model, which the architect can turn and move about on a computer-generated building site to find the most efficient placement for the location. (Courtesy Intergraph Inc.)

line drawings, or "blueprints." With the help of a CAD system, an architect can draw a high-rise office block on a graphics screen and then later rearrange floor plans, air ducts, or wiring plans by moving lines and objects around. Creative design requires both two- and three-dimensional views of an object, and a CAD system can produce a three-dimensional (3D) model from two-dimensional (2D) drawings. Realistic views of buildings and their surroundings can thus be simulated, and multiple views can be displayed on a screen. The designer can then use these views to evaluate alternative designs within the constraints imposed by planning regulations and user requirements. Design data on building structure, interior layout, and the routing of wiring and plumbing lines can be stored in different layers in a computer data base. Design changes by one architect can be used to update the data base, and these changes are then available to the other architects and engineers who are working on the project.

Several architectural CAD systems, including some that run on personal computers (pc's), are available today. It's expected that time-consuming and expensive architectural drafting procedures will be largely automated in the years ahead. Construction of elaborate scale models will then often be replaced by dramatic pictures presented on color display screens. And cost estimates, lists of materials needed, project schedules, and construction reports will likely be generated directly from the CAD data base.

Industrial Engineering   **Industrial engineering** deals with the design, implementation, and improvement of integrated systems of people, materials, and equipment. A main objective of industrial engineering is to optimize the productivity of people and machines. In manufacturing businesses, industrial engineers specify how a product is to be made, the layout of the workplace, the methods to be used at each stage of production, and the work measurement standards to be employed. Computer-aided industrial engineering systems are designed to help engineers perform these tasks. For example, CAD systems allow engineers to design each production task interactively and determine the most efficient manufacturing methods to use. Data about the tools and people available for use and a 3D model of the workplace can also be considered in the design effort. The efficiencies made possible by computer-aided industrial engineering systems are helping to keep many manufacturing businesses profitable in today's fiercely competitive marketplace.

VLSI Chip Design You'll recall from Chapter 1 that many electronic components and connections are packaged in a single integrated circuit chip. Only a few components were placed in early circuits—an example of small-scale integration. But component density increased over the years so that now *very large scale integration* (VLSI) is possible. VLSI technology now permits the placement of over 500,000 transistors in an electronic circuit design that fits into a single tiny package.

The greater the circuit density of a VLSI chip, the longer the time needed to perfect its design, and the greater its design cost. Chip producers are naturally interested in reducing design time and expense, and these results can be achieved only through the use of powerful CAD systems. Such systems allow designers to analyze, draw, and edit circuits and check design rules and circuit layout procedures. Special CAD programs are used to check for design errors in circuit networks containing thousands of components and connections. The layout of these networks is the most time-consuming stage in the VLSI chip design process. Minimizing the chip area is still a human function, but CAD systems are widely used to verify the feasibility of proposed layouts. After a chip design has been completed, CAD systems are also used to plan for the placement of chips on circuit boards and for the routing of the necessary connections between chips.

3D Parts by Solid Modeling The design process required to produce mechanical parts begins with conceptual ideas and sketches, followed by detailed

Powerful, specialized CAD systems enable designers to speed the process of designing and checking integrated circuit chips that pack half a million transistors or more onto a thumbnail-sized chip. (© Alvis Upitis/The Image Bank)

drawings, design analysis, and final drawings, and concludes with prototype construction, revision, and final manufacture. Earlier CAD programs produced computerized versions of detailed drawings to speed up the drawing process. But humans still had to interpret these drawings to generate the necessary manufacturing information. Today's programs take over additional design steps. In these **solid modeling programs,** a machined part is represented as a 3D object, complete with volume and geometric information. The computerized solid model can be used to analyze stress capabilities and other design characteristics of the part. The model can also be used to generate tool paths for machining and fabricating operations, and it can supply programming details needed by robots and other computer-controlled machines that produce parts to design specifications.

The use of a solid modeling system may eliminate the need to construct prototypes because design errors can be detected and corrected by experimenting with the model on a graphics screen. Solid modeling programs for design and manufacturing are currently restricted to a few types of mechanical parts, but their capabilities will certainly increase in the near future.

Robotics and Computer-Aided Manufacturing Applications

Robotics refers to the study of robot technology, and you saw in Chapter 3 that a *robot* is a computer-controlled machine used in manufacturing. The operations performed by a robot can be changed simply by changing its program of instructions. Businesses already use thousands of robots to perform tasks that are unpleasant, unhealthy, or monotonous. Robots appear in many shapes and sizes. For example, an industrial robot may be a spray-painting device as big as the cars it paints, or it may be a small mobile delivery cart that distributes parts or mail.

In addition to a computer, most industrial robots also have an arm, wrist, and hand or gripper. The arm is powered by hydraulic, electric, or pneumatic methods. Most robots are built to move in five or six independent ways, but

This factory robot picks up kitchen sink stampings, moves them over a fixed polishing brush until every corner gleams, and passes them on to the next production station. Because it lacks sensors, it must be reprogrammed before it can polish a part that is of a different shape or size. (Courtesy ASEA Robotics, Inc.)

WINDOW 15-1

A ROBOT SUB ACHIEVES NEW DEPTHS

When an Air India jumbo jet crashed off the coast of Ireland in mid-1985, the deep-diving submarine that retrieved the voice recorder from the wreckage was really a robot of many talents. Most of the time, this robot is busy repairing and maintaining undersea telephone cables, but it has also gone down to photograph a crashed helicopter off Norfolk, Va., and to locate and examine rockets that sank off Cape Canaveral, Fla.

To retrieve the Air India flight recorder, the remote-controlled craft, known as Scarab, plunged to 6,700 feet and scored the most impressive achievement in its 5-year operation. Two Scarabs searched the crash site to help investigators determine whether the plane was destroyed by a bomb.

Although many small specialized submarines are used regularly in scientific exploration and offshore oil operations, they normally have crews and cannot stay submerged for long. Few of them can go to depths of more than a mile or maneuver over extensive stretches of ocean floor. Scarab, for Submersible Craft for Assisting Repair and Burial, was developed by Bell Telephone Laboratories to overcome these limitations. It was modeled after the Navy submersible Curv, which is used to recover torpedoes and other ordnance.

The telecommunications industry wanted a durable and versatile craft to deal with the costly problem of damage to undersea cables, primarily from the trawling lines of fishing vessels on the continental shelves. Cables are now buried at least 3 feet under the sea floor as protection from such damage. But once the cables were buried, there was a problem of finding them and retrieving them for repairs.

This was the need that Scarab addressed. The two Scarabs weigh 6,300 pounds and are the size of a small truck. They have been in operation since 1980. Scarab was designed to operate down to depths of 6,000 feet. AT&T engineers allowed for a comfortable margin of safety, so there was little doubt that the craft could withstand the pressures of 6,700 feet, where the plane wreckage lay. The craft could probably descend 9,000 feet.

The Scarab that recovered the voice recorder was operated remotely from a control room on its mother vessel, a French cable ship. A 10,000-foot umbilical cable linked the two, carrying electrical power and commands to Scarab and feeding back data and television signals to the ship.

According to a description of Scarab operations published in the Bell Laboratories Record, three people monitor and control Scarab's every move. One person operates the propulsion controls, firing electrical and hydraulic thrusters to maneuver the craft. Another operates the craft's television cameras and jointed mechanical arms. A third person tends the craft's minicomputer.

In this manner, Scarab investigated the corridor 10 miles by 1 mile where investigators thought the plane's wreckage would be. At first, Scarab had no success in locating the plane. Scarab's sonar "ear" failed to pick up any of the pinging signals that should have been emanating from the plane's two flight data and voice recorders. Only after engineers made a fine adjustment in the sonar, permitting it to detect signals at a slightly higher frequency, did the robot begin hearing signals. Then it moved closer, maneuvering on sledlike runners, and saw the recorder with its television "eyes."

After the Scarab grasped the "black box" with its mechanical claw, controllers on the surface ship winched the craft up from the bottom. It was immediately submerged again to look for the other recorder.

"Scarab never gets tired," the Bell Laboratories Record says. "It will work as long as its operators want and isn't vulnerable to life-threatening hazards, as human divers would be. It can go deeper, stay longer and do a job in less time."

Adapted from John Noble Wilford, "A Robot Sub Is Achieving New Depths," *The New York Times*, July 11, 1985. Copyright © 1985 by The New York Times Company. Reprinted by permission.

---

some have greater freedom of movement. The gripper at the end of the robot arm may use a vicelike mechanism, a vacuum suction cup, an electromagnet, or fingers and hooks.

Robots with vision, speech, and speech recognition capabilities are currently under development. These machines will respond to touch and will have sensors that can detect pressure, heat, magnetic fields, and acceleration forces. Such sensors will enable future robots to respond more flexibly and to perform tasks that aren't completely predictable. The automobile industry is the largest user of robots today, but the electronics industry is catching up.

The prices of robots are dropping, so the robot population will grow rapidly in the future. Let's look now at a few specific ways that robots are being used.

Flexible Manufacturing Systems As you saw in Chapter 3, a **fixed automation system** is one that follows a preset series of steps to produce a product. Such a system is effective if the product design is stable and spans a long time period and if the volume produced is high. But we're living now in a society where consumers want customized products, and as a result product life cycles are becoming shorter. Many businesses are thus finding that a **flexible manufacturing system (FMS),** which can be programmed to alter its procedures to suit different production needs, is the key to manufacturing profitability. The robots in an FMS can produce several parts simultaneously, and they can also be quickly reprogrammed to handle design changes and produce customized and individualized items in response to changes in the marketplace. For example, the heater and air conditioner control panels for Ford cars and trucks are assembled by an FMS that uses seven robots. The same assembly line is used to produce six different types of control panels, and the system can quickly change from producing one type to another. And the Yamazaki machine tool factory in Japan uses an FMS to produce 74 different parts. Only six people work in this unit during the day, and the night shift is unmanned.

Material Handling The purpose of **material handling** in a factory is to provide the right material at the right place and at the right time. The success of any automated manufacturing business depends on a material handling system that can accurately transport parts to the proper workstations. The movement of these parts from station to station may involve robots, conveyors, carts on tracks, or other automatic devices, and all these devices may be under computer control. The design of the material handling system should be such that the failure of one system component shouldn't halt the entire manufacturing process. For example, if one cart breaks down, there must be alternative paths available to reroute the remaining carts. Depending on the manufacturing process, the system must be able to manage hot, cold, heavy, fragile, or hazardous materials at different handling speeds.

Companies using computerized material handling systems include General Motors and Volvo, where computer-controlled carts carry automobile assemblies to and from workstations. In Finland, a handling system comprised of conveyors and robots moves fragile color picture tubes in a manufacturing plant. And at John Deere & Company, tractor parts are automatically retrieved from storage and forwarded by conveyors to any workstation with a few commands from a computer terminal.

Automated Assembly The assembly of discrete parts is usually done by humans today, but this operation can also be performed by robots that can be programmed to grasp, insert, and align various components in an assembly. In fact, robots are much better than humans at tasks such as stuffing printed circuit boards with components. But a current problem in robotic assembly is that robots usually aren't able to properly select randomly oriented components from a bin of parts. This limitation restricts the use of automated assembly today, but the development of cost-effective sensor-based robots will permit the widespread automation of assembly work in the future.

The "Factory of the Future"   The future automated factory is likely to use an FMS, an automated material handling system, and a complex computerized management information and control system. The computer obviously plays a central role in such a factory. The Fanuc factory at Mount Fuji in Japan has been called a prototype "factory of the future." This factory produces parts for robots and other machines. Some 250 components are manufactured in batches of 5 to 20 units using computer-controlled robots and machine tools. Materials are delivered from an automated warehouse to workstations by robot trucks. When the robots at the various workstations have finished their work, the material handling system once again takes over. Finished parts are automatically stored, and other materials are moved to their next destinations by the robot trucks. During the day shift, humans adjust machine tools, repair machines, and get raw materials ready for the other two shifts. Although the assembly of parts into complete machines isn't fully automated today, many of the other Fanuc factory operations are carried out without human intervention.

Control Applications

Let's look now at a few engineering and business control applications.

Operational Control   In an engineering or business setting, input resources in the form of materials, energy, labor, capital, and information are supplied, and goods or services are produced. An **operational control system** is one that monitors the day-to-day transformation of these input resources so that the output of goods or services meets preplanned quality and quantity standards. In some operational control systems, humans read instruments, take measurements, and adjust production methods so that output standards are maintained. In other control systems, however, computers monitor output quality and automatically make production adjustments when abnormalities are detected. Since computers can sense output deviations and react to those deviations much faster than any human and since computers don't get bored doing repetitive tasks while people do, it's no wonder that computers are now found in *process control, production control, inventory control,* and *space shuttle launch operations.*

Process control   Computerized **process control systems** are being used to monitor *continuously operating* facilities, such as oil refineries, chemical plants, steel and paper mills, and electric power generating stations. These processes are similar in that they convert a continuous flow of input materials and energy into output materials, products, converted energy, and waste. During the process, instruments measure such variables as pressure, temperature, flow rate, and so on. If the process is deviating from an acceptable standard, regulating devices are adjusted to bring the process back into control. In an **open-loop process control** operation, the computer records instrument readings, compares the readings against standards, and notifies process control personnel of needed manual adjustments in regulating devices.

In a more complex **closed-loop process control** operation (Figure 15-2), the computer receives measurements, makes comparisons, and, *in addition,* signals the regulatory devices to make the necessary changes. Of course, human operators may monitor the overall process and instruct the computer to

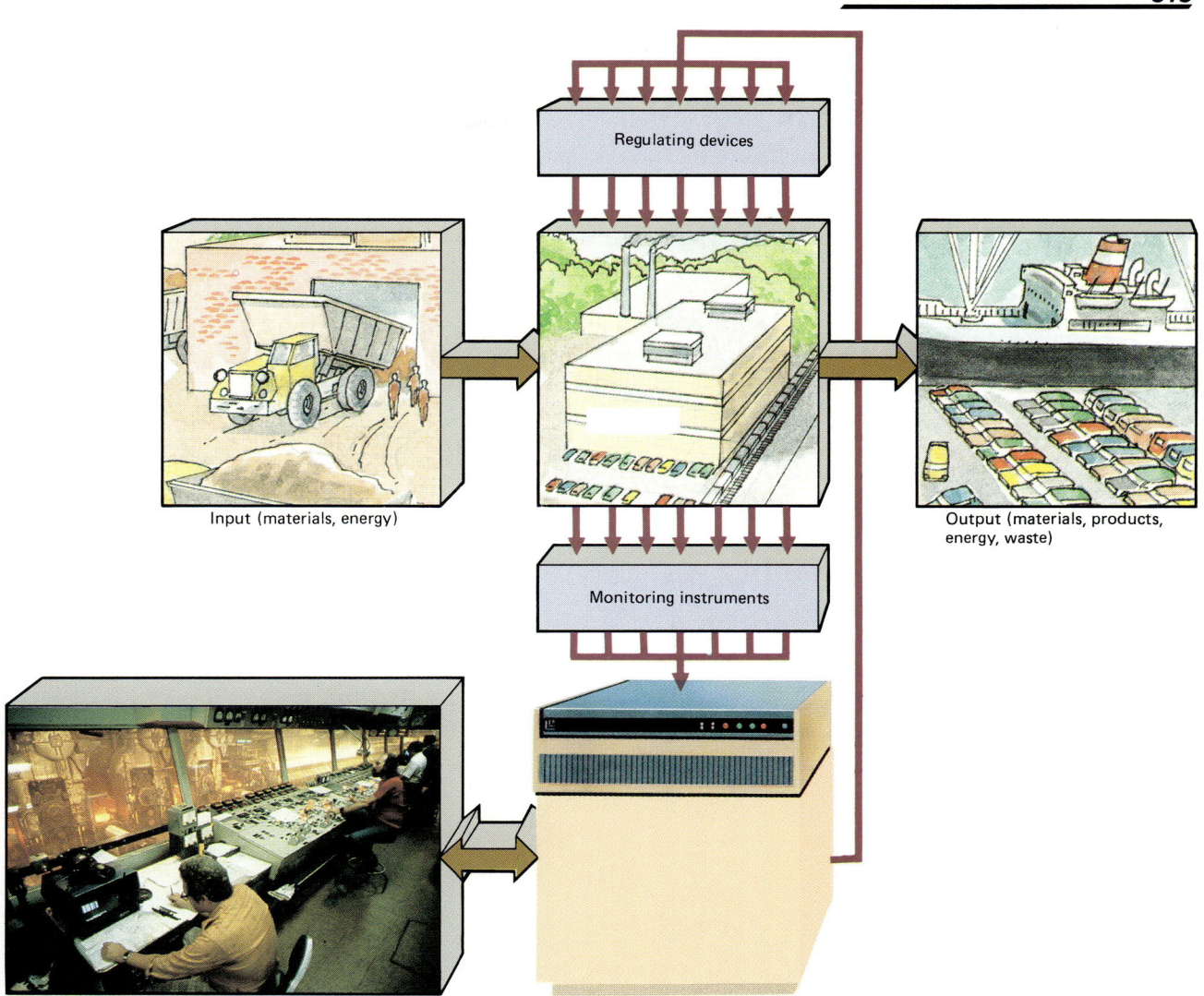

FIGURE 15-2

A computerized closed-loop process control operation. (© Fred Ward/Black Star, 1982)

make occasional changes in control parameters in particular situations, but the control operation is essentially automatic. Use of the computer in this way permits quicker-responding and more accurate control than would otherwise be possible. The use of minicomputers and microcomputers for process control applications is expanding rapidly.

Two process control examples are:

1 *The generation of electricity.* The Southern California Edison Company's Solar One project (Figure 15-3) collects solar energy that's used to turn water into the steam needed to run electric generators. A system of 1,818 reflective mirrors, each with a surface area of 432 square feet, concentrates the sun's rays on a central collector. Each of the mirror assemblies has a microprocessor-based controller that tracks the sun's position, and the entire

MODULE 4

516

FIGURE 15-3

Solar One's computer-controlled mirrors look toward the dawn's early light (*top*) and focus the midday sun's rays on the central energy collector (*bottom*). (Courtesy Southern California Edison Co.)

mirror field is controlled by a central computer. The operation of the system obviously depends on weather conditions. When excess heat is produced, it's stored in a tank filled with gravel, sand, and a special oil. On cloudy days, this stored heat is used to supplement the solar energy. Complete coordination between the collector system, the thermal storage system, and the power generating system is achieved through computer control.

2 *The production of chemical compounds.* A desired compound may be produced by mixing two chemicals at a particular temperature in a sealed vessel or reactor. The vessel's temperature is controlled by the circulation of hot and cold water through a surrounding jacket. The production process consists of a sequence of operations. The two chemicals are fed through valves into the vessel and stirred, while hot- and cold-water valves are adjusted to achieve and then maintain the desired temperature for a specified time period. The stirring stops and the vessel is cooled at the end of this

CHAPTER 15

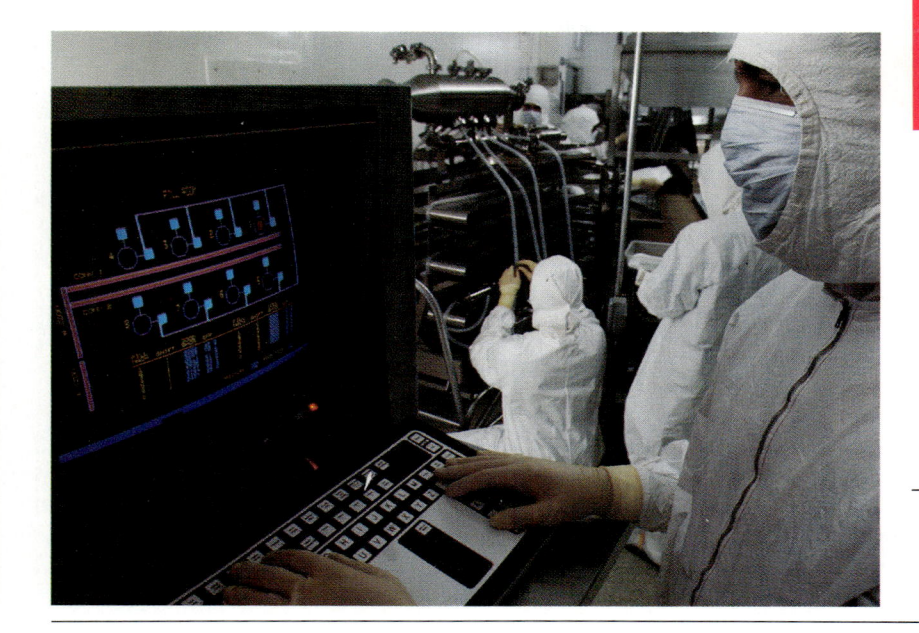

517

Computer-controlled production processes greatly increase productivity in drug manufacturing, where chemical compounds must be mixed precisely under sterile conditions. (© Arnold Zann/Black Star, 1984)

period, and the vessel contents are removed through a product exit valve. As you can see, the production process depends on a sequence of monitoring, decision making, and controlling operations, and these operations can be complex in large plants where many reaction vessels must be controlled. Manual control of such plants is usually out of the question, and computer control is a necessity.

Production control Manufacturing activities in a factory must be carefully planned, scheduled, and controlled. **Production control** is the activity that ensures that production schedules and deadlines are met and production costs are minimized. Computers play an important role in most production control systems in use today. For example, during the actual production in a factory, data entry stations may be used to transmit such facts as the time spent on an operation, the status of a machine tool, the size of a queue requiring work, or the need for machine setup or repair. The computer may then be used to compare the actual conditions against the production plan to determine if appropriate control action is required. A production control example from Chapter 5 is illustrated in Figure 15-4. In addition to controlling the overall production process, computers are often used to control individual production tools such as shapers, milling machines, and drill presses. Automated machine tools directed by computer-produced tapes or computerized machine tools controlled by programmable microcomputers can be used to produce precision parts meeting design specifications automatically. An early use of these **numerical control (NC) machines** was in the aircraft industry to cut precise and intricate airplane sections from solid metal. But NC machines are now employed for such dissimilar tasks as constructing prefabricated house walls, building robots, and producing hydraulic presses. Rapid operation and low scrap losses are two advantages of these automatic machines. And as we've seen, robots with built-in computers can sense the need for assembly tasks and can then take steps to perform those tasks. The use of robots rather

FIGURE 15-4

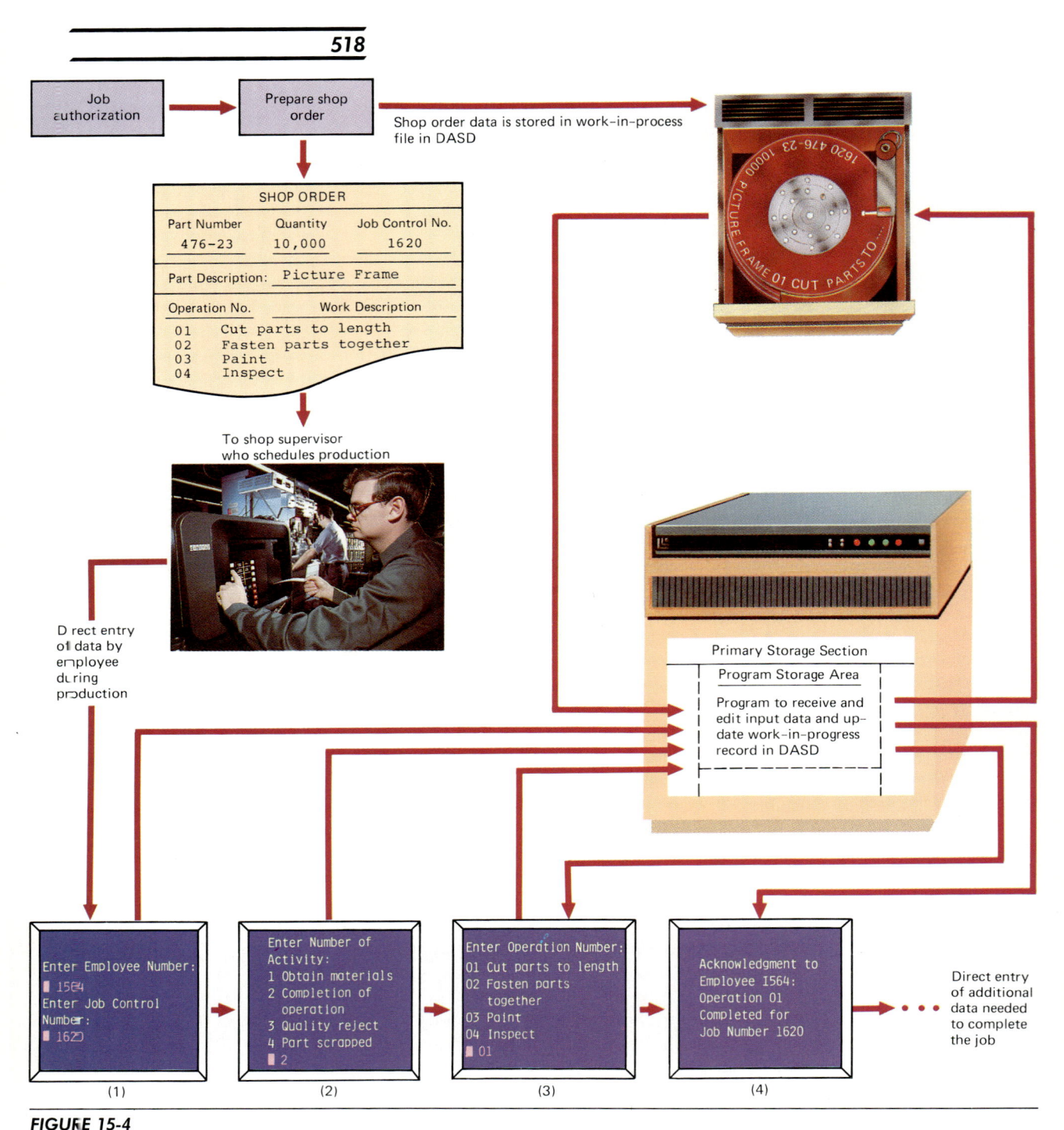

A computerized production control system.
(© Ellis Herwig/The Data Bank)

than humans may result in improved quality control. If a tired human welder on an automobile assembly line leaves out a couple of welds, a consumer gets a car that rattles. A tireless robot programmed to do the same welding operation may produce more consistent quality.

Inventory control **Inventory control** involves tracking and accounting for the parts and materials used in businesses and other organizations. In a factory, transaction recorders are often used to keep control of the inventory of parts and supplies used in production. Let's assume, for example, that an employee needs a dozen hinges to complete a job. The employee gets the hinges from a supply station and then keys such data as the part number, unit price, number of hinges taken, and the job number into the transaction recorder. These data are sent to the computer where they're checked for accuracy and then accepted to update the proper record in the inventory file. If an error is detected, a signal may be relayed back to the recording station.

Numerous other inventory control systems are used in businesses. For example, a computerized system is used by Martin-Brower Corporation, a Chicago-based distributor of paper products, nonperishable food products, and service supplies to drive-in restaurants specializing in fast service. Martin-Brower has 10 warehouses and a 5,000-item inventory to control. The system estimates future demand by computing current market trends and seasonal fluctuations for items like bags and cups. A forecast is prepared for each warehouse. The system also reports two or three times a week on the demand rate for each item in the inventory. Items that appear to be in short supply are flagged by the system, which also recommends reorder quantities. Business managers then make the reorder decision based on their knowledge of the situation.

Space shuttle launch control The reusable space shuttle provides an economical means of carrying people, equipment, and satellites to and from low earth orbit. Many space shuttle flights are likely to be scheduled each year in the future, and a computer-controlled launch processing system (LPS) is now used to oversee shuttle checkout and launch operations. The LPS continuously monitors the shuttle and the associated ground equipment that loads liquid fuels and measures temperatures, pressures, flow rates, valve and switch settings, and hundreds of other variables. Data are compared with predefined tolerance levels almost instantaneously, and abnormal conditions are displayed on color graphics screens. In many situations the LPS will automatically respond to abnormal conditions. In addition to its checkout and launch functions, LPS is also used to compute and display status reports on shuttle-related activities performed away from the launch site. The complexity of the system requires the use of about a hundred minicomputers and four mainframes for a typical shuttle launch.

Traffic Control Many businesses must provide service on demand to randomly arriving objects or people (such as automobiles pulling into a gas station, airplanes arriving at an airport, or customers entering a bank). This demand for service has to be balanced against the limited resources available to satisfy the demand. A **traffic control system** is one designed to satisfy this service demand in an efficient way. Computers are an integral part of the traffic control systems used to regulate transportation activities. For example, some of the first transportation control applications dealt with vehicle traffic on freeways. Computer-controlled signals at entrance ramps help motorists enter freeways. Sensors on the freeway transmit traffic information to a computer, which uses the information to locate gaps in the traffic flow. Such

Modern airliners like the Boeing 767 carry their own flight management computer systems, which can select the shortest, most fuel-efficient route to the destination, fly the airplane there, and even land it and taxi it to the terminal. The computer gives the pilots constant readouts of important information on the two CRT screens in the center of the instrument panel. (Courtesy Boeing Commercial Airplane Co.)

systems work well with skilled drivers, but they are less effective with inexperienced and timid drivers who often ignore them.

Another important transportation control system is used by the railroad industry to make efficient use of freight cars. Computer studies are used to relocate cars to areas where the future demand is likely to be high. And transportation control is also needed at sea where, in spite of sophisticated radar systems, ships are still involved in collisions each year. The problem is that radar doesn't differentiate obstacles in a ship's path. To overcome this problem of possibly mistaking an oil tanker for a buoy, computers with collision assessment programs have been installed on the bridges of ships. The assessment program can automatically differentiate between ships, debris, and land masses. In addition, the bridge computer can plan the ship's route to conserve fuel. Once the ship is in port, computers can help in controlling the warehousing, inventory, and distribution services offered to shippers. Finally, if you've read Chapter 8, you know that computer-aided control systems are indispensable tools for air traffic controllers at the world's airports.

FEEDBACK

FEEDBACK AND REVIEW 15

The following *matching questions* will test and reinforce your understanding of the material presented in this chapter. A number of terms are listed below. Place the letter of the appropriate term beside the definition or concept to which it belongs.

A) satellite B) CAD C) set standards D) simulation E) robotics F) FEM
G) inventory control H) industrial engineering I) computer models
J) production control K) identify problem L) pollution M) process control N) solid modeling O) weather forecasting P) FMS Q) robot

1. The first step in planning.
2. The art of building and testing a computer model of some real or theoretical object or system.
3. Many variables can be entered into ____, where they can then be examined under a variety of experimental conditions.
4. The current ____ programs that tax the capabilities of the world's largest computers are crude models of what meteorologists would use if only more powerful computers were available.
5. An earth-orbiting device that's used in many different types of scientific research.
6. The first step in the control function.
7. The Empire State System of New York is designed to monitor air and water ____.
8. An acronym for a general term that refers to the integration of computers and graphics-oriented software in order to automate the design process.
9. An acronym for a technique used by engineers to analyze stress.
10. The field of engineering that deals with the design, implementation, and improvement of integrated systems of people, materials, and equipment.
11. A machined part is represented in a ____ program as a 3D object, complete with volume and geometric information.
12. A general term that refers to the study of the types of computer-controlled machines that are often used in manufacturing.
13. A machine that usually has an arm, a wrist, and a hand.
14. The acronym for a manufacturing system that can be programmed to alter its procedures to suit different production needs.
15. A system that monitors continuously operating facilities.
16. The activity that ensures that production schedules are met and production costs are minimized.
17. The activity that involves tracking and accounting for the parts and materials used in organizations.

LOOKING BACK

1. Computers are helping scientists plan research efforts, make decisions, and control activities on a daily basis. Scientific planning and decision-making topics presented in this chapter include weather forecasting, water planning, agricultural planning, satellite usage, and applications in medical research and the social sciences. In many of these applications, scientists use simulation models to test real or theoretical objects or systems.

2. The control function is a follow-up to planning, and computers help scientists, engineers, and others measure the performance of an activity, compare the performance with preset standards, and then take appropriate control action. Scientific control topics presented in this chapter include pollution control and the conservation of natural resources.

3. Several computer-aided design (CAD) applications found in engineering and business settings have also been examined. These applications deal with structural, architectural, and industrial engineering topics and with the design of integrated circuits and machined parts.

4. Robotics is a general term that refers to the study of robot technology. Examples of how robots are being used in flexible manufacturing systems, material handling systems, and automated assembly work are presented in the chapter. The factory of the future is likely to utilize these concepts.

5. An operational control system in an engineering or a business setting is one that monitors the day-to-day transformation of input materials, energy, labor, and other resources so that the output of goods or services meets preplanned quality and quantity standards. Such systems are found in process and manufacturing industries. In process industries, for example, computerized process control systems monitor continuously operating facilities that refine oil, produce chemicals and steel, and generate electricity. The process control systems may be open- or closed-loop operations. And in manufacturing industries, computerized production control systems monitor the overall production process and control individual production tools. Inventory control systems are found in all types of operations, and a specialized operational control system is used to monitor space shuttle launches. Traffic control systems also use computers to balance the demand for service against the limited resources available to satisfy the demand.

CHAPTER 15

KEY TERMS AND CONCEPTS

planning steps 502
computer models 502
control steps 507
computer-aided design (CAD) 508
finite element method (FEM) 508
industrial engineering 509
solid modeling programs 511
robotics 511
fixed automation system 513
flexible manufacturing system (FMS) 513
material handling 513
operational control system 514
process control systems 514
open-loop process control 514
closed-loop process control 514
production control 517
numerical control (NC) machines 517
inventory control 519
traffic control system 519

TOPICS FOR REVIEW AND DISCUSSION

1. (a) What is the planning function? (b) What are the planning steps followed by scientists, engineers, managers, and others?
2. "Computer models are expressed as symbols that lend themselves to quantitative analysis." Discuss this statement and give three examples of computer models used by scientists.
3. Why aren't weather forecasting programs more accurate?
4. (a) How can computers help scientists make better use of water resources? (b) How can they help in agricultural planning?
5. Give three examples of ways that computers and satellites can be used to further scientific research efforts.
6. (a) How are computers being used in medical research? (b) In the social sciences?
7. (a) What is the control function? (b) What are the control steps followed by scientists, engineers, managers, and others?
8. (a) How can computers help control pollution? (b) How can they help conserve natural resources?
9. (a) What is computer-aided design (CAD)? (b) How are CAD techniques used in structural, architectural, and industrial engineering?
10. (a) How can CAD systems be used to design integrated circuits? (b) To design machined parts?
11. (a) What is robotics? (b) How can robots be used in a flexible manufacturing system? (c) In a material handling system?
12. What components are likely to be found in the "factory of the future"?
13. What's the difference between an open-loop and a closed-loop process control system?
14. How are computers used to monitor space shuttle launches?
15. "Computers are an integral part of the traffic control systems used to regulate transportation activities." Discuss this statement.

PROJECTS/ISSUES TO CONSIDER

1. Go to your library and identify five examples of computer usage in the sciences that weren't discussed in this chapter. Research these examples and present your findings to the class.

2. While you're at the library, look up five engineering/business examples of computer usage that weren't mentioned in this chapter. Research these examples and report your findings to the class.

ANSWERS TO FEEDBACK AND REVIEW SECTION

1. K   2. D   3. I   4. O   5. A   6. C   7. L   8. B   9. F   10. H   11. N   12. E
13. Q   14. P   15. M   16. J   17. G

A CLOSER LOOK

INFORMATION POWER

Although computers have been an indispensable part of the business world since the 1960s, they have traditionally been used to perform repetitive or tedious clerical tasks—reports, analyses, payroll, billing—that could be accomplished, if less quickly, by human employees. Now, however, companies are beginning to utilize computers in a variety of new and vastly different functions, serving markets and providing services that would be impossible without them. Linked to telecommunications, computers are making new steps in market research, customer service, and many other business applications.

These new applications are only partially due to technological advances. According to a *Business Week* cover story on this phenomenon, as computers become part of everyday life, more people are perceiving more ways to use them. What becomes essential is a fresh mind-set, a new way of perceiving the role of information technology in business.

The ability to use computers and telecommunications creatively to collect, make sense of, and distribute information is already spelling the difference between success and mediocrity in a wide range of businesses, and the competition to keep abreast of these creative advances is fierce. "The difference between now and 5 years ago is that technology had limited function. You weren't betting your company on it," said William H. Gruber, president of Research and Planning Inc., a Cambridge (Mass.) consulting firm, in 1985. "Now you are."

Information management experts speak in almost legendary terms of three "classic cases" as examples of the advantages of computer technology and telecommunications in the business world.

(1) Merrill Lynch & Co. introduced a new service in 1978 called the Cash Management Account. This combines a customer's checking, savings, credit card, and securities accounts into one monthly statement and automatically transfers any "extra" money into an interest-bearing money market account. Less than eight years later, the Cash Management Account system was managing approximately $85 billion. And while competing firms have introduced similar systems into the field, Merrill Lynch still controls nearly 70% of the market.

(2) American Hospital Supply Corp., which distributes products from 8,500 manufacturers to more than 100,000 health-care providers, saw its market share soar in the 1970's after it set up computer links to its customers and suppliers. Hospitals could enter orders themselves via AHS terminals. The technology let the company cut inventories, improve customer service, and get better terms from suppliers for higher volume. More importantly, AHS's continuous direct link from hospitals made ordering so convenient that competing supply companies barely stood a chance.

(3) American Airlines Inc. has used computer and communications technology to build an entirely new business with sky-high profit margins. This innovation is American's Sabre reservation system, which lists the flight schedules of every major airline worldwide. Almost half of the automated travel agents in the United States subscribe to Sabre, and American gets about $1.75 on every Sabre reservation made for other carriers. AMR Corp., American's parent corporation, estimated that Sabre alone would bring in $170 million in 1985. "We are now in the data processing as well as the airline business," says President Robert L. Crandall, a data processing expert who conceived Sabre in 1975, when he was American's marketing chief.

Such success stories have sent companies in every industry scrambling to find ways to harness the power of information technology—from computers and telephones to communications satellites and videodisks. Security Pacific National Bank has spun its data processing department off into an independent division with freedom to contract itself out to other banks; conversely, if Security Pacific receives a better bid on an internal project, it can choose to hire an outside contractor for the job. Red Lion Inns, a motel chain with 11,000 rooms in eight Western states, uses a computer not only to make reservations, but to flag the motels with low occupancy rates and quickly announce discount rates at those locations. The Norton Co. of Worcester, Mass., has set up an information network called the Norton Connection and given distributors terminals so they can enter orders electronically and get details in seconds on the status of orders, pricing, and catalog items. When a customer calls, the distributor can promise a delivery date in seconds, a process which used to take days. And on the international front, Holland's Akzo Systems and its sister subsidiary, Akzo Coatings, have developed a computerized estimate system for use in automobile body shops. Employees punch in a description of the car and the parts and repair work it needs, and the system spits out a parts-and-labor calculation. Sales of Akzo Coatings's paints, as well as requests for the estimate system, have been impressive in northern Europe.

But even with the incentive of lucrative profits to be reaped, many managers find it difficult to make the transition from traditional data processing. "The technically sound people are often not creative [in business strategy]," notes Peter Keen, a former Massachusetts Institute of Technology professor who now consults on how to use information technology. Formerly trained to think of their jobs as a support function rather than as a strategic business tool, data processing managers will need to change their approach. "They will have to delight in solving the business problem, not the crossword puzzle that was programming," notes John F. Rockart, a professor at MIT's Sloan School of Management. The employee who can talk management's language and explain how to launch a preemptive attack in the marketplace is an invaluable asset, and salaries are generous for the rare individuals who fit this description.

Sometimes, whole new enterprises grow out of systems put in place just to provide information. Citibank, which offers financial services and data, has teamed up with McGraw-Hill Inc., which collects data on commodities, to create a 24-hour commodity trading venture called Global Electronic Markets Co. Now, traders can not only get information instantly but also make deals and transfer money in minutes.

In other cases, a unique idea may fail when it hits the market, only to be picked up and improved upon by a competitor. Chemical Bank, for example, was first to offer automated teller machines to its New York City customers. The response was lukewarm, and Chemical pulled back. Seeing the customer service possibilities of the idea, rival Citibank carefully researched the market and then created much "friendlier" machines. By blanketing the city with them in the late 1970s, it more than doubled its checking and deposit balances and almost tripled its market share, from 5% to about 13% today. So, too, American's Sabre reservation system was developed in response to United Airlines's announcement of its Apollo on-line reservation service. While Apollo listed only United's flights, American realized that travel agents would make full-time use of a system that listed the flights of all airlines. (Today, under government pressure, both Sabre and Apollo list all airlines, and don't give preference to their own flights.)

The long-term implications of this information technology arms race scare some observers, who feel that business may ignore its own welfare in the rush to innovate. Computerized airline reservations, for example, have made it easier for passengers to choose the cheapest and most convenient flight—as a result fares have stayed low and airline stocks have not performed as well as other investments in recent years.

According to *Business Week*'s story on the subject, "just as Star Wars-style programs are likely to proceed even though they may escalate the chances of nuclear war, business is so competitive that companies are likely to do anything to gain an edge, even though in some cases their industries may be the ultimate victims. And competitors have got to be willing to follow. So businesses must gird themselves for the information technology revolution. The ones who understand how to use the new tools will be the survivors."

Catherine L. Harris, "Information Power," *Business Week*, October 14, 1985. Copyright © 1985 by McGraw-Hill, Inc. Reprinted by special permission.

MODULE 5

In our quest to discover what computers are, what they do, how they're put to work, and how they affect people, we've looked in earlier modules at hardware components, applications software, system/software development concepts, and the impact of computer applications throughout our society. In this module, we learn about the steps needed to make a computer perform a particular task, first by analyzing problems to be solved with computer assistance and then by writing the instructions to produce those results.

PROGRAMMING

16 PROGRAMMING ANALYSIS: CONCEPTS AND EXAMPLES

17 A BASIC BEGINNING

18 MORE ABOUT BASIC

CHAPTER 16

PROGRAMMING ANALYSIS:
CONCEPTS AND EXAMPLES

THE PUBLIC LIBRARY: PUBLIC-DOMAIN SOFTWARE

The extensive public-domain collections for personal computers are a valuable resource. It is easily possible to build an extensive software library and incorporate the utilities into your home projects. Most programs in the public domain provide source code; you can learn from the code and, more important, you can customize the routines for your own requirements. Undoubtedly, some of the software will fill your needs, and even the more obscure programs may trigger your imagination.

The notion that "free means shoddy" does not apply to this software. The typical piece of public-domain software starts out as a program written for someone's personal use. Having written the program, the author may decide not to invest the additional time and energy required to market it. So, instead of copyrighting it, the author allows the program to be copied; the program consequently becomes part of the public domain. Programs that are developed and produced by commercial software vendors bear a copyright notice; it is against the law to copy and distribute such programs. A legitimate user must purchase these programs and register his or her name with the vendor, an activity that usually results in program support and updates.

Some programs commonly thought of as public domain are only quasi-public domain. They are available from the usual public-domain sources, but they are supported by their authors; the authors may fix bugs and add enhancements from time to time. Programs of this sort typically have required a much larger investment in programming time than has the average public-domain program, and they could possibly have been marketed through traditional channels had their authors wanted to go that route. Therefore, the authors request that if you try their programs and decide to use them, you send an amount of money suggested in the documentation.

What kind of programs are available in the public domain? Short utilities for use in DOS or BASIC constitute the majority of public-domain software. The programs adequately fill many needs, and they have a tendency, as the user community modifies and expands them, to become more and more bug-free and sophisticated. Most public-domain programs provide limited functionality, and their user interfaces and documentation are generally less polished than commercial products, but it is amazing how many commercial products do very little more than integrate the capabilities of programs that already exist in the public domain. If nothing else, exposure to these programs will make you more aware of what to look for and expect from the products you buy. And who knows, you may find software that's perfectly suited to your needs. Public-domain programs can be found at local users groups and in regional and national bulletin board services.

Adapted in part from Jon R. Edwards, "Public Domain Utilities," *Byte,* Fall 1985, Copyright © 1985 by McGraw-Hill, Inc. Reprinted with permission. All rights reserved.

Adapted in part from Nelson Ford, "The Public Library," *Softalk for the IBM Personal Computer,* May 1985. Copyright © 1985 by Nelson Ford. Used by permission.

CHAPTER 16

531

LOOKING AHEAD

This chapter is the first of three that deal with analyzing problems and preparing computer applications programs to solve them. After a brief introduction to some programming analysis concepts, you'll see how programmers use flowcharts to help them analyze computer problems. (Solutions for the problems presented in this chapter are coded in the BASIC programming language in Chapter 17.) The final pages of the chapter then give you a summary of the logic structures and concepts used in structured programming and introduce you to other programming analysis tools. The information in this chapter will enable you to:

- Define the programming process and understand programming analysis concepts

- Identify the symbols used in program flowcharts, construct a simple flowchart to meet a set of problem specifications, and outline the benefits and limitations of flowcharts

- Create the logic needed to process multiple records and understand the use of accumulators and counters

- Summarize the structured logic patterns used to solve programming problems

- Identify and discuss alternative analysis tools that may be used to replace or supplement program flowcharts

CHAPTER OUTLINE

LOOKING AHEAD
PROGRAMMING ANALYSIS CONCEPTS
A Program Analysis Approach
General Flowcharting Concepts
PROGRAMMING ANALYSIS EXAMPLES
A Simple Input/Process/Output Example
Feedback and Review 16-1
Gaining Flexibility with Decisions and Loops
Feedback and Review 16-2
A Multiple-Decision Situation
The Use of Accumulators
The Use of Counters

Feedback and Review 16-3
Benefits and Limitations of Flowcharts
LOGIC STRUCTURES AND
STRUCTURED PROGRAMMING
Three Logic Structures
Structured Programming Concepts
Some Benefits of Structured Programming
OTHER PROGRAMMING ANALYSIS TOOLS
Structured Pseudocode
Decision Tables
LOOKING BACK

PROGRAMMING ANALYSIS CONCEPTS

You'll recall from Chapter 2 that people who develop software generally follow a six-step approach:

1 *Define the need.* Software development typically starts when a person or an organization decides to write (or acquire) a computer program in order to perform a task more efficiently. A personal computer user may work alone to complete this and other steps in the development process, but people in organizations often work in system study teams.

2 *System analysis.* Data pertaining to the problem must be gathered and analyzed.

3 *System design.* Alternative approaches to satisfy the need are considered, and specifications for the chosen solution are drafted. These specifications include the output desired, the input data needed, and the general procedures required to convert input data into output results. (It's often possible at this point to select a prewritten software package that will satisfy the need.)

4 *Programming analysis.* If custom-made software is required to solve the problem, the design specifications are broken down into the necessary input/output, calculation/text manipulation, logic/comparison, and storage/retrieval operations.

5 *Program preparation.* The programmer then codes these specific operations using a programming language acceptable to a particular computer system.

6 *Implementation and maintenance.* The new software is tested for errors by programmers and users, put into use, and maintained (modified and improved) as necessary to meet changing conditions.

The *first three steps*—the **system analysis/design stage**—are discussed at length in Chapter 11. The **programming process** consists of the *last three* of the six listed steps. Chapter 12 describes programming languages and the implementation and maintenance of programs. Our purpose in this chapter is to analyze a number of typical programming problems (step 4). We'll then see in Chapters 17 and 18 how specific operations may be coded using the BASIC programming language (step 5).

A Program Analysis Approach

Part of the challenge of programming is that recommended programming techniques can be applied in flexible ways. Thus different programmers can, and do, use different strategies to develop solutions for programming applications. Regardless of the **program analysis approach** used, however, a programmer must answer a number of questions. The following checklist of these questions should be helpful to you as you develop your own programs:

1 *Have the problem specifications been spelled out clearly and completely?* A specification to "Write a program to prepare customer bills" is not enough. Before the programmer can make any significant progress, specifics such as these must be available:

- The program must print a number of bills.

- Each bill must contain the customer's name, local address, city, state, Zip code, and net amount owed.

- For each bill, the input data to be processed are customer name, local address, city, state, Zip code, quantity of a product purchased, and unit price of the product.

2 *Am I familiar with a solution method that will solve the problem?* An **algorithm** is a finite number of step-by-step directions that solve a particular problem. The algorithm to compute the acreage in a rectangular lot, for example, consists of the following steps: (*a*) Multiply the length (in feet) of the lot by the width (in feet) to get the square footage of the property and (*b*) divide this square footage figure by 43,560—the number of square feet in an acre—to get the acreage of the property. When a programmer knows an algorithm or procedure that will solve the problem at hand, the solution may then be coded in a selected programming language. If this isn't the case, the next question should be considered.

3 *Can I locate a solution method to solve the problem from other people or from books or journals?* Full or partial solutions to problems are often available. After all, the programmer who's given the task of writing a billing program today is certainly not the first one to have faced that problem. If other resources can provide the solution method, the necessary program may then be coded in a selected language. If a solution method is unavailable, the next question must be considered.

4 *How can I develop an algorithm or procedure that will solve this problem?* This is the creative problem-solving question that often challenges programmers. An effective approach to follow in the programming analysis stage of program development is to *break down a large* (and seemingly unmanageable) *problem into a series of smaller and more understandable tasks* or subproblems. The programmer can apply each of the above questions in the checklist to the individual subproblems. For example, the billing program specification listed in question 1 can be broken down into the following major tasks:

(**a**) Enter customer name, local address, city, state, Zip code, quantity purchased, and unit price into the processor.

(**b**) Compute net amount owed by customer.

(**c**) Print customer name, local address, city, state, Zip code, and net amount owed.

(**d**) If there's another bill to process, branch program control back to **a**. Otherwise, continue to next task.

(**e**) Stop processing.

In many (perhaps most) cases, it will be desirable to break some of the initially identified tasks into still smaller units. For example, task **b** must be refined as follows:

(b) Compute net amount owed by customer.

(b1) Compute net amount owed by the formula $A = Q \times P$ (where A is net amount, Q is quantity purchased, and P is unit price).

Programming analysis continues until every small task or subproblem has been reduced to the point that the programmer is confident he or she does have a solution method that will solve the task. Effective program coding can begin only after the programmer has this confidence. Note that it's not necessary that the first solution method be *the* best possible method. Improvements can often be added to functioning programs, and the best possible method may never be discovered.

WINDOW 16-1

USEFUL USER GROUPS

For those who are new to the pc scene and aren't sure what a user group is for or about—here's a partial answer.

User groups are an invaluable source of practical information for new computer users. Magazines do what they can to answer questions and to provide communication between readers. But they do so rather inefficiently, because of the number of subscribers they serve and because of the production time they require. Hardware and software vendors may be chary of support for some of the same reasons, including the number of supplicants. For many kinds of nuts-and-bolts problems—problems about how to make software work with hardware, hardware work with software, software work with software—your best hope for help is your local user group. Quite apart from their value as problem-solving agencies, moreover, user groups play a vital educational role.

Many user groups include SIGs; these are special-interest groups, subdivisions of a user group comprised of members interested in a particular topic. Many groups have SIGs for beginners. Others have SIGs that focus on particular programming topics (Pascal, BASIC, Forth, etc.) or applications (word processing, data management, graphics, for example). Various groups have SIGs focused on pc-mainframe communications.

Many user groups maintain libraries of public-domain software that they make available to members either for free or at a nominal cost. And some groups offer dial-up bulletin-board services that facilitate the exchange of public-domain materials.

Groups range in size from a handful of members to a multitude. Among the latter category are the Silicon Valley Users' Group, the New York pc Users' Group, and the Boston-area group (actually a SIG of the gigantic Boston Computer Society). Small groups are probably new groups; rapid growth is the rule.

Groups typically meet once a month. SIG meetings in some places are held on the same evening or day as the full session; elsewhere they're separate events entirely. Meetings often feature a software or hardware presentation by a group member or by a representative of an outside vendor.

In addition to all the other forms of support they provide, most user groups offer their members a monthly newsletter. This may be anything from a couple of pages of photocopied computer printout containing minutes of the most recent meeting to a miniature magazine, professionally typeset and printed, complete with paid advertisements, illustrations, feature articles, short programs, patches to existing programs, book reviews, surveys of computer magazines, letters, question-and-answer columns, and you name it. A subscription to the club newsletter is likely to be worth the annual membership dues, all by itself.

Perhaps the best way to summarize the spirit of user-group activity is to quote the March 1984 issue of *Bits and Bytes*, the newsletter of the Borderline IBM PC User's Group (Bellingham, Washington). Its editor writes:

> What you are reading here are the things the members of our group have found out. No hype, no egos, just ground floor, grass roots information straight from the source—you—the members of the Borderline IBM PC User Group that gather the information together and get it to the newsletter editor. I encourage any of you that think that the things you learn are not important enough to share to think again. Someone wants to be where you are now. Help yourself via helping others by sharing what you are learning about your PC now.

Adapted from Kathy Talley-Jones, "Users Do It in Groups," *Softalk for the IBM Personal Computer*, May 1984. Copyright © 1984 by Kathy Talley-Jones. Used by permission.

There are a number of programming analysis tools to help the programmer break a problem down into smaller tasks in order to arrive at a solution method. One frequently used tool is the *program flowchart*.

General Flowcharting Concepts

Flowcharts are generally classified into system and program categories.

System Flowcharts   If you've read Chapter 11, you know that a **system flowchart** is a diagram that shows a *broad overview* of the flow and sequence of operations in a processing system. A system flowchart emphasizes input documents and output reports, but it *doesn't* go into detail about how input data are used to produce output information. Standard symbols are used in these charts. The symbols representing input/output and processing are shown in Figure 16-1a. Although the input/output (I/O) symbol stands for any medium or device, it's often replaced in system charts by other symbols whose shape suggests the particular medium or device being used. (A few of these alternative symbols are shown in Figure 16-1b; you'll find many other system flowchart symbols in Figure 11-10, page 383.)

Program Flowcharts   A **program flowchart** is a *detailed graph* that represents steps to be performed within the computer to produce the needed output. Thus, as Figure 16-2 shows, the program flowchart evolves from the system chart.

Levels of Program Flowcharts   There are no standards on the amount of detail that should be provided in a program flowchart. The billing program outlined in Figure 16-2b could easily have been shown in a single chart. But as you've seen, it's often desirable in more complex situations to break major **program segments,** or **modules,** into still smaller and more manageable units. Figure 16-2c illustrates how a smaller flowchart can evolve from a higher-level chart. A chart that outlines the main segments of a program is called a **main-control,** or **macro, flowchart.** One that details the steps in a module is called a **micro,** or **detail, flowchart.**

Symbols Used in Program Flowcharts   Only a few symbols are needed in program flowcharting to indicate the necessary operations. These symbols, which have been adopted by the American National Standards Institute (ANSI), are shown here and their descriptions follow. (Most of them have already been used in Figure 16-2, and many have been used throughout the book).

Input/output   The **input/output symbol** used in system charts is also used in program charts to represent any I/O function. The special symbols designating disks, documents, etc., that are used in system charts are generally not used with program diagrams. In the program flowchart section of Figure 16-2, the same I/O symbol designates:

● The *input data* to be read into the processor (customer name, address, quantity purchased, and unit price)

The basic system-charting symbols for input/output and processing
(a)

A few of the system flowchart symbols used as substitutes for the basic I/O symbol
(b)

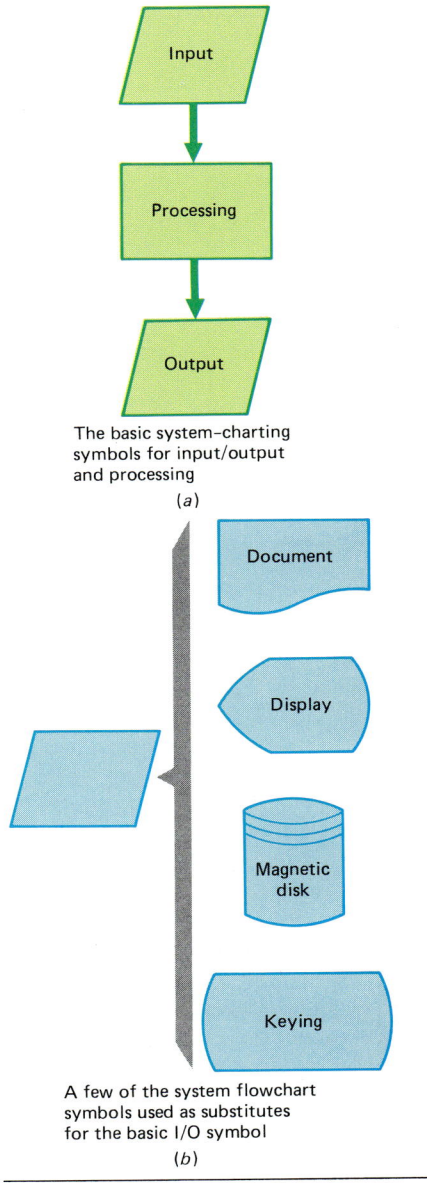

FIGURE 16-1

A few of the symbols used in system flowcharts. Other system-charting symbols are found in Chapter 11.

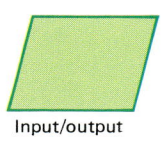

Input/output

MODULE 5

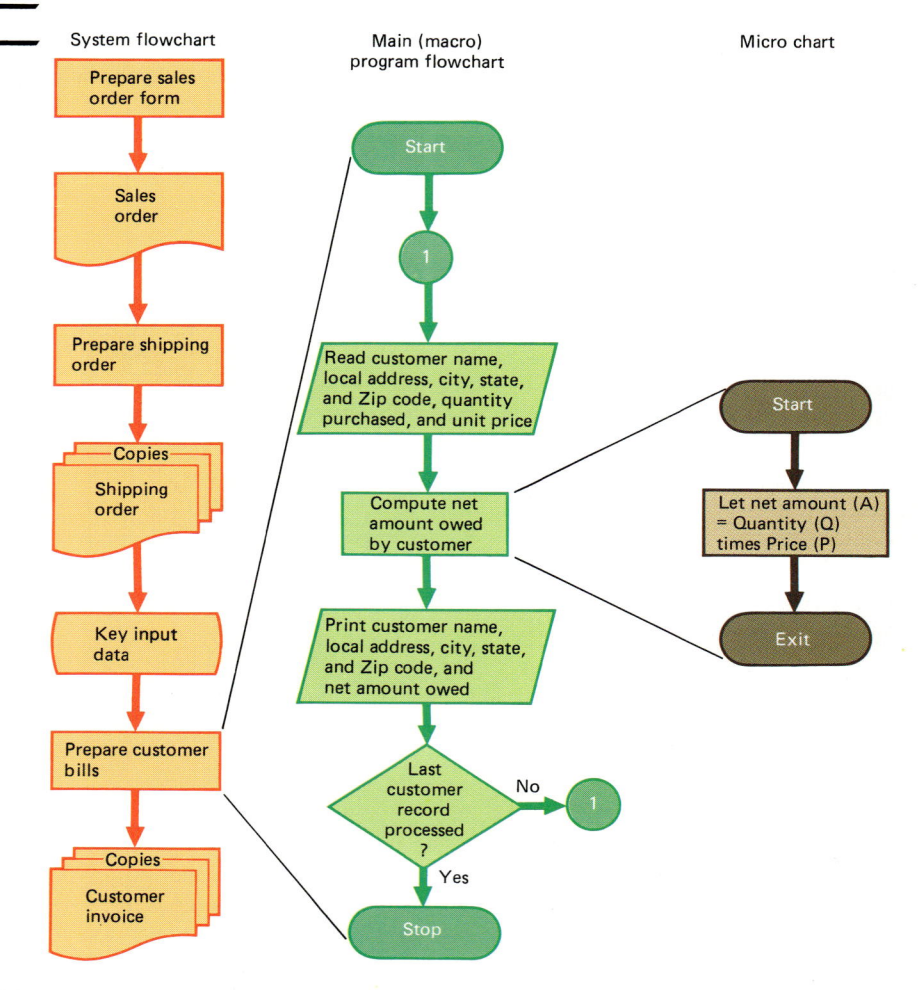

536

FIGURE 16-2

A program flowchart evolves from a system chart. In many cases, a main (or macro) program chart identifies the major tasks or modules to be performed, and then detailed micro charts are used to show the processing steps within specified modules. Thus programmers may prepare one macro program chart and several micro charts during programming analysis.

System flowchart

Prepare sales order form → Sales order → Prepare shipping order → Copies / Shipping order → Key input data → Prepare customer bills → Copies / Customer invoice

Main (macro) program flowchart

Start → 1 → Read customer name, local address, city, state, and Zip code, quantity purchased, and unit price → Compute net amount owed by customer → Print customer name, local address, city, state, and Zip code, and net amount owed → Last customer record processed? — No → 1 ; Yes → Stop

Micro chart

Start → Let net amount (A) = Quantity (Q) times Price (P) → Exit

(a) System flowchart for an order entry/shipping/billing system

(b) A program flowchart evolves from a system chart. This program flowchart shows the major tasks called for in a billing program specification

(c) In many cases it may be desirable to break down major program tasks into smaller units and chart the functions performed in these smaller segments

- The *output information* to be printed on the customer's bill (customer name, address, and amount owed)

[Processing symbol]

Processing

Processing The rectangle used in system charts is again used in program charts to represent processing operations. Of course, the processing described in the rectangle of a program chart is only a small segment of a major processing step called for in a system chart. Arithmetic and data movement instructions are generally placed in these boxes. A **processing symbol** is shown in the micro chart in Figure 16-2c. The net amount of a customer's bill is computed by multiplying the quantity purchased by the unit price.

Terminal The **terminal symbol,** as the name suggests, represents the beginning (START) and the end (STOP) of a program. It may also signal a program interruption point when information may enter or leave. For example, to detect certain errors in input data, the programmer may provide a special program branch ending in a terminal symbol labeled ''HALT.''

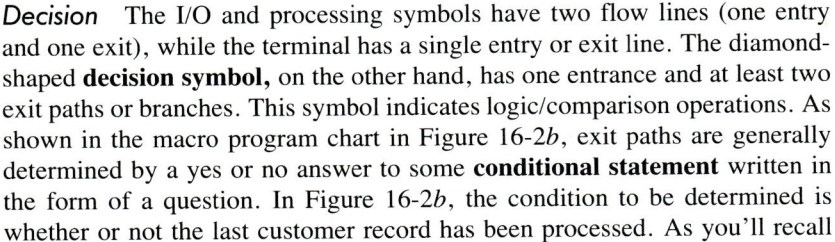

Decision The I/O and processing symbols have two flow lines (one entry and one exit), while the terminal has a single entry or exit line. The diamond-shaped **decision symbol,** on the other hand, has one entrance and at least two exit paths or branches. This symbol indicates logic/comparison operations. As shown in the macro program chart in Figure 16-2*b*, exit paths are generally determined by a yes or no answer to some **conditional statement** written in the form of a question. In Figure 16-2*b*, the condition to be determined is whether or not the last customer record has been processed. As you'll recall from Chapter 2, a dummy record can be placed at the end of the customer file so that the computer program will know when the last valid record has been processed. So long as valid records remain, program control will exit from the conditional branch of the decision symbol labeled ''NO.'' When the last valid record has been processed and the dummy record is then read, the ''YES'' branch is followed and processing stops.

Connector A circular **connector symbol** labeled ''1'' is used in Figure 16-2*b* when program control exits from the decision symbol along the ''NO'' branch. This connector symbol is used when additional flow lines might cause confusion and reduce understanding. Two connectors with identical labels serve the same function as a long flow line. That is, they show an exit to some other chart section, or they indicate an entry from another part of the chart. How's it possible to determine if a connector is used as an entry or an exit point? It's very simple: If an arrow *enters but doesn't leave* a connector, it's an exit point and program control is transferred to the identically labeled connector that does have an outlet. Thus, in Figure 16-2*b*, the connector to the right of the decision symbol is an exit point, and program control loops back to the entry connector at the top of the chart when another record is to be processed.

Offpage connector Some programmers prefer to substitute an **offpage connector symbol** for the circular connector to show that program flow is entering from or going to a separate flowchart page.

Preparation And some programmers also prefer to use the **preparation symbol** rather than the general-purpose processing symbol to control, initiate, or perform some other operation on the program itself. For example, the processing symbol is used to load the initial values in accumulators and counters in Figures 16-9, 16-10, 16-11, and 16-12. But the preparation symbol could also have been used to present these initial values.

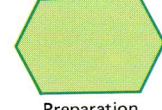

Predefined process Programmers frequently find that certain processing operations are repeated in their programs. Instead of rewriting a module each time it's needed, the programmer can prepare it once and then integrate it into other programs as required. Libraries of these predefined processes, or **sub-**

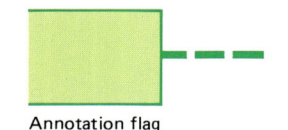

routines, are often maintained to reduce the time and cost of programming. Thus a single **predefined process symbol** replaces a number of operations that need not be detailed at that particular point in a chart. (Of course, a detailed micro flowchart of the subroutine should be available if needed.) In short, the subroutine is a commonly used module that during program execution receives input from the main-control program, performs its limited task, and then returns the output to the primary program.

Annotation Annotation flags are used to add clarifying comments to other flowchart symbols. They can be drawn on either side of another symbol.

Annotation flag

We'll use most of these flowchart symbols in the next section to analyze a number of program applications. Beginning with several very simple problems, we'll gradually develop these situations into more realistic examples. The problems that are flowcharted in this chapter are all coded in the BASIC programming language in Chapter 17.

Although the program flowchart is a popular programming analysis tool, it's not the only one. Others are available that can be used to replace or supplement flowcharts. We'll look at some of these other analysis tools later in the chapter.

PROGRAMMING ANALYSIS EXAMPLES

You were introduced to the Byter family in the Background Module, and our programming analysis examples will produce computer solutions to their needs. You're already familiar with many of the examples presented here, but others are new.

A Simple Input/Process/Output Example

Programming analysis converts problem specifications into I/O, calculation/text manipulation, logic/comparison, and storage/retrieval operations. Of course, not every type of operation may be needed for every problem solution.

Problem 1: Elm Creek Charges, Single Property Owner You'll recall from Chapter 1 that when the city of Calvin decided to beautify its property along Elm Creek, some owners of adjacent land (including the Byters) agreed to participate in the project. An agreement was reached: Property owners bought additional plants from the city and paid the city a planting charge equal to 6 percent of the price of the plants. Let's assume that the following specifications are drawn up in the city manager's office for a program to prepare charge statements:

● Input data to be processed are the name of the property owner, the quantity planted, and the unit price of plants.

● The net amount owed by the property owner for the plants should be computed.

● Planting charges equal to 0.06 of the amount of the plants should be computed.

- The planting charges should be added to the amount owed for the plants to get the total charges to the property owner.

- The printed output should be a charge statement giving the property owner's name, the net amount owed for the plants, the planting charge, and the total charge.

The flowchart shown in Figure 16-3 satisfies these specifications and illustrates a simple input/process/output procedure. You'll notice that convenient abbreviations have been assigned by the programmer to identify the input data and the result of processing. The programmer has considerable freedom in selecting abbreviations, but as you'll learn in Chapters 17 and 18, the selections must conform to the rules of a programming language. As you can see, the net amount of the plants purchased by a property owner is found by multiplying the quantity planted by the unit price. In flowcharts and programs, the asterisk is used to indicate multiplication. Other operation symbols include + (addition), − (subtraction), and / (division).

FEEDBACK

Feedback AND REVIEW 16-1

Lisa, the youngest Byter, is enrolled in a computing class offered by her school. She has a class assignment to prepare a program that will compute the gasoline mileage of the family car during a trip. Lisa has received the following specifications for this program:

- Input data to be processed are the odometer readings at the beginning and end of a trip and the amount of gasoline used. (The family car leaves on a trip with a full fuel tank, the Byters keep a record of any fuel purchased, and they fill the tank at the end of the trip to determine the amount used.)

- The gasoline mileage should be computed.

- The printed output should be a mileage report showing the input data and the computed gas mileage.

To test your understanding of the program analysis and flowcharting concepts you've just read, prepare a program flowchart to help Lisa with this assignment.

Gaining Flexibility with Decisions and Loops

You've probably already noticed what an employee in the Calvin city manager's office quickly discovered: The initial Elm Creek charges program computes a statement for one property owner and then stops! After each statement is printed, the program has to be reloaded before the next one can be prepared—hardly an efficient use of the employee's or the computer's time. Furthermore, the prepared statement doesn't include the property owner's address.

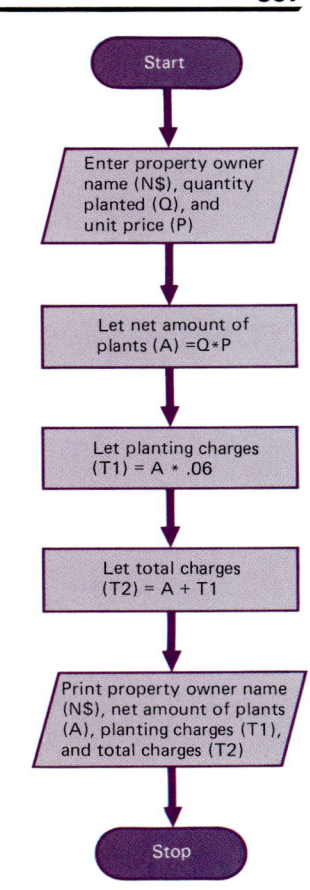

FIGURE 16-3

Program flowchart for Problem 1: Elm Creek Charges, Single Property Owner. You'll notice that the programmer has assigned convenient abbreviations, such as N$, Q, and A, to identify input data and processing results.

Problem 2: Elm Creek Charges, Multiple Property Owners In order to modify the program charted in Figure 16-3, the employee prepared the following revised specifications:

- Input data to be processed are property owner's name, local address, city, state, and Zip code; quantity planted; and unit price of plants.

- The net amount owed for the plants should be computed.

- Planting charges equal to 0.06 of the amount of the plants should be computed.

- Planting charges should be added to the amount owed for the plants to get the total charges to the property owner.

- The printed output should be a charge statement giving the property owner's name, local address, city, state, and Zip code; net amount owed for the plants; the planting charge; and the total charge.

- The program should be able to process statements for any number of property owners!

The flowchart shown in Figure 16-4 satisfies these requirements. (A program prepared from this flowchart will produce results similar to those shown in Figure 1-12, page 25, but a few more output details have been included here.) Although the property owner's address has been added, I/O operations and computations are similar to those shown in Figure 16-3. But this program design is much more flexible. It can follow a controlled loop, repeat processing steps, and print any number of statements. A **loop** consists of a sequence of instructions that can be executed repetitively. Included in these instructions must be a test to determine when program control should exit from the loop and a provision to return control to the beginning of the loop. Without the ability to execute loops, computers would be little more than toys.

The loop in our example that makes repetition possible is found between the two connector symbols labeled ''A.'' The repetitive processing of charge statements continues until the last valid statement has been printed and the program encounters a ''sentinel value.'' This value is the quantity-planted amount of −99.9 that's shown in the decision symbol in Figure 16-4. It will appear in a last dummy record at the end of the property owners file. A **sentinel value,** then, is simply some *arbitrary* data item that's placed at the end of a file to indicate that all valid data have been processed. (In our example, the sentinel could easily have been a unit price of −999.9 rather than a quantity value of −99.9). Of course, the sentinel must have a value that *couldn't possibly occur* as a valid data item. A negative number consisting of a string of 9s is often used as the sentinel value because the 9s stand out and are generally understood to be artificial, or ''dummy record numbers.''

In summary, then, as long as valid records are being processed, the answer to the **test for exit condition** shown in the decision symbol in Figure 16-4 will be ''NO.'' The charges will then be calculated, the statement will be printed, and program control will loop back to read the next record to be processed. When all statements have been printed and the dummy record is read, the answer to the conditional statement is ''YES.'' The exit path out of the loop is then followed and processing stops. Such an exit path must, of

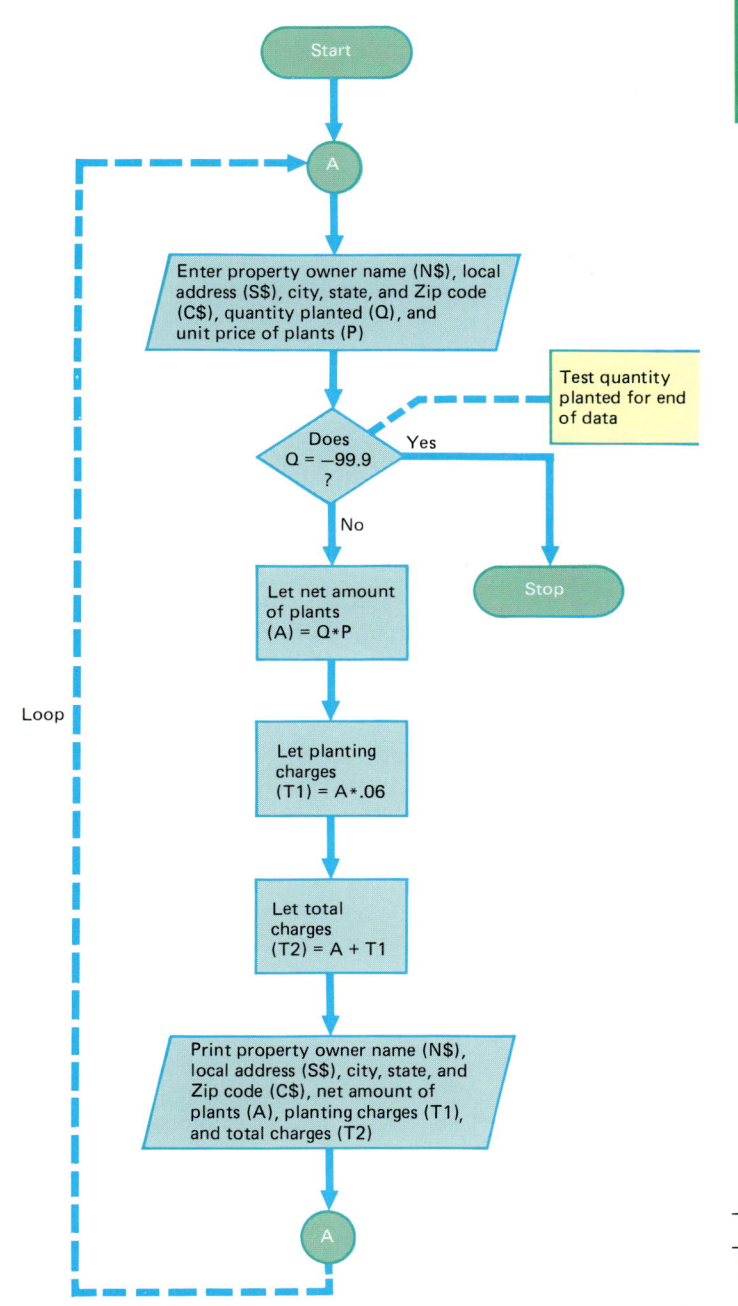

FIGURE 16-4

Program flowchart for Problem 2: Elm Creek Charges, Multiple Property Owners.

course, exist when loops are used. **Endless**, or **infinite**, **loops** (Figure 16-5) result from failure to provide an exit path and are a common and troublesome problem that programmers often run into.

Problem 3: Meals Compensation Report   You'll recall from Chapter 2 (and from Figure 2-6, page 61) that Marie Byter is in charge of an experimental program to deliver meals to needy families with preschool children. Part-time workers prepare and deliver these meals, and Marie uses a Meals Compensation Report to keep track of employee earnings and the number of meals prepared. The following specifications were used to produce this report:

● The report should have headings indicating the employee name, the cold and hot meals produced, and the employee earnings.

● Input data to be processed are the name of each employee and the cold and hot meals produced by each employee.

● Earnings of each employee are computed as follows: The amount earned for preparing and delivering each cold lunch is $0.75, and $1.50 is received for each hot meal.

● Under the report headings should be printed the name, quantities of cold and hot meals produced, and earnings of each employee.

● The program should be able to include any number of employees in the report.

Figure 16-6a shows a flowchart drawn to these specifications; Figure 16-6b shows the report output. The headings are printed first, and the loop that processes the report data is located between the connector symbols labeled "A." If the printing of the headings has been included in the loop, there would be a separate—and redundant—heading for each employee. In this example, the dummy record inserted at the end of the employee file has "END OF DATA" as the employee's name. The exit path out of this loop will be followed only when the dummy record satisfies the exit condition test.

Problem 4: Student Payment Report   Jill Byter is enrolled in her college's work-study program. Her current assignment is to write a program that will produce a report for a department head. This report should show the hours worked and earnings received over a 4-week period by the student assistants allocated to the department. The department head has given Jill the following specifications:

● The report should have headings indicating the student name, total hours worked for the 4-week period, and the earnings received for that period.

● Input data to be processed for each student are the student's name, hourly pay rate, and hours worked each week for the 4-week period.

● The program should compute the total hours worked by each assistant during the period and the total earnings each has received for the period.

● Each student's name, total hours worked, and total earnings should be printed under the report headings.

● The program should be able to include any number of assistants in the report.

Jill has prepared the flowchart in Figure 16-7 to meet these specifications. The headings are printed first. The loop is then located between the connector symbols labeled "1." The exit path out of the loop is followed after the computer reads a record—the last dummy record—that has an hourly rate of pay of −99.9.

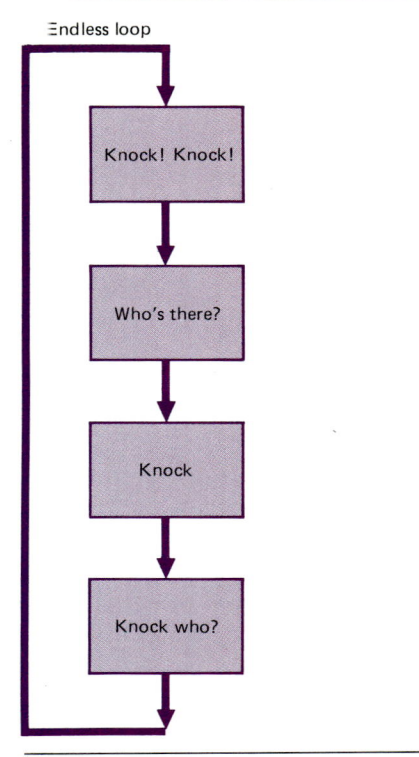

FIGURE 16-5

An irrelevant example of an endless loop. (From Stan Kelly-Bootle, *The Devil's DP Dictionary*, New York, McGraw-Hill Book Company, 1981. Used with the permission of the McGraw-Hill Book Company)

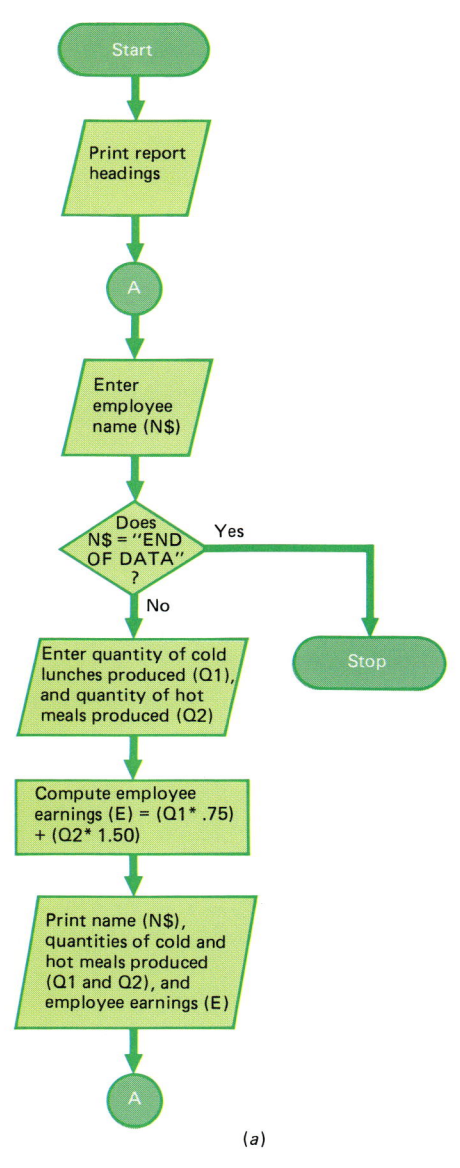

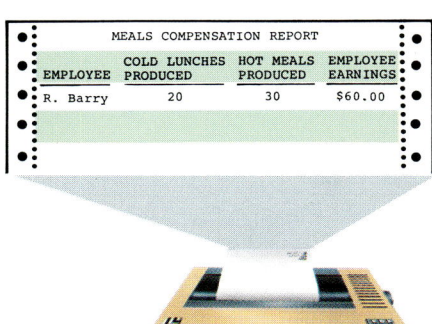

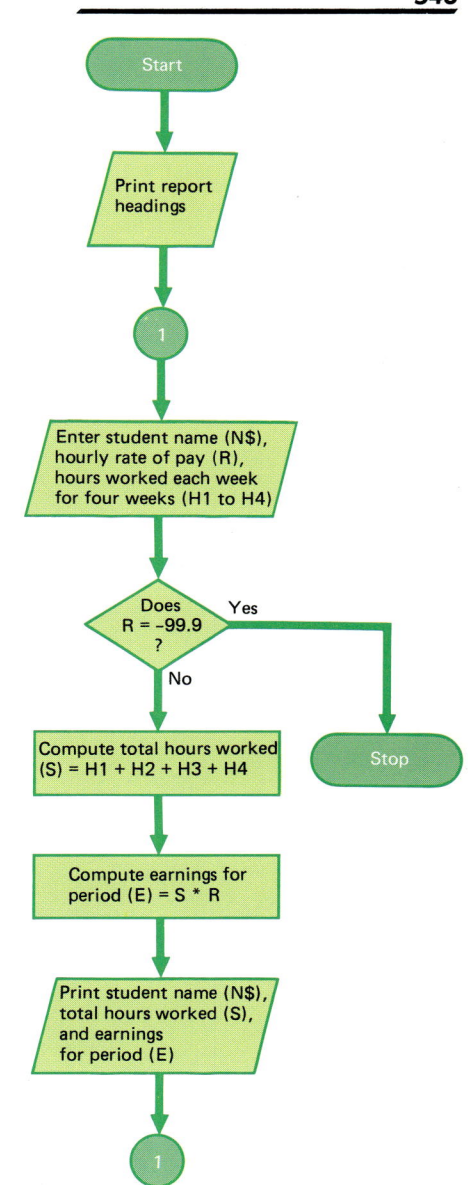

FIGURE 16-7

Program flowchart for Problem 4: Student Payment Report.

FIGURE 16-6

(a) Program flowchart for Problem 3: Meals Compensation Report. (b) The output produced by the Meals Compensation Report.

FEEDBACK

FEEDBACK AND REVIEW 16-2

You can now use the concepts that we've examined to help Lisa Byter improve the mileage program flowchart prepared in Feedback and Review 16-1. Lisa feels that the program should meet the following specifications:

- Input data are odometer readings at the beginning and end of each trip and the amount of fuel used.

- The program should be *interactive*—it should ask the user to supply it with the input data.

- The gasoline mileage should be computed.

- The printed output should be a line giving the miles per gallon for a trip.

- The program should ask the user if data for another trip are to be processed, and it should then respond appropriately to either a yes or no answer.

- Finally, when no additional trips are to be processed, the program should send the user a polite "sign-off" message.

A Multiple-Decision Situation

Each flowchart for the preceding problems used only a *single* decision symbol. But programmers must provide *many* decision paths when intricate logic is needed to solve complex problems. The following problem gives an example of the use of multiple decisions. Several later examples in this module also will use a series of logic decisions.

Problem 5: Plant Control Report—Elm Creek Project Bill Byter works in the Calvin City Planning Office, and you saw in Chapter 2 that he has been given the job of managing the inventory of plants that the city is buying and using to beautify its property along Elm Creek. Before writing the program to produce the Plant Control Report shown in Figure 2-12, page 70, Bill drafted the following specifications:

- Report headings are needed, and the input data consist of the name of each plant and the beginning inventory, quantity received, and quantity planted figures for each item. Any number of plants can be processed.

- The inventory available for planting during a period is found by adding the quantity received during the period to the inventory at the beginning of the period.

- The inventory at the end of the period is found by subtracting the quantity planted from the available inventory.

- The name of each plant is printed on the report along with its beginning inventory, quantity received, quantity planted, and ending inventory.

Figure 16-8a shows the flowchart for this plant control report. The loop begins after the report headings shown in Figure 16-8b are printed. Input data are entered, a test is made to see if all valid records have been processed, and the inventory available for planting is determined. The available inventory *should* be found by adding receipts to the beginning inventory. If a data error causes quantity received to be less than zero, a program provision keeps the available inventory equal to the beginning figure. The ending inventory *should* be found by subtracting the quantity planted from the quantity available. But if a data error causes quantity planted to be less than zero, no change is made to the available inventory. The output shown in the chart is then printed under the report headings.

The Use of Accumulators

The use of an accumulator is an important programming technique. An **accumulator** is a programmer-designated storage location in the processor that accepts and stores a *running total* of individual values as they become available during processing. The programmer *must* initially set the contents of the storage location to some value, and that value is usually zero. After this first step, each successive value placed in the accumulator is added to the value already there.

Problem 6: Meals Compensation Report with an Accumulator Marie Byter has decided to use an accumulator in her Meals Compensation Report. This accumulator will add the amounts entered into the "EMPLOYEE EARNINGS" column of Figure 16-6b to produce the total employee compensation. To produce this value, Marie has added the following specifications to those we've already seen in problem 3:

● The earnings for each employee should be accumulated to get the total amount of earnings for all workers during the report period.

● After all valid employee records have been processed, a "TOTAL EMPLOYEE COMPENSATION" subheading and the accumulated total amount should be printed at the bottom of the report.

The flowchart in Figure 16-9 is a revision of Figure 16-6a that incorporates these additional specifications. You'll notice that the first operation is to set a total employee earnings accumulator (G) to zero. The report headings are then printed, and the loop that processes the input data for each employee begins at the connector labeled A. An employee's name is entered, an exit test is made, meal production data are entered, and the employee's earnings are computed (no change has been made in these program steps). But we do encounter a change when we come to the processing symbol that reads LET $G = G + E$, where G equals the value in the accumulator and E is the earnings of an employee. If the *first* worker's earnings are $60, then $60 will be added to the initial value in the accumulator (0), and the new total of $60 will now be stored in the accumulator. If the *next* employee's earnings are $195, the total in the accumulator will then be $255 ($60 + $195), and so it goes.

After the accumulator has been updated, the worker's name, quantities of cold and hot meals produced, and earnings are printed under the report head-

MODULE 5

546

```
                    ┌───────┐
                    │ Start │
                    └───┬───┘
                        ▼
            ┌─────────────────────┐
            │ Print report headings│
            └──────────┬──────────┘
                       ▼
                      (1)
                       ▼
        ┌────────────────────────────────┐
        │ Read name of this plant (P$),  │
        │ beginning inventory (B), quantity│
        │ received (R), and quantity planted (S)│
        └──────────────┬─────────────────┘
                       ▼
                  ╱ Does ╲       Yes
                 ╱ R = -99.9 ╲─────────────┐
                 ╲    ?     ╱              │
                  ╲───┬────╱               ▼
                      │ No              ┌──────┐
                      ▼                 │ Stop │
                   ╱ Is ╲    Yes        └──────┘
                  ╱ R ≥ 0 ╲──────────────┐
                  ╲   ?   ╱              │
                   ╲──┬──╱               │
                      │ No               ▼
┌──────────────┐  ┌──────────────┐  ┌──────────────────┐
│Data error:   │  │Let available │  │Let available     │
│quantity      │──│inventory     │  │inventory (A)=B+R │
│received (R)<0│  │(A) = B       │  └────────┬─────────┘
└──────────────┘  └──────┬───────┘           │
                         ▼◄──────────────────┘
                      ╱ Is ╲    Yes
                     ╱ S ≥ 0 ╲──────────────┐
                     ╲   ?   ╱              │
                      ╲──┬──╱               │
                         │ No               ▼
┌──────────────┐  ┌──────────────┐  ┌──────────────────┐
│Data error:   │  │Let ending    │  │Let ending inventory│
│quantity      │──│inventory     │  │(E) = A − S       │
│sold (S)<0    │  │(E) = A       │  └────────┬─────────┘
└──────────────┘  └──────┬───────┘           │
                         ▼◄──────────────────┘
        ┌────────────────────────────────┐
        │ Print name of this plant (P$), │
        │ beginning inventory (B), quantity│
        │ received (R), quantity planted (S),│
        │ and ending inventory (E)       │
        └──────────────┬─────────────────┘
                       ▼
                      (1)
```

(a)

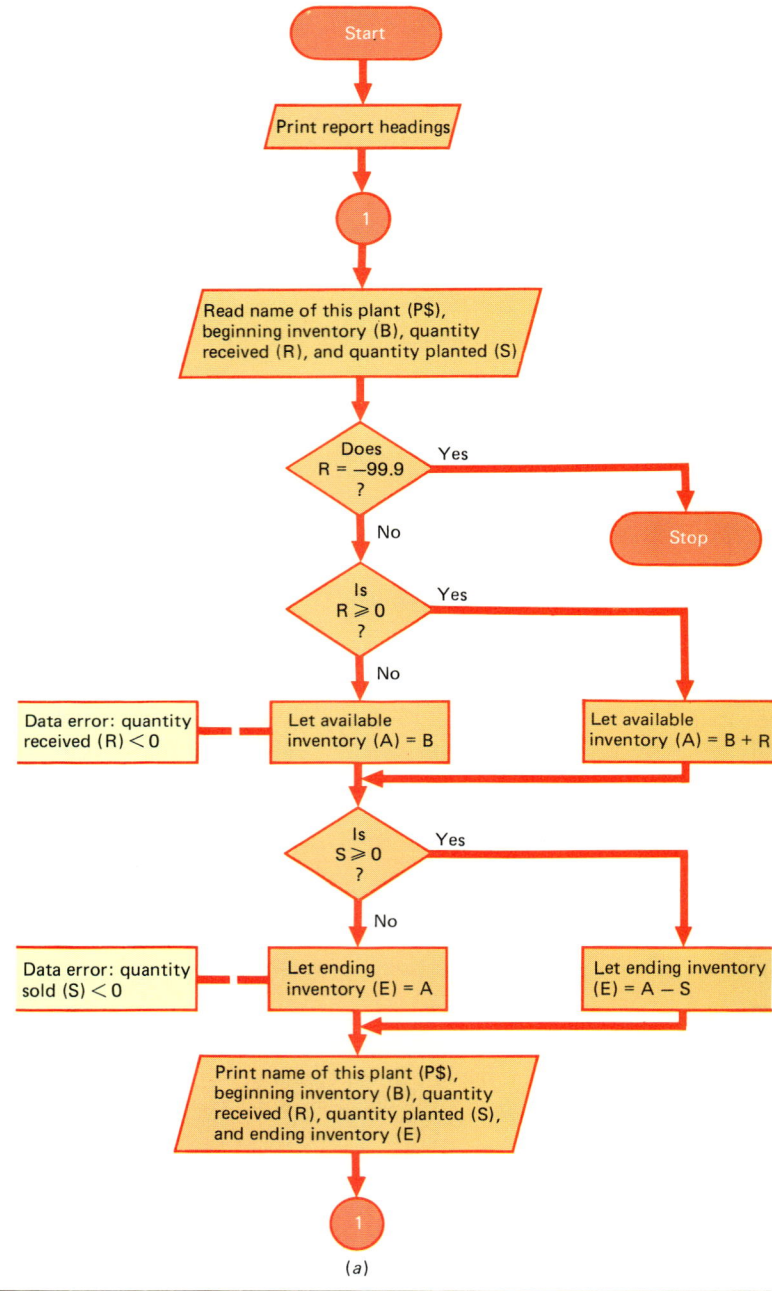

	PLANT CONTROL REPORT			
PLANT	BEGINNING INVENTORY	QUANTITY RECEIVED	QUANTITY PLANTED	ENDING INVENTORY
Azalea	200.0	150.0	289.0	61.0
Boxwood	165.0	118.0	203.0	80.0
Daffodil (Doz)	188.5	144.0	176.5	156.0
Honeysuckle	35.0	225.0	200.0	60.0
Juniper	76.0	150.0	132.0	94.0
Peony	92.0	100.0	160.0	32.0

(b)

FIGURE 16-8

(a) Program flowchart for Problem 5: Plant Control Report—Elm Creek Project. (b) Output produced by the Plant Control Report.

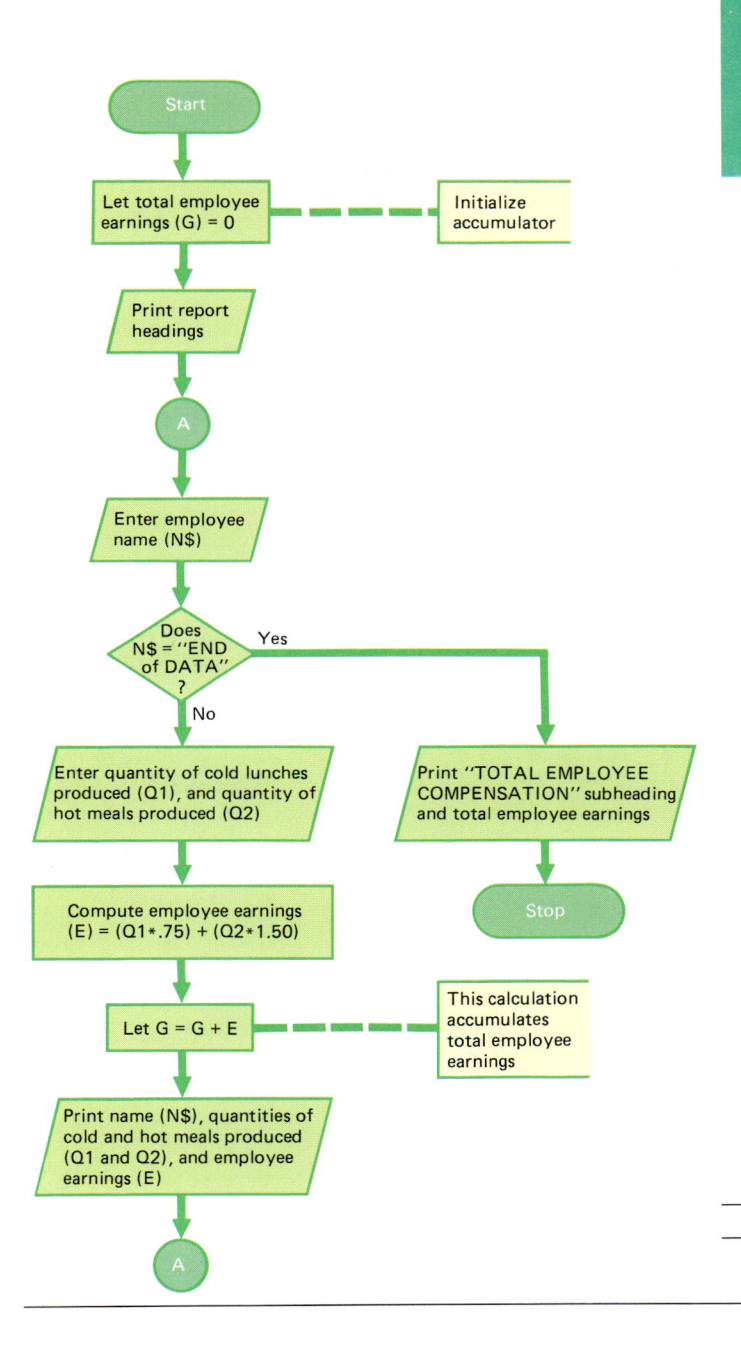

FIGURE 16-9

Program flowchart for Problem 6: Meals Compensation Report with Accumulator.

ings. When the last worker's record has been processed, the total of all earnings is stored in the accumulator. Once the dummy record has been read and the exit condition has been met, a "TOTAL EMPLOYEE COMPENSATION" subhead and the amount stored in the accumulator are printed. (As you'll see in the programming language used in Chapters 17 and 18, characters that are bounded by quotation marks in a printing operation are reproduced in exactly that way when a program is run.)

Problem 7: Elm Creek Planting Summary To help keep track of the planting activities of the Elm Creek beautification project, Bill Byter decided to prepare a report that summarizes the type and quantity of plants used and the net charges levied for these plants. The following specifications were drawn up for this summary report:

● The report should be prepared with an "ELM CREEK PLANTING SUMMARY" heading followed by a line of "PLANT," "UNIT PRICE," "QUANTITY," and "NET CHARGES" subheadings.

● Input data to be processed should include the name of each plant, the quantity planted, and the unit price. The program should process all plants used.

● The net charges levied for each plant should be computed.

● The total net charges for all plants should be accumulated.

● The name, unit price, quantity planted, and net charges for each plant should be printed on the report below the appropriate subheadings.

● After all plants have been processed, a "TOTAL NET CHARGES" subheading and the amount of the accumulated total charges should be printed at the bottom of the report.

The flowchart in Figure 16-10 shows how these specifications can be met. Report headings are printed and the accumulator is set to zero. The loop then begins with the reading of input data about a particular plant. The net charges for this plant are computed, and the amount is added to the total in the accumulator. The plant name, unit price, quantity planted, and net charge values are then printed, and the program loops back to read the data for the next plant. When all plants have been processed, the total of their charges is stored in the accumulator. Once the condition needed to exit the loop is met through the reading of a last dummy record, a "TOTAL NET CHARGES" subheading and the accumulated total charges are printed.

The Use of Counters

You've now seen how accumulators may be used. Another important programming aid is the use of a counter. A **counter** is a special type of accumulator that's often used to record the number of times a loop has been processed. For example, if a programmer wants to process the procedure in a loop a fixed number of times, that number can be specified in the program. A counter can then keep track of the number of passes through the loop. When the counter value reaches the predetermined number, an exit condition based on the value of the counter is satisfied, and program control follows an exit path out of the loop.

Problem 8: Elm Creek Charges with a Counter Let's modify the situation described in problem 2 (and flowcharted in Figure 16-4) to see how a counter can control a loop. The following specifications apply in this example (you'll notice that we've simplified the input data and the output results):

● Input data are the number of property-owner records to be processed and the name, quantity planted, and unit price data for each property owner.

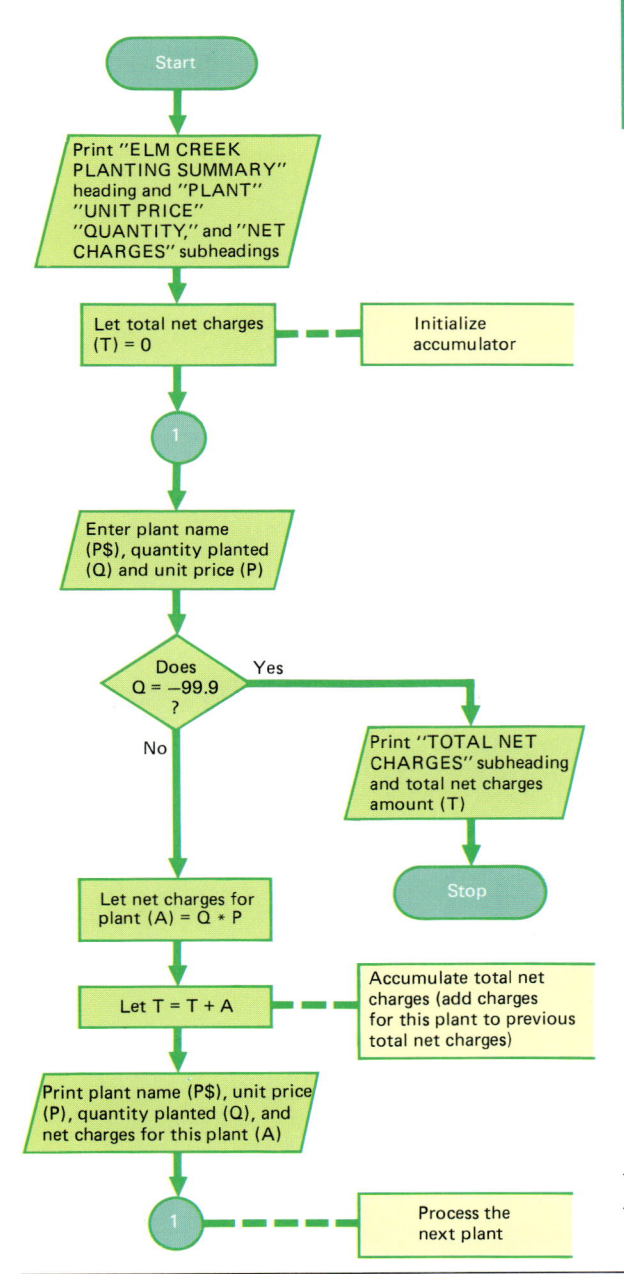

FIGURE 16-10

Program flowchart for Problem 7: Elm Creek Planting Summary.

- The net amount owed for the plants, the planting charges, and the total charges should be computed for each owner.

- The printed output should be a statement for each property owner giving the owner's name and the total amount of the charges to be paid.

- Processing should stop after all records have been processed.

A chart meeting these specifications is shown in Figure 16-11. A counter is *initialized* (or initially set) at 1 in our example, and the number of records to

MODULE 5

550

```
                        Start
                          │
                          ▼
                  ┌───────────────┐
                  │ Let counter   │┄┄┄┄┄┄  Initialize
                  │ (K) = 1       │        counter
                  └───────────────┘
                          │
                          ▼
                 ╱─────────────────╲
                ╱ Enter number of   ╲
               ╱  property-owner     ╲
               ╲  records (N) to be  ╱
                ╲ processed         ╱
                 ╲─────────────────╱
                          │
                          ▼
                         (A)
                          │
                          ▼
                 ╱─────────────────╲
                ╱ Enter property-   ╲
               ╱  owner name (N$),   ╲
              ╱   quantity planted    ╲
              ╲   (Q), and unit       ╱
               ╲  price (P)          ╱
                ╲─────────────────╱
                          │
                          ▼
                  ┌───────────────┐
                  │ Let net amount│
                  │ of plants     │
                  │ (A) = Q*P     │
                  └───────────────┘
                          │
                          ▼
                  ┌───────────────┐
                  │ Let planting  │
                  │ charges       │
                  │ (T1) = A*.06  │
                  └───────────────┘
                          │
                          ▼
                  ┌───────────────┐
                  │ Let total     │
                  │ charges (T2) =│
                  │ A + T1        │
                  └───────────────┘
                          │
                          ▼
                 ╱─────────────────╲
                ╱ Print property-   ╲
               ╱  owner name (N$),   ╲
               ╲  and total charges  ╱
                ╲ (T2)              ╱
                 ╲─────────────────╱
                          │
                          ▼                      The value of the counter
                        ╱     ╲     Yes          is compared to the number
                       ╱ Does  ╲───────────┐     of records to be processed
                      ╱  K = N  ╲          │
                      ╲    ?   ╱           ▼
                       ╲      ╱         ┌──────┐
                        ╲    ╱          │ Stop │
                         ╲  ╱           └──────┘
                          │ No
                          ▼
                  ┌───────────────┐
                  │ Let K = K + 1 │┄┄┄┄┄┄┄  Increment counter
                  └───────────────┘          (Add 1 to the
                          │                  counter contents)
                          ▼
                         (A)
```

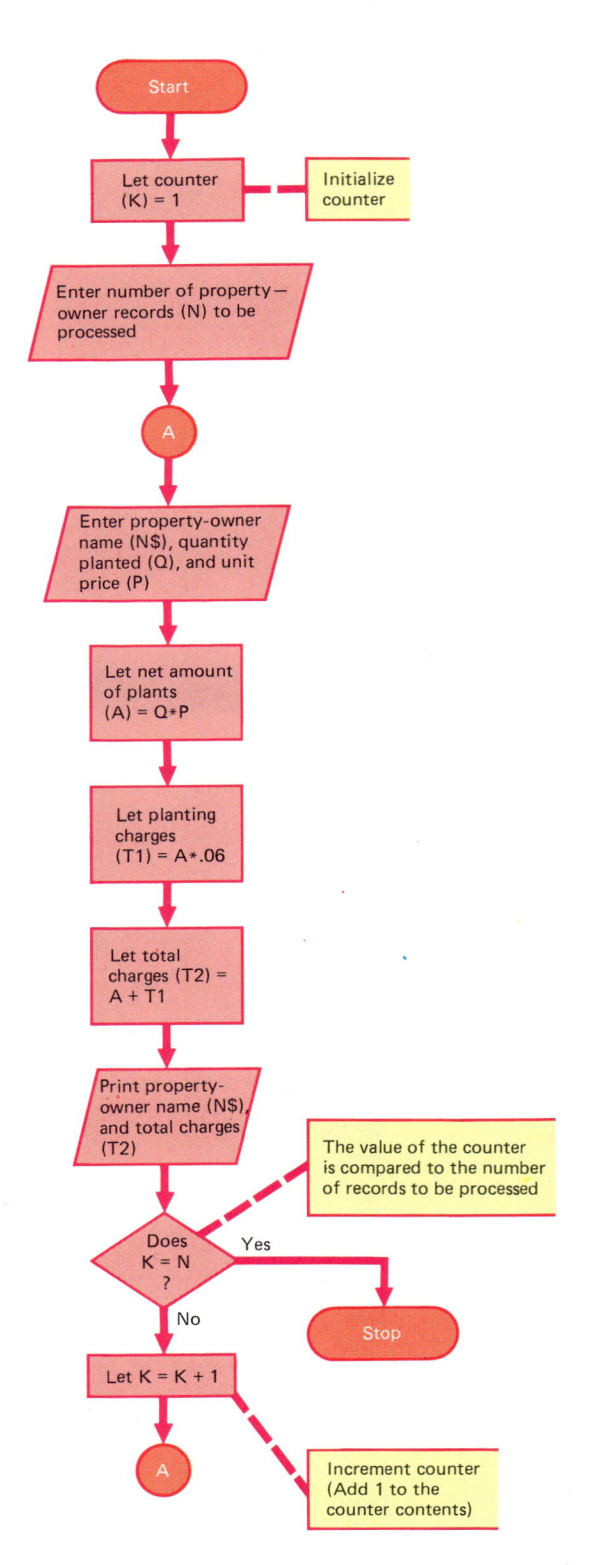

FIGURE 16-11

Program flowchart for Problem 8: Elm Creek Charges with a Counter.

be processed is entered. After the first property-owner record has been processed, a test for exit condition is made. The initial value of the counter (1) is compared to the number of records to be processed. Since the counter value does not yet equal this number of records, program control moves to the next operation. In this step, the counter is *incremented* (or added to) by a value of 1, and so the counter's value is now 2. When the last owner record has been processed and when K = N, the exit path out of the loop will be followed without any need for a dummy record at the end of the file.

Problem 9: Sam's Savings Simulator

Sam Byter has done some part-time programming work after school and on weekends. He's also a "landscape consultant" during the summer. From these activities, Sam has accumulated some income and has decided that he needs a savings simulation program like the one shown in Figure 1-2, page 13. Sam's specifications for this program are:

```
***SAVINGS ACCUMULATION SIMULATOR***
 INITIAL SAVINGS AMOUNT? 2000
 INTEREST RATE ON SAVINGS (PERCENT)? 10
 NUMBER OF YEARS? 3
       SAVINGS ACCUMULATION MODEL
    YEAR            SAVINGS
    NO.             BALANCE

     1               2,200
     2               2,420
     3               2,662
 MORE DATA (YES, NO)?
```

• It should be an *interactive* program that queries users about the initial savings amount to be invested, the interest rate percentage paid on savings, and the number of years to be simulated.

• The user should be able to answer "what if" questions by varying the responses to all input queries while producing any number of simulations.

• After each simulation run, the program should print a message asking the user if more data are to be processed. If Sam wants another simulation, the program should repeat the input queries; if he's finished, the program should stop.

The flowchart in Figure 16-12 satisfies these requirements and produces results similar to those shown back in Figure 1-2. There are two loops in Sam's program. The one found between the two connector symbols labeled A processes each simulation run; the one between the connectors labeled B processes the data for each of the years specified by the user. Let's assume that Sam wants to see how much his savings will grow in 3 years at some specified rate of interest. A counter is initialized, the program asks Sam to enter the input data, and Sam responds to the queries. The program then produces headings and begins to process the first of three passes through the B loop. The interest earned in year 1 is computed and added to the initial savings amount to get the new savings balance. The next step is to print the value of K—which is 1 in this first pass through the loop—and the new savings balance. The program then tests to see if the B loop should be terminated. Since K *doesn't* equal N in this first pass (K is 1 and N is 3), the program adds 1 to the counter and another pass is made through the B loop.

FIGURE 16-12

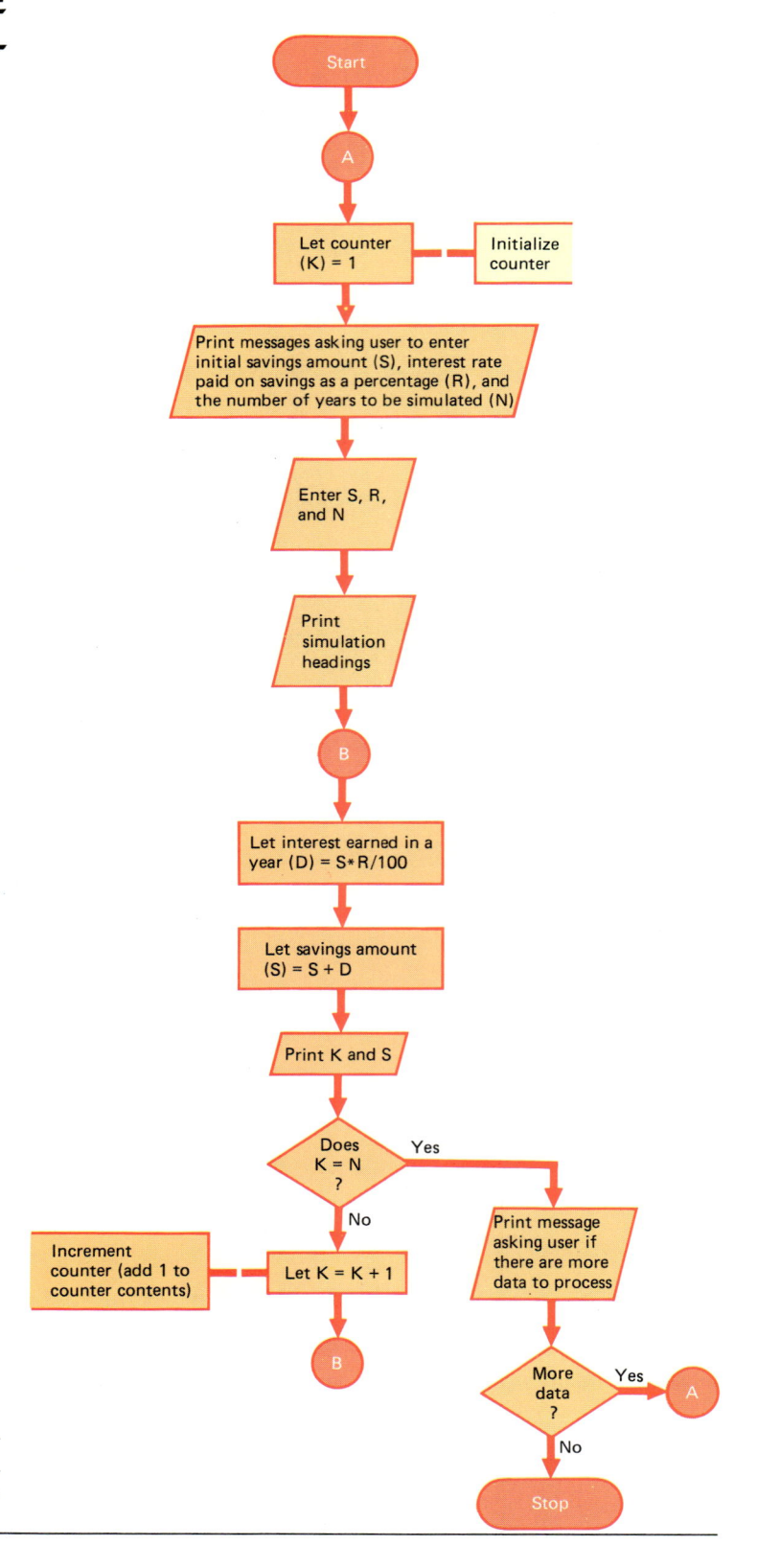

Program flowchart for Problem 9: Sam's Savings Simulator.

When K *does* equal N at the completion of the three passes specified by Sam, the first simulation run is completed, and program control branches out of the B loop. A message is sent to the user to see if additional simulations should be run. If Sam wants to see *what* will happen *if* he increases his initial savings amount and the number of years to be simulated, he can answer "YES" to the "more data?" question. The program will then branch back to the A connector at the top of the flowchart, the counter is reset to 1, and another run will begin. If Sam is through for now with his financial planning, he can answer "NO" to the "more data?" question, and processing will stop.

FEEDBACK

FEEDBACK AND REVIEW 16-3

How would you like to convert the charge program in problem 8 into a program that produces a summary report of owners and their charges? (Don't tell me your answer, it might depress me.) Anyway, that's what we're going to do, and the chart in Figure 16-11 will help you get started. Let's suppose this time that the program should meet these specifications:

- Program looping should be controlled by a counter, and the total amount charged to all property owners should be accumulated.

- The report should have a "REPORT OF OWNERS AND CHARGES" heading line and a second line with "OWNERS" and "CHARGES" subheadings.

- Input data are the number of property-owner records to be processed and the name, quantity planted, and unit price data for each property owner.

- The net amount owed for the plants, the planting charges, and the total charges should be computed for each owner.

- Under the report headings should be printed the name and the total amount of charges for each property owner.

- After all records have been processed, a "TOTAL AMOUNT OF CHARGES" subheading and the total charges accumulated for all owners should be printed at the bottom of the report, and the processing should stop.

Benefits and Limitations of Flowcharts

A programmer may benefit from using flowcharts during programming analysis in the following ways:

1 *Quicker grasp of relationships.* Current and proposed procedures may be understood more rapidly through the use of charts.

2 *Effective analysis.* The flowchart becomes a model of a program or system that can be broken down into detailed parts for study.

3 *Effective synthesis.* Synthesis is the opposite of analysis; it's the combination of the various parts into a whole entity. Flowcharts may be used as working models in the design of new programs and systems.

4 *Communication.* Flowcharts aid in communicating the facts of a problem to those whose skills are needed in the solution. The old adage that "a picture is worth a thousand words" rings true when the picture happens to be a flowchart.

5 *Proper program documentation.* **Program documentation** involves collecting, organizing, storing, and otherwise maintaining a complete historical record of programs and the other documents associated with a system. Good documentation is needed because (*a*) documented knowledge belongs to an organization and does not disappear with the departure of a programmer; (*b*) if projects are postponed, documented work will not have to be duplicated; and (*c*) if programs are modified in the future, the programmer will have a more understandable record of what was originally done. From what we've seen of the nature of flowcharts, it's obvious that they can provide valuable documentation support.

6 *Efficient coding.* The program flowchart acts as a guide or blueprint during the program preparation phase. Instructions coded in a programming language may be checked against the flowchart to help ensure that no steps are omitted.

7 *Orderly debugging and testing of programs.* If the program fails to run to completion when submitted to the computer for execution, the flowchart may help in the "debugging" process. That is, it may help in detecting, locating, and removing mistakes.

In spite of their many obvious advantages, flowcharts have several *limitations:*

1 Complex and detailed charts are sometimes laborious to plan and draw, especially when a large number of decision paths exist.

2 Although branches from a *single* decision symbol are easy to follow, the actions to be taken, given certain specified conditions, can be difficult to follow if there are *several* paths.

3 There are no standards determining the amount of detail that should be included in a chart.

LOGIC STRUCTURES AND STRUCTURED PROGRAMMING

We've now analyzed and flowcharted several problems. As you examined the logic of these problems, you may have noticed that a few patterns were frequently repeated. What you probably didn't realize unless you've read Chapter 12, however, is that any problem can be solved through the repeated use of just a few logic structures.

Three Logic Structures

Three standard logic patterns are all that are necessary to prepare any pro-

(a) Simple sequence structure

(b) Selection structure

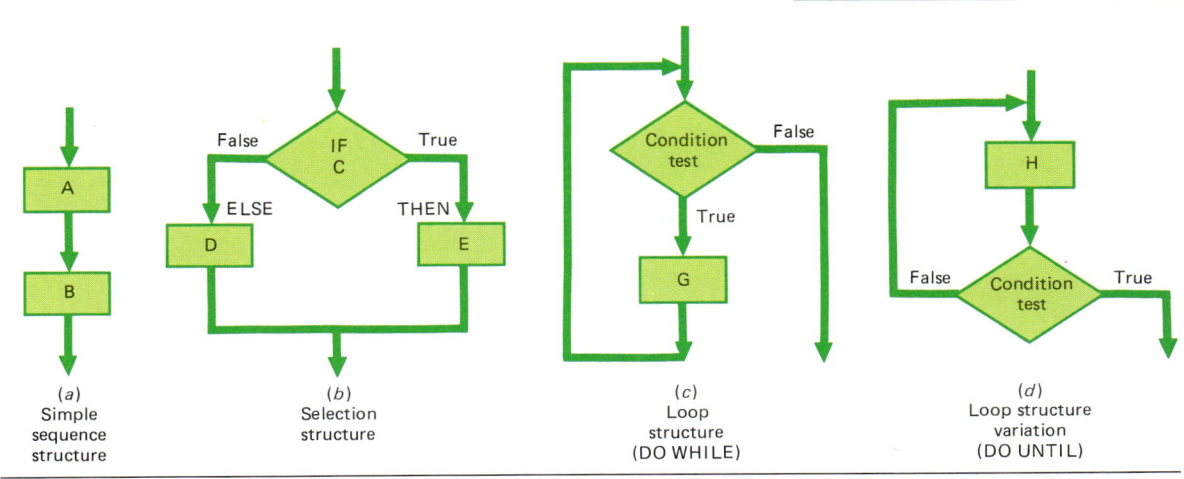

(c) Loop structure (DO WHILE)

(d) Loop structure variation (DO UNTIL)

FIGURE 16-13

Logic patterns used in structured programming.

gram. These patterns are shown in Figure 16-13. The **simple sequence structure** (Figure 16-13a) merely consists of one step followed by another. The **selection structure** (Figure 16-13b) requires a test for some condition followed by two alternative program control paths. As you know, the path selected depends on the results of the test. This pattern is sometimes referred to as an **IF-THEN-ELSE structure.**

The **loop structure** causes the program to execute one or more operations *while* a condition is *true* (Figure 16-13c). When the condition becomes false, the looping process is ended. If the condition is initially false, the operation found in this **DO WHILE structure** isn't executed. A variation of this third basic pattern is one in which the operation is repeated *until* a condition is found to be true (Figure 16-13d) after which the exit path is followed. This variation is called a **DO UNTIL structure.** You'll notice that the condition test is made at the beginning of a DO WHILE loop and at the end of a DO UNTIL loop.

Structured Programming Concepts

In the mid-1960s, programmers were writing ever-larger programs, and they were using mazes of branches to alter the sequence of processing operations. The **branch structure** shown in Figure 16-14, for example, causes control to branch away from a sequence and GOTO operation K if the condition is false. Although complex programs with excessive branches worked at first, they were often difficult to understand and maintain. In an attempt to tame needless program complexity and confusion, researchers began to look at how programs were being organized and produced. The discovery at this time that only three structures are needed to produce programs quickly led to the development of new programming concepts and tools.

The term **structured programming** initially described the disciplined use of the three standard logic structures. Although the logic patterns can be combined, or "nested," in actual practice as shown in Figure 16-15, each pattern has a **single entry point** and a **single exit point.** Each pattern is also readable from *top to bottom*. This inherent simplicity leads to more understandable program logic. Rules on indenting the coding structures written on

FIGURE 16-14

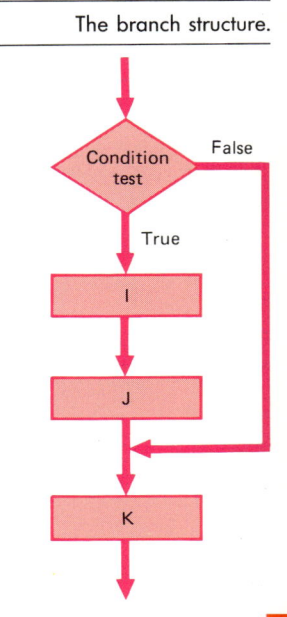

The branch structure.

MODULE 5

556

FIGURE 16-15

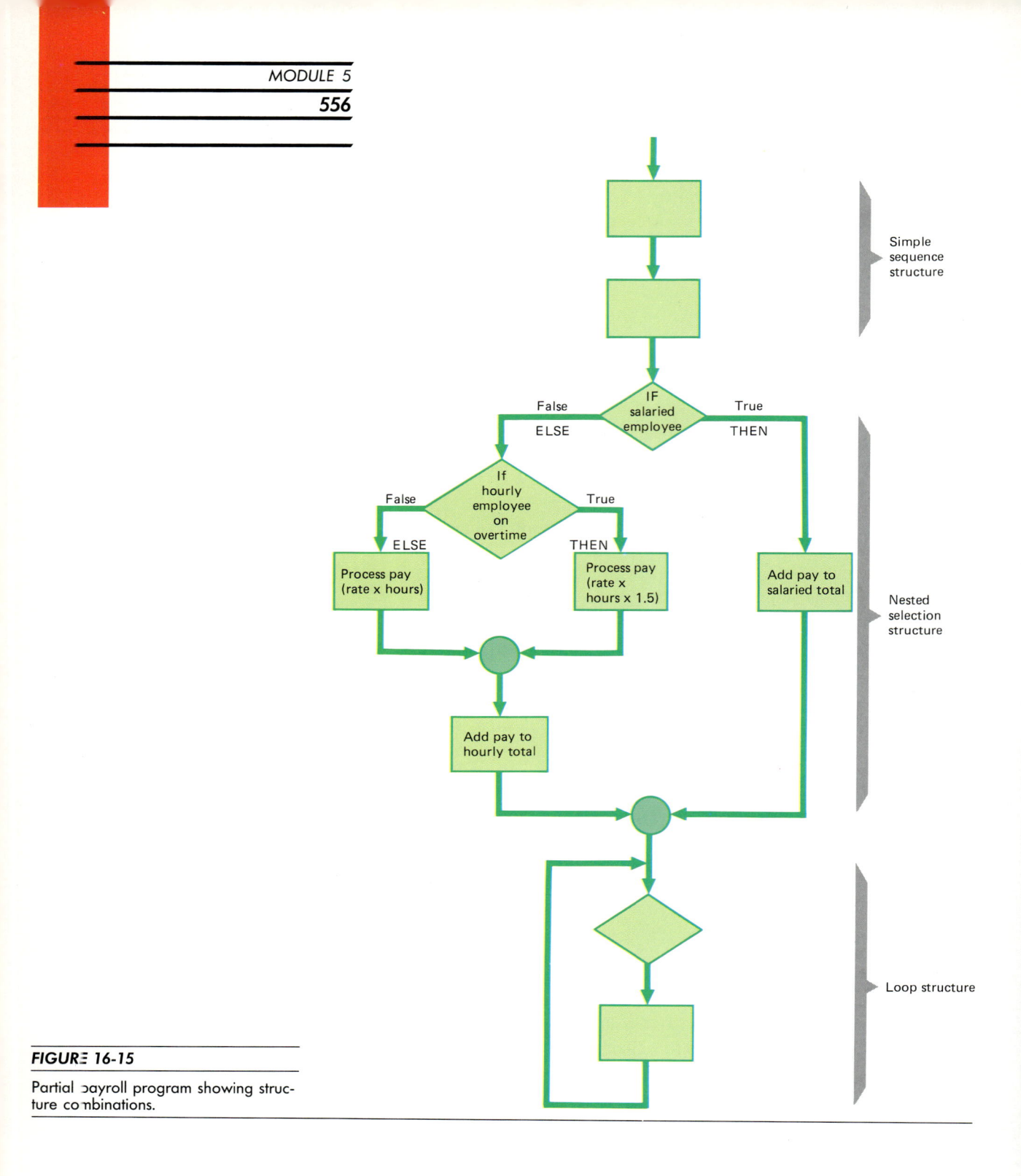

Partial payroll program showing structure combinations.

program coding sheets were also established to give a clearer picture of the coding logic.

Since these original concepts were developed, however, a number of other techniques have been added under the structured programming banner.

Thus many now expand the definition of structured programming to include the following practices (all of which are discussed in Chapter 12):

- A *modular (top-down) approach* is used to identify main program functions and then break them down into lower-level logical units. This aids in program analysis and preparation.

- *Peer reviews* or *structured walkthroughs* allow programmers to review the work of their colleagues to detect and correct programming and logic errors.

- Programmers may be organized into teams, and a *chief programmer* may assign module development to different team members.

Some Benefits of Structured Programming

Some of the advantages of using structured programming practices are:

1 Proven techniques may be used to attack a problem, and programmers can avoid needless complexity and confusion.

2 Programs can be broken up into modules and assigned to several people to speed up the programming process.

3 Since they represent only a portion of a program that may be lengthy and complex, these modules may be easier to understand, test, and debug.

4 Fewer errors are likely to get through the development process, program implementation is likely to be speeded up, and later program maintenance efforts may be easier and less expensive.

A possible limitation of structured programming practices is that the time needed to run a structured program consisting of numerous modules might be a little longer than the time required to run a comparable nonstructured program. But the costs of running hardware to process a given amount of work are dropping every day while programming costs are increasing. Thus the improvement in programmer productivity made possible by structured practices more than makes up for any extra running costs that may be incurred.

OTHER PROGRAMMING ANALYSIS TOOLS

Because of the limitations listed earlier, program flowcharts may be replaced or supplemented by alternative programming analysis tools.

Structured Pseudocode

One such tool is structured pseudocode. Since ''pseudo'' means imitation and ''code'' refers to instructions written in a programming language, **pseudocode** is a counterfeit and abbreviated version of actual computer instructions. These pseudo instructions are phrases written in ordinary natural language (English, French, Spanish). A pseudocode version of the Elm Creek

FIGURE 16-16

Pseudocode for Problem 5: Plant Control Report—Elm Creek Project.

```
Print report headings
Read first plant record
DOWHILE there are more records
    IF quantity received ⩾ 0
        Let available inventory = beginning inventory + receipts
    ELSE
        Let available inventory = beginning inventory
    ENDIF
    If quantity planted ⩾ 0
        Let ending inventory = available inventory − quantity planted
    ELSE
        Let ending inventory = available inventory
    ENDIF
    Print line on report
    Read next record
ENDDO
Stop
```

Plant Control Report problem charted in Figure 16-8 is shown in Figure 16-16.

As you can see in Figure 16-16, pseudocode is compact and is thus easy to revise. A few terms, or "key words," are often written in uppercase letters in a pseudocode problem solution. These key words identify the *sequence, selection,* and *loop structures* that we've just discussed. Figure 16-17 presents some of these common key words and shows you how they identify the three structured logic patterns. Figure 16-18 summarizes many of the concepts outlined in Figure 16-17 and shows a pseudocode solution for Sam's savings simulator problem charted in Figure 16-12.

Computer professionals who write structured programs often prefer to use pseudocode in preparing a detailed plan for a program. However, there are no standard rules to follow in using pseudocode, and, of course, a graphic representation of program logic isn't available.

Decision Tables

A **decision table** can be a powerful tool for tracing complex program logic. The decision table format is shown in Figure 16-19*a*. The table is divided into two main parts: The upper part contains the *conditions* and questions to be tested in reaching a decision, and the lower part describes the *actions* taken for a given set of conditions. The contents of the condition stub correspond to the conditions contained in the decision symbols of a flowchart, and the condition entries correspond to the paths leading out from decision symbols. Action statements corresponding to the statements located in nondecision symbols of a chart are listed in the action stub.

A decision table version of the Elm Creek Plant Control Report problem that we've now charted and put in a pseudocode format is shown in Figure 16-19*b*. Each decision rule column is the equivalent of one path through the flowchart. Decision tables may thus be used in place of program flowcharts for the following reasons:

● Tables are easier to draw and change than flowcharts, and they provide

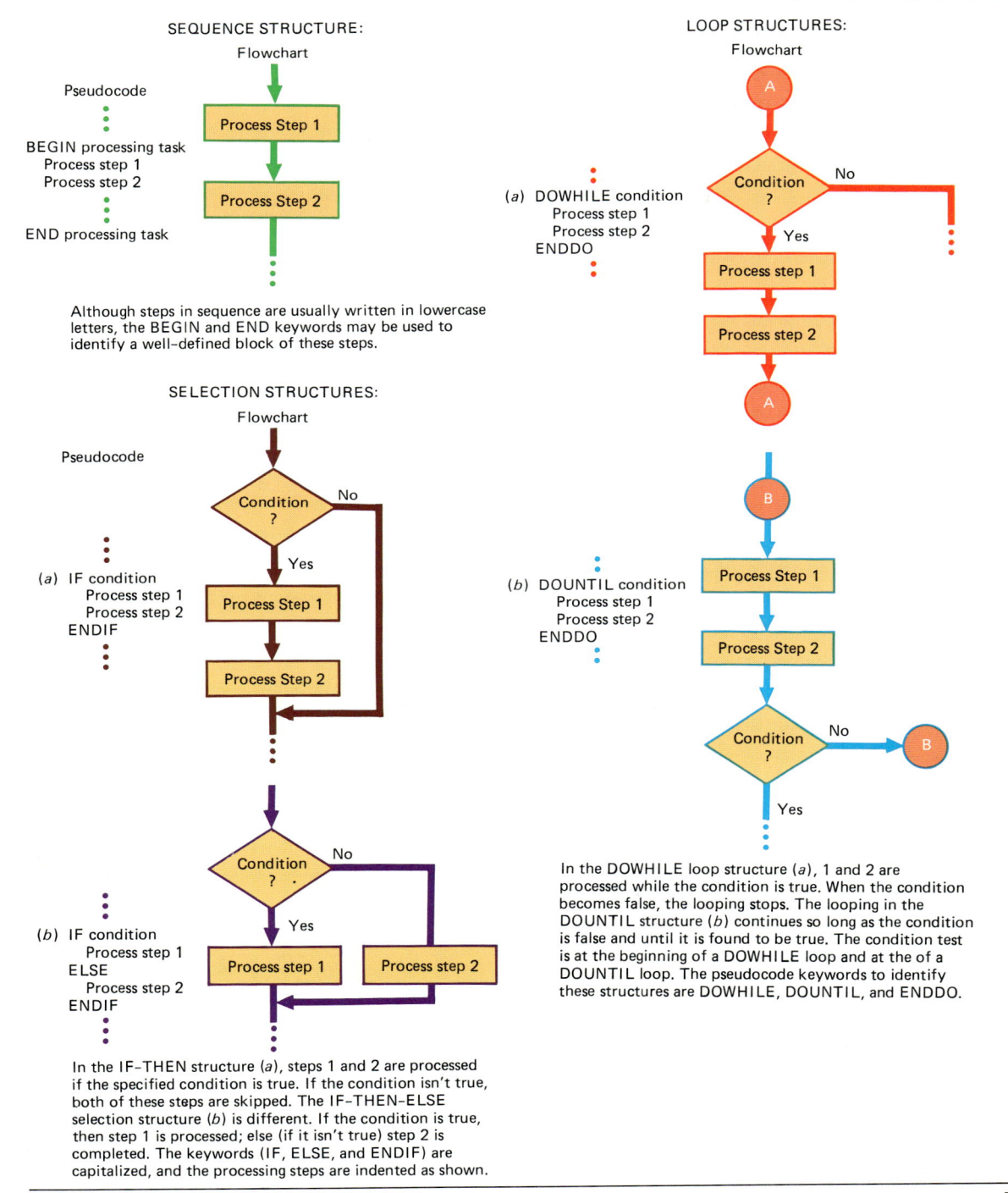

SEQUENCE STRUCTURE:

Pseudocode

```
    ⋮
BEGIN processing task
    Process step 1
    Process step 2
    ⋮
END processing task
```

Flowchart: Process Step 1 → Process Step 2

Although steps in sequence are usually written in lowercase letters, the BEGIN and END keywords may be used to identify a well-defined block of these steps.

SELECTION STRUCTURES:

Pseudocode

```
    ⋮
(a) IF condition
        Process step 1
        Process step 2
    ENDIF
    ⋮
```

```
    ⋮
(b) IF condition
        Process step 1
    ELSE
        Process step 2
    ENDIF
    ⋮
```

In the IF-THEN structure (a), steps 1 and 2 are processed if the specified condition is true. If the condition isn't true, both of these steps are skipped. The IF-THEN-ELSE selection structure (b) is different. If the condition is true, then step 1 is processed; else (if it isn't true) step 2 is completed. The keywords (IF, ELSE, and ENDIF) are capitalized, and the processing steps are indented as shown.

LOOP STRUCTURES:

```
    ⋮
(a) DOWHILE condition
        Process step 1
        Process step 2
    ENDDO
    ⋮
```

```
    ⋮
(b) DOUNTIL condition
        Process step 1
        Process step 2
    ENDDO
    ⋮
```

In the DOWHILE loop structure (a), 1 and 2 are processed while the condition is true. When the condition becomes false, the looping stops. The looping in the DOUNTIL structure (b) continues so long as the condition is false and until it is found to be true. The condition test is at the beginning of a DOWHILE loop and at the of a DOUNTIL loop. The pseudocode keywords to identify these structures are DOWHILE, DOUNTIL, and ENDDO.

FIGURE 16-17

Pseudocode key words and concepts.

```
DOWHILE there are more data
    Let counter (K) = 1
    Print messages asking for simulation run data
    Accept run data
    Print simulation headings
        DOUNTIL counter = number of years (N) to be simulated
            BEGIN processing savings data for year K
                Let interest earned = savings amount * rate/100
                Let savings amount = savings amount + interest earned
                Print counter value and savings amount
            END processing savings data for year K
            Add 1 to counter (K)
        ENDDO
    Print message asking if there are more data to process
ENDDO
Stop
```

FIGURE 16-18

Many of the concepts outlined in Figure 16-17 are shown in this pseudocode for Problem 9: Sam's Savings Simulator. This problem is flowcharted in Figure 16-12.

FIGURE 16-19

(a) Decision table format. (b) Decision table for Problem 5: Plant Control Report—Elm Creek Project.

	Table Heading	Decision Rules
Condition	If And stub And	entries
Action	Then And stub And	entries

(a)

Inventory Control Report		Decision Rule Number				
		1	2	3	4	5
Condition	Quantity received = −99.9	N	N	N	N	Y
	Quantity received ≥ 0	Y	N	Y	N	
	Quantity sold ≥ 0	Y	N	N	Y	
Action	Let available inventory = B + R	X		X		
	Let available inventory = B		X		X	
	Let ending inventory = A − S	X			X	
	Let ending inventory = A		X	X		
	Print line on report	X	X	X	X	
	Read next record	X	X	X	X	
	Stop					X

(b)

more compact documentation (a small table can replace several pages of flowcharts).

- It's also easier to follow a particular path down one column than through several flowchart pages.

But tables aren't as widely used as flowcharts because:

- Flowcharts are better able to express the total sequence of events needed to solve a problem.

- Flowcharts are more familiar to, and are preferred by, many programmers.

LOOKING BACK

1. People must usually follow six steps in order to put computers to work. The first three (defining the need, gathering and analyzing data, and designing and preparing specifications to solve the problem) are included in the systems analysis and design process. The last three steps (programming analysis, program preparation, and program implementation and maintenance) make up the programming process. Included among the questions that must be considered during program analysis are, (a) Are problem specifications clear and complete? (b) Is a solution method now known? (c) If not, can such a method be obtained from other sources? (d) If a solution method must be created, what approach should be used?

2. A system flowchart shows a broad overview of the flow and sequence of operations in a processing system, but it doesn't go into detail about how input data are used to produce output information. That task is left to the program flowchart which does present a detailed picture of how steps are to be performed within a processor to produce the needed output. A single flowchart may be used to represent a problem solution, or the major program modules in a main-control flowchart can be drawn separately in a series of micro flowcharts. Standard symbols used in system and program flowcharts are introduced and explained in this chapter.

3. Nine problems are analyzed and flowcharted in this chapter. These same applications are coded in the BASIC language in Chapter 17. The specifications for each problem were presented, and a flowchart was drawn to meet these specifications. After examining a simple input/process/output chart, we moved to problems that required the flexibility made possible by the use of decisions and loops. Charts with multiple decision symbols were presented, and then the use of accumulators and counters was discussed.

4. Flowcharts enhance communication and understanding between programmers and others, contribute to effective problem

analysis and synthesis, provide good documentation, and are useful during program coding and debugging. However, complex and detailed charts can be hard to draw, and following the actions taken in specific cases can be difficult when many decision paths are available.

5. The logic of all programs written for computers can be described using just the simple sequence, selection, and loop structures. A branch structure may also be employed, but some computer professionals believe that its use can lead to complex and confusing programs. The term "structured programming" initially described the disciplined use of the three logic structures, but a number of other practices have now been included under its banner. Included in these practices are the use of top-down concepts to decompose main functions into lower-level components for modular coding. Structured programming may reduce needless complexity, allow several people to work on modules simultaneously, and produce modules that are easier to understand, test, debug, and maintain.

6. Other programming analysis tools such as pseudocode and decision tables sometimes are used to replace or supplement program flowcharts. Pseudocode is a counterfeit and abbreviated version of actual computer instructions. It's compact, easy to change, and popular with programmers who use a structured approach. But there are no standard rules governing its use. A decision table is compact and is easy to draw and change. It's a powerful tool for defining complex program logic because a single table column can represent a maze of lines through several pages of flowcharts. Flowcharts are more frequently used, however, because they are better able to express the total sequence of events needed to solve a problem.

KEY TERMS AND CONCEPTS

system analysis/design stage 532
programming process 532
program analysis approach 532
algorithm 533
system flowchart 535
program flowchart 535
program segments (modules) 535
main-control (macro) flowchart 535
micro (detail) flowchart 535
input/output symbol 535
processing symbol 536

terminal symbol 537
decision symbol 537
conditional statement 537
connector symbol 537
offpage connector symbol 537
preparation symbol 537
subroutines 537
predefined process symbol 538
annotation flag 538
loop 540
sentinel value 540
test for exit condition 540
endless (infinite) loop 541

accumulator 545
counter 548
program documentation 554
simple sequence structure 555
selection structure (IF-THEN-ELSE structure) 555
loop structure (with DO WHILE and DO UNTIL variations) 555
branch structure 555
structured programming 555
single entry and single exit points 555
pseudocode 557
decision table 558

Topics for Review and Discussion

1. (a) What are the steps in the system analysis and design process? (b) What are the steps in the programming process?
2. "Although different programmers use different strategies to develop program solutions, certain questions must usually be considered regardless of the strategy used." Identify and discuss these questions.
3. In computer science, the term "stepwise refinement" is given to the process of breaking down a large problem into a series of smaller and more understandable tasks. How can the use of program flowcharts help in this process?
4. (a) What's the purpose of a program flowchart? (b) How does it differ from a system flowchart? (c) What symbols are used in program charts?
5. What features must be included in any program loop?
6. (a) What's a sentinel value? (b) Why must the sentinel be a value that couldn't occur as a valid data item?
7. (a) What's an accumulator? (b) How is an accumulator initialized and then updated to compute a running total?
8. (a) What's a counter? (b) How can a counter be used to keep track of the number of times a loop has been executed?
9. Using the flowchart for problem 5 in Figure 16-8, identify the simple sequence, selection, and loop structures in the program logic.
10. Discuss the benefits and limitations of flowcharts.
11. Why is proper program documentation a necessity?
12. (a) What is pseudocode? (b) Prepare a pseudocode solution for the Elm Creek Planting Summary problem charted in Figure 16-10.
13. What are the advantages and limitations of decision tables?
14. Review the flowchart for problem 2 in Figure 16-4. How could you modify it so that the user could interact with the program and supply the input data at the time of processing?
15. After studying the Feedback and Review 16-1 chart solution found at the end of this chapter, how could you modify it so that Lisa could interact with the program and supply the input data at the time of processing?
16. Let's assume Sam Byter wants to write a program that will compute the amount of grass seed needed to complete various landscaping projects. Input data for this program should be the length and width (in feet) of a rectangular lot. The program should interact with Sam and request this input. It should then compute the number of bags of seed that will be needed for the lot. Each bag contains enough seed to cover 5,000 square feet of lot surface. The output should be a line showing the number of bags needed for the job.
17. As a continuation of question 16, let's now revise Sam's program so that he can compute the number of bags of seed needed for any number of lots. After completing one pass through the steps charted in question 16, the program should now ask Sam this question: "DO YOU WANT TO STOP (Y/N)"? Provision should then be made to accept "Y," "N," or incorrect responses. Prepare a flowchart for this revision.
18. Let's assume that you need to prepare a program that will compute the number of acres in any number of rectangular lots. The program should interact with the user and request the length (in feet) and width (in feet) of each lot prior to computing its acreage and printing out the result. There are 43,560 square feet in an acre. After computing the acreage in a first lot, the program should then determine from the user if there are any additional lots to process. When the processing is completed, the program should print a "GOOD-BYE" message. Draw a flowchart for this program.
19. Let's assume Lisa's teacher has found a student guilty of chewing gum in class. The punishment is to write "I will not chew gum in class" 10 times. Prepare a flowchart for a program that will (a) accept any "naughty student" message and (b) reproduce this message any designated number of times.
20. Let's now assume that a state has decided to impose a one-time tax on new cars in an effort to (a) raise additional revenue and (b) encourage citizens to buy more fuel-efficient cars. The tax on each car is based on its current overall Environmental Protection Agency (EPA) mileage rating. The EPA mileage rating categories and the tax payment due on purchase are indicated below:

EPA Mileage Rating	Tax Due
Less than 15 mpg	$450
15 and less than 20 mpg	250
20 and less than 25 mpg	100
25 mpg and over	5

Prepare a flowchart for a program that meets the following specifications: (a) It should produce the amount of tax due, given a car's EPA mileage rating as input, and (b) it should interact with the user by requesting the necessary input data.
21. Now let's revise the chart prepared for question 20. After completing one pass through the steps charted in question 20, the program should then ask the user this question: "ANOTHER TAX COMPUTATION (Y/N)"? Provision should be made to accept "Y," "N," or incorrect responses. Prepare a flowchart for this revision.
22. After reviewing Figure 2-3, page 57, prepare a flowchart for Jill Byter's mailing list program.
23. Sam Byter has been hired to prepare a length conversion program for a carpet store. This program should meet the following specifications: (a) It should process without interruption the carpet lengths (in yards) of all customer orders to be filled during the day. (b) It should print an output report converting the yardage in each order into the corresponding lengths in feet and in inches. (c) After processing all orders

and preparing the output report, the processing should stop. Prepare a flowchart to meet these specifications.

24. Let's assume that you've owned your car for 6 months and it has been in the shop for numerous repairs. Suspecting that you may have a lemon, you're thinking of trading it for another model. The price of your car was $9,875, and you've been offered $9,295 for it. You would like to know the annual rate of depreciation on the car before making a decision. The annual rate of depreciation is calculated by the following formula:

$$\text{Depreciation rate} = 1 - \left(\frac{\text{resale price}}{\text{original price}}\right)^{1/\text{age in years}}$$

Prepare a flowchart for a program that will (a) request that the user supply it with the original and resale prices and the age of the investment in years, (b) compute the annual depreciation rate and convert it into a percentage, and (c) be able to repeat these operations as needed.

25. After reviewing the chart for Jill's Student Payment Report in Figure 16-7, prepare a new version that accumulates (a) the total hours worked and (b) the total earnings for all students. The new program should first print "TOTAL HOURS" and "TOTAL EARNINGS" subheadings at the bottom of the report, and it should then print the accumulated amounts.

26. Jill Byter is still running for a seat in the student house of representatives. Let's assume she wants to print a message on gummed labels that can then be attached to the campaign letters she has written with her word processing program (see Figure 2-10, page 66). Prepare a flowchart for a program that achieves the following objectives: (a) The number of labels to be printed is specified in the program and (b) the message to be printed on each label is:

THE STUDENT HOUSE OF REPRESENTATIVES
ELECTION WILL BE HELD NEXT TUESDAY.
PLEASE REMEMBER TO VOTE FOR JILL BYTER.
THANKS FOR YOUR SUPPORT!

27. Sam Byter has another idea for an investment planning tool. This time he wants an interactive program to compute the future value of an investment. The input data are supplied in response to a series of questions posed by the program. These questions appear in the first four lines below the heading in the program output. The fifth line gives the future value computation produced by the program. The formula needed to produce this result is:

$$T = P * [1 + (I/100)/N]^{(N \cdot Y)}$$

where:
T = value of investment after Y years
P = initial investment
I = nominal interest rate (percent)
N = number of compounding periods per year
Y = number of years in the future

Here is an output example:

FUTURE VALUE OF AN INVESTMENT

WHAT IS THE NOMINAL INTEREST RATE (PERCENT)? 6
HOW MANY COMPOUNDING PERIODS PER YEAR? 4
WHAT IS THE INITIAL INVESTMENT (DOLLARS)? 10000
HOW MANY YEARS BEFORE WITHDRAWAL? 10
FUTURE VALUE IS $18140.15

DO YOU WANT ANOTHER RUN (Y/N)? Y
WHAT IS THE NOMINAL INTEREST RATE (PERCENT)? 6
HOW MANY COMPOUNDING PERIODS PER YEAR? 4
WHAT IS THE INITIAL INVESTMENT (DOLLARS)? 20000
HOW MANY YEARS BEFORE WITHDRAWAL? 10
FUTURE VALUE IS $36280.3

DO YOU WANT ANOTHER RUN (Y/N)? NO
TYPE A 'Y' OR AN 'N'
DO YOU WANT ANOTHER RUN (Y/N)? N

Prepare a flowchart for a program that will produce this output.

28. Several student assistants work for Jill's economics professor. The professor must prepare a report each pay period authorizing the school business office to pay the assistants for the hours they have worked during that period. It's also the professor's responsibility to keep track of the total amount paid to the assistants each period so that she will not exceed the budget the dean has given her. The professor has asked Jill to prepare a program that will meet the following specifications: (a) It should supply, when needed, the name and hourly pay rate of each assistant from a stored data file, and it should also supply the number of such assistants in the file. (b) During processing, it should permit the user to enter the number of hours worked by each student during the period. (c) Given the above input data (name, hourly pay rate, and number of hours worked), it should (1) print each student's name and (2) compute and print out the amount of pay authorized for each student during the period. (d) It should accumulate the total amount paid to the assistants for the period, and it should print this total amount after all assistants have been processed. (e) As a further aid to her record keeping, the professor would also like the program to compute and print out the average (arithmetic mean) amount paid during the period. Prepare a flowchart to meet these specifications.

Project to Consider

1. Contact an organization of interest to you, and determine the programming analysis approach or approaches used by the organization. Also, inquire about the procedures used to acquire software applications packages. Present your findings to the class.

Answers to Feedback and Review Sections

Possible flowcharts for Feedback and Review Sections 16-1 through 16-3 follow. Your versions may differ in some respects (variable abbreviations and so on) and still be correct.

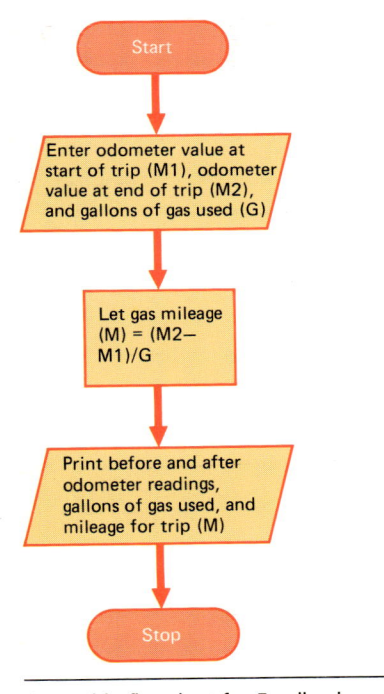

A possible flowchart for Feedback and Review 16-1.

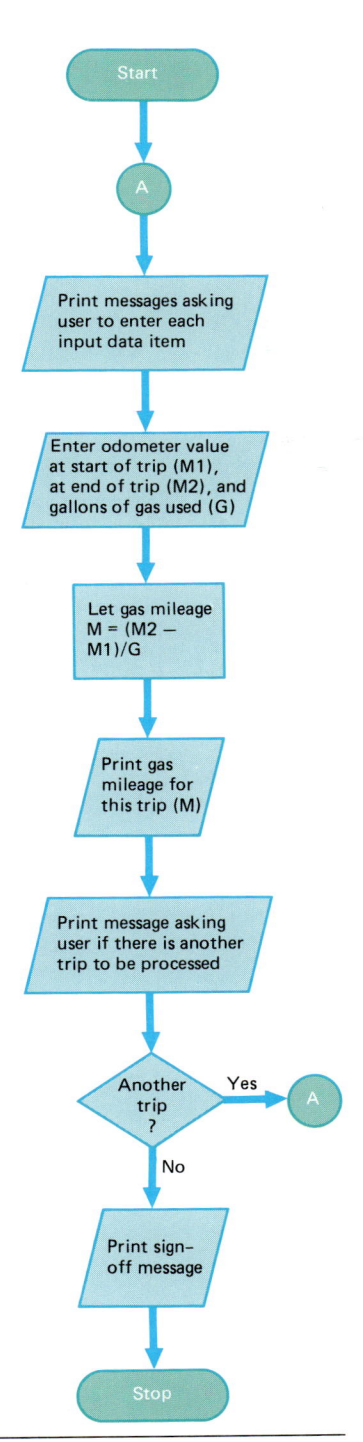

A possible flowchart for Feedback and Review 16-2.

MODULE 5

566

```
Start
  ↓
[Let counter (K) = 1] ----- Initialize counter
  ↓
[Let total amount accumulator (T) = 0] ----- Initialize accumulator
  ↓
[Print report headings]
  ↓
[Enter number of property owner records (N) to be processed]
  ↓
 (A)
  ↓
[Enter property-owner name (N$), quantity planted (Q), and unit price (P)]
  ↓
[Let net amount of plants (A) = Q*P]
  ↓
[Let planting charges (T1) = A*.06]
  ↓
[Let total charges (T2) = A + T1]
  ↓
[Let T = T + T2] ----- Accumulate total amount charged to all property owners
  ↓
[Print property-owner name (N$), and total charges (T2)]
  ↓
<Does K = N ?> ----- The value of the counter is compared to the number of records to be processed
  │Yes → [Print "TOTAL AMOUNT OF CHARGES" Subheading and total amount accumulated (T)] → Stop
  │No
  ↓
[Let K = K + 1] ----- Increment counter (Add 1 to counter contents)
  ↓
 (A)
```

A possible flowchart for Feedback and Review 16-3.

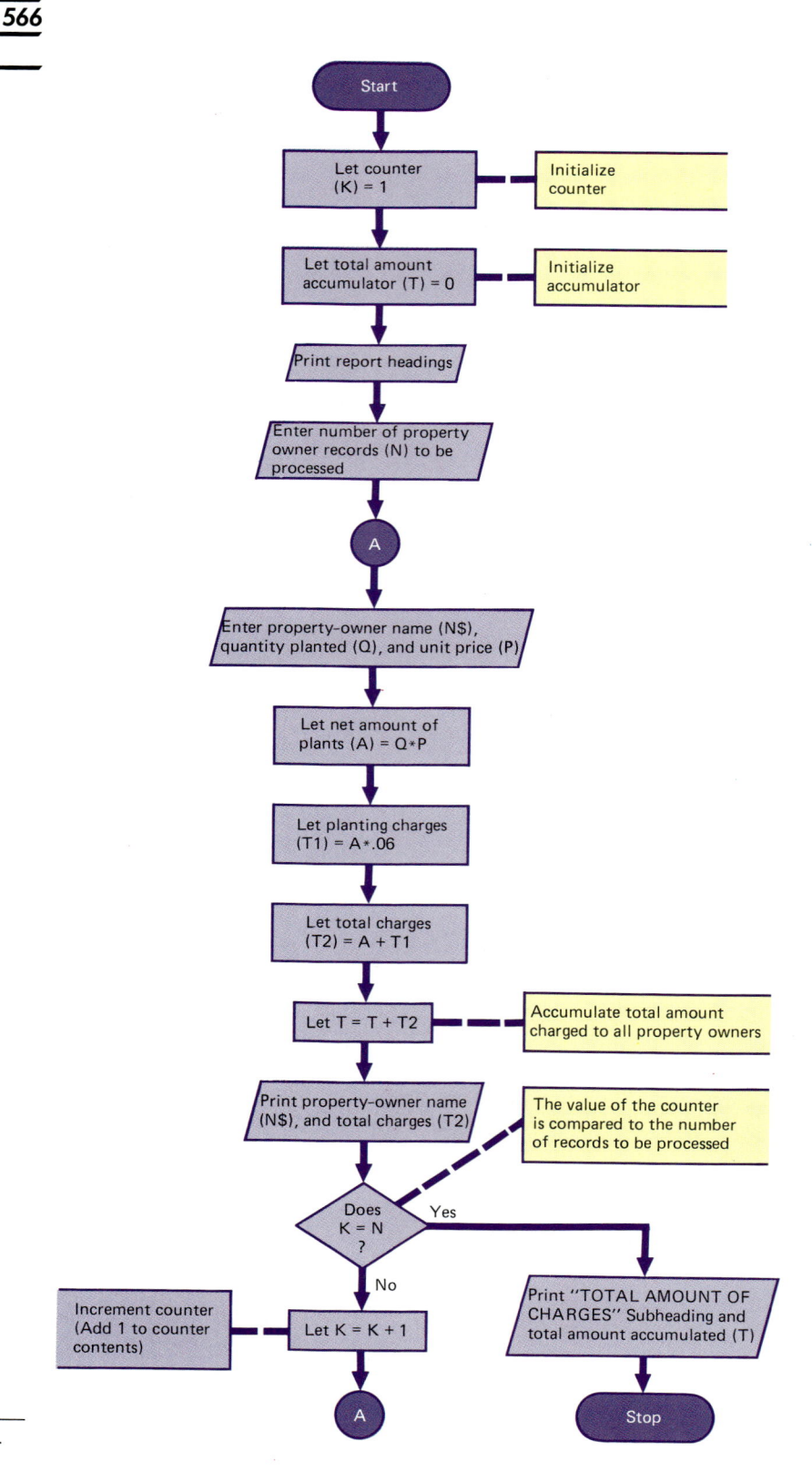

A CLOSER LOOK

HOW ABOUT A COMPUTER PROGRAM FOR DINNER?

The first task in programming is to be realistic about what the computer can cope with. People often think that a computer would be useful in the home, managing things like menus. It is a nice idea, but it is unrealistic. You would like it to look in the larder and the fridge and report that you had three tins of sardines, a half-used jar of mayonnaise, and some rice, so the best supper you could manage would be a sort of salad.

But all this is what the computer cannot do. The poor, legless, eyeless thing cannot go poking about in the larder. To get the information into it, *you* would have to be its eyes and legs and then type in the data. While you were doing that, your own perfectly good menu-producing computer—driven by hunger as the silicon one is not—would have planned a meal and have it half ready.

The second step in writing a program is to find some data that you and the computer can both make some sense of. Space Invaders is an excellent example—people see the little shapes on the screen as alien monsters that have to be killed; the computer sees them as neat little shapes that can be drawn here and there as the player wants. When the coordinates of the missile coincide with the coordinates of the monster the machine replaces the monster by a different picture of exploding rubbish and outputs a tone to the loudspeaker.

So, having settled on some mutually convenient symbols, you then have to ask whether the computer's commands can do anything useful to them. Languages that will run on micros are quite clever in some ways and very stupid in others. They can do logarithms and sines and cosines, which many intelligent adults cannot do, but they cannot work out how to organize a problem at all.

Even though there are many things that a computer cannot do, there are still plenty that it can—if you take enough trouble. Let us look at what might be involved in writing a simple program. Written in a hitherto unknown language called "FOODGOL," the following program illustrates basic programming concepts of steps, decisions, and loops.

Let us look at the steps needed to eat your dinner.

Adapted from Peter Laurie, *The Joy of Computers*, Little, Brown, & Co., 1983. Reprinted by permission of Century Hutchinson Publishing, Ltd., London.

Eating Program 1

1. Pick up knife and fork
2. Cut off a morsel of food
3. Stick it with fork
4. Put in mouth
5. Cut off a morsel of food
6. Stick it with fork
7. Put in mouth
8. Cut off a morsel of food
9. Stick it with fork
10. Put in mouth
11. Cut off a morsel of food
12. Stick it with fork

This looks sensible enough, if a bit tedious to write. But we could make the program much simpler by incorporating a loop:

Eating Program 2

1. Pick up knife and fork
2. Cut off a morsel of food
3. Stick it with fork
4. Put in mouth
5. Goto 2

Now, each time you have put some food in your mouth the program makes you go to step 2. "Cut off a morsel of food," followed by "Stick it with fork," etc. Hold on—what will happen when the food on your plate is all eaten up?

Eating Program 3

1. Pick up knife and fork
1a. Is there any food on plate? If not, put knife and fork down, stop
2. Cut off a morsel of food
3. Stick it with fork
4. Put in mouth
5. Goto 1a

What was missing was a test to see whether the actions should continue. This is now a complete programming loop. It will make you start eating, continue eating, and stop eating when there is nothing left. In fact, it is difficult to see how you would write the program without using a loop. Look at Eating Program 1 again. How do you know in advance how many times to repeat the cycle? Do you write 10 of them and hope you do not get served any banquets? Or 100, and put up with scraping an empty plate, maybe dozens of times? There has to be a test to see if you have finished.

We can enlarge the program to let you have some pie:

> **Eating Program 4**
>
> 1. Pick up knife and fork
> 1a. Is there any food on plate? If not, goto 6
> 2. Cut off a morsel of food
> 3. Stick it with fork
> 4. Put in mouth
> 5. Goto 1a
> 6. Ask for pie
> 7. Is there any food on plate? If not, put knife and fork down, stop
> 8. Cut off a morsel of food
> 9. Stick it with fork
> 10. Put in mouth
> 11. Goto 7

We have changed the program in three ways. First, when the first course is finished, step 1a takes us to step 6 which makes us ask for pie. There is a new loop to cope with eating the pie, with a new test to see if it has been finished.

However, lines 8, 9, 10 are exact copies of 2, 3, 4. Lines 11 and 5 are very similar. We can make the same chunk of program control eating both courses with a "subroutine."

> **Eating Program 5**
>
> 1. Pick up knife and fork
> 1a. Is there any food on plate? If not, goto 6
> 2a. Gosub 100
> 5. Goto 1a
> 6. Ask for pie
> 7. Is there any food on plate? If not, put knife and fork down, stop
> 8. Gosub 100
> 11. Goto 7
> 100. Cut off a morsel of food
> 101. Stick it with fork
> 102. Put in mouth
> 103. Return

"Gosub" is a computing command borrowed from BASIC which means "Goto the step ordered (in this case, 100), do the steps that follow, and come back when you meet the command RETURN." Having jumped from step 2a to the subroutine at step 100, executed the steps there, and returned, the program does the next step, which is 5, just as before. When the test at 1a shows there is no more first course, the program jumps—as before—to step 6, and uses the subroutine at step 100 to eat the pie.

What is the point? First, it saves program space. Secondly, it means that all the eating is carried out by the same bit of program. If eating is to be done in a different way, say, by using chopsticks rather than a knife and fork, it is easy to change the way the program works. In this case we have to, because we have forgotten to tell the unfortunate eater to chew and swallow. As the program stands, he will stuff his mouth with food until he suffocates:

> **Eating Program 6**
>
> 1. Pick up knife and fork
> 1a. Is there any food on plate? If not, goto 6
> 2a. Gosub 100
> p5. Goto 1a
> 6. Ask for pie
> 7. Is there any food on plate? If not, put knife and fork down, stop
> 8. Gosub 100
> 11. Goto 7
> 100. Cut off a morsel of food
> 101. Stick it with fork
> 102. Put in mouth
> 102a. Chew
> 102b. Swallow
> 103. Return

It would have been much more difficult to alter Eating Program 1—we would have had to add two new steps every three steps. A mistake would have been easy. We have also just fixed a "bug"—a bit of the program which did not do what it was meant to. Professional programmers spend most of their time doing that.

CHAPTER 17

A BASIC BEGINNING

Computer Software: Today's Shooting Stars

The art of developing computer software has attracted many practitioners. This hot new field draws some people with promises of overnight fortunes; others are intrigued with the endless possibilities of programming. But like most artistic ventures, software authorship offers no guarantees.

Of course, some software authors become instant millionaires and inspire us all. Tom Frye, a 26-year-old high school dropout and Berkeley panhandler, converted the Pac-Man arcade game into an Atari videocassette and earned a million dollars in royalties. Bill Gates, who at 28 was featured on a 1984 cover of *Time* magazine, developed a $100+ million empire through his software company, Microsoft. And Mitch Kapor, a former radio disc jockey, grossed over $50 million in 1 year with Lotus's 1-2-3. Still, the total number of software millionaires is less than twenty out of thousands.

Everyone would like to have a hit program and be a millionaire, but this goal has remained out of reach for most programmers. It's easy to conclude that those who make it big are more intelligent—they have the right concepts and know how to implement them—whereas the others are simply coding up the wrong tree. But even those who catch the big wave usually have only one glory ride.

With the exception of Bill Gates, most of today's software gurus have made it on the basis of one successful program. Dan Bricklin and Bob Frankston transformed the personal computer from a hobbyist's toy into a serious business machine when they unveiled VisiCalc, but their subsequent TK!Solver failed to attract as great an audience. Rob Barnaby wrote WordStar in 1977 but has not been heard from since.

As reported in *Time* magazine, Bill Gates seldom, if ever, writes code any more. Although he is a brilliant programmer, his success as chairman of Microsoft is primarily derived from his astute business sense. Gates, after all, has built a successful company of more than 500 people, including a regiment of brilliant programmers.

So the question is, if the software princes are smarter than the software paupers, why do so many of them hit the jackpot only once?

The secret to successful software is a delicate balance of creative vision and functional skills. Snappy techniques are important, and software developers have learned to use techniques such as windows, mice, and menu commands to captivate their audience. But harmonizing these factors into one final product is a tough job. Aspiring software authors have to develop an ear for the user's needs and abilities.

Meanwhile the search for the next software star continues. The great program that will point out the new direction for personal computing has yet to be written.

Excerpted from David Bunnell, "Computer Software: Today's Shooting Stars," *PC World*, July 1984, Vol. 2, issue 7, published at 555 De Haro Street, San Francisco, 94107. Reprinted by permission.

CHAPTER 17

571

LOOKING AHEAD

This chapter gives you an introduction to BASIC—a popular programming language that allows personal computer and terminal users to interact with their machines. After you've mastered the language rules and programming techniques presented in this chapter, you'll have the tools needed to write programs that can solve complex problems. BASIC is a rich and powerful language, and Chapter 18 contains additional instruction in using it. The information in this chapter will enable you to:

- Identify and discuss the parts of a BASIC statement
- Understand and use the BASIC statements discussed in the chapter to prepare programs
- Write programs that incorporate input operations, calculations, decisions, loops, accumulators, counters, and output operations to achieve specified goals

CHAPTER OUTLINE

SOME BASIC NECESSITIES
Using Your System
System Commands and Program Statements
Program Entry Elements
Arithmetic Operations
Correcting Errors
PROGRAM PREPARATION EXAMPLES
A Simple Input/Process/Output Example
Feedback and Review 17-1
Gaining Flexibility with Decisions and Loops
Feedback and Review 17-2
A Multiple-Decision Situation
The Use of Accumulators
The Use of Counters
Feedback and Review 17-3
LOOKING BACK

SOME BASIC NECESSITIES

When Professors John Kemeny and Thomas Kurtz developed BASIC at Dartmouth College in the mid-1960s, their goal was to create an *interactive language* that (1) would be easy to learn and (2) would thus be used regularly by students. BASIC was a success on both counts, and its popularity quickly spread around the world. Over the years, BASIC has been improved, its scope has been extended, and millions of personal computer (pc) and timesharing terminal users have written programs in the language (Figure 17-1).

There are now so many versions or dialects of BASIC that a program that works on one manufacturer's equipment may not run without modification on another system. In the pages that follow, we'll discuss certain BASIC program statements that permit the computer to perform input, data movement, and output. The statements used in the example programs found in the chapter follow the rules of many BASIC dialects. Any differences that exist between the BASIC version that your computer system uses and the version used in this chapter should be relatively easy to resolve.

Using Your System

Since BASIC is a language that's meant to be used for interactive computing, the user typically writes programs and enters some or all of the necessary data from the *keyboard* of a pc or timesharing terminal. Data also may be entered through floppy- and hard-disk drives and magnetic tape cassette units attached to pc or terminal systems. The *output* information usually appears on a visual display screen or is printed by a character printer. Output may also be recorded on magnetic disks or tapes if the computer is equipped with appropriate pc or terminal attachments.

Sign-on Procedures Let's assume that you glanced ahead in this chapter to get an idea of what's involved in preparing a BASIC program. Since we are supposing, let's also assume that at the first opportunity you then rushed to an available keyboard to try your hand at writing a program. Alas, banging on

FIGURE 17-1

BASIC is a second language that millions have now learned. Classes are given by schools, computer clubs, and even by retailers. (Courtesy Computerland)

the keyboard produced no results—because you didn't turn the computer on, or you didn't follow the proper sign-on (or "log-on") procedure required to get access to the system.

In a *personal computing environment,* the sign-on "procedure" may simply involve turning on the power. The BASIC translating software—usually called an *interpreter*—may be permanently stored in integrated circuit chips inside the processor, instantly ready for use. Alternatively, the BASIC interpreter may be stored on a disk, and you'll need to insert this disk into a disk drive, turn on the power, and then press a few keys on the keyboard to gain access to it.

In a *timesharing environment,* the terminal must be turned on first. The computer user must then establish communication between the terminal and the central processor. This procedure typically consists of typing specified words—such as HELLO or LOGIN—or pressing specified keys on the terminal. It may also involve dialing a number on a phone next to the terminal and using a communications device called a modem to make a connection with the processor.

Once hooked up, the computer may automatically send a sign-on request to the terminal in the form of a message or special character. The user must then follow a prescribed sign-on procedure, supplying one or more of the following: an account or project number, a user name or identification, and/or a password. After this information has been supplied, some systems that support multiple languages also require that the user name the programming language that will be used. Thus, it may also be necessary to type BASIC so that the computer can call up the BASIC translating software.

There's no standard sign-on procedure, but there are no difficult ones either. The procedures for signing on the particular system you'll be using are easy to learn and are available from manuals and local sources.

System Commands and Program Statements

System commands and program statements are both found in a BASIC programming environment, and both make use of certain designated words. Let's make sure we know the difference between these two categories. We've seen that some computer systems require the user to type key words like HELLO or LOGIN as a part of the sign-on procedure. Such words are called **system commands.** They are entered by the user into the system, and they direct the computer to take immediate action to accomplish a specific task. A number of system commands are found in every BASIC programming environment, but the words vary with the system being used. Some typical system commands are:

- RUN (to execute the user's program of current interest)
- LIST (to list the contents of a current program)
- SAVE (to store a current program—which must be given a name—in online secondary storage for later access)
- NEW (deletes program from memory)

As with sign-on procedures, the system commands for the particular equipment you'll be using are available from manuals and local sources.

WINDOW 17-1

THE ACRONYM: A USER'S LAMENT

"What's in a name?" wrote W.S.;
What's in acronyms is anyone's guess.
With acronyms, one does save space,
But loses hope—as one tries to trace
Back through the pages, perhaps to glean,
Just what in heck the darn things mean.
Acronyms help our technicians
Avoid the verbal repetitions.

But how 'bout us, the uninitiated—
Those whose code books are outdated?
We float alone, and too pathetic,
In a soup that's alphabetic.
Our overload becomes more terrific
With each new high-tech hieroglyphic.
A "ROM" or a "RAM" or even "DISOSS"
Keeps us from sounding too verbose.
But to me, it seems beyond belief
That we'd go to such lengths to try to be brief.

From Jo Ann Oravec in "Readers' Forum," *Datamation*, Nov. 1, 1985. Copyright © 1985 by Technical Publishing Company, a Dun and Bradstreet Company. All rights reserved.

Designated words such as READ, INPUT, LET, and END are also found in the sequence of numbered individual instructions, or **program statements,** that make up a BASIC program. We'll discuss the meanings and uses of these key words later in the chapter.

You've seen that when a system command is entered, it causes the computer to take *immediate action*. When a program statement is initially keyed in, however, the computer may take *no apparent action at all*. Of course, the machine is probably checking the statement for syntax errors and storing it with other statements, but the program instruction in the statement is not immediately executed at the time of entry. Rather, the individual statements are stored until a complete program is formed and until the user turns the control of the computer over to the program through the use of a RUN command. The statements are then executed to process the input data and produce the output results.

We are about ready to write the programs needed to solve the problems discussed (and flowcharted) in Chapter 16. Only a few *program entry, arithmetic*, and *error-correcting* necessities stand in our way.

Program Entry Elements

Key words are used in constructing program statements, and statements are then put together to form a BASIC program. A typical BASIC statement takes the following form:

Line number   Type of statement   Value(s)

Let's look at each of these statement elements.

Line Numbers   Each statement in a BASIC program begins with a **line number (ln).** Depending on the equipment used, the ln can be any integer (whole number) beginning at 1 (and going to four or five digits) that *you* select. The *order* of these line numbers is used by the computer during the execution of the program. Beginning with the lowest ln, statements will be processed in ascending order until the processor encounters conditional or unconditional transfer statements that cause a change in the sequence. It's generally desirable to number your statements in increments of 5 or 10. That way you'll have room later to include any additional instructions or modifications that may be needed, and you won't have to renumber the lines that follow the insertion. For example, let's assume that you've written a BASIC program that looks like this:

```
10   LET A=5
20   LET B=8
30   LET C=A+B
40   END
```

This program will add the values of A and B, but since you've forgotten to tell the computer to print out the result of this tough computation, it will forever remain a mystery. To remedy this oversight, you can type the following statement at the bottom of the program:

```
35   PRINT C
```

The computer will then know that you want to print the value of C after line 30 has been executed. If you enter a system command to LIST the program, you'll see that ln 35 has been correctly positioned between statements 30 and 40.

Types of BASIC Statements   Every statement in BASIC has a *statement type*, and learning the language is mainly a matter of learning the rules that apply to these statement types. Computer instructions are found in all languages to permit input/output, calculation, logic/comparison (to permit transfer of program control), and storage/retrieval and data movement operations. In the simple program we've just encountered, the LET statement was used to initially *assign* values to storage locations labeled "A" and "B" in the computer. The LET statement was also used to look up the values of the contents of A and B, calculate the sum of those values, and assign the total to a storage location labeled "C" (30   LET C=A+B). Thus the LET, or *assignment*, type of statement can be used to assign input values to locations, perform calculations, and move processed results to other locations. The PRINT type of statement, of course, is used for *output*. An END statement is typically the highest-numbered statement in a program and simply indicates the completion of the program. In the pages that follow, we'll examine a number of other types of BASIC statements.

Values in BASIC   BASIC manipulates values that are either constants or variables. A *constant* is a value that is provided explicitly by the program and *cannot* be changed by the computer at any time during program execution. Valid **numeric constants** include such values as 55, −16.5, 3.14159, and 1.09E+8. The 55 could represent a constant rate of speed, that is, 55 miles per hour. The −16.5 could represent the constant amount of dollars to be deducted from paychecks for a group insurance plan. And the 3.14159 could be the approximation of pi used in calculations.

The E (exponential) notation used in the constant 1.09E+8 is needed because there's only a limited amount of space available to store a value in the computer's memory. Thus 1.09E+8 can be used to represent 1.09×10^8, or 109,000,000. Also, 1.26E−6 can be used to represent 1.26×10^{-6}, or

0.00000126. (Don't worry too much about this E notation shorthand for expressing very large or very small quantities. It's mentioned here so that if you receive some output in E notation form, you'll understand what it means.) Valid constants may also include strings of alphanumeric characters. **Character string constants** may be any string of characters enclosed in quotation marks, such as ''4009 SARITA DRIVE'' or ''BILL BYTER''.

Unlike a constant, a **numeric variable** is a quantity that can be referred to by name and that *can* change values at different stages during the running of a program. Although it's true that the *location* in storage that holds the variable (and the *name* given by the programmer to that location) *doesn't change*, the *contents* of the storage location (like the contents of a post office box) may be altered many times during the program's processing of the available data. For example, you may recall from Chapter 16 that a counter can be used to record the number of times that a loop has been executed. To do this, a storage location with the **variable name** K can be established by the programmer and assigned an initial value of 1. An appropriate BASIC statement to do this is

    10   LET K=1

where K names a variable. After each pass through the loop, the contents of the counter will change or be incremented by a value of 1. That is,

    100   LET K=K+1

Obviously, in this BASIC statement the equals sign (=) does not mean the same as it does in algebra. Rather, the numeric variable value stored at the location identified by ''K'' is retrieved from storage, a value of 1 is added to it, and the new variable quantity replaces the previous contents in the location named ''K.'' Thus, if a loop is executed 30 times, there will be 30 different values for K.

It will be up to you to name the variables that are needed in the programs you write. The rules in BASIC that govern the naming of variables are easily remembered, but they're often more restrictive than the rules that apply to other languages. This is a shortcoming of some BASIC dialects. For example, in some established versions of the language a numeric variable is restricted to a name that consists of a single letter or a single letter followed by a single digit. Thus, in these dialects A, X, B1, and T2 are all valid numeric variable names, but 7G, AB, RATE, and B24 are not. Other dialects allow programmers to use longer names—a feature that makes programs easier for people to understand—but the computer ignores all characters beyond the first two letters or the first letter/number combination. And some newer versions of BASIC permit the full use of longer variable names. For example, the version of Microsoft BASIC used with the IBM Personal Computer family permits these names to have up to 40 characters, but the first character must still be a letter. We'll use one- or two-character numeric variable names in our examples because they are accepted by all BASIC dialects.

In addition to numeric variables, there are also **string variables**—strings of alphanumeric and special characters—that can be referred to by name and that can change during the running of a program. For example, the contents of the storage space that contains a customer's name will change constantly during the processing of a billing program. When naming a string variable in many established versions of BASIC, people must choose a single letter followed by a dollar sign ($). In those dialects, E$, B$, and N$ are all valid, but AB$, $X, and XYZ$ are not. Some other BASIC systems allow a string variable name to be any valid numeric variable name followed by a dollar sign. Thus, A1$ and TN$ are valid examples in such systems. But newer versions of BASIC are less restrictive. For instance, the Microsoft BASIC used with the IBM PC family permits string variable names to have up to 40 characters, but the first character must still be a letter and the last character must still be a dollar sign. In our examples we'll use the two-character string variable names that are accepted by all BASICs.

Arithmetic Operations

You'll use five arithmetic operations in writing BASIC programs: addition, subtraction, multiplication, division, and exponentiation (raising to a power). The symbols representing these operations (and examples of their use) are shown in Figure 17-2. Note that in BASIC the multiplication symbol must be present, even though it can be omitted in algebra. Failure to use the asterisk is a common error, and the computer will probably send you an error message if you forget it.

A formula in a program may include several operations. You must understand the order in which the computer handles these operations so that you may avoid errors. What value will be assigned to A, for example, when the computer encounters this statement that you've written?

50   LET A=4+6∧2/10−2

If the computer simply started at the left and performed operations in sequence, the result would be 4 plus 6 (or 10), raised to the second power (giving 100), divided by 10 (10), minus 2, giving a value of 8 to assign to A. But the computer follows a different set of rules in determining the order of operations. Moving from left to right in a formula *without parentheses:*

1   All exponentiation is performed first.

2   All multiplication and division operations are then completed.

3   Finally, all addition and subtraction takes place.

Operation	BASIC Symbol	BASIC Examples	Algebraic Equivalent
Addition	+	A + B 2 + 8	A + B 2 + 8
Subtraction	−	B − C 6 − 3	B − C 6 − 3
Multiplication	* (asterisk)	D * E 4 * F	DE or D(E) or D × E 4F or 4(F) or 4 × F
Division	/ (slash)	G/H 8/2	G ÷ H or $\frac{G}{H}$ 8 ÷ 2 or $\frac{8}{2}$
Exponentiation	∧ or ↑	J ∧ 2 (or J ↑ 2) 3 ∧ 3	J^2 3^3

FIGURE 17-2
Arithmetic operations: Symbols and examples in the BASIC language.

Following these priority rules, then, what value would the computer assign to A in our example? The *first* operation performed would be to square 6 (6∧2), giving 36. *Next,* the value of 36 would be divided by 10, giving 3.6. Your formula now looks like this:

$$4+3.6-2$$

Finally, moving from left to right, 4 is added to 3.6, giving 7.6, and 2 is then subtracted from 7.6 to give the final value of 5.6 to assign to the variable name A.

If parentheses are used, the computations within the parentheses are handled first, using the above order rules. If several sets of parentheses are nested within one another, the operations in the innermost group are performed first. For example, suppose your assignment statement had looked like this:

50 LET A=(8+(6*4)/2)/2

The first part of the formula evaluated is (6*4) in the innermost set of parentheses. The result is

50 LET A=(8+24/2)/2

Within the remaining set of parentheses, the division operation is performed first, and the resulting value of 12 is then added to 8. This total of 20 is then divided by 2 to get a value of 10 to assign to A.

Correcting Errors

In entering your program statements at the keyboard, you'll probably make errors that will have to be corrected. A very common error, of course, is to strike the wrong key or keys during program or data entry. If, as is often the case, you immediately detect your mistake, you need correct only one or two characters and then continue on with the line you are typing. For example, let's assume that the correct entry should be

50 LET A=(4*G)/2

but you type

50 LEG A

and then catch your error. How can you "erase" the G and enter the T? Different BASIC systems use different approaches, but generally a special correction key (such as RUBOUT, DELETE, or ← key) is used for this purpose. Each time you strike this **correction key** (CK), you erase one character in the typed line and move to its left. Thus to change the G to a T, you would need to press the CK three times: once to erase A, once to erase the blank character, and once to erase the G. You could then enter the T and complete the line.

Suppose, however, you discover that you've typed

50 LTE A=(4*G)/2

before you press the RETURN key that will cause the computer to analyze the statement. In this case you *could* backtrack with the correction, but it would probably be easier to delete the *entire line* and start over. The method to do this varies with the system being used, but on many systems the procedure is to hold down the CONTROL, or CTRL, key and then press either the U or the X key.

Finally, let's assume that you've typed

50   LTE A=(4+G)/2

instead of

50   LET A=(4*G)/2

and you *have pressed* the RETURN key. In this case, the computer will probably detect the *syntax error* in the spelling of LET, reject the statement, and send you an error message. You'll then have to reenter the statement. If in retyping the statement you repeat the mistake of *adding* 4 to the quantity stored in G rather than *multiplying* these values, the computer will accept the statement because it contains no syntax errors, but, of course, a *logical error* still remains. To correct this statement that has now been stored in the computer, you need only reenter the same line number with the correct information, and this second entry will completely erase the previous contents of the line (a very nice feature). If you want to delete a program line that has already been stored, you simply type the line number and then hit the RETURN key, and the previous entry will be deleted.

Now that you have a grasp of some of the details of program entry, arithmetic operation, and error correction, it's time to look at some example programs that illustrate the various BASIC statements.

PROGRAM PREPARATION EXAMPLES

Several problems were analyzed and flowcharted in Chapter 16. As you know, these examples are linked to the Byter family. Let's now see how programs for these examples can be prepared in BASIC.

A Simple Input/Process/Output Example

Program 1: Elm Creek Charges, Single Property Owner   The program to compute the total amount owed by a single Elm Creek property owner, along with the output charge statement produced by this program, is shown in Figure 17-3. (The flowchart for this program is found in Figure 16-3, page 539.) A system command has been used to list the program steps, which are the numbered lines in Figure 17-3. After completing a task, the computer typically produces a **BASIC prompt symbol** to let the user know that the system is waiting for the user's next command or statement. The prompt symbol shown in Figure 17-3 is "Ok," but other symbols such as] or > are often used.

The output of the program is produced at the bottom of Figure 17-3. In

```
100 REM *ELM CREEK BEAUTIFICATION CHARGES
110 REM *
120 REM *VARIABLE NAMES
130 REM * N$   NAME OF PROPERTY OWNER
140 REM * Q    QUANTITY PLANTED
150 REM * P    UNIT PRICE OF PLANTS
160 REM * A    NET AMOUNT OF PLANTS
170 REM * T1   PLANTING CHARGES
180 REM * T2   TOTAL AMOUNT OF CHARGES
190 REM *
200 REM *READ NAME, QUANTITY PLANTED AND PRICE
210       READ N$,Q,P
220 REM *COMPUTE NET AMOUNT OF PLANTS
230       LET A=P*Q
240 REM *COMPUTE PLANTING AND TOTAL CHARGES
250       LET T1=A*.06
260       LET T2=A+T1
270 REM *PRINT NAME, NET AMOUNT, PLANTING AND TOTAL CHARGES
280       PRINT N$
290       PRINT "NET = ";A;" PLANTING = ";T1;" TOTAL = ";T2
300 REM *INPUT DATA
310       DATA "BILL BYTER",33.0,4.50
320       END
```

> Computer listing of the program

```
Ok
RUN
BILL BYTER
NET =  148.5   PLANTING =   8.91   TOTAL =   157.41
Ok
```

> Output produced by the computer in response to the system command RUN

FIGURE 17-3
BASIC Program 1: Elm Creek Charges, Single Property Owner.

response to the RUN command, the computer has executed the program to produce the results shown.

Before we examine the program in Figure 17-3 in more detail, we should digress briefly for a few words about **programming style.** "Style" may be defined as the way in which something is said or done, as distinguished from its substance. An objective of this chapter is to present the programs in a style that will make them *easier to read and understand*. For this reason, you'll see a lot of program statements in this chapter that begin with REM—a BASIC abbreviation for REMark. A **REM statement** is used for program documentation and is provided *solely* for the benefit of people who want to read and understand the program. Whenever the computer encounters the letters REM, it ignores the rest of the statement and moves on to the next line number!

Every program in this chapter (and in Chapter 18) uses REM statements to (1) identify the program, (2) define the variable names used in the program, (3) place explanatory headings throughout the body of the program, and (4) add spacing within the program to aid readability. Indentation of statements is also used to aid readability. Of course, the disadvantages of these stylistic features are that they add to program length, are harder to type, and take up more storage space. After all, 15 of the 23 lines in the program in Figure 17-3 are "unnecessary" REM statements. Usually, though, the merits of REM documentation will far outweigh their inconvenience in the programs you write.

The first 11 lines in Figure 17-3 are self-explanatory REM statements.

The program is identified, variable names used in the program are defined, and a heading explains the purpose of line number (ln) 210. The statement in ln 210 is an input **READ statement** that *must be used in conjunction* with a **DATA statement.** The general form of these statements is

    ln READ list of variable   ln DATA list of data
                names   values

where the values to be assigned to the variable names identified in a READ statement are found in a DATA statement. Thus, when the computer encounters

    210   READ N$,Q,P

it looks for a DATA statement (which it finds at ln 310) and reads the first three data values it finds. In other words, it "uses up" the data by assigning them to the variable names, as follows:

    210   READ   N$,   Q,   P
    310   DATA   "BILL BYTER",   33.0,   4.50

You'll notice that since the property owner's name is a string variable, it's referred to as N$ in the program to conform to the rules for naming string variables discussed earlier. The numeric variable names given to quantity planted (Q) and unit price (P) also follow these rules. These variables are named by the programmer and are arbitrary choices. The property owner name variable, for example, could just as easily have been C$ or (A$, B$, . . .) as N$.

Each of our data items could have been placed in a separate DATA statement. It's common, however, to compress multiple data items into a single statement as shown here to save memory and data entry time. But the data must always be typed in the DATA statement(s) in the *order indicated by the READ statement*. The computer doesn't care how many DATA statements there are because before it executes the program it will arrange in order, in a single long list, all the values contained in all the DATA statements. A *pointer* is set internally in the system at the *first* value in the list, and, as we've seen, the first variable name encountered in a READ statement during program execution is assigned the value indicated by the pointer. The pointer then shifts to the next value, which will be "used up" by the next variable name encountered in a READ statement. And so it goes throughout the entire data list. Although DATA statements may be typed anywhere in the program except after the END statement, it's common practice to locate them near the end of the program, as shown in Figure 17-3.

Once the *data-input* operation has been accomplished, the next step in the program is to compute the net amount owed for the plants. This *processing* is carried out by using the **LET statement** in ln 230. The net amount owed for plants is found by multiplying the 33 items planted (Q) by the unit price of $4.50 (P). The net amount owed is assigned the variable name A. The next steps are to compute the planting charges (ln 250) and the total charges owed by the property owner (ln 260). In ln 250, the LET statement is used to multiply the net amount owed for the plants by a 6 percent (0.06) planting charge. The result of this computation is assigned to a storage location identified by the variable name T1. The total charges are then found in ln 260 by adding this planting charge value stored in T1 to the plant amount stored in A. This sum is assigned to the storage location named T2.

A **PRINT statement** is used to display program results. (Such commands, when found at the end of very long programs, may account for the expression "Some day your PRINTs will come.") The program *output* in our example consists of two printed lines. The *first* output line names the property owner (BILL BYTER), and is produced by the PRINT statement in ln 280. You'll notice that the N$ variable name shown in ln 280 isn't printed in the output. Rather, the *contents stored* in N$ are printed.

The *second* output line is produced by the PRINT statement in ln 290. This line begins with

290   PRINT "NET = ";A

The first things you'll notice are the *quotation marks*. Characters (including blank spaces) that are bounded by these marks in a PRINT statement are printed exactly as they appear in the statement when the program is executed. The marks themselves, however, aren't printed. Thus, NET = is printed, beginning at the left margin, when this program is run. You'll also notice a semicolon in ln 290. *Semicolons* are used in PRINT statements to cause items to be printed close together. Otherwise, the next item might be printed some distance across the page. Here, the value of the variable name A following the semicolon (the net amount owed for the plants in our example) is printed with just a little additional spacing. You should now be able to interpret the results generated by the remainder of the PRINT statement found in ln 290. The '' PLANTING = '' and '' TOTAL = '' explanations are printed, and the planting and total charge amounts are produced.

Commas are also used in PRINT statements to serve a specific function. A statement that reads

350   PRINT A,B,C,D,E

will cause the values of the five variable names to be printed across the page, with A beginning at the left margin, B beginning (perhaps) 14 spaces to the right, C beginning 28 spaces to the right, etc. The width of some terminal or pc printers is 72 or 80 characters, and the use of commas in the PRINT statement may *automatically* establish a format of five columns or zones. The automatic spacing can vary from one system to another. This implicit-specification feature of BASIC is especially appreciated by problem-solvers who are not professional programmers, because it allows them to receive output in a usable form without getting bogged down in output formatting details.

A PRINT statement can also produce *vertical spacing* in the output. If, for example, you write the following statement:

120   PRINT

the computer will follow your wishes—it will fill a line with blank spaces and advance the output page to the next line. Any number of empty PRINT statements can thus be used to control output line spacing.

The last program statement in Figure 17-3 is the **END statement.** It's generally the last statement in a BASIC program, and it includes only a line number. Some versions of BASIC don't require an END statement. But it's a good idea to use it because you might someday want to run your programs on other systems that do require its use.

FEEDBACK

Feedback and Review 17-1

You'll remember that in Feedback and Review 16-1, page 539, you were asked to help Lisa Byter prepare a flowchart for a program that will compute the gasoline mileage achieved by the family car during a trip. A possible flowchart for this program is shown at the end of Chapter 16. The variable names used in that chart are:

M1	Odometer reading at start of trip
M2	Odometer reading at end of trip
G	Gallons of gas used
M	Gas mileage

Using these variable names (or others of your own choosing), write a BASIC program to produce output results that are similar to these:

```
ODOMETER READING AT START OF TRIP : 2300
ODOMETER READING AT END OF TRIP   : 4500
GALLONS OF GAS USED DURING TRIP   : 150
MILEAGE FOR TRIP (MILES PER GALLON) : 14.66667
```

Gaining Flexibility with Decisions and Loops

As you saw in Chapter 16, the Calvin city employee wasn't happy with a program that stopped after it had computed Elm Creek beautification charges for just one property owner. And so the program was revised.

Program 2: Elm Creek Charges, Multiple Property Owners The program shown in Figure 17-4 processes charge statements for any number of property owners. (The logic of this program was charted in Figure 16-4, page 541.) This flexibility is achieved by adding a loop controlled by a logic/comparison statement.

The REM statements from ln 100 through ln 220 are similar to those in program 1. Since program 2 will also process an owner's local address (S$) as well as a city and state address (C$), names have been included for these variables. (The Zip code is part of variable C$).

The READ statement in ln 230 and the DATA statements in ln 400 through ln 520 provide the program with the input data. The first time the READ statement is executed in our example, the input data in ln 400 (''BILL BYTER'') are assigned to N$, the data in ln 410 (''622 HYATT ROAD'') are assigned to S$, the data in ln 420 (''CALVIN, INDIANA 47631'') are assigned to C$, and the data in ln 430 (33.0 plants and $4.50 per plant) are the quantity and price assigned to Q and P.

```
100 REM *ELM CREEK BEAUTIFICATION CHARGES
110 REM *
120 REM *VARIABLE NAMES
130 REM * N$   NAME OF PROPERTY OWNER
140 REM * S$   ADDRESS
150 REM * C$   CITY AND STATE
160 REM * Q    QUANTITY PLANTED
170 REM * P    UNIT PRICE OF PLANTS
180 REM * A    NET AMOUNT OF PLANTS
190 REM * T1   PLANTING CHARGES
200 REM * T2   TOTAL AMOUNT OF CHARGES
210 REM *
220 REM *READ NAME, ADDRESS, QUANTITY PLANTED AND PRICE
230       READ N$,S$,C$,Q,P
240 REM *TEST QUANTITY FOR LAST INPUT
250       IF Q=-99.9 THEN 530
260 REM *COMPUTE NET AMOUNT OF PLANTS
270       LET A=P*Q
280 REM *COMPUTE PLANTING AND TOTAL CHARGES
290       LET T1=A*.06
300       LET T2=A+T1
310 REM *PRINT NAME, ADDRESS, NET AMOUNT, PLANTING AND TOTAL CHARGES
320       PRINT N$
330       PRINT S$
340       PRINT C$
350       PRINT TAB(3);"NET =";A;" PLANTING =";T1;" TOTAL =";T2
360       PRINT
370       PRINT
380       GOTO 230
390 REM *INPUT DATA
400       DATA "BILL BYTER"
410       DATA "622 HYATT ROAD"
420       DATA "CALVIN, INDIANA 47631"
430       DATA 33.0,4.50
440       DATA "CHARLES CRAVENS"
450       DATA "1515 BLOCK DRIVE"
460       DATA "CALVIN, INDIANA 47631"
470       DATA 28.0,5.25
480       DATA "DELTA DESIGNS, INC."
490       DATA "26 STRAWBERRY STREET"
500       DATA "BROOKLYN, NEW YORK 11202"
510       DATA 63.0,5.75
520       DATA "L","L","L",-99.9,0.
530       END
```

Computer listing of the program

```
Ok
RUN
BILL BYTER
622 HYATT ROAD
CALVIN, INDIANA 47631
   NET = 148.5   PLANTING = 8.91   TOTAL = 157.41

CHARLES CRAVENS
1515 BLOCK DRIVE
CALVIN, INDIANA 47631
   NET = 147   PLANTING = 8.82   TOTAL = 155.82

DELTA DESIGNS, INC.
26 STRAWBERRY STREET
BROOKLYN, NEW YORK 11202
   NET = 362.25   PLANTING = 21.735   TOTAL = 383.985
```

Output produced by the computer in response to the system command RUN

On ln 250 we find a new statement type—the **IF . . . THEN conditional branching statement.** IF . . . THEN statements take the following form:

ln IF (logical assertion) THEN ln

For example, in

120 IF A < 10 THEN 30

the computer is told that if the logical assertion is *true*—i.e., if A is *less* than 10—program control is transferred to line number 30. If, however, the condition expressed in the assertion isn't met, the program moves to the next statement in the line number sequence. Other examples of logical assertions are:

```
A = B
B > C
D < =0     (D is less than or equal to 0)
M > =N     (M is greater than or equal to N)
S < >T     (S is not equal to T)
3*Z > X/T
```

As you can see, a "logical assertion" consists of a first expression (a constant, a variable name, or a formula), a relational (=, <, >, or some combination of these), and a second expression.

In the statement on ln 250 of our example program,

250 IF Q=-99.9 THEN 530

the value assigned to the quantity purchased field (Q) of the input record is compared to a sentinel value of −99.9. (A *sentinel value,* you'll recall, is an arbitrary data item placed at the end of a file to indicate that all valid data have been processed.) Since the value of Q during the first pass through the loop is the 33.0 plants charged to Bill Byter, the logical assertion is false and the program moves on to ln 270. You'll notice, however, that a last dummy record has been placed in ln 520 with a sentinel value of −99.9 for Q. When this record is finally read, the logical assertion will be true, the exit condition will be met, program control will be transferred to ln 530, and processing will end.

The statement in ln 270 computes the net amount for the plants charged to each property owner. Next, the statements in lines 290 and 300 compute planting and total charges. Finally, the PRINT statements in lines 320 through 370 produce the output shown in Figure 17-4. The three PRINT statements in ln 320 through ln 340 cause the system to print the property owner's name, local address, city, state, and Zip code. These three lines of print begin at the left margin of the page.

The **PRINT TAB function** in ln 350 is a little different. In the first part of this statement,

← **FIGURE 17-4**

BASIC Program 2: Elm Creek Charges, Multiple Property Owners.

350   PRINT TAB(3);"NET=";A

the TAB(3) part of the instruction controls the *spacing on the print line* much as a tabulator setting controls the spacing on a typewriter. When the computer encounters this part of the statement, it knows that it's to move three spaces *from the left margin* and then begin printing the heading enclosed in quotes. After NET = is printed, the net amount owed for the plants is also supplied, as you can see in the output of Figure 17-4. The remainder of the PRINT statement in ln 350 is like the one we saw in Figure 17-3. But suppose the following PRINT statement had been encountered:

180   PRINT TAB(18);M;TAB(28);N

The value of the variable name M would be printed beginning 18 spaces from the left margin, and the value of N would be printed starting at 28 spaces *from the left margin* (not from M).

The two empty PRINT statements in ln 360 and ln 370 cause the output page to advance two lines before printing the next property owner's charges. In ln 380, we find another new BASIC statement type. There's nothing difficult about this **GOTO unconditional branching statement.** It simply transfers program control to the line specified in the statement. Thus

380   GOTO 230

causes program control to branch back to the READ statement on ln 230 to begin processing the next owner's charges.

An Interactive Alternative to Program 2   Let's assume that instead of using READ . . . DATA statements, the user of the Elm Creek program would rather *interact* with the computer and give the necessary input data in the form of responses to questions and messages supplied by the program. The program in Figure 17-5 shows us how this might be done. The first 13 line numbers in this program are about the same as those in Figure 17-4.

In the PRINT statements in ln 230 and ln 240, however, things start to change. As you know, the messages enclosed in quotes in these PRINT statements will be produced as output. In this case, the output messages are requesting input data from the program user. As you'll notice in Figure 17-5, when the program is run, these two message lines are printed immediately. Line number 250 is

250   INPUT N$,S$,C$,Q,P

This is a new type of BASIC statement that causes the computer to (1) print a question mark (?) and (2) stop executing the program until the user supplies it with the necessary input data for the variable names listed in the **INPUT statement.** INPUT is always followed by one or more variable names separated by commas. Therefore, the *first* result of ln 250 is to cause a ? to be printed, as shown in the output of Figure 17-5. The *second* result of the INPUT statement is to halt the program until the user types in the property owner's name (N$), complete address (S$ and C$), quantity planted (Q), and unit price (P) and then presses the RETURN key. The first output is produced as shown at the bottom of the opposite page.

587

```
100 REM *ELM CREEK BEAUTIFICATION CHARGES
110 REM *
120 REM *VARIABLE NAMES
130 REM * N$   NAME OF PROPERTY OWNER
140 REM * S$   ADDRESS
150 REM * C$   CITY AND STATE
160 REM * Q    QUANTITY PLANTED
170 REM * P    UNIT PRICE OF PLANTS
180 REM * A    NET AMOUNT OF PLANTS
190 REM * T1   PLANTING CHARGES
200 REM * T2   TOTAL AMOUNT OF CHARGES
210 REM *
220 REM *INPUT NAME, ADDRESS, QUANTITY PLANTED AND PRICE
230      PRINT "ENTER NAME, ADDRESS, CITY/STATE, QUANTITY AND PRICE"
240      PRINT "(ENTER -99.9 FOR QUANTITY PLANTED TO INDICATE END OF DATA)"
250      INPUT N$,S$,C$,Q,P
260      IF Q=-99.9 THEN 410
270 REM *COMPUTE NET AMOUNT OF PLANTS
280      LET A=P*Q
290 REM *COMPUTE PLANTING AND TOTAL CHARGES
300      LET T1=A*.06
310      LET T2=A+T1
320 REM *PRINT NAME, ADDRESS, NET AMOUNT, PLANTING AND TOTAL CHARGES
330      PRINT
340      PRINT N$
350      PRINT S$
360      PRINT C$
370      PRINT TAB(3);"NET =";A;" PLANTING =";T1;" TOTAL =";T2
380      PRINT
390      PRINT
400      GOTO 230
410      END
```

Computer listing of the program

```
Ok
RUN
ENTER NAME, ADDRESS, CITY/STATE, QUANTITY AND PRICE
(ENTER -99.9 FOR QUANTITY PLANTED TO INDICATE END OF DATA)
? "BILL BYTER","622 HYATT ROAD","CALVIN, INDIANA 47631",33.0,4.50

BILL BYTER
622 HYATT ROAD
CALVIN, INDIANA 47631
   NET = 148.5  PLANTING = 8.91   TOTAL = 157.41


ENTER NAME, ADDRESS, CITY/STATE, QUANTITY AND PRICE
(ENTER -99.9 FOR QUANTITY PLANTED TO INDICATE END OF DATA)
? "L","L","L",-99.9,0
Ok
```

Output produced by the computer in response to the system command RUN

FIGURE 17-5

An alternative to program 2 using the INPUT statement.

ENTER NAME, ADDRESS, CITY/STATE, QUANTITY AND PRICE
(ENTER −99.9 FOR QUANTITY PLANTED TO INDICATE END OF DATA)

Produced by the PRINT statements on ln 230 and ln 240

?

Caused by INPUT statement on ln 250

"BILL BYTER", "622 HYATT ROAD", . . .

Keyed in by user

Before moving on, let's consider one other aspect of PRINT and INPUT statements. Suppose a program contains the following statements:

    100   PRINT "ODOMETER READING AT START OF TRIP";
    110   INPUT M

The effect of placing a semicolon *at the end of a PRINT statement* is to suppress the automatic printer carriage return that usually takes place when the computer reaches the end of a PRINT instruction. Thus the printing (or display) mechanism does not return to the left margin. So when the computer encounters the INPUT statement in ln 110, the ? caused by this statement will be printed to the right of the message produced by ln 100. The output would then look like this:

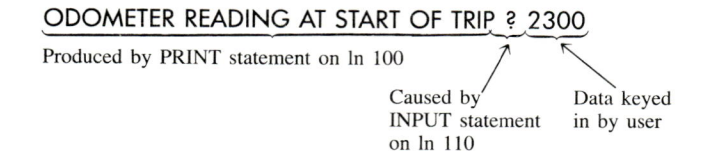

ODOMETER READING AT START OF TRIP ? 2300

   Produced by PRINT statement on ln 100

                                        Caused by   Data keyed
                                        INPUT statement in by user
                                        on ln 110

Once the user has supplied the input data for a property-owner record in our example and has pressed the RETURN key, the program takes over to print the owner's charges as shown in the output of Figure 17-5. The remaining steps in this example are exactly like those shown in Figure 17-4.

Program 3: Meals Compensation Report Marie Byter's program to track the number of meals prepared for needy families, and the earnings of the workers who produced and delivered those meals, is shown in Figure 17-6. (The logic for this program was charted in Figure 16-6, page 543.) The REM statements in the first nine program lines are self-explanatory. The PRINT statements in lines 190 through 210 produce the report headings shown in the output section of Figure 17-6. We've already discussed the use of commas in PRINT statements, and ln 190 illustrates this usage. Marie's system automatically divides the output line into print zones of 14 spaces each. A comma in a PRINT statement causes the next item in that statement to be printed at the beginning of the next zone. You'll notice in ln 190 that nothing is placed in front of the first comma, and so nothing is printed in the first zone of the first line of the report heading. The printing of COLD LUNCHES begins in the first space of the second zone, HOT MEALS begins in the first space of the third zone, and so on. The PRINT statement in ln 200 produces the second heading line. Since "EMPLOYEE" appears before the first comma in ln 200, that item is printed beginning at the left margin (which is the first space of the first zone). The printing of PRODUCED begins in the first space of the second zone, and so it goes until the second heading line is printed. You should now be able to see how commas are used in ln 210 to complete the heading.

    The next step in Marie's program is to read the name of the first worker (ln 230) from the DATA statement in ln 330. The loop in the program is controlled by the IF . . . THEN statement in ln 240. If the name of the worker is "END OF DATA," program control will go to ln 400 and processing will end. Since N$ in the first pass through the program is "R. BARRY," how-

```
100 REM *MEALS COMPENSATION REPORT
110 REM *
120 REM *VARIABLE NAMES
130 REM *   N$   NAME OF WORKER
140 REM *   Q1   QUANTITY OF COLD LUNCHES PRODUCED
150 REM *   Q2   QUANTITY OF HOT MEALS PRODUCED
160 REM *   E    EMPLOYEE EARNINGS
170 REM *
180 REM *PRINT REPORT HEADINGS
190       PRINT ,"COLD LUNCHES","HOT MEALS","EMPLOYEE"
200       PRINT "EMPLOYEE","PRODUCED","PRODUCED","EARNINGS"
210       PRINT "_____","_____","_____","_____"
220 REM *READ EMPLOYEE NAME AND TEST FOR END OF DATA
230       READ N$
240       IF N$="END OF DATA" THEN 400
250 REM *READ QUANTITIES OF MEALS PRODUCED
260       READ Q1,Q2
270 REM *COMPUTE EMPLOYEE EARNINGS
280       LET E=Q1*.75+Q2*1.5
290 REM *PRINT NAME, MEALS PRODUCED, AND EARNINGS
300       PRINT N$,Q1,Q2,"$";E
310       GOTO 230
320 REM *INPUT DATA
330       DATA "R. BARRY"
340       DATA 20.,30
350       DATA "T. LOPEZ"
360       DATA 60.,100.
370       DATA "A. MARTIN"
380       DATA 50.,150
390       DATA "END OF DATA"
400       END
```

Computer listing of the program

```
Ok
RUN
                 COLD LUNCHES   HOT MEALS    EMPLOYEE
EMPLOYEE         PRODUCED       PRODUCED     EARNINGS
_____       _____     _____   _____
R. BARRY         20             30           $ 60
T. LOPEZ         60             100          $ 195
A. MARTIN        50             150          $ 262.5
Ok
```

Output produced by the computer in response to the system command RUN

FIGURE 17-6

BASIC Program 3: Meals Compensation Report.

ever, program control moves to ln 260. The program reads the quantities of cold and hot meals produced by the first employee from the DATA statement in ln 340. Employee earnings are computed in ln 280 by (1) multiplying the cold and hot meal quantities by the constant amounts—$0.75 and $1.50—shown in the program and (2) adding these products to get the total earnings for the worker. The first line under the report headings is then produced by the PRINT statement in ln 300. The employee name (N$) is printed in the first zone, the quantities of meals produced (Q1 and Q2) are printed in zones 2 and 3, and a dollar sign ("$") is printed at the beginning of zone 4. A semicolon follows the dollar sign in ln 300 to keep the spacing tight, and the employee earnings figure (E) is also printed in zone 4. The GOTO statement in ln 310 then sends program control back to ln 230 to read the name of the next employee in the file.

Program 4: Student Payment Report You'll remember from Chapter 16 that Jill Byter has been asked to write a program that shows the hours worked and earnings received by student assistants over a 4-week period. Jill's flowchart for this job is shown in Figure 16-7, page 543, and the BASIC program for the application is shown in Figure 17-7.

The REM statements in the first 10 program lines require no explanation. The report heading is printed by the statements in lines 200 through 220. The instruction in ln 240 then causes the program to read the input DATA for the first student from lines 350 and 360. A test is made in ln 260 to see if the hourly rate of pay (R) is equal to −99.9 (the value in the last dummy record). The total hours worked by the student and the student's earnings for the period are then computed in lines 280 and 290. Finally, the first line below the report heading is produced by the PRINT statements in lines 310 and 320, and ln 330 causes program control to branch back to ln 240 to read the next student record.

The only thing new in this program is the use of a **PRINT USING function** in lines 310 and 320. In ln 310

310   PRINT USING "\   \";N$;

The backslash symbols (\) tell the computer that characters from a string are to be printed in the space allotted. If the backslashes are typed with no spaces, two characters are printed; if there are two spaces between the slashes, four string characters are printed, and so on. Since there are 19 spaces between the slashes in ln 310, there's room for a string variable with 21 characters. The *first* semicolon in ln 310 is used to separate the string format from the item to be printed. As you can see, the string variable that's printed in the allocated space is N$. Thus, space has been allocated to print a student name with up to 21 characters. The *second* semicolon in ln 310 suppresses the automatic printer carriage return/line feed operation.

In ln 320,

320   PRINT USING " #####.##   #####.##";S,E

the number sign (#) characters can be thought of as "place holders" for the numeric data identified by the variables S and E. Each number sign represents one printed digit. Thus space is provided by ln 320 for two numeric fields, each of which consists of five positions, a decimal point, and two more positions. If the numbers to be printed have fewer digits than the positions specified—as they do in our example—the unused positions are filled with blank spaces. Values are automatically rounded to two decimal places. The semicolon in ln 320 again separates the numeric field formats from the items to be printed. In this example, the items are the sum of the hours worked by a student (S) and the earnings of that student for the period (E).

PRINT USING statements allow programmers to exercise strict control over the output format. We've only touched on a few of the PRINT USING features available in the BASIC dialect used to produce Jill's program. But not all dialects have PRINT USING statements, and the details of usage in those which do can vary. You should check the operating manual of your particular system for possible differences.

```
100 REM *STUDENT PAYMENT REPORT
110 REM *
120 REM *VARIABLE NAMES
130 REM * N$       STUDENT NAME
140 REM * R        HOURLY RATE OF PAY
150 REM * H1-H4    HOURS WORKED FOR WEEKS 1-4
160 REM * S        SUM OF HOURS WORKED
170 REM * E        STUDENT EARNINGS FOR PERIOD
180 REM *
190 REM *PRINT HEADING
200     PRINT "STUDENT NAME          TOTAL HOURS          EARNINGS"
210     PRINT "_____          _____          _____"
220     PRINT
230 REM *READ NAME,RATE OF PAY AND HOURS WORKED EACH WEEK
240     READ N$,R,H1,H2,H3,H4
250 REM *TEST R FOR END OF DATA
260     IF R=-99.9 THEN 440
270 REM *COMPUTE TOTAL HOURS WORKED AND EARNINGS FOR PERIOD
280     LET S=H1+H2+H3+H4
290     LET E=S*R
300 REM *PRINT NAME,TOTAL HOURS AND EARNINGS
310     PRINT USING "\                    \";N$;
320     PRINT USING "   #####.##            #####.##";S,E
330     GOTO 240
340 REM *INPUT DATA
350     DATA "JACOB ALTMAN       ",   5.50
360     DATA  22.0,  21.5,  15.0,  16.0
370     DATA "JACK ARMSTRONG     ",   5.00
380     DATA  20.0,  14.5,  13.0,  12.5
390     DATA "SALLY JACOBSON     ",   6.00
400     DATA  20.0,  11.0,  15.0,  18.5
410     DATA "ALFRED NEWMAN      ",   5.00
420     DATA  18.0,  10.0,  23.5,  16.0
430     DATA "END OF DATA",-99.9,0.,0.,0.,0.
440     END
```

Computer listing of the program

```
Ok
RUN
STUDENT NAME          TOTAL HOURS          EARNINGS
_____          _____          _____

JACOB ALTMAN             74.50              409.75
JACK ARMSTRONG           60.00              300.00
SALLY JACOBSON           64.50              387.00
ALFRED NEWMAN            67.50              337.50
Ok
```

Output produced by the computer in response to the system command RUN

FIGURE 17-7

BASIC Program 4: Student Payment Report.

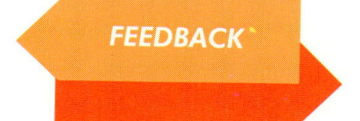

FEEDBACK AND REVIEW 17-2

Using what you've now learned of the BASIC language, update the program prepared for Feedback and Review 17-1 so that it will interact with the user to produce output results similar to these:

```
RUN
ODOMETER READING AT START OF TRIP ?  2300
ODOMETER READING AT END OF TRIP   ?  4500
GALLONS OF GAS USED DURING TRIP   ?  230
MILEAGE FOR TRIP(MILES PER GALLON) :  9.565217

ANOTHER TRIP (Y/N)? Y
ODOMETER READING AT START OF TRIP ?  4700
ODOMETER READING AT END OF TRIP   ?  5700
GALLONS OF GAS USED DURING TRIP   ?  98
MILEAGE FOR TRIP(MILES PER GALLON) :  10.20408

ANOTHER TRIP (Y/N)? NO
TYPE A 'Y' OR AN 'N'
ANOTHER TRIP (Y/N)? N
GOOD BYE
```

A Multiple-Decision Situation

Program 5: Plant Control Report—Elm Creek Project   The logic for Bill Byter's Plant Control Report was flowcharted in Figure 16-8, page 546, and the program that produces this report is shown in Figure 17-8. Since there are no new types of BASIC statements used in this program, you should be able to follow the coding steps.

The body of the program loop begins in ln 270 after the report headings are printed (using the statements in lines 210 through 240). Input plant data are read (ln 270), a test is made to see if all valid records have been processed (ln 290), and the inventory available for planting is determined (lines 310 through 340). The ending inventory is then found (lines 360 through 390). An output line for a plant is printed (lines 420 and 430), and program control then branches back to ln 270 to read and process another plant record.

The Use of Accumulators

You saw in Chapter 16 that an *accumulator* is a programmer-designated storage location in the processor that's used to accept and store a *running total* of individual values as they become available during processing. The contents of the accumulator location must initially be set to a programmer-designated value that's usually zero. Each successive value placed in the accumulator is

```
100 REM *PLANT CONTROL REPORT--ELM CREEK PROJECT
110 REM *
120 REM *VARIABLE NAMES
130 REM * P$    PLANT NAME
140 REM * B     BEGINNING INVENTORY
150 REM * R     QUANTITY RECEIVED
160 REM * S     QUANTITY PLANTED
170 REM * A     AVAILABLE INVENTORY
180 REM * E     ENDING INVENTORY
190 REM *
200 REM *PRINT HEADINGS
210     PRINT "                    PLANT CONTROL REPORT"
220     PRINT
230     PRINT "PLANT           BEGINNING    QUANTITY    QUANTITY      ENDING"
240     PRINT "                INVENTORY    RECEIVED    PLANTED    INVENTORY"
250 REM *READ PLANT NAME, BEGINNING INVENTORY, QUANTITY RECEIVED,
260 REM * AND QUANTITY PLANTED
270     READ P$,B,R,S
280 REM *TEST QUANTITY RECEIVED FOR END OF DATA
290     IF R=-99.9 THEN 530
300 REM *COMPUTE AVAILABLE INVENTORY
310     IF R>=0 THEN 340
320     LET A=B
330     GOTO 360
340     LET A=B+R
350 REM *COMPUTE ENDING INVENTORY
360     IF S>=0 THEN 390
370     LET E=A
380     GOTO 420
390     LET E=A-S
400 REM *PRINT PLANT NAME, BEGINNING INVENTORY, QUANTITY RECEIVED,
410 REM * QUANTITY PLANTED, ENDING INVENTORY, AND THEN RETURN
420     PRINT USING "\                \";P$;
430     PRINT USING "######.##     #####.##    #####.##    ######.##";B,R,S,E
440     GOTO 270
450 REM *INPUT DATA
460     DATA "AZALEA         ",   200.0,   150.0,   289.0
470     DATA "BOXWOOD        ",   165.0,   118.0,   203.0
480     DATA "DAFFODIL (DOZ)",   188.5,   144.0,   176.5
490     DATA "HONEYSUCKLE    ",    35.0,   225.0,   200.0
500     DATA "JUNIPER        ",    76.0,   150.0,   132.0
510     DATA "PEONY          ",    92.0,   100.0,   160.0
520     DATA "END OF DATA    ",     0.0,   -99.9,     0.0
530     END
```

```
Ok
RUN
                PLANT CONTROL REPORT

PLANT           BEGINNING    QUANTITY    QUANTITY      ENDING
                INVENTORY    RECEIVED    PLANTED    INVENTORY
AZALEA             200.00      150.00      289.00       61.00
BOXWOOD            165.00      118.00      203.00       80.00
DAFFODIL (DOZ)     188.50      144.00      176.50      156.00
HONEYSUCKLE         35.00      225.00      200.00       60.00
JUNIPER             76.00      150.00      132.00       94.00
PEONY               92.00      100.00      160.00       32.00
Ok
```

FIGURE 17-8

BASIC Program 5: Plant Control Report—Elm Creek Project.

```
100 REM *MEALS COMPENSATION REPORT WITH ACCUMULATOR
110 REM *
120 REM *VARIABLE NAMES
130 REM *   N$   NAME OF WORKER
140 REM *   Q1   QUANTITY OF COLD LUNCHES PRODUCED
150 REM *   Q2   QUANTITY OF HOT MEALS PRODUCED
160 REM *   E    EMPLOYEE EARNINGS
170 REM *   G    TOTAL EMPLOYEE EARNINGS
180 REM *
190 REM *INITIALIZE ACCUMULATOR
200       LET G=0
210 REM *PRINT REPORT HEADINGS
220       PRINT ,"COLD LUNCHES","HOT MEALS","EMPLOYEE"
230       PRINT "EMPLOYEE","PRODUCED","PRODUCED","EARNINGS"
240       PRINT "_____","_____","_____","_____"
250 REM *READ EMPLOYEE NAME AND TEST FOR END OF DATA
260       READ N$
270       IF N$="END OF DATA" THEN 370
280 REM *READ QUANTITIES OF MEALS PRODUCED
290       READ Q1,Q2
300 REM *COMPUTE EMPLOYEE EARNINGS AND ACCUMULATE TOTAL EARNINGS
310       LET E=Q1*.75+Q2*1.5
320       LET G=G+E
330 REM *PRINT NAME, MEALS PRODUCED, AND EARNINGS
340       PRINT N$,Q1,Q2,"$";E
350       GOTO 260
360 REM *PRINT TOTAL EARNINGS HEADING AND ACCUMULATED AMOUNT
370       PRINT ,,,"TOTAL EMPLOYEE"
380       PRINT ,,,"COMPENSATION"
390       PRINT ,,,"_____"
400       PRINT ,,,"$";G
410 REM *INPUT DATA
420       DATA "R. BARRY"
430       DATA 20.,30
440       DATA "T. LOPEZ"
450       DATA 60.,100.
460       DATA "A. MARTIN"
470       DATA 50.,150
480       DATA "END OF DATA"
490       END
```

Computer listing of the program

```
Ok
RUN
                COLD LUNCHES    HOT MEALS       EMPLOYEE
EMPLOYEE        PRODUCED        PRODUCED        EARNINGS
_____      _____    _____       _____

R. BARRY        20              30              $ 60
T. LOPEZ        60              100             $ 195
A. MARTIN       50              150             $ 262.5
                                                TOTAL EMPLOYEE
                                                COMPENSATION
                                                _____
                                                $ 517.5

Ok
```

Output produced by the computer in response to the system command RUN

FIGURE 17-9

BASIC Program 6: Meals Compensation Report with Accumulator.

then added to the value already there. Accumulators are used in the following two programs.

Program 6: Meals Compensation Report with Accumulator
Marie Byter has decided to add an accumulator to the program you've already studied in Figure 17-6. The logic for the revised program shown in Figure 17-9 is charted in Figure 16-9, page 547. The accumulator adds the amounts entered into the "EMPLOYEE EARNINGS" column in the output report to produce a total employee earnings figure.

The storage location that's used to accumulate employee earnings is given the variable name G in Marie's program, and G is initially set to zero in ln 200. The next several program steps are exactly like those in Figure 17-6. Report headings are printed (lines 220–240), an employee name is read (ln 260), a test for exit condition is made (ln 270), the quantities of cold and hot lunches are entered (ln 290), and an employee earnings figure is computed (ln 310). We can see from the output results shown in Figure 17-9 that the first employee—R. BARRY—earned $60. When ln 320 is executed for the first time, this $60 amount is added to the previous amount (0) stored in the accumulator. The new total of $60 is then assigned to the accumulator (G) thereby erasing the previous value of 0. When the next record for T. LOPEZ is processed, the $195 earnings for this worker will be added to the $60 now in the accumulator to get a new total of $255 ($60 + $195). This procedure to update the accumulator continues until all records have been processed. After the accumulator has been updated for the first time, however, the first line is printed under the report headings by the statement in ln 340 and program control than branches back (ln 350) to read the next employee record.

When the last valid record has been processed, the exit condition in ln 270 is satisfied, and program control branches to ln 370. The PRINT statements in lines 370 through 390 create the "TOTAL EMPLOYEE COMPENSATION" subheading at the bottom of Marie's report. The statement in ln 400 prints a dollar sign and the total earnings amount stored in the accumulator. The next executable statement in the program sequence is then the END instruction in ln 490. But Marie could have inserted the following statement into her program to clarify program logic:

405   STOP

The **STOP statement** is commonly used in more complex programs that incorporate subordinate program modules or subroutines. It functions much like a "GOTO the END" instruction. There can be several STOP statements placed wherever a program should logically end, but there's only one END statement in a program.

Program 7: Elm Creek Planting Summary
Bill Byter has prepared the program in Figure 17-10 to summarize Elm Creek plantings and charges. (The logic for this program is charted in Figure 16-10, page 549.)

After the headings shown in the output portion of Figure 17-10 are printed by lines 200 through 220, the accumulator is set to zero (ln 240). Input data are read (ln 260), a test for exit condition is made (ln 280), the net charges for a plant are computed (ln 300), and the net charges are accumulated (ln 310). A line on the output report is printed for the plant (lines 330

```
100 REM *ELM CREEK PLANTING SUMMARY
110 REM *
120 REM *VARIABLE NAMES
130 REM * P$   PLANT NAME
140 REM * Q    QUANTITY PLANTED
150 REM * P    UNIT PRICE OF PLANT
160 REM * A    NET CHARGES FOR PLANT
170 REM * T    TOTAL NET CHARGES
180 REM *
190 REM *PRINT HEADING
200     PRINT "              ELM CREEK PLANTING SUMMARY"
210     PRINT
220     PRINT "PLANT              UNIT PRICE      QUANTITY     NET CHARGES"
230 REM *INITIALIZE ACCUMULATOR
240     LET T=0
250 REM *READ PLANT, UNIT PRICE, AND QUANTITY PLANTED
260     READ P$,Q,P
270 REM *TEST QUANTITY FOR END OF DATA
280     IF Q=-99.9 THEN 370
290 REM *COMPUTE NET CHARGES AND ACCUMULATE TOTAL NET CHARGES
300     LET A=Q*P
310     LET T=A+T
320 REM *PRINT PLANT, PRICE, QUANTITY, NET CHARGES, AND THEN RETURN
330     PRINT USING "\                \";P$;
340     PRINT USING "#######.##    #######.##   $$##,###.##";P,Q,A
350     GOTO 260
360 REM *PRINT TOTAL NET CHARGES AND STOP
370     PRINT
380     PRINT
390     PRINT "                                        TOTAL"
400     PRINT "                                     NET CHARGES"
410     PRINT TAB(48);
420     PRINT USING "$$###,###.##";T
430 REM *INPUT DATA
440     DATA "AZALEA"
450     DATA 515.0, 5.75
460     DATA "BOXWOOD"
470     DATA 823.0, 3.95
480     DATA "DAFFODIL (DOZ)"
490     DATA 212.5, 5.25
500     DATA "HONEYSUCKLE"
510     DATA 364.0, 4.50
520     DATA "JUNIPER"
530     DATA 388.0, 3.85
540     DATA "PEONY"
550     DATA 414.0, 2.90
560     DATA "END OF DATA",-99.9,0.
570     END
```

Computer listing of the program

```
Ok
RUN
              ELM CREEK PLANTING SUMMARY

PLANT              UNIT PRICE      QUANTITY     NET CHARGES
AZALEA                  5.75         515.00      $2,961.25
BOXWOOD                 3.95         823.00      $3,250.85
DAFFODIL (DOZ)          5.25         212.50      $1,115.63
HONEYSUCKLE             4.50         364.00      $1,638.00
JUNIPER                 3.85         388.00      $1,493.80
PEONY                   2.90         414.00      $1,200.60


                                        TOTAL
                                     NET CHARGES
                                     $11,660.13
Ok
```

Output produced by the program in response to the system command RUN

← FIGURE 17-10

BASIC Program 7: Elm Creek Planting Summary.

and 340), and the program loops back to read another record (ln 350). The two dollar signs ($) in the PRINT USING statement in ln 340 will cause a dollar sign to "float" in the designated field. That is, a "$" will appear immediately to the left of the first digit that appears in the field, regardless of its location. The comma between the # symbols in ln 340 punctuates within the field as shown in the output of Figure 17-10; it *doesn't* indicate the beginning of a print zone in this situation.

After all valid records have been processed, the exit condition in ln 280 is satisfied, and program control branches to ln 370. Two empty PRINT statements (lines 370 and 380) are used for output line spacing, and two more PRINT statements (lines 390 and 400) produce the subheading at the bottom of the summary report. The statement in ln 410 moves the print mechanism 48 spaces from the left margin, and the statement in ln 420 then specifies the print format for the total net charges amount (T) that has been accumulated during the running of the program. After ln 420 has been processed, the next executable statement in the program sequence is the END instruction in ln 570.

The Use of Counters

Another important programming technique discussed in Chapter 16 is the use of a counter. A *counter,* you'll recall, is a special type of accumulator that's often used to record the number of times a loop has been processed. The counter is incremented with each pass of the program through the loop. When the counter value reaches a predetermined number, an exit condition based on the value of the counter is satisfied, and the program follows an exit path out of the loop.

Program 8: Elm Creek Charges with a Counter The program listing in Figure 17-11 shows how a counter controls a loop. (The logic for this program to process Elm Creek beautification charges—which modifies the one shown in Figure 17-4—is found in Figure 16-11, page 550.)

The counter (K) is initialized at 1 in ln 220, and the number of records to be processed (and thus the number of passes to be made through the program loop) is read in ln 230. In our example, the number of records to be processed (N) is set at 4 by the first DATA item in ln 410. After the first property-owner record has been processed (ln 250 through ln 340), a test for exit condition is made in ln 360. In the first pass through the program loop, this statement

```
360  IF K=N THEN 500
```

compares the initial value of the counter (1) to the number of records to be processed (4). Since the counter value obviously doesn't equal 4, program control moves on to ln 380. In this step,

```
380  LET K=K+1
```

```
100 REM *ELM CREEK BEAUTIFICATION CHARGES
110 REM *
120 REM * N$   NAME OF PROPERTY OWNER
130 REM * Q    QUANTITY PLANTED
140 REM * P    UNIT PRICE OF PLANTS
150 REM * A    NET AMOUNT OF PLANTS
160 REM * T1   PLANTING CHARGES
170 REM * T2   TOTAL AMOUNT OF CHARGES
180 REM * N    NUMBER OF RECORDS TO BE PROCESSED
190 REM * K    COUNTER
200 REM *
210 REM *INITIALIZE COUNTER AND READ NUMBER OF RECORDS
220       LET K=1
230       READ N
240 REM *READ NAME, QUANTITY PLANTED AND PRICE
250       READ N$,Q,P
260 REM *COMPUTE NET AMOUNT OF PLANTS
270       LET A=Q*P
280 REM *COMPUTE PLANTING AND TOTAL CHARGES
290       LET T1=A*.06
300       LET T2=A+T1
310 REM *PRINT NAME AND TOTAL CHARGES
320       PRINT N$;TAB(30);"TOTAL =   $";T2
330       PRINT
340       PRINT
350 REM *TEST FOR END OF DATA
360       IF K=N THEN 500
370 REM *INCREMENT COUNTER AND RETURN
380       LET K=K+1
390       GOTO 250
400 REM *INPUT DATA
410       DATA   4
420       DATA "BILL BYTER"
430       DATA  33.0,  4.50
440       DATA "CHARLES CRAVENS"
450       DATA  28.0,  5.25
460       DATA "DELTA DESIGNS, INC."
470       DATA  63.0,  5.75
480       DATA "JOHNSON FOOD MARTS, INC."
490       DATA 180.0,  2.90
500       END
```

Computer listing of the program

```
Ok
RUN
BILL BYTER                    TOTAL =   $ 157.41

CHARLES CRAVENS               TOTAL =   $ 155.82

DELTA DESIGNS, INC.           TOTAL =   $ 383.985

JOHNSON FOOD MARTS, INC.      TOTAL =   $ 553.32

Ok
```

Output produced by the computer in response to the system command RUN

FIGURE 17-11

BASIC Program 8: Elm Creek Charges with a Counter.

the counter is incremented by a value of 1, and so its new value is 2. When the last property-owner record has been processed, and when K=N, the exit path out of the loop will be followed to ln 500, and processing will end without any need for a dummy record at the end of the file.

Program 9: Sam's Savings Simulator   The program listing for Sam Byter's interactive savings simulation program that processes savings amount, interest rate, and time data is shown in Figure 17-12. (The flowchart for this program is found in Figure 16-12, page 552.) The counter (K) is initialized at 1 in ln 210.

Since this program is designed to *interact* with the user, the series of PRINT and INPUT statements found in lines 230 through 290 produce input queries and accept user responses. The output headings are then printed (lines 310–350). There are two loops in Sam's program, and the one that processes the data for each of the years in a particular simulation run begins with ln 370. In the first pass through this loop, the interest earned in the first year (D) is computed (ln 370), and this interest amount is added to the initial savings balance (S) to get the new savings balance (ln 380). The next step in ln 400 is to print the value of K—which is 1 in the first pass through the loop—and the new savings balance. The program then tests to see if this simulation run should be terminated (ln 420). The value of K at this time is 1, and this value is compared to the number of years (N) specified by the user in ln 280. Let's assume that Sam wants to produce savings results for 3 years. In that case, K is 1 and N is 3 so program control moves to ln 430. A value of 1 is added to the counter, and control is then transferred back to ln 370 by the unconditional branching statement in ln 440. Another pass through the simulation is then processed.

When K *does* equal N in ln 420, the first simulation run is completed, and program control branches out of the simulation loop to ln 460. A blank line is added to the output (ln 460), and the program then asks the user if more data are to be processed (ln 470). The user's response is accepted (ln 480) and tested (lines 490 and 500). If the response is "YES" (ln 490), control loops back to reset the counter and start a new simulation run. If the response is "NO" (ln 500), processing ends. And if the user's response is given incorrectly, a prompt message is sent (ln 510), and the user is given another chance.

Built-in Looping with an Automatic Counter   Since using a counter to control a loop is such a useful technique, most programming languages have instructions that can be used to establish an automatic counter. The program listing in Figure 17-13 shows how an automatic counter can be set up in BASIC. This program is an alternative to the version of Sam's savings simulator that we've just examined in Figure 17-12.

The statements from lines 190 through 330 are exactly like lines 220 through 360 in Figure 17-12. But this program then uses a pair of statements—the **FOR statement** on ln 340 and the **NEXT statement** on ln 390—that you're not familiar with. These FOR and NEXT statements must always be used together. The FOR statement *opens* a loop, and the loop is *closed* with the NEXT statement. That is, a FOR statement sets up a loop and is placed at the beginning of the loop, while the NEXT statement is located at the end

```
100 REM *SAM'S SAVINGS SIMULATOR
110 REM *
120 REM *VARIABLE NAMES
130 REM * S     SAVINGS
140 REM * R     YEARLY INTEREST RATE PAID ON SAVINGS(PERCENT)
150 REM * D     INTEREST EARNED IN A YEAR
160 REM * N     NUMBER OF YEARS TO BE SIMULATED
170 REM * X$    USER RESPONSE TO END OF DATA INQUIRY
180 REM * K     COUNTER
190 REM *
200 REM *INITIALIZE COUNTER
210       LET K=1
220 REM *ENTER DATA FOR SIMULATION
230       PRINT "INITIAL SAVINGS";
240       INPUT S
250       PRINT "INTEREST RATE ON SAVINGS(PERCENT)";
260       INPUT R
270       PRINT "NUMBER OF YEARS";
280       INPUT N
290       PRINT
300 REM *PRINT HEADINGS
310       PRINT "SAVINGS ACCUMULATION SIMULATOR"
320       PRINT
330       PRINT "YEAR";TAB(18);"SAVINGS"
340       PRINT "NO.";TAB(18);"BALANCE"
350       PRINT "____";TAB(18);"_____"
360 REM *CALCULATE SAVINGS BALANCE FOR EACH YEAR
370       LET D=S*R/100
380       LET S=S+D
390 REM *PRINT YEARLY SUMMARY
400       PRINT K;TAB(18);S
410 REM *TEST FOR END OF THIS SIMULATION
420       IF K=N THEN 460
430       LET K=K+1
440       GOTO 370
450 REM *END OF DATA INQUIRY
460       PRINT
470       PRINT "MORE DATA (YES,NO)";
480       INPUT X$
490       IF X$="YES" THEN 210
500       IF X$="NO" THEN 530
510       PRINT "PLEASE TYPE 'YES' OR 'NO'"
520       GOTO 470
530       END
```

Computer listing of the program

```
Ok
RUN
INITIAL SAVINGS? 2000
INTEREST RATE ON SAVINGS(PERCENT)? 10
NUMBER OF YEARS? 3

SAVINGS ACCUMULATION SIMULATOR

YEAR              SAVINGS
NO.               BALANCE
____              _____
 1                2200
 2                2420
 3                2662

MORE DATA (YES,NO)? NOT
PLEASE TYPE 'YES' OR 'NO'
MORE DATA (YES,NO)? NO
Ok
```

Output produced by the computer in response to input data supplied by the user

of the loop. The program line or lines that are *between* the FOR and NEXT statements are executed repeatedly and form the *range,* or *body,* of the loop.

The general form of these statements is

```
ln  FOR v=i TO t STEP n
ln    .
ln    .
ln    .
ln  NEXT v
```

where ln is a line number, v is a variable name acting as an automatic counter or index, i is the initial value or expression given to the counter, t is the terminal value or expression of the counter when the looping is completed, and n is the amount by which the counter should be stepped up or down after each pass through the loop. (If the step value is omitted in the FOR statement, the computer will automatically use a step size of 1.) Some examples of valid FOR . . . NEXT statements are:

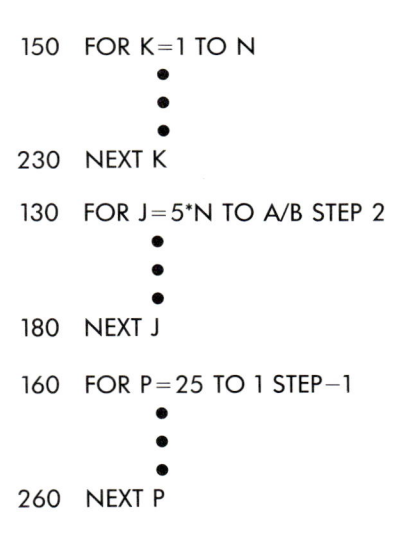

```
150   FOR K=1 TO N
        .
        .
        .
230   NEXT K

130   FOR J=5*N TO A/B STEP 2
        .
        .
        .
180   NEXT J

160   FOR P=25 TO 1 STEP-1
        .
        .
        .
260   NEXT P
```

The first of these FOR . . . NEXT examples is found in our program in Figure 17-13. In our example, the automatic counter (K) is initially set at 1 in the FOR statement (ln 340), and the interest earned in the first year is computed (ln 350) and added to the initial savings balance (ln 360). An output line is printed with the initial value of K and the new savings balance (ln 380), and the end of the loop is reached at the NEXT statement (ln 390). An *automatic* test is made to determine if the counter value is greater than N (the number of years specified by the user). If K *isn't* greater than N, the counter is automatically stepped up by 1 and the next pass through the loop occurs. When the savings results have been simulated for the number of years designated by the user, the value of K *will* be greater than N and program control will exit from

← FIGURE 17-12

BASIC Program 9: Sam's Savings Simulator.

```
100 REM *SAM'S SAVINGS SIMULATOR
110 REM *
120 REM *VARIABLE NAMES
130 REM * S    SAVINGS
140 REM * R    YEARLY INTEREST RATE PAID ON SAVINGS(PERCENT)
150 REM * D    INTEREST EARNED IN A YEAR
160 REM * N    NUMBER OF YEARS TO BE SIMULATED
170 REM * X$   USER RESPONSE TO END OF DATA INQUIRY
180 REM *
190 REM *ENTER DATA FOR SIMULATION
200       PRINT "INITIAL SAVINGS";
210       INPUT S
220       PRINT "INTEREST RATE ON SAVINGS(PERCENT)";
230       INPUT R
240       PRINT "NUMBER OF YEARS";
250       INPUT N
260       PRINT
270 REM *PRINT HEADINGS
280       PRINT "SAVINGS ACCUMULATION SIMULATOR"
290       PRINT
300       PRINT "YEAR";TAB(18);"SAVINGS"
310       PRINT "NO.";TAB(18);"BALANCE"
320       PRINT "____";TAB(18);"_____"
330 REM *CALCULATE SAVINGS BALANCE FOR EACH YEAR
340       FOR K=1 TO N
350          LET D=S*R/100
360          LET S=S+D
370 REM *PRINT YEARLY SUMMARY
380          PRINT K;TAB(18);S
390       NEXT K
400 REM *END OF DATA INQUIRY
410       PRINT
420       PRINT "MORE DATA (YES,NO)";
430       INPUT X$
440       IF X$="YES" THEN 200
450       IF X$="NO" THEN 480
460       PRINT "PLEASE TYPE 'YES' OR 'NO'"
470       GOTO 420
480       END
```

Computer listing of the program

```
Ok
RUN
INITIAL SAVINGS? 2000
INTEREST RATE ON SAVINGS(PERCENT)? 10
NUMBER OF YEARS? 3

SAVINGS ACCUMULATION SIMULATOR

YEAR           SAVINGS
NO.            BALANCE
____           _____
 1             2200
 2             2420
 3             2662

MORE DATA (YES,NO)? NOT
PLEASE TYPE 'YES' OR 'NO'
MORE DATA (YES,NO)? NO
Ok
```

Output produced by the computer in response to input data supplied by the user

WINDOW 17-2

GAUSS'S PUNISHMENT

A couple of hundred years ago there lived a great mathematician named Carl Friedrich Gauss. At age 7, legend goes, Gauss committed some minor behavioral infraction and was punished. He had to find the sum of the first 500 natural numbers, that is, to add 1 + 2 + 3 + ... + 499 + 500.

Nowadays we get a bit smug about solving problems like this. After all, we can just write a simple program, for instance,

```
10    For N=1 to 500
20    Sum=Sum+N
30    Next
40    Print "The sum is";Sum
```

and in a second or two, out comes:

The sum is 125250

But 200 years ago there were no Apples, IBMs, Commodores, TRS-80s, or even hand calculators. So what did young Gauss do? Well, remember, he was a genius, so you certainly would not expect him to laboriously add up the 500 numbers, would you?

Gauss argued as follows: Sum = 1 + 2 + ... + 499 +500. Then he wrote the equation as: Sum = 500 +499 + ... + 2 + 1. Next he added the two sides of the equations but added the numbers down rather than across. This gives 2 × Sum = 501 + 501 + ... + 501 + 501. Because there are 500 columns, 2 × Sum = 500 × 501. Hence, Sum = 500 × 501 ÷ 2 = 125250. Not bad for a 7 year old!

If you study Gauss's reasoning, you see that the technique works because the sequence is an "arithmetic" one; that is, one in which successive terms differ by a constant. Another example of an arithmetic sequence or progression is the series of odd numbers (successive terms differ by the constant 2). An example of a nonarithmetic sequence is the set of perfect squares, 1, 4, 9, 16, 25, ..., as the terms differ by varying amounts. If you tried to duplicate Gauss's trick with perfect squares, it would fail because the column sums (501 in the above example) are not constant.

So whenever you want to add an arithmetic series, a useful technique is to write the series in reverse order, set up equations to get twice the sum on the left, add the columns on the right, then divide by 2 to get the sum. The only possible difficulty with this technique is knowing how many terms the sequence has or what the last term is. I leave that for you to ponder. Try writing a program to add the first 1,000 odd numbers. Then try to duplicate what Gauss did.

Adapted from Michael Ecker, "Gauss's Punishment," *Popular Computing*, June 1984. Copyright © 1984 by McGraw-Hill, Inc. All rights reserved. And from Jo Ann Oravec, "The Acronym: A User's Lament," *Datamation*, November 1, 1985. Reprinted with permission of *Datamation*® magazine, copyright © 1985 by Technical Publishing Company, a Dun and Bradstreet company. All rights reserved.

← FIGURE 17-13

An alternative to program 9, Figure 17-12, showing built-in looping with an automatic counter.

Gauss's Punishment

```
10  REM   Sum of 1st 1000 odd numbers
20  REM
30  SUM=0
40  FOR J=1 TO 1000:  REM Count to 1000
50  ODD=2*J−1:  REM ODD is the Jth odd number
60  SUM=SUM+ODD
70  NEXT J
80  PRINT "Sum is ";SUM
90  END
```

the FOR . . . NEXT loop structure to the next executable line number in sequence. In our example, this is the PRINT statement in ln 410. The remaining program steps in Figure 17-13 are identical to those explained in Figure 17-12.

As this example illustrates, the built-in looping capability available through the use of FOR . . . NEXT statements gives the programmer a relatively simple and powerful repetitive processing tool.

FEEDBACK

Feedback and Review 17-3

It's time once again for you to become a programmer. Your assignment is to prepare a summary report that names Elm Creek property owners and lists their charges. The specifications for this program are spelled out in Feedback and Review 16-3, page 553, and the flowchart drawn to these specifications is shown at the end of Chapter 16. The program in Figure 17-11 will help you get started with this assignment. The input data to be processed are given in Figure 17-11, and some variable names to use in the program are suggested. The program you write should produce output results similar to these:

REPORT OF OWNERS AND CHARGES

OWNERS	CHARGES
BILL BYTER	157.41
CHARLES CRAVENS	155.82
DELTA DESIGNS, INC.	383.985
JOHNSON FOOD MARTS, INC.	553.32
TOTAL AMOUNT OF CHARGES	$ 1250.535

LOOKING BACK

1. BASIC is a popular programming language used with personal computers and timesharing processors, because it makes it easy for people to interact with their computers. Sign-on procedures, the key words used in systems commands, and other details of language usage vary from one system to another.

2. Key words are used in constructing BASIC statements, and these statements are then put together to form a program. Each statement in a BASIC program begins with a line number, and each type of statement has certain rules that must be followed. A number (but certainly not all) of these rules have been discussed in the chapter for the following types of statements and functions:

    REM
    READ . . . DATA
    LET
    PRINT
    END
    IF . . . THEN
    PRINT TAB
    GOTO
    INPUT
    PRINT USING
    STOP
    FOR . . . NEXT

3. The values contained in BASIC statements may be constants or variables. There are numeric constants and character string constants, and there are also numeric variables and string variables. Specific rules for naming and using these numeric and string values must be followed.

4. The computer handles arithmetic operations in a specific order. The rules used in determining the order of these operations have been spelled out in the chapter. Some common procedures for correcting errors that may occur during program and data entry have also been discussed.

5. Solutions have been written in BASIC for all the problems analyzed and flowcharted in Chapter 16. All programs have been written in a programming style that makes them easier to read and understand. Beginning with some short programs to accomplish simple input, processing, and output, we have moved on to more detailed examples that use decisions, loops, accumulators, and counters. The language rules and programming techniques that we've considered during the discussion of these programs can be used to solve very complex problems. Of course, BASIC has many additional features that are not considered in this chapter. Some (but again not all) of these additional features are presented in Chapter 18.

MODULE 5
606

KEY TERMS AND CONCEPTS

system commands 573
program statements 574
line number (ln) 574
numeric constants 575
character string constants 576
numeric variable 576
variable name 576
string variables 576
correction key 578

BASIC prompt symbol 579
programming style 580
REM statement 580
READ . . . DATA statements 581
LET statement 581
PRINT statement 582
END statement 582
IF . . . THEN conditional branching statement 585

PRINT TAB function 585
GOTO unconditional branching statement 586
INPUT statement 586
PRINT USING function 590
STOP statement 595
FOR . . . NEXT statements 599

TOPICS FOR REVIEW AND DISCUSSION

1. Explain the procedures required to sign on the system you are using.
2. (a) How do system commands and program statements differ? (b) Which typically causes the computer to take immediate action?
3. Identify and discuss the elements that may be found in a BASIC statement.
4. "BASIC manipulates values that may be constants or variables." Discuss this sentence.
5. Define and give examples of a (a) numeric constant, (b) character string constant, (c) numeric variable, (d) variable name, (e) string variable, and (f) string variable name.
6. (a) Why is it important to understand the order in which the computer handles the arithmetic operations in a formula? (b) What is this priority order in a formula without parentheses? (c) What changes are made in this order when parentheses are used?
7. Explain the procedures required by the system you are using to correct the errors that may occur in program and data entry.
8. "Diagnostic messages detect syntax errors but not logical errors." Discuss this statement.
9. What will the computer do in executing the following BASIC statements:

```
(a)  010  READ A,B,C,D,E
     200  DATA 025,200,300
     210  DATA 060,150 175, . . . ,125
(b)  120  PRINT A,B,C
(c)  020  PRINT TAB(10);"HELP"
(d)  050  IF N < =50 THEN 100
(e)  130  FOR J=1 to 10 STEP 2
     170  NEXT J
(f)  60   INPUT S$
(g)  20   REM GIVE THE USER A SHOCK
(h)  40   LET A=(K*P/G)/2
(i)  60   PRINT "WHAT IS YOUR AGE";
     70   INPUT A
     80   PRINT
```

10. Write a "grass seed" program for the specifications outlined in question 16 at the end of Chapter 16 (page 563).
11. Let's now revise the grass seed program you've just written for question 10 to include the additional features specified in question 17 at the end of Chapter 16 (page 563).
12. Write a program for the rectangular lot problem outlined in question 18 at the end of Chapter 16 (page 563).
13. Write a program for the "naughty student" problem discussed in question 19 at the end of Chapter 16 (page 563). Use FOR . . . NEXT statements in your program.
14. Prepare a program to process the mileage tax problem outlined in question 20 at the end of Chapter 16 (page 563).
15. Now let's revise the mileage tax program you've written for question 14 so that it will meet the specifications outlined in question 21 at the end of Chapter 16 (page 563).
16. Write a program to process Jill Byter's mailing list application. (See Figure 2-3, page 57, and question 22 at the end of Chapter 16.)
17. Write a program for Sam Byter's length conversion problem that was described in question 23 at the end of Chapter 16 (page 563).
18. Prepare a program to solve the depreciation problem outlined in question 24 at the end of Chapter 16 (page 564).
19. After reviewing Jill's Student Payment Report program in Figure 17-7 and after reading the revised specifications for

this program outlined in question 25 at the end of Chapter 16 (page 564), write a program that will meet the revised specifications.

20. The specifications for Jill Byter's message labels program, and the output message to be produced by this program are given in question 26 at the end of Chapter 16 (page 564). Prepare a program to these specifications that will produce the desired message. Use FOR . . . NEXT statements in your program.

21. The specifications for Sam Byter's program to compute the future value of an investment, along with the type of output desired, are presented in question 27 at the end of Chapter 16 (page 564). Write a program that meets those specifications and produces the output shown at the end of Chapter 16.

22. After reviewing the specifications for Jill's student pay authorization program discussed in question 28 at the end of Chapter 16 (page 564), write a program that will meet those specifications. Use the following input data:

Student	Pay Rate per Hour	Hours Worked
Jack Armstrong	$5.00	20
Jacob Altman	5.50	22
Sally Jacobson	6.00	30
Alfred Newman	5.50	25

23. After you've reviewed program 4, Figure 17-7, prepare a revision using FOR . . . NEXT statements that will use the same input data to produce the same output results.

24. Revise Sam's savings simulator program in Figure 17-13 so that it will produce the following output results:

YEARLY DEPOSIT? 2000
INITIAL SAVINGS? 20000
INTEREST RATE ON SAVINGS(PERCENT)? 6
NUMBER OF YEARS? 4

SAVINGS ACCUMULATION SIMULATOR

YEAR NO.	YEARLY DEPOSIT	INTEREST EARNED	SAVINGS BALANCE
1	2000	1200	23200
2	2000	1392	26592
3	2000	1595.52	30187.52
4	2000	1811.251	33998.77

MORE DATA (YES,NO)? N
PLEASE TYPE 'YES' OR 'NO'

MORE DATA (YES,NO)? NO

25. Sam's savings simulator program in Figure 17-13 can also be used as a starting point for another simulation program. The desired output is shown below. You'll note that the program only produces one simulation run. Write a program to produce this output:

INITIAL TAKE HOME PAY? 20000
YEARLY PAY INCREASE(PERCENT)? 5
INITIAL YEARLY LIVING EXPENSES? 15000
YEARLY COST OF LIVING INCREASE(PERCENT)? 8
INITIAL SAVINGS? 20000
INTEREST RATE ON SAVINGS(PERCENT)? 6
NUMBER OF YEARS? 5

SAVINGS ACCUMULATION SIMULATOR

YEAR NO.	YEARLY EARNINGS	INTEREST EARNED	YEARLY EXPENSES	SAVINGS BALANCE
1	21000	1200	16200	26000
2	22050	1560	17496	32114
3	23152.5	1926.84	18895.68	38297.65
4	24310.12	2297.859	20407.34	44498.29
5	25525.62	2669.897	22039.93	50653.88

26. In running the grass seed programs identified in questions 10 and 11, Sam has noticed that they produce results that are often incorrect for the particular situation. The problem is that the programs compute the number of bags of seed needed to plant a *vacant* lot, but many of Sam's jobs involve seeding lots that have buildings. And since the buildings occupy space that can't be planted on the lots, Sam has been buying too much grass seed. Revise the grass seed program prepared in question 11 so that it will (a) accept the dimensions of any buildings located on a lot and (b) subtract the area of these buildings from the total lot area in order to get the appropriate planting area. Your program output should look like this:

LENGTH OF LOT (FEET)? 400
WIDTH OF LOT   (FEET)? 500

HOW MANY BUILDINGS ON THE LOT? 2

LENGTH OF BUILDING 1 (FEET)? 100
WIDTH OF BUILDING   1 (FEET)? 150
LENGTH OF BUILDING 2 (FEET)? 20
WIDTH OF BUILDING   2 (FEET)? 70
BAGS OF GRASS SEED NEEDED: 36.72

DO YOU WANT TO STOP (Y/N)? YES
TYPE Y OR N
DO YOU WANT TO STOP (Y/N)? Y

Project to Consider

1. The salaries of programmers and systems analysts vary according to skill levels and geographic locations. Salary scales are published annually by several magazines, including *Infosystems* and *Datamation*. Locate a recent salary survey published by such a source and note the salary scales for programmers/analysts and other occupations of interest to you in your geographic area. Call the personnel offices of a few area organizations and find out how their salary figures for programmers/analysts and other job categories compare with those reported in the survey. Present your findings to the class.

Answers to Feedback and Review Sections

Possible programs for Feedback and Review Sections 17-1 through 17-3 follow. Your versions may differ in several ways and still be correct. For example, PRINT statements with different tab spacings can easily be substituted for the ones shown in the answer to Feedback and Review 17-3. And, of course, different REM statements and different variable names will cause a difference in appearance without making any significant difference in content.

A possible BASIC program for Feedback and Review 17-1.

```
100 REM *MILEAGE PROGRAM
110 REM *
120 REM *VARIABLE NAMES
130 REM *   M1 ODOMETER READING AT START OF TRIP
140 REM *   M2 ODOMETER READING AT END OF TRIP
150 REM *   G  GALLONS OF GAS USED
160 REM *   M  GAS MILEAGE
170 REM *
180 REM *READ ODOMETER DATA AND GALLONS OF GAS USED
190         READ M1,M2,G
200 REM *COMPUTE MILEAGE
210         LET M=(M2-M1)/G
220 REM *PRINT RESULTS AND STOP
230         PRINT "ODOMETER READING AT START OF TRIP :";M1
240         PRINT "ODOMETER READING AT END OF TRIP   :";M2
250         PRINT "GALLONS OF GAS USED DURING TRIP   :";G
260         PRINT "MILEAGE FOR TRIP(MILES PER GALLON):";M
270 REM *INPUT DATA
280         DATA    2300, 4500, 150
290         END
```

Computer listing of the program

```
Ok
RUN
ODOMETER READING AT START OF TRIP : 2300
ODOMETER READING AT END OF TRIP   : 4500
GALLONS OF GAS USED DURING TRIP   : 150
MILEAGE FOR TRIP(MILES PER GALLON): 14.66667
Ok
```

Output produced by the computer in response to system command RUN

```
100 REM *MILEAGE PROGRAM
110 REM *
120 REM *VARIABLE NAMES
130 REM *   M1 ODOMETER READING AT START OF TRIP
140 REM *   M2 ODOMETER READING AT END OF TRIP
150 REM *   G  GALLONS OF GAS USED
160 REM *   M  GAS MILEAGE
170 REM *   A$ OPERATOR RESPONSE TO END OF DATA QUESTION
180 REM *
190 REM *INPUT ODOMETER READINGS AND GALLONS OF GAS USED
200       PRINT "ODOMETER READING AT START OF TRIP ";
210       INPUT M1
220       PRINT "ODOMETER READING AT END OF TRIP   ";
230       INPUT M2
240       PRINT "GALLONS OF GAS USED DURING TRIP   ";
250       INPUT G
260 REM *COMPUTE MILEAGE
270       LET M=(M2-M1)/G
280 REM *PRINT RESULTS
290       PRINT "MILEAGE FOR TRIP(MILES PER GALLON):";M
300       PRINT
310       PRINT
320 REM *ENTER RESPONSE TO END OF DATA INQUIRY
330       PRINT "ANOTHER TRIP (Y/N)";
340       INPUT A$
350 REM *TEST OPERATOR RESPONSE FOR END OF DATA
360       IF A$="Y" THEN 200
370       IF A$="N" THEN 410
380       PRINT "TYPE A 'Y' OR AN 'N'"
390       GOTO 330
400 REM *PRINT SIGN OFF MESSAGE AND STOP
410       PRINT "GOOD BYE"
420       END
```

Computer listing of the program

```
Ok
RUN
ODOMETER READING AT START OF TRIP ? 2300
ODOMETER READING AT END OF TRIP   ? 4500
GALLONS OF GAS USED DURING TRIP   ? 150
MILEAGE FOR TRIP(MILES PER GALLON): 14.66667


ANOTHER TRIP (Y/N)? Y
ODOMETER READING AT START OF TRIP ? 4700
ODOMETER READING AT END OF TRIP   ? 5700
GALLONS OF GAS USED DURING TRIP   ? 76
MILEAGE FOR TRIP(MILES PER GALLON): 13.1579


ANOTHER TRIP (Y/N)? NO
TYPE A 'Y' OR AN 'N'
ANOTHER TRIP (Y/N)? N
GOOD BYE
Ok
```

Output produced by the computer interacting with the user

A possible BASIC program for Feedback and Review 17-2.

A possible BASIC program for Feedback and Review 17-3 (*on following page*).

```
100 REM *SUMMARY OF ELM CREEK CHARGES
110 REM *
120 REM * N$   NAME OF PROPERTY OWNER
130 REM * Q    QUANTITY PLANTED
140 REM * P    UNIT PRICE OF PLANTS
150 REM * A    NET AMOUNT OF PLANTS
160 REM * T1   PLANTING CHARGES
170 REM * T2   TOTAL AMOUNT OF CHARGES
180 REM * N    NUMBER OF RECORDS TO BE PROCESSED
190 REM * K    COUNTER
200 REM * T    TOTAL AMOUNT ACCUMULATED
210 REM *
220 REM *INITIALIZE COUNTER AND ACCUMULATOR
230       LET K=1
240       LET T=0
250 REM *PRINT HEADINGS
260       PRINT "          REPORT OF OWNERS AND CHARGES"
270       PRINT
280       PRINT "OWNERS";TAB(40);"CHARGES"
290       PRINT
300 REM *READ NUMBER OF RECORDS TO BE PROCESSED
310       READ N
320 REM *READ NAME, QUANTITY PLANTED, AND PRICE
330       READ N$,Q,P
340 REM *COMPUTE NET AMOUNT OF PLANTS
350       LET A=Q*P
360 REM *COMPUTE PLANTING AND TOTAL CHARGES, AND ACCUMULATE TOTAL
370       LET T1=A*.06
380       LET T2=A+T1
390       LET T=T+T2
400 REM *PRINT NAME AND TOTAL CHARGES
410       PRINT N$;TAB(40);T2
420 REM *TEST FOR END OF DATA
430       IF K=N THEN 480
440 REM *INCREMENT COUNTER AND RETURN
450       LET K=K+1
460       GOTO 330
470 REM *PRINT TOTAL AMOUNT AND STOP
480       PRINT
490       PRINT "TOTAL AMOUNT OF CHARGES";TAB(38);"$";T
500 REM *INPUT DATA
510       DATA    4
520       DATA "BILL BYTER"
530       DATA  33.0,   4.50
540       DATA "CHARLES CRAVENS"
550       DATA  28.0,   5.25
560       DATA "DELTA DESIGNS, INC."
570       DATA  63.0,   5.75
580       DATA "JOHNSON FOOD MARTS, INC."
590       DATA 180.0,   2.90
600       END
```

Computer listing of the program

```
Ok
RUN
          REPORT OF OWNERS AND CHARGES

OWNERS                                  CHARGES

BILL BYTER                              157.41
CHARLES CRAVENS                         155.82
DELTA DESIGNS, INC.                     383.985
JOHNSON FOOD MARTS, INC.                553.32

TOTAL AMOUNT OF CHARGES              $ 1250.535
Ok
```

Output produced by the computer in response to the system command RUN

A CLOSER LOOK

PROGRAMMING STYLE

A good writer writes clearly and persuasively. This is true whether the writer wants the reader to ax a political opponent or fall in love. It's also true when the writer wants the reader to believe that a computer program functions correctly.

To write persuasively, it's important to master spelling, syntax, and semantics. But correct spelling, syntax, and semantics are insufficient for persuasive memoranda and persuasive love letters. They're also insufficient for persuasive computer programs. The meanings of memoranda, love letters, or computer programs are always expressed by their written texts, but it is the manner in which they're written—i.e., their style—that determines their readability and their persuasiveness.

Clear and compelling memoranda are regrettably scarce in Washington, D.C. The same is probably true—just as regrettably—of love letters, and it's also true of computer programs. There is a simple reason for all three scarcities: Writing well is hard.

It would be nice if we could depend on our language to guarantee good writing, but we can't. For example, French is said to be the best language for love letters. Perhaps this is true, but it doesn't stop English lovers. There are good English love letters and bad French love letters, just as there are good PL/1 programmers and bad Pascal programmers. A language can facilitate and encourage good writing, but it can't offer any guarantees.

Indeed, there are no guarantees. There are, however, some good guides. One favorite is William Strunk, Jr., and E. B. White's famous little book, *The Elements of Style*, in which Strunk and White preach and practice such pithy commandments as those in Figure A. The commandments come complete with helpful explanations and discussions, as well as examples of sins and redemption.

Just as there are guides for writing clear and compelling English, there are guides for writing clear and compelling computer programs. A good one is Brian W. Kernighan and J. P. Plauger's book, *The Elements of Programming Style*, which is similar to *The Elements of Style*, not just in title, but in form and intent. Kernighan and Plauger offer such pithy commandments as those in Figure B. And, like the commandments in Strunk and White, these too come complete with helpful explanations and discussion, as well as examples of programming sins and their redemption.

A language is a tool for expression, but even a good tool can be used badly. Well-written prose depends on the writer. And, no matter how well the designers of a programming language do their job, well-written programs depend on the programmer. Consider one last commandment:

Do not take shortcuts at the cost of clarity.

Did it come from Strunk and White or from Kernighan and Plauger? You decide.

From John E. Shore, *The Sachertorte Algorithm and Other Antidotes to Computer Anxiety*, Viking Press, 1985. Copyright © 1985 by John E. Shore. Reprinted by permission.

FIGURE A

Advice from Strunk and White.

Omit needless words.
Be clear.
Avoid fancy words.
Use definite, specific, concrete language.
Enclose parenthetic expressions between commas.
Avoid a succession of loose sentences.
Express coordinate ideas in similar form.
Keep related words together.
Choose a suitable design and hold to it.
Revise and rewrite.

FIGURE B

Advice from Kernighan and Plauger.

Avoid temporary variables.
Write clearly—don't be too clever.
Choose variable names that won't be confused.
Say what you mean, simply and directly.
Parenthesize to avoid ambiguity.
Use the fundamental control flow constructs.
Avoid unnecessary branches.
Follow each decision as closely as possible with its associated action.
Make your program read from top to bottom.
Don't stop with your first draft.

CHAPTER 18

MORE ABOUT *BASIC*

A BRIEF HISTORY OF MICROSOFT BASIC

Microsoft BASIC (MBASIC) is an industry standard for BASIC languages simply because it was the first—and for many years the only—version of BASIC available for microcomputers. Thus, MBASIC introduced a whole new generation to the esoteric art of writing instructions for computers.

The first microcomputer BASIC interpreter was written in 1974 by two college students, Paul Allen and Bill Gates, on a PDP-8 minicomputer for an Intel 8080 microprocessor emulator. Allen and Gates were intrigued by the first microcomputer to be produced in quantity, the Altair 8800, which had just been brought to market by Micro Instrumentation and Telemetry Systems (MITS). They realized that the new device required a language interpreter and they quickly filled the need. Their first BASIC interpreter required 4K bytes of RAM and was crude by today's standards—but then, so was the Altair.

MITS licensed the Allen/Gates BASIC for the Altair in 1975, and the

Microsoft Corporation was born. By the end of 1976, over 10,000 Altairs had been sold with MBASIC. Microsoft's work on an expanded version of BASIC using 8K bytes was spurred by a new machine under development by Commodore, Ltd. The Commodore PET debuted in 1976 with a licensed version of the 8K-byte MBASIC.

The 8K-byte MBASIC is commonly referred to as version 2.0; the 4K-byte version is 1.0. In early 1978, Microsoft sold a license to Tandy Corporation for the TRS-80 Model I. This machine originally used a BASIC written in-house, called Level I BASIC, a limited product that soon gave way to Level II, or MBASIC version 2.0. At the same time, the company licensed version 2.0 to another recent entry into the computer business, a West Coast-based garage operation dubbed Apple Computer Inc.

By early 1979, a new version of the language was under development. Version 3.0 of MBASIC provided extended functions for program development plus graphics and sound commands. These enhancements were made at the request of potential new licensees who wanted software that showed off the newest hardware capabilities.

On the heels of version 3.0 came a version of MBASIC that supported floppy-disk drives. Though Microsoft named it version 4.0, the rest of the world called it Disk BASIC and its popularity spread quickly.

Late 1980 brought IBM and Microsoft together, an event that catapulted Microsoft into a leadership position in the microcomputer-software industry. Working with Seattle Computer, Microsoft created version 5.0, or GW (Gee Whiz) BASIC. Version 5.0, finally released in 1981, was designed to take advantage of 16-bit processor environments and added many enhancements for sophisticated color graphics, windows and ports, music, softkeys, and other features.

Microsoft claims an installed base of 2 million machines licensed to run the various versions of its BASIC interpreter. Considering the explosive sales of microcomputers, this estimate is doubtless conservative.

Reprinted from Brig Elliott, "A Brief History of Microsoft BASIC," *Byte*, April 1984. Copyright © 1984 by McGraw-Hill, Inc. Reprinted with permission. All rights reserved.

CHAPTER 18

LOOKING AHEAD

Our study of BASIC continues here with programs that demonstrate its additional features. Once again, our examples apply to the Byter family. The information in this chapter will enable you to:

- Write BASIC programs using nested FOR . . . NEXT loops and selected library functions
- Create one- and two-dimensional arrays and use these arrays in BASIC programs
- Follow the program logic used to sort data items into a predetermined order
- Explain the use of the additional BASIC statements presented in the last section

CHAPTER OUTLINE

LOOKING AHEAD
NESTED FOR . . . NEXT LOOPS
FOR . . . NEXT Loops: A Review
Flowcharting FOR . . . NEXT Loops: A Dilemma
Inner and Outer Loops
THE USE OF LIBRARY FUNCTIONS
The SQR Function
INT and RND Functions
ONE-DIMENSIONAL ARRAYS
Entering Data into Arrays
Printing Arrayed Data
The DIM Statement
Example Programs Using One-Dimensional Arrays
Feedback and Review 18-1
TWO-DIMENSIONAL ARRAYS
Example Program Using Two-Dimensional Array
Feedback and Review 18-2
LET'S SORT THIS OUT
Bubble Sorts
Feedback and Review 18-3
ADDITIONAL BASIC STATEMENTS
Statements to Facilitate Structured Programming
A Few Other Statements
LOOKING BACK

NESTED FOR . . . NEXT LOOPS

FOR . . . NEXT Loops: A Review

You saw in Chapter 17 how a FOR statement opens a loop and establishes an automatic counter and how the loop is then closed with a NEXT statement. The program lines located between FOR and NEXT statements are executed repeatedly and form the range, or body, of the loop. A simple example of the FOR . . . NEXT structure is shown in the program in Figure 18-1. Jill Byter, still campaigning for a seat in her college's Student House of Representatives, wrote this program to print a message on gummed labels. The message reminds voters of the forthcoming election and of Jill's candidacy. Jill attaches these labels to campaign letters and flyers.

FIGURE 18-1
An example of a FOR . . . NEXT loop.

```
100 REM *MESSAGE LABELS PROGRAM
110 REM *
120 REM *VARIABLE NAMES
130 REM * N  NUMBER OF LABELS TO BE PRINTED
140 REM *
150 REM *READ NUMBER OF LABELS TO BE PRINTED
160       READ N
170 REM *PRINT LABELS
180       FOR K=1 TO N
190          PRINT TAB(5);"THE STUDENT HOUSE OF REPRESENTATIVES"
200          PRINT TAB(5);"ELECTION WILL BE HELD NEXT TUESDAY."
210          PRINT TAB(5);"PLEASE REMEMBER TO VOTE FOR JILL BYTER."
220          PRINT TAB(5);"   THANKS FOR YOUR SUPPORT !"
230          PRINT
240          PRINT
250       NEXT K
260 REM *LABELS TO BE PREPARED
270       DATA 3
280       END
```
Computer listing of the program

```
Ok
RUN
    THE STUDENT HOUSE OF REPRESENTATIVES
    ELECTION WILL BE HELD NEXT TUESDAY.
    PLEASE REMEMBER TO VOTE FOR JILL BYTER.
       THANKS FOR YOUR SUPPORT !


    THE STUDENT HOUSE OF REPRESENTATIVES
    ELECTION WILL BE HELD NEXT TUESDAY.
    PLEASE REMEMBER TO VOTE FOR JILL BYTER.
       THANKS FOR YOUR SUPPORT !


    THE STUDENT HOUSE OF REPRESENTATIVES
    ELECTION WILL BE HELD NEXT TUESDAY.
    PLEASE REMEMBER TO VOTE FOR JILL BYTER.
       THANKS FOR YOUR SUPPORT !

Ok
```
Output produced by the computer as the program is executed

The REM statements in line number (ln) 100 through ln 150 of Figure 18-1 are clear enough. In ln 160, a READ statement determines from the DATA statement in ln 270 that the program should print three labels. The FOR statement in ln 180 opens the loop and specifies printing N (or 3 in this case) labels. The PRINT statements on lines 190–240 form the body of the loop. These lines produce the message and control line spacing. The NEXT statement on ln 250 closes the loop. Each pass through the loop causes an automatic test to take place to determine if the counter value (K) is greater than N. When three labels have been printed, the value of K is greater than N, printing stops, and program control exits from the FOR . . . NEXT loop structure to the next executable line number in sequence. In our example, this is the END statement in ln 280.

Flowcharting FOR . . . NEXT Loops: A Dilemma

It's a simple matter to prepare a flowchart for the program given in Figure 18-1. In fact, *each* of the three charts in Figure 18-2 presents the logic of Jill's message label program. But the dilemma illustrated in Figure 18-2 is that there's little agreement on the approach to use in flowcharting FOR . . . NEXT loops. Version (*a*) uses standard symbols but is somewhat more tedious to prepare than versions (*b*) and (*c*). Version (*b*) is compact and convenient, but it uses a rather cryptic and nonstandard symbol. Since version (*c*) uses standard symbols and is also relatively compact, we'll use this flowcharting approach to represent FOR . . . NEXT loops. But the other versions are equally acceptable.

Inner and Outer Loops

Efficient programs often include one or more **inner loop** structures within the body of an **outer loop.** That is, it's common to find one or more **nested FOR . . . NEXT loops** within the range of an outer FOR . . . NEXT structure. Consider the following example:

```
 ┌─190    FOR X=1 TO 2
 │  ┌─210    FOR Y=1 TO 4
 │  │
 │  └─230    NEXT Y
 └───300    NEXT X
```

In this example, the *Y,* or *inner loop,* is executed four times each time there is a pass through the *outer,* or *X, loop*. That is, when program control first moves to ln 190, the X loop is established and the first pass through the X loop begins. In ln 220, the inner Y loop is created and is then executed four times. After the fourth pass through the Y loop, program control moves in sequence to ln 300 to complete the first of two passes through the X loop. In the second iteration through the outer loop, the Y loop is again executed four times. Thus when the two passes of the outer loop have been completed, the inner loop has been executed a total of eight times.

It's desirable during programming to *indent inner loops* to make them easier to identify and understand. The indentation of inner loops also helps to

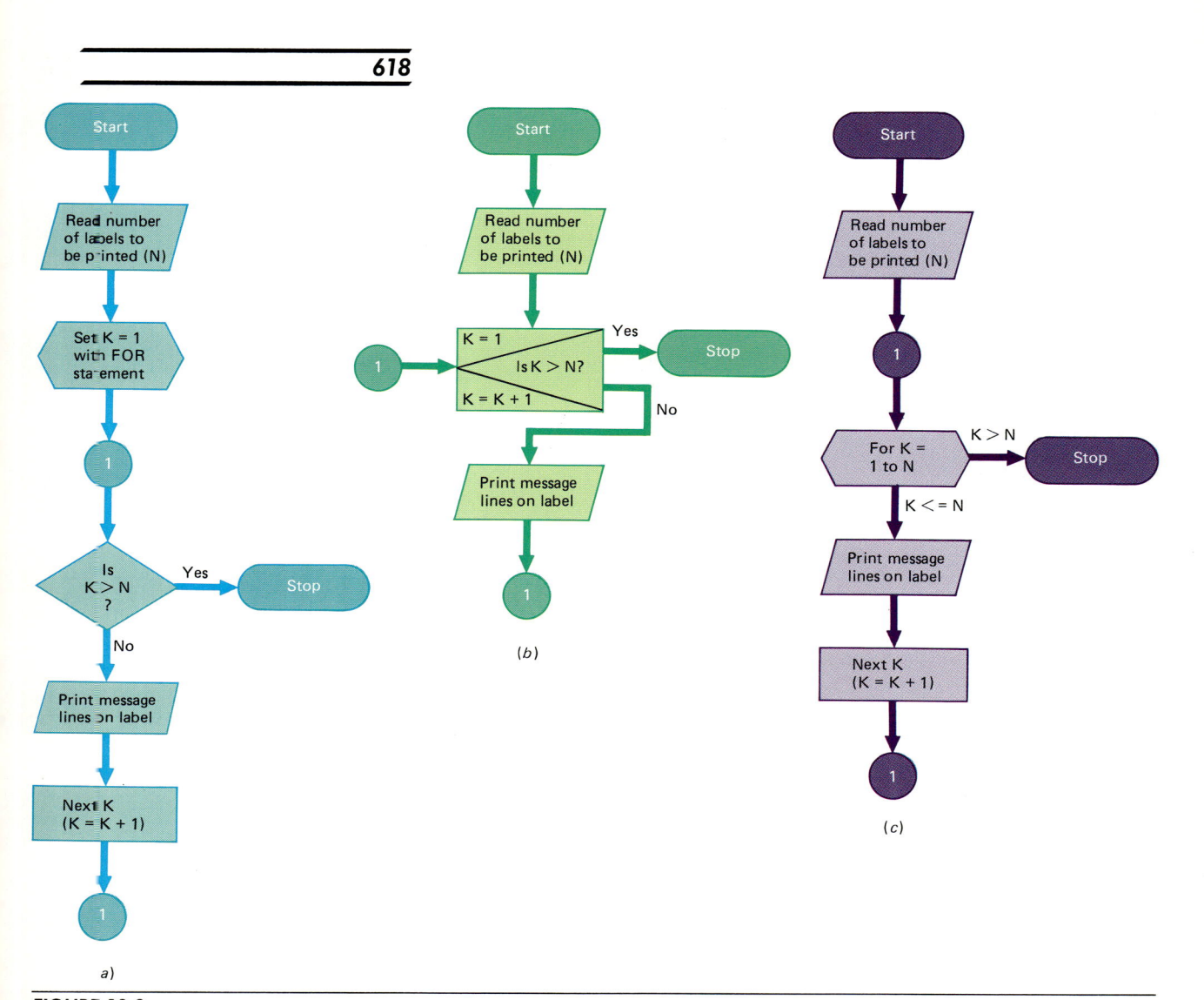

FIGURE 18-2

Three flowcharts for the program shown in Figure 18-1. Since there's little agreement on charting FOR . . . NEXT loops, we'll use the approach shown in version (c). The other versions are equally correct.

prevent the creation of **crossed loops**—a logic error that prevents the computer from correctly executing the program. Examples of valid and invalid loop structures follow:

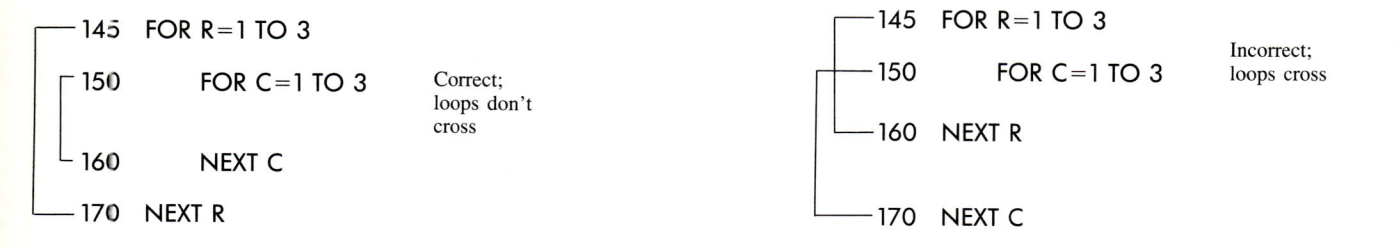

```
 ┌── 145   FOR R=1 TO 3
 │                                   Correct;
 │   150       FOR C=1 TO 3          loops don't
 │                                   cross
 │   160       NEXT C
 └── 170   NEXT R
```

```
 ┌── 145   FOR R=1 TO 3
 │                                   Incorrect;
 │ ┌ 150       FOR C=1 TO 3          loops cross
 │ │
 └─┼ 160   NEXT R
   │
   └ 170   NEXT C
```

Let's take a look now at a simple program that shows how nested loops work. Jill received many favorable comments about her campaign labels, and so she and some other nursing students decided to use labels to remind voters to support a bond election called to raise money for a hospital construction project. The flowchart showing the logic of the reminder labels program is presented in Figure 18-3a, and the program written for this purpose is shown in Figure 18-3b.

Following the initial REM statements in Figure 18-3b, the READ statement in ln 170 and the DATA statement in ln 320 determine the number of labels to print and the number of "Happy Holiday" greetings to produce on each label. The outer (or X) FOR . . . NEXT loop is established on ln 190 to control the number of labels to print. In this case, A is 2, so the outer loop will be executed twice, and two labels will be printed. The inner (or Y) FOR . . . NEXT loop is created on ln 210, and this loop is programmed to print "HAVE A HAPPY INDEPENDENCE DAY" B (or 4) times on each label. After the inner loop has been executed four times on the first pass through the outer loop, program control passes to lines 250–290 and a reminder message is printed on the first label. The first label is now printed, and the first pass through the outer loop is completed on ln 300. Program control is then automatically transferred back to ln 190 to begin another execution of the outer loop. As the output in Figure 18-3b shows, the outer loop is executed twice, and the inner loop is executed (2 × 4 or) eight times.

THE USE OF LIBRARY FUNCTIONS

Since several common computing tasks are frequently needed in BASIC programs, these tasks have been *preprogrammed* by BASIC developers and are available to the BASIC user as built-in **library functions.** Among them are sophisticated trigonometric and exponentiation functions and three functions which we'll consider now: SQR (square root); INT (integer); and RND (randomize).

The SQR Function

We can illustrate SQR simply; for example,

    100   LET Y=SQR(X)

tells the computer to look up the value of X, take the *square root* (**SQR**) of that value, and then assign the result to the variable name Y. If X has a value of 36, then 6 is the result that will be assigned to Y.

Let's look now at a more challenging example. The *economic order quantity (EOQ)* is a term often encountered in inventory management. It refers to the order size for some item in inventory (e.g., tee shirts) that results in the lowest total inventory cost for a period. Managers often use an EOQ model to plan inventory levels and make ordering decisions. If the assump-

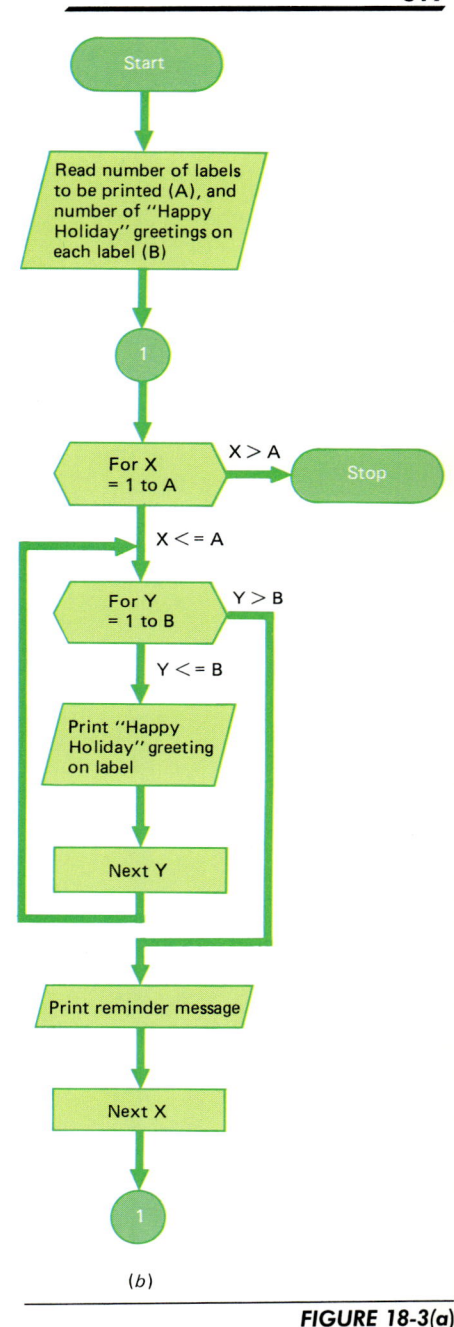

(b)

FIGURE 18-3(a)

A flowchart showing a nested FOR . . . NEXT loop.

```
100 REM *REMINDER LABELS PROGRAM
110 REM *
120 REM *VARIABLE NAMES
130 REM * A   NUMBER OF REMINDER LABELS TO BE PRINTED
140 REM * B   NUMBER OF "HAPPY INDEPENDENCE DAY" GREETINGS ON EACH LABEL
150 REM *
160 REM *READ NUMBER OF LABELS AND NUMBER OF GREETINGS ON EACH LABEL
170      READ A,B
180 REM *SET UP OUTER LOOP TO CONTROL NUMBER OF LABELS
190      FOR X=1 TO A
200 REM *SET UP INNER LOOP TO CONTROL NUMBER OF GREETINGS
210         FOR Y=1 TO B
220            PRINT TAB(10);"HAVE A HAPPY INDEPENDENCE DAY"
230         NEXT Y
240 REM *MESSAGE PRINTED ON EACH LABEL AFTER INNER LOOP IS PROCESSED
250         PRINT TAB(5);"BUT PLEASE REMEMBER TO SUPPORT THE NEW WING"
260         PRINT TAB(5);"FOR THE HOSPITAL WHEN THE BOND ELECTION IS"
270         PRINT TAB(5);"HELD ON JULY 10. ******THANKS*******!"
280         PRINT
290         PRINT
300      NEXT X
310 REM *NUMBER OF LABELS AND GREETINGS
320      DATA 2, 4
330      END
```

Computer listing of the program

```
Ok
RUN
         HAVE A HAPPY INDEPENDENCE DAY
         HAVE A HAPPY INDEPENDENCE DAY
         HAVE A HAPPY INDEPENDENCE DAY
         HAVE A HAPPY INDEPENDENCE DAY
    BUT PLEASE REMEMBER TO SUPPORT THE NEW WING
    FOR THE HOSPITAL WHEN THE BOND ELECTION IS
    HELD ON JULY 10. ******THANKS*******!

         HAVE A HAPPY INDEPENDENCE DAY
         HAVE A HAPPY INDEPENDENCE DAY
         HAVE A HAPPY INDEPENDENCE DAY
         HAVE A HAPPY INDEPENDENCE DAY
    BUT PLEASE REMEMBER TO SUPPORT THE NEW WING
    FOR THE HOSPITAL WHEN THE BOND ELECTION IS
    HELD ON JULY 10. ******THANKS*******!

Ok
```

Output produced by the computer as the program is executed

FIGURE 18-3(b)

A program showing a nested FOR . . . NEXT loop.

tions underlying the model are valid, then the following formula will produce the economic order quantity:

$$Q = \sqrt{\frac{2AP}{UI}}$$

where:

Q = economic order quantity

A = quantity of inventory required for a period

P = cost of placing one order

U = unit cost of item ordered

I = inventory carrying costs expressed as a percentage of the unit cost

Instead of writing a detailed sequence of instructions to perform the square root function, the programmer can use the SQR function to determine the EOQ value with a single line:

420   LET Q=SQR((2*A*P)/(U*I))

INT and RND Functions

INT ("integer") and **RND** ("randomize") **functions** are presented in the example shown in Figure 18-4. The flowchart to help you trace through the logic of this example is found in Figure 18-4a, and the program coding is shown in Figure 18-4b.

The example in Figure 18-4b is a multiplication drill and practice program. Lisa and Sam Byter wrote this program to help students in the lower grades at Lisa's school learn the multiplication tables. The program specifications were:

● It should interact with the student and supply the necessary instructions on the purpose and use of the drill.

● It should give students 20 pairs of numbers to multiply, and it should keep track of the number of correct and incorrect responses.

● Each number to be multiplied should be a *random number;* that is, it should be any whole number (integer) from 0 through 9, and each of these numbers should have an equal chance of being selected in a single trial.

● It should provide immediate feedback after each student's response; that is, it should acknowledge a correct answer, or if the answer is incorrect, it should provide the correct response.

● After the 20 pairs of numbers have been multiplied, the program should compute the student's test score. A score of 85 or better is "passing."

● The program should produce an immediate test-score feedback message to the student.

The helpful documentation found in the REM statements in lines 100 through 230 needs no explanation. The LET statements in lines 240 and 250 initialize the accumulators that will be used to total the number of correct (Q1) and incorrect (Q2) student responses during a program run. PRINT statements giving instructions to the student, along with an INPUT statement requesting the student's name so that student-program communication can be more "personal," occupy lines 270 through 380.

The PRINT statements in lines 400–420 are instructions that show the student how to enter a **random number seed value.** In the BASIC dialect used at Lisa's school, a seed is any whole number between −32768 and +32767. The seed is used as a starting value for the random number generator

FIGURE 18-4(a)

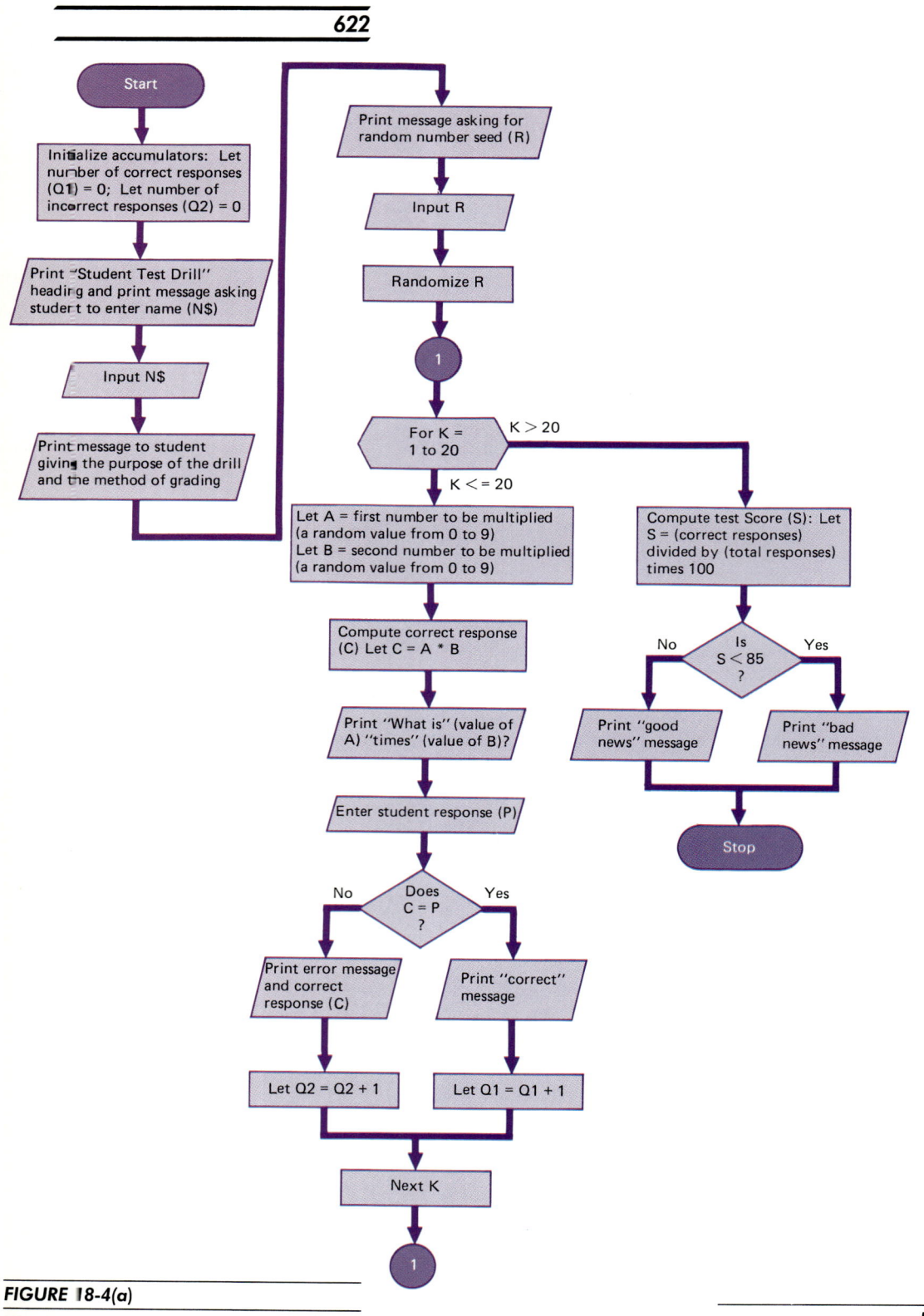

Flowchart for multiplication drill and practice program [Figure 18-4(b)].

FIGURE 18-4(b)

Multiplication drill and practice program.

```
100 REM *MULTIPLICATION DRILL AND PRACTICE PROGRAM
110 REM *
120 REM *VARIABLE NAMES
130 REM * N$     STUDENT NAME
140 REM * A      FIRST FACTOR
150 REM * B      SECOND FACTOR
160 REM * C      CORRECT RESPONSE
170 REM * P      STUDENT RESPONSE
180 REM * Q1     NUMBER OF CORRECT RESPONSES
190 REM * Q2     NUMBER OF INCORRECT RESPONSES
200 REM * S      PRACTICE SESSION SCORE
210 REM * R      RANDOM NUMBER SEED
220 REM *
230 REM *INITIALIZE ACCUMULATORS
240         LET Q1=0
250         LET Q2=0
260 REM *OBTAIN STUDENT'S NAME AND SUPPLY DRILL INSTRUCTIONS
270         PRINT "     STUDENT TEST DRILL"
280         PRINT
290         PRINT "WHAT IS YOUR NAME";
300         INPUT N$
310         PRINT
320         PRINT "PLEASE RELAX AND GET COMFORTABLE ";N$;"."
330         PRINT "THIS IS A DRILL OF YOUR KNOWLEDGE OF THE"
340         PRINT "MULTIPLICATION TABLES.  YOU'LL BE ASKED"
350         PRINT "TO MULTIPLY 20 PAIRS OF NUMBERS.  CONSIDER"
360         PRINT "YOUR ANSWERS CAREFULLY ";N$;"."
370         PRINT "YOU SHOULD TRY TO SCORE 85 OR BETTER ON THIS DRILL."
380         PRINT
390 REM *GET RANDOM NUMBER SEED AND INITIALIZE RANDOM NUMBER GENERATOR
400         PRINT "PLEASE INPUT A RANDOM NUMBER SEED.  THIS SEED CAN"
410         PRINT "BE ANY WHOLE NUMBER FROM -32768 TO +32767."
420         PRINT "RANDOM NUMBER SEED";
430         INPUT R
440         RANDOMIZE R
450 REM *LOOP THROUGH THE SEQUENCE OF TEST QUESTIONS
460         FOR K=1 TO 20
470 REM *GENERATE TWO RANDOM INTEGERS IN THE INTERVAL FROM ZERO TO NINE
480            LET A=INT(RND*10)
490            LET B=INT(RND*10)
500 REM *COMPUTE CORRECT RESPONSE
510            LET C=A*B
520 REM *OBTAIN STUDENT RESPONSE
530            PRINT "WHAT IS ";A;" TIMES ";B;
540            INPUT P
550 REM *TEST STUDENT RESPONSE
560            IF C=P THEN 620
570 REM *INCORRECT RESPONSE MESSAGE:
580            PRINT "SORRY ";N$;", THE CORRECT ANSWER IS ";C;"."
590            LET Q2=Q2+1
600            GOTO 640
610 REM *CORRECT RESPONSE MESSAGE:
620            PRINT "CORRECT!"
630            LET Q1=Q1+1
640         NEXT K
650 REM *COMPUTE DRILL SCORE, EVALUATE PERFORMANCE, AND STOP.
660         LET S=(Q1/(Q1+Q2))*100
670         IF S<85 THEN 740
680 REM *PASSING SCORE MESSAGE:
690         PRINT
700         PRINT "GOOD WORK, ";N$;" YOUR SCORE WAS ";S;", AND 85"
710         PRINT "IS CONSIDERED PASSING."
720         STOP
```

Computer listing of the program

```
730 REM *FAILING SCORE MESSAGE:
740      PRINT
750      PRINT "TOO BAD, ";N$;" A SCORE OF 85 OR BETTER WAS THE"
760      PRINT "GOAL, AND YOUR SCORE WAS ";S;"."
770      END
```
```
Ok
RUN
          STUDENT TEST DRILL

WHAT IS YOUR NAME? LISA

PLEASE RELAX AND GET COMFORTABLE LISA.
THIS IS A DRILL OF YOUR KNOWLEDGE OF THE
MULTIPLICATION TABLES.  YOU'LL BE ASKED
TO MULTIPLY 20 PAIRS OF NUMBERS.  CONSIDER
YOUR ANSWERS CAREFULLY LISA.
YOU SHOULD TRY TO SCORE 85 OR BETTER ON THIS DRILL.

PLEASE INPUT A RANDOM NUMBER SEED.  THIS SEED CAN
BE ANY WHOLE NUMBER FROM -32768 TO +32767.
RANDOM NUMBER SEED? 521
WHAT IS   0   TIMES   2 ?  0
CORRECT!
WHAT IS   6   TIMES   6 ?  36
CORRECT!
WHAT IS   0   TIMES   6 ?  6
SORRY LISA, THE CORRECT ANSWER IS   0 .
WHAT IS   7   TIMES   6 ?
                 •
                 •
                 •
                 •
WHAT IS   9   TIMES   6 ?  54
CORRECT!
WHAT IS   4   TIMES   2 ?  8
CORRECT!
WHAT IS   4   TIMES   4 ?  16
CORRECT!
WHAT IS   3   TIMES   8 ?  24
CORRECT!

GOOD WORK, LISA YOUR SCORE WAS   95 , AND 85
IS CONSIDERED PASSING.
Break in 720
Ok
```

Output produced by the computer as the program is executed

used in that BASIC dialect. Complex mathematical calculations generate a series of pseudo-random values that simulate the unpredictability of true random numbers, but different BASIC dialects use different approaches. If the random number generator in the BASIC used at Lisa's school isn't reseeded or if the same seed (starting value) is used for each student drill session, the same sequence of random numbers will be repeated each time the program is run. For example, you'll notice that in the output section of Figure 18-4*b* Lisa has used a seed value of 521. If she should use this same value again in another run, she'll have to answer the same set of questions. But students at Lisa's school can avoid the repeating sequence problem by supplying a different seed value (R) to the INPUT statement in ln 420 each time they use the program. The **RANDOMIZE statement** in ln 440 will then use these student-supplied values to generate different sequences of random numbers. Note, however, that other BASIC dialects may or may not use RANDOMIZE statements, and if they do, the usage can vary.

After the random number generator in Lisa's BASIC has been seeded, program control moves to the FOR . . . NEXT loop in ln 460 that causes the program to process 20 pairs of random numbers. (The NEXT statement to close this loop is found on ln 640.) The random numbers from 0 to 9 are generated in lines 480 and 490 and are assigned to the variable names A and B. The numbers generated are equally likely to occur, they typically fall in a range from 0.000000 . . . to 0.999999 . . . , and they are available for use in a BASIC program when the RND library function is called up by the programmer. In our example,

```
480   LET A=INT(RND*10)
```

the RND function produces numbers such as 0.1064710 and 0.6817323. Unfortunately, these numbers aren't in the 0 to 9 range needed by the program. To get around this problem, the program multiplies each random number generated by 10. Thus 0.1064710 becomes 1.064710. Finally, the INT (integer) function simply deletes everything following the decimal point. Thus 1.064710 simply becomes 1. (The value 0.6817323 called up by the RND function first becomes 6.817323 and then simply 6 in this program.)

Once random integers from 0 to 9 have been assigned to A and B in lines 480 and 490, the program performs the following steps:

1   The pair of random numbers is multiplied, and the result is assigned to C (ln 510).

2   The student is asked to multiply A times B, and the student's response is assigned to P (lines 530 and 540).

3   If the student's response is *correct*, a reinforcement message is printed, the "correct response" accumulator (Q1) is incremented, and the loop is repeated (lines 560, 620, 630, and 640).

4   If the student's response is *wrong*, the correct answer is given, the "incorrect response" accumulator (Q2) is incremented, and the loop is repeated (lines 560, 580, 590, 600, and 640).

When the loop has been executed 20 times, program control passes to ln 660, which computes the student's test score. If the test score is "passing"—*not* < 85 in ln 670—line numbers 690 through 720 are executed; if a "failing" grade is made, lines 740 through 770 are processed.

The INT and RND functions are often used in game programs to make the games less predictable and thus more interesting. You'll find an extrasensory perception game example discussed in question 26 at the end of this chapter.

ONE-DIMENSIONAL ARRAYS

An **array** is any collection of data items that are generally related in some way and are stored in a computer under a *common name*. If the array consists of a single *list* of items, it's called a **one-dimensional array.**

You may recall from Chapter 17 that the plants used in the Elm Creek beautification project and the prices of those plants are as follows (see Figure 17-10, page 596):

PLANT	UNIT PRICE
AZALEA	$5.75
BOXWOOD	3.95
DAFFODIL (DOZ)	5.25
HONEYSUCKLE	4.50
JUNIPER	3.85
PEONY	2.90

This list of plants is a one-dimensional array, and this array can be stored in a computer under a common variable name. The same rules that govern the naming of simple variables also apply in naming arrays. Since the plant list consists of character string values, an **array name** of P$ may be selected. Each item (or *element*) in this P$ array is then identified by a *subscript* as shown below:

P$ ARRAY	SUBSCRIPT
AZALEA	(1)
BOXWOOD	(2)
DAFFODIL (DOZ)	(3)
HONEYSUCKLE	(4)
JUNIPER	(5)
PEONY	(6)

Each subscript merely identifies one element or plant in the array. Thus, P$(1) identifies the first plant in the P$ array which in this case is AZALEA. The identification needed by the computer to locate the PEONY element in the P$ array is P$(6). This plant array is called *one-dimensional* because only a *single* subscript is needed to locate an element in the array.

Another one-dimensional array can be set up to store the unit-price list for the plants. This array may be named P, and the elements of this array may be identified as follows:

P ARRAY	
$5.75	P(1)
3.95	P(2)
5.25	P(3)
4.50	P(4)
3.85	P(5)
2.90	P(6)

It's best not to use the same name for both an array and a simple variable in a program even though BASIC will permit this confusing practice. Why?

Because P1 and P(1) in a BASIC program look alike but they represent different variables. The P1 name is given to a simple variable found in a single storage location, while the P(1) variable refers to the first element in an array named P.

Entering Data into Arrays

FOR . . . NEXT loops may be used to enter data into arrays. *Character string elements* can be entered as shown below:

```
260   FOR H=1 TO 6
270      READ P$(H)
280   NEXT H
290   DATA "AZALEA","BOXWOOD","DAFFODIL (DOZ)"
300   DATA "HONEYSUCKLE","JUNIPER","PEONY"
```

In ln 260, the FOR statement sets up a loop and creates an automatic counter or index (H) to control the reading of six data items. In the first pass through the loop, the value of H is 1. When the READ statement in ln 270 is executed for the first time, the computer reads AZALEA from the DATA statement in ln 290 and stores it in P$(1), the first location in the array named P$. The NEXT statement on ln 280 is then encountered and the next loop begins. This time, the value of H is 2, and BOXWOOD is read into the P$(2) location in the array. And so it goes until all six data items have been entered into the array.

Numeric values are entered into an array in the same way. The following program segment shows how the unit-price list for the plants may be entered:

```
320   FOR I=1 TO 6
330      READ P(I)
340   NEXT I
350   DATA 5.75,3.95,5.25,4.50,3.85,2.90
```

In this case, the $5.75 price of an azalea plant will be identified by P(1), the first item stored in the array named P. The value of P(2) will be $3.95, and the other prices will be stored in sequence as P(3), P(4), P(5), and P(6).

Printing Arrayed Data

How can we get the computer to print the items that we've now entered into the arrays named P$ and P? It's very simple:

```
420   FOR N=1 TO 6
440      PRINT P$(N);TAB(25);P(N)
450   NEXT N
```

As the loop index (N) goes step by step from 1 to 6, the PRINT statement on ln 440 prints the elements stored in locations 1 to 6 in both the P$ and P arrays. The following output is produced when all the program segments listed above are executed:

```
AZALEA           5.75
BOXWOOD          3.95
```

DAFFODIL (DOZ)	5.25
HONEYSUCKLE	4.5
JUNIPER	3.85
PEONY	2.9

The DIM Statement

A computer must know how many elements there are in an array so that provision can be made to store and properly manipulate these elements. When the size of an array is *not* specified in a program, the BASIC interpreter or compiler usually will automatically provide storage space for 10 elements. This automatic feature of BASIC was used when the six elements in the P$ and P arrays mentioned above were entered into the computer. It would *not* be possible, however, to enter an array of 20 items without reserving space in advance for 20 elements.

Space is reserved for a specific number of elements in an array by the use of a **DIM** (for **DIM**ension) **statement.** It's good programming practice to use DIM statements in all programs regardless of the size of the arrays so that adequate storage space is available. And since these DIM statements must precede any other program statements that deal with the arrays they describe, it's also good practice to place the DIM statements immediately after the introductory REM statements.

The general form of the DIM statement is:

> ln   DIM   array name1(limit 1),array name2(limit 2), . . .

Each limit is an integer (whole number) that specifies the *maximum* number of storage locations to be reserved for the preceding array name. (A subscript of zero is possible in some BASIC dialects, and this will add one additional element to the maximum number that can be stored.) Thus, in the following statement,

> 90   DIM   P$(20)

space is reserved for 20 elements in an array named P$. Fewer than 20 elements can be read into P$, but element P$(21) cannot be stored. A single DIM statement can also be used to specify the number of elements to be stored in multiple arrays. Thus,

> 200   DIM   P$(6),P(6),Q(6),A(6)

identifies P$, P, Q, and A as array names and specifies that six is the maximum number of elements that can be stored in each array.

Example Programs Using One-Dimensional Arrays

Figure 18-5 presents an example that incorporates the array concepts that we've now covered. The flowchart in Figure 18-5*a* will help you trace through the logic of this example, and the program listing for the example is shown in Figure 18-5*b*. This program produces Bill Byter's Elm Creek Planting Summary Report—a document that Bill uses to keep track of the planting activities along Elm Creek. Another program approach to produce this report was flowcharted in Figure 16-10, page 549, and a listing of this alternative program appears in Figure 17-10, page 596. (Since PRINT USING statements found in Figure 17-10 aren't used here, the output of Figure 18-5b differs somewhat from the program output shown in Figure 17-10.)

Following the preliminary REM statements, you'll notice in ln 200 that a DIM statement specifies the storage space needed for arrays P$, P, Q, and A.

FIGURE 18-5(a)

Flowchart for the Elm Creek Planting Summary program [Figure 18-5(b)].

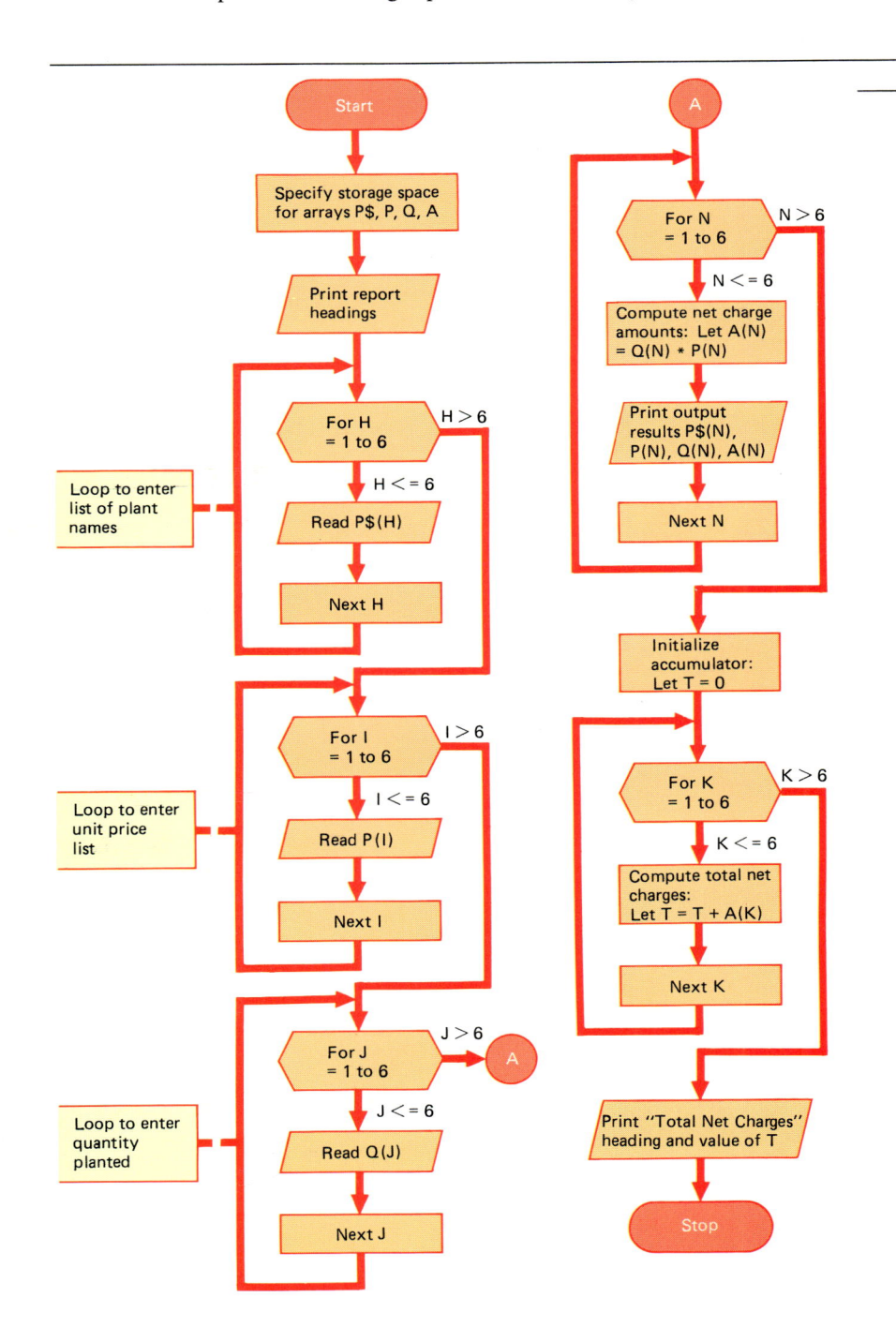

```
Start
  ↓
Specify storage space
for arrays P$, P, Q, A
  ↓
Print report
headings
  ↓
For H = 1 to 6  ──H>6──┐
  ↓ H<=6              │
Read P$(H)            │
  ↓                   │
Next H ───────────────┘
  ↓
For I = 1 to 6  ──I>6──┐
  ↓ I<=6              │
Read P(I)             │
  ↓                   │
Next I ───────────────┘
  ↓
For J = 1 to 6  ──J>6──→ A
  ↓ J<=6
Read Q(J)
  ↓
Next J
```

Loop to enter list of plant names

Loop to enter unit price list

Loop to enter quantity planted

```
A
↓
For N = 1 to 6  ──N>6──┐
  ↓ N<=6              │
Compute net charge    │
amounts: Let A(N)     │
= Q(N) * P(N)         │
  ↓                   │
Print output          │
results P$(N),        │
P(N), Q(N), A(N)      │
  ↓                   │
Next N ───────────────┘
  ↓
Initialize
accumulator:
Let T = 0
  ↓
For K = 1 to 6  ──K>6──┐
  ↓ K<=6              │
Compute total net     │
charges:              │
Let T = T + A(K)      │
  ↓                   │
Next K ───────────────┘
  ↓
Print "Total Net Charges"
heading and value of T
  ↓
Stop
```

```
100 REM *ELM CREEK PLANTING SUMMARY
110 REM *
120 REM *VARIABLE NAMES
130 REM * P$   PLANT NAME
140 REM * Q    QUANTITY PLANTED
150 REM * P    UNIT PRICE OF PLANT
160 REM * A    NET CHARGE TO PROPERTY OWNER
170 REM * T    TOTAL NET CHARGES
180 REM *
190 REM *SPECIFY STORAGE SPACE FOR ARRAYS
200        DIM P$(6),P(6),Q(6),A(6)
210 REM *PRINT HEADING
220        PRINT "                    ELM CREEK PLANTING SUMMARY"
230        PRINT
240        PRINT "PLANT                UNIT PRICE      QUANTITY     NET CHARGES"
250 REM *ENTER LIST OF PLANT NAMES
260        FOR H=1 TO 6
270          READ P$(H)
280        NEXT H
290        DATA "AZALEA","BOXWOOD","DAFFODIL (DOZ)"
300        DATA "HONEYSUCKLE","JUNIPER","PEONY"
310 REM *ENTER UNIT PRICE LIST FOR PLANTS
320        FOR I=1 TO 6
330          READ P(I)
340        NEXT I
350        DATA 5.75, 3.95, 5.25, 4.50, 3.85, 2.90
360 REM *ENTER QUANTITY PLANTED
370        FOR J=1 TO 6
380          READ Q(J)
390        NEXT J
400        DATA 515.0, 823.0, 212.5, 364.0, 388.0, 414.0
410 REM *COMPUTE NET CHARGE AMOUNTS AND PRINT OUTPUT RESULTS
420        FOR N=1 TO 6
430          LET A(N)=Q(N)*P(N)
440          PRINT P$(N);TAB(25);P(N);TAB(40);Q(N);TAB(50);"$";A(N)
450        NEXT N
460 REM *INITIALIZE ACCUMULATOR AND COMPUTE TOTAL NET CHARGES
470        LET T=0
480        FOR K=1 TO 6
490          LET T=T+A(K)
500        NEXT K
510 REM *PRINT TOTAL NET CHARGES AMOUNT AND STOP
520        PRINT
530        PRINT TAB(55);"TOTAL"
540        PRINT TAB(49);"NET CHARGES"
550        PRINT TAB(49);"$";T
560        END
```

Computer listing of the program

```
Ok
RUN
              ELM CREEK PLANTING SUMMARY

PLANT               UNIT PRICE      QUANTITY     NET CHARGES
AZALEA                 5.75           515         $ 2961.25
BOXWOOD                3.95           823         $ 3250.85
DAFFODIL (DOZ)         5.25           212.5       $ 1115.625
HONEYSUCKLE            4.5            364         $ 1638
JUNIPER                3.85           388         $ 1493.8
PEONY                  2.9            414         $ 1200.6

                                                   TOTAL
                                                 NET CHARGES
                                                 $ 11660.13

Ok
```

Output produced by the computer as the program is executed

← FIGURE 18-5(b)
Use of one-dimensional arrays to produce Bill Byter's Elm Creek Planting Summary Report.

Report headings are then printed (lines 220–240), and the plant names' list is read into the P$ array using lines 260–300. The unit-price list for these plants is stored in the array named P in lines 320–350. (Do you get the feeling that you've seen this program before?) And the quantities of each item planted during the period are stored in array Q in lines 370–400.

The net charges for each plant are computed in lines 420 and 430. In the first execution of the loop initiated in ln 420, the net charges for the first plant—AZALEA—are determined by multiplying Q(1) times P(1). Since Q(1) is 515 plants and P(1) is $5.75, the net charges amount assigned to A(1) is $2,961.25. The PRINT statement in ln 440 is then used to print the first element in arrays P$, P, Q, and A. In each of the remaining five passes through the loop in lines 420–450, another line will be printed on the output report.

Line 470 establishes an accumulator to total the net charge amounts stored in array A. Line 480 initiates another loop. In the first execution of this loop, the value of A(1), which is $2,961.25, is added to the initial value of T, which is zero, to produce a new total for T (ln 490). In each of the remaining five passes through this loop, the other elements in array A are added to the accumulator. The remaining program lines (520–550) then print a "TOTAL NET CHARGES" heading and the amount accumulated in T.

You'll find another example that uses one-dimensional arrays flowcharted in Figure 18-6a. The program listing for this example is shown in Figure 18-6b. Sam and Lisa wrote this "poetry" generating program to amuse the students at Lisa's school at the same time they were writing the multiplication drill and practice program. They named this program "Lord Byron" in honor of the poet father of Lady Augusta Ada Lovelace. (If you've read Chapter 12, you know that some people consider Ada to be the world's first programmer.)

The variable names assigned to the arrays are shown in the early REM statements, and the storage spaces for these arrays are assigned by the DIM statement in ln 210. Line 230 requests a random number seed (R), and the program user enters this value in line 240 to initialize the random number generator (ln 250). These steps are exactly like those used in Figure 18-4b. The number of "poems" to be produced is entered next (lines 260 and 270), and the arrays of title words (T$), nouns (N$), verbs (V$), and adjectives (A$) are loaded by the four FOR . . . NEXT loops in lines 290–400.

An outer (J) FOR . . . NEXT loop is established in ln 420 to produce the number of poems requested by the user. (This outer loop is closed by the NEXT statement in ln 580.) Each poem title is generated by lines 440 and 450. The statement in ln 440

```
440   LET J1=INT(RND*20)+1
```

produces random values ranging from 1 to 20. At one extreme, when the RND function generates a value of 0.000000 . . . , ln 440 will produce this

FIGURE 18-6(a)

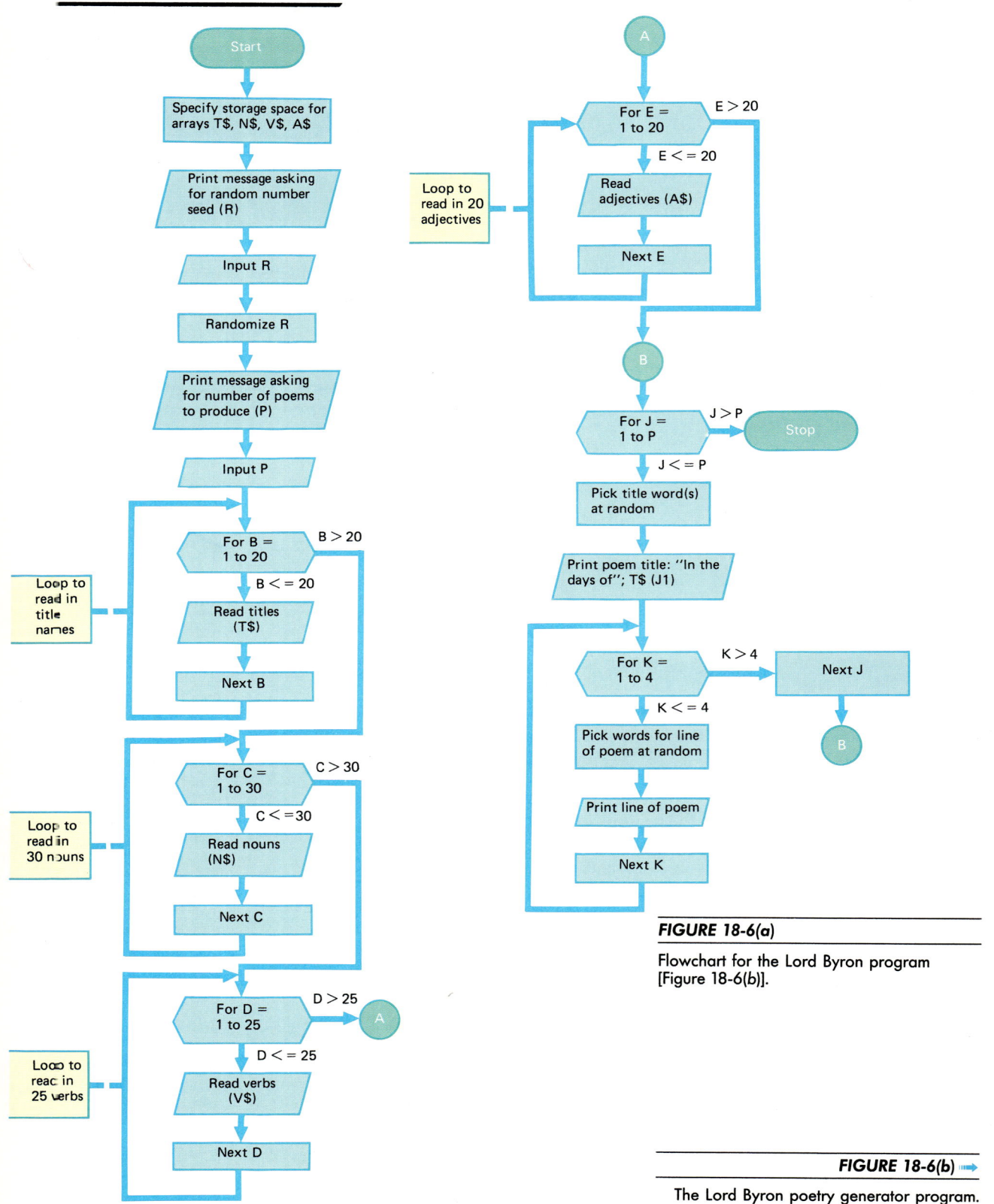

Flowchart for the Lord Byron program [Figure 18-6(b)].

FIGURE 18-6(b)

The Lord Byron poetry generator program.

```
100 REM *LORD BYRON
110 REM *
120 REM *VARIABLE NAMES
130 REM * T$   ARRAY OF TITLES
140 REM * N$   ARRAY OF NOUNS
150 REM * V$   ARRAY OF VERBS
160 REM * A$   ARRAY OF ADJECTIVES
170 REM * R    RANDOM NUMBER SEED
180 REM * P    NUMBER OF POEMS
190 REM *
200 REM *SPECIFY STORAGE SPACE FOR ARRAYS
210         DIM T$(20), N$(30), V$(25), A$(20)
220 REM *ENTER RANDOM NUMBER SEED AND NUMBER OF POEMS TO BE COMPOSED
230         PRINT "RANDOM NUMBER SEED (-32768 TO +32767)";
240         INPUT R
250         RANDOMIZE R
260         PRINT "NUMBER OF POEMS TO BE GENERATED";
270         INPUT P
280 REM *READ IN STRING DATA
290         FOR B=1 TO 20
300            READ T$(B)
310         NEXT B
320         FOR C=1 TO 30
330            READ N$(C)
340         NEXT C
350         FOR D=1 TO 25
360            READ V$(D)
370         NEXT D
380         FOR E=1 TO 20
390            READ A$(E)
400         NEXT E
410 REM *GENERATE SEVERAL POEMS
420         FOR J=1 TO P
430 REM *COMPOSE THE TITLE
440            LET J1=INT(RND*20)+1
450            PRINT TAB(10);"IN THE DAYS OF ";T$(J1)
460            PRINT
470 REM *WRITE A FOUR LINE MASTERPIECE
480            FOR K=1 TO 4
490               LET K1=INT(RND*20)+1
500               LET K2=INT(RND*30)+1
510               LET K3=INT(RND*25)+1
520               LET K4=INT(RND*20)+1
530               LET K5=INT(RND*30)+1
540               PRINT A$(K1);N$(K2);V$(K3);A$(K4);N$(K5)
550            NEXT K
560            PRINT
570            PRINT
580         NEXT J
590         STOP
600 REM *INPUT DATA
610         DATA "NIGHT","PLEASE","NO","MAUDE","STRIFE"
620         DATA "NEVER","BEAUTY","RAPTURE","WOOL","LOVE"
630         DATA "HELL","SNOW","YES","MUSIC","LIFE"
640         DATA "WATER","FAST-FOOD FRANCHISES","MILK","TIME","DREADFUL"
650 REM *
660         DATA "YEAR ","FIRE ","TREE ","TIME ","TOWN "
670         DATA "CHILDREN ","SUMMER ","BRIDE ","FLOWER ","HEART "
680         DATA "MIND ","BODY ","BED ","KEY ","DEW-DROPS "
690         DATA "BEAR ","SAND ","PATH ","PLACE ","HOUR "
700         DATA "SOLDIER ","COMRADES ","GRAVES ","DEVIL ","ANGELS "
710         DATA "VINE-CLAD HILLS ","BIG BAD WOLF ","BEASTS ","GODS ","RIVERS "
720 REM *
730         DATA "RUNS ","SWIMS ","DIES ","TALKS ","WORKS "
```

Computer listing of the program

```
740        DATA "PLAYS ","WALKS ","FEELS ","SEES ","NODS "
750        DATA "MOURNS ","ENTANGLES ","GASPS ","EBBS ","FLOWS "
760        DATA "FADES ","BURIES ","BEATS ","RETURNS ","BITES "
770        DATA "LIVES ","THREATENS ","YELLS ","SCREAMS ","WHINES "
780 REM *
790        DATA "THE STRONG ","PLAYFUL ","THE SPRY ","A LIVELY ","ONE LAZY "
800        DATA "A HAIRY ","THE FAT ","THE SAD ","A TINY ","YOUNG "
810        DATA "THE SACRED ","THE BOLD ","DELICATE ","CHEERFUL ","A GALLANT "
820        DATA "PRETTY ","GOOD ","THE GREAT ","LONELY ","MOURNFUL "
830        END
```

```
Ok
RUN
RANDOM NUMBER SEED (-32768 TO +32767)? 12
NUMBER OF POEMS TO BE GENERATED? 2
          IN THE DAYS OF MUSIC

A TINY TOWN PLAYS A TINY PATH
MOURNFUL GODS ENTANGLES CHEERFUL GODS
THE FAT HOUR FEELS THE SAD HEART
GOOD RIVERS GASPS PLAYFUL ANGELS


          IN THE DAYS OF BEAUTY

A GALLANT HOUR NODS THE GREAT MIND
PLAYFUL MIND WORKS CHEERFUL BED
THE BOLD VINE-CLAD HILLS WHINES PRETTY DEVIL
THE SAD PATH TALKS THE GREAT BODY


Break in 590
Ok
```

Output produced by the computer as the program is executed

result: J1 = INT(.000000∗20)+1 = 0+1 = 1. And at the other extreme, J1 = INT(.999999∗20)+1 = 19+1 = 20. After ln 440 has assigned a random value from 1 to 20 to J1, this random number is used in ln 450 to select 1 of the 20 terms contained in the T$—or title—array. Thus if J1 has a value of 1, then the title will be "IN THE DAYS OF" NIGHT, since NIGHT is the T$(1) element in the title array. (NIGHT was the first element on ln 610 that was read into the T$ array (ln 300), when the array elements were stored.)

After the title has been printed, an inner (K) FOR . . . NEXT loop is established on lines 480–550. The purpose of this K loop is to randomly assemble the terms used to produce each of the four lines found in a poem. Each pass through the loop produces one line of the poem. If there are three poems to be generated, this loop will be executed (3 × 4 or) 12 times. The values of K1 through K5 are randomly generated in each pass through the loop (lines 490–530), and these values become the array subscripts that select and print words from the arrays of nouns, verbs, and adjectives (ln 540). After the creation of a four-line masterpiece, program control loops back to ln 420 and an automatic test is made to see if the specified number of poems has been written. If J is <=P, the program generates another poem; if J > P, then the program stops (ln 590).

Two poems produced by this program are shown following the program listing in Figure 18-6b. The "Break in 590" comment at the end of the program output in Figure 18-6b is produced by Sam and Lisa's BASIC interpreter when it encounters the STOP statement in ln 590. You might want to modify this program (use more arrays with larger and better vocabularies) to create a superior poetry generator—a "William Shakespeare" perhaps?

FEEDBACK

FEEDBACK AND REVIEW 18-1

A portion of a program that produces a weekly welfare applications report for Marie Byter, along with the output produced by this program, is shown below. As you can see, this report shows the number of welfare applications that have been processed by the workers in Marie's department in a recent week. Explain the purpose of lines 180–240 in this program.

```
100 REM *WEEKLY WELFARE APPLICATIONS REPORT
110 REM *
120 REM *VARIABLE NAMES
130 REM * N$   ARRAY OF CASEWORKER NAMES
140 REM * W    ARRAY OF WEEKLY APPLICATIONS PROCESSED
150 REM * N    NUMBER OF CASEWORKERS
160 REM *
170 REM *SPECIFY STORAGE SPACE FOR ARRAYS
180        DIM N$(8),W(8)
190 REM *READ IN NUMBER OF CASEWORKERS
200        READ N
210 REM *READ CASEWORKER NAME AND WEEKLY APPLICATIONS PROCESSED
220        FOR I=1 TO N
230           READ N$(I),W(I)
240        NEXT I
```
Program segment

```
RUN
                        WEEKLY APPLICATIONS
CASEWORKER NAME            PROCESSED

V. BARON                       10
G. CONRAD                      15
R. DAVIS                       21
F. GARCIA                       8
J. HUANG                       25
D. MOLINA                      21
P. QUINCY                      11
S. YAMAMOTO                    16
Ok
```
Program output

TWO-DIMENSIONAL ARRAYS

We've been discussing arrays consisting of lists of items. But an array can also be a *table,* or *matrix.* Let's suppose, for example, that the director of the research bureau in the School of Education at Jill's college wants to analyze the personal computer (pc) purchases made by different schools in different regions of the state. Let's also assume that the following table presents the available purchase data for a particular period:

PURCHASES OF PERSONAL COMPUTERS

SCHOOL REGION	COMMUNITY COLLEGES	VO-TECH SCHOOLS	HIGH SCHOOLS
EASTERN	195	40	85
CENTRAL	185	25	60
WESTERN	155	65	45

As you can see, this table consists of data organized into rows and columns. Each row gives the purchase data for a region of the state, and each column shows the purchases made by a particular type of school. Thus, you can see that 65 pc's were bought by vo-tech schools in the western region (third row, second column).

You'll notice that there are nine elements in the table (3 rows × 3 columns). A particular element in a table is identified by a *pair* of subscripts. Thus, the 65 pc's bought by vo-tech schools in the western region are indicated by the subscript (3,2), where the *first number indicates the row* and the *second the column.* This table is called a **two-dimensional array** because two numbers (row, column) are needed to locate the element.

A two-dimensional array is named just like other BASIC variables, but the same name can't be used in the same program to identify both one- and two-dimensional arrays. If the array name S in our example stores the table data in the computer, then the pc systems bought by the different schools can be identified by the subscripts shown below:

S ARRAY

S(1,1)	195	S(1,2)	40	S(1,3)	85
S(2,1)	185	S(2,2)	25	S(2,3)	60
S(3,1)	155	S(3,2)	65	S(3,3)	45

We can also store the names of the school regions or districts, and the types of schools, in the following one-dimensional arrays:

D$ ARRAY		S$ ARRAY	
EASTERN	D$(1)	COMMUNITY COLLEGES	S$(1)
CENTRAL	D$(2)	VO-TECH SCHOOLS	S$(2)
WESTERN	D$(3)	HIGH SCHOOLS	S$(3)

The BASIC interpreter usually also contains instructions that automatically provide storage space for a two-dimensional array with up to 10 rows and 10 columns. But as noted earlier, it's good practice to use DIM statements in all programs regardless of the size of the arrays. The following statement

100 DIM B(15,8)

will reserve storage space for a two-dimensional array named B that has 15 rows and 8 columns. And this statement

230   DIM D$(3),S$(3),S(3,3)

will provide space for the one- and two-dimensional arrays discussed above.

Example Program Using Two-Dimensional Array

Let's assume that the research-bureau director hires Jill and Sam to write a program that computes pc purchases by region and by type of school. These results are printed in a report, and the total pc purchases for the period also are accumulated and printed. Figure 18-7a is a flowchart that shows the logic of this program, and the program listing to produce this report is shown in Figure 18-7b.

Following the initial REM, the DIM statement in ln 230 specifies the storage space needed for the arrays. Then the D$ (school regions) and S$ (types of schools) arrays are entered into storage (lines 250–330). Lines 360 through 410 employ a nested FOR . . . NEXT loop structure to enter the purchase data from the table into the two-dimensional array named S. The outer (or R) loop initiated in ln 360 controls the table rows, and the inner (or C) loop set up in ln 370 controls the table columns. In the first pass through the outer loop, R has a value of one, and the inner loop is executed three times. In these three executions of the C loop, the values of 195, 40, and 85 are read from the DATA statement in ln 410 and are assigned to storage as array elements S(1,1), S(1,2), and S(1,3) by the READ statement in ln 380. The six remaining elements in the S array are stored in the second and third executions of the R loop.

After the first set of report headings is printed in lines 430–450, another nested FOR . . . NEXT loop structure accumulates and prints the purchases of each region. Lines 470 and 480 set up the outer (I) loop and initialize the "row total" accumulator (T1). The first execution of the inner (C) loop in lines 490–510 adds the purchase data in the three columns of row 1 of the table to the accumulator. [These are elements S(1,1), S(1,2), and S(1,3) in the S array.] The PRINT statement in ln 520 then prints (1) the name of the first school region stored in the D$ array (EASTERN) and (2) the total purchases (T1) for that region. In the second iteration through the outer loop, the accumulator is reset to zero and the procedure is repeated for the next school region.

After region purchases have been computed and printed, another heading is printed on the output report (lines 550–570). Program control then moves to the nested FOR . . . NEXT structure in lines 590–650. The purpose of this structure is to accumulate and print the pc purchases of each type of school. Lines 590 and 600 set up the outer loop (J) and initialize the "column total" accumulator (T2). The first execution of the inner (R) loop in lines 610–630 adds the purchase data in the three rows of column 1 of the table to the accumulator. [These are elements S(1,1), S(2,1), and S(3,1) in the S array.] The PRINT statement in ln 640 then prints (1) the name of the first type of school stored in the S$ array (COMMUNITY COLLEGES) and (2) the total purchases (T2) for that type of school. This procedure is repeated for the other types of schools in the next two executions of the outer loop.

MODULE 5

638

Finally, the total purchases of pc's for the period is produced in lines 670–720. A "total purchases" accumulator (T3) is initialized in ln 670, and an outer loop (R) is set up by the FOR statement in ln 680. The elements S(1,1), S(1,2), and S(1,3) are added to the accumulator in the first execution of the inner (C) loop in lines 690–710. The second and third passes through the outer loop add the remainder of the elements in the S array to the value of T3. The PRINT statement in ln 750 then prints on the output report a summary line and the total purchases amount accumulated in T3.

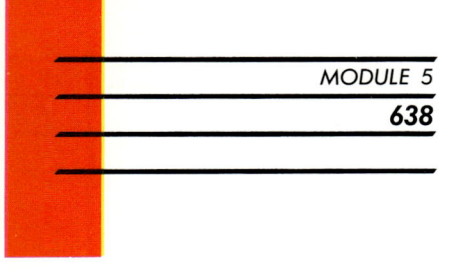

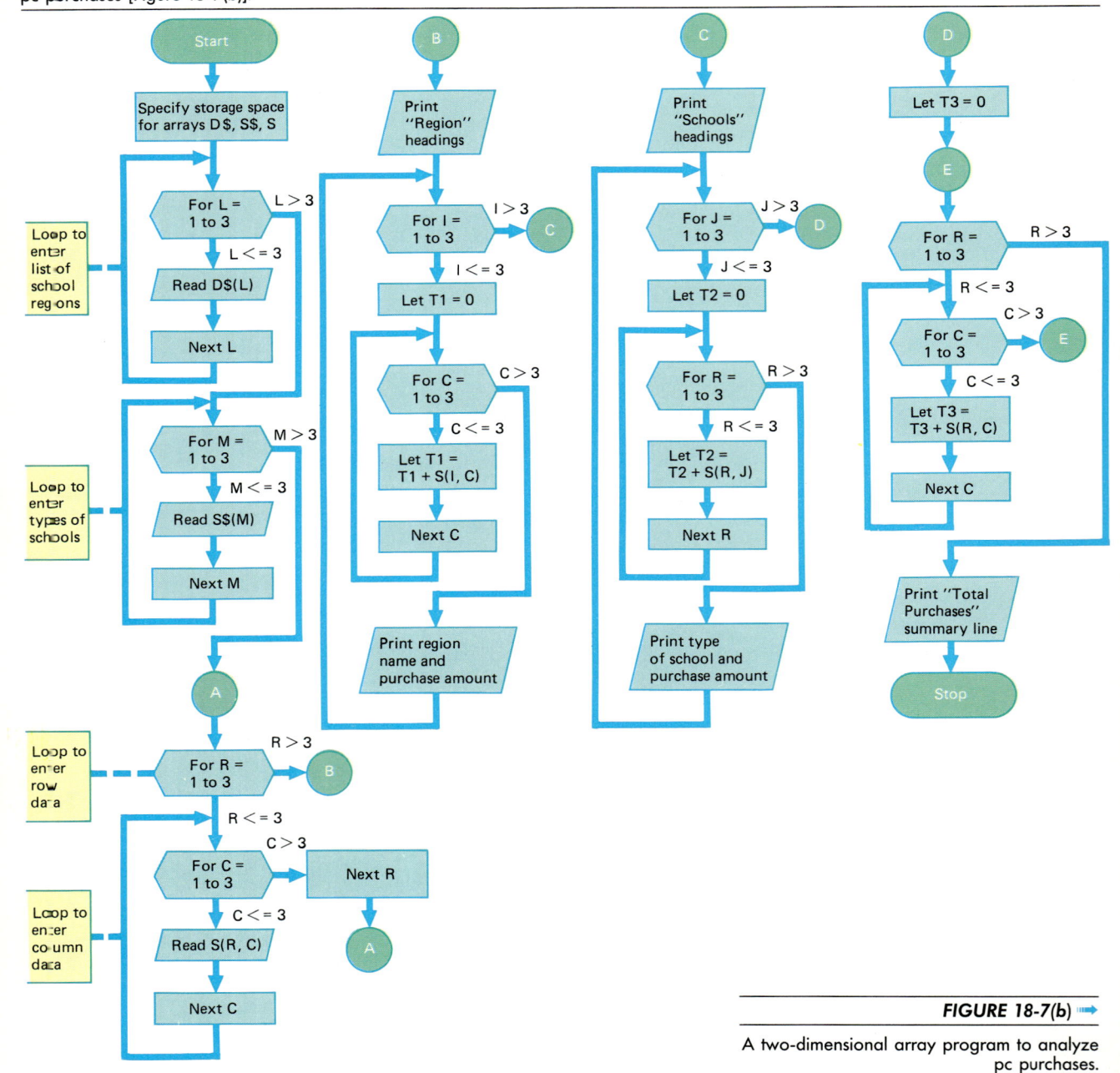

FIGURE 18-7(a)

Flowchart for the program to analyze school pc purchases [Figure 18-7(b)].

FIGURE 18-7(b)

A two-dimensional array program to analyze pc purchases.

```
100 REM *ANALYSIS OF PERSONAL COMPUTER PURCHASES
110 REM *
120 REM *VARIABLE NAMES
130 REM * D$   SCHOOL REGIONS
140 REM * S$   TYPES OF SCHOOLS
150 REM * S    PURCHASE DATA FOR PC SYSTEMS
160 REM * R    SUBSCRIPT TO CONTROL TABLE ROWS
170 REM * C    SUBSCRIPT TO CONTROL TABLE COLUMNS
180 REM * T1   ROW TOTALS
190 REM * T2   COLUMN TOTALS
200 REM * T3   TOTAL PURCHASES FOR THE PERIOD
210 REM *
220 REM *SPECIFY STORAGE SPACE FOR ARRAYS
230        DIM D$(3), S$(3), S(3,3)
240 REM *ENTER LIST OF SCHOOL REGIONS
250        FOR L=1 TO 3
260           READ D$(L)
270        NEXT L
280        DATA "EASTERN REGION","CENTRAL REGION","WESTERN REGION"
290 REM *ENTER TYPES OF SCHOOLS
300        FOR M=1 TO 3
310           READ S$(M)
320        NEXT M
330        DATA "COMMUNITY COLLEGES","VO-TECH SCHOOLS","HIGH SCHOOLS"
340 REM *ENTER PURCHASE DATA FROM TABLE.  THE R LOOP CONTROLS THE TABLE
350 REM *ROWS AND THE C LOOP CONTROLS THE TABLE COLUMNS.
360        FOR R=1 TO 3
370           FOR C=1 TO 3
380              READ S(R,C)
390           NEXT C
400        NEXT R
410        DATA 195, 40, 85, 185, 25, 60, 155, 65, 45
420 REM *PRINT HEADINGS
430        PRINT TAB(22);"SCHOOL RESEARCH BUREAU"
440        PRINT TAB(12);"PURCHASE OF PERSONAL COMPUTERS BY REGION"
450        PRINT TAB(12);"-------- -- -------- --------- -- -------"
460 REM *INITIALIZE ACCUMULATOR AND COMPUTE REGION PURCHASES
470        FOR I=1 TO 3
480           LET T1=0
490              FOR C=1 TO 3
500                 LET T1=T1+S(I,C)
510              NEXT C
520           PRINT D$(I);" PURCHASES";TAB(30);" = ";T1
530        NEXT I
540 REM *PRINT HEADING
550        PRINT
560        PRINT TAB(12);"PURCHASE OF PERSONAL COMPUTERS BY SCHOOLS"
570        PRINT TAB(12);"-------- -- -------- --------- -- -------"
580 REM *INITIALIZE ACCUMULATOR AND COMPUTE SCHOOL PURCHASES
590        FOR J=1 TO 3
600           LET T2=0
610              FOR R=1 TO 3
620                 LET T2=T2+S(R,J)
630              NEXT R
640           PRINT S$(J);" PURCHASES";TAB(30);" = ";T2
650        NEXT J
660 REM *COMPUTE TOTAL PURCHASES OF PERSONAL COMPUTERS FOR PERIOD
670        LET T3=0
680        FOR R=1 TO 3
690           FOR C=1 TO 3
700              LET T3=T3+S(R,C)
710           NEXT C
720        NEXT R
```

Computer listing of the program

```
730 REM *PRINT SUMMARY LINE AND STOP
740         PRINT
750         PRINT TAB(10);"**TOTAL PURCHASES FOR PERIOD = ";T3
760         END
```

```
Ok
RUN
                    SCHOOL RESEARCH BUREAU
            PURCHASE OF PERSONAL COMPUTERS BY REGION
            -------- -- -------- --------- -- ------
EASTERN REGION PURCHASES       =   320
CENTRAL REGION PURCHASES       =   270
WESTERN REGION PURCHASES       =   265

            PURCHASE OF PERSONAL COMPUTERS BY SCHOOLS
            -------- -- -------- --------- -- -------
COMMUNITY COLLEGES PURCHASES   =   535
VO-TECH SCHOOLS PURCHASES      =   130
HIGH SCHOOLS PURCHASES         =   190

         **TOTAL PURCHASES FOR PERIOD =   855
Ok
```

Output produced by the computer as the program is executed

FEEDBACK AND REVIEW 18-2

A portion of a program that generates a monthly welfare applications report for Marie Byter, and the output produced by this program in a recent period, is shown at the top of the facing page. Explain the purpose of lines 190–250 in this program.

```
100 REM *MONTHLY WELFARE APPLICATIONS REPORT
110 REM *
120 REM *VARIABLE NAMES
130 REM * N$   ARRAY OF CASEWORKER NAMES
140 REM * W    ARRAY OF WEEKLY APPLICATIONS PROCESSED
150 REM * M    ARRAY OF MONTHLY APPLICATIONS PROCESSED
160 REM * N    NUMBER OF CASEWORKERS
170 REM *
180 REM *SPECIFY STORAGE SPACE FOR ARRAYS
190       DIM N$(8),W(8,4),M(8)
200 REM *READ IN NUMBER OF CASEWORKERS
210       READ N
220 REM *READ CASEWORKER NAME AND WEEKLY APPLICATIONS PROCESSED
230       FOR I=1 TO N
240         READ N$(I),W(I,1),W(I,2),W(I,3),W(I,4)
250       NEXT I
```

Program segment

```
RUN
NAME              W1      W2      W3      W4      TOTAL

V. BARON          10      16      12      19       57
G. CONRAD         15      18      16      21       70
R. DAVIS          21      25      19      22       87
F. GARCIA          8      10      12       9       39
J. HUANG          25      12      13      14       64
D. MOLINA         21      24      22      29       96
P. QUINCY         11       9      13      16       49
S. YAMAMOTO       16      22      19      25       82
Ok
```

Program output

LET'S SORT THIS OUT

You learned way back in Chapter 1 that people often prefer to work with data that have been arranged in some logical sequence. The sequence may be from first to last, from largest to smallest, from oldest to newest. Arranging data in such a predetermined order is called **sorting.** Names are often put in alphabetical order, and numeric data are often sorted into an ascending or descending sequence. In fact, you've seen in Chapter 2 that the records in sequential files are stored in an ascending or descending order determined by a record key before sequential processing is carried out. When there are only a few data items to deal with, people can quickly examine these items and then mentally place them in a desired order. But what if there are hundreds, thousands, or even millions of items to consider? Fortunately for people, the computer easily handles these large sorting tasks.

Example Before we examine one way that a computer can be used to sort data items, let's first look at the example program in Figure 18-8. This program—used to produce Marie Byter's Weekly Welfare Applications Report—shows the number of welfare applications that have been processed each week

```
100 REM *WEEKLY WELFARE APPLICATIONS REPORT
110 REM *
120 REM *VARIABLE NAMES
130 REM * N$   ARRAY OF CASEWORKER NAMES
140 REM * W    ARRAY OF WEEKLY APPLICATIONS PROCESSED
150 REM * N    NUMBER OF CASEWORKERS
160 REM *
170 REM *SPECIFY STORAGE SPACE FOR ARRAYS
180       DIM N$(8),W(8)
190 REM *READ IN NUMBER OF CASEWORKERS
200       READ N
210 REM *READ CASEWORKER NAME AND WEEKLY APPLICATIONS PROCESSED
220       FOR I=1 TO N
230         READ N$(I),W(I)
240       NEXT I
250 REM *PRINT REPORT HEADING
260       PRINT TAB(25);"WEEKLY APPLICATIONS"
270       PRINT "CASEWORKER NAME";TAB(30);"PROCESSED"
280       PRINT "_____";TAB(25);"_____"
290 REM *PRINT OUT REPORT
300       FOR I=1 TO N
310         PRINT N$(I);TAB(30);W(I)
320       NEXT I
330 REM *INPUT DATA
340       DATA 8
350       DATA "V. BARON    ", 10
360       DATA "G. CONRAD   ", 15
370       DATA "R. DAVIS    ", 21
380       DATA "F. GARCIA   ",  8
390       DATA "J. HUANG    ", 25
400       DATA "D. MOLINA   ", 21
410       DATA "P. QUINCY   ", 11
420       DATA "S. YAMAMOTO ", 16
430       END
```

Computer listing of the program

```
OK
RUN
                          WEEKLY APPLICATIONS
CASEWORKER NAME           PROCESSED
_____           _____
V. BARON                  10
G. CONRAD                 15
R. DAVIS                  21
F. GARCIA                  8
J. HUANG                  25
D. MOLINA                 21
P. QUINCY                 11
S. YAMAMOTO               16
OK
```

Output produced by the computer as the program is executed

FIGURE 18-8

A program to produce Marie Byter's Weekly Applications Report.

by the caseworkers in Marie's department. There's nothing new in this program. (In fact, you may recognize part of it from Feedback and Review 18-1.) The FOR . . . NEXT loop in lines 220–240 loads two arrays with worker names and applications processing totals for a recent period. You should now be able to trace through the rest of this program to see how the program output is produced.

Bubble Sorts

Notice that the output produced in Figure 18-8 is in alphabetical order because that's the way the input data file is organized. However, Marie believes that the report would be more useful if the program sorted and then printed the weekly processing or production totals in a *descending order*. That way, it would be easier to identify the top producers.

Although there are several approaches that we could use to accomplish this sorting assignment, we'll only consider one here. A **bubble sort** compares two adjacent elements in an array and then immediately interchanges them if they aren't in the desired ascending or descending sequence. The program example presented in Figure 18-9 uses the same data found in Figure 18-8, but this new version uses a bubble sort to arrange the weekly processing totals in a descending order. The flowchart presented in Figure 18-9*a* will help you trace through the logic of this program, and the program listing is shown in Figure 18-9*b*.

Although three new variable names have been defined in the early REM statements in Figure 18-9*b*, there are no other differences between this program and the one you've just studied in Figure 18-8 until you get to the REM statement in ln 280 that announces the beginning of the sorting procedure. In ln 310, a variable named F$ is set up as a "flag," or value, that's used to detect when certain processing steps are completed. As you'll see, this variable—initially set to "DONE"—is used later to determine if the entire sorting process has been completed.

The *first sorting pass* through the array of weekly processing totals (W) is established with the FOR statement in ln 330. You'll notice that this FOR . . . NEXT loop (lines 330–470) will be executed N−1 times during this first sorting pass. Since N is 8 in our example, the FOR . . . NEXT loop will be executed seven times to complete one sorting pass. In the first execution of this loop I = 1, and in ln 340 the first item in the W array of caseworker production figures is compared to the second item in that array. Since the value of W(1) is 10 and since the value of W(1+1) is 15, the IF . . . THEN statement in ln 340 causes program control to branch to ln 380. The F$ flag is set to "NOT DONE" in ln 380 to indicate that the sorting hasn't been completed, and lines 390–410 are used to interchange the weekly production values of W(1) and W(1+1). This exchange is accomplished by first creating a working storage space (S) so that the switch can be made. In ln 390, the value of W(1), or 10 at this time, is stored in the location named S. In ln 400, the value of W(1+1), or 15 at this time, is transferred to W(1), thereby erasing the value of 10 previously stored there. And the switch is completed in ln 410 when the previous value of W(1) that's stored in S is assigned to W(1+1), thereby erasing the value of 15. Thus W(1) now has a value of 15 and W(1+1) contains a value of 10. The same procedure is then followed in the next three program lines (lines 430–450) to interchange the caseworker names so that they correctly match the data in array W. Note that an S$ working storage space has been created in ln 430 to permit this switch.

Having now switched the first two values in the W and N$ arrays, the computer encounters the NEXT statement in ln 470, and program control is transferred back to ln 330 for a second iteration through the FOR . . . NEXT loop. Note that we *haven't* completed the *first sorting pass* through the data. All we've done is complete the *first iteration* through the loop in lines 330–470. In the *second iteration*, the value of W(2) is compared to W(2+1) in ln

FIGURE 18-9(a)

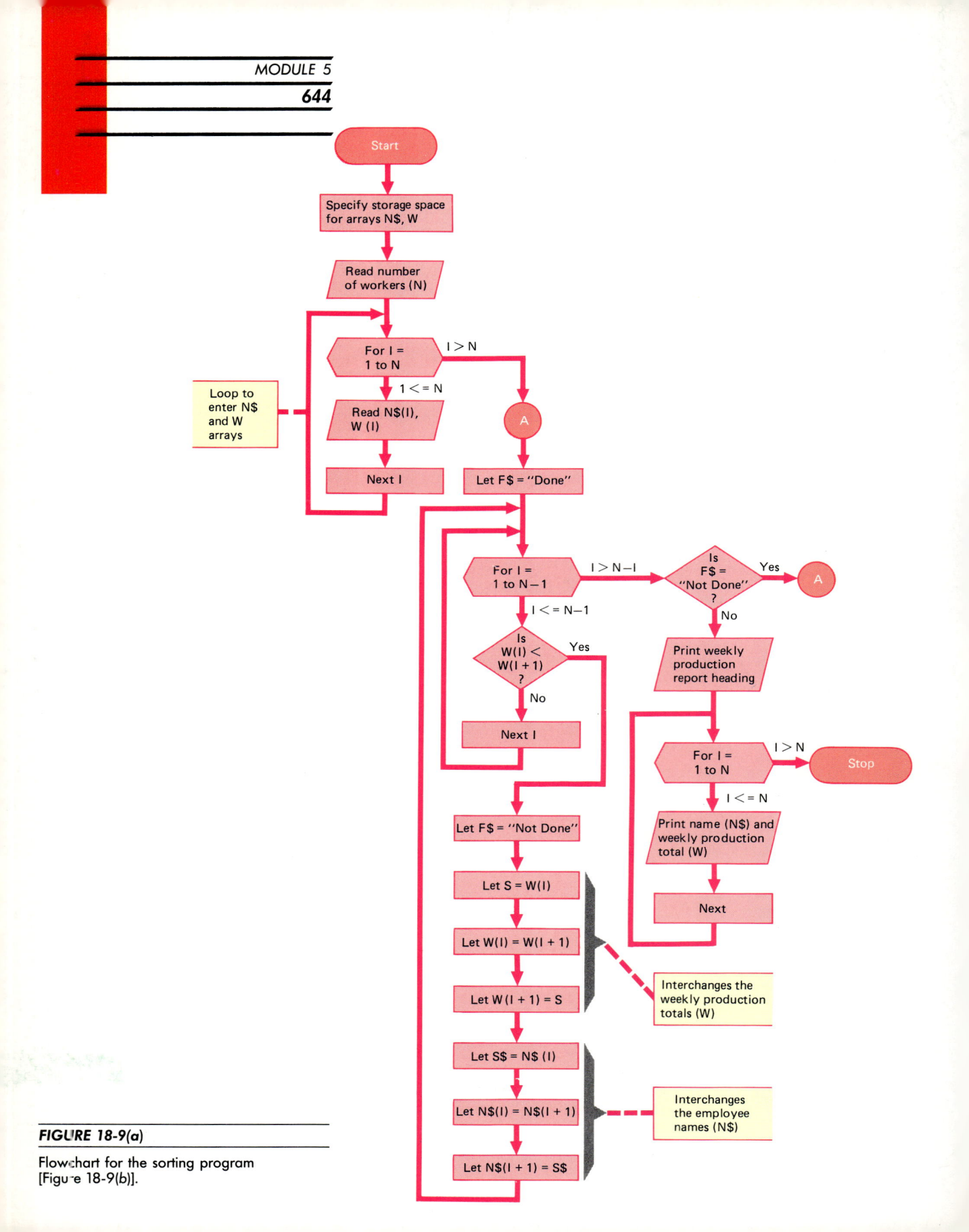

Flowchart for the sorting program [Figure 18-9(b)].

```
100 REM *WEEKLY WELFARE APPLICATIONS REPORT
110 REM *
120 REM *VARIABLE NAMES
130 REM * N$    ARRAY OF CASEWORKER NAMES
140 REM * W     ARRAY OF WEEKLY APPLICATIONS PROCESSED
150 REM * N     NUMBER OF CASEWORKERS
160 REM * F$    FLAG INDICATING COMPLETION OF SORTING
170 REM * S     WORKING STORAGE SPACE--CASEWORKER PROCESSING TOTAL
180 REM * S$    WORKING STORAGE SPACE--CASEWORKER NAME
190 REM *
200 REM *SPECIFY STORAGE SPACE FOR ARRAYS
210       DIM N$(8),W(8)
220 REM *READ IN NUMBER OF CASEWORKERS
230       READ N
240 REM *READ CASEWORKER NAME AND WEEKLY APPLICATIONS PROCESSED
250       FOR I=1 TO N
260          READ N$(I),W(I)
270       NEXT I
280 REM *SORT CASEWORKERS ON BASIS OF PRODUCTIVITY
290 REM *
300 REM *SET FLAG TO "DONE" INITIALLY
310       LET F$="DONE"
320 REM *EXAMINE DATA TO SEE IF THEY ARE IN ORDER
330       FOR I=1 TO N-1
340          IF W(I)<W(I+1) THEN 380
350          GOTO 470
360 REM *IF DATA ARE NOT IN ORDER THEN SET FLAG
370 REM *TO "NOT DONE" AND INTERCHANGE ORDER
380          LET F$="NOT DONE"
390          LET S=W(I)
400          LET W(I)=W(I+1)
410          LET W(I+1)=S
420 REM *
430          LET S$=N$(I)
440          LET N$(I)=N$(I+1)
450          LET N$(I+1)=S$
460 REM *
470       NEXT I
480 REM *IF FLAG INDICATES "NOT DONE" THEN REPEAT
490       IF F$="NOT DONE" THEN 310
500 REM *PRINT REPORT HEADING
510       PRINT TAB(25);"WEEKLY APPLICATIONS"
520       PRINT "CASEWORKER NAME";TAB(30);"PROCESSED"
530       PRINT "_____";TAB(25);"_____"
540 REM *PRINT OUT REPORT
550       FOR I=1 TO N
560          PRINT N$(I);TAB(30);W(I)
570       NEXT I
580 REM *INPUT DATA
590       DATA 8
600       DATA "V. BARON      ", 10
610       DATA "G. CONRAD     ", 15
620       DATA "R. DAVIS      ", 21
630       DATA "F. GARCIA     ",  8
640       DATA "J. HUANG      ", 25
650       DATA "D. MOLINA     ", 21
660       DATA "P. QUINCY     ", 11
670       DATA "S. YAMAMOTO   ", 16
680       END
```

Computer listing of the program

FIGURE 18-9(b)

A program that sorts the weekly production of welfare applications in a descending order.

```
Ok
RUN

CASEWORKER NAME          WEEKLY APPLICATIONS
                             PROCESSED

J. HUANG                         25
R. DAVIS                         21
D. MOLINA                        21
S. YAMAMOTO                      16
G. CONRAD                        15
P. QUINCY                        11
V. BARON                         10
F. GARCIA                         8
Ok
```

Output produced by the computer as the program is executed

340. Since W(2) was changed to a value of 10 in the first iteration, 10 is now compared to W(2+1) which now has a value of 21. Since 10 < 21 in ln 340, program control branches to ln 380 and the values of W(2) and W(2+1) are switched in lines 390–410. The employee names in N$(2) and N$(2+1) are also switched in lines 430–450.

Figure 18-10 shows the results of the comparisons made by the FOR . . . NEXT loop in lines 330–470 during the *first sorting pass* through the arrays. As you can see, N−1, or 7, comparisons were made as specified by the FOR statement in ln 330. (If the FOR statement had read FOR I=1 TO N, the computer would have tried to compare item 8 to item 9 in ln 340, and the W array doesn't have an item 9!) When the first sorting pass through the W array is completed, the order of the W array will be as shown in column 4 of Figure

FIGURE 18-10

Values of the W array before sorting and after each pass through the sorting loop.

(1) Original values of W array	(2) Iteration of FOR . . . NEXT loop	(3) Data items being compared	(4) Values of the W array resulting from the first sorting pass	(5)	(6)	(7)
				\multicolumn{3}{c}{Values of the W array resulting from these subsequent sorting passes:}
				2	3	4
10	1	10 / 15	15	21	21	25
15	2	10 / 21	21	15	25	21
21	3	10 / 8	10	25	21	21
8	4	8 / 25	25	21	15	16
25	5	8 / 21	21	11	16	15
21	6	8 / 11	11	16	11	11
11	7	8 / 16	16	10	10	10
16			8	8	8	8

18-10. Program control then branches to ln 490, and a test is made of the contents of the F$ storage location. If F$ = "NOT DONE", then program control branches back to ln 310, F$ is set to "DONE", and another sorting pass is processed. Since F$ was changed to "NOT DONE" by the sorting carried out in the first pass discussed above, there will be a second pass. The values of the W array at the end of this *second sorting pass* are shown in column 5 of Figure 18-10. Since additional sorting took place in this second pass, the F$ flag is once again set to "NOT DONE", a *third* pass is carried out, and the results are shown in column 6 of Figure 18-10.

At the end of each sorting pass, the largest value of 25 in the W array has "bubbled up" by one position (see columns 4–7 of Figure 18-10). Thus, after the *fourth pass,* the value of 25 is at the top of the array and all the other values are in a descending order. (If 25 had been the last value in the original W array, N−1, or 7, sorting passes would have been required to put the array in a descending order.) At the end of the fourth pass, the F$ flag is set to "NOT DONE" so a fifth pass is made. In this pass, the computer goes through the entire array and makes no switches. Thus, the value of F$ remains set to "DONE" at the end of the pass. Program control then moves to ln 510, and the report headings are printed. The contents of the sorted N$ and W arrays are then printed by the FOR . . . NEXT loop in lines 550–570, and the processing stops.

FEEDBACK

FEEDBACK AND REVIEW 18-3

We've seen that Marie prefers to have the weekly caseworker production report sorted in a descending order so that it will be easier to spot the top producers. But what if she wants a report in an ascending sequence (the smallest weekly production total is printed first and the largest total is printed last) so that those who may have lighter workloads are prominently displayed at the top of the report?

1. How would you modify the program in Figure 18-9*b* so that the output is sorted in an ascending order?
2. Using the same input data shown in Figure 18-9*b*, how many sorting passes would be needed to place the largest value of 25 at the bottom of the W array?

ADDITIONAL BASIC STATEMENTS

There are many statements included in the BASIC language that we haven't discussed so far in this book. A few of these additional statements are summarized here.

Statements to Facilitate Structured Programming

Many professional programmers are now using the *structured programming* techniques discussed in Chapter 16 to handle and tame needless program complexity and confusion. Two important concepts that fall under the structured programming banner are (1) the use of a modular, or top-down, approach to identify main program functions and then to break these functions down into lower-level modules for analysis and program preparation and (2) the use of the three basic logic structures (simple sequence, selection, and loop) discussed in Chapter 16. **GOSUB** and **RETURN statements** in BASIC smooth the way for the use of a top-down approach. And the **WHILE/WEND** and **IF-THEN-ELSE statements** available in newer BASIC dialects facilitate the use of basic loop and selection structures.

Let's look at the example in Figure 18-11 that demonstrates all these BASIC statements. This example is another program used to prepare Bill Byter's Plant Control Report for the Elm Creek beautification project. The logic used to prepare this report was flowcharted in Figure 16-8, page 546, and you've seen an earlier program to prepare Bill's report in Figure 17-8, page 593. The program version in Figure 18-11 uses the same input data and produces the same output results as Figure 17-8, but it also introduces BASIC statements that facilitate the use of structured programming concepts.

GOSUB and RETURN Statements   You'll notice in Figure 18-11 that there's a *main program module* (located in lines 210–290) at the top of the listing and several *subordinate modules,* or *subroutines,* located below this main routine. You'll also notice in the main program module that a REM statement introduced by a colon (:) can be placed on the same line as another statement in the BASIC dialect used here. The first line (ln 210) in the main program module uses a GOSUB statement. This statement

   210   GOSUB 320

transfers program control from the main program sequence to a subroutine beginning at ln 320. After the steps in lines 320–350 of the "print heading" subroutine have been executed, the program reaches the RETURN statement in ln 360. As you might expect, this statement sends program control back to the main program location that *follows* the initial GOSUB statement. Thus program control branches from ln 360 to ln 220. Another GOSUB statement

FIGURE 18-11

An example of the use of statements that facilitate structured programming.

```
100 REM *PLANT CONTROL REPORT-ELM CREEK PROJECT
110 REM *
120 REM *VARIABLE NAMES
130 REM * P$   PLANT NAME
140 REM * B    BEGINNING INVENTORY
150 REM * R    QUANTITY RECEIVED
160 REM * S    QUANTITY PLANTED
170 REM * A    AVAILABLE INVENTORY
180 REM * E    ENDING INVENTORY
190 REM *
200 REM *MAIN PROGRAM*********************************************
210        GOSUB 320      :REM   PRINT REPORT HEADINGS
220        GOSUB 400      :REM   READ FIRST PLANT RECORD
230        WHILE R<>-99.9
240           GOSUB 450   :REM   COMPUTE AVAILABLE INVENTORY
250           GOSUB 560   :REM   COMPUTE ENDING INVENTORY
260           GOSUB 670   :REM   PRINT LINE ON REPORT
270           GOSUB 400   :REM   READ NEXT PLANT RECORD
280        WEND
290        END
300 REM ****************************************************************
310 REM *PROCEDURE TO PRINT HEADING
320        PRINT "              PLANT CONTROL REPORT"
330        PRINT
340        PRINT "PLANT        BEGINNING    QUANTITY    QUANTITY       ENDING"
350        PRINT "             INVENTORY    RECEIVED    PLANTED     INVENTORY"
360        RETURN
370 REM ****************************************************************
380 REM *PROCEDURE TO READ PLANT NAME, BEGINNING INVENTORY, QUANTITY RECEIVED
390 REM * AND QUANTITY PLANTED
400        READ P$,B,R,S
410        RETURN
420 REM ****************************************************************
430 REM *PROCEDURE TO COMPUTE AVAILABLE INVENTORY
440        REM *IF BLOCK
450        IF R>=0 THEN 470 ELSE 500
460        REM *CONDITION TRUE
470          LET A=B+R
480          GOTO 510
490        REM *CONDITION FALSE
500          LET A=B
510        REM *END IF BLOCK
520        RETURN
530 REM ****************************************************************
540 REM *PROCEDURE TO COMPUTE ENDING INVENTORY
550        REM *IF BLOCK
560        IF S>=0 THEN 580 ELSE 610
570        REM *CONDITION TRUE
580          LET E=A-S
590          GOTO 620
600        REM *CONDITION FALSE
610          LET E=A
620        REM *END IF BLOCK
630        RETURN
640 REM ****************************************************************
650 REM *PRINT PLANT NAME, BEGINNING INVENTORY, QUANTITY RECEIVED,
660 REM * QUANTITY PLANTED, ENDING INVENTORY, AND RETURN
670        PRINT USING "\            \";P$;
680        PRINT USING "######.##    #####.##    #####.##    ######.##";B,R,S,E
690        RETURN
700 REM ****************************************************************
710 REM *INPUT DATA
720        DATA "AZALEA        ",    200.0,    150.0,    289.0
730        DATA "BOXWOOD       ",    165.0,    118.0,    203.0
```

Computer listing of the program

```
740      DATA "DAFFODIL (DOZ)",    188.5,   144.0,   176.5
750      DATA "HONEYSUCKLE  ",      35.0,   225.0,   200.0
760      DATA "JUNIPER      ",      76.0,   150.0,   132.0
770      DATA "PEONY        ",      92.0,   100.0,   160.0
780      DATA "END OF DATA  ",       0.0,   -99.9,     0.0
Ok
RUN
                    PLANT CONTROL REPORT
PLANT              BEGINNING    QUANTITY    QUANTITY    ENDING
                   INVENTORY    RECEIVED    PLANTED    INVENTORY
AZALEA                200.00      150.00      289.00       61.00
BOXWOOD               165.00      118.00      203.00       80.00
DAFFODIL (DOZ)        188.50      144.00      176.50      156.00
HONEYSUCKLE            35.00      225.00      200.00       60.00
JUNIPER                76.00      150.00      132.00       94.00
PEONY                  92.00      100.00      160.00       32.00
Ok
```

Output produced by the computer as the program is executed

in ln 220 sends program control to another subroutine beginning on ln 400, and another RETURN statement in ln 410 transfers control back to ln 230 in the main module.

WHILE and WEND Statements The WHILE statement in ln 230 establishes the type of basic DO WHILE loop structure discussed in Chapter 16. The condition expressed in the WHILE statement may be any condition that's valid in an IF statement. In our example, the condition is that R (the quantity of plants received) *isn't* equal to −99.9. In the first pass through the program this condition is *true,* and so the steps within the DO WHILE loop that are located in the subroutines identified in lines 240–270 are executed in the sequence called for in the main program module.

A second plant record is read when the GOSUB statement in ln 270 transfers program control to ln 400. The RETURN statement in ln 410 transfers control back to ln 280. The DO WHILE loop structure ends with this WEND (While END) statement in ln 280. When the WEND statement is encountered, control branches back to ln 230 and another test of the WHILE condition is made. This looping process will continue until the WHILE condition becomes *false*—that is, until the R value of −99.9 in the last (dummy) record is read. Program control then exits the loop and goes to the first instruction following the WEND statement. In our example, that is the END statement in ln 290. The END statement is often placed at the end of the main routine in a structured program since this is where the program logically ends.

IF-THEN-ELSE Statement Let's back up a moment and look at the execution of the first subroutine following the WHILE statement on ln 230. This subroutine (identified in ln 240) is a procedure to compute the available inventory of plants. The steps in this procedure begin in ln 450 with an IF-THEN-ELSE selection statement:

450   IF R > =0 THEN 470   ELSE 500

The action to be selected is determined by the condition following the IF part of the statement. If the condition is *true*—if R *is* >=0—then the program carries out the activity prescribed by the THEN part of the statement. But if the condition is *false*, then the program selects and processes the ELSE part of the statement.

If the condition is true in our example, the program moves to carry out the step found in ln 470, and if the condition is false, the step found in ln 500 is executed. But other BASIC commands can follow the words THEN and ELSE. For example, this is a valid IF-THEN-ELSE statement:

    220   IF J=N THEN LET B=20   ELSE LET B=10

There's another IF-THEN-ELSE statement in ln 560 that you should now be able to interpret.

A Few Other Statements

MAT Statements   The word "matrix" is another term for a list or a table of data elements, and some BASIC dialects have a number of **MATrix statements** to carry out array activities. For example, this statement

    150   MAT A=ZER

stores zeros in all the elements of an array named A. And these line numbers

    100   DIM A(2,2)
    110   MAT READ A
    120   DATA 15.00,6.25,8.00,5.00

will read the data items indicated into a two-dimensional array named A. Thus the element in A(1,1) is 15.00, the A(1,2) element is 6.25, and the A(2,1) and A(2,2) elements are 8.00 and 5.00.

The following statements will permit a user to interact with the program and enter data into a two-dimensional array from a keyboard:

    100   DIM A(3,4)
    110   MAT INPUT A

Of course, the first four data items entered must be in the proper row order. That is, they must be the elements in the first row of the array. The next four elements must be those in the second row, and so on.

Finally,

    200   MAT PRINT A

will print the elements in the array in a row order. Although these and other MAT statements are very convenient, they are not yet available in the BASIC dialects used with many popular personal computers.

ON . . . GOTO Statement   This statement serves as a multiple-path branching instruction. In this example,

    100   ON B GOTO 150, 180, 210

if the variable name B has a value of 1, program control is transferred to ln 150. If the value of B is 2, program control branches to ln 180. And control goes to ln 210 if B equals 3. There could have been additional line numbers specified in our example statement to accommodate B values of 4, 5, etc. If B isn't one of the values provided for, control may move to the next executable statement in the program sequence or an error message may be printed.

The **ON . . . GOTO statement** is useful in routing program control to different parts of a program in response to a user's selection of option 1, 2, 3, 4, etc., in a menu of possible alternatives. Let's assume, for example, that Sam Byter decides to combine his savings simulator, future value, and grass seed programs into a single program package. If he did that, the program segment shown below would enable him to choose the part of the package that he wished to have executed.

```
100   PRINT "ENTER 1 TO RUN SAVINGS SIMULATOR"
110   PRINT "ENTER 2 TO COMPUTE FUTURE VALUE OF INVESTMENT"
120   PRINT "ENTER 3 TO COMPUTE BAGS OF GRASS SEED NEEDED"
130   PRINT "WHAT IS YOUR SELECTION";
140   INPUT C
150   ON C GOTO 200, 700, 1000
              •
              •
              •
```

RESTORE Statement   As you know, when the first READ statement is encountered in a BASIC program, the computer looks for the first DATA statement and assigns the first data value(s) it finds in the DATA statement to the variable(s) specified in the READ statement. And subsequent READ statements "use up" the values found in the later DATA statements. But it's sometimes desirable to *reuse* the same data items several times during the execution of a program. When this is the case, duplicate DATA statements *could* be entered on different lines as needed. But there's an easier way.

The **RESTORE statement** resets the internal data pointer to the *first item* found in the *first DATA statement* in the program. Thus, when the READ statements following the RESTORE statement are encountered, the computer reassigns the data values beginning with the first DATA statement.

In this program segment, for example,

```
110   READ N$,R
          •
          •
430   RESTORE
435   READ P$,X
          •
          •
620   DATA "LISA BYTER", 25
          •
          •
```

the first READ statement in ln 110 looks to the first DATA statement in ln 620 and assigns "LISA BYTER" to the variable named N$ and 25 to the location named R. Later in the program, the RESTORE statement is used to reset the internal data pointer once again to the DATA statement in ln 620. Then "LISA BYTER" and 25 are reassigned by ln 435, but this time to the variable names P$ and X.

LOOKING BACK

1. We've considered several example programs that show additional features of the BASIC language in this chapter. Some new programming techniques—using arrays and sorting data—have also been demonstrated. We've reviewed loops and seen how one or more inner FOR . . . NEXT loops may be nested within the body of an outer FOR . . . NEXT loop. And we've seen how preprogrammed library functions such as SQR, INT, and RND may be called up and used in BASIC programs.

2. An array is a collection of data elements that are generally related in some way and are stored in a computer under a common array name. A one-dimensional array consists of a single list of items, and only a single subscript is needed to identify a particular item. A two-dimensional array, on the other hand, consists of data arranged in columns and rows. An item in an array with three columns and two rows is identified by the array name and two subscripts. Thus N(1,2) identifies the item located in row 1 and column 2 of the N array. Example programs have been presented to show you how to enter alphanumeric data into one- and two-dimensional arrays with the help of DIM statements, how to call up and manipulate array elements during processing, and how to print the contents of arrays.

3. An example program that uses the bubble sort technique has also been presented. A bubble sort compares two adjacent elements in an array and then immediately interchanges them if they aren't in the desired ascending or descending sequence.

4. Finally, a few additional BASIC statements (GOSUB and RETURN, WHILE and WEND, IF-THEN-ELSE, MAT, ON . . . GOTO, and RESTORE) are briefly summarized in the last section of the chapter.

KEY TERMS AND CONCEPTS

inner loop 617
outer loop 617
nested FOR . . . NEXT loops 617
crossed loops 618
library functions 619
SQR function 619
INT function 621
RND function 621
random number seed value 621
RANDOMIZE statement 625
array 626
one-dimensional array 626
array name 626
DIM statement 628
two-dimensional array 636
sorting 641
bubble sort 643
GOSUB and RETURN statements 648
WHILE and WEND statements 648
IF-THEN-ELSE statement 648
MAT statements 651
ON . . . GOTO statement 652
RESTORE statement 652

Topics for Review and Discussion

1. "It's common to find one or more nested FOR . . . NEXT loops within the range of an outer FOR . . . NEXT structure." What is meant by the term "nested loop"?
2. In the following program segment,

```
180   FOR M = 1 TO 10
190      FOR N = 1 TO 5
             •
             •
             •
220      NEXT N
240   NEXT M
```

how many times will the N loop be executed?
3. (a) Is it necessary to indent the inner loops in a nested structure? (b) Is it desirable to indent the inner loops? Why or why not?
4. (a) What is a BASIC library function? (b) Give three examples of these functions and explain the purpose of each.
5. (a) What is an array? (b) How are arrays named?
6. (a) What is a one-dimensional array? (b) What is a two-dimensional array?
7. (a) How may data be entered into arrays? (b) How may arrayed data be printed?
8. Explain the purpose of this line in a BASIC program:

    80   DIM   N$(8), M(8), W(8,4)

9. "Since the BASIC interpreter will usually contain instructions that will automatically provide storage space for arrays, the use of the DIM statement is generally a waste of time." Discuss this sentence.
10. Why must computers be able to sort data into predetermined sequences?
11. (a) What approach is followed when a bubble sort places data items in a predetermined sequence? (b) How does this technique get its name?
12. In a bubble sort, what's the maximum number of sorting passes that would be needed before eight items are put in a descending sequence?
13. Summarize some of the functions of the following BASIC statements: MAT statements; ON . . . GOTO statement; GOSUB and RETURN statements; RESTORE statement; IF-THEN-ELSE statement; WHILE and WEND statements.
14. After reviewing the "Lord Byron" poetry generator in Figure 18-6b, write your own version (a "William Shakespeare"?) to produce four-line masterpieces.
15. Write a program that (a) uses INPUT statements to receive data and (b) employs the SQR function to produce the following economic order quantity results: (Hint: See "The SQR Function" section in the chapter.)

```
QUANTITY OF INVENTORY REQUIRED FOR PERIOD? 12000
COST OF PLACING ONE ORDER? 300
UNIT COST OF ITEM? 100
INVENTORY CARRYING COST FOR ITEM FOR PERIOD? 10

                    EOQ OUTPUT

ECONOMIC ORDER QUANTITY = 848.528
MORE DATA (YES,NO)?
```

16. Two versions of Bill Byter's Elm Creek Planting Summary program are shown in Figures 17-10, page 596, and 18-5b, page 630. Your assignment now is to prepare a third version of this same program using the structured programming approach shown in this chapter.
17. The Monthly Welfare Applications Report for Marie Byter (introduced in Feedback and Review 18-2) is a monthly summary of the Weekly Applications Report shown in Figure 18-8. After reviewing Figure 18-8 and the program segment shown in Feedback and Review 18-2, prepare a program that will produce the monthly production output shown in Feedback and Review 18-2.
18. Modify the Monthly Welfare Applications Report program prepared for question 17 so that the monthly production total is sorted into a descending order as shown below:

NAME	W1	W2	W3	W4	TOTAL
D. MOLINA	21	24	22	29	96
R. DAVIS	21	25	19	22	87
S. YAMAMOTO	16	22	19	25	82
G. CONRAD	15	18	16	21	70
J. HUANG	25	12	13	14	64
V. BARON	10	16	12	19	57
P. QUINCY	11	9	13	16	49
F. GARCIA	8	10	12	9	39

19. Jill Byter is working in a hospital during the summer, and the hospital administrator asks her to conduct a survey among hospital personnel. The purpose of the survey is to determine which of five fabrics—silk, wool, cotton, nylon, or burlap—is preferred as a material for hospital uniforms. Jill selects eight people, gets them to use garments made of the five fabrics, and asks them to rank the fabrics in order of preference from 1 to 5. The input data for a "clothing survey" program is shown below. (The numbers refer to the rankings of the materials in the order mentioned above—the first number is for the ranking of silk, the second is for wool, and so on.)

```
470  REM *SURVEY DATA
480      DATA 1,2,3,4,5
490      DATA 4,2,1,5,3
500      DATA 2,3,1,5,4
510      DATA 1,3,2,4,5
520      DATA 3,5,4,1,2
530      DATA 5,3,1,2,4
540      DATA 3,5,1,2,4
550      DATA 5,4,3,2,1
560      DATA 0,0,0,0,0
```

Using these input values, prepare a clothing survey program to produce the following output:

HOSPITAL CLOTHING SURVEY

RANKING BY FIRST PREFERENCE
SILK   2
WOOL   0
COTTON 4
NYLON   1
BURLAP 1

20. The output for the program prepared in question 19 lists the "first-place" votes but doesn't give an overall ranking. Jill now feels that it would be better if the program gave such a ranking value to each fabric. She has thus decided to assign a value of 5 to each first choice, 4 to each second choice, 3 to a third choice, and so on. Using the same input data found in question 19, modify the program prepared for question 19 so that it produces the following output results:

HOSPITAL CLOTHING SURVEY

RANKING BY FIRST PREFERENCE
SILK   2
WOOL   0
COTTON 4
NYLON   1
BURLAP 1

OVERALL RANKING
SILK   24
WOOL   21
COTTON 32
NYLON   23
BURLAP 20

21. After reviewing the mileage program for Feedback and Review 17-1 listed on page 608, write a version of this program that utilizes a main routine and subroutines organized in a top-down manner. Use GOSUB and RETURN statements in your program.

22. A mileage tax program is discussed in question 20 at the end of Chapter 16 and in question 14 at the end of Chapter 17. Write a version of this program that utilizes a main routine and subroutines.

23. Review the specifications for Sam Byter's grass seed program presented in question 16 at the end of Chapter 16 (page 563). Now write a top-down program meeting these specifications that utilizes GOSUB and RETURN statements.

24. As a continuation of question 23, prepare another top-down program that meets the revised "grass seed" specifications spelled out in question 17 at the end of Chapter 16 (page 563).

25. Moving right along with our grass seed problems, now write another top-down program to meet the specifications and produce the output shown in question 26 at the end of Chapter 17 (page 607).

26. After they had written their multiplication drill and practice program (Figure 18-4b), Sam and Lisa decided to use some of the same concepts to prepare a game program. The output of their game—an E.S.P test—is shown below. Write a program to produce this output. (The program should respond with a "YOU GUESSED IT!" message when a correct choice is made, and E.S.P. ability should be assumed if the correct guesses represent more than 20 percent of the total guesses.)

E.S.P. TEST
THIS IS A TEST OF YOUR POWERS OF EXTRA-SENSORY PERCEPTION (E.S.P.). THE COMPUTER GENERATES A SERIES OF RANDOM INTEGERS IN THE RANGE FROM ZERO TO NINE AND YOU ARE REQUIRED TO TRY AND GUESS WHAT THEY ARE. ON THE BASIS OF PURELY RANDOM GUESSING ONE WOULD EXPECT TO GUESS CORRECTLY ABOUT TEN PERCENT OF THE TIME. IF YOU ARE ABLE TO GUESS SIGNIFICANTLY MORE THAN TEN PERCENT OF THE ANSWERS THEN PERHAPS YOU HAVE SOME POWERS OF E.S.P.

TO BEGIN PLEASE RELAX AND CONCENTRATE ON AN APPROPRIATE RANDOM NUMBER SEED. WHEN YOU FEEL INSPIRED PLEASE ENTER THE NUMBER YOU ARE THINKING OF.

RANDOM NUMBER SEED? 235

I'M THINKING OF A NUMBER. WHAT IS IT? 4

TOO BAD THAT WASN'T THE NUMBER I WAS THINKING OF. PERHAPS YOU'RE NOT CONCENTRATING HARD ENOUGH.
            T R Y T O R E L A X ! ! !
•
•
•
I'M THINKING OF A NUMBER. WHAT IS IT? 7

TOO BAD THAT WASN'T THE NUMBER I WAS THINKING OF. PERHAPS YOU'RE NOT CONCENTRATING HARD ENOUGH.
            T R Y T O R E L A X ! ! !

YOU GUESSED 10 PERCENT OF THE NUMBERS CORRECTLY. BASED ON THIS PERCENTAGE E.S.P. ABILITY IS NOT INDICATED.

27. Pleased with her work on the clothing survey, the hospital administrator has now asked Jill for a program to summarize, in graphic form, the charitable donations that the hospital has received over the past year. The input data (in thousands of dollars) and the desired output results are

shown below. Write a program that Jill can use to produce this output.

```
380  REM *INPUT DATA
390      DATA "JAN ",20
400      DATA "FEB ",25
410      DATA "MAR ",29
420      DATA "APR ",27
430      DATA "MAY ",35
440      DATA "JUN ",45
450      DATA "JUL ",15
460      DATA "AUG ",20
470      DATA "SEP ",30
480      DATA "OCT ",25
490      DATA "NOV ",40
500      DATA "DEC ",50
Ok
RUN
                 HARPER HOSPITAL
                RECEIPTS OF DONATIONS
                      (000 OF $$)

        1         10        20        30        40        50
JAN   $$$$$$$$$$$$$$$$$$$$
FEB   $$$$$$$$$$$$$$$$$$$$$$$$$
MAR   $$$$$$$$$$$$$$$$$$$$$$$$$$$$$
APR   $$$$$$$$$$$$$$$$$$$$$$$$$$$
MAY   $$$$$$$$$$$$$$$$$$$$$$$$$$$$$$$$$$$
JUN   $$$$$$$$$ $$$$$$$$$$$$$$$$$$$$$$$$$$$$$$$$$$$$
JUL   $$$$$$$$$$$$$$$
AUG   $$$$$$$$$$$$$$$$$$$$
SEP   $$$$$$$$$$$$$$$$$$$$$$$$$$$$$ $
OCT   $$$$$$$$$$$$$$$$$$$$$$$$$
NOV   $$$$$$$$$$$$$$$$$$$$$$$$$$$$$$ $$$$$$$$$$
DEC   $$$$$$$$$$$$$$$$$$$$$$$$$$$ $$$$$$$$$$$ $$$$$$$$$$$$
```

ANSWERS TO FEEDBACK AND REVIEW 18-1

Line 180 sets up 2 one-dimensional arrays named N$ and W and reserves storage space for eight elements in each of these arrays. Line 200 reads the number of caseworkers (N) from a DATA statement located later in the program. As you can see from the output, the value of N is 8 for this period. The FOR . . . NEXT loop in lines 220–240 loads the N$ and W arrays with data taken from later DATA statements. In the first pass through this loop, the first employee name (N$) encountered in a DATA statement is assigned to storage location N$(1), and the first weekly applications total found in a DATA statement is assigned to storage location W(1) in the W array. This process continues until the other names and processing totals are loaded into the N$ and W arrays. By the way, this segment comes from Figure 18-8, a program considered later in the chapter.

Answers to Feedback and Review 18-2

Line 190 sets up 2 one-dimensional arrays named N$ and M and reserves storage space for eight elements in each of these arrays. A two-dimensional array (W) is also specified for a table with eight rows and four columns (see output). Line 210 reads the number of caseworkers (N) from a later DATA statement. The FOR . . . NEXT loop in lines 230–250 is used to load the N$ and W arrays with data items found in later DATA statements. For example, if ln 240 reads the following DATA line

770   DATA "V. BARON",10,16,12,19

it will assign V. BARON to N$(1), 10 to W(1,1), 16 to W(1,2), 12 to W(1,3), and 19 to W(1,4). This process continues in lines 230–250 until the other names and production figures are loaded into the N$ and W arrays. As you can see in the output, the program later adds these weekly production figures to produce a monthly total. (Question 17 at the end of the chapter asks you to complete the program steps needed to produce the output shown.)

Answers to Feedback and Review 18-3

1. A small portion of the modified version of Figure 18-9b that produces a production report sorted in an ascending order is shown below. The output of this version is also presented. To save you some eye strain, look at ln 330 in this program. In Figure 18-9b, this line was

   330   IF W(I) < W(I+1) THEN 380

And in the modified version this line is

   330   IF W(I) > W(I+1) THEN 380

That's it. Changing < to > is all it takes to convert the sorting program from a descending order to an ascending sequence.

2. After the first sorting pass, the item with the largest value will always be in the last position in an ascending sequence.

```
320 REM *EXAMINE DATA TO SEE IF THEY ARE IN ORDER
330       FOR I=1 TO N-1
340         IF W(I)>W(I+1) THEN 380
350       GOTO 470
```
A partial computer listing of the program

```
RUN
                         WEEKLY APPLICATIONS
CASEWORKER NAME              PROCESSED
-------------------      -------------------
F. GARCIA                        8
V. BARON                        10
P. QUINCY                       11
G. CONRAD                       15
S. YAMAMOTO                     16
R. DAVIS                        21
D. MOLINA                       21
J. HUANG                        25
Ok
```
Output produced by the computer as the program is executed

A CLOSER LOOK

PROGRAM DEBUGGING
A "bug" is a fault of some kind, either in the computer hardware or in the software program that will not work properly. And the process of rectifying a fault is known as "debugging."

What Can Go Wrong?
When your computer suddenly stops doing what you think it should, or stops working altogether, it is very tempting to blame the hardware immediately—it is, after all, the part of the system you see and touch. But, more often than not, it is the software that is at fault.

Even the most experienced programmers make mistakes and when you are first learning to program, mistakes are inevitable. Some of these errors will be easy to find, but there is always going to be the elusive variety, and tracking these down is simply a matter of going over the program listing time and time again.

There are two types of software bugs: syntax errors and logic errors. Of the two, syntax errors are by far the easier to find, especially as the majority of computers will detect them and throw up on the screen a suitable error message, such as "SYNTAX ERROR IN LINE 1240", for example. Some computers will display an error code, which you can look up in the user's manual.

Syntax Errors
Generally, syntax errors are due to simple typing mistakes ("PRIMT" instead of "PRINT", for example), and they are both easy to make and to rectify. Some typing mistakes, though, are more difficult to find: "/" (the symbol for division) instead of "*" (the symbol for multiplication) would cause some interesting and difficult-to-find errors if it was hidden somewhere within a long program listing.

Another type of syntax error is the result of using a BASIC word incorrectly. Consider the following example:

LET A = (K*P/G)/2

It is very easy in this sort of expression to type the brackets incorrectly—either leaving one out or putting one in the wrong place—and this is not easy to spot.

"Falling into" subroutines can cause absolute chaos. It is easily done, too—either by leaving out the END statement before a group of subroutines at the bottom of the listing or, even worse, by leaving the RETURN statement from one subroutine. This causes you to fall into the next subroutine below it and execute that one, returning only when you hit the RETURN at the end of that one, by which time all sorts of interesting things could have happened for no immediately obvious reason.

While you are writing a complex program, you will almost certainly be adding and deleting lines throughout the listing. During this process it is surprisingly easy to erase a line to which you have, elsewhere, specified a GOTO or GOSUB. Again, this will be reported when you run the program and the computer finds that it is supposed to GOTO a line that does not exist, but it is nevertheless annoying. For example, take a program statement like:

120   IF A$ = "Y" THEN GOTO 500
       .
       .
       .
500   REM This is a comment
510   PRINT "GOOD BYE"
etc.

If you are running out of memory space with a long program, you can save some space by deleting all of the REM statements. In this case, with line 500 there, it does not matter that you GOTO it from line 120—any line beginning with REM is ignored by the computer, and the program itself will in this case carry on from line 510. But if you subsequently delete line 500 as part of a REM purge, you will see an error message when you try to GOTO it.

Most versions of BASIC are quite good at reporting syntax errors, with messages of varying degrees of helpfulness. These range from a curt error code (which you have to look up in a manual) to (in at least one case) a display of the offending line with the error marked for your attention. What your computer cannot do, however, is detect an error in the logic of a program.

Logic Errors
Logic errors are those in which you have the syntax perfect but you have told the machine to do the wrong thing. A simple example of this type of mistake would be to ask the computer to PRINT the value of the variable X when you really meant X$.

It can be immensely frustrating when you know what you want the computer to do and you are certain that you have programmed it correctly, but the machine will still not do it. The computer, obviously, has no way of knowing or guessing what you are trying to do. It merely follows the instruction you have given it and—assuming there are no syntax errors in your program—will do exactly as it is told. If you have given it a program that contains logic errors but is perfect in its syntax, it will execute it—but as far as you are concerned, the result will not be correct.

The other major problem is to ensure that variables are given the values they are supposed to receive while the program is being executed. You can usually check this by inserting extra lines to print out the value of any suspicious variables in areas where you expect trouble. You can also insert END or STOP commands at appropriate places. This is slightly cruder but it does take advantage of BASIC's interactive nature by asking it to print the variables' values directly from the keyboard.

Finding out if the computer is executing the right part of the program can sometimes be difficult. Some machines have a TRACE facility. By typing TRACE ON or TRON before you RUN the program you will see a display of the line numbers as the program is executing. Usually, if your BASIC allows it, it is more convenient to put TRON and its opposite, TROFF, around the section you suspect is not being reached. If no line numbers appear on the screen while the program is running, you know the section is not being used. If you do not have TRACE facilities, you can simulate them by inserting messages at the start of each section of the program: PRINT "NOW IN RANDOM NUMBER SUBROUTINE", for example. Do not forget, however, to take them out again once the program is working correctly.

The process of debugging is made easier if you take care with the design and layout of your programs. Start by drawing up at least a written flowchart, which divides the program into functional sections and describes what each is supposed to do. And take care over the design of screen displays—what is to appear on the screen and the choice of color or graphics, for example. When you actually write the program, keep to these sections as far as possible and separate them with a few blank REM lines. And begin each section with one or more REM statements that describe briefly what the section does and what variables it uses or affects elsewhere in the program.

From Peter Rodwell, *The Personal Computer Handbook,* London, Dorling Kindersley Ltd., 1983. Used by permission.

WINDOW 18-1

THE 10111'RD PSALM

The Computer is my taskmaster; I need not think.
He maketh me to write flawless reports
    He leadeth me with Computer-Aided Instruction
He restoreth my jumbled files
He guideth me through the program with menus.
Yea, though I walk through the valley of
    the endless GOTO,

I will fear no error messages;
    For thy User's Manual is with me.

Thy disk drive and thy Pac-Man—they comfort me.
Thou displayest a spreadsheet program before me
    in the presence of my supervisor.

Thou enableth the printout;
    the floor runneth over (with paper).
Surely good jobs and good pay shall follow me
    All the days of my life;

And I shall access your CPUs, forever.

(P.S. Please note that 10111 is the binary equivalent of 23.)

Revised by Charles P. Rubenstein, with apologies to King David. From Charles P. Rubenstein, Pratt Institute, "The 10111'rd Psalm," *Digital Deli,* Workman Publishing, New York, 1984. Reprinted with permission of the publisher.

Glossary

The communication of facts and ideas in any field is dependent on a mutual understanding of the words used. The purpose of this section, then, is to present definitions for some of the terms that are often used in the field of computers and data processing.

access To locate the desired data. See *direct-access, random access, remote access, serial access.*

access arm The disk-drive component used to position read/write heads over a specified track.

access time The elapsed time between the instant when data are called for from a storage device and the instant when the delivery operation is completed.

accumulator A register or storage location that forms the result of an arithmetic or logic operation.

ACM Acronym for Association for Computing Machinery, a professional group dedicated to advancing the design, development, and application of information processing.

acoustic coupler A type of modem which permits data communication over regular telephone lines by means of sound signals.

acronym A word formed from the first letter(s) of the words contained in a phrase or name.

Ada A high-level programming language developed by the Department of Defense for use in military systems.

address An identification (e.g., a label, name, or number) that designates a particular location in storage or any other data destination or source.

ADP Automatic data processing.

ALGOL (ALGOrithmic Language) An algebraic, high-level language similar to FORTRAN that is widely used in Europe.

algorithm A set of well-defined rules for solving a problem in a finite number of operations.

alphanumeric Pertaining to a character set that includes letters, digits, and, usually, other special punctuation character marks.

analog computer A device that operates on data in the form of continuously variable physical quantities.

analyst See *system analyst.*

annotation symbol A symbol used to add messages or notes to a flowchart.

ANSI (American National Standards Institute) An organization that develops and approves standards in many fields.

APL (A Programming Language) A mathematically oriented high-level language.

application program Software designed to perform tasks such as word processing, billing, or inventory control.

applications packages Prewritten computer programs designed for special- or general-purpose tasks. Some applications packages perform single functions, while others integrate several functions in a single package.

architecture The organization and interconnection of computer system components.

arithmetic-logic unit The part of a computing system containing the circuitry that does the adding, subtracting, multiplying, dividing, and comparing.

artificial intelligence (AI) A computer science branch that's involved with using computers to solve problems that appear to require human imagination or intelligence.

ASCII (American National Standard Code for Information Interchange) A standard code used to exchange information among data processing and communications systems.

assembler program A computer program that takes nonmachine-language instructions prepared by a programmer and converts them into a form that may be used by the computer.

assembly language A means of communicating with a computer at a low level. This language lies between high-level languages (such as BASIC and COBOL) and machine language (the 1s and 0s the computer understands).

asynchronous transmission The transmission of data a character at a time, with each character identified by start and stop bits; characters can be sent at irregular intervals (contrast with *synchronous transmission*).

automated office A general term that refers to the merger of computers, office electronic devices, and telecommunications technology in an office environment.

auxiliary storage A storage that supplements the primary internal storage of a computer. Often referred to as *secondary storage.*

back-end processor A computer that serves as an interface between a larger processor and data bases stored on direct-access storage devices.

background processing The automatic execution of lower-priority (background) computer programs during periods when the system resources are not required to process higher-priority (foreground) programs.

backup Alternate programs or equipment used in case the original is incapacitated.

bank-switched memory The use of software-controlled switches that allow a central processor to switch between memory locations in primary and supplementary memory banks so that the apparent size of primary storage is increased.

bar code A machine-readable code consisting of vertical bars of varying widths that are used to represent data.

BASIC (Beginners All-Purpose Symbolic Instruction Code) A high-level interactive programming language frequently used with personal computers and in timesharing environments.

batch processing A technique in which a number of similar items or transactions to be processed are collected into groups and periodically processed (contrast with *interactive processing*).

baud A unit for measuring data transmission speed.

BCD (Binary-Coded Decimal) A method of representing the decimal digits zero through nine by a pattern of binary 1s and 0s (e.g., the decimal number 25 is represented by 0010 0101 in 8-4-2-1 BCD notation).

binary digit Either of the characters 0 or 1. Abbreviated "bit."

binary number system A number system with a base or radix of two.

bit See *binary digit*.

block Related records, characters, or digits that are grouped and handled as a unit during input and output. A section of program coding treated as a unit.

branch An instruction that transfers program control to one or more possible paths.

broadband channels Communications channels such as those made possible by the use of laser beams and microwaves that can transmit data at high speed.

buffer A storage device used to compensate for the difference in rates of flow of data from one device to another—e.g., from an I/O device to the processor.

bug An error in a system or program.

bus Circuits that provide a communication path between two or more devices, such as between a CPU, storage, and peripherals.

byte A group of adjacent bits, usually eight, operated on as a unit.

cache A very high speed storage device.

CAD/CAM (Computer-Aided Design/Computer-Aided Manufacturing) A general term applied to the efforts being made to automate design and manufacturing operations.

CAI (Computer-Assisted Instruction) A general term that refers to a learning situation in which the student interacts with (and is guided by) a computer through a course of study aimed at achieving certain instructional goals.

call A transfer of program control to a subroutine.

canned programs Programs prepared by an outside supplier and provided to a user in a machine-readable form (see *applications packages*).

cathode-ray tube (CRT) An electronic tube with a screen upon which information may be displayed.

central processing unit (CPU) The component of a computer system with the circuitry to control the interpretation and execution of instructions. The CPU includes arithmetic-logic and control sections.

channel (1) A path for carrying signals between a source and a destination. (2) A track on a magnetic tape.

character string A string of alphanumeric characters.

chip A tiny sliver (usually made of silicon) on which integrated electronic components are deposited.

clock A device that generates the periodic signals used to control the timing of all processor operations.

COBOL (COmmon Business-Oriented Language) A high-level language developed for business data processing applications.

code A set of rules outlining the way in which data may be represented; also, rules used to convert data from one representation to another. To write a program or routine.

collate To combine items from two or more sequenced files into a single one.

COM (Computer Output Microfilm) A technology that permits the output information produced by computers to be stored on microfilm.

common carrier A government-regulated organization that provides public communications services.

communications channel A medium for transferring data from one location to another.

compiler A computer program that produces a machine-language program from a source program that's usually written in a high-level language by a programmer. The compiler is capable of replacing single source program statements with a series of machine-language instructions or with a subroutine.

computer An electronic symbol manipulating system that's designed and organized to automatically accept and store input data, process them, and produce output results under the direction of a detailed step-by-step stored program of instructions.

computer network A processing complex consisting of two or more interconnected computers.

computer operator One whose duties include setting up the processor and peripheral equipment, starting the program run, checking on processor operation, and unloading equipment at the end of a run.

concentrator A communications device that receives input from many low-speed lines and then concentrates and transmits a compressed and smooth stream of data on a higher-speed and more efficient transmission channel. Multiplexers also perform this function.

concurrent programming See *multiprogramming*.

conditional transfer An instruction that may cause a departure from the sequence of instructions being followed, depending upon the result of an operation, the contents of a register, or the setting of an indicator.

connector symbol Used in a flowchart to represent a junction in a flow line, this symbol is often used to transfer flow between pages of a lengthy chart.

console The part of a computer system that enables human operators to communicate with the computer.

constant A value that doesn't change during program execution.

control program Generally part of an operating system, this program helps control the operations and management of a computer system.

control unit The section of the CPU that selects, interprets, and sees to the execution of program instructions.

counter A device (e.g., a register) used to represent the number of occurrences of an event.

CPU See *central processing unit*.

crash A hardware or software failure that leads to an abnormal cessation of processing.

CRT See *cathode-ray tube*.

cursor A symbol on a visual display screen that highlights the location(s) to be affected by the next character or command that is entered.

cybernetics The branch of learning which seeks to integrate the theories and studies of communication and control in machines and living organisms.

cylinder All tracks on magnetic disks that are accessible by a single movement of the access mechanism.

DASD Acronym for direct-access storage device.

data Facts; the raw material of information.

data bank See *data base*.

data base A stored collection of the libraries of data that are needed by organizations and individuals to meet their information processing and retrieval requirements.

data base administrator One responsible for defining, updating, and controlling access to a data base.

data base management system (DBMS) The comprehensive software system that builds, maintains, and provides access to a data base.

data communications The means and methods whereby data are transferred between processing sites.

data entry operator One who transcribes data into a form suitable for computer processing.

data processing One or more operations performed on data to achieve a desired objective.

debug To detect, locate, and remove errors in programs and/or malfunctions in equipment.

decision support system (DSS) A computer-based system that backs up and assists those engaged in planning and decision-making activities.

decision symbol This diamond-shaped symbol is used in flowcharts to indicate a choice or branch in the processing path.

decision table A programming analysis tool that shows all the conditions to be considered in a problem as well as the actions to be taken when a given set of conditions is present.

default data Values (correct most of the time) that are automatically provided by software to reduce keystrokes and improve a computer user's productivity; however, the user has the option of replacing default data with other values when such action is needed.

diagnostics Error messages printed by a computer to indicate system problems and improper program instructions.

digital computer A device that manipulates discrete data and performs arithmetic and logic operations on these data. Contrast with *analog computer*.

digital PBX A private branch exchange system that may be used to automatically manage thousands of communications lines without human assistance. Both voice and data transmissions can be handled simultaneously over telephone lines, and no modems are needed for local data exchanges.

direct-access Pertaining to storage devices where the time required to retrieve data is independent of the physical location of the data.

direct processing The technique of directly locating, retrieving, and updating any file record without the need to read preceding or succeeding file records (contrast with *sequential processing*).

disk A revolving platter upon which data and programs are stored.

disk drive An electromechanical device that writes data onto and reads data from a floppy or rigid magnetic disk.

disk pack A removable direct-access storage medium containing multiple magnetic disks mounted vertically on a single shaft.

diskette A floppy disk. A low-cost magnetic medium used for I/O and secondary storage purposes.

distributed data processing (DDP) A general term describing the processing of a logically related set of information processing functions through the use of multiple, geographically separated, computing and communications devices.

DO UNTIL loop structure A control structure in which one or more operations in a loop are repeated until a condition is found to be true, after which the exit path out of the loop is followed.

DO WHILE loop structure A control structure in which one or more operations in a loop are continued while a condition is true. When the condition becomes false, the exit path out of the loop is followed.

documentation The preparation of documents, during system analysis and subsequent programming, that describe such things as the system, the programs pre-

pared, and the changes made at later dates.

downtime The length of time a computer system is inoperative due to a malfunction.

EBCDIC (Extended Binary-Coded Decimal Interchange Code) An 8-bit code used to represent data in modern computers.

edit To correct, rearrange, and validate input data. To modify the form of output information by inserting blank spaces, special characters where needed, etc.

editor A program used to interactively review and alter text materials and other program instructions.

EDP Acronym for electronic data processing.

EEPROM An electrically erasable and programmable read-only memory chip that can be reprogrammed with special electrical pulses.

electronic funds transfer (EFT) A general term referring to a cashless approach used to pay for goods and services. Electronic signals between computers are often used to adjust the accounts of the parties involved in a transaction.

electronic mail A general term to describe the transmission of messages by the use of computing systems and telecommunications facilities.

electronic spreadsheet program A software package that permits users to quickly create, manipulate, and analyze data organized in columns and rows.

emulator A stored logic device or program that permits one computer to execute the machine-language instructions of another computer of different design.

EPROM An erasable and programmable read-only memory chip that can be reprogrammed under limited conditions.

executive routine A master program in an operating system that controls the execution of other programs. Often referred to as the supervisor or kernel.

executive workstation Special desktop computer-based units designed for busy people who may not like to type. They have special function keys, and may accept input through the use of a mouse or a touch screen. They have the ability to perform word/data processing, manage data bases, produce graphics, and support many other activities.

expert system A software package that includes (1) a stored base of knowledge in a specialized area and (2) the capability to probe this knowledge base and make decision recommendations. Expert systems are the products of research in the field of artificial intelligence.

facsimile system A system used to transmit pictures, text, maps, etc., between geographically separated points. An image is scanned at a transmitting point and duplicated at a receiving point.

fiber-optic cable A data transmission medium made of tiny threads of glass or plastic that is able to transmit huge amounts of information at the speed of light.

field A group of related characters treated as a unit—such as an item or data element in a record.

file A collection of related records treated as a unit.

file processing The updating of master files to reflect the effects of current transactions.

floppy disk See *diskette*.

flowchart A diagram that uses symbols and interconnecting lines to show (1) a system of processing to achieve objectives (system flowchart) or (2) the logic and sequence of specific program operations (program flowchart).

FORTRAN (FORmula TRANslator) A high-level language used to perform mathematical computations.

front-end processor A computer programmed to function as an interface between a larger host and assorted peripheral devices.

full-duplex transmission The simultaneous sending and receiving of data over a communications path.

generator A computer program that constructs other programs to perform a particular type of operation—e.g., a report program generator.

graphic display unit A visual device that is used to project graphic images.

half-duplex transmission The sending and then receiving of data over a communications path during alternating periods of time. Data may not be sent in both directions at the same time.

hard copy Printed or filmed output in humanly readable form.

hard disk A rigid metal platter coated with a magnetizable substance. Contrast with *floppy disk*.

hardware Physical equipment such as electronic, magnetic, and mechanical devices. Contrast with *software*.

heuristic A problem-solving method in which solutions are discovered by evaluating the progress made toward the end result. A directed trial-and-error approach. Contrast with *algorithm*.

hierarchical data structure A logical approach to structuring data in which a single-root data component or "parent" may have subordinate elements or "children," each of which, in turn, may "own" one or more other elements (or none). Each element or branch below the parent has only a single owner.

high-level language A programming language oriented toward the problem to be solved or the procedures to be used. Instructions are given to a computer by using convenient letters, symbols, or English-like text, rather than by using the 1s and 0s code that the computer understands.

HIPO charts (Hierarchy plus Input/Process/Output charts) Charts used in the analysis, design, and programming of computer applications.

Hollerith Code A particular type of code used to represent alphanumeric data on 80-column punched cards.

host computer A main control computer in a network of distributed processors and terminals.

hybrid computer A data processing

device using both analog and discrete data representation.

IF-THEN-ELSE selection structure A basic program control structure that requires a test for some condition followed by two alternative program paths. The path selected depends on the results of the test.

indexed sequential access method See *ISAM*.

information Meaning assigned to data by humans.

information retrieval The methods used to recover specific information from stored data.

input/output (I/O) Pertaining to the techniques, media, and devices used to achieve human-machine communication.

input/output symbol A figure in the shape of a parallelogram that's used to indicate both input and output operations in a flowchart.

instruction A set of characters used to direct a data processing system in the performance of an operation—i.e., an operation is signaled and the values or locations of the instruction operands are specified.

integrated software package A software product that combines several applications—e.g., word processing, spreadsheet operations, the creation of graphs—into a single package so that it's possible to share data and move material among these functions.

intelligent terminal A terminal with a built-in processor that can be programmed to perform specific functions such as editing data and controlling other terminals.

interactive processing A processing approach that starts immediately after input data are entered into a computer system, and the output results of the processing are quickly produced (contrast with *batch processing*).

interactive system One that permits direct communication and dialog between system users and the operating program in the processor.

interface A shared boundary—e.g., the boundary between two systems or devices.

internal storage The addressable storage in a digital computer directly under the control of the CPU.

interpreter A computer program that translates each source language statement into a sequence of machine instructions and then executes these machine instructions before translating the next source language statement.

I/O See *input/output*.

ISAM (Indexed Sequential Access Method) A method whereby records organized in a sequential order can be referenced directly through the use of an index based on some key or characteristic.

item A group of related characters treated as a unit. (A record is a group of related items, and a file is a group of related records.)

job A collection of specific tasks constituting a unit of work for a computer.

job-control language (JCL) A language that permits communication between programmers and an operating system. A job-control program written in this language can be translated into requests for action that can be executed by the computer.

jump A departure from sequence in executing instructions in a computer. See *conditional transfer*.

K In computer science, an abbreviation for a value equal to 2^{10}, or 1,024; in other contexts, an abbreviation for "kilo," meaning 1,000.

key A unique item that's used to identify a record.

label One or more characters used to identify a program statement or a data item.

language A set of rules and conventions used to convey information.

leased line A permanent or semipermanent communications service provided by a common carrier to link sending and receiving units in an organization.

library routine A tested routine maintained in a library of programs.

light pen An electrical device that permits people to provide input to computers by writing or sketching on the screen of a cathode-ray tube.

local-area network (LAN) A privately owned communications system that links computers, terminals, word processing stations, and other devices located within a compact area such as an office building or a campus.

logic diagram See *flowchart*.

LSI (Large-Scale Integration) The process of integrating a large number of electronic circuits on a single small chip of silicon or other material.

machine language A language used directly by a computer.

macro instruction A source language instruction that's equivalent to a specified number of machine-language instructions.

magnetic ink character recognition (MICR) The recognition of characters printed with a special magnetic ink by machines.

magnetic storage Utilizing the magnetic properties of materials to store data on such devices and media as disks, tapes, and chips.

main control module The highest level in a hierarchy of program modules. This module controls others below it.

mainframe A large computer system that has the capability to support many powerful peripheral devices.

maintenance programming The act of changing and modifying existing programs to meet changing conditions.

management information system (MIS) A computer-based information system designed to supply organizational managers with the necessary information needed to plan, organize, staff, direct, and control the operations of the organization.

master file A file containing relatively

permanent data. This file is often updated by records in a transaction file.

memory Same as *storage*.

menu A set of programmed choices provided to a computer user.

message switcher A communications processor that receives messages and forwards them to appropriate locations.

MICR See *magnetic ink character recognition*.

micro-to-mainframe linkage A hardware/software product that permits communication between a mainframe system and the personal computer systems located on the desks of users.

microcomputer The smallest category of computer, consisting of a microprocessor and associated storage and input/output elements.

microfiche A sheet of film (usually 4 by 6 inches) that may be used to record the results of computer processing.

microprocessor A CPU on a chip; a device that provides the basic arithmetic, logic, and control circuits required for processing.

microprogram A sequence of elementary instructions that is translated by a micrologic subsystem residing in the processor.

microsecond One-millionth of a second.

millisecond One-thousandth of a second.

minicomputer A relatively fast but small and inexpensive computer with somewhat limited input/output capabilities.

MIS See *management information system*.

mnemonic Pertaining to a technique used to aid human memory.

modem A device that modulates and demodulates signals transmitted over voice-grade communication facilities.

modular approach Dividing a project into a hierarchy of segments and smaller units in order to simplify analysis, design, and programming efforts.

monitor routine See *executive routine*.

mouse An input device about the size of a tape cassette that rolls on a small bearing and has one or more buttons on the top. When rolled across a flat surface, the mouse guides the cursor on a visual display screen in the direction of the mouse's movement.

multiplex To simultaneously transmit messages over a single channel or other communications facility.

multiplexer A communications device that receives messages from low-speed lines and then sends these messages along a single high-speed transmission channel. Concentrators also perform this function.

multiprocessing The simultaneous execution of two or more sequences of instructions by a single computer network.

multiprocessor A computer network consisting of two or more central processors under a common control.

multiprogramming The simultaneous handling of multiple independent programs by interleaving or overlapping their execution (same as *multitasking* and *concurrent programming*).

multitasking See *multiprogramming*.

nanosecond One-billionth of a second.

narrow bandwidth channels Communications channels that can only transmit data at slow speeds—e.g., telegraph channels.

natural language A human language such as English, French, German, etc.

network An interconnection of computer systems and/or peripheral devices at dispersed locations that exchange data as necessary to perform the functions of the network.

network data structure A logical approach to structuring data that permits network nodes to be connected in a multi-directional manner. Each node may have several "owners," and may, in turn, own any number of other data units.

node An end point of a branch in a network, or a common junction of two or more network branches.

nonvolatile storage A storage medium that retains its contents in the absence of power.

object language The output of a translation process. Contrast with *source language*.

object program A fully compiled or assembled program that's ready to be loaded into the computer. Contrast with *source program*.

OCR (Optical Character Recognition) The recognition of printed characters through the use of light-sensitive optical machines.

octal Pertaining to a number system with a base of eight.

offline A term describing persons, equipment, or devices not in direct communication with the processor (contrast with *online*).

offpage connector symbol A flowchart symbol used to show that program flow is entering from or going to a separate flowchart page.

online A term describing persons, equipment, or devices that are in direct communication with the computer (contrast with *offline*).

operand The data unit or equipment item that's operated upon. An operand is usually identified by an address in an instruction.

operating system An organized collection of software that controls the overall operations of a computer.

operation code The instruction code used to specify the operations a computer is to perform.

optical disk A medium used with laser reading/writing devices to store huge quantities of data.

overlapped processing An approach that permits the computer to work on several programs instead of one.

parallel interface An electrical interconnection that permits 8 or more bits of data to be moved in the same instant in time (contrast with *serial interface*).

parity check A method of checking the accuracy of binary data after those data have been transferred to or from storage. The number of 1 bits in a binary character is controlled by the addition or deletion of a parity bit.

Pascal A popular high-level programming language that facilitates the use of structured programming techniques.

patch The modification of a program in an expedient way.

peripherals The input/output devices and auxiliary storage units of a computer system.

personal computer (pc) A single-user-oriented and general-purpose microcomputer processing system that can execute program instructions to perform a wide variety of tasks.

picosecond One-thousandth of a nanosecond.

pixel A picture element on the screen of a visual display used for graphics work that is controlled by the contents of a specific location in storage. By turning each pixel on or off, the processor is able to paint a graphic image.

PL/1 (Programming Language 1) A high-level language designed to process both scientific and file processing applications.

plotter A device that converts computer output into a graphic, hard-copy form.

point-of-sale (POS) terminal An I/O device capable of (1) immediately updating sales and inventory records at a central processor and (2) producing a printed sales transaction receipt.

pointer A data item in one record that contains the location address of another logically related record.

port An electrical interconnection. See *parallel interface, serial interface*.

preparation symbol A flowchart symbol used to indicate the control, initiation, or performance of some other operation on the program itself.

primary storage section Also known as *internal storage* and *main memory*, this section of the processor holds program instructions, input data, intermediate results, and the output information produced during processing.

printer A device used to produce humanly readable computer output. A wide range of impact and nonimpact printers is available.

processing symbol A rectangular figure used in flowcharts to indicate a processing operation—e.g., a calculation.

program (1) A plan to achieve a problem solution; (2) to design, write, and test one or more routines; (3) a set of sequenced instructions to cause a computer to perform particular operations.

program flowchart See *flowchart*.

program library A collection of programs and routines.

programmer One who designs, writes, tests, and maintains computer programs.

programming language A language used to express programs.

PROM (Programmable Read-Only Memory) A read-only storage device that can be programmed after manufacture by external equipment. PROMs are usually integrated circuit chips.

pseudocode A programming analysis tool. Counterfeit and abbreviated versions of actual computer instructions that are written in ordinary natural language.

radix The base number in a number system—e.g., the radix in the decimal system is 10. Synonymous with base.

RAM (Random Access Memory) (1) A storage device structured so that the time required to retrieve data is not significantly affected by the physical location of the data. (2) The *primary storage section* of a personal computer.

random access See *direct-access*.

real time Descriptive of online computer processing systems which receive and process data quickly enough to produce output to control, direct, or affect the outcome of an ongoing activity or process.

record A collection of related items of data treated as a unit.

register A device capable of storing a specific amount of data.

relational data structure An approach to structuring data in such a way that the logical relationships are represented in interrelated tables.

relational symbols Symbols such as > ("greater than"), < ("less than"), or = ("equal to") that are used to compare two values in a conditional branching situation.

remote access Relating to the communication with a computer facility by a station (or stations) that is distant from the computer.

report program generator (RPG) Software designed to construct programs that perform predictable report-writing operations.

robot A computer-controlled manipulator that's designed to move materials, parts, tools, or other specialized devices through a series of programmed steps.

robotics A general term that refers to the study of robot technology.

ROM (Read-Only Memory) Generally a solid-state storage chip that's programmed at the time of its manufacture and may not be reprogrammed by the computer user.

routine An ordered set of general-use instructions. See *program*.

run time The time required to complete a single, continuous execution of an object program.

scratchpad storage A memory space used for the temporary storage of data. Typically, scratchpad memories are high-speed integrated circuits. See *cache*.

semiconductor storage A memory device whose storage elements are formed as solid-state electronic components on an integrated circuit chip.

sequential processing The technique of retrieving and processing the first record stored in a file sequence, then the second record in the order, and so on, until the entire file has been searched (contrast with *direct processing*).

serial access Descriptive of a storage device or medium where there is a sequential relationship between access time and data location in storage—i.e., the access time is dependent upon the location of the data. Contrast with *direct-access* and *random access*.

serial interface An electrical interconnection that permits data to be moved one bit at a time over a single path. Contrast with *parallel interface*.

simplex transmission The movement of data along a path that permits communication in only one predetermined direction.

simulation To represent and analyze properties or behavior of a physical or hypothetical system by the behavior of a system model. (This model is often manipulated by means of computer operations.)

software A set of programs, documents, procedures, and routines associated with the operation of a computer system. Contrast with *hardware*.

solid-state Descriptive of electronic components whose operation depends on the control of electric or magnetic phenomena in solids, such as transistors and diodes.

sort To arrange data into a predetermined sequence.

source language The language that is an input for statement translation.

source program A computer program written in a source language such as BASIC, FORTRAN, COBOL, etc.

spooler program Software that allows the processor to alternate between processing a user's ongoing activity and controlling another activity such as printing.

spreadsheet program See *electronic spreadsheet program*.

statement In programming, an expression or generalized instruction in a source language.

storage Descriptive of a device or medium that can accept data, hold them, and deliver them on demand at a later time. Synonymous with *memory*.

structured programming An approach or discipline used in the design and coding of computer programs. The approach generally assumes the disciplined use of a few basic coding structures and the use of top-down concepts to decompose main functions into lower-level components for modular coding purposes.

supercomputer Computer systems characterized by their very large size and very high processing speeds. Generally used for complex scientific applications.

supervisor See *executive routine*.

synchronous transmission The transmission of data in blocks of characters at timed intervals (contrast with *asynchronous transmission*).

system (1) A grouping of integrated methods and procedures united to form an organized entity; (2) an organized grouping of people, methods, machines, and materials collected together to accomplish a set of specific objectives.

system analysis A detailed step-by-step investigation of related procedures to see what must be done and the best way of doing it.

system analyst One who studies the activities, methods, procedures, and techniques of organizational systems in order to determine what actions need to be taken and how these actions can best be accomplished.

system commands The means by which programmers communicate with the operating system of the computer.

system design The creation of alternative solutions to the problems uncovered in system analysis. The final design recommendation is based on cost effectiveness and other factors.

system flowchart See *flowchart*.

systems programming The development and maintenance of operating system software.

telecommunications Transmission of data between computer systems and/or terminals in different locations.

telecommuting Substituting work performed on computer-based workstations and telecommunications networks in homes and neighborhood work centers for tasks performed in central office locations.

teleconferencing The electronic linking of geographically scattered people who are all participating at the same time.

terminal A device that performs I/O operations in a computer system.

terminal symbol An oval-shaped figure used in a flowchart to indicate starting and termination points.

throughput The total amount of useful work performed by a computer system during a given time period.

timesharing The use of specific hardware by a number of other devices, programs, or people simultaneously in such a way as to provide quick response to each of the users. The interleaved use of the time of a device.

top-down methodology A disciplined approach to organizing complexity by identifying the top-level functions in a system and then decomposing these functions into a hierarchy of understandable lower-level modules.

unconditional transfer An instruction that always causes a branch in program control away from the normal sequence of executing instructions.

UPC (Universal Product Code) A machine-readable code of parallel bars used for labeling products found in supermarkets.

user-friendly software A phrase that presumably describes a program or system that people with limited computing backgrounds will find easy to learn and/or use.

utility routine Software used to perform some frequently required process in the operation of a computer system—e.g., sorting, merging, etc.

value-added network (VAN) A communications network operated by an organization that leases the facilities of a common carrier and then offers additional services to its customers.

videotex systems A general term used to describe personal computing/communications networks that permit interaction between people and stored data bases.

virtual storage Descriptive of the capability to use online secondary storage devices and specialized software to divide programs into smaller segments for transmission to and from internal storage in order to significantly increase the effective size of the available internal storage.

visual display terminal A device capable of displaying keyed input and processor output on a screen.

VLSI (Very Large Scale Integration) The packing of hundreds of thousands of electronic components on a single semiconductor chip.

voice-grade channels Medium-speed data transmission channels that use telephone communications facilities.

volatile storage A storage medium that loses its contents in the event of a power interruption.

von Neumann bottleneck A reference to the fact that processing speed in a von Neumann machine is limited by the speed of (1) the circuits in the single channel used to carry instructions from primary storage to the control section and (2) the circuits in the single data path between primary storage and the arithmetic-logic section.

von Neumann machine A computer system whose processor has a single control, primary storage, and arithmetic-logic section. Such a machine follows the design approach developed by John von Neumann and others in the mid-1940s.

Winchester technology The name given to those types of rigid magnetic disk storage systems that are permanently housed (along with their access arms and read/write heads) in sealed, contamination-free containers. Winchester disk systems come in many sizes and storage capacities.

window A portion of the visual display screen used to show the current status of an application of interest. The display screen can be separated into several windows to simultaneously show the status of the different applications in an integrated software package.

word A group of bits or characters considered as an entity and capable of being stored in one storage location.

word length The number of characters or bits in a word.

word processing The use of computers to create, view, edit, store, retrieve, and print text material.

zone bits Used in different combinations with numeric bits to represent alphanumeric characters.

INDEX

INDEX

Abacus, 43
Abuses of computers:
  of data, 311
  by governments, 104–106
  of law-enforcement data bases, 457
  in organizations, 115–116
  privacy and, 107–109
  smart cards and, 193
  systems security and, 106–107
  vote fraud, 472
Access:
  to data on magnetic disks, 205–209
  to direct files, 235–236
  to indexed sequential files, 236
  on magnetic tape, 214
  to sequential files, 235
Access arms on disk drives, 203, 207
Access speed, 208–209
Access time, 198
Accounts receivable (A/R) applications, 165
Accumulators, 152, 154, 545–548, 592–597
Accuracy:
  of collected data, 106
  of computers, 12–13
  of input data, 167–168
Acoustic couplers (modems), 280–281
Ada (language), 402, 420
Adders, 154
Address buses, 246, 247
Address registers, 156
Addresses, 132–135, 150
  in commands, 154
  on disks, 206
  for documents on microfiche, 223
  symbolic, 407
Agricultural planning, 503–504
Aiken, Howard, 44, 239
Air traffic control systems, 292
Airline reservation systems, 524
ALGOL (language), 418–419

Algorithms, 533
Allen, Paul, 49, 613
Alphanumeric output, 224–226
Altair 8800 computer, 48, 613–614
Alternatives in system design, 388–390
American National Standards Institute
    (ANSI):
  Ada standard by, 420
  BASIC standard by, 411
  COBOL standard by, 414
  flowchart symbols adopted by, 535
  FORTRAN standard by, 413
  Pascal standard by, 420
  PL/1 standard by, 417
American Standard Code for Information
    Interchange (ASCII), 137
American Telephone and Telegraph
    Company (AT&T), 110, 277, 282
Animation, 102
Annotation flags, 538
Apple Computer, Inc., 49, 614
  Macintosh computer by, 49, 247, 345–346, 487
Application packages (programs), 29
Applications, 6–9, 54–56, 100–101
  artificial intelligence and, 94–99
  business, 524–525
  calculation, 60–64
  data entry for, 163–167
  educational, 476–483
  engineering, 508–520
  examples of, 51–52
  of expert systems, 395–396
  governmental, 111, 447–458
  for handicapped people, 125, 465–466
  health-care, 112, 458–467
  home control, 89
  in humanities, 483–492
  input/output, 56–59
  integrated packages, 348–350

Applications (*Cont.*):
  interactive and batch processing of, 67–69
  legal, 111–112, 455–458
  limitations upon, 36
  logic/comparison, 69–71
  of mainframe computers, 268–269
  of personal computers, 254–256
  for police work, 17
  prewritten software for, 318
  of public data bases, 301–302
  in purchasing decisions, 251
  of real time processing systems, 292
  scientific, 502–507
  selection of packages for, 350–353
  of spreadsheets, 326
  storage/retrieval, 71–78
  of supercomputers, 270–272
  text manipulation, 64–67
  (*See also* Programs; Software)
Applications programmers, 436
Archeological applications, 491–492
Architectural engineering, 508–509
Architecture (design) of computers, 34
Archival applications, 195–196
Arithmetic-logic section (ALU) of processor
    units, 22, 48, 144–145, 152–154
Arithmetic operations in BASIC, 577–578
Arrays in BASIC:
  one-dimensional, 626–635
  two-dimensional, 636–640
Art applications, 483, 488
Artificial intelligence (AI), 94–99
  expert systems and, 375, 395–396, 460
  "softer" software and, 370
ASCII (American Standard Code for
    Information Interchange), 137
ASCII-8 code, 138
Asimov, Isaac, 91–92
Assembly languages, 406–408
Assembly programs (assemblers), 407

INDEX

AT&T (American Telephone and Telegraph), 110, 277, 282
Atanasoff, John Vincent, 44–45
Atanasoff-Berry computer (ABC), 45
Audio-response systems, 228
Audit trails, 300
Authoring languages, 479
Authors of software, 569–570
   styles used by, 611
Authorship identification, 483–485
Automated assembly applications, 513
Automated teller machines (ATMs), 178–179, 193
Auxiliary (secondary) storage devices, 22, 198
   (See also Secondary storage)

Babbage, Charles, 44, 420
Bach, Richard, 104
Backgammon, 95, 97
Backslashes (\), 590
Backup copies of disks, 205
Backus, John, 412, 418
Band printers, 221–222
Bank of America, 293
Bank-switched memory, 249
Banking applications, 64, 524
   financial transaction terminals for, 178–179
   magnetic ink character recognition used for, 184–185
   of personal computers, 303
   service systems for, 302
   smart cards for, 193
   surveillance in, 108
Bar codes, 177, 178
Barnaby, Rob, 570
BASIC (language), 411, 572–573
   accumulators in, 592–597
   arithmetic operations in, 577–578
   arrays in: one-dimensional, 626–635
      two-dimensional, 636–641
   commands and statements in, 573–574
   counters in, 597–602
   error correction in, 578–579
   history of, 48, 49, 613–614
   I/O processing in, 579–583
   library functions in, 619–625
   loops and decisions in, 583–591
   nested FOR . . . NEXT loops in, 616–619
   program entry elements in, 572–577
   sorting in, 641–647
   statements in, 648–652
Batch processing, 48, 67–69
   applications of, 163–165
   job control language for, 357
   on mainframe computers, 269
Begin-sector hole, 206
Bell, Alexander Graham, 276

Berliner, Hans, 95, 97
Berry, Clifford, 44–45
Bible studies, 484
Bibliographic Retrieval Services (BRS), 301
Binary coded decimal (BCD), 137
Binary numbering system, 45, 135–136
   used in machine languages, 406
Biochips, 129–130, 141
Biosensors, 143
Bipolar semiconductor chips, 140
Bits, 134
Blackboards, 224
Blind people, 465–466, 505
Blocks on magnetic tape, 214
Boeing Aerospace Company, 395–396
Boilerplate language, 455
Braille systems, 466
Branching statements, 555, 585, 586, 651–652
Branchpoints in programs, 26
Brandeis, Louis, 109
Bricklin, Dan, 49, 570
Broadband channels, 281
BRS (Bibliographic Retrieval Services), 301
Bubble sorts, 643–647
Budget applications, 443–445, 447
Buffers, 142, 221, 264, 358–360
Bugs in programs, 423–424, 658–659
Burks, A. W., 45
Bus LANs (networks), 288
Buses, 243, 246
Business applications, 102, 113–114, 524–525
   COBOL for, 414
   data entry for, 163–167
   for engineering, 508–520
   of expert systems, 395–396
   management information systems, 372–376
   of personal computers, 255–256, 258–259
   (See also Applications)
Buying (see Purchasing)
Bytes, 134

Caches (buffers), 142, 264
Caduceus (medical diagnostic program), 98
Calculating, 15, 17
   applications of, 60–64
Campaign (political) management software, 51–52, 320, 506
   (See also Elections)
Card readers, 173
Careers in computing, 435–439
Carlos, Walter, 487
Cartoons, 487
Cartridges (disk), 200
Cassette tapes, 178
CAT (computerized axial tomography) scanning, 460–461

Cathode-ray tubes (CRTs; monitors; VDTs; video display terminals), 169–171
   health hazards associated with, 225
   output displayed on, 224–226
   for personal computers, 250
   user-friendly interfaces for, 171–176
Cells in spreadsheets, 60–62, 324
Cellular telephones, 274
Census data, 43
Central processing units (CPUs), 22
   microprocessor chips, 48, 242, 246–249
   (See also Processor units)
Centralized data entry, 163
Centronics printer interface, 250–251
Channels (data transmission), 281–282, 287
Channels (I/O), 358
Channels (magnetic tape), 213
Character addressable computers, 133
Character printers, 217–219
Character readers, 184–186, 465
Character strings:
   in arrays, 627
   constants, 576
Characters:
   kanji and kana, 158
   optical recognition of, 185–186
   stored in sectors on disks, 206
Charts, graphics programs for, 62–64
Check bits, 138
Checkers, 94
Checks, magnetic ink character recognition used for, 184–185
Chess, 36, 94–97
Chief programmer teams, 401, 437
City governments, 447–450
Classifying data, 14
Clock speeds, 145, 248
Clocks, 145, 156
Closed captioning on television, 466
Closed-loop process control, 514–515
Coaxial cables, 281
COBOL (language), 414–417
CODASYL (Conference of Data Systems Languages), 414
Coding, 422
   flowcharts and, 554
   pseudocode in, 557–558
Coding data, 135–138
Coding structures, 404–405
Colons (:), 648
Color displays, 172
Combinatorial explosion, 36
Command-driven programs, 174
Command-line interfaces, 367
Commands:
   in BASIC, 573–574
   control section operations on, 154–156
   in machine languages, 406
   for operating systems, 367
Commas (,) in BASIC, 582

INDEX

Commodore PET (computer), 614
Common carriers, 282–283
Communicating word processing stations, 297–299
Communication satellites, 281–282
Communications, 15, 276–278
   for banking systems, 302, 303
   coordination of, 285–291
   data base retrieval systems, 301–302
   data transmission channels for, 281–282
   data transmission techniques for, 278–281
   distributed data processing networks for, 265, 293–296
   educational applications of, 473–474
   electronic mail and message systems, 296–300
   for handicapped people, 465–466
   real time processing systems on, 291–292
   service organizations for, 282–285
   software for, 71–72, 332–334
   telecommunications specialists for, 437
   for telecommuting, 302
   timesharing and remote computing service systems on, 292–293
Communications processors, 285–288
Comparison operations, 17–18
   applications of, 69–71
Compatibility, 250–252, 267
Compilers, 410, 422, 424
Computer-aided design (CAD), 114, 395, 508–511
Computer-aided manufacturing (CAM), 114, 511–514
Computer-aided prosthetics, 466
Computer animation, 102
Computer art, 486–488
Computer-assisted instruction (CAI), 320–321, 477–482
Computer-assisted retrieval (CAR), 223–224
Computer-assisted testing, 482–483
Computer-based education (CBE), 476
Computer codes, 137–138
Computer graphics (*see* Graphics)
Computer literacy, 9
Computer-managed instruction (CMI), 477
Computer models, 502–503
Computer operations personnel, 437–439
Computer-output-to-microfilm (COM), 222–223
Computer stylistics, 484
Computer Workers of America, 225
Computerized axial tomography (CAT) scanning, 460–461
Computerized conferences, 299–300
Computers:
   advances in, 27–31
   applications of, 7–9, 51–52
   artificial intelligence and, 94–99
   definition of, 12
   differences among, 31–34

Computers (*Cont.*):
   ease of use of, 367
   educational applications of, 476–483
   employment opportunities involving, 435–439
   in government, 447–454
   health hazards associated with, 225
   history of, 5–6, 43–49
   humanities applications of, 483–492
   impact of, on organizations, 109–116
   limitations upon, 34–36
   linked to telephones, 277
   in local-area networks, 288–291
   mainframes, 267–269
   minicomputers, 264–266
   modems to connect telephones with, 278–281
   operating systems for, 353–363
   outputs from, 215–228
   personal computers, 242–259
   potential dangers in, 104–109
   processing by, 13–18
   social impact of, 99–109
   software for communications between, 332–334
   speed and accuracy of, 12–13
   supercomputers, 270–272
   as systems, 18–24
   voting using, 472
Concurrent programming (multiprogramming; multitasking), 245, 360
Conditional branching statements, 585
Conservation applications, 507
Constants, 575–576
Control applications, 507
   in engineering and business, 514–520
   in homes, 89
Control Data Corporation (CDC), 271, 449
Control programs, 355–360
Control section of processor units, 22, 145, 154–156
Control totals, 168
Copyrights on software, 529–530
Core storage, 139–140
Correction key, 578
Counters, 548–553, 597–604
County governments, 447–450, 472
CP/M-80 operating system, 253
CP/M-86 operating system, 254
CPUs (*see* Central processing units; Processor units)
Crashes of read/write heads, 204
Cray Research, 271
Credit cards, 193
Critical paths, 72
Crossed loops, 618–619
Cursors, 170, 173–174, 342
Custom-made software, 80–82, 318
   hospital information systems, 376–378

Custom-made software (*Cont.*):
   make or buy decisions on, 401
   management information systems, 372–376
CYBER 205 computers, 271
Cycle times, 270
Cylinders on disks, 207–208

Daisy-wheel printers, 217–219
Danziger, Jeff, 487
Data:
   coding of, 135–138
   entered into arrays, 627
   information distinguished from, 14
   inputting, 160–168
      offline devices for, 180–186
      online devices for, 168–180
   organization of, 54
   potential dangers in gathering, 104–106
   privacy rights in, 107–109
   security for, 311
   sequential and direct storage and retrieval of, 74–78
   software for communications of, 332–334
   sorting of, 641–647
   stored on magnetic disks, 203–205
   stored on magnetic tape, 213–214
Data banks, 71–72, 301
Data base administrators, 435–436
Data base management systems (DBMSs), 57–59, 100, 328–332, 410–411
Data bases, 54
   legal and law enforcement, 455–457
   on mainframe computers, 269
   museum and historical applications of, 490–491
   retrieval systems for, 301–302
   security for, 311
Data buses, 246
Data collection stations, 161
Data communications, 15, 276–278
   service organizations for, 282–285
   (*See also* Communications)
Data density, 181
Data entry methods, 161–167
   in BASIC, 572
Data entry operators, 437–439
Data fields, 54
Data integrity, 106, 107, 311, 332–334
Data items, 54
Data processing, 14–15
DATA statements, 581, 652
Data transmission channels, 281–282
Debugging, 423–424, 554, 658–659
Decimal numbering system, 135, 137
Decision-making applications, 447
   information for, 372–374
   scientific, 502–507

INDEX

Decision support systems (DSSs), 374–376, 395–396
Decision tables, 558–561
Decision trees, 396
Decisions:
 in BASIC programs, 583–591
 flowchart symbol for, 537
 in programs, 539–542, 544–545
Decoders 156
Dedicated (leased) lines, 281
Default data, 163–165
Demonstration disks, 352
Design reports, 390
Design walkthroughs, 387
Desk-checking programs, 424
Detail (micro) flowcharts, 535
Detail reports, 216–217
Devices (*see* Hardware; Peripheral devices)
Dialects of BASIC, 572
Dialog Information Services, 301
Dialogues, 479–480
Digital Equipment Corporation (DEC), 47
Digital Research, 253, 254
Digital subtraction angiography (DSA), 462–463
Digitizer tablets, 174
Digitizing cameras, 196
DIM (dimension) statements, 628
Direct access, 199–212
Direct-access storage devices (DASD), 75, 161, 198, 235
Direct-connect modems, 279
Direct (random) files, 75, 235–236
Direct input devices, 14
Direct processing (direct-access; random processing), 75–78
Direct storage and retrieval, 74–78
Discovery learning environments, 482
Disk addresses, 206
Disk cartridges, 200
Disk drives, 200
Disk operating systems (DOS), 31, 253
Disk packs, 200
Disks:
 floppy, 20, 22, 178, 183–184
 magnetic, 199–209
 optical, 196, 210–211, 490
 for sequential access, 212–213
Displays, 172–173, 224–226
 for personal computers, 250
 visual interfaces for, 367
 windows in, 31, 49, 176, 259
Distributed data entry, 161
Distributed data processing (DDP) networks, 265, 269, 293–296
DNA synthesis, 467
DO UNTIL structure, 555
DO WHILE loops, 55, 650
Documentation, 425–426
 flowcharts in, 554
 REM statements for, 580

Documents:
 boilerplate language in, 455
 "hypertext," 337
 natural language translation of, 485–486
 outlining packages for, 334–336
 transmission of, 297–299
 (*See also* Word processing)
Dollar sign ($) in BASIC, 577
DOS (disk operating systems), 31, 253
Dot-addressable graphics, 227
Dot-matrix printers, 217, 219, 227
Double-sided disks, 203
Drill and practice, 320, 478–479
Driver programs, 251
Drug research, 505
Drum printers, 222, 227
Dumb terminals, 169
Dummy records, 60, 69, 150, 540, 585
Dynamic RAM chips, 140

EBCDIC (Extended Binary Coded Decimal Interchange Code), 137–138
Eckert, J. Presper, 45, 239–240
Economic analysis, 505–506
Economic order quantity, 619–621
Edit checks, 168
EDSAC computer, 45
Educational applications, 102, 103, 112–113, 320–322, 476
 computer-assisted instruction, 477–482
 computer-assisted testing, 482–483
 computer-managed instruction, 477
 Electronic University, 473–474
 Logo used for, 420–421
 Writing to Read program, 497
EDVAC computer, 45
"Egoless" programming teams, 401–403, 437
8-bit code, 137–138
8-bit microprocessor chips, 246, 248–249, 253
8/16-bit microprocessor chips, 247
8010 Star Information System (Xerox), 49
Elections, 472
 (*See also* Political campaign packages)
Electronic clocks, 145, 156
Electronic funds transfer (EFT) systems, 108, 178–179, 193
Electronic Information Exchange System, 300
Electronic mail/message systems (EMMSs), 296–300
Electronic offices, 322–324
Electronic spreadsheet packages (*see* Spreadsheet programs)
Electronic University, 473–474
Electronically erasable programmable read-only memory (EEPROM) chips, 143
Electrostatic printers, 227
Eliza (program), 96

Employment:
 benefits of computers for, 100–101
 in computer fields, 435–439
 future of, 52
 potential dangers of computers for, 104
 telecommuting and, 302
Emulators (alternate input devices), 125
Encryption systems, 300
END statements, 575, 582–583
End users, 81
Endless loops, 541
Engineering applications, 113–114, 395–396, 508–520
ENIAC computer, 45, 139
Entertainment applications, 103, 321
Equals sign (=) in BASIC, 576
Erasable and programmable read-only memory (EPROM) chips, 143
Ergonomics, 171–173, 225
Error detection, 71
 by compilers and interpreters, 424
 in data entry, 167–168
 parity checking for, 138
 in software development, 405
Errors:
 correction of, in BASIC, 578–579
 dangers of, 91–92
 of inaccurate and incomplete data, 106
 operating system handling of, 361–362
 syntax and logical, 424, 658–659
Ethernet (network), 290
Exception reports, 217
Execution cycles, 156, 248
Expert systems, 97–99, 336, 395–396
 in decision support systems, 375
 for medical diagnosis, 460
Exponential notation, 575–576
Extended Binary Coded Decimal Interchange Code (EBCDIC), 137–138
External direct-connect modems, 279
External output, 216, 217

Facsimile (fax) transmission, 297
Fault-tolerant systems, 28
Federal Bureau of Investigation (FBI), 111, 456
Federal Communications Commission (FCC), 277
Federal government:
 actions against AT&T and IBM by, 277
 computers used by, 452–454
 General Services Administration of, 443–445
 voting systems and, 472
Federalist Papers, 484
Fiber-optic cables, 282
Fifth-generation computers, 99, 110
File maintenance (updating), 59
File management systems (FMSs), 57–59, 328

INDEX

677

Files, 54
    master and transaction, 163
    during system conversions, 426–427
    types of, 235–237
Film recorders, 227
Filmed output, 222–224
Financial management packages, 322
Financial transaction terminals, 178–179
Fine art applications, 486–488
Fingerprints, 17
Fixed automation systems, 513
Fixed-head-per-track devices, 209
Fixed word-length storage, 133–134
Flags in programs, 643
Flatbed plotters, 227
Flexible manufacturing systems (FMS), 113–114, 513
Floppy-disk readers, 184
Floppy disks (diskettes), 20, 22, 178, 183–184, 200–203
Flowcharts, 382, 383, 535–538, 553–554
    decision tables versus, 558–561
    FOR . . . NEXT loops in, 617
Flutie, Doug, 79
FOR . . . NEXT loops, 599–604
    to enter data into arrays, 627
    nested, 616–619
Formats, disk, 207
FORTRAN (language), 412–414
Fourth-generation languages (4GLs), 410–411
Frames on magnetic tape, 213
Frankston, Bob, 49, 570
Front-end processors, 287, 360
Frye, Tom, 569
Full-duplex communications, 281
Function keys, 170, 171
Functions in BASIC, 619–625
Future of computers:
    direct-access storage for, 211–212
    health-care applications, 467
    industrial, 514
    of microprocessor chips, 248
Fuzzy logic, 97

Gallium arsenide (GaAs) chips, 141
Games:
    artificial intelligence and, 94–97
    educational, 321, 481–482
Gates, Bill, 49, 369–370, 569, 570, 613
Gauss, Carl Friedrich, 603
General-purpose packages, 80, 318
    communications, 332–334
    data base management systems, 328–332
    electronic spreadsheets, 324–325
    graphics, 325–328
    "mindware," 336
    outlining, 334–336
    word processing, 322–324

General Services Administration (GSA), 443–445, 453–454
General Telephone and Electronics (GTE), 282, 284
Genetic engineering, 467
Geology package, 98
Goldstine, H. H., 45
GOSUB statements, 648–650
GOTO statements, 555, 586, 658
Governmental applications, 101–102, 111–112
    conservation and pollution control, 507
    federal, 443–445, 452–454
    law enforcement, 455–458
    local, 447–450
    potential dangers in data gathering by, 104–106
    of real time processing, 292
    "recycling" used software for, 402
    state and regional, 450–452
    voting, 472
Graphics, 224–227
    cartoons, 487
    computer-aided design, 508–511
    computer art, 486–487
    enhanced, for displays, 172
    in integrated software packages, 30
    in interfaces, 367
    light pens and tablets for, 174
    as output, 217
    paint systems for, 321
    on personal computers, 250
    software for, 62–64, 325–328
    transmission of, 287–299
Grid charts, 384–385
GTE Telenet, 284

Half-duplex communications, 281
Handicapped, computer aid for, 102, 125, 465–466
Handwriting, machines to read, 158, 185
Hard (rigid) disks, 22, 200–205
Hard-sectored disks, 207
Hardware:
    advances in, 27–28
    communications processors, 285–288
    for handicapped people, 125
    input devices, 19–20, 168–186
    modems, 278–281
    output devices, 22–24
    of personal computers, 246–252
    printers, 217–222
    processor units, 20–22
    secondary storage devices, 22
    (See also Peripheral devices)
Health-care applications, 100, 102, 111–112, 458–467
    home-based software for, 322
    hospital information systems, 376–378
Health hazards of computers, 225

Hearing-impaired people, 466, 505
Heuristics, 96, 396
Hewlett-Packard Company, 293
Hierarchical (tree) structures, 332
High-speed buffers (caches), 142, 264
High-speed networks, 288
Higher-level languages, 47, 408–410
    [See also Languages (programming)]
History, computer applications for, 490–491
History of computers, 5–6, 43–49
    of Microsoft BASIC, 613–614
Hobby applications, 103, 321
Hoff, Marcian "Ted," 48
Hollerith, Herman, 43–44, 173
Home use of personal computers, 257
    applications of, 254–255
    for banking applications, 303
    for control applications, 89
    software for, 321–322
HomeMinder (program), 89
Hospital applications, 458–467
    information systems, 376–378
Host computers, 265, 269, 287, 360
Housekeeping applications:
    in government, 447
    in health-care organizations, 458
Humanities, applications in, 112–113, 483–492
"Hypertext," 337

IBM (see International Business Machine Corporation)
Icons, 49, 175–176, 350, 367
Ideal (language), 397, 398
IEEE-488 parallel interface standard, 250
IEEE-696 parallel interface standard, 250
IF . . . THEN statements, 585
IF-THEN-ELSE statements, 555, 650–651
Impact of computers:
    in humanities, debate over, 492
    upon organizations, 109–116
    potential dangers in, 104–109
    social, 99–109
Impact printers, 217–219
Implementation of programs, 423–426
Index holes, 206
Indexed sequential access method (ISAM), 236
Indexed sequential files, 236
Indexes, 236
Industrial applications, 511–520
Industrial engineering, 509–510
Infomedia Corporation, 300
Information:
    business applications of, 524–525
    data distinguished from, 14
    in expert systems, 395
    hospital information systems for, 376–378
    management information systems for, 372–376

INDEX

Information (*Cont.*):
  potential dangers in gathering, 104–106
  privacy rights in, 107–109
  (*See also* Data)
Information centers, 375–376
Information processing industry, 110
Information Revolution, 9
Information system managers, 435
Inkjet plotters, 227
Inkjet printers, 219, 227
Input buffers, 359
Input devices, 19–20
  for handicapped, 125
  Japanese keyboards, 157–158
  offline, 180–186
  online, 168–180
  for personal computers, 249
  smart cards, 193
Input/output operations, 17
  applications of, 56–59
  in BASIC, 579–583
  flowchart symbol for, 535–536
  operating systems for, 355
  programming analysis example of, 538–539
INPUT statements, 586–588
Input storage area of processor units, 20, 132, 150
Input tablets, 174
Inputs, 14, 160–168
  in BASIC, 572
Instruction cycles, 156, 248
Instruction registers, 154–156
Instruction sets, 249
Instructions:
  arithmetic-logic unit operations on, 152–154
  control section operations on, 154–156
  in high-level languages, 408–409
  multiprocessing of, 360
INT (integer) function, 621, 625
Integrated software packages, 29–31, 49, 80, 259, 318, 348–350
Integrity of data, 106, 107, 311, 332–334
Intel Corporation, 48
  microprocessor chips by, 246–247
Intelligent modems, 279
Intelligent terminals, 170–171
Intensive care units, patient monitoring in, 463–465
Interactive languages, 411, 572
Interactive processing, 67, 69, 161, 276
  internal and external output generated by, 216
  real time, 291–292
Interface elements in networks, 278
Interfaces:
  ease of use in, 367
  standards for, 250–251
  user-friendly, for VDTs and personal computers, 171–176
Internal direct-connect modems, 279

Internal output, 216
International Business Machine Corporation (IBM):
  federal suit against, 277
  history of, 44, 46
  mainframe computers by, 47, 268
  Microsoft and, 614
  personal computers by, 49, 246–247, 253
  revenues of, 110
  Writing to Read program of, 497
Interpreters, 410, 421–422, 424, 573
Interrecord gaps, 214
Interrupts, 361
Inventory control, 519
Inventory control applications, 167
ITT World Communications, 284

Jacquard, Joseph Marie, 43
Japan, 99, 110, 270, 271
Japanese keyboards, 157–158
Jazz (program), 346
Job control language (JCL), 357
Job control programs, 356–358
Jobs, Steve, 49
Jobs (*see* Employment)
Joysticks, 174

K (kilobits), 141
Kana characters, 158
Kanji characters, 158
Kapor, Mitch, 569
Kemeny, John, 48, 572
Kernels (monitors; supervisors; program), 355
Kernighan, Brian W., 611
Key fields, 328
Key-to-disk stations, 182
Keyboard enhancer programs, 349
Keyboard macros, 370
Keyboards, 20, 171–172, 249
  Japanese, 157–158
  memory-resident software and, 349
  used with video display terminals, 169, 170
Keys, record, 74–75
Knowledge-based systems (expert systems), 97–99, 395–396
Kurtz, Thomas, 48, 572
Kurzweil Reading Machine (KRM), 465

Languages (natural):
  command-line interfaces for, 367
  Japanese, 157–158
  translation of, 485–486
  voice input systems for, 180
Languages (programming), 28, 47
  ALGOL, Pascal, and Ada, 418–420
  authoring, 479
  BASIC (*see* BASIC)
  COBOL, 414–417

Languages (programming) (*Cont.*):
  FORTRAN, 412–414
  Logo, 420–421
  PL/1, 417
  RPG, 418
  selection of, 421–422
  translation programs for, 256, 319
  types of, 405–411
Laser printers, 219–221
Laser recording systems, 210–211
Lasers used for communications, 282
Latency (search time), 208
Law-enforcement applications, 17, 111, 316, 447, 455–458
Leased (dedicated) lines, 281
Legal applications, 100–112, 320, 455–458, 485
Legal issues:
  data security, 311
  in law-enforcement data bases, 457
  privacy, 109
Leibniz, Gottfried von, 43
LET statements, 581
Levy, David, 95, 96
LEXIS, 301–302, 455
Librarian programs, 363
Library functions in BASIC, 619–625
Library programs, 362–363
Light pens, 174
Limit checks, 168
Line numbers in BASIC programs, 574–575
Line printers, 221–222
Liquid-crystal displays (LCDs), 226
Lisa (computer), 49, 245
List structures, 330–332
Live Aid concert, 345–346
Liveboard, 224
Local-area networks (LANs), 288–291
Local governments, 447–450, 472
Log-on and log-off procedures, 72, 573
Logic/comparison operations, 17–18
  applications of, 69–71
Logic structures, 554–555
Logical errors, 424, 579, 658–659
  crossed loops, 618–619
LOGIN (Local Government Information Network), 449–450
Logo (language), 420–421
Loops, 539–542, 555, 567–568
  in BASIC programs, 583–591
  DO WHILE, 650
  FOR . . . NEXT, 599–604
  nested FOR . . . NEXT, 616–619
  in sorting programs, 643–646
Lotus 1-2-3 (program), 445, 569
Lovelace, Lady Augusta Ada, 44, 420, 631
Low-speed digital PBX networks, 290–291
Low-speed personal computer networks, 290

M (megabits), 141
McCarthy, John, 95

INDEX

Machine languages, 406
Macintosh computer (Apple), 49, 247, 345–346, 487
Macro (main-control) flowcharts, 535
Macro instructions, 408–409
Magnetic bubble storage, 210
Magnetic disks, 199–209
   floppy, 20, 22, 178, 183–184
Magnetic ink character recognition (MICR), 184–185
Magnetic tape, 20, 181–183
   for backup of hard disks, 205
   for sequential access, 213–215
   on tape strip devices, 211
Mail-order distributors, 353
Mailing-list applications, 56–57
   abuses of, 108
Main circuit boards (motherboards), 242–243
Main-control (macro) flowcharts, 535
Main memory (see Primary storage)
Main menus, 175
Mainframe computers, 33–34, 267–269, 332
Maintenance of software, 404, 427, 428
Management information systems (MISs), 372–376
   directors of, 435
Mark I digital computer, 44
Markkula, Mike, 49
Master files, 163, 167
MAT (matrix) statements, 651
Material handling applications, 513
Matrixes (two-dimensional arrays), 636–641
Mauchly, John W., 45, 239
MBASIC (Microsoft BASIC language), 49, 576, 577, 613–614
MCI Communications Corporation, 283
Mead Data Central, 301–302
Media:
   floppy disks, 20, 22, 178
   magnetic disks, 199–209
   for offline data entry, 180–186
Medical applications, 103, 320, 460–465
   diagnostic packages, 98
   research, 466–467, 505
   (See also Health-care applications)
Medical imaging systems, 460–463
Medium-speed networks, 290
Megahertz (MHz), 145
Memory:
   programs resident in, 349
   RAM disks in, 209–210
   random access, 140–141
   read-only, 142–144
   on smart cards, 193
   virtual, 361
   (See also Primary storage; Storage)
Memory-resident software, 349
Menu-driven programs, 173–175
Menu lines, 176
Menus, 58, 175, 350, 367
Message distribution services, 297

Message switchers, 287
Metal-oxide semiconductor (MOS) chips, 140
MHz (megahertz), 145
Mice, 173–174
Micro (detail) flowcharts, 535
Microcomputers, 31–33, 242
   intelligent terminals and, 170–171
   software to link mainframes with, 332
   (See also Personal computers)
Microfiche, 223
Microfilm as output, 222–223
Microprocessor chips, 48
   biochips, 129–130
   performance of, 248–249
   in personal computers, 242, 245–248, 253
   on smart cards, 193
   in smart terminals, 170
Microprograms, 142
Microsoft Corporation, 49, 569, 570, 614
   BASIC by, 49, 576, 577, 613–614
   MS-DOS operating system by, 253, 349
Microtomography, 467
Microwave systems, 281
Military systems, 292
"Mindware" packages, 336
Minicomputers, 33, 264–266
   history of, 47
   superminis, 34
Minspeak emulator, 125
MITS (Micro Instrumentation and Telemetry Systems), 48–49, 613
Mnemonic code, 406
Modeling, 374–375, 502–503
Modems, 278–281
Modular (top-down) program design, 403–404, 557
Monitors (cathode-ray tubes; CRTs; VDTs; video display terminals), 169–171
   health hazards associated with, 225
   output displayed on, 224–226
   user-friendly interfaces for, 171–176
Monitors (kernels; supervisors; program), 355
Monochrome displays, 172, 173
Motherboards (main circuit boards), 242–243
Motorola 68000 microprocessor chip, 247, 248
Mouse, 173–174
MS-DOS operating system, 253, 349
Multifunction integrated packages, 350
Multiplexers, 287
Multiprocessing, 360
Multiprocessor systems, 34, 267
Multitasking (concurrent programming; multiprogramming), 245, 360
Multiuser systems, 243, 245, 264
Museum applications, 195–196, 483, 488–490
Music, computers and, 487–488
MYCIN (medical diagnostic system), 460

Narrowband channels, 281
National Crime Information Center (NCIC), 111, 456–457
Nested FOR . . . NEXT loops, 616–619
Network structures, 332
Networks, 277–278, 285–291
   data communications service organizations, 282–285
   for distributed data processing, 265, 269, 293–296
   local-area, 288–291
   portable computers linked to, 273–274
   (See also Communications)
New York Statewide Police Information Network (NYSPIN), 111
NEXT statements, 599–604
   in nested loops, 616–619
Nine-track magnetic tape, 213
Node (satellite) processors, 265
Nonimpact printers, 219, 222, 227
Nonvolatile storage, 139, 210
Notecards (program), 337
Nuclear accident simulations, 499–500
Nuclear magnetic resonance (NMR), 461–462
Number sign (#) in BASIC, 590
Numbering systems, 135–136
Numeric keypads, 171
Numeric values:
   in arrays, 627
   constants, 575–576
   variables, 576
Numerical control (NC) machines, 517–518

Oasis-16 operating system, 254
Object programs, 407, 424
Octal numbering system, 135
Office uses of personal computers, 255–256, 258–259
Offline data entry devices, 180–186
Offline storage, 22, 198
ON . . . GOTO statements, 651–652
One-dimensional arrays, 626–635
Online data entry devices, 168–180
Online storage, 22
Open-loop process control, 514
Operands, 406
Operating systems (OS), 31, 318, 353–363
   ease of use of, 367
   for personal computers, 252–254
   systems security in, 107
Operation code (op code), 406
Operational control systems, 514–519
Optical character readers, 177, 185–186, 465
Optical disks, 196, 210–211, 490
Optical mark readers, 185
Order of operations in BASIC, 577–578
Order entry/shipping/billing systems, 163–165

INDEX

Organizational impact of computers, 109–110
  benefits of, 101–104, 111–114
  potential dangers in, 104–109, 115–116
Organizational stress, 116
Organizations:
  data base management systems used by, 323–330
  for data communications, 282–285
  internal and external output generated for, 215
  management information systems for, 372–376
  special-purpose software for, 320–321
  system conversions and changeovers in, 425–427
Outlining packages, 59, 334–337
Output buffers, 359
Output devices, 22–24
  for graphics, 227
  for personal computers, 250
  printers, 217–222
Output storage area of processor units, 21, 132, 152
Outputs, 15, 215–217
  displays and graphics, 224–227
  film, 222–224
  print, 217–222
  voice, 227–228

p-System, 254
Packaged programs, 29, 401
Packet-switching networks, 284
Page printers, 219–222
Pages of programs, 361
Paint systems, 321
Paper, programs on, 178
Papert, Seymour, 420
Parallel assemblies, 34
Parallel interfaces, 250–251
Parallel running conversions, 427
Parentheses [( )] in BASIC, 578
Parity bits, 138
Parity checking, 138
Pascal, Blaise, 43, 419
Pascal (language), 419–420
Passwords, 193, 311, 362
PBX (private branch exchange) networks, 290–291
Peer reviews in program construction, 405, 557
Pen plotters, 227
People's Firehouse, 315–316
Peripheral devices, 24
  for graphic outputs, 227
  for handicapped people, 125
  modems, 278–281
  for offline data entry, 180–186
  for online data entry, 168–180
  for personal computers, 249–250

Peripheral devices (*Cont.*):
  printers, 217–222
  (*See also* Hardware)
Perpendicular recording techniques, 211–212
Personal computers, 31–33, 242–246
  Asimov on, 91–92
  banking applications for, 303
  BASIC used in, 411
  benefits of, 103–104
  Eckert on, 239–240
  examples of, 257–259
  hardware of, 246–250
  history of, 6, 48–49
  home control applications for, 89
  intelligent terminals and, 170–171
  mainframes linked with, 332
  microcomputers and, 31–33
  multiuser systems using, 245
  in networks, 290
  output devices for, 23
  public-domain software for, 529–530
  software for, 252–256, 350–353
  standards and purchasing considerations for, 250–252
  used by governments, 447–448
  user-friendly interfaces for, 171–176
  user groups for, 534
"Personalized" letters, 64–65
PET (positive emission tomography), 462
Phares, David, 326
Pick OS (operating system), 254
Pictures (*see* Graphics)
PILOT, 479
Pilot conversions, 427
Pixels, 172, 250
PL/1 (language), 417
Planning applications, 502–507
PLATO, 479
Plauger, J. P., 611
Plotters, 227
Poetry-generation program, 631–635
Point-of-sale (POS) terminals, 177
Pointer fields, 235
Pointers, 330–332, 581
Police applications, 17, 111, 316, 447
Political campaign packages, 51–52, 320, 506
  (*See also* Elections)
Pollution control applications, 450–451, 507
Poor, Victor, 48
Portable computers, 243, 273–274
  liquid-crystal displays on, 226
Portable data entry terminals, 179–180
Portable telephones, 273–274
Ports, 251
Positive emission tomography (PET), 462
Post-implementation reviews, 427–428
Power supplies, 141
President (U.S.), computers used by, 454
Prewritten software packages, 29, 79–80, 318, 401

Primary storage (main memory):
  available to microprocessor chips, 248–249
  in processor units, 20–22, 132–135, 139–144, 150–152, 198
  programs resident in, 349
  on supercomputers, 270
Print chains, 221
Print spoolers, 349
PRINT statements, 582, 588
  for arrays, 627–628
PRINT TAB function, 585–586
PRINT USING function, 590
Printed output, 217–222
Printer buffers, 221
Printers, 217–222, 227
  Centronics parallel interface standard for, 250–251
Priorities in processing, 361
Privacy, 107–109
Problem definition surveys, 378–380
Process control systems, 514–517
Processing, 13–18
  flowchart symbol for, 536
  interactive and batch, 67–69
  of programs, in operating systems, 362–363
  sequential and direct, 75–78
  timesharing in, 48
Processor units (central processing units; CPUs), 20–22
  arithmetic-logic and control functions of, 144–145, 152–156
  communications processors, 285–288
  design differences in, 34
  in mainframes, 267
  microprocessor chips, 242, 246–249
  multiprocessing by, 360
  primary storage in, 132–135, 150–152
  storage components in, 139–144
  (*See also* Microprocessor chips)
Production control, 517–518
Productivity, 101, 113
Program and media librarians, 439
Program coding, 422
Program flowcharts, 382, 383, 535–538, 553–554
Program interrupts, 361
Program statements (*see* Statements)
Program storage area of processor units, 21, 132, 150
Programmable read-only memory (PROM) chips, 143
Programmed instruction, 477–478
Programmers, 401–403, 436–437
Programming:
  structured, 404–405, 555–557, 648–651
  style in, 580, 611
  [*See also* BASIC; Languages (programming)]

INDEX

Programming analysis, 82, 532–535
  examples of, 538–554
  flowcharting in, 535–538
  logic structures and structured programming in, 554–557
  tools for, 557–561
Programming languages [see Languages (programming)]
Programs, 6
  accumulators in, 545–548
  on bar codes, 178
  in BASIC, 574–577
  coding of, 422
  counters in, 548–553
  custom-made, 80–82
  debugging of, 658–659
  definition of, 12
  development of, 400–405
  educational, 103
  implementation of, 423–426
  loops and decisions in, 539–542
  maintenance of, 427, 428
  multiple decisions in, 544–545
  operating system processing of, 362–363
  packaged, 29
  public-domain, 529–530
  reliability of, 35–36
  spoolers, 221
  stored, 24–26
  used, "recycling" of, 402
  (See also Applications; BASIC; Software)
Project management packages, 72, 334
Prompts, 175, 579
Proprietary operating systems, 253
Prospector (geology program), 98
Prosthetics, computer-aided, 466
Prototyping, 388
Pseudocode, 557–558
Pseudo-disks (RAM disks), 209–210
Pseudorandom numbers, 624–625
Public-domain software, 529–530, 534
Pull-down menus, 176, 350, 367
Punched cards, 43, 44, 173, 181
Purchasing:
  personal computers, 250–252
  software, 350–353, 401
Pyle, Harry, 48

Quotation marks ('') in BASIC, 582

Radiation produced by VDTs, 225
Radio, portable computers linked using, 273–274
RAM disks, 209–210
Random access memory (RAM), 140–141
  "disks" in, 209–210
  in personal computers, 243
Random (direct) files, 75, 235–236
Random processing (direct processing), 75–78

Randomization, 621–625
RANDOMIZE statements, 625
Range checks, 168
Read-only memory (ROM) chips, 142–144, 243
Read operations, 132
READ statements, 581, 652
Read/write heads, 199–200, 208–209
Reader-sorter units, 184–185
Reading applications, 497
  (See also Educational applications)
Real time processing systems, 291–292
Record keys, 74–75
Records, 54
  in data base management systems, 328
  in direct files, 235–236
  dummy, 60, 69, 150, 540, 585
  recorded on magnetic tape, 213–214
  in sequential files, 235
Recreational applications, 102
Reels, magnetic tape on, 213
Regional organizations, 450–451
Registers, 152–156
REJIS (Regional Justice Information System), 457
Relational structures, 332
Relative (direct, random) files, 75, 235–236
Reliability:
  of computers, 28
  of programs, 35–36
REM (remark) statements, 580, 648
Remote batch stations, 163
Remote computing service systems, 292–293
Remote concentrators, 287
Reports, 216–217
  analysis, 385–386
  design, 390
  RPG used for, 418
Reproduction of data, 15
RESTORE statements, 652
Retail stores, 353
Retrieval operations, 15, 18
  from microfiche, 223–224
  in primary storage, 132
  from public data bases, 301–302
  sequential and direct, 74–78
RETURN statements, 648–650
Reverse video, 172
Reviews of software, 352
Richardson, Lewis, 491
Rigid metal disks, 22, 200, 204–205
Ring LANs (networks), 288
RND (randomize) function, 621–625
Robotics and robots, 101, 104, 511–514
RPG (language), 418
RS-232C serial interface, 251

S-100 bus, 250
Saenz, Michael, 487

Safety applications, 102–103
Sales applications, 100–101, 167
SAT preparation programs, 51
Satellite (node) processors, 265
Satellites, 281–282, 503–505
Scelbi-8H computer, 48
Scientific applications, 113, 502–507
  FORTRAN used for, 412
  nuclear accident simulations, 499–500
Screens (see Displays)
SDC Information Services, 301
Search-and-replace capabilities, 324
Search time (latency), 208
Second-generation computers, 46–47
Secondary storage, 198
  devices for, 22
  for direct access, 199–212
  for personal computers, 250
  for sequential access, 212–215
Sectors on disks, 206–207
Security of computer systems, 106–107, 115–116
  communications software and, 332–334
  for data, 311
  operating system monitoring of, 362
Seek time, 208
Segments of programs, 361
Semicolons (;) in BASIC, 588, 590
Semiconductor chips, 140–141
  in magnetic bubble storage, 210
Sensors:
  for patient monitoring in intensive care units, 463–465
  "smelling," 143
Sentinel values, 540, 585
Sequence register, 154–156
Sequential access, 212–215
Sequential-access storage media, 198–199
Sequential files, 74–75, 235
Sequential processing, 75
Sequential storage and retrieval, 74–78
Serial interfaces, 251
Service bureaus, 293
7-bit code, 137–138
Shells:
  for expert systems, 395
  for integrated applications, 348–350
Shockley, William, 47
Sidekick (program), 349
Sign-on procedures in BASIC, 572–573
Silicon chips, 27
Silicon disks (RAM disks), 209–210
Silicon Valley, 47
Simplex circuits, 281
Simulations, 374
  educational, 321, 480–481
  for medical research, 466
  of nuclear accidents, 499–500
  social welfare applications of, 506
  in weather forecasting, 502

INDEX

Single-function applications programs, 79, 318
  general-purpose packages, 322–336
  special-purpose packages, 319–322
Single-sided disks, 203
Single-user computers, 243
6-bit code, 137
16-bit microprocessor chips, 245–248, 253
16-bit minicomputers, 264
16/16-bit microprocessor chips, 247
16/32-bit microprocessor chips, 247
64-bit microprocessor chips, 248
Size of computers, 31–34, 243
Skinner, B. F., 478
Smart cards, 192–193
Smart terminals, 170
Smarthome (program), 89
"Smelling" sensors, 143
Social impact of computers, 99–100
  Eckert on, 240
  positive, 100–104
  potential dangers in, 104–109
Social science applications, 505–507
Social welfare applications, 506–507
Soft-sectored disks, 207
Softstrip, 178
Software:
  advances in, 28–31
  authors of, 569–570
  compatibility of, in mainframes, 267
  conversions of, 426–427
  custom-made, 372–378
  development of, 378–390, 400–405
  educational, 103
  general-purpose packages, 322–336
  for handicapped people, 125
  history of, 48
  implementation of, 422–426
  integrated packages, 348–350
  maintenance of, 427–428
  memory-resident, 349
  obtaining, 78–82
  operating systems, 353–363
  for personal computers, 252–256
  public-domain, 529–530
  selection of, 350–353
  "softer," 369–370
  special-purpose packages, 319–322
  systems security in, 107
  types of, 318–319
  used, "recycling" of, 402
  user-friendly, 171, 174–176
  word processing, 342–343
  (*See also* Applications; Programs)
Software engineering, 401
Software shells, 348–350
Solid modeling programs, 510–511
Sorting, 15, 641–647
Sound synthesis:
  of music, 487–488
  of speech, 125, 227–228, 465

Source code, 529
Source data entry, 161
Source documents, 14
Source programs, 407, 424
Southern Pacific Communications Corporation, 284
Spaceflight applications, 458, 519
Speaker-dependent and -independent voice input systems, 180
Special interest groups (SIGs), 534
Special-purpose packages, 79, 318–322
Speech recognition, 125, 180
Speech synthesis, 125, 227–228, 465
Speed of computers, 12–13, 27
  access speed, 208–209
  access time, 198
  architecture to improve, 34
  clock speeds, 145
  of microprocessor chips, 248
  of RAM disks, 210
  of supercomputers, 270
Spelling checkers, 324
Spooler programs, 221, 349
Spreadsheet programs, 60–62, 100, 324–325
  in integrated software packages, 30
  VisiCalc, 49
SQR (square root) function, 619–621
Star LANs (networks), 288
State governments, 451–452
Statements:
  in BASIC, 573–575, 648–652
  in FORTRAN, 413–414
  in Pascal, 420
  in PL/1, 417
Static RAM chips, 141
Stibitz, George, 276
STOP statements, 595
Storage, 18, 198–199
  advances, in, 28
  areas in processor units for, 20–22
  coding data in, 135–138
  of data, 15
  offline media for, 180–184
  for personal computers, 249–250
  primary (*see* Primary storage)
  processor components for, 139–144
  in processor units, 150–152
  secondary (*see* Secondary storage)
  sequential and direct, 74–78
  virtual, 361
Storage dumps, 425
Storage hierarchy, 198–199
Storage/retrieval applications, 71–74
Stored programs, 24–26, 45
Strategic Air Command (SAC), 452
Streaming tape drives, 205
Stress, organizational, 116
String variables, 576–577
Structural Design Language (STRUDL), 395–396
Structural engineering, 508

Structured programming, 404–405, 421, 555–557, 648–651
Structured pseudocode, 557–558
Structured walkthroughs, 405, 557
Strunk, William, Jr., 611
Style in programming, 580, 611
Submarines, robot, 512
Submenus, 175
Subroutines, 403, 537–538, 568, 648–650, 658
Subscripts, in array names, 626
Summarizing data, 15
Summary reports, 217
Supercomputers, 34, 270–272
Supermicrocomputers, 243
Superminicomputers, 34, 264
Supervisors (monitors; kernels; program), 355
Surveillance, 108
Symbolic addressing, 407
Symbols in flowcharts, 535–538
Synergy, 99
Syntax errors, 424, 579, 658
Synthesizers (music), 487
System analysis, 82, 318–386
System analysts, 82, 436
System commands, 573–574
System design, 82, 386–390
System flowcharts, 382, 383, 535
System integrators (software shells), 349–350
System interruptions, 361
System scheduling, 358–361
System software, 318–319, 353–363
  (*See also* Operating systems)
System studies, 81–82, 378–381
System 360 (mainframe), 47
Systems, 19
  conversions and changeovers in, 426–427
  custom-made, 372
  development of, 378–390
  (*See also* Software)
Systems modeling simulations, 481
Systems programmers, 436, 437
Systems security, 106–107, 115–116
  communications software and, 332–334
  for data, 311
  operating system monitoring of, 362

Tables (two-dimensional arrays), 636–641
Tablets, 174
Tape, magnetic, 20, 181–183, 213–215
  for backup of hard disks, 205
Tape drives (transports), 183
Tape strip devices, 211
Telecommunications, 276
Telecommunications specialists, 437
Telecommuting systems, 302
Teleconferencing, 300
Telegraph lines, 276, 277, 281, 282

INDEX

TeleLearning Systems, 473–474
Telenet, 284
Telephones, 276
   common carriers for, 282–283
   computers linked to, 277
   electronic mail versus, 296
   for hearing impaired, 466
   modems to connect computers with, 278–281
   portable, 273–274
   synthesized voice over, 227–228
   voiceband channels for, 281
Teleprinter terminals, 179–180
Teletext systems, 284
Templates for spreadsheets, 325
Terminals:
   financial transaction, 178–179
   flowchart symbol for, 537
   health hazards associated with, 225
   in minicomputer systems, 264
   in multiuser systems based on microcomputers, 245
   point-of-sale, 177
   teleprinters and portable data entry, 179–180
   video display (*see* Video display terminals)
Testing:
   computer-assisted, 482–483
   of programs, 424–425
Texas Instruments, 48
Text manipulation operations, 17
   applications of, 64–67
Thermal-transfer printers, 227
Thernstrom, Stephen, 491
Thesaurus programs, 324
"Thinking," 96
Third-generation computers, 47
32-bit mainframe computers, 267
32-bit microprocessor chips, 248, 253
32-bit superminicomputers, 264
32/32-bit microprocessor chips, 247–248
Time management packages, 72–74, 334
Timesharing, 47–48, 292–293, 573
Top-down analysis methodology, 385
Top-down design methodology, 386–387
Touch screens, 173
TRACE facilities, 659
Trace programs, 425
Tracks:
   on cylinders, 207–208
   on magnetic disks, 203
   on magnetic tape, 213

Traffic control systems, 519–520
Transaction files, 163, 167
Transaction processing, 67
Transfer rates, 181
Transforms, 235
Transistors, 47
Translation of natural languages, 485–486
Translation programs, 28, 256, 319, 362, 410
Transmission channels, 281–282
Transmissions, 278–281
Transportable computers, 243
TROFF (trace off) statements, 659
TRON (trace on) statements, 659
Troubleshooting and repair programs, 98–99
TRS-80 Model I (computer), 614
Turing, Alan, 96
Turtles in Logo, 420–421
Two-dimensional arrays, 636–640
Tymnet, Inc., 284
Tymshare Network, 296
Typing errors, 658

Ultrasound, 462
Unconditional branching statements, 586
Unemployment, 104
Uninet, 284
Uninterruptible power systems (UPSs), 141
UNIVAC computer, 45–46
Universal Product Code (UPC), 177
UNIX operating systems, 253–254
Urban planning applications, 506–507
User-friendly interfaces, 171–176
User groups, 534
Utility programs, 362, 530

Value-added carriers, 284
Value-added networks (VANs), 284
Values in BASIC, 575–577
"Vaporware," 352
Variable word-length storage, 133–134
Variables, 576–577
Versabraille system, 466
Very large scale integration (VLSI), 510
Video display terminals (cathode-ray tubes; CRTs; monitors; VDTs), 169–171
   health hazards associated with, 225
   output displayed on, 224–226
   user-friendly interfaces for, 171–176
Videodisks, 196
Videotex systems, 284–285

Virtual storage, 361
VisiCalc, 49, 570
Visual arts, computers in, 488
Visual interfaces, 367
Visually handicapped people, 465–466, 505
Voice input systems, 180
Voice mail, 297
Voice response systems, 227–228
Voice store-and-forward systems, 297
Voice synthesis, 125, 227–228, 465
Voiceband channels, 281
Volatile storage, 140, 210
Von Neumann, John, 45
Von Neumann machines, 34, 45
Voting by computer, 472
   (*See also* Political campaign packages)

Walkthroughs, 387, 405, 557
Wands, 177
Water planning, 503
Watson, Thomas J., Jr., 46
Weather forecasting, 271, 502–503
Weizenbaum, Joseph, 36, 96
WEND (while end) statements, 650
Western Union, 282
WESTLAW, 455
WHILE statements, 650
White, E. B., 611
Whiteboards, 224
Winchester disk drives, 200, 204–205
Windows, 31, 49, 176, 259
Wirth, Nicklaus, 419
Word addressable computers, 133
Word processing:
   communicating stations for, 297–299
   in integrated software packages, 29
   in Japan, 158
   outlining packages for, 334–336
   software for, 64–67, 322–324, 342–343
   used by lawyers, 455
   (*See also* Documents)
Words, 133
WordStar, 570
Working storage space of processing units, 20–21, 132, 150
Wozniak, Steve, 49
Writing to Read program, 497

X-rays, 225, 460–463

Zilog Z80 microprocessor chip, 249